LET'S GO

CHILE
including Easter Island

DANIEL SPITZER EDITOR
LUCAS TATE ASSOCIATE EDITOR

RESEARCHER-WRITERS
BEN COWAN
MELISSA CRONIN
MARK WARNER KIRBY
DANNY KOSKI-KARELL
LUIS REGO
FRED G. SYKES, JR.

TALI MAZOR MAP EDITOR
LAUREN TRUESDELL MANAGING EDITOR

ST. MARTIN'S PRESS ✹ NEW YORK

Maps by David Lindroth copyright © 2005 by St. Martin's Press.

Let's Go: Chile Copyright © 2005 by Let's Go, Inc. All rights reserved. Printed in the United States of America. No part of this book may be used or reproduced in any manner whatsoever without written permission except in the case of brief quotations embodied in critical articles or reviews. Let's Go is available for purchase in bulk by institutions and authorized resellers. For information, address St. Martin's Press, 175 Fifth Avenue, New York, NY 10010, USA. www.stmartins.com.

Distributed outside the USA and Canada by Macmillan, an imprint of Pan Macmillan Ltd. 20 New Wharf Road, London N1 9RR
Basingstoke and Oxford
Associated companies throughout the world
www.panmacmillan.com

ISBN: 0-312-33560-1
EAN: 978-0312-33560-1
First edition
10 9 8 7 6 5 4 3 2 1

Let's Go: Chile is written by Let's Go Publications, 67 Mount Auburn Street, Cambridge, MA 02138, USA.

Let's Go® and the LG logo are trademarks of Let's Go, Inc.
Printed in the USA.

LET'S GO

■ THE RESOURCE FOR THE INDEPENDENT TRAVELER

"The guides are aimed not only at young budget travelers but at the indepedent traveler; a sort of streetwise cookbook for traveling alone."

—The New York Times

"Unbeatable; good sight-seeing advice; up-to-date info on restaurants, hotels, and inns; a commitment to money-saving travel; and a wry style that brightens nearly every page."

—The Washington Post

"Lighthearted and sophisticated, informative and fun to read. [Let's Go] helps the novice traveler navigate like a knowledgeable old hand."

—Atlanta Journal-Constitution

"A world-wise traveling companion—always ready with friendly advice and helpful hints, all sprinkled with a bit of wit."

—The Philadelphia Inquirer

■ THE BEST TRAVEL BARGAINS IN YOUR PRICE RANGE

"All the dirt, dirt cheap."

—People

"Anything you need to know about budget traveling is detailed in this book."

—The Chicago Sun-Times

"Let's Go follows the creed that you don't have to toss your life's savings to the wind to travel—unless you want to."

—The Salt Lake Tribune

■ REAL ADVICE FOR REAL EXPERIENCES

"The writers seem to have experienced every rooster-packed bus and lunar-surfaced mattress about which they write."

—The New York Times

"Value-packed, unbeatable, accurate, and comprehensive."

—The Los Angeles Times

"[Let's Go's] devoted updaters really walk the walk (and thumb the ride, and trek the trail). Learn how to fish, haggle, find work—anywhere."

—Food & Wine

LET'S GO PUBLICATIONS

TRAVEL GUIDES

Australia 8th edition
Austria & Switzerland 12th edition
Brazil 1st edition
Britain & Ireland 2005
California 10th edition
Central America 9th edition
Chile 2nd edition
China 5th edition
Costa Rica 2nd edition
Eastern Europe 2005
Ecuador 1st edition **NEW TITLE**
Egypt 2nd edition
Europe 2005
France 2005
Germany 12th edition
Greece 2005
Hawaii 3rd edition
India & Nepal 8th edition
Ireland 2005
Israel 4th edition
Italy 2005
Japan 1st edition
Mexico 20th edition
Middle East 4th edition
Peru 1st edition **NEW TITLE**
Puerto Rico 1st edition
South Africa 5th edition
Southeast Asia 9th edition
Spain & Portugal 2005
Thailand 2nd edition
Turkey 5th edition
USA 2005
Vietnam 1st edition **NEW TITLE**
Western Europe 2005

ROADTRIP GUIDE

Roadtripping USA **NEW TITLE**

ADVENTURE GUIDES

Alaska 1st edition
New Zealand **NEW TITLE**
Pacific Northwest **NEW TITLE**
Southwest USA 3rd edition

CITY GUIDES

Amsterdam 3rd edition
Barcelona 3rd edition
Boston 4th edition
London 2005
New York City 15th edition
Paris 13th edition
Rome 12th edition
San Francisco 4th edition
Washington, D.C. 13th edition

POCKET CITY GUIDES

Amsterdam
Berlin
Boston
Chicago
London
New York City
Paris
San Francisco
Venice
Washington, D.C.

HOW TO USE THIS BOOK

ORGANIZATION. *Let's Go: Chile* is united by a single principle: traveler utility. Our coverage begins in Santiago, the point of entry for most overseas travelers. From there, coverage is laid out north to south from Arica, the jumping-off point for travelers from Peru, to Puerto Williams, the southernmost settlement on earth. Coverage progresses from large city to large city, each followed by smaller sights and towns in the area. The book closes with a new chapter on Easter Island.

TRANSPORTATION. In planning itineraries, travelers should first consult the city from which they will be departing in order to find out potential destinations. Also consult the Transportation section of the nearest regional capital. For a list of regions and capitals, see the **Regions of Chile** map in the **Discover** chapter of the book. In general, information in parentheses in Transportation sections appears in the format (trip duration, times of departure, price).

COVERING THE BASICS. The first three chapters of this guide provide readers all the information they will need to know before arriving in Chile (or can refer them to the proper source for such information). The **Essentials** chapter has helpful tips on issues such as safety, health, money, packing, and other travel concerns for before and during your trip. **Life and Times** is designed to help travelers familiarize themselves with Chilean culture. **Alternatives to Tourism** is for those wishing to get further involved through work and volunteering opportunities in Chile.

FEATURES AND SCHOLARLY ARTICLES. Along with safety, utility, and accuracy, *Let's Go* places high emphasis on ensuring travelers as authentic and exciting a travel experience as possible. As such, we have included several small articles, written by researchers on the road, or by experts on various aspects of Chilean culture. Smaller features are found throughout the book in black sidebars. Four longer articles also appear. See the "Scholarly Articles" listing in our index to locate them. In addition, *Let's Go: Chile* has added useful travel tips into the text, brought straight to you from our researchers out in the field.

PRICE DIVERSITY. Researchers for *Let's Go* list establishments in order of value from best to worst, with standouts receiving the *Let's Go* thumbs-up (🔼). In addition, the series has instituted a series of price ranges to help give visitors a feel for the price they can expect to spend at an accommodation or restaurant. For a full list of ranges, see p. xii. Price ranges are slightly different on Easter Island. See **Easter Island Essentials** (p. 486) for these ranges.

LANGUAGE. Occasionally, readers will encounter italicized words. The italicization reflects that these words are taken from another language (usually Spanish, with some references to Mapudungun, the Mapuche tongue, and Rapa Nui, the native language on Easter Island). If a translation is not provided immediately following the word or phrase, the phrase should appear in the **Life and Times** chapter of this guide, or in the **Spanish Quick Reference**, located in the **Appendix**.

A NOTE TO OUR READERS. The information for this book was gathered by *Let's Go* researchers from January through August of 2004. Each listing is based on one researcher's opinion, formed during his or her visit at a particular time. Those traveling at other times may have different experiences since prices, dates, hours, and conditions are always subject to change. You are urged to check the facts presented in this book beforehand to avoid inconvenience and surprises.

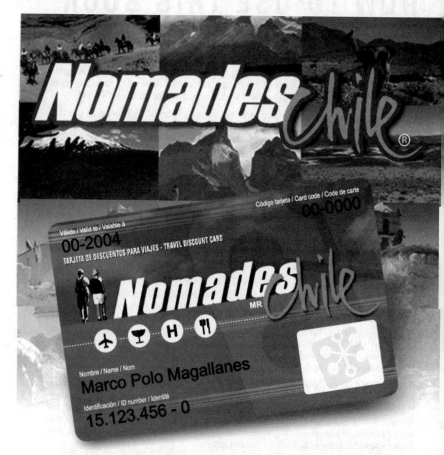

CONTENTS

Chile: Chapters

PERU

BOLIVIA

Lago Titicaca

Tacna
Arica

Uyuni

Iquique

Norte Grande
pp. 135-194

San Pedro
de Atacama

Antofagasta

Easter Island
pp. 481-498

Easter Island
Hanga Roa

PACIFIC OCEAN

Copiapó

Norte Chico
pp. 195-240

La Serena

CHILE

Viña del Mar
Valparaíso
Santiago

Mendoza

Santiago
pp. 93-134

Rancagua

Curicó
Talca

Middle Chile
pp. 241-322

ARGENTINA

Concepción

Temuco

Valdivia

La Araucanía
and Los Lagos
pp. 323-393

Puerto Montt

San Carlos
de Bariloche

Castro

Chiloé
pp. 394-420

Aisén and the
Carretera Austral
pp. 421-439

PACIFIC
OCEAN

Coyhaique

ATLANTIC
OCEAN

El Chaltén

Magallanes and
Tierra del Fuego
pp. 440-480

El Calafate

Puerto
Natales

Estrecho de
Magallanes

Punta
Arenas

Isla Grande de
Tierra del Fuego

Ushuaia

Cabo de
Hornos

0   200 miles
0   200 kilometers

RESEARCHER-WRITERS

Ben Cowan   *Los Lagos and Chiloé*

This California boy has found his nirvana wandering far from home. A noted world traveler, Ben explored Europe for a year after editing *Let's Go: Central America* in 2002—which he took on after years of travel through Nicaragua, Costa Rica, and Honduras. His veteran skills came to bear on his insightful and exhaustive research. A former leader of adventure trips, Ben long ago acquired a love of good food and tough hikes, and gives the scoop on both.

Melissa Cronin   *Santiago, Easter Island, and the Route to Mendoza*

Melissa didn't let her status as a *Let's Go* newbie hold her back, taking on an ambitious journey over the Andes, across the Pacific Ocean, and into the heart of Santiago's most vibrant *barrios*. A writing talent *par excellence*, Melissa attacked her tour with verve and resolve, sending home gushing reviews of tangerine-and-iris sunsets over Easter Island and jagged, scarred peaks on the route to Mendoza. Her wit will charm readers and inspire them to explore.

Mark Warner Kirby   *Aisén and Tierra del Fuego*

An adventure hound who cut his teeth on *Let's Go: New Zealand*, *Southwest USA*, and *Alaska*, Mark found peace in the stark, open territory of Patagonia. His years of mountain-climbing and guiding wilderness trips gave Mark the know-how to attack every route and give *Let's Go* readers the the straight story. To catch more of Mark's mastery, pick up the latest issue of *National Geographic Adventure*, where he's now an Assistant Editor.

Danny Koski-Karell   *Middle Chile, La Araucanía, and Los Lagos*

With an iron will hardened by elite-level crew racing and ropeless mountain climbing, DKK pushed through a knee injury to give readers an unsparing account of the most rugged national parks in Chile's classic adventure zone—including some we had never even heard of. After *Let's Go: Germany* and *Vietnam*, he was ready for a more visceral challenge, and his love of Chile's grand landscapes is impossible to miss in his coverage. Danny, we love you too.

Luis Rego   *Valparaíso, Viña del Mar, and surroundings*

Luis's experience in beautiful Valparaíso changed him, giving him a chance to learn Spanish with only a knowledge of Portuguese. When he wasn't dodging stray dogs, he was churning out copy reminiscent of his tours of duty with *Let's Go: Brazil* and *Spain & Portugal*. We'll never forget this faithful low-season RW. As we've learned from his hilarious copybatches, Luis is a really lighthearted individual, a researcher leaving us in stitches.

Fred G. Sykes, Jr.   *Norte Grande and Norte Chico*

A regular James Bond, Freddy was excited to research because of the opportunity to "do spy work" on Chilean hotels and "fight evil" on secret island hideaways. An agent with an amazing ability to find undocumented deals and tasty lunch specials, Mr. Sykes managed to evade the giggling schoolgirls tracking him through northern Chile. We're proud of him for breaking hearts along with records for copy turned in—thanks for writing half the book, Freddy!

CONTRIBUTING WRITERS

Victor Tan Chen   *Researcher-Writer*, Let's Go: Chile 2003

Alex Leary   *Researcher-Writer*, Let's Go: Chile 2003

Tom Mercer   *Researcher-Writer*, Let's Go: Chile 2003

Sarah Kenney was the editor of *Let's Go: Barcelona 2002*.

Brian Milder was a Researcher-Writer for *Let's Go: New Zealand 2000*. He spent a year in Chile as a Rockefeller Fellow living in La Victoria and volunteering at the Non-profit Enterprise and Self-sustainability Team (NESsT).

Manuela Zoninsein is the editor of *Let's Go: Central America*. She majors in Social Studies at Harvard University. She spent six months living in Santiago while attending the Universidad de Chile and the Pontificia Universidad Católica.

Amity Wilczek was a graduate student in evolutionary biology at Harvard University.

ACKNOWLEDGMENTS

TEAM CHILE THANKS: Our incredible RWs, who always amazed and surprised us; August, Lindsay, and Ashley for making us laugh; Emma and Teresa for answering our questions and putting up with our antics; Kirkie, Elizabeth, Jeremy, Christina, Clay, Adam, Vicki, Matt, Anne, and Jenn for providing experience and resources; our proofers and our typist, Emily; and Lauren, our Let's Go "Big Mama," who guided us with a firm hand, a warm heart, and the occasional sarcastic edit. We love you, LT.

DAN THANKS: The SAM pod; the ME staff; E/T; Teresa for helping without making me cry once; Tali for putting up with everything I threw at her—and throwing it right back at me, perfectly; Melissa and Freddy for giving me an incredible summer, and for being my loving Let's Go son and daughter, sort of; my family and friends; LT, for taking a chance on me and helping me succeed; 🗺 Luke, my co-editor and my friend, without whom I could not have done this; and Chile, for challenging and inspiring me.

LUKE THANKS: Dan for his talent, friendship, and leadership; LT for her excellence; Teresa for her guidance; August for his perspective and the SAM pod for the good times; Jeremy for setting the tone; Freddy and Melissa for making work a joy; Tali for her patience; my parents, brother, and grandma for their care and encouragement; Tony, Steve Reifenberg, Aníbal, Marcela, and my friends in Chile, for helping me find this path; and my wife, Kristi, for her unending love, support, and wisdom.

TALI THANKS: Dan and Luke for loving these maps as much as I do, keeping me on my toes, and bribing me with jellybeans; LT, for making sure I'm feeling okay each week; my family, who supported me in every way possible; and my friends, who through their own insanity, ensured that I remained sane this summer (at least, by comparison).

Editor
Daniel Spitzer
Associate Editor
Lucas Tate
Managing Editor
Lauren Truesdell
Map Editor
Tali Mazor
Typesetter
Adam R. Perlman

Publishing Director
Emma Nothmann
Editor-in-Chief
Teresa Elsey
Production Manager
Adam R. Perlman
Cartography Manager
Elizabeth Halbert Peterson
Design Manager
Amelia Aos Showalter
Editorial Managers
Briana Cummings, Charlotte Douglas, Ella M. Steim, Joel August Steinhaus, Lauren Truesdell, Christina Zaroulis
Financial Manager
R. Kirkie Maswoswe
Marketing and Publicity Managers
Stef Levner, Leigh Pascavage
Personnel Manager
Jeremy Todd
Low-Season Manager
Clay H. Kaminsky
Production Associate
Victoria Esquivel-Korsiak
IT Director
Matthew DePetro
Web Manager
Rob Dubbin
Associate Web Manager
Patrick Swieskowski
Web Content Manager
Tor Krever
Research and Development Consultant
Jennifer O'Brien
Office Coordinators
Stephanie Brown, Elizabeth Peterson

Director of Advertising Sales
Elizabeth S. Sabin
Senior Advertising Associates
Jesse R. Loffler, Francisco A. Robles, Zoe M. Savitsky
Advertising Graphic Designer
Christa Lee-Chuvala

President
Ryan M. Geraghty
General Manager
Robert B. Rombauer
Assistant General Manager
Anne E. Chisholm

PRICE RANGES >> CHILE

Our researchers list establishments in order of value from best to worst; our favorites are denoted by the Let's Go thumbs-up (🖑). Since the best value is not always the cheapest price, however, we have also incorporated a system of price ranges, based on a rough expectation of what you'll spend. For **accommodations,** we base our range on the cheapest price for which a single traveler can stay for one night. For **restaurants** and other dining establishments, we estimate the average amount a traveler will spend. The table tells you what you'll *typically* find in Chile at the corresponding price range; keep in mind that no system can allow for every individual establishment's quirks.

ACCOMMODATIONS	RANGE	WHAT YOU'RE *LIKELY* TO FIND
❶	under US$6 under CH$4000	Camping; most dorm rooms, such as HI or other hostels. Expect bunk beds and a communal bath. Hot water is not a guarantee. No credit cards accepted.
❷	US$6-12 CH$4000-7600	Upper-end hostels or small hotels. You may have a private bathroom, or a sink in your room and communal shower in the hall. Breakfast may be included.
❸	US$12-24 CH$7600-15,000	A small room with a private bath. May have decent amenities, such as phone and TV. Breakfast often included in the price. Credit cards may be accepted.
❹	US$24-36 CH$15,000-23,000	Similar to ❸, but with more amenities or in a more touristed area. Phones, hot water, cable TV, and breakfast included.
❺	over US$35 over CH$23,000	Large *cabañas*, hotels, and upscale chains. Will almost definitely include private bathroom with hot water, maid service, cable TV, phones. Most major credit cards accepted.

FOOD	RANGE	WHAT YOU'RE *LIKELY* TO FIND
❶	under US$3 under CH$2000	Mostly street-corner food and juice stands and fast-food joints; more specifically, *empanada* or chicken-and-fries restaurants.
❷	US$3-5.50 CH$2000-3500	Small restaurants with limited or outside seating. Meals may include beef, *churrasco*, chicken, fish, or *lomo* with a small side of rice or salad. Credit cards rarely accepted.
❸	US$5.50-8 CH$3500-5000	Mid-priced entrees, seafood, and pasta dishes. Tip will bump the price up a bit, since you will have a waiter. Many of the same food options as lower-priced options, but in a more sit-down atmosphere. Credit card acceptance is unpredictable.
❹	US$8-11 CH$5000-7000	A somewhat fancier restaurant, with more ambience than ❸, but less expensive dining options, and a less extensive wine list than ❺. Credit cards likely to be accepted.
❺	over US$11 over CH$7000	Often will have a unique design or ambience. Expect dishes with foreign names and a decent wine list. Waiters should be tipped at least 10%. Credit cards almost always accepted.

DISCOVER CHILE

Chile is quite possibly Latin America's best kept secret. While at its widest point, Chile spans only 365km, its 6435km of coastline traverse a number of geographically diverse regions, providing the country with a unique diversity of climates, terrain, and wildlife. In the far north, near the highest volcano in the world, flamingo-filled lakes surround the driest place on earth. In the south, enormous glaciers flow down into national parks, which protect trees thousands of years old. Between all that, world-renowned vineyards share Chile's rolling valleys with rheas, *guanacos*, and *pudús*. And halfway across the Pacific Ocean, ancient stone giants on Easter Island beg travelers to come and explore one of the most isolated and intriguing isles on Earth.

Yet Chile offers more than incredible natural attractions. Its culture and history are a fusion of Spanish, English, and German influences. This unmistakably European feel is augmented by Chile's indigenous roots, which add a unique flavor to the cultural mix. The diversity of terrain and climate are echoed in this diverse culture. The desert landscape of the north is inhabited by a laid-back population, while the rolling, fertile hills of the Central Valley host a frantic, high-energy urban lifestyle. And farther south, the rugged, untamed forests and mountains are home to a cultural heritage that mixes the fierce independence of the Mapuche and the resilience of rural farmers. Wherever you go, however, a distinctly Chilean way of life is perceptible—characterized by a rapid, rhythmic incarnation of Spanish, and, even more importantly, a strong sense of national identity.

Even from its isolated perch between the Andes mountain range and the Pacific Ocean, Chile has managed to distinguish itself among its sibling nations. It is a country with a long democratic tradition, still struggling to deal with a brutal interlude of authoritarian rule. Yet it has managed to return to steady democracy despite the serious political and social challenges it faces. In fact, over the last few decades, Chile has gained a level of economic stability and development that well surpasses its neighbors to the north and east.

On the verge of taking its place among the leading countries of the world with modern social programs and stronger economic and political ties to both Europe and Asia, Chile offers many of the conveniences and reliability of a developed nation while maintaining the amazing sights and fascinating culture that make Latin America an increasingly popular tourist destination.

CHILE: AT A GLANCE

OFFICIAL NAME: República de Chile	**DIVISIONS:** 13 regions (I-XII, plus the Región Metropolitana; see map, p. 7)
CAPITAL: Santiago	
POPULATION: 15,800,000	**RELIGIONS:** Roman Catholic 82%, Protestant 10%, Secular 7%, Other 1%
AREA: 756,950 sq. km (99,069 sq. mi.)	
TERRITORIES: Isla de Pascua (Easter Island), Archipiélago Juan Fernández	**CURRENCY:** Chilean Peso (CH$)
	AVERAGE AMOUNT OF WINE CONSUMED PER YEAR: 20L per person

1

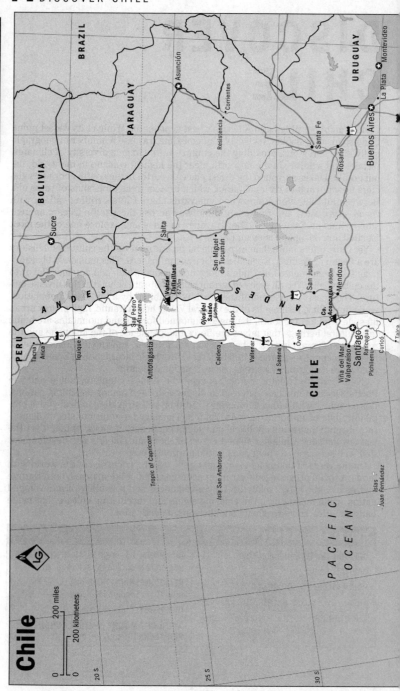

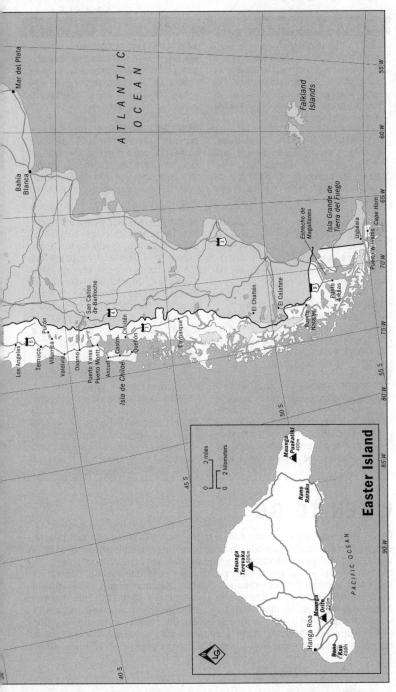

ATLANTIC
OCEAN

Mar del Plata

Bahía
Blanca

Falkland
Islands

Los Angeles
Temuco
Villarrica
Pucón
Valdivia
Osorno
Puerto Varas
Puerto Montt
Ancud
Castro
Chaltén
Quellón
Isla de Chiloé

San Carlos
de Bariloche

Coyhaique

El Chaltén

El Calafate

Puerto
Natales

Punta
Arenas

Estrecho de
Magallanes

Isla Grande de
Tierra del Fuego

Ushuaia

Puerto Williams Cape Horn

55 W
60 W
65 W
70 W
75 W
80 W

40 S
45 S
50 S
55 S

Easter Island

PACIFIC OCEAN

0   2 miles
0   2 kilometers

Maunga
Puakatiki
400m

Rano
Raraku

Maunga
Terevaka
506m

Maunga
Orito
220m

Hanga Roa

Rano
Kau
410m

85 W
90 W

DISCOVER

BEST CABIN HIDEAWAY: Those who can't resist gorgeous sunsets should rent a *cabaña* in the small town of **Ensenada** on the tranquil **Lago Llanquihue**. Sit back, relax, and enjoy as the slopes of **Volcán Osorno** reflect the bright orange of the sun across the lake.

BEST PLACE TO SEE PLUTO: Mamalluca, an observatory outside **La Serena**, was built especially for non-scientists. Wonder at the beauty of the night sky, or make a wish on a shooting star as you watch it fly by.

BEST PLACE TO EAT IN CHILE: While Chile is certainly not known for the complexity or delectability of its cuisine, nearby **Mendoza, Argentina** serves visitors choice cuts of beef, prepared with that old, secret, Argentine recipe: flavor.

BEST PLACE TO SEE CHINCHILLAS: Appropriately, Chile's **Parque Nacional Chinchilla** protects the last remaining wild colonies of—sure enough, chinchillas. You'll go crazy over the cute, little critters, and they'll go crazy over you.

BEST WINE TOUR: As the world's fifth-largest wine producer, Chile is home to gorgeous, fertile valleys, perfect for cultivating flavorful grapes. Check out one of the myriad tours—or all, depending on your tolerance—especially the tour of **Viña Concha y Toro**, Chile's largest vineyard.

BEST FLOWERING DESERT: Although it's the driest desert in the world, the **Atacama Desert** never ceases to surprise visitors. Once every 5 years or so a surge of rain brings out its hidden floral beauty, especially around **Vallenar**.

BEST URBAN OASIS: Visit the **Parque Japonés Kokoro No Niwa** in downtown **La Serena**. You'll marvel at the singularity of this clean and gorgeous Japanese-style park, sheltered from the hustle and bustle of everyday metropolitan business.

BEST PLACE TO DANCE WITH A CHAP IN A TUX: Those who can't get enough of Chile's crazy mix of wildlife, or visitors with an odd penchant for penguins, should check out the tour of **Islas Chañaral, Choros,** and **Damas** in **Reserva Nacional Pingüino de Humboldt**. The little black-and-white birds dot the islands, making you question whether you are at a national park, or a fancy ball where upscale gents bring their ladies for a special dance: the Humboldt Waddle.

BEST WAY TO HAVE AN EXISTENTIAL MOMENT: Take a bus ride across the **Andes Mountains**, on your way to many different destinations in both Chile and neighboring Argentina. The trip itself, with gorgeous views of looming snow-tipped peaks, is enough to make you appreciate their mighty majesty.

WHEN TO GO

Chile's different climatic zones ensure that a variety of weather conditions prevail year-round, making a wide array of activities available at any time of the year. Chile is divided into three significant climatic areas: the arid north; the cool and damp south; and the temperate, almost Mediterranean, Central Valley, which experiences heavy rainfall between May and August and bright sunshine the rest of the year. The spring and summer seasons in Chile (between October and March, as in all countries of the Southern Hemisphere) tend to see the most tourist traffic, as foreigners and Chileans from far and wide flock to the white-sand beaches of the glamorous Viña del Mar and other coastal resorts. Santiago is warm and sunny this time of year (25°C/77°F Dec.-Mar.), trekking is pleasant in Los Lagos (13°C/55°F Oct.-Apr.), and the erratic weather of Patagonia simmers down to warmer days (daytime highs 15°C/59°F Oct.-Mar.). The peak tourist season that ushers in fully-booked hotels, packed *discotecas*, and exorbitant prices is between the end of December and the beginning of February, when locals are on summer vacation.

The Chilean winter, however, is not an altogether unpleasant time to travel—ski slopes among the Andes are at their best, the Atacama desert in northern Chile offers warm and sunny days on beautiful beaches, and almost all prices are discounted by 5-30%. The downside? Many smaller towns in Middle Chile and Los Lagos are practically deserted, temperatures in the Far South are frigid, and heating is not always provided in budget accommodations, leaving you shivering under thin sheets. Consider heading to Chile during "shoulder season" travel periods (Oct.-Nov. and Mar.-Apr.), when extremes of weather are less frequent, prices are moderate, and neither ghost towns nor overcrowded hostels get you down.

THINGS TO DO

Chile's natural and geographical idiosyncrasies are a godsend for its tourism industry. The diversity of climate and terrain throughout the country makes possible a wide array of exciting and gratifying adventures for the budget traveler. The healing *termas* in Chillán will soothe your trail-hardened muscles, the laid-back culture of Chiloé or Easter Island will move you to abandon your frenzied work life, and the still, mirrored surface of Lago Llanquihue will offer you a chance to see yourself in the simpler light of a reflected sunset.

TO DO	THE NORTH	MIDDLE CHILE	LOS LAGOS	CHILOÉ	THE SOUTH
Biking	Year-round		Nov.-Apr.		Nov.-Mar.
Volcano tours	Year-round		Nov.-Mar.		Nov.-Apr.
History tours	Year-round	Year-round	Year-round	Nov.-Mar.	Year-round
Archaeology	Year-round				
Lake tours			Nov.-Apr.	Nov.-Apr.	Nov.-Mar.
Mountaineering	Year-round	Nov.-Apr.	Oct.-Apr.		Nov.-Mar.
Skiing		June-Oct.	June-Oct.		
Trekking	Year-round	Nov.-Apr.	Oct.-Apr.	Dec.-Mar.	
Hot springs	Year-round	Year-round	Year-round		Nov.-Apr.
Festivities	Year-round	Year-round	Year-round	Oct.-Apr.	

EAT

While Chile's cuisine is not internationally renowned, the proliferation of cheap and fresh fruits, vegetables, and seafood at Chile's many open-air markets will keep your interest piqued and your wallet full. Fill up on the catch of the day in the open-air fresh fish market, **La Recova,** in **La Serena** (p. 214), or

TOP TEN UNREAL VISTAS

From the deserts of the north to the ice fields of the south, Chile's terrain is marked by a diversity of natural wonders unlike those in any other country. You'll stand gaping in awe as you wonder both how these marvels came to be, and how Chile is home to them all. Don't forget your camera.

1. Fields of steaming geysers at **El Tatio (p.** 179), near **San Pedro de Atacama** (p. 170).
2. Rows of mammoth, man-made *moai* at the various *ahu* on **Easter Island** (p. 481).
3. Hard-bodied surfers and majestic waves crashing on the shores of **Pichilemu** (p. 285), Chile's premier surf town.
4. Enormous chunks of ice calving off **Glaciar Perito Moreno** (p. 461) into Lago Argentino.
5. The roiling, churning Class IV rapids of the fearsome **Río Futaleufú** (p. 426).
6. The stark, granite **Torres del Paine** (p. 452), shrouded in clouds and tormented by violent winds and rain.
7. Massive groves of green *alerce* in **Parque Pumalín** (p. 426), near **Chaitén** (p. 423).
8. The smoldering crown of **Volcán Villarrica** (p. 345), South America's most active volcano.
9. The eerie, moon-lit terrain of **Valle de la Luna** (p. 181).
10. The bright, snow-covered slopes of the internationally renowned **ski resorts** (p. 123) outside **Santiago.**

head south to **Dalcahue** (p. 403) for decadently delicious oysters. Lobsters cost next to nothing and taste even better among the hustle and bustle of the chaotic *caleta* in **Coquimbo** (p. 229). Indulge in mackerel at every restaurant in **Mejillones** (p. 189), spiced up with dreamy sauces. Gorging on a hearty *paila marina* for a pittance in **Antofagasta** (p. 183) is a real treat as well. However, if you are looking for an especially hearty and satisfying banquet, head east over the peaks of the Andes to **Mendoza, Argentina** (p. 268) and dine on some of the finest cuisine in South America.

DRINK

Bold and flavorful, rich and fruity, sweet and subtle; world-famous Chilean wines will flirt with your palate and leave you begging for more. Satiate the oenophile within by going right to the source and enjoying informative tours and free tastings of wine from the cellars of the largest producer in Chile—**Concha y Toro** (p. 131). Or venture deeper into Middle Chile, the original wine country, to enjoy a truly tongue-titillating experience on **La Ruta del Vino Valle de Curicó** (p. 292). Sip in style at **Pica** (p. 161), a luscious, too-good-to-be-true desert oasis, legendary for its overpowering wines. However, if you prefer guzzling to savoring, knock back a few *pisco* sours at **Planta Capel** (p. 226), the largest *pisco* plant in Chile. And if you enjoy that, you can pay homage to the rife Chilean beverage at **Pisco Elqui** (p. 227), a town named in honor of the drink. Decided not to ply yourself with poison? Be content drinking in the beauty of a sublime sunrise at the ethereal **El Tatio Geysers** (p. 179). Chances are, however, that if you go white-water rafting on the **Futaleufú** (p. 426), the heart in your throat won't prevent you from swallowing down gallons of river water.

BE MERRY

Salsa, salsa, and more salsa is the name of the game in Chile's plentiful *discotecas* and *salsatecas*. Dance till dawn in **Iquique** (p. 152), splurge on a night on the town in **Valparaíso** (p. 243), and shake it in the hottest spots on the continent in **Barrio Bellavista** and **Suecia** in **Santiago** (p. 93). Applaud *los huasos*, Chilean cowboys, at the rough-'n'-tumble rodeo in **Rancagua** (p. 275), right in the heart of *la tierra huasa*. Cheer on the Talca

Rangers with other *fútbol* fanatics in the enormous stadium in **Talca** (p. 295), or laugh wholeheartedly at the embarrassing bray of "jackass" penguins at the **Monumento Natural Los Pingüinos** (p. 447). For a more relaxing night, kick back with a *refresco* and stare out as the sun serenely sets over **Tahai** on **Easter Island** (p. 481).

PRAY

With over 80% of the population perpetuating Chile's Catholic fervor, the atmosphere is set for exploration of the divine. Stir your spirituality by gazing upon vivid depictions of the Holy Trinity in the grand **Iglesia Catedral de Concepción** (p. 311). If you're moved to get physically closer to the heavens above, just ride the elevator to the top of the 28m (93 ft.) tall **Cruz del Tercer Milenio** in Coquimbo (p. 231)—South American Catholicism's answer to Disneyland. On a more sophisticated note, the **Iglesia Catedral de La Serena** (p. 220), famed for its colonial architecture, is definitely worth a visit. Meanwhile, Chilean Catholicism takes on a Buddhist flavor at the elaborate shrine to the Virgin Mary, the **Mirador la Virgen,** in **Vicuña** (p. 226). If you need more help than that, join the pilgrims from far and wide who crawl on hands and knees to **Andacollo** to benefit from the miraculous powers of the sacred **Virgen de Andacollo** (p. 223).

WONDER

One of Chile's most endearing features is its assortment of quaint museums harboring odd, miscellaneously mismatched collections. After checking the polished cosmopolitan exhibits at the **Museo de Bellas Artes** and **Museo de Arte Contemporáneo** (p. 121) in **Santiago,** consider the irony of the life-sized

poster of Walt Whitman in Pablo Neruda's **Valparaíso** home, **La Sebastiana** (p. 248), now one of the most popular museums in the country. For a more unusual exhibit, stop by the **Museo Bomberil Benito Riquelme** (p. 298) in **Talca** for a different sort of art—the museum is an extensive tribute to firefighters and the artwork on display has been inspired by the valiant efforts of several Chilean firemen. Taking it up a notch is the eccentric and largely eclectic **Museo de la Alta Frontera** (p. 316) in **Los Angeles,** where animals are presented alongside exquisite displays of ornate Mapuche silver jewelry. If you're bitten by the anthropological bug, mosey on over to the **Museo Regional de la Araucanía** (p. 329) in **Temuco,** where all displays are labeled with signs written in Mapudungun, the original Mapuche tongue. Finally, arrive at the archaeological capital of Chile, **San Pedro de Atacama,** where the **Museo Arqueológico Gustavo le Paige** (p. 177) features ancient mummies and an impressive exhibit detailing the history of the region.

CONQUER

Stunning natural expanses and a mind-blowing diversity of flora and fauna are standard features of Chile's world-famous *parques nacionales.* Ignore the rumblings of the still-active **Volcán Llaima** in the **Parque Nacional Conguillío** (p. 332) during your ascent, or grab a gas mask and trek to the top of the turbulent **Volcán Villarrica** in **Parque Nacional Villarrica** (p. 345). If you're looking for a more serene ascent, slide along gorgeous glaciers in the **Parque Nacional Los Glaciares** (p. 466). If you need a little help getting uphill, head out of the parks and turn to the oldest lift in Chile, the **Ascensor Concepción** in **Valparaíso** (p. 243). However, if your definition of conquering a peak entails coming downhill rather than up, head to **Valle Nevado** (p. 123), known to have some of the best skiing in Chile. If mountains aren't your cup of tea, conquer the temperamental waves at **Pichilemu** (p. 285), the mecca for persistent *surfistas.* Finally, refute the claim of a pompous British colonizer who declared that even a monkey would have trouble scampering to the top of an *araucaria,* as you scamper to the tops of Chile's "monkey puzzle" trees, conquering the quirks of Chilean flora, in **Parque Nacional Nahuelbuta** (p. 322).

BURN

Sunburn, that is. Rub shoulders with the bronzed and beautiful on the whitesand beaches of ritzy, resorty **Viña del Mar** (p. 251). But if you just don't feel that glamorous when languishing in the sun, escape to the more secluded, yet just as beautiful, nearby beach towns of **Reñaca** (p. 256), **Concón** (p. 257), **Quintero** (p. 258), and **Zapallar** (p. 258). Or head south several kilometers and sunbathe on the shores of **Algarrobo** (p. 259). The Chilean coast is never-ending, so even if you're sauntering through the *altiplano* deserts of Norte Grande, you can catch some sun at the trendy beaches of **Iquique** (p. 152). And if all of this endless frolicking in the clear blue waters still isn't enough, head to **Bahía Inglesa** (p. 205), a haven of unadulterated beach nirvana. The views, the fishing, the strolls, the kayaking, the camping, and the warm sands of the picturesque beach resort are unrivaled in all of Chile—except maybe by stunning sandy coves in the **Parque Nacional Pan de Azúcar** (p. 208), where beaches are enclosed by luscious patches of forest. Finally, for those who want to be whisked away from it all, treat yourself to a trip across the Pacific and lounge on the beautiful white sands of **Anakena** (p. 498).

SUGGESTED ITINERARIES

**FROM GRANDE TO CHICO:
THE MOUNTAINS AND SANDS OF THE NORTH**

PERU

Arica **START**

RN Lauca

BOLIVIA

RN Las Vicuñas

Iquique

RN Pampa del Tamarugal

El Tatio

San Pedro de Atacama

Antofagasta

RN Los Flamencos

PN Nevado Tres Cruces

Bahía Inglesa

Copiapó

RN Pingüino de Humboldt

La Serena

Pisco Elqui

ARGENTINA

CHILE

Santiago

FROM GRANDE TO CHICO: THE MOUNTAINS AND SANDS OF THE NORTH (4 WEEKS)

Before exposing yourself to the most extreme environs of Chile, you might as well soak up some sun in the relaxed beach town of **Arica** (p. 137). As the major international gateway from Peru and Bolivia, and an important regional transport hub, it's an easy place to start. From there, head east to **PN Lauca** (p. 147) to enjoy vast alpine fields, snow-capped mountains, and diverse wildlife. Be sure to plan a trek through neighboring **RN Las Vicuñas** (p. 150) to see the brilliant white salt plains of the **Salar de Surire.** After walking in the clouds with the reserve's *vicuñas* and *guanacos,* find another slice of heaven in **Iquique** (p. 152). Often called the Miami Beach of South America, this coastal city is an interesting contrast of 19th-century colonial port and 21st-century luxury beach resort, complete with a nightly wildlife of its own. Heading south, you'll enter the vast **Atacama Desert,** the driest place on earth, via an otherworldly forest of strange trees—**RN**

Pampa del Tamarugal (p. 160), protector of the last of the tenacious *tamarugo* trees, which manage to thrive even in the dry, saline soils at the edge of the desert. Head on to the heart of the desert, **San Pedro de Atacama** (p. 170), an oasis village that is the jumping-off point for some of the best sights of the region. From here, you can head on over to watch the steaming explosions of **El Tatio Geysers** (p. 179), catch a sunrise over the eerie landscape of **Valle de la Luna** (p. 181), and frolic with flamingos in **RN Los Flamencos** (p. 181). When you are ready to get back to civilization, catch a bus to **Antofagasta** (p. 183), the largest city in the northern region, where you'll find plenty of urban excitement. After a short break to relax on the beaches in **Bahía Inglesa** (p. 205), head on to **Copiapó** (p. 197). From Copiapó, conquer **PN Nevado Tres Cruces** (p. 201), home to some of the best hiking and climbing the Andes have to offer, including **Ojos del Salado,** the highest volcano in the world. Just don't fall in, because you will want to be on the road again to reach **La Serena** (p. 214), from where you can jump around with the penguins in nearby **RN Pingüino de Humboldt** (p. 222), before toasting yourself for finishing your journey at the *pisco* plant in **Pisco Elqui** (p. 227).

HISTORY, MYSTERY, AND BEACHES: MILLING ABOUT THE MIDDLE (3 WEEKS)

The incredible number of sights and activities packed into Middle Chile make it a must-see area, and there's no better place to start than the thriving metropolis of **Santiago** (p. 93). Enjoy the wide boulevards and bustling crowds of *el centro* or groove into the early morning hours in **Barrio Bellavista.** Escape the urban insanity to indulge in the internationally recognized wines of **Concha y Toro** (p. 131) or ski the slopes of **Valle Nevado** (p. 123). Finally, take in a piece of Chilean history at Santiago's myriad museums before hopping a flight across the Pacific to **Hanga Roa, Easter Island** (p. 488). Spend a few days traversing the island trying to solve the mystery of the *moai,* while

DISCOVER

HISTORY, MYSTERY, AND BEACHES: MILLING ABOUT THE MIDDDLE

taking some time to lounge around on the beaches of **Ovahe** and **Anakena**. Upon your return, get moving to the coastal resorts, starting with **Valparaíso** (p. 243). Spend time wandering through picturesque neighborhoods surrounding downtown and check out one of Pablo Neruda's houses, before briefly heading to **Isla Negra** (p. 260) to see even more of his eclectic collection of artifacts and curios. After getting your fill of culture, it's time to see the other side of beach life in **Viña del Mar** (p. 251). One of the hottest resort towns in South America, Viña will have you relaxing on white-sand beaches and jumping in clubs until dawn. If the high life gets to be too much, continue your beach travels in the less-touristed town of **Reñaca** (p. 256). Next, recreate the cross-country journey of García Hurtado de Mendoza, riding through the Andes to **Mendoza, ARG** (p. 268), where you can reward yourself and your stomach with some of the finest dining in South America. After all that beaching, you're bound to be hungry.

OVER THE RIVER AND THROUGH THE WOODS: THE LAKES (3 WEEKS) Get ready to roll through one of the most beautiful regions of Chile. Beginning in the urban transport hub of **Temuco** (p. 325), head south to **Villarrica** (p. 333), a good place to spend the night while daytripping to the more expensive **Pucón** (p. 338). This popular lakeside town is great not only for relaxing on black-sand beaches, but also for organizing trips into nearby **PN Villarrica** (p. 345) to climb the majestic Volcán Villarrica. When you are finished playing on the snow-capped peak, it's time to move on to the Siete Lagos. Head-

ing back toward the Pacific coast, head to the capital of Los Lagos, **Valdivia** (p. 350). Set among rolling farmlands, Valdivia is not only the rainiest place in Chile, it is also often considered the most attractive city in all Chile, with its Germanic heritage lending the city a little extra *sabor*. Next head on down to **Puerto Varas** (p. 367), on the shores of **Lago Llanquihue.** Varas is a fun place to kill a day or two while enjoying the sparkling blue waters of Llanquihue, as well as the imposing backdrop of Volcanes Osorno, Calbuco, and Puntiagudo. Then move on from the residential suburb to the larger **Puerto Montt** (p. 386). The only major city for miles, Puerto Montt is the meeting point of the Panamerican Highway out of Los Lagos, the Carretera Austral out of Aisén, and the ferry from the Island of Chiloé. Before finishing up your tour, rent a cabin for a few days on the shores of the lake in the small mountain hideaway of **Ensenada** (p. 372), before tackling the *alerce* groves of **PN Alerce Andino** (p. 393), which protects several-millennia-old *alerce* trees. Finally, catch a bus from Puerto Montt over the border to **Bariloche, ARG** (p. 377), from where you can

OVER THE RIVER AND THROUGH THE WOODS: THE LAKES

experience some of South America's finest skiing before heading home, or continue on to Patagonia.

ICE AND FIRE: TACKLING TIERRA DEL FUEGO (3 WEEKS)

Looking for some rugged adventure and don't mind a little cold and wind? Head to Tierra del Fuego. Start off in **Punta Arenas** (p. 442), a sheep-herding town that has managed to

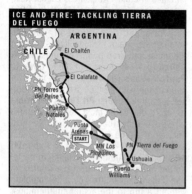

ICE AND FIRE: TACKLING TIERRA DEL FUEGO

survive and grow while keeping its quiet origins. From here you can head over to **MN Los Pingüinos** (p. 447) and waddle around with some of the playful, tuxedoed birds. When you're ready to get down to business, head north to **Puerto Natales** (p. 448), a quiet city that serves as a jumping-off point for some of the most incredible parks in South America. At the top of that list is **PN Torres del Paine** (p. 452). Vast forests, alpine fields, rocky ravines, and blue-green lakes surround the impossibly steep and smooth torres that give the park its name. While you could easily spend weeks wandering this incredible park, keep pushing on—your next stop is **El Calafate, ARG** (p. 456). This tiny town in Argentine Patagonia sits at the base of some of the largest glaciers in the world. Walk within a few feet of the towering **Glaciar Perito Moreno** (p. 461) or take a boat up to an estancia perched over the vast **Glaciar Upsala** (p. 462). If you're looking for terrain more suited to hiking, continue north to **El Chaltén, ARG** (p. 462), where you can climb the well-known Mt. Fitz Roy; but don't be in too

much of a rush to leave Chile's more flamboyant neighbor. First trek on down to the touristy **Ushuaia, ARG** (p. 470). The "Land of Fire" isn't quite the burning place you thought it would be—**PN Tierra del Fuego** (p. 476) is actually the best place from which to arrange trips to Antarctica. Before wrapping up this short jaunt, be sure to visit **Puerto Williams** (p. 478) on **Isla Navarino**, allowing you to finish up your trip at the southernmost human settlement in the world.

THE BEST OF CHILE (1 MONTH)

So you want big cities, rugged wilderness, burning deserts, towering glaciers, and gorgeous beaches? Sounds like you want all of Chile—or, at least as much as you can cram into a month of travels. Your first stop (and likely entry point) is the bustling metropolis of **Santiago** (p. 93). Gape at the soaring skyscrapers of Santiago Centro and get your groove on in the hip Barrio Bellavista. Then jump to the far north, landing in **Arica** (p. 137), gateway to Peru and Bolivia, as well as to some of the north's most fascinating sights, including **PN Lauca** (p. 147), home to llamas, alpacas, vicuñas, and guanacos, as well as the blindingly white salt plains of the **Salar de Surire.** From alpine plains and snow-capped mountains to the barren desert, **San Pedro de Atacama** (p. 170) is your next stop. Try catching the sunset at **Valle de la Luna** (p. 181) and the sunrise over **El Tatio Geysers** (p. 179). When you're ready to head back to civilization, continue to **Antofagasta** (p. 183), the region's largest city. This is a great place to rest up before attacking the highest volcano in the world, **Ojos del Salado,** in **PN Nevado Tres Cruces** (p. 201). Back on the Pacific coast, **Valparaíso** (p. 243) is a great place to take in a little culture and see Pablo Neruda's old haunts. Or swing over to Valpo's sister city, **Viña del Mar** (p. 251), one of the hottest, wildest beach resorts in South America. If you haven't had enough of beaches and waves, head on to Chile's premier surf town, **Pichilemu** (p. 285), a growing mecca for surfers and young travelers alike. However, if sand isn't your favorite thing, head on to **Curicó** (p. 289), from where you can feel free to hop around on the **Ruta del Vino Valle de**

THE BEST OF CHILE

PERU
Arica
PN Lauca
BOLIVIA

San Pedro
de Atacama
Antofagasta

PN Nevado
Tres Cruces

CHILE

Viña del Mar
Valparaiso
Pichilemu
Curicó

Santiago
START

ARGENTINA

Pucón

Puerto Varas
Puerto Montt
Castro

PN Torres
del Paine

Punta
Arenas
Ushuaia

Puerto
Williams

Curicó (p. 292) and sample some of Chile's finest. Don't drink too much, because soon, it's off to beautiful **Pucón** (p. 338), near the shores of **Lago Villarrica.** From here, you can take a tour out to the imposing **Volcán Villarrica,** or enjoy the increasingly popular town, before heading on to **Puerto Varas** (p. 367). With a laid-back atmosphere and incredible views of the Andes, beautiful Puerto Varas is slowly becoming one of the more popular cities in Chile's Región Los Lagos. Next, catch a ferry from **Puerto Montt** (p. 386) to **Castro** (p. 406) on the isle of Chiloé. Be sure to spend time wandering through some of the quaint fishing villages that dot the coast and drop by the picturesque **PN Chiloé** (p. 414). After that, head down to **Punta Arenas** (p. 442), where you can spend time with penguins and prep yourself for a trek through **PN Torres del Paine** (p. 452), one of the most well-known parks in South America. When you've had enough of alpine fields, blue-green lakes, and craggy peaks, move on to **Ushuaia, ARG** (p. 470). Although it claims to be "*el fin del mundo*" (the end of the world), no pan-Chilean adventure would be complete without a trip to the actual southernmost human settlement in the world, **Puerto Williams** (p. 478), on Isla Navarino. Finally, head on back to Santiago, and kick back with a *pisco* sour. You've earned it.

ESSENTIALS

PLANNING YOUR TRIP

BEFORE YOU GO

Passport (p. 14). Required for all visitors, except for citizens of Argentina, Brazil, Paraguay, or Uruguay, who may simply use their national identity cards.

Visa (p. 15). Visas not required for citizens of Australia, Canada, New Zealand, the United Kingdom, or the United States for stays under 90 days. Citizens of Ireland must contact the Chilean consulate for a visa application. Travelers also need to pay a tax upon arrival.

Work Permit (p. 15). Required for all foreigners planning to work in Chile.

Required Vaccinations (p. 25). No inoculations are required to enter Chile.

Recommended Vaccinations (p. 25). The following vaccinations are recommended for travelers going to Chile: Hepatitis A, Hepatitis B (for all infants and children who have not completed the series), and typhoid.

Other Health: Malaria pills are recommended for those traveling to malaria risk areas (p. 25). If your regular **medical insurance policy** (p. 25) does not cover travel abroad, you may wish to purchase additional coverage.

EMBASSIES AND CONSULATES

CHILEAN CONSULAR SERVICES ABROAD

Australia: 390 St. Kilda Rd., Level 13, **Melbourne** VIC 3004 (☎61 03 9866 4041; fax 61 03 9866 7977; www.chile.com.au). Open M-F 9am-2pm.

Canada: 50 O'Connor Street, Ste. 1413, **Ottawa,** ON K1P 6L2 (☎1 613-235-4402; fax 235-1176; www.chile.ca). **Consulate:** 2 Bloor St. W, Ste. 1801, **Toronto,** ON M4W 3E2 (☎416-924-0106; fax 924-2627; www.congechiletoronto.com). Consular services also available in **Montreal, Vancouver,** and **Winnipeg.** All offices open M-F 9am-5pm.

Ireland: 44 Welington Rd., Ballsbridge, Dublin 4 (☎353 1 667 5094; embachileirlanda@eircom.net). Open M-F 9am-5pm.

New Zealand: 19 Bolton St., **Wellington** (☎64 471 62 70; fax 473 53 24; www.embchile.co.nz). Consular services available in **Auckland, Christchurch,** and **Wellington.** Open M-Th 9am-5pm, F 9am-2pm.

UK: 12 Devonshire St., **London** W1G 7DS (☎44 20 7580 6392; fax 7436 5204; www.echileuk.demon.co.uk). **Consulate** (☎7580 1023). Embassy open M-F 9:30am-5:30pm. Consulate open M-F 9:30am-1pm.

US: Massachusetts Ave. NW, Washington D.C. 20036 (☎1-202-785-1746; fax 887-5579; www.embassyofchile.org); **Consulate:** 866 United Nations Plaza, Ste. 601, 1st Ave. and 48th St., New York, NY 10017 (☎212-980-3366; fax 888-5288; www.chileny.com). Consular services also available in **Chicago, Houston, Los Angeles, Miami, Philadelphia, San Francisco,** and **San Juan, Puerto Rico.** Open M-F 9am-1pm.

13

CONSULAR SERVICES IN CHILE

Australia: Isidora Goyenechea 3621, 12th and 13th fl., Las Condes, Santiago (☎56 2 550 3500; fax 331 5960; www.chile.embassy.gov.au). Open M-F 9am-12:30pm and 1:30-5pm.

Canada: Nueva Tajamar 481, 12th fl., Torre Norte, Edificio World Trade Center, Providencia, Santiago (☎56 2 362 9660; fax 56 2 362 9663; www.dfait-maeci.gc.ca/chile). Open M-F 9-11am and 2-4pm.

Ireland: Isidora Goyenechea 3162, 8th fl., Las Condes, Santiago (☎56 2 246 6616; fax 245 6636; aylwin@netline.cl).

New Zealand: El Golf 99, Of. 703 (Casilla 112), Las Condes, Santiago (☎56 2 290, 9800; fax 56 2 458 0949; embajada@nzembassy.cl). Open M-Th 9am-1pm and 2-5pm; F 9am-1:30pm.

UK: El Bosque Norte 0125, Santiago (☎56 2 370 4100; fax 335 5988; www.britemb.cl). Open M-Th 9am-5:30pm, F 9am-1pm.

US: Andrés Bello 2800, Las Condes, Santiago (☎56 2 232 2600; fax 330 3710; www.usembassy.cl). Open M-F 8:30-11:30am.

TOURIST OFFICES

With representative offices in almost all cities and smaller towns across Chile, the National Tourism Board, **Sernatur,** is a helpful resource for travelers. The head office, located in Santiago (p. 102), offers an additional facility specializing in adventure tourism and ecotourism. For further information, check out local branches of **LanChile,** located throughout Chile, as well as in **Australia, Canada, New Zealand,** the **UK,** and the **US.** Visit www.lan.com to find the branch closest to you. Once in Chile, for information on national parks, camping, and environmental concerns, check out the local office of the **Corporación Nacional Forestal** (Conaf, p. 50).

DOCUMENTS AND FORMALITIES

PASSPORTS

REQUIREMENTS

Citizens of Australia, Canada, Ireland, New Zealand, the UK, and the US need valid passports to enter Chile and to re-enter their home countries. In order to exit Chile, children under the age of 18 traveling alone in Chile will require a document, to be notarized by a domestic Chilean consular office, to certify that they have parental permission to travel in Chile. Chile does not allow entrance if the holder's passport expires in less than six months; returning home with an expired passport is illegal, and may result in a fine. Citizens living abroad who need a passport or renewal should contact the nearest passport office of their home country.

NEW PASSPORTS

Citizens of Australia, Canada, Ireland, New Zealand, the UK, and the US can apply for a passport at any passport office and many post offices and courts of law. Any new passport or renewal applications must be filed well in advance of the departure date, though most passport offices offer rush services for a very steep fee.

PASSPORT MAINTENANCE

Photocopy the page of your passport with your photo, as well as your visas, traveler's check serial numbers, and any other important documents. Carry one set of copies in a safe place, apart from the originals, and leave another set at home. Consulates also recommend that you carry an expired passport or an official copy of your birth certificate in a part of your baggage separate from other documents.

If you lose your passport, immediately notify the local police and the nearest embassy or consulate of your home government. To expedite its replacement, you will need to know all information previously recorded and show ID and proof of citizenship. In some cases, a replacement may take weeks to process, and it may be valid only for a limited time. Any visas stamped in your old passport will be irretrievably lost. In an emergency, ask for immediate temporary traveling papers that will permit you to re-enter your home country.

VISAS, INVITATIONS, AND WORK PERMITS

VISAS
Citizens of Ireland need a visa in addition to a valid passport for entrance to Chile; citizens of Australia, Canada, New Zealand, the UK, the US, and most Western European countries do not need visas. Foreigners traveling without a visa for pleasure or on business trips are allowed to enter Chile for a period of 90 days. Additionally, a fee, known as a reciprocity tax, must be paid in cash by travelers at the immigration booth upon entrance to Chile, at which point a tourist card will be issued. The fee is US$34 for Australian citizens, US$55 for Canadian citizens, and US$100 for citizens of the United States. This administrative fee is paid only once and is valid until the expiration of the passport.

Double-check entrance requirements at the nearest embassy or consulate of Chile (**Embassies and Consulates Abroad**, p. 13) for up-to-date info before departure. US citizens should also consult the US State Department website at http://travel.state.gov/foreignentryreqs.html.

WORK PERMITS
Admission as a visitor does not include the right to work, which is authorized only by a work permit. Entering Chile to study requires a special visa. For more information, see **Alternatives to Tourism** (p. 81).

IDENTIFICATION
When you travel, always carry at least two forms of identification on your person, including a photo ID; a passport and a driver's license or birth certificate is usually adequate. Never carry all of your IDs together; split them up in case of theft or loss, and keep photocopies of all of them in your luggage and at home.

STUDENT, TEACHER, AND YOUTH IDENTIFICATION
The **International Student Identity Card (ISIC),** the most widely accepted form of student ID, provides discounts on some sights, accommodations, food, and transport; access to a 24hr. emergency helpline (North America ☎877-370-ISIC; elsewhere US collect 1 715-345-0505); and insurance benefits for US cardholders (**Insurance**, p. 25). Sample discounts in Chile range from 15% off bus tickets with **Buses Tas Choapa** to a free Whopper Jr. at **Burger King;** on Easter Island, **Museo Sebastián Englert** offers 50% off adult tickets. For further info on discounts, check out www.istcnet.org/DiscountDatabase. Applicants must be full-time secondary or post-secondary school students at least 12 years of age. Because of the proliferation of fake ISICs, some services (particularly airlines) require more proof of student identity.

The **International Teacher Identity Card (ITIC)** offers teachers the same insurance coverage as the ISIC and similar but limited discounts. For travelers who are 25 years old or under but are not students, the **International Youth Travel Card (IYTC)** also offers many of the same benefits as the ISIC.

ESSENTIALS

Each of these identity cards costs US$22 or equivalent. ISIC and ITIC cards are valid through the academic year in which they are issued; IYTC cards are valid for one year from the date of issue. Many **student travel agencies** (p. 31) issue the cards; for a list of issuing agencies or more information, see the **International Student Travel Confederation (ISTC)** website (www.istc.org).

CUSTOMS

Upon entering Chile, you must declare certain items from abroad and pay a duty if their value exceed US$500. The importation of flowers, fruits, vegetables, and meat products is prohibited. Travelers may bring up to 400 cigarettes, 500g of tobacco, 50 cigars, and up to 2.5 liters of alcohol. Do *not* bring firearms. Note that goods and gifts purchased at **duty-free** shops abroad are not exempt from duty or sales tax; "duty-free" merely means that you need not pay a tax in the country of purchase. Upon returning home, you must declare all articles acquired abroad and pay a duty on the value of goods in excess of your home country's allowance. In order to expedite your return, make a list of any valuables brought from home and register them with customs before traveling abroad, and keep receipts for all goods acquired abroad. In addition, Chile charges an 19% **Value Added Tax (VAT)**, resembling the US sales tax, on merchandise (see **Taxes**, p. 20). For additional info, check out the Government of Chile National Customs Service website at www.aduana.cl.

MONEY

CURRENCY AND EXCHANGE

The unit of currency in Chile is the Chilean *peso* (CH$). Denominations of *pesos* include coins worth CH$1, 5, 10, 50, 100, and 500, as well as banknotes of CH$500; 1000; 2000; 5,000; 10,000; and 20,000. Take some time to familiarize yourself with the relative value of each. It is best to carry around small denominations, for safety reasons, and because many Chilean establishments cannot give change for large bills, especially in small towns. In addition, some Chileans may try to fool foreigners by telling them they do not have change. It is therefore best to head to a large, reputable establishment (such as a supermarket) to break larger bills.

The currency chart below is based on August 2004 exchange rates between local currency and Australian dollars (AUS$), Canadian dollars (CDN$), European Union euros (EUR€), New Zealand dollars (NZ$), British pounds (UK£), and US dollars (US$). Check the currency converter on websites like www.xe.com or a large newspaper for the latest exchange rates. For exchange rates in Argentina, consult the **Mendoza** section of this guide (p. 268).

CURRENCY	
AUS$1 = CH$454.14	CH$1000 = AUS$2.20
CDN$1 = CH$484.17	CH$1000 = CDN$2.06
EUR€1 = CH$782.17	CH$1000 = EUR€1.28
NZ$1 = CH$416.20	CH$1000 = NZ$2.41
UK£1 = CH$1169.28	CH$1000 = UK£0.86
US$1 = CH$638.80	CH$1000 = US$1.57

As a general rule, it's cheaper to convert money in Chile than at home. While currency exchange will probably be available in your arrival airport, it's wise to bring enough foreign currency to last for the first 24-72 hours of your trip.

When changing money abroad, head first to banks or *casas de cambio* that have at most a 5% margin between buy and sell prices. Since you lose money in each transaction, **convert large sums** (unless the currency is depreciating rapidly), **but no more than you'll need.** In general, foreign currency is not accepted in Chile, apart from some hotels that may waive the VAT for foreigners using US dollars.

If you use traveler's checks or bills, carry some in small denominations (the equivalent of US$50 or less) for times when you are forced to exchange money at disadvantageous rates, but bring a range of denominations since charges may be levied per check cashed. Store money in a variety of forms; ideally, at any given time you will be carrying some cash, traveler's checks, and an ATM/credit card. All travelers should also consider carrying some US dollars (about US$50 worth).

TRAVELER'S CHECKS

Traveler's checks are one of the safest and least troublesome means of carrying funds. **American Express** and **Visa** are the most recognized brands. Many banks and agencies sell them for a small commission. Check issuers provide refunds if the checks are lost or stolen. They are readily accepted throughout Chile. Ask about toll-free refund hotlines and the location of refund centers when purchasing checks, and always carry emergency cash.

American Express: Checks available with commission at select banks, at all AmEx offices, and online (www.americanexpress.com; US residents only). American Express cardholders can also purchase checks by phone (☎800-721-9768). Checks available in Australian, Canadian, European, Japanese, British, and US currencies. For purchase locations or more information contact AmEx's service centers: in Australia ☎800 68 80 22; in Canada and the US 800-221-7282; in New Zealand 0508 555 358; in the UK 0800 587 6023; elsewhere, call the US collect at 1 801-964-6665.

Visa: Checks available (generally with commission) at banks worldwide. AAA (p. 39) offers commission-free checks to its members. For the location of the nearest office, call Visa's service centers: in the UK ☎0800 51 58 84; in the US 800-227-6811; elsewhere, call the UK collect at 44 173 331 8949. Checks available in Canadian, Japanese, European, British, and US currencies.

CREDIT, DEBIT, AND ATM CARDS

Where they are accepted, credit cards often offer superior exchange rates—up to 5% better than the retail rate used by banks and other currency exchange establishments. Credit cards may also offer services such as insurance or emergency help, and may even be required to reserve hotel rooms or rental cars. **MasterCard** and **Visa** are the most welcomed, as well as **Diners Club** and **Discover; American Express** cards work at some ATMs and at AmEx offices and major airports. Once in Chile, if you lose your credit card, call: American Express (☎800 361 002); Diners Club International (☎800 220 220); MasterCard International (☎1230 020 2012); Visa International (☎1230 020 2136)

ATM cards are widespread in Chile. Depending on the system that your home bank uses, you can most likely access your personal bank account from abroad. ATMs get the same wholesale exchange rate as credit cards, but there is often a limit on the amount of money you can withdraw per day (usually around US$500). There is typically a surcharge of US$1-5 per withdrawal.

Debit cards can be used wherever the associated credit card company (usually MasterCard or Visa) is accepted. Debit cards may be used to withdraw cash from associated banks and ATMs throughout Chile. Ask your local bank about obtaining one.

The two major international money networks are **Cirrus** (US ☎ 800-424-7787 or www.mastercard.com) and **Visa/PLUS** (US ☎ 800-843-7587 or www.visa.com). Most ATMs charge a transaction fee that is paid to the bank that owns the ATM.

GETTING MONEY FROM HOME

If you run out of money while traveling, the easiest and cheapest solution is to have someone back home make a deposit to the bank account linked to your credit card or ATM card. For additional info, check out the online **International Money Transfer Consumer Guide** (http://international-money-transfer-consumer-guide.info). Other options include the following.

WIRING MONEY

It is possible to arrange a **bank money transfer,** which means asking a bank back home to wire money to a bank in Chile. This is the cheapest way to transfer cash, but also the slowest, usually taking several days. Note that some banks may only release your funds in Chilean pesos, potentially sticking you with a poor exchange rate; inquire about this in advance. Money transfer services such as **Western Union** are faster and more convenient than bank transfers, but are also more expensive. Western Union has many locations worldwide. To find one, visit www.western-nunion.com, or call in Australia ☎ 800 501 500, in Canada 800-235-0000, in Ireland 66 947 5603, in New Zealand 0800 005 253, in the UK 0800 83 38 33, or in the US 800-325-6000. In Chile, Western Union services may be found in most **Correos de Chile** and **Tur Bus** offices. Call **Chile Express** (toll-free ☎ 800 800 102) for locations. Money transfer services are also available at **American Express** offices.

US STATE DEPARTMENT (US CITIZENS ONLY)

In serious emergencies only, the US State Department will forward money within hours to the nearest consular office, which will then disburse it according to instructions for a US$30 fee. If you wish to use this service, you must contact the Overseas Citizens Service division of the US State Department (☎ 317-472-2328; nights, Sundays, and holidays 202-647-4000).

COSTS

The cost of your trip will vary considerably depending on where you go, how you travel, and where you stay. The largest expenses will probably be your round-trip **airfare** to Santiago (**Getting to Chile: By Plane,** p. 30) and intercity bus tickets, if you plan to travel outside of Santiago. Before you go, calculate a reasonable daily **budget.**

STAYING ON A BUDGET

To give you a general idea, a bare-bones day in Chile (camping or sleeping in hostels/guesthouses, buying food at supermarkets) would cost about US$10-15 (CH$6400-9600); a slightly more comfortable day (sleeping in hostels/guesthouses and the occasional budget hotel, eating one meal per day at a restaurant, going out at night) would cost US$25-45 (CH$16,000-29,000); and for a luxurious day, the sky's the limit. Don't forget to factor in emergency reserve funds (at least US$200) when planning how much money you'll need.

TIPS FOR SAVING MONEY

Some general ways to save money include buying food in supermarkets rather than eating out, splitting accommodation and food costs with other trustworthy travelers, and doing your **laundry** in the sink (unless you're explicitly prohibited from doing so). On the other hand, since public transportation can be somewhat erratic in much of South America—with Chile as no exception—some travelers prefer to put their budget concerns behind their safety concerns, and stick with big-name transportation companies.

TIPPING AND BARGAINING

Tipping and especially bargaining in the developing world is a quite different and much more commonplace practice than you may be accustomed to; there are many unspoken rules to which tourists must adhere.

THE ART OF THE DEAL. Bargaining in Chile is a given: no price is set in stone, and vendors and drivers will automatically quote you a price that is several times too high; it's up to you to get them down to a reasonable rate. With the following tips and some finesse, you might be able to impress even the most hardened hawkers:

1. Bargaining needn't be a fierce struggle laced with barbs. Quite the opposite: good-natured wrangling with a cheerful face may prove your best weapon.

2. Use your poker face. The less your face betrays your interest in the item the better. If you touch an item to inspect it, the vendor will be sure to "encourage" you to name a price or make a purchase. Coming back again and again to admire a trinket is a good way of ensuring that you pay a ridiculously high price. Never get too enthusiastic about the object in question; point out flaws in workmanship and design. Be cool.

3. Know when to bargain. In most cases, it's quite clear when it's appropriate to bargain. Most private transportation fares and things for sale in outdoor markets are all fair game. Don't bargain on prepared or pre-packaged foods on the street or in restaurants. In some stores, signs will indicate whether *precios fijos* (fixed prices) prevail. When in doubt, ask tactfully, "Is that your lowest price?" or whether discounts are given.

4. Never underestimate the power of peer pressure. Bargaining with more than one person at a time always leads to higher prices. Alternately, try having a friend discourage you from your purchase—if you seem to be reluctant, the merchant will want to drop the price to interest you again.

5. Know when to turn away. Feel free to refuse any vendor or driver who bargains rudely, and don't hesitate to move on to another vendor if one will not be reasonable about the final price he offers. However, to start bargaining without an intention to buy is a major *faux pas*. Agreeing on a price and declining it is also poor form. Turn away slowly with a smile and "thank you" upon hearing a ridiculous price—the price may plummet.

6. Start low. Never feel guilty offering a ridiculously low price. Your starting price should be no more than one-third to one-half the asking price.

Although it is not necessary to tip when using taxis, a small gratuity may be expected with other services. It is customary to tip 10% at restaurants, even at smaller, more casual establishments. When staying at upper-range accommodations, a CH$1000 tip will suffice for porters and bell-boys, but maids in upscale hotels should be tipped CH$1500-2000 for a two-night stay. Meanwhile, bargaining is not only permissible, but expected in markets and fairs throughout Chile. Most foreigners will initially be told the *gringo* price for goods, so bargain with vendors in open markets where the price of merchandise is not displayed, particularly in the case of *artesanías* and *ferias*. The same rules apply with tour operators and taxi drivers—try and shop around to get an estimate of current price ranges, haggle for the best value, and always agree upon an amount before embarking on a trip. Bargain at hotels and hostels, especially if traveling during the low season.

TAXES

Travelers should remember to account for the 19% **Impuesto valor añadido (IVA),** or **Value Added Tax (VAT)** on merchandise. IVA/VAT refunds are not granted in Chile. However, most hotels, and many other establishments, including restaurants and tour guides, allow foreigners to circumvent the IVA tax by paying for stays or other services in cash, more specifically, in US dollars. Ask about the IVA discount for foreigners when checking in.

PACKING

Pack lightly: Lay out only what you absolutely need, then take half the clothes and twice the money. The Travelite FAQ (www.travelite.org) is a good resource for tips on traveling light. The online **Universal Packing List** (http://upl.codeq.info) will generate a customized list of suggested items for your trip. If you plan to do a lot of hiking, also consult **Camping and the Outdoors,** p. 49.

Luggage: If you plan to cover most of your itinerary by foot, a sturdy **frame backpack** is unbeatable. (For the basics on buying a pack, see p. 51.) Toting a **suitcase** or **trunk** is fine if you plan to live in one or two cities and explore from there, but not a great idea if you plan to move around frequently. In addition to your main piece of luggage, a **daypack** (a small backpack or courier bag) is useful.

Clothing: Chile's diverse and sometimes erratic climate calls upon travelers to be prepared for anything. No matter when you're traveling, it's a good idea to bring a warm jacket or wool sweater, a rain jacket (Gore-Tex® is both waterproof and breathable), sturdy shoes or hiking boots, and thick socks. Flip-flops or waterproof sandals are must-haves for grubby hostel showers. You may also want one outfit for going out, and maybe a nicer pair of shoes. If you plan to visit religious or cultural sites, remember that you will need modest and respectful dress.

Sleepsack: Some hostels require that you either provide your own linen or rent sheets from them. Save cash by making your own sleepsack: fold a full-size sheet in half the long way, then sew it closed along the long side and one of the short sides.

Converters and Adapters: In Chile, electricity is 220 volts AC, enough to fry any 120V North American appliance. Americans and Canadians should buy an adapter (which changes the shape of the plug; US$5) and a converter (which changes the voltage; US$20-30). Don't make the mistake of using only an adapter (unless appliance instructions explicitly state otherwise). Australians and New Zealanders (who use 230V at home) won't need a converter, but will need a set of adapters to use anything electrical. For more on all things adaptable, check out http://kropla.com/electric.htm.

Toiletries: Toothbrushes, towels, cold-water soap, talcum powder (to keep feet dry), deodorant, razors, tampons, and condoms are often available, but may be difficult to find; bring extras. **Contact lenses** are likely to be expensive and difficult to find, so bring enough extra pairs and solution for your entire trip. Also, bring your glasses and a copy of your prescription in case you need emergency replacements.

First-Aid Kit: For a basic first-aid kit, pack bandages, a pain reliever, antibiotic cream, a thermometer, a Swiss Army knife, tweezers, moleskin, decongestant, motion-sickness remedy, diarrhea or upset-stomach medication (Pepto-Bismol or Imodium), an antihistamine, sunscreen, insect repellent, and burn ointment.

Film: Film and developing in Chile are fairly reasonable (about US$5 to purchase and US$7 to develop a roll of 36 exposures). Less serious photographers may want to bring a disposable camera or two. Despite disclaimers, airport security X-rays can fog film, so buy a lead-lined pouch at a camera store or ask security to hand-inspect it. Always pack film in your carry-on luggage, since higher-intensity X-rays are used on checked luggage.

ESSENTIALS

Other Useful Items: For safety purposes, you should bring a **money belt** and small **padlock.** Basic **outdoors equipment** (plastic water bottle, compass, waterproof matches, pocketknife, sunglasses, sunscreen, hat) are also useful. **Quick repairs** of torn garments can be done on the road with a needle and thread; also consider bringing electrical tape for patching tears. If you want to do laundry by hand, bring detergent, a small rubber ball to stop up the sink, and string for a makeshift clothes line. **Other things** you're liable to forget are sealable **plastic bags** (for damp clothes, soap, food, shampoo, and other spillables); an **alarm clock;** safety pins; rubber bands; a flashlight; earplugs; garbage bags; and a small **calculator.** A **cell phone** can be a lifesaver on the road; see p. 44 for information on acquiring one that will work at your destination.

Important Documents: Don't forget your **passport, traveler's checks, ATM and/or credit cards, adequate ID, and photocopies** of all of the aforementioned in case these documents are lost or stolen (p. 15). Also bring all of the following that apply: Hostelling International (HI) membership card (p. 46); driver's license (p. 15); travel insurance forms; and ISIC card (p. 15).

SAFETY AND HEALTH

EMERGENCIES	The emergency numbers for all Chile are **Ambulance ☎ 131,** **Fire ☎ 132,** and **Police ☎ 133.**

GENERAL ADVICE

In any type of crisis situation, the most important thing to do is **stay calm.** Your country's embassy abroad (p. 14) is usually your best resource when things go wrong; registering with that embassy upon arrival in Chile is a good idea. The government offices listed in the **Travel Advisories** box below can provide information on the services they offer their citizens in case of emergencies abroad.

LOCAL LAWS AND POLICE

While Chilean police, known as *carabineros*, are generally known as being friendly, honest, and reliable, the penalties for breaking certain laws are often harsher, including arrest, imprisonment, or expulsion from the country. Do not attempt to bribe a *carabinero*. Be prepared to present proper identification should you be stopped by a Chilean police officer in the street. While this practice is very rare, it is legal. In addition, Chilean laws on financial affairs are very strict, and heavily enforced—bouncing a check, for example, can lead to incarceration.

DRUGS AND ALCOHOL

Although Chilean wines are considered South America's finest, don't get carried away. Only travelers over the age of 18 may consume alcohol. Driving while under the influence of alcohol is severely penalized in Chile, and may lead to incarceration if the driver is involved in an accident. Similarly, the possession, use, or trafficking of illegal drugs, including marijuana, is strictly prohibited. Convicted offenders can expect heavy fines and imprisonment.

SPECIFIC CONCERNS

NATURAL DISASTERS

EARTHQUAKES. Chile is prone to earthquakes. In 1960, Chile experienced what has come to be known as "The Big One," in which a quake off the coast of Chile caused a tsunami that destroyed much of the coastal area between Concepción and southern Chiloé. In 2004, both the northern regions and Santiago experienced rather strong quakes. In the event of a quake, open a door to provide an escape route and protect yourself by moving underneath a sturdy doorway, table, or desk.

FLOODS. Heavy rainfall is not uncommon throughout central and southern Chile. In 2000, rainstorms flooded much of Chile between Valparaíso and the southern Lakes Region. The rainy season in Chile is between May and August.

DEMONSTRATIONS AND POLITICAL GATHERINGS

Public demonstrations are quite common in Chile, especially in larger cities such as Santiago and Valparaíso, especially around September 11, the anniversary of the 1973 military coup that deposed Salvador Allende. Political protests are known to occur near government buildings as well as some universities. In the past, many protests have ended in violence. Visitors are encouraged to unconditionally avoid such protests and demonstrations. For additional info, contact your local Chilean embassy or your embassy in Chile.

TERRORISM

Since the retaliatory actions of the United States after September 11, 2001, there has been a general international air of resentment toward American travelers. While Chileans are generally friendly to travelers, the US State department nonetheless advises American travelers to travel with extreme caution, to be constantly aware, and to take all necessary measures to ensure their personal safety (as should all travelers). In addition, while terrorist organizations are suspected to reside along the Tri-Border Area of Argentina, Brazil, and Paraguay, terrorist attacks against Chile or foreigners in Chile are considered to be less likely.

Of additional concern in Chile are **land mines,** which may pose a threat to hikers in less-traveled, remote sections of national parks. In the northern border areas, Parque Nacional Lauca, Monumento Natural Salar de Surire, and Reserva Nacional Los Flamencos are at risk, while in the south, demarcated land mine fields in Parque Nacional Torres del Paine and Parque Nacional Tierra del Fuego should be avoided. Check with park authorities before wandering into less-frequented areas and always heed warning signs. For up-to-date information about potential threats to tourists, consult the US State Department's report on Chile, http://travel.state.gov or www.usembassy.cl. In addition, the box on **travel advisories** (see below) lists offices to contact and web pages to visit to get the most updated list of your home country's government's advisories about travel.

TRAVEL ADVISORIES. The following government offices provide travel information and advisories by telephone, by fax, or via the web:

Australian Department of Foreign Affairs and Trade: ☎ 13 00 555135; faxback service 02 6261 1299; www.dfat.gov.au.

Canadian Department of Foreign Affairs and International Trade (DFAIT): In Canada and the US ☎ 800-267-8376, elsewhere 1 613-944-4000; www.dfait-maeci.gc.ca. Call for their free booklet, *Bon Voyage...But.*

New Zealand Ministry of Foreign Affairs: ☎ 04 439 8000; fax 494 8506; www.mft.govt.nz/travel/index.html.

United Kingdom Foreign and Commonwealth Office: ☎ 020 7008 0232; fax 7008 0155; www.fco.gov.uk.

US Department of State: ☎ 202-647-5225, faxback service 647-3000; http://travel.state.gov. For *A Safe Trip Abroad,* call ☎ 512-1800.

PERSONAL SAFETY

EXPLORING AND TRAVELING

To avoid unwanted attention, try to blend in as much as possible. Respecting local customs (in many cases, dressing more conservatively than you would at home) may placate would-be hecklers. Familiarize yourself with your surroundings before setting out, and carry yourself with confidence. Check maps in shops and restaurants rather than on the street. If you are traveling alone, be sure someone at home knows your itinerary, and never admit that you're by yourself. When walking at night, stick to busy, well-lit streets and avoid dark alleyways. If you ever feel uncomfortable, leave the area as quickly and directly as you can.

There is no sure-fire way to avoid all the threatening situations you might encounter while traveling, but a good **self-defense course** will give you concrete ways to react to unwanted advances. **Impact, Prepare,** and **Model Mugging** can all refer you to local self-defense courses in the US (☎ 800-345-KICK). Visit www.impactsafety.org for a list of nearby chapters. Workshops (1½-3hr.) start at US$75; full courses (20-25hr.) run US$350-400.

Driving in Chile can be easy and convenient, if somewhat stressful. Make sure to have an **international driving permit** (p. 39) and your **vehicle registration** available at all times. While drivers in general strictly respect traffic rules, do not be surprised if the pace seems fast. The speed limit in Chile, unless otherwise indicated, is 100km/hr (65 mph), except in urban areas, in which the speed limit is 50km/hr (30 mph). Those caught speeding will be severely penalized. Similarly, drivers found not wearing seatbelts may have their licenses taken away and are sent before a judge. Children under 40 lbs. should ride only in specially-designed carseats, available for a small fee from most car rental agencies. Study route maps before you hit the road, and if you plan on spending a lot of time driving, consider bringing spare parts. If your car breaks down, wait for the police to assist you. For long drives in desolate areas, invest in a cellular phone and a roadside assistance program (p. 44). Park your vehicle in a garage or well-traveled area, and use a steering wheel locking device in larger cities. **Sleeping in your car** is one of the most dangerous (and often illegal) ways to get your rest. For info on **hitchhiking** concerns, see p. 40.

POSSESSIONS AND VALUABLES

Never leave belongings unattended; crime occurs in even the most reputable-looking hostel or hotel. Bring your own **padlock** for hostel lockers, and don't ever store valuables in any locker. Be particularly careful on **buses** and **trains**; horror stories abound about determined thieves who wait for travelers to fall asleep. Carry your backpack in front of you where you can see it. When traveling with others, sleep in alternate shifts. When alone, use good judgment in selecting a train compartment: never stay in an empty one, and use a lock to secure your pack to the luggage rack. Try to sleep on top bunks with your luggage stored above you (if not in bed with you), and keep important documents and other valuables on your person.

There are a few steps you can take to minimize the financial risk associated with traveling. First, **bring as little with you as possible.** Second, buy a few combination **padlocks** to secure your belongings either in your pack or in a hostel or train station locker. Third, **carry as little cash as possible.** Keep your traveler's checks and ATM/credit cards in a **money belt**—not a "fanny pack"—along with your passport and ID cards. Fourth, **keep a small cash reserve separate from your primary stash.** This should be about US$50 (US$ are best) sewn into or stored in the depths of your pack, along with your traveler's check numbers and important photocopies.

In large cities, **con artists** often work in groups and may involve children. Beware of certain classic sob stories that require money, rolls of bills "found" on the street, or mustard spilled (or saliva spit) onto your shoulder to distract you while they snatch your bag. **Never let your passport or bags out of your sight.** Street crime is a problem in metropolitan Santiago, and reports of thefts of purses, wallets, backpacks, and briefcases are not uncommon. Beware of **pickpockets** in city crowds, especially on public transportation. Also, be alert in public telephone booths: if you must say your calling card number, do so very quietly; if you punch it in, make sure no one can look over your shoulder. While you must always be on your guard throughout the country, pay special attention to personal safety in larger cities, such as Santiago, as well as Valparaíso and Viña del Mar, which are more crowded during the height of the Chilean summer season.

If you will be traveling with electronic devices, such as a laptop computer or a PDA, check whether your homeowner's insurance covers loss, theft, or damage when you travel. If not, you might consider purchasing a low-cost separate insurance policy. **Safeware** (US ☎ 800-800-1492; www.safeware.com) specializes in covering computers and charges US$90 for 90-day comprehensive international travel coverage up to US$4000. If you can, try not to bring electronic devices of major value. As a general rule in Chile: anything that can get stolen *will* get stolen if you let it out of your sight for even a moment.

PRE-DEPARTURE HEALTH

In your **passport,** write the names of any people you wish to be contacted in case of a medical emergency, and list any allergies or medical conditions you may have. Matching a prescription to a foreign equivalent is not always easy, safe, or possible, so if you take prescription drugs, consider carrying up-to-date, legible prescriptions or a statement from your doctor stating the medication's trade name, manufacturer, chemical name, and dosage. While traveling, be sure to keep all medication with you in your carry-on luggage. For tips on packing a basic **first-aid kit** and other health essentials, see p. 20. To obtain common over-the-counter drugs in Chilean pharmacies, be sure to know the name of the drug, and not just the brand name (e.g. ibuprofen and *not* Advil).

IMMUNIZATIONS AND PRECAUTIONS

Travelers over two years old should make sure that the following vaccines are up to date: MMR (for measles, mumps, and rubella), DTaP or Td (for diphtheria, tetanus, and pertussis), IPV (for polio), Hib (for *haemophilus* influenza B), and HepB (for Hepatitis B). Adults traveling to Chile on trips longer than four weeks should consider the following additional immunizations: Hepatitis A vaccine and/or immunoglobulin (IG), an additional dose of polio vaccine, and typhoid and cholera vaccines, particularly for rural travelers. For those who will venture into the wild, a rabies vaccination is recommended as well. For recommendations on immunizations and prophylaxis, consult the Center for Disease Control (see below) in the US or the equivalent in your home country, and check with a doctor for guidance.

INSURANCE

Travel insurance covers four basic areas: medical/health problems, property loss, trip cancellation/interruption, and emergency evacuation. Though regular insurance policies may well extend to travel-related accidents, you may consider purchasing separate travel insurance if the cost of potential trip cancellation, interruption, or emergency medical evacuation is greater than you can absorb. Prices for travel insurance purchased separately generally run about US$50 per week for full coverage, while trip cancellation/interruption may be purchased separately at a rate of US$3-5 per day depending on length of stay.

Medical insurance (especially university policies) often covers costs incurred abroad; check with your provider. **US Medicare** does not cover foreign travel. **Canadian** provincial health insurance plans increasingly do not cover foreign travel; check with the provincial Ministry of Health or Health Plan Headquarters for details. **Homeowner's insurance** often covers theft during travel and loss of travel documents (passport, plane ticket, railpass, etc.) up to US$500.

ISIC and **ITIC** (p. 15) provide basic insurance benefits to US cardholders, including US$100 per day of in-hospital sickness for up to 60 days and US$5000 of accident-related medical reimbursement (see www.isicus.com for details). Cardholders have access to a toll-free 24hr. helpline for medical, legal, and financial emergencies overseas. **American Express** (US ☎800-528-4800) grants most cardholders automatic collision and theft car rental insurance and ground travel accident coverage of US$100,000 on flight purchases made with the card.

INSURANCE PROVIDERS

STA (p. 31) offers a range of plans that can supplement your basic coverage. Other private insurance providers in the US and Canada include: Access America (☎800-284-8300; www.accessamerica.com); Berkely Group (☎800-797-4514; www.berkely.com); Globalcare Travel Insurance (☎800-821-2488; www.globalcare-cocco.com); Travel Assistance International (☎800-821-2828; www.europassistance.com); and Travel Guard (☎800-826-4919; www.travelguard.com). Columbus Direct (☎020 7375 0011; www.columbusdirect.co.uk) operates in the UK and AFTA (☎02 9264 3299; www.afta.com.au) is in Australia.

USEFUL ORGANIZATIONS AND PUBLICATIONS

The US **Centers for Disease Control and Prevention** (**CDC;** ☎877-FYI-TRIP; fax 888-232-3299; www.cdc.gov/travel) maintains an international travelers' hotline and an informative website. The CDC's comprehensive booklet *Health Information for International Travel* (The Yellow Book), an annual rundown of disease, immunization, and general health advice, is free online or US$29-40 via the Public Health Foundation (☎877-252-1200; http://bookstore.phf.org). Consult the appropriate government agency of your home country for consular information sheets on health, entry requirements, and other issues for various countries (see the listings in the box on **Travel Advisories,** p. 23). For quick information on health and other travel warnings, call the **Overseas Citizens Services** (M-F 8am-8pm ☎888-407-4747; after-hours 202-647-4000; from overseas 317-472-2328), or contact a passport agency, embassy, or consulate abroad. For information on medical evacuation services and travel insurance firms, see the US government's website at http://travel.state.gov/medical.html or the **British Foreign and Commonwealth Office** (www.fco.gov.uk). For general health info, contact the **American Red Cross** (☎800-564-1234; www.redcross.org).

STAYING HEALTHY

Common sense is the simplest prescription for good health while you travel. Drink lots of fluids to prevent dehydration and constipation, and wear sturdy, broken-in shoes and clean socks.

ENVIRONMENTAL HAZARDS

Heat exhaustion and dehydration: Heat exhaustion leads to nausea, excessive thirst, headaches, and dizziness. Avoid it by drinking plenty of fluids, eating salty foods (e.g. crackers), abstaining from dehydrating beverages (e.g. alcohol and caffeinated beverages), and always wearing sunscreen. Continuous heat stress can eventually lead to heatstroke, characterized by a rising temperature, severe headache, delirium and cessation of sweating. Victims should be cooled off with wet towels and taken to a doctor.

Sunburn: Always wear sunscreen (SPF 30 is good) when spending excessive amounts of time outdoors. If you are planning on spending time near water, in the desert, or in the snow, you are at a higher risk of getting burned, even through clouds. If you get sunburned, drink more fluids than usual and apply an aloe-based lotion. Severe sunburns can lead to sun poisoning, a condition that affects the entire body, causing fever, chills, nausea, and vomiting. Sun poisoning should always be treated by a doctor.

Hypothermia and frostbite: A rapid drop in body temperature is the clearest sign of overexposure to cold. Victims may also shiver, feel exhausted, have poor coordination or slurred speech, hallucinate, or suffer amnesia. *Do not let hypothermia victims fall asleep.* To avoid hypothermia, keep dry, wear layers, and stay out of the wind. When the temperature is below freezing, watch out for frostbite. If skin turns white or blue, waxy, and cold, do not rub the area. Drink warm beverages, stay dry, and slowly warm the area with dry fabric or steady body contact until a doctor can be found.

High Altitude: Allow your body a couple of days to adjust to less oxygen before exerting yourself. If you visit the Andes Mountains, ascend gradually to allow time for your body to acclimatize to prevent insomnia, headaches, nausea, and altitude sickness. Note that alcohol is more potent and UV rays are stronger at high elevations.

INSECT-BORNE DISEASES

Many diseases are transmitted by insects—mainly mosquitoes, fleas, ticks, and lice. Be aware of insects in wet or forested areas, especially while hiking and camping; wear long pants and long sleeves, tuck your pants into your socks, and use a mosquito net. Use insect repellents such as DEET and soak or spray your gear with permethrin (licensed in the US only for use on clothing). **Mosquitoes**—responsible for dengue fever, among other illnesses—can be particularly dangerous in wet, swampy, or wooded areas of Chile's many national parks. **Ticks**—responsible for Lyme and other diseases—can be particularly dangerous in rural and forested regions of the North as well.

Dengue fever: An "urban viral infection" transmitted by *Aedes* mosquitoes, which bite during the day rather than at night. The incubation period is 3-14 days, usually 4-7 days. Early symptoms include a high fever, severe headaches, swollen lymph nodes, and muscle aches. Many patients also suffer from nausea, vomiting, and a pink rash. If you experience these symptoms, see a doctor immediately, drink plenty of liquids, and take fever-reducing medication such as acetaminophen (Tylenol). *Never take aspirin to treat dengue fever.* There is no vaccine available for dengue fever.

Hantavirus Pulmonary Syndrome (HPS): This respiratory disease, found primarily in rural and camping areas, caused by a virus carried in rats and mice, was of epidemic status in 1993, but is no longer considered a significant risk to tourism in affected zones. To avoid contracting this disease, use common sense when traveling outdoors. Stay away from rodents, and avoid sleeping on the floor without protection.

Lyme disease: A bacterial infection carried by ticks and marked by a circular bull's-eye rash of 2 in. or more. Later symptoms include fever, headache, fatigue, and aches and pains. Antibiotics are effective if administered early. Left untreated, Lyme can cause problems in joints, the heart, and the nervous system. If you find a tick attached to your skin, grasp the head with tweezers as close to your skin as possible and apply slow, steady traction. Removing a tick within 24 hours greatly reduces the risk of infection. Do not try to remove ticks with petroleum jelly, nail polish remover, or a hot match. Tick bites usually occur in moist, shaded environments and heavily wooded areas. If you are going to be hiking in these areas, wear long clothes and DEET.

Other insect-borne diseases: Lymphatic filariasis is a roundworm infestation transmitted by mosquitoes. Infection causes enlargement of extremities and has no vaccine. **Leishmaniasis,** a parasite transmitted by sand flies, can occur throughout South America. Common symptoms are fever, weakness, and swelling of the spleen, as well as skin sores weeks to months after the bite. There is a treatment, but no vaccine. **CHAGAS disease (American trypanomiasis)** is another relatively common parasite transmitted by the cone nose and kissing bug, which infest mud, adobe, and thatch. Its symptoms are fever, heart disease, and later on an enlarged intestine. There is no vaccine and limited treatment.

FOOD- AND WATER-BORNE DISEASES

Prevention is the best cure: be sure that your food is properly cooked and the water you drink is clean. While tap water in Chile is generally considered safe to drink, unaccustomed travelers with delicate dispositions are advised to drink mineral water. Buy bottled water or purify your own by boiling it or treating it with **iodine tablets;** note, however, that some parasites such as *giardia* have exteriors that resist iodine treatment, so boiling is more reliable. Watch out for food from markets or street vendors that may have been cooked in unhygienic conditions. Other culprits are raw shellfish, unpasteurized milk, and sauces containing raw eggs. Always wash your hands before eating or bring a quick-drying purifying liquid hand cleaner.

Traveler's diarrhea: Results from drinking fecally contaminated water or eating uncooked and contaminated foods. Symptoms include nausea, bloating, and urgency. Try quick-energy, non-sugary foods with protein and carbohydrates to keep your strength up. Over-the-counter anti-diarrheals (e.g. Imodium) may counteract the problems. The most dangerous side effect is dehydration; drink 8 oz. of water with ½ tsp. of sugar or honey and a pinch of salt, try decaffeinated soft drinks, or eat salted crackers. If you develop a fever or your symptoms don't go away after 4-5 days, consult a doctor. Consult a doctor immediately for treatment of diarrhea in children.

Dysentery: Results from a serious intestinal infection caused by certain bacteria in contaminated food or water. The most common type is bacillary dysentery. Symptoms include bloody diarrhea (sometimes mixed with mucus), fever, and abdominal pain and tenderness. Bacillary dysentery generally only lasts a week, but it is highly contagious. Amoebic dysentery, which develops more slowly, is a more serious disease and may cause long-term damage if left untreated. A stool test can determine which kind you have; seek medical help immediately. Dysentery can be treated with the drugs norfloxacin or ciprofloxacin (commonly known as Cipro). If you are traveling in high-risk areas, especially the rural regions of the North, consider obtaining a prescription before you leave home. Dehydration can be a problem; be sure to drink plenty of water or eat salted crackers.

Cholera: An intestinal disease caused by a bacteria found in contaminated food. Symptoms include severe diarrhea, dehydration, vomiting, and muscle cramps. See a doctor immediately; if left untreated, it may be deadly, even within a few hours. Antibiotics are available, but the most important treatment is rehydration. There is no vaccine available in the US, so those needing vaccination should seek it upon arrival to Chile.

Hepatitis A: A viral infection of the liver acquired primarily through contaminated water, including through shellfish from contaminated water. Symptoms include fatigue, fever, loss of appetite, nausea, dark urine, jaundice, vomiting, aches and pains, and light stools. The risk is highest in rural areas and the countryside, but it is also present in urban areas. Ask your doctor about the Hepatitis A vaccine (Havrix or Vaqta) or an injection of immunoglobulin (IG; formerly called gamma globulin).

Giardiasis: Transmitted through parasites (microbes, tapeworms, etc. in contaminated water and food) and acquired by drinking untreated water from streams or lakes. Symptoms include diarrhea, abdominal cramps, bloating, fatigue, weight loss, and nausea. If untreated it can lead to severe dehydration. Giardiasis occurs worldwide.

Typhoid fever: Caused by salmonella bacteria; common in villages and rural areas in South America. While mostly transmitted through contaminated food and water, it may also be acquired by direct contact with another person. Early symptoms include a persistent, high fever, headaches, fatigue, loss of appetite, constipation, and sometimes a rash on the abdomen or chest. Antibiotics can treat typhoid, but a vaccination (70-90% effective) is recommended.

Leptospirosis: A bacterial disease caused by exposure to fresh water or soil contaminated by the urine of infected animals. Able to enter the human body through cut skin, mucus membranes, and through ingestion, it is most common in tropical climates. Symptoms include a high fever, chills, nausea, and vomiting. If not treated it can lead to liver failure and meningitis. There is no vaccine; consult a doctor for treatment.

OTHER INFECTIOUS DISEASES

Rabies: Transmitted through the saliva of infected animals; fatal if untreated. By the time symptoms (thirst and muscle spasms) appear, the disease is in its terminal stage. If you are bitten, wash the wound thoroughly, seek immediate medical care, and try to have the animal located. A rabies vaccine, which consists of 3 shots given over a 21-day period, is available and recommended for developing world travel, but is only semi-effective. Rabies is found all over the world, and is often transmitted through dogs.

Hepatitis B: A viral infection of the liver transmitted via blood or other bodily fluids. Symptoms, which may not surface until years after infection, include jaundice, loss of appetite, fever, and joint pain. High-risk activities for transmission include unprotected sex, IV drug use, and unprotected health work. A 3-shot vaccination sequence is recommended for health-care workers, sexually-active travelers, and anyone planning to seek medical treatment abroad; it must begin 6 months before traveling.

AIDS and HIV: For detailed information on Acquired Immune Deficiency Syndrome (AIDS) in Chile, call the US Center for Disease Control's 24hr. hotline at ☎800-342-2437, or contact the Joint United Nations Programme on HIV/AIDS (UNAIDS), 20 Ave. Appia, CH-1211 Geneva 27, Switzerland (☎41 22 791 3666; fax 791 4187). Note that in order to obtain a visa for work or study, travelers will need a health certificate from a doctor confirming the applicant's good health that includes an HIV test. Contact the Chilean consulate for information.

Sexually transmitted diseases (STDs): Gonorrhea, chlamydia, genital warts, syphilis, herpes, and other STDs are more common than HIV and can cause serious complications. **Hepatitis** B and C can also be transmitted sexually. Though condoms may protect you from some STDs, oral or even tactile contact can lead to transmission. If you think you may have contracted an STD, see a doctor immediately.

OTHER HEALTH CONCERNS

MEDICAL CARE ON THE ROAD

Generally, medical care in Chile is good, though it may not always meet the standards that travelers might be accustomed to. Doctors and hospitals often expect immediate cash for services, and US medical insurance is not always valid.

If you are concerned about obtaining medical assistance while traveling, you may wish to employ special support services. The *MedPass* from **GlobalCare, Inc.,** 6875 Shiloh Rd. East, Alpharetta, GA 30005, USA (☎ 800-860-1111; fax 678-341-1800; www.globalcare.net), provides 24hr. international medical assistance, support, and medical evacuation resources. The **International Association for Medical Assistance to Travelers** (**IAMAT;** Canada ☎519-836-0102; New Zealand www.cybermall.co.nz/NZ/IAMAT, US 716-754-4883) has free membership, lists English-speaking doctors worldwide, and offers detailed info on immunization requirements and sanitation. If your regular **insurance** policy does not cover travel abroad, you may wish to purchase additional coverage (p. 25).

Those with medical conditions (such as diabetes, allergies to antibiotics, epilepsy, or heart conditions) may want to obtain a **Medic Alert** membership (first year US$35, annually thereafter US$20), which includes a stainless steel ID tag, among other benefits, such as a 24hr. collect-call number. Contact the Medic Alert Foundation, 2323 Colorado Ave, Turlock, CA 95382, USA (☎888-633-4298; outside US 209-668-3333; www.medicalert.org).

WOMEN'S HEALTH

Women traveling in unsanitary conditions are vulnerable to **urinary tract (including bladder and kidney) infections.** Over-the-counter medicines can sometimes alleviate symptoms, but if they persist, see a doctor. **Vaginal yeast infections** may flare up in hot and humid climates. Wearing loosely fitting trousers or a skirt and cotton underwear will help, as will over-the-counter remedies like Monostat or Gynelotrimin. Bring supplies from home if you are prone to infection, as they may be difficult to find on the road. And, since **tampons, pads,** and reliable **contraceptive devices** are sometimes hard to find when traveling, bring supplies with you, unless you are spending most of your time in major cities. **Abortion** is illegal in Chile, except when the pregnant woman's life is in danger. **Emergency contraception** is also illegal.

GETTING TO CHILE

BY PLANE

When it comes to airfare, a little effort can save you a bundle. If your plans are flexible enough to deal with the restrictions, courier fares are the cheapest. Tickets bought from consolidators and standby seating are also good deals, but last-minute specials, airfare wars, and charter flights often beat these fares. It's important is to hunt around, to be flexible, and to ask persistently about discounts. Students, seniors, and those under 26 should never pay full price for a ticket.

AIRFARES

Airfares to Chile peak between June and August, and December and January, with fares often soaring to US$1200 and up; holidays are also expensive. The cheapest times to travel are February to May and September to November. Midweek (M-Th morning) round-trip flights run US$40-50 cheaper than weekend flights, but they are generally more crowded and less likely to permit frequent-flier upgrades. Not fixing a return date ("open return") or arriving in and departing from different cities ("open-jaw") can be pricier than round-trip flights. Patching one-way flights together is one of the most expensive ways to travel. Flights between Santiago and regional hubs—Antofagasta, Arica, and Concepción—will tend to be cheaper.

If Chile is only one stop on a more extensive globe-hop, consider a round-the-world (RTW) ticket. Tickets usually include at least five stops and are valid for about a year; prices range US$3400-5000. Try **Northwest Airlines/KLM** (US ☎800-447-4747; www.nwa.com) or **Star Alliance,** a consortium of 22 airlines including United Airlines (US ☎800-241-6522; www.staralliance.com).

Fares for roundtrip flights to Santiago from the US or Canada cost US$600-1200; from the UK, UK£500-800; from Australia, AUS$1700-3000; from New Zealand, NZ$1700-3000.

BUDGET AND STUDENT TRAVEL AGENCIES

While knowledgeable agents specializing in flights to Chile can make your life easy and help you save, they may not spend the time to find you the lowest possible fare—they get paid on commission. Travelers holding **ISIC** and **IYTC cards** (p. 15) qualify for big discounts from student travel agencies. Most flights from budget agencies are on major airlines, but in peak season some may sell seats on less reliable chartered aircraft.

> **STA Travel,** 5900 Wilshire Blvd., Ste. 900, Los Angeles, CA 90036, USA (24hr. reservations and info ☎800-781-4040; www.sta-travel.com). A student and youth travel organization with over 150 offices worldwide (check their website for a listing of all their offices), including US offices in Boston, Chicago, L.A., New York, San Francisco, Seattle, and Washington, D.C. Ticket booking, travel insurance, railpasses, and more. Walk-in offices are located throughout Australia (☎03 9349 4344), New Zealand (☎09 309 9723), and the UK (☎0870 1 600 599).

> **CTS Travel,** 30 Rathbone Pl., London W1T 1GQ, UK (☎020 7209 0630; www.ctstravel.co.uk). A British student travel agent with offices in 39 countries including the US, Empire State Building, 350 Fifth Ave., Ste. 7813, New York, NY 10118 (☎877-287-6665; www.ctstravelusa.com).

> **Travel CUTS (Canadian Universities Travel Services Limited),** 187 College St., Toronto, ON M5T 1P7 (☎416-979-2406; www.travelcuts.com). Offices across Canada and the US including Los Angeles, New York, Seattle, and San Francisco.

> **usit.,** 19-21 Aston Quay, Dublin 2 (☎01 602 1777; www.usitworld.com), Ireland's leading student/budget travel agency has 22 offices throughout Northern Ireland and the Republic of Ireland.

COMMERCIAL AIRLINES

The commercial airlines' lowest regular offer is the **APEX** (Advance Purchase Excursion) fare, which provides confirmed reservations and allows "open-jaw" tickets. Generally, reservations must be made seven to 21 days ahead of departure, with seven- to 14-day minimum-stay and up to 90-day maximum-stay restrictions. These fares carry hefty cancellation and change penalties (fees rise in summer). Book peak-season APEX fares early. Use **Microsoft Expedia** (http://msn.expedia.com) or **Travelocity** (www.travelocity.com) to get an idea of the lowest published fares, then use the resources outlined here to try and beat those fares. Low-season fares should be appreciably cheaper than the high-season (Jan.-Feb. and July-Aug.) ones listed here.

TRAVELING FROM NORTH AMERICA

Basic round-trip fares to Chile range roughly US$600-1200. Standard commercial carriers like American and United will probably offer the most convenient flights, but they may not be the cheapest, unless you manage to grab a special promotion or airfare war ticket. You will probably find flying one of the following "discount" airlines a better deal, if any of their limited departure points is convenient for you. (Discount airlines include Grupo TACA, Aero Continente, and Avianca.)

> **American Airlines** (US ☎800-433-7300; www.aa.com) is one of the most reliable and popular American carriers to South America.

FLIGHT PLANNING ON THE INTERNET. The Internet may be the budget traveler's dream when it comes to finding and booking bargain fares, but the array of options can be overwhelming.

Many airline sites offer special last-minute deals on the Web. American Airlines (www.aa.com), British Airways (www.britishairways.com), Delta Airlines (www.delta.com), LanChile (www.lanchile.com), Lufthansa (www.lufthansa.com), and Swiss (www.swiss.com) are just a few.

STA (www.sta-travel.com) and **StudentUniverse** (www.studentuniverse.com) provide quotes on student tickets, while **Orbitz** (www.orbitz.com), **Expedia** (www.expedia.com), and **Travelocity** (www.travelocity.com) offer full travel services. **Priceline** (www.priceline.com) lets you specify a price, and obligates you to buy any ticket that meets or beats it; **Hotwire** (www.hotwire.com) offers bargain fares, but won't reveal the airline or flight times until you buy. Other sites that compile deals for you include www.bestfares.com, www.flights.com, www.lowestfare.com, www.onetravel.com, and www.travelzoo.com.

Increasingly, there are online tools available to help sift through multiple offers; **SideStep** (www.sidestep.com; download required) and **Booking Buddy** (www.bookingbuddy.com) let you enter your trip information once and search multiple sites.

An indispensable resource on the Internet is the **Air Traveler's Handbook** (www.faqs.org/faqs/travel/air/handbook), a comprehensive listing of links to everything you need to know before you board a plane.

Delta (US ☎800-221-1212; www.delta.com) is another major American carrier with regular flights to Chile.

United (US ☎800-538-2929; www.united.com), a member of the Star Alliance, flies from their major hubs to Santiago.

LanChile (US ☎866-435-9526, Santiago 600 526 2000; www.lanchile.com) is one of the largest airlines in Latin America. Partnered with some of the largest international airlines, including American Airlines, it serves six continents.

Grupo TACA (US ☎800-400-8222; www.grupotaca.com) is an alliance of several Central American airlines with TACA Peru. With direct flights from most major cities in the US, Grupo TACA is one of the more convenient airlines for flying within the Americas.

Avianca (US ☎800-284-2622; www.avianca.com) is a Colombian airline with flights to major cities throughout Latin America. Most flights connect through Bogotá.

TRAVELING FROM THE UK AND IRELAND

Lufthansa (UK ☎0 870 1288 737, Germany 49 0 1803 33 66 33; www.lufthansa.com) generally has the best prices on flights from the UK.

Air France (☎0820 820 820; www.airfrance.com) usually has cheap rates from France and the UK.

Iberia (☎93 401 3131; www.iberia.com) also routes flights through London to Santiago.

Aerolíneas Argentinas (☎93 401 3131; www.aerolineasargentinas.com) offers competitive fares and stops in Buenos Aires on the way to Santiago.

TRAVELING FROM AUSTRALIA AND NEW ZEALAND

Qantas Airlines (☎1300 650 729; www.qantas.com.au) is based in Sydney.

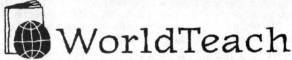

Air New Zealand (☎0800 737 000; www.airnewzealand.com) can get you there from home in New Zealand.

AIR COURIER FLIGHTS

Those who travel light should consider courier flights. Couriers help transport cargo on international flights by using their checked luggage space for freight. Generally, couriers must travel with carry-ons only and deal with complex flight restrictions. Most flights are round-trip only, with short fixed-length stays (usually one week) and a limit of a one ticket per issue. Most of these flights also operate only out of major gateway cities, mostly in North America. In order to fly courier flights, one must usually join the courier association first. Round-trip courier fares from the US to Chile run about US$300-500. Most flights leave from Los Angeles, Miami, New York, or San Francisco in the US; and from Montreal, Toronto, or Vancouver in Canada. Generally, you must be over 21 (in some cases, 18). In summer, the most popular destinations usually require an advance reservation of about two weeks (you can usually book up to two months ahead). Super-discounted fares are common for "last-minute" flights (3 to 14 days ahead). See www.aircourier.org or www.courier.org for more information.

STANDBY FLIGHTS

Traveling standby requires considerable flexibility in arrival and departure dates and cities. Companies dealing in standby flights sell vouchers, not tickets, along with a promise to get you to your destination (or nearby) within a certain window of time (typically 1-5 days). You call in before your specific window of time to hear your flight options and the probability that you will be able to board each flight. You can then decide which flights you want to try to make, show up at the appropriate airport at the appropriate time, present your voucher, and board if space is available. Vouchers can usually be bought for both one-way and round-trip travel. You may receive a monetary refund only if every available flight within your date range is full; if you opt not to take an available (but perhaps less convenient) flight, you can only get credit toward future travel. Carefully read agreements with any company offering standby flights as tricky fine print can leave you in the lurch. To check on a company's service record in the US, call the Better Business Bureau (☎703-276-0100). It is difficult to receive refunds, and clients' vouchers will not be honored when an airline fails to receive payment in time.

TICKET CONSOLIDATORS

Ticket consolidators, or **"bucket shops,"** buy unsold tickets in bulk from commercial airlines and sell them at discounted rates. The best place to look is in the Sunday travel section of any major newspaper (such as the *New York Times*), where many bucket shops place tiny ads. Call quickly, as availability is typically extremely limited. Not all bucket shops are reliable, so insist on a receipt that gives full details of restrictions, refunds, and tickets, and pay by credit card (in spite of the 2-5% fee) so you can stop payment if you never receive your tickets. For more info, see www.travel-library.com/air-travel/consolidators.html.

Travel Avenue (☎800-333-3335; www.travelavenue.com) searches for best available published fares and then uses several consolidators to attempt to beat that fare. **NOW Voyager,** 315 W. 49th St. Plaza Arcade, New York, NY 10019 (☎212-459-1616; www.nowvoyagertravel.com) arranges discounted flights, mostly from New York. Other consolidators worth trying are **Rebel** (☎800-732-3588; www.rebel-tours.com) and **Cheap Tickets** (☎800-652-4327; www.cheaptickets.com). Yet more consolidators on the web include **Flights.com** (www.flights.com) and **TravelHUB** (www.travelhub.com). Keep in mind that these are just suggestions to get you started in your research; *Let's Go* does not endorse any of these agencies. As always, be cautious, and research companies before you hand over your credit card number.

TRAVELING FROM AUSTRALIA, NEW ZEALAND, AND THE UK
From Australia and New Zealand, look for consolidator ads in the travel section of the *Sydney Morning Herald* and other papers. In London, the **Air Travel Advisory Bureau** (UK ☎ 02 7 636 5000; www.atab.co.uk) can provide names of reliable consolidators and discount flight specialists.

BY LAND

In 1925, a multinational coalition initiated a project that would make the road tripper's ultimate fantasy come true—the Panamerican Highway, more commonly known as the *Panamericana*. Running from Alaska to Chile, the route was supposed to connect an entire hemisphere. Unfortunately, the underdeveloped and highly dangerous Panama-Colombia border proved too much to overcome. Nevertheless, road warriors can still embark on a shorter version from almost anywhere in South America and arrive in Chile.

BORDER CROSSINGS

Border crossings in Chile range in their quality and accessibility. Except in the far south, most crossings are high up in the Andes. Accessibility is dependent in all cases on the weather, since heavy snow can close many of the passes. To travel into Peru and Bolivia, Arica is the best city from which to leave. There are several routes to Bolivia farther south, but they tend not to be as well-maintained and service is not as regular. Options for entering Argentina abound; the most popular route is from Santiago to Mendoza. Buses run frequently to Mendoza, and from there, service extends to locations throughout South America, including Buenos Aires, São Paulo, and Río de Janeiro. Farther south, passes become more common as the Andes descend. However, snow and ice also become more of a problem.

INTO ARGENTINA
Visitors from Australia, Canada, Ireland, New Zealand, the United Kingdom, and the United States do not need to obtain a visa ahead of time. Free tourist visas are issued upon arrival for 90 days and can be extended for another 90 days. Numerous border crossings interrupt the long border between Argentina and Chile. The crossover into Mendoza (p. 268) beginning from Santiago, Valparaíso, or Viña del Mar allows thousands of buses and cars to pass through the renowned mile-long tunnel through the Andes. Crossings in the north include the route from Copiapó through Paso de San Francisco (p. 203). Boats between Puerto Williams and Ushuaia (p. 478) are a popular choice among locals and tourists alike. The roads from Osorno to Bariloche (p. 469), Chile Chico to Los Antiguos (p. 437), Puerto Natales to Villa Cerro Castillo (p. 457), also see heavy tourist traffic, and are the most frequently used routes in the south.

INTO BOLIVIA
Travelers from Australia, Canada, New Zealand, the United Kingdom, and the United States do not need to pay for a visa for stays shorter than 90 days. However, tourist visas (issued upon arrival) generally expire after 30 days and can only be renewed in La Paz. There is a US$25 airport fee when flying out of the country. The most common crossing to Bolivia is from Arica to La Paz (p. 146).

The road over the Andes has recently been renovated and makes for a fairly comfortable trip. Many travelers also cross from San Pedro de Atacama through Hito Cajón (p. 179), on their way to see the spectacular Salar de Uyuni.

INTO PERU
Visas are not required for stays shorter than 90 days for travelers from Australia, Canada, Ireland, New Zealand, the United Kingdom, and the United States. However, there is a US$25 airport fee when flying out of the country. The easiest and most common Chile-Peru border crossing is between Arica and Tacna (p. 145). The road is well maintained and heavily traveled by buses and cars.

GETTING AROUND CHILE

BY PLANE

Although flying is generally not as cheap as taking the bus, Chile does have one of the best air transit systems in South America. Dominated by LanChile, a former state-owned enterprise that has become one of the most successful international airlines in Latin America, service between major cities is frequent and competitively priced when purchased in advance.

From Santiago, you can almost always fly direct to most of the major cities including Antofagasta, Arica, Concepción, Copiapó, Iquique, La Serena, Puerto Montt, Punta Arenas, and Temuco; those that aren't direct may include intermediary touch-downs that do not require switching planes. Other smaller cities such as Balmaceda, Calama, Coyhaique, El Salvador, Osorno, and Valdivia can be reached with a local connecting flight. **LanChile** (Chile ☎600 526 2000; www.lanchile.com), its subsidiary **LanExpress** (formerly Ladeco; Chile ☎600 526 2000; www.lanexpress.com) and, to a lesser extent, **Aero Continente** (Chile ☎600 242 4242; www.aerocontinente.com) are the major airlines with domestic flights. All three airlines have offices in major cities and have online reservation services.

Airfares vary depending on how far in advance tickets are purchased. Buying tickets three to seven days in advance is almost always cheaper than buying last minute, saving you US$30-40. Purchasing tickets more than a week in advance can be even cheaper. However, LanChile often does have special last-minute fares available that can often be up to 50 percent off. They publish drastically discounted *"último minuto"* fares every Tuesday evening for flights departing on the following three days. Round-trip tickets are also much cheaper than two one-way tickets. If you are traveling from anywhere in central or northern Chile to the southern regions around Punta Arenas and Tierra del Fuego, air travel is always the most economical way of arriving there.

BY BUS

Buses are the cheapest and most convenient way of traveling relatively smaller distances. The quality of buses varies depending on the route, but the system as a whole is one of the best in Latin America and, by US and European standards, is fairly inexpensive. All of Chile's major roads are paved and usually in good condition with the exception of the Carretera Austral in the southern region of Aisén—the road is rough and, in many places, incomplete. Secondary roads in rural areas tend to be gravel and sometimes dirt.

The bus system in cities and large towns is generally very well-organized. Most buses leave from central terminals at regularly scheduled times. For common routes, you can simply show up and purchase tickets from the offices at the time you wish to travel; you may, however, want to call in advance during holidays and some summer weekends. Smaller towns without specific bus terminals often have a central street or block with bus company offices where passengers are picked up. In rural areas, bus stops are generally along the road, and travelers must flag down the bus they want and purchase tickets on board.

Fares depend on how far you go as well as how you travel. Buses in Chile have several different classes. For major routes, the cheapest available is **Pullman,** a standard 44-seat bus similar to those used in the US and Europe that is being phased out. For longer routes, **semi-cama** is a more comfortable but more expensive option that is now becoming the norm. These buses have partially reclining seats and serve drinks and snacks. **Salón cama** is the most luxurious, with fully reclining seats (almost bed-like) and meal service. Although this costs considerably more than standard service, it can be worth the expense for long trips. Shorter routes tend to use smaller buses and sometimes oversized vans. Fares are generally fixed when departing from a station or a company's office, although there are occasionally student discounts for longer trips. In more rural areas, when catching buses from a road-side bus stop, fees are up to the discretion of the driver, so there is often room for negotiation.

BY TRAIN

Chile's train service is very limited. Starting in Santiago, trains only serve major cities in the south, such as Chillán, Concepción, Rancagua, and Temuco. Rates are moderate (US$15-18 one-way). However, the late schedule of many trains can make a sleeping compartment (US$35-50 one-way) worth the money. Round-trip fares are cheaper. In general, though, buses are more frequent and less expensive.

BY CAR

Despite the quality of Chile's bus system, travelers may find that, at times, having a car can be a good option. Especially in the desert areas of the north and the Lakes Region in the south, a car may be the only way to reach some remote sites. Driving in Chile is not as much of a challenge as you might think. Road conditions are very good on main roads, and four-wheel-drive vehicles are available to rent for people headed into more rural areas. Chileans also drive on the right side of the road and follow similar traffic laws to those of the United States (although they are known for changing lanes quickly without signaling).

Technically, the only thing a tourist needs to drive in Chile is a valid license from their home country. However, it is highly recommended that travelers obtain an **International Driving Permit** (p. 39). Although car rental companies do not require it, *carabineros* (police) in rural areas have been known to detain drivers who do not have one. (Unlike in some of its neighboring countries, Chile's *carabineros* strictly enforce traffic laws such as speed limits and cannot be bribed.) Drivers should also double-check that their insurance will cover them while abroad, as many companies have special rules concerning the developing world.

RENTING

A rented car can be invaluable in Chile's more rural and underdeveloped areas. However, rentals are not cheap and the various costs of renting, insuring, and operating a car add up quickly. In most cases, negotiating a deal with a taxi service or local tour agency is more economical and much less hassle. If you are going to rent, keep in mind the region in which you will be driving. Most rural areas have roads in good enough shape that a normal sedan can handle them. However, in the desert area of the north, the Carretera Austral, and many of the national parks, a four-wheel-drive vehicle is strongly recommended, if not necessary. Also, when negotiating with rental agencies, remember that cheaper cars tend to be less reliable and harder to handle on difficult terrain. Less expensive four-wheel-drive vehicles in particular tend to be more top heavy, and are more dangerous when navigating particularly bumpy roads.

RENTAL AGENCIES

Almost every major city in Chile has at least a few car rental companies. Arrangements can be made the day of, although during the Chilean summer it is often necessary to call ahead in order to guarantee you get the type of car you want. Arrangements for many rental companies can now be made over the Internet, and all places accept advance reservations over the phone. For major international renters like Hertz, you can also call the office in your home country and have them make the reservation, but prices and availability can vary greatly. Numbers for these local offices are included in city listings; for home-country numbers, call your toll-free directory.

To rent a car from most establishments in Chile, you need to be at least 25 years of age with a valid license or International Driving Permit. However, many agencies will rent to travelers as young as 23 or 21, although there is sometimes an additional charge or insurance fee.

Large national and international chains often allow one-way rentals, picking up in one city and dropping off in another. There is usually a minimum hire period and sometimes an extra drop-off charge that varies with the distance between the two points. Major rental agencies in Chile include:

Hertz (Santiago ☎ 2 496 1111; www.hertz.cl) has locations in almost every major city in Chile.

Budget (Santiago ☎ 2 362 3200; www.budget.cl) is another international rental agency in Chile.

Thrifty (Santiago ☎ 2 225 6328; www.thrifty.com) is more limited in its coverage, serving only a few cities.

COSTS AND INSURANCE

Rental car prices start at around US$50 a day from national companies and US$40 from local agencies, with significant discounts when renting for six days or more. Expect to pay US$30-50 more for larger cars and for four-wheel-drive vehicles. Cars with **automatic transmission** can cost up to US$10 a day more than standard manuals (stick shift), and in some places, automatic transmission is hard to find in the first place. It is virtually impossible, no matter where you are, to find an automatic four-wheel-drive vehicle.

Most rental packages offer unlimited kilometers, although smaller businesses tend to give you a certain allowance per day. Return the car with a full tank of gas to avoid high fuel charges at the end. Be sure to ask whether the price includes **insurance** against theft and collision. Remember that if you are driving on an **unpaved road** in a rental car, you are almost never covered by insurance; ask about this before leaving the rental agency. Beware that cars rented on an **American Express** or **Visa/MasterCard Gold or Platinum** credit cards in Chile might *not* carry the automatic insurance that they would in some other countries; check with your credit card company. Insurance plans almost always come with an **excess** (or deductible) of around US$350-500 for conventional vehicles;

excess can be higher for younger drivers and four-wheel-drive vehicles. This means you pay for all damages up to that sum, unless they are the fault of another vehicle. The excess you will be quoted applies to collisions with other vehicles; collisions with non-vehicles, such as trees ("single-vehicle collisions"), will cost you even more. The excess can often be reduced or waived entirely if you pay an additional charge.

DRIVING PRECAUTIONS. When traveling in the summer or in the desert, bring substantial amounts of water (a suggested 5L of **water** per person per day) for drinking and for the radiator. For long drives to unpopulated areas, register with police before beginning the trek, and again upon arrival at the destination. Check with the local automobile club for details. When traveling for long distances, make sure tires are in good repair and have enough air, and get good maps. A **compass** and a **car manual** can also be very useful. You should always carry a **spare tire** and **jack, jumper cables, extra oil, flares, a flashlight (torch),** and **heavy blankets** (in case your car breaks down at night or in the winter). If you don't know how to **change a tire,** learn before heading out, especially if you are planning on traveling in deserted areas. Blowouts on dirt roads are exceedingly common. If you do have a breakdown, **stay with your car;** if you wander off, there's less likelihood trackers will find you.

ON THE ROAD

Driving in the populated areas of Chile is not difficult. More rural areas, however, tend to have gravel and dirt roads. Drivers should be extra cautious when traveling through the mountains and parks area, as roads are generally narrow and winding and are often covered by fog. The strictly-enforced speed limit is generally 50km/hr. in towns and cities and 100km/hr. on the highway. **Petrol (gasoline)** prices vary, but average about US$0.50 per liter in cities and US$0.60 per liter in outlying areas; gas stations generally sell unleaded *(sin plomo)*, leaded *(con plomo)*, and diesel fuel, so pay attention to what type of fuel your car requires. Also, when traveling through remote areas such as the desert region in the north, be sure to carry an extra container of gas, since stations are few and far between.

DANGERS. In unpopulated and highly rural areas, storms, lack of maintenance, and disuse can cause unpaved roads to fall into dangerous disrepair. Be sure to consult with your rental company over all planned routes before venturing into unknown areas.

CAR ASSISTANCE. The Automóvil Club de Chile (Santiago ☎2 431 1000; www.aclub.cl) has locations in most major cities and offers a variety of services, including car insurance and towing. Purchasing coverage from them gives you free towing for up to 120km from anywhere in the country. Some of the larger rental agencies like Hertz also offer roadside assistance.

DRIVING PERMITS AND CAR INSURANCE

INTERNATIONAL DRIVING PERMIT (IDP)

If you plan to drive a car while in Chile, you should obtain an International Driving Permit (IDP). While you can rent a car with only a valid license from your home country, it may be a good idea to get an IDP anyway, in case you are in a situation (e.g. an accident or stranded in a small town) where the police do not know English; information on the IDP is printed in ten languages, including Spanish. Chilean police will appreciate an IDP in addition to your home license.

Your IDP, valid for one year, must be issued in your home country before you depart for Chile. An application for the permit usually needs to include one or two photos, a current local license, an additional form of identification, and a fee. To apply, contact the national or local branch of your home country's automobile association. Be careful when purchasing an IDP online or anywhere other than your home automobile association. Many vendors sell permits of questionable legitimacy for higher prices.

Most credit cards cover standard insurance. If you rent, lease, or borrow a car, you will need a **green card,** or **International Insurance Certificate,** to certify that you have liability insurance and that it applies abroad. Green cards can be obtained at car rental agencies, car dealers (for those leasing cars), some travel agents, and some border crossings. Rental agencies may require you to purchase theft insurance in countries such as Chile, in which auto theft is a valid concern.

BY BOAT

Ferries are not a very common mode of transportation except in the southern region of Aisén. In this rugged country, the Carretera Austral is in rough condition and incomplete. Boats are often the only way to continue moving. The route from Puerto Montt to Puerto Natales (p. 392) has become fairly popular since it avoids the hassle of multiple bus and ferry lines while passing through the islands and fjords that dominate the region.

BY BICYCLE

For those hardcore travelers who want to set their own pace and keep in shape, bicycling through Chile can be a very rewarding experience. Cyclists should be careful though, as main roads like the Panamerican, although well maintained, have heavy traffic. Secondary and rural roads can also be a problem due to their narrowness and lack of paved shoulders. Travelers should look for a sturdy mountain bike to carry them through these regions.

When traveling by bike, be sure to carry extra supplies. These include tools for bike repairs such as replacement inner tubes for the tires and also food and drink. In remote areas where water is difficult to come by, carrying extra is a necessity. Wind can also be a major problem, especially in the Patagonia region—try and do most of your biking during periods of the day when the wind has subsided.

BY THUMB

 Let's Go never recommends hitchhiking as a safe means of transportation, and none of the information presented in this book is intended to do so.

While travelers in Chile may find that hitchhiking is fairly common, *Let's Go* strongly urges you to consider the risks before you choose to hitchhike. In summer months, some travelers see Chileans themselves (generally students) hitting the road with their packs on and their thumbs out. Those who choose to hitchhike report that it's easiest to find rides by asking around at service stops along a main highway and that truck drivers are the most likely to pick up passengers. They also report that in rural areas, individuals and families are more likely to take on extra passengers, though thin traffic in those areas can result in long waits.

If you choose to hitchhike, use common sense. If somethign does not feel right then don't do it; you are better off waiting. Women traveling alone should never hitchhike. Despite the fact that it is a popular mode of travel, because of safety concerns, *Let's Go* does not recommend hitchhiking and urges you to consider all possible risks before doing so.

KEEPING IN TOUCH

BY MAIL

SENDING MAIL HOME FROM CHILE

Airmail is the best way to send mail home from Chile. Write "airmail" and *"por avión"* on the front. Regular mail takes between two and three weeks to reach Europe or the US, whereas Chile Express is the most common, reliable, and inexpensive way to send mail within a few days. DHL Worldwide Express (in the US ☎800-800-345; www.la-reg.dhl.com) also provides express service.

Post offices in larger cities tend to have the quickest and most consistent service. If you need something to reach its destination in a reasonably short time period, don't send it from a tiny post office in a remote town.

SENDING MAIL TO CHILE

Mark envelopes "air mail" and *"por avión"* to ensure timely delivery. In addition to the standard postage system whose rates are listed below, **Federal Express** (www.fedex.com; Australia ☎13 26 10; Canada and the US ☎800-463-3339; Ireland 1800 535 800; New Zealand 0800 733 339; UK 0800 123 800) handles express mail services from most countries to Chile—a fairly pricey but efficient service. For example, a letter sent by FedEx from New York to Chile would typically take 1-3 business days and cost US$48; one from London to Chile would average 1-3 days for UK£37. DHL is less common in the US, but offers similar rates and services and has more locations in Chile than FedEx, making it a more convenient alternative.

Australia: Allow 6-7 days for regular airmail. Postcards and letters up to 20g cost AUS$1; packages up to 1kg AUS$26, up to 3kg AUS$66. EMS can get a letter to Chile in 4-5 days for AUS$35. www.auspost.com.au.

Canada: Allow 6-10 days for regular airmail. Postcards and letters up to 30g cost CDN$1.40; packages up to 1kg CDN$37, up to 3kg CDN$56. www.canadapost.ca.

Ireland: Allow approximately one week for regular airmail. Postcards and letters up to 50g cost €0.65; packages up to 1kg €10, up to 2kg €16. www.letterpost.ie.

New Zealand: Allow approximately one week for regular airmail. Postcards NZ$1.50; letters up to 200g NZ$3; parcels up to 1kg NZ$32, up to 3kg NZ$81. www.nzpost.co.nz.

UK: Allow 5-8 days for airmail. Letters up to 40g cost UK£1; packages up to 1kg UK£9.50, up to 2kg UK£18.50. International Signed For puts parcels on the first available flight for UK£3.30 more. www.consignia-online.com.

US: Allow 5-7 days for regular airmail. Postcards cost US$0.70; letters under 4 oz. US$3; packages up to 1 lb. US$16; up to 3 lbs. US$22. **Global Express Mail** takes 2-5 days and costs US$22.25/24.75 (0.5/1 lb.). **Global Priority Mail** delivers small/large flat-rate envelopes to Chile in 4-7 days for US$5/9. www.usps.com.

RECEIVING MAIL IN CHILE

There are several ways to arrange pick-up of letters sent to you by friends and relatives while you are abroad. Mail can be sent to Chile through **Lista de Correos** (or by using the international phrase **Poste Restante**) to almost any city or town with a post office. Address *Poste Restante* letters to:

> Firstname LASTNAME
> Lista de Correos
> City, Chile

The mail will go to a special desk in the central post office, unless you specify a post office by street address or postal code. It's best to use the largest post office, since mail may be sent there regardless. Bring your passport (or other photo ID) for pick-up; there may be a small fee (if there is, it should not exceed the cost of domestic postage). If the clerks insist that there is nothing for you, have them check under your first name as well. *Let's Go* lists post offices in the **Practical Information** section for each city and most towns.

BY TELEPHONE

CALLING HOME FROM CHILE

A **calling card** purchased before you leave for Chile is probably your cheapest bet, but cheap cards are available in Chile as well. Cards can be purchased for collect, billed, or pre-paid calls. You can frequently call collect without even possessing a company's calling card just by calling their access number and following the instructions. Before settling on a calling card plan, be sure to research your options in order to pick the one that best fits both your needs and your destination. **To obtain a calling card** from your national telecommunications service before leaving home, contact the appropriate company listed below. To **call home with a calling card,** contact the operator for your service provider in Chile by dialing the appropriate toll-free access number.

COMPANY	TO OBTAIN A CARD, CONTACT:	TO CALL ABROAD FROM CHILE, DIAL:
AT&T (US)	www.consumer.att.com/prepaid-card/	☎800 225 288 or 800 360 311
British Telecom Direct	☎0800 34 51 44; www.pay-phones.bt.com	☎800 360 066 or 800 800 044
Canada Direct	☎800 668 6878; www.mts.mb.ca/	☎800 360 280 or 800 800 226
MCI (US)	☎800-955-0925; http://consumer.mci.com/prepaid_cards/	☎800 360 180
Sprint (US)	https://prepaid.sprint.com/	☎800 360 777
Telstra	http://telstra.com.au/callingcard-shop/	☎800 360 150 or 800 800 287

You can usually also make direct international calls from pay phones, but if you aren't using a calling card, you may need to drop your coins as quickly as your words. Where available, prepaid phone cards purchased in Chile (**Calling within Chile**, p. 43) and occasionally major credit cards can be used for direct international calls. (See the box on **Placing International Calls**, p. 43, for directions on how to place a direct international call.)

Placing a **collect call** *(llamada con cobro revertido)* through an international operator is even more expensive, but may be necessary in case of emergency. You can typically place collect calls through the service providers listed above even if you don't have one of their phone cards.

In order to dial out from any phone in Chile, you can choose a **carrier service** by dialing one of the numbers below. To call within Chile, dial the carrier code and then the regional area code and number; for international calls, dial the carrier code followed by a 0 and the country code and phone number. If you wish simply to use the default carrier for the phone you are using, for calls within Chile, dial zero followed by the area code and phone number; for international calls, dial 00 followed by the country code and phone number.

CARRIER	DIAL
Bell South	181 + 0 + Country Code + Area Code + Number
Chilesat	171 + 0 + Country Code + Area Code + Number
CNT Carrier	121 + 0 + Country Code + Area Code + Number
Entel	123 + 0 + Country Code + Area Code + Number
Manquehue LD	122 + 0 + Country Code + Area Code + Number
Telefónica (CTC)	188 + 0 + Country Code + Area Code + Number
Transam Comunicaciones	113 + 0 + Country Code + Area Code + Number
VTR	120 + 0 + Country Code + Area Code + Number

CALLING WITHIN CHILE

PLACING INTERNATIONAL CALLS. To call Chile from home or to call home from Chile, dial:

1. The **international dialing prefix.** To dial out of out of **Chile,** dial 00 or specific carrier number (see above chart); **Australia,** dial 0011; **Canada** or the **US,** 011; the **Republic of Ireland, New Zealand,** or the **UK,** 00.

2. The **country code** of the country you want to call. To call **Chile,** dial 56; **Australia,** 61; **Canada** or the **US,** 1; **Ireland,** 353; **New Zealand,** 64; the **UK,** 44.

3. The **city/area code.** *Let's Go* lists the city/area codes for cities and towns in Chile opposite the city or town name, next to a ☎. If the first digit is a zero (e.g., 02 for Santiago), omit the zero when calling from abroad (e.g., dial 2 from Canada to reach Santiago).

4. The **local number.**

The simplest way to call within the country is to use a phone at a **locutorio,** a grouping of phones, which enables you to pay after you have made your calls. **Prepaid phone cards** (available at newspaper kiosks and tobacco stores) carry a certain amount of phone time depending on the card's denomination, and usually save time and money in the long run. The computerized phone will tell you how much time in units (minutes), you have left on your card. Another kind of prepaid telephone card comes with a Personal Identification Number (PIN) and a toll-free access number. Instead of inserting the card into the phone, you dial the access number and follow the directions on the card. These cards can often be used to make international as well as domestic calls. International calling cards from Entel or CTC offices (generally in denominations of CH$1000-3000, CH$5000, and CH$10,000) tend to be cheaper than using *centro de llamadas* services, which in turn are cheaper than public pay phones. Phone rates typically tend to be highest in the morning, lower in the evening, and lowest on Sunday and late at night.

CELLULAR PHONES

For students and other travelers who will spend extended amounts of time in Chile, cellular phones will prove useful. **Entel** and **Telefónica** are the main competitors, and both provide prepaid options. Prepaid cards to fill the phone's allotment of minutes can be purchased at kiosks and convenience stores across the country.

The international standard for cell phones is **GSM,** a system that began in Europe and has spread to much of the rest of the world. If you would like to bring your own cellular, you will need a **GSM-compatible phone** and a **SIM (subscriber identity module) card,** a country-specific, thumbnail-sized chip that gives you a local phone number and plugs you into the local network. Many SIM cards are **prepaid,** meaning that they come with calling time included and you don't need to sign up for a monthly service plan. Incoming calls are frequently free. When you use up the prepaid time, you can buy additional cards or vouchers (usually available at convenience stores) to get more. For more information on GSM phones, check out www.telestial.com, www.telefonicamovil.cl, www.entel.cl, www.roadpost.com, or www.planetomni.com. Companies like **Cellular Abroad** (www.cellularabroad.com) rent cell phones that work in a variety of destinations around the world, providing a simpler option than picking up a phone in-country.

 GSM PHONES. Just having a GSM phone doesn't mean you're necessarily good to go when you travel abroad. The majority of GSM phones sold in the United States operate on a different **frequency** (1900) than international phones (900/1800) and will not work abroad. Tri-band phones work on all three frequencies (900/1800/1900) and will operate through most of the world. As well, some GSM phones are **SIM-locked** and will only accept SIM cards from a single carrier. You'll need a **SIM-unlocked** phone to use a SIM card from a local carrier when you travel.

TIME DIFFERENCES

Chile is four hours behind **Greenwich Mean Time (GMT),** one hour ahead of New York time, and four hours ahead of San Francisco. Chile **ignores Daylight Saving Time,** so when the US "springs forward," New York and Chile are on the same time.

The following chart is applicable from **late October** to **early April**.

4AM	6AM	7AM	8AM	NOON		10PM
Vancouver Seattle San Francisco Los Angeles	Galápagos Chicago Easter Island	New York Toronto Boston	New Brunswick Chile	London (GMT)		Sydney Canberra Melbourne

Because Chile and Australia ignore Daylight Saving Time, the following table is applicable from **early April** to **late October**.

4AM	5AM	6AM	7AM	8AM	NOON	9PM
Vancouver Seattle San Francisco Los Angeles	Galápagos Denver Easter Island	Chicago	New York Toronto Boston Chile	New Brunswick	London (GMT)	Sydney Canberra Melbourne

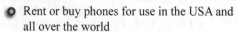

BY EMAIL AND INTERNET

Internet cafes are the easiest and most reliable way to access the Internet in Chile. You can find them in every major city and even in most smaller cities and towns. Rates are generally US$1-4 per hour, with other services such as printing and sometimes CD burning provided for an extra charge. Though in some places it's possible to establish a remote link with your home server, in most cases this is a much slower (and thus more expensive) option than taking advantage of free **web-based email accounts** (e.g., www.hotmail.com and www.yahoo.com). Internet cafes and the occasional free Internet terminal at a public library are listed in the **Practical Information** sections of major cities.

ACCOMMODATIONS

HOSTELS

Many hostels are laid out dorm-style, often with large single-sex rooms and bunk beds, although private rooms that sleep up to four are becoming more common. They sometimes have kitchens and utensils for your use, bike or moped rentals, storage areas, transportation to airports, breakfast and other meals, laundry facilities, and Internet access. There can be drawbacks: some hostels close during certain daytime "lockout" hours, have a curfew, don't accept reservations, impose a maximum stay, or, less frequently, require that you do chores. In Chile, a dorm bed in a hostel will average around US$5-10 (CH$3000-6000) and a private room around US$10-25 (CH$6000-15,000).

A HOSTELER'S BILL OF RIGHTS. There are certain standard features that we do not include in our hostel listings. Unless we state otherwise, you can expect that every hostel has no lockout, no curfew, a kitchen, free hot showers, some system of secure luggage storage, and no key deposit.

HOSTELLING INTERNATIONAL

Joining the youth hostel association in your own country (listed below) automatically grants you membership privileges in **Hostelling International (HI),** a federation of national hosteling associations. Non-HI members are often allowed to stay in some hostels but will have to pay extra to do so. There are 14 participating hostels scattered through Chile, in locations including Ancud, Arica, Chillán, Easter Island, Frutillar, Isla de Pascua, Pucón, Puerto Montt, Punta Arenas, Salto de Laja, San Pedro de Atacama, Santiago, Temuco, Valdivia, and Viña del Mar. The HI umbrella organization's web page (www.hihostels.com), which lists the web addresses and phone numbers of all national associations, can be a great place to begin researching hosteling in a specific region. For hosteling information specific to Chile, check www.hostelling.cl.

A new membership benefit is the FreeNites program, which allows hostelers to gain points toward free rooms. Most student travel agencies (p. 31) sell HI cards, as do all of the national hosteling organizations listed below. All prices listed below are valid for **one-year memberships.**

Australian Youth Hostels Association (AYHA), 422 Kent St., Sydney, NSW 200 (☎02 9261 1111; fax 9261 1969; www.yha.com.au). AUS$52, under 18 AUS$19.

Hostelling International-Canada (HI-C), 205 Catherine St. #400, Ottawa, ON K2P 1C3 (☎613-237-7884; fax 237-7868; www.hihostels.ca). CDN$35, under 18 free.

HostellingChile, Hernando de Aguirre 201, Of. 602, Providencia, Santiago, Chile (☎56 2 233 3220; fax 233 2555; www.hostelling.cl). CH$16,000; under 30 CH$14,000.

An Óige (Irish Youth Hostel Association), 61 Mountjoy St., Dublin 7 (☎830 4555; fax 830 5808; www.irelandyha.org). €20, under 18 €10.

Youth Hostels Association of New Zealand (YHANZ), Level 1, Moorhouse City, 166 Moorhouse Ave., P.O. Box 436, Christchurch (☎0800 278 299, outside NZ 03 379 9970; fax 365 4476; www.yha.org.nz). NZ$40, under 18 free.

Hostelling International Northern Ireland (HINI), 22 Donegal Rd., Belfast BT12 5JN (☎02890 31 54 35; fax 43 96 99; www.hini.org.uk). UK£13, under 18 UK£6.

Scottish Youth Hostels Association (SYHA), 7 Glebe Cres., Stirling FK8 2JA (☎01786 89 14 00; fax 89 13 33; www.syha.org.uk). UK£6, under 17 £2.50.

Youth Hostels Association (England and Wales), Trevelyan House, Dimple Rd., Matlock, Derbyshire DE4 3YH, UK (☎0870 770 8868; fax 770 6127; www.yha.org.uk). UK£14, under 18 UK£6.

Hostelling International-USA, 8401 Colesville Rd., Ste. 600, Silver Spring, MD 20910 (☎301-495-1240; fax 495-6697; www.hiayh.org). US$28, under 18 free.

BOOKING HOSTELS ONLINE. One of the easiest ways to ensure you've got a bed for the night is by reserving online. Click to the **Hostelworld** booking engine through **www.letsgo.com,** and you'll have access to bargain accommodations from Argentina to Zimbabwe with no added commission.

OTHER TYPES OF ACCOMMODATIONS

HOTELS, RESIDENCIALES, AND HOSPEDAJES

The terms hotel, *residencial*, and *hospedaje* are sometimes used ambiguously to refer to similar establishments in Chile. **Residenciales,** sometimes called *hostales*, however, are the most common accommodations—they are usually established businesses offering simple, short-term lodging, often with shared bathrooms and up to four beds in a room. A bed in a *residencial* tends to cost US$10-20 a night, although single rooms and rooms with special amenities such as television cost slightly more. **Hospedajes,** which run about US$10-15 per night, are modest accommodations with shared bathrooms and are usually family-run and located in a few spare rooms of the family's home. **Hotels** are generally more expensive than *residenciales* and *hospedajes*, offering more amenities, especially in the larger cities. Hotels are rated on a scale of one to five stars by the Chilean national tourist board, **Sernatur** (p. 14), but the rating system is based on facilities and not upkeep; ask to see a room before you spring for a pricey four-star. **Hotel singles** in Chile cost about US$20-40 per night, **doubles** cost slightly more. You'll typically share a hall bathroom; a private bathroom will cost extra, as may hot showers. Some hotels offer "full pensión" (all meals) and "half pensión" (no lunch). If you make **reservations** in writing, indicate your night of arrival and the number of nights you plan to stay. The hotel will send you a confirmation and may request payment for the first night. Not all hotels take reservations, and few accept checks in foreign currency. Enclosing two International Reply Coupons will ensure a prompt reply (US$1.05 each; available at any US post office).

HOSPITALITY CLUBS

Hospitality clubs link their members with individuals or families abroad who are willing to host travelers for free or for a small fee to promote cultural exchange and general good karma. In exchange, members usually must be willing to host travelers in their own homes; a small membership fee may also be required. **Global-Freeloaders.com** (www.globalfreeloaders.com) and **The Hospitality Club** (www.hospitalityclub.org) are good places to start. **Servas** (www.servas.org) is an established, more formal, peace-based organization, and requires a fee and an interview to join. An Internet search will find many similar organizations, some of which cater to special interests (e.g., women, gay and lesbian travelers, or members of certain professions). As always, use common sense when planning to stay with or host someone you do not know.

LONG-TERM ACCOMMODATIONS

Travelers planning to stay in Chile for extended periods of time may find it most cost-effective to rent an apartment. A basic one-bedroom (or studio) **apartment** in Santiago will range US$250-500 per month. Besides the rent itself, prospective tenants usually are also required to front a security deposit (frequently one month's rent), which can sometimes be difficult to retrieve, and the last month's rent. Students and those planning to stay in the country for shorter periods of time will appreciate the availability of *departmentos amoblados*, or furnished apartments. The online portal of Santiago's major newspaper, *El Mercurio* (www.elmercurio.cl), provides searchable apartment listings in many neighborhoods.

CAMPING AND THE OUTDOORS

Camping is one of the most accessible and enjoyable outdoor activities in the many **parques nacionales** and **reservas nacionales** in Chile. Sites vary from the most rustic grounds to swankier private-owned venues offering restrooms, water supply, cooking facilities, and hot showers. Official campsites charge about CH$4000-CH$10,000 (US$7-16) per tent, although it is more economical to look for the occasional grounds that charge CH$4000-CH$10,000 (US$7-16) for an entire site and share the cost with a few other campers. Private campgrounds in and around smaller towns offer more services and are generally cheaper than official **Conaf** administered campsites (p. 50). Most national parks prohibit camping outside of designated areas, and camping in the wild is not suggested except for the most experienced campers with their own transportation and a knowledgeable guide.

Spanish-speakers planning on camping and trekking should check out the Chilean **Turistel** website (www.turistel.cl) for information about Turistel's meticulous maps of camping spots and comprehensive camping guides such as *Guía Turística Turistel: Rutero Camping*. Another excellent general resource for travelers planning on spending time in the outdoors is the **Great Outdoor Recreation Pages** (www.gorp.com). This site includes a section entitled *Chile: 20 Best Adventures* (www.gorp.com/gorp/location/latamer/chile/top_twenty.htm), with some useful information about outdoor activities in Chile. Gochile.com also has detailed descriptions of most parks in both English and Spanish (www.gochile.com).

USEFUL PUBLICATIONS AND RESOURCES

A variety of publishing companies offer hiking guidebooks to meet the educational needs of novice or expert. For information about camping, hiking, and biking, write or call the publishers listed below to receive a free catalog.

LEAVE NO TRACE. Let's Go encourages travelers to embrace the "Leave No Trace" ethic, minimizing their impact on natural environments and protecting them for future generations. Trekkers and wilderness enthusiasts should set up camp on durable surfaces, use cookstoves instead of campfires, bury human waste away from water supplies, bag trash and carry it out with them, and respect wildlife and natural objects. For more detailed information, contact the **Leave No Trace Center for Outdoor Ethics,** P.O. Box 997, Boulder, CO 80306, USA (☎800-332-4100, 303-442-8222; www.lnt.org).

Sierra Club Books, 85 Second St., 2nd fl., San Francisco, CA 94105, USA (☎415-977-5500; www.sierraclub.org). Publishes general resource books on hiking and camping.

The Mountaineers Books, 1001 SW Klickitat Way, Ste. 201, Seattle, WA 98134, USA (☎206-223-6303; www.mountaineersbooks.org). Boasts over 600 titles on hiking, biking, mountaineering, natural history, and conservation. Check out *Mountaineering in Patagonia* (Mountaineers Books, US$22.95) for information about outdoor adventures in Chile and Argentina.

Wilderness Press, 1200 5th St., Berkeley, CA 94710, USA (☎800-443-7227, 510-558-1666; www.wildernesspress.com). Carries over 100 hiking guides and maps, mostly for the western US.

Woodall Publications Corporation, 2575 Vista Del Mar Dr., Ventura, CA 93001, USA (☎877-680-6155; www.woodalls.com). Annually updates campground directories.

NATIONAL PARKS

The national parks system in Chile is controlled by the **Corporación Nacional Forestal (Conaf),** a government-run corporation that aims to use resources responsibly to preserve the country's flora, fauna, and spectacular natural environments. Conaf runs administration offices in Chile's national parks and national reserves, offering information, maps, and rescue services for hikers and other visitors. The conserved spaces in Chile—totaling a whopping 140,000 sq. km, 18% of the country's territory—include 31 **parques nacionales** (PN), 48 **reservas nacionales** (RN), and 15 **monumentos naturales** (MN). *Parques nacionales* are extensive areas generally used only for recreation and study, and are intended to preserve Chile's threatened or endangered plants, creatures, and environments. The *reservas* are meant to ensure the country's proper use of essential natural resources, but are also used for recreational purposes. *Monumentos naturales* tend to be smaller areas set aside to preserve specific native species of flora and fauna or geological sites that have particular cultural or scientific importance. Chile's preserved areas are representative of the extreme natural environments of the country, including the towering volcano in **Parque Nacional Lauca** in Norte Grande; the scenic waterfalls and pools of **Reserva Nacional Radal Siete Tazas** in Middle Chile; and the striking granite pillars and glaciers of **Parque Nacional Torres del Paine** in the far south.

Parques Nacionales (PN), *Reservas Nacionales* (RN), and *Monumentos Naturales* (MN) are often accessible by inexpensive public transportation from nearby cities or towns. Some charge no entrance fee, while others charge as much as US$15 during peak season. Visitors to both *reservas nacionales* and *parques nacionales* should start by checking out the **Centro de Información Ambiental** run by Conaf for maps, educational talks and other orientating information—ask for suggestions about hiking routes and local guides. Conaf also often runs campsites for approximately US$10-15 per tent. Contact the central office for general information. (Bulnes 285, Of. 501, Santiago. ☎56 2 390 0000 or 390 0208; www.conaf.cl.)

ENVIRONMENTALLY RESPONSIBLE TOURISM. The idea behind responsible tourism is to leave no trace of human presence behind. A camp stove is the safer (and more efficient) way to cook than using vegetation, but if you must make a fire, keep it small and use only dead branches or brush rather than cutting vegetation. Make sure your campsite is at least 150 ft. (50m) from water sources or bodies of water. If there are no toilet facilities, bury human waste (but not paper) at least four inches (10cm) deep and above the high-water line, and 150 ft. or more from any water supplies and campsites. Always pack your trash in a plastic bag and carry it with you until you reach the next trash receptacle. For more information on these issues, contact one of the organizations listed below.

Earthwatch, 3 Clock Tower Place #100, Box 75, Maynard, MA 01754, USA (☎800-776-0188, 978-461-0081; www.earthwatch.org).

International Ecotourism Society, 28 Pine St., Burlington, VT 05402, USA (☎802-651-9818; fax 802-651-9819; www.ecotourism.org).

National Audubon Society, Nature Odysseys, 700 Broadway, New York, NY 10003 (☎212-979-3000; fax 212-979-3188; www.audubon.org).

Tourism Concern, Stapleton House, 277-281 Holloway Rd., London N7 8HN, UK (☎020 7753 3330; fax 020 7753 3331; www.tourismconcern.org.uk).

WILDERNESS SAFETY

THE GREAT OUTDOORS

Staying **warm, dry, and well-hydrated** is key to a happy and safe wilderness experience. For any hike, prepare yourself for an emergency by packing a first-aid kit, a reflector, a whistle, high-energy food, extra water, raingear, a hat, and mittens. For warmth, wear wool or insulating synthetic materials designed for the outdoors. Cotton is a bad choice since it dries painfully slowly.

Check **weather forecasts** often and pay attention to the skies when hiking, as weather patterns can change suddenly. Always let either a friend, your hostel, a park ranger, or a hiking organization, know when and where you are going. Know your physical limits and do not attempt a hike beyond your ability. See **Safety and Health,** p. 22, for information on outdoor ailments and medical concerns.

Earthquakes are not uncommon in Chile. Although the possibility of natural disasters should not keep you away, it is a good idea to be informed before heading out into Chile. Consult the website for the **Oficina Nacional de Emergencia de Chile (ONEMI)** for information on Chilean earthquakes (www.onemi.cl). For more general information about earthquake awareness, check out the **US Federal Emergency Management Agency** site at www.fema.gov.

WILDLIFE

Luckily for travelers in Chile, no poisonous snakes or insects in the country pose a common threat to humans. The **puma,** or mountain lion, is the only large feline in the country, but it generally avoids humans and is elusive in its natural habitat. Nevertheless, travelers should always be cautious of fauna in the wild and should not disturb their natural environments. For more information, consult *How to Stay Alive in the Woods,* by Bradford Angier (Macmillan Press, US$8).

CAMPING AND HIKING EQUIPMENT

WHAT TO BUY

Good camping equipment is both sturdy and light. North American suppliers tend to offer the most competitive prices.

Sleeping Bags: Most sleeping bags are rated by season; "summer" means 30-40°F (around 0°C) at night; "four-season" or "winter" often means below 0°F (-17°C). Bags are made of **down** (warm and light, but expensive, and miserable when wet) or of **synthetic** material (heavy, durable, and warm when wet). Prices range US$50-250 for a summer synthetic to US$200-300 for a good down winter bag. **Sleeping bag pads** include foam pads (US$10-30), air mattresses (US$15-50), and self-inflating mats (US$30-120). Bring a **stuff sack** to store your bag and keep it dry.

Tents: The best tents are free-standing (with their own frames and suspension systems), set up quickly, and only require staking in high winds. Low-profile dome tents are the best all-around. Worthy 2-person tents start at US$100, 4-person at US$160. Make sure your tent has a rain fly and seal its seams with waterproofer. Other useful accessories include a **battery-operated lantern,** a plastic **groundcloth,** and a nylon **tarp.**

Backpacks: Internal-frame packs mold well to your back, keep a lower center of gravity, and flex adequately to allow you to hike difficult trails, while **external-frame packs** are more comfortable for long hikes over even terrain, as they carry weight higher and distribute it more evenly. Make sure your pack has a strong, padded hipbelt to transfer weight to your legs. There are models designed specifically for women. Any serious backpacking requires a pack of at least 3000 in.^{3} (49,000cc), plus 500 in.^{3} (8200cc) for sleeping bags in internal-frame packs. Sturdy backpacks cost US$125-420—your pack is an area where it doesn't pay to economize. On your hunt for the perfect pack, fill up a prospective model with something heavy, strap it on correctly, and walk around the store to get a sense of how it distributes weight. Either buy a **rain cover** (US$10-20) or store all of your belongings in plastic bags inside your pack.

Boots: Be sure to wear hiking boots with good **ankle support.** They should fit snugly and comfortably over 1-2 pairs of **wool socks** and a pair of thin **liner socks.** Break in boots over several weeks before you go to spare yourself blisters.

Other Necessities: Synthetic layers, like those made of polypropylene or polyester, and a pile jacket will keep you warm even when wet. A **space blanket** (US$5-15) will help you to retain body heat and doubles as a groundcloth. Plastic **water bottles** are vital; look for shatter- and leak-resistant models. Carry **water-purification tablets** for when you can't boil water. Although most campgrounds provide campfire sites, you may want to bring a small **metal grate** or **grill.** For those places that forbid fires or the gathering of firewood, you'll need a **camp stove** (the classic Coleman starts at US$50) and a propane-filled **fuel bottle** to operate it. Also bring a **first-aid kit, pocketknife, insect repellent,** and **waterproof matches** or a **lighter.**

WHERE TO BUY IT

The mail-order/online companies listed below offer lower prices than many retail stores. A visit to a local camping or outdoors store will give you a good sense of the look and weight of certain items. It's also possible to wait until arriving in Chile, and pick up gear at **La Cumbre** or other area outfitters.

Campmor, 28 Parkway, P.O. Box 700, Upper Saddle River, NJ 07458, USA (US ☎888-226-7667; www.campmor.com).

Discount Camping, 880 Main North Rd., Pooraka, South Australia 5095, Australia (☎08 8262 3399; fax 8260 6240; www.discountcamping.com.au).

Eastern Mountain Sports (EMS), 1 Vose Farm Rd., Peterborough, NH 03458, USA (☎888-463-6367; www.ems.com).

La Cumbre, Apoquindo 5258, Las Condes, Santiago, Chile (☎/fax 56 2 220 9907; www.lacumbreonline.cl).

L.L. Bean, Freeport, ME 04033 USA (Canada and US ☎800-441-5713; UK ☎ 891 297; www.llbean.com).

Mountain Designs, 51 Bishop St., Kelvin Grove, Queensland 4059, Australia (☎07 3856 2344; www.mountaindesigns.com).

Recreational Equipment, Inc. (REI), Sumner, WA 98352, USA (Canada and US ☎800-426-4840, elsewhere 253-891-2500; www.rei.com).

YHA Adventure Shop, 19 High St., Staines, Middlesex, TW18 4QY, UK (☎1784 458625; www.yhaadventure.com).

ORGANIZED ADVENTURE TRIPS

Organized adventure trips offer another way of exploring the wild, placing individual travelers or small groups on trips with other adventurers of similar experience levels. Tourism bureaus often can suggest parks, trails, and outfitters. Organizations that specialize in camping and outdoor equipment like REI and EMS (see above) also are good source for info. Activities include hiking, biking, skiing, canoeing, kayaking, rafting, climbing, photo safaris, and archaeological digs.

There are many agencies that organize adventures abroad, but if you'd rather arrange trips once you've arrived in Chile, local tourism bureaus can often suggest parks, trails, and outfitters. Look for local tour operators in the **Practical Information** section of major outdoor destinations under the **Tours** heading. Local operations are generally reliable, and provide a safer and more informative means of seeing the best of the Chilean outdoors than going it alone. Many operations are staffed with helpful, experienced, English-speaking guides and include equipment and/or meals within the price of the tour. The supervision of a trained tour guide is often a good idea in remote, possibly uncharted, terrain in many parts of Chile including Norte Grande, Chiloé, and the Far South—remember, solo attempts to traverse trails or ascend peaks that require you to be accompanied by a guide is not only unnecessarily reckless; it is illegal and potentially fatal.

Bíobío Expeditions Worldwide, P.O. Box 2028, Truckee, CA 96160, USA (☎800-246-7238; US fax 530-550-9670, Chile fax 56 2 334 3012; www.bbxrafting.com/adventure/chile). Kayaking and whitewater rafting expeditions in Chile.

Expediciones Chile (☎888-488-9082; www.exchile.com). Offers kayaking, fly fishing, and multi-sport trips in Chile.

GORPtravel, P.O. Box 1486, Boulder, CO 80306, USA (US ☎877-440-GORP; international 1 720-887-8500; http://gorptravel.gorp.com). Adventure tours to Chile and Argentina include mountain biking, hiking, walking, whitewater rafting, and kayaking.

Specialty Travel Index, 305 San Anselmo Ave., Ste. 309, San Anselmo, CA 94960 (US ☎888-624-4030, elsewhere 415-455-1643; www.specialtytravel.com). Listings for tours worldwide, including Chile.

SPECIFIC CONCERNS

SUSTAINABLE TRAVEL

As the number of travelers on the road continues to rise, the detrimental effect they can have on natural environments becomes an increasing concern. With this in mind, *Let's Go* promotes the philosophy of **sustainable travel.** Through a sensitivity to issues of ecology and sustainability, today's travelers can be a powerful force in preserving and restoring the places they visit.

Ecotourism, a rising trend in sustainable travel, focuses on the conservation of natural habitats and using them to build up the economy without exploitation or overdevelopment. Travelers can make a difference by doing advance research and by supporting organizations and establishments that pay attention to their impact on their natural surroundings and strive to be environmentally friendly.

Ecotourism websites are expanding on the Internet. Planeta (www.planeta.com) has Chile-specific suggestions for sustainable travel, and Earthfoot (www.earthfoot.org) provides opportunities for environmental work there (see **Alternatives to Tourism,** p. 82).

ECOTOURISM RESOURCES. For more information on environmentally responsible tourism, contact one of the organizations below:

The Centre for Environmentally Responsible Tourism (www.c-e-r-t.org).

Earthwatch, 3 Clock Tower Pl., Ste. 100, Box 75, Maynard, MA 01754, USA (☎800-776-0188, 978-461-0081; www.earthwatch.org).

International Ecotourism Society, 733 15th St. NW, Washington, D.C. 20005, USA (☎202-347-9203; www.ecotourism.org).

RESPONSIBLE TRAVEL

The impact of tourist pesos on the destinations you visit should not be underestimated. The choices you make during your trip can have potent effects on local communities—for better or for worse. Travelers who care about the destinations and environments they explore should become aware of the social and cultural implications of the choices they make when they travel.

Community-based tourism aims to channel tourists' money into the local economy by emphasizing tours and cultural programs that are run by members of the community and that benefit disadvantaged groups. A resource for general information on community-based travel is *The Good Alternative Travel Guide* (UK£10), a project of **Tourism Concern** (☎020 7133 3330; www.tourismconcern.org.uk).

Especially in areas with highly indigenous populations, tourists must take care to be respectful of customs and not intrude where they are unwanted. Indiscriminately throwing around money or taking pictures of "different"-looking natives, or giving gifts of candy and trinkets to their children, can unsettle cultural mores that are valuable and important to indigenous groups.

TRAVELING ALONE

There are many benefits to traveling alone, including independence and greater interaction with locals. On the other hand, solo travelers are more vulnerable targets for harassment and street theft. If traveling alone, try not to stand out, look confident, and be especially careful in deserted or very crowded areas. Never admit that you are traveling alone. Maintain regular contact with someone at home who knows your itinerary. For more tips, pick up *Traveling Solo* by Eleanor Berman (Globe Pequot Press, US$18), visit www.travelaloneandloveit.com, or subscribe to **Connecting: Solo Travel Network,** 689 Park Rd., Unit 6, Gibsons, BC V0N 1V7, Canada (☎604-886-9099; www.cstn.org; membership US$28-45).

WOMEN TRAVELERS

Women exploring on their own inevitably face some additional safety concerns, but it's easy to be adventurous without taking undue risks. If you are concerned, consider staying in hostels which offer single rooms that lock from the inside or in religious organizations with rooms for women only. Stick to centrally located accommodations and avoid solitary late-night treks or metro rides.

Always carry extra money for a phone call, bus, or taxi. **Hitchhiking** is never safe for lone women, or even for two women traveling together. Look as if you know where you're going and approach older women or couples for directions if you're lost or uncomfortable. Generally, the less you look like a tourist, the better off you'll be. Dress conservatively, especially in rural areas. Wearing a conspicuous **wedding band** sometimes helps to prevent unwanted overtures.

Chile, like most Latin American countries, has a very *machista* culture. Men will often make comments about passing women, especially in front of other men, although public violence against women is rare. To lessen unwanted attention, dress conservatively, especially in rural areas, and try to blend in. Your best answer to verbal harassment is no answer at all; feigning deafness, sitting motionless, and staring straight ahead at nothing in particular will do a world of good that reactions usually don't achieve. If the man is extremely persistent or you are in a situation where you cannot move away (i.e., on a bus or metro) then a firm, loud, and very public *"¡Déjame en paz!"* (DAY-ha-may en pas; "Leave me alone!") or *"¡No me moleste!"* (no may mole-EST-ay; "Don't bother me!") should be enough to dissuade him. If harassment does not subside, do not hesitate to turn to an older woman for support or seek out a police officer. Memorize the emergency numbers in places you visit, and consider carrying a whistle on your keychain. A self-defense course will both prepare you for a potential attack and raise your level of awareness of your surroundings (see **Self Defense**, p. 24). Also be sure you are aware of the health concerns that women face when traveling (p. 30).

GLBT TRAVELERS

As in most of Latin America, the strong Catholic tradition in Chile is still fairly intolerant of homosexuality. The tactile nature of Chilean culture is helpful in some ways, since it is not uncommon for women to hold hands and men to embrace. However, actions beyond that are often met with suspicion.

Despite this obstacle, there is a growing, vocal gay, lesbian, and bisexual community, especially in Santiago. There is also a small but thriving gay rights movement led by the Movimiento Unificado de Minorías Sexuales (MUMS; www.orgullogay.cl). Their website has links to other gay community resources, including organizations like Gay Chile (www.gaychile.cl) and www.lesbianas.cl. *Let's Go* tries to list gay-friendly nightlife wherever possible.

Transgendered travelers will most likely encounter similar intolerance, especially outside of Santiago. To avoid hassles at airports and border crossings, transgendered travelers should make sure that all their travel documents consistently report the same gender. Many countries (including Australia, Canada, Ireland, New Zealand, the UK, and the US) will amend passports of post-operative transsexuals, though governments are generally less willing to amend documents for pre-operative transsexuals and other transgendered individuals.

Listed below are contact organizations, mail-order bookstores, and publishers that offer materials addressing some specific concerns. **Out and About** (www.planetout.com) offers a bi-weekly newsletter addressing travel concerns and a comprehensive site addressing gay travel concerns. The online newspaper **365gay.com** also has a travel section (www.365gay.com/travel/travelchannel.htm).

ESSENTIALS

FURTHER READING: GLBT

Spartacus 2003-2004: International Gay Guide. Bruno Gmunder Verlag. (www.spartacusworld.com, US$33.)

Ferrari Guides' Gay Travel A to Z, Ferrari Guides' Men's Travel in Your Pocket, Ferrari Guides' Women's Travel in Your Pocket, and *Ferrari Guides' Inn Places.* Ferrari Publications (US$16-20).

The Gay Vacation Guide: The Best Trips and How to Plan Them, Mark Chesnut. Kensington Books (US$15).

Gay's the Word, 66 Marchmont St., London WC1N 1AB, UK (☎44 20 7278 7654; www.gaystheword.co.uk). The largest gay and lesbian bookshop in the UK, with both fiction and non-fiction titles. Mail-order service available.

Giovanni's Room, 1145 Pine St., Philadelphia, PA 19107, USA (☎215-923-2960; www.queerbooks.com). An international lesbian/feminist and gay bookstore with mail-order service (carries many of the publications listed below).

International Lesbian and Gay Association (ILGA), 81 rue Marché-au-Charbon, B-1000 Brussels, Belgium (☎32 2 502 2471; www.ilga.org). Provides political information, such as homosexuality laws of individual countries.

TRAVELERS WITH DISABILITIES

Traveling with through Chile a disability may be difficult. The more upscale hotels will generally be able to meet your needs, but public transportation and most hostels are ill-equipped. Those with disabilities should inform airlines and hotels of their disabilities when making reservations; some time may be needed to prepare special accommodations. Call ahead to restaurants, museums, and other facilities to find out if they are handicapped-accessible. **Guide dog owners** should inquire to consulates or customs agents as to the quarantine policies of each destination country on their South American journey.

USEFUL ORGANIZATIONS

Access Abroad, www.umabroad.umn.edu/access. A website devoted to making study abroad available to students with disabilities. The site is maintained by Disability Services Research and Training, University of Minnesota, University Gateway, Ste. 180, 200 Oak St. SE, Minneapolis, MN 55455, USA (☎612-626-1333).

Accessible Journeys, 35 W. Sellers Ave., Ridley Park, PA 19078, USA (☎800-846-4537; www.disabilitytravel.com). Designs tours for wheelchair users and slow walkers. The site has tips and forums for all travelers.

Directions Unlimited, 123 Green Ln., Bedford Hills, NY 10507, USA (☎800-533-5343). Books individual vacations for the physically disabled; not an info service.

Flying Wheels, 143 W. Bridge St., P.O. Box 382, Owatonna, MN 55060, USA (☎507-451-5005; www.flyingwheelstravel.com). Specializes in escorted trips to Europe for people with physical disabilities; plans custom accessible trips worldwide.

Mobility International USA (MIUSA), P.O. Box 10767, Eugene, OR 97440, USA (☎541-343-1284; www.miusa.org). Provides a variety of books and other publications containing information for travelers with disabilities.

Society for Accessible Travel and Hospitality (SATH), 347 Fifth Ave. #610, New York, NY 10016, USA (☎212-447-7284; www.sath.org). An advocacy group that publishes free online travel info and the travel magazine *OPEN WORLD* (annual subscription US$13, free for members). Annual membership US$45, students and seniors US$30.

MINORITY TRAVELERS

Most of the Chilean population is white or *mestizo*, having fairer skin than the populations of most South American countries. This general homogeneity means that any minority traveler—regardless of skin color—is bound to stick out, particularly in rural parts of the country. Indeed, the elements of racism that some Chileans harbor are often directed toward their darker-skinned neighbors from Bolivia or Peru. In general, the whiter your skin, the better treatment you'll receive. Beware, however: light-skinned travelers are viewed as wealthier, and may be more likely to be the targets of crime or subjected to inflated prices at markets.

Travelers of African or Asian descent will likely attract more attention from curious locals and their gawking children, who may point, giggle, and stare. Asians may find themselves called *chinos*, while African Americans may be called *morenos* or *negros*. None of these words are meant to be offensive; to Chileans they are simply descriptive terms and are uttered as expressions of surprise upon sighting someone of a different ethnicity.

In many rural areas, non-Spanish speakers may be viewed by some as a threat, and generally, natives are not accommodating or patient with non-Spanish speakers. It helps to try to speak Spanish and get accustomed to words and phrases particular to Chilean Spanish—it'll put the locals at ease and probably make you many friends. Check out the **Spanish Quick Reference** in the **Appendix** for a useful on-the-road guide (p. 499).

DIETARY CONCERNS

Vegetarians should not have too much trouble finding decent culinary options in Chile's major cities, especially in Santiago, which has several vegetarian restaurants. It is more difficult in rural areas, however, where meat and fish reign. However, many dishes can easily be altered by asking for them *sin carne* (without meat) or requesting vegetables. For information, check out the North American Vegetarian Society, P.O. Box 72, Dolgeville, NY 13329 (☎518-568-7970; www.navs-online.org), which publishes information about vegetarian travel, including *Transformative Adventures: A Guide to Vacations and Retreats* (US$15).

The travel section of the The Vegetarian Resource Group's website, at www.vrg.org/travel, has a comprehensive list of organizations and websites that are geared toward helping vegetarians and vegans traveling abroad. For more information, visit your local bookstore or health food store, and consult *The Vegetarian Traveler: Where to Stay if You're Vegetarian, Vegan, Environmentally Sensitive*, by Jed and Susan Civic (Larson Publications; US$16). Vegetarians will also find numerous resources on the web; try www.vegdining.com, www.happycow.net, and www.vegetarianismo.com.br, for starters.

Travelers who keep kosher should contact synagogues in larger cities for information on kosher restaurants. Your own synagogue or college Hillel should have access to lists of Jewish institutions across the nation. Also, check http://shamash.org/kosher/ for a list of kosher restaurants in most countries—Chile included. If you are strict in your observance, you may have to prepare your own food on the road. A good resource is the *Jewish Travel Guide*, edited by Michael Zaidner (Vallentine Mitchell; US$18). Travelers looking for halal restaurants may find www.zabihah.com a useful resource.

ESSENTIALS

OTHER RESOURCES

Let's Go tries to cover all aspects of budget travel, but we can't put *everything* in our guides. Listed below are books and websites that can serve as jumping-off points for your own research.

USEFUL PUBLICATIONS

Hippocrene Books, Inc., 171 Madison Ave., New York, NY 10016, USA (☎718-454-2366; www.hippocrenebooks.com). Publishes foreign-language dictionaries and language-learning guides.

Hunter Publishing, 470 W. Broadway, fl. 2, South Boston, MA 02127, USA (☎617-269-0700; www.hunterpublishing.com). Has a large catalog of travel and adventure guides.

Rand McNally, P.O. Box 7600, Chicago, IL 60680, USA (☎847-329-8100; www.randmcnally.com), publishes road atlases.

Adventurous Traveler Bookstore, P.O. Box 2221, Williston, VT 05495, USA (☎800-282-3963; www.adventuroustraveler.com) sells hiking and travel guides.

Travel Books & Language Center, Inc., 4437 Wisconsin Ave. NW, Washington, D.C. 20016, USA (☎800-220-2665; www.bookweb.org/bookstore/travelbks/). Over 60,000 titles from around the world.

WORLD WIDE WEB

Almost every aspect of budget travel is accessible via the web. From your keyboard, you can make a hostel reservation, get advice on travel hot spots from other travelers, or find out how much a train costs. Listed below are travel-related sites to begin your surfing; other relevant sites are listed throughout the book. Since website turnover is high, use online search engines to research on your own.

 WWW.LETSGO.COM Our freshly redesigned website features extensive content from our guides; community forums where travelers can connect with each other and ask questions or advice—as well as share stories and tips; and expanded resources to help you plan your trip. Visit us soon to browse by destination, find information about ordering our titles, and sign up for our e-newsletter!

THE ART OF TRAVEL

How to See the World: www.artoftravel.com. A compendium of great travel tips, from cheap flights to self defense to interacting with local culture.

Travel Library: www.travel-library.com. A fantastic set of links for general information and personal travelogues.

Travel Intelligence: www.travelintelligence.net. A large collection of travel writing by distinguished travel writers.

World Hum: www.worldhum.com. An independently produced collection of "travel dispatches from a shrinking planet."

BootsnAll.com: www.bootsnall.com. Numerous resources for independent travelers, from planning your trip to reporting on it when you get back.

INFORMATION ON CHILE

CIA World Factbook: www.odci.gov/cia/publications/factbook/index.html. Tons of vital statistics on Chile's geography, government, economy, and people.

Go Chile: www.gochile.cl. The main Chile-based website for tourist information.

Geographia: www.geographia.com. Highlights, culture, and people of Chile.

Atevo Travel: www.atevo.com/guides/destinations. Detailed introductions, travel tips, and suggested itineraries.

World Travel Guide: www.travel-guides.com. Helpful practical info.

PlanetRider: www.planetrider.com. A subjective list of links to the "best" websites covering the culture and tourist attractions of Chile.

LIFE AND TIMES

LAND

Bounded by the Andes to the east and the Pacific Ocean to the west, Chile is one of the most isolated, yet environmentally diverse countries in South America. Spanning over 4300km (2700 mi.) from north to south (nearly half the length of South America), Chile averages only 177km (100 mi.) in width. Nevertheless, the range of geographic formations packed into this narrow country gives rise to an incredible mix of environments from the arid desert regions of the north to the lush rolling farmland of the Central Valley to the rocky glacial fields of the south.

GEOGRAPHY AND CLIMATE

THE ANDES. Stretching along the entire eastern border, the **Andes** are an omnipresent feature of the Chilean landscape. Highest in the far north, they contain peaks reaching well over 6000m (20,000 ft.). **Ojos del Salado** (6893m) is the highest peak in the country and the highest active volcano in the world. **Aconcagua** (6959m), the highest peak in the world outside the Himalayas, lies just across the border in Argentina. Toward the south, the mountains gradually decrease in elevation, while mountain passes occur more frequently and are easier to negotiate.

The creation of the Andes due to the collision of two tectonic plates also makes this region a hotbed of seismic activity. Some 2000 volcanoes are scattered throughout the range, about 50 of which are still active. **Earthquakes** have also had a major impact on the country—in 1960, one of the biggest quakes in Chile's history (8.75 on the Richter Scale) decimated cities throughout Chiloé and the Central Valley and sunk some parts of the coast nearly two meters into the ocean.

NORTE GRANDE AND NORTE CHICO. The far north of Chile is arid and rugged, dominated by the **Atacama Desert,** one of the driest deserts in the world. To the west, cold air brought up by the Humboldt current meets the steep cliffs of the **Cordillera Domeyko** that line the coast and forms banks of fog that roll down into the desert valley. This cold air current significantly moderates the climate in the region, with the average temperature ranging between 14°C (58°F) and 21°C (70°F). Despite the relative coolness, the Atacama region still receives little rain and, in some parts of the desert, there has never been any recorded precipitation.

Despite the desert conditions, Norte Grande boasts some of Chile's most fantastic landscapes. Sublime sunsets highlight an incredible range of earthy colors derived from the rich mineral deposits that cover the area. These mineral deposits, especially the vast salt plains, also make Norte Grande one of Chile's most valuable regions. The **copper exports** that have formed the foundation of the Chilean economy for decades all come from this region.

THE CENTRAL VALLEY AND LOS LAGOS. Just north of the capital city, the scrublands of Norte Chico break into the beginnings of the Central Valley. This region, stretching from Santiago south to the island of Chiloé, is the most populated and most fertile part of Chile, home to Chile's lucrative wine industry. The vast tracts of grapes that make their white wine famous grow well in the seasonal rain and mild, almost Mediterranean climate. The region is also home to some of Chile's largest cities, including **Santiago, Valparaíso,** and **Concepción.**

As you head south from the Central Valley, the climate becomes progressively rainier. The city of **Valdivia** in the heart of Los Lagos, for example, receives over 253cm (115 in.) of rain a year. Dozens of beautiful lakes dot this damp region and the ever-present background of mountains makes this one of the most picturesque parts of Chile. Industry has also capitalized on its grassy pastures and vast forests, making it Chile's center for lumber production and cattle ranching.

AISÉN, THE FAR SOUTH, AND TIERRA DEL FUEGO. Beyond the port city of Puerto Montt, the Central Valley drops below sea level, creating a perplexing maze of islands, inlets, and fjords. The sheer cliffs of the Andes move closer and closer to the water's edge until they too disappear into the ocean. The landscape is dominated by alpine forests and grasslands that break into tundra plains in the far south. The frigid Humboldt Current flowing north from Antarctica brings with it cold temperatures and bitter winds; in many places enormous **glaciers** cover the mountains and plains below. The rugged nature of this part of the country has made it difficult to develop. Nevertheless, the region is important in Chile's overall economy, as lumber and livestock are in abundant supply, and petroleum is also an important product in the area surrounding the **Strait of Magellan.** The Strait is an important connection between the Atlantic and Pacific Oceans that allows both passengers and cargo ships to avoid the dangerous trip around Cape Horn.

FLORA AND FAUNA

Due to its relative physical isolation and its diversity of geographic regions, Chile boasts an incredible variety of plants and animals, many of which are found only in Chile. Many of these species such as the **vicuñas** and **guanacos** of the northern *altiplano* or the **alerce** and **monkey puzzle** *(araucaria)* trees of Los Lagos are characteristic of Chile's varied and unique wildlife. Unfortunately, most of these are also in serious danger of extinction. Unchecked hunting, trapping, logging, and clearing have pushed dozens of once-widespread plants and animals onto the endangered species list. Weak or non-existent environmental laws have facilitated serious environmental damage from industrial pollution and overpopulation. Despite these problems (and partially in response to them), the government has built one of the largest and most successful national park systems in the world.

PLANTS

The diversity and uniqueness of Chile's plant life can be seen in every part of the country. Some of the most interesting and rare species are found in the most sparsely populated regions, a phenomenon seen most vividly in the case of the northern desert region. Although what little life there is in the desert and *altiplano* is, as expected, dominated by various types of cacti, the area is also home to the **tamarugo,** a spiny acacia tree, and the **queñoa,** which lives at slightly higher altitudes. Shrubs cover most of the land to the south, although the Santiago area has vestiges of the previously extensive **Southern Beech** forests (also called the Chilean palm). The climate becomes more tolerable for wildlife in the Central Valley and Los Lagos. The increase in rain and milder temperatures support a wide variety of trees, flowers, and grasses. Most notable among these are the national flower, the **Chilean Bell Flower,** and the national tree, the **monkey puzzle.** One of the other well-known species in this region is the **Alerce,** a relative of the sequoia tree that can survive for over 4000 years. Heavy logging of these enormous trees, however, has brought critical attention from international conservation groups.

ANIMALS

Although Chile's severe climate zones and relative isolation has limited the breadth of animal species that populate the country, it has allowed for the development of a number of rare and interesting species. In the highlands surrounding the northern deserts live a large number of the **llamas** and **alpacas** so well-known in Peru and Bolivia. However, Chile also is home to two other members of the llama family, **guanacos** and the endangered **vicuñas.** The soft fine coat of the vicuña made it the fabric of choice for the ancient Incan royalty and nearly drove it to extinction when it became widely popular at the turn of the century. Similarly, the rodent-like **chinchilla** was hunted so thoroughly that almost none exist today except as household pets. Its close cousin, the mountain **vizcacha,** has survived, although only in the southern highlands.

The **rhea,** or *ñandú,* is Chile's version of the ostrich, and makes its home in the southern highlands, along with the **Andean condor.** With a wing span of over three meters, the condor is often spotted floating lazily on the updrafts that blow through the mountain peaks. The endemic **huemul,** an endangered Chilean deer, lives within the rocky Patagonia. In the more hospitable temperate regions, Chile boasts a richer diversity of wildlife: look for **pumas** and other wild cats; the **pudú,** a small deer-like mammal; and a wide range of birds.

Although Chile's terrestrial wildlife is somewhat limited, its assorted and abundant marine life more than compensates. The shores of the country are teeming with the incredible variety the Pacific offers. **Penguins, sea lions, seals,** and **otters** can be found along Chile's extensive coastline. The coastal waters are home to a wide range of **whales** and **dolphins** and produce the enormous selection of fish and shellfish that are such an important part of the Chilean cuisine.

HISTORY

PRECOLONIAL TIMES AND SPANISH COLONIZATION (1460-1550). Think twice before arguing with a Chilean—considering their history of unrelenting resistance, they're bound to put up quite a fight. When the Incas attempted to conquer Chile in 1460 and 1491, they encountered fierce resistance from the indigenous **Araucanians,** specifically members of the **Mapuche** tribe, and were only able to establish some forts in the Central Valley.

The Araucanians, a fragmented tribal society consisting primarily of hunters and farmers, constituted the largest Amerindian group in Chile. The Araucanians' almost mythical ability to withstand foreign attempts at colonization of their land served them well when the Spanish conquest of Chile began in 1536-37. **Francisco Pizarro** invaded Chile in search of "Otro Perú" (Another Peru). Disappointed at not finding gold, Pizarro returned to Peru immediately, but in 1540-41 agreed to **Pedro de Valdivia's** request to conquer and colonize the region.

Santiago was founded on February 12, 1541, but Valdivia did not undertake the conquest of the southern regions until 1550, and the conquest of Chile was consolidated in the late 1550s under **Governor Don García Hurtado de Mendoza.** This time, to resist colonization, the Araucanians added horses and European weaponry to their arsenal, and were able to hinder the Spaniards until the late 19th century, by which time a century of European conquest and disease had decimated about half of the original A'raucanian population of over one million.

COLONIAL PERIOD (1550-1759). Despite the corruption of the political system and the Spanish officials posted in Chile, Chileans exhibited loyalty to crown authority for three centuries of colonial rule. Ironically, the colonizers themselves often circumvented royal laws—in the countryside, local landowners and military officials often established their own rules.

Over time, Chile became accepted primarily as an agricultural colony due to the scant amounts of precious metals available. As a result, Chile came to depend on coerced labor. However, maintaining officials and an army in Chile, which was regarded as a "deficit area" of the Spanish empire, proved a cumbersome task. Meanwhile, Chileans resented their reliance on Peru for governance and trade. Although the economy expanded under Spanish rule, Chileans found taxation, and particularly, the restrictions on trade and production, stifling.

In addition, the stratification of colonial Chilean society on the basis of race, ethnicity, and class irked many. *Peninsulares* (recently arrived Spaniards) and *criollos* (Chilean-born children of Spanish immigrants) dominated the upper class. The increasing population of *mestizos* (mixed European and Indian blood) were next, followed by indigenous populations and African slaves. Most Spaniards were in favor of the subjugation and extermination of *indígenas*, forcing the Roman Catholic Church to serve as the main defender of the indigenous population from Spanish atrocities.

As home to one of the largest standing armies in the Americas, Chile became a garrison to protect against both potential Araucanian and European encroachment (including the invasion of Valparaíso by **Sir Francis Drake** in 1578). However, it was not until the Wars of Independence (1810-18) that Chile involved itself in international affairs.

THE ROAD TO INDEPENDENCE (1759-1818). The **French Bourbon** monarchs came to power after the **Habsburg** dynasty's rule over Spain ended in 1700. The **Bourbon Reforms** of 1759-96, introduced by French Bourbon monarchs, allowed for more independence for Chile from the Viceroyalty of Peru. Eventually, Irish-born Governor O'Higgins's promotion of self-sufficiency in economic production and public administration initiated Chile's movement toward independence.

After the authority of the crown was undermined by Napoleon's invasion of Spain, loyalists began to form cliques to govern both Spain and her colonies until the king was restored. This turn left many Chileans wondering who the regional authority was now—the French monarch, the Spanish rebels, or local leaders? Therefore, on **September 18, 1810** (a date now celebrated as Chile's independence day), *criollo* leaders of Santiago declared that they would govern the colony until order was restored in Spain, and immediately opened the ports to all traders. This initial experiment in self-government was led by a new president, **José Miguel Carrera Verdugo** (1812-13). However, Carrera's militaristic tendencies provoked a response from **Bernardo O'Higgins Riquelme,** an advocate for complete independence, who opposed Carrera's ideas by launching a rival

50,000-9000 BC
Adventurous Chileans-to-be cross the Bering Strait

12,000 BC
Araucanian natives set up shop in the foothills of the Andes

AD 1460
Incas invade Chile and are driven out by the inhabitants

1491
Incas attack again, but still can't subdue the mighty Araucanians

1536
After defeating the Incas, the Spanish try their hand at conquering Chile... and fail.

1541
Pedro de Valdivia leads Spaniards back into Chile and founds Santiago

1578
Sir Francis Drake loots and pillages Valparaíso

1544-1759
Chile develops as a farming colony

1759-1796
Bourbon reforms give Chileans new ideas of indepence

1807
Napoleon's army invades Spain

1810
Loyalists declare independence until "real" Spanish government restored

LIFE AND TIMES

LIFE AND TIMES

faction. As a result, civil war broke out among the *criollos*. However, troops in Peru seized opportunity and reasserted control in Chile in 1814 with a victory at the **Battle of Rancagua.**

The harsh rule of Spanish loyalists after *La Reconquista* (the Reconquest) of 1814-17 only served to increase the Chilean desire for independence. In 1817, O'Higgins, who was in exile in Argentina, joined forces with José de San Martín and launched a daring attack on the Spaniards over the Andes, ultimately defeating the colonizers at the **Battle of Chacabuco** on February 12. Chilean independence was formally granted after San Martín crushed the last Spanish force on Chilean soil at the **Battle of Maipú** on April 5, 1818.

BUILDING THE REPUBLIC (1818-1879). Although Bernardo O'Higgins seemed to have a tight hold over Chile after the war, his position as a dictator was soon challenged. By 1823, his attempts to draw more of the oligarchy into his administration had been thwarted and he was ousted from power.

For Chile, the fall of O'Higgins set the stage for seven years of bad luck. From 1823 to 1830, 30 different governments tried to establish themselves. Finally, in 1830, **Diego Portales** stepped into that void of solid power. By hammering out a compromise amongst the most powerful elites, Portales was able to catapult **José Tomás de Ovalle** into the presidency and establish an incredibly strong conservative government. This new government was further strengthened by the adoption of a new constitution in 1833 that called for a powerful central presidency and a parliament controlled by the oligarchy.

In the subsequent military skirmishes with Peru and Bolivia and the domestic economic boon, Chile's new regime was able to militarily and economically earn its legitimacy. However, as the number and power of new economic elites began to grow, so did the push for secularization and the diminishment of the role of the Roman Catholic Church in government, as well as the liberalization of the Chilean political process. As a result, after nearly two decades of stability and unity, the late 1850s and early 1860s brought a hint of impending upheaval.

WAR OF THE PACIFIC AND THE NEW PARLIAMENT (1879-1920). The massive influx of investment and industrial goods from Europe caught up to Chile in the 1870s. Faced with a serious balance-of-payments crisis, the government began looking toward the region north of Antofagasta for revenue. Although the incredible mineral wealth of the area was extracted by Chilean-European conglomerates, the territory was still claimed by Bolivia and Peru. In 1879, Chile found just the excuse it was looking for to change all that.

In 1878, Bolivia tried to impose a series of new taxes on the mining companies. When they refused to pay, the Bolivian government seized the firms, infuriating the Chilean elites, and causing Chile to declare war. In 1879, Peru announced its intention to honor a secret alliance and support Bolivia, and a war between three totally unprepared states with virtually no armies (and standing navies of two ships on each side—Bolivia had no navy) began. When Chile managed to sink one of Peru's and capture the other, Chile thought itself the victor. However, Peru did not give up the fight. In 1881, the Chilean army was forced to land troops in central Peru and capture the capital city of Lima. Even then, the Peruvians refused to give up and fought a bloody land war for two more years. Chile made huge territorial gains as a result of the War of the Pacific, much of which was rich in valuable minerals. However, these economic gains led to different problems. In 1886, when **José Balmaceda** was elected president, Chile found itself under the rule of a leader trying to exploit this new mineral wealth for his own purposes. Enraged by his heavy-handed rule, the Chilean congress raised an army and overthrew Balmaceda.

Under the new government, the presidency was eliminated entirely and the parliament became the ruling body. However, this new parliamentary government had a variety of new issues to tackle. As the Chilean economy had changed, so had the social structure. Business, trade, and industrialization facilitated the growth of the middle class and the working class. Both classes became increasingly aware that their urban orientation and social concerns were not in any way linked with the landed oligarchy and that they had to get politically involved. The first widespread strikes occurred around the turn of the century, and the old conservative elite were suddenly contending not only with the traditional liberal party but also a new wave of Radicals, including Democratic Socialists and even Communists. As the country headed into the 20th century, the elite-dominated parliament was becoming progressively more isolated and out-of-touch.

A NEW CONSTITUTION AND THE RISE OF THE LEFT. In 1920, widespread discontent among the middle class catapulted the reformist **Arturo Alessandri Palma** into the presidency. However, the powerful, elite-controlled parliament blocked most of his initiatives. Four years later, frustrated by the deadlock, middle-class military officers led a military coup. Alessandri was kept as president and the parliament was forced to pass the reform measures. However, conflicts within the new government forced the president to flee to Argentina and set the stage for another more sweeping set of changes.

Soon after Alessandri's flight, another group of military officials, led by **Carlos Ibáñez del Campo,** staged a second coup and invited the ex-president to return. With their support, Alessandri drafted a new constitution that strengthened the presidency and instituted a number of welfare guarantees and reforms not present in the original document. Following his own ambitions, however, Ibáñez soon forced the president to resign, setting himself up to be elected in 1927. Due to the effects of Ibáñez's brutal, autocratic style of rule and his leftist reform policies, the next five years of Chile's history were somewhat chaotic. Nevertheless, most of the ensuing troubles arose from the Great Depression of the 1920s and 30s.

Order was finally restored after the elections of 1932 and the return of Alessandri. This time, however, he faced a very different political landscape. The government was no longer domi-

1879
Chile, beset by revenue trouble, invades Bolivia and Peru

1881
After Peruvian resistance, Chilean forces sack Lima

1883
Peru admits defeat; Chile landlocks Bolivia and claims mineral resources

1886
José Balmaceda tries to gain control of mineral wealth and enhance presidential power

1890
Congress raises an army to oust Balmaceda

1891
Balmaceda is booted, presidency abolished, and parliamentarism established

1920
President Allessandri ushers in middle-class reform

1924
Military intervenes to push through reforms

1925
Chile's 2nd constitution established

1925-1932
Chile relapses into political schizophrenia

LIFE AND TIMES

nated by the parties of the old elite, the Conservatives and Liberals. Instead, radicals now held the center and a multitude of groups had formed on the left, including the Socialist and Communist Parties. By 1958, the political discontent and divisions were growing. The candidate of the old oligarchy, **Jorge Alessandria Rodríguez** (the son of Arturo), just barely obtained a plurality above the leftist **Salvador Allende** and **Eduardo Frei Montalva,** representing the newly formed, centrist Christian Democratic party. The power of Allende's leftist coalition, the *Frente de Acción Popular* (Popular Action Front), frightened the elites. The working class had been gaining rights and benefits slowly but continuously over the last few decades and each new addition only made them more demanding. This well-organized coalition posed a serious threat to the elite's dominance.

In an effort to ensure the defeat of Allende in the 1964 election, the Liberal and Conservative parties, now united as the National Party, along with many foreign interests (including the United States), threw their support behind the Christian Democrat, Eduardo Frei Montalva. They got far more than they bargained for. Hoping to solidify support both with the middle class and the lower class, Frei instituted a serious of major reforms attacking the power of the elites. By the time the next elections rolled around in 1970, the National Party was significantly weaker and the peasants and working-class were suddenly highly active.

THE DEATH AND REBIRTH OF DEMOCRACY. In response to the independent efforts of both the National Party and the Christian Democrats to recapture the presidency, the Socialists, Communists, and Liberals in both the Radical and Christian Democrat parties formed a coalition called *La Unidad Popular* (Popular Unity). Allende, under their banner, just beat the other candidates, but not by enough to win outright. The decision had to be ratified by Congress. In exchange for his promise to respect the democratic institutions of the country and continue elections, the Christian Democrats gave him the support he needed to become president. For the first time in its history, Chile had a socialist president.

The goals of Allende's government were not much more radical than Frei's. He wanted to nationalize major industries, speed up agrarian reform, and institute a massive redistribution of wealth, efforts for which the foundations had already been laid. However, the speed with which these changes were implemented shocked supporters and critics alike. Within a year, dozens of major industries were nationalized and all of the large *haciendas* were disbanded. Allende had ended an economic system that had dominated Chile for centuries.

As the initial steps of the reforms were completed, the government began to encounter problems. The immense financial burden of the nationalizations and a ballooning public sector threatened to evolve into an unpayable debt. This burden combined with both a fall in world copper prices and the complexity introduced by state-management industry to form the beginnings of a serious economic crisis.

At the same time, support for the government began to waver. The seizures and nationalizations had produced a powerful alliance between the landed elites and foreign investors (especially the United States). On the reverse side, radical leftists frustrated by the continued moderation of reforms became increasingly violent. Meanwhile, within the UP itself internal disagreements about the pace and direction of reforms were dividing the party. Middle-class backing eroded as the economic and social situation deteriorated and when an elite- and US-supported truckers' strike paralyzed the country, popular support evaporated. The country became unstable, and as upper class alliances pushed for change, the Chilean military launched an offensive on their behalf.

In 1973, the army launched a major coup, ending decades of stable democracy with a raid on the government palace led by tanks and bombers that ended in the death of President Allende. At first, the new military regime was proclaimed to be a temporary solution. It enjoyed widespread support from wealthy citizens who believed that its main goals were to regain economic and social stability while rebuilding the political institutions that had been severely weakened. However, it soon became evident that **General Augusto Pinochet**, who had emerged as the head figure of the junta, had no such intentions.

In order to garner a strong grip on his newfound power, Pinochet quickly embarked on a large-scale suppression campaign, arresting and executing thousands of political activists, journalists, professionals, union leaders, and anyone else considered subversive. Tens of thousands more were imprisoned and tortured or forced to flee the country. Newspapers and other media were shut down or taken over, trade unions were disbanded, all political parties were suspended, and the Communist and Socialist parties were banned. Soon after, the national congress was dissolved and Pinochet appointed himself dictator. To consolidate his rule, the general created the *Directoria de Inteligencia Nacional* (DINA), which was in charge of "homeland security" and became one of the most atrocious state-sponsored terrorist groups in the world.

Along with this brutal oppression came an new economic orientation. With the help of the "Chicago Boys" (economists trained at the University of Chicago in the US), Pinochet introduced a series of radical, market-oriented reforms. All state-owned industries were privatized, public spending and employment were slashed, and trade and investment were liberalized. This "shock treatment" was designed to halt inflation and eliminate state-created inefficiency, and its effects were brutal and immediate. Unemployment jumped to well over 20 percent and salaries plummeted, hitting the middle and lower classes the hardest. Although the policies were successful in controlling inflation and sparking major economic growth among the wealthy, the costs were enormous. Public services deteriorated, unemployment remained high, and the radical shift in income distribution impoverished huge portions of the population.

LIFE AND TIMES

1970
Marxist Popular Unity candidate Salvador Allende elected President

1971
Nationalization of the copper industry

March 1973
PU gains seats in mid-term elections despite country-wide turmoil

September 1973
General Augusto Pinochet launches a bloody military coup; Allende is assassinated

1973-1975
Violent period of "social stabilization" led by DINA, Pinochet's secret police

1975
Initiation of "economic stabilization" with Chicago Boys' austerity plan

1977
Pinochet disbands political parties, crushing hopes for democracy

1980
New constitution passed, giving Pinochet 8 more years in power

1982
Debt crisis sweeps through Latin America; Pinochet implements austerity measures

1983
Opposition to Pinochet demonstrated in major labor protests

LIFE AND TIMES

Nonetheless, by 1980, international experts began talking about the "Chilean miracle," that a Latin American country had managed to escape the chaos and poverty of a radical government and build a stable economy. Pinochet felt confident enough in his standing that he decided it was time to create a new constitution to silence the rising criticism of his dictatorship and to secure his position as leader. In 1980, he called for a plebiscite to approve a new constitution that would guarantee his position for at least eight more years and allow for another eight-year extension in the future. Manipulating the constitution to ensure himself a long-term, authoritative role in Chilean government, Pinochet was able to mask his intentions and push through his veiled policy, attaining a seemingly impossible two-thirds ratifying vote.

Soon after the installation of the new constitution, Chile's national situation suddenly deteriorated. In 1982, international credit vanished as the US spiraled into a major recession, plunging countries all across Latin America into serious debt crises. Although Chile's public debt had not traditionally been high, many of its private firms and banks were in trouble. Faced with a serious economic setback, Pinochet once again instituted austerity policies. This second wave of salary cuts and unemployment seriously undermined the remaining support for the regime.

By 1983, serious signs of the regime's weakness were visibly manifesting themselves. For the first time in nearly a decade, leftist groups were successfully staging massive demonstrations. Even more worrisome for the military government was that militant opposition groups were beginning to form in the urban shantytowns created by high rates of unemployment and poverty. The outwardly stable environment (for those who had not had family members disappear with the secret police) that had been one of Pinochet's few sources of legitimacy was fading rapidly. Political activists didn't take long to capitalize on this uncertainty—the Christian Democratic Party, Chile's largest political party, was resurrected along with others, and a center-left coalition, the Democratic Alliance, was formed to put pressure on the regime. By the middle of 1984, even the Catholic Church had swung behind the democratization movement and, in August, a church-mediated accord was signed by center-right parties to move for immediate elections.

Despite this growing protest movement, Pinochet refused to yield and intensified his ban on political activity instead. There was to be no discussion of elections until after the constitutionally-prescribed plebiscite in 1988 decided whether or not Pinochet would be granted another eight years as the nation's leader. Nevertheless, the opposition he faced was more than just a leftist uprising. Conservative business leaders and foreign investors were becoming more and more nervous about the increasing instability in Chile. International pressure, especially from the normally reticent United States, increased as a trend towards democracy swept through Latin America. Confronted by such broad-based opposition, the General was not able to control the plebiscite and, in October of 1988, 55% voted "No" to extending his rule. In December of 1989, **Patricio Aylwin** led the **Concertación,** a coalition of the major centrist parties, to electoral victory, defeating the Pinochet-backed candidate Hernán Büchi Buc. For the first time in 16 years, Chile had a democratic government.

THE DEMOCRATIC 90S. The return to democracy has been neither a simple nor quick process for Chile. In many ways, the peacefulness of the transition has made it even harder. Because so much of the torture and killing had happened secretly, many members of the upper echelons of society—allegedly unaware of Pinochet's corrupt and violent practices—did not immediately rescind their support for the dictator. Because of this support, the compromises that were reached in order to guarantee military cooperation with democracy made the task of dealing with the Pinochet legacy complicated.

One of the most significant compromises was that all of the top military officials were granted immunity from prosecution and were given the option to become senators for life. General Pinochet remained the commander of the armed forces and the civilian government was prohibited from replacing him until he chose to retire. Another major concession was that military officials would be granted a major presence in the new cabinet and play a role in executive decision-making.

The effects of these agreements go beyond simply protecting those responsible for the decade and a half of oppression. They have allowed conservative groups to remain a force to be reckoned with. Aylwin's four years in office were fairly uneventful as a result. Without the two-thirds majority needed for constitutional changes, he could not push through major reforms and was forced to continue with most of Pinochet's economic policies. Fortunately for the Concertación, the world economy had stabilized and export prices were on the rise. The resulting economic boom, combined with a few successful social programs, helped Eduardo Frei (son of the ex-President Eduardo Frei) win the 1993 election.

During his six-year term, Frei was able to make even more progress on many fronts. Economically, many of the liberal reforms were developed, allowing for a diversification in Chile's export profile. Frei was also able to push through major social reforms aiming to reduce the extreme levels of poverty and lower the unemployment from the Pinochet regime. On the human rights side, a Chilean judge finally sent General Manuel Contreras to jail for his role in several assassinations.

Chile experienced more volatility in 1998 than any year since the democratic transition. The nation had developed strong ties with its neighbors across the Pacific and the Asian financial crisis hit it hard. After 10 years of sustained growth averaging over 6 percent annually, the Chilean economy slipped into recession. On top of that, General Pinochet finally retired and took up his position as life senator, only to be indicted by a Spanish judge and arrested in London for the torture and murder of Spanish citizens during his rule. The resulting controversy became a major issue in Chile. Still unable to incur the wrath of the military and other conservative groups, the Frei government lodged a formal protest, saying that Pinochet should be tried in Chile if he was to be tried anywhere. With this issue still unresolved and the economy still struggling to recover, the Concertación faced a serious challenge from conservative candidate Joaquín Lavín. Ultimately, however, their candidate **Ricardo Lagos** managed to sneak by in a run-off election.

LIFE AND TIMES

TODAY

The last few years for Chile have been years of new challenges and old issues. The presidency of Ricardo Lagos, the first socialist president since Salvador Allende, has marked a serious political shift. Already, following a decade of liberal leaders, Lagos has shaken things up by appointing women and liberal activists to important positions, enacting constitutional reforms, and increasing funding for social reforms and protection programs. Nevertheless, divisions in the Concertación have allowed the conservative Right to gain ground. This has been clearly shown through the continued inability of the government to rid the Senate of the nine Pinochet-appointed senators.

Martial-civil relations are still somewhat volatile, but have been improving in recent years. The prosecution of the officers responsible for Pinochet's "Caravan of Death" and the first sentencing of an active-duty officer have been key events in the country's effort to not only rehabilitate its scarred past, but also to ease social tensions.

Economically, the country is still trying to get back on its feet. Although the economy has returned to positive growth, improvement has been slow due to the troubled economies of Argentina and the US. Lagos and his government have worked to counter this by solidifying and diversifying the nation's economic ties. The President was part of the Asian trade talks and recently signed a free trade agreement with the European Union. Additionally, Lagos has signed the US-Chile Free Trade Agreement, which took effect in January 2004. Nevertheless, unemployment has continued to remain high and the combination of volatile financial markets and slumping export prices may mean Chile is in for a rough ride.

Throughout all of these controversies and issues, social reform has remained one of most pressing national issues. At the end of Pinochet's regime, over 40 percent of the population was living in poverty, with 13 percent in absolute destitution. Through increased investment in education, health services, and social protection, those numbers have been reduced to 17 and 4 percent respectively, an incredible feat for any country; unfortunately, problems still remain. Unemployment is still high and is especially prevalent among young adults. Levels of inequality are also very high. Despite the economic growth of the last decade, the gap between rich and poor has expanded significantly, raising serious concerns about the effectiveness of current social programs.

Chile has come a long way since authoritarianism, politically, economically, and socially. Nevertheless, some of the country's most difficult issues remain unresolved. Combined with a turbulent international scene, these will make the next couple of years vitally important to the future direction and success of the nation.

PEOPLE

DEMOGRAPHICS

Mestizaje, the blending of races resulting from centuries of migration, explains why over 70% of Chile's 15 million residents are *mestizos,* a racial mixture of Europeans and *indígenas.* Unfortunately, Chileans maintain an ambivalent attitude towards their native heritage—while indigenous culture is celebrated, Chileans tend to consider indigenous people inferior and instances of neglect, disrespect, and mistreatment are not rare. Indigenous communities still constitute about 3% of the population: 40,000 **Aymara** inhabit the northern areas bordering

Bolivia; **Araucanians** reside in the south of the country, especially around Temuco; and several thousand **Mapuche** populate the Central Valley. In recent years, the Mapuche have been organizing to preserve their language and traditions—prepare to be engulfed in traditional ceremonial rituals like the *ñgillatun* celebration, the great festival of crops and fertility. If passing through Osorno and Temuco, look out for the most visible members of Chile's society—cowboys. Intent on maintaining a separate identity from Argentina's mythical *gauchos*, Chilean cowboys, *huasos*, still work on ranches and sport impressive attire.

Descendants of 19th-century European migrants—most notably **German** settlers—make up a significant portion of the residents of Los Lagos. Valdivia, with its own German newspaper, resembles a German city and brews German beer, while Osorno manifests distinct German influences. Arrivals from the former **Yugoslavia** also populate a good portion of Chilean society. Chile's **Croatian** population is the fifth largest in the world, consisting of both a native and first-generation population. **Middle Eastern** migrants are now respected members of the Chilean business community, and dominate financial circles and manufacturing operations. Christian communities from Lebanon, Syria, and Palestine escaped to Chile at the time of the devolution of the Ottoman Empire. Consequently, since their ports of embarkation were under Turkish control, migrants with a Middle Eastern heritage are commonly, although incorrectly, referred to as *turcos* (Turks). Since a tropical plantation economy never developed, Chile was removed from the African slave trade, and there is little significant black population or culture in Chile.

Despite these multi-faceted demographics, there is a strong sense of a unified Chilean identity, provided by the homogenizing influence of the prevalent Spanish language, the Roman Catholic religion, a pride in the Chilean literary tradition, and Chile's relative isolation from bordering South American countries.

LANGUAGE

Spanish is the official language of Chile. However, peppered with terms from Indian languages, English, German, Italian, and even Serbo-Croatian, Chilean Spanish is a vital cultural expression reflecting the varied ancestry of the people that call Chile home. That Chileans remain implicitly aware of the singularity of their spoken Spanish is evident, as people prefer to say **castellano** rather than *español*. In Chile, the question "*¿Habla español?*" seems to ask "Do you speak Spanish (like a Spaniard)?," so say "*¿Habla castellano?*" and curry Chilean favor. Besides contending with the speed of spoken Chilean Spanish, the uninitiated tourist will not find the language incomprehensible, but stay attuned to quirky regionalisms and peculiar pronunciation, or refer to the Appendix (p. 499) for common words and phrases unique to Chilean Spanish. Other languages you may encounter while in Chile include **Aymara,** spoken in the mountains of the extreme north, around Arica and Iquique; **Huilliche,** spoken by several thousand Chileans between Valdivia and Chiloé; **Rapa Nui,** spoken mainly on Easter Island; and **Mapudungun,** the language of the Mapuche. English speakers don't abound (even among tourist office staff, hostel owners, waiters, and bus and taxi drivers), so brush up on basic Spanish and don't feel self-conscious trying it out on amiable Chileans.

RELIGION

Eighty-five percent of Chileans identify themselves as **Roman Catholic,** and rather than remain allied with conservative elements, the Roman Catholic Church exists as a religious body that is representative of Chilean society as a whole. Chilean Catholics, whether practicing or not, tend to respect the tenets of their Church (although some reject the more rigidly conservative views of the Vatican on several issues, including artificial birth control, marriage of the clergy, and abortion). Chileans maintain ties to the Church through sacraments such as baptism, marriage, and last rites, while attendance at Sunday Mass varies across the country. The movement to support social change with religious backing, known as Liberation Theology, appeals to Chileans primarily concerned with social issues.

Protestant sects, such as the **Anglican** and **Lutheran** churches, mainly serve members of the small English and German communities that remain in Chile. Chileans dissatisfied with the Roman Catholic Church prefer to embrace Evangelical denominations that were introduced to Chile through missionaries from the United States during the 20th century. Other Christian groups that are now established include **Baptists, Evangelicals, Methodists, Mormons, Presbyterians,** and **Seventh-Day Adventists.**

CULTURE

FOOD AND DRINK

MEALS AND MEALTIMES. Chileans take their time with food, as evidenced by the fact that they usually eat four leisurely meals a day. Though typical Chilean food is fairly bland, opportunities to explore cuisine exist. Moreover, Chileans pay more attention to the conversation of the meal than the food being eaten.

Desayuno (breakfast) has a southern-European flair, and standard breakfast fare usually consists of *café con leche* (strong coffee and hot milk) and toast with butter and jam. **Almuerzo** (lunch), the main meal of the day, is taken between 1 and 3pm. A generation ago, Chilean employees were given up to 2½ hours off to return home, partake of an unhurried *almuerzo*, and even sneak in a quick *siesta* before returning to work. While rampant capitalism and longer commutes have made this traditional midday break implausible in Santiago and other major cities, lunch remains an elaborate and comparatively elongated affair, and it is not unusual for smaller offices to close their doors during this time. However, for motivated Chileans and tourists on the go, quick options are available at the food stalls, delis, and convenience stores embedded in nooks and crannies across cities.

Even the most copious lunch will, however, be followed by "tea time" in the illustrious manner of the British. This light meal referred to as **el té** or **las onces** (elevens—named for the letters in *aguardiente*, the brandy that can spice up the tea) is taken at anytime between 4 and 6pm. *Café con leche, café helado* (iced coffee), or hot tea (Brit-style with milk) are normally served along with either toast, *marraqueta* (a traditional bread loaf), or fancier cakes and pastries. Restaurants cater to this cultural habit and remain open for tea, while some establishments identify specifically as tea rooms. **La comida** (dinner, or literally, the meal) is typically eaten at 9pm, and is served even later at social events. The meal resembles lunch but is generally less opulent. Try not to use the Spanish word *la cena* (supper) to refer to this meal, for although it's universally understood, it immediately identifies you as a non-Chilean.

CHILEAN CUISINE. Chilean cuisine is a simple melange of fare from native Indian, Spanish, French, German, English, Italian, Mexican, and Asian origins. Chileans also fully relish their natural resources through the generous use of fruits and vegetables in their recipes and innovative preparation of the varied supply of fresh seafood. As in the rest of the region, **corn** (*maíz* in Spanish, but *choclo* in Chile) is the basic ingredient of most Chilean foods.

Traditional national foods commonly enjoyed for *almuerzo* include **humitas** (akin to Mexican *tamales*), **pastel de choclo** (a corn casserole containing beef, chicken, raisins, onions, olives, and spices, and reflecting both Indian and European origins), and **cazuela** (a clear broth with rice, potato, corn, and chicken or beef). Particularly voracious eaters have *cazuela* as an appetizer and continue with **empanadas** (flour tortillas filled with cheese, meat, or seafood and fried).

Other well-known Chilean dishes include **porotos granados** (cranberry beans with squash and corn), **pan amasado** (a common heavy bread), and **pernil de chanco a la chilena** (braised fresh ham with chili sauce). Although dishes with less meat and more vegetables are typical of rural Chilean cuisine, **parrillas** (a popular type of restaurant that serves a variety of meat cuts and sausages) abound. **Lomo a la pobre** (poor man's steak—meat covered with eggs) is filling and widespread.

With its 4300km coastline, an abundance of **seafood** is available in Chile, and is commonly incorporated into local cuisine. Popular dishes to look out for are: **budín de centolla** (a pudding of crab, butter, onions, flour, cream, egg yolks, and cheese); **chupe de marisco** or **chupe de locos** (sea scallops or abalone with white wine, butter, cream, cheese, and spices); **paila marina** (a soup made from various shellfish); **caldillo de congrio** (an eel and vegetable soup); and the ever popular **curanto** (a hearty stew of fish, shellfish, chicken, pork, lamb, beef, and potato). Unusual seafood dishes to try are **picoroco** (a dish using a barnacle with white crab-like meat) and the overwhelmingly flavorful **piure**. Many recommend that fish should be had **al vapor** (steamed) or **a la plancha** (grilled), rather than **frito** (fried). While enjoying marine munchables, keep in mind that *marea roja* (red tide), a deadly seaborne toxin, has been detected off the southern coast of Chile. Since the Chilean government is carefully supervising the sale of shellfish so as to screen for the toxin, the threat posed by *marea roja* remains minimal; however, be cautious and only consume seafood purchased from reliable sources.

As these plentiful offerings are difficult to find outside of restaurants, most visitors will eat increasingly popular **lunchtime snacks** instead. Prevalent sandwiches are the **churrasco** (steak) and **jamón y queso** (ham and cheese). Sandwich combos to try are the **Barros Luco** (beef and cheese), named for the Chilean president Ramón Barros Luco (1910-1915), and the **Barros Jarpa** (containing ham, and consequently named after the 19th-century Chilean writer-lawyer-diplomat-politician, Ernesto Barros Jarpa). The **chacarero,** named after Chilean farm workers, contains beef, tomato, chili, and green beans, and comes highly recommended. An **ave palta** (chicken and avocado) sandwich is largely considered a staple of the corporate luncheon crowd.

You'll definitely come across **pebre,** a varyingly mild or spicy sauce, that can accompany any or all of the listed victuals. Traditionally an accompaniment to red meat and rice, Chileans generally like *pebre* with most of their food.

If you have any room left, partake of the rare **Chilean sweets.** Diverse fresh fruit options from the Central Valley aside, try out Chile's most distinctive desserts that originated with German immigrants. **Kuchen** is a delicious pastry loaded with fruits like raspberries and apricots. **Macedonia** is another offering dripping fruit syrup. **Alfajor,** a common Chilean pastry, consists of an excess of *dulce de leche* (caramelized milk, also known as *manjar*) sandwiched between thin pastries and powdered sugar. Or try **arroz con leche** (chilled rice with milk, sugar, and cinnamon), and *semola con leche* (a *flan* with sweet corn flour and caramel). Simpler *tortas* and *queques* (cakes) abound in pastry shops across the country.

While the cosmopolitan Santiago offers food to suit even the most finicky palate (the German culinary influence is evident, vegetarian options are not lacking, and Chinese restaurants abound), other regions are not diverse in their offerings. The best restaurants are restricted to resort towns such as Viña del

Mar, La Serena, and Puerto Varas, while Arica and Iquique boast good **chifas** (Chinese restaurants). Nevertheless, good Chilean food is available throughout the country, and most establishments oblige **vegetarians** on request. Make sure that you articulate your desire for vegetarian entrees, because many so-called vegetarian dishes in rural Chile include ham.

DRINKS. Neither occupation, nor age, nor economic background, nor locality, can prevent Chileans from having **vino** (wine) with their meals. It is not surprising that this essential element of the Eucharist is universally enjoyed throughout Chilean society. The abundance of **vineyards** (Chile's wine country stretches for 875km from just north of Santiago to Concepción) producing excellent **reds** and **whites** for both domestic and foreign markets ensures that fine, inexpensive varieties remain readily available. Notable vineyards include Undurraga, Santa Carolina, Cousiño Macul, and particularly, Concha y Toro, Chile's largest wine maker with 19 sq. km of land just south of Santiago. Concha y Toro's reds, especially the **Cabernet Sauvignon** and **Merlot,** have won international critical acclaim, while their *Casillero del Diablo* and *Trío* series are considered among Chile's finest wines. Consider daytrips to vineyards around Santiago (p. 131) for tours and tastings.

When in the mood for something with more of a punch, Chileans drink **pisco,** a grape-based distilled spirit produced in northern vineyards in the Limarí and Elqui valleys. Pisco sour, Chile's answer to the Mexican margarita, is notorious for its ability to intoxicate and inflict severe hangovers on uninitiated tourists. *Pisco* can also be added to Coca-Cola to produce the popular *piscola.* If your tolerance level is low, try **chicha** instead. A punch made from grapes beginning to ferment, this beverage is common during Independence Day celebrations on September 18.

If passing through Chile around Christmastime, check out the Chilean equivalent of eggnog. **Cola de mono** is an enjoyable mixture of milk, coffee, sugar, and *aguardiente,* a clear Chilean brandy. While **beers** are commonly available on tap, Chile is not known for its ales or lagers, outside of the Valdivia-produced Kuntsmann. A full-bodied beer to try is Escudo; otherwise, stick to popular draft beers (know in Chile as *schop*) such as Cristal.

If you're hoping to stay hydrated, **non-alcoholic** options abound as well. Delectable juices of in-season fruits are available at most restaurants year-round, but remember that Chileans have a penchant for added sugar, and specify that you'd prefer *"puro jugo sin azúcar"* (pure juice without sugar) if that is indeed the case. American soft drinks, both of the regular and diet variety, are readily available, as is water. Tap water in Chile is usually potable, but err on the side of caution, and drink bottled water whenever possible. Chileans enjoy both still *(sin gas)* and carbonated *(con gas)* water. Both are available throughout the country.

CUSTOMS AND ETIQUETTE

GREETINGS AND PUBLIC BEHAVIOR. South Americans are generally warm, tactile people who converse in close proximity. Get used to being cozy with your Chilean companions, because backing away is considered offensive. When greeting a group of Chileans, it is important to smile, make eye contact, and shake hands firmly with everyone present, as a group greeting can seem standoffish. Closer male friends may hug and pat each other's backs affectionately; women often greet each other by touching cheek to cheek and quickly cheek-kissing. Men and women follow this practice as well, but only in non-professional situations

Smoking at social functions is pretty standard, but if you are going to light up, offer a cigarette to your companions first. Always arrive fashionably late for social functions—15 to 30 minutes after the invitation time is customary. If you get there on time or early, you may catch your host or hostess off-guard. (Promptness is essential, however, for business functions—see **Business Etiquette,** below.)

HOUSEGUEST CUSTOMS. Bringing a **gift** to a home you are visiting is an appropriate gesture, as long as you don't choose anything too expensive that might seem flashy. Gifts from your home country that aren't available in Chile, such as your country's native handicrafts, candy, or liquor, are a good bet. You'll also score points if you bring small tokens, such as candy or games, to any children in the household that you are visiting.

Flowers are acceptable gifts, but send them before your arrival or bring them with you so that they don't seem an afterthought. Avoid yellow roses, a sign of contempt, and black and purple flowers, which symbolize death. If you receive a gift, open it immediately in front of your host and express enthusiastic thanks.

TABLE MANNERS. Chilean manners can be a bit more formal than those of other South American countries, but keeping a few things in mind will help you make a good impression on your Chilean acquaintances. Be sure that you know the correct utensils for each course—eating anything with your hands, even french fries, is a definite faux pas. Placing your hands in your lap while at the table is a sign of deception, so keep both hands above the table at all times. It is polite to sample everything that served and to compliment the host or hostess on all of the eats.

Meals in Chile are often more about conversation and visiting than the food itself. Enjoy leisurely meals with your Chilean friends—stay for conversation rather than taking off when your plate is clean.

If you go out to eat, the person who makes the invitation often pays. Don't expect to share in the bill, but plan to reciprocate with a similar invitation at a later date. Arrange ahead of time to pay the bill in a restaurant if you made the invitation. You will have to ask for *la cuenta* (the bill) at the end of the meal—the waiter won't rush you out by bringing it automatically.

BUSINESS ETIQUETTE. Chilean businesspeople are big on exchanging business cards, so it's a good idea to have yours translated into Spanish on the back of your standard card; the swap of cards usually occurs after the ritual handshake.

Meetings and business gatherings begin with chit-chat. Arrive on time, but don't be surprised if others, especially the seniors of the meeting, arrive half an hour late. Status at meetings is important, and an age hierarchy is assumed. If you are unsure who is the eldest, keep an eye on the behavior of others at the meeting, and defer to that person. Be aware that feelings are often the driving force in business interactions. A respectful and humble approach to discussion is your best bet—attempting forceful negotiations, cracking excessive jokes, or putting people down will lead only to embarrassment among your Chilean colleagues.

TABOOS. If you make some gestures common in other areas of the world, you may unintentionally offend your new Chilean friends. Be careful not to slap your right fist into a left open palm—this is a strong insult in Chile. Displaying an open palm with fingers splayed is taken to mean "stupid." Make sure to point and beckon with your entire hand instead of your index finger. Also, do not raise your right fist near your head—this is a communist-associated taboo in Chile.

THE ARTS

HISTORY AND THE CURRENT SCENE

ARCHITECTURE. Due to Chile's frequent earthquakes, many **architectural monuments** from the colonial period are no longer standing. In **Valparaíso,** Chile's oldest city, for example, no colonial buildings remain as the result of a 1730 earthquake that leveled all of the city's colonial structures. The city, however, was rebuilt immediately and has continued to develop architecturally, with a mix of imposing professional buildings and older residential structures in the north of the city. Southern cities, including **Valdivia** and **Osorno,** reflect the impact of their German heritage in the few buildings that have survived earthquakes.

In **Santiago,** the architecture is a merging of remains from ancient monuments, colonial buildings, and modern skyscrapers. The perfectly calibrated city blocks of old Santiago are centered around the **Plaza de Armas,** which is flanked with several significant historical buildings in the **colonial** style. In the early 20th century, the plaza was embellished with several new buildings in the **Art Nouveau** style, including the **Cousiño Palace,** the **Church of the Sacramentinos,** the **Palace of Fine Arts,** and the **Tribunal.** The city expands out from the original center to include additional buildings and homes in the **Neo-Gothic, modern,** and **California** styles.

FINE ARTS. Colonial art from the 17th and 18th centuries in Chile is composed almost entirely of religious images. Early colonial sculptures, paintings, and murals depict dramatic images of Christ, the Virgin Mary, and the Catholic saints. Toward the end of Spanish domination in Chile, colonial artists became increasingly interested in depicting the most wealthy and influential citizens, especially those of Santiago, in their work.

Romanticism, which ruled the Chilean art scene at the beginning of the 19th century, was created primarily by European artists who came to Chile after it gained its independence. The classic landscapes and portraits of Romanticism replaced the predominantly sacred images of the previous colonial period.

Chile's premier 20th-century painter, **Roberto Matta,** is a pioneer in the style of **abstract realism.** Matta is noted for his abstract style that "has one foot in architecture and the other in dreams."

LITERATURE. Latin America's first **epic poem,** La Araucana, was penned by the Chilean soldier-poet **Don Alonso de Ercilla** in the late 16th century. This poem, which illuminated the beauty of the Chilean countryside, paved the way for Latin American poets to come, and is ranked by Chileans among the epics of Homer, Virgil and Lucano.

Alonso de Ovalle, often referred to as Chile's "first writer," is considered the finest poet of 17th-century Chile. The friar composed his best-known work, Histórica relación del reino de Chile, while abroad in Rome—distance allowed him to capture the country with nostalgia and insight. His poems map the cities, valleys, rivers, lakes, and mountains of Chile to perfection. Much of 18th-century Chilean poetry is narrow in focus, composed mainly by male members of the Catholic Church. In the later 18th and 19th centuries, Chilean **romanticism** flourished in the wake of the Spanish romantics.

Chile's literary pride lies, however, in its two 20th-century **Nobel Laureates** who secured Chile's reputation as "the land of poets." **Gabriela Mistral,** a Vicuña native, worked as a schoolteacher until her poems of mourning, Sonetos de la muerte (Death Sonnets), made her famous throughout Latin America. Mistral won the Nobel Prize for Literature in 1945 and continued to publish poetry while serving in the League of Nations, helping to reform the Chilean and Mexican school systems, and teaching Spanish literature at reputed North American universities.

World-renowned poet **Pablo Neruda,** influenced by Mistral during his youth in Temuco, published poetry on a wide range of political, social, and sentimental subjects and experimented with many literary styles, including the "esoteric surrealism" of his 1933 breakthrough Residencia en la tierra (Residence on Earth). After returning to Chile from political exile due to his alliance with the Communist party, Neruda was awarded the Nobel Prize for Literature in 1971.

Perhaps Chile's best-known 20th-century novelist is **Isabel Allende**—niece of former Chilean president **Salvador Allende**—whose works of **magical realism** are best-sellers in both Latin America and in translation in the United States. Her classic novel, *La casa de los espíritus (The House of the Spirits)*, follows in the path of the novel *Cien años de soledad (One Hundred Years of Solitude)*, by Colombian Nobel Laureate Gabriel García Márquez, adopting its cyclic storytelling and magical possibilities while introducing new ideas about gender and social movements. Allende's work is also said to be influenced by 20th-century novelist **José Donoso,** known for his epic novel of family, *Casa del campo*. Allende continues to pen novels today; her latest work, published in 2003, is entitled *Mi país inventado (My Invented Country)*.

MUSIC. Chile's **folkloric music** is rich and diverse, influenced by Spanish, Argentine, Peruvian, and Mexican traditions. Music for the **cueca,** the national dance of Chile, is one of the country's classic styles, featuring exact, quick rhythms sung with accompaniment from guitar, piano, and accordion. Other styles such as the **Tonada,** a more improvisational folkloric style, and the **Chilean Waltz,** a melding of Peruvian and Argentine waltzes, are traditional throughout the country.

Popular music tends to be prevalent on the radio and in *discotecas*. Prepare to be regaled with Latin pop from celebrities such as Juanes and Shakira. Successful Chilean acts to look for include Los Prisoneros, Los Jaivas, a Chilean pop band, classical composer Luis Advis, and Illapu, a group specializing in folkloric music.

DANCE. The national dance of Chile, **la cueca,** is widely considered the best expression of the Chilean spirit, despite the fact that there is some controversy as to whether the dance originated in Chile or in Lima, Peru. Regardless, the dance has been appropriated by Chileans since colonial times and is a time-honored component of Chilean culture. The tranquil and hesitant movements that define *la cueca* are meant to evoke the behavior of the rooster and chicken during an amorous conquest. Partners brandishing handkerchiefs and accompanied by musicians on guitar, piano, accordion, or harp, dance separately, never touching, yet remaining connected through fluid movements, eye contact, and facial expressions. The flirtatiousness of the dance is gradually intensified through complex footwork that steadily brings the male dancer closer to his female partner. *La cueca* is still an integral part of any celebration or festival in the Chilean countryside and is performed year-round by *huasos* around Temuco and Osorno. But don't expect to practice your rooster imitation in a hip urban nightclub. Known as *discotecas* in Chile (the term "nightclub" refers to strip clubs or other shadier operations), dance clubs blast popular Top 40 American hits and Latin-pop numbers while youngsters groove and gyrate on crowded dance floors.

FILM AND TELEVISION. Pinochet's military regime was not kind to the **Chilean film industry,** but the current dearth of a national cinema has not always been the case in Chile. Cinema originated in Chile before World War I, and although film production was initially spasmodic and the introduction of talkies dealt an early blow to the industry, in 1958, a new Chilean cinema emerged.

Developed by the *cineclub* at the University of Chile and the Film Institute at the Universidad Católica in Santiago, cinema became an integral mode of popular cultural expression that vigorously supported the socialist cause. Rather than be harmed by the introduction of television to Chile in 1962, the film industry benefited from increased distribution through made-for-TV films. Thematically, Chilean cinema of the 1960s echoes the history of the Popular Unity government, and became particularly influenced by politics during the cultural upheaval of the Allende years. Director Miguel Littin's famous film *El chacal de Nahueltoro (The Jackal of Nahueltoro)* is regarded as a prophetic, national allegory, while his 1972 film *La tierra prometida (The Promised Land)* eerily anticipates the *coup d'état* of September 11, 1973.

Although Chilean films developed specifically as aesthetic and ideological products, they were not embraced by the public until positively reviewed in European journals. However, the popular socialist bent of the new Chilean cinema made it one of the main targets for the military's repression, and strict film censorship policies were implemented after Pinochet established military rule.

After the destruction of the national film institute of the Popular Unity government, the Chilean film industry basically disappeared. The distribution of films in Chile came under the control of companies such as Warner Brothers, Paramount, Columbia Pictures, and 20th Century Fox. Similarly, if you turn on the TV for an authentic Chilean visual experience, you're in for a disappointment. Today, Chile's 350 theaters exhibit European and especially American Hollywood films with Spanish subtitles. Recently, the growing film industry has featured the work of directors such as Gonzalo Justiniano, whose most recent film, "B-Happy," earned international recognition. Meanwhile, increasingly popular cable TV packages bring CNN, MTV, Discovery Channel, and American shows such as *Friends* and *Seinfeld* into millions of homes. Chilean soap operas, however, are the one exception—*telenovelas* (several-month-long soap operas) consistently get good ratings and are watched by men and women alike.

SPORTS AND RECREATION

SOCCER. Soccer, known in South America as **fútbol,** is undoubtedly the most important sport in Chile—almost all Chilean men and many women take pride in their *fútbol* skills. Don't be surprised to see young children playing in blocked-off parking lots and entire families playing in their yards during their free time.

Although the national team tends to fall in the shadows of star South American teams such as Argentina, Brazil, and Uruguay, Chile is proud of having hosted the World Cup in 1962, when its national team made it to the semi-finals for the first (and only) time. Many Chileans enthusiastically follow the ongoing competition between rival teams from the **Universidad de Chile** (University of Chile), **Colo Colo,** and the **Universidad Católica** (Catholic University). If visiting Santiago, make suer to check out a professional game at the **Estadio Nacional.**

TENNIS. Although Chile's enthusiasm for **tenis** (tennis) never quite matches its love of soccer, the country is proud of its world-renowned tennis players. The current Chilean tennis stars are **Nicolas Massú** and **Fernando González,** both ranked among the top twenty tennis players in the world.

SKIING. Chile's **ski season** lasts from June to October, so skiing and snowboarding fanatics from the Northern Hemisphere flock to the country each winter to join the many South Americans who hit Chile's famous slopes. **Portillo Ski Resort** is the oldest and perhaps most widely known ski establishment in South America, but its steep prices and exclusivity make it inaccessible for many budget travelers. **Valle Nevado, La Parva,** and **Farellones/El Colorado,** all within 60km of Santiago, are perhaps the best choices for extended stays or daytrips from the capital.

SURFING. During the summer months, Chileans trade their skis for surfboards, hitting the numerous **surf spots** along the coast in northern and central Chile. The type of surfing available varies by location—in the **northern region,**

between Arica and Iquique, the waves are small, but the water is warm and there are many unexplored beaches for the adventurous surfer to navigate. The **central region** of the country, particularly near **Pichilemu**, boasts larger waves, but the waters are colder and the surf season is consequentially slightly more limited.

HOLIDAYS AND FESTIVALS

Most of Chile's **nationally observed holidays** are religious, despite the official separation of church and state that occurred in 1925. Traditional Catholic holidays are generally solemn, and include Mass, street processions, elaborate costuming, and reenactments of Bible stories. Secular holidays, such as Independence Day, often involve dancing and the preparation of traditional foods.

CHILEAN FESTIVALS

DATE	NAME AND LOCATION	DESCRIPTION
January 1	*Año Nuevo* (New Years Day)	Family and social celebrations, often held outdoors.
March 1	*Día del Trabajo* (Labor Day)	Schools and businesses closed; parades and worker demonstrations throughout the country.
March 20-27 (varies)	*Semana Santa* (Holy Week)	Week leading up to Easter; schools and businesses closed in many places. Precessions and masses.
March 27 (varies)	*Día de Pascua* (Easter Sunday)	Masses held and time spent with family.
April 3 (varies)	*Domingo de Cuasimodo* (Middle Chile only)	Sunday after Easter; houses are decorated and costumes worn; parade in the streets—priests, accompanied by *huasos*, or cowboys, give communion to the poor and elderly.
May 21	*Glorias Navales*	Commemoration of the 1879 naval battle at Iquique; celebrations, military parades, and speeches.
June 23	*Corpus Christi*	Streets are lined with decoration; costumed performances in or near churches.
June 29	*Día de San Pedro y San Pablo* (St. Peter and St. Paul)	Masses held; schools and businesses closed—homage paid to St. Peter and St. Paul.
August 15	*Asunción de la Virgen* (Assumption of the Virgin Mary)	National Holiday; masses held.
September 3	National day of Reconciliation/National Unity Day	Celebration of national unity after Pinochet's regime.
September 18	*Día de Independencia* (Independence Day)	Eating, drinking, and dancing the national dance "cueca" are customary; unofficial beginning of summer.
September 19	Army Day	Military celebration of independence, parade in Santiago draws crowds and is watched on TV throughout Chile.
October 12	*Día de la Raza* (or *Día de la Hispanidad*)	Originally established by Franco's regime in Spain to celebrate Spain's former colonies, now commemorated with school and office closings.
November 1	*Todos los Santos* (All Saints Day)	Religious holiday observed by churches; the following day flowers are placed on loved ones' graves.
December 8	*Inmaculada Concepción* (Immaculate Conception)	People attend church and gather to honor the Virgin Mary.
December 24	Christmas Eve	Many attend *Miso de Gallo*—midnight mass—and await *Viejo Pascuero* (old man Christmas).
December 25	*Navidad* (Christmas Day)	Time spent with family, preparation of traditional foods.

ADDITIONAL RESOURCES

GENERAL HISTORY

Culture and Customs of Chile, by Guillermo I. Castillo-Feliú.

The Breakdown of Democratic Regimes, ed. Juan Linz, et al. A great compilation of Latin American political thinkers on the fall of Chilean democracy in the 1970s.

Chilean Democracy, by Arturo Valenzuela. Written by one of Chile's foremost political theorists, it looks at the country's political history.

Chile Since Independence, by Leslie Bethell. General history of Chile.

A Nation of Enemies, by Pamela Constable and Arturo Valenzuela. Chronicle of the Pinochet dictatorship.

FICTION AND NON-FICTION

A Gabriela Mistral Reader, by Gabriela Mistral. A Mistral compilation, in English.

The House of the Spirits, by Isabel Allende. Allende's best-known magical realism novel.

La Araucana, by Alonso de Ercilla y Zâuäniga. The classic Chilean epic poem.

My Invented Country, by Isabel Allende. The author's latest novel, in English translation.

Residence on Earth, by Pablo Neruda. The poet's breakthrough work of surrealism.

Twenty Love Poems and a Song of Despair, by Pablo Neruda. One of Neruda's most famous collections.

ALTERNATIVES TO TOURISM

A PHILOSOPHY FOR TRAVELERS

Let's Go believes that the connection between travelers and their destinations is an important one. We've watched the growth of the "ignorant tourist" stereotype with dismay, knowing that many travelers care passionately about the communities and environments they explore—but also knowing that even conscientious tourists can inadvertently damage natural wonders and harm cultural environments. With this "Alternatives to Tourism" chapter, *Let's Go* hopes to promote a better understanding of Chile and enhance your experience there.

There are several different options for those who seek to participate in Alternatives to Tourism. Opportunities for **volunteering** abound, both with local and international organizations. **Studying** can also be instructive, either in the form of direct enrollment in a local university or in an independent research project. **Working** is a way to both immerse yourself in the local culture and finance your travels.

As a **volunteer** in Chile, you can participate in a program that truly helps those you serve, whether working with orphans in Santiago or building homes for farmers in the *campo*, either on a short-term basis or as the main component of your trip. The disparity of wealth between rich and poor in Chile, as in other countries, provides the opportunity for volunteers to apply their skills either at a high level with advanced teaching positions, or on a simpler level, counseling the homeless on elements of leading a stable life. Later in this section, we recommend organizations that can help you find the opportunities that best suit your interests, whether you're looking to pitch in for a day or a year.

Studying at a college or language program is another option. Chile's universities, especially Universidad Católica and Universidad de Chile, are some of the finest in Latin America, and attract the world's most accomplished scholars of Latin American studies. The language programs offered in Chile have been honed by this higher level of academic expectations, so expect the best from them (along with higher prices).

Many travelers also structure their trips by the **work** that they can do along the way—either odd jobs as they go, or full-time stints in cities where they plan to stay for some time. Full-time work for professionals is most easily found from your home country, with the many governmental organizations or multinational corporations that are established in Chile. For those who seek short-term work teaching English or while traveling, it's sometimes possible to coordinate a position before arriving, but travelers often find it easier to get work when they're on the ground in Chile and able to meet with possible employers directly.

 Start your search at ▨ **www.beyondtourism.com**, Let's Go's brand-new search able database of Alternatives to Tourism, where you can find exciting feature articles and helpful program listings divided by country, continent, and program type.

VOLUNTEERING

Since Chile has low volunteer participation within the country (a meager 4% of the adult Chilean population volunteers, against 56% in the US, 34% in Germany, and 34% in neighboring Peru that leads in the region), there are endless volunteer programs open to foreigners in Chile. Many of these services charge you a fee to participate in the program and to do work. These fees can be surprisingly hefty (although they frequently cover airfare and most, if not all, living expenses). Try to do research on a program before committing—talk to people who have previously participated and find out exactly what you're getting into, as living and working conditions can vary greatly. Different programs are geared toward different ages and levels of experience, so make sure that you are not taking on too much or too little. The more informed you are and the more realistic expectations you have, the more enjoyable the program will be.

Most people choose to go through a parent organization that takes care of logistical details, and frequently provides a group environment and support system. There are two main types of organizations—religious (often Catholic) and non-sectarian—although there are rarely restrictions on participation for either.

URBAN ISSUES

Chile's urban centers, though more developed than many in Latin America, still have large populations working through issues of poverty, homelessness, and familial instability. Volunteers working with those issues have often found their experiences in Chile to provide them with a new perspective on those issues that stayed with them long after departing the country. The following organizations are seeking volunteers.

Nuestra Casa, Huérfanos 2832, Santiago (☎02 689 0157; fax 681 9765; www.nuestra-casa.cl), provides their formerly homeless residents with a stable place to live. The mostly college-aged volunteers work with the residents to help them get back on their feet independently.

One World Nursery School, 6 Norte 767, Viña del Mar (☎32 479 831). This bilingual Montessori preschool looks for volunteers who can bring unique talents and abilities to work for the children of this seaside city.

Spanish Immersion Programs in Latin America, Tomás Andrew 074, Providencia Santiago (☎02 635 4776), connects volunteers with opportunities to work in homeless shelters, children's organizations, public hospitals, and environmental groups.

Voluntarios de la Esperanza, Trinidad Oriente 3400 Casilla 9702, La Florida, Santiago (☎/fax 02 267 0014; www.voluntariosesperanza.org), recruits volunteers to live and work in their orphanages. Opportunity for direct service to impoverished Chilean children dealing with the loss of their families and often histories of abuse.

ENVIRONMENTAL CONSERVATION

The wide range of flora and fauna along Chile's coastline has drawn tourists from all over the world to this natural wonder wedged between the mountains and the sea. As Chile has developed into an industrial and consumer nation, however, that rich biodiversity has come under attack. Environmental groups have sprung up to protect the flora and fauna, and the following are looking for volunteers.

El Canelo de Nos, Portales 3020 Casilla 380, San Bernardo (☎02 857 1943; fax 857 11 60; canelo@rdc.cl). An NGO founded in 1985, El Canelo de Nos works with environmental sustainability, social development and poverty eradication.

Earthwatch, 3 Clocktower Pl., Ste. 100, Box 75, Maynard, MA 01754, USA (☎800-776-0188 or 978-461-0081; www.earthwatch.org). Arranges 1- to 3-week programs in Chile to promote conservation of natural resources. Costs average $1700 plus airfare.

Save the Wild Chinchillas, Casilla 302, Illapel (☎09 471 4953; www.wildchinchillas.org). This group sticks to its point—an entire non-profit organization devoted to the chinchilla, a furry rodent that could face extinction within 25 years without positive intervention now.

RURAL AND SUBURBAN DEVELOPMENT

Life in the Chilean countryside flows at a slower pace than most visitors will be used to, but relaxing *almuerzos* unfortunately don't translate into an idyllic, worry-free existence for *campesinos*. The following organizations work in small towns, poor suburbs, and the *campo* to fight housing problems, encourage agricultural development, and encourage community development.

CEDELCOOP, Orompello 586 Dept. 202, Concepción (☎41 247 283), promotes education in modern agricultural technology for rural farmers. Works with government agencies to equalize socioeconomic conditions for those farmers.

Fundación Chol-Chol, Casilla 14, Nueva Imperial, Novena Region, Temuco (☎45 197 4864; www.cholchol.org). Offers volunteer opportunities for a minimum of 3 months to Spanish speakers possessing an undergraduate degree to work in local health clinics, in the field of agricultural development, within the forestry program, and as grant writers or computer programmers.

Habitat for Humanity International, 121 Habitat St., Americus, GA 31709, USA (☎229-924-6935 ext. 2551, in Chile 56 2 264 1868; www.habitat.org, in Chile www.habitatparalahumanidad.cl). Volunteers build houses in over 83 countries including Chile for anywhere from 2 weeks to 3 years. Short-term program costs range US$1200-4000.

Mondo Challenge, Galliford Building Gayton Road Milton Malsor, Northampton NN7 3AB UK (☎1604 858225; fax 1604 859323; www.mondochallenge.org), provides opportunities for volunteering in teaching and community development positions, especially in northern Chile.

United Planet, 41 Appleton St., Boston, MA 02116 USA (☎617-292-0711; fax 617-292-0712; www.unitedplanet.org). Join one of their Quests for US$995 plus airfare to spend 2 weeks constructing much-needed housing in Chile's poorer sectors.

Volunteers for Peace, 1034 Tiffany Rd., Belmont., VT 05730, USA (☎802-259-2759; www.vfp.org). Arranges placement in work camps in Chile. Membership required for registration. Annual *International Workcamp Directory* US$20. Programs average US$200-400 for 2-3 weeks.

FAITH-BASED PROGRAMS

Chile's Catholic heritage comes to bear on its volunteer opportunities. Groups from the United States and Chile have created these faith-based service programs, which tend to require a longer commitment and place more of an emphasis on service and the integration of spirituality into service than other volunteer programs.

Hogar de Cristo, Santiago (☎02 540 9100; www.hogardecristo.com) selectively recruits volunteers to work in branches scattered throughout Chile. Volunteers can be assigned to one of several programs, including working with street children, orphans, or pre-schoolers; monitoring the organization's Chile-wide crisis hotline; and ministering to the elderly, sick, and dying. The organization is predominantly Catholic in membership as well as mission. Consult the bilingual website to apply.

Holy Cross Associates, P.O. Box 668 Notre Dame, IN 46556 (☎574-631-5521; fax 631-9233; http://holycrossassociates.nd.edu/), recruits young Catholic volunteers to join a two-year faith-based service program with an emphasis on community, simple living, and solidarity with the poor.

ILADES, Almirante Barroso 6, Santiago (☎02 671 7499 or 695 177; fax 698 6873; www.ilades.cl). A Chile-based service program with Jesuit roots, ILADES provides numerous opportunities for short- and long-term service.

Jesuit Volunteers International, P.O. Box 3756, Washington, D.C. 20027 (☎202-687-1132; fax 687-5082; www.jesuitvolunteers.org). A Catholic organization that promotes spiritual growth through service, community living, and solidarity with the poor.

San Marcos Church, 599 Padre Hurtado, Las Condes, Santiago (☎02 220 2228; www.sanmarcoschurch.cl). For travelers already living or working in Santiago, San Marcos provides opportunities to work in a Christian (non-Catholic) setting at an orphanage, halfway house for young women, and camp for children with disabilities.

GENERAL COMMUNITY SERVICE

For volunteers who are unsure of their calling, Chile's umbrella service organizations and speciality programs offer new avenues for devoting volunteers' time and energy to service of others.

Elderhostel, Inc., 11 Avenue de Lafayette, Boston, MA 92111, USA (☎877-426-8056; fax 877-426-2166; www.elderhostel.org). Sends volunteers aged 55 and over around the world to work in construction, research, teaching, and many other projects. Costs average $100 per day plus airfare.

En Todo Amar y Servir, Santiago (☎02 511 5283; fax 525 3943; www.entodoamaryservir.cl), connects volunteers to projects in Chile. Has links to over 50 institutions and non-profit organizations that work for social welfare.

Programa Universidad del Adulto Mayor, Arlegui 119, Viña del Mar (☎32 465 197; fax 465 197; programas.especiales@uv.cl), provides educational activities for the elderly and works with women's issues and disability issues. Based at the Univ. of Valparaíso.

Raleigh International, 27 Parsons Green Ln., London SW6 4HZ, UK (☎020 7371 8585; fax 7371 5116; www.raleighinternational.org). Prince William spent his gap year working on sustainable environmental and community projects in Tortel, Chile through Raleigh. If that doesn't commend it enough, surf the website to learn more about 3-month expeditions that are part of a longer program including training weekends and workshops. With an emphasis on personal development and cultural awareness, Raleigh volunteers in Chile track endangered species with the financial support of government ministries, international development groups, and the Millennium Commission.

US Servas, 11 John St., Rm. 505, New York, NY 10038 (☎212-267-0252; fax 267-0292; www.usservas.org), provides an international network of hosts for travelers building peace by providing opportunities for mutually arranged individual visits, typically for 2 nights, between people of diverse cultures and backgrounds. Year-round. US$85 per adult for 1 year of travel. Contact Program Associate Katrina Grigg-Saito.

CLOSE, BUT NOT TOO CLOSE
The Challenges of Integration into Chilean Society

I'll admit it: going into my semester abroad in Santiago, I had the naïve expectation that within six months I would be fully integrated into Chilean society. I'd have the requisite group of Chilean friends, a host family as close as my biological one, and maybe even a boyfriend. I expected to have a string of bars I frequented. I wanted to run into people I knew on the street (forget that over 6 million people live in Santiago). I wanted to have a routine, a niche that I would create for myself in a matter of months. However, now, after half a year of retrospection, I'm starting to accept the difficulties I met in making Chilean friends and building that niche. Even now, I wonder how many real Chilean friends I had and how successful I was in terms of "integrating" myself.

Yo no caché nada...

Aforementioned "integration" faces particular challenges in Chile. It's a country whose physical, geographical boundaries made cross-border travel a near impossibility until air travel developed. As a result, access to the world of ideas, trends, and happenings in the global arena only arrived with television, which to this day is still controlled and censored—imagine a place where the most fashionable and "experimental" TV station is the one owned by the Catholic University. Even then, the world beyond the Pacific and the Andes became accessible only as the Internet began to spread.

Moreover, most Chileans live at their parents' home from birth through university all the way until marriage. The friends they had in pre-school are the same ones they will have at least until their wedding day. This limits possibilities for social exchange or interaction across class, geographic, and familial borders. It also makes it particularly difficult for any foreigner to break into social circles. Add to the mix a murderous dictatorship that embedded a culture of fear of speaking out or expressing one's opinions, and you've got the makings of a conservative and insulated country, where people are largely not open to things that are different or new. Suffice to say, culturally speaking, Chile is not porous to outsiders.

In addition to the closed nature of Chilean society, the people are somewhat serious and reserved. While Argentines announce Italian and fashionable European undertones, Brazilians sing of indigenous and African roots, and Peruvians pay homage to a strong Andean Incan population, Chile is a country whose main cultural influences since Spanish settlement were Germany and England, making Chile, if not the most serious Latin American culture, certainly the most punctual. People don't smile or laugh too loudly in the street. Their dancing is subdued; their music, respectful.

Upon introduction, Chileans were always warm, welcoming, and willing to engage in surface-level socialization. Yet, when it came time to open up to a newcomer, it was another story. Since most lived at home, the family and its rules still came first. Many university-age students, if they didn't have curfews, either didn't have their own cars to get around, had no place of their own to which they could invite friends, or simply weren't willing or able to pay for drinks at bars.

I cannot, however, forget the hospitality with which I was met throughout Chile. My host mother opened up her home and life to me. Chileans also, surprisingly, were very quick to help if I had a problem. Never did I want for directions when I was lost, or confused on the *micro*. Whenever they learned I was from abroad, they wanted to engage in conversation, hear my opinion of their country, and listen to stories of life beyond. Though reserved, they are considerate and reflective. It is clear that they spend much time discussing and thinking. In fact, Chile has one of the most vibrant black markets for pirated books, which Chileans devour.

Signs point to recuperation, albeit slow, after the dictatorship. The first generation that was not alive during Pinochet's rule is growing up, and it is clear that they are learning to take advantage of their new liberties. My advice to any foreigner who spends an extended period of time in Chile, however, is to be patient. It will still take a long time to get to know Chileans, to understand their cultural symbols and interpersonal style, and to figure out how to become a part of their lives. Also, be sensitive to the subtleties of Chilean culture. For Chile, like any country, has its own social codes and rules, which take time to learn—and accept. *Cachai?*

Manuela Zoninsein is the editor of Let's Go: Central America 2005. She currently majors in Social Studies at Harvard University. She spent six months living in Santiago while attending the Universidad de Chile and the Pontificia Universidad Católica.

STUDYING

VISA INFORMATION

US citizens planning on studying in Chile need to apply for a visa before embarking. Check the US Embassy website (www.chile-usa.org) for the consulate that has jurisdiction over your state. The process of collecting the necessary documentation, sending it to the consulate, and receiving approval may take several weeks, so begin far in advance of your departure. **Student Visas** require: a) a passport that will be valid until after the expected end date, b) a health certificate stating that you are in good health and have been HIV tested, c) a police certificate confirming that you are a citizen in good standing, d) four recent passport photos, e) US$100 fee, f) proof of acceptance from the university or program you will be attending in Chile, and g) a statement from your bank or parents showing that you are financially solvent.

Study abroad programs range from basic language and culture courses to college-level classes, often for credit. In order to choose a program that best fits your needs, you will want to find out what kind of students participate in the program and what sort of accommodations are provided. In programs that have large groups of students who speak the same language, there is a trade-off. You may feel more comfortable in the community, but you will not have the same opportunity to practice a foreign language or to befriend other international students. For accommodations, dorm life provides a better opportunity to mingle with fellow students, but there is less of a chance to experience the local scene. If you live with a family, there is a potential to build lifelong friendships with Chileans and to experience day-to-day life in more depth, but conditions can vary greatly from family to family, and some students report feeling smothered by Chilean home life and the experience of having parents as rulemakers again.

UNIVERSITIES

Those relatively fluent in Spanish may find it cheaper to enroll directly in a Chilean university, although getting college credit may be more difficult. Some American schools still require students to pay them for credits they obtain elsewhere. Most university-level study-abroad programs are meant as language and culture enrichment opportunities, and therefore are conducted entirely in Spanish. Still, many programs do offer classes in English and beginner- and lower-level language courses. A good resource for finding programs that cater to your particular interests is www.studyabroad.com, which has links to various semester abroad programs based on a variety of criteria, including desired location and focus of study. The following is a list of organizations that can help place students in university programs abroad, or have their own branch in Chile.

AMERICAN PROGRAMS

The following is a list of several US-based programs that organize study abroad opportunities. There also a number of universities that run their own programs in Chile, including Clemson University, Harvard University, Stanford University, State University of New York (SUNY), Syracuse University, Tufts University, University of Miami, and University of Wisconsin.

Institute for Study Abroad—Butler University (IFSA-Butler), Butler University, 1100 W. 42nd St., Ste. 305, Indianapolis, IN 46208 (☎888-344-9299; www.ifsa-butler.org), runs programs in conjunction with the **Cooperating Opportunities Program of America (COPA)** in Santiago, Valparaíso, and Viña del Mar.

Council on International Educational Exchange (CIEE), 7 Custom House St., 3rd fl., Portland, ME 01401, USA (☎800-407-8839; www.ciee.org/study). Sponsors work, volunteer, academic, and internship programs in Chile.

School for International Training, College Semester Abroad, Admissions, Kipling Rd., P.O. Box 676, Brattleboro, VT 05302 (☎888-272-7881 or 802-258-3212; www.sit.edu). Semester- and year-long programs in Chile US$13,100-13,225. Also runs the **Experiment in International Living** (☎800-345-2929; www.usexperiment.org), 4-week summer programs that offer high-school students cross-cultural homestays, community service, ecological adventure, and language training in Chile and cost US$4300.

State University of New York (SUNY) at Plattsburgh, 101 Broad St., Plattsburgh, NY 12901 (☎518-564-5827; www.plattsburgh.edu/academics/studyabroad/), runs study abroad programs in several major Chilean cities.

Institute for International Education of Students, 33 North LaSalle St., 15th fl., Chicago, IL 60602 (☎800-995-2300; www.iesabroad.org), provides opportunities for course study, internships and service work.

CHILEAN PROGRAMS

Studying in Chile is common for students and is easy to arrange. A convenient way is to apply to a program in your home country (for Americans, those listed above or others). For a flat fee they will generally take care of enrolling you in your selected university, arrange housing, and provide important resources and support while you are living there. When selecting a program, pay attention to what kind of living and studying situation they offer. Depending on your preferences, you will have to decide whether to stay with a family or in a dormitory, to study in the actual university classes or in special program classes, and to have a very supportive program or a more flexible, independent one. This varies greatly from program to program, so be sure to talk with other students who have previously participated in them or with university study-abroad advisors.

If you are looking for a more independent immersion experience, you may want to enroll directly in Chilean universities with international exchange programs. This is a much more difficult task since you have to negotiate your application to the university and arrange housing on your own, but is often more rewarding. These universities regularly enroll foreign students.

Pontificia Universidad Católica de Chile, Alameda Bernardo O'Higgins 340, Santiago (☎02 354 2000; www.ucatolica.cl). One of Chile's leading institutions, a private Catholic university with a strong academic reputation.

Universidad de Chile, Diagonal Paraguay 265, Of. 1703, Santiago (☎02 678 2300; www.uchile.cl). The largest public university in Santiago, "U Chile" has a more liberal history than Universidad Católica, and a wide range of course offerings.

Universidad Adolfo Ibáñez, Diagonal Las Torres 2640, Peñalolén, Santiago (☎02 369 3500; www.uai.cl). A technologically advanced university on the cutting edge of flexible liberal arts curriculum in Chile.

LANGUAGE SCHOOLS

Language schools are often run by international or local organizations or divisions of foreign universities. They rarely offer college credit, but are a good alternative to university study if you want a deeper focus on the language or a slightly less rigorous course load. These programs are also good for high school students who may not feel comfortable with older students in a university program.

ALTERNATIVES TO TOURISM

Bridge-Linguatec International, 915 South Colorado Blvd., Denver, CO 80246, USA (Canada and US ☎303-777-7783 or 800-724-4210; www.bridgelinguatec.com). Offers group or private classes from US$540-1290 per week.

Casa Aventura, Gálvez 11, Valparaíso (☎32 755 963; www.casaventura.cl), offers Spanish lessons to travelers. 1hr. lesson CH$5000. 1-week introductory class CH$75,000. 2-week intensive course CH$250,000, with homestay CH$360,000.

¡école!, General Urrutia 592, Pucón (☎45 441 675; www.ecole.cl), offers Spanish classes in southern Chile's adventure zone. Package rates available for long-term study.

Facultad de Filosofía de la Universidad de Chile, Ignacio Carrera Pinto 1025, Ñuñoa, Santiago (☎02 678 7040). Offers semester-long Spanish courses for foreign students at the university. Semesters run late Aug.-early Dec. and Mar.-July (US$600). Monthly homestays available (US$350 per month). Open M-F 9am-6pm.

Instituto de Letras (☎56 2 354 7882), on the San Joaquín campus of the Universidad Católica in Santiago. Offers shorter Spanish language courses and arranges homestays. Private lessons US$25 per hr., group courses US$85 per hr. for groups up to 12. Open M-F 9am-6pm.

Natalis Language Center, Vicuña Mackenna 6, 7th fl. (☎02 222 8721; www.natalis-lang.com), in Santiago. Customized course offerings available, ranging 20-25hr. per week with up to 5 students. 3-week, 75hr. courses are the most popular offering (US$365), and private lessons are available as well (US$8-13 per hr.).

Universidad Austral de Chile, Casilla 567, Valdivia (☎63 213 911). Students interested in learning Spanish can enroll directly in the university or arrange private lessons.

WORKING

VISA INFORMATION

US citizens planning on working in Chile need to apply for the appropriate visa before embarking. Check the US Embassy website (www.chile-usa.org) for the consulate that has jurisdiction over your state. The process of collecting the necessary documentation, sending it to the consulate, and receiving approval may take several weeks, so begin well before your departure. If you have been hired by a Chilean company for long-term work, you may have to apply for a **Working Visa.** This requires a contract signed by both you and your employer that is notarized in Chile plus a recommendation from a past employer.

There are two main schools of thought about working abroad. Some travelers want long-term jobs that allow them to get to know another part of the world in depth (e.g., teaching English or working in the tourist industry). Other travelers seek out short-term jobs to finance their travel. They usually seek employment in the service sector or in agriculture, working for a few weeks at a time to finance the next leg of their journey. This section discusses both short- and long-term opportunities for working in Chile. Make sure you understand Chile's **visa requirements** for working abroad.

To find casual, private employment, it helps to post an ad in a local store or pay for an advertisement in the classified sections of newspapers such as *El Mercurio* (☎02 330 1111; www.elmercurio.cl) or *La Tercera* (☎02 550 7000; www.tercera.cl). *El Rastro* (☎02 672 2051; www.elrastro.cl), a paper that publishes free advertisements, is also a good resource.

To acquire an official work permit once in Chile, visit the *Extranjeria* section of the State *Intendencia* (☎02 676 5800), on the corner of Calle Moneda and Morande in Santiago, for information about applying for a one-year work permit. The permit can usually be updated later with little difficulty to a *visación de residencia*, which allows an unlimited stay in Chile.

LONG-TERM WORK

If you're planning on spending a substantial amount of time (more than three months) working in Chile, search for a job well in advance. International placement agencies are often the easiest way to find employment abroad, especially for teaching English. **Internships,** usually for college students, are a good way to segue into working abroad, though they are often unpaid or poorly paid (many say the experience, however, is well worth it). Be wary of advertisements or companies that claim they will get you a job abroad for a fee—often the listings are out of date or readily available online or in newspapers. It's best, if going through an organization, to use one that's reputable. Some good ones include:

GoAbroad.com, 8 E. 1st Ave., Ste. 102, Denver, CO 80203, USA (☎720-570-1702; fax 720-570-1703; www.goabroad.com). Lists jobs in Chile and has specific sites for teaching, interning, and general working abroad.

Southern Cone Internships, Apoquindo 2818 #30, Las Condes, Santiago (☎1294, US fax 866-726-5705; www.sc-internships.com), arranges unpaid professional internships, Spanish classes, and homestays.

INTERNships INTERNational, LLC, 1612 Oberlin Rd., Raleigh, NC 27608, USA (Dec.-May ☎919-832-1575, June-Jan. 207-442-7942; www.internshipsinternational.org). Offers unpaid internships and connections to language schools around the world, including in Santiago. US$1100 fee guarantees internship placement.

TEACHING ENGLISH

Teaching jobs abroad are rarely well-paid, although some elite private American schools can pay somewhat competitive salaries. Volunteering as a teacher in lieu of getting paid is also a popular option, and even in those cases, teachers often get some sort of a daily stipend to help with living expenses. In almost all cases, you must have at least a bachelor's degree to be a full-fledged teacher, although college undergraduates can often get summer positions teaching or tutoring. There are a wealth of jobs available teaching English in Chile—it is perhaps the most accessible employment for those looking to work in the country for an extended period of time.

Many schools require teachers to have a **Teaching English as a Foreign Language (TEFL)** certificate. Not having one does not necessarily exclude you from finding a teaching job, but certified teachers often find higher paying jobs. Native English speakers working in private schools are most often hired for English-immersion classrooms where no Spanish is spoken. Those volunteering or teaching in public, poorer schools, are more likely to be working in both English and Spanish. Placement agencies or university fellowship programs are the best resources for finding teaching jobs in Chile. The alternative is to make contacts directly with schools or just to try your luck once you get there. If you are going to try the latter, the best time of the year is several weeks before the start of the school year. The following organizations are extremely helpful in placing teachers in Chile.

Amity Institute, Amity Volunteer Teachers Abroad Program, 10671 Roselle St., Ste. 100, San Diego, CA 92121, USA (☎858-455-6364; fax 455-6597; www.amity.org). Offers both full-year and semester-long positions. US$25-50 processing fee and US$500 placement fee. For anyone with at least 2-3 years of teaching experience, **AVTA** also offers positions with **Teacher Workshops Abroad,** a program that conducts pedagogical workshops for local teachers. Same fees.

English First, Hernando de Aguirre 215, Providencia, Santiago (☎02 374 2180; www.english-first.com), is probably the best place in Chile to start seeking a job teaching English. The establishment is well respected and prefers to hire candidates with a TEFL certificate and/or prior teaching experience. Compensation begins at CH$3000-7000 per hr. Also provides information on other programs hiring teachers.

Bridge-Linguatec International, 915 South Colorado Blvd., Denver, CO 80246, USA (☎303-777-7783 or 800-724-4210; www.bridgelinguatec.com). Places chosen applicants in positions teaching English to businesspeople in Santiago. Certification is required for all teachers; preference given to those who certify with Bridge-Linguatec. Pay starts at US$7 an hour. Contact Catherine Amaro at teachers-chile@bridgelinguatec.com with an email expressing interest; attach résumé.

International Schools Services (ISS), 15 Roszel Rd., Box 5910, Princeton, NJ 08543, USA (☎609-452-0990; fax 452-2690; www.iss.edu). Hires teachers for more than 200 overseas schools including in Chile; candidates should have experience teaching or with international affairs; 2-year commitment expected.

Office of Overseas Schools, US Department of State, Room H328, SA-1, Washington, D.C. 20522, USA (☎202-261-8200; fax 261-8224; www.state.gov/m/a/os). Keeps a comprehensive list of schools abroad and agencies that arrange placement for Americans to teach abroad.

TeachAbroad.com, 8 E. 1st Ave., Ste. 102, Denver, CO 80203, USA (☎720-570-1702; fax 570-1703; www.teachabroad.com). Part of the umbrella company GoAbroad.com, this service allows you to search listings for teaching positions around the world, and has numerous listings for Chile.

Teaching English in Chile (http://lauca.usach.cl/~mfarias/index.html). Website offers links to resources and opportunities for English teachers in Chile.

World Teach, Center for International Development, 79 John F. Kennedy St., Cambridge, MA 02138, USA (☎800-483-2240 or 617-495-5527; www.worldteach.org). Teach English, math, science, and environmental education for 6 months in Chile.

SHORT-TERM WORK

Traveling for long periods of time can get expensive; therefore, many travelers try their hand at odd jobs for a few weeks at a time to make some extra cash to carry them through another month or two of touring around. Although a notarized contract of employment and contract visa is required to remain legally employed in Chile, since short-term placements usually offer free or discounted room and/or board in exchange for work, some travelers report that a work permit is not necessarily required for obtaining temporary employment. Short-term job opportunities are occasionally listed at www.gonomad.com/alternatives/alternatives.html. Most often, these short-term jobs are found by word of mouth, or simply by talking to the owner of a hostel or restaurant. Many places, especially due to the high turnover in the tourism industry, are always eager for help, even if only temporary. *Let's Go* tries to list temporary jobs like these whenever possible; check the practical information sections in larger cities, or check out the list below for some of the available short-term jobs in popular destinations.

Ancud: Fundación Con Todos, Eleuterio Ramírez 207, 2nd fl., (☎65 622 604; contodos@entelchile.net). The Fundación deals with projects available among a growing network of farmers in Chiloé making individual farms available for accommodations under the premise that visitors will participate in farm activities. Longer-term volunteer projects can be arranged.

Chillán: Hostal Canada, Libertad 269 (☎42 234 515), hires 1 English-speaking tour guide to take hostel guests on 4hr. excursions on bicycle around the Chillán area from Dec.-Mar. Trips include visits to the city's historic neighborhoods and parks. Guide must lead two 4hr. tours every weekday and one 4hr. tour on Saturday. Compensation includes a low salary (CH$9000 per day) and lunch; greater compensation possible for experienced candidates. Contact owner Mariela Albornoz for more information.

Concepción: Restaurant Da Giovanni, Caupolicán 346, local 3 (☎41 241 936), hires up to 2 waiters for work in Dec. and Jan. Work is M-F 48hr. per week. Contact the owner, Gilda Carnese, for information. **Havana Club,** Barros Arana 1356 (☎41 224 006), hires up to 5 waiters and 4 bouncers to work 8hr. per day W-Sa. Pay is CH$116,000 per month. Call the office during business hours for more information.

Los Ángeles: Restaurant El Alero, Colo Colo 235 (☎43 320 058), hires waiters and kitchen helpers, usually between Nov. and Mar. Pay is CH$116,000 per month plus tips for a 48hr. work week (12hr. shifts). Contact the administrator for more information. **Hotel y Hostería Salto del Laja** (☎43 321 706 or 313 956; fax 313 996), in Salto del Laja, 27km north of Los Angeles. Needs waiters, cooks, receptionists, laundry washers, and other staff for its hotel and restaurant during the summer. Monetary compensation. Contact general manager Martinentel Puff by Dec. for the following summer.

Pucón: Turismo M@yra hires secretaries and salespeople to work in their office Dec.-Feb. **Hostel Backpackers** looks for speakers of both English and Spanish to act as sales representatives.

Rancagua: Max Sabor San Martín 422, 2nd fl. (☎220 088) hires waiters for 2-3 month periods, especially when business picks up in Nov. **Granja Amanda,** Carrelea de la Fruta, El Manzano (☎198 2346), hires long-term, full-time workers in landscaping.

San Fernando: Hotel Termas del Flaco (☎72 711 832) needs as many as 70 seasonal workers in various hotel jobs from Dec. to Apr. Monthly salary of CH$116,000. Contact Don Miguel Guzmán (☎711 832) for more information.

Villarrica: Politur Villarrica, O'Higgins 635 (☎/fax 45 441 373; www.politur.com), looks for up to 2 guides or office workers to help out Dec.-Feb. and possibly at other times of the year. Candidates must speak English and Spanish. Duties range from leading tours in parks or on river rapids to regular office tasks. The position pays about CH$120,000 per month and is geared toward university students doing 3-month *practica*. Contact Ema Avello Aedo.

FOR FURTHER READING ON ALTERNATIVES TO TOURISM

Alternatives to the Peace Corps: A Directory of Third World and U.S. Volunteer Opportunities, by Joan Powell. Food First Books, 2000 (US$10).

How to Live Your Dream of Volunteering Overseas, by Collins, DeZerega, and Heckscher. Penguin Books, 2002 (US$17).

International Directory of Voluntary Work, by Whetter and Pybus. Peterson's Guides and Vacation Work, 2000 (US$16).

International Jobs, by Kocher and Segal. Perseus Books, 1999 (US$18).

Overseas Summer Jobs, by David Woodworth. Peterson's Guides and Vacation Work, 2003 (US$18).

Work Abroad: The Complete Guide to Finding a Job Overseas, by Hubbs, Griffith, and Nolting. Transitions Abroad Publishing, 2000 ($16).

Work Your Way Around the World, by Susan Griffith. Worldview Publishing Services, 2001 (US$18).

Invest Yourself: The Catalogue of Volunteer Opportunities, published by the Commission on Voluntary Service and Action (☎718-638-8487).

SANTIAGO

In many ways, Santiago is what you would expect from the capital city of a rapidly emerging, economically successful nation. Its six million inhabitants, one-third of the country's population, crowd its bustling streets each day. Carried through the city by the modern subway system or extensive bus line, they head to work at the governmental, financial, and commercial institutions that are the heart of the country's growing power. Department store windows all over the city boast sparkling displays of electronics, fashion, and home decor, reflecting the level of growth and prosperity that the country has recently achieved.

With so many indicators of prosperity in the thriving metropolis, it's hard to believe that the nation has only just emerged from totalitarian rule. What's more, Santiago has flourished in the difficult political and economic environment of South America, emerging as a beacon of civil order and economic success on a struggling continent. Santiago has been a surprise to the world, and continues to defy all kinds of expectations today.

Despite its urban sprawl, for example, residents harbor an almost small-town pride, and government-sponsored fairs and performances bring them together to enjoy the city. As for cultural influences, European and indigenous roots are expressed through the venues of architecture, music, and *artesanía*. Anomalies like the prevalence of German beerhalls and the strangely Italian tendency to say "ciao" instead of "adiós" are uniquely Chilean. They've even adopted the all-American hot dog as the city's favorite dish, smothering it in locally grown avocado.

Visitors to the city are always amazed to see the ways in which Santiago tends to move beyond the usual presuppositions. But really, a visit to this city is all about finding your own surprises. It's about glancing up at a skyscraper in Las Condes and seeing the jagged outline of the Andes reflected against its surface. It's about taking a chance on an unmarked door in Barrio Bellavista and finding a throbbing, glittering nightclub inside, or listening to the Chilean military band on the Plaza de Armas segue seamlessly from a national march to the *Rocky* theme song.

The city offers different sounds, sights, and sensations to everyone who walks its streets. It's like a present that you have to unwrap and uncover. The city's waiting, its predictable facades hiding countless quirks and surprises. Go find them.

HIGHLIGHTS OF SANTIAGO

GORGE on fresh seafood and juicy fruit in the wrought-iron **Mercado Central** (p. 113).

INVESTIGATE the castles, crypts, and gardens of **Cerro Santa Lucía** (p. 119).

VIEW the sparkling Andes from high above Santiago on **Cerro San Cristóbal** (p. 119).

WONDER about the origins of Pablo Neruda's eccentric collection of odds and ends in the eclectic **Museo La Chascona** (p. 121).

SAMPLE some of Chile's finest wines in the lush vineyards of **Concha y Toro** (p. 131).

FLY on skis or with a hang-glider over **Valle Nevado** (p. 123).

SANTIAGO

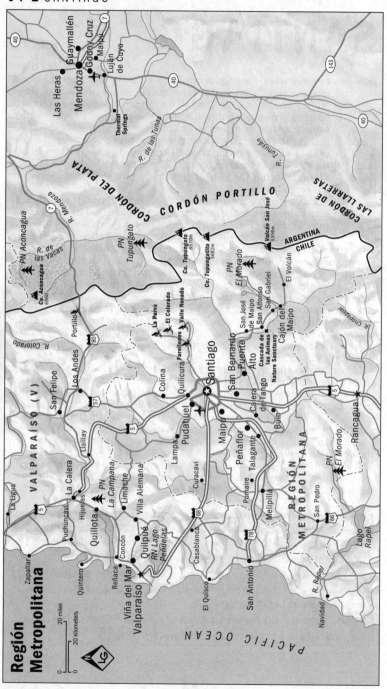

Región Metropolitana

Around Santiago

TO LA SERENA (474km)
TO LOS ANDES (80km) & MENDOZA (342km)
Américo Vespucio Norte
Cardenal J. M. Caro
Independencia
Panamericana Norte
5 57
Costanera Norte
Santa María
Martín E. de Balaguer
TO ✈ AEROPUERTO ARTURO MERINO BENITEZ
Apostol Santiago
Dorsal
Recoleta
Vitacura
Alonso de Córdova
Pres. Kennedy
Las Condes
TO ⛷ SKI CENTERS (40km)
Río Mapocho
Carrascal
SEE SANTIAGO OVERVIEW MAP pp. 96-97
Parque Metropolitano
Club de Golf, Los Leones
Apoquindo
Cuarto Centenario
Manquehue
Mapocho
J.J. Pérez
Gamero Santos Dumont
Gen. Velásquez
Santa María Balmaceda
Cerro ▲ San Cristóbal
Providencia
Eliodoro Yáñez
Cristóbal Colón
Pocuro
Américo Vespucio
Príncipe de Gales
San Pablo
Parque Quinta Normal
TO VIÑA DEL MAR (120km) & VALPARAÍSO (120km)
68
Las Rejas
O'Higgins
Estación Central
Almirante Latorre
Blanco Encalada
Vicuña Mackenna
Santa Isabel
Pedro de Valdivia
Senador Jaime Guzmán E.
Irarrázaval
Larraín
José Arrieta
Américo Vespucio
R. Freire
Autopista del Sol
Pte. S. Allende
Parque O'Higgins
Club Hípico
Rondizzoni
Estadio Nacional
Grecia
I. Riquelme
C. Valdovinos
R. de Araya
José Pedro Alessandri
Camino a Melpilla
Aeropuerto Los Cerrillos
Cerrillos
Pres. Jorge Alessandri Rodríguez
Santa Rosa
Departamental
Marathón
Tobalaba
Lo Ovalle
W. Martinez
La Florida
Lo Espejo
5
El Parrón
Américo Vespucio
78
TO MELPILLA (67km) & SAN ANTONIO (109km)
Panamericana Sur
J. M. Carrera
TO RANCAGUA (87km)

N
LG

0   2 miles
0   2 kilometers

SANTIAGO

✈ INTERCITY TRANSPORTATION

Airport: Aeropuerto Arturo Merino Benítez, Casilla 61 Correo Central (☎676 3227 or 676 3275; www.aeropuertosantiago.cl), is the hub for all international and domestic flights. **Taxis** from the airport to Santiago Centro cost CH$7000-10,000. **Tur Bus Aeropuerto,** is cheaper, and drops off at M: Los Héroes, M: Universidad de Santiago, Alameda 3750, and M: Pajaritos ("601 9883 or 601 0549; every 15min. 6am-10:30pm, CH$1200). Minibuses are more expensive but will drop at your hotel. **Transfer** has a booth near the baggage terminal (☎677 3030; reservas@turtransfer.cl. CH$3200 to Santiago Centro, CH$3700-4500 to Providencia, Ñuñoa, and Las Condes). **TransVip,** will take you to the airport 3hr. before departure (☎677 3000; CH$3200). Other options include **Chile Transfer** (☎817 2882) and **Transporte Ejécutivo** (☎457 0607). **Tur Bus Aeropuerto** also makes pickups for trips back to the airport at M: Los Héroes and their headquarters at Moneda 1529, just west of San Martín.

International and Domestic Airlines:

LanChile, Huérfanos 926, Santiago Centro (☎526 2000; www.lanchile.com). M: Plaza de Armas. Some fares drop dramatically in winter. To: **Arica** (3hr., CH$82,000-198,000); **Buenos Aires, ARG** (2hr., CH$65,000-117,000); **Mendoza, ARG** (2hr., CH$95,000); **Puerto Montt** (2hr., CH$100,000). Open M-F 9am-6:45pm, Sa 10am-12:45pm.

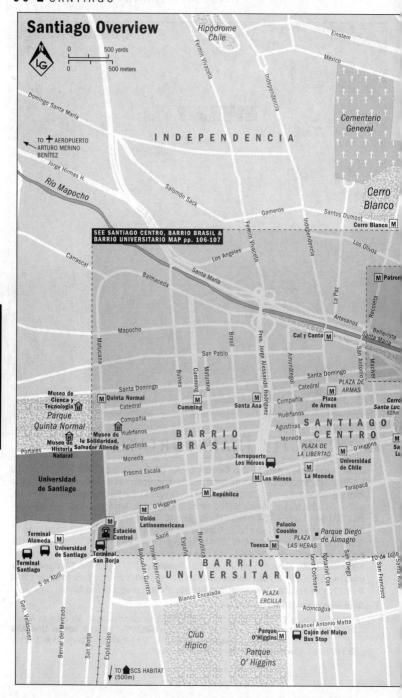

Santiago Overview

N LG

| 0 | 500 yards |
| 0 | 500 meters |

Hipódrome Chile

Einstein

México

Fermín Vivaceta

Independencia

Cementerio General

Domingo Santa María

I N D E P E N D E N C I A

TO ✈ AEROPUERTO ARTURO MERINO BENÍTEZ

Jorge Hirmas H.

Río Mapocho

Salomón Sack

Cerro Blanco

Santos Dumont

Cerro Blanco M

Gameros

Santos Dumont

Los Olivos

SEE SANTIAGO CENTRO, BARRIO BRASIL & BARRIO UNIVERSITARIO MAP pp. 106-107

Carrascal

Los Angeles

Fermín Vivaceta

Independencia

La Paz

Balmaceda

Santa María

M Patron

Recoleta

Artesanos

Bellavista

Santa María

Mapocho

Brasil

Pres. Jorge Alessandri Rodríguez

Cal y Canto M

Amunátegui

San Antonio

Machver

San Pablo

Cal y Canto M

Santa Domingo

PLAZA DE ARMAS

Matucana

Bulnes

Maturana

Cumming

Catedral

Plaza de Armas

Cerro Santa Luc 628m

Museo de Cienca y Tecnología 🏛

Santa Domingo

M Quinta Normal

Catedral

Cumming

Santa Ana M

Compañía

Huérfanos

S A N T I A G O

C E N T R O

M Sa Lu

Parque Quinta Normal

Museo de Historia Natural 🏛

Compañía

Museo de la Solidaridad, Salvador Allende

Huérfanos

Agustinas

Agustinas

Moneda

B A R R I O

B R A S I L

Moneda

PLAZA DE LA LIBERTAD

M O'Higgins

Universidad de Chile

Portales

Terrapuerto Los Héroes 🚌

M La Moneda

Universidad de Santiago

Erasmo Escala

Romero

M Los Héroes

Tarapacá

O'Higgins

M República

Terminal Alameda M

Unión Latinoamericana

Palacio Cousiño

Parque Diego de Almagro

Universidad de Santiago

M Estación Central

Sazié

PLAZA LAS HERAS

10 de Julio

Terminal Santiago

Terminal San Borja

España

Toesca M

Ñataniel Cox

San Diego

Santa Ros

San Francisco

5 de Abril

Basculán Gurrero

Unión Americana

República

B A R R I O

U N I V E R S I T A R I O

Lord Cochrane

Gen. Velásquez

Bernal del Mercado

San Borja

Exposición

Blanco Encalada

PLAZA ERCILLA

Aconcagua

Manuel Antonio Matta

Club Hípico

Parque O'Higgins M

Cajón del Maipo Bus Stop 🚌

Parque O' Higgins

TO 🏠 SCS HABITAT (500m)

SANTIAGO

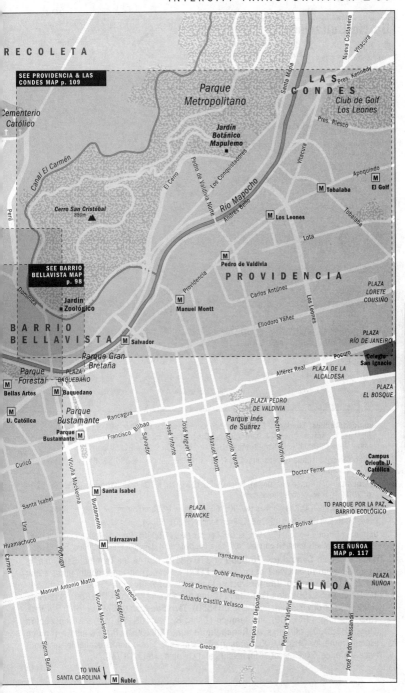

RECOLETA

SEE PROVIDENCIA & LAS CONDES MAP p. 109

Cementerio Católico

Parque Metropolitano

LAS CONDES

Pres. Kennedy

Club de Golf Los Leones

Pres. Riesco

Santa María

Nueva Costanera

Vitacura

Jardín Botánico Mapulemo ■

Canal El Carmén

El Cerro

Pedro de Valdivia Norte

Los Conquistadores

Río Mapocho

Andrés Bello

Vitacura

Apoquindo

M El Golf

M Tobalaba

Perú

Cerro San Cristóbal 390m ▲

M Los Leones

Tobalaba

Lota

M Pedro de Valdivia

Providencia

PROVIDENCIA

SEE BARRIO BELLAVISTA MAP p. 98

Dominica

Jardín ■ Zoológico

Carlos Antúnez

Los Leones

PLAZA LORETE COUSIÑO

M Manuel Montt

Eliodoro Yáñez

BARRIO BELLAVISTA

M Salvador

PLAZA RÍO DE JANEIRO

Parque Gran Bretaña

Pocuro

Colegio San Ignacio

Parque Forestal

PLAZA BAQUEDANO

Alférez Real

PLAZA DE LA ALCALDESA

M Bellas Artes

M Baquedano

PLAZA EL BOSQUE

M U. Católica

Parque Bustamante

Rancagua

PLAZA PEDRO DE VALDIVIA

Curicó

Parque Bustamante M

Francisco Bilbao

Salvador

José Infante

José Miguel Claro

Parque Inés de Suárez

Manuel Montt

Antonio Varas

Pedro de Valdivia

Campus Oriente U. Católica

Vicuña Mackenna

Doctor Ferrer

Sen. J. Guzmán E.

M Santa Isabel

TO PARQUE POR LA PAZ, BARRIO ECOLÓGICO

Santa Isabel

Bustamante

PLAZA FRANCKE

Simón Bolívar

Lira

Huamachuco

Portugal

M Irárrazaval

SEE ÑUÑOA MAP p. 117

Carmen

Irarrázaval

PLAZA ÑUÑOA

Manuel Antonio Matta

Vicuña Mackenna

San Eugenio

Grecia

Dublé Almeyda

José Domingo Cañas

Eduardo Castillo Velasco

ÑUÑOA

Campos de Deporte

Pedro de Valdivia

José Pedro Alessandri

Sierra Bella

Grecia

TO VIÑA SANTA CAROLINA ▼ M Ñuble

SANTIAGO

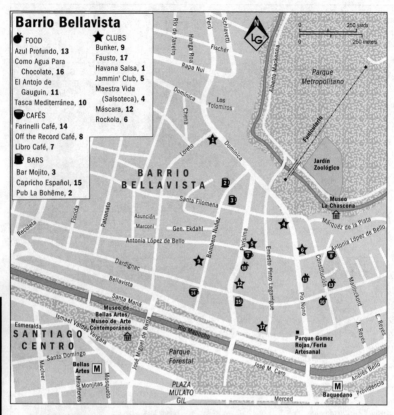

Barrio Bellavista

⭐ FOOD
Azul Profundo, **13**
Como Agua Para
  Chocolate, **16**
El Antojo de
  Gauguin, **11**
Tasca Mediterránea, **10**

☕ CAFÉS
Farinelli Café, **14**
Off the Record Café, **8**
Libro Café, **7**

🍺 BARS
Bar Mojito, **3**
Capricho Español, **15**
Pub La Bohème, **2**

⭐ CLUBS
Bunker, **9**
Fausto, **17**
Havana Salsa, **1**
Jammin' Club, **5**
Maestra Vida
  (Salsoteca), **4**
Máscara, **12**
Rockola, **6**

American Airlines, Huérfanos 1199, Santiago Centro (☎679 0000 or 601 9272; www.aa.com). M: Plaza de Armas. Open M-F 9am-6:30pm. Other offices may be found in Providencia at Santa Magdalena 090 and El Bosque Norte 0107 (also open Sa 9:30am-12:30pm).

British Airways, Isidora Goyenechea 2934, Of. 302, Las Condes (☎330 8600). M: El Golf. Open M-F 9am-6pm.

Continental (in alliance with **Copa**), Fidel Oteíza 1921, 7th fl., Of. 703, Providencia (☎200 2100 or 200 2101; www.continental.com).

Delta, Vitacura 2700, Las Condes (☎690 1555). Open M-F 9am-7pm.

Taca, Dr. Barros Borgoño 105, 2nd fl., Providencia (☎235 5500).

United, El Bosque Norte 0177, 9th fl., Las Condes (☎337 0000). Open M-F 9am-6pm, Sa 9am-12:45pm. Tickets must be purchased 7 days in advance. 4-day min. stay, including Sa.

Trains: Estación Central (☎376 8500 or 376 8312), next to the Terminal San Borja, is west of downtown on Line 1 of the Metro. **EFE** (www.efe.cl) only runs south, and the line terminates at **Temuco**. The **Metrotren Line** goes to: **Rancagua** (9 per day 7:50am-10:45pm, CH$1200); **San Fernando** (10 per day 8am-11:20pm, CH$1650); **San Francisco** (22 per day 7:35am-midnight, CH$850). **TerraSur** goes to **Chillán** (5hr.; 7:45am, 1:45, 6:45pm; CH$6500) and **Temuco** (13hr.; 8, 9pm; CH$14,000) via **Concepción** (9hr., CH$8000); all trains via **Rancagua** (1¼hr., CH$2000). There's also a **Temuco** express route for CH$50,000. Fares are for standard seats; bunks available for about twice the price. 20% discount for seniors and children. AmEx/DC/MC/V.

Buses: The 4 main terminals in Santiago are located on the southwestern side of the city. **Tur Bus** is the largest and most reputable company in Chile, but is often slightly more expensive. **Pullman** is the second-largest company, with numerous regional-based franchises. These 2 companies have frequent departures to most locations. **Buses Ahumada** and **Tas Choapa** are two other sizable companies.

 THE ART OF BUS TRAVEL. Beware super-cheap bus tickets—they will likely lack the space and comfort that make 25hr. bus rides palatable. For those willing to spend a few bucks, the luxury coaches with beds—*camas, semi-camas,* or suites—are worth the price on longer journeys.

Terminal San Borja, San Borja 184, Santiago Centro (☎776 0645). M: Estación Central. Serves northern and central Chile. **Tur Bus** (☎778 7836 or 778 7338) goes to: **Arica** (29hr.; 7:15, 10am, 4, 10:45pm; CH$18,500); **Copiapó** (12hr., 17 per day 7:25am-11:40pm, CH$7500); **Iquique** (24hr., 5 per day 8am-8:30pm, CH$18,500); **Valparaíso** (1¾hr.; every 10min. 7:10am-10pm; CH$2400); **Viña del Mar** (1¾hr.; every 10min. 7:10am-10pm; CH$2700).

Terminal Alameda, Alameda 3714 (☎776 1038). M: Universidad de Santiago. **Tur Bus** (☎270 7500 or 270 7425) and **Pullman** (☎778 1185 or 776 2424) depart from this smaller locale. **Tur Bus** goes to: **Mendoza, ARG** (7hr., CH$14,500); **Quilpué** (1½hr., 7 per day 12:15-5:40pm, CH$2200); **Valparaíso** (1¾hr.; every 30min.; CH$2400); **Viña del Mar** (1¾hr.; every 30min.; CH$2700). **Pullman** goes to **Los Andes/San Felipe** (CH$1900), **Quilpué** (CH$2300), **Valparaíso** (CH$2300), and **Viña del Mar** (CH$2600). **Pullman del Sur** has routes to **Rancagua** (CH$1300), **San Fernando** (CH$2000), and **Talca** (CH$3000).

Terminal Santiago (Terminal Sur), Alameda 3848 (☎779 1385), next to Terminal Alameda. M: Universidad de Santiago. Has trips to southern Chile and international destinations, including **Mendoza, ARG. Pullman del Sur** runs to: **Arica** (CH$23,000); **Buenos Aires, ARG** (M-F 1pm, CH$25,000); **Calama** (CH$22,000); **Copiapó** (CH$10,000); and **Ovalle** (CH$6000). **Crucero del Norte** (☎482 2256; www.crucerodelnorte.com.ar) makes international trips, including to **Río de Janeiro, BRA.** (36hr., Th noon, CH$75,000. 46hr.; M and Sa-Su noon; CH$65,500.)

Terrapuerto Los Héroes, Tucapel Jiménez 21 (☎420 0099; www.terrapuertolosheroes.co.cl). M: Los Héroes. **Pullman del Sur International** goes to **Buenos Aires, ARG** (20hr., M and F 1:15pm, CH$25,000) and **Pullman del Sur** has overnight coaches to **Temuco** (9hr.; 10, 10:30pm; CH$8000) and **Valdivia** (12hr.; 9:30, 10:15pm; CH$15,000). **Buses Ahumada** (☎696 9337) goes to: **Buenos Aires, ARG** (20hr., W-Th and Sa-Su 11am, CH$25,000); **Los Andes** and **San Felipe** (1½hr., every 30min. 6:30am-10:30pm, CH$2000); **Mendoza, ARG** (7hr.; 9:30am, 1, 3:30pm; CH$7000). **Tas Choapa** (☎696 9326 or 697 0062) goes to several destinations in the north and south, including: **Antofagasta** (18hr., 6pm, CH$18,000); **Chillán** (4hr.; 8:30am, 8:35pm; CH$3500); **Copiapó** (12hr.; 8:45am, 9:30pm; CH$6000); **Lima, PER** (50hr., 4pm, CH$50,000); **Mendoza, ARG** (8:50am, CH$7000); **Ovalle** (5½hr.; 9:15am, 2:30, 4:30, 11pm; CH$4000); **Puerto Montt** (14hr.; 8:30, 10:35pm; CH$7000). **Cruz del Sur** also services southern destinations like **Ancud** (7pm, CH$16,500), **Puerto Montt** (14hr.; 8:30, 9:20pm; CH$14,000), **Temuco** (9hr., 9:15pm, CH$8500), and **Valdivia** (9:30pm, CH$10,000).

■ ORIENTATION

The heart of the capital is **Alameda,** the main street which runs from Barrio Brasil in the southwest (where it's called **O'Higgins**) to Barrio Bellavista in the northeast. Across the **Río Mapocho,** it's named **Avenida Providencia,** which cuts through the middle of the neighborhood of the same name, heading northeast to Las Condes where it turns into **Avenida Apoquindo** and then **Avenida Las Condes** up into Vitacura. When visible, the Andes are a good reference point to the east and southeast. Santiago is a sprawling metropolis, with 34 *comunas.*

Santiago Centro, located along central Alameda, is home to governmental and commercial institutions that keep it all running. Tourists and *Santiaguinos* alike frequent the area's museums, plazas, and malls, making it a bustling, people-watching mecca.

Santiago Metro

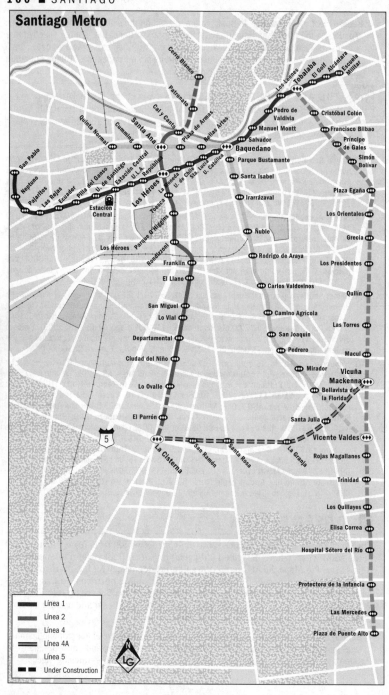

Línea 1
Línea 2
Línea 4
Línea 4A
Línea 5
Under Construction

Providencia, northeast of Santiago Centro, stretches east along the south side of the Río Mapocho. Fancy hotels and cafes line Av. Providencia and the parallel street, 11 de Septiembre, making it a convenient place to window-shop and wander. At night, its cafes and bars are crowded, with **Suecia** thumping until dawn.

Las Condes, located at the very northeast of the city, is a well-to-do residential zone with interesting colonial architecture. Its modern shopping malls, gourmet restaurants, and premier hotels are nestled along the backdrop of the Andes.

Barrio Brasil, located north of Alameda and west of Vía Norte Sur, and **Barrio Universitario,** south of Alameda, are full of small universities, institutes, and cafes that lend the area an authentic, bohemian feel. Students lounge on benches, talking and playing music, and municipal signs throughout ask, "Are you in Santiago or in Paris?"

Barrio Bellavista, located southwest of Cerro San Cristóbal along the north side of the Río Mapocho, is notorious for the late-night revelry that ensues here year-round. Darkness makes the decrepit neighborhood more palatable, but remain aware of your safety as you sample the offerings of Santiago's hottest nightspot.

Ñuñoa, far from the urban hub of Alameda, is tucked within the expanse of elementary schools and doctor's offices that fill Santiago's more residential areas. As a whole, the neighborhood is relatively tame, but on weekends, its center explodes with crowds that gather at Plaza Ñuñoa for its bars, cafes, and theatrical performances.

☲ LOCAL TRANSPORTATION

Metro: The incredibly modern, spotless, fast, and quiet subway is an absolute pleasure to take. It runs M-Sa 6:30am-10:30pm, Su 8am-10:30pm. **Line 1** (red) is the most heavily used, and travels roughly east-west, following Providencia/Alameda/O'Higgins. **Line 2** (yellow) runs north-south, beginning near the Río Mapocho, and ending in the southern suburb of La Cisterna. **Line 5** (green) also runs north-south, beginning at Parque Quinta Normal, and extending to the community of La Florida. Several extensions of Metro service are underway, with expected completion by the end of 2005. Individual fares vary (rush hour 6-7:30pm CH$370; all other times CH$310). If traveling much during commuting hours, it's best to buy a **multiviaje** ticket good for 10 trips (CH$3300). During off-peak times, the **valor** ticket (CH$3300) is a better deal, subtracting the value of each trip at the time of travel. Customer Service Centers with lost and found and senior discount sales are located at Estación La Moneda (☎250 3234), Estación Cal y Canto (☎250 3232), and Estación Irarrázaval (☎230 3206). All open M-F 7:30am-10pm, Sa-Su La Moneda open 9am-6pm.

Buses: Known as *micros*, these can be found anywhere, especially along **O'Higgins/ Alameda/Providencia.** Routes are marked on the windshield, with most buses traveling along Alameda and passing Plaza Italia. Buses run M-F until 1am, Sa-Su 24hr. (CH$300). Blue **Metrobuses** depart from the end of Metro lines or busy stops like Escuela Militar and Pajaritos to neighborhoods that don't have Metro service (CH$250).

 STOP THE MICRO—I WANT TO GET ON! Taking *micros* in Santiago is urban adventuring at its best. Buses don't always make their designated stops, but slow down enough at the curb for people to read the route listings in their windshields. If the one you need passes by, flag it down and hop on! You'll pay the driver or the cashier sitting just behind, who will give you a little ticket as a receipt. Save the ticket, as control officers often board buses to check the slips of everyone aboard. Keep an eye out for your destination and pull the cord on the ceiling or walk up to the door if you want to get off.

S A N T I A G O

Colectivos: These vehicles look similar to taxis, but are actually a kind of taxi/bus hybrid. The neon signs on the roof list the fixed routes that they run, picking up passengers who flag them down along the way. They cost less than taxis, but more than buses (CH$350-800). You can catch one anywhere, especially Plaza Italia or in front of La Moneda.

Taxis: Metered taxis are black with yellow roofs. Standard rate CH$150, plus CH$80 every 200m, CH$180 at night. **"Radio taxis,"** which you call for pickup instead of waiting to flag down, are a more reliable choice at night: **Andes Pacífico** (☎ 225 3064), **Monumental**, (☎ 687 3752), and **Providencia** (☎ 209 0445) each charge CH$500 per km, CH$1500 min. None can legally enter the downtown area without a passenger, and even though some drivers ignore this law, it's best to walk to Alameda or Parque Forestal in Santiago Centro to catch one.

Car Rental: You must be 21 to rent a car in Chile, and have a credit card, International Driving Permit (see p. 39), and passport or Chilean ID card. Most branches are represented at the airport. National chains are more efficient and allow drop-off flexibility, but for those planning to return their cars to Santiago, local companies are cheaper. National chains include: **Alamo,** Bilbao 2846 (☎ 233 4117); **Avis,** Guardia Vieja 255, Of. 108 and at the airport (☎ 601 9966 and 609 1382; www.avischile.cl); **Budget,** Bilbao 1439, Of. 201 (☎ 362 3200; www.budget.cl); **Chilean,** Bellavista 0183 (☎ 737 9650); **Dollar,** Kennedy 8292 (☎ 202 5510; dollar@ctcinternet.cl); **Hertz,** Andrés Bello 1469 (☎ 420 5200 or 420 5222; www.hertz-chile.cl).

WAKE UP AND SMELL THE... The winter blues generally cut across national boundaries, and *Santiaguinos* in particular have a reason to feel down. From March to October, the changes in temperature cause a cloud of *microbus* smog to settle over the city. Visitors with respiratory problems should avoid the city during these months, as the smog can make it quite difficult to breathe. When others visit, however, they can travel in a manner that will make the air more breathable for future guests. Aside from the Metro, the government offers a service called *Ciclocarros*, which consists of a number of red and yellow carts with black roofs driven around by men dressed in similar colors riding bikes. The service is free. Find *Ciclocarros* anywhere in Santiago Centro, though the main depot is at the Monjitas side of the Plaza de Armas. Open M-Sa 9am-6pm.

⁊ PRACTICAL INFORMATION

PHONE CODE	The regional phone code for Santiago is ☎ 02.

TOURIST AND FINANCIAL SERVICES

Tourist Offices: Sernatur, Providencia 1550 (☎ 731 8336 or 731 8337), M: Manuel Montt, with offices in the Arturo Merino Benítez Airport, Mall Parque Arauco, and Terminal San Borja. Sernatur provides detailed brochures and helpful maps, with coupons for discounts at local restaurants and discos. Open Dec.-Mar. daily 9am-6:30pm; Apr.-Nov. M-F 8:45am-6:30pm, Sa 9am-2pm. **Municipalidad de Santiago,** Merced 860 (☎ 632 7783 or 632 7785). M: U. de Chile. 1 block from the Plaza de Armas in historic Casa Colorado. Another location at Cerro Santa Lucía. Open M-Th 10am-6pm, F 10am-5pm.

Tours: LanChile (p. 95) has package deals to **Calama** (CH$150,000 for 3 days), and **Easter Island** (US$1500 for 5 days). Most travel centers in Santiago generally offer similar lineups at similar prices, including daytrips to **Isla Negra, Pomaire, Valparaíso,** and **Viña del Mar,** as well as to the surrounding **ski resorts** and **vineyards** (CH$2500-$35,000). **Chilean Expeditions and Travels,** Hernando Aguirre 128, Of. 507, Providencia (☎ 232 0745; chilexp@123mail.cl), offers this basic selection. **Melentour,** Moneda 772, local 406B (☎ 638 9865; www.melentour.cl), in Santiago Centro, offers a trip to **Parque Rancagua** over the border in Argentina (CH$49,000). **Turistour,** Alonso de Córdova 4227 (☎ 488 0444;

www.turistour.com), runs overnight winery trips (CH$88,000) and a few dinner show options in Santiago (CH$20,000-$50,000). However, the most unique option by far is found at **El Cementerio General**, Zañartú 951 (☎ 737 9469; cementeriogrl@netline.cl), which offers themed tours of the cemetery, with stops at the graves of historical, political, literary, and art world luminaries. Call for reservations.

Adventure Tours: Altue, Encomenderos 83, 2nd fl., Las Condes (☎ 232 1103 or 233 2964; www.chileoutdoors.com). M: El Golf. Offers sea kayaking, trekking, rafting and horseback riding trip deals, as well as day tours to the ancient forests of **PN La Campana** (US$90) and rafting down the wild **Maipo River** (US$50). Open M-F 9:30am-2pm and 3:30pm-7pm. DC/MC/V. **Cascada Expediciones,** Orrego Luco 040, 2nd fl., Providencia (☎ 234 2274 or 861 1777; www.cascada-expediciones.com). M: Pedro de Valdivia. Runs an all-inclusive rafting trip on the **Maipo** daily (US$79), a 6-day sea kayaking trip in the southern fjords (Nov.-Mar. US$990), and a 6-day nature tour of **Easter Island** (US$1100). Or contact their main office in the Cajón del Maipo, Camino El Volcán 17710, San José de Maipo (☎861 1777 or 861 2244). **Continentur** (☎373 0876; www.continentur.cl) offers a 4-day trip to **San Pedro de Atacama** and **Valle de la Luna** by air (from US$480), as well as a 5-day excursion to southern Chile's **Torres del Paine** (from US$520). **KL Chile,** Av. Las Condes 12207 (☎217 9101; www.kladventure.com), has backcountry skiing, trekking, and serious mountaineering trips (US$2700-$3500). **Yak Expediciones,** Nocedal 7135 (☎227 0427; www.yakexpediciones.cl), has various sea kayaking courses and trips (from US$310).

Embassies and Consulates (see **Consular Services in Chile,** p. 14): **Argentina,** Miraflores 285 (☎639 8617 or 638 0890); **Australia,** Gertrudis Echeñique 420, Providencia (☎228 5065); **Bolivia,** Santa María 2796, Providencia (☎232 8180 or 232 4997); **Brazil,** Alonso Ovalle 1665, Santiago Centro (☎698 2486); **Canada,** World Trade Center Building, Nueva Tajamar 481, 12th fl., Providencia (☎362 9660); **Ecuador,** Providencia 1979, 5th fl. (☎231 5073); **Ireland,** Isidora Goyenechea 3162, Of. 801, Las Condes (☎245 6616); **New Zealand,** El Golf 99, Of. 703 (☎290 9802); **Peru,** Andrés Bello 1751, Providencia (☎235 6451 or 235 2356); **UK,** El Bosque Norte 0125, 3rd fl., Providencia (☎370 4100); **US,** Andrés Bello 2800, Providencia (☎232 2600; www.usembassy.cl).

Immigration Office: Extranjería, Agustinas 1235, 2nd fl. (☎550 2400 or 737 4687; www.extranjeria.gob.cl). Report lost tourist cards here. Open M-F 8:30am-2pm.

Currency Exchange: Casas de cambio are scattered throughout the city, especially along Agustinas and Huérfanos. Reputable companies include **Cambios Inter, ChilExpress S.A., DHL,** and **Entel. Citibank,** at Ahumada 40, Huérfanos 770, and Teatinos 180, with offices throughout Santiago, doesn't charge a service fee. (Main office Providencia 2653, 3rd fl.; ☎338 3000. Open M-F 9am-2pm and 3-5:30pm.) You can also change money in the **Correo Central** and other post offices, as well as in most hotels.

Banks: Widespread and easily accessible, most banks have **24hr. ATMs.** Many banks cluster in the city center along O'Higgins, to the east of M: Baquedano. **Banco de Chile,** O'Higgins 140 (☎638 5102 or 637 1111). **BancoEstado,** O'Higgins 1111 (☎670 7000). Open M-F 9am-2pm and sometimes 3pm-5pm.

ATMs: Called **Redbanc,** these are found mostly in supermarkets, malls, bus stations, and along the busiest pedestrian stretches. Open 24hr. AmEx/MC/V.

American Express: Andrés Bello 2711, 9th fl., Providencia (☎636 9100). M: Tobalaba. Open M-Th 9am-6:30pm, F 9am-5pm.

Western Union: Providencia 2309 (☎335 2314). Branches available in **Correos de Chile** locations and **Tur Bus** terminals (see **Emergency and Communications,** p. 105).

Teaching English: English First, Hernando de Aguirre 215, Providencia (☎374 2180) is probably the best place to start if seeking a job teaching English as a foreign language. (See **Alternatives to Tourism,** p. 89)

Language Schools: Instituto de Letras (☎354 7882); **Natalis Language Center,** Vicuña Mackenna 6, 7th fl. (☎222 8721; www.natalislang.com). All offer a variety of Spanish-language courses. For more details, see **Alternatives to Tourism,** p. 87.

SANTIAGO

LOCAL SERVICES

Luggage Storage: The *custodia* is located in the western wing of the Estación Central terminal in the Paseo Estación Mall. (☎589 2354. CH$600-800 per piece per day. Electronic equipment can be stored for CH$1500. Open daily.) Most hotels will also store bags. Terrapuerto Los Héroes stores bags for CH$400-800. Open 6:30am-10:30pm. Terminal San Borja (p. 99) also offers storage (CH$300-1100). Open 6am-midnight.

Lost Property: Metro Customer Service Centers in Estación La Moneda (☎250 3234), Estación Cal y Canto (☎250 3232), and Estación Irarrázaval (☎230 3206), each have a lost and found. Open M-F 7:30am-10pm, La Moneda also open Sa-Su 9am-6pm. For items lost above ground, try the police station at General Mackenna 1314. Open 24hr.

Outdoor Equipment: Find ski and trekking shops in **Mall Alto de Las Condes** (p. 126). Also find equipment at **La Cumbre,** Apoquindo 5258 (☎220 9907; www.lacumbreonline.cl), which has boots, pads, packs, fishing equipment, and more, at lower prices than most competitors. Open M-F 11am-8pm, Sa 11am-4pm. **Rod & Gun,** Av. Las Condes 9607 (☎371 0334; www.chilerivers.cl), has much of the same equipment, at slightly higher prices. Open M-F 10am-10pm. **Patagonia,** Helvecia 210, Las Condes, (☎335 1796; patagoni@entelchile.net), has water bottles, gloves, shoes, and packs.

Bookstores: Bookstores are easily found along Alameda and Huérfanos. Texts in languages other than Spanish, however, can be hard to find.

   📖 **English Reader,** Los Leones 116, Providencia (☎334 7388; www.englishreader.cl). M: Los Leones. Not only the best English bookstore in Santiago, this bright spot is also a lively gathering place for young expats. The cozy cafe hosts conversation nights (45min. English, 45min. Spanish; Tu and Th 7:30pm). Their huge selection is full of best-sellers and more practical choices (around CH$4000). W buy 2, get 1 free. Open M-F 9:30am-8pm, Sa 10:30am-5pm. AmEx/DC/MC/V.

   Librería Australis, Providencia 1670, local 5A (☎236 8054). M: Manuel Montt. Has a wide range of materials for travelers, including guides to flora and fauna, maps, books about indigenous history, and copies of *Let's Go: Chile* for your friends. Open M-F 9:30am-8pm, Sa 9:30am-3:30pm.

Library: Biblioteca Nacional, Alameda 651 (☎260 5200; www.dibam.cl/biblioteca_nacional). M: Santa Lucía. Contains English-language books and magazines housed in its impressive stone and marble quarters. Visitors can read in the library if they show passport ID. Open M-F 9am-7pm, Sa 9am-2pm.

GLBT Organizations: There are a host of websites providing information for GLBT travelers regarding safety and GLBT-friendly establishments in Santiago and beyond. The most comprehensive are **www.gaychile.com** (☎898 6033) and **www.lesbianas.cl** (see **GLBT Travelers,** p. 55). Organizations and public action groups include **Movimiento Unificado de Minorias Sexuales (MUMS),** Alberto Reyes 63, Providencia (☎737 0892), **Movil Movimiento de Liberación Homosexual,** San Ignacio 1263, Casa Dos (☎554 8015), and **Redes de Orientación en Salud Social (REOSS),** Calle Melpilla 3432 (☎736 5542). **Radio Tierra,** AM1300 (☎442 9585; www.radiotierra.cl), has a radio show for sexual minorities called Triángulo Abierto. Sa 7-10:30pm.)

Laundromat: Lavandería Echaurren, Echaurren 164, Barrio Brasil (☎671 3420), is the de facto choice for travelers and students in the area because of its low prices. Wash or dry CH$1000, both CH$1700. Open M-Sa 9am-8pm, Su 11:30am-2pm and 3-8pm. In Santiago Centro, check out **Lavaseco,** Huérfanos 1980 (☎673 3575) or **Sandrico,** Alameda 949, local 152 (☎671 5782).

GLBT SAFETY. Despite the number of resources available for GLBT travelers in Santiago, be aware that Chile's strong Catholic foundation pervades even the most GLBT-friendly neighborhoods, including **Barrio Bellavista.** Attitudes toward sexuality remain conservative. It is advisable not to dress or act in a flamboyant manner in order to avoid instances of verbal harassment or physical violence.

EMERGENCY AND COMMUNICATIONS

Emergency: Ambulance ☎131. **Fire** ☎132. **Police** ☎133. **Information** ☎103.

Police: General Mackenna 1314 (☎544 5000). M: Cal y Canto. Open 24hr. Also, find stationed guards at **Centros de Seguridad e Información,** along Alameda, including at the intersections with Vicuña Mackenna and Juan A. Ríos. Maps posted.

Crisis Lines: Drug Helpline ☎135. **Poison Control** ☎635 3800. **Fonosida** (☎800 202 120) is a confidential, anonymous, and free AIDS hotline. Open Su-Th 2pm-midnight, F-Sa noon-9am. **Domestic Violence Hotline** ☎800 220 040.

Pharmacies: Pharmacies are everywhere in Santiago. **Farmacias Ahumada,** Providencia 2132 (☎222 1121), is only one of several 24hr. pharmacies on the main drag of Providencia. In Santiago Centro, find these frequently along Alameda. Other reputable chains include **Cruz Verde** and **SalcoBrand.**

Medical Services: Recommended by the US embassy for quality and service are the **Clínica Alemana,** Vitacura 5951 (☎212 9700), and the **Clínica Las Condes,** Lo Fontecilla 441 (☎210 4000). Both open 24hr. and accessible only by cab or ambulance.

Telephones: Card- and coin-operated **Entel** and **Manquehue Net** phones are everywhere, but users report that these phones often don't accept coins, or worse, eat them.

Internet Access: Cyber cafes have popped up all over Santiago, especially in Barrio Brasil, in Providencia, and throughout Santiago Centro. **Red Café,** Echaurren 127, Barrio Brasil. CH$500 per hr. Open M-Th 9:15am-11:30pm, F 10am-11:30pm, Sa 10:30am-11:30pm. **Biblioteca Nacional,** Alameda 651, Santiago Centro (☎260 5200) also has access. Passports sometimes required. 18+. CH$600 per hr.

Post Office: Empresa Correos de Chile (☎274 7799 or 269 2866; www.correos.cl), has many locations, including the **Correo Central** at the southwest corner of the Plaza de Armas. Open M-F 8am-7pm, Sa 9am-2pm. **Branch,** Providencia 1466 (☎235 7086) has a **Federal Express.** Open M-Sa 9am-6:30pm, Su 9am-12:30pm. **Federal Express** main office, Providencia 1951 (☎361 6000). Open M-F 9am-1:30pm and 2:30-7pm. The office at Camilo Henríquez 190 is open later (M-F 9am-8pm).

⌂ ACCOMMODATIONS

Santiago boasts a range of accommodations whose quality and price vary almost as much as the city's sprawling neighborhoods. Prices are listed in US currency when payment is accepted in US dollars in order to circumvent the 19% VAT (see **Taxes,** p. 20). For longer stays, check out the newspaper, *El Mercurio,* which has a section on rooms for rent (around CH$80,000-100,000 per month).

UNDER CH$4000 (❶)		Hotel Paris (108)	CEN
▨ La Casa Roja (110)	BRA	Residencial Alemana (110)	BRA
▨ SCS Habitat (110)	BRA	Residencial José Estay (108)	CEN
		Residencial Mery (110)	BRA
CH$4000-CH$7600 (❷)			
Hotel Olicar (108)	CEN	**CH$15,000-CH$23,000 (❹)**	
Residencial Londres (108)	CEN	Hotel Foresta (108)	CEN
Residencial San Patricio (112)	BRA	Hotel Montecarlo (108)	CEN
CH$7600-CH$15,000 (❸)		**OVER CH$23,000 (❺)**	
Hostal Río Amazonas (110)	BRA	Hotel Conde Ansúrez (112)	BRA
Hostelling International (112)	BRA	Hotel Diego de Velázquez (110)	PRV

BRA Barrio Brasil and Barrio Universitario **CEN** Santiago Centro **PRV** Providencia and Las Condes

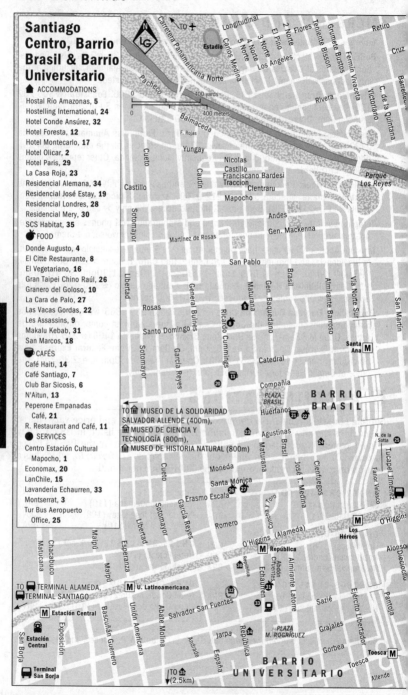

Santiago Centro, Barrio Brasil & Barrio Universitario

⌂ ACCOMMODATIONS
Hostal Río Amazonas, **5**
Hostelling International, **24**
Hotel Conde Ansúrez, **32**
Hotel Foresta, **12**
Hotel Montecarlo, **17**
Hotel Olicar, **2**
Hotel Paris, **29**
La Casa Roja, **23**
Residencial Alemana, **34**
Residencial José Estay, **19**
Residencial Londres, **28**
Residencial Mery, **30**
SCS Habitat, **35**

◖ FOOD
Donde Augusto, **4**
El Citte Restaurante, **8**
El Vegetariano, **16**
Gran Taipei Chino Raúl, **26**
Granero del Goloso, **10**
La Cara de Palo, **27**
Las Vacas Gordas, **22**
Les Assassins, **9**
Makalu Kebab, **31**
San Marcos, **18**

◗ CAFÉS
Café Haiti, **14**
Café Santiago, **7**
Club Bar Sicosis, **6**
N'Aitun, **13**
Peperone Empanadas Café, **21**
R. Restaurant and Café, **11**

● SERVICES
Centro Estación Cultural Mapocho, **1**
Economax, **20**
LanChile, **15**
Lavandería Echaurren, **33**
Montserrat, **3**
Tur Bus Aeropuerto Office, **25**

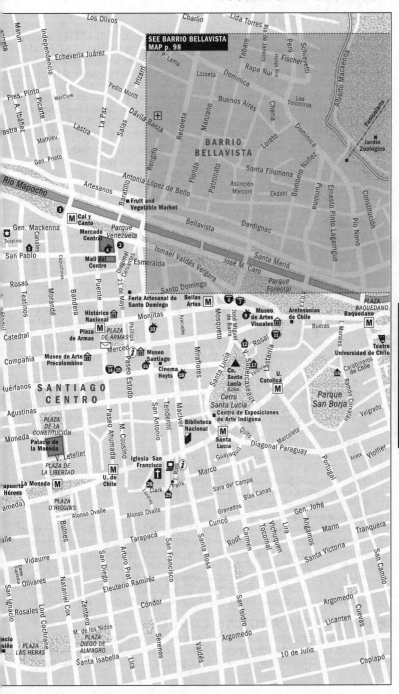

SEE BARRIO BELLAVISTA
MAP p. 98

BARRIO
BELLAVISTA

SANTIAGO
CENTRO

SANTIAGO

SANTIAGO CENTRO

As the heart of the capital, Santiago Centro is home to the bulk of lodging offerings. Truly budget accommodations are clustered west of the Mercado Central in the neighborhood Estación Mapoch. Carefully evaluate the security of these establishments before paying, as reassuring safety signs like locked doors at night can be few and far between. Prices here tend to be the lowest in town, but the lack of perks or amenities as well as the questionable safety of the area make longer stays here rather uncomfortable. Very little English is spoken in these establishments. Hotels tucked along Alameda are just as close to the *centro*, but in a quieter, cleaner locale. While more expensive, they are substantially more comfortable.

Hotel Paris, Paris 813 (☎664 0921; carbott@latinmail.com). M: U. de Chile. With clean, comfortable rooms and lots of amenities, the Hotel Paris is the best choice in the Centro area. Right off Alameda, its location is central but quiet, and after a day of sightseeing, you'll come back to a private bath, TV, and bar. A small lending library is located in the dining area on the 2nd fl. Continental breakfast CH$1000. Singles CH$8000; Doubles with king *(matrimonial)* CH$12,000, 2 twins CH$16,000. AmEx. ❸

Hotel Olicar, San Pablo 1265 (☎698 3683; hotel_olicar@chile.com). M: Cal y Canto. 2 blocks west of the Mercado Central, this clean, well-maintained hotel is the best budget option in this part of town. The high ceilings and spiral stairs to the common kitchen give the place a hint of old-world grandeur, though a view of trash-filled backyards slightly detracts from the overall ambience. All its open space can also make Olicar a little chilly in winter. The front door is locked and security cameras are running 24hr. Singles CH$4000-$6000; doubles CH$8000; triples CH$10,000. ❷

Residencial Londres, Londres 54 (☎633 9192; www.lula.cl/residencial). M: U. de Chile. This *residencial* is a little dark and singles are very cramped, but everything is kept very clean by the friendly and helpful owner. The doubles with bath are the best choice—they are more spacious and overlooking the quiet cobblestoned street below. Luggage storage CH$300 per day. Breakfast CH$800. Singles CH$7000; doubles CH$14,000, with bath CH$16,000; triples CH$21,000/CH$24,000. ❷

Hotel Montecarlo, Victoria Subercaseaux 209 (☎633 9905 or 638 1176; www.hotel-montecarlo.cl). M: Santa Lucía. With 24hr. room service, premium cable, free Internet, breakfast, and private baths, the Hotel Montecarlo offers superior amenities for a slightly higher cost. Nondescript rooms with matching decor are cleaned every day. Rooms on the west side have lush views of Cerro Santa Lucía. Singles US$30; doubles US$38; double suites with couch US$49. AmEx/MC/V. ❹

Hotel Foresta, Victoria Subercaseaux 353 (☎639 6261 or 639 4862). M: Santa Lucía. Eclectic touches like a suit of armor in the lobby and carousel horse pillows in some rooms make Hotel Foresta stand out from other upscale hotels in Santiago Centro. The 7th fl. restaurant is a hidden treat. Some rooms can be dark—for more sun, ask for a view of Cerro Santa Lucía. Premium cable included. Private bath. Singles US$35; doubles US$45; junior suites US$50. AmEx/DC/MC/V. ❹

Residencial José Estay, Ramón Corvalán 37, local 112 (☎247 2272; joseestay@hotmail.com). M: Baquedano, in the "Don Bernardo" building. Offers 2 rooms in the quiet and kitschy apartment of the eponymous José, an English speaker and helpful guide for tourists. The huge collection of Coca-Cola merchandise and paraphernalia crowding the kitchen is a sight in itself. Free Internet M-F after 8pm, Sa after 2pm, and Su all day. Both rooms with private bath. Breakfast included. Call or email 5-7 days before arriving in Santiago; no walk-ins accepted. Rooms CH$11,000, discounts for longer stays. ❸

PROVIDENCIA AND LAS CONDES

These two neighborhoods are where the rich set down their roots in Santiago, whether on vacation or all year long, and are home to high-end hotels like the **Park Plaza,** Ricardo Lyon 207 (☎372 4000; www.parkplaza.cl) and the **Hyatt Regency,**

Providencia and Las Condes

▲ ACCOMMODATIONS
Hotel Diego de Velazquez, 16

● FOOD
Bar Normandie, 23
El Club, 1
El Patio Restaurante, 19
El Huerto/La Huerta, 13
New York Bagel Bakery, 4
Panadería Costaño, 22

🍺 BARS
Babble, 10
Bar Liguria, 24
Flannery's Irish Geo Pub, 7

★ CLUBS
Entre Negros, 9
ilé Habana, 8
Infierno Discoteque, 11

■ SHOPPING
Mundo del Vino, 2

● SERVICES
Altue, 6
Books, 20
Federal Express, 15
Instituto Cultural de
  Providencia, 18
LanChile, 14
Librería Australis, 17
Patagonia, 3
Santa Isabel, 12
Sernatur, 21
Unimarc, 5

SANTIAGO

Kennedy 4601 (☎218 1234; www.santiago.hyatt.com). As quality accommodations at cheaper prices are available in other nearby neighborhoods, most travelers are better off staying elsewhere and taking the Metro in to mingle with the million-aires. Save your money for buying *completas* in bulk.

Hotel Diego de Velázquez, Diego de Velázquez 2141 (☎234 4400; www.hoteldie-godevelazquez.com). M: Pedro de Valdivia. In a classy Providencia neighborhood. The impeccable interior is marked by adobe themes. Ask for a new room, as the most recently renovated units are better-kept and much brighter, but cost the same as old rooms. Pricey Internet (CH$35 per min.). Cable TV and A/C in every room. Heated pool and spa. Buffet breakfast included. Singles US$110; doubles US$125; triples US$145; 2-room. apt. US$175; 3-room. apt. US$215. Online rates US$40-$60 cheaper. ❺

BARRIO BRASIL AND BARRIO UNIVERSITARIO

Lodging in Brasil caters to the young and cash-strapped, with hostels often making up for lacking amenities with ambience.

▨ **La Casa Roja,** Agustinas 2113 (☎696 4241; www.lacasaroja.cl). M: Los Héroes. La Casa Roja is a veritable backpacker's haven. Stunning bathrooms, large common spaces, impromptu barbecues, and ping-pong tournaments are the norm here. Ski trips to Valle Nevado (CH$5500), free tours of the city, backpacking bus trips, and a huge kitchen are available. Internet free 20min. per day, then CH$600 per hr. Break-fast CH$1700. Key deposit CH$2000. 8-bed dorms CH$4500 per person; singles with bath CH$15,000; doubles CH$12,000 per person. ❶

▨ **SCS Habitat,** San Vicente 1798 (☎683 3732; scshabitat@yahoo.com). From Est-ación Central, take buses #335, 358, or 360 for 18 blocks and get off before the underpass; walk to the end of Exposición, turn left on Subercaseaux, and go east 3 blocks to San Vicente. The friendly and helpful American owner offers camping equip-ment, trekking maps, bike rental, a food store, and the nicest kitchen in town. Great source of information about Chile for independent, resourceful backpackers. Free phone for receiving long-distance calls. Internet CH$600 per hr. Breakfast CH$1000 includes fresh fruit and occasional baked goodies. Camping CH$2500. Dorms CH$4000 per person. ❶

Residencial Alemana, República 220 (☎671 2388; ralemana@entelchile.net). This house seems from another time. The facade is antique and curlicued, while inside, lace and animal paintings abound. High ceilings and plenty of windows keep every-thing light and airy. Clean, shared baths. TV available. Breakfast included. Singles CH$6000-9000; doubles CH$10,000-11,000, with bath CH$13,000. AmEx/DC/MC/V. ❸

Residencial Mery, Pasaje República 36 (☎696 8883 or 699 4982; residencialmery@yahoo.com). M: República. The lacquered wood, pink bedspreads, and flowered wallpaper of this little *residencial* might remind you of your grandmother's house. Coupled with the coziness of familiarity, firm beds, and the quiet, back-alley location ensure a good night's sleep. Clean rooms come with towels and cable TV. Reserva-tions recommended in the summer. Singles CH$9500; doubles CH$16,000, with bath CH$22,000; triples CH$24,000; quads CH$28,000. ❸

Hostal Río Amazonas, Rosas 2234 (☎671 9013). This cozy hostel's brightly painted walls and leafy plants will make you feel like you're in a tropical paradise, while the attentive owners will make you feel at home. Breakfast included. Singles CH$13,500, with bath CH$15,000; doubles CH$20,000/CH$23,000. AmEx/DC/MC/V. ❸

THE TIMES, THEY ARE A-CHANGIN'

Conflicting Social and Political Mores in Santiago's La Victoria

"Y por qué vives allá?" The taxi driver refused to drive me home until I convinced him that if I could live in Santiago's infamous *barrio*, La Victoria, he could certainly take me there. This reluctance to venture into La Victoria is not unusual, though. Many Chileans have strong reactions to the mere mention of its name, ranging from extreme glorification to scathing condemnation. A look into prevailing attitudes toward La Victoria and its tumultuous history helps explain the sharp political divisions of Chile's past, the changing social landscape of its present, and the vast uncertainty of its future.

Communism in Chile has had a controversial history. Marxist ideas pouring out of Europe at the turn of the century galvanized mine workers and by 1922, the Communist Party was thriving. The Great Depression strengthened the radical left, increasing tension with the ruling elite and provoking widespread social turbulence. The presidential victory of the Radical Party brought a new era of social reform until the advent of the Cold War sparked a backlash. Still, Communists led nearly two decades of protest that only intensified until the bloody coup of 1973.

During this period, La Victoria became a symbol of popular struggle. Founded by *pobladores* (colonizers) in 1957 through a *toma de terreno* (land takeover), La Victoria became a model for *tomas* throughout Chile. In the months leading up to the *toma*, communists and students organized hundreds of families who had become resigned to squatting on the banks of a river on the periphery of Santiago. Under the guidance of the Communist Party, the group identified a few large plots of land held by wealthy landowners and planned their future community. The present-day site of La Victoria was to be a self-sufficient commune with roads, a school, a health clinic, and a home for every family. On October 30, 1957, the group seized the land and prepared to defend themselves against those who would try to expel them from the property. The *pobladores* stalwartly stood their ground, and after several days of resistance, declared victory, naming their new community La Victoria in honor of the occasion.

The taxi turns onto 30 de Octubre, whose name commemorates the date of the *toma*. On this street, months earlier, I watched the annual reenactment of the *toma*, as a few hundred *victorianos*, marching to chants of *"El pueblo unido jamás será vencido"* (the town united will never be conquered), proudly followed in the steps of the *pobladores* 44 years before. Accompanied by a police escort, the crowd stopped pointedly in the middle of the main thoroughfare to block traffic before triumphantly continuing on.

However, this historical celebration of La Victoria's founding was dwarfed by the celebration a few nights later, when over 1000 people crowded the street for a night of music and dance. The program was a mix of traditional Chilean music, including homages to legendary folk singers Victor Jara and Violeta Parra. More trendy groups such as Amerikan Sound, a Chilean version of the Backstreet Boys, also performed.

The obvious distinctions between the two events are good indicators of the competing social and cultural traditions of La Victoria. Hearing the youthful crowd's frenzied response to the heartthrobs of Amerikan Sound, one may think that the the *barrio*'s future is clear. However, as we pass the Communist Party building, I notice a group of middle-aged men deep in discussion under the intense gaze of Che Guevara. Two murals of the communist revolutionary and a conspicuous mural of Salvador Allende, the only declared Marxist to rule Chile before the coup, preside over the room as if to urge on the communist struggle. In 1983, *victorianos* took to the streets in the first massive protest against the Pinochet regime, setting off a series of nationwide protests that led to the eventual decline of the military regime. For years, *victorianos* suffered the consequences of their valor—detention, torture, and death—but still remained resolute.

Ironically enough, present-day democracy has done what years of repression could not—weakened the *barrio*'s social solidarity and ideological homogeneity. Without a unifying force to oppose, the *victorianos* remain preoccupied with the economic pressures of providing for their families. Within this social and political vacuum, other forces have taken to the streets as well—at night, drug dealers on the corner of 30 de Octubre brazenly hawk their wares to passersby, causing the district's reputation to devolve from famous to infamous in recent years.

We arrive at the house, which seems no more than a pile of wood and scrap metal, where I live with a family of ten. The driver has already asked me to have exact change ready so he can speed off. I enter the living room where I find the eldest daughter copying a Neruda poem to distribute at an event celebrating the Communist poet's birthday. Meanwhile, her sister mimics the suggestive movements of scantily clad dancers on TV. The conflicting social, cultural, and political mores of La Victoria are here, in these sisters. I can't help wondering which is La Victoria's future.

Brian Milder was a Researcher-Writer for Let's Go: New Zealand 2000. He spent a year in Chile as a Rockefeller Fellow living in La Victoria and volunteering at the Nonprofit Enterprise and Self-sustainability Team (NESsT).

Hostelling International, Cienfuegos 151 (☎671 8532; www.hostelling.cl). M: Los Héroes. HI's efficiency and cleanliness speak to its membership status, but it's consequently lacking in the quirky ambience of some of its neighbors. Cafeteria, patio, lockers, off-street parking, and luggage storage (CH$500 per day per piece) available. Breakfast CH$500. Dorms CH$6000 per person; singles CH$12,000, with bath CH$16,000; doubles CH$18,000/CH$24,000; triples CH$24,000; quints CH$37,500. CH$1500 discount with ISIC; HI members save CH$500-1000. AmEx/DC/MC/V. ❸

Residencial San Patricio, Catedral 2235 (☎671 9045 or 695 4800). Although rooms are a bit dingy, bright lighting, cable TV, private baths, and heaters are compensation enough. The guests' kitchen is in a courtyard, under a fiberglass roof. Internet CH$500 per hr. All rooms CH$5000 per person, with bath CH$6000. ❷

Hotel Conde Ansúrez, República 25 (☎696 0807 or 671 8376; www.ansurez.cl). M: República. This old-world hotel might seem out of place in the youth-oriented atmosphere of Barrio Universitario, but its many amenities are welcome after a night of pool or pub-hopping nearby. Cable TV, security boxes, A/C, and private bath in every room. Breakfast included. Singles US$50; doubles US$60; triples US$80; quads US$90; quints US$100. AmEx/DC/MC/V. ❺

◧ FOOD

ASIAN		**ITALIAN**	
Gran Taipei Chino Raúl (116)	BRA ❸	Diego Pizzería (115)	LC ❷
		La Taverna della Piazza (118)	ÑUÑ ❷
BAKERIES		La Tecla (118)	ÑUÑ ❷
New York Bagel Bakery (115)	LC ❶	San Marcos (113)	CEN ❸
Panadería Costaño (114)	PRV ❶		
		MEDITERRANEAN	
CAFES		La Terraza Restorán (117)	BEL ❶
Café de la Isla (119)	ÑUÑ	Tasca Mediterránea (117)	BEL ❹
Café Santiago (119)	CEN		
Club Bar Sicosis (118)	CEN	**MIDDLE EASTERN**	
El Cuarto Café (119)	ÑUÑ	El Antojo de Gauguin (116)	BEL ❸
La Casa en el Aire (119)	BEL	⊠ Qatir (115)	LC ❷
Libro Café (118)	BEL		
N'Aitun (118)	BRA	**NEW AMERICAN**	
Off the Record Café (118)	BEL	El Club (115)	LC ❷
Peperone Empanadas Café (118)	BRA		
R. Restaurant and Café (119)	CEN	**ORGANIC**	
		El Patio Restaurante (115)	PRV ❸
FAST FOOD		Granero de Goloso (113)	CEN ❶
Doña Isabel (114)	PRV ❶		
Makalu Kebab (116)	BRA ❶	**ROMANTIC**	
		⊠ Como Agua Para Chocolate	CEN ❸
FRENCH			
Bar Normandie (115)	PRV ❶	**SEAFOOD**	
El Amor Nunca Muere (117)	ÑUÑ ❶	Azul Profundo (117)	BEL ❹
Les Assassins Restaurant (113)	CEN ❸	Donde Augusto (114)	CEN ❹
		El Citte Restaurante (116)	BRA ❸
GRILLS		Mercado Central (113)	CEN ❶
⊠ Bar Liguria (114)	PRV ❷		
La Cara de Palo (116)	BRA ❸	**VEGETARIAN**	
Las Vacas Gordas (116)	BRA ❸	El Huerto/La Huerta (114)	PRV ❷
		⊠ El Vegetariano (113)	CEN ❷

BEL Barrio Bellavista **BRA** Barrio Brasil and Barrio Universitario **CEN** Santiago Centro
LC Las Condes **ÑUÑ** Ñuñoa **PRV** Providencia

SANTIAGO CENTRO

If you have access to kitchen facilities, or just want to buy a huge squeeze tube of Chile's favorite dish, mayonnaise, **Montserrat**, 21 de Mayo 819, is an easy stop. The aisles are wide, well-stocked, and organized. (☎638 4339. M: Cal y Canto. Open 10am-8pm. AmEx/DC/MC/V. Also at Monjitas 739, closer to Alameda.) For fruits and veggies dirt cheap, try the low-lying corrugated-roof **market** across the river from the Mercado Central via the footbridge from 21 de Mayo. (Open 7am-9am.)

▨ **El Vegetariano,** Huérfanos 827, local 18, in the Galería Imperia. M: U. de Chile. If the displays of neon-lit *completas* in Santiago Centro start to turn your stomach, El Vegetariano certainly provides a welcome retreat. Dine under a high stained-glass ceiling and Renaissance-style murals on deliciously mayo-free food like spinach crepes (CH$2850), Spanish tortilla with vegetables and potatoes (CH$2790), or a soy burger (CH$2350). Open M-F 8am-8pm, Sa 10-4. AmEx/DC/MC/V. ❷

San Marcos, Huérfanos 618 (☎633 6880). M: Santa Lucía. In Santiago, Italian means pizza, and San Marcos follows fashion, with higher-end hearth-cooked pies (from CH$2950). Their homemade pastas, however, are the real specialty. The *gnocchi bolognese* (CH$4180) and seafood ravioli (CH$4900) are delicious rarities. Happy hour 4-5pm has 2-for-1 entrees. Open M-Sa 8am-midnight. AmEx/DC/MC/V. ❸

Mercado Central, on the corner of Paseo Ahumada and San Pablo. M: Cal y Canto. With miles of coastline, Chile serves some of the best seafood in the world, and the Mercado is a great place to sample it, as long as the aggressive hawkers and fish-gut floor don't turn your stomach. Even if you don't indulge, the visit is a thrilling sensory experience. Fresh *erizo* (sea urchin; CH$500 per kg), and half-shell oysters (25 for CH$1500) can be cut right from the shell to slurp as you wander. Sit-down restaurants offer similar seafood delights. Open M-Th 7am-4pm, F-Sa 7am-8pm, Su 7am-5pm. ❶

Granero de Goloso, Santo Domingo 49 (☎638 6289). M: Santa Lucía. A clean and quiet little oasis that sells natural foods from Chilean farms. Here in the self-billed "corner of delights," you can pick up Chilean virgin olive oil (CH$2290) or natural honey (CH$2500 per 600g). If you want to buy wheat (CH$500 per kg), there's a huge grinder right out front where pigeons like to snack. Open M-Sa 10am-7:30pm. ❶

Les Assassins, Merced 297B (☎638 4280). M: U. Católica. The staff at this snug little restaurant speaks Spanish, English, and French, and the menu reflects this triple influence. Though the French touch is emphasized, and the menu is written in the language,

THE BIG SPLURGE

AS THE RESTAURANT TURNS: EL GIRATORIO

At El Giratorio, it's not the tall *pisco* sours (CH$1500) or shockingly beautiful views of the Andes that make diners feel like the room is spinning. Here, 19 stories high above Santiago, the restaurant's really moving. The treat at this rotating restaurant, however, is the view. El Giratorio looks out over the sprawl of Santiago's expanse below, with verdant Cerro San Cristóbal looming close by, and the sparkling Andes acting as a backdrop. What's more, it's the only such restaurant in the world whose speed isn't locked—though management usually keeps it on a standard speed.

Beyond the gimmick, however, El Giratorio serves some of the best food around. The mostly Chilean fare like "escalopa," a lightly fried steak accompanied by spinach creme crepes (CH$6200), is well-executed, and desserts like *manjar* crepes (CH$1600) are positively sedating. The combination of delicious meals, impeccable service, and singular location once made the Giratorio a favorite of the ruling elites: Pinochet's wife used to take her tea here each afternoon. Now, though, you'll find middle-class families, as well as tourists from the world over, splurging on the most unique meal in Santiago.

11 de Septiembre 2250, Providencia (☎232 1827 or 251 5789). Open daily noon-1:30am. AmEx/DC/MC/V. ❸ you'll still find Chilean favorites like *bife al lomo* (CH$3600) mixed in with French dishes such as *crème brûlée* (CH$1980), French onion soup (CH$3100), and *Filet Roquefort* (CH$4980). Open M-Sa noon-11pm. AmEx/DC/MC/V. ❸

Donde Augusto, in the Mercado Central (☎672 2829). Offers everything the market stands have, plus cooking, chairs, and a higher cost. Specialties include seafood *paella* (CH$9900) and fish in a chowder-like *salsa de mariscos* (from CH$7000). Photos of celebrity diners line the walls and waiters wear jackets, but you're still sitting in the middle of a screaming, stinking fish market, and the wine list is too short to help you forget. Open M-Th 7am-4pm, F 7am-8pm, Sa 7am-6pm, Su 7am-5pm. AmEx/DC/MC/V. ❹

 VEGGIE TALES. Among the range of *completas, churrascos*, and beef that are offered at most of Santiago's restaurants, a vegetarian plate is usually offered as well. In Santiago, however, vegetarianism generally means abstinence from red meat. Said vegetarian dishes often come with tuna or ham, so ask about the ingredients before ordering.

PROVIDENCIA

If you're not eating out, but have kitchen access or a need to amass a munchies stash, check out **Santa Isabel,** Providencia 2188. This supermarket is well-lit, clean, and staffed by efficient checkers. (☎233 0092. M: Los Leones. Open M-Sa 9am-10pm, Su 10am-8pm.) For those too hungry to make it home, the second floor houses **Doña Isabel ❶,** a fast-food place with offerings like *lomo al pobre* (CH$2900) and a quarter of a chicken (CH$1300).

For restaurants, the gastronomic heart of Providencia, aside from Barrio Bellavista, radiates outward from **Avenida Suecia** and **Avenida Providencia.** Here, you'll find themed restaurants and American-style bars in such concentration that locals call the area "Gringolandia." True to its name, the area is often teeming with expatriates. Those feeling overloaded on *bife al lomo* need only wander a few minutes to find a traditional burger and fries. If you're looking for a more unique dining experience, however, there are several excellent options.

■ **Bar Liguria,** Providencia 1373 (☎235 7914). M: Pedro de Valdivia. This bright little bistro is a fun place to spend a lunch hour or an evening (see **Bars,** p. 128). The short menu changes daily, but expect to find creative dishes like vegetable polenta (CH$2750) alongside traditional Chilean fare like *cazuela de vacuno* (CH$4600). The passing crowds and retro decor will keep you entertained; the attentive and attractive staff will keep you happy. Open M-W 10am-midnight, Th-Sa 10am-2am. ❷

El Huerto/La Huerta, Orrego Luco Norte 054 (☎233 2690). M: Pedro de Valdivia. Due to its wide variety of dishes and calm, comfortable dining area, El Huerto has long been known as the best vegetarian restaurant in Santiago. To accommodate more diners and to offer a cheaper choice, the owners opened a smaller adjoining cafe, **La Huerta.** The original serves creative and filling dishes like vegetable curry with rice and fresh fruit (CH$4300), cheese fondue (CH$4500), and spinach calzones (CH$4500) in a cozy dining nook. The patio cafe at La Huerta offers quicker service and smaller portions of simpler fare like soup and salad deals (CH$2000). El Huerto open M-Sa noon-midnight, Su 7pm-midnight; La Huerta open M-Sa 8am-4pm. AmEx/DC/MC/V. ❷

Panadería Costaño, Providencia 1401 (☎235 3798). M: Manuel Montt. Smells seeping out from this Providencia bakery lure in countless passersby each day. Cookies (CH$240 per 100g), *empanadas* (CH$550), and fresh breads (CH$800) are laid out around the spacious, warmly-lit store in woven baskets and on rustic wooden shelves. Some are shipped to this chain's other locations, but here there's a dining area where you can sit and bask in the warm, heady air. Open M-F 7am-9pm, Sa 7am-8pm. ❶

Bar Normandie, Providencia 1234 (☎236 3011). M: Manuel Montt. The glossy wood furnishings, ancient photographs, and French menu give the place the feel of a portside European cafe, and the delectable *crepe suzette* (CH$300), sauteed eggplant (CH$1200), or *coq au vin* (CH$3000) seem worth more pesos than you pay. Open M-Th 11am-11pm, F-Sa noon-1am. ❶

El Patio Restaurante, Providencia 1670 (☎236 1251), at the back of Galería el Patio. M: Manuel Montt. All of the veggies at this El Patio are organically grown, ensuring crisp freshness, albeit at higher prices. Enjoying the tofu stir-fry (CH$4500) or fruit salad with yogurt (CH$4000) in the glassed-in patio might make you feel like you've escaped to the country, but the adjoining sushi bar and black-clad staff keep it all from getting too rustic. Open M-Th noon-midnight, F-Sa noon-1:30am, Su 12:30pm-4pm. DC/MC/V. ❸

LAS CONDES

The cheapest food in Las Condes is found at its supermarket, **Unimarc,** Apoquindo 2770. (☎96 621 7502. M: Tobalaba. Open M-Sa 9am-10pm, Su 10am-8pm.) Most sit-down restaurants in Las Condes are geared toward guests of the nearby Ritz or Hyatt, and are consequently overpriced. On the other hand, the area along Isidora Goyenechea west of Calle Carmencita is dotted with American chain restaurants.

🗹 **Qatir,** Las Verbenas 9183 (☎342 0479). M: Escuela Militar. Most people think you can only have dancers at your table in one of the shady cafes of Santiago Centro. Well, you can at this Middle Eastern restaurant, though they come clothed in scarves and flowing skirts. Falafel CH$1400. Kebab CH$3500. Baklava CH$900. *Pisco* CH$1500. Open M-Sa 10:30am-1am, Su 10am-5pm. AmEx/DC/MC/V. ❷

El Club, El Bosque Norte 0580 (☎246 1222). M: Tobalaba. The luxurious hardwood decor, delicious food, and ritzy clientele at this intimate spot don't seem to correspond with the low prices. Grilled chicken breast CH$2200. French onion soup CH$3100. Caramel nut tart CH$2900. Open daily noon-12:30am. AmEx/DC/MC/V. ❷

New York Bagel Bakery, Roger de Flor 2894, Las Condes (☎246 3060). One of the only places in the city where you can get breakfast food without *manjar* (caramelized milk) You'll see lots of Americans snacking on cheesecake (CH$3300), bagels (CH$650), and croissants (CH$710). Open M-F 7:30am-8:30pm, Sa-Su 7am-9pm. ❶

Diego Pizzería, El Bosque Norte 0160. M: Tobalaba. This big, boisterous pizzeria serves some of the quickest and cheapest food in Las Condes, including spinach fettucine (CH$1800) and individual pizzas (CH$4000). The dessert menu and their happy hour 4-10pm, are both inordinately long. Open 12:30pm-12:30am. ❷

NO WORK, ALL PLAY

THAT'S WHAT I CALL FAST FOOD!

¡Cuídate! ¡Garzones! ("Look out! Waiters!")

That's a phrase that you'll never find in most guidebooks, but *Let's Go* knows that it could come in really handy in Santiago. On the 20th or 21st of October, it'll be all but essential, when downtown Santiago hosts the annual Waiter's Marathon. The Confederation of National Food Workers initiated this event to promote vocational pride, and each year, it grows in popularity.

Time trials throughout the country precede the big day, when over 50 waiters descend upon the city, dressed in the mandatory race gear of white vest, dress shirt, black pants, shined shoes, and bow tie (jackets optional). Racers must carry a tray with a bottle of wine and a glass that cannot be secured by any means, including the glue and sashes that previous contestants have attempted to sneak in. Spectators fill the Plaza de la Constitución, around which the race takes place. The course is 6.5km long, with an incredible record of 14.7 minutes. Just remember: seeing them move incredibly quickly during the day doesn't give you license to be impatient at dinner.

For additional info about the race, call La Confederación Nacional de Trabajadores de los Alimentos (Cotiach), ☎672 4302.

BARRIO BRASIL AND BARRIO UNIVERSITARIO

The cheap, greasy fare of most restaurants in the area is geared toward the packs of ravenous college students that roam the streets every day and late into the night. More refined ethnic and seafood restaurants can also be found, especially Chinese restaurants, which are common in Barrio Brasil. Ricardo Cummings, north of Alameda, hosts clusters of quality eateries. For groceries, try **Economax,** at the corner of Ricardo Cummings and Santo Domingo. (Open daily 8:30am-10pm.)

Las Vacas Gordas, Cienfuegos 280 (☎697 1066 or 673 6962). The pervasive aroma of the open grill might make the happy cartoon heifers on this restaurant's facade seem a little out of place. Luckily, the decorative guilt trip ends at the door. Meats including steak (CH$3100), pork (CH$2500), and chicken (CH$2390) are empha-sized, but the asparagus salad (CH$1590) is just as delicious. Wash it all down with a smooth *pisco* sour (CH$850). Open daily noon-4pm and 8pm-midnight. AmEx/DC/MC/V. ❸

La Cara de Palo, Ricardo Cummings 97 (☎671 8184), means "the wooden face," and the dark wood exterior and inner walls are both carved with crazy Polynesian-style smiles, among other things. The Basque trout (CH$3290) or grilled chicken (CH$2990) are delicious deals. Open M-Sa 1pm-1am, Su 11am-6pm. AmEx/DC/MC/V. ❸

Makalu Kebab, Salvador San Fuentes 2249 (☎698 4956). A favorite hangout for uni-versity students for its casual, hip atmosphere and bargain food. The jukebox plays familiar English songs and TVs let sports fans keep up on their *fútbol.* Kebab and fries CH$650. 6 *empanadas* with drink CH$1000. *Churrasco* CH$900. Beer CH$1000-1400. Open M-Th 10am-12:30am, F 10am-2:30am, Sa noon-10pm. ❶

El Citte Restaurante, Ricardo Cummings 635 (☎698 4877). This little hole in the wall is popular with older locals for its cheap but well-cooked fare. Among the fish options (CH$3000-4000), the *corvina* (sea bass) is especially good, but choose your sauce (CH$1100-1300) wisely. Open M-Sa noon-midnight, Su 11am-4pm. ❸

Gran Taipei Chino Raúl, Ricardo Cummings 78 (☎699 1809). Chefs from Shanghai, Guangdong, and Taiwan ensure an authentic culinary experience. They also cook by request. Sautéed bamboo and mushroom CH$3250. 4-course *menú* CH$5250. Lunch *menú* CH$2100. Karaoke on weekends. Open daily 11am-1am. AmEx/DC/MC/V. ❸

BARRIO BELLAVISTA

For a little extra money, you can treat yourself to a memorable meal in Bellavista. This bohemian *barrio* features specialty restaurants that prepare dishes with an artistic flair commensurate with the multicultural surroundings. The best culinary strip resides on Constitución.

▓ **Como Agua Para Chocolate,** Constitución 88. (☎777 8740). M: Baquedano. Beware: the menu prepared in the "magic kitchen" and the Mexican villa interior inspire an ambi-ence of aphrodisia, and the ingredients like oysters and asparagus are meant to inspire *amor.* If that's your plan, call ahead to reserve the "mesa-cama," a table that's really a double bed, and a giant hint. Date-friendly dishes include *Salad Seducción* (CH$4100) and *Ave de la Pasión* (CH$5900). Romantic meals for 2 CH$13,000. The namesake dessert (CH$3300) may seem like a chocolate overload, but it certainly takes consum-ers to decadent heights. Open daily 12:30pm-5pm and 8pm-1am. DC/MC/V. ❸

El Antojo de Gauguin, Pío Nono 69 (☎737 0398). M: Baquedano. We can't say what a French painter's monocle has to do with Middle Eastern cuisine, but it's definitely a wel-come addition to the vibrant mix of Bellavista dining. The *baba ghanoush* (CH$2800), chicken kebab pita (CH$2400), and stuffed grape leaves (CH$3900) are authentic and flavorful. Open M-Th 9am-4pm and 7-11pm, F-Sa 7pm-2am. AmEx/DC/MC/V. ❸

SANTIAGO

Tasca Mediterránea, Purísima 161 (☎ 735 3901); also at Domínica 35. The Mediter-ranean menu is fashioned after some of Pablo Neruda's favorite recipes, and dishes like seasoned chicken *tapas* (CH$7500) illustrate the icon's impeccable taste. The ambience follows suit, with a decisively poetic and alluringly romantic flavor from theater and live music performances W-Sa. A slightly more economical choice for those on an artist's budget is the grilled fish with vegetables (CH$4500). 3-course lunch *menú* CH$3500. Open M-F 1pm-1am, Sa 7pm-2:30am. AmEx/DC/MC/V. ❹

Azul Profundo, Constitución 111 (☎ 738 0288). M: Baquedano. Though the maritime decorating scheme borders on cheesy, this restaurant takes seafood seriously. Many kinds of marine life, including salmon (CH$5800), conger eel (CH$5600), and shark (CH$5600) are available. "Lifeguards," such as beef medallions (CH$5800), keep it all from getting too overwhelming. Wine CH$4500-38,000. Beer CH$1600-3000. Reservations recommended F-Sa. Open M-Sa 1-3:30pm and 7:30pm-1am. AmEx/DC/MC/V. ❹

ÑUÑOA

Ñuñoa's small cafes provide for an easy stop for locals on the way home after a day of work, but for visitors, dozens of delightfully distinct and varied options abound, providing an interesting meal at any time of day.

El Amor Nunca Muere, Humberto Trucco 43 (☎ 274 9432). M: Baquedano. At this lit-tle French bistro, you can entertain yourself reading the scrawlings on the walls or the strangely amorous names of the dishes. Meals like the "Naked," a green bean, tomato and curry wrap, or "Passionate Crepes" (CH$3100) will have you wondering if sex really does sell (and for only CH$2500). A/C. Creative dessert menu includes apple crepes (CH$1200). *Pisco* sour CH$1600. Open M-Th 5pm-2am, F-Sa 5pm-4am. ❶

La Terraza Restorán, Jorge Washington 58, (☎ 223 3987). As the name suggests, this bistro is fronted by an open-air terrace where you can watch nighttime crowds passing by. Chilean favorites like *churrasco* (CH$3200) are available, and the respectable *tapas* offerings (CH$2000-2400) and heady sangria (CH$2100) are a delectable Spanish touch. Happy hour 6-9pm. Open daily 11am-midnight. AmEx/DC/MC/V. ❶

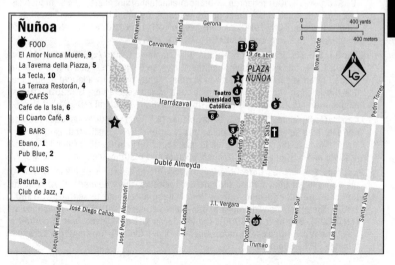

Ñuñoa

● FOOD
El Amor Nunca Muere, **9**
La Taverna della Piazza, **5**
La Tecla, **10**
La Terraza Restorán, **4**
● CAFÉS
Café de la Isla, **6**
El Cuarto Café, **8**
■ BARS
Ebano, **1**
Pub Blue, **2**
★ CLUBS
Batuta, **3**
Club de Jazz, **7**

La Tecla, Doctor Johow 320 (☎274 3603; www.latecla.cl). True to its name, this restaurant's distinctive facade is marked by a huge, twisting keyboard. Luckily, the food is just as unique, with offerings like a chicken and ricotta wrap (CH$3300) or Hawaiian pizza (CH$2900-3900). All drinks ½-price during happy hour M-Sa 7-9pm. Open M-F 12:30-3:30pm and 7pm-midnight, Sa 12:30-3:30pm and 7pm-2am. AmEx/DC/MC/V. ❷

La Taverna della Piazza, on Plaza Ñuñoa (☎223 4414; www.latavernadellapiazza.cl). A wide range of delicious Italian dishes are offered, including pastas (CH$3000-4100), paninis (CH$3000), and pizzas (CH$4100). The huge selection of drinks is especially inviting—see if you can keep a straight face while ordering the "Italian Banana" (CH$2800). Open Su-Th 11am-midnight, F-Sa 11am-2am. AmEx/DC/MC/V. ❷

⌗ CAFES

In Santiago, the *schop* (beer) houses and *comida típica* joints are the locals' favorite places to relax and argue about *fútbol*. A quieter, more intellectual atmosphere, however, pervades the city's cafes, whose unassuming presence gives them the air of an underground scene. On the other end of the cafe spectrum, Santiago Centro's pedestrian walkways are littered with establishments like the inescapable **Café Haiti.** These "*cafés con piernas*" (cafes with legs), draw an ogling, suit-clad corporate clientele with young, busty female waitstaff decked out in slinky evening wear. Tinted and blacked-out windows on other "cafe" fronts suggest that even more is revealed inside.

N'Aitun, Ricardo Cummings 453, Barrio Brasil (☎671 7837; www.naitun.co.cl). Named after the Mapuche word for "rest," this artsy cafe instructs patrons to "Relax, let it go," and provides books, magazines, and nightly shows for that purpose. Schedules change weekly, so call ahead. Salads CH$700. Dessert CH$700. *Pisco* sour CH$1100. Drinks up to CH$300 more expensive on weekends. Open M-Th 10am-2am, F-Sa 10am-4am.

Off the Record Café, Antonia López de Bello 0155, Barrio Bellavista (☎777 7710). Fusion dishes named after great thinkers and artists from Neruda to Bogart (CH$10,000-12,000) reflect the vibrant intellectual atmosphere, where intense discussion, movie screenings, and poetry readings are often held. To save cash, consider a tiramisu (CH$1900) or cappuccino (CH$1200). Open M-F 9am-2am, Sa 10am-2am, Su 10am-1am. AmEx/DC/MC/V.

Club Bar Sicosis, José Miguel de Barra 544, Santiago Centro (☎632 4462). M: Bellas Artes. Right down the street from the Museo de Bellas Artes, this intimate cafe is seeped in artistic influences. Artwork covers brightly painted walls and sandwiches like the Picasso (goat cheese, lettuce, and mixed vegetables; CH$2500) are all named after artists. Coffee CH$650. Open daily 8am-3am. AmEx/DC/MC/V.

Libro Café, Purísima 165, Barrio Bellavista (☎735 3901). With its candlelit red interior and large selection of old books, this is a perfectly sophisticated place to sip a glass of wine (CH$1500) and listen to jazz. *Tapas* CH$2500-3850. Open M-Th noon-4:30pm and 6:30pm-2am, F-Sa noon-4:30pm and 6:30pm-4am. AmEx/DC/MC/V.

Peperone Empanadas Café, Huérfanos 1954, Barrio Brasil (☎687 9180). Though the name might be a turn-off for cafe connoisseurs, the *empanada* choices at this tiny cafe are superior and varied—from vegetarian cuisine to seafood (CH$600-1000). There's also a wide range of drinks like cappuccino (CH$850), hot chocolate (CH$1000), and beer (CH$900). The interior is just as eclectic, with a portrait of Dalí, poetry by Borges, and more. Open M 6pm-midnight, Tu-Th and Sa 12:30pm-midnight, F 12:30pm-1am.

Café Santiago, José Miguel de Barra 405, Santiago Centro (☎638 8982). M: Santa Lucía. The soft light of the beaded lamps reflecting off the warm wood of this cafe makes it a comfortable place to relax in the middle of Santiago Centro. The creative menu is a standout, with mixed drinks like Iced Caramel (CH$1800) or Espresso BonBon (CH$1000). Sandwiches served baked or cold CH$1500. Open daily 11am-10pm.

La Casa en el Aire, Antonia López de Bello 0125, Barrio Bellavista (☎ 777 9985). M: Baquedano. Named after a Neruda poem, this cafe keeps its literary flavor with occasional poetry readings. It's a quiet and mellow place to have a drink—like a cafe but with alcohol. *Pisco* CH$990. Open daily 8pm-2am.

El Cuarto Café, Humberto Trucco 35, Ñuñoa (☎225 1495). This cozy cafe serves a variety of creative dishes that, while small, seem worth more than you pay. Ham, cheese, and olive *panqueques* (CH$2300) go great with cream of tomato soup (CH$1300). A wide range of dessert offerings like caramel-orange pancakes (CH$1200), Edy's ice cream (CH$850), or banana milk frappes (CH$900) are a great ending to a meal. Open M-Th 9:30am-12:30am, F 9:30am-2am, Sa 10:30am-1:30am. AmEx/DC/MC/V.

R. Restaurant and Café, Lastarría 307, Santiago Centro (☎664 9844). M: U. Católica. Located in Plaza Mulato Gil, this refuge is great for coffee and dessert. Espresso drinks CH$620-1100. Excellent cheesecake CH$2320. Dinner pastas from CH$5000. Cafe open M-Th 11:30am-midnight, F-Sa 11:30am-2am. Restaurant open M-Th 12:30-4pm and 7:30pm-midnight. AmEx/DC/MC/V.

Café de la Isla, Irarrázaval 3465, Ñuñoa (☎341 5389). This cafe has its own garden, which stocks the 100% organic kitchen and fills meals like goat cheese brochettes (CH$8200). Some eat in the formal dining area out back, while drinks in the smaller cafe are a much cheaper option. Excellent fruit shakes CH$1300, piña colada CH$2700. Open M-Th 10am-1:30am, F 10am-3am, Sa 7am-3am. AmEx/DC/MC/V.

◎ SIGHTS

▨**CERRO SANTA LUCÍA.** Santiago spent over 300 years trying to solve an unusual municipal problem: what can you do with a pile of rock and dirt in the middle of the capital city? In 1872, Santiago's mayor, **Benjamin Vicuña Mackenna,** took action, and transformed the immovable eyesore into a public park whose winding paths lead to hidden turrets, plazas, and fountains, with a view of the Andes that grows more impressive as you ascend. The lack of guard railings makes the Cerro difficult for children or the elderly. *(☎664 4216. M: Santa Lucía. Open daily Jan.-Feb. 9am-8pm; Mar.-Dec. 9am-6pm; 2hr. tours Th 11am. Sign-in required. Free.)*

▨**PARQUE METROPOLITANO DE SANTIAGO/CERRO SAN CRISTÓBAL.** A lush escape from urban life, this park offers over 7 sq. km of sharp hills and breathtaking views of Santiago below. When weather permits, especially after rain, you can also catch spectacular views of the Andes in the background. The main entrance to the park at the end of **Pío Nono** (in Barrio Bellavista) houses the base of a **funicular** (cable railway) that lurches up an almost vertical track to the top of **Cerro San Cristóbal.** From there you can soar over the park in a **teleférico** (cable car) to **public swimming pools** and botanical **gardens.** If you get hungry, the park has lots of choices, big and small—but make sure not to feed the animals in the **zoo.** *(☎730 1300 or 730 1386; www.parquemet.cl. Pío Nono entrance open daily 8am-10pm. Funicular open M-Sa 10am-8pm, Su 10am-5pm. Round-trip CH$1200, children 3-13 CH$700. Cable car open M-F 2:30-6:30pm, Sa-Su 10:30am-7:30pm. Zoo open Tu-Su 10am-7pm. CH$2000/$700, seniors CH$1300. Combined funicular, cable car, and zoo CH$4300/CH$1900. Taxi to the top CH$500 per person. Pools open Nov.-Mar. 10am-7pm. Free yoga at the Botanical Gardens Su at 10am. Free concerts in the cultural house Su noon.)*

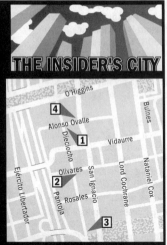

THE INSIDER'S CITY

MANSIONS OF SANTIAGO

While the department stores and neon signs of Santiago Centro make the city seem like a recent construction, the area southwest of Alameda features European-style mansions that bring the stately glory of Santiago past into concert with the bustling present. From M: Los Héroes, walk east toward the city center and turn right onto Dieciocho. You won't be able to miss these grand dames.

1 Dieciocho 102: **Residencia Eguiguren** (1906) has curli-cued balconies that reflect a strong French influence.

2 Dieciocho 190: The Neogothic **Subercaseaux Mansion,** built in 1913 with money from the family's successful vineyard, Concha y Toro.

3 At the end of Dieciocho, enjoy the intricate facades of **Palacio Cousiño (1878),** the only mansion open to the public.

4 **Iglesia San Ignacio's** pink Neoclassical Italian exterior makes it quite a contrast Santiago's many other cathedrals.

PLAZA DE ARMAS. This traditional center of Santiago's municipal life is still a core of urban vitality. Especially on weekdays during the 6-7pm rush hour, *Santiaguinos* and tourists alike flood the square. Street performers, artists, vigorous chess players, and the beautiful landscaping and architecture of the Plaza are sure to hold your attention. If not, then one of the many amorous couples nearby might. *(M: Plaza de Armas. Bounded by Monjitas, Paseo de la Puente, Merced, and Paseo Estado.)*

PALACIO COUSIÑO. The ornate and stately decor of this gorgeous colonial mansion is a prime example of the European influence that permeates Santiago. In the warm, yellow light that filters through the paned glass of the Winter Patio, you can practically see the original inhabitants at *onces*. *(Dieciocho 438. ☎698 5063. M: Toesca. Required tours in Spanish or English last about 40min. Open Tu-F 9:30am-1:30pm and 2:30-5pm, Sa-Su 9:30am-1:30pm. CH$1500, children CH$500.)*

CATEDRAL DE SANTIAGO. Just steps from the bustle of the Plaza and the stand-up comedian telling dirty jokes out front, the Catedral seems shockingly out of place. Inside, dimly lit statues of saints line the ceiling, giving the church an ethereal air. As you wander through, you'll find countless hidden nooks, pieces of art, and historical relics. You'll also come across more modern additions—discarded lottery tickets and pictures of loved ones—that are almost as haunting. *(At the corner of Calle Monjitas and 21 de Mayo. M: Plaza de Armas. Open daily 10am-7pm. Mass offered M-Sa 11am, 12:30, and 7pm; Su 10, 11am, noon, and 7pm. Confessions M-F 10:30am-1pm and 5-7pm, Sa-Su 10am-1pm.)*

PALACIO DE LA MONEDA. Located north of Alameda at the corner of Teatinos and Moneda, this just might be the most impressive building in Santiago. The host of alert, sharply dressed *carabineros* probably doesn't hurt. Free tours on the last Sunday of every month take visitors to the inner plaza and wishing fountain to get a real insider's perspective on Chilean history and government. The crisp precision of the changing of the guard is equally impressive. *(M: La Moneda. Courtyard open daily 10am-6pm. Changing of the guard every 48hr. at 10am.)*

PARQUE QUINTA NORMAL. This lush 16-acre park is an urban oasis in Santiago Centro. Popular among Santiaguinos, it's perfect for bike rides, strolls, picnics, and summer boating on the pond. Those seeking more intellectual stimulation can find it at the various **museums** (see below) nearby. *(4 blocks north of M: Estación Central at Matucana 502. Open daily Nov.-Mar. 8am-7pm; Apr.-Oct. Tu-Su 8am-8:30pm. Free.)*

IGLESIA DE SAN FRANCISCO. Here, in the oldest building in Santiago, the exposed rock walls and rusty medieval candelabras call to mind the older days and forgotten stories of Santiago. With visual references to those who were crucified in the 19th century, the atmosphere is decidedly eerie. It gets even creepier if you move up close to the walls, where *Santiaguinos* have left dozens of golden plates and handmade labels with messages such as "Thank you for fixing my daughter's knee." There's also a glass display that looks like a carnival fortune teller but holds a graphic model of a bloodied *Jesus de la Caña. (Bernardo O'Higgins 834, Londres 4. ☎ 639 8737. M: U. de Chile. Mass Tu-Sa every 2 hr. 8am-noon and 7:30pm, Su every hr. 9am-1pm and 7:30pm. Confession Tu-Sa 10am-2pm and 6pm-8pm. Free.)*

🏛 MUSEUMS

As the capital of a nation that has long been home to diverse cultures, Santiago is home to a variety of especially rich museums. In its art galleries and historical centers, the contributions of the Mapuche, the Rapa Nui, and the Spanish *conquistadores* all coexist, fusing into the dynamic works of modern Chileans. Major museums are scattered throughout the city, making a day of full exploration more like a public transportation scavenger hunt. Many of the museums are small, and require less of a time investment than you might anticipate. **Sernatur** (see **Tourist Office**, p. 102) provides a complete listing of museums in central Santiago.

MUSEO NACIONAL DE BELLAS ARTES/MUSEO DE ARTE CONTEMPORÁNEO. The gorgeous Neoclassical monument on the edge of Parque Forestal houses both the Museo Nacional de Bellas Artes and the Museo de Arte Contemporáneo (MAC), making it the home of the largest concentration of collected art in Chile. The Museo de Bellas Artes displays both classic and contemporary artwork by Chilean and international artists. There's also a cafe serving coffee (CH$800) and sandwiches (CH$900-1200), whose smells will distract you as you wander. The MAC sits in the shadow of its more formidable twin, and carries a range of pieces mostly by Latin artists. *(M: Bellas Artes, Parque Forestal. Bellas Artes: ☎ 639 1946; www.mnba.cl. Open in summer Tu-Su 11am-8pm, in winter Tu-Su 10am-6:50pm. Free tours Sa-Su 12:30 and 4:30pm. CH$600; students, children, and seniors CH$300. MAC: ☎ 639 5486 or 639 1675; www.mac.uchile.cl. Open Tu-Sa 11am-7pm, Su 11am-4pm. CH$300, students CH$200.)*

MUSEO LA CHASCONA. While this museum's name refers to the unruly hair of Pablo Neruda's widow, it could just as easily refer to the eccentric and sprawling design of the famed poet's house. La Chascona is one of three Neruda houses that have been turned into museums (see **La Sebastiana**, p. 248, and **Isla Negra**, p. 260). The blue exterior reflects Neruda's obsession with the sea, while the design motifs of the two main buildings represent a ship and a lighthouse. Pre-Columbian pottery, Russian dolls, and wooden African statues reflect his diplomatic and personal world travel. *(Fernando Márquez de la Plata 0192, Barrio Bellavista. ☎ 777 8741. Open Tu-Su 10am-6pm. Required tours in English CH$3000, in Spanish CH$2000, students and seniors CH$900.)*

MUSEO DE ARTE PRECOLOMBINO. This museum is truly unique, not just in Chile, for its focus on indigenous artwork. The size and variety of the collection pays homage to the cultural contributions of Latin America's first inhabitants, including a large wooden statue crafted by the Mapuche people to commemorate their dead. *(Bandera 361, 1 block west of the southwest corner of the Plaza de Armas. ☎ 688 7348; www.precolombino.cl. Open Tu-Su 10am-6pm. Free guided tours available but require a call ahead for reservation. CH$2000, students and children free.)*

MUSEO DE SANTIAGO/CASA COLORADA. From Santiago's beginnings as a colonial outpost to the construction of the Puente Cal y Canto, this museum outlines the city's history until the 19th century. You'll be wishing it went further after exploring fascinating exhibits on the development of the tram and the building of Cerro Santa Lucía. The Casa Colorada, which houses the museum, a library, and a municipal tourist office, is a historical site of its own. The home of Chile's first president and the location of the first government *junta* of 1810-11, it remains beautifully preserved. All signs are in Spanish. *(Merced 860, just east of the southeast corner of the Plaza de Armas. ☎ 633 0723; www.munistgo.cl/colorada. Open Tu-F 10am-6pm, Sa 10am-5pm, Su 11am-2pm. CH$500, students and seniors CH$300, children CH$200, Su free.)*

MUSEO HISTÓRICO NACIONAL. The chronological layout of this museum makes it a good crash course in early Chilean history—at least for those who understand enough Spanish to read the extensive placards. While artifacts like Mapuche weapons and Spanish religious paintings are amazingly well-preserved, eyeless mannequins dressed as "a typical woman" or "a child in the colonial era" are somewhat laughable. In the end, the museum might not impress less-than-diehard historians. *(Plaza de Armas 951, on the north side of the plaza near the post center. M: Plaza de Armas. ☎ 633 0462 or 638 1411; www.museohistoriconacional.cl. Open Tu-Su 10am-5:30pm. CH$600, children 8-12 and students CH$300, seniors and children under 8 free. Su free.)*

MUSEO DE ARTES VISUALES. Since 2001, this museum has been home to six floors of post-1960s modern Chilean art, including a mural by Roberto Matta that is typically huge and frenetic. The self-proclaimed mission of the museum is to bring art to the traditionally disenfranchised. As such, they welcome tourists and children, and are fully handicapped-accessible. *(Lastarría 307, in Plaza Mulato Gil. From M: U. Católica, walk up Lastarría; the plaza is ahead on the right. ☎ 638 3502; www.mavi.cl. Open Tu-Su 11:30am-7:30pm. CH$1000, students CH$500; free Tu after 3:30pm and all day Su.)*

MUSEO COLONIAL. Its billing as a museum of ecclesiastical art might not seem appealing to all travelers, but mixed in are weird and wonderful pieces that constantly surprise the wandering visitor. **Gabriela Mistral's** Nobel Prize medal resides next to a room filled floor to ceiling with rusty old locks and keys. Next door, hidden inside a window nook, is a collection of 18th-century scourges with blood still visible on the tips. *(Alameda 834. ☎ 639 8737. M: U. de Chile. Open Tu-Sa 10am-1:30pm and 3-6pm, Su 10am-2pm. CH$1000, children and students with ID CH$300.)*

MUSEO DE LA SOLIDARIDAD, SALVADOR ALLENDE. Built in 1971, this museum showcases pieces of contemporary art donated by international artists who expressed solidarity with President Allende and later supported Chile's return to democracy. Despite this background, the pieces are only occasionally political in nature. Of the seven rooms around the peaceful courtyard, the "Finnish room" and "Spanish room" are the most impressive. *(Herrera 360A. From Estación Central, walk 6 blocks north to Compañía, then 2 blocks east. ☎ 681 7542 or 681 4954. www.mssa.cl. Open Tu-Su 10am-7pm. CH$500, students CH$250. Guides available with 4 days advance registration.)*

USACH PLANETARIUM. Even though smog and city lights often blur Santiago's night sky, you can still do your star-gazing within its confines. Usach offers shows Fridays at 7pm and Saturdays and Sundays at 11am, noon, 3:30, and 5pm. *(Alameda 3349. From M: Estación Central look for its orange dome to the left along Alameda. ☎ 778 1325; www.planetariochile.cl. CH$2000; children, students, and seniors CH$1300.)*

PARQUE QUINTA NORMAL MUSEUMS. Parque Quinta Normal, Matucana 502, near M: Estación Central, is home to a cluster of small museums. Taken as a group, they could make for a fun afternoon. The **Museo Nacional de Historia Natural** is the most famous of the Quinta Normal museums. Founded in 1830, it is one of the oldest museums in Latin America. Its skeletons and taxidermy are standard, but the copper exhibit, run by the copper industry's public relations branch, is amusing. Seemingly designed to transform children into copper-loving fanatics, it's an testament to the power of propaganda. *(☎ 681 4095; www.mnhn.cl. Open Tu-Sa*

10am-6pm; Su 10am-6pm, low season noon-6pm. CH$600, students and seniors CH$300. Su free.) The **Museo de Ciencia y Tecnología** has interactive astronomy, geology, and multimedia exhibits that are a big hit with kids and antsy adults. *(☎681 8808. Open Tu-F 10am-5:15pm, Sa-Su 11am-5:15pm. Adults CH$800, students and children CH$600.)* Another favorite across generations is the **Museo Ferroviario,** whose exhibits showcase over a dozen steam engines and carts. *(☎681 4627. Open Tu-F 10am-5:30pm, Sa-Su 11am-5:30pm. Adults CH$650, children and students CH$300.)* At **Museo Artequín,** home to reproductions of masterworks like those of Van Gogh, you might catch yourself wondering if an afternoon with an art book would be just as beneficial. The real attraction is the cast-iron building, which was Santiago's contribution to the 1889 Parisian Centenary Fair. *(☎681 6022. Open Tu-Su 10am-5pm. CH$800, students and children CH$300).*

SMALLER MUSEUMS. Museo Ralli rewards the public transportation pilgrimage with a collection of Latin American and European contemporary art that is perhaps the most impressive in Santiago. Featured artists include Dalí, Chagall, Miró, and Matta. *(Alonso de Sotomayor 4110. ☎206 4224. From M: Los Leones, take any bus headed up Av. Vitacura, get off right after Alonso de Córdova, and go 3 blocks north on Candelaria Goyenechea to its intersection with Alonso de Sotomayor. Open May-Sept. Tu-Su 10:30am-4pm; Oct.-Apr. Tu-Su 11am-5pm. Free.)* Mummy lovers should check out **Museo Arqueológico de Santiago,** home to once-buried artifacts and anthropological exhibits. Its small size might not merit an individual visit, so stop by on your way out of the Museo de Artes Visuales. *(Lastarría 321, 2nd. fl., next to Museo de Artes Visuales. ☎638 3975. Open M-F 10am-2pm and 3:30-6:30pm, Sa 10am-2pm. Free.)* Children's museum junkies will want to make the trek all the way to La Florida for the ultra-modern **Museo Interactivo Mirador (MIM),** a huge chunk of geometrically sculpted cement on an expansive esplanade. It's typical of the genre, with brightly colored, interactive exhibits and games that are a welcome counterpart to the austere and instructive exhibits of other museums. *(Sebastopol 90. From M: Mirador, follow Mirador Azul 3 blocks west to Punta Arenas, go left, then immediately right onto Sebastopol and follow the signs into the park. ☎294 3955; www.mim.cl. Open daily 10am-7pm, low season 9:30am-5:30pm. CH$3000; students, seniors, and children 4-12 CH$2000; children under 4 free.)*

⛷ SKIING

Only 90 minutes up an extremely curvy road from Las Condes, the ski resorts of **Valle Nevado, El Colorado/Farellones,** and **La Parva** beckon from Santiago's horizon. In the winter, snow collects in thick layers, pleasing ski bums and daytrippers alike. During the summer months, these stark ski villages draw mountain bikers and trekkers with their convenient access to the high Andes peaks. During the ski season, **SkiTotal,** Apoquindo 4900, local 39-42 (☎246 0156; www.skitotal.cl), three blocks east of M: Escuela Militar, offers equipment rental and transport to any of the ski resorts. (Buses depart from the Las Condes office and Mall Parque Arauco daily 8:30am; depart ski areas 5:30pm. Skis, boots, and pole rental CH$13,000 per day. Transport US$13.) **KL Adventure,** Av. Las Condes 12207 (☎217 9101; www.kladventure.com), offers similar services on a more limited scale. To get there, take *micros* #229, 637, or others going up Av. Las Condes to Cantagallo; the office is across from IMAC. (Leaves daily 8:30am, returns 5:30pm. Complete rentals US$18. Transport US$10.) **Ski Van,** Nicholas Gogol 1483, Vitacura (☎219 2635 or 218 6914), also runs vans (CH$6000). For avid skiers, a **combined lift ticket** is available from any of the resort sites, as trails and lifts can be linked. Inquire at the ticket office.

VALLE NEVADO. Valle Nevado is primarily acclaimed by beginning and intermediate skiers due to its emphasis on easier terrain, but Heli-Ski capacity keeps experts just as happy. Facilities are top-notch. Lodging is quite expensive during the peak season, but the best bet if you're desperate is **Hotel Tres Puntas ❾**. (July 2-July 15 and July 30-Aug. 26 singles US$274; doubles US$400; June 18-July 1 and Aug. 27-Oct. 10 singles US$128; doubles US$200; includes meals, lift tickets, access to amenities.) In summer, lifts carry hang-gliders up to their point of departure, and mountaineers can use the resort as a staging ground of their own. *(55km up the road from Lo Barneachea. ☎ 206 0027 or 477 7700; www.vallenevado.com. 12 lifts service 35 trails totaling 24 mi.: 15% beginner, 40% intermediate, 35% advanced, 10% expert. Over 23,000 skiable acres. Elev. 2860-3670m. Rentals available. Tickets July and Sa-Su CH$20,000, children CH$12,000; June and Aug.-Sept. M-F CH$15,000/ CH$9500.)*

EL COLORADO/FARELLONES. These resort towns offer visitors two separate base towns, but the lifts and trails are all interconnected and inseparable. *(39km up the valley road. ☎ 246 3344; www.elcolorado.cl. 18 lifts service 20 trails totaling 23½ mi. 2471 skiable acres. Elev. 2430-3333m. Open June 15-Oct. 12. Rentals available. Tickets in July and Sa-Su CH$20,000, children CH$12,000; June and Aug.-Sept. M-F CH$15,000/ CH$10,000.)*

LA PARVA. Higher than El Colorado and generally considered to be better for experts, La Parva offers Heli-Ski as well as an efficient ski school. Summer brings great trekking opportunities. *(40km up the valley road. ☎ 264 1466; www.laparva.cl. 14 lifts service 30 trails totaling 23½ mi.: 10% beginner, 45% intermediate, 30% advanced, 15% expert. 1730 skiable acres. Elev. 2670-3630m. Rentals available. Tickets in July and Sa-Su CH$20,000, children CH$15,000; June and Aug.-Sept. M-F CH$16,000/CH$12,000. Joint ticket with Valle Nevado CH$26,000/CH$22,000, children CH$16,500/CH$13,500.)*

PORTILLO. A bit farther from the city of Santiago, northeast past the city of Los Andes (p. 267), Portillo gets the most attention abroad for its fabulously isolated location and dry snow. Only 450 skiers are issued lift tickets each day, and daytrippers are frequently excluded during peak season. Coupled with its distance from any major city, this might make you want to consider staying. Most of the lodging is beyond deluxe, but they do offer two very affordable annexes, the **Octagon Lodge** and the **Inca Lodge.** Geared more toward backpackers, the dorm rooms with shared bath are quite a deal, running about US$420 per week, including lift tickets and lessons. Week-long stays are really pushed, though you can officially stay shorter periods. *(159km from Santiago. ☎ 361 7000 or 263 0606; www.skiportillo.com. 12 lifts serve 15 trails of varied terrain: 18% beginner, 25% intermediate, 35% advanced, 22% expert. Open June 12-Oct. 9. Tickets CH$17,000, children CH$12,500.)*

🎵 ENTERTAINMENT

SPORTS

FÚTBOL. Seeing dazed *Santiaguinos* stand in frozen packs all over town, you might think that a strange epidemic has hit. More likely, there's a TV somewhere nearby and they're transfixed by Chile's national pastime: soccer. Natives call it *fútbol* with a loving lilt, and follow the exploits of the capital's three most popular clubs—**Colo Colo,** Cienfuegos 41, Barrio Brasil (☎ 698 0806); **Universidad Católica,** Andrés Bello 2782, Las Condes (☎ 231 2777); and **Universidad de Chile,** Campos de Deportes 565, Ñuñoa (☎ 239 2793)—with the fervor of an anxious parent. The national team is just as popular, and you can gauge their success by parades of honking cars that flood the streets after each victorious game. *(Tournaments in the Estadio Nacional, Grecia 2001, Ñuñoa. ☎ 238 8102. Seats CH$3000-5000.)*

HORSE RACING. Hipódromo Chile, Av. Hipódromo Chile 1715, (☎270 9200; www.hipodromo.cl), hosts races Thursday and Saturday 2:30-10pm. *(Take an Independencia-Plaza Chacabuco bus from the Mapocho station or the #303 bus from Calle Bandera in town.)* **Club Hípico,** Blanco Encalada 2540 (☎693 9721), also has races on Sundays and Fridays 2:30-10pm. *(7 blocks south of M: Unión Latinoamericana on Unión Americana.)* If you prefer to watch from a screen, there are several tele-tracks throughout Centro and in Barrio Brasil that satiate betting appetites. **Telesport,** Av. Providencia 1214 and elsewhere, is a popular chain for off-track betting.

RODEO. Rodeo, the proclaimed "national" sport (some *fútbol* fans would debate this point), is especially popular in September, when the season coincides with other national festivities. The season continues into May, but the most important event, the **Campeonato Nacional de Rodeo,** takes place in Rancagua the last weekend in March (see p. 280). For more information, contact the Federación del Rodeo Chileno, Moneda 1040, Piso 13. (☎699 0115; www.caballoyrodeo.cl. CH$5000-40,000.)

PERFORMING ARTS

Bellavista has the highest concentration of theaters in the city, many offering avant-garde productions (Th-Su, CH$4000-8000). While most theaters tend to be pricier on weekends, they offer student discounts on Thursday and Sunday.

Teatro Municipal, Agustinas 794 (☎463 8800, www.municipal.cl), is Chile's official artistic center and features concerts, ballets, and operas by prestigious national and international groups with prices CH$500-77,000.

Teatro Universidad de Chile, Providencia 043 (☎634 5295). M: Baquedano. Houses the national Chilean ballet company and hosts world-renowned Latin American musicians for weekly concerts. Shows from CH$1000.

Teatro Universidad Católica, Jorge Washington 26, Ñuñoa (☎205 5652), is a center of artistic life far from Alameda. Shows Th-Su. CH$7000; students, seniors, and children CH$4000. Su 2-for-1. Ticket office open 11am-8pm show days.

CINEMA

Hollywood films, rivaled by an excellent collection of independent films, come to Santiago soon after their US release. Most are in their original language with Spanish subtitles. (Tickets CH$1600-2800; nearly all theaters give student discounts.) Check the entertainment center of *El Mercurio* and other papers for showtimes.

SANTIAGO CENTRO

Cinema Hoyts, at Huérfanos 735 (☎664 1861). M: U. de Chile. Shows mainstream US, art house, and Chilean flicks on 6 screens. CH$2600-2800. For more options, check out their other location with 9 screens at San Antonio 144 (☎632 9566).

Centro de Extensión Universidad Católica, Alameda 390 (☎686 6516). M: U. Católica. Offers country- and director-specific film showings in conjunction with local embassies. Call ahead for schedules. Tickets from CH$2000.

Cine Arte Alameda, Bernardo O'Higgins 139 (☎664 8890). M: U. Católica. Features international art house films and old films. The foyer is full of flyers advertising artistic events in the city and rotating art exhibits adorn the walls. There's also a cafe. Screenings 1-9:30pm. Adults CH$2500, students and seniors CH$1900. W all shows CH$1500. Those who have *multivía* Metro cards can see two shows M-F for CH$2500.

PROVIDENCIA AND LAS CONDES

Both **Mall Parque Arauco** and **Mall Alto Las Condes** provide those in search of films modern, multi-screen cinemas. See **Shopping,** below, for details.

CULTURAL INSTITUTES

Santiago's cultural institutes offer the Chilean artistic and creative community a number of smaller venues for exhibiting and performing their work. Activities include plays, workshops, exhibitions, film screenings, readings, and more. The largest and most significant institutes are the old train station, **Centro Cultural Estación Mapocho** (☎787 0000; M: Cal y Canto), and **Plaza Central Centro de Extensión Universidad Católica,** Alameda 390 (☎686 6518 or 222 0275; M: U. Católica). Smaller ones include **Biblioteca Nacional,** Alameda 651 (☎633 8957; M: Santa Lucía), and the **Instituto Cultural del BancoEstado de Chile,** Alameda 123 (☎639 2624 or 639 7785; M: Baquedano). Feel free to stop by: the foyers are filled with flyers announcing various artistic performances throughout the city.

SHOPPING

Santiago has shopping of all varieties: pedestrian ways, gargantuan malls, and fun *ferias artesanales.* Window-shopping is a great way to walk off a gelato binge.

> **TIP**
>
> **SHOP 'TIL YOU DROP.** For some visitors to Chile, navigating the interior of a store might prove a more difficult task than traversing its streets. Buying is actually a two- or three-step process. First, order your item from a person behind a counter who will give you a receipt. Bring the receipt to a cashier, who will stamp it once you've paid. Exchange this for the item. In some food establishments, you order and pay at the cashier. It's best to watch patrons for a minute before starting to wait in what might be the wrong line.

MALLS AND COMMERCIAL GOODS

SANTIAGO CENTRO

◪ **Ahumada and Huérfanos.** These 2 streets, north of Alameda, have been pedestrian-only since 1977 and are filled with department stores and small malls called *galerías.* Street performers and piped-in Muzak versions of American light rock will keep you laughing.

Mall del Centro, Puente 689 (☎361 0011). M: Plaza de Armas. This mall is home to a blend of 85 boutiques and department stores, as well as a food court. There's a guard and information desk at the entrance. Open M-F 10am-9pm, Su 11am-9pm.

PROVIDENCIA

Av. Providencia and 11 de Septiembre. From their intersection with Pedro de Valdivia in the west to Tobalaba in the East, these streets each present great routes for the wandering shopper, with both small boutiques and larger shopping centers including **Mall Panorámico** (11 de Septiembre; open M-Sa 10am-9pm), and **Centro Comercial Dos Providencia,** Providencia 2237. (Open M-F 10am-1:15pm and 4pm-6pm.)

LAS CONDES

Mall Alto Las Condes, Kennedy 9001 (☎299 6965). Catch a bus along Alameda or take a cab from M: Escuela Militar. The biggest and most modern mall in Chile, with 245 shops and department stores, a 12-screen cinema, and many dining options. Open daily 11am-8pm.

Mall Parque Arauco, at the intersection of Kennedy and Américo Vespucio (☎299 0500; www.parquearauco.cl). M: Escuela Militar. A close second to Mall Alto Las Condes, with over 200 stores, a 14-screen cinema, restaurants, a food court, and art galleries. Open M-Sa 10am-9pm, Su 11am-9pm.

Mundo del Vino, Isidora Goyenechea 2931 (☎293 9955; www.elmundodelvino.cl). M: El Golf. This chain of stores has perhaps the largest selection of Chilean wines on the planet, as well as liquors, champagnes, and some international brands. Open M-Sa 10:30am-8:30pm, Su 10:30am-8pm.

LOCAL CRAFTS

Ferias artesanales (craft fairs) are ubiquitous in Santiago, but their amazing variety and low prices mean you'll enjoy each one you cross. They feature everything from lapis lazuli jewelry (CH$100-$500) to llama wool sweaters (CH$7500) to tarot readings (CH$1750). Well-endowed wooden figurines are a tourist favorite.

 SEE DEEP BLUE? The deep blue stones, lapis lazuli, are very rare, and Chile is one of the only nations in which they may be found. In the commercial hub of Santiago, *artesanía* stores and *ferias* are often brimming with jewelry and decor crafted from the stone. However, many merchants capitalize upon its popularity with unsuspecting tourists. Close replicas, painted darker blue to merit a higher price, are sometimes mixed in among the genuine items. For a quick check, use a tissue dipped in nail polish remover on the top of the stone. If your tissue turns blue, it's a fake.

In **Santiago Centro**, the **Feria Artesanal de Santo Domingo**, Santo Domingo 831, sells typical *feria* wares. (Open M-F 10am-8:30pm, Sa 10am-9pm.) For specifically indigenous fare of the Mapuche or Rapa Nui, the **Centro de Exposiciones Arte Indígena** on the Santa Lucía side of Cerro Santa Lucía offers very cheap but beautiful handicrafts. (Open M-Sa 10am-6pm. AmEx/MC.) For a more organized and sheltered craft-shopping atmosphere, try **Artesanías de Chile**, Lastarria 305, #107 (☎ 633 0081), in Plaza Mulato Gil, next to the Museo de Artes Visuales.

In **Providencia**, the *artesanía* experience is less pervasive, with many smaller shops scattered about the neighborhood. The specialty is lapis lazuli, with boutiques like **Artesanía en Lapis Lazuli**, Providencia 1998 (☎ 233 3469; open M-F 10am-8pm, Sa 10:30am-2:30pm), and **Rentsen y Sagrado Lapis Lazuli**, Ricardo Lyon 146 (☎ 234 2363; open M-F 10am-8pm, Sa 10am-2pm), selling this Chilean rarity.

Las Condes has fewer *artesanía* options, unless you consider a handmade Gucci purse folk art. One option is **Pueblito de los Domínicos**, Apoquindo 9085 (☎ 245 5142), next to the Cathedral of the Dominicans. The Pueblito features some quirky handicrafts that you might not see elsewhere, such as intricately carved matchsticks. To get to the Pueblito, take a bus marked "Apoquindo" from Alameda, or a cab from M: Estación Militar for about CH$5000. (Open Tu-Su 10:30am-7pm.)

Barrio Bellavista's Parque Gómez Rojas, at the corner of Pío Nono and Santa María, has a permanent, convenient *feria artesanal*. If you're looking for lapis lazuli in particular, try **Artesanía Chile en Lapis Lazuli**, Bellavista 0918, which has a wide and well-organized selection. (☎ 738 0275. Open M-F 10am-7pm, Sa 10am-3pm.)

⬛ NIGHTLIFE

If you're awake yourself, you'll find that very few places in the city open much before 10am. That's because the owners are probably sleeping in, for Santiago is home to a varied and vibrant nightlife that doesn't even start until midnight, and rages on to dawn.

 WHERE TO GO BUMP IN THE NIGHT. While all of Santiago's neighborhoods have their own specific character during the day, they are equally different by night. **Barrio Bellavista** is the notorious local favorite. Virtually deserted during the day, its streets and bars are packed at night. **Providencia** harbors a more upscale bar scene, and is also home to **Suecia**, which is more popular among tourists and expatriates. **Santiago Centro's** occasional options are strong stalwarts of area nightlife. **Las Condes** is generally littered with ritzy bars where businessmen and yuppies relax after a long week. **Ñuñoa** is really only a tourist destination because of its nighttime ambience. Bars and cafes are clustered tightly around the town plaza in a layout ideal for a pub crawl.

ON THE MENU

ABOVE AND BEYOND
PISCO SOURS

From taxi drivers to sidewalk vendors everyone will tell you that the *pisco* sour is the specialty drink of Santiago. A few bars in the city, however, have moved beyond the traditional lineup of *pisco* peers, inventing unique concoctions that are all their own.

The Earthquake (CH$950), at **El Hoyo,** San Vicente 375, Santiago Centro (☎689 0339), at the corner with Gorbea el Centro. M: Estación Central. This mix was devised by a patron who found the wine too warm. The consummate "girly drink," it's a chilled glass of wine with a layer of pineapple ice cream on top.

The Nagasaki Sour (CH$1800), at **Zen,** Dardignac 0175, Bellavista (☎737 9520). M: Baquedano. Tired of plain old *pisco*? Try the Nagasaki Sour, a Japanese variation on the traditional Chilean liqueur, served with an eye-watering splash of wasabi.

The Auracan Bitter (CH$1100), at **Bar Nacional,** Bandera 317, Santiago Centro (☎695 3368). M: U de Chile. Meant to ease the digestive strain of eating the restaurant's *completos* and *papas fritas*, this indigenous, 60-proof "herbal mix" will help ease your stress too.

BARS

Phone Box Pub, Providencia 1652, Providencia (235 9972). M: Pedro de Valdivia. Patrons enter the trellised patio of this rowdy pub through a phone box. Over 30 beers (from CH$1000) and 50 liquors (CH$1500) are ½-price during the absurdly long happy "hour" M-W 4pm-9pm and Th-Sa 4pm-10pm. Open M-Th 11am-1am, F-Sa noon-3am.

Bar Liguria, Providencia 1373, Providencia (☎235 7914). M: Pedro de Valdivia. While Suecia hosts the raging club-goers in Providencia, Bar Liguria is a more relaxed, but no less funky, place to grab a drink. Dinner is served as well (p. 114). *Pisco* CH$1200. Open M-W 10am-midnight, Th-Sa 10am-2am.

Flannery's Irish Geo Pub, Encomenderos 83, Las Condes. They say that everyone's Irish on St. Patrick's Day, and everyone's Irish at Flannery's, a raucous Irish pub where stout (CH$1450) and potatoes abound. For holdouts, some international dishes like fajitas (CH$4100) are offered. Open M-F noon-3am, Sa-Su 6pm-2am. AmEx/DC/MC/V.

Pub Blue, 19 de Abril 3526, Ñuñoa (☎223 7132). Compared to other themed nightspots in Santiago, the concept of this Ñuñoa bar seems laughable. Luckily, patrons and cheesy 80s music bring the ambience, and cheap, no-frills choices make up the difference. *Pisco* sours CH$1800. Happy hour M-Th 5-7pm, F-Sa 6-10pm. Open M-W 4pm-1am, Th 4pm-2am, F-Sa 6pm-3am. AmEx/DC/MC/V.

Bar Mojito, Santa Filomena 104, Barrio Bellavista (☎732 3805). Just off the main drag of Suecia, this spicy Cuban/Creole joint serves great cajun chicken salads (CH$3100) and jambalaya (CH$4520), but the focus is on the drinks, like *mojitos* (CH$1900). Open M-Th 6pm-2am, F-Sa 6pm-5am.

Pub La Bohême, Bombero Nuñez 336, Barrio Bellavista (☎737 4110). With walls covered in depictions of bodies and a young crowd, the atmosphere here exudes sex and all of the pretentions that it involves. Not crowded until late. *Pisco* sour CH$1300, margarita CH$3100, amaretto coffee CH$800. Min. drink order F-Su CH$6000. Techno weekends, softer stuff on weekdays. Open M-Sa 8:30pm-5am. AmEx/DC/MC/V.

Babble, General Holley 2337, Providencia (☎223 8433). The site of many bachelorette parties, Babble is "Where women rule." If the reserved parties leave room, passersby are let in to enjoy the festive atmosphere. Beers from CH$2000. Cover CH$3000, women free. Open Tu-Th 9pm-4am, F-Su 9pm-5am. AmEx/DC/MC/V.

Ebano, Jorge Washington 176, Ñuñoa. (☎453 4665). This "cocina soul" (soul kitchen) is technically a restaurant, and moderately sized dishes like sushi (CH$4000) and red wine risotto (CH$6500) don't disappoint. What's really emphasized, though, is the alcohol. Enjoying a drink to the sounds of 70s soul music in the intimate atmosphere is a veritable aphrodisiac. Wine CH$1500-2000. Half-price mixed drinks during happy hour M-Sa 7:30-9:30pm. Open M-Th 7pm-1am, F-Sa 7pm-3am. AmEx/DC/MC/V.

CLUBS AND DISCOS

 BEWARE THE BARE. Though nighttime dance spots are referred to as "nightclubs" in many other countries, be aware: in Chile, "clubs" and "nightclubs" refer to strip joints. Those wishing to dance should head to "Discotecas."

From the expected presence of Latin beats, to the sounds of pop, jazz, reggae, trance, and even Britpop, the clubs of Santiago offer something great for every traveler. Nightlife options are spread throughout the city, but the neighborhoods of Bellavista and Suecia are world-renowned flashpoints of activity. Bellavista has more character than sanitized Suecia, and consequently attracts more locals, but Suecia's dance floors are always packed, with a more international crowd. As a rule of thumb in Santiago, the cheaper the cover, the younger the crowd.

Infierno Discoteque, Suecia 019, Providencia (☎234 2320 or 242 8007). It would be nearly impossible to visit Santiago and miss this spot. The huge, decaying hand on its roof, with a green fingernail pointing down to the dungeon door, can be seen throughout Providencia. Failing that, any *Santiaguino* will tell you that this is the place to go (assuming that they're not insulting you, since the name means "hell" in Spanish). 3 floors host more than 1000 dancers and private parties in a VIP area. Drinks aren't too expensive—beer CH$1000, shots CH$1500. Cover F CH$2000 for men, CH$1000 for women; Sa CH$3000/CH$2000. Open F-Sa 10:30pm-5am, disco midnight-5am.

Blondie, Alameda 2879, Santiago Centro (☎681 7793; www.blondie.cl). If your hips start to hurt from all of the salsa and merengue played at Santiago's clubs, Blondie offers a welcome departure. This stalwart of the night scene plays Britpop, cyberpunk and new wave in 3 giant rooms spanning 4 floors. Theme nights feature the videography and discography of particular artists. Cover CH$3000. Open F-Sa midnight-5am.

Ilé Habana, Bucarest 95, Providencia (☎231 5711). The bright stucco walls, potted palms, and live beats lend Habana an authentic Cuban atmosphere. Its dance floor is generally packed, and gets so earlier than nearby locales. Mambo, cha-cha, and *bacheta* classes, as well as other cultural programs, are occasionally offered. Beer CH$1500-1900. *Pisco* CH$2300. Cuban drinks CH$3200. Cover F-Sa after 8pm CH$5000. Open M-F noon-4am, Sa-Su 7:30pm-5am.

Rockola, Antonia López de Bello 56, Barrio Bellavista (☎735 1167 or 777 0717). This location has been home to many different nightspots. Now, it's trying to make its mark as one of the only places in Santiago exclusively playing trance. Its stage occasionally hosts local alternative acts. Cover CH$4000. Open Th-Sa 10:30pm-5am.

Entre Negros, Suecia 0188, Providencia (☎334 2094 or 917 2427). Though this club's gimmick—African tribal art and blackface statues—borders on offensive, it's not too obvious within the club. Beyond that, Entre Negros offers a solid mix of varied tunes and drinks (beer CH$1000). Live music Th-Sa 10pm-midnight. Cover CH$3000 weekends only. Open Tu-Sa 8pm-5am. Disco midnight-5am.

Batuta, Jorge Washington 52, Ñuñoa (☎274 7096). Good live acts grace this nightlife standout in the Ñuñoa area. Acts vary from rock to funk and everything in between. There's also a small dance floor if the mood strikes. Cover CH$2000-4000. Open M and W 9pm-2am, Th-Sa 11pm-3am.

THE INSIDER'S CITY

ÑUÑOA AT NIGHT

Removed from the main axis of Santiago's cultural life, the area of Plaza Ñuñoa is an artistic oasis in a residential desert. The variety of establishments here lend themselves to a well-rounded evening. Thursday through Saturday nights are always the most vibrant.

1 Cruise on over to the **Teatro Universidad Católica** and catch a show before dinner.

2 Follow the curious keyboard into **La Tecla,** the perfect place for a light dinner of pizza or *panqueques* under a faux city skyline.

3 Enjoy the real outdoors with a stroll on Plaza Ñuñoa's paths to the **fountain,** a favorite among amorous couples.

4 Move along to the **Club de Jazz,** where live tunes will put you in the mood for...

5 A late-night snack at **El Amor Nunca Muere,** a French-style eatery whose unique, tasty crepes will send you off to bed delightfully stuffed.

Jammin' Club, Antonia López de Bello 49, Barrio Bellavista (☎777 9985). This laid-back bar is the granddaddy of Santiago's growing reggae scene. Incense, Bob Marley, and lots of red, yellow, and green make it a chill spot to escape the frenetic salsa beats of most other places. Cover CH$3000. Open Th-Sa 10:30pm-5am.

Club de Jazz, Alessandri 85, Ñuñoa (☎274 1937). This mansion features local and foreign jazz musicians. A nice escape from the rest of Santiago's salsa- and cover-heavy live music scene. Cover CH$3000, students CH$2500. Open Th-Sa 10:30pm-2am.

Maestra Vida (Salsateca), Pío Nono 380, Barrio Bellavista (☎777 5325, www.maestravida.cl). This raging salsa machine is the pinnacle of Pío Nono's salsa establishments. Classes offered Th-F 9pm, Su 7pm, CH$2000-2500. Cover CH$2500. Open Tu-W and Su 8pm-2:30am, Th 8pm-4am, F-Sa 9pm-4:30am. AmEx/DC/MC/V.

La Asociación Cristiana Feminina, Moneda 1640, Santiago Centro (☎696 1608), is far from a nightclub, but is a great place to forget your self-consciousness when it comes to salsa. M tango classes, Th salsa; samba, merengue, and cumbia rotate throughout the week. CH$1000 per session, CH$4000 per month. Open daily 5-11pm.

Havana Salsa, Domínica 142, Barrio Bellavista (☎737 1737 or 777 5829). Behind a faux storefront facade, gorgeous professional Cuban dancers gyrate to merengue, salsa, hip-hop, tango, flamenco, and more. After downing a few *cervezas,* try dancing yourself. CH$7500 includes buffet dinner before 11pm and 1 drink after. Show 11:30pm-1am. Cover after 11pm CH$5000. Open W-Sa 8:30pm-4am.

GAY AND LESBIAN FOOD AND NIGHTLIFE

Although Santiago still has a great deal of discrimination against homosexuals, the gay and lesbian community does have access to a vibrant nightlife, primarily in Barrio Bellavista. Establishments are usually unmarked and inconspicuous from the outside, but inside, they host some of the city's best parties.

Bunker, Bombero Nuñez 159, Barrio Bellavista (☎737 1716). The premier gay and lesbian club, and one of the best clubs in the city. Great house and techno, 3 bars, deck, catwalk, and plenty of cages. Black-lit specters on the walls and dismembered parts of ana-tomically-correct mannequins adorn the bars and walls. Sells its own CD mix. Pricey mixed drinks from CH$1700, beers CH$1200-1800. 2-for-1 before 1am. The only club with its own cabaret drag show (2:30am). Cover CH$6000. Open F-Sa 11:30pm-5am.

▨ **Capricho Español,** Purísima 65, Barrio Bellavista (☎777 7674). The name of this bar means "Spanish fling," and the atmosphere conveys the same feelings of intimacy and excitement. Small nooks abound, and there's a secret system of inter-table phones disguised as little angels. *Tapas* CH$3500. *Paella* CH$3800. Beef carpaccio CH$5500. Whiskey sour CH$2500. Open M-Th 8pm-2am, F-Su 8pm-3am. AmEx/DC/MC/V.

Fausto, Santa Maria 0832, Providencia (☎777 1041). The oldest gay nightspot in Chile, and still, some would argue, the best. Classic elegance is the norm here, where the dark wood walls are covered with mirrors and classic artwork, and one room houses a piano bar. Cover CH$3500. Open W-Su 11:30pm-late.

Farinelli Café, Bombero Nuñez 68, Barrio Bellavista (☎732 8966). A twist on the infamous *cafés con piernas,* with lots of *pierna.* Well-toned waiters flaunt tight shirts and thong underwear. Tea, coffee, and cakes CH$800-1200. Open daily 5pm-2am.

Máscara, Purísima 129, Barrio Bellavista (☎737 4123). This disco draws a lesbian crowd and is run mostly by women. Music from salsa to pop to techno. Internet, darts, and pool. Cover CH$4000 per couple. Open Th-Sa 8pm-2am.

▶ DAYTRIPS FROM SANTIAGO

WINE OF THE MAIPO VALLEY

With dozens of international awards to its credit, the Chilean wine industry is emerging as a world power in oenology. New hybrid blends and innovative techniques have followers looking toward the country's future in the field. Yet just as warranted is a look at its past. Wine is a centuries-old tradition throughout all of Chile. Its grapes, in fact, are the only pre-phylloxera vines remaining in the world—the only survivors of a 19th century beetle onslaught that forced European viticulturists to graft their grapes onto North American varieties. In any case, there is no better way to get a feel for the trajectory of Chilean wine than by touring one of its many vineyards. Particularly in the Maipo Valley region, the climate makes each vineyard a lush feast for the eyes. Tours celebrate the history of the industry, emphasizing family structures and *haciendas,* but quickly proceed to the technological centers, where anticipated achievements are stressed. At the visit's end, however, you will revel in the present, sampling a free taste of your hosts' wares.

VIÑA CONCHA Y TORO

To get to Viña Concha y Toro, take Metro Line 5 to Bellavista de la Florida. From there, take blue Metrobus #72, 73, 74, 80, or 85, which pass by the entrance to Concha y Toro (40min.; CH$260).

The scale of Concha y Toro's nationwide operation is no less than impressive. As the country's largest wine producer, Concha y Toro has vines covering 45.3 sq. km in 21 vineyards over 6 valleys of central Chile, producing grapes for 100,000,000L of finished product. Concha y Toro has won international recognition for its wines and proudly offers tours of its Maipo Valley vineyard to show how it's all done. Here, the gallery of guests, including Bono and Mick Jagger, is further proof of their superstar status. (☎821 7069 or 821 1063; www.conchaytoro.cl. Tours 45min. *English M-F 11:30am and 3pm, Sa 10am and noon; Spanish M-F 10:30am and 4pm, Sa 11am. US$6 per person. Reservations required at least 4 days in advance.)*

VIÑA SANTA CAROLINA

Take Metro Line 5 to Bellavista de la Florida and take a colectivo *to the Viña.*

SANTIAGO

Viña Santa Carolina is one of the oldest vineyards in Chile, dating back to 1875. Its original wine cellar is actually a national monument, as the only remaining representative of a once-popular construction material—*cal y canto*—egg whites and limestone. Tours of the estate and *bodegas* are not regularly scheduled, so call at least 24hr. ahead. *(Located on Rodrigo de Araya. ☎450 3000; www.vscwine.com.)*

VIÑA DE MARTINO
To get to Martino, take a bus from Terminal San Borja to Isla de Maipo (1hr.).

This boutique winery operates on a smaller scale than many others in the area, lavishing grapes with personal attention that directs the products more to the premium market. While Martino didn't open to the public until 2001, it has since directed the same attention to detail to their visitors, offering an in-depth multipart tour. *(Manuel Rodríguez 229. Call ☎819 2959 for hours and tour times.)*

VIÑA SANTA RITA
Take Metro Line 2 to Lo Ovalle, and then Metrobus #74 to the vineyard.

With helpful tours, a gourmet restaurant called La Casa de Doña Paula, and a substantial wine shop, the owners have made it easy for tourists to explore this historic winery, founded in 1880. *(☎800 367 482, tour reservations 362 2594; www.santarita.com. 45min. bilingual tours Tu-F 10:30, 11:30am, 12:15, 3, 4pm, Sa-Su noon and 3:30pm; free tasting not included. **Restaurant ❺** open daily 1-4:30pm.)*

VIÑA UNDURRAGA
From Terminal San Borja, take Buses Melipilla to 6km from Malloco exit.

Undurraga is famous for being the first Chilean winery to export, in 1903, but more so for the little round bottles—*caramayolas*—in which the wine was and still is sold. *(Camino a Melipilla, Km34. ☎372 904 or 372 2850. Tours M-F at 10, 11am, 2, 3:30, 4:30pm. Undurraga's wine shop, La Sacristia, open M-F 9:30am-5:30pm.)*

CAJÓN DEL MAIPO
*To get to the Cajón del Maipo, take Metrobus #72 from M: Bellavista de la Florida to San José del Maipo. Going up the canyon beyond San José, the more convenient blue-and-white **Buses Cajón del Maipo** (☎850 5769) leave from just to the right of the M: Parque O'Higgins exit on Matta. From there, buses leave to: Baños Morales (2hr., daily Jan.-Mar. and Oct.-Nov. 7:15am; CH$2000); San Alfonso (1½hr., every 30min. 7am-10pm, CH$1500); San José (1hr., every 10min. 7am-10pm, CH$1200). Colectivos (CH$350) also run from San José up to San Alfonso, and on to San Gabriel if weather allows.*

Squeezed down between lumbering mountain ranges, the Cajón del Maipo was originally developed as a housing area for nearby mine workers. Today, it's a retreat from the pressures of the working life, just about 25km from Santiago. The scenery is postcard-perfect, the fragrant air is smog-free, and there are a host of outdoor activities by which to enjoy them. Its capital is the southernmost San José de Maipo, from which the Camino al Volcán winds up through the peaks to the towns of San Alfonso and tiny San Gabriel. Transportation slows as you move along on dirt roads to El Volcán, a small bridge to the hot springs of Baños Morales, and finally a path to the popular **Parque Nacional El Morado.**

The municipal capital of the Cajón, **San José,** is an essential stopover for travelers to the region. It's home to the last tourist office, supermarket, gas station, and ATM for miles. **Sernatur,** Comercio 1900-788, has friendly staff and a free (if cartoony) map of the area. (☎861 1275; www.sernatur.cl. Open M-Th 8:30am-5:30pm, F 8:30am-4:30pm, Sa-Su 9am-6pm.) Find the **Redbanc ATM** attached to the right side of the supermarket on the corner of 2 Sur. **Abasto Super,** Comercio 19909, is a good place to stock up on essentials for your trip. (☎861 1032; info@abastosuper.cl. Open M-Sa 8am-2pm and 4-10pm, Su 9am-2pm. AmEx/DC/MC/V.)

There's not much else to hold a visitor's interest in San José. However, up the road in **San Alfonso** is some of the best outdoor activities you can find. There's whitewater rafting on the **Río Maipo,** horseback rides or trekking through the **Cascada de las Animas** Nature Sanctuary, and the beauty of its eponymous waterfall. Cajón tours from the city (see **Adventure Tours,** p. 103) regularly stop here, but renting a quaint cabin in one of the many complexes is the best way to immerse yourself in the area's beauty and discover it on your own schedule.

For dinner, check out **Café Nerudiano ❶,** Camino al Volcán 30466, a neighborhood hangout whose walls are covered with residents' artwork depicting the Cajón. It's a great place to enjoy *comida típica* like *churrasco* (CH$1800) or quesadillas (2 for CH$1500) while sipping a beer (CH$800) and soaking up the local flavor. (☎09 047 4127; cafenerudiano@hotmail.com. Open Th-F 7pm-11pm, Sa-Su 11am-11pm.) Staying in the Cajón is not cheap, but if you do plan to stay, check out **Cascada de las Animas ❹,** Camino al Volcán 31086, by far the best lodging in the Cajón, as you'll be spending most of your time here anyway. Rafting trips depart from here (CH$17,000), and cabins (CH$35,000-$80,000, sleeping 3-10), campsites (CH$20,000 for one person, CH$25,000 for two), and horseback tours of the nature sanctuary (CH$3000-10,000) are also available.

MAIPÚ

Located 10km southwest of Santiago Centro, this suburb is about 30min. away. The easiest transportation to Maipú is to take a micro from the Alameda at Teatinos, in front of the Palacio Moneda. Don't get on one marked only "Maipú," as several go to more residential areas of the town; look at the route listing on the windshield for one marked "Templo." You'll see the impossible-to-miss temple on your right after about 30min. Colectivos are also available at Armunátegui, for a slightly less bumpy ride to the suburb.

High above the treeline of this largely residential suburb, a concrete spire pierces the sky. Presiding over a wide, dusty plaza and encircled by a span of ominous concrete columns, the gargantuan structure almost looks like a UFO traffic control center, or an abandoned site of mass worship. In a way, the latter is true, for this futuristic building is the **Templo Votivo de Maipú,** a church designed in 1944 and operating to this day. The church is built on the site of an 1818 military rout of the Spanish Royalists. The commander-in-chief of the victorious liberating army, Bernardo O'Higgins, constructed a little temple in recognition of the event, and the outer walls of the **Basílica del Carmen** remain today, framing the alien descendant behind it. (Open daily 8:30am-7pm; Mass M 6:30pm, Tu-Sa noon and 6:30pm, Su 10am, noon, 6:30pm.) The empty and echoey interior of the Templo is much less distinctive than its facade, but plan to spend some time in the **Museo del Carmen de Maipú,** which is attached to its right side. This hidden treasure is full of amazingly well-preserved artifacts from the religious, military, and social life of early Chile. Pieces like huge engraved sabres, sparkling satin dresses, and mother-of-pearl hair combs are superior to artifacts you'll find in Santiago. The collection of over 20 giant horse-drawn carriages, in particular, is overwhelmingly opulent. If this doesn't interest you, however, kiosks line the sidewalk in front of the temple, selling snacks and economy packs of votive candles. (☎942 9669. Open Tu-F 9am-1pm and 3-6pm, Sa-Su 10am-1pm and 3-6pm. CH$500, students and children CH$250.)

POMAIRE

To get to Pomaire, take a bus from the Terminal San Borja. At Ticket Office 1 (Rut. 78 Santiago-Melipilla) or 3 (Buses Melipilla), ask for the loading spot of the bus to Melipilla. When you board the bus to purchase your ticket (CH$800), ask them to leave you at "la cruz," the cross of the main road and the path to Pomaire. Buses depart every 30min. When the driver lets you off, walk up the road a little to the first street on your right, where *you'll see a small bus stand. Wait here for a smaller, local bus that says "Pomaire" on the windshield. It will take you right into the town (CH$300). You can also take a less frequent colectivo for about CH$400.*

On the trip to Pomaire, a little town nestled up against verdant hills and mountains, you'll feel like you're moving not just through the countryside, but back through time itself. Horses, not *micros*, crowd the streets, and friendly residents wear ponchos and straw hats instead of suits. Despite its agricultural surroundings, Pomaire is geared toward tourists, with its one main street sporting a line of *artesanía* shops and *tienditas*. The crafts here are of a better quality than those you'll find in Santiago, and extremely cheap. The town's famous pottery, which they claim doesn't break in suitcases, can be purchased for CH$650-2000. The largest and most formal spot to grab a bite is **Los Naranjos ❶**, 44A Roberto Rodríguez, whose spacious roofed terraces host *cueca* shows for tour groups that call ahead. The fare is *comida típica*, with beer (CH$1000), a perfect accompaniment for huge *empanadas* (CH$2000) or *cazuela* (CH$1800). *Empanadas* are really the town's specialty, with nameless little places along the main drag selling ½ lb., oven-baked monsters that are of a completely different variety than the pockets you get in Santiago. (☎ 831 1791. Open daily 9am-9pm).

NORTE GRANDE

While Norte Grande, home to the world's driest desert, is often seen as nothing more than a stretch of *altiplano* (highland) desolation, this northernmost region of Chile is actually vibrantly alive. Home to an amazing variety of relaxing beaches, exciting *parques nacionales*, steamy geysers, and even steamier night-clubs, Norte Grande seems a microcosm of the best that Chile has to offer. Because Norte Grande is not as touristed as some of its neighboring regions to the south, it affords visitors the opportunity to experience the best of Chile in a less-crowded and more thrilling kind of way.

As the crossroads between Chile, Peru, and Bolivia, Norte Grande is also characterized by a unique history of enmeshed cultures. However, this cultural blend is not merely a thing of the past. The region's diverse prehistorical roots converge with the frenzied present every day on the streets of Norte Grande's cities. The ancient **Gigante de Atacama,** the world's largest geoglyph, towers high above the Panamerican Highway. Tourists cruise on over to **Socoroma,** a charming Aymaran farming village centered a around a traditional Andean bell tower, in shiny 4WD vehicles. The sound of clinking glasses in the swanky restaurants of **Arica** echoes in halls of traditional Chinchorro relics in the **Museo Arqueológico San Miguel de Azapa.** Hip beats from *discotecas* in **Iquique** and **Antofagasta** threaten to awaken the carefully preserved mummies in the museums of **San Pedro de Atacama.** And in the five-star hotels of Norte Grande's growing cities, visitors can expect to find all the comforts and amenities of 21st-century life, right down the road from natives in traditional costume celebrating ancient rites.

While Norte Grande is in the process of being brought out of its prehistoric shell, many of the region's major sights are indeed entrenched in a history that predates and will undoubtedly outlast the region's human inhabitants. And while at first glance, the primary natural wonders of the region seem to be nothing more than desert landscapes at the mercy of an arid climate, visitors who look closer will find that Norte Grande also possesses a richness of biodiversity characteristic of the more fertile valleys of Middle Chile. **Parque Nacional Lauca** exists as an elegant synopsis of Chilean wildlife: llamas, alpacas, and *vicuñas* scamper among soothing thermal baths while flamingos soar toward the peaks of mist-covered mountains. Endangered *tamarugo* trees stretch to mighty heights in the **Reserva Nacional Pampa del Tamarugal.** The earth explodes in a mystical fog at **El Tatio Geysers,** while legendary wine flows freely in **Pica,** allowing visitors to raise a glass to millennia of natural history as they take advantage of the primitive comforts of a lush oasis in the middle of the driest place on earth.

HIGHLIGHTS OF NORTE GRANDE

MOONWALK through the **Valle de la Luna,** near **San Pedro de Atacama** (p. 170).

GYRATE Greek-god-style in Pharos, one of the hottest nightclubs in **Iquique** (p. 152).

LANGUISH under date palms while enjoying the fine wines of **Pica** (p. 161).

GASP for air and at the breathtaking views at the world's highest lake, **Lago Chungará,** in **Parque Nacional Lauca** (p. 147).

COWER before the massive scale of the copper mine at **Chuquicamata** (p. 168).

HANG TEN on the wicked waves of **Playa Chinchorro** (p. 143) in **Arica.**

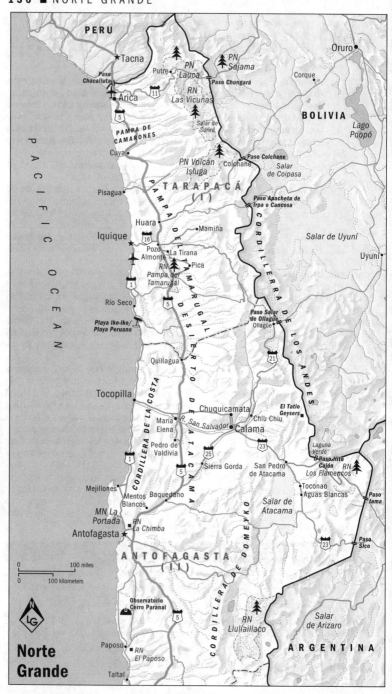

ARICA
☎58

Developed as a port for the inland mining industries under the Spanish settlers, the formerly Peruvian territory of Arica (pop. 215,000) became part of Chile only after an heroic battle on the massive Morro de Arica, a mountain that overlooks the city. Chile's victory in that battle, part of the War of the Pacific (1879-1884), is still celebrated annually during Semana Ariqueña in early June. Today, Arica's beaches offer some of the best waves in the country and draw tourists from all over Chile and Bolivia, while the town itself serves as a base for excursions into the hauntingly beautiful *altiplano* landscape of Parque Nacional Lauca, Reserva Nacional Las Vicuñas, and Monumento Natural Salar de Surire.

▐▀ TRANSPORTATION

As a transportation hub for travelers going to and from Peru and Bolivia, Arica has reliable international flights as well as bus connections to Tacna, Peru on the Panamerican, and to La Paz, Bolivia on Ruta 11. It is also a starting point for trips along Ruta 11 to *pre-cordillera* and *altiplano* desert destinations of Chile's far north, including Parque Nacional Lauca.

Flights: Aeropuerto Internacional Chacalluta (☎211 116), 20km north of Arica, near the Peruvian border. There is no shuttle bus, so use **Radio Taxi Aeropuerto** (☎291 000), which runs regular service to and from Arica (CH$6000; CH$2000 in a *colectivo*). **LanChile,** 21 de Mayo 439 (☎231 641, 251 641, or 252 725), is located between Colón and Baquedano and at the airport. Flies to: **Antofagasta** (2½hr., 7:25 and 11:55am, CH$45,000) via **Iquique** (30min., US$45); **La Paz, BOL** (30min., 11:45am, US$114); **Santiago** (4hr., 4 per day 8am-6:55pm, US$140) via **Iquique** (30min., US$45). Open M-F 10am-1:30pm and 5-9pm, Sa 10am-1pm. **Mar y Tour,** Colón 301 (☎232 913), sells **LanPeru** tickets. Call for flight times and price info.

Buses: There are two **bus terminals** in Arica—the **Terminal de Buses** and the **Terminal Internacional.** Most international buses to **Bolivia** and **Argentina** leave from the Terminal de Buses, while the Terminal Internacional is used mostly for buses and *colectivos* to **Peru.** There are many bus companies, all with their own schedules and fares. Differences in fares can be substantial, so it is worth shopping around. To get to **Tacna, PER,** it's better to go by *colectivo*, as it is faster and only slightly more expensive than by bus. It's also cheaper to buy tickets to destinations in Peru once in Tacna.

Terminal de Buses, Diego Portales 948 (☎241 390). The **information office** (open 7am-midnight) can help you find the best company for your destination.

Tur Bus (☎222 217 or 241 059; www.turbus.cl) goes to: **Calama** (8hr., 4 per day 12:30pm-10pm, CH$7000); **Iquique** (4hr., 9 per day 7:30am-9pm, CH$3000); **San Pedro de Atacama** (12hr., 10pm, CH$9000); **Santiago** (26hr., 7 per day 9:30am-11:15pm, CH$19,000) via **Antofagasta** (10hr., CH$8000), **Copiapó** (15hr., CH$14,500), and **La Serena** (23hr., CH$17,700).

Flota Barrios (☎223 587) sends buses to: **Calama** (8hr., 10:30pm, CH$6000); **Santiago** (28hr., 10:30 and 11pm, CH$15,000) via **Antofagasta** (10hr., CH$7000), **Copiapó** (16hr., CH$11,000), **La Serena** (24hr., CH$6000), and **Valparaíso** (28hr., CH$15,000).

Zesal goes to destinations in **Peru,** including: **Arequipa, PER** (8hr., 6 per day 7am-4:30pm, CH$10,000) via **Moquegua, PER** (6hr., CH$6000) and **Tacna, PER** (1-2hr., CH$2000); **Cuzco, PER** (18hr., 7am and 4:30pm, CH$18,000) via **Puno, PER** (13hr., CH$12,000); **Lima, PER** (20hr., 1pm, CH$13,000).

Pullman Cuevas Internacional (☎ 241 090) has daily departures to: **Chungará** (in **PN Lauca;** 5hr., CH$2500); **La Paz, BOL** (8hr., 9:30 and 2:30am, CH$7000) via **Socoroma** (3hr., CH$1500); **Putre** (3¾hr., CH$2000).

Terminal Internacional (☎ 261 092), next door to the Terminal de Buses. Numerous **colectivos** go to **Tacna, PER** (1-2hr., CH$1500-2000), including **San Remo** (☎ 260 509; CH$2000), which also goes to: **Arequipa, PER** (8hr., every hr. 8am-9:45pm, CH$10,000); **Cuzco, PER** (18hr., 11am, CH$19,000) via **Puno, PER** (13hr., 11am and 7pm, CH$10,000); **Lima, PER** (20hr., 4 per day 2:30-7pm, CH$21,000).

Local Buses: Public buses run 5:30am-11:30pm (CH$250).

Taxis: Try **RadioTaxi Estrellas del Norte** (☎ 266 000; available 24hr.) or **Pucarani Radio-Taxis** (☎ 255 907; available 24hr.) Taxis from downtown to town outskirts (beaches, *discotecas,* etc.) cost CH$1000-1500. *Colectivos* cost CH$300 per person before 8pm and CH$350 after 8pm to anywhere inside the city.

Car Rental: Budget, Comandante San Martín 599 (☎/fax 258 911; www.budget.cl), inside Hotel Arica and at the airport. Compact sedan CH$34,500. 4WD CH$77,000. Cheaper weekly rates. **Hertz,** Baquedano 999 and at the airport (☎ 231 487, at airport 219 186; www.hertz.cl), has similar rates. **Cactus Rent A Car,** Baquedano 635 (☎ 257 430; cactusrent@latinmail.com), at the corner of Maipú inside the shopping arcade, is a more economical alternative (CH$28,000-40,000).

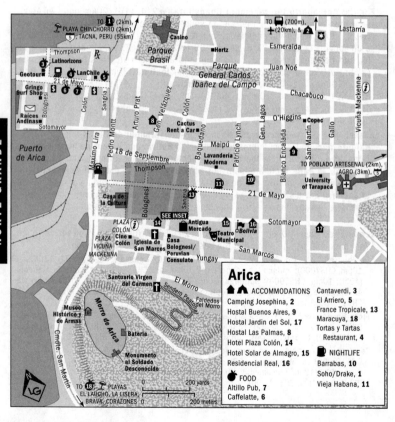

Arica

🏠 **ACCOMMODATIONS**
Camping Josephina, **2**
Hostal Buenos Aires, **9**
Hostal Jardin del Sol, **17**
Hostal Las Palmas, **8**
Hotel Plaza Colón, **14**
Hotel Solar de Almagro, **15**
Residencial Real, **16**

🍴 **FOOD**
Altillo Pub, **7**
Caffelatte, **6**

Cantaverdi, **3**
El Arriero, **5**
France Tropicale, **13**
Maracuya, **18**
Tortas y Tartas Restaurant, **4**

🎵 **NIGHTLIFE**
Barrabas, **10**
Soho/Drake, **1**
Vieja Habana, **11**

Bike Rental: Cactus Rent A Car (see above) also rents bicycles (CH$2000 per hr., CH$8000 per day). Open 8am-9pm.

◼ ⏻ ORIENTATION AND PRACTICAL INFORMATION

The main thoroughfare, **21 de Mayo**, runs east-west and forms a pedestrian mall between **Baquedano** and **Prat**. **El Morro de Arica**, a rocky mountain located some 100m from the beach on the town's southwestern corner, towers over the rough, rectangular grid of downtown Arica and its surrounding coastal desert landscape. The picturesque **Plaza Colón**, with palm-fringed lawns and the **Iglesia San Marcos**, sits close to the waterfront at the foot of El Morro. Beaches surround downtown Arica, with **Playas Chinchorro** and **Las Machas** to the north and **Playas Brava, Corazones, El Laucho**, and **La Lisera** to the south.

Tourist Offices: Sernatur (☎232 101; fax 254 506), on Prat near the corner with San Marcos, offers brochures on all of northern Chile. Open M-F 8:30am-5:30pm. The municipally-run **Dirección de Turismo**, Sotomayor 415 (☎206 245), between Baquedano and Colón, has English-speaking staff. Open M-F 8:30am-5:30pm. **Conaf,** Vicuña Mackenna 820 (☎250 207 or 250 570), on the corner with Chacabuco, provides information on weather, camping, hiking, and driving conditions in the national parks and reserves. Also makes reservations for stays in Conaf's *refugios* inside local parks. Register here if you plan on visiting a national park. Open M-F 8:30am-5:20pm.

Tours: There are common tours run by most agencies. The first is an **archaeological trip** around Arica and the **Lluta Valley** including a stop at **Museo Azapa**. The most common tour is the 1-day trip to **PN Lauca**, including stops at **Lago Chungará** and various **Andean villages** including **Socoroma** and **Putre**. Longer tours include 2- and 3-day jaunts to **PN Lauca** and **RN Las Vicuñas**, which reach the **Salar de Surire** before turning back to Arica along the same roads. The king of tours is the 4-day loop starting in Arica and meandering through **Museo Azapa**, the **Lluta Valley, Socoroma, Putre, PN Lauca, RN Las Vicuñas, PN Volcán Isluga, Humberstone**, and **El Gigante de Atacama** before ending in **Iquique** or returning to Arica. All tours to Lauca include at least 1 meal, and most carry emergency oxygen and serve coca tea, which is supposed to help with altitude acclimatization. There are many agencies in Arica, but the 3 listed below are known to be among the most reputable and well-established.

Raíces Andinas, Sotomayor 195 (☎233 305; www.raicesandinas.com), near Iglesia San Marcos, is run by a few veteran Arica tour operators that combine the best guides, service, local knowledge, and off-the-beaten-path trips in Arica. Each tour is all-inclusive, featuring meals, lodging, park fees, and wine with dinner. English-, French-, and German-speaking guides available. Raíces offers a 1-day tour to **PN Lauca** (CH$12,000), a 2-day tour of the **Lluta Valley** and **PN Lauca** (CH$47,000; min. 2 people), a 3-day tour to **Lluta Valley, PN Lauca,** and **RN Las Vicuñas,** including the **Salar de Surire** (CH$90,000), and a 4-day trip including **PN Volcán Isluga, Colchane,** and **Humberstone** (CH$130,000). Open daily 9am-10pm. AmEx/D/MC/V.

Latinorizons, Bolognesi 449 (☎/fax 250 007; www.latinorizons.com), on the pedestrian walkway off 21 de Mayo. This Belgian-owned tour operator has English- and French-speaking staff and offers a straightforward version of the standard area tours. Staff is very helpful in outlining exactly what each tour entails. Reputable company popular with foreigners. They offer a 1-day tour to **PN Lauca** (CH$12,000), 2-day tour to the **Lluta Valley** and **PN Lauca** (CH$50,000), 3-day tour to **PN Lauca** and **RN Las Vicuñas** (CH$90,000), and 4-day tour including **PN Volcán Isluga** (CH$145,000). Open 9am-10pm. AmEx/D/MC/V.

Geotour, Bolognesi 421 (☎253 927; www.geotour.cl), on the pedestrian walkway off 21 de Mayo. A reputable agency popular with Chileans and tourists. Offers a ½-day tour of **Arica,** the **Lluta Valley,** and **Museo Azapa** (CH$10,000) along with the other standard 1-, 2-, 3-, and 4-day tours. Prices vary depending on amount of people. AmEx/D/MC/V. Open daily 9am-10pm.

Global Tours, 21 de Mayo 260 (☎232 909), between Colón and Bolognesi, sells airplane tickets and package tours. Open M-F 9am-1:30pm and 4-8:30pm, Sa 10am-1pm.

THE LOCAL STORY

ARICA'S ENDLESS SUMMER

A few kilometers from Arica, die-hard surfers head out every afternoon for a few hours of consistent swells. The waves in Arica are biggest at the end of winter, when it's common to have 3-4m sets, so locals are out in force every July. But they never could have expected that in 2003, some of the world's best surfers would show up on the shores of Arica as part of the Billabong Odyssey, a challenge to find and surf the world's biggest waves.

On the morning of July 5th, a team of 16 filmmakers, writers, jet-ski drivers, and the world's best surfers swept into the city and headed straight for the ocean. They set a series of jet skis in the water, and, with the aid of the Chilean navy, journeyed past the shore waves to the massive 14m waves breaking on off-shore reefs. As modern surfing legends like Mike Parsons and Ken Bradshaw rode perfect tubes, crowds of local surfers gathered to watch surfing like Chile had never seen.

During the Billabong crew's second day in Arica, Chile's surf underground came out in force. Local TV crews, the Chilean surf magazine *Marejada*, tourist officials, the mayor of Arica, and dozens of young surfers took the day off to watch the pros in action. The Billabong crew returned the favor and showed a number of 10- to 14-year-old surfers tricks like riding to the back of a tube

Consulates: Bolivian Consulate, Patricio Lynch 292 (☎231 030). Open M-F 9am-2pm. **German Consulate,** Prat 391 (☎254 663 or 231 655). Open M-F 10am-noon. **Peruvian Consulate,** San Martín 235 (☎231 020). Open M-F 8:30am-1pm.

Currency Exchange and Banks: Atlas Citybank, 21 de Mayo 170 (☎231 720), between Prat and Bolognesi, also **exchanges currency.** Open M-F 9am-2pm and 4-6:30pm. There is a **24hr. ATM** on 21 de Mayo at **BancoEstado.**

Supermarkets: There are no major supermarkets in the downtown area, but there are smaller local markets on Patricio Lynch and Colón off of 21 de Mayo. A **Lider** (☎248 192), Diego Portales 2291, is next to the bus terminals on the outskirts of town.

Outdoor Equipment: Gringo Surf and Skate Shop, Bolognesi 440 (☎09 849 5524; gringosurf@hotmail.com), sells surf and skateboard equipment and rents surfboards (US$10 per day). Open daily 10am-10pm. **Din S.A.,** 21 de Mayo 451 (☎252 719), sells fishing gear and wet-suits. **CM Prat,** 21 de Mayo 161 (☎225 067), sells gear.

Laundromat: There are no coin-operated public laundries in Arica—you leave your laundry to be washed at a *lavandería.* Try **Lavandería La Moderna S.A.,** 18 de Septiembre 457 (☎232 006). Open M-Sa 10am-1:30pm and 5-9pm.

Police: ☎133. Local *carabineros* on Lastarria between Gallo and San Martín.

24hr. Pharmacy: There are many in town, especially on 21 de Mayo. **Farmacias Redfarma** (☎232 155), at the corner of Colón and 18 de Septiembre, is open 24hr.

Hospital: Ambulance ☎131. **Hospital Dr. Juan Noe,** 18 de Septiembre 1000 (☎229 200), east of downtown. Open 24hr.

Internet Access: Internet cafes abound, especially on and around 21 de Mayo. Try **Galera Internet,** 21 de Mayo 211 (☎251 388), inside the shopping arcade. CH$100 per 10min., CH$350 per hr. Open M-Sa 8:30am-12:30am, Su and holidays 10am-10pm.

Post Office: Prat 305 (☎231 326), next to Sernatur. Offers **Lista de Correos** and **Western Union.** Open M-F 8:30am-2pm and 3:30-6:30pm, Sa 9am-12:30pm. **DHL,** Colón 351 (☎256 753; www.dhl.com), between Sotomayor and 21 de Mayo, has courier service and functions as a **Western Union.** Open M-F 9am-6:30pm, Sa 10am-1pm.

ACCOMMODATIONS

Arica has some of the best budget options in northern Chile, with a number of hostels that feature private bath and cable TV for very low prices. There's no shortage of solid mid-range and high-range hotels, either, but they don't offer much more than their less expensive neighbors. Although camping is free on the beaches north of town, good campgrounds with swimming pools, BBQ, kitchen, and shower facilities are available in Villa Frontera north of town and in the Azapa Valley southeast of town. Prices go up during holiday seasons (Dec.-Feb., Easter, and mid-Sept.) but can be bargained down during the rest of the year.

Hostal Las Palmas, Velásquez 730 (☎255 753; laspalmas-lascondes@tie.cl), between Maipú and O'Higgins, is easily the best hostel in town. Painted brick walls flank spotlessly clean rooms with cable TV. Relax on the 3rd fl. terrace to enjoy a great harbor view. Laundry CH$1000 per kg. All rooms CH$4000 per person, with bath CH$6000. ❷

Hotel Plaza Colón, San Marcos 261 (☎/fax 231 244 or 254 424; www.hotelplazacolon.cl), across from Iglesia San Marcos. This pink building with blue balconies has comfortable rooms with bath, A/C, cable TV, and fridge. All rooms have views of El Morro and the ocean. The restaurant on the top floor has a harbor view. Breakfast included. Singles CH$21,000; doubles US$29,000; triples US$37,500. AmEx/D/MC/V. ❹

Residencial Real, Sotomayor 580 (☎253 359), between Lynch and Lagos. Look for the crown to find this clean, spacious, and very affordable hostel. Rooms have clashing bed covers but showers are hot and beds are big. Every room has cable TV. Locked front door provides extra security. Singles CH$3500; doubles CH$6000; triples CH$9000. ❶

Hostal Jardín del Sol, Sotomayor 848 (☎232 795; hostaljardindelsol@hotmail.com), between San Martín and Arturo Gallo. Set in tranquil surroundings with a plant-filled white common area and balcony. Features laundry facilities (CH$2000 per kg), a kitchen with microwave, and small concrete rooms with bath and ceiling fans. Indoor common area has satellite TV. Free Internet and bike rental. Breakfast included. CH$7000 per person. AmEx/D/MC/V. ❷

Hotel Solar de Almagro, Sotomayor 490 (☎224 444; almagroarica@hotmail.com), on the corner with Lynch. Friendly staff and large, comfortable rooms with bath, red triangular balcony, cable TV, fridge, and phone. Breakfast included. Singles CH$18,500; doubles CH$21,500; triples CH$27,500. AmEx/D/MC/V. ❹

without riding their backs into reef. The pros were amazed at the untapped waves Chile had to offer, and the Ariqueños couldn't believe their waves had attracted the world's best.

The off-shore surfing of the Billabong crew isn't the day-to-day surfing one can expect in Arica. They had the aid of the Chilean navy, a fleet of 4 jet skis, and a slew of on-site medical personnel.

But pedestrian surfers and enthusiasts alike can be found every morning at Playas Chinchorro and Las Machas, and you'll likely see their silhouette at sunset. In Arica, the waves are rideable even out of season. Whenever you go, be careful to adhere to surf etiquette—stealing the local crowd's waves will likely buy you more trouble than it's worth.

With recent events, Chile's surfing scene is destined to explode. The global publicity of the Billabong Odyssey, with daily ESPN coverage, has put Arica on the map, but the real boom will come when Californians realize they don't have to settle for bad July surfing conditions when they can surf in northern Chile's best season. When that day comes, grab your boards, duck the tourists, and find a new South American paradise. Until then, hop on the plane. Arica's surf is waiting.

For more on the Billabong Odyssey, check out their new website at www.billabongodyssey.com with movies, pictures, and a day-to-day log of events.

Hostal Buenos Aires, Maipú 740 (☎253 111), between Blanco Encalada and San Martín. Small but adequate rooms with bath and cable TV enclose a peaceful, flower-filled inner courtyard. Beds are new with thick, comfortable mattresses. Singles CH$5000; doubles CH$9000; triples CH$12,000. The owner will lower prices for students. ❷

Camping Josephina, Pedro Lagos 14 (☎213 995), in Villa Frontera near the airport. From Arica, go north on Panamericana Norte past the turnoff for Ruta 11 (to La Paz) and exit at Villa Frontera. Follow the signs for camping. One of the better campgrounds in the Villa, it has a swimming pool, tennis court, BBQ, kitchen, and a hot water shower. 5min. walk to the beach. Camping CH$2000 per person. House with 15 beds: triples CH$12,000; entire house CH$30,000. ❶

🍴 FOOD

In addition to the typical *chifas* (Chinese restaurants), pizzerias, and chain eateries such as Bavaria, Arica has a lively gastronomical scene with several fine restaurants offering signature Chilean seafood cuisine. There's a strip of inexpensive eateries along 18 de Septiembre between Prat and General Lagos.

🍽 **Maracuya,** Comandante San Martín 321 (☎227 600; fax 255 448), on the beach near the pier. Waiters in formal attire serve up excellent seafood in a romantic seaside setting. Everything on this sophisticated international menu is likely to satisfy the most discerning palate—try the *corvina salsa amazónica* (steak with mango salsa; CH$6800), the *camarones ecuatorianos al ajillo* (shrimp in garlic cream sauce; CH$13,500), or the *crema de salmón* (salmon with cream and curry; CH$3000). Open-air seating available. Open 12:30-2pm and 8pm-1:30am. AmEx/D/MC/V. ❹

🍽 **Cantaverdi,** Bolognesi 453 (☎258 242), between Thompson and 21 de Mayo. Jazzy, mellow space with soft colors and a sunburst motif. Locals and tourists alike flock to this hip bar/restaurant for a light meal. Popular before the *discotecas* on weekends. Sandwiches CH$1800-4000. Pizzas CH$3200-4000. Beer CH$900-1000. Mixed drinks CH$1500-3500. Open M-Sa 9am-5am. AmEx/D/MC/V. ❷

Altillo Pub, 21 de Mayo 260 (☎231 936), between Bolognesi and Colón. With its candle-lit tables and glam-goes-slumming Hollywood interior, this pub caters to a yuppie crowd. Drinks are served with sass by the fun waitresses. The bar food includes rare finds like nachos (CH$1200) and chocolate cheesecake (CH$1900). Stocks 24 brands of beer (CH$900-2400). Open M-Sa 6pm-3am. AmEx/DC/MC/V. ❷

Tortas y Tartas Restaurant, 21 de Mayo (☎258 538), between Bolognesi and Colón. Patrons fill this trendy eatery with pedestrian walkway seating to sample from the chic menu. Specialities include the chicken pancakes in white sauce (CH$2900), salads (CH$2100), and vegetarian options (CH$2700). Breakfast CH$1200-2500. Pasta CH$3500. Fish CH$3200-4500. Open daily 9:30am-11pm. AmEx/D/MC/V. ❸

El Arriero, 21 de Mayo 385 (☎/fax 232 636), between Baquedano and Colón. Wind through the long corridor and step down into the main dining room adorned with paintings, maps, photos, wooden wheels, and musical instruments. The *Arriero* (CH$7000) and *Gaucho* (CH$13,000) are enormous meat samplers. Has an extensive wine list. Fish CH$4500-6000. Open daily noon-3:30pm and 7-11pm. AmEx/D/DC/MC/V. ❸

Caffelatte, 21 de Mayo 248 (☎231 881), between Colón and Velásquez. Crowded cafe/restaurant with penthouse seating overlooking the street. Try the 3-course *menú* (CH$1500). Sandwiches CH$1300-1900. Pizzas CH$2000-2500. Milk shakes CH$1500. Open M-Sa 8am-midnight, Su 10am-3pm and 6pm-midnight. ❶

France Tropicale, 21 de Mayo 384 (☎/fax 257 217), between Colón and Baquedano. Dark tropical decor, candlelit tables, and Christmas lights along the ceiling make this upstairs bar/restaurant a fun after-hours hangout for a *gringo*-dominated crowd. Music features lots of Michael Jackson. Large pizzas CH$2100-3500. Beer CH$1000-1200. Open Su-Th 6:15pm-2:30am, F-Sa 6:15pm-4am. ❷

🔯 SIGHTS

A climb to the top of **El Morro de Arica,** the impossible-to-miss mountain in the middle of Arica, offers a panoramic vista of the city, ocean, and surrounding desert landscape. This is also the perfect spot to watch a glorious Chilean sunset. To reach the top of El Morro, walk up the easy zigzagging footpath at the southern end of Colón or take a taxi (CH$1000 per person). At the top of El Morro you will also find the **Museo Histórico y de Armas** (built in 1974 by the Pinochet regime), filled with military paraphernalia and miniature model enactments of the victory of Chile's army over Peru in the **War of the Pacific.** There is an extensive gun collection from the 1870s to the 1960s. (Open 8:30am-8pm. CH$500, children CH$250)

After a trip to El Morro, descend the footpath and check out **Casa Bolognesi,** on the corner of Colón and Yungay, a two-story mansion that houses the Peruvian Consulate General. A block northwest, on the **Plaza Colón,** is the colorful quasi-Gothic **Iglesia San Marcos,** a small, beige, prefabricated building designed by Gustave Eiffel, of Parisian tower fame. The church is not as impressive as El Morro looming overhead, but it adds a unique flavor to Plaza Colón.

Another Eiffel creation is the **Casa de la Cultura,** the ex-customs house dating back to 1874, next to Sernatur and across San Marcos from Plaza Colón. The small, elegant brick building seems out of place amidst modern buildings, but the marble facade, wood-paneled ceiling, corrugated metal columns, and spiral staircase are architecturally interesting. There are some permanent displays of photos and mementos, but most space is used for rotating art and cultural exhibitions. (☎206 366. Open M-F 8:30am-8pm, Sa-Su and holidays 9am-9pm. Free.)

🏖 BEACHES

From the foot of **El Morro,** it is a 20min. walk to the beaches south of downtown (**Playa El Laucho** is the nearest, followed by **Playas La Lisera** and **Brava; Corazones** is farther south). Enclosed by a rock embankment, La Lisera is the most convenient beach in the area, but it is often packed in the summer. Clean public toilets with showers, changing rooms, and a children's playground make a day spent here even more enjoyable. To get to La Lisera, take Bus #8 or pay CH$1000 for a taxi. The waves at Brava and Corazones are too strong for swimming, but Corazones features the occasional seal, as well as coves and pools for bathing, making it a delightful hiking, biking, or fishing trip from downtown. No buses go to Corazones, but *colectivos* cost CH$2000.

The beaches north of town, **Chinchorro** and the more distant **Las Machas** (locals often lump these together, calling both Chinchorro), stretch for miles to the Peruvian border. Chinchorro has a few rocky areas beyond the swim zone where waves break and surfers gather. Miles of coast provide uncrowded surfing year-round. These beaches also have areas that are good for swimming, and camping is permitted. To get to Chinchorro, take Bus #12 or a *colectivo* for CH$350.

▐ SHOPPING

A good bet when shopping for **Andean handicrafts** is the **Poblado Artesanal,** Hualles 2825, a mock *altiplano* village of whitewashed stone houses with thatched roofs. During the summer, the Poblado Artesanal hosts cultural events and folk music performances on Friday and Saturday evenings. During the winter, the village closes early. Numerous *colectivos* (#7 and 8; CH$300 per person) and buses (#3, 7, and 9) come here from downtown. (☎ 222 683. Open in summer M-Su 9:30am-1:30pm and 3:30-8:30pm; in winter M-Su 9:30am-1:30pm and 3:30-6pm.)

A great place to buy fresh produce from all over Chile and Peru is **Terminales Agropecuarios,** referred to by locals as **Agro,** located 15-20min. northeast of downtown by bus (CH$250). *Colectivos* with "Agro" written on them cost CH$300 per person. Agro sells the usual fruits and vegetables, such as apples and avocados, but also has hard-to-find items like alpaca jerky. Agro also sells many items other than produce, including secondhand clothes, all for reasonable prices.

The narrow alley of **Bolognesi,** between 21 de Mayo and 18 de Septiembre, also has stalls where locals sell arts and crafts (open 6am-6pm). The **Antigua Mercado,** on Sotomayor, two blocks from Plaza Colón, has a fish market on Saturday and Sunday mornings.

▐ ▐ ENTERTAINMENT AND NIGHTLIFE

Arica has a hopping nightlife, one of the liveliest in northern Chile, focused more on laid-back bars than raging *discotecas* (though there's no shortage of those either). A good place to hang out on summer nights is the **Isla de Alacrán.** Jutting out from the foot of El Morro, it's the hot spot where local youths park their cars to party and socialize without a cover charge into the wee hours of the morning. **Cine Colón,** 7 de Junio 190 on Plaza Colón, shows recent flicks from Hollywood and Europe. (☎ 231 165. M-Tu and Th-Su CH$3200, W CH$2200. Shows 2-10pm.)

◪ **Vieja Habana,** 21 de Mayo 485, between Lynch and Baquedano. Salsa experts and amateur backpackers come here to make things hot with the opposite sex. A long, candle-it hallway ends in an exotic, low-lit dance area with a candle-covered bar. Latin music and dark lounge areas are almost as sexy as the dancing. Dance classes for all levels Th-Sa 7-9pm. Live salsa F and Sa. Open Th-Sa 9pm-3am.

Barrabas, 18 de Septiembre 524 (☎ 230 928), close to the corner with Lynch, has a dark interior with a number of lounge areas on 2 floors. College bar atmosphere, with 90s rock blaring through the speakers. Occasional live music Sa-Su. Cover Th-Sa CH$1000. Open M-W 9pm-1am, Th-Sa 9pm-6am.

Drake, Buenos Aires 209 (☎ 215 891), near the beaches north of downtown. Wooden statues of Santa María hover over a two-story dance floor with a young crowd dancing to house music. Beer CH$1200. Erotic show on Th. Cover CH$2500 for Chileans, CH$4000 for foreigners; includes a drink. Open Th-Sa midnight-5am. AmEx/D/MC/V.

Soho, Buenos Aires 209 (☎ 215 891), in the same building as Drake. This steamy 2-story meat market of youngsters is incongruous with the industrial, minimalist structure. Connected to Drake after 2am—roam through both clubs for 1 cover charge. Beer CH$1200. Mixed drinks CH$1500-3000. Occasional live music. Cover F CH$1500, Sa CH$2000. Open Th-Sa 11pm-5am. AmEx/D/MC/V.

DAYTRIP FROM ARICA

MUSEO ARQUEOLÓGICO MIGUEL DE AZAPA. A visit to this superb regional museum, administered by the University of Tarapacá, is a must for an overview of the area's archaeological heritage. The arid climate of this northernmost area of Chile has ideal conditions for the preservation of relics. The mummies exhibited from the Chinchorro culture are thought to be among the oldest ever uncovered. Guided tours in Chinese, English, French, German, Japanese, and Portuguese are available free of charge. Arica's tour operators include a visit to this museum and nearby geoglyphs in tour itineraries. You can also get there from downtown Arica by *colectivo*. *(☎205 555; www.uta.cl/masma.* Colectivos *depart from the corner of Chacabuco and Lynch 10am-6pm; CH$700. Private tour including stops along the way at geoglyphs CH$5000. To return to Arica, walk to the main road and flag down a* colectivo. *Open Nov.-Apr. 9am-8pm; May-Oct. 10am-6pm. CH$1000, children CH$300.)*

BORDER CROSSING INTO PERU: CHACALLUTA

The road from Arica to **Tacna, Peru,** a major launching point for travelers into Peru, is well-maintained and heavily traveled. The best way to cross the border is in one of the big American sedans that leave, when full, from either the Terminal Internacional in Arica, or the Tacna bus terminal (CH$1500-3000). From Arica, the road runs 20km north through Chacalluta before crossing the border. Customs open 8am-midnight. The process is simple and involves no more than a passport stamp and a brief search of your luggage for contraband and various food products (see **Essentials: Border Crossings,** p. 35, for info on visas and fees). Early in the morning the process takes 15min., but after 10am the crossing could take 1-2hr. For more information on Tacna, see **Let's Go: Peru.**

PUTRE ☎58

Putre (pop. 1800), the capital of the Parinacota Province, sits 3500m high at the base of the Nevados de Putre. A popular overnight acclimatization stop for travelers heading to nearby destinations in the national parks, Putre is similar in feel to Socoroma, though somewhat bigger and blander. As one might expect from a town at this altitude, it gets very cold at night—warm clothes are a must for visitors. The town comes alive during the February *Carnaval* and the September-October Ferán *(Feria Regional Andino)*, a three-day fair with animals, fresh produce, crafts, and musicians from Chile, Bolivia, and Peru.

The town's 17th-century **Iglesia de Putre,** on the **Plaza de Armas,** was damaged by an earthquake in 2001, but the whitewashed stone church with an exceptionally elaborate facade has been fully restored. For those more interested in birds than churches, **Alto Andino Nature Tours** (www.birdingaltoandino.com) is the only tour operator in town. Run by Alaskan biologist Barbara Knapton, Alto Andino Nature Tours specializes in conducting bird-watching and natural history tours throughout northern Chile, including visits to coastal marine mammal colonies.

La Paloma Restaurant ❶ serves great breakfasts with simple meals. (Breakfast CH$800; lunch and dinner CH$1800.) **Restaurant Apacheta ❶,** Arturo Pérez Canto 540, serves simple but satisfying meals. (Breakfast CH$800, lunch or dinner CH$1400.) The real jewel of the nightlife scene is **Kuchu Marka,** Baquedano 351, on the main thoroughfare. The funky, rustic pub, decorated with murals of the Andean highlands, showcases alpaca dishes (CH$1500), assorted beers (CH$1000-1500), and *tumbo* sours (CH$1500) as their regional specialities. (Occasional live music. Open daily noon-2am or until last customer.)

Northern Parks and Reserves

Hotel Kukuli ❸ has new beds in rooms with sparkling bathrooms. Rooms are simple, but have patios. (Singles CH$13,000; doubles CH$23,000; triples CH$25,000.) **La Paloma ❷**, the biggest *residencial* in town, has rooms that get cold at night, but the concrete complex offers a sunbathing area on the terrace. (☎222 710. CH$5000 per person, with bath CH$8000.) Contact the Arica Conaf office (p. 139) for information about the **Conaf station ❷** in Putre. It offers two simple triples and one 6-bed dorm. (☎250 207 or 250 570. CH$3000 per person for Chileans, CH$4000 for foreigners.) **Hostería Las Vicuñas ❺**, on the outskirts of town under the distant snow-capped Cerro Putre, provides a pleasant *chalet*-like setting with free Internet, satellite TV, and private bath, if you're willing to shell out the cash. (☎224 466. Breakfast and dinner included. Doubles US$57; triples US$72. AmEx/D/DC/MC/V.)

Most services are clustered around the Plaza de Armas, including the **bank**, which only exchanges money to Chilean *pesos* and cashes traveler's checks, and has **no ATM** (☎355 420; open M-F 9am-11:30am), and a number of small **supermarkets** (open daily 8am-10pm). The **police station, paramedic clinic,** and the Entel **centro de llamadas/post office** (open daily 8am-1pm and 4-10pm) are near the plaza.

Departing from Arica, **Pullman Cuevas Internacional** buses stop at Putre on their way to La Paz, BOL (daily 5am and noon). **La Paloma** buses depart for Arica (2¾hr., 1:30pm, CH$1500). To reach PN Lauca from Putre without taking a car or guided tour, go to **Cali Supermarket** to book a reservation on the Arica-La Paz international bus. To return, catch a bus on Ruta 11.

BORDER CROSSING INTO BOLIVIA: CHUNGARÁ

Ruta 11, the road that runs from Putre to Parque Nacional Lauca, continues through the park to Chungará, 7km from the border. This frontier town is home to the Chilean customs office. Just over the border is Tambo Quemado and Bolivian customs. The road then continues on to La Paz. Although this route is heavily traveled and well-maintained, the pass can be closed in winter due to inclement weather, so it's best to double-check with Conaf or the authorities in Arica before attempting the crossing. The customs office at Chungará is open daily 8am-8pm. The process is fairly simple and involves no more than a passport stamp and a brief search of your luggage for contraband and various food products (see **Essentials: Border Crossings,** p. 35, for info on visas and fees).

SOCOROMA

A charming Aymara farming village, **Socoroma** (pop. 120) lies 5km down from Ruta 11. Lined with cobbled streets, Socoroma's picture-perfect mini square is complete with a quintessential Andean bell-tower church, red and white geranium flowers, and the towering snow-capped Cerro Putre in the background. There are few amenities in town, but the peaceful valley streams, fruit-filled terraces, and abundant flowers around the plaza make Socoroma a worthy diversion from neighboring Putre. Pullman Cuevas International stops in Socoroma daily.

LLUTA VALLEY AND POCONCHILE

The fascinating Lluta Valley geoglyphs, dating from the 12th century and restored in the 1980s, are included in the trips to PN Lauca run by Arica's tour operators. **Geo Tour** (p. 139) in Arica covers both the Lluta and Azapa Valleys in its day tour. East of the Lluta Valley along Ruta 11 sits the tiny village of **Poconchile** with its 17th-century **Iglesia de San Gerónimo.** Damaged by an earthquake in 2001, this atypical Andean church has wooden towers that were added in the 19th century. A small shop and restaurant are across the road from the church. After Poconchile, Ruta 11 climbs steeply and one begins to see the bizarre **cactus candelabras** that dot the landscape and grow 3-4cm a year on the moisture they get from the coastal mist known as *camanchaca* or *garua.* In the summer the cacti bloom, and for a day the desert landscape is dotted with vivid purple flowers.

Just before you reach the **Pukará de Copaquilla,** a circular pre-Inca stone fortress erected to protect trade caravans and restored in 1987, you can stop at **Pueblo de Maillku ❷,** the solar-powered abode of a Chilean couple with their small children, for a cup of coca leaf tea and homemade bread. The couple offers a plain room for lodging. (maillku@latinmail.com. CH$1500 for tea and bread. Rooms CH$5000 per person; camping CH$2500 per person. Acclimatization tour provided.) The lookout point for the Pukará is a good place to let out a shout and hear the valley echo. **Bus Lluta** serves this area on its buses to Molinos (1hr. to Poconchile, 7 per day from corner of Chacabuco and Vicuña Mackenna in Arica, CH$600).

PARQUE NACIONAL LAUCA

Parque Nacional Lauca is the undisputed jewel of tours in Chile's Region I. Visitors to the area come for some of the world's highest lakes and volcanoes, or to experience the brain-alteringly high altitudes. The park encompasses 1380 sq. km of *altiplano* desert at 4000-6300m above sea level, and boasts a variety of landscapes, including pristine lakes, vast stretches of grasslands, snow-capped volcanic peaks, hot springs, and thermal baths. Additionally, PN Lauca's flora and fauna are as diverse as its terrain. The park features four species of camelids (llamas, alpacas, *vicuñas*, and *guanacos*), a wide variety of birds (giant coots, Andean geese, three species of flamingo, and *nadus*), and diverse plants found in dense forests (*quenoa*, *llareta*, and *portulaca*). Several peaks in the park offer hikers and alpinists easy access to the otherwise elusive 6000m mark.

▐ TRANSPORTATION. Parque Nacional Lauca lies on the border with Bolivia, an easy 3hr. drive from Arica on the paved Ruta 11 to La Paz. A high-clearance 4WD vehicle is strongly recommended for driving on the gravel roads inside the park, especially during the wet months in summer when roads get flooded or washed away. Although some people choose to navigate the park alone with a good map, a hired guide often facilitates the trip and is a necessity for those going on to Reserva Nacional Las Vicuñas and Monumento Natural Salar de Surire. For information on **public transportation** to the park, see **Tours** in Arica, p. 139.

ORIENTATION AND PRACTICAL INFORMATION. The park is flanked in the south by RN Las Vicuñas and MN Salar de Surire, which were once part of the park, but became separate in the 1980s to permit mining.

There are **Conaf** ranger stations, located at **Las Cuevas** (the park's western entrance), **Parinacota,** and **Chungará,** which can provide information concerning hiking trails and the latest conditions for climbing nearby peaks. (Open daily 9am-5:30pm.) There is also a **police station** in Chucuyo village. Registering with the Arica Conaf office is not necessary unless you plan to go hiking in the park. To climb **Volcán Parinacota** (6342m), **Volcán Guallatire** (6060m), or other peaks adjacent to the Bolivian border, you need a special permit from the **Dirección de Frontera y Límites** in Santiago, which can also be obtained at **Gobernación Provincial** in Putre or Iquique (if you go with a guided tour, the guide will take care of this paperwork). Although it's possible for experienced climbers with proper equipment to tackle Volcán Parinacota or Volcán Guallatire on their own, it is strongly recommended that everyone climb with an experienced guide. Jorge Barros has been hiking Chile's peaks for over a decade and is an extremely experienced, Arica-based mountain guide. (☎ 220 269 or 09 866 2030; www.suritrek.cl.)

It is important to note that you cannot get **fuel, cash,** or **provisions** in the park, so it's necessary to stock up in Arica or Iquique. Driving inside the park after sunset is certainly not recommended, as it is easy to get lost in the frigid darkness, and it is almost impossible for Conaf or the police to find broken-down cars. Those who

---

AT A GLANCE

AREA: 1380 km sq.

CLIMATE: Dry climate; average of 28cm of annual precipitation, some rain in the summer and snow in the winter. Temperature ranges 12°C to 20°C during the day; -3°C to -10°C at night.

GATEWAYS: Putre.

HIGHLIGHTS: Remarkable variety of wildlife, including llamas, alpacas, *vicuñas,* and flamingos; mountain climbing, hot springs, thermal baths.

FEES: Free.

CAMPING: Conaf's campsite at Chungará; free camping possible throughout the park but risky.

plan on hiking or climbing in the park should remember that altitude sickness can have devastating consequences, and even a seemingly easy hike can turn into a major exertion at this altitude. Be careful to eat and drink moderately, carry plenty of water, and avoid more physical activity than your body can handle.

ACCOMMODATIONS AND FOOD. Unlike most Conaf stations, the locations at Las Cuevas, Parinacota, and Chungará don't offer hot water, kitchens, or indoor accommodations, but they do allow **camping** and have **picnic areas.** Most of the campsites only offer open-air, dirt-floor, unprotected areas, except the Lago Chungará site, which has 1.2m-high stone walls protecting each camping area from the elements. Campers have access to the bathroom facilities during the Conaf office's hours (9am-5:30pm). Those brave enough to camp should bring an insulated sleeping bag and warm clothing, since the nights are frigid at 4500m. (CH$5500 per tent.) Though many visitors make the most of the park's vast size and camp without permission, it is a highly discouraged practice, as most of the land belongs to Aymara owners who reserve the right to ask campers caught on their land to leave.

Restaurante Copihue de Oro ❶, in Chucuyo village, serves simple meals (CH$1500) and maintains a basic 6-bed dorm with hot showers for lodgers. (Dorms CH$3000.) Chucuyo has several other restaurants that offer similarly priced meals; most of these cater to truck drivers stopping en route to and from La Paz, Bolivia. **Florentina Álvarez ❶,** in Parinacota village, offers a no-frills, 6-bed room. (No hot water. CH$2500.) There is no place to eat in Parinacota or the park.

SIGHTS. Beyond the Las Cuevas entrance, the first stop is a brief walking path near the lonely Conaf station. The path has a number of bridge-aided stream crossings and provides a chance to get up close and personal with hundreds of wild *vicuñas* and the incredibly cute *vizcacha.* Among the rarer animal sightings are the Andean fox and *nedus.* Putre-based **Alto Andino Nature Tours** (p. 145) offers detailed nature tours. Continuing along Ruta 11, Volcán Parinacota and other peaks are visible from the road. The tiny village of Chucuyo is next with its **police station,** a couple of **restaurants,** and a family of tourist-friendly **llamas** that will eat out of your hand. There are a few **artisanal stands** selling alpaca sweaters, gloves, and scarves, but there is a wider selection at Lago Chungará.

The tiny village of **Parinacota** (pop. 20) has a beautiful **church** and stalls where the Aymaran residents sell their **crafts.** Ask for permission before photographing the Aymaran villagers. Enclosed within a walled compound, the 17th-century stone church features a thatched roof, a bell tower, an otherworldly interior, a fine display of gold and silver from Bolivian mines, and wonderfully preserved murals. No flash photography of the murals is permitted. Ask for caretaker Cipriano Morales Huanca to open the door (he has held the church key for over 30 years). Parinacota is a good place to start a **hike** to the top of nearby **Cerro Guane Guane** (5097m), which offers expansive views over the park. There is no marked trail to the top, but the hike from the Conaf *refugio* takes only a few hours. Although climbing gear is not necessary, some people prefer to travel with a local guide.

Past Las Cuevas along Ruta 11 is **Laguna Cotacotani,** a shallow lake near Parinacota, with a series of small snow-capped hills jutting up from the middle of the icy body of water. From the Cotacotani viewing area along the side of the road there is a path down to the lake, around the lake, through small hills, and finally ending in Parinacota. The path is often overlooked by tour agencies but the hour-long walk provides peaceful views of small waterfalls and icy mountain streams. Shortly after Cotacotani, you reach **Lago Chungará** (4500m), the highest lake in the world, flanked by twin volcanoes. Formed out of lava from the neighboring (and now-dormant) **Volcán Parinacota** (6342m) and **Volcán Pomerape** (6280m), the 37m deep lake is a wonder of nature. The Conaf campsite offers a cold but beautiful

NORTE GRANDE

location for spending a night and is also a base for hiking the nearby Cerro Choquelimpie. (5228m. There's no marked trail, but it's a straightforward 4hr. hike to the top; 2hr. down. No climbing gear is necessary. Conaf rangers can get you a local guide.)

RESERVA NACIONAL LAS VICUÑAS

Once part of Parque Nacional Lauca until separated for mining purposes, Reserva Nacional Las Vicuñas, home to Monumento Natural Salar de Surire, although less accessible than PN Lauca, remains beautifully undisturbed. The reserve and the monument offer equally stunning landscapes with immense *pampas*, verdant *cienegas* (swamps), dramatic mountains, an ominously smoking volcano, and eerie, bubbling pools along the borax plains of the Salar de Surire. Wildlife includes great herds of over 21,000 *vicuñas*, llamas, and alpacas, as well as three species of pink flamingo. This area offers hikers and alpinists breathtaking opportunities to climb to particularly high altitudes.

AT A GLANCE	
AREA: 2090 sq. km	**GATEWAY:** Arica
CLIMATE: Temperatures oscillate between 5°C and 15°C during the day, and -5°C and -15°C at night. The annual rainfall average is 26cm.	**HIGHLIGHTS:** Salar de Surire, Volcán Guallatire, Río Lauca. Diverse fauna including *vicuñas*, llamas, and alpacas at Chilcaya; 3 species of flamingo and hot springs at Polloquere; spectacular views from the peak of the volcano.
CAMPING: No sites available; *refugios* in Surire (CH$5500).	

⊟ TRANSPORTATION. Seeing this sublime territory takes some effort, as the only way to get here is by means of a guided tour (see **Arica: Tours,** p. 139) or by driving a rental car along the bumpy reserve road. 4WD is a must, and the road is often impassable during the summer rains and winter snow. Most visitors to this area come south from PN Lauca on the gravel road (Ruta A232) that turns into Ruta 235 as it reaches the Río Lauca and enters RN Las Vicuñas.

> **!** It's recommended to drive in **RN Las Vicuñas** and **MN Salar de Surire** with a guide, as even good maps are of little help in areas where there are no road signs and you could end up illegally in Bolivia. Be careful not to walk off the beaten path near the Bolivian border, as there are **land mines** to prevent drug trafficking.

 ORIENTATION AND PRACTICAL INFORMATION. A high-clearance **4WD** is strongly recommended for driving on the gravel roads inside RN Las Vicuñas and Salar de Surire. Upon arrival at **Guallatire,** visitors are required to register their car information and passport numbers at the **police station,** given the proximity to the Bolivian border and the high frequency of stolen cars and drug traffickers that use this area to cross the border. The **Conaf office** at Surire has plenty of **gas** available for prices not much higher than in Arica and Iquique.

⌐◖ ACCOMMODATIONS AND FOOD. Palina Sánchez, a resident of Guallatire, offers simple **rooms ❶** and **food ❶** for passing truck drivers and sleep-deprived tour groups. Ask for Palina at the police station. (CH$3000 per person, with bath CH$6000. *Menú* CH$1500.) The **Conaf refugio ❷,** in Surire, located on a hill overlooking MN Salar de Surire, is an absolutely terrific place to spend a night—an oasis of warmth and comfort with a breathtaking view of the surrounding landscape. In the building where the ranger lives, there's a 4-bed room that has a hot shower, a fireplace, and a kitchen. Bring a sleeping bag in case the room is full and you have to sleep on the floor. (CH$5500 per person.) Another building next door offers 5 rooms and a kitchen.

🔆 **SIGHTS.** Located at the foot of the world's tallest dormant volcano, Volcán Guallatire (6060m), the small town of **Guallatire** has little more than a 17th-century church and a defunct Conaf station. Climbing Volcán Guallatire, which last erupted in 1961, is not technically challenging, but given the emissions of poisonous gas and changing wind directions, climbing with a guide is recommended.

Beyond Guallatire, you can cross the **Río Lauca** on a bridge. Avoid it during the wet summer months, as the bridge often floods and becomes impassable, even with a high-clearance 4WD. The nearby **police station** in **Chilcaya** affords a magnificent view of the Salar de Surire. At sunset, this landscape is particularly beautiful and eerie, with glowing purple mountains, warm hues of the salt and borax sediments, and blue pools. No trees, only scrub bushes, survive at this altitude.

After traveling around the Salar for some 15km, you reach the Conaf station/*refugio* in **Surire** on a hill overlooking the salt pan. After a night in the *refugio*, nearby peaks (about 5000m high), which have no trails, offer climbs lasting a few hours.

A 12km drive past the Conaf *refugio* will take you to **Polloquere**, also called **Aguas Calientes**, which is close to a lookout point for watching colonies of three species of flamingos. Polloquere is a magnificent place, with several **thermal pools** and steaming **hot springs** overlooking the endless stretches of white Salar. Bathing in one of the more tepid thermal pools (beware: some pools are almost at boiling temperature) is a euphorically relaxing experience. Camping next to the pools is not recommended, as the sulfuric gases can give you a bad headache overnight.

Most tours of Surire end at Polloquere, but those who wish to press farther south can continue on toward the Conaf station and *refugio* at **Enquelga** inside **Parque Nacional Volcán Isluga,** another pristine expanse of *altiplano* desert with an active volcano similar to that in RN Las Vicuñas. Although it can be impassable in the wet season and snow often blocks the way on the gravel road from Polloquere to Enquelga, the road travels through sweeping *pampas* and steep mountain passes (4800m) and ranks as one of the most stunning scenic drives in the world. If the pass is closed, some tour groups will make a brief, illegal pass on the low road through Bolivia. The pass requires only 5min. in Bolivia, but if you're caught, the authorities will leave you with an impounded car and a South American police record. *Let's Go* does not recommend breaking local laws.

PARQUE NACIONAL VOLCÁN ISLUGA

Seven kilometers north of Colchane, the tiny settlement of Isluga guards the southern entrance to Parque Nacional Volcán Isluga. Sprawled across 1800 sq. km, the park's expansive *altiplano* wilderness, **Valle Arabia,** is interrupted only by a beautiful 17th-century church. This quintessential Andean colonial *iglesia* fits perfectly in its surroundings. The stunning landscape, unfolding leisurely beneath towering snow-capped peaks, features vast green plains dotted with llamas, alpacas, and *vicuñas*. Nearby, at the base of the active volcano, **Volcán Isluga** (5530m), lies another small settlement called **Enquelga.** The park exit lies north of Enquelga; from there you can continue north to the Salar de Surire and PN Lauca. Much of the land in the park belongs to the local Aymaran Indian community, so there is no admission fee. However, camping within the park is not recommended, due to its proximity to the Bolivian border, the threat of drug traffickers, and a lack of security supervision. In general, when tackling altitudes over 3500m, it is wise to spend up to three days acclimatizing—you should not attempt to climb the peaks here until you have successfully adjusted to the altitude and taken precautions against altitude sickness. The path through the park is often impassable during the summer rainy season and during the occasional winter snowstorm.

Climbing Volcán Isluga is not as challenging as climbing other peaks in surrounding parks but most hikers will still benefit from the help of an experienced guide. The climb takes 6hr. from the Conaf *refugio* to the peak. Start early in the morning, as you cannot camp on the soft volcanic soil. Hiking boots and ski poles or walking sticks are recommended for this mildly strenuous climb, which should be avoided during wet summer weather and can be extremely cold and snow-covered during the winter. The **refugio ❷** offers basic accommodations as well—two 4-bed rooms are complemented by a hot shower, kitchen facilities, and a comforting fireplace (CH$5500 per person). If you call Conaf in Arica in advance, even if the *refugio* is full, basic rooms can be arranged in houses in Enquelga (CH$3500, including use of the *refugio*'s shower and kitchen). **Raíces Andinas** in Arica (p. 139) arranges 3-day trips through Parque Nacional Volcán Isluga, Parque Nacional Lauca, and the Salar de Surire.

Other than a **paramedic clinic** staffed with a nurse in Enquelga, no amenities are available in Parque Nacional Volcán Isluga. Since Volcán Isluga is located very close to the Bolivian border, you need a special permit from the **Dirección de Frontera y Límites** in Santiago or **Gobernación Provincial** in Putre or Iquique.

COLCHANE

Past the red and yellow clays of Valle Incahuasi, deep canyons and interesting cacti indicate your arrival at Colchane. The turnoff point for PN Volcán Isluga, this wind-swept, almost deserted town lies on the Bolivian border. Basic accommodations include **Pensión Gómez/Residencial Camino del Inca ❶**, with humble rooms, hot water, and breakfast for CH$3000, and **Residencial Choke ❶**, which offers sparse rooms with hot water for CH$3000 and simple meals for CH$1200. Colchane is cold at night, and the concrete walls of accommodations don't provide much insulation, so bring warm clothes. You must stop at the **customs office** (open 8am-8pm) if planning to cross the border. Colchane provides some amenities, including a **police station**, a **paramedic clinic**, and a **centro de llamadas** (open 9am-8pm). Expensive **gas** is available from Andrés García (ask a villager to direct you to him). There are **no banks or ATMs in Colchane,** so get cash before you leave Iquique. The international **bus** to and from Iquique arrives and departs at irregular hours (5hr., CH$4000). When making travel plans, remember that the wet season can render this road impassable.

IQUIQUE ☎ 57

A popular beach town drawing visitors from all over Chile and neighboring countries, Iquique has a mild and dry year-round climate that makes its beaches among the best in South America. Perfect surfing waves break outside the swim zone, making the beaches accessible for everyone. Moreover, the steep mountains surrounding town make Iquique *the* spot for paragliding. Victorian houses, from Iquique's British capitalist origins, seem incongruous beside miles of white-sand beaches flecked with palm trees, Floridian high-rise hotels, and a large casino. But Iquique is not all beaches and history; it flexes its modern industrial muscle as a major port with a thriving fishing industry. Zona Franca, a bustling duty-free import/export zone, is a haven for trade, attracting hordes of businessmen and shoppers from the world over for great deals on everything from automobiles and electronics to clothes and perfumes.

🔁 TRANSPORTATION

Flights: Aeropuerto Diego Aracena (☎426 350; fax 420 037), 40km south of town on Ruta 1, is connected to downtown by **Taxis Aeropuerto** (☎419 004 or 415 916). CH$7000 to the airport, CH$8000 from the airport. 3 major airlines serve Iquique:

LanChile, Tarapacá 465 (☎427 600), with a branch in Mall Las Américas. To: **Arica** (30min., 4 per day 7am-10:30pm, CH$18,800); **Santiago** (3hr., 7 per day 9:10am-8:10pm, CH$93,000) via **Antofagasta** (50min., CH$29,600); **La Paz, BOL** (1hr., at least 1 per day, US$131).

Sky Airlines, Ramírez 411 (☎415 013). Offers comparatively cheaper flights to: **Antofagasta** (50min., 8am and 2pm, CH$16,000); **Arica** (35min.; 7, 11am, 1, 10:30pm; CH$12,000); **Santiago** (3hr.; 7:30am; CH$118,000, CH$75,000 if booked a week in advance).

TAM, Tarapacá 451 (☎390 600; fax 390 604). Open M-F 9am-6pm, Sa 9am-1pm. Flies to **Sao Paulo, BRZ** (M, W, F 2:50pm; round-trip US$413) via **Asunción, PAR** (one-way US$212).

Iquique

🔼 **ACCOMMODATIONS**
Hostal Catedral, **1**
Hotel Bellavista, **12**
Hotel Caiti, **13**
Hotel Carani, **6**
Hotel Carlos Condell, **14**
Hotel de la Plaza, **17**
Hotel Dona Genoveva, **7**
Residencial J.J. Pérez, **18**

🍴 **FOOD**
Amaretto, **10**
Barracuda, **15**
Boulevard, **8**
Cafetería Vizzio, **2**
Casino Español, **3**
La Protectora, **5**
Restaurant-Cafeteria Colonial, **4**
Restaurant la Carreta de Antonio, **19**
Ta Chang, **11**

🎵 **NIGHTLIFE**
Aqua, **22**
Canavans, **21**
Kamikaze, **23**
Pharos, **20**
Taberna Van Gogh, **9**
Tennessee Bar, **16**

NORTE GRANDE

Buses: Most bus companies have offices along **Barros Arana** across from the **Mercado Central.** Buses either leave from in front of the office or at the company's terminal.

Tur Bus (☎472 984 or 472 986) goes to: **Arica** (4hr., 6 per day 8:30am-3:15am, CH$3000); **Calama** (9hr., 5 per day 8:30am-11:30pm, CH$6000); **Santiago** (24hr., 4 per day 10am-9:35pm, CH$18,500) via **Antofagasta** (6hr., CH$8000), **Copiapó** (12hr., CH$13,000), **La Serena** (18hr., CH$13,800), **Tocopilla** (3hr., CH$3500), and **Valparaíso** (23hr., CH$18,500). Ticket office on Barros Arana, across the street from the Mercado Central. Buses leave from the terminal on Patricio Lynch north of town.

Ramos Cholele (☎411 650), **Pullman Carmelita** (☎412 227), and **Pullman Santa Rosa** (☎431 796), on Barros Arana between Sargento Aldea and Latorre, send buses to: **Arica** (4hr., 25 per day, CH$3000-3500); **Calama** (9hr., 10:45pm, CH$4500); **Santiago** (24hr., 7 per day 8am-9:30pm, CH$20,000-23,000) via **Antofagasta** (6hr., CH$4500-7000), **Chañaral/Copiapó** (12hr., CH$15,0000-17,000), and **La Serena** (14hr., CH$18,000).

Pullman Santa Angela: (☎423 751), on Barros Arana between Sargento Aldea and Latorre, has frequent departures to **Pica/Matilla** (2hr., every hr. 8am-9:30pm, CH$1500) via **Humberstone/Santa Laura** (45min., CH$800), **Pozo Almonte** (1hr., CH$1000), **Huayca** (1hr., CH$1200), and **La Tirana** (1¾hr., CH$1200).

Agencia Barreda, Barros Arana 965 (☎411 425), goes to **Pica** (8am-9:30pm, CH$1500) and **Mamiña** (2¾hr., 8am and 4pm, CH$2500). Buses leave from company office.

Pullman Cuevas, Juan Martínez 922 (☎517 897), goes to **Oruro, BOL** (14hr., M-F 10pm, CH$7000) via **Colchane** (8hr., CH$4000).

Taxis and Colectivos: *Colectivos* cost CH$400 within Iquique and CH$440 to the outskirts of town. Radio taxis cost at most CH$800 anywhere in town during the day, CH$1500 after 10pm—try **Pacífico** (☎451 111) or **Rocar** (☎446 768). **Taxi Tour,** San Andrés 783 (☎414 875), and **Turis Cargo,** Barana 295 (☎412 191), go to **Arica** (CH$7000 per person). Taxis to **Mamiña** (CH$32,000), **Pica** (CH$26,000), **Pozo Almonte** (CH$15,000), and **La Tirana** (CH$18,000) leave from Mercado Centenario.

Car Rental: Hertz, Aníbal Pinto 1303 (☎/fax 510 432, airport 410 924; www.hertz.cl). **Budget,** Bulnes 542 (☎416 332, airport 407 034; fax 416 095; www.budget.cl). Both charge between CH$34,000 (small sedan) and CH$59,000 (4WD) per day.

✴ ⑦ ORIENTATION AND PRACTICAL INFORMATION

Historic **Plaza Prat,** flanked by a white-washed clock tower, is at the center of town. **Baquedano,** the main thoroughfare, runs north-south from Plaza Prat's southeastern corner down to the beach, providing a pedestrian zone between Thompson and Zegers. The streets between Plaza Prat and **Plaza Condell** are lined with large stores and are always crowded with eager shoppers. Beaches, including **Playa Cavancha** and **Playa Brava,** lie south of downtown along **Avenida Balmaceda.**

Tourist Office: Sernatur, Aníbal Pinto 436 (☎312 238), between Serrano and San Martín. Offers information and can provide brochures, but lacks English speaking staff. Open M-F 9am-2pm and 4-6pm, Sa 10am-1pm. English-speaking Darinka Goravica at **Croacia Tours,** 18 de Septiembre (☎422 122 or 09 543 0347; autotek@entelchile.net), between S. Aldea and Latorre, is friendly and well informed.

Tours: The most common offerings in the area are full-day tours to the thermal baths in **Mamiña,** or to the desert oasis towns of **Pica** and **Matilla.** The ghost towns of **Humberstone** and **Santa Laura,** the **Pintado geoglyphs,** and **La Tirana** also tend to be popular destinations. Daytrips to **Gigante de Atacama, Pisagua,** and **PN Volcán Isluga** via Colchane are available as well. Iquique is also famous for its excellent **paragliding,** and many tour agencies provide links with individual instructors. **Surfing lessons** and **sandboarding** on Cerro Dragón are also available. All tours run at least every week during the summer but filling the minimum is near impossible in the winter.

Mane Tour, Baquedano 1067 (☎/fax 473 032 or 09 543 2485; www.iqq.cl/manetour), between Zegers and O'Higgins. Runs full-day tours to Mamiña (CH$18,000 per person, min. 4 people). Tours to Humberstone, La Tirana, Matilla, Pica, Pintados, and Santa Laura available (CH$15,000 per person, min. 4 people). The Pisagua daytrip (stopover at Gigante de Atacama; CH$20,000 per person, min. 4 people) and PN Volcán Isluga daytrip (CH$35,000 per person, min. 5 people) are popular choices. Also set up surfing, paragliding, and sandboarding lessons. Open M-F 9am-1:30pm and 4:30-8pm, Sa 9:30am-1pm.

Avitours, Baquedano 997 (☎473 775 or 519 135; www.avitours.cl), on the corner with Zegers. Offers similar daytrips to Mamiña (CH$22,000 per person, min. 4 people); Humberstone, La Tirana, Matilla, Pica, Pintados, and Santa Laura (CH$18,000 per person, min. 4 people); PN Volcán Isluga (CH$40,000 per person, min. 4 people); and a 3-day journey through PN Volcán Isluga, Salar de Salire, RN Las Vicuñas, and PN Lauca (CH$130,000; includes all meals, water, oxygen tanks, and lodging). Open M-F 9am-7:30pm, Sa 10am-2pm.

Turismo Unita, Baquedano 1054 (☎450 422; turismounita@terra.com), runs a 3-day tour of PN Lauca, PN Volcán Isluga, and the Salar de Surire.

Altazor Skysports, Diego Portales 920 (☎/fax 437 437, 431 382, or 09 886 2362; altazor@entelchile.cl), outside of town, specializes in paragliding (CH$25,000 for 3-4hr. instruction and flight). The best way to organize a jump is to call Altazor 1-2 days in advance.

Turismo Jaws, Latorre 324 (☎418 336; www.iqq.cl/transjaws), on the corner with Baquedano, offers a daytrip to Arica (CH$15,000 per person, min. 10 people).

Consulates: Bolivia, Gorostiaga 215 (☎/fax 421 777). **Peru,** Zegers 570 (☎411 466).

Currency Exchange and Banks: These are widespread, especially around Plaza Prat. Most banks have **24hr. ATMs. Wall Street Money Exchange,** Serrano 391 (☎422 011), changes dollars, euros, and traveler's checks. Open M-F 8:30am-6:30pm, Sa 10am-1pm. Also try **BankBoston,** Serrano 372 (☎472 141; www.bankboston.cl). Open M-F 9am-2pm and 3-7pm.

Supermarket: Downtown, try **Rossi Supermercados,** Tarapacá 579 (☎412 567), on the southeastern corner of Plaza Condell. Open daily 9am-10pm. Or try **Lider,** Héroes de la Concepción 2653 (☎480 480), next to Mall Las Américas. Open 10am-11pm.

Outdoor Equipment: Lombardi (☎390 037), on Héroes de la Concepción, in Mall Las Américas, sells camping, surfing, and other sports and outdoor equipment. Open daily 11am-10pm.

Laundromats: Lavazul, Juan Martínez 2025 (☎475 263; www.iqq.cl/lavazul), offers wash and dry for CH$1100 per kg.

Police: ☎133. In town ☎413 110.

Pharmacies: There are many on Plaza Condell. **Farmacias Ahumada,** Tarapacá 599 (☎412 269), on the corner with Vivar. Open daily 9am-midnight.

Hospital: Ambulance ☎131. **Hospital Ernesto Torres Galdames,** Héroes de la Concepción 502 (☎415 555).

Internet Access: Internet access is readily available all over town. **Mundo-Clic,** Latorre 370 (☎517 895), between Lynch and Baquedano (CH$500 per hr.). Open M-Sa 9am-2am, Su 9am-midnight. For cheaper rates but shorter hours try **Baquedano 909,** 2nd fl. (☎519 711), 3 blocks east of the Plaza de Armas. CH$350 per hr.

Post Office: Bolívar 458 (☎422 148 or 417 212), between Lynch and Labbe. Also handles Western Union service. Open M-F 8:30am-1pm and 3-7pm, Sa 9am-noon. **DHL/Western Union,** Arturo Prat 540 (☎220 510; www.dhl.com), on Plaza Prat, offers courier services. Open M-F 9am-7pm, Sa 10am-1pm.

ACCOMMODATIONS

Iquique's lodging varies drastically, from humble *residenciales* to restored colonial mansions and luxury beachfront hotels. Public camping is permitted on beaches south of Playas Cavancha and Brava (20km or more away from downtown). However, camping is advisable only in summer, when the beaches furnish a guard house with a police officer 24hr.

Residencial J.J. Pérez, J.J. Pérez 650 (☎421 820), between Ramírez and Vivar. Seek out the wooden doorway and "Residencial" sign that lead into a comfortable, amenity-packed hideaway. This newly renovated, multi-story building offers great proximity to the beach, and the staff is ready and willing to aid any tourist. Private bath and TV. Singles CH$6000; doubles CH$10,000; triples CH$12,000. ❷

Hotel Doña Genoveva, Latorre 458 (☎411 578 or 391 116; fax 390 405), between Lynch and Labbe, off Plaza Prat, is among the town's best medium-priced accommodations. The distinctive wood exterior houses comfortable rooms with private bath, cable TV, fridge, and laundry service in a welcoming family atmosphere. Breakfast included. Singles CH$12,500; doubles CH$18,000; triples CH$24,000. AmEx/D/MC/V. ❸

Hotel de la Plaza, Baquedano 1025 (☎419 339), 3 blocks south of Plaza Prat. This former mansion offers cable TV, rooms with private bath, and breakfast. The real attractions, however, are the high stained-glass atrium above the reception area and the 2nd fl. balcony with views of the boardwalk traffic. Singles CH$9000; doubles CH$14,000; triples CH$17,500; quads CH$24,000. ❸

Hotel Carani, Latorre 426 (☎399 999 or 399 996; fax 399 998), between Lynch and Labbe. A good bet for business travelers desiring a comfortable, centrally located hotel. The pink 5-story building has a quiet backyard garden and well-lit lobby area. Rooms equipped with private bath, cable TV, fridge, laundry, and phone. Breakfast included. Singles CH$17,000; doubles CH$24,000; triples CH$30,000. AmEx/D/MC/V. ❹

Hotel Caiti, Gorostiaga 483 (☎/fax 423 038), between Lynch and Labbe, near the center of town. A decent mid-range option with a serene inner patio and lots of fluorescent lights. Rooms have good beds, private bath, cable TV, and fridge. Breakfast included. Singles CH$10,500; doubles CH$16,500; triples CH$21,500. ❸

Hotel Carlos Condell, Baquedano 964 (☎/fax 313 027), between Zegers and Wilson. Iquique's colonial history comes alive in this newly renovated wooden building hearkening back to the 19th century. The sparkling Neoclassical facade encloses a meticulous interior decorated with miniature ship models, steering wheels, and mounted period photos. The grandeur of some rooms is accentuated by high ceilings. Breakfast included. Singles CH$15,000; doubles $20,000; triples $25,000. AmEx/D/MC/V. ❸

Hostal Catedral, Labbe 253 (☎426 372), opposite the cathedral. Despite the location, there is nothing religious about this hostel except the cleanliness of its rooms and open-air courtyard. A peaceful and pleasant alternative to the cheapest options in town. Breakfast included. Rooms with shared bath CH$5500 per person. Singles with bath CH$9800; doubles CH$14,500; triples CH$21,500. ❷

Hotel Bellavista, Bellavista 106 (☎517 979 or 517 980), on the corner with Covadonga. The proximity to the beaches increases the value of the clean pink stucco rooms with big glass windows significantly. Views of the sunset from the rooftop sitting area are gorgeous. Rooms within this red 5-story building contain private bath, cable TV, fridge, and security box. Breakfast included. Singles CH$15,000; doubles CH$20,000; triples CH$25,000. AmEx/D/MC/V. ❹

FOOD

Iquique's Parisian flavor emerges in its many cafes, where residents assume a cosmopolitan air at outdoor tables, balancing their newspapers, cigarettes, and espressos like old pros.

■ **Boulevard,** Baquedano 790 (☎413 695), between Latorre and Gorostiaga. A colorful taste of France behind a sea-blue street facade with a drawing of the Eiffel Tower. Enjoy a perfect *café* and snack on fondue while taking advantage of the charming outdoor seating, or come at night for a glass of wine and engaging conversation. The food is creatively prepared and the main course and dessert crepes (CH$4000-4800) are rich. 3-course lunch specials with drink CH$3000. *Profiteroles* CH$2000. Open daily 10:30am-4pm and 6pm-2am. AmEx/DC/MC/V. ❸

Casino Español and Restaurant Carlos Flambeau's (☎423 284), at the northeast corner of Plaza Prat next to Club Croata. Don't let this impressive Moorish building, reminiscent of Spain's Alhambra, intimidate you—it's not that expensive here, the service is exceptional, and the food is notably good. An older clientele regularly enjoys tasty soup (CH$1800-3700), seafood (CH$5800-10,300), and the house special, *paella* (CH$7900). Beer CH$1000. Open daily 10:30am-2am. AmEx/DC/MC/V. ❸

Restaurant La Carreta de Antonio, Playa Brava 1858 (☎442 909 or 323 209), across from the Shell Station. One of the better eateries in town, pleasantly located on the beach. Excellent seafood (CH$2500-6000) and meat dishes (CH$4700-6600) are served with panache. Open daily 10am-7am. AmEx/DC/MC/V. ❸

Barracuda, Gorostiaga 601 (☎427 969; www.tabernabarracuda.cl), on the corner of Ramírez. This pub and restaurant features an oak bar, gas lamps, wooden ceiling fans, and walls plastered with pictures of US presidents. Sandwiches and entrees have nicknames like the "Hemingway," a huge cut of swordfish with a cheddar cheese potato (CH$7300) or the "Titanic," a cheese *churrasco* on a baguette (CH$3200). Appetizers CH$1400-7300. Cheesecake CH$1900. Open M-Sa 6pm-2:30am. AmEx/D/MC/V. ❸

La Protectora (☎421 923), inside La Sociedad Protectora de Empleados de Tarapacá on Plaza Prat. The impressive building houses a collection of old mining relics and plays Frank Sinatra tunes. The food is inexpensive, and occasional live music spices up the plaza. Chilean crab cake CH$3000. Salads CH$1100-2500. Pizza CH$1100-2600. Beer CH$800-1200. Open daily 1-4pm and 8pm-midnight. AmEx/D/MC/V. ❷

Cafetería Vizzio, Tarapacá 400 (☎390 271 or 09 543 1293), on the corner with Lynch. A good bet for a satiating cup of coffee (CH$500-950) or light sandwiches (CH$1900-2200). Popular with locals, this cafe/restaurant also serves breakfast (CH$2000) and has a good *menú* (soup, entree, and coffee; CH$2500). Open daily 8am-midnight. ❷

Ta Chang, Sargento Aldea 765 (☎317 625), between Barros Arana and Vivar. Despite the nondescript interior, the portions at this top-notch *chifa* are huge and tasty. Some authenticity is ensured by the fact that the owners are a couple from Guangdong, China. Chicken CH$1800-2100, beef CH$2000-2400, fish CH$2500-3500. 4-course meals for 2-4 people CH$4000-9000. Open daily noon-4pm and 6:30pm-midnight. ❷

Restaurant-Cafetería Colonial, Baquedano 702 (☎312 502), on the southeast corner of Plaza Prat. Stained glass windows, photos of old Iquique, and thick red seats provide a homey atmosphere. The charming street seating is between the boardwalk and plaza and has a beautiful view at night. The 3-course lunch specials (CH$2200) are a value. Veal *milanesa* CH$4000. Open M-Sa 11am-4pm and 6:30pm-midnight. ❷

Amaretto, Sargento Aldea 753, between Barros Arana and Vivar. Locals pile into this simple pizza, *churrasco*, and breakfast sandwich hole-in-the-wall for low prices and quality food served with a smile. Low-priced daily specials are dished out by the dozen. Pizza and glass of homemade juice CH$1100. Egg and cheese sandwich with tea, coffee, or soda CH$850. *Churrasco* CH$900. Open daily 9am-4pm and 6pm-1am. ❶

📷 SIGHTS

PLAZA PRAT. Plaza Prat is a great place to sit among soaring fountains and shaded benches, but the buildings on the plaza are the real attraction. The **Torre del Reloj,** the prominent white clock tower in the middle of the plaza, is an architectural melange of Gothic and Moorish elements, and looks beautiful amidst the flowers and fountains of the plaza. The prominent white Neoclassical building with a harp crest on its pinnacle is the **Teatro Municipal,** the cultural center of Iquique since 1890. Until the 1920s, European companies performed to the wealthy mining barons of Iquique's economic heyday. Now everything from local comedians to ballet and classical music grace the incredible, copper-infused theater. The large yellow building next door is **La Sociedad Protectora de Empleados de Tarapacá,** the former quarters of one of Chile's first labor unions. Today, this opulent mansion with Corinthian friezes and stone balustrades is home to a popular bar/restaurant, **La Protectora** (see above), and hosts a collection of mining relics. The **Casino Español** (p. 157), a colorful rendition of the Alhambra in Granada, Spain, is a 1904 restaurant/museum with paintings of scenes from Spanish history and two life-sized bronze sculptures of Don Quixote and his sidekick, Sancho Panza. The Moorish arches and posh, domed interior house intricate sabres and knights' armor from Spain. *(Theater entrance CH$300. Open daily 11am-2pm and 4-6pm.)*

PARAGLIDING. Due to the smog trapped over the city by the surrounding mountains, Iquique mornings are often foggy. However, the natural mountain walls also force offshore winds upward, creating one of the world's best environments for paragliding. Paragliding, the offspring of hang-gliding and parachuting, involves soaring through the air beneath a rectangular parachute while performing spins and directing the glider. Iquique's upward-moving drafts are strong enough to keep a paraglider aloft all day long. Tours, including instruction, safety preparation, and a tandem jump (a jump strapped to an instructor) last 3-4hr. and are offered by a number of tour agencies along Baquedano, including **Mane Tour** (p. 155). It's important to remember that rapidly shifting wind directions and the fact that you're jumping off a cliff make this a dangerous sport.

BEACHES. There are plenty of places to sunbathe, swim, and surf on Iquique's beautiful white-sand beaches. Near downtown, Playa Cavancha is the most popular choice with locals and tourists alike, due to the kitschy boardwalk lined with cacti, palm trees, and fountains and the wide clean beach area. Farther south, Playa Brava and other beaches along Ruta 1 aren't as wide or sandy, but crowds are smaller during the summer, making for better surfing and quieter sunbathing. A guard house on Brava watches over a series of public campgrounds with volleyball nets. *(Playa Cavancha is within walking distance of the center of town. Colectivos to Playa Brava are CH$400; camping is free.)*

MUSEO REGIONAL. Two blocks south of Plaza Prat on Baquedano, an old judicial building, consistent with the 19th century architecture typical of Baquedano, now houses the Museo Regional. Inside, petroglyphs from Pica, fishing spears, and descriptions of Inca hallucinogenic drug use intrigue visitors. Well-preserved mummies and an impressive collection of mining relics surround a courtyard containing a recreation of the living quarters of a 19th-century miner. Conditions were generally harsh and the museum does a good job detailing the lives of the miners. There is also a room devoted to local bird and sea life. *(Baquedano 951. ☎411 214. Free. Open M-F 9am-5:30pm, Sa-Su 10am-5pm.)*

CASINO IQUIQUE. A far cry from historic, Casino Iquique is a large one-room warehouse with a tacky dulled-down red carpet and tropical bar amidst a sea of CH$100-500 slot machines. Blackjack, poker, and roulette tables further offer the thrill of chance for a minimum CH$5000 and maximum CH$50,000 bet, while servers offer free drinks to those playing the tables. *(Prat 2755. Colectivos to the casino CH$400. Open 24hr. Entrance CH$300.)*

🛍 SHOPPING

Iquique offers everything from duty-free shopping in **Zona Franca** (known in the vernacular as Zofri) to quaint handmade products available at decent *artesanías.* The new **Mall Las Américas,** an American-style shopping mall, and small "Mom and Pop" stores add to the array of shopping options. Established in 1975, Zona Franca is a veritable beehive of wholesalers and retailers. The retail mall next door to Zona Franca harbors smaller stores. *(☎515 600 or 515 405; www.zofri.cl. Open M-Sa 11am-9pm.)* Any *colectivo* going north from downtown takes you to Zofri for CH$400 per person. Prices tend to be slightly higher in Mall Las Américas (open 11am-10pm), on Héroes de la Concepción, south of town, but there is a **CineMark** megaplex that plays new releases on 8 big screens. *(☎432 500. Open daily 11am-11pm. M-Tu and Th-Su CH$2500, W CH$1700.)* The **Mercado Centenario,** east of Plaza Prat, offers a wide range of local fruits, vegetables, and fish including delicious mangos and hulking cuts of swordfish. *(Open daily 8am-3pm and 5-11pm.)*

🎵 NIGHTLIFE

Iquique is the nightlife hot spot of northern Chile—most bars and clubs stay rockin' all night long. Because of Iquique's higher-than-average concentration of gay and lesbian residents, the scene is big and inviting, despite the few openly gay or lesbian nightlife establishments that exist. Near the center of Iquique are many bars good for warming up before heading to the dance clubs along Playa Brava, south of downtown. A taxi from downtown to the clubs costs CH$1500.

IN RECENT NEWS

BOLIVIAN BEACHES?

A 120-year-old dispute over an arid stretch of Pacific coast annexed from Bolivia by Chile has recently flared up anew. The 180 miles of coastline, taken by Chile after the War of the Pacific (1879-1883), has been a growing source of resentment for land-locked Bolivians. Bolivia wants access to the coast in order to export natural gas, a plan many Bolivians hope will change the country's position as one of South America's poorest nations.

The issue has been contentious for decades. Bolivia and Chile haven't enjoyed full diplomatic relations for 25 years because of the border dispute. Chilean President Ricardo Lagos granted Bolivia permission to use land to export gas without paying taxes, but asserted that the area would remain a part of Chile. In response, Bolivian President Carlos Mesa took the issue to the hemisphere-wide Monterrey Summit, held in Mexico in Jan. 2004.

Since the summit, the rhetoric on both sides has escalated, with Bolivia demanding the territory and Chile refusing, claiming that a 1904 peace treaty legally established the current border. Pressing the issue, Bolivian indigenous-rights leader Evo Morales suggested a trade embargo be imposed by Bolivia against Chile to pressure Lagos to back down. With Chilean-Bolivian relations so rapidly disintegrating, those traveling between the two should stay abreast of developments.

■ **Taberna Van Gogh,** on the corner of Ramírez and Latorre (☎319 847). This laid-back bar has Van Gogh as their centerpiece, from the worked wooden rafters above the 2nd fl. seating area to the starry night painted on the ceiling. A great place for those who want to be social, unwind to mellow music, and like their liquor with a twist of culture. Try a "Starry Night" (kahlua and amaretto; CH$2000). Beer CH$1000-1500. Open M-Sa 7:30pm-4am. AmEx/D/MC/V.

■ **Pharos,** Arturo Prat (☎381 682), on Playa Brava south of downtown. If the triumphant entrance lined with commanding statues of Zeus, Poseidon, centurions, centaurs, and chariots isn't enough to get you going, the 2 large dance floors surrounded by imposing Greco-Roman columns will probably inspire you to new heights of revelry and rambunctiousness. Groove with the mostly 20s crowd to house DJ tunes. Beer CH$1000. Cover CH$4000, women CH$3000. Open F-Sa 11pm-5am. AmEx/D/MC/V.

Tennessee Bar, Gorostiaga 663 (☎09 545 0334), between Ramírez and Vivar. This whiskey-pouring watering hole has adopted the Jack Daniel's label as its sign, but don't be fooled. The clientele is mostly tame night-owls who come to pre-game and chill in live music before cutting loose at the discos. 10 mini *empanadas* CH$1000. 2-for-1 *pisco* sours (CH$2000) 9-10pm. Pitcher of beer CH$2500. Open M-Sa 8pm-2am.

Aqua, on Playa Brava (☎09 148 0531). The dance floor over the ocean and endless blue bar has a young crowd boiling F and Sa nights. The club plays mostly *pachenga*, pop, and rap music that blaze on this *discoteca's* huge sound system. Dance with a view of the sunrise through the rear wraparound window overlooking Playa Brava. Beer CH$800-1200. Cover CH$3000, women CH$1000. Open F-Sa 11:30pm-5am.

Canavans, Bajo Molle, Km7 (☎381 167). Although the 3 giant plastic toucans over this bar/*discoteca*/theater look more like something for a daycare center, Canavans is the best option for the late 20s crowd. Arrive around 11:30pm to catch Chilean dance groups perform until 1am, when the stage and dance floor open. Cover CH$3000. Open F-Sa 11:30pm-5am. AmEx/D/MC/V.

Kamikaze, Bajo Molle, Km7 (☎315 322; www.kamikaze.cl). Look for the large plane lodged into a red building to find Kamikaze. This bar/*discoteca* offers 2 fl. of bass-infused partying. Downstairs, the 18-25 crowd dances away to loud pop, salsa, and *pachenga*, while others chill at the tables and bamboo-bar upstairs. Cover CH$6000, women CH$4000; includes a drink. Open F-Sa midnight-5am. AmEx/D/MC/V.

La Caldera del Salón, Vía 3, Km7 (☎385 066), at Bajo Molle, farther south from Pharos. This glitzy 2-story *salsateca* whips up salsa, salsa, and more salsa. An older, more upscale crowd jives among brightly-lit artificial palm trees below the glowing circular ceiling. Cover CH$6000; includes a drink. Open F-Sa 11pm-5am.

RESERVA NACIONAL PAMPA DEL TAMARUGAL ☎57

South of Pozo Almonte, the Reserva Nacional Pampa del Tamarugal sprawls across 1000 sq. km. The first sector, a wooded area featuring the *tamarugo* tree, a weak-looking desert tree with white branches and green leaves, as well as mice, lizards, and reptiles, is a less-than-thrilling stop for most visitors. The *tamarugo* is a native tree species that once covered a vast area of Norte Grande but is now nearly extinct due to waterlogging that occurred during the area's nitrate boom. The *tamarugo* scattered throughout the reserve today are a result of Conaf's restoration efforts. Buses between Iquique and Antofagasta/Calama stop at the **Conaf office** at the Reserva Nacional (1¾hr. from Iquique, CH$2500). The Conaf office, 25km south of Pozo Almonte, just off the Panamerican, offers exhibits about the reserve's ecology. (☎751 055. Open M-F 8am-6pm but staffed during the daytime on weekends as well.) Conaf also has four **cabins** ❸ with four rooms each, kitchen facilities, a refrigerator, and shared hot-water bath (CH$8000-10,000 per cabin). **Camping** ❶ is also permitted (CH$4000 per site).

Although the campgrounds here are complete with barbecue facilities, picnic tables, sinks, and power outlets, the only reason to stay overnight is to visit the amazing **geoglyphs** at the **Salar de Pintados** in the Reserva Nacional. The Salar de Pintados is world famous for the 390 geoglyphs that can be viewed here. Drawn between AD 800 and 1300, these fascinating depictions of human and animal figures and geometric shapes aren't Velásquez-quality works of art, but the figures are clearly discernible. Historically, the figures were used to mark everything from trade sights to water and good hunting grounds. The geoglyphs also served as the signposts of this 9th-century desert, directing nomads toward the coast and mountains. Some geoglyphs were restored by the Universidad de Tarapacá in 1982. Look out for the souvenir shop at the entrance to the geoglyphs. (To reach the Pintados geoglyphs, drive south from the Conaf office for a few minutes or walk for an hour. From Pozo Almonte, hire a taxi for CH$12,000. Pay CH$1000 admission at the Conaf office.)

PICA   ☎ 57

In addition to being the home of calming rock pools and charming *artesanías*, Pica (pop. 1200) also offers visitors luscious wines and fruits, including its limes, which reputedly make the best *pisco* sours in all of Chile. The picturesque **Plaza de Armas** is home to the **Iglesia de San Andrés**, with its beige classical facade and twin bell towers. The present building dates from 1886 after earlier 17th- and 18th-century buildings were destroyed by earthquakes. A visit to the **municipal museum,** Balmaceda 178, is worth a glance because it's free, but it doesn't have much to offer. Exhibits of large concrete blocks and "fossils" require a vivid imagination to enjoy, but the small collection of mining relics provide an interesting glimpse into the past. For a more impressive prehistoric collection look out for the dinosaur footprints found near Chacrialla and the 1500-year-old mummy. (☎ 741 665 or 741 156; www.pica.cl. Open Tu-F 9am-1pm and 4-8pm, Sa 9am-1pm. Free.) In the northern part of town, the local municipality runs Pica's **natural rock pool,** open for swimming, tanning, and pure relaxation. Naturally heated mountain streams flow from underground into this small rock quarry, providing a fun bathing excursion complete with small underwater caves and waterfalls. The pool is crowded on weekends year-round, but during the week it's easy to find peace and quiet. There are showers and changing rooms at the pool. (☎ 741 310 or 741 340. CH$1000 per person, children CH$500. Open daily 9am-5pm.)

Make sure you sample ✪RAH **Alfajores ❶**, on the corner of the plaza. The sweet pastries made with a homemade mango jam are delicious. For heartier meals, try **Café y Hostal Suizo ❷**. (Breakfast CH$3250. Pizzas CH$3900. Sandwiches CH$2000. Open daily 8am-4pm. AmEx/D/MC/V.) **Guayito ❶** serves a delicious *menú* (CH$2000) with three courses and a drink. (Open daily 11am-midnight.) **Restaurant La Palmera ❶**, Balmaceda 115 on the plaza, serves simple meals for CH$1800. (☎741 144. Open daily 8pm-11pm.) **El Socavón ❷** offers a thatched roof and a romantic setting for those important meals. They serve *empanadas* (CH$500) and the CH$3000 house special, the *Socavón* salad, with crab, *ceviche*, and greens. (☎741 576. Open daily 11am-2am. AmEx/D/MC/V.) For a hoppin' Saturday night, try dancing at **El Palmear**, Balmaceda 414. (☎741 026. Open daily midnight-5am.)

The best to place to stay in Pica is **Cafe y Hostal Suizo ❸**, at General Ibáñez, a short walk from the rock pool. The Danish owners have set up a delightful Swiss-style two-story lodge that offers freshly painted, comfortable, clean rooms with satellite TV and private bath. (☎741 551. Breakfast included. Doubles CH$17,000; triples CH$20,000; quads CH$22,000. AmEx/D/MC/V.) **Guayito ❷**, General Ibáñez 69, is a tourist complex that has simple "bed and a lightbulb" rooms with private bath. This complex also has a swimming pool, wooded picnic area, conference

NORTE GRANDE

room, and campground with grills. (☎741 663 or 741 358; fax 741 270. Camping CH$1500 per person. Singles CH$7000; doubles CH$10,000; triples CH$15,000.) Other lodgings include **Hostería O'Higgins ❷**, Balmaceda 6, whose clean and new rooms with cable TV and private baths with hot water more than make up for the small beds. (☎741 524. Breakfast included. CH$5000 per person.) Although not in Pica proper, **◪Hostal Agua Santa ❹**, 2km on the road toward Matilla, has a pool with waterfall, rooms with cable TV and private baths, a large garden of mango, orange, and lime trees, and cabins with small kitchenettes and room for 10 people. The included breakfast features a fruit platter prepared before your eyes. (Rooms CH$24,000 per person; cabin for up to 10 CH$50,000. AmEx/D/MC/V.)

Pica's amenities include a **tourist office**, on Balmaceda at the entrance to Cocha Resbaladero. (☎741 310 or 741 340; www.pica.cl. Open Tu-Sa 11am-1:30pm and 3-7pm.) Other services include a **gas station**, small **supermarkets, Internet access** on the plaza, and a courier service, **Chile Express**, at Balmaceda 255 (☎741 378), which also serves as a **Western Union** and a **centro de llamadas.** (Open daily 9am-10:30pm.) Numerous **fruit vendors** and *artesanías* along General Ibañez sell mangos, dried fruit, and various handicrafts. (Mangos CH$1000 per kg. Open daily 10am-9pm.) The **post office** is at Balmaceda 371. (Open M-F 9am-12:45pm and 2:30-5pm.) Frequent **buses** run between Iquique and Pica (2hr., CH$1500) via Pozo Almonte (CH$800). A taxi to Iquique costs CH$40,000.

LA TIRANA   ☎57

La Tirana (pop. 500) occupies an important place in Chilean religious consciousness. During the town's annual religious feast of **Virgen del Carmen** (July 12-18), tens of thousands of pilgrims from all over Chile overflow this tiny village, which is virtually deserted through the rest of the year. The festivities revolve around the **Santuario de la Tirana,** the large town square housing a church with a faux night-sky ceiling painted dark blue with hundreds of raised golden stars. The spectacular dancing in colorful costumes during the celebration awakens the magnificent church. Constructed in the 1930s on the ruins of an earlier church destroyed by an earthquake, the yellow wooden exterior incongruously recalls a Masonic Temple. Opposite the church, the **Museo Regional del Salitre** (☎751 601) is a single-room exhibit containing an odd collection of paraphernalia including radios, stuffed birds, a movie projector, and a piano made in 1840.

While some pilgrims crawl from Iquique on their knees to express their praise to la Virgen de Carmen's religious devotion, a less spiritual means of arrival is available—buses connecting Iquique and Pica stop in La Tirana on a daily basis (1hr., CH$500). There are no accommodations in La Tirana except during the celebration, when local residents open their doors and offer cheap lodging and the local police convert the area outside town into free campsites. Small shops that serve basic meals are scattered throughout town.

EL GIGANTE DE ATACAMA

Ninety-five kilometers northeast of Iquique, El Gigante de Atacama, standing tall at 85m, is the largest geoglyph of a human figure in the world. The geoglyph is inscribed upon **Cerro Unita,** a lone barren hill that eerily interrupts the consistent flatness of the terrain. This bizarre figure is comprised of a large, apparently crowned, head and a long-limbed body with outstretched arms. The peculiarity of El Gigante is augmented by his equally bizarre companion, a smaller, unidentifiable creature sporting a long protuberance. The giant is impressively gigantic but public transport to the figures is not available, so you'll have to take a guided tour from Iquique, hire a taxi, or drive yourself. *(To see the geoglyphs, walk 1km off the road to reach the side of the hill that displays the giant. The side of the hill visible from the road features geometric geoglyphs resembling airport landing strips.)*

TARAPACÁ ☎ 57

Nine kilometers east of Cerro Unita and 7km farther along the road, the town of Tarapacá, a dusty town littered with deteriorating adobe houses, was the capital of the northernmost region of Chile when the area was under Peruvian rule. Sadly, for a town with such an illustrious history, there is little reason to stop here anymore unless a visit to the **Iglesia San Lorenzo** strikes your fancy. A national monument built in 1717, the church holds its annual festival on August 10. The church has recently finished renovations from a 1987 earthquake. To get in, ask at the shop on the corner of the plaza for the key. At the entrance to Tarapacá is a small monument dedicated to a battle fought here in 1879 during the War of the Pacific. Tarapacá offers no accommodations and no amenities other than a small **grocery store** and a **centro de llamadas**. Since international buses do not pass by here, arrange a guided tour or hire a taxi to see Tarapacá.

MAMIÑA ☎ 57

Mamiña (pop. 250) has long been famous for its smelly yet reviving thermal baths, but this tiny town at 2500m is also home to pre-Hispanic ruins, petroglyphs, and geoglyphs. Mamiña is a great place to relax and let the outside world melt away.

▐▪▌ TRANSPORTATION AND PRACTICAL INFORMATION. Buses leave regularly to Iquique (2¾hr., 8am and 6pm, CH$3000) via Pozo Almonte (1¾hr., CH$1500). As you enter Mamiña, the paved road becomes cobblestone around the upper section of town and gravel in the lower section. The upper section centers around the **Iglesia de Nuestra Señora del Rosario**, a brick building built in the 17th century, and the Plaza de Armas. The lower section of town houses most accommodations and sights. Mamiña has **no bank, ATM, gas station, or Internet access;** however, a few **grocery** stores (open daily 9am-11pm), a **paramedic clinic**, and a **centro de llamadas** (open daily 9am-1pm and 2:30-10:30pm) are available.

▐▪▌ ACCOMMODATIONS AND FOOD. Besides staying with a local family, there are no cheap options for lodging in this spa town. If you're looking to spoil yourself, head down to the lower section of town, to **Hotel Los Cardenales ❺**, a colorful chalet overlooking the valley. This four-star complex boasts a large indoor thermal swimming pool, terraces ideal for sunbathing, and tastefully decorated rooms that include a Jacuzzi, satellite TV, and three meals a day. Guests are invited to luxuriate in the owners' spacious and elegant living room. Make sure to book ahead, or you may just have to settle for lunch and the use of the swimming pool for a day. (☎517 000; fax 517 777. CH$25,000 per person; lunch option CH$8000. AmEx/D/MC/V.) If Cardenales is outside your budget, visit **Hotel Niña de Mis Ojos ❷**. Clean rooms with private bathrooms and chipping paint flank the dining hall where breakfast (CH$1200) and four-course lunches (CH$2500) are served. (☎420 451. CH$15,000 per person including all meals; without meals CH$7000.) **Hotel Tamarugal ❷**, next to Baños de Ipla, offers a view of the valley from intimate, white-washed rooms with private baths and three meals a day included. A ping-pong table and plastic pool help prolong relaxation after time in the thermal baths. (☎/fax 519 937. All meals included. CH$15,000 per person.) Another luxurious, yet affordable, alternative to Hotel Los Cardenales is **Hotel Llama Inn ❸**, with comfortable rooms, thermal baths, and two-room cabins that sleep four to six people. A large hall with a lounge and bar, satellite TV, and a sizable outdoor swimming pool are great and their adorable pet llamas are good for hours of entertainment. (☎420 451. Singles CH$19,000 including all meals. AmEx/D/MC/V.) **Restaurant Cerro Morado ❸** is a hotel with comfy rooms in a chalet-style wooden building. All cabins have thermal baths. The restaurant serves breakfast (CH$1200), and the hearty lunch is usually a local recipe like rabbit or alpaca meat and salad. (☎09 244 6093. Singles CH$12,000 including all meals.)

◪ SIGHTS. While most hotels have private thermal baths, a dip in public baths is possible at **Baños de Ipla**. The smell of sulfur is pungent, but at 40 degrees Celsius it's hard not to feel relaxed. (☎751 298. Open daily 8am-2pm and 3-9pm. CH$1000 per 20min.) **Baños el Chino,** located 20m past Hotel Cardenales, is a public mud bath in an outdoor setting named after a Chinese visitor in the 19th century who was miraculously cured of all ailments after covering himself in the mud. The attendant brings a bucket of mud to your own private room and when you're done covering yourself in the skin-enhancing goo, there are benches for baking in the sun. The couples' rooms allow pairs to enjoy the natural mud baths together. (Open daily 9am-3pm. CH$1000 per day, children CH$500.) **Kespikala Centro de Arte y Artesanía Indígena** (☎09 364 4762) is housed in a rustic stone building with a straw-covered ceiling in the lower part of town. A space for the promotion, display, and sale of indigenous arts and crafts, including pink volcanic rock, the *centro* also functions as the unofficial tourist office for the village.

CALAMA   ☎ 55

Although the copper mining town of Calama (pop. 123,000) isn't much of a tourist hot spot, it's an important transportation hub for travelers. Much of the tourist traffic that passes through is en route to nearby San Pedro de Atacama, stopping in briefly for the amenities (banks with ATMs, car rentals, and an airport) that tiny San Pedro lacks. Calama is conveniently near San Pedro (only an hour away on the paved Ruta 23) and has spectacular attractions in the surrounding area, including some interesting archaeological ruins, Andean villages perched high in the mountains, and the beautiful landscape of the Atacama. Set in the middle of the Atacama desert, San Pedro has the world's largest sustained oasis population. Within the next couple of years, however, Calama anticipates an influx of more than eager tourists—the entire population of neighboring Chuquicamata (p. 168), a company town of some 15,000 people, is scheduled to relocate here.

▐ TRANSPORTATION

Flights: Aeropuerto El Loa, 5km from downtown, is serviced by **radio taxis** (CH$3500 to town; see **Taxis and Colectivos,** below). **LanChile,** Latorre 1726 (☎343 466), between Sotomayor and Vicuña Mackenna. Open M-F 9am-1pm and 3-7:30pm, Sa 9:30am-1pm. Flies to **Santiago** (3hr.; 5 per day 7:30am-6:50pm; one-way CH$88,500, round-trip CH$144,500) via **Antofagasta** (30min.; one-way CH$23,805, round-trip CH$33,610). **Sky Airline,** Latorre 1497 (☎310 190), on the corner with León Gallo, has cheap last-minute flights to **Santiago** (3hr.; M, W, F 7:30am, Th-Sa 6:30pm; one-way CH$124,579, round-trip CH$129,800).

Trains: The **train station** (☎348 901) is on the corner of Balmaceda and Sotomayor. A British company runs a weekly train service to **Uyuni, BOL** (24hr., W 11pm, CH$7000), where you can connect to trains continuing onto **Oruro, BOL** or **La Paz, BOL.** Book a ticket on the day of departure, 3-10pm. At Ollagüe on the Bolivian border, the train changes to a Bolivian locomotive—a slow, old train with very basic seats (no first class available). Unless you are a railway aficionado, it is better to go with the faster and more comfortable bus service to Uyuni, BOL.

Buses: There is no central bus station in Calama, and the various bus companies leave from their own offices or terminals.

Tur Bus (☎317 699), on the corner of Balmaceda and Ramírez. Buses leave from the terminal at Granaderos 3048, several blocks north of downtown. Daily buses to: **Antofagasta** (3hr., every 30min. 7am-9:45pm, CH$2500); **Arica** (9hr., 10:05pm, CH$7000) via **Iquique** (7hr., 4 per day 7am-11:15pm, CH$6000), **María Elena** (2hr., CH$2000), and **Tocopilla** (3hr., CH$3100); **San Pedro** (1½hr., 8 per day 7am-6:20pm, CH$1000); **Santiago** (22hr., 9 per day 7:45am-10pm, CH$18,000) via **Copiapó** (11hr., CH$12,000) and **La Serena** (16hr., CH$13,500).

Pullman Bus (☎311 410) leaves from the corner of Balmaceda and Sotomayor. Daily departures to: **Arica** (9hr., every hr. 9:30am-10:30pm, CH$8000) via **Iquique** (7hr., CH$7000); **Santiago** (22hr., every 30min. 7:30am-9:45pm, CH$18,000) via **Antofagasta** (3hr., CH$2500), **Baquedano** (2hr., CH$2100), **Copiapó** (10hr., CH$11,000), **La Serena** (15hr., CH$13,000), and **Valparaíso** (20hr., CH$18,000).

Flota Barrios (☎341 643) departs daily from Santa María near the corner with Ramírez. To: **Antofagasta** (3hr., 5 per day 7:45am-8:15pm, CH$2000) via **Baquedano** (2hr., CH$1500); **Santiago** (24hr., 7:45am, 3, 7:15pm; CH$20,000).

Ramos Cholele (☎317 989), at the corner of Vargas and Balmaceda, also has daily departures to **Antofagasta, Arica, Iquique,** and **Santiago.** Call ahead for prices and times.

Regional Buses: Smaller, regional companies serve nearby destinations. **Buses Frontera** (☎318 543) leaves from its office on Antofagasta between Abaroa and Latorre for: **San Pedro** (1½hr.; 7 per day 8:30am-8:30pm; one-way CH$1300, round-trip CH$2300); **Socaire** (2½hr.; M, W, F 6pm; CH$3000); **Toconao** (2hr., 4 per day 8:30am-6pm, CH$1800). **Atacama 2000** (☎364 295) leaves from the corner of Antofagasta and Abaroa daily to **Peine** (3½hr., 12:30 and 6pm, CH$2300) via **Toconao** (2¼hr., CH$1500) and **San Pedro** (8:30am, 12:30, 6pm; CH$1000). **Camus** (☎342 800), on Balmaceda between Vargas and Espinoza, also has infrequent daily departures to **María Elena** and **Toconao.**

Micros: *Micros* run daily 7am-10pm. CH$200, CH$250 to outskirts of town.

Taxis and Colectivos: A few taxi companies head to the airport, including **Radio Taxi Afluentes del Loa** (☎316 824) and **Taxi Abant** (☎346 769). **Taxi LM,** Balmaceda 1974 (☎346 069), goes to **Tocopilla** for CH$3500 per person. **Colectivos** cost CH$300-350 in and near downtown. **Colectivo 80** (☎362 523) goes to **Chiu Chiu** (CH$1300 per person).

Car Rentals: Try the reputable **Hertz,** Granaderos 1418 (☎341 380; www.hertz.cl).

ORIENTATION AND PRACTICAL INFORMATION

The downtown area is pretty compact, with most shops and services concentrated within a **rectangular grid** bound by Vargas to the north, Vicuña Mackenna to the south, Granaderos to the west, and Vivar to the east. Try not to venture beyond this square at night. **Ramírez** is a pedestrian street, between Abaroa and Vivar, with a bunch of pharmacies, 24hr. ATMs, Internet stores, and upscale hotels. **Sotomayor** is the main banking and commercial street for everything money-related.

Tourist Office: Oficina de Información Turística, Latorre 1689 (☎345 345; calamainfotour@entelchile.net), on the corner with Vicuña Mackenna, provides great information on Calama and San Pedro. Open M-F 9am-12:50pm and 3-7:30pm.

Tours: There are several tour operators in town, but the same tours are offered for less by more experienced travel agencies in San Pedro. Your best bet is to inquire at the **Oficina de Información Turística** (see above), which offers guided tours to **El Tatio Geysers,** with visits to Chiu Chiu, Caspana, and other villages and archaeological ruins. (Departs 4am, returns 6pm. Call for prices.) Trips to **San Pedro de Atacama, Lago Chaxa** in Salar de Atacama, **Toconao,** and **Valle de la Luna** also available. (Departs 7am, returns 10:30pm. Entry fee to Lago Chaxa and the museum in San Pedro extra. Call for prices.) The **Chuquicamata Division of Codelco Chile** runs the must-see tour of the Chuquicamata mine (see **Chuquicamata,** p. 168).

Consulates: Bolivian Consulate, Latorre 1395 (☎344 413 or 341 976), on the corner with Latorre. Open M-F 9am-3pm.

Banks and Currency Exchange: There are tons of **banks** and **24hr. ATMs** on Sotomayor and Ramírez between Abaroa and Vivar. **Moon Valley,** Vivar 1818 (☎361 423), cashes traveler's checks. Open M-Sa 9:30am-2pm and 4:30-9:30pm.

Camping and Outdoor Equipment: Mall Calama (☎368 300), on Balmaceda, a 10min. walk north of downtown, harbors a few stores that sell camping and outdoor equipment. Try **Ripley** (☎368 100), on the 2nd fl., for camping gear, and **Maui and Sons** (☎319 415), on the 1st fl., for surfboards and warm jackets. Open daily 11am-9pm.

Supermarket: The biggest is **Lider,** Balmaceda 3242 (☎368 200), next to Mall Calama, north of downtown. Lider is also a department store. Open daily 9:30am-10pm.

Laundromat: There are several in town, including **Lavandería Gallardo** (☎316 541), on Latorre near the corner with León Gallo. CH$1300 per kg. Open M-Sa 10am-9pm.

Police: ☎133.

Pharmacy: There are many in the center of town, including **Farmacia Cruz Verde,** Sotomayor 1898 (☎341 468). Open daily 9am-10pm.

Hospital: Ambulance ☎131. **Hospital Carlos Cisternas,** Carlos Cisternas 2253 (☎342 347), near the corner with Granaderos.

Internet Access: The heaviest concentration of Internet places is north of the plaza along Granaderos, but **Ciber Café Internet,** Ramírez 1917 between Abaroa and Latorre, has the most central location. CH$500 per hr. Open daily 10am-11pm.

Post Office: 2 locations: downtown at Vicuña Mackenna 2197, on the corner with Granaderos, and in Mall Calama. (Downtown: ☎342 536. Open M-F 9am-1:30pm and 3:30-7:30pm, Sa 9am-2pm. Mall: ☎343 304. Open M-F 10:30am-2pm and 4-8pm.) Both also function as **Western Union.**

▐ ACCOMMODATIONS

Due to Calama's mining-derived wealth, prices for accommodations are significantly higher here compared to those in Arica or Iquique. Despite a few good values, most middle- and upper-range lodgings are overpriced. The lodging experience screams "get to San Pedro."

El Mirador, Sotomayor 2064 (☎/fax 340 329 or 310 294), between Abaroa and Latorre. A worthwhile splurge, El Mirador boasts a sitting room with antique furniture and a big-screen TV, a distinctive wooden lookout tower (hence the name "El Mirador"), and spacious rooms with private bath and cable TV. Parking and breakfast included. Singles CH$28,000; doubles CH$35,000. AmEx/D/DC/MC/V. ❺

Gran Chile, Latorre 1474 (☎317 455 or 331 829), on the corner with León Gallo. The motel-like concrete building has newly furnished rooms with private bath and cable TV. Singles CH$9500; doubles CH$13,500; triples CH$19,000. ❸

Hostal San Sebastián, Aníbal Pinto 1902 (☎343 810), on the corner with Ramírez. One of the better budget options. San Sebastián has matching sheets and bedspreads in small but comfortable rooms. The friendly staff makes the stay here even more enjoyable. Rooms enclose a dining area with cable TV. Breakfast included. Singles CH$5000, with bath CH$9000; doubles CH$12,000; triples CH$15,000. ❷

Hotel Punakora, Santa María 1640 (☎344 955 or 344 958), near Vicuña Mackenna. This 2-story building with an inner atrium has appealing and new, thick-mattressed rooms with private bath, cable TV, phone, fridge, free Internet, and airport pickup. Breakfast included. Singles CH$36,500; doubles CH$42,500. AmEx/DC/MC/V. ❺

Hostal El Arriero, Ramírez 2262 (☎315 556), between Granaderos and Santa María. Enter through the red fence with yellow railings. Rooms have low ceilings with low beds, but the bright hallway is a mood lifter. Cheap price and cheap rooms close to the center of town. CH$4000 per person. ❷

Hotel John Kenny, Ecuador 1991 (☎341 430 or 310 400; fax 340 069), on the corner with Latorre, a 10min. walk south of downtown. A flower-laden peach interior can't hide the bizarre lookout tower. The well-designed interior also can't help the small rooms, but cable TV and private baths compensate. Singles CH$14,000; doubles CH$26,000. ❹

📭 FOOD

Despite its size and significance for travelers, Calama presents a gastronomical challenge. It takes some effort to find a decent eatery with a good atmosphere.

Club Croata, Abaroa 1869 (☎342 126), on the east side of Plaza 23 de Marzo. Its walls are covered by posters of the Dalmatian coast and Croatian coats of arms. The leather lounge surrounding the bar is a great place to party late nights. Try the *almuerzo del día* (4-course lunch special; CH$2500) or sample from the Croatian-Chilean menu that includes sandwiches (CH$1500-2000), fish (CH$4000-4800), and salads (CH$1500-2000). Open daily 9:30am-4pm and 7:30pm-midnight. ❷

El Pollo Scout, Vargas 2102 (☎341 376), on the corner of Vargas and Latorre. Quick and easy Chilean food, great for a cheap dinner or snack. The ¼-chicken with fries (CH$1500) is the house special and locals swarm here until the place closes. *Churrasco* and other sandwiches CH$1000-1400. Open daily 11pm-1am. ❸

Barlovento, Granaderos 2030-2034 (☎342 848), between Antofagasta and Vargas. Don't let the gaudy mirrored exterior deter you—Barlovento is a great restaurant with attentive service that makes dishes right before your eyes. They have a tasty variety; from crab (CH$3800) to vegetarian dishes (CH$2500-3800) to the daily *menú* (CH$2000). Beer CH$600-1200. Open daily 8am-1am. AmEx/DC/MC/V. ❸

Restaurant La Paila, Vargas 1905 (☎09 394 2795), on the corner with Vivar. Enter the nondescript interior to be greeted by a "welcome" plaque in 7 languages. Paila doesn't look like much but this place knows seafood. *Paila marina* CH$3500. Fish CH$3000-4500. *Mariscos* CH$3500-5000. Sandwiches CH$1000-2000. Beer CH$1000. Open daily noon-5am. ❷

Restaurante Grande Chung Hwa, Latorre 1415 (☎363 826), south of León Gallo. Steaming wonton soup (CH$1500) and chop suey (CH$3000) are served in an imposing Buddhist temple facade. Waitresses clad in red silk serve in front of an aquarium of giant goldfish. Dinner for 2 CH$9800. Chicken dishes CH$3500-4000. Open daily noon-4pm and 8pm-1:30am. AmEx/D/MC/V. ❸

👁 🕭 SIGHTS AND ENTERTAINMENT

One of the best things to do in Calama is to take a tour of the ⚐**Chuquicamata mine,** the world's biggest open-pit copper mine. **Chuquicamata Division of Codelco Chile,** the large state-owned copper producer, runs the tour, starting in Chuquicamata. Take any yellow *colectivo* from the corner of Abaroa and Ramírez. (20min., CH$800), tell the driver "Chuquicamata Codelco Tour," and they'll drop you off right at the front door of the tour office. The tour starts with presentations in the tour office, followed by a bus ride to the copper mine (long pants and closed shoes are required). If the first bus is full, then another bus is usually organized. (☎327 550; www.codelco.com. Tours start 2pm; participants should arrive 1-1:30pm. Free; donations accepted.)

On a lazy afternoon, the **Plaza 23 de Marzo** offers a relaxing place to sit while enjoying the pink exterior of **Iglesia Catedral San Juan Bautista,** which was built in 1906 and remodeled in 2000. Another spot to visit is **Parque El Loa,** just south of downtown on O'Higgins next to the Río Loa, which has a riverside swimming pool, museums, and *artesanía* stalls. (Open daily 8am-10pm.) Within the park grounds, two museums, the **Museo de Historia Natural y Cultural** and the **Museo Arqueológico y Etnográfico,** provide encyclopedias of information on the Atacama region. The Museo de Historia is across Parque Loa's stream and has everything from insects of the world to one hundred years of Chilean currency. The Museo Arqueológico is smaller and the exhibits of local textile work, past and present, are only worth a quick look. (To reach Parque El Loa take *colectivo* #18 from downtown. Museo de Historia open Tu-Su 10:30am-1pm and 3-7pm. CH$500, children CH$200. Museo Arqueológico open M-Th 10am-12:45pm and 3-7pm, Sa-Su 2-6pm. Free.)

There are numerous **artesanías** selling crafts and souvenirs in town, including the **Feria Artesanal** on Ramírez, but you are better off buying these in San Pedro. For recent Hollywood movies and other flicks, you can try **Cine Mundo** in Mall Calama. (☎349 480. CH$3000, W CH$2400. Open daily 11am-10:30pm.)

▶ DAYTRIPS FROM CALAMA

CHUQUICAMATA   ☎55

Yellow colectivos to Calama leave from the Plaza de Armas down the street from the tour office. (One-way CH$800).

Superlatives abound in describing the mining town of Chuquicamata, simply called "Chuqui" by locals—it is home to the biggest open-pit copper mine in the world, owned and operated by the biggest copper producer in the world, **Codelco,** the biggest single contributor to Chile's Gross Domestic Product. Copper created Chuqui, but copper is currently destroying it as well. Air contamination and ground pollution from the refinery process, as well as a recently discovered stash of copper, mean Codelco is relocating the city's entire population by 2006. Chuqui feels more like a ghost town every day as lines of houses are left empty, but still standing. School is still in session and banks are still operating, but that will all change soon as Chuqui becomes part of the projected 15km long, 5km wide, 2000m deep expansion of the copper mine, expected to be completed by 2052.

The **◼tour** of the state-of-the-art facilities that produce refined copper makes the vast importance of the mining industry in Chile really hit home. **Codelco,** the Corporación Nacional del Cobre de Chile, is the world's foremost copper producer, churning out 16% of the total world production, and controlling 20% of the total identified copper reserves worldwide. Codelco has tried to maintain a sound environmental policy, utilizing a system of dust control and water purification, but the cumulative effect of years of pollution has clearly taken its toll. The tour of Chuquicamata begins in Calama (see **Sights and Entertainment,** above) and is an absolute must-do. A bus brings guests to a lookout point over the 2.7 mi. long, 1.9 mi. wide, and 2400 ft. deep mine. Beyond the mine, the tour includes a chance to climb around one of the massive mine trucks.

Chuquicamata still has a few restaurants, a **gas station, bank, minimarket,** and **police station,** but people and stores are disappearing rapidly. There are no accommodations here, but there is no reason to stay overnight anyway, given the air pollution and the proximity of Calama with its abundance of accommodations.

CHIU CHIU

There is no bus service between Calama and Chiu Chiu, so grab a colectivo—call Línea 80 in Calama. (☎343 400. 45min., CH$1300.)

Chiu Chiu (pop. 800) is a small village smack-dab in the middle of miles of desert. The only things in between Chiu Chiu and the mountains miles away are sand, more sand, and one small stream. Fortunately, this stream carries fresh mountain run-off, and the inhabitants of Chiu Chiu have a bustling agricultural system. Carrots, potatoes, and onions run about CH$1000 per 100kg. Roam the sunny **Plaza de Armas** or shop around at the plentiful **artesanía** in town.

A couple of simple restaurants are available, including **Muley ❷**, which has a daily *menú* (CH$2500 for 2 plates) and expensive *churrasco*. (☎09 451 7743; muley@chile.com. *Churrasco* CH$1800. Open daily 9am-11pm.) For those too tired to head back to Calama, comfortable beds in a simple concrete complex are available at **Hotel Tujina ❷**, which provides a steady supply of hot water. (☎09 566 4589. Rooms with shared bath CH$5000 per person, with private bath CH$9000.) Chiu Chiu also has a few small **grocery stores**, a **centro de llamadas** (open daily 9:30am-1pm and 3:30-5:30pm), and a **paramedic station.**

CASPANA

To get to Caspana, you need to come with a tour group or drive on your own, as there is no public transportation. The drive from El Tatio has spectacular altiplano scenery, with sweeping vistas of snow-capped peaks, herds of llamas and vicuñas on vast punas, and steep canyons with scattered petroglyphs.

A series of Andean villages and pre-Hispanic archaeological ruins dot the rugged landscape between Calama and the geysers at El Tatio. The most significant of these is Caspana (pop. 600), some 40km from El Tatio via a network of gravel roads. In this charming, pre-*cordillera* village nestled in a fertile river valley, villagers can be spotted herding sheep on green pastures watered by the Río Caspana. Many of the quaint houses are made of stone, with straw roofs, mud reinforcement, and cactus suspension beams. The rustic town also features the agricultural terraces of pre-Hispanic origins and the whitewashed **Iglesia de San Lucas.** Next to a stone bridge straddling the Río Caspana is the **Museo Etnográfico,** which houses a significant collection representing the local cultural and archaeological heritage. (Open Tu-Su 10am-1pm and 2-5pm. CH$600, students CH$400.)

Humble accommodations are available in a run-down dorm room at **Comite Artesanas de Caspana ❶.** (No hot water. CH$1500 per person.) There are a couple of eateries in town featuring basic meals, and the Comite also doubles as a tiny **grocery store.** (Open daily 9am-1pm and 5-8pm.) No other services exist except for a **paramedic station** and a **centro de llamadas** (open 9am-1pm and 5-8pm).

Near Caspana, heading farther north, is the even tinier village of **Toconce** (pop. 100), with a small *iglesia* and agricultural terraces, and the similarly diminutive **Alquina** (pop. 50), which has a nice lookout point over the Río Salado. Situated between Alquina and Toconce is **Pukará de Turi,** the ruins of a pre-Inca city, and the nearby **Baños de Turi,** a natural thermal spring.

PUKARÁ DE LASANA

The only way to get to Pukará de Lasana is via a tour group or by colectivo—try Línea 80. (☎343 400. CH$1800 for the 1hr. ride from Calama; CH$500 from Chiu Chiu.)

Farther west, 33km from Turi, is **Pukará de Lasana,** the ruins of a 12th-century village restored between 1951 and 1953. Built on a hill that rises above the valley of the Río Loa, the longest river in Chile, Pukará de Lasana is an intricate maze of rooms and passages enclosed by gray stone walls. There is an entrance at the foot of the hill with a small exhibition room featuring ancient

NORTE GRANDE

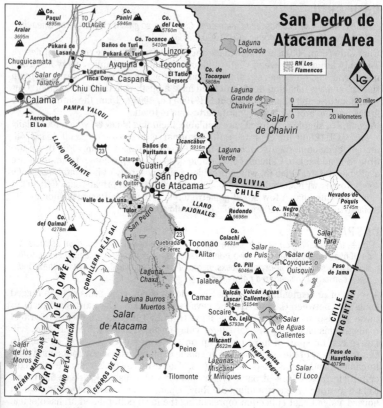

tools, pottery, and other archaeological findings. The climb up the hill is an easy 5min. walk—you can tour the whole Pukará in 20min. if you are in a hurry. (Open daily 10am-6pm. CH$1000.) In the summer, **camping** is possible along the Río Loa. If you pay the CH$1000 admission fee, you can even use the super-clean bath/shower during office hours in the entrance to the Pukará building.

SAN PEDRO DE ATACAMA   ☎ 55

In the past decade, the tiny desert oasis village of San Pedro de Atacama (pop. 3000), with its dusty streets and quaint adobe houses, has been transformed into the tourist mecca of northern Chile. A hip, pre-*cordillera* town packed with trendy eateries, bars, and accommodations, San Pedro de Atacama contains an endless variety of adventure tours into the surrounding Atacama desert, the driest in the world. The adventurer can sandboard in moonlight, the academic can visit uncovered Incan ruins, and those with older, weaker joints can enjoy a posh breakfast while watching dozens of geysers explode at nearby El Tatio. San Pedro has something for everyone—and it shows in the crowded, tourist-packed streets.

San Pedro de Atacama

🏠 ACCOMMODATIONS

Hostal Camping Puritama, 9
Hostal Camping Takha Takha, 8
Hostal Katarpe, 6
Hostaría San Pedro de Atacama, 17
Hotel Kimal, 10
Hotel Tulor, 18
Residencial Chiloé, 1
Residencial Corvatsch, 2
Residencial Rayco, 3
Residencial Florida, 4

🍴 FOOD

Café Adobe, 14
Café Étnico, 5
Café Export, 7
Casa de Piedra, 13
La Estaka, 15
Milagro, 12
Restaurante La Casona, 11
Restaurante Paacha, 16

▐ TRANSPORTATION

Flights: Calama airport is the closest airport. **Transfer Licancábur** (☎/fax 334 194) runs a minibus from the airport to San Pedro (1½hr., CH$6000 per person). Call for schedules. There is no taxi *colectivo* between Calama and San Pedro.

Buses: San Pedro does not have a central bus terminal; most buses leave from the area on Licancábur between Calama and the Feria Artesanal. Note that **Frontera** buses are often used by **Pullman** for the same routes, and tickets can be purchased at the Frontera office for Pullman buses connecting to **Antofagasta, Arica, Calama, Iquique, Santiago,** and other cities.

Tur Bus (☎ 851 549), on the corner of Licancábur and Calama, goes to: **Arica** (11hr., 8:30pm, CH$9000) via **Iquique** (8hr., CH$7000); **Calama** (1hr., 8 per day 8:50am-10:30pm, CH$1000); **Santiago** (22hr., 4 per day 8:50am-7:30pm, CH$19,500) via **Antofagasta** (4hr., CH$3800), **Copiapó** (15hr., CH$12,200), and **La Serena** (17hr., CH$14,400).

Buses Frontera (☎ 851 117), on Licancábur near Tocopilla, goes to: **Calama** (1hr., 7 per day 8am-8:30pm, CH$1000); **Socaire** (1¾hr., M and Th-F 7:30pm, CH$1700); **Toconao** (30min., 5 per day 10am-7:30pm, CH$500).

Buses Atacama 2000 (☎ 851 501), on Licancábur opposite the Feria Artesanal, goes to: **Calama** (1hr.; 8am, 1:30, 7pm; CH$1100); **Peine** (1¾ hr.; M-F 7:40pm, Su-Tu 2:30pm; CH$1800) via **Toconao** (30min., CH$500).

Geminis (☎ 851 538), on Le Paige off the plaza, offers service to **Jujuy, ARG** (13hr.; Tu, F, Su 11:30am; CH$13,000).

Taxis: Taxis leave from the general bus stop area on **Licancábur,** opposite the Feria Artesanal. **Radio taxi** goes to destinations in or near San Pedro, including **Calama** (CH$25,000), **Catarpe** (CH$6500), **Pukará de Quitor** (CH$3000), **Toconao** (CH$16,000), and **Tulor** (CH$6000).

Rentals: There are no car rental agencies in San Pedro. **Colque Tours** (see **Tours,** p. 173) sells and rents camping and mountaineering equipment. **H20** (☎ 851 013), on Caracoles between Toconao and Tocopilla, sells mineral water and rents **bikes** (CH$1000 per hr., CH$3000 per half-day, CH$5000 per day) and **sandboards** (CH$3500 per half-day, CH$5000 per day). There are many other bike and sandboard rental agencies on Caracoles that offer the same rates.

ORIENTATION AND PRACTICAL INFORMATION

San Pedro is located 1½hr. east of Calama by bus, on the paved **Ruta 23,** which continues south to Socaire. Most destinations in town are within 10-15min. walking distance, and although most addresses are *sin número* (without a number), the village is small enough to search out what you are looking for on foot. The church and many services are on the **Plaza de Armas,** but **Caracoles** is the main drag where most restaurants, tour operators, and shops reside.

Tourist Office: Sernatur, on the northeast corner of the Plaza de Armas. Open M-W and F-Sa 9:30am-1pm and 2-7pm, Su 9:30am-1pm and 3-7pm.

> **TIP**
>
> **LEARNING FROM OTHERS' MISTAKES.** While the San Pedro de Atacama branch of Sernatur has no English-speaking staff, and minimal information and brochures, it does maintain a log containing visitors' experiences and criticisms of tour agencies, hotels, and hostels in San Pedro. Previous tourists have cited everything from drunk van drivers to attempted assaults, so be sure to **look through the book before making reservations** with agencies or hostels. Virtually every company has at least one criticism—be wary of those with an impressive collection.

Tours: Most agencies offer the same tours and will often work together to fill up available slots. The "Big Three" tours are offered daily by every operator, going to: **Valle de la Luna** (includes visit to Valle de la Muerte and other nearby sights; in summer 4pm and evening full-moon trip, in winter 2pm; CH$4000-5000, entrance fee CH$1500); **El Tatio Geysers** (breakfast included; 4am, CH$10,000-12,000); **Laguna Chaxa,** in the Salar de Atacama (includes visit to Toconao; 3pm, CH$5000-6000, entrance fee CH$2000). A full-day trip is **Geysers y Pueblos Altiplánicos,** which visits El Tatio Geysers and a series of Andean villages and archaeological sites between El Tatio and Calama, including **Caspana** and **Pukará de Lasana** (breakfast and lunch included; 4am, CH$20,000-25,000). **Lagunas Altiplánicas y Salar de Atacama** covers Laguna Chaxa, Toconao, Socaire, and a series of *altiplano* lakes further south such as Lagunas Miscanti, Miñiques, and Lejia (breakfast and lunch included; 7am, CH$20,000-25,000, 3 entrance fees CH$5000 each). Many operators also offer half-day **archaeological tours** around San Pedro that go to Pukará de Quitor, the ruins in Catarpe, and Tulor (8am, CH$6000-7000, entrance fee CH$3000). Full-day trips and archaeological tours usually require a minimum of 4 people. A few operators offer specialized tours, such as mountaineering trips to nearby peaks and a 3-day trip to **Uyuni, BOL.** Completing the fantastic San Pedro tours will free up time for possibly taking a 2-, 3-, or 4-day tour to Uyuni, BOL, including a visit to the world's largest salt flat, the **Salar de Uyuni.** There are numerous biking, horseback riding, sandboarding, trekking, and astronomical tours available as well (see **Outdoor Activities,** p. 178).

Desert Adventure (☎851 067 or 851 181; www.desertadventure.cl), on the corner of Caracoles and Tocopilla. A reputable tour agency with tours in English, French, German, and Spanish. Desert Adventure is one of the only agencies in town with traveler's insurance for every customer and personally contracted guides and vehicles. Their tours of the Big Three include surprises like geyser-cooked eggs and funny, informative guides. Other tourists have called Desert Adventure reliable, consistent, and informative. They also have a series of 2-, 3-, and 4-day all-inclusive tours that include lodging, numerous tours, and pick-up and drop-off at the airport in Calama (see website for details). Open M-F 9am-9:30pm, Sa-Su 10am-9:30pm. AmEx/D/MC/V.

Cosmo Andino Expeditions (☎/fax 851 069; cosmoandino@entelchile.net), across the street from Desert Adventure on the corner of Caracoles and Tocopilla. Has the most proficient French-, German-, and English-speaking staff in town. Cosmo tours generally cost a few thousand *pesos* more for the reliability of their vans and a well-trained staff of trilinguists. Their main forays include the Big Three and popular daytrips (El Tatio Geysers CH$12,000; *altiplano* lakes CH$25,000; Valle de la Muerte CH$5000). Open daily 9:30am-9pm. AmEx/D/MC/V.

Vulcano Expediciones (☎/fax 851 023 or 851 373; www.vulcanochile.cl), on Caracoles near Toconao. If all the talk about the Big Three has you tired, Vulcano is a great cure. Vulcano offers a number of off-the-beaten-path excursions, including the chance to climb the monstrous Volcán Llullaillaco (6760m). Their difficult mountain hikes require good physical condition and are only available during the summer, but the local guides have a good reputation for knowing the area. Vulcano offers the traditional tours and the traditional tours on steroids: for example, see El Tatio Geysers then hike parts of the surrounding mountain range. For more information on sandboarding trips (CH$15,000), hikes of Licancábur (CH$60,000), and other 4-day trips, visit their website. Open daily 9:30am-10pm. AmEx/D/MC/V.

Corvatsch Expediciones (☎851 087; corvatsch@sanpedroatacama.com), on the corner of Le Paige and Tocopilla. For those in dire need to save a few *pesos*, Corvatsch is a good option. Their tours are cheaper than most other agencies and of the budget travel agencies they have one of the better reputations. Corvatsch does not, however, have its own guides, buses, or any English-, French-, or German-speaking staff. They hire independent guides or put customers with other agencies. There's nothing wrong with going on a Cosmo Andino tour for CH$2000 less than Cosmo Andino customers pay. Valle de la Muerte CH$3000. Full-day *altiplano* trip CH$20,000. El Tatio Geysers CH$10,000. Open daily 10am-10pm. AmEx/D/MC/V.

Rancho Cactus (☎851 506; ranchocactus@sanpedroatacama.com), on Toconao across the street from Hostería San Pedro de Atacama. Horse enthusiasts or newcomers are welcome at this small San Pedro ranch. The English-, French-, and Spanish-speaking owner gives a 2hr. tour of Pukará de Quitor (CH$10,000) and longer full-day tours of many sights in the area (CH$35,000 per person). No experience is needed for the shorter trips. Open daily 9am-8pm. AmEx/D/MC/V.

Colque Tours (☎851 109), on the corner of Caracoles and Calama. Colque is the best bet for multi-day trips to Uyuni, BOL. (US$80-90 per person; US$100 for the 4-day trip returning to San Pedro. All meals and lodging included. 4-day English-speaking guide US$95.) The company has offices in Uyuni and La Paz, so you don't need to change to a different Bolivian company when you reach the border. Also offers half-day trips to Laguna Verde and Laguna Blanca in Bolivia (CH$7000 per person, min. 4 people; CH$3000 entrance fee) in addition to the usual trips. Open daily 10am-8:30pm. AmEx/D/MC/V.

Currency Exchange: There are several exchanges in town, including **Valle de la Luna** (☎315 981), on the corner of Toconao and the Plaza de Armas, which cashes traveler's checks and exchanges euros, US dollars, and other South American currencies. Open M-Sa 10am-11pm, Su 11:30am-9:30pm.

Bank: There will be a **BancoEstado** in San Pedro as of October 2004, but until then, there is **no bank in town.** BancoEstado has installed a portable **ATM** truck in the plaza next to the police stations for the time being. The money supply is limited, so bring an extra supply of cash before coming to San Pedro. Open daily 9am-10pm.

BIKE-IT-YOURSELF TOURS

Doing a tour in San Pedro can be expensive and difficult to plan. What's more, most tours are so close to the beaten path that it's impossible to see the amazing sights without hearing dozens of German, French, British, and American tourists complaining about having to dust their $600 digital zoom lens. But there is a cheap, less-traveled way to get to know the famous San Pedro archeological sites and it's great exercise too.

For CH$5000 per day, a shock-absorbing, cushion-seated, multi-speed mountain bike can carry the active traveler on an historical jaunt through San Pedro's past. So tie your shoes tight, pack three bottles of water and lunch, and take a bike ride through history:

8-10am
Pick a bike rental agency among the many along Caracoles and rent a bike for the day (CH$5000). Grab a copy of their bike map before you leave. Hop on and head along Licancábur for the 10km ride along paved roads to **Tulor**. Explore 2800-year-old deteriorating Atacamenian structures, buried under 1.5m of sand. (1hr. ride; Tulor entrance CH$1000.)

10-11:30am
Go back the way you came and make a beeline to **El Museo**

Supermarket: There are only a few small stores, including the one on the corner of Caracoles and Tocopilla. Open daily 8:15am-10pm.

Laundromat: Alaja (☎09 776 9194), on Caracoles between Calama and Atienza. CH$1500 per kg. Open daily 9am-2pm and 5-9pm.

Police: ☎133. *Carabineros* (☎851 003), on the Plaza de Armas opposite the church.

Pharmacy: There are no pharmacies in town, but **Mario Ramos** (☎851 013), next to H2O on Caracoles, between Toconao and Tocopilla, has some medication, though no antibiotics. Open daily 9am-10pm.

Hospital: Ambulance ☎133. A paramedic clinic, **Posta Médica** (☎851 010), on the Plaza de Armas, is next to Sernatur. Open M-Th 8am-12:45pm and 1:45-4:45pm, F 8am-12:45pm and 1:45-3:45pm. Call for medical assistance during off-hours.

Internet Access: There are a few places to connect in town, including **Valle de la Luna** (see **Currency Exchange,** above). **Café Adobe** (p. 177). CH$1000 per hr. Also try **Café Étnico** (p. 177), which has cheaper rates and offers 15min. free with any purchase and 30min. free with the *menú* of the day.

Post Office and Courier Service: Post office (☎851 954), on the plaza, across from Valle de la Luna. Open M-F 9am-12:30pm and 2:30-6pm, Sa 8:30am-12:30pm. Postcards CH$240 to US, CH$320 to Europe. **Chile Express** (☎851 434), on the corner of Calama and Caracoles, also functions as a **centro de llamadas.** Open M-F 8:30am-10pm, Sa-Su 10am-10pm.

ACCOMMODATIONS

San Pedro is full of accommodations that run the gamut from simple camping and *residenciales* to posh hotels with jacuzzis and swimming pools. Most budget and medium-range accommodations don't have heaters, which is problematic because it can get cold inside these rooms at night, especially in winter.

Hotel Kimal (☎851 152; www.kimal.cl), on the corner of Caracoles and Atienza. Though there aren't many rooms, the small, personal Hotel Kimal offers rooms with private bath, satellite TV, and thick comforters centered around a pool and jacuzzi with a flowing waterfall. Tree cover makes the hotel feel like a peaceful garden far away from the dry, barren desert. The accompanying restaurant is one of the best in town and rooms come with a small Kimal gift bag. Internet and breakfast buffet included. Singles CH$51,000/US$83; doubles CH$71,000/US$115;

triples CH$85,000/US$137. Checks, traveler's checks, and AmEx/D/MC/V. ❺

Residencial Rayco (☎851 008), on the corner of Le Paige and Calama. Rayco offers similar quality to other budget options, for less. The rooms have simple wooden floors and are clean. An open-air sitting area is great for relaxing after an early morning tour. Light the heater for instant and long-lasting hot water. Dorms CH$3500; singles CH$5000; doubles CH$10,000; triples CH$15,000. ❶

Hostería San Pedro de Atacama, Toconao 460 (☎851 011; www.diegodealmagrohoteles.cl), south of Caracoles. Enter through the open gate with the large sign. The spacious rooms here lack the aesthetic touch of Hotel Kimal, but the big swimming pool and view of nearby peaks can't be beat. Free Internet. Private baths, cable TV, space heaters. Breakfast included. Singles and doubles CH$62,000/US$100; triples CH$80,000/US$130. AmEx/D/MC/V. ❺

Residencial Chiloé (☎851 017), on the corner of Antofagasta and Atienza. Chiloé's main complex is on the other side of a small bridge over a flowing river. Each room has its own plastic table and chairs on the roofed balcony. Rooms are simple, without bath or TV, but are clean. The sitting area around the grounds are a big draw. Singles CH$6000; doubles CH$12,000; triples CH$18,000. ❷

Hostal Camping Puritama (☎851 540), on the corner of Caracoles and Atienza. Rooms are simple, with only beds and sheets, but the outdoor sitting area with a grill makes for a good time with friends. Bike rentals available. Singles CH$5000; doubles CH$10,000; triples CH$12,000. ❷

Hostal Camping Takha Takha (☎851 038), on Caracoles near Atienza, has rustic rooms with straw-mat ceilings and a stone shower. Rooms have clean, new sheets, and hot water is never a problem. The camping area is guarded by a wooden wall between a few big pine trees and has a fire pit. Camping CH$4000 per person. Singles CH$9000; doubles CH$17,000; triples CH$21,000. AmEx/D/MC/V. ❷

Hotel Tulor (☎/fax 851 027; www.tulor.cl), on Atienza south of Caracoles, where the lack of buildings allows for a great view. Tulor has spotless rooms with fully stocked bathrooms in an adobe, thatched-roof building. There is a central, big-screen TV with satellite and a small bean-shaped pool with a view. Rooms have heaters, hot water, and telephones. Breakfast included. Singles CH$60,000/US$100; doubles CH$72,000/US$120; triples CH$90,000/US$150. AmEx/D/MC/V. ❺

Gustavo Le Paige in San Pedro proper (CH$2000, students and children CH$1000). Take a close at the exhibits, pick-up clues about Tulor, and be your own guide for the rest of the day. (1hr. ride)

11:30am-1pm
Time to get back on the bike. This time head out on Calama. Cross a few low streams and follow the 3km dirt path to the 12th-century Atacamenian fortress, **Pukará de Quitor.** Enjoy the crumbling fortress and the incredible views of the fertile valley. (20min. ride, Quitor entrance CH$1500.)

1-1:30pm
Grab that bagged lunch and chow before doing anything else. Drink lots of water; the desert is hot, high, and dry.

1:30-2:30pm
Venture farther along the dirt path, deeper into the valley. After a fun 5km ride with a few more stream crossings, look left for **Katarpe,** the remnants of a 14th-century Incan administration center. (30min. ride)

2:30-3:30pm
Head home along the 8km path, rest your buns, and grab a drink just in time for a 4pm tour of the majestic Valle de la Luna. Now that's cost-efficient traveling. (45min. ride)

Residencial Florida (☎851 021), on Tocopilla near the corner with Antofagasta, has spartan rooms along a social courtyard with hammocks, tree swings, and a ping-pong table. Popular among the younger crowd for the low prices and proximity to bars along Caracoles. Florida is a fun, cheap option, but watch out for the 10:30am check out. Book exchange. Singles CH$4000; doubles CH$8000; triples $12,000. ❶

Residencial Corvatsch (☎ 851 101), on Antofagasta between Calama and Atienza. The old rooms have shared baths and come with bed, sheets, and light. The new annex out back has new bathrooms and beds with thick comforters. It also has free Internet and a leather-clad lounge area. Rooms with shared bath CH$6000 per person, low-season CH$4000; annex rooms CH$35,000; doubles CH$39,000; triples CH$45,000. ❷

Hostal Katarpe (☎851 033; katarpe@sanpedroatacama.com), on Atienza between Antofagasta and Caracoles. Excellent rooms with clean sheets, professional photos of the area, and private bath. The courtyard sitting area under a thatched roof on high wooden posts is relaxing. Doubles CH$26,000; triples CH$32,000. ❸

🄲🄽 FOOD AND NIGHTLIFE

Rustic bar/restaurants are the highlight of San Pedro, featuring stylish wall-paintings of geoglyphs and petroglyphs, bonfires in their inner court-yards, and thatched ceilings. Most restaurants offer daily specials (3- or 4-course meals for CH$3000-6000) and **happy hours** (buy-1-get-1-free). Nightlife revolves around these eateries, many which stop serving dinner and start serving break-beats and dance music around 11pm. Most aren't cheap, so if you need to save some money, there are good, inexpensive *empanadas* (CH$350) and chicken near the bus stations.

▣ **Café Export** (☎851 547), on the corner of Caracoles and Toconao. With its hip interior, mouth-watering daily specials, and amazing bottle-acrobat-bartenders, Export is one of the hottest places in town. The pastas (CH$3000) and pizzas (CH$3000-3500) are big and made fresh daily. But the real draw are the singing bartenders, dancing waitresses, and live local music. *Menú* of the day includes wine, salad, main course, and dessert (CH$5000). Open daily 11am-4pm and 6:30pm-very late. AmEx/D/MC/V. ❷

▣ **Restaurante Paacha** (☎851 152; www.kimal.cl), on the corner of Caracoles and Atienza, in the Hotel Kimal. Paacha is the most elegant, romantic, and delicious dining experience in town. Simple tables covered with lone candles and peach tablecloths surround the pool and waterfall of Hotel Kimal. Inside, the dark wooden bar has a large variety of expensive liquors and wines to serve with original dishes like steak with pesto served with a goat-cheese-filled potato with a carrot glaze. And that's just a standard daily option. Desserts include crepes with a chestnut-coffee sauce and a raspberry tart with chantilly cream drizzled with caramel. Entrees CH$5500-7500. *Menú* CH$8000 (includes soup or salad, main course, glass of wine, and dessert). Open 11:30am-4:30pm and 7pm-midnight. AmEx/D/MC/V. ❹

La Estaka (☎851 201; www.laestaka.cl), on Caracoles near Tocopilla. Easily the best combination of price and quality in town. Dishes like curry chicken with basmati rice and vegetable bruschetta are artistically prepared in the entertaining interior with adobe walls, colorful tiles, and a swanky bar. An example of a typical *menú* is cream of asparagus soup, salted salmon, caramel flan, and a *pisco* sour (CH$4500). Breakfast CH$2500. Open daily 9am-3:30pm and 6:30pm-2am. AmEx/D/MC/V. ❷

Restaurante La Casona (☎851 004; www.restaurantlacasona.com), on Caracoles between Calama and Atienza. One of the bigger eateries in town, but candlelight creates one of the most intimate atmospheres. After patrons enjoy the spaghetti carusso (CH$3500) and the delicious papaya and *dulce de leche* crepes, the open-air bar turns into a hip bar scene. Casona has the most extensive wine collection in San Pedro (CH$5000-22,000). *Menú* CH$5500. Open daily 8am-3am. AmEx/D/MC/V. ❸

Café Adobe (☎851 132; www.cafeadobe.cl), on Caracoles between Calama and Toco-pilla, has the biggest bonfire in its lively, open-air seating area. Come here to munch on tasty fare, exchange travel stories, check your e-mail (CH$1000 per hr.), and do a little dancing. Prices are bit high, but the food is great. Pizzas CH$4500-4700. *Menú* CH$6500 (includes soup or salad, main course, dessert, and drink). Open Su-Th 8:30am-1am, F-Sa 8:30am-3am. AmEx/D/MC/V. ❸

Milagro (☎851 515; www.milagro.cl), on the corner of Caracoles and Calama. Milagro does things a bit louder and with a little more attitude than most of the mellower restau-rants in San Pedro. Techno and 80s hits blare through doorways while people dip meat and fruit in the only fondue pots in town. Late nights, the steps around the central firepit are great for enjoying an after-dinner drink or dancing. Cheese fondue for 2 people CH$7000, for 4 CH$11,000. Chocolate fondue for 2 CH$6000, for 4 CH$9000. Greek salad CH$2000. Open daily 11:30am-4pm and 6pm-very late. AmEx/D/MC/V. ❷

Casa de Piedra (☎851 271; www.restaurantcasapiedra.cl), on Caracoles between Calama and Tocopilla. The outdoor seating area is warm with a nightly bonfire. Come for Italian, Chilean, and other international fare. Vegetarians will enjoy the Gruyère *empan-ada* (CH$2500), and meat eaters can dive into Piedra's well-grilled variety (CH$3500-5000). *Empanadas* CH$2000-2500. Open daily 8am-1:30am. AmEx/D/MC/V. ❷

Café Étnico (☎851 377), on Tocopilla between Caracoles and Le Paige. Patrons check e-mail (CH$800 per hr.) while munching on Frisbee-sized sandwiches (CH$1300-2500) and delicious quiches (CH$2000). Buy anything and Étnico gives you 15min. free; buy the *menú* (CH$2500), including delicious freshly squeezed juice, and type e-mails for 30min. free of charge. Étnico also has a great variety of good books for a hefty 2-books-for-1 exchange. Open Su-Th 8:30am-1am, F-Sa 8:30am-2:30am. AmEx/D/MC/V. ❷

🜁 SIGHTS

MUSEO ARQUEOLÓGICO GUSTAVO LE PAIGE. A visit to this museum, on Le Paige near the Plaza de Armas, is a must. Although this regional museum is housed in a circular, one-story building, the quality of the exhibits is nothing less than world-class. The museum exhibits the work of Father Gustavo Le Paige, who arrived in Chile in 1953. Two years later, he accidentally stumbled onto an Indian tomb, which led to a lifetime of work devoted to collecting, cataloging, and pre-serving 380,000 artifacts representing Atacama heritage from 9000 BC to the 16th century. The museum is a summary of his work, and the collection is renowned for its incredibly well-preserved mummies. (*☎851 002. Written guide in English available. Open M-F 9am-noon and 2-6pm. CH$2000, students CH$1000. Chileans free.*)

PLAZA DE ARMAS. On the eastern side of the white, adobe-style benches in the Plaza de Armas is a modest, 16th-century adobe house known by two names: La Casa de Pedro de Valdivia, since it is believed that Valdivia slept here, and La Casa Incaica, because of its trapezoidal window with Incan features. Unfortunately, vis-its inside are not possible yet, but the *municipalidad* has started a reconstruc-tion process set to finish within two years. Next to the plaza is a white-washed colonial church, the **Iglesia San Pedro.** Built in the early 18th century, the church, large for a village of this size, has colorful altarpieces and a roof made of wood and cactus tied together with llama leather—a style typical of the *altiplano* area.

🜂 SHOPPING

There are trendy *artesanías* all over San Pedro, but the best place to find a bar-gain is at the **Feria Artesanal,** the pedestrian shopping center on the street extend-ing north from the Plaza de Armas. Both the *feria* and the area north of it on

Licancábur are full of stalls selling a wide range of memorabilia ranging from wool garments, carved wood ashtrays (CH$1000-3500), and llama dolls (CH$2000), to hats and *guanaco* pashminas (CH$6000).

■ OUTDOOR ACTIVITIES

San Pedro offers a wide range of outdoor activities, such as biking, hiking, horseback riding, sandboarding, trekking, and mountaineering. Many tour operators in town rent outdoor equipment (see **Rentals**, p. 172). **Colque Tours** and **Vulcano** have camping packages with different equipment depending on the difficulty of a trek (see **Tours**, p. 172). A number of agencies offer **horseback riding** trips to surrounding sights. For **mountaineering**, you need to be acclimatized to the high altitude of the peaks you want to climb, usually by spending at least three days at similar altitudes. **Trekking** trails include half-day trips to **Valle de la Luna**, the **Mars Valley**, and **Puritama**. Among the easier peaks to climb near San Pedro are **Lascar** (5154m), an active volcano, and **Toco** (5604m). More difficult ones include **Sairecábur** (6050m), **Pili** (6040m), **Colorado** (5748m), and **Licancábur** (5916m). **San Pedro** (6150m) and the more distant **Llullaillaco** (6723m) are only for hard-core veterans with special climbing gear. Llullaillaco requires a guide and a permit from Santiago. All peaks except for Lascar have no marked trails, so it is best to climb with a local guide, even if you are an experienced alpinist. Most peaks can be climbed year-round except in wet weather from January to early March.

■ DAYTRIPS FROM SAN PEDRO DE ATACAMA

PUKARÁ DE QUITOR AND CATARPE

3km northwest of San Pedro de Atacama. CH$1200 fee at the base of Pukará.

Taken together, the ruins at **Quitor** and **Catarpe** make an excellent half-day trip from San Pedro on foot, bike, or horse. There are two paths to the sights. One includes stream crossings along a dirt path and the other follows the paved road. Ask a rental agent what roads to take and they will direct you. The pre-Incan hilltop fortress of **Pukará de Quitor** is the first stop along the way. Flanked by two steep gorges and overlooking far reaches of plains, the fortress has always presented a challenge to powerful invading armies. The main hill of ruins is a 5min. hike through hundreds of adobe houses, most of which have been reconstructed, but a few that were uncovered intact. Next to Quitor is an easy 30min. hike up El Mirador for incredible views of the Valle de la Muerte and the surrounding valley. Next, the Incas await you at **Tambo de Catarpe**, a ruin 8km from Quitor by way of a dried-up riverbed and a few stream crossings. In the wet season, this route is impassable even with a 4WD, so it is better to get here on foot or by bike. Built around AD 1450 on a hill a bit higher than Quitor, this was an administrative center used for the collection of tributes that were sent to Cuzco, the Incan capital. The stone walls are similar to those at Quitor, but there are scattered fragments of ceramics hidden along the structure floors. The climb up is 5min. from the sign at the bottom.

TULOR

40min. cycling from San Pedro. For directions to Tulor, ask at any agency in San Pedro that rents bicycles. Huts open daily 9am-6pm. Free. There is a map of the village at the entrance.

No archaeological tour of San Pedro would be complete without a visit to the prehistoric village of **Tulor**, 10km southwest of San Pedro. Built by the first Atacaman farmers between 800 BC and AD 500, this large village on an exposed plain was a web of clay huts inside a walled compound, erected for protection from the sandy winds. There isn't much left of the once-important village, as the same sand the huts were built to protect against has worn away most of the structures. At the entrance to the site are two huts administered by Conaf that are reconstructions of the originals, which are now mostly submerged in the earth, with only their top parts visible above the sand. Not many guided tours include Tulor, as it is so close to town, but an archaeological tour from San Pedro may include Tulor, Pukará de Quitor, Catarpe, and the Museo Gustavo Le Paige.

EL TATIO GEYSERS

The best way to get to El Tatio from San Pedro is with a tour group (tours daily 4am), as the unpaved roads are very hard to follow after dark, and it is best to arrive here by sunrise. If you go alone, a 4WD is strongly recommended. No camping is allowed at El Tatio, and the nearby CORFO refugio is not open to travelers. Allow yourself a few days to acclimatize in San Pedro before taking this tour. Be aware of the danger of altitude sickness.

The mystically beautiful ◪**El Tatio Geysers** (4321m), 90km northeast of San Pedro, compose the highest geyser field in the world. Although El Tatio's geysers have less powerful and less frequent eruptions than those in New Zealand's Rotorua or in Yellowstone National Park in the United States, seeing dozens of columns of steam and water vapor exploding against the surrounding snow-peaked mountains is unforgettable, especially at dawn, when the fumes are most visible. Be forewarned: the high altitude means that temperatures are below 0°C year-round.

Lying between towering peaks on a *puna* (arid, flat stretch of land) marked with yellow-green shrubs and crystal-clear streams, the landscape around El Tatio is similar to that of the national parks to the north. Colorful stretches of red and yellow minerals cross the field, left behind by the evaporation of the mineral-rich geyser' water, which turns to steam upon contact with the air, leaving the piggybacking minerals behind.

The geysers are visited by crowds of people everyday, but it is possible to get away from the crowds on the massive field. If you choose to venture off on your own, be very careful when walking around the field, as some spots have soft surface crust, and cracking into the underlying geyser pool could result in severe burns. Several hundred meters from the geyser field, there is a sizable thermal pool shielded by a stone fence where you can bathe in the soothing water (about 28°C). The stream of water that heats the pool is very hot, but sitting 2m from where the water enters allows for hot, but not too hot, water. Most tours from San Pedro stop here for a dip after serving you breakfast on the geyser field.

BORDER CROSSING INTO BOLIVIA: HITO CAJÓN

Frequent snowfalls close the Hito Cajón border crossing, and travelers without tour groups or permission from the government are often turned away, so it's recommended that you contact a tour agency to arrange good transportation and check weather conditions beforehand. The customs office is open 9am-noon and 2-4pm. The process is fairly simple and involves no more than a passport stamp and a brief search of your luggage for contraband and various food products (see **Essentials: Border Crossings,** p. 35, for info on visas and fees).

SALAR DE UYUNI, BOLIVIA

One of the most spectacular and popular trips from San Pedro, the 10,000 sq. km **Salar de Uyuni,** the world's highest and biggest salt flat, is the focus of the town's most extensive (and expensive!) adventure tours. Tours from San Pedro to the expansive wonder are offered in 3- to 4-day trips, with the fourth day left for the option to return from Uyuni to San Pedro.

The trek starts early the first day with the precarious **Hito Cajón** border crossing into Bolivia. The tour then visits the incandescent emerald-green **Laguna Verde** at the base of **Volcán Lincancábur** (5868m), followed by a dip in the warm waters of **Laguna Chalviri** in the **Salar de Chalviri**, before heading to borax-lined shores and crystal blue-green waters of **Laguna Colorada** (4121m). After watching the hundreds of Andean, Chilean, and rare James flamingoes, travelers bundle up for a cold night in the lakeside *refugio*. Day two starts with a 4am trip to the geysers of **Sol de Mañana** (5000m) to watch 50-100m columns of steam shoot through the air. The explosions are followed by a jaunt through the **Eduardo Avaroa Bird Reserve** (Bs35), a stop at the crystal-clear **Lagunas Cañapa**, a quick stop with a view of **Volcán Ollague** (5865m), and finally a short drive to **San Juan** for a night in one of the five **alojamientos ❷**. (Singles with warm shower Bs20; doubles Bs40.)

The last day of the trip focuses on a drive right through the Salar itself, heading first to an earthen oasis in the middle of the sea of salt, **Isla Inkawari,** where travelers often disembark to hike and grab a quick snack at the on-site **restaurant ❷**. Forty minutes north of the Isla, tours stop at the now-defunct **Hotel Playa Blanca** and **Hotel Palacio de Sal**, where everything (beds, tables, chairs, and walls) is constructed entirely of salt and salt mortar. From here, the ride to Uyuni offers incredible views of the *salar*, where salt deposits extend to 4m deep, and a look at the **ojos de sal**—weak areas in the *salar* where salt has worn away to reveal underground wells with bright pink hues and frigidly cold bubbling waters. Most tours then stop in Uyuni to drop off some passengers, then return to San Pedro.

Colque Tours (p. 173) offers the most frequent and reliable tours of the Salar, and has offices throughout Bolivia that help ease any problems during the journey. Other agencies offer tours of the Salar, but be sure to check the travelers' opinion book at **Sernatur** in San Pedro (p. 172) and ask for a detailed itinerary and reimbursement policy before finalizing plans. If the pass to Bolivia is blocked, trips can be delayed for days or canceled. **Altitude sickness** is a serious risk at the 5000m heights around the Salar, so acclimatize before going and drink lots of water.

TOCONAO

About 40km south of San Pedro is the idyllic oasis village of Toconao (pop. 900), similar to San Pedro, though much smaller. The village's brownish-gray volcanic stone houses are less aesthetically appealing than San Pedro's adobe ones, but the surrounding scenery is stunning. The **Río Toconao** flows next to the village, cutting a gorge through the desert called the **Quebrada de Jerez**, a century-old forest of fruit trees, including apple, pomegranate, and grape. Wine from Toconao's grapes is renowned, as the rich mountain waters that nourish the trees create a unique taste. The wine is only available in very limited supply around the San Pedro area during the summer (entrance CH$1500).

In Toconao proper is the trimmed-stone **Iglesia de San Lucas** (built in 1744), on the **Plaza de Armas.** The church has a straw ceiling and a colonial bell tower, which has come to be recognized as the town's symbol. Legend has it that if a woman sits in the bell tower, she will be pregnant in exactly one year. For the key to the church, ask at the shop next door. Toconao has a few basic accommodations and restaurants, including **El Valle de Toconao ❶**, with clean rooms with shared baths, hot water and electricity until midnight, and a self-catering kitchen. (☎852 009. Singles CH$4000; doubles CH$7000.) Also check out the **restaurant ❷** on the premises, which serves simple meals. (Breakfast CH$1200. Lunch *menú* CH$2500. Open daily 7am-1pm and 5-10pm.) In town, you will also find a **Conaf office** (open M-F 8:30am-12:30pm and 2-6pm), **police station, paramedic clinic,** and a small **grocery store.**

There are also several **artesanías** in the village. There is **no gas station, bank, or ATM**. From town, **Buses Frontera** goes to San Pedro (30min., 6 per day 7am-7pm, CH$500), as does **Buses Atacama 2000** (30min.; 7am, 1, 6pm; CH$500). A round-trip **taxi** from San Pedro to Toconao costs around CH$15,000.

RESERVA NACIONAL LOS FLAMENCOS

The Reserva Nacional los Flamencos is actually made up of seven distinct patches of protected land around the San Pedro de Atacama area, each with a unique land-scape and set of flora and fauna. The *reserva* encompasses an amazing variety of attractions, including ◼**Valle de la Luna** (Valley of the Moon), with its eerie, lunar-looking terrain; the **Salar de Atacama**, a giant desert salt plain containing the breathtaking ◼**Lago Chaxa,** whose micro-organisms sustain three species of fla-mingos; and **Lagunas Miscanti** and **Miñiques,** whose lookout points provide vistas of some of the most beautiful sunsets imaginable.

AT A GLANCE	
AREA: Total of about 740 sq. km, in 7 separate sectors.	**HIGHLIGHTS:** Valle de la Luna, Salar de Atacama, Lago Chaxa, Lagunas Miscanti and Miñiques; 3 species of flamingos.
CLIMATE: Each of the 7 areas has a distinct climate; rainy periods Dec.-Mar.	**FEES:** CH$1500, children CH$300.
GATEWAYS: San Pedro, Toconao, Tulor.	**CAMPING:** Official camping not allowed in most places.

◻◼ **TRANSPORTATION AND PRACTICAL INFORMATION.** As the road to RN Los Flamencos is well-maintained, it is possible to visit on your own in a rented car. Many tour companies also run daytrips to various sites in the reserve (see **Tours,** p. 172). For up-to-date information on conditions in RN Los Flamencos, stop in at the **Conaf** office in Solcor, located 10min. south of San Pedro on the way to Toconao, or the Conaf office in Toconao (p. 180). Both offices are open M-F 8:30am-12:30pm and 2-6pm.

◻◼ **SIGHTS AND OUTDOOR ACTIVITIES.** One of the best and closest day-trips from San Pedro de Atacama is to **Valle de la Muerte** (Valley of Death), 15km southwest of San Pedro. Valle de la Muerte and accompanying Valle de la Luna (Valley of the Moon) comprise one of the seven distinct pockets that make up RN Los Flamencos. Two theories have arisen to explain Valle de la Muerte's macabre name. The first tale was started by cattle herders who had to pass through the life-less sand dunes and jagged rock formations of the valley. Supposedly, falling rocks killed hundreds of cows—and many of the herders as well. The other, more widely accepted story, originates with archaeologist Gustavo Le Paige, of San Pedro fame. The red, rocky landscape of Valle de la Muerte looks very similar to the land-scape of Mars, but when the French Le Paige tried to pronounce Mars (in Spanish *Marte*), the people of San Pedro justifiably misunderstood. Most tours from San Pedro take you to the salt mines and a sculpture-like natural salt outwelling called **Las Tres Marías,** which evokes an image of the Virgin Mary standing in prayer. Camping is not allowed in this sector of the park.

Near Valle de la Muerte is ◼**Valle de la Luna** (Valley of the Moon), a desolate salt highland surrounded by massive sand dunes and other natural rock boundaries. The circular flat looks like a sunken lunar crater. A trip to the valley involves hik-ing up and walking across the narrow ridge atop the mountainous sand dune. At the end of the 15min. hike, a rock outcropping with man-made stairs provides a viewing platform for incredible sunsets. The valley lights up in varying shades of reds and yellows until darkness falls and the crater is filled with the bright glow of the moon. Following an evening sunset at Valle de la Luna, head back to the salt mines and Las Tres Marías in Valle de la Muerte. Bring a flashlight to light up the salt crystals inside the caves and watch them glow.

South of San Pedro lies the largest salt deposit in Chile, the **Salar de Atacama**, in a 3000 sq. km tectonic basin. Although the *salar* is small in comparison to Bolivia's awesome Salar de Uyuni, it is nevertheless a spectacular natural wonder. The average annual rainfall here amounts to a mere 20-30cm, falling mostly in summer, making the *salar* one of the driest desert areas in the world. What little water there is comes from underground sources that evaporate rapidly, leaving shallow, scattered ponds filled with salt-saturated waters high in lithium (the *salar*'s lithium deposit allegedly makes up 40% of the world reserves). In some of the ponds, there are enough micro-organisms to keep three breeds of flamingo nourished: James, Andean, and Chilean. The water in one of the small lakes in the *salar* has enough salt content to produce natural buoyancy, similar to Israel's Dead Sea.

Only 4km south of Toconao, Ruta 4 meets a turnoff that leads some 28km southwest to ■**Lago Chaxa,** inside the Salar de Atacama. Here, a marked trail leads into the *salar*, with viewing stations along the way for breathtaking vistas of the vast *salar* and numerous flamingos. Like Valle de la Luna, Lago Chaxa is a great spot for one of the most sublimely beautiful sunsets in the world. At night, the low *altiplano* temperatures freeze the small lakes; the flamingos, asleep with one leg in the water, have to use their other leg to break free when the sun rises and begins to melt the ice. The pink of the flamingos against the white and black snow-capped volcanoes and endless stretches salt provide a view only Dalí could imagine. The small Conaf office at the park entrance is in the process of building a two-room museum about the *salar* and flamingos. *(No public transportation is available to Lago Chaxa; come with a tour group or in your own car. Park at the entrance to the lake. Open daily 7am-7pm. CH$2000, children CH$500.)*

If you have access to a car, another good daytrip from Toconao is a drive south along Ruta 23, into the **Lagunas Miscanti-Miñiques** sector of the reserve. Forty kilometers south along the paved section of the route is the village of Socaire (pop. 280), a small farming and cattle-breeding community. All of Socaire's major buildings, even the 200-year-old church, are made with white volcanic rock, and most have cactus wood ceilings. The majority of the population works at the local lithium refinery company, Soquimich, but a few farmers use the same irrigation terraces introduced and built by the Incas over 500 years ago. A small valley of large dirt platforms burst with mineral-rich vegetables during the summer, the same platforms that provide the area's best onions, corn, couscous, and potatoes.

Continuing along **Ruta 23** 31km south, the road turns to gravel and a turnoff loops east toward **Laguna Miscanti** and **Laguna Miñiques,** two spectacular, crystal-blue *altiplano* lakes (4200m). Miñiques, or "frog" in old Atacaman, was once home to a large population of green jumping critters. However, once local miners introduced trout to the lake and the trout finished off the fish, starvation set in, wiping out the population. As a result, no large organisms live in the lakes, although they receive frequent visits from birds.

Surrounding the lakes are their namesake peaks, **Cerro Miscanti** (5622m) and **Cerro Miñiques** (5910m). The loop continues past a few salt pans and small lakes, including the beautiful **Laguna de Tuyajito,** toward **Paso Sico** on the Argentine border, but no organized tours pass through here. Be careful, as driving on the unpaved roads south of Toconao can be dangerous, if not impossible, in the wet season, when the roads are washed away. *(No public transportation to Lagunas Miscanti and Miñiques; come with a tour group or in your own car. Entrance CH$2000. Conaf* *has 2 cabins available between the 2 lakes for CH$3000 per person, max. 6 people. Cabins have stove, bathroom, beds, and electricity, but bring your own water and warm clothes. Contact the Conaf office in Toconao for reservations.)*

ANTOFAGASTA ☎ 55

As the capital of Chile's Region II, dry and sunny Antofagasta (pop. 300,000) welcomes visitors with its pleasant beaches and enormous, strikingly efficient port, the biggest on South America's Pacific coast. Like Iquique, Antofagasta came into its own as a port city during the nitrate boom of the late 19th and early 20th centuries, a legacy reflected in the Neoclassical buildings of the waterfront Barrio Histórico. Once part of Bolivian territory, the city was conquered by Chile during the War of the Pacific (1879-1884). Today, Antofagasta remains the main export platform for copper from Chuquicamata and other minerals of the Atacama desert. Although the beaches here are not as warm or suitable for surfing as those in Arica or Iquique farther north, and parts of downtown can seem rather gray and unappealing, the traveler will nevertheless find a well-connected transportation hub with all the conveniences of a large city. The proximity of stunning coastal sights such as La Portada, the most photographed site on Chile's northern coast, add beauty to the utility of Antofagasta.

▇ TRANSPORTATION

As a major transportation hub, Antofagasta offers transportation to important destinations across Chile.

Flights: Aeropuerto Cerro Moreno (☎296 077), 25km north of downtown off Ruta 1, is connected to downtown by **radio taxis** (CH$6000) and **minibuses.** For minibuses, try **Aerobus,** Baquedano 328 (☎262 727), which provides door-to-door service (CH$2500 per person; 4 or more people CH$2000 per person). The main flight provider, **LanChile,** Prat 445 (☎265 151), is open M-F 9am-7pm, Sa 10am-1:30pm. Flies to: **Arica** (1½hr.; 12:05 and 9:25pm; CH$34,500) via **Iquique** (45min.; CH$29,500); **La Serena** (1hr.; 10:20am and 5:35pm; CH$91,600); **Santiago** (3hr., 10 per day 8:35am-9:55pm, CH$83,000).

Buses: Major intercity bus companies and a regional minibus company have their own offices/terminals from which their buses leave, but a few smaller companies leave from **Terminal de Buses Rurales,** on the corner of Latorre and Riquelme.

Tur Bus, Latorre 2751 (☎220 240), between Bolívar and Sucre, departs for: **Arica** (10hr., every hr. 4am-10:15pm, CH$8000) via **Iquique** (6hr., CH$7000) and **Tocopilla** (3hr., CH$3000); **Calama** (3hr., every hr. 5am-10pm, CH$2500) via **Baquedano** (1hr., CH$1400); **Mejillones** (1hr., 10 per day 11am-11:30pm, CH$1100); **San Pedro de Atacama** (5hr., 7 per day 6:15am-3:15pm, CH$3800); **Santiago** (20hr., every hr. 10am-11:45pm, CH$17,000) via **Chañaral** (5hr., CH$6000), **Copiapó** (9hr., CH$8500), and **La Serena** (14hr., CH$11,500); **Taltal** (4hr., 6 per day 8am-7:30pm, CH$3200).

Pullman Bus, Latorre 2805 (☎268 838), on the corner of Bolívar, goes to: **Arica** (10hr.; 10am, 8:45, 10:30pm; CH$8000) via **Iquique** (7hr., CH$7000); **Calama** (3hr., 9 per day 7:15am-9pm, CH$2500); **Santiago** (20hr., 12 per day 10:45am-12:45am, CH$20,000) via **Copiapó** (7hr., CH$10,000) and **La Serena** (14hr., CH$15,000).

Flota Barrios, Condell 2764 (☎351 410), has daily departures to most major destinations.

Megatur, Latorre 2748 (☎450 819), opposite Tur Bus, is a minibus company that departs for **Mejillones** (1hr., every 30min. 6:30am-10:30pm, CH$1000) via **La Portada** (25min., CH$600).

Local Buses and Colectivos: Buses in town run daily 6am-2am and cost CH$300. **Microbus 15** makes frequent runs to La Portada (CH$800). *Colectivos* anywhere in town cost CH$300-350. *Colectivos* serving La Portada from Antofagasta depart from corner of Bolívar and Latorre (20min., CH$6000 per person).

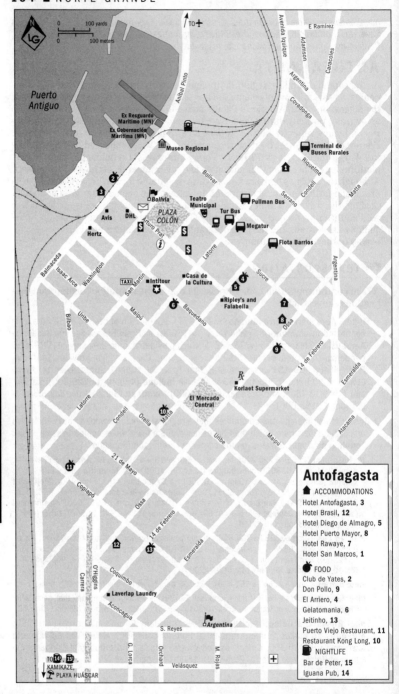

Antofagasta

ACCOMMODATIONS

Hotel Antofagasta, **3**
Hotel Brasil, **12**
Hotel Diego de Almagro, **5**
Hotel Puerto Mayor, **8**
Hotel Rawaye, **7**
Hotel San Marcos, **1**

FOOD

Club de Yates, **2**
Don Pollo, **9**
El Arriero, **4**
Gelatomania, **6**
Jeitinho, **13**
Puerto Viejo Restaurant, **11**
Restaurant Kong Long, **10**

NIGHTLIFE

Bar de Peter, **15**
Iguana Pub, **14**

Radio Taxis: There are numerous companies, including **Abece** (☎244 222), **Antofagasta** (☎268 726), **Gran Vía** (☎240 505), and **Servitaxi** (☎251 222).

Car Rentals: Hertz, Balmaceda 2492 (☎269 043; www.hertz.cl), and **Avis,** Balmaceda 2556 (☎226 153), have a wide variety of cars. (Compact CH$25,000-36,000; 4x4 CH$40,000-57,000).

■ ⍰ ORIENTATION AND PRACTICAL INFORMATION

Similarly to Iquique, Antofagasta sits on a narrow coastal strip surrounded by a backdrop of abruptly rising mountains. While the city is a big jumble of neighborhoods sprawling north to south, the downtown area next to the port is a compact rectangular grid bound by **Bolívar** and **Maipú** running northwest to southeast, and **Balmaceda** (which turns into Aníbal Pinto farther north) and **Ossa** southwest to northeast. **Plaza Colón** is the heart of downtown, while **Arturo Prat** between San Martín and Matta is the main shopping street. South of the city center, the expanse narrows and restaurants, clubs, and hotels line the beach. The Panamerican passes 20km east of town. Coastal Ruta 1 connects the city north to Iquique.

Tourist Office: Sernatur (☎451 818; www.sernatur.cl), on the corner of San Martín and Prat, on the ground floor inside the *Intendencia* (Regional Government) building. The helpful staff speaks some English, and photo displays of the region's tourist attractions include explanations in English and Spanish. Open M-F 8:30am-5:30pm.

Tours: Rutas de Sal, Jose Miguel Carrera 1485 c-1 (☎/fax 386 827; www.rutasdesal.cl), south of downtown, and **Intitour,** Baquedano 460 (☎266 185; intitour@dtl.net) organize tours to La Portada and other attractions in and around Antofagasta.

Consulates: Argentina, Blanco Encalada 1933 (☎220 440; fax 378 707). Open M-F 9am-1pm. **Bolivia,** Washington 2675, Of. 1301 (☎259 008; fax 221 403). Open M-F 9am-1pm.

Banks, ATMs, and Currency Exchange: There are many banks around the central **Plaza Colón. BankBoston,** Prat 427 (☎220 066) is near the plaza on the corner of Prat and San Martín. Also try **Banco Santander,** San Martín 2628 (☎269 271), **Banco de Chile,** Prat 356 (☎205 712), and **BancoEstado,** Prat 400 (☎268 948). All these banks are on the plaza and have **24hr. ATMs.**

Supermarkets: There are several in town, including the centrally located **Korlaet,** Ossa 2445 (☎263 631). Open M-Sa 7am-11pm, Su 9am-3pm. The giant **Lider** megastore, in **Antofagasta Shopping** (☎642 200), about 1km north along Aníbal Pinto, sells almost anything available in Chile. Open daily 9am-11pm.)

Laundromat: South of town, **Laverlap Laundry,** 14 de Febrero 1802 (☎251 085), offers same-day laundry and dry cleaning service. CH$3700 per basket.

Police: ☎133 or ☎269 069. Office at Baquedano 450.

Pharmacies: These are abundant all over town, especially on Prat between Matta and San Martín. Try **Farmacias Cruz Verde** (☎490 708), attached to Korlaet supermarket. Open 9am-11pm.

Hospital: Hospital Regional de Antofagasta Dr. Leonard Guzmán, Argentina 1962 (☎204 648 or 204 571), near the corner with Velásquez, south of downtown.

Internet Access: Easily available in any part of town. There are a few that stay open late near the **Tur Bus** terminal on Latorre. Try **Ciber de Com,** Sucre 485 (☎371 851). Open M-Sa 10am-2pm and 4pm-midnight, Su 11am-7pm.

Courier Services: DHL, Prat 260 (☎252 001; www.dhl.com), between Balmaceda and Washington. Also functions as a **Western Union.** Open M-F 9am-2pm and 3-7pm, Sa 10am-1pm.

NORTE GRANDE

Post Office: At Washington 2623 (☎410 631), on Plaza Colón. Also functions as a **Western Union.** Open M-F 9am-7pm, Sa 9am-2:30pm.

◤ ACCOMMODATIONS

There are surprisingly few good budget options in this large city. The best bang for the buck is down near the bars, discos, and beach in the southern end of town. In the summer, free camping on beaches further south of town is popular with independent travelers.

Hotel Diego de Almagro, Condell 2624 (☎268 331; fax 251 721), at the corner of Prat and Condell. Resembles a medieval castle. Thick wooden doors and torch-imitating lights make this a unique option. Big rooms with big beds also have a sitting area. Cable TV, minibar, private bath. Breakfast included. Singles CH$24,000; doubles CH$33,000; triples CH$44,500. AmEx/D/MC/V. ❹

Hotel Brasil, Ossa 1978 (☎267 268). The 38 rooms with cable TV are big and brown. Brasil is far away from town but across the street from the beach. Shield your eyes from the sparklingly clean shine of the floors and bathrooms. Prices are great when the staff is up front about room availability. Singles CH$6000, with bath CH$11,000; doubles CH$9000/CH$15,000; triples CH$12,000/CH$20,000. ❷

Hotel Antofagasta, Balmaceda 2575 (☎228 811; fax 268 415; www.hotelantofagasta.cl), along the coast, a few blocks down from the port. Part of the Panamerican chain of hotels, Hotel Antofagasta features a beachside pool and flower shop. Both city view (CH$38,500) and ocean view (CH$45,000) rooms have cable TV, mini bathroom kit, minifridge, and balconies. A stay at Hotel Antofagasta is a stay in luxury. Pool and private beach. Concierge can organize tours to surrounding area. AmEx/D/MC/V. ❺

Hotel San Marcos, Latorre 2946 (☎251 763 or 226 303), up Latorre from Tur Bus and Pullman Bus and close to the center of town. A good bet on the edge of the middle price range with clean, comfy rooms with bath and cable TV. Orange sheets, orange shades, and orange towels somehow avoid being tacky. Breakfast included. Singles CH$14,500; doubles CH$20,500; triples CH$24,000. AmEx/D/MC/V. ❹

Hotel Rawaye, Sucre 762 (☎225 399), is the cheapest option close to town. The beds are low, bathrooms are shared, and TV is spotty—but it's cheap. The neon signs from strip joints along the street are soothing night lights. Singles CH$4000; doubles CH$7000; triples CH$10,000. ❶

Hotel Puerto Mayor, Ossa 2643 (☎410 066 or 410 188), between Prat and Sucre. The new building, motel-like super comfy rooms, and friendly staff make this a great choice. Its central downtown location and free parking make it even better for motorists. Rooms include bath, cable TV, and breakfast. Singles CH$15,000; doubles CH$20,000; triples CH$30,000. AmEx/D/MC/V. ❹

◖ FOOD

Antofagasta offers a range of good cheap stops to upscale trendy restaurants. Near the plaza, chicken-and-fries joints are plentiful. The **Mercado Central** is particularly fun, with fresh fish, fruit, and veggies of all sorts. For more restaurant options check out the culinary guide to Antofagasta offered at the **Sernatur** office.

◪ **Jeitinho,** Copiapó 900 (☎410 780 or 495 851). The heart of Brazil in northern Chile? This gem is far enough away from downtown to avoid overcrowding and close enough to the coast to enjoy a beachside, after-dinner stroll. Lunch and dinner meals are CH$3000 and CH$6000 and include 2 to 4 meats, a salad bar, a bowl of black beans, rice, and a fruit dessert. Attentive service and mellow Bossa Nova guitar complete the mood. Open daily noon-1:30am. AmEx/D/MC/V. ❸

El Arriero, Condell 2644 (☎264 371). Dried *jamón serrano*, wine casks, and red flowers are the perfect decor for this traditional restaurant. The chef prepares all the meat on a large grill behind a glass window for everyone to see. The solo and 2-person *parrilla* offer an excellent variety of meats from *chorizo* to cuts of T-bone steak. Live piano. Filet mignon CH$7000. Salads CH$2000. Fish CH$6500. *Jamón serrano* CH$3000. Open daily 11am-5pm and 7:30pm-midnight. AmEx/D/MC/V. ❹

Don Pollo, Ossa 2594 (☎252 691), on the corner with Prat. Red-uniformed waitresses serve grilled chicken with ruthless efficiency on 2 floors of parasoled red plastic tables. Good for a quick bite, as evidenced by the crowds of locals. Chicken CH$900-1500, with fries CH$1500. Open M-Sa 11am-4pm and 6-11pm, Su noon-6pm. ❶

Club de Yates, on Aníbal Pinto (☎263 942), on the waterfront next to Hotel Antofagasta. Dine in style while taking in the harbor view on the wooden deck next to moored yachts. The maritime decor ranges from white-and-blue tableware to real, peckish seabirds. 3-course lunch specials CH$4800. Chicken CH$5500-6500. Steak CH$7500-12,000. Seafood CH$7000-30,000 (the lobster). Open M-Sa 10am-1:30am, Su 10am-5pm. AmEx/DC/MC/V. ❹

Puerto Viejo Restaurant, Copiapó 597 (☎252 272), between Esmeralda and 14 de Febrero. One of the best seafood joints in town. Enjoy savory ocean dishes amid a slightly older clientele in this intimate interior with a seafaring theme that includes ship steering wheels, anchors, and lifesavers. Fish CH$4800-8200. *Mariscos* CH$3200-6500. Meat CH$4500-5800. Open M-Sa 8pm-5am. AmEx/DC/MC/V.❸

Restaurant Kong Long, Matta 2269 (☎495 964), a block off the Mercado Central. Attentive service and good Asian cuisine add to the pleasing nature of this dragon-themed restaurant. As far as Chilean Chinese goes, the Xin Xang is surprisingly good. Spring rolls CH$800. Seafood CH$3500-5000. Chicken CH$2500-3500. Chop suey CH$2300-3500. Open daily noon-4pm and 7pm-12:30am. AmEx/DC/MC/V. ❷

Gelatomania, on the corner of Baquedano and Latorre, 2 blocks south of Plaza Colón. After all the eating is done, Gelatomania's 40-odd flavors make the perfect dessert. This restaurant serves basic Chilean fare and doubles as a currency exchange, but the real appeal is the ice cream, with exotic Swiss chocolate, *dulce de leche*-almond, and banana split. Huge single scoop CH$300, massive double scoop CH$450. AmEx/D/MC/V. ❶

⚙ SIGHTS

PLAZA COLÓN. The large central plaza of Antofagasta is not much more than a fun place to people-watch, but it is home to two of the best sights in town. The **Torre del Reloj** is a small clock tower that might look familiar to British travelers. It's not Big Ben, but this little replica of London's great monument is the world's closest equivalent to "Little Ben." The British and Chilean flags unite at the bottom as a symbol of the important British role in the city's development as a port. Also on the plaza, the tall and narrow Gothic **Iglesia Catedral San José** has three lofty entrances below tall spires. It looks big from the outside and inside, and impressive murals and a long stretch of gray pillars make the church seem even bigger.

BARRIO HISTÓRICO. One block northeast of the plaza along the coast, this collection of turn-of-the-century government structures has examples of Chile's coastal architecture during the nitrate boom. Four buildings, the Ex-Estación Ferrocarril, Resguardo Marítimo, Gobernación Marítima, and Ex-Customs House, along with the large pier, Muelle Salitrero Melbourne Clark, make up the attractive *barrio.* Only the Ex-Customs House and Ex-Estación Ferrocarril are open for tours, but take a good look at the wooden designs: the style dominates in nearby beach towns. Although not part of the *barrio*, the massive ships loading and unloading cargo along the pier often put on an impressive show.

MUSEO REGIONAL. Across the street from the train station and also part of the Barrio Histórico, Antofagasta's regional museum is housed in the Ex-Customs House. The museum has great exhibits on the ecology, geology, history, and archaeology of the Antofagasta region. Explanations of geoglyphs and the mysterious geographic features of San Pedro are simple and provide good background to any traveler heading that way. A mix-and-match display of spinning wheels with different climatic, geographic, and historic characteristics is informative and addictive fun. *(North along Balmaceda. Open Tu-F 9am-5pm, Sa-Su 11am-2pm. CH$600, students CH$300.)*

LOCAL BEACHES. After a historical tour of downtown, head south along Balmaceda for a little *siesta* and a memorable sunset along the recently refurbished oceanside walkway. A 20min. walk along the coast ends at Antofagasta's beach, Balneario Municipal. The beach is crowded during the summer months but fine sand and a protected bathing area are great for laying out. If the McDonald's surrounding the area is too much, Balneario Huascar and Playa Amarilla are a short bus ride south. Both Huascar and Amarilla are less crowded and offer fishing, camping, and volleyball as well as fine white sand. Huascar is also the nightlife center of Antofagasta and live DJs perform every weekend. *(From downtown, CH$300 by bus or CH$400 by colectivo to Balneario Municipal. During the summer, colectivos run to Huascar and Amarilla for CH$800.)*

📷 🎵 SHOPPING AND ENTERTAINMENT

Department stores like **Ripley** and **Falabella** are located close to the corner of Prat and Condell. The **Feria Artesanal** sells souvenirs and beaded leather jewelry outside the Mercado Central, housed in an impressive building set on the large plaza occupying the block bounded by Matta, Ossa, Maipú, and Uribe. The Mercado is host to a number of juice stands and has great fresh fish, fruit, and vegetables. For entertainment and cultural performances, check out the **Teatro Municipal** in the large concrete building, which stages ballet, concerts, plays, and other shows. (☎264 919. Ticket office open M-F 9am-1pm and 3:30-7pm.) About 1km north of the city along Balmaceda, **Antofagasta Shopping** is a mall with an 8-screen **Cinemark** cineplex. (☎490 348. Showings 3-10pm. CH$3000; M-W CH$2000.)

🎵 NIGHTLIFE

Nightlife rocks near Playa Huáscar south of town, but you'll have to take a cab to get there. It's worth the trip.

Kamikaze (☎245 138), on Camino Coloso. Part of a popular chain, this club features an oddly morbid decor using World War II paraphernalia. However, the crowd of 18- to 25-year-olds are too caught up dancing to care. The mix ranges from *salsateca* to rap, pop, and techno—all good for dancing. Occasional live music. Beer CH$1500. Cover CH$6000, women CH$5000, includes a drink. Open Th-Sa 11pm-5am. AmEx/D/MC/V.

Iguana Pub and Disco Box, on Camino Coloso, opposite Kamikaze. A little less crowded than its neighbor, Iguana is a lively 2-in-1 deal. Cover gets you inside the bar and the *discoteca*, both featuring energetic dance floors and a happy crowd of young locals. Beer CH$1500. Occasional live bands. Cover CH$6000, women CH$5000, includes a drink. Open Th-Sa 11pm-5am. AmEx/D/MC/V.

Bar de Peter, on Camino Coloso also across the street from Kamikaze. When famous DJs come to Antofagasta, they go to Bar de Peter first. The crowd includes anyone from 18-year-olds to DJ-enlightened thirty-somethings. Fluorescent lights flash in time with the music and drunken interpretive dance is popular. Hosts live DJs almost every weekend. Cover is normally CH$2500 but changes with different performers. Open Th-Sa 11pm-5am. AmEx/D/MC/V.

▶ DAYTRIPS FROM ANTOFAGASTA

From Antofagasta, Ruta 1 extends 385km to Iquique, offering spectacular coastal scenery with white sand beaches below sharply rising mountains. Fifteen kilometers north of Antofagasta, ▧**Monumento Natural La Portada** sticks out of the ocean like an elephant in a herd of sheep. It seems that the raging Pacific is quite a sculptor, as it has pounded and shaped a giant arch out of the sedimentary rock of the coastal cliffs. The Conaf-managed site offers great photo ops as well as serene afternoons tanning, fishing, or strolling along the sandy coves and beautiful beaches. Check the cover of almost any travel brochure of the area and you'll see the heavily photographed wonder. The current is too strong for swimming or surfing, but the seals frolicking through the waves can put on quite a show.

From La Portada, it is another 16km west to **Juan López,** a beach village that is popular in the summer. A couple of hotels and restaurants are near the beach. **Microbus 29** makes the trip for CH$300 between December and March, otherwise jump in a taxi for CH$7000. Another major sight between La Portada and Antofagasta is **Reserva Nacional La Chimba,** 25 sq. km of coastal wilderness including beaches for swimming. (Take Micro #2 or 3 for CH$300 from the corner of Sucre and Latorre in Antofagasta. Open in the summer.)

South of Antofagasta, the **European Space Organization's astronomical observatory** on Cerro Paranal (2644m) offers tours of the the four cleverly-named "Very Large Telescopes." The tour does not involve any stargazing—just seeing and learning about the world's largest telescopes is well worth the trip. Free tours by ESO run Saturday and Sunday of the last two weekends of every month. No public transportation is available, but ESO may accept visitors on its own buses. (☎ 435 000 or 435 001; www.eso.org/paranal/sepe/visito. Call or email ahead.) Not far from Cerro Paranal, off the Panamerican, is **Mano del Desierto,** the 1992 work of Mario Irarrázaval, an Antofagasta-based sculptor. Made of an iron-cement mix, this 11m-tall hand, half-buried in the desert plain, points upward toward the clear sky. The Mano is visible from the highway, on the right when leaving Antofagasta northbound, on the left heading south into the city.

MEJILLONES ☎ 55

This small, protected port town is proud of its history, centered around the three late 18th-century houses built along the coast. What were once the customs house, a naval office, and town hall now stand as monuments to the past while retaining modern functionality. Just beyond the city limits, the towering hydroelectric plant and giant copper mine contrast starkly with the quiet, historic town. The plant's towers light up the night sky and loom over the city during the day. However, the plant and mine are far enough away that the opportunity to enjoy the peace and history of this small town is not lost.

📠 **TRANSPORTATION. Tur Bus** (☎ 622 816), on Latorre between Rodríguez and Las Heras, goes to Antofagasta (1hr.; 7:30am, 5:15, 11:15pm; CH$1100) and Iquique (8hr.; 12:15, 6:15, 10:15pm; CH$6900) via Tocopilla (2hr., CH$2400). **Megatur** (☎ 621 528), on Latorre between Borgoño and O'Higgins, has departures to Antofagasta

(1hr., every 30min. 7:15am-9:45pm, CH$1000). **Corsal** (☎ 623 110) also provides service to Antofagasta (1hr., every 30min. 6:40am-10pm, CH$1000). **Radio taxis** wait on the municipal plaza on the corner of Latorre and Borgoño, 24hr. (☎ 623 040 or 621 204. CH$500 inside Mejillones, CH$1000 to outskirts of town, CH$12,000 to Antofagasta/La Portada.)

■ ☑ **ORIENTATION AND PRACTICAL INFORMATION.** Mejillones has three streets running east-west parallel to the beach that host most shops and services: **Andalicán, Latorre,** and **San Martín.** San Martín runs along the coast, and Latorre and Andalicán follow inland. Mejillones has most amenities, including **Banco Santander** (☎ 621 532) with a **24hr. ATM** on Borgoño between San Martín and Latorre. A **Copec service station** runs along San Martín 525 (☎ 621 588). The **police station** (☎ 621 516) is on O'Higgins near the **hospital** (☎ 621 575 or 621 486). An **Entel** *centro de llamadas* at Latorre 529 (☎ 410 202) lets you make domestic and international calls. An Internet cafe, **Cyber Play,** is on Andalicán 859, a block away from the hospital (☎ 623 732. CH$400 per hr. Open M-F 2pm-midnight, Sa-Su 11:30am-midnight). The **post office** is on the corner of Las Heras and Ongolmas one block up from Latorre. (☎ 621 510. Open M-F 10am-noon and 4-6pm, Sa 9am-1pm.)

▐ ▐ **ACCOMMODATIONS AND FOOD.** There are a few accommodations and restaurants in town, including **Residencial Doña Juanita** ❷, Latorre 441, which has big rooms with cable TV along a stretch of hallway almost longer than Mejillones itself (☎ 623 026. Dorms CH$4500; doubles with bath CH$10,000; triples CH$12,000.) The most expensive option is **Hotel Mejillones** ❺, on the corner with San Martín, which has excellent deluxe rooms with private bath, satellite TV, refrigerators, phones, and a buffet breakfast. If your room isn't one of those with a great ocean view then head up to the top floor and chill in the plush bar/restaurant which overlooks the coast. (☎ 621 244 or 621 590. Singles CH$34,800; doubles CH$38,100; triples CH$49,000. AmEx/D/MC/V.) **Hotel Capitania** ❸, San Martín 410, on the corner with Pinto, with its second-floor wooden veranda, looks like an upscale bed-and-breakfast with a view. But the purple walls and chipping paint make it more of a mid-range hotel. (☎ 621 542 or 621 276. Singles CH$15,000; doubles CH$20,000; triples CH$24,000. AmEx/D/MC/V.) **Residencial Don Eduardo** ❷, San Martín 670, offers six rooms with cable TV and private bathrooms, as long as you don't mind the posters of naked women on the back wall. (Singles CH$4500; doubles CH$8000.)

There are an abundance of seafood restaurants on San Martín and Latorre, but the following few stand above the pack. **Casino Municipal de Mejillones** ❷, in the spacious building on the beach next to Hotel Mejillones, has a great seafood platter made for three but cheap enough for two. (☎ 623 113. *Bandeja* seafood platter for three CH$8000. *Pescados* CH$3500-4500. *Mariscos* CH$3000-4300. Open daily noon-1am.) **Restaurante Zlatar** ❷, on Borgoño between Latorre and San Martín, has great grilled swordfish (CH$4500) and other local fish options. (Open daily 11am-11pm.) In the center of town, **Maxi Pizza** ❶, Latorre 710, has mini *empanadas* (CH$150) and cheap (CH$2900-3100) fresh pizzas. (☎ 621 685. Open M-Sa noon-3pm and 7pm-1am.) Cheap *empanada* stands fill the area near the **Copec Station** on San Martín.

◙ **SIGHTS.** The **Capitania del Puerto** (Port Authority), built in 1906, is a Tudor two-story flanked by British and American fighter jets propped up on posts. The area around the building on Latorre has live bands or DJs every Saturday night. **Ex Aduana,** the white building with a red roof across the street, now houses the **Museo Histórico y Natural de Mejillones,** on the corner of Pinto and San Martín. The museum has detailed information on Mejillones from a step-by-step illustration of the Battle of Angamos (a decisive naval battle during the War of the Pacific) to a mock burial of an indigenous woman from 2000 years in the past. (CH$300. Children free. Open M-F 10am-2pm and 3-6pm, Sa-Su 10am-2pm and 3-5pm.) Up the street from the museum, at Latorre and Pinto, the third Tudor building is home to the local **municipalidad.** The beach in Mejillones is part of a 20km stretch of untouched sand, but is narrow and often plagued with red algae. A more secluded, hidden beach is at **Hornitos,** 40km north of Mejillones just off Ruta 1. During the summer months a **minibus** picks up beachgoers on Latorre near the plaza and makes five daily runs to and from Hornitos. (Runs 10am-6pm. CH$800.) The beach is protected by cliffs and, like Mejillones, is guarded from the Pacific currents that make other beach areas rough and dangerous.

TOCOPILLA ☎55

Behind a rust-filled port and in front of tall mountains, Tocopilla looks like it is about to fall into the ocean. Walking through town is not aesthetically pleasing— large ships that service the nearby hydroelectric plant leave trash along the shore. Tocopilla is not the beach town that its northern and southern neighbors can claim to be. What Tocopilla (pop. 25,000) does have is an abundance of supermarkets, Internet access points, hostels, and enough restaurants to make it a good stopping point between Antofagasta (185km) and Iquique (638km). A stay in Tocopilla is a stay along the main street, and a conscious decision to avoid the beach.

F TRANSPORTATION. Tocopilla is well-connected by bus to major destinations. **Tur Bus,** on the corner of 21 de Mayo and Bolívar (☎811 122), departs daily for: Antofagasta (3hr., every hr. 7am-11:10pm, CH$3000); Calama (3hr.; noon, 7, 8:30pm, CH$3100) via María Elena (1hr., CH$1800); Iquique (3hr., every hr. 7am-10:30pm, CH$3500); Santiago (21hr., 12:35pm and 1am, CH$20,500). **Pullman Bus** (☎815 340), on the corner of 21 de Mayo and Washington, goes daily to Antofagasta (3hr., 5 per day 12:30-11pm, CH$3000); Calama (3hr., 11:15am, CH$3000) via María Elena (1hr., CH$1500); Iquique (3hr., 5 per day 11am-6:30pm, CH$3000). There is also frequent service by **Flota Barrios,** on 21 de Mayo between Washington and Colón (☎813 224); **Pullman Carmelita,** 21 de Mayo 1654 (☎813 269), next to the *municipalidad;* and **Buses Camus** (☎813 102), on 21 de Mayo between Freire and Rodríguez. **Colectivos** depart from Rodríguez and 21 de Mayo for Calama (CH$5000 per person) via María Elena (CH$2400 per person).

■ 🚩 ORIENTATION AND PRACTICAL INFORMATION. Most shops and services are on the main street, **21 de Mayo.** Passing traffic runs along **Prat,** along with minimal shops and services. The small **Plaza Condell** is on 21 de Mayo between Pinto and Bolívar. **Torre del Reloj** (erected in 1800), on the corner of Baquedano and Prat, is a stocky wooden clock tower with an atypical dome. Just a block south on the corner of Prat and Serrano is the small glass and metal **Iglesia Parroquial Nuestra Señora del Carmen** with its smog-stained exterior. The **municipalidad,** on the corner of 21 de Mayo and Pinto, offers tourist information in a pink Art Deco building.

The travel agency, **Travel Pacífico Tour,** 21 de Mayo 1524, serves as an unofficial tourist office with its knowledgeable and helpful staff. (☎811 127. Open M-F 10am-1:30pm and 5-9pm, Sa 10am-noon.) Other amenities Tocopilla offers include: **BancoEstado,** 21 de Mayo 1901 and Freire (☎813 012 or 811 791), with a **24hr. ATM;** a **Shell service station** at the northern end of town; and **Supermercado Colón,** Colón 1704 at the corner with 21 de Mayo. (Open M-Sa 9am-2am, Su 9am-2pm.) The **police station** is at 21 de Mayo 1666 (☎813 202). Look for **Mega Farmacia Victoria,** 21 de Mayo 1705, on the corner of Colón (open M-Su 10am-2pm and 5-10pm) and **Hospital Marcos Macuada** (☎812 839 or 814 558) uphill from 21 de Mayo, on Santa Rosa. **Internet access** is available at **Incart.** Look for the street sign, on 21 de Mayo between Colón and Freire. (☎811 289. CH$300 per hr. Open M-Su 11pm-midnight.) Find the **post office** along 21 de Mayo 1653. (☎813 257. Open M-F 9am-2pm and 4-6pm, Sa 9:30am-1:30pm.)

⌐ ACCOMMODATIONS. The cheapest hotels in town are down 21 de Mayo toward the Parochial Church. **Residencial Royal ❶,** 21 de Mayo 1988, flatters itself by including royal in the title, but cable TV and private bath options are royally cheap. (☎811 488. Singles CH$3000, with bath and cable TV CH$6000; doubles CH$6000/CH$8000; triples CH$8000/CH$10,000. Prices can be bargained.) **Hotel Casablanca ❷,** 21 de Mayo 2054, is one block farther but prices are higher than Royal for broadcast TV and no private bath. (☎09 313 9832. Singles CH$5000; doubles CH$10,000, with bath CH$12,000.) The most upscale hotels are next door to each other on 21 de Mayo between Bolívar and Baquedano. **Hotel Atenas ❹** rolls out a red carpet, and has rooms with bath, cable TV, phone, fridge, and breakfast included. (☎813 650 or 813 651. Singles CH$15,000; doubles CH$20,000; triples CH$24,000.) Its next-door neighbor, **Hotel Chungará ❸,** has 22 rooms with private bath and cable TV along a corridor with a mountain view. (☎811 036. Breakfast included. Singles CH$11,750; doubles CH$14,750; triples CH$16,750.)

❸ FOOD. The restaurant scene is a bit better, with **Casa de Don Julio ❸,** Serrano 1336, topping the list with its excellent international menu and attentive service. (☎816 129. 2-person *paradilla* CH$12,000. Mexican entrees CH$3000-5000. Pastas CH$3000-8000. Open daily noon-3pm and 8pm-1am. AmEx/D/MC/V.) Also good is the pink **Club de la Unión ❷,** on Prat between Baquedano and Serrano, with its spacious interior and difficult-to-find street entrance. (☎813 198. Entrees CH$2000-4500. Open daily noon-4pm and 8:30-11pm.) Other choices include **Restaurant Echikhouse ❶,** 21 de Mayo 2132, in the three-story building, which offers a *menú* (CH$1600) and sandwiches (CH$1000-2000). The third floor of Echikhouse is a bar with live music or mixing on weekends. (☎813 172. Beer CH$500-1200. Drinks CH$1500-2500. Open daily 10am-3am.) For faster service and food, **Pollo Spiedo ❶,** on the corner of Prat and Colón, is a chain that churns out chicken and fries. (¼ chicken with fries CH$1400. Open M-Sa 11am-11pm, Su 11am-7pm.)

❹ NIGHTLIFE. There are a number of options for nightlife near the corner of 21 de Mayo and Serrano. The scene is mostly the 17- to 22-year-olds in Tocopilla, but the variety is good. **Puerto Pelicano,** Serrano 1329, is a combination bar/*salsoteca*/*discoteca* with a kitschy, bright-colored, palm-studded interior, dominated by the youngest of the drinking crowd. (☎815 587. Beer CH$2000. Cover with drink CH$4000. Bar open M-Sa midnight-5am, dancing F-Sa midnight-5am.) **Tequila Pub,** at the corner of 21 de Mayo and Serrano, is the local watering hole frequented by soccer fans and people wanting to sing along to classic rock and pop. **Lukas,** a block down Serrano from Pelicano, is a two-story club/lounge with seating areas to chat while having a drink. Both Tequila Pub and Lukas are open F-Su only.

MARÍA ELENA ☎ 55

In the desert between Tocopilla and its larger neighbor Calama, María Elena sits as the lone survivor of the 20th-century nitrate busts. Hundreds of other nitrate company towns (*oficinas salitreras*) in the area have been abandoned, but the 7000 or so residents of María Elena are still going strong. Street signs are nonexistent, but all major roads lead to the central plaza.

▐ **TRANSPORTATION.** All bus companies have offices on Balmaceda near the plaza. **Tur Bus** (☎ 639 431) goes daily to: Antofagasta (3hr., 7am and 6:20pm, CH$2500); Calama (1½hr.; 5:45am, 1, 8:15, 9:45pm; CH$2000); Iquique (5hr.; 8:45am, 6:15pm, 1am; CH$5300) via Tocopilla (1hr., CH$1800); Santiago (22hr.; 7am, 6:20, 11:15pm; CH$17,500). **Pullman Bus** (☎ 639 839) also goes to Antofagasta (3hr.; 7am, 2:15, 8pm; CH$2500) and Calama (12:30pm, CH$1800). **Buses Camus** (☎ 413 619) and **Flota Barrios** (☎ 639 153) have regular service to Antofagasta, Calama, and Tocopilla as well. **Taxis** can be caught from the plaza to around town, as well as to the Chug Chug geoglyphs (CH$12,000) and Tocopilla (CH$15,000).

▐ **PRACTICAL INFORMATION.** Most amenities are available in María Elena. **BancoEstado,** on the plaza, has a **24hr. ATM.** (Open M-F 9am-2pm.) The local **municipalidad,** four blocks east of the plaza, offers a few insights on staying out of trouble. **Supermarcado As** is on Prat across from the plaza. (☎ 639 107. Open M-Sa 8am-2pm and 4:30-10pm, Su 11am-5pm.) A **lavandería,** O'Higgins 280, offers quality service with a smile. (Open M-Su 1pm-11pm.) In case of an emergency, make use of the helpful **police** office near the plaza (☎ 633 839) and **hospital** across the street from the *municipalidad* (☎ 413 738). A combination **Internet, Chile Express,** and **calling center,** O'Higgins 207, is under the guise of a Telefónica store. (☎ 639 684. Internet CH$800 per hr. Open daily 8:30am-11pm. AmEx/D/MC/V.) The town also has a **post office.** (☎ 639 355. Open M-F 9am-12:30pm and 3-6pm, Sa 9am-noon.)

▐▐ **ACCOMMODATIONS AND FOOD.** There are only two accommodations in which to rest your nitrate-weary head. **Residencial Jor ❷,** three blocks east and four blocks north of the plaza, has 30 rooms with baths, and a communal kitchen in a rustic, amiable atmosphere. (☎ 639 104. Singles CH$5000; doubles CH$8000; triples CH$9000; quads CH$10,000. AmEx/D/MC/V.) The humbler **Residencial Chacance ❷** has pink painted rooms, some with TV and private bath. The ping-pong table provides a great opportunity to warm up on cold desert nights. (☎ 639 524. CH$3000-4000 per person.) If you get hungry, the best bet is making your own meal from the grocery stores, but **Restaurant El Rinconcito ❶,** inside the mini-mall on the plaza, offers a filling *menú* for CH$2000. (☎ 639 427. Open 9am-5pm.) **Schopería Scorpions ❶,** on the plaza, will be the saving grace for those rolling in late; they're open until the wee hours of the morning. (Lunch CH$1500-1700. Open daily noon-3am.)

▐ **SIGHTS.** María Elena has many old, prominent buildings, including the Teatro María Elena and elementary school, which are now barren but make interesting sights for those having lunch in the plaza. Prominent attractions like **Chacabuco** and the **Chug Chug geoglyphs** are more easily accessible from Antofagasta and Calama but taxis are always available. The **Museo Arqueológico e Histórico,** on the plaza, exhibits prehistoric relics, turn-of-the-century cigarette boxes and food cans, and a thick collection of 1930s Chilean magazines. The museum also features a mock archaeological dig. The curator gives great advice on trips through the surrounding area. (☎ 639 172. Open M-F 9am-1pm and 4-8pm, Sa-Su 9am-2pm and 4-10pm. Free.) Large plumes of dust rising from the edge of town come from the **nitrate plant.** Tour scheduling is erratic, so admiring the huge chutes and massive machine processes from a distance is recommended to keep you out of the smog. (Call the Sociedad Química Mineral de Chile for tour availability. ☎ 413 756.)

Although there are no agencies that offer tours of Chacabuco, María Elena is a good place to catch an intercity bus to the Chacabuco junction. Where the Panamerican and Ruta 25 meet, hop off and walk 1km to the offices. As one of the most well-preserved mining towns in the area, Chacabuco is worth the short walk. Not only was it the largest *oficina* equipped with the Shanks system, it was also used as a Pinochet concentration camp for 3-4 years. During that time, Pinochet's henchmen locked all the doors and windows in town so that no outsiders could witness the daily torture, executions, and illegal trials used on over 3000 prisoners. Roberto Zaldivar, an ex-prisoner, gives tours of the site, with information about both the mine and the concentration camp. To fully understand the impact of Pinochet's camp, watch the reaction of local residents in María Elena. (From María Elena, take an intercity bus to Antofagasta and tell the driver to stop at Chacabuco; the 1km walk is almost directly at the intersection of Ruta 25 and the Panamerican, over 100km south of María Elena. Roberto Zaldivar's tour CH$1200, children CH$600.) Closer to town, **Pedro de Valdivia,** established in 1931 by the Guggenheim brothers, still functions as an office and mine, but no residents live there. The old mine produced 1,220,000 tons of salt and nitrate in its heyday, and a walk around the site gives a clear look into the history of the mining *oficinas.*

NORTE CHICO

Between the desolate, beautiful landscapes of Norte Grande and the bustling urban centers and lush valleys of Middle Chile, rests Norte Chico. Often ignored, bypassed, and overlooked, it is left out of the tourist's picture of Chile. However, those who skip over this region also miss out on a land marked by a unique and intriguing fusion of both geographical and human influences. The southern extent of the Atacama desert, vast scrub plains, and a sandy, moist coastline combine to form a fascinating mix of terrain. Pristine white-sand beaches lie surrounded by eerie, rugged landscapes, cloudforests hide amidst rolling fog banks in the barren plains, and soaring volcanoes hurl themselves skyward at the edges of glistening, white salt plains.

The prehistoric era comes alive in Norte Chico. Small men may not run around with spears, but regional museums include everything from information on Diaguita skull deformation to a lonely runaway *moai* from Easter Island which managed to traverse the Pacific Ocean and end up in an archaeological museum in **La Serena**. Furthermore, Norte Chico features enormous observatories at **El Tololo** where researchers push into the cutting-edge theory of the accelerating universe (ask them about it!) and its smaller, more tourist-friendly neighbor, **Mamalluca**, which takes visitors back in time, watching the same skies as their ancestors, with clear views of Jupiter's moons, the stars of Scorpio, and long stretches of cloudy nebulas.

North from Santiago, **Ovalle** and the coastal beach city of **La Serena** are the first major stopovers in Norte Chico, providing travelers not only with modern malls and movie theaters, but also with historical museums that give visitors a glimpse into the mysteries surrounding the **Valle del Encanto** and **Parque Nacional Fray Jorge.** East of La Serena, the small, tranquil town of **Vicuña** provides an opportunity to learn more about the heart of Chilean revelry—*pisco*—in addition to letting visitors take a journey into the center of the earth's magnetic energies in the comfortable cabins of **Pisco Elqui.** Farther north, visitors can take hiking trips from **Vallenar** as well as journeys into the nearby **Valle de Elqui.** Even farther north, away from the mountains along the coast is **Bahía Inglesa,** a hidden gem where families can set out a picnic and watch their children roam, exploring along clear green and blue waters. For those interested in wildlife, make sure to check out the penguins at **Reserva Nacional Pingüino de Humboldt** and **Parque Nacional Pan de Azúcar** as well as the flamingo sanctuaries of **Parque Nacional Nevado Tres Cruces.** Finally, adventurous travelers should make sure to climb the world's tallest volcano, and Latin America's second tallest peak, **Ojos del Salado.**

HIGHLIGHTS OF NORTE CHICO

GASP in awe at the rare transformation of the desert around **Vallenar** (p. 211) into a striking, flower-filled Eden.

PILGRIMAGE to the immense **Cross of the Third Millennium** (p. 197) in **Coquimbo** (p. 229) and marvel at this starkly modern religious icon.

CONQUER the grueling slopes of the highest active volcano in the world, **Ojos del Salado,** just outside **Parque Nacional Nevado Tres Cruces** (p. 201).

WANDER through the majestic cloudforests of **Parque Nacional Fray Jorge** (p. 237), mysteriously nourished by a coastal fog.

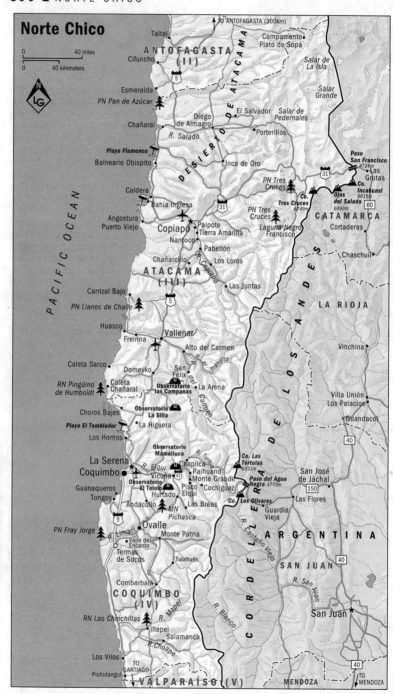

Norte Chico

0 ├─────────┤ 40 miles
0 ├─────────┤ 40 kilometers

ANTOFAGASTA (II)

↑ TO ANTOFAGASTA (300km)

Taltal
Cifuncho
Campamento
Plato de Sopa
Salar de
La Isla
Salar
Grande
Esmeralda
PN Pan de Azúcar
El Salvador
Salar de
Pedernales
Chañaral
Diego
de Almagro
R. Salado
Porterillos
Paso
San Francisco
4726m
Las
Grutas
Playa Flamenco
Balneario Obispito
Inca de Oro
PN Tres
Cruces
Co.
Incahuasi
6615m
Caldera
Bahía Inglesa
PN Tres
Cruces
Co.
Tres Cruces
6749m
Ojos
del Salado
6893m
CATAMARCA
Angostura
Puerto Viejo
Copiapó
Paipote
Tierra Amarilla
Laguna Negro
Francisco
Cortaderas
Nantoco
Pabellón
Chaschuil
Chañarcillo
Los Loros
ATACAMA (III)
Las Juntas
LA RIOJA
Carrizal Bajo
PN Llanos de Challe
Vinchina
Huasco
Freirina
Vallenar
Alto del Carmen
Caleta Sarco
Domeyko
San
Félix
La Arena
Villa Unión
Los Palacios
RN Pingüino
de Humboldt
Caleta
Chañaral
Observatorio
las Campanas
Guandacol
Choros Bajos
Observatorio
La Silla
Playa El Temblador
La Higuera
Los Hornos
Observatorio
Mamalluca
Co. Las
Tórtolas
6332m
La Serena
Coquimbo
Chapilca
Vicuña
Paihuano
Monte Grande
Pisco
Elqui
Cochiguaz
Paso del Agua
Negra 4779m
San José
de Jáchal
Guanaqueros
Tongoy
Observatorio
El Tololo
Hurtado
Las Breas
Co. Los Olivares
Guardia
Vieja
Las Flores
Andacollo
MN
Pichasca
PN Fray Jorge
Ovalle
Monte Patria
ARGENTINA
Valle del
Encanto
Termas
de Socos
Tulahuén
SAN JUAN
R. San Juan
Combarbalá
COQUIMBO (IV)
San Juan
RN Las Chinchillas
R. Mapel
R. Blanco
Illapel
Salamanca
R. Choapa
Los Vilos
TO
SANTIAGO
Pichidangui
VALPARAÍSO (V)
MENDOZA
TO
MENDOZA

DESIERTO DE ATACAMA

PACIFIC OCEAN

CORDILLERA DE LOS ANDES

COPIAPÓ ☎ 52

Though Copiapó was named after a Diaguita word meaning "cup of gold," it was silver that made Copiapó home to South America's first railroad. While present-day Copiapó feels more like a bustling city, its mining past still resonates in the University of Atacama's mineralogical studies and the mining paths still visible in surrounding mountains. The railroad station, mining museum, and extensive mineralogical museum make Copiapó a great city to learn about Chile's mining past. There are not many things to see in Copiapó, but it has all the modern amenities of any big city. Residents of Vallenar and nearby beach towns Caldera and Bahía Inglesa come to stock up on groceries and new movies. Even though the closest parks are over 200km away, Copiapó is the starting point for visits to Parque Nacional Nevado Tres Cruces and Volcán Ojos del Salado.

▐ TRANSPORTATION

Flights: Chamonate Airport (☎214 360), 15km west of Copiapó. **LanChile,** Colipí 484 (☎213 512 or 262 000), just off the plaza. Open M-F 9am-1:30pm and 3-7pm, Sa 9:30am-1:30pm. Daily flights to **La Serena** and **Santiago.**

Buses: Terminal de Buses, Chacabuco 112 (☎212 577), by the Panamerican. Though most companies depart from here, several have their own terminals. **Tur Bus,** Chañarcillo 680 (☎238 612), serves: **Antofagasta** (7½hr., every hr. 4am-11pm, CH$13,000); **Arica** (17hr., 6 per day 4am-10:45pm, CH$13,500); **Caldera** (1hr., 12 per day 4am-10:45pm, CH$1000); **Chañaral** (2½hr., every hr. 4am-11:30pm, CH$2000); **Iquique** (14hr., 9 per day 4am-11pm, CH$13,000); **La Serena** (5hr., every 30min. 8:15am-10:45pm, CH$4000); **Santiago** (12hr., 16 per day 4am-10:45pm, CH$8900). **Pullman Bus,** Colipí 109 (☎212 977), 1 block from the terminal, goes to: **Antofagasta** (15 per day, CH$11,600); **Arica** (5 per day, CH$18,000); **Iquique** (5 per day, CH$27,000); **Santiago** (every hr., CH$13,000). **Regional Buses** are near the Terminal de Buses on the corner of Chacabuco and Esperanza, though many regional destinations can also be reached using Tur Bus or Pullman Bus. **Buses Recabarren** (☎216 991) and **Casther** (☎218 889) go to **Caldera** (1hr., every 30min., CH$1000).

Taxis and Colectivos: Find taxis at Plaza Prat. *Colectivos* to Diego de Almagro can be caught at Chacabuco 151, where the regional buses pull in, across the street from the Terminal de Buses. *Colectivos* to **Caldera** (CH$1000), **Chañaral** (CH$3000), **Huasco,** and **Vallenar** (CH$3000) can be found there or at the Terminal de Buses.

Car Rental: Avis, Peña 102 (☎213 966; copiapo@avischile.cl), off the Panamerican. **Budget,** Freire 50 (☎216 272; copiapo@budget.cl), on the Panamerican. Both offer a variety of 4x4s (CH$42,000-60,000) for adventurers going to PN Nevado Tres Cruces.

✈ ▐ ORIENTATION AND PRACTICAL INFORMATION

At the center of Copiapó's downtown grid is **Plaza Prat.** Most accommodations and restaurants are within a few blocks of the plaza. To the west, the town squeezes between dusty hills and stretches thin in the area where there are several museums and the University of Atacama. The southern boundary of the city is the **Panamerican,** called **Freire** westbound and **Copayapu** eastbound. Northern **Infante** has most amenities, and the eastern boundary is at **Henríquez.**

Tourist Office: Sernatur, Los Carrera 691 (☎231 510), on the northeast side of the plaza, is very helpful. English spoken. Open daily 9am-5:30pm. **Conaf,** Martínez 55 (☎210 282 or 237 104), a 15min. walk west of the plaza, across the street from the

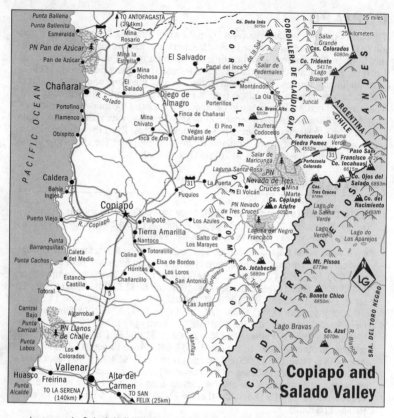

large purple Splash building, has good information about nearby Parques Nacionales Nevado Tres Cruces and Pan de Azucar, including updates on trail conditions. Open M-Th 8:30am-5:30pm, F 8:30am-4:30pm.

Bank: There are several **banks** and **24hr. ATMs** off the plaza, down either O'Higgins or Colipí. **Banco Santander** is west of the plaza at O'Higgins 521 (☎213 993).

Emergency: ☎ 131.

Police: ☎133. Local police, O'Higgins 753 (☎212 627).

Pharmacies: Farmacia Ahumada has 2 locations, Chacabuco 201 (☎231 828) and O'Higgins 561 (☎236 712).

Hospital: Hospital San José (☎212 023), on Los Carreras at the corner with Vicuña, several blocks east of the plaza.

Internet Access: Cyber Chat, Vallejos 431 (☎09 553 9139). CH$500 per hr. Open daily 9am-midnight.

Post Office: Los Carreras 691 (☎213 398), behind Sernatur. Open M-F 9am-2pm and 4-6pm, Sa 9:30am-1pm.

NORTE CHICO

Copiapó

▲ ACCOMMODATIONS
Hotel Chagall, **8**
Hotel Copa de Oro, **3**
Hotel Montecatini I, **4**
Residencial Casa Grande, **1**
Residencial Chañarcillo, **13**
Residencial Nuevo Chañarcillo, **5**

● FOOD & NIGHTLIFE
Di Tito, **2**
El Corsario, **12**
El Sanguchon, **10**
Empanadopolis, **9**
Estoril, **6**
Splash, **11**

Henríquez
Matta
Los Carrera
Mackenna
Salas
Infante
Manuel Rodríguez
Vallejos
Atacama
Ramón Freire
Copayapu
Río Copiapó
Diego Portales
Colipi
Museo Mineralógico
LanChile
Chacabuco
PLAZA PRAT
Iglesia Catedral
Tur Bus
Rodaggio
Pullman Bus
Maipu
Decams
Esperanza
TAXI
Budget
O'Higgins
Cine Alhambra
Chañarcillo
La Paz
Cementerio
Yerbas Buenas
Circunvalación
Yumbel
Los Carrera
Talcahuano
Museo Regional Casa Matta
Iglesia San Francisco
Jotabache
Rancagua
Cerro La Cruz
Matta
Río Copiapó
Junín
Luz Torre
Blanco
Museo Ferroviario y Estación
Batallón Atacama
Martinez
Las Heras
Ramón Freire
Copayapu
Avis
Rómulo Peña
Palaceta Viña de Cristo
Ayacucho
Locomotura Copiapó
TO CHAMONATE (15km),
CALDERA, CHAÑARAL (167km)
TO + SAN JOSÉ

0   200 yards
0   200 meters

ACCOMMODATIONS

Given the lack of things to do in Copiapó, there are a surprising number of options for lodging. Most hostels are off the northwest corner of the plaza on **Rodríguez** and **Infante** but there are also some easy budget options near the bus stations. Whatever your price range, there won't be a shortage of options.

■ **Hotel Montecatini I,** Infante 766 (☎211 516 or 214 552). A large slice of peace and quiet with healthy portions of beautiful interior design. White hallways with white pillars surround a central courtyard of lime and pomegranate trees. Light blue rooms are soothing VIP rooms have cable TV and are bigger. Breakfast included. Singles CH$12,700, VIP CH$17,000; doubles CH$17,500/CH$24,500; triples CH$22,800. ❸

Hotel Chagall, O'Higgins 760 (☎213 775 or 211 454), is an upscale, modern hotel with high prices as proof. Front lobby has a new marble floor with a well-furnished sitting area and bar. Large rooms with cable TV, A/C and heat, alarm clocks, minibars, shampoo and soap, and big beds. Breakfast included. Singles CH$31,900; doubles CH$35,000; triples CH$39,000. Prices increase Dec.-Mar. AmEx/D/MC/V. ❺

Hotel Copa de Oro, Infante 530 (☎216 309). The gold exterior fits the name and makes the hotel stand out. Some room entries are outside, and cold during the winter. Main lounge with leather couches and pink interior is comfortable. Cable TV, private bath. Singles CH$20,000; doubles CH$25,000; triples CH$35,000; quads CH$40,000. Prices around CH$5000 lower in low season. ❹

Residencial Nuevo Chañarcillo, Rodríguez 540 (☎217 105). The owner is an animal lover and has covered the walls with posters of cute little kittens. Some rooms have cable TV, some only antennae. Bathroom tiles cover the bottoms of room walls. Almost everything but the large plastic collie is green. Singles CH$4700, with bath CH$9500; doubles CH$8300/CH$13,100; triples CH$12,500/CH$16,100. ❷

Residencial Casa Grande, Infante 525 (☎244 450). A big, old house with wooden columns surrounding a courtyard. Rooms between the main door and the locked door to the courtyard are a potential security risk. Airy rooms with TV. Some long-term renters stay in this good budget option, so it's best to book in advance. CH$3500 per person. ❶

Residencial Chañarcillo, Chañarcillo 741 (☎213 281), near the bus station. Although it's very basic and the rooms are small, Chañarcillo is one of the better choices for lodging near the bus station. Not to be confused with the Residencial Nuevo Chañarcillo. Indoor windows don't lock on all the rooms, so be careful with your property. Singles CH$4100, with bath CH$7000; doubles CH$11,000; triples CH$15,000. ❷

FOOD AND ENTERTAINMENT

There are a couple of discos in Copiapó for those who wish to cut loose. Try **Splash,** Martínez 46, across from the Conaf offices. The movie theater, **Cine Alhambra,** Atacama 455 (☎212 187), downtown, shows a couple of first-run movies on its one screen. A few restaurants are close, for an excellent dinner and a movie.

■ **Empanadopolis,** Colipí 320 (☎216 320). If all the Greek gods joined to create the best budget *empanada* stop in Chile, it would be almost as good as Empanadopolis. 21 unique *empanadas*, including the Hercules (cheese and olive; CH$400), Poseidon (ham, cheese, tomato sauce, oregano; CH$400), and the Plato (meat, green pepper, "tooth of dragon"; CH$700) are made fresh upon order. Personal pizzas (CH$900) also make great meals. Open M-Th 11am-3pm and 6-10pm, F-Sa 11am-midnight. ❶

El Sanguchon, Atacama 407 (☎231 872), 1 block from the movie theater. Red stucco walls and dark carpeting help the dining atmosphere. The menu is Chilean food well executed. The candlelight doesn't come cheap. *Churrasco completo* CH$2500. Grilled chicken and meat dishes CH$3500. Desserts CH$1500. Open 10am-midnight. ❷

Di Tito, Chacabuco 710 (☎240 253), on the corner of Infante. A cartoon Italian smiles on this stereotypical Italian restaurant's sign. Great pizzas (small CH$2800; large CH$4800) and a long pasta list (CH$3400-3800). Open 11am-4pm and 6pm-1am. ❷

El Corsario, Atacama 245 (☎233 659). The outside seating is in a patio with a plant-filled stone fountain. A romantic setting. The pirate on the wall outside the restaurant should be a fisherman, with the quality of seafood served here. Open M-Sa noon-4pm and 7:30-midnight, Su noon-4pm. May not be open consistently during the winter. ❸

Fábrica Helados Cuello, Maipú 519. This little soft-serve ice cream shop delights with its sweet treats. The machinery looks like it's got at least 20 years on it, but the ice cream still tastes great. CH$200-300 for a swirl. ❶

Estoril, Maipú 542, across the street from Cuello. This small mom-and-pop joint squeezes out the best fresh juices in Copiapó. Blend orange, papaya, kiwi, tuna (a native Chilean cactus fruit), mango, and many other fruits in ½L (CH$600) or 1L glasses (CH$900-1200). Open 10am-1pm and 3-6pm. ❶

📷 SIGHTS

IGLESIA SAN FRANCISCO. Built in 1872, this towering, red-walled church was the sight of the first Franciscan convent in the area. The church was one of the first non-Catholic churches in Chile, and the unique dark red paint with white trim helps it stand out. If you are in Copiapó on a Friday morning, tear yourself away from the busy center and head over to the *iglesia*, where the **farmers' market** will be in full swing. *(Near the Panamerican on the western edge of town, between Matta and Rancagua. Market open F 7am-3pm.)*

CASA MATTA AND THE MUSEO REGIONAL. Like most of the regional museums in major cities in Chile, **Casa Matta** traces the changes between indigenous and Spanish cultures. However, Casa Matta also has a unique plastic mine that illustrates the evolution of mining technology. The plastic shaft is realistically dark and enhances the lackluster displays of picks and mining helmets. *(Atacama 98, on the corner of Rancagua. Open M 2-5:45pm, Tu-F 9am-5:45pm, Sa 10am-12:45pm and 3-5:45pm, Su 10am-12:45pm. CH$600, children CH$300, Su free.)*

MUSEO MINERALÓGICO. Mining was the backbone of this city, and this museum is good proof. There are thousands of rocks divided by category. If there is a rock type in Chile, they have it. One highlight of this "rockfest" is the collection of fluorescent rocks behind little glass viewers. Hit a switch and watch them glow. The complex crystals are particularly beautiful. You don't need to know about mineralogy to enjoy the bright colors or wonder how valuable the exotic rocks are. *(On the corner of Colipí and Rodríguez, a block from the plaza. ☎206 606. Open M-F 10am-1pm and 3:30-7pm, Sa 10am-1pm. CH$500, children CH$200.)*

UNIVERSIDAD DE ATACAMA. A 25min. walk west of the plaza, across the Panamerican, the Universidad de Atacama serves the region's higher educational needs while preserving historical artifacts. Visitors can walk into the elegant mansion, the **Palacete Viña de Cristo,** head up the staircase with marble handrails, and twist around the two-story spiral staircase to the cupola for a view of the surrounding mountains. The university is also the final resting place of the **Locomotura Copiapó,** the first railcar in South America and one of the oldest steam engines in the world. *(The Palacete is on University grounds at the end of Romulo Peña. Open Mar.-Dec. M-F 9am-6pm. The Locomotura is outside, a few blocks farther on, also within the school grounds.)*

PARQUE NACIONAL NEVADO TRES CRUCES   ☎52

Parque Nacional Nevado Tres Cruces, 180km from Copiapó, is quickly becoming one of Chile's most desired new adventure destinations. Founded in 1995 on 590 sq. km of land deep in the *cordillera* of the Atacama region, the park is known for the flamingos that feed in the saline waters of its several lakes. The best flamingo-watching periods are from December to February. It's possible to navigate the rocky roads of the park on your own, but it's highly recommended to travel with one of the many tour agencies that serve the park (see **Tourist Office,** p. 197).

The larger sector of the park comprises the Salar de Maricunga and the Laguna Santa Rosa. The **Salar de Maricunga** is a large, brilliant, white salt flat surrounded by tall mountains. Flamingos fill the salt-saturated pools that stretch across a large plain. The pools seem metallic, reflecting the sky and surrounding mountains. The ponds also serve as salty habitats for ducks, geese, and other animals. The blue waters of **Laguna Santa Rosa** begin in the southeast end of the Salar de Maricunga and also help sustain a population of *guanacos* and other Chilean flora and fauna. The **Refugio Conaf** near Laguna Santa Rosa offers temporary shelter for the wet, cold, or sleepy. The refuge is little more than a wooden hut (no water, electricity, or bathrooms), so pack accordingly. (Open all year. Free.) Conaf has also another, ritzier refuge to the south in the smaller sector.

The southern sector of the park, a few hours south of the larger sector on a well-labeled road off International Highway 31, encircles the **Laguna del Negro Francisco,** a striking, deep blue-green lake at 4500m above sea level. The water has an incredible variety of aquatic organisms that draw a diverse group of land animals. Flamingos linger in both the salty and freshwater parts, dotting the entire lake with color. Most wildlife can be observed between September and April, before the animals migrate. The **Refugio Conaf** of Laguna del Negro Francisco offers electricity, hot water, toilets, and mattresses in a wooden hut, but travelers must bring their own drinking water and food. (Open year-round. CH$6000 per person.)

To reach the park from Copiapó, drivers should take International Highway 31 east out of the city. At Sector de la Puerta, take the east fork, Route C-31, to get to Laguna Santa Rosa. Allow several hours for the 166km trip. Laguna del Negro Francisco is another 85km south of this sector. Visitors should be sure to have good 4WD vehicles to drive anywhere in the park or if crossing into Argentina (see **Border Crossing,** p. 203). 4x4 vehicles can be found at most car rental agencies in Copiapó and generally cost CH$42,000-60,000 per day. **Atacama Expeditions,** off the northeast corner of Plaza O'Higgins 640 in Copiapó (☎216 981; www.atacamaexpeditions.cl), offers a daytrip to **Laguna Santa Rosa, Salar de Maricunga,** and other areas in the larger section of the park for CH$86,000 for up to four people. Tours leave year-round, although from June to October there are fewer people to divide the cost, and conditions are often too snowy. For more information, contact **Conaf** (☎210 282 or 237 104) or **Sernatur** (☎231 510) in Copiapó. Entrance CH$2000 for nationals, CH$4000 for foreigners; children CH$500/CH$1500.

OJOS DEL SALADO   ☎ 52

Volcán Ojos del Salado lies just outside of Parque Nacional Nevado Tres Cruces, and rivals its neighbor as one of the hottest regional destinations for adventurous travelers. At 6890m, Ojos del Salado is the Chilean Andes' tallest peak, the world's highest active volcano (with eruptions in 1937 and 1956), and the third-highest peak in the Americas. The name "Eyes of Salt" is derived from the large salt deposits that are scattered throughout the area. At the base of the volcano sits the emerald **Laguna Verde,** a picturesque sight in such striking surroundings. Temperatures range from -10°C to -40°C year-round, so extremely warm clothing is vital.

Guided excursions to the base of the mountain and Laguna Verde are available through **Conaf, Atacama Expeditions,** and **Sernatur** in Copiapó (see **Tourist Office,** p. 197). Atacama Expeditions offers a two-day tour to Laguna Santa Rosa and the Salar de Maricunga in Nevado Tres Cruces the first day and Ojos del Salado and Laguna Verde the second day (CH$150,000 for up to 4 people). Guided hikes of Ojos del Salado are also available but prices vary depending on the time of year and conditions. Climbing is only permitted between October and May because of heavy winter snowfall. Acclimatization is necessary before and after the hike, and is normally started at the base shelter of the **Universidad de Atacama** at 5100m (room for 6 people; no extra charge) and then continued at the **Refugio Cesar Tejos,** at 5800m, which is a little larger and better equipped. The whole process takes about eight days, with six days devoted to the actual hike. The main challenge of the hike is dealing with the extreme cold and altitude. Otherwise, the climb is not overly technical until the last stretch before the peak. Because the volcano straddles the border with Argentina, hikers must obtain special permission to attempt the trek. Contact the **Frontier and Limits Office** (Bandera 54, 4th fl., Santiago. Fax 56 2 697 1909; www.difrol.cl.) or visit the **Sernatur** office in Copiapó. It is not difficult to gain permission and does not take much time, but the documentation is necessary for emergencies and border disputes. Any hike done through a travel agency will take care of permission as part of the hike preparations.

To get to Ojos del Salado, continue another hour or so along the international highway from Parque Nacional Nevado Tres Cruces. From Copiapó, it is about 260km to the base of the mountain.

BORDER CROSSING INTO ARGENTINA: PASO DE SAN FRANCISCO
To the north of Volcán Ojos del Salado is Paso de San Francisco, the route from Chile into Argentina. Several *ripio* roads from Copiapó and the surrounding area meet in PN Nevado Tres Cruces, passing by stretches of salt flats, flocks of flamingos, and high, barren peaks. Chilean customs is at the Salar de Maricunga, 105km from the pass. The route continues across the border to **Tinogasta** in Argentina. The pass may be closed in winter due to inclement weather, so check with Conaf before attempting the crossing. The customs office at Maricunga station is open 8:30am-6:30pm. The process is fairly simple and involves no more than a brief search of your luggage for contraband and various food products followed by a passport stamp. 98km past the Chilean border is the Cortaderas Frontier Control, where your stamp and luggage may go through another simple check (see **Essentials: Border Crossings,** p. 35, for info on visas and fees).

CALDERA   ☎ 52

Unlike many of its mining neighbors, Caldera (pop. 12,000) has remained unscathed by industrial blight—the sun is plentiful on the fine sandy beaches here, and the tranquil bays are perfect for a leisurely afternoon of swimming, kayaking, and windsurfing. Although Caldera was developed as a port for the region's silver and copper mines, it still manages to project a relaxed holiday-town atmosphere. The bay outside one of the main beaches, Playa Copiapina, is full of fishing boats that bring a pungent smell to the small town every morning.

TRANSPORTATION. Tur Bus, Gallo 149 (☎316 832), near Vallejos, departs from its office for: Antofagasta (7hr., 6 per day 9:15am-11:45pm, CH$7000) via Chañaral (1hr., CH$1400); Arica (17hr., 11:55am and 10:15pm, CH$14,000) via Iquique (14hr., CH$13,000); Calama (10hr., 9:15 and 10:45pm, CH$9300); Santiago (13hr., 8:15 and 9:15pm, CH$11,200) via Copiapó (1hr., 5 per day, CH$1100); Taltal (3hr., 12:15 and 5pm, CH$3200). **Pullman Bus** (☎316 585), just across Gallo from Tur Bus on the corner with Vallejos, goes to: Arica (16hr., 7 per day 8:45am-11:40pm, CH$17,000) via Antofagasta (7hr., CH$8000); Chañaral (1hr., 6 per day 8:30am-7:45pm, CH$1000); Copiapó (1hr., 6 per day 10am-9:30pm, CH$1000); Santiago (12hr., 6 per day 5-11:30pm, CH$12,000). During the summer, **minibuses** run between Caldera (from the Plaza de Armas) and Bahía Inglesa (from Chañaral) for CH$200. **Colectivos** leave from the Plaza de Armas in Caldera and run between Caldera and Bahía Inglesa (10min.; Nov.-Apr. CH$1000, May-Oct. CH$400) and Copiapó (CH$1000). **Taxis** between Caldera and Bahía Inglesa cost CH$1400.

⚡🚻 ORIENTATION AND PRACTICAL INFORMATION. The commercial center surrounds the central plaza up the street from the **Tur Bus** and **Pullman Bus** stations on **Gallo.** Around the plaza, **Ossa Cerda, Gana,** and **Gallo** host city essentials. The **municipalidad** is along the plaza and can provide minimal tourist information. A **tourist information center** is underneath the gray walkway of the plaza. (Open M-Sa 9am-2pm and 6-11pm, Su 10am-2pm; low season M-F 9am-1:30pm and 3-5pm.)

Caldera has most necessary services, including **BancoEstado** with a **24hr. ATM** on Gallo and Tocomal, between the bus station and the plaza; **Inca Supermarket,** Carvillo 480 (☎315 214); a **police** station, Ossa Cerda 274 (☎616 289); and **Farmacia Cruz** at Cousiño 325. (☎315 830. Open M-Sa 9:30am-2pm and 5-10pm, Su 10:30am-5pm.). **Bianchi,** Edwards 520-A (☎315 748), sells camping gear. **Internet** is available at **Globalcel,** Carvallo 370 (☎316 213) and small locations around the plaza. (CH$500 per hr. Open daily 10am-2pm and 5-9pm.) There is also a **Chile Express,** Carba Local 1 (☎315 707) and a **post office,** Edwards 325 (☎315 285).

🚻🏠 ACCOMMODATIONS AND FOOD. In Caldera and Bahía Inglesa, prices are much lower between May and September. Accommodations are plentiful in Caldera, and although it is not as beautiful as Bahía Inglesa, it has access to the outside world. **Hotel Pucara ❸,** Ossa Cerda 460, opposite the church, is good option. With a self-serve kitchen, and clean rooms with bath, TV, and breakfast, it's almost too good to be true. The plain patio and old leather chairs will motivate you to get out and go to the beach. (☎319 886. Singles CH$12,000; doubles CH$15,000. Low-season singles CH$8000; doubles CH$12,000.) **Hotel Terra del Sol ❷,** Gallo 370, between the bus station and the plaza at Gallo, is a steal in the winter with free Internet, TV, breakfast, and a summer beach house atmosphere. (☎319 885. Dorms CH$9000; singles with bath CH$12,000. Low-season dorms CH$4000; singles with bath CH$6000.) **Comercial Jandy ❸** has ocean views and a crisp, clean, new feeling for half the price of the beachside hotels. To top it off, Internet, TV, private bath, and breakfast are included. (☎316 640. Singles CH$15,000; doubles CH$30,000. Low-season singles CH$8000; doubles CH$15,000. AmEx/D/MC/V.)

Caldera cuisine features quality fresh seafood. For freshly made, cheap seafood options, head down behind the green train station along the pier. No-name restaurants along the water serve crab and scallop *empanadas* (CH$800) and *paila marina* (CH$1000). The established restaurants are more expensive but a few blocks closer to the town center. **The New Charles Restaurante ❸,** on Ossa Cerda on the plaza, is crowded during the summer and empty all winter. They offer fresh seafood in a canteen-like atmosphere. (☎315 348. Entrees CH$3000-4500. Open 9am-midnight.) **Restaurante Estella Mary ❷,** on the corner of Ossa Cerda and Gallo, is decorated like a Mexican tequila joint but is fresh and clean. The outdoor bar is great for having a few drinks and enjoying the CH$1500 *menú* with fresh fish. (Open M-Sa noon-5pm and 7pm-midnight.)

🎦 🎵 **SIGHTS AND ENTERTAINMENT.** The **Ex-Estación Ferrocarril** has exhibits of work by local artists, as part of the **Centro de Desarrollo Cultural,** and a small exhibit about the history of South America's first railway. (Open M-F 10am-1pm and 3-9pm, Sa 11am-1pm and 3-8pm. Free.) A few blocks inland, on the **Plaza de Armas,** is the **Iglesia de San Vincente** (built in 1862) with a yellow exterior and a tall Gothic bell tower that can be seen from almost any point in Caldera. **Playa Brava** lies within Caldera but it is dirtier and the harbor boats obstruct the view. There are a couple of better beaches 10km north, including **Playas Rodillo** and **Ramada,** which are both crowded in summer. The best beaches, however, are in nearby Bahía Inglesa. In the summer, there are a couple of **discotecas** that blare mixes of popular Spanish and English pop, rap, and dance, including **Takeo** and **Loreto Bar,** both on Camino Caldera-Bahía Inglesa between Caldera and Bahía Inglesa. The walk to the *discotecas* is manageable, but a ride home will probably be necessary.

BAHÍA INGLESA   ☎52

Just 5km south of Caldera is the little beach resort of Bahía Inglesa, an unadulterated beach nirvana. Named the "English Bay" due to the landing of British privateer Edward Davis in 1687, the fine sand and azure waters attract more than just lonely sailors. During the summer holiday season, the sweeping coastal desert setting draws vacationers from all over Chile, making advance reservations for the fabulous camping and *cabañas* a must.

The beaches of Bahía Inglesa are divided by large rock outcroppings. Las Machas is the widest and longest stretch of beach, while Las Piscinas and El Chuncho y Blanca offer crystal green and blue water with volcanic rock and fine white sand. At the end of Morro, the main road along the beach, **Morro Ballena Expediciones Marítimas** offers **kayak rentals, fishing excursions** with local fishermen, and other aquatic activities. (Single kayak CH$2000; double CH$4000. Fishing CH$3000-7000 per person.) The tourist information center in Caldera (p. 204) offers excursions to Bahía Inglesa and beaches farther south.

Considering its size, Bahía Inglesa has incredible accommodations ranging from rustic camping and *cabañas* to ritzy hotels. Among the former is **Camping Bahía Inglesa ❶,** a fenced campground on Playa Las Machas, which offers 56 *cabañas,* all with kitchen facilities, bath, and living room, as well as 90 sandy campsites with clean communal baths and a swimming pool. Like any place in Bahía Inglesa, the prices are sky-high during the summer and a bargain during the winter. Camping Bahía Inglesa has A-E rated cabañas that vary in size, look, and location. (☎315 424 or 316 399. 6-person *cabañas* CH$9,000-45,000; 6-person campsite CH$18,000, low-season CH$8000.) **Los Jardines de Bahía Inglesa ❸** offers more privacy for their 35 dark wood *cabañas* with TV, parking, and a small patio. The main complex is weighed down by hundreds of anchors of all shapes and sizes, as well as a game room and two poolside bars. (☎315 359, in Santiago 02 698 2650. *Cabañas:* small CH$42,000; medium CH$56,000; large CH$66,000; extra-large CH$94,000. Low-season *cabañas:* small CH$20,000; medium CH$25,000; large CH$35,000; extra-large CH$40,000. AmEx/D/MC/V.) **Hotel Rocas de Bahía ❺,** El Morro 888 on Playa El Chuncho y Blanca, has whitewashed rooms, all with a view of the beach and sunset. Rocas de Bahía is extremely social and all the room balconies have foot-high dividers for easy party hopping. The pyramid-like building, set against the blue ocean water and the white sand, resembles an Aegean resort. On the top floor are a beautiful swimming pool and bar/restaurant with a wraparound view of the horizon. (☎316 005; www.rocasdebahia.cl. Free bike usage. Singles CH$60,000; doubles CH$66,000; triples CH$66,000. Low-season singles CH$29,300; doubles CH$39,000; triples CH$47,000. AmEx/D/MC/V.)

NORTE CHICO

PRESIDENT'S BRAVE OCEAN SWIM GETS GLOWING REVIEWS

On December 31, 2003, Ricardo Lagos made good on a promise and visited Chañaral for a swim at the beach outside of town. The President of Chile interrupted his vacation, flew into the city's small airport, and went for a quick dip accompanied by his bodyguards on the otherwise empty beach—a not altogether notable occurence, except that Chañaral's beach and waters were the sight of toxic waste dumping for 40 years.

The story starts in 1938 when an American copper mining company began disposing of toxic excess in the Río Solado. From there, the sulfuric acid and metallic waste flowed out to the Pacific in front of Chañaral's beach, damaging the local tourism and fishing industries. In 1971, copper mining was nationalized under Codelco, but the mega-corporation maintained the same waste disposal methods, furthering contamination of Chañaral's coast.

In the late 1980s, however, Codelco changed its waste disposal method, initiated a number of local building and social programs, and began a campaign to clean the beaches.

On March 11th, 2003, President Lagos promised to swim at

After an exhausting morning of baking in the sun, lunch at **el Plateao** ❷ is a must. This Thai, Indian, Vietnamese, and Peruvian fusion restaurant does all of the above in a bamboo house with peppers and seashells lining the wall. Most of the dishes include fresh local seafood in a number of combinations, from Vietnamese coconut *pad thai* to tandoori scallops and Peruvian baked chicken in Thai peanut sauce. Meals are enormous; five crab claws and two fish with a steaming pile of rice is the average size, and the food is worth every peso. (Chilean seafood dishes CH$4000. Fusion dishes CH$6000.) For a cheaper snack, **Bahía House** ❶, El Morro 1038, a block down from Hotel Rocas de Bahía, has filling seafood *empanadas* (CH$600-900) and cheap Chilean fare. (☎09 348 7204. Open 8am-10pm.) The town's one fancier restaurant is in the **Hotel Rocas de Bahía** ❸, where excellent food is matched with an incredible view. (Pasta CH$2500-3800. Seafood CH$4000-6800. *Lomo* CH$3900-4000. Open 12:30-4pm and 8pm-midnight. AmEx/DC/MC/V.)

During the summer, **minibuses** run between Bahía Inglesa (from Av. Chañaral) and Caldera (from the Plaza de Armas) for CH$300. **Colectivos** from Bahía Inglesa to the Plaza de Armas in **Caldera** run past Hotel Rocas de Bahía all the time during the summer but have to be called during the winter (5-10min.; summer CH$400, winter CH$1000). **Taxis** cost CH$1500 between Bahía Inglesa and Caldera.

CHAÑARAL ☎ 52

A visit to Chañaral will have you looking slim and buff in no time. This small fishing and mining port of 14,000 is built into the side of a mountain, so going across town means climbing uphill. Hiking past town to the Faro del Milenio, a large lighthouse on the surrounding hills, provides a great view of the surrounding area. With the mountains in the distance, the buildings of Chañaral stretching into the desert, and green wisps of grass behind the long sandy beach, the town consistently provides lovely panoramas. But those wisps of grass aren't what they seem. The greenish glow is the environmental treat provided by local copper mining and refinery stations: arsenic and copper contamination. Fortunately, the Chilean government has contained the contamination and is in the process of completely eliminating any possible threats. The riptide in this area can be very strong—be careful while enjoying the long stretches of breaking waves.

TRANSPORTATION. Tur Bus (☎481 012), on the Panamerican opposite the Copec station, departs from its office for: Antofagasta (5hr., every hr. 7:30am-11:55pm, CH$6000); Copiapó (2hr., CH$2000); Santiago (13hr., 8 per day 6am-9:15pm, CH$12,700) via Caldera (1hr., CH$1400); Taltal (2hr., 1:45 and 6:10pm, CH$1800). **Pullman Bus** (☎480 213), on Los Baños across from the *municipalidad*, departs from its office for: Arica (14hr.; 2:45, 11:15pm, 12:15am; CH$15,000); Copiapó (2hr., every hr. 8:45am-10:30pm, CH$2500); Iquique (12hr., 9pm and 3am, CH$14,000) via Antofagasta (5hr., CH$5000); Santiago (14hr., 4 per day 3:45pm-12:15am, CH$15,000) via La Serena (7hr., CH$6000), Ovalle (9hr., CH$6500) and Valparaíso (13hr., CH$15,000). **Flota Barrios,** Merino Jarpa 567 (☎480 894), opposite the fire station, goes to similar destinations with varying frequency.

There are **minibuses** to Parque Nacional Pan de Azúcar during the summer, run by local tourist agencies. Local **colectivos** to Parque Nacional Pan de Azúcar run during the summer for CH$2000 one-way.

ORIENTATION AND PRACTICAL INFORMATION. Most of the hostels, restaurants, and amenities in Chañaral are on **Merino Jarpa.** The area up the hill is mostly residential, but the **Plaza de Armas** is in that area, along **Buin.** The Panamerican runs one block down from Merino Jarpa and along it are the **Tur Bus** and **Pullman Bus** centers. The main beach is past the Panamerican, away from town. On the hillside above town, the **Foro del Milenio,** a new local lighthouse, and a small graffiti-covered amphitheater are a 15min. walk from the city center.

Chañaral has no tourist office, so inquire at the *municipalidad*'s **Oficina de Relaciones Públicas** on the corner of Merino Jarpa and Los Baños. (☎480 142 ext. 209. Open M-F 8am-2pm and 3-7pm.) There is a **souvenir kiosk** next to the *municipalidad* on Merino Jarpa, where you may book tours to Parque Nacional Pan de Azúcar run by **Souvenir Tour Chile.** (☎09 555 4454. Full-day trip to El Mirador CH$26,000; full-day trip to Las Lomitas CH$44,000. Open M-Sa 9am-2pm and 6:30-10pm, in summer also Su 6:30pm-10pm.) Souvenir Tour Chile also provides taxis to Parque Nacional Pan de Azúcar (CH$7000 one-way).

BancoEstado, with a **24hr. ATM,** is at Buin 801. (☎480 000. Open M-F 9am-2pm.) **Supermercado Zamora,** at the corner of Buin and Maipú, is open 24hr. and also has an ATM (☎480 352). The **police** station is on Carrera (☎480 133). Buy essentials at **Farmacia Varas,** Zuleta 150. (☎481 105. Open M-Sa 10am-10pm, Su 10am-noon.) The **Hospital Doctor Luis Her-**

Chañaral before the end of the year, once Codelco had finished decontamination. Lagos held true, and 11 days after Codelco announced the complete recovery of the beach's swimming area, the President showed up.

By the next day, local residents were swimming for the first time in years. But environmentalists claim that the beach is still contaminated and presents a hazard to public health. The vice-president of the Red Nacional de Acción Ecológica, Manuel Cortés, fears that the President's publicity stunt will do more damage than good, saying "To go for one swim isn't going to have notable effects, but without a doubt it is going to convince the poorest members of the community to use the beach and to turn this true toxic dump into a swimming area."

The debate as to how contaminated the beach is remains unresolved, but judging from Codelco's history of contamination at other mining sites, most notably the soon-to-be-relocated town of Chuquicamata, there may still be cause for concern. Chañaral's beach is beautiful and could someday be a tourist haven, but in the meantime, the thick green layer of metallic dust that stretches for miles behind the beach is a sign that Codelco has a lot more work to do before residents' concerns are swept away.

rera is at Prat and Carrera (☎480 107). For smaller needs, a **doctor's office** is at the corner of Merino Jarpa and Domeyko. (☎500 301. Open M-F 7am-4pm.) Bikes, camping, and fishing gear are available through **Don Álvaro**, Merino Jarpa 1101. (☎480 083. Open M-Sa 10am-9pm.) **Internet** access is available at a **Telefónica** call center, Merino Jarpa 506, and various Internet centers near the *municipalidad* (☎480 571. CH$800 per hr. Open M-W 8:30am-11pm, Th 9am-2pm and 5-10pm, Su 11am-2pm and 5-10pm.) A **Chile Express** with **Western Union** services are located opposite the *municipalidad*, at Los Banos 202. (☎480 187. Open M-F 9am-2pm and 4-7pm, Sa 10:30am-1pm.) The **post office** is at Comercio 172. (☎489 041. Open M-F 9am-1pm and 3-6:30pm, Sa 9am-12:30pm.)

⌂🛏 ACCOMMODATIONS AND FOOD. Chañaral does not have ritzy hotels or dirt-cheap, dirty hostels; most options fall somewhere in between. Like other beach towns in the area, prices double from December to February. **Hostal Los Aromos ❷**, Los Aromos 7, is a new setup with the most comfortable rooms in town, all with cable TV. (☎489 636. Singles CH$5000, with bath CH$7000; doubles CH$10,000/CH$15,000; triples $15,000.) Another good option is **Hostería Chañaral ❹**, Muller 268, with a big open-air courtyard overflowing with flowers, and a beach view from the comfy lounge area. The concrete rooms don't match the quality of the courtyard, but include TV, bath, and breakfast. (Singles CH$30,000; doubles CH$40,000; triples CH$48,000. Low-season singles CH$18,000; doubles CH$22,000; triples CH$24,000. AmEx/D/MC/V.) More basic accommodations are found at **Hotel La Marina ❶**, Merino Jarpa 562, the cheapest option in town, with clean rooms and shared baths. The metal doors give La Marina a submarine-adventure feel. (☎09 340 8464. CH$3500 per person.) Across the street, **Hotel Jiménez ❷**, Merino Jarpa 551, offers clean rooms, some with TV. (☎480 328. Breakfast included. Singles CH$4000, with bath CH$5500; doubles CH$11,000/CH$12,500; quads CH$16,500.)

Dining in town is overpriced, but the options along the Panamerican offer similar food for cheaper prices. Seafood is good in Chañaral and **Acuarium Parador ❷** offers the best view in town. Across the Panamerican from the center of town, the aquarium is on the beach and has small fish tanks around the main dining area. (Seafood dishes CH$2000-3500. Open noon-1am.) The restaurant at **Hostería Chañaral ❸** offers great seafood and a wide ocean view. (Sandwiches CH$900-CH$1600. Fish CH$3500-CH$6500. Steaks CH$3600-CH$5500. Open daily noon-3pm and 7-11pm. AmEx/DC/MC/V.) Downtown, the popular **Restaurant Rincón Porteño ❷**, Merino Jarpa 567, offers simple meals in front of a big TV in a canteen-style setup (☎480 071. Open M-Sa 9am-10pm, Su noon-9pm.) A few good seafood restaurants are off the Panamerican opposite the Copec gas station. These include **La Querencia ❶** (☎480 222; *congrio* CH$2500, *paila marina* CH$2500, fish sandwiches CH$900; open 24hr.) and **Los Arbolitos ❷** (open 24hr.). The clientele is mostly truck drivers and motorists, but the food is good for a quick bite.

PARQUE NACIONAL PAN DE AZÚCAR

Created in 1985 on 440 sq. km of coastal desert, Parque Nacional Pan de Azúcar is a sanctuary for a wide range of Chilean wildlife. Humboldt penguins waddle up paths along Isla Pan de Azucar; unique desert fauna flourish; and sea otters, seals, foxes, and condors roam free. This splendor has made Pan de Azúcar one of Chile's premier national parks, and with its miles of hiking trails, it's accessible to many. The beaches within the park territory are pristine, but public access there is limited. Tens of thousands of visitors flock here during the summer, but during the winter, the lack of visitors can make ocean attractions much easier to see. With the camping and *cabaña* options available through **Conaf** (p. 209), visitors can stay for a day or a week to explore the desert, mountain, and ocean treks.

AT A GLANCE

AREA: 440 sq. km.

CLIMATE: Mediterranean. Hot in the summer, with temperatures upwards of 90°F. Winters average 55°F.

GATEWAYS: Chañaral.

FEES: CH$3500, children CH$2000.

HIGHLIGHTS: Pristine white-sand beaches and desert landscapes. Hiking, camping, and fishing. Refuge to hundreds of Humboldt penguins, sea lions, seals, and a large variety of wildlife.

CAMPING: Various *refugios* along the beaches; *cabañas* near Caleta.

▣ TRANSPORTATION. For active tourists, the best way to get here is by **biking** from Chañaral (2hr.). In the summer, **Turismo Chango,** along the Panamerican (☎480 484 or 480 668; www.pandeazucar.com), in Chañaral, runs a minibus service to and from the park (30min.; 4 per day 8:30-9am, returns 6pm; CH$1000-2000.) **Taxis** from Chañaral to Caleta depart from the *municipalidad* area (CH$14,000 round-trip). Usually, during the summer, there are tourists willing to split the cost of a taxi. During the winter, cheap transportation is nonexistent without a group. Biking along the 22km paved road is not difficult, with only one small hill along the way. Bikes can be rented at **Don Álvaro** (p. 230) in Chañaral. See **Chañaral Transportation** (p. 207) for additional transportation information.

▦ ORIENTATION. The park is located 22km north of Chañaral on a new paved road. It is illegal to camp on **Playa Refugio,** the beach just before the park's southern entrance, but you can walk on its fine sand and admire the stunning scenery without the fishing boats or trash prevalent on many of the area's other beaches. Enter from the south to approach three adjacent beach sights beneath the base of towering **Cerro Soldado—Playa Blanca, Playa Piqueros,** and nearby **Playa Soldado.** All three are pristine and white, but only **Piqueros** offers camping. A couple of hundred meters away is a bulbous island that resembles a mound of sugar. This is **Isla Pan de Azúcar,** home to 3000 Humboldt penguins, seals, sea otters, pelicans, cormorants, and other rare wildlife. Visitors cannot step foot on the island, but can approach it in a number of vehicles to observe the animals at close range. Although the strong currents make swimming along the beaches hazardous, they are great for sunbathing and fishing. Among the more worthwhile vantage points in the park are **El Mirador,** a lookout point 300m high and about 8km from the Conaf office, and **Las Lomitas,** a peak 800m high that is 30km from the office. Everyone from out-of-shape desk workers to expert mountaineers can enjoy the hikes. A couple of kilometers farther north of the Conaf office is **Caleta Pan de Azúcar,** a ramshackle village of 20 fishermen. Buy fresh seafood directly from the fishermen or stop in at one of the small stores nearby.

▨ PRACTICAL INFORMATION. The **Conaf office** at the southern entrance is home to a Conaf ranger who collects entrance fees (CH$3500, Chileans CH$2000) and provides maps, brochures, and up-to-date information about the park. (Open 24hr. Copiapó Conaf office ☎210 282 ext. 33. Open daily 8:30am-12:30pm and 2-6:30pm.) To get a close look at the penguins on Isla Pan de Azúcar, there are two options. A number of local fishermen, including Manuel Silva (☎02 196 5300; CH$40,000 per boat, max. 7 people) and Rodrigo Carvajal (☎480 563 or 09 429 2132; www.galeon.com/pinguitour; CH$40,000) run 2hr. boat trips around the island. **Chango Turismo** has a small fleet of 10-12 kayaks that circle the island in calm seas. (☎480 484; www.pandeazucar.com. CH$10,000 per boat.) Surprisingly enough for such a small hamlet, there is a satellite telephone in the village for international phone calls (☎09 196 5300).

ACCOMMODATIONS AND CAMPING. There are several Conaf camping **refugios ❶** on Playas Piqueros and Soldado and north of Caleta, all with a rock shelter, picnic tables, BBQ equipment, and communal bathroom facilities (4-person site CH$8000). A restaurant and communal showers are around the Caleta campsite. Also close to Caleta are four Conaf **cabañas ❷**, which are an excellent value in beautiful settings. Baths, a living room, kitchen facilities, solar power, and hot water are included. Reserve a month in advance in high season at the Copiapó Conaf office (p. 197; 6-person *cabaña* CH$35,000-40,000). Camping in the park is allowed only at the designated Conaf camping *refugios*. During the low season, *cabaña* prices can be negotiated with the Conaf office in Copiapó.

TALTAL   ☎ 55

The small stopover point between Chañaral and Antofagasta is the hidden town of Taltal. Taltal doesn't have a spectacular beach, but rather offers a simple life; residents don't have to lock their doors at night. The community is tight, and the mayor's niece, brother, and other family members are important local figures who love to show visitors around. Arturo Prat is the main street, running past two beautiful plazas. The **Plaza de Armas** is lined with rows of antique street lamps that light up the center of town, and the **Plaza de la Cultura** has ping-pong tables, tennis courts, a skating park, and a long series of waterfalls running past small sitting areas overlooking the ocean. On the edge of town, **Museo Augusto Capdeville** offers a very small look at Diaguita artifacts and town history. (At the corner of Prat and Moreno. Open M-F 10am-2pm and 4-6pm. Free.)

There are only a few options for food or accommodations in Taltal, so a budget establishment is hard to find. **Residencial Karime ❷**, Ramírez 371, has an almost nonexistent front door and a loud metal staircase, but the new rooms, hot showers, table lamps, and included breakfast are all great for the price. (☎ 613 262. CH$4500 per person.) **Hotel San Martín ❷**, Martínez 279, has smaller, older rooms, all with TV. (☎ 611 088. Singles CH$5000, with bath CH$10,000; doubles CH$10,000/CH$15,000; triples CH$15,000/CH$25,000.) Two more expensive options on the beach along Esmeralda are **Hotel Mi Tampi ❹**, O'Higgins 138, and **Hostería Taltal ❹**, Esmeralda 671. Hotel Mi Tampi is a new, cute bed-and-breakfast with a blue-and-yellow bordeaux motif, satellite TV, and private bath. (☎ 613 605. Singles CH$19,500; doubles CH$21,500; triples CH$24,000. AmEx/D/MC/V.) Hostería Taltal and the accompanying **Restaurant Taltal ❸** have beachside views with a large patio that juts out over the breaking waves. The rooms are clean and have TV and private bath, but are not as new as Tampi's. (☎ 611 625 or 611 173. Singles CH$18,500; doubles CH$19,800. AmEx/D/MC/V.)

For food, **Caberna 87 ❶**, Martínez 247, offers the town's main budget stop. (Fresh fish with salad CH$2000. *Menú* CH$1500.) **Club Social Taltal ❸**, Torreblanca 162, across the street from the *municipalidad*, has well-prepared crab cakes, mushroom steak, lobster, and grilled tuna, depending on the season. After dinner, homemade ice cream is a few blocks away at **Capri ❶**, Ramírez 217. The owner is proud of the massive metal ice cream maker on the counter and has a long list of fruity ice creams. (☎ 611 273. 2 scoops CH$300.)

Taltal seems small in the shadows of its large northern neighbor, Antofagasta, but it has all the necessary amenities. Most everything can be found along Prat, including the **municipalidad,** Prat 515 (☎ 611 139 or 611 028), which eagerly offers information to tourists. **BancoEstado** and a **24hr. ATM** are off Prat on Ramírez 247 (☎ 611 060). **Perucci Supermarket** (☎ 426 878) is at the corner of Prat and San Martín. **Almacén Farmacia Prat,** Prat 845, can handle basic needs. (☎ 09 874 6166. Open M-Sa 10am-1:30pm and 5-9:30pm.) The **hospital,** O'Higgins 450 (☎ 611 077) and **police station,** Sargento Aldea 502 (☎ 611 133 or 613 393), are both in the hills around town, away from the water. There's also **Internet** at a **Telefónica** call center, Prat 635. (☎611 812. CH$600 per hr. Open M-F 9am-10pm, Su 11am-2pm and 5-10pm.) A **Chile Express,** San Martín 409, with **Western Union,** is four blocks up. (☎612 073. M-Sa 9am-2pm and 3:30-7pm.) A **post office,** in the *municipalidad,* can handle non-rushed mail. (☎611 123. Open M-F 9am-1:30pm and 3-5pm, Sa 9am-noon.)

The **Tur Bus** station, Prat 631, is the only transportation in and out of town (☎611 426). Buses run north to Antofagasta (3½hr., 4 per day 3:30am-8:10pm, CH$2500) and south to Chañaral (2hr.; 1:45, 4, 6pm; CH$2000). Long-distance buses are available from the larger hubs in Antofagasta and Chañaral.

VALLENAR   ☎51

Though Vallenar lacks a famous church or thriving artisan's market, it is a sunny, quaint town that will help ease you into a slower pace. The main street narrows into a pedestrian-only walkway and makes for peaceful after-dinner strolls. Vallenar is a great place to visit for a day or live the rest of your life, but its lack of exciting activities doesn't really encourage longer vacations.

▐ TRANSPORTATION

The **Terminal de Buses** is found on the western edge of town at the corner of Prat and Matta. For longer trips and more travel times, you may have to wait for the frequent buses to La Serena or Copiapó. Both **Tur Bus** (☎616 331) and **Pullman Bus** (☎612 461) go to Copiapó (every hr. 5:30am-2:30am, both CH$2000) and La Serena (every hr. 5:30am-2:30am; Tur Bus CH$2300, Pullman CH$2500). Not all buses passing by Vallenar stop in Vallenar, so it is advisable to check at the ticket booth.

Local bus service within the Huasco Valley, as well as **taxi colectivo** service, is localized on Maranon between Verdaguer and Ercilla (CH$2000). The nameless *colectivo* company goes to Los Altos del Carmen (1hr., 8 per day 7:30am-6:30pm, CH$1000) and San Felix (1½hr., 3 per day 11am-5:30pm, CH$1200).

▗▘ ▐ ORIENTATION AND PRACTICAL INFORMATION

Buses drop off passengers on the west side of town, after descending from the Panamerican. The city is laid out in a very regular grid and navigation is easy. **Plaza O'Higgins** makes a good reference point. The plaza is centered in town, interrupting **Prat,** the main thoroughfare. The bus station is several blocks west of the plaza on Prat, and east of the plaza Prat becomes a pedestrian walkway where many of the shops and restaurants are situated. The northern boundary of town is **Maranon,** while **Sargento Aldea** marks the southern edge.

A small souvenir stand, Prat 898 (☎660 360), doubles as a **tourist kiosk,** but they have little information. Visitors can ask for information at the bus terminal or at the **municipalidad,** on the northwest corner of the plaza. Several **banks** and **ATMs** are also conveniently located along Prat. The **Centro Cultural de Vallenar,** Prat 1094), has a theater for local shows and exhibits of local artists. **Farmacia Ahumada,** Prat 1100, is on the corner of Prat and Colchagua. (☎614 476. Open 8am-midnight.) The **hospital** (☎611 202) is on the northwest side of town, at the corner of Merced and Talca. **International calls** can be made at **Don Victor,** Prat 865 (☎612 798), and there is fast **Internet access,** Prat 862, in the middle of town. (☎342 946. CH$400 per hr. Open 10am-9pm.) The **post office,** 51 JJ Vallejos, is off the northwest corner of the plaza. (☎614 539. Open M-F 9am-1pm and 3-6:30pm, Sa 9:30am-1pm.)

ACCOMMODATIONS

There are no spectacular deals in Vallenar, but most accommodations are pretty acceptable. Most of the budget lodging is a few blocks off Prat in either direction. There are a couple of upscale locations in the southern part of the town.

Hostal Camino del Rey, Merced 943 (☎610 449). Big cable TVs and big beds fill an itty-bitty living space. Bathroom surfaces are so clean they double as mirrors. Rooms are brightly lit with windows onto the courtyard. Breakfast included. Singles CH$7800, with bath CH$13,800; doubles CH$13,800/CH$18,000. ❸

Hotel Cecil, Prat 1059 (☎614 071; www.hotelcecil.cl). The entryway is dark wood that looks warm and inviting, but in the courtyard, a pockmarked plastic roof covers a leafy patio. Rooms are spacious with a chair and table, some with couches. The pool comes in handy during hot summers. Cable TV. Breakfast included. Singles CH$20,000; doubles CH$25,000; triples CH$30,000. Prices negotiable. ❹

Residencial Oriental, Serrano 720 (☎613 889), near the plaza. Sherbet-colored parakeets chirp from their courtyard cage. The rooms are similarly cheerful despite a little chipped paint. Bathroom stalls are low enough to offer a show. Singles CH$3500, with bath CH$6500; doubles CH$7000/CH$12,000. ❶

Hotel Garra de León, Serrano 1052 (☎613 753). The *garra de león* flower is unique to Chile; its namesake hotel is not. Very roomy hallways with huge bedrooms. Thin carpets, fake flowers, and wholesale furniture attempt to create an upscale facade. Minibar, A/C, parking, and cable TV available. Breakfast included. Singles CH$28,000; doubles CH$34,100; triples CH$38,500. AmEx/D/MC/V. ❺

Hostería de Vallenar, Ercilla 848 (☎614 379). The most modern hotel in Vallenar, featuring cable TV, alarm clocks, stocked minibars, a pool table, international cuisine, free buffet breakfast, and even mints for your pillow. Heated pool. Singles CH$35,000; doubles CH$40,300; each extra person CH$13,650. AmEx/D/MC/V. ❺

Residencial Mary 2, Ramírez 631 (☎610 322). Enter through the restaurant and a parking lot, just north of and parallel to the plaza. Two long fluorescent lights brighten the white walls and fogged windows. Paint chip piles accumulate in corners. Private baths and spacious rooms. One lightbulb in most rooms. CH$5000 per person. ❷

FOOD

Excellent diners and coffee stops line Prat. The one-lane road and pedestrian walkway make for excellent people-watching while you're enjoying a surprising variety of menu options. A supermarket under the guise of a bakery, **Panadería Santo's Pan,** Prat 1356 (☎611 465), has enough Pringles and cereal to sink a ship.

Arriero, Prat 1061 (☎09 887 4620), is an underpriced Argentine steakhouse transported to Chile. Horseshoes, aged wooden tables, and swinging doors are a perfect fit for a carnivorous *guacho*. BLTs (CH$1400) and club sandwiches (CH$1800) are rare finds in Chile. With their ambience and quality food, the prices should be twice as high. Beef carpaccio CH$3200. 9oz. filet mignon CH$3800. Open 11am-3pm and 5pm-very late. ❷

Bar Bogart, Serrano 976 (☎342 904). This 50s-style bar lives up to its name. Dark red carpeting, a leather bar, and black walls are accented by posters of Marilyn Monroe and James Dean. The sandwiches are cheap and the drinks aren't, but of all the gin joints in the world, this is a good one to check out. Open M-Sa 10am-4am, Su 7pm-2am. ❷

Il Boccato, Prat 750 (☎614 609), has wraparound windows on the plaza with great views of palm trees and passing people. Pizzas (CH$3000-3500) and pastas such as ravioli with alfredo sauce (CH$2600) won't disappoint. Attentive waiters will bring banana splits

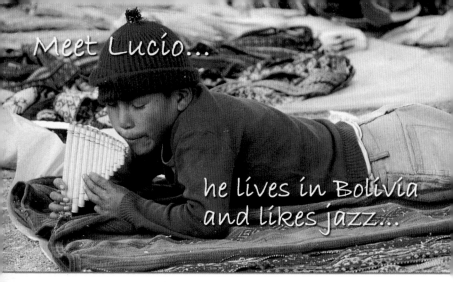

Meet Lucio...

he lives in Bolivia
and likes jazz...

Destinations

Join one of our 1 to 24
week volunteer projects
in over 20 countries
worldwide that need your
help with conservation,
care work, media,
teaching, building,
and health care.

Immersion

Live and work among
locals for an experience
like no other. Touch a
child's life at a Brazilian
Youth Outreach Center or
feed a recovering penguin
in South Africa - the
options are endless.

Impact

In Bolivia, 70% of the
people live in poverty
and many children dro
out of school. i-to-i
volunteers give a boos
to nearly 1000 childre
every year by teaching
life skills and literacy.

i-to-i Volunteer Travel

Extraordinary people
Amazing places
Meaningful travel

i-to-i

Request a free brochur
www.i-to-i.com/lg
800.985.7527

(CH$1650) or papaya with cream (CH$1650) faster than you can eat it. Open Su-Th 10am-midnight, F-Sa 10am-1am. AmEx/D/MC/V. ❷

Café del Centro, Prat 1121 (☎611 117), looks like a diner, feels like a diner, and serves diner food. Sandwiches "from Chicago, Singapore, and New York" (CH$2000-2800) are really just your standard Chilean favorites in disguise. Impressive tea selection. Peach Melba CH$1800. Open daily 10am-3pm and 5-10pm. ❶

DAYTRIPS FROM VALLENAR

ALTO DEL CARMEN   ☎51

Deep into the Huasco Valley are the secluded towns of Alto del Carmen and San Felix, 45km and 70km, respectively, from Vallenar. On the way to Alto del Carmen is the new dam, **Embalse Santa Juana,** which has created a crystal blue mountain lake with limited camping, sailing, and water activities during the summer. Farther along, the road forks just before reaching Alto del Carmen. The right branch leads to the small town of El Tránsito, but the road is not well paved and public transportation is infrequent. The left-hand fork leads into downtown Alto del Carmen, known mostly for its *pisco* plant, which of course makes "Alto del Carmen" *pisco*. The plant is a scaled-down version of larger plants in Vicuña, and the actual production of *pisco* only happens during the summer, but the tour is worth its CH$0 entry fee any time. (Open M-F 8:30-12:30pm and 2-6pm. Free.) Down the hill from Alto del Carmen's town plaza is a riverside hike that offers beautiful views of the valley and serene, rushing waters. There is only one main street, featuring a church with an impressive modern mural covering its belltower, and small unnamed *pensiones* for food. Buses run frequently back to Vallenar for a place to stay (1hr., 6 per day 7:30am-7:30pm, CH$800).

SAN FELIX   ☎51

Farther down the line is a secluded town with one public telephone and the best damn watering hole this side of the equator. Their small specialty brand of *pisco,* **Horcón Quemado,** is made with the same equipment used by the company's founder 50 years ago. To get to the Horcón Quemado plant from the town entrance, take a left on Matta, continue to the end, and take a right on an unnamed street. The plant is about 100m up the street. Eduardo Alfonso Mulet, the owner and grandson of the founder, will show you around the plant, talking about San Felix and the company's history. He's also known to challenge

THE BIG SPLURGE

LIKE A FINE WINE

Pisco, the ubiquitous Chilean liquor, isn't pisco if it doesn't come from Regions III or IV of Chile. Of all the pisco in this fertile land, however, the world's finest is hidden deep within the Huasco Valley: Horcón Quemado 30-year-old pisco.

Sr. Mulet, the founder of Horcón Quemado, made a stash from a particularly good year of grapes 40 years ago, and that harvest has produced one of the rarest bottles of pisco on the market. Only 250 bottles are distributed worldwide each year, and for US$100 it's a steal. Most pisco is aged only six months to a year, but 30 years has given the Horcón Quemado a distinctively mature aroma and flavor to go with its dark amber coloring.

With Capel poised to put pisco on the map with a global marketing campaign, Sr. Mulet's batch could be a great investment. Buyers must be proactive, however, as there are only two places to find the handful of bottles produced: at the Horcón Quemado plant in Huasco, and in a few upscale stores in Santiago. Though it's expensive for the budget traveler, drinking in high style is more than worth five days without food, water, or shelter.

For information on Horcón Quemado, contact Agrícola El Dain Ltda., El Churcal San Felix, III Region Chile or ☎51 610 985, or contact owner Eduardo Alfonso Mulet, sanfelixsa@hotmail.com guests to test their drinking limits by trying all of the Horcón Quemado products, except their 30 year reserve. You'll smile for the sweet Horcón Quemado wine aperitif, and feel the 15-year-old aged *pisco* slide down smoothly. (Tours 10am-6pm. Free.)

San Felix also offers a great selection of day-hikes through the surrounding mountains. Don't miss the legendary trail from San Felix to **El Tránsito,** in the neighboring valley, a moderately challenging 20km day-hike. (Camping free. Take the road past the Horcón Quemado plant, which becomes the trail.) If heading out of town doesn't excite your passions, you can also explore the garden-like plaza, with layers of big plants leading into a hidden sitting area.

With the lack of tourist infrastructure in San Felix, it's no surprise that there is only one low-priced accommodation and small (though delicious) *pensiones* for dining. There are many **personal residences ❶** that serve lunch to visitors, bus drivers, and locals, but they can only be found by asking around. **Residencial San Felix ❶** offers inexpensive, under-decorated bedrooms with rustic bathrooms. (Along Matta in front of the main plaza. CH$2500 per person.) This *residencial* also offers a small restaurant with a varied *menú* of the day (CH$1500). Sr. Mulet has a few beautiful new **cabins ❷** in the hills around his Horcón Quemado plant. They overlook the valley, and tangerines fall off fruit trees onto the front doorstep. Kitchens, large rooms, and a warm feeling make these *cabañas* complete. (☎610 985. CH$35,000 for 6-person *cabaña*.)

Rest assured, in San Felix you will escape all the trappings of the modern world, like **banks, ATMs,** and the **Internet. Buses** leave Vallenar to San Felix by way of Alto del Carmen (3 per day 7:30am-4:30pm, CH$1500).

LA SERENA ☎51

The capital of Region IV and the second-oldest city in Chile, La Serena is one of the nation's most popular summer resorts. Pristine beaches, stately churches, tree-lined avenues, and a relaxed atmosphere attract throngs of visitors. Founded in 1544 by the Spaniard Juan de Bohón, the city was burned down by the indigenous Diaguita tribe and had to be reconstructed five years later. The city's growth was relatively slow until the 1940s, when Don Gabriel González Videla, the much-revered governor and later president of Chile, instituted the "Plan Serena," aimed at boosting the economic and cultural significance of the city. The recent growth of the tourism industry here has taken advantage of the often sunny weather, expanding La Serena past its somewhat dilapidated downtown. It's now a great place to relax on beaches all day and party all night. However, given the city's popularity, it can get expensive quickly for those on a tight budget.

▐ TRANSPORTATION

Flights: Aeropuerto La Florida (☎271 812, flight information 200 900), 5km east of town by way of Juan de Díos Peni. Taxis between the airport and the Plaza de Armas CH$2500-3000. **LanChile,** Balmaceda 406 (☎221 531; fax 219 496), offers frequent service to most major Chilean cities, including Antofagasta, Arica, Iquique, and Santiago. Open M-F 9am-1:30pm and 3-7pm, Sa 10am-1pm. Branches at the airport (☎200 993) and in Mall Plaza La Serena, Alberto Solari 1400 (☎200 904).

Intercity Buses: Terminal de Buses (☎224 573), on the corner of El Santo and Amunátegui, a 20min. walk from the Plaza de Armas. **Luggage storage** CH$400-1000. Open 7am-11:45pm. The station houses over 10 bus companies, each of which post their destinations and fares in their office windows. Fares are usually identical, but it can pay to shop around before buying a ticket. The 2 most reputable and far-reaching carriers are Tur Bus and Pullman. Open 24hr.

Tur Bus (☎215 953 or 225 823) goes to: **Arica** (22hr., 6 per day 6am-10:30pm, CH$15,300); **Iquique** (20hr., every 2hr. 6:15am-12:15pm, CH$13,800) via **Antofagasta** (12hr., CH$11,500), **Calama** (15hr., CH$13,500), and **Copiapó** (5hr., CH$5000); **Ovalle** (1hr., every hr. 8am-10pm, CH$1500); **Santiago** (7hr., every hr. 7am-2am, CH$4500); **Valparaíso** (6hr., every 2hr. 9am-11pm, CH$4500) via **Viña del Mar** (6hr., CH$4500).

Pullman Bus (☎212 941). Has another station 2 blocks away at Panamericana Norte (☎225 157 or 212 941), across from Plaza España. Sends buses to: **Antofagasta** (13hr., every hr. 8am-3:15am, CH$10,000; *salón cama* 9:30pm, CH$25,000); **Arica** (24hr., 4 per day 3:15pm-midnight, CH$18,000); **Calama** (16hr., CH$14,000); **Copiapó** (6hr., every hr. 7:15am-10:30pm, CH$4500); **Iquique** (20hr., 4 per day 2-11:30pm, CH$15,000); **Santiago** (6hr., every hr., CH$9000; *salón cama* 2 per day 2pm and 11:30pm, CH$14,000-18,000); **Valparaíso** (6hr., 5 per day 8:45am-11pm, CH$7000) via **Viña del Mar** (6hr., CH$7000).

Local Buses: *Colectivos* function like local buses in La Serena, and are the easiest way to get around town (CH$250) or to **Coquimbo** (30min., every 10min. 7:30am-11:30pm, CH$250). Destinations are prominently posted on *colectivos*. They congregate on Pedro Pablo Muñoz between Prat and Cordovez, on Aguirre between Matta and Los Carrera, and on Domeyko off Balmaceda.

Taxis: Taxis line the stretch of Aguirre between Matta and Los Carrera. **Serena Ltda.** (☎223 344) is at the main bus station. **Taxi Scontat** (☎271 699) handles the airport. Taxis between Aeropuerto La Florida and the Plaza de Armas run CH$2500-3000.

Car Rental: Avis, Aguirre 63 (☎227 171; fax 227 049; www.avischile.cl). **Budget,** Libertad 875 (☎218 272; fax 218 308; www.budget.cl).

Bike Rental: Talinay Adventure Expeditions (p. 216) rents mountain bikes (CH$1000 per hr.).

◼◼ ORIENTATION AND PRACTICAL INFORMATION

La Serena's grid-like layout makes it easy to navigate. The center of downtown is the **Plaza de Armas,** bordered by Prat, Matta, Cordovez, and Los Carrera. Most sights and accommodations are within easy walking distance of the Plaza. Two blocks past the tourist office from the corner of Prat and Matta is the southern tip of the large **Parque Pedro de Valdivia.** The western border of the park is the **Panamerican Highway** (known locally as Juan Bohón), which runs parallel to the ocean. Perpendicular to the Panamerican, two blocks from the Plaza de Armas, is **Francisco de Aguirre,** from which it's a 40min. walk to the city's beaches and the gaudy, resort-lined **Avenida del Mar.**

The main bus terminal is a 20min. walk south of the Plaza de Armas. To get to the plaza, exit through the main station doors and turn left to get to Amunátegui. Turn left on Amunátegui, cross the street, and walk until the Panamerican. Turn right at the Panamerican and walk three blocks, passing Plaza España on the right and crossing Aguirre. Turn right on Aguirre and walk for three blocks. Turn left on Matta and walk two blocks to enter the Plaza de Armas.

Tourist Office: Sernatur, Matta 461 (☎225 199; www.sernatur.cl), across from the Plaza de Armas. The staff has free maps of La Serena and information on accommodations and tour companies offering excursions to **Valle de Elqui.** Open Jan.-Feb. M-F 8:30am-9pm, Sa-Su 10am-8pm; Mar.-Dec. M-Th 8:30am-5:30pm, F 8:30am-4:30pm.

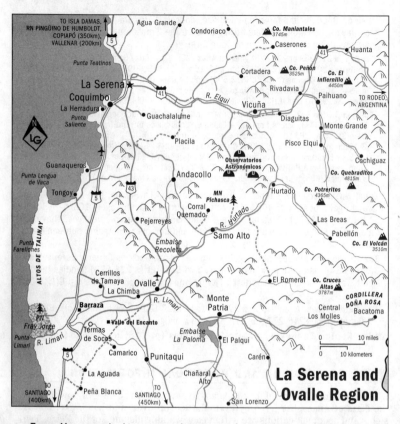

La Serena and Ovalle Region

Tours: Many organized tour companies compete for tourist attention in La Serena. The most popular guided tours run to **Isla Damas** and the **Reserva Nacional Pingüino de Humboldt,** the **Valle de Elqui,** and the world-renowned **Mamalluca Observatory.** Jan.-Feb. tours daily; low season most tours weekends only.

Gira Tour, Prat 689 (☎223 535 or 09 165 8120; giratour@tie.cl). Tours to: **Isla Damas** (10½hr., 8:30am, CH$23,000); **Mamalluca Observatory** (4hr., 8:30pm, CH$12,000); **Valle de Elqui** (9hr., 9:30am, CH$13,000). Open M-F 9am-2pm and 3:30-7pm. Sa 10am-1pm. AmEx/MC/V.

Tour Andes, Prat 595 (☎ 211 739 or 09 765 919; www.tourandes.cl). Popular tours to: **Isla Damas** (10hr., 8am, CH$25,000); **Mamalluca Observatory** (5hr., 7pm, CH$12,000); **Valle de Elqui** (9hr., 9:30am, CH$13,000). Open M-F 9am-6pm, Sa 10am-2pm. AmEx/MC/V.

Talinay Adventure Expeditions, Prat 470 (☎218 658 or 09 623 5481; xtrimfun@yahoo.com or talinay@turismoaventura.net), in the same building as Café del Patio (p. 221). Friendly staff provides tons of information on La Serena. Popular tours to: **Isla Damas** (12hr., 7:45am, CH$25,000); **Mamalluca Observatory** (2hr., 7pm, CH$12,000); **Valle de Elqui** (10½hr., 9am, CH$13,000). Adventure tours include: **mountain biking** (half-day CH$22,000, full-day CH$32,000), **sandboarding** (CH$28,000), and **surfing** (CH$25,000). **Bike rental** CH$1000 per hr. Open Jan.-Feb. M-Sa 9:30am-midnight; Mar.-Dec. M-F 9:30am-2pm and 4-8pm. AmEx/MC/V.

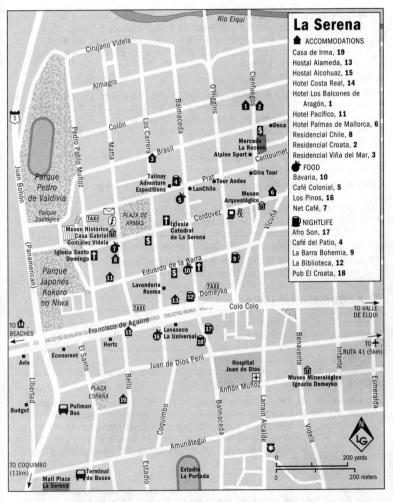

La Serena

♠ ACCOMMODATIONS
Casa de Irma, **19**
Hostal Alameda, **13**
Hostal Alcohuaz, **15**
Hotel Costa Real, **14**
Hotel Los Balcones de
    Aragón, **1**
Hotel Pacífico, **11**
Hotel Palmas de Mallorca, **6**
Residencial Chile, **8**
Residencial Croata, **2**
Residencial Viña del Mar, **3**
🍴 FOOD
Bavaria, **10**
Café Colonial, **5**
Los Pinos, **16**
Net Café, **7**
🍸 NIGHTLIFE
Afro Son, **17**
Café del Patio, **4**
La Barra Bohemia, **9**
La Biblioteca, **12**
Pub El Croata, **18**

Currency Exchange: Gira Tour (see above) exchanges euros, US$, and traveler's checks without commission.

Banks: BancoEstado, Brasil 506 (☎222 936), on the corner of Cienfuegos at La Recova, and **Banco Santander,** Cordovez 351 (☎230 000), on the Plaza de Armas, have **24hr. ATMs.** Open M-F 9am-2pm. MC/V.

Markets: Mercado La Recova (☎213 888; p. 220). **Deca,** Brasil 750 (☎207 400), on the side of La Recova parallel to Cantournet and Prat, has all you could hope for in a supermarket. Open M-Sa 8:30am-12:30am, Su 9am-9pm. AmEx/MC/V.

Camping Supplies: Alpine Sport, Cienfuegos 361 (☎224 544), across from La Recova. Sells camping supplies, backpacks, tents, and hiking boots. Open M-F 9:45am-2:15pm and 4:30-9:15pm, Sa 10am-2:30pm and 5-9pm. AmEx/MC/V.

Laundromats: Lavandería Rooma, Los Carrera 654 (☎225 620). Wash and dry CH$3800 per 5½kg. Same-day service. Open Jan.-Feb. M-F 8:30am-8pm, Sa 8:30am-1:30pm; Mar.-Dec. M-F 8:30am-1pm and 4-8pm, Sa 8:30am-1:30pm. **Lavaseco La Universal,** Aguirre 411 (☎222 845). Wash and dry CH$1000 per kg. Same-day service. Open M-F 9am-1pm and 4-8:30pm, Sa 9am-1:30pm.

Police: ☎ 133. Also, in town at Larrain Alcalde 700 (☎224 488 or 225 504).

Pharmacies: Farmacia Ahumada, Cordovez 651 (☎218 065 or 217 616), has the longest hours of La Serena's pharmacies. Open M-F 8am-midnight, Sa-Su 9am-midnight. AmEx/MC/V. **Farmacia Homeopática Caribú,** Cordovez 672 #105 (☎224 348), in the Centro Comercial Serena Oriente. Open M-F 9:30am-2pm and 4-9pm, Sa 10am-2pm. AmEx/MC/V.

Hospital: Ambulance ☎131. **Hospital Juan de Dios,** Balmaceda 916 (☎225 569 or 200 500). Entrance at Larrain Alcalde and Anfion Muñoz.

Telephones and Internet Access: *Centros de llamadas* line Cienfuegos and Prat (CH$500 per hr.). **Conecta,** Cordovez 607 (☎209 000), provides cheap Internet access (CH$500 per hr.), phone and fax services, and pre-paid cell phones. Open M-Sa 8:30am-10pm. **Net Café** (p. 220) offers 15min. free with any CH$600 purchase and 1hr. with meal combos (CH$2700-5100; CH$300 per additional hr.). **Talinay Adventure Expeditions** (p. 216) has Internet access (CH$350 per 30min., CH$600 per hr.).

Post Office: ☎213 753. On the corner of Matta and Prat, across from the Plaza de Armas. Open M-F 8:30am-6:30pm, Sa 9:30am-1pm.

⛰ ACCOMMODATIONS

La Serena's budget accommodations are concentrated downtown on the streets surrounding the Plaza de Armas and along Aguirre, near the bus station. Prices reflect the city's popularity as a summer resort, and most budget places still feel a bit pricey. Budget-conscious travelers may want to consider staying nearby in La Serena's less expensive sister city, Coquimbo. Higher-end accommodations are available in La Serena along the beachfront Avenida del Mar.

Residencial Croata (HI), Cienfuegos 248 (☎224 997 or 216 994; www.hostalcroata.cl), 2 blocks left past Mercado La Recova when coming from the Plaza de Armas. Friendly staff, sunny rooms, and free Internet access draw crowds of budget travelers. All rooms have cable TV and private bath. Breakfast included. Jan.-Feb. singles CH$15,000; doubles CH$18,000; triples CH$21,000. Mar.-Dec. singles CH$12,000; doubles CH$15,000; triples CH$18,000. ❸

Hostal Alcohuaz, Aguirre 307 (☎217 088 or 09 549 0292), on the corner of Andres Bello. Run by a friendly family eager to make visitors comfortable. Conveniently located near the bus station, but some noise filters in from the busy avenue. All rooms have cable TV, and bathrooms are spotless. Internet access CH$300 per 30min. Breakfast CH$800. Laundry service. Singles CH$4000, with bath CH$8000; doubles CH$9000/CH$12,000; triples CH$12,000/CH$15,000; quads CH$16,000/CH$20,000. ❷

Hotel Pacífico, Eduardo de la Barra 252 (☎225 674), near the entrance to the Parque Japonés. The regal facade reveals a faded elegance inside, with old, faded Chilean and US maps peeling from the walls. The large, airy rooms are comfortable and bright, but they feature saggy mattresses. Ideal for groups. Breakfast included. Singles CH$6000, with bath CH$10,000; doubles CH$11,000/CH$15,000; triples with bath CH$19,000; quads with bath CH$23,000. ❸

Casa de Irma Mura Vargas, Andres Bello 951 (☎223 735). The owner of this unnamed *residencial* spends her days gathering unsuspecting travelers from the bus and bringing them to her house for free Internet and TV, big beds, and a warm atmosphere. A quick walk down

Andres Bello and up Matta to the Plaza de Armas. Irma is a great substitute mother for any weary traveler. She likes to chat over coffee and will check in to make sure everything is just like home, because for her, it is home. CH$4000 per person. ❷

Hotel Costa Real, Aguirre 170 (☎221 010; www.regiondecoquimbo.cl/costareal). If you're looking for a hotel with a stocked mini-bar, a gourmet hotel restaurant, and mints on the bed, head to Costa Real. It's an admirable imitation of other upscale chain hotels. Services include a gym, pool, laundry, 24hr. room service, and the chance to hobnob with the rich and famous of La Serena. Breakfast included. Singles CH$40,000; doubles CH$45,000. AmEx/D/MC/V. ❺

Hotel Palmas de Mallorca, Cordovez 750 (☎210 399). The yellow color scheme can be overwhelming, but the sumptuous sitting room with mellow red columns and the hotel's amenities more than make up for the canary coloring. All rooms have cable TV and private bath; some have verandas, stereos, and telephones. Breakfast included. Jan.-Feb. singles CH$14,000; doubles CH$16,000; triples CH$19,000. Mar.-Dec. singles CH$11,000; doubles CH$14,000; triples CH$19,000. MC/V. ❸

Hotel Los Balcones de Aragón, Cienfuegos 289 (☎212 419). Its decor makes Los Balcones more campy than classy, but also less stodgy than other higher-end hotels in town. All rooms have cable TV, alarm clocks, telephones, mini-bars, and private bath. Room service available. Breakfast included. Singles CH$25,000; doubles CH$31,000; triples CH$36,000. Negotiate discounts in the low season. AmEx/MC/V. ❺

Residencial Viña del Mar, Brasil 423 (☎212 349). Rooms are bland, but big. Breakfast included. Singles CH$6000, with bath CH$7500; doubles CH$10,000/CH$13,000; triples CH$15,000/CH$18,000; quads CH$20,000/CH$24,000. ❷

Hostal Alameda, Aguirre 452 (☎213 052). Rooms are small but likeable, and the small open-air patio creates a comfortable atmosphere. Travelers making an early-morning exit to the bus station might want to stay here. Breakfast included. Singles CH$6000, with bath CH$9000; doubles CH$13,000/CH$15,000; triples CH$15,000/CH$18,000; quads with bath CH$22,000. Prices negotiable. ❸

Residencial Chile, Matta 561 (☎211 694). Its great location, welcoming owner, and chirping parakeets offset the small size and stuffiness of the rooms. Breakfast CH$1500. Singles CH$6000; doubles CH$10,000; triples CH$15,000. ❷

FOOD

Discerning eaters will be pleased with La Serena's eateries. Standard cafes and tourist-oriented restaurants abound near the Plaza de Armas, but the real treasures lie farther afield, away from the ocean. Seafood is best at **Mercado La Recova** (p. 220). Papaya is a regional specialty, used to make liqueurs, candy, and pastries which can be bought from vendors at the Plaza de Armas.

Los Pinos, Los Carrera 831 (☎224 737). The sign outside promises friendly home-cooked meals, and Los Pinos delivers just that. There's no listed menu, just the fixed lunch (called *menú*—confusing, isn't it?), which locals devour on their midday break. Check out the bar lined with beer cans. The *menú* (CH$1200) includes soup, salad or rice, and an entree. Open M-F 10am-10pm; Sa and Su 12am-8pm. ❶

Café Colonial, Balmaceda 475 (☎216 373), between Prat and Cordovez. A sanctuary of North American food, with pancakes, ham-and-cheese omelettes, and orange juice for breakfast. The friendly Australian owner, vegetarian options, and airy interior make this a popular choice with backpackers. Pizzas CH$2000-4500. Sandwiches CH$1300-2800. Pasta CH$2000-2500. *Menú* CH$3000. 2-for-1 happy hour F-Sa 8-11pm. Open Jan.-Feb. M-F 8am-midnight, Sa 9am-midnight, Su noon-8pm; Mar.-Dec. M-F 8am-midnight, Sa 9am-midnight. AmEx/MC/V. ❷

Net Café, Cordovez 285 (☎212 187), on the corner of Matta across from the Plaza de Armas. Delicious sandwiches (CH$650-1990) and tropical fruit smoothies (CH$890-2200) make pricey Internet combo meals well worth it. Combos include a sandwich, fruit smoothie, and 1hr. Internet access (CH$2700-5100; CH$300 per additional hr.). Coffee CH$500-1090. 15min. free Internet access with any CH$600 purchase. Open daily 10:30am-midnight. ❷

Bavaria, Eduardo de la Barra 489 (☎228 894), on the corner of Balmaceda. Bavaria is a chain restaurant best known for its *parrilladas* (CH$9800-13,000 for 2 people), but vegetarians should check it out for its long list of salad options (CH$1400-2600). *Menú* CH$3600. Open daily noon-4pm and 6:30pm-midnight. AmEx/MC/V. ❸

◎ SIGHTS

▨PARQUE JAPONÉS KOKORO NO NIWA. Also known as the *Jardín del Corazón*, this enclosed Japanese garden has over 80 species of plants, including bamboo groves and many exotic flowers. Small Japanese temples provide shade for the wandering swans. On sunny days, turtles sun themselves on the pond banks, keeping watch over the goldfish. Couples cuddle on the benches and singles curl up with books. This is the perfect spot to take an afternoon stroll—or to sneak off to the side for a *siesta*. *(Between Juan Bohón, Aguirre, and Pedro Pablo Muñoz, 2 blocks from the Plaza de Armas. Open daily 10am-6pm. CH$600, children CH$300.)*

MUSEO ARQUEOLÓGICO. Visitors walk around this horseshoe-shaped museum traveling through time, beginning with the origins of life on Earth. Cultural artifacts from indigenous groups are displayed throughout the halls. A sea-lion-hide boat is well preserved and an Easter Island *moai* is strikingly presented. Other highlights include mummies and shrunken heads. The museum does not have English translations, but the artifacts are intriguing enough to speak for themselves. *(At the corner of Cordovez and Cienfuegos. ☎224 492. Open Tu-F 9:30am-5:45pm, Sa 10am-1pm and 4-7pm, Su 10am-1pm. CH$600, seniors and children ages 8-18 CH$300, children under 8 free.)*

IGLESIA CATEDRAL DE LA SERENA. Built in 1844 in the Neoclassical style and now a national monument, the cathedral lords over the other *iglesias* from its prime location on the Plaza de Armas. Inside the cool, stone building, the soft songs of pious monks can usually be heard from deep inside the cloisters—but don't be fooled, they're on stereo. Still, the mood inside is somber, from the cool, checkered marble floor to the stone columns rising toward the magnificent, curved ceiling. Through a door to the left of the altar is the Sala de Arte Religioso, where appropriately serious faces peer out of classical paintings. *(Los Carrera 450, on the corner of Cordovez. Sala open M-F 10am-1pm and 4-7pm, Sa 10am-1pm. Mass Su-F noon, Sa noon and 6pm. CH$400.)*

MERCADO LA RECOVA. This large market and artisanal fair is an excellent place to get acquainted with the regional specialties in food and handicrafts. Sweets made from papaya are especially popular, but there are also musical instruments, alpaca clothing, and all sorts of edible delicacies. Artists set up kiosks outside of the market, making this a perfect place to bargain for gifts. Dozens of seafood restaurants are upstairs in the marketplace, selling some of the freshest fish in town. *(At the corner of Cienfuegos and Cantournet. ☎213 888. Open daily 10am-8pm. Free.)*

IGLESIA SANTO DOMINGO. Also known as Iglesia Padres Carmelitas Descalzos, this is the most beautiful of La Serena's many churches. First built in 1673, Santo Domingo had to be reconstructed after being sacked by pirates a century later. Natural light streams through stained glass windows onto the beautiful stone walls. On the right-hand side, climbing vines and red flowers are visible, as tinted shadows dance upon the opaque glass. *(Cordovez 235, on the corner of Pedro Pablo Muñoz. ☎ 211 276. Mass M-Sa 7:30pm, Su 11:30am and 7:30pm.)*

CASA GABRIEL GONZÁLEZ VIDELA. This old house, built in 1894, has been the home of La Serena's main historical museum since 1984. The museum exhibits regional historical artifacts upstairs and has several rooms dedicated to Chilean art, but the front of the house is reserved for homage to González Videla, a La Serena native who served as President of Chile from 1946 to 1952. The tribute to his life in this museum includes his desk, old radio, and life-sized models wearing his and his wife's clothing. *(Matta 495, on the corner of Cordovez, across from the Plaza de Armas. ☎ 215 052. Open Tu-F 10am-6pm, Sa-Su 10am-1pm. CH$600, seniors and children ages 8-18 CH$300, children under 8 free.)*

🏖 BEACHES

The stretch of sand between La Serena and Coquimbo is serenely beautiful, as long as you're looking toward the ocean. Running parallel to the beaches is **Avenida del Mar,** lined with a host of high-rise resorts and high-rolling tourists. From the corner of Prat and Matta at the Plaza de Armas, walk three blocks on Matta past the tourist office. Turn right on Aguirre and follow it straight for about 40min. until it hits the beachfront Avenida del Mar; the beaches extend to the left. Alternatively, grab a taxi and ask for the beach. The beaches between Aguirre and Cuatro Esquinas are known for their rough tides and are better suited to sunbathing than swimming. For a dip, the beaches past Cuarto Esquinas toward Coquimbo are best. As a general rule, the farther south down Avenida del Mar you go, the smoother and wider the beaches become. Look for signs saying "Playa Apta" for security before you jump in the water.

🎵 🍸 ENTERTAINMENT AND NIGHTLIFE

Nightlife in La Serena centers on the stretch of Aguirre between Los Carrera and Larrain Alcalde. There is a **Cinemark** movie theater (☎ 600 600 2463 or 212 144) in the Mall Plaza La Serena, Alberto Solaril 1400, next to the bus station.

Pub El Croata, Balmaceda 871 (☎ 214 713). El Croata's variety can cover any group's plans. In this pub, it's tough to choose between the candlelit dining room and packed full bar. Cocktails CH$1800-4000. Beer CH$150-1500. Wine CH$4000-8500. Entrees CH$1800-5000. Live blues Th 11pm, classic rock F 11pm. Cover F-Sa CH$3000 for men, includes a drink; women free. Open M-W 7pm-3am, Th-Su 7pm-5am. ❷

Café del Patio, Prat 470 (☎ 212 634), 1 block from the Plaza de Armas. This bar is a popular backpacker hangout, with a laid-back atmosphere and good food. Cocktails CH$1900-4000. Beer CH$1000-1500. Wine CH$4900-9000. Sandwiches CH$1400-2900. Pizzas CH$2100-3500. Entrees CH$1500-4500. Live music F-Sa nights. Open M-Th 10am-2am, F-Sa 10am-4am, Su 7pm-2am. ❸

Afro Son, Balmaceda 824 (☎ 229 344), in the Centro Latinoamericano de Arte y Cultura. A great place for a quiet lunch or a raucous Saturday night. Beer CH$200-1500. Wine CH$4500-8000. Menú CH$1500. Live jazz and Latin W-Su 11pm. Open Mar.-Dec. M-Tu 9am-5pm, W-Sa 9am-5pm and 8pm-2am, Su 9pm-2am. ❷

La Biblioteca, Aguirre 600 (☎ 218 789). Come to study at this "library" and leave drunk with new friends. A small bookshelf sits out of reach behind the bar. Vintage posters of new classics like Star Wars, Indiana Jones, and Homer Simpson line the walls. The jukebox has an extensive collection of both Spanish and English crowd-pleasers. Students from the University of La Serena like to start their nights here to discuss socialism and drink Cristal. Open daily 6pm-3am. ❷

La Barra Bohemia, O'Higgins 624 (☎219 682), on the corner of Eduardo de la Barra. The corner doorway opens into a dark room lit by green light bulbs hanging in copper pots, and a long strip of green neon lighting illuminates the underside of the bar. Popular for a drink in the evenings. Sandwiches CH$1600-2800. Cocktails CH$1900-4000. Live music Th-Sa 11pm. Open daily 6pm-2am. ❷

▶ DAYTRIP FROM LA SERENA

RESERVA NACIONAL PINGÜINO DE HUMBOLDT

Gira Tour, Tour Andes, and Talinay (p. 216) offer all-inclusive tours (CH$23,000) from La Serena. Alternatively, you can head to the rotary at the end of Aguirre to catch a colectivo Th-Sa at 9am (☎ 253 206; CH$6000 round-trip). Going without a tour, you can hire a fishing boat for CH$20,000-35,000 to take you on the water. The small tour and fishing boats sail only in good weather. Reserve open daily 9am-6pm. Entrance Dec. 15-Mar. 15 CH$1600, students and children CH$600; low season free.

At this 86-acre National Reserve, the rare Humboldt penguin is easy to find. Hundreds sprawl on rocks in the early summer morning on all three islands within the reserve: **Isla Choros, Isla Chañaral,** and **Isla Damas.** All contain similar wildlife, but Isla Choros is where the majority of penguins pass their time. The reserve isn't only for penguin-watching; **bottle-nosed dolphins, sea lions,** and dozens of unique birds make appearances throughout the year. Most of the animals are playful and jump and frolic around passing seacraft. Boats stop for a short time on tours to allow passengers to climb around and explore **Islas Damas.** Although there normally isn't much wildlife on the island, the view of the Pacific is breathtaking from its highest point. During the summer, campers can stay on the island and hope to catch some early morning penguin or dolphin sightings.

There aren't many options for accommodations around the reserve. **Punto de Choros,** a town about 10km before the park's entrance, is the only settlement near the reserve, and it is devoid of camping or overnight options. However, visitors can camp on the mainland by the park's welcome center (CH$2000). From December 15 to March 15, **camping ❷** is permitted on Isla Damas at **Playa la Poza** (CH$12,000). Payment and permission should be taken care of at the park administration at Caleta de Choros. Campers need to bring their own equipment, food, and water, and be sure to remove their trash when they leave.

There are many tour companies in La Serena that provide transportation to the reserve and once at the reserve. **Gira Tour** and **Talinay Adventure Expeditions** have an all-inclusive tour (CH$23,000) including transport to and from the reserve and between the islands, a guide, and lunch. For those who want to go without a tour, a *colectivo* minibus picks up passengers in La Serena near the rotary at the end of Aguirre. (☎253 206; runs Th-Sa 9am; CH$6000 round-trip). Once at the reserve, hiring a fishing boat could cost CH$20,000-35,000. By car, the turnoff for the reserve is 70km north of La Serena at the Coleta de Choros turnoff on the Panamerican. From the turnoff, the park entrance is another 44km along labeled but rugged dirt roads. Here, visitors register with **Conaf** and pay the entrance fee.

ANDACOLLO

☎ 51

The small mining town of Andacollo lies in a dramatic gorge midway between Ovalle and La Serena. The ride there is an adventure in itself, on a road that makes hairpin turns through undulating foothills. Views of La Serena and the beach are beautiful below, above, and inside the clouds along the route. As the road dips toward the entrance to the town, the white peaks of the *cordillera* emerge menacingly in the distance. However, the visitor's eye is quickly drawn from the jagged peaks to the pointed spires of Andacollo's two awe-inspiring churches.

Numerous abandoned pits and mineral deposits tell the story of Andacollo's history as a copper and gold mining town. Over 100,000 tourists visit this small, economically challenged mountain town every Christmas to see the town's main attraction: the 103cm wood statue of the Virgen de Andacollo. According to locals, for close to five centuries the Virgen has been hearing prayers and curing illnesses. During the annual Fiesta Grande from December 23 to 26, the town swells with devout pilgrims and on most Sundays during the year a visitor can count on large celebrations and mass congregations.

🖥🛈 TRANSPORTATION AND PRACTICAL INFORMATION. To get to Andacollo, catch a **colectivo** on Domeyko in La Serena (1½hr., CH$1500). Local bus company **Turis Ranch** picks up and drops off in La Serena on the corner of Balmaceda and Eduardo de la Barra. (☎217 567. Every 30min. 7am-9:30pm, CH$800) **Urmaneta** is the main thoroughfare through town hosting everything from a **24hr. ATM**, *colectivos*, and numerous lodging and eating options. There is **no tourist kiosk, public Internet access, or large post office,** so contacting the outside world before leaving La Serena is a good idea.

🛏🍴 ACCOMMODATIONS AND FOOD. Andacollo is best seen as an easy daytrip from La Serena, but if you decide to stay in town, there are several decent *residenciales* on Urmaneta, the only main street in town. During Fiesta Grande, there is **camping** across the bridge from the plaza and several homes become short-term hotels as they open their doors and rent out beds. Free camping is allowed M-Sa behind the **Basílica.** Year-round, try **Residencial Las Vegas ❶,** close to the plaza on Urmaneta. Although it is a little dark and dusty, it's a good budget option. (CH$2000 per person; CH$6000 with 3 meals a day.) Most other *residenciales* in town offer the same quality for CH$5000. The best restaurants in town are the striking, red-adobe **La Casona De Tomás ❶,** and the miniature airplane hangar next door, **La Chilenita ❶.** Both are a block up Urmaneta from the plaza and offer similar Chilean *menús*, like *pollo asado* with french fries (CH$1500) or beefsteak with rice (CH$1500). The high-ceilinged green dining room with stained-glass windows of Casona de Tomás is slightly more subdued, while the sunlit ceiling and warehouse dining room of La Chilenita is more appropriate for larger, louder groups.

🎴 SIGHTS. The small town is centered around the newly laid stones of **Plaza Pedro Nolasco Videl,** which stretches out in front of the large churches and the town hall. **Iglesia Chica,** a national monument, was built in the 1600s and protects the **Virgen de Andacollo** for most of the year in an ornate silver-plated altar. The rest of the church is much more modest, with simple wooden benches and three small chapels off to the side. Attached to the church is a small **Museo de Ofrendas a la Virgen,** where gifts for the Virgen, ranging from Chinese dragon masks, a boomerang, diplomas, military metals, and model ships, have been collected over the years. (Open M-Sa 10am-1pm and 3-5pm; Su 10am-6:30pm.) Around the corner, also on the plaza, is the huge **Basílica,** a Byzantine-style wood church painted a bright salmon-pink. Two tall, imposing towers out front balance the interior of the church that has seating room for over 10,000 people. Spiral staircases lead to the balcony of the church, while huge wooden pillars, impressively painted to resemble marble, hold up the entire structure.

VICUÑA ☎51

Don't be frightened by the giant funeral mask in the center of this city's Plaza de Armas. It's the face of this town's most famous resident, Spanish poet and mystic Gabriela Mistral. Her legacy is everywhere in this town, from the main thoroughfare which bears her name to her own restaurant, and soon, her own line of poetry guides. Travelers with a history of strained necks or bad backs be forewarned: you may spend most of your time looking up on this trip. Whether straining to see the snow-tipped peaks high above the valley roads or arching your head back to catch shooting stars while visiting Mamalluca Observatory, you may need to bring a few aspirin. When it's time to relax, Vicuña is the perfect town to recover: peaceful, sunny, and full of free samples of the local booze, *pisco*, to relax your muscles.

⌂ TRANSPORTATION

Vicuña's bus terminal, **Terminal Rodoviario,** is on the corner of Prat and O'Higgins. **Via Elquí** (☎ 411 642) offers hourly service to **Coquimbo** (CH$1300), **La Serena** (CH$1300), **Molle** (CH$800), **Monte Grande** (CH$900), and **Pisco Elquí** (CH$1000). **Tur Bus** (☎ 472 727) goes to **Santiago** (8hr., 2 per day 7:30 and 9:30pm, CH$7500). It's better to catch long distance buses in La Serena, where there are more choices, destinations, and departures.

The terminal for **colectivos** is directly across from the bus station. *Colectivos* go frequently to **La Serena** (CH$1600), as well as to other towns in the **Valle de Elquí,** including **Monte Grande** and **Pisco Elquí** (CH$900). Local **taxis,** and the men who drive them, lounge on the north side of the Plaza de Armas.

✚ 🛈 ORIENTATION AND PRACTICAL INFORMATION

Vicuña sits on the northern bank of the **Río Elquí** and is laid out in a grid pattern centered around the **Plaza de Armas. Mistral** runs east-west and is the major thoroughfare. The Río Elquí borders the city to the south and access to the city from Ruta 41 is across two narrow bridges. Both roads lead to the plaza.

The municipal **tourist office,** San Martín 275, is in the Torre Bauer on the corner on the plaza. The helpful staff is happy to give away their many pamphlets. (☎ 209 125. Open M-Sa 8:30am-9pm; low season M-Sa 8:30am-5:30pm.) **BancoEstado,** Chacabuco 384, on the plaza, has an ATM, but does not give cash for foreign cards, so visitors should plan to use traveler's checks or exchange money in a larger city. The **Casa de Cultura,** Chacabuco 334 (☎ 411 283), on the plaza, has a library and seasonal exhibitions. **Cruz Verde** (☎ 411 223) is the **pharmacy** on Prat between the bus terminal and the plaza. **Hospital San Juan de Dios** (☎ 411 263) is at the very end of Prat, four blocks north of the Plaza. **Internet access** is available at **Ciberbook,** Mistral 571 (☎ 412 099). The post office, **Correos de Chile,** is on the plaza on the corner of San Martín and Mistral, alongside the *municipalidad.*

⌂ ACCOMMODATIONS

Vicuña's diversity of accommodations is baffling for such a small city. The variety of living styles and standards, from little cabins to rooms with finely detailed interiors, provides options for all budget ranges. Most of the hostels line up along Mistral at the northern end of the plaza.

Hostal Valle Hermoso, Mistral 706 (☎ 411 206), past the Museo Mistral. Honoring its neighbor, this hostel has portraits of the poet on its wall. All rooms have showers, TV, and faux roses to make visitors feel at home. The hostel is very quiet, with spacious rooms off a boxy Spanish courtyard with red tiles and a large decorative stone ball. Singles CH$6000; doubles CH$10,000; triples CH$15,000. ❷

Hotel Halley, Mistral 542 (☎ 412 060). This perfect bed-and-breakfast pulls out all the stops. Room interiors have cute wooden makeup tables with intricately carved wooden jewelry boxes. Antique furniture matches the dark staircase. The courtyard is a beautiful garden. Cable TV, private bath, and breakfast included. Singles CH$14,000; doubles CH$24,000; triples CH$30,000. AmEx/D/MC/V. ❹

Hostal Michal, Mistral 573 (☎411 060). The rooms are reminiscent of college dormitories, but are quite comfortable, with TV and bath. The yard has a swing set. May be closed low-season. Singles CH$8000; doubles CH$10,000; triples CH$12,000. ❸

Hotel Restaurant los Olmos, Prat 148 (☎411 124). Big no-frills rooms include large beds. The hotel is adjacent to a funeral home, which might explain the dark front hallway. The location across the street from the bus station is helpful, though. Rooms have TV and private bath. CH$4000 per person. ❶

Yunkay, O'Higgins 72 (☎411 593). The sole *cabaña* option in Vicuña. Each little cabin offers two rooms, a small kitchen, and bathroom. The grill and swimming pool outside create a great setting for a Sunday barbecue. A little bit of a trailer-park vibe. Two rows of tables under a thatched roof provide for a sociable eating area. Doubles CH$20,000; *cabañas* CH$45,000. AmEx/D/MC/V. ❹

Residencial la Elquina, O'Higgins 65 (☎411 317), west of the plaza. This *residencial* has a fertile garden with a large orange tree and bright red pepper plants. Triples are matchbox-sized. Hammocks and love seats fill the backyard garden. Great for couples or quiet introspection. Singles CH$5000, with private bath CH$6000; doubles CH$8000/CH$10,000; triples CH$12,000/CH$15,000. Prices can be bargained, especially during the low season. ❷

Residencial Mistral, Mistral 180 (☎411 278), west of the plaza. Walking through the entryway and restaurant challenges the olfactory senses. Cheap option with the best view in town. Look out over the mountains and rooftops from the wooden balcony. Breakfast included. CH$3500 per person. ❶

FOOD

Despite its prime location in Chile's culinary heartland, Vicuña is not known for its food. Choices are limited, but it is possible to do better than a sandwich or pizza at some of the high-class restaurants on Mistral. The one consistency is that *pisco* goes well with all the food at all the Vicuña eateries.

Restaurant Yo y Soledad, Los Carrera 320 (☎419 002). The wall of vines in the middle of the entryway is the mask in front of Vicuña's cheapest option. Green walls aid the garden atmosphere, but a big-screen TV and the dim lighting kill that quickly. Good portions. *Menú* CH$1500 for 2 plates, CH$2500 for 4 plates. Open daily 10am-11pm. ❷

Restaurante Halley, Mistral 404 (☎411 225). By far the most luxurious option in town. The back room is large, airy, and decorated with care. A thatched roof, nuts hanging in bundles, and a large carriage wheel set the tone. Food is common Chilean beef and chicken, but is cooked by experienced chefs. The *pastel de choclo* (CH$2950) is the house specialty and is deliciously filling. Rabbit with salad $3500. Appetizers CH$1400-2800. Open 10am-midnight. AmEx/D/MC/V. ❸

Timbao, San Martín 203 (☎412 732). A laid-back pizza joint that best fits with the 300 or more days of sun Vicuña receives every year. Old men play chess on worn-out chairs in the corner. The food is basic *churrasco* (CH$1300) and baked chicken ($1600), but the pizzas (CH$1900-2600) are excellent. Open daily 10am-10pm. ❷

SIGHTS

MUSEO GABRIELA MISTRAL. This small exhibit is the crown jewel of the Mistral museums in the Elqui Valley. A replica of the two-room house where the world-renowned poet was raised shows her modest upbringing. The main museum holds personal letters, diary entries, and her life story. Quotes from her poetry are engraved under every bust and are presented with pictures from the surrounding Elqui Valley. No prior knowledge is necessary to enjoy this tour. (*Mistral 579, several* *blocks east of the plaza. ☎411 223. Open Jan.-Feb. M-Sa 10am-7pm, Su 10am-6pm; Mar.-Sept. M-F 10am-1pm and 2:30-5:45pm, Sa 10am-1pm and 3-4:45pm; Oct.-Dec. M-F 10am-1pm and 3-7pm, Sa 10am-1pm and 3-6pm. CH$600, students CH$300.)*

OBSERVATORIO CERRO MAMALLUCA. This stargazer is a gift from the United States to Chile for their active participation as a global telescope hub. The telescope is not as big as its 8m neighbors at El Tololo, but nighttime tours allow visitors to gaze through the telescope to search the sky for world-ending meteors. At 12 in., the Mamalluca telescope is perfect for seeing the rings of Saturn, giant Jupiter, and craters dotting the moon's surface. Tours are given in both Spanish and English and are run by astronomer-comedians. The guides explain the southern constellations, point out nebulae and distant galaxies, and insist that "they're out there." A new planetarium is set to open for summer 2005. The whole trip takes about 2½hr. *(Tickets can be purchased at Mistral 260, over the phone at ☎411 352, or at www.mamalluca.org; tour and transportation cost CH$5000. Summer tours: 4 starting at 10:30pm; winter: 3 starting at 6:30pm.)*

PLANTA CAPEL. Welcome to the *pisco* capital of the world. Like region-specific beverages champagne and scotch, *pisco* is only *pisco* if it comes from Region III or IV of Chile. The Capel plant just outside Vicuña is the largest producer of this strong grape liquor. The tour includes a walkthrough and explanation of all the main facilities including fermentation casks, the grape processor, and the bottling plant. The icing on the cake is the free *pisco* bar at the end of the tour where the tour guide has to bully people to try free shots of *pisco*. The tour is best during the harvest from February to May. *(Across the river from the main area of Vicuña. Taxis leave from the Plaza de Armas, but the walk is only about 20min. Walk east on Chacabuco, away from the plaza. Eventually the road curves around and crosses the river. After the bridge turn left. The plant will be visible about 300 yards ahead. ☎411 251. Open in summer 10am-6pm; in winter 10am-12:30pm and 2:30-6pm. Tours in English Mar.-Dec. Call ahead. Free.)*

PLAZA DE ARMAS. Vicuña's main square is a friendly, palm-filled meeting place for the town. In the late afternoons, teenagers practice guitar and children play tag around the center square, a blue pool of water over a stone model of Gabriela Mistral. Plastic cars are available for children to pedal around, or for adults who want to frighten locals. On the northwest side of the plaza the red **Torre Bauer,** built in 1905 in Germanic style for Mayor Adolfo Bauer, is tall enough to make finding the tourist office on the first floor easy. Diagonally across from the tower on Mistral is the main church, the **Iglesia Inmaculada Concepción,** also red and built around the same time as the tower. Just down from the church is the **Pueblito de los Artisanos,** an ideal spot to shop for Elqui Valley artwork and gifts.

MUSEO ENTOMOLÓGICO E HISTORIA NATURAL. Entomophobes might want to sit this one out. Menacing tarantulas and giant African beetles are safely pinned inside giant display cases inside this randomly placed museum. Other displays include fluorescent butterflies and fossils with papier-mâché models that make it clear that the rock-like fossils are not rocks. Descriptions are in both Spanish and English. *(Chacabuco 334, on the plaza. Open 10:30am-1:30pm and 3:30-6pm. CH$400, students and children CH$200.)*

MIRADOR LA VIRGEN. From the bus coming into town, the view of the valley is beautiful. But nothing can compare to the view of the valley from the Mirador la Virgen. The quick hike provides a panoramic view of the Elqui River, Vicuña, and the surrounding grape fields. It's an easy morning or evening hike to catch the sun coming or going. Snow-capped mountains in the distance catch the eye, but the radio transmission tower in front of them stands out as an eyesore. Offerings are encouraged at the small shrine to the Virgin Mary. *(Walk east on Mistral away from town, past the Museo Mistral. At the end of town, when the road ends, turn left. Follow this road as it winds* *around until you hit a dirt road with a sign indicating the mirador. Turn left here and walk along the road until you reach a path with a handrail. This will wind up the hill to the top. The entire walk from the plaza to the top takes no more than 45min. at a leisurely pace. It is also possible to drive to the top by following the same directions and continuing along the dirt road.)*

EL SOLAR DE LOS MADARIAGA. The sign outside advertises a glimpse into the past, and the man who runs this small museum seems to come right out of the past himself. The original Señor Madariaga was a wealthy businessman from Valparaíso who made a home in Vicuña on a friend's recommendation. This 15-room *solar* was his home, and it has been preserved in its original state, with elegant furniture, faded family photographs, and fruit trees blooming in the courtyard. The very old man who oversees this house was married to the granddaughter of the original Madariaga. Likely to be dressed in an impeccable suit, he is happy to invite visitors to take a seat on one of the antique chairs while he explains the family history. The sign on the front is right; this is less a museum and more like a step back through time. *(Mistral 683, several blocks east of the plaza. Open 10am-7pm, low season 10am-1pm and 3-7pm. CH$400.)*

■ DAYTRIP FROM VICUÑA

MONTE GRANDE

Buses leave hourly from Vicuña and drop passengers in the town center (CH$800). Ask the driver to let you know when to get off. Buses continue on to Pisco Elqui before returning along the same road.

On the way up to Pisco Elqui there is a very small town that Gabriela Mistral chose as her burial place. The poet's grave, **la tumba de la poetisa**, is a 200m walk up the hill toward Pisco Elqui and provides a valley view along with one of Mistral's many messages: "What the soul does for the body, the artist does for the community." Another Mistral monument, directly off the small plaza, has been made out of what is now called **Casa Escuela**, or Mistral's childhood schoolroom. The museum is small and contains maps, books, and other artifacts from the poet's childhood. The Museo Gabriela Mistral in Vicuña is more informative, but **Casa Escuela** does provide insight into the poet's work. (Open Tu-Su 10am-1pm and 3-6pm. CH$300.) There is another *pisco* plant in Monte Grande that makes a less widely distributed brand of *pisco:* **Los Artesanos de Cochiguaz.** The *pisco* may taste better for the personal attention it receives, but the tour is small and lackluster when compared to the tours offered in Pisco Elqui and Vicuña. (Open 10am-1pm and 2:30-6pm. Tours and tastings free.) The highlight of this small mountain town is the **Galería de Arte Zen,** about 400m downhill along the main road. Inside, soothing meditation music plays over the barely audible rushing stream in the back. A few rooms with pebble floors showcase the owner's personal artwork and provide a relaxing environment. Massage oils (CH$5000), organic fruit (CH$5000), tarot readings (CH$7500), Zen readings (CH$10,000) and astrology readings (CH$15,000) are all offered by the Zen master that runs this series of stone huts.

There are no lodging options in Monte Grande, so it's best to wait until reaching Pisco Elqui. If your hunger can't wait, **Mesón del Fraile ❷,** a yellow restaurant across the street from the main square, serves excellent sandwiches. The papaya sour is the house special. (Open 9am-10pm; low season 9am-1pm and 3-6pm).

PISCO ELQUI   ☎ 51

Four kilometers deeper into the valley from Monte Grande is the wonderful village of Pisco Elqui. There are no museums, no hectic tours, just peace and quiet, welcoming residents, and a few of the most relaxing *cabañas* in Chile. From the white roses that grow in the plaza, the town is mostly uphill. Artisans and local growers have permanent kiosks set up selling honey, jam, bracelets, and all sorts of local artwork. The

NORTE CHICO

views from the higher points in the city show endless rows of growing grapes. There is another *pisco* plant to tour with free samples—just don't let the bus driver wander over during his break.

Raise a glass after a tour of the **Solar de Pisco Tres Erres,** the *pisco* plant at the edge of the plaza. (English tours daily 11:30am-12:30pm and 2:30-6:30pm; low season open Tu-F and every other Su and M. Free.) For an adventure into the valley, **Rancho Rodríguez** is the place to go. The ranch offers a horseback ride through the valley (CH$2500 per hr.) and a 2hr. stargazing tour (CH$4000). In the winter, masochists or fans of the intense cold can ride horseback through the snowy valleys for the same reasonable CH$2500 per hr. To get to the ranch, walk up the main road from the plaza, past Mandarino, and take a right onto Prat at the top of the hill. The ranch is down the hill on the left, across from El Tesoro.

The most unique restaurant in town is the cave-like pizza and juice stand, **Los Jugos ❷** and **Mandarino ❸.** The two tuck under the same thatched roof off of the plaza and offer a wide array of vegetarian options. Los Jugos makes thick juices with fresh papayas, kiwis, apples, oranges, and more. They aren't cheap, but they justify the CH$1300 price. Mandarino serves homemade pizza and an especially delicious vegetable pizza made with fresh local veggies. The atmosphere is unique: the restaurant has a dirt floor and the clay benches are strewn with sheepskins as cushions. In the winter, the fireplace roars.

The town lies on a steep incline along the side of the valley. Walking up hill to the right from the plaza there is a municipal pool and **campground ❷.** (Swimming CH$1500. Camping CH$5500.) At the top of the hill, this road ends and is intersected by Prat. Turning left on Prat leads to the **Hotel Gabriela Mistral ❸,** where fluorescent colored *cabañas* contrast sharply with the colors of the valley, but second-floor balconies overlooking the street offer an impressive view. (☎ 198 2525. Singles CH$6000; doubles CH$12,000; 3-person *cabañas* CH$18,000; 4-person *cabañas* CH$24,000.) Farther along Prat is the hippie **Hostería los Datiles ❹,** which offers new cabins, a pool, and a peaceful, flowing stream. They also have meditation pyramids that help channel meditative energy and seem out of place in the otherwise lovely garden. In addition, the *hostería* offers yoga meditation and Mayan horoscope charts. (☎ 198 2540. Singles CH$15,000; doubles CH$25,000; *cabañas* CH$40,000-45,000. AmEx/D/MC/V.) Turning right on Prat leads to the **Tesoro de Elqui ❺,** the most luxurious cabin option in town. *Cabañas* sit on a hill in a colorful garden with a pool at the base of the hill and a great view of the valley. Hammocks, on-site massage and reflexology are available, in addition to a warm dining area converted from a greenhouse. The neighbors offer psychic readings and meditation classes. (☎ 451 069. Dec.-Mar. *cabaña* singles CH$30,000; doubles CH$35,000; triples CH$40,000; big cabin CH$49,000. Apr.-Nov. *cabaña* singles CH$25,000; doubles CH$30,000; triples CH$34,000; big cabin CH$40,000.)

To get to Pisco Elqui, take a local **bus** from the terminal in Vicuña (CH$800) or pick it up as it passes by Monte Grande (CH$100).

COCHIGUAZ   ☎ 51

If the Elqui Valley were a train track, Cochiguaz would be the end of the line. Cochiguaz is as deep into the valley as dirt roads go. A 19km stretch of dirt road, Cochiguaz features a string of individual houses, upscale and low-priced camping grounds, and the most unique *cabaña* resorts in Chile. The two consistencies shared by all the properties along the road are the views of waterfalls flowing into a mountain river and the belief that the valley holds healing powers. According to the local brochures, NASA found the highest level of electromagnetism in the world in the deep Elqui Valley. According to locals, this is a sign that the Andes are the current focal point of global energy, a privilege that gives the valley its healing powers.

Many of the resorts try to capitalize on this myth with meditation, yoga classes, and revitalizing massages. About 11km along the road is **Alma Zen** ❹, a solar-powered group of *cabañas*, quiet meditation grounds, massage therapy, and a unique circular pool watched over by a giant Buddha. Houses are two-tiered, contain a kitchen and heater, and prices include breakfast. (☎473 861; www.valledeelqui.cl. Singles CH$20,000; doubles CH$35,000; *cabañas* CH$40,000. AmEx/D/MC/V.) At the end of the road is the most luxurious of the Cochiguaz *cabaña* hot spots, **Casa del Agua** ❹, a quartz-strewn, serene property. Horse tours are led by the activity head, Ziggy, a Bavarian who will explain in detail the specificities of the powers of the Elqui Valley. Massages, a perfectly cooked *pollo asado*, and heated pools relax the mind, body, and soul. (☎321 371; www.casadelagua.cl. 4-person *cabañas* CH$45,000; 6-person CH$55,000. AmEx/D/MC/V.) A cheaper, but equally eye-pleasing, option is **Cabañas El Albaricoque** ❸. The first of the three along the road, El Albaricoque has the biggest, most spacious *cabañas* with heaters, kitchenettes, and fireplaces great for winter or even summer in the mountains. The streamside sitting areas are perfect for finishing a good book while soaking up some rays. (☎198 2565. *Cabañas* CH$27,000. AmEx/D/MC/V.)

To get to Cochiguaz, either hike the well-labeled road on the left after Monte Grande or ask Hernán, the owner of the local restaurant **Los Paltos** for a ride (one-way CH$5000; round-trip CH$10,000).

COQUIMBO ☎51

Coquimbo lies on the southern tip of the Bahía de Coquimbo, just south of the popular summer resort city of La Serena. While there's less going on in Coquimbo than in its sister city, Coquimbo's bargain accommodations draw visitors here during January and February. Others make the pilgrimage from far-off lands to see the monolithic **Cruz del Tercer Milenio,** an enormous cement cross that towers over the city and can be seen for miles. Coquimbo is an important regional port, once the stomping ground of the infamous pirate-turned-explorer Sir Francis Drake. A large blue and black ship, the *Margot Maria Stengel,* used to lie near Coquimbo's beach, but has been pulled to shore and tethered along the seawall near the bus terminal. Coquimbo is not a must-see, but makes an interesting blue-collar contrast to the glitz lining La Serena's Avenida del Mar.

◪ TRANSPORTATION. Long-distance buses arrive at the **Terminal Rodoviario de Coquimbo,** Varela 1300 (☎326 651), at corner of Garriga, four blocks from the central Plaza de Armas. **Pullman** (☎328 388) sends buses to **Copiapó** (5hr., every hr. 7:30am-10:45pm, CH$5000), **Santiago** (6hr., every hr., CH$10,000), and **Valparaíso** (6hr., 5 per day 9am-11:15pm, CH$9500) via **Viña del Mar** (6hr., CH$9500). **Tur Bus** (☎327 293; www.turbus.cl) goes to **Ovalle** (1hr., every hr. 8:15am-10:15pm, CH$1100), **Santiago** (6hr., every hr. 7:15am-2:15am, CH$8900), and **Valparaíso** (6hr., every 2hr. 9:15am-11:15pm, CH$8900) via **Viña del Mar** (6hr., CH$8900).

Colectivos provide the easiest way to get between Coquimbo and sister city **La Serena.** *Colectivos* coming from La Serena stop along Varela. *Colectivos* departing for **La Serena** (30min., every 10min. 7:30am-11:30pm, CH$350) or the **Cruz del Tercer Milenio** (10min., every 15min. 9am-9pm, CH$250; labeled "#10" or "Cruz") line up along the Plaza de Armas. **Alfa Mar,** office #24 at the bus station (☎391 165), sends *colectivos* to **Guanaqueros** (45min., CH$1400) and **Tongoy** (1hr., CH$1600). **Radio Taxis,** at the Terminal Rodoviario (☎323 214), run all over the city (CH$500-1000).

■ **ORIENTATION AND PRACTICAL INFORMATION.** Coquimbo sits on the northern edge of a wide peninsula overlooking the **Bahía de Coquimbo.** Most services are downtown, in the area immediately surrounding the central **Plaza de Armas** and along the main commercial strip Aldunate. To get downtown from the bus station, take a right on Varela. Walk three blocks and turn left onto Bilbao; the Plaza de Armas is one block ahead on the right. **Costanera** runs along the shore; parallel to it are **Melgarejo** and **Aldunate**, which border the main plaza. The bus station is two blocks from the shore, a short walk from the Plaza de Armas. The city's only major sight, the **Cruz del Tercer Milenio,** is in the hilly *parte alta* of the city, away from the ocean. To orient yourself in town, look for the towering cross.

The **Casa de la Cultura y el Turismo,** Costanera 701, on the corner of Freire, gives out free maps of Coquimbo. (☎313 971. Open daily Mar.-Dec. 8:30am-5:30pm.) During the summer, **Museo de Sitio,** a tiny gazebo in the Plaza de Armas, gives limited information to tourists and exhibits some pre-Colombian bones discovered in Coquimbo in 1981. (Jan.-Feb. open M-Sa 9:30am-8:30pm, Su 9:30am-2pm.) Countless banks line Aldunate and there are two **24hr. ATMs** off the Plaza de Armas: **Banco de Chile,** at the corner of Las Heras and Melgarejo, and **BancoEstado,** at the corner of Bilbao and Melgarejo. **Luggage storage** is available at the **Terminal Rodoviario** (see **Transportation,** above. CH$300-1000, open daily 6am-midnight.) **Farmacia Abraham Peralta,** Aldunate 947, refills prescriptions and has over-the-counter medications. (☎321 000. English spoken. Open M-Sa 9:30am-9pm, Su 11am-2pm. AmEx/MC/V.) **Hospital de Coquimbo,** Videla (☎206 246 or 206 242), is accessible by *colectivos* labeled "Hospital" (CH$250). **Conecta,** Aldunate 1196, sells pre-paid cell phones and provides Internet access (CH$500 per hr.), telephones, and fax service. (☎203 948. Open M-Sa 9am-10pm.) The **post office,** Aldunate 951, is housed in the building that stands in the middle of the Plaza de Armas. (☎311 524. Open M-F 9am-1pm and 3-6pm, Sa 9:30am-1pm.)

■ **ACCOMMODATIONS.** Most hotels and hostels in Coquimbo are more reasonably priced than those in La Serena. Although the town itself has less to offer visitors, Coquimbo can be a cheaper place to stay for those commuting just to La Serena's beaches. Budget accommodations cluster on or around Aldunate. From the bus station, head away from the shore and go toward the Plaza de Armas. **Hotel Lig ❸,** Aldunate 1577, a few blocks inland from the bus station, has bright, airy, well-decorated rooms, all with private bath, cable TV, and telephone. (☎311 171. Breakfast included. Singles CH$11,450; doubles CH$18,500; triples CH$23,100.) **Hotel Ibérica ❷,** Lastra 400, on the corner of Aldunate overlooking the Plaza de Armas, is an old, colonial-style hotel in a great location. Rooms have a view and cable TV with true international diversity. (☎312 141. Breakfast CH$300-900. Jan.-Feb. singles CH$5500, with bath CH$7500; doubles CH$9000/CH$13,000; triples with bath CH$17,000; quads with bath CH$19,000. Mar.-Dec. singles CH$4000, with bath CH$6500; doubles CH$8000/CH$10,000; triples with bath CH$15,000; quads with bath CH$17,000. MC/V.) **Hotel Vega Mar ❸,** Las Heras 403, at the corner of Aldunate just off the Plaza, has sunny, airy rooms with private bath that compensate for the building's peeling paint. (☎311 773. Breakfast CH$500. Jan.-Feb. singles CH$5000; doubles CH$8000; triples CH$9000. Mar.-Dec. singles CH$4000; doubles CH$6000; triples CH$7000.) **Hotel Restaurant Bilbao ❷,** Bilbao 471, one block uphill off Aldunate, offers clean rooms, all with private bath and TV. Some rooms have the luxury of verandas overlooking the busy avenue, which can make for some noise at night. (☎315 767. Breakfast included. Singles CH$6000; doubles CH$12,000; triples CH$18,000.)

◻ FOOD. Seafood is the name of the game in Coquimbo, and it's generally fresh, tasty, and fairly inexpensive. Restaurants line Aldunate, and street vendors set up shop in the Plaza de Armas and along the waterfront. **Feria del Mar ❷**, on the waterfront between Costanera and Parque O'Higgins, across the park from the bus station, is a lively seafood market with dozens of stalls to which vendors eagerly try to woo customers. All the fish and shellfish here are fresh, well-prepared, and pretty cheap. (Entrees CH$3500-5000. Open daily 10am-8pm.) **Restaurant Sal y Pimienta del Capitán Denny ❶**, Varela 1301, across the street from the bus station, is a popular lunch spot with locals. (*Menú* CH$1200. Seafood entrees CH$800-2500. Open M-Sa 11am-3pm and 6-9pm.) **Roka Pizza ❶**, Juan Antonio Río 43, at the end of Aldunate near the bus station, serves fast, filling meals, including some vegetarian options. (☎320 533. Fried chicken CH$900-2900. Pizza CH$1200-5300. Sandwiches CH$700-1500. Open M-Th 11am-2am, F-Sa 11am-6pm.) **Santa Isabela**, Aldunate 1390, sells groceries. (☎317 570. Open M-Th 8:30am-10:30pm, F-Sa 8:30am-11pm, Su 8:30am-3pm. AmEx/MC/V.)

◙ SIGHTS. There's not a lot to see downtown, but a leisurely stroll around town can nonetheless be a pleasant way to spend an afternoon. From the bus station, walk toward the shore through **Parque O'Higgins**, where families picnic during the summer months. Directly in front of the park on Costanera is the lively **Feria del Mar**. To the right, **Playa de Coquimbo** stretches to La Serena. While it's not as beautiful as the beaches in La Serena, the calm water is perfect for swimming. Walking left along Costanera, there is a **Catamarán Mistral** booth (☎315 295 or 09 548 2369), organizing harbor tours that pass sea lion and penguin colonies (1hr., 7 per day noon-7:30pm, CH$1000). Turning left on Bilbao leads to the central **Plaza de Armas,** which houses an artisan's market (M-Th 8am-8pm, F-Sa 8am-midnight) and live music on weekend nights (F-Sa 8pm-midnight).

Towering over Coquimbo is the city's biggest sight, the imposing **Cruz del Tercer Milenio,** a 93m tall cement cross commemorating the 2000th birthday of Jesus Christ. To get there from the Plaza de Armas, catch a *colectivo* labeled "Cruz" on Aldunate across from the Plaza (CH$250). Construction began in May 2000 and the ambitious project aims to be completed by 2007. As of January 2004 only the first phase—the cross—has been completed; further plans include large parks surrounding the cross for meditation, confessionals, and vivid depictions of the Ten Commandments. The cross itself is an amazing, if not bizarre, sight and well worth a visit. With its cement spiral staircase and three columns symbolizing the Father, the Son, and the Holy Spirit, the cross looks more like the realization of a science fiction novella than a religious icon. And the regular but invisible banging of hammers adds to the surreal atmosphere. There are galleries in the base of the cross and an elevator that takes visitors up to the third floor viewing area (CH$700). From there, a second elevator (CH$1900) goes 70m up the cross into the glass-enclosed arms, affording visitors an awe-inspiring view of the entire valley. (Open M-F 9:30am-8pm, Sa-Su 10:30am-9pm. Ground-level pavilion free.)

◪ ENTERTAINMENT. Locals generally spend evenings having leisurely meals or a few drinks in the restaurants along Aldunate. The **Plaza de Armas** hosts live music on weekend nights (F-Sa 8pm-midnight). However, since Coquimbo's waterfront can feel abandoned at night, it's advisable that solo travelers go in a group if spending a night on the town. Those looking for something a little more exciting should head to La Serena, where most of the area's nightlife takes place. **Restaurante El Callejón,** Pasaje los Artesanos 21, off Malgarejo three blocks from the Plaza de Armas toward the bus station, is a popular evening hangout for watching *fútbol* matches and downing a few beers. (☎315 765. Entrees CH$1000-2500. Beer CH$1000-1500. Open M-Th 10am-midnight, F-Sa 10am-3am.) **Club de Jazz de Coquimbo,** Aldunate 739, has live music weekend nights. (☎288 784 or 09 425 2159. Cocktails CH$2000-4000. Open Th-Sa 10pm-3am.)

TONGOY   ☎51

Unlike larger beach towns like **La Serena** (p. 214) and **Valparaíso** (p. 243), Tongoy has a slower pace and less crowded beaches, which make it the perfect place to escape city life for a few days. **Playa Grande,** on the right at the end of Fundición Sur, is popular with sunbathers, while the smaller **Playa Socos,** running alongside Costanera, off Fundición Norte, is best suited for swimming.

⬛ TRANSPORTATION. Buses and *colectivos* stop at the central **Plaza Victor Domingo Silva,** between Fundición Norte and Fundición Sur. **Serena Mar,** on Fundación Norte at the corner of Costanera (☎09 161 2034), sends buses to **La Serena** (1hr., every 20min. 8am-midnight, CH$1100) and **Ovalle** (1½hr., 7 per day 8am-7:30pm, CH$4000). **Alfa Mar,** Fundición Sur 590 (☎391 165), five blocks from the plaza up Fundición Sur walking with traffic, sends *colectivos* to **Coquimbo** (1hr., CH$1600) and **Guanaqueros** (15min., CH$300).

⬛⬛ ORIENTATION AND PRACTICAL INFORMATION. The main road in town is **Fundición. Fundición Sur** heads into town, while **Fundición Norte** heads north to La Serena, making it easy to orient yourself in town. To get to Playa Grande from the plaza, walk up Fundición Sur against traffic. To get to Playa Socos, walk with the traffic down Fundición Norte and take a right on Costanera. The **tourist office,** on Fundición Norte at the corner of Gomez Carreño, on the plaza, has limited information on Tongoy. (☎391 860. Open daily 10am-2pm and 4-8pm.) **There are no banks, ATMs, or currency exchanges in Tongoy.** The **police** (☎391 258) are located two blocks from the plaza walking against traffic on Fundición Norte. **Tambo,** Fundición Sur 64, across from the plaza, is a **pharmacy** with a *centro de llamadas* inside. (☎391 635. Open daily Jan.-Feb. 9:30am-11pm; Mar.-Dec. 9:30am-1:30pm and 4-9pm. MC/V.) **Consultorio de Tongoy,** Fundición Norte 127 (☎391 270), offers **emergency medical care,** but the nearest hospital is in Coquimbo. **Nexus,** Costanera 6, at the corner of Galvez, has **Internet access.** (☎391 668, 245 522, or 09 504 9408. CH$350 per 15min., CH$600 per 30min., CH$1000 per hr. Open daily 10am-10pm.) The **post office,** on Fundición Norte, is in the same building as the tourist office. (☎391 860 or 392 397. Open M-F 8:30am-1pm and 2-6pm, Sa 8:30-noon.)

⬛ ACCOMMODATIONS. In the low season, you may have to hunt around for a budget option that remains open, but if you don't mind splurging a bit, there are numerous hotels and *residenciales* that stay open year-round. **◪Hotel Agua Marina ❸,** Fundición Sur 92, has well-decorated rooms, all with private bath. (☎391 870. Breakfast included. Jan.-Feb. doubles CH$20,000; triples CH$25,000; quads CH$30,000. Mar.-Dec. doubles CH$13,000; triples CH$18,000; quads CH$25,000.) **Residencial de Rosario ❷,** La Serena 58, three blocks up off Fundición Sur, has modest rooms that lead straight to Playa Grande, all with shared baths. If you don't see their sign, ask around for Rosario, the owner. (☎392 953. Singles CH$4000; doubles CH$8000; triples CH$12,000.) **Hostal Rincón de Pierro ❸,** La Serena 28, offers rooms off a courtyard, all with private bath and TV. (☎392 532. Breakfast included. Singles CH$9000; doubles CH$18,000; triples CH$27,000; quads CH$36,000.) **Hostería Tongoy ❺,** Costanera 10, is an upscale hotel with views of the beach. (☎391 203 or 391 900; www.hoteltongoycosta.cl.

NORTE CHICO

Breakfast included. Jan.-Feb. doubles CH$38,000, with cable TV and mini-bar CH$48,000; triples CH$63,000. Mar.-Dec. doubles CH$31,000/CH$39,000; triples CH$51,000. MC/V.)

🖬 **FOOD.** Seafood dominates Tongoy's culinary scene, but there are a few notable exceptions. **Restaurant Aquário ❶**, Costanera 56, one block off Fundición Norte, serves lighter fare in a bright and breezy dining room overlooking Playa Socos. (☎391 850. *Menú* CH$2800. Sandwiches CH$300-2200. Beer CH$500-800. Open Jan.-Feb. daily 9am-1am, Mar.-Dec. F-Su 10am-10pm.) **Restaurant Sin Rival ❷**, Fundición Sur 60, has a wide range of salad options and a huge TV where loyal fans gather to watch *fútbol* matches. (☎287 359. Salads CH$1000-1800. Soups CH$2500-3500. Entrees CH$1000-4800. Beer CH$500-1200. Open Jan.-Feb. Tu-Su 9:30am-midnight.) **Restaurant El Rey II ❸**, Lord Cochrane 47, is a good option for seafood on Playa Grande. (☎391 129. Omelettes CH$2500-3400. *Empanadas* CH$2200-550. *Ostiones* CH$3200-4000. Open daily Jan.-Feb. 9:30am-midnight, Mar.-Dec. 11am-10pm.) The small open-air **market**, on Fundición Sur at the corner of Barnes, sells fresh fruits and vegetables. (Open M and F 8am-4pm.)

GUANAQUEROS ☎51

Surrounded by mountains and situated on the edge of Bahía de Guanaqueros, this town's long beach and calm waters attract daytrippers from the surrounding area during the summer. Few choose to spend the night, and there are few services available, but Guanaqueros is nonetheless a relaxing place to spend a few days.

The few restaurants in Guanaqueros specialize in seafood, and there are very few vegetarian options in town. **Molokai Restaurant ❷**, Costanera 2597, serves mostly meat entrees and has an outdoor patio. (☎260 2448 or 09 689 6296. Entrees CH$2900-5500. *Emparedados* CH$1200-1400. Open Jan.-Feb. daily 9am-midnight, Mar.-Dec. W-Su 9am-midnight.) **Restaurant Mediterráneo ❶**, Costanera 2205, is a popular local lunch spot during the summer. (*Menú* CH$1600. Sandwiches CH$400-1400. Entrees CH$1700-3000. Open daily Jan.-Feb. 8am-midnight.)

Accommodations in Guanaqueros are limited. If everything is full, look for signs reading "arrienda" (rent) in windows around town. **Hotel La Bahía ❸**, Prat 58, at the corner of El Suizo and Costanera, has comfortable rooms right off the main strip. (☎/fax 395 380. Breakfast CH$1000. Jan.-Feb. singles CH$10,000, with bath CH$15,000; doubles CH$12,000/CH$18,000; triples CH$15,000/CH$22,000. Mar.-Dec. singles CH$7000, with bath CH$10,000; doubles CH$9000/CH$12,000; triples CH$12,000/CH$15,000.) **Apart-Hotel El Pequeño ❹**, Maria Ibsen 1130, off El Suizo one block uphill at Restaurant El Pequeño, has private bath, TV, and telephone. (☎395 125; aparthotel-elpequeno@entelchile.net. Breakfast included with basic rooms. Suites include kitchen but no breakfast. Singles CH$15,000; doubles CH$21,000; triples CH$24,000; quads CH$28,000; quints CH$29,900. AmEx/MC/V.)

Colectivos stop in the center of town on El Suizo, on the two blocks before it turns into Costanera. **Alfa Mar** (☎391 165 or 323 719) sends *colectivos* to **Coquimbo** (45min., CH$1400) and **Tongoy** (15min., CH$300). El Suizo runs along the beach and curves with it to become Costanera; going uphill at the curve is Prat. **There are no banks, ATMS, or currency exchanges in Guanaqueros.** The closest hospital is in Coquimbo, although there is an emergency room in Tongoy. **Centro de llamadas**, Prat 25, at the corner of El Suizo and Costanera, is a telephone office. (☎395 775. Open daily Jan.-Feb. 9:30am-1am.)

NORTE CHICO

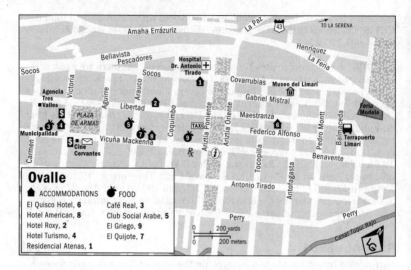

Ovalle

▲ ACCOMMODATIONS
El Quisco Hotel, **6**
Hotel American, **8**
Hotel Roxy, **2**
Hotel Turismo, **4**
Residencial Atenas, **1**

🍴 FOOD
Café Real, **3**
Club Social Arabe, **5**
El Griego, **9**
El Quijote, **7**

OVALLE ☎ 53

Perched on the banks of the vigorous Río Limarí, Ovalle (pop. 97,514), also known as the "Pearl of Limarí," is the capital of the Limarí province of Chile's Region IV. Ovalle is a good base for delving into ancient attractions like the Valle del Encanto, and exploring the surrounding idyllic countryside of fertile valleys. Produce growers congregate in Ovalle four times a week to sell the fruits of those valleys in the colorful Feria Modelo. Ovalle may be a non-tourist town, but it also provides you the opportunity to witness Chilean life freer from global influences.

▋ TRANSPORTATION

Buses: Terrapuerto Limarí, on the corner of Maestranza and Balmaceda, is Ovalle's main bus hub. Buses en route to or from La Serena stop here. Local buses go to **La Serena** (8 per day 10am-12:30am, CH$1000). **Tur Bus** (☎623 659) has several buses to **Santiago** (6hr., 7:45am-12:45am, CH$4500), as does **Tas Choapa** (☎626 820). **Pullman Bus** (☎626 825) and **Pullman Carmelita** (☎316 749) go north to **Arica** (23hr., 2 per day 10:30am-2:30pm, CH$15,000) via **Iquique** (18hr., CH$14,000). Buses also run to: **Antofagasta** (4 per day 9am-8pm, CH$12,500) **Calama** (8 per day 6:30am-12:30am, CH$12,000); **Valparaíso** (3 per day 2:15pm-4:40pm).

Taxis: Taxi *colectivos* wait on Ariztía Poniente and go frequently to **La Serena** (1½hr., CH$12,000). For CH$35,000 a *colectivo* will take you or a group to **Parque Nacional Fray Jorge, Valle del Encanto,** and **Termas de Socos.**

✱ ▋ ORIENTATION AND PRACTICAL INFORMATION

Ovalle's bus station, the **Terrapuerto Limarí,** sits at the eastern edge of town near the **Feria Modelo.** To get to the heart of town, turn left on Maestranza from the bus terminal and continue to the **Plaza de Armas.** The action is bordered by **Ariztía Oriente** to the east and **Carmen** to the west. Ariztía Oriente and **Ariztía Poniente,** two one-way streets divided by a grassy strip, bisect the town in a north-south direction.

Tourist Office: A **tourist information kiosk** sits along Vicuña Mackenna on the grass divider between Ariztía Oriente and Ariztía Poniente. Hours vary.

Tours: Agencia Tres Valles (☎629 650), on the corner of Libertad and Carmen, leads trips into the surrounding areas. They also do **currency exchange** at reasonable rates.

Bank: Banco Santander, Victoria 322 (☎622 056), and **Banco de Chile,** Victoria 261 (☎620 003), both have **24hr. ATMs.**

Police: Aguirre 641 (☎133).

Pharmacy: Farmacia Ahumado, Mackenna 72 and 90 (☎630 720). Open 24hr.

Hospital: ☎131. **Hospital Dr. Antonio Tirado,** Ariztía Poniente 7 (☎620 042), on the northern end of Ariztía.

Post Office: On Vicuña Mackenna, on the plaza.

▐ ACCOMMODATIONS

Lodging in Ovalle offers a range of price options but lacks variety and unique hotel amenities. The inexpensive choices are more interesting, with the open air garden of Hotel Roxy and the El Quisco Hotel hat trick of convenient location, greenhouse interior, and friendly service.

▨ **El Quisco Hotel,** Maestranza 161 (☎620 351). Not only is El Quisco the best deal in Ovalle, but if you roll into town late at night, this is one of the best places to stay because of its proximity to the bus station. This family-run hotel has all the amenities of an upscale hotel for half the price. The plastic roofing over the main hallway (which is not as sketchy as it sounds) gives the place a cool greenhouse feel without the wind and rain of the outdoors. All rooms have TV. Singles CH$6000, with bath CH$8000; doubles CH$10,000/CH$12,000; triples with bath CH$18,000. AmEx/ MC/V. ❷

Residencial Atenas, Socos 12 (☎620 424). An 8-table bar and eating area great for groups line this *residencial's* entryway. The mirror-backed bar adds space to the common area. Cheapest deal in town. Warm shower CH$500. Broadcast TV CH$1000. Singles CH$4700; doubles CH$7000; triples CH$10,500. ❷

Hotel Roxy, Libertad 155 (☎620 080). This quiet hotel is built around a big courtyard with small gardens of cacti and other colorful desert plants. During the daytime, it's a relaxing place to catch some peaceful rays. By night, the starry sky is breathtaking. Getting to the shared bathrooms involves walking outside. Singles CH$6500, with bath CH$13,000; doubles CH$10,000/CH$13,500; triples CH$12,000/ CH$17,500. ❷

Hotel Turismo, Victoria 295 (☎623 258; www.hotelturismo.cl), overlooking the plaza, offers all the bells and whistles of expensive hotels: cable TV, free parking, breakfast, a large restaurant, and private baths. However, even when combined with the hotel's central location and tremendous views, Turismo cannot make up for its high prices. The hotel offers few unique qualities, apart from the clashing triangular designs on the comforters, which combine with peach-toned hallways to create an unmistakable 90s feel. Singles CH$21,500; doubles CH$31,000; triples CH$36,000. AmEx/MC/V. ❹

Hotel American, Mackenna 169 (☎620 159; www.hotelamerican.cl). The only thing that stands out about the American is the cutesy toilet cover in the bathroom. The bright sunlight that fills the entryway emphasizes the wall-to-wall white tile flooring and lack of carpeting. Big cable TVs in all the rooms make up for the lackluster views. Breakfast included. Singles: first floor CH$15,900, second floor CH$19,500; doubles CH$23,500/CH$28,000; triples CH$26,500/CH$33,500. AmEx/MC/V. ❹

NORTE CHICO

☐ FOOD

Ovalle's few restaurants are scattered around the Plaza de Armas and on Mackenna. The regional speciality, river prawns, are worth a try when in season. Fresh fruits and vegetables are abundantly available at the **Feria Modelo** near the bus station. Backpackers and others on long journeys will enjoy the Feria's high-quality dried fruits and nuts, which combine to make a high-energy trail mix.

Café Real, Mackenna 419b (☎624 526), just off the plaza. Coffee shop by day, pub by night, and movie theater on the weekend, Café Real is certainly Ovalle's hippest spot. Slide along the shiny blue floors to a secluded table and let one of the waitresses serve you a *leche con fruta* while George Michael croons on the stereo. Café Real manages to be trendy with a non-commercial feel, a coffee shop with alcohol and a pool table (CH$2000 per hr.). Bands occasionally perform live on F and Sa nights. Open M-Th 9am-8:30pm, F 9am-1:30am, Sa 10am-1:30am. AmEx/D/MC/V. ❷

Club Social Árabe, Arauco 225 (☎620 015), off Mackenna, offers standard Chilean fare and spicier, more interesting Middle Eastern food in a spacious room. The cupola on the top is enclosed by windows, lighting up the peach-colored walls. Count on the great service to bring some *kuppe* (CH$3200) or a sweet *caipiriña* (CH$2500). Open M-Sa 10am-1am, Su 10am-4pm. AmEx/D/MC/V. ❸

El Quijote, Arauco 284 (☎620 501), on the corner of Mackenna. Quijote feels like a 1960s commune. Politically-themed posters and iconic images of figures such as Pablo Neruda and Salvador Allende line the walls, towering over tables tucked into dimly-lit corners. On weekdays, there aren't many customers and service can be leisurely, but the owner has more than enough fascinating stories to pass the slow hours. A great weekend meeting spot. The mixed drinks are a better bet than the standard Chilean fare. Open M-Th 9am-1am, F-Sa 9am-3am. ❷

El Griego, 79 Mackenna (☎620 541). There is no Greek food here—only freshly made Chilean treats, pastries, and bread. The owner and two bakers make *cachitos* packed with *dulce de leche* (CH$300), *alfajores* (CH$250), chocolate cake (CH$380), and fresh breads in the back of this small dessert haven. Open M-Sa 7am-4:30pm.

◉ SIGHTS

The **Museo del Limarí,** at the corner of Covarrubias and Antofagasta, is a great place to start a trip through the unique cultural offerings of Ovalle. This archaeological museum, located in an old train station, has three rooms displaying Diaguita pottery and artifacts in bright glass displays. Be sure to check out the display describing the process of Diaguita head deformation. As shrunken heads go, it's a small collection, but worth a look. (☎620 029. Open Tu-F 9am-6pm, Sa 10am-1pm, 5-8pm, Su 10am-1pm. CH$600, children and students CH$300. Free on Su.) Down a couple of blocks behind the bus station is the **Feria Modelo,** a large-scale farmer's market held in a huge train hangar. The fertile fields around Ovalle offer up a wide variety of fruits and vegetables that provide sweet eye candy and even sweeter Chilean fruits. The market is replete with the standard tomatoes (CH$300 per kg), apples, and oranges (CH$350 per kg) but also contains fruits unique to Chile like *pepinos de fruta* (CH$200 per kg), and *maneaqui* (CH$200 per kg). The fresh avocados (CH$600 per kg) and almonds (CH$900 per kg) are full of rich flavor. In addition to the food, there is also a miscellaneous goods section where vendors sell everything from pots and pans to watchbands and baby pacifiers. (Open M, W, F 6am-6pm, Su 10am-2pm.) If a day at the market isn't thrilling enough, catch the latest American action flick at **Cine**

Cervantes, Mackenna 370, right next to the post office on the plaza. (☎620 267. Shows daily 3:30, 6:30, 9pm; CH$1500.)

▶ DAYTRIPS FROM OVALLE

VALLE DEL ENCANTO

From Ovalle, Route 43 heads northeast 88km to La Serena through endless fields of grapes, artichokes, and mandarin orange groves interspersed with flat scrubby land dotted with cacti. Twenty kilometers from Ovalle is a sign for Valle del Encanto, a remote archaeological monument. It's a dusty 5km walk from Route 43 to the park entrance, but it's often possible to get a ride with other visitors. The park is comprised of about eight acres of **petroglyphs** (images carved into stone) and **pictographs** (images painted onto stone) dating back at least 2000 years to the pastoral Molle people. The images are best observed on sunny afternoons and appear to depict religious images. The collection also contains hundreds of *tacitas* (small, manmade bowls dug in large stones, used for grinding). *Guardaparques* Salvador Araya and Clemen Pizarro are happy to explain prevailing archaeological theories, including Pizarro's theory that aliens created the rock engravings. Visitors are able to scramble around the boulders while seeking out the ancient images which are helpfully pointed out by white arrows.

Free **camping** is permitted at three spots within the park. The sites are marked with picnic benches and signs. Ask at the entrance for a map. Park guides are learning English slowly; a knowledge of Spanish will enhance your experience.

From Ovalle, ask any **bus** heading to La Serena to drop you at the turn-off for Valle del Encanto, 19km north on Route 43. Do the same if heading out from La Serena. It's a flat 5km to the park. Alternatively, you can hire a **cab** (CH$15,000) in Ovalle. (Park open 8:15am-8:30pm, low season 8:15am-6pm. CH$300.)

PARQUE NACIONAL FRAY JORGE

A World Biosphere Reserve since 1977, Parque Nacional Fray Jorge is renowned for its most unique section: four square kilometers of Valdivian cloud forest, where fauna common to the cool, rainy regions of Valdivia and Patagonia in the south are surrounded by the cacti and sand more typical of the semi-arid desert conditions of Norte Chico. The cloud forest is sustained by the *camanchaca*, the dense fog that descends over the trees and provides the park with nearly 10

THE LOCAL STORY

A SNAKEBIT ROMANCE

Women: bored of a male traveling buddy? Bring him to the Valle del Encanto, turn yourself into a snake, and scare him away.

The Valle del Encanto, or "Valley of Enchantment," was named after one of the most mystical events in Chilean history. Back in the early 1800s, a local pastor was herding his goats when he was brought to a sudden stop on a ridge overlooking the valley. Below, in a well, the pastor saw a truly beautiful girl. He was mesmerized by her from the second he saw her in that well, bathing nude and juggling oranges. In an instant, he fell completely in love.

The pastor ran down the hill, goats in tow, scrambled over a large boulder, and pulled himself to the rock directly above the well. When he peered in, the girl had vanished. His heart sank as his dreams of a lifetime with the beauty disappeared.

Looking into the water, the pastor saw something moving, and again froze in shock. Beneath him, a 3 ft. viper slithered between two oranges. The snake looked into the man's eyes and began moving toward him as if to attack. Terrified of the rapidly approaching serpent, the priest forced himself to break away. He sprinted back to his village, where he told his story and proclaimed his love for the juggler. His legend gave a name to this enchanted place, and the Valle del Encanto lives on today.

AT A GLANCE	
AREA: 100 sq. km	**FEATURES:** 4 sq. km of Valdivian cloud-forest sustained by the mysterious *camanchaca*.
CLIMATE: Temperate; Feb. average 7°C, July average 23°C; annual rainfall 100cm, rainier in the cloud forest.	
	HIGHLIGHTS: Hiking Sendero el Bosque.
CAMPING: *Cabañas* and camping sites available at El Arrayancito.	**FEES:** CH$1600; children and students CH$600.
GATEWAYS: Ovalle, La Serena.	

times the average annual rainfall for the region (which averages around 10cm), and drops even more within the cloud forest. Although scientists have not been able to explain fully the presence of southern plant species in the deserts of Norte Chico, it is suspected that the cloud forest once stretched 800km along the Chilean coast but has disappeared due to climate change and/or human interference. The park encompasses 100 sq. km and extends from sea level to 600m. Temperatures average 7°C in July and 23°C in February at the coast. The cloud forest is cooler and quite wet—warm waterproof clothing is essential in the park.

Sendero el Bosque, a 1km trail through a forest speckled with labeled trees, is accessible just past the park administration. Past the hairpin turns on the road up is a 40min. walk up through the clouds and the moist cloud forest. The wooden platforms, funky rare trees, and seclusion within the clouds make the trail seem like something out of a fairy tale. Amidst the clouds it's almost impossible to see the ocean cliffs at the base of the mountain.

Camping is possible at **El Arrayancito ❷,** which consists of 13 sites administered by **Conaf** (CH$8000 per site). There are bathroom facilities and potable water at the campsite 5km from the **info center.** A cabaña ❸ that houses five people is also operated by Conaf. (CH$22,000; low season CH$18,000.)

Although there is no public transportation to get you to Fray Jorge, taxis offer fixed rates to and from the park. More conveniently, several travel agencies in La Serena lead daytrips to the park. If you're driving yourself, the turn-off for the park is at 389km on the Panamerican. From the turn-off, it's another 22km west to the park entrance. The drive to the park is very bumpy and rough on a car, and the drive from the park entrance to the top of the mountain on which the cloud forest resides is worse. (Park open M-Su 9am-4:30pm. CH$1600, children CH$600.)

TERMAS DE SOCOS

Thirty-four kilometers from Ovalle, where Route 43 meets the Panamerican, lies the **thermal spa** known as Termas de Socos. These thermal baths are said to have therapeutic healing properties, but are in reality just a relaxing indulgence. **Hotel Socos ❺** manages the baths and provides luxurious accommodations along with an **on-site camping area ❷.** A stay at the hotel is an expensive option, especially given that non-guests can use the **thermal baths.** While these baths are really just glorified bathtubs, their heat is immediately soothing. The hotel **pool** is at air-temperature and filled with the spring water for those who need cooler miracle healing to contrast the hot miracle healing of the thermal baths. The well-manicured gardens are a great place to sit after a thermal bath massage and the whole complex seems designed to make you forget your worries and relax in the soothing water. (☎982 505, in Santiago 2 363 336; www.termasocos.cl. 30min. in thermal baths CH$3700. Pool access CH$3600.

Dry massage CH$6500; underwater massage CH$9400. Camping with pool access and services CH$4500. Singles with full board, thermal baths, and access to the pool CH$40,000; doubles CH$74,000; triples CH$102,000.)

The turn-off for the Termas de Socos is at 370km on the Panamerican. **Buses** on the Panamerican heading to La Serena from Ovalle can drop off or pick up passengers. From the turn-off, it's another 1km to the spa. *Colectivos* from Ovalle will make the drive for CH$5000 if you want a private car. Hotel staff will pick up and drop off guests who call ahead.

LOS VILOS ☎53

Los Vilos's white-sand beach attracts visitors north from Valparaíso in the summer. Tourism brings much-needed income to Los Vilos, one of Chile's poorest cities. Its blue-collar residents are some of the nicest on the coast. Although the city's hustle and bustle is as chaotic as it is lively, Los Vilos is a pleasant place to spend a day or two before escaping to some of the area's quieter beach towns.

Most restaurants are on Caupolicán and along the beach on Allende/Costanera. **Restaurant Roma ❷,** Caupolicán 712, serves Italian food, including some vegetarian options, as well as ice cream. (☎542 701. Sandwiches CH$600-1700. Pizzas CH$1400-3000. Pastas CH$1900-2900. Ice cream CH$850-1600. Open daily 7am-2am. AmEx/MC/V.) **Restaurant Costanera ❸,** Puren 80, off Caupolicán one block toward the beach, has a wide selection of seafood and a dining room overlooking the beach. (☎541 257. Soups CH$600-3600. Appetizers CH$1990-3800. Omelettes CH$2100-3600. Entrees CH$1990-4690. Open daily 11am-midnight. AmEx/MC/V.) An **open-air market** on Galvarino, at the end of the street toward the Panamerican, two blocks from Caupolicán away from the ocean, sells fruits and vegetables. (Open Tu and Th 9am-2pm.)

Budget accommodations line Caupolicán and its side streets, providing plenty of inexpensive places to stay near the beach. ◪**Hostal El Conquistador ❸,** Caupolicán 210, at the end of the street near the dock, offers spacious rooms with private bath and TV that are almost like *cabañas*. Kitchen and laundry facilities available. (☎542 724. English and French spoken. Breakfast included. Jan.-Feb. singles CH$12,000; double CH$18,000; triples CH$24,000. Mar.-Dec. singles CH$10,000; doubles CH$16,000; triples CH$22,000.) **Hotel Bellavista ❷,** Rengo 20, off Caupolicán one block toward the beach, has cheaper digs close enough to the beach to hear the waves crash from the rooms. (☎541 073. Breakfast included. Singles CH$4000, with bath CH$5000; doubles CH$8000/CH$10,000; triples CH$12,000/CH$15,000; quads CH$16,000/CH$20,000.)

Los Vilos is connected to the Panamerican by **Caupolicán,** the town's main road where most services are located. One block toward shore, running along the beach parallel to Caupolicán, is **Allende/Costanera** (randomly known as either Allende or Costanera by locals and street signs alike). There is no tourist office in Los Vilos, but limited information on the city can be found at the *municipalidad,* Caupolicán 309. (☎541 105. Open M-F 8:45am-1pm and 2:15-6pm.) **BancoEstado,** Guacolda 98, at the corner of Caupolicán, has the only **ATM** in town. (☎541 060. Open M-F 10am-2pm.) The **police,** on Tucapel (☎540 028), can be reached from Caupolicán by walking four blocks up Rengo away from the beach and turning left onto Tucapel. **Lavandería Victoria,** Lautaro 350, is at the end of Guacolda one block off Caupolicán away from the ocean. (☎548 006. Wash, dry, and press CH$3000. Open M-Sa 9:30am-1:15pm and 3:30-7:15pm.) **Farmacia Nueva Estrella,** Caupolicán 789, sells basic supplies. (☎541 085. Open daily 9:30am-10:30pm.) **Hospital San Pedro,** on Arauco at the corner of Rengo (☎540 061), is five blocks away, walking off Caupolicán away from the ocean. **Barlett@.net,**

Guacolda 110, one block off Caupolicán away from the ocean, has **Internet access.** (☎541 055 or 09 612 7235. CH$600 per hr. Open M-F 9am-9pm, Sa 10am-9pm, Su 3-9pm.) The **post office** is at the corner of Galvarino and Lincoyan, across from the Plaza de Armas. From Caupolicán, walk one block up Guacola away from the ocean, turn right on Lautaro, and then left on Lincoyan.

The **Terminal de Buses,** on the corner of Allende and Costanera (☎541 197), is on the dock at the end of town, two blocks past the end of Caupolicán. **Pullman Bus,** at the bus station (☎541 108), runs to Pichidangui (15min., noon, CH$150). **Tur Bus,** Panamericana Norte Km225 (☎542 814), runs to La Serena (3hr., every hr. 10:40am-9:30pm, CH$4500) and Santiago (3hr., every hr. 7am-7:40pm, CH$3000) via Pichidangui (15min., CH$500). Buses following the Panamerican typically drop passengers off on the highway across from Tur Bus, where *colectivos* wait to take them to the center of town (CH$800). **Taxis** (☎542 724) line up on Caupolicán and also make the trip to Pichidangui (CH$1000).

PICHIDANGUI   ☎53

Pichidangui is a dusty small town that attracts as many horses as it does people. Just outside of Los Vilos, it certainly is a worthwhile detour from the Panamerican. Pichidangui's calm white-sand beach runs parallel to Costanera, the town's main road, and is accessible from the *caleta* at the end of Costanera. The *caleta* also hosts an artisan's fair. (Open daily 10am-6pm.)

Restaurants serve mainly seafood, but vegetarians can find cheese empanadas (CH$500) at the stands along the *caleta* on Costanera. **Restaurant Antulauquen ❸,** on the corner of Costanera and Atún, has a large dining room offering ocean views. (☎531 105. Appetizers CH$1800-4000. Soups CH$2400-3200. Seafood entrees CH$3000-5400. Meat entrees CH$2300-4800. *Menú* CH$3800. Open daily Jan.-Feb. 9am-midnight.) **Restaurant Pichidangui ❷,** on Costanera at the bus stop, is a popular local lunch spot with an outdoor patio. (☎531 138. Soups CH$2300-3000. Appetizers CH$2500-4000. Seafood entrees CH$2300-6000. Meat entrees CH$2000-11,000. Open daily Jan.-Feb. 9am-midnight; Mar.-Dec. 10am-11pm.)

Lodging options are limited; if there's no vacancy, look for "arrienda" signs. **Residencial Lucero ❸,** on the corner of El Dorado and Albacora, has clean, simple rooms tended by a kind elderly woman. (☎531 106. Breakfast included. CH$6000 per person, with bath CH$7000.) **Motel Cabañas El Marino ❹,** on the corner of El Atún and El Toyo, rents luxurious *cabañas*, all with kitchen, private bath, and three beds. (☎531 287. *Cabañas* Jan.-Feb. CH$35,000, Mar.-Dec. CH$20,000.)

Buses either arrive in town at the end of Costanera, by the *caleta* and the beach, or on the Panamerican, where *colectivos* shuttle to town (CH$250). **Pullman Bus,** on Costanera at the bus stop, departs from the Panamerican. (☎531 138. Open daily 10:30am-10pm.) Pullman runs to **Santiago** (2½hr., every hr. 6:30am-8:30pm, CH$3500), via **La Ligua** (1hr., CH$1000). **Tur Bus,** on El Escorpión off Costanera, departs from the bus stop on Costanera (☎531 800; open daily 8am-11pm) and sends buses to **Los Vilos** (15min., 5 per day 7:10am-7:40pm, CH$500) and **Santiago** (2½hr., 2 per day noon-6:50pm, CH$3500) via La Ligua (1hr., CH$1000). There are **no banks, ATMs, or currency exchange** in Pichidangui. Services in town include: **police,** on La Aguia (☎531 109), and a small **clinic,** on La Tunina (☎531 023) off Costanera. A **centro de llamadas,** El Dorado 198, one block away from the beach up Costanera, has **Internet access.** (☎09 342 4048. CH$500 per hr. Open daily 4-10pm.)

MIDDLE CHILE

Between the dusty desert landscapes and rural villages of the north and the harsh, rocky terrain of the south lies a region characterized by fertility. As the geographic and economic heart of the nation, rife with bustling metropolises, resplendent valleys, peaceful beaches, not to mention plentiful *turistas*, Middle Chile stands as not only a firm reminder of Chile's geographical wondrousness, but also as a staunch figurehead for the rapid economic development experienced by Chile in recent years. As a result of this rapid economic development, Middle Chile has ventured forth into the realm of tourism, putting much of its tourist-generated wealth back into the very industries that sustain this new rapid and growing influx of visitors.

In addition to being the richest, most populated, and most developed region in the country, Middle Chile is also perhaps the most diverse in its array of activities and opportunities for travelers. From the snowy slopes of **Chapa Verde**—perfect for skiing—to the hot springs at the **Termas de Chillán**—perfect for relaxing—the region's myriad attractions cater to both thrill-seekers and chill-seekers alike. The plethora of beaches along the coast reflect this phenomenon as well—beach-goers can catch a powerful wave at the **Punta de Lobos** near **Pichilemu,** or work on their tans on the more serene and less-touristed beaches of the *litoral central*.

As a cultural centerpiece, Middle Chile is also home to a variety of sights whose significance has stood the test of time. Middle Chile provides visitors the opportunity to view the personal collections of Chile's literary legend, Pablo Neruda, while traversing the streets of **Valparaíso,** or travel to the resting place of the signed Act of Independence in the **Museo O'Higginiano** in **Talca.** Many travelers even choose to re-enact the historic journey of explorer García Hurtado de Mendoza, and take a journey from the Pacific coast, through the Andes, and into **Mendoza, Argentina.**

Yet, while Middle Chile is indeed a place to appreciate the present and the past, in the end, it is more the future that seems to be Middle Chile's concern—the future of the nation as a whole. While in the past, the nation's economy has focused largely upon mining, agriculture, and fishing, the industries of tourism and wine production have grown lately in size and importance. And from the tourist-grabbing "vineyard of the sea," **Viña del Mar,** to the wine-producing vineyards of the Central Valley, Middle Chile has taken this fact to heart. So toast the past and the future with a glass of Chilean wine from the **Colchagua Valley** and put on your dancing duds for a night on the town—after all, it's important not to forget that Middle Chile is bound to show you a good time in the present.

HIGHLIGHTS OF MIDDLE CHILE

WANDER through the eclectic collections of famed poet Pablo Neruda at **La Sebastiana** (p. 248) in **Valparaíso,** as well as in his house on **Isla Negra** (p. 260).

ZOOM down the slopes of **Volcán Chillán** or relax in the soothing, mineral-enriched waters at the **Termas de Chillán** (p. 305).

FLOAT in the teacup pools of **Reserva Nacional Radal Siete Tazas** (p. 293).

CUT through the vicious waves of the **Punta de Lobos** near **Pichilemu** (p. 285).

GRAB a thick slice of history or an even thicker slice of choice beef in **Mendoza, Argentina** (p. 268).

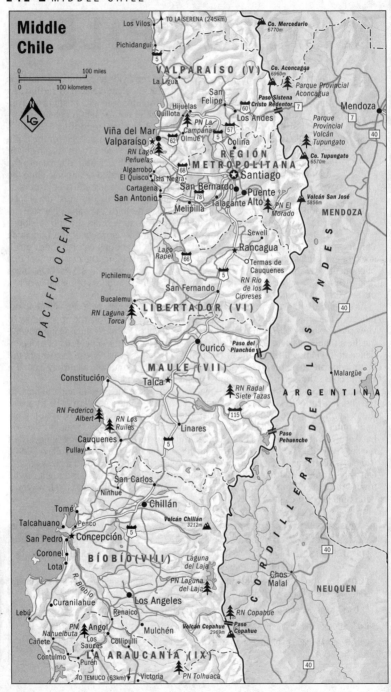

Middle Chile

0   100 miles

0   100 kilometers

N
LG

VALPARAÍSO (V)

TO LA SERENA (245km)

Los Vilos

Pichidangui

Co. Mercedario
6770m

Co. Aconcagua
6960m

Parque Provincial
Aconcagua

La Ligua

San
Felipe

Paso Sistena
Cristo Redentor

7

Mendoza

Hijuelas   60

Quillota   Los Andes   7

PN La
Campana   57   Parque
Provincial
Viña del Mar ★   Olmué   5   Volcán
Valparaíso ★   Colina   Tupungato

RN Lago   62
Peñuelas   **REGIÓN**

Algarrobo   68   **METROPOLITANA**   Co. Tupungato
6570m
El Quisco Isla Negra   ✪ Santiago

Cartagena   San Bernardo   **MENDOZA**

San Antonio   78   Puente
Melipilla   Talagante Alto
Volcán San José
5856m

PN El
Morado

Sewell

Lago
Rapel   66   ★ Rancagua

Termas de
Cauquenes

Pichilemu   5

San Fernando   RN Río
de los
Cipreses

Bucalemu

RN Laguna   **LIBERTADOR (VI)**
Torca

Curicó   Paso del
Planchón

MAULE (VII)   **A R G E N T I N A**

Constitución

Talca ★   Malargüe

RN Radal
Siete Tazas

RN Federico   115
Albert   RN Los
Ruiles   Paso
Pehuenche
Linares

Cauquenes

Pullay   5

San Carlos

Ninhue

Tomé   Chillán

Talcahuano   Penco

San Pedro ★ Concepción   Volcán Chillán
5   3212m

Coronel   40

Lota   **BÍOBÍO (VIII)**   Laguna
del Laja

R. Bíobío   PN Laguna
del Laja

Curanilahue   Los Ángeles   Chos
Lebú   Renaico   Malal   **NEUQUEN**

PN   Angol   Mulchén   RN Copahue
Nahuelbuta
Cañete   Los
Sauces   Collipulli   Volcán Copahue   Paso
2969m   Copahue
Contulmo   Purén   **LA ARAUCANÍA (IX)**

TO TEMUCO (63km)   Victoria   PN Tolhuaca   40

P A C I F I C   O C E A N

C O R D I L L E R A   D E   L O S   A N D E S

THE COASTAL RESORTS

VALPARAÍSO ☎ 32

Valparaíso (pop. 275,000), Chile's principal port city, has a contrasting character: old and new, high hills and low beaches, rich patrons and poor workers walk its streets. At first glance, Valpo (as it is affectionately known) looks like a haphazard collection of buildings and ships. Houses cling precariously to hillsides, upscale hotels surround *El Congreso*, and small fishing boats fight for harbor space between looming Chilean naval vessels. Despite the opening of the Panama Canal, Valpo has remained vibrant—it is the proud home of Chile's navy and the keeper of its naval history. A major earthquake devastated the city in 1906, but luckily, Valparaíso's signature system of *ascensores* (funicular lifts), which shuttle people between the lowlands and the city's many hills, managed to remain intact. *Porteños*, Valparaíso's residents, are proud of their heritage and work hard to preserve their diverse cultural monuments. Backpackers are drawn here by the city's chaotic beauty and its active arts scene, and many find it difficult ever to leave.

⌐ TRANSPORTATION

Flights: There is no airport in Valparaíso; visitors fly into Santiago's airport and get to and from Valparaíso by shuttle bus (☎212 028; 2hr., daily 5:20am, CH$2700). **Lan-Chile,** Esmeralda 1048 (☎251 441), has an office near Plaza Aníbal Pinto. Open M-F 9am-6:30pm and Sa 10am-1pm. AmEx/MC/V.

Trains: Estación Puerto, Errázuriz 711 (☎214 562), at Muelle Prat, facing Plaza Sotomayor. Open daily 6:30am-10:30pm. Trains go to **Limache** (1½hr., every 30min. 6:30am-10pm, CH$550) via **Viña del Mar** (CH$250).

Buses: Estación Rodoviario, Pedro Montt 2800 (☎939 646), at the corner of Rawson. Valparaíso's main terminal is at the western end of El Plan across from the Congreso Nacional. Open daily 5:30am-11:30pm. A second **bus station,** Molina 380 (☎210 273), serves the northern towns of La Ligua and Los Vilos.

Tur Bus, in Estación Rodoviario (☎212 028 or 221 973), goes to: **Antofagasta** (18hr., 2 per day 7:45am-11pm, CH$18,000) via **La Serena** (7hr., CH$8900); **Arica** (30hr., 7:45am, CH$10,000) via **Iquique** (27hr., CH$20,000); **Concepción** (9hr., 3 per day 9am-10pm, CH$9900); **Pucón** (11hr., 9pm, CH$16,400) via **Villarrica** (10½hr., CH$16,000); **Santiago** (2hr., every 15min. 5:30am-10pm, CH$2700); **Temuco** (10hr., 3 per day 7:45-11pm, CH$15,500). Open M-F 5am-10pm, Sa 6am-10pm, Su 6:30am-10pm. MC/V.

Pullman Bus, in Estación Rodoviario (☎253 125 or 216 163), sends buses to: **Antofagasta** (12hr., 4 per day 7:30am-10:30pm, CH$23,000) via **Copiapó** (9hr., CH$13,000); **Arica** (28hr., 9:30am, CH$25,000); **Cartagena** (2hr., every 20min. 6:20am-10pm, CH$2000) via **Algarrobo** (1½hr., CH$1500), **El Quisco** (1½hr., CH$1500), **Isla Negra** (1½hr., CH$1500), **Peñuelas** (30min., CH$500), and **Punta de Tralca** (1½hr., CH$1500); **Concepción** (9hr., 9:45am, CH$8000); **Iquique** (24hr., 3 per day 7:15am-5:15pm, CH$24,000); **La Serena** (6hr., 7 per day 7:30am-10:45pm, CH$8000); **Puerto Montt** (13hr., 6pm, CH$16,000) via **Osorno** (12hr., CH$14,000); **Santiago** (2hr., every 15min. 6:15am-10:30pm, CH$2600). Open daily 6am-10pm. MC/V.

 Travelers report petty crime in the area around Plaza Sotomayor. Pickpocketing can happen at any time, day or night, as do classic cons (see **Possessions and Valuables,** p. 24). Leave valuables locked up somewhere safe, keep to well-lit areas, and, if at all possible, walk with someone else when going out at night.

MIDDLE CHILE

Valparaíso

TO VIÑA DEL MAR (9km)

400 yards
400 meters

Bahía de Valparaíso

TO PLAYA ANCHA

SEE VALPARAÍSO OLD CITY DETAIL MAP pp. 245

Baron Dock

Estación Baron

Recintos Portuarios

Prat Dock

Streets and features:

Yolanda, Castro, Toconal, Blanco Viel, Gonzáles, Nelson, Diego Portales, España, Errázuriz, Brasil, Ercilla, Mitre, Atralia, Santa Justina, Santa Clarissa, Eduardo Jenner, 12 de Febrero, Casablanca, Argentina, Almirante Simpson, Rancagua, Retamo, Almirante Barroso, Colón, Van Buren, Garibaldi, Independencia, Francia, Freire, Rodríguez, Yungay, Chacabuco, Pedro Montt, Cruz, Parque Italia, Las Heras, Buenos Aires, Carrera, Edwards, Molina, Huito, Yerbas Buenas, Mackenna, Guillermo Rivera, Condell, Bellavista, Pudeto, Donoso, Ramírez, Esperanza, Cumming, O'Higgins, Pajonto, Papudo, Templeman, San Enrique Montt, Monte Alegre, Lautaro Rosas, Urriola, Almirante Montt, Cienfuegos, Blanco, Cochrane, Prat, Serrano, Bustamante, Wheelwright, Echaurren, Santo Domingo, Sucre, J. Ortuzar, Paseo 21 de Mayo, Artillería, Cabrales, Castillo, Jara, Vivera, Merlet, Aduanilla, Millanne, Cintura, José Tomás Ramos, William Lyon, Boccacio, Tomás Pérez, Mackay, Guillermo Munich, Alemania, L. Leona, Cumming, Newman, A D'Halmar, Ferrari, L. La Torre, Señoret

Cerros (hills):

CERRO BARÓN, CERRO LECHEROS, CERRO RODRÍGUEZ, CERRO POLANCO, CERRO DE LA MERCED, CERRO MONJAS, CERRO MARIPOSA, CERRO FLORIDA, CERRO BELLAVISTA, CERRO PANTEON, CERRO CARCEL, CERRO LA LOMA, CERRO BISMARK, CERRO MIRAFLORES, CERRO CHAPARRO, CERRO CORDILLERA, CERRO SANTO DOMINGO, CERRO ARTILLERÍA, CERRO ALEGRE, CERRO CONCEPCIÓN

Points of interest:

Ascensor Polanco, Ascensor Larraín, Ascensor Lechero, Ascensor Baron, Iglesia Doce Apostoles, Congreso Nacional, Estación Rodoviario, Rawson, PLAZA O'HIGGINS, Best Rent A Car, Teatro Municipal, Victoria, Hospital Carlos van Buren, Uruguay, Morris, Simón Bolívar, Cine Hoyts, San Ignacio, Colón Rent A Car, Ascensor Monjas, Ascensor Mariposa, Ascensor Florida, Inglesa, Museo del Aire Abierto, Santa Isabel, VICTORIA Market, PLAZA ECUADOR, Cementerio Católico, CEMENTERIO DISIDENTES, TO LA SEBASTIANA, Ascensor El Peral, Estación Puerto, Mercado Puerto, PLAZA SOTOMAYOR, PLAZA DE LA JUSTICIA, Museo Naval y Marítimo, Inf. Hyatt

TAXI

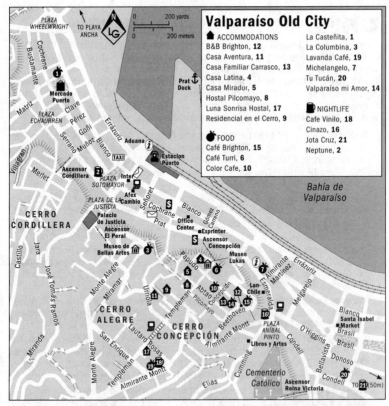

Valparaíso Old City

■ ACCOMMODATIONS
B&B Brighton, **12**
Casa Aventura, **11**
Casa Familiar Carrasco, **13**
Casa Latina, **4**
Casa Mirador, **5**
Hostal Pilcomayo, **8**
Luna Sonrisa Hostal, **17**
Residencial en el Cerro, **9**

● FOOD
Café Brighton, **15**
Café Turri, **6**
Color Cafe, **10**

La Casteñita, **1**
La Columbina, **3**
Lavanda Café, **19**
Michelangelo, **7**
Tu Tucán, **20**
Valparaíso mi Amor, **14**

▮ NIGHTLIFE
Cafe Vinilo, **18**
Cinazo, **16**
Jota Cruz, **21**
Neptune, **2**

Bahía de
Valparaíso

Ascensores: The city's lifts are either municipal (CH$100 up, CH$100 down) or private (CH$120 up, CH$100 down). Municipal lifts include Barón, El Peral, Polanco, Reina Victoria, and San Agustín. The others (see above) are private. Open daily 7am-11pm.

Buses: Valparaíso is small enough to get around easily on foot, but local buses are plentiful. Destinations and fares are prominently posted in front windows. *Micros* to **Viña del Mar** (20min., CH$330) leave along Errázuriz; look for a sign reading "Viña." Buses labeled "Puerto Montt" or "Rodoviario" pass by the main bus station (CH$170); those also saying "Aduana" will pass through downtown and Plaza Sotomayor all the way to the red customs house (CH$170). Green "Verde Mar" buses labeled "D" or "O" will head up Alemania to **La Sebastiana,** Pablo Neruda's house (CH$170).

Taxis: *Colectivos* have set routes and fares, functioning just like local buses; these cabs wait until they are full before leaving and are cheaper than normal taxis. Both *colectivos* and normal taxis can be found at Valparaíso's many plazas. Regular taxis can be called from the following places around town: **Estación Rodoviario** (☎253 451 or 222 960), **Pedro Montt** (☎217 400), **Plaza Aduana** (☎256 215), **Plaza Aníbal Pinto** (☎214 695), **Plaza O'Higgins** (☎214 624), and **Plaza Sotomayor** (☎214 706).

Ferries: Boat tours of the bay leave from Muelle Prat. Schedules vary depending on the weather and the season. 30min. tours CH$1000-1500 per person.

Car Rental: Best Rent A Car, Victoria 2681 (☎212 885 or 250 868). Open M-F 8:30am-7:30pm, Sa 9:30am-6pm, Su 10am-1pm. MC/V. **Colón Rent A Car,** Colón 2581 (☎256 529 or 250 868). Open M-F 9am-7:30pm, Sa 9:30am-2pm. MC/V.

MIDDLE CHILE

✦ 🔂 ORIENTATION AND PRACTICAL INFORMATION

Getting around Valparaíso's confusing streets can be a bit intimidating. Valparaíso is wedged between hills and the ocean, so the easiest way to stay oriented is to find one or the other. The bus station is on the eastern edge of town in the business district, **El Plan,** which follows a grid. All of the city's downtown hills can be reached by a system of 15 *ascensores* (funicular lifts) or winding roads and staircases. Most budget accommodations are on **Cerro Concepción,** accessible from **Prat,** and **Cerro Alegre,** accessible from the end of Prat on Plaza de la Justicia.

Tourist Office: Condell 1490 (☎939 108), near Plaza Aníbal Pinto, has free maps. Open M-F 8:30am-2pm and 3:30-5:30pm. The **branch** office, on Muelle Prat (☎939 489), has longer hours, free maps, and information on sights, tours, nightlife, and more. English spoken. Open daily 10am-2pm and 3-6pm. Another **branch,** Pedro Montt 2800 (☎939 669), at Estación Rodoviario. Open M-Sa 10am-6pm, Su 10am-1pm.

Tours: Casa Aventura, Gálvez 11 (☎755 963; www.casaventura.cl), p. 247, offers city tours (2hr.; 2 per day 10am-3pm; CH$5000 per person) and **horseback riding** (departs 9am, returns 7pm; CH$25,000 per person).

Bank: Banks lie on Prat near Plaza Sotomayor. **BancoEstado,** Prat 656 (☎265 000), has good exchange rates and a **24hr. ATM.** Open M-F 9am-2pm. **Scotiabank,** Prat 762 (☎600 670 0500; fax 209 722). Open M-F 9am-2pm. More **24hr. ATMs** are at **Banco Edwards,** Cochrane 785, and **BCI,** Cochrane 820, both at the corner of Urriloa, 1 block from Plaza Sotomayor.

Currency Exchange: Exprinter, Prat 895 (☎217 010), where Prat and Cochrane converge, across from Ascensor Concepción. Open M-F 9am-2pm and 3-6pm. **Inter,** Plaza Sotomayor 11 (☎255 892). Open M-F 9am-6pm, Sa 10am-1pm.

Language Classes: Casa Aventura (p. 247), offers Spanish lessons to travelers. 1hr. lessons CH$5000. 1-week introductory classes CH$75,000. 2-week intensive course CH$250,000, with homestay CH$360,000; 3-week intensive course CH$375,000/ CH$545,000; 4-week intensive course CH$500,000/CH$725,000.

English-Language Bookstore: Cummings 1 Libros y Artes, Subida Cummings 1 (☎09 606 1665; www.cummings1.cl), at Plaza Aníbal Pinto, has books in English, French, German, and Spanish, and holds small art exhibitions. Open M-Th noon-2:30pm and 3:30-9pm, F noon-2:30pm and 5-10pm, Sa 11am-2pm and 7-10pm.

Market: Santa Isabel, Pedro Montt 1819 (☎212 640) and Brasil 1449 (☎215 659), sell groceries. Open daily 8:30am-10pm. MC/V.

Laundromat: Inglesa, Pedro Montt 2065 (☎255 625). Open M-F 9am-1:30pm and 4-8:30pm, Sa 9am-1:30pm. **Lavanda Café** (p. 248), on Cerro Alegre, also has a cafe/art gallery. Wash and dry small load CH$3200, large load CH$3800.

Police: ☎133. Buenos Aires 750 (☎217 864). **Policía de Investigaciones de Chile,** Uruguay 174 (☎253 001), and Plazuela San Francisco (☎220 850), are better suited to handle any problems travelers may encounter.

Pharmacies: Cruz Verde, Pedro Montt 1903 (☎233 361). Open 24hr. MC/V. **Farmacias Ahumada,** Pedro Montt 1881 (☎215 524). Open 24hr. MC/V.

Hospital: Ambulance ☎131. **Hospital Carlos Van Buren,** San Ignacio 725 (☎204 000).

Fax Office: Office Center, Cochrane 841 (☎254 717). Open M-F 8:30am-7:30pm, Sa 10am-1pm.

Internet Access: World Next Door Café, Blanco 692 (☎459 555; www.valparaiso.worldnextdoorcafe.com), 1 block off Plaza Sotomayor. 10am-1pm CH$350 per hr.; 1-8pm CH$900 per hr. Open M-F 10am-8pm, Sa 10am-4pm. **Infinito Empresas,** Templeman 612 (☎963 552), on Cerro Concepción. CH$150 per 15min., CH$400 per hr. Open M-F 11am-9pm, Sa noon-9pm, Su noon-8pm.

Post Office: Prat 856 (☎256 786). Open M-F 8:30am-6pm, Sa 8:30am-1pm. **Branch,** Plaza Sotomayor 95 (☎213 654). Open M-F 8:30am-6pm, Sa 8:30am-1pm.

ACCOMMODATIONS

For a major city, Valpo's prices are surprisingly reasonable. High-end hotels, catering to visiting government officials, can be found near **El Congreso** and the bus terminal. Most budget accommodations are on **Cerro Concepción** and **Cerro Alegre.** For a more scenic setting, try staying on one of the *cerros.*

Luna Sonrisa Hostal, Templeman 833 (☎734 117; www.lunasonrisa.cl), on Cerro Alegre. There's no sign, so look for the door number. The private lockers in the dorms, the open kitchen, and the breakfast with homemade jam and real coffee make you feel right at home. The location on a quiet street makes this a great place to get some rest. Bright rooms, most with shared bath. English spoken. Breakfast included. Dorms CH$6000; singles CH$8000; doubles CH$14,000, with bath CH$19,000. ❷

Casa Aventura, Gálvez 11 (☎755 963; www.casaventura.cl), off Urriola on Cerro Concepción. Casa Aventura's owners go out of their way to provide opportunities for their guests, organizing tours and language classes (p. 246). Quirky and comfortable region-themed rooms, all with shared bath. Kitchen for guest use. English spoken. Breakfast included. Reception 8am-8pm. Dorms CH$6000; doubles CH$12,000. ❷

Casa Mirador, Abtao 457 (☎257 098), off Templeman on Cerro Concepción. Comfortable mattresses and good water pressure make Mirador a crowd pleaser. All rooms have shared bath. Breakfast included. Singles CH$8000; doubles CH$16,000; triples CH$24,000; quads CH$32,000. ❸

Casa Latina, Papudo 462 (☎494 622; casalatina@vtr.net), on Cerro Concepción. A great location, bright rooms, and soft pillows make Casa Latina a beacon for backpackers. Kitchen available. Breakfast included. Singles CH$9000. AmEx/MC/V. ❸

Residencial en el Cerro, Pierre Loti 51 (☎495 298; alekos_@hotmail.com), off Templeman on Cerro Concepción. Has quiet rooms closest to all the action on Concepción and Alegre. 10min. free Internet per day; CH$600 per additional hr. Breakfast CH$1000. Jan.-Feb. dorms CH$9000; singles CH$9000; doubles CH$18,000. Mar.-Dec. dorms CH$7000; singles CH$7000; doubles CH$14,000. ❸

Hostal Pilcomayo, Pilcomayo 491 (☎251 075; www.hostalpilcomayo.cl), at the corner of Templeman on Cerro Concepción. Decent rooms, all with shared bath, on the scenic *cerro.* Free Internet. Kitchen for guest use. Breakfast included. Singles CH$6000; doubles CH$12,000; triples CH$18,000. AmEx/MC/V. ❷

Casa Familiar Carrasco, Abtao 668 (☎210 737), off Templeman on Cerro Concepción. Bright rooms in a quiet family home, all with shared bath. Breakfast included. Singles CH$8000; doubles CH$16,000; triples CH$24,000; quads CH$32,000. ❸

B&B Brighton, Paseo Atkinson 151-153 (☎223 513 or 598 802; www.brighton.cl), on Cerro Concepción. A great choice for an upscale splurge, with exceptional rooms, some with views of the lower city and the port, all with private bath and cable TV. Breakfast included. Doubles CH$30,000. AmEx/MC/V. ❺

FOOD

Most mid- and upper-range restaurants specialize in seafood, and even the most basic establishments carry their fair share of clams *a la macha.* Yet seafood isn't the only option; many places have creative menus with vegetarian options. Fresh vegetables and cheap seafood are easily found at **Mercado Puerto** (p. 249).

Michelangelo, Esmeralda 1099 (☎232 918), at the corner of Almirante Martinez, 1 block from Plaza Aníbal Pinto. The traffic in Michelangelo testifies to the popularity of its delicious

Italian food. It's easy to enjoy the culinary magic with the relaxed but elegant atmosphere. Pasta CH$2500-3500. Meat entrees CH$2900-4500. Salads CH$1200-2900. Open M-F 2pm-1:30am, Sa 1pm-2am, Su 1-9:30pm. AmEx/MC/V. ❷

Valparaíso mi Amor, Papudo 612 (☎749 992), off Templeman on Cerro Concepción. Art gallery, bookstore, Internet cafe, bar—this place does it all. The owner, an amateur cinematographer, also shows foreign films (daily 9:30pm; CH$1000 includes 1 drink). Internet CH$700 per hr. Entrees CH$2000-5000. Live music F-Sa 10:30pm. Open daily Jan.-Feb. noon-5pm and 8pm-3am; Mar.-Dec. Th-Sa 8pm-3am. ❷

La Columbina, Pasaje Apolo 77-91 and Paseo Yugoslavo 15 (☎236 254 or 236 226), across from the Museo de Bellas Artes in Cerro Alegre. This 3-story restaurant/bar built into the hillside is one of Cerro Alegre's gems, with deliciously simple dishes. Oysters with olive oil, garlic, and goat cheese CH$7400. *Tapas* CH$8000 for 2 people, CH$12,000 for 4. Entrees CH$6200-8500. Live music F-Su 11pm. Open Su-M 9am-4pm, Tu-Th 9am-midnight, F-Sa 9am-2am. AmEx/MC/V. ❸

Color Café, Papudo 526 (☎09 007 0217), off Templeman on Cerro Concepción. A small *salón de té* serving by the cup (CH$500-700) and by the pot (CH$2000-2500). *Tabla vegetariana* CH$4500. Open Tu-Th 9am-10pm, F-Sa 9am-1am, Su 9am-10pm. ❸

Café Brighton, Paseo Atkinson 151-153 (☎223 513 or 598 802; www.brighton.cl), off Concepción on Cerro Concepción. Looking down over city, the cafe's outdoor patio offers wonderful views. Coffee CH$600-1200. Crepes CH$2500-3000. Entrees CH$4800-5200. *Menú* (includes drink, appetizer, entree, dessert, and coffee) CH$6200. *Menú turístico* (includes drink, entree, and dessert) CH$4200. Live music F-Sa midnight. Open Su-Th 10am-1am, F-Sa 10am-3am. AmEx/MC/V. ❷

Café Turri, Templeman 147 (☎259 198), on Cerro Concepción, left of the exit of Ascensor Concepción. Turri is a lively place to take *onces* (CH$4200 for fruit juice, ice cream, sandwich, cake, and tea or coffee) after a day walking in the hills. The attentiveness of the officious staff corresponds to the price tag on some of the dishes. Salads CH$1100-3600. Sandwiches CH$2300-2950. Entrees CH$5550-10,050. AmEx/MC/V. ❸

Lavanda Café, Almirante Montt 454 (☎591 473), on Cerro Alegre. This laundromat/cafe is a great place to sip coffee and look at art while you wait for your clothes to dry. Coffee CH$400-1000. Fruit juices CH$500. Wash and dry small load CH$3200, large load CH$3800. Open M-Sa 10am-2pm and 4-8pm. ❶

La Casteñita, Blanco 86 (☎591 945), at the corner of Valdivia near the Mercado Puerto. Chefs prepare the seafood here in a palm-covered *cabaña* in the center of the room. Entrees CH$4500-6500. Open daily 9am-8pm. ❸

Tu Tucán, Condell 1391 (☎253 406), and Pedro Montt 1639 (☎596 163). A relaxed restaurant serving lighter fare. Each intimate booth is adorned with a stained glass hanging lamp. Sandwiches CH$690-1990. Entrees CH$1250-1950. Pizzas CH$1450-2150. Open daily 9am-1am. AmEx/MC/V. ❷

⊙ SIGHTS

Typical for haphazard Valparaíso, the houses hanging from the *cerros* are a sight themselves, as are the 15 *ascensores* rising among them. Not to be overshadowed by these encroaching hills, the port is an area of constant activity, and features the **Museo Naval y Marítimo** on the Cerro Artillería overlooking the port. (*☎283 749. Open Tu-Su 10am-5:30pm. CH$500, children and seniors CH$200*)

▧ **LA SEBASTIANA.** Pablo Neruda's *casa en el aire* (house in the air) sits high above the city on Cerro Florida. From here, the grime and noise of downtown melt away and what remains is the essence of Valparaíso's colorful architecture and sprawling port. Neruda moved here in 1961 and named his home after the architect who built it. Although he spent more time at his other homes (see **Isla Negra,** p. 260, and **Museo La Chascona,** p. 121), La Sebastiana is filled with his odd collections and eclectic furniture. There are no guided tours, but ask at the entrance for an English explanation of the rooms. *(Ferrari 692, off the 6900 block of Alemania, on Cerro Florida. From Plaza Sotomayor take any Verde Mar bus labeled "D" or "O" and ask to be let off at the "Casa de Neruda."* ☎ *256 606 or 233 759. Open Mar.-Dec. Tu-F 10:30am-2pm and 3:30-6pm, Sa-Su 10:30am-6pm. CH$2000, students and seniors Tu-F CH$1000, children free.)*

MUSEO DEL AIRE ABIERTO. Started by art students and finished by professional artists, the 20 abstract murals painted on Cerro Bellavista's stone walls, known as the "open sky museum," have seen better days. The murals are weather-worn, and the neighborhood is a bit dilapidated. Still, this is one of Valparaíso's signature sights—a testament to its active arts scene. Note that Cerro Bellavista is reportedly unsafe at night, and the small streets can be confusing, so it's best to visit during the day. *(The murals are on a series of paseos and subidas off Aldunate and Ferrari.)*

MUSEO LUKAS. This museum houses the art of renowned newspaper satirist and cartoonist LUKAS (originally Renzo Antonio Giovanni Pecchenino Raggi), who moved from Italy to Valparaíso at age one and remained here for most of his life. If you understand Spanish, the cartoons will make you smile, but even without the captions, they are amusing. They sell an explanatory book (CH$5000) in English and Spanish. *(Paseo Gervasoni 448, on Cerro Concepción, across from Ascensor Concepción.* ☎ *221 344. Open Tu-Su 10:30am-2pm and 3-6pm. CH$500.)*

PLAZA SOTOMAYOR. This plaza is probably Valparaíso's most recognizable tourist destination. The blue facade of the ex-*Intendencia* of Valparaíso (now the naval headquarters) encloses one end of the plaza. Facing it is the main attraction, the **Monumento a los Héroes de Iquique.** The statue is dedicated to the martyrs of the War of the Pacific, paying particular homage to national hero Arturo Prat, whose remains are interred beneath the statue and for whom an eternal flame burns at all times. *(Opposite the train station and Muelle Prat. Flag lowering ceremony daily 6pm.)*

MERCADO PUERTO. This two-story market is a great place to grab a cheap lunch at one of the seafood restaurants upstairs or to ogle the variety of shellfish and fish culled from the bay that sit glistening in beds of ice. There are also stalls with other foods such as cheeses and fresh vegetables. *(Entrances on Cochrane and Blanco between San Martín and Valdivia. Open M-Th 8am-7pm, F-Sa 8am-7:30pm, Su 8am-5pm.)*

🎭 ENTERTAINMENT

Arguably the cultural capital of Chile, Valparaíso has something for everyone— from those looking to check out a *fútbol* match or watch international films to aficionados who want to catch some live music.

Santiago Wanderers (www.santiagowanderers.cl), Valparaíso's *fútbol* team, play in the Estado Municipal, on González de Hontaneda, northwest of town in Playa Ancha. To get there, catch any Verde Mar bus labeled "N," "P," "L," or "M" from anywhere along Blanco or Pedro Montt. Buses labeled "N" and "P" stop directly in front of the stadium; those labeled "L" and "M" stop a block away from the stadium. For schedules and prices, check out the website.

Valparaíso mi Amor (p. 248) is an art gallery that screens international cinema, and also serves as a cafe and bar. Movies daily 9:30pm; CH$1000 includes 1 drink.

Cine Hoyts, Pedro Montt 2177 (☎ 594 709), has eight screens playing first-run American movies with Spanish subtitles. Shows noon-10pm. CH$5500. MC/V.

Teatro Municipal, Uruguay 410 (☎ 214 654 or 218 462), on Plaza O'Higgins, frequently hosts plays and concerts. Check the tourist office for calendar of events. Prices vary.

🔌 NIGHTLIFE

Neighboring Viña del Mar has a reputation for hot nights that Valparaíso just can't touch, but, as with all else, nightlife in Valparaíso has character. Most restaurants become pubs at night, where locals and backpackers mingle over beer.

■ **Jota Cruz,** Condell 1466 (☎211 225), 3 blocks from Plaza Victoria down a small alley at the big green Corona sign. The birthplace of Valparaíso's signature dish, *chorrillana* (french fries topped with beef, onions, and hard-boiled eggs), Jota Cruz is a lively place where you can write on the walls and tables. Highly recommended by locals, and with good reason. Live music all day. *Chorrillana* for 2 CH$3500, for 3 CH$5000. *Menú* CH$1400. Beer CH$600. Wine CH$2400-45,000. Open daily noon-5am.

■ **Café Vinilo,** Almirante Montt 448 (☎230 665), between Lautaro Rosas and San Enrique, on Cerro Alegre. Named for its collection of vinyl, from which customers can make requests (CH$400), this restaurant/bar also sells one-of-a-kind articles of clothing designed by the owner. Creative menu with an abundance of vegetarian options. Coffee CH$500-1200. Beer CH$500-1500. Mixed drinks CH$1300-3500. Wine CH$2300-4300. *Tapas* CH$2300-4300. Open Jan.-Feb. M-Th 9am-1am, F-Sa 9am-3:30am. Mar.-Dec. M-Th 9am-midnight, F-Sa 9am-3:30am.

Cinzano, Plaza Aníbal Pinto 1182 (☎213 043). A great place to listen to live tango. Entrees CH$3600-4900. Mixed drinks CH$1800-4500. Wine CH$4500-45,000. Live music Tu-Sa 9pm. Open M-Th 10am-2am, F-Sa 10am-4:30am.

Neptune, Blanco 558 (☎224 761), 1 block off Plaza Sotomayor. Dark wood, dim lighting, and cheap pitchers of beer (CH$2700) make Neptune a popular bar with backpackers. *Menú* CH$1500. Sandwiches CH$900-2000. Beer CH$600-900. Mixed drinks CH$1700-3000. Open M-Th 10am-10pm, F-Sa 10am-8am.

🔌 DAYTRIPS FROM VALPARAÍSO

QUINTAY   ☎32

Micros *to Quintay leave from Valparaíso's main bus station (1hr., 4 per day 7:50am-6pm, CH$1000). Colectivos depart much more frequently from 12 de Febrero, between Pedro Montt and Chacabuco. Colectivos will leave when there are 3 or 4 passengers, and can drop visitors at any of the town's three sections (1hr.; to plaza CH$1300, to beach CH$1500).*

An hour south of Valparaíso, the remote fishing village of Quintay is a quiet town known for its serene white-sand beach. Surrounded by mountains, the peaceful Playa Grande feels very secluded. There is a small plaza in the center of town where *colectivos* congregate. The *caleta* can be reached by walking down the dirt road to the east. The dirt road to the west leads to the beach. Follow the road downhill as it veers to the right, past a wire barricade with a tiny door in it. From there, follow the rocky shore, keeping it on the left until you hit the beach. Hikers should make sure to wear sturdy shoes and long pants, since portions of the hike run through cactus fields. A better option is to ask a *colectivo* driver to stop at the beach. **Hostería Quintay ❸,** La Playa 449, a 3min. walk up the road from the beach, has luxurious rooms in a rustic house, all with private bath and a queen-sized mattress. The tranquil backyard is perfect for lazy afternoons. There's also an attached **restaurant ❶.** (☎09 563 9719. Breakfast included. Jan.-Feb. doubles CH$14,000; Mar.-Dec. CH$12,000. Entrees CH$1500-1800. Restaurant hours vary.)

Because Quintay is easily accessible only from Valparaíso, it is best done as a daytrip. There are no services in town, and very few food options near the beach; buy supplies before heading out. To return to Valparaíso, catch a *colectivo* from the plaza or from along the beach, or call (☎362 669) to request one.

VIÑA DEL MAR ☎ 32

Valparaíso's sister city Viña del Mar (pop. 300,000) is a vacationer's paradise. Sometimes called the "Garden City" because of the exotic trees in the Quinta Vergara, Viña is best known as one of the hottest coastal resorts in South America—and it lives up to its reputation. Luxury condominiums tower over streets crowded with people day and night. Families spend the day on the coast, couples stroll along white-sand beaches in the evening, and the young and hip pack the *discotecas* all night long. Most establishments remain open outside the busy summer months, making the spring and fall, when the weather is pleasant and the crowds aren't so thick, great times to visit.

⌐ TRANSPORTATION

Trains: Estación Viña del Mar, on the corner of Bohn and Grove (☎ 680 501). Open daily 6:30am-10:30pm. Trains run to: **Limache** (1hr., every 30min. 6:50am-10:20pm, CH$450) and **Valparaíso** (20min., every 30min. 7:20am-10:05pm, CH$250).

Buses: Terminal de Buses, Av. Valparaíso 1050 (☎ 710 658 or 710 696), at the corner of Quilpué, 3 blocks from Plaza Vergara. A dozen companies have offices in the bus station; **Pullman** and **Tur Bus** have the broadest selection of destinations. **Luggage storage** is available in the station's basement (CH$600-800). Open daily 7am-11pm.

Tur Bus, in the bus station (☎ 750 203), goes to: **Antofagasta** (18hr., 2 per day 8am-11:15pm, CH$18,000) via **La Serena** (7hr., CH$8900); **Arica** (30hr., 8am, CH$10,000) via **Iquique** (27hr., CH$20,000); **Concepción** (9hr., 3 per day 8:45am-9:35pm, CH$9900); **Pucón** (11hr., 8:35pm, CH$16,400) via **Villarrica** (10½hr., CH$16,000); **Temuco** (10hr., 3 per day 7:20-10:35pm, CH$15,500); and **Santiago** (2hr., every 15min. 5:40am-10pm, CH$2700). Open M-F 5am-10pm, Sa 6am-10pm, Su 6:30am-10pm. MC/V.

Pullman Bus, in the bus station (☎ 752 088), sends buses to: **Antofagasta** (12hr., 4 per day 7:45am-10:45pm, CH$23,000) via **Copiapó** (9hr., CH$13,000); **Arica** (28hr., 10am, CH$25,000); **Concepción** (9hr., 9:30am, CH$8000); **Iquique** (24hr., 3 per day 7:45am-5:40pm, CH$24,000); **La Serena** (6hr., 7 per day 7:45am-11pm, CH$8000); **Puerto Montt** (13hr., 5:45pm, CH$16,000) via **Osorno** (12hr., CH$14,000); and **Santiago** (2hr., every 15min. 6:15am-10:30pm, CH$2600). Open daily 6am-10pm. MC/V.

Ahumada International, in the bus station (☎ 752 005), runs buses to: **Buenos Aires, ARG** (21hr., W and Th 9am, CH$30,000) and **Mendoza, ARG** (7hr., 6:20am, CH$7000).

Micros: *Micros* are all over the city. Fares and destinations are plastered all over the windshield and side, but don't hesitate to ask the driver before hopping on. *Micros* labeled "Puerto" or "Aduana" go south to **Valparaíso** (CH$330); those labeled "Libertad" run north to **Mall Arauco Marino** (CH$170); and the one marked "Plaza Viña" goes to the central **Plaza Vergara.**

Taxis/Colectivos: *Colectivos* and taxis wait at the train station, Plaza Vergara, and the casino. **Radio Taxis** (☎ 970 201, 680 444, or 687 136). *Colectivos* run to **Concón** (CH$500) and **Reñaca** (CH$300).

Car Rental: Hertz, Quillota 766 (☎ 381 025; www.aspillagahornauer.cl), off 8 Norte. Open M-F 8:30am-7pm, Sa 9:30-1pm. **Mach Viña del Mar,** Libertad 1080 (☎ 381 080; www.mach.cl). Open M-F 9am-1:30pm and 3:30-7:30pm, Sa 9am-1pm.

◢✦⁊ ORIENTATION AND PRACTICAL INFORMATION

Viña's neatly ordered layout makes it easy to get around. The **Estero Marga Marga,** runs east to west bisecting the city. South of the river, downtown stretches six blocks from **Plaza Vergara** to **Von Schroeders** between **Arlegui** and **Avenida Valparaíso.** The only beach south of the river, **Playa Caleta Abarca,** is easily reached on **Marina.** North of the Marga Marga, the streets conform to a grid. Streets running east-west,

MIDDLE CHILE

Viña del Mar

▲ ACCOMMODATIONS
Hotel Ankara, 1
Hotel Asturias, 13
Hotel Bahía Casino, 10
Hotel Capric (HI), 11
Hotel Jardine del Mar, 12
Residencial Ona-Berri, 15

♦ FOOD
Cap Ducal, 8
Club Unión Arabe, 9
Deli Planet, 3
Fellini, 6
Samoiedo Restaurant, 14

▮ NIGHTLIFE
Alcazaba Pub, 4
Barlovento, 7
Bartolo, 5
Café Journal, 16
The Happy Viking, 2

PACIFIC OCEAN

Laguna Sausalito
El Bosque
Sausalito
Valparaiso Sporting Club
Sporting
Los Castaños
Estero Marga Marga
Simón Bolívar
Cancha
Hospital Gustavo Fricke
Alvarez

TO MALL MARINA ARAUCO (300m)

12 Norte
11 Norte
10 Norte
4 Oriente
3 Oriente
2 Oriente
1 Oriente
9 Norte
8 Norte
7 Norte
6 Norte
Quillota
Hertz
Valparaiso Travel
Palacio Rioja
5 Oriente
6 Oriente
4 Oriente
Arlegui
Puente Mercado
Quilpué
Terminal de Buses
Quillota
Puente Quillota
Central
Limache

Libertad
Museo Fonck
Palacio Carrasco
Terranova Turismo
Valparaiso
Santa Isabel
Teatro Municipal
Bohn
QUINTA VERGARA
Estación Viña del Mar
Anfiteatro

Mach Viña del Mar
TO RENACA (8km)
1 Poniente
2 Poniente
3 Poniente
8 Norte
5 Norte
4 Norte
3 Norte
2 Norte
1 Norte
Puente Libertad
Puente Peatonal Quinta
PLAZA VERGARA
Cine Arte
Grove
Cousiño
Quinta
Palacio Vergara

Playa Los Marineros
Playa Blanca
Playa El Sol
Playa Acapulco
Vergara Dock
San Martin
Peru
4 Poniente
5 Poniente
6 Poniente
Puente Villanelo
Puente Ecuador
Puente Casino
Etchevers
Villanelo
Traslaviña
Arlegui
Ecuador
Von Schroeders
Viana
Alvarez
Errázuriz
Agua Santa
Portales

Casino Viña del Mar
LOS HÉROES
TAXI
Berger
Palacio Presidencial
Iberia
Castillo
Callao
Balmaceda
Alamos
Vista Hermosa
Cementerio

Castillo Wolfe
Reloj de Flores
CERRO CASTILLO
Libertad
Marina
Playa Caleta Abarca
Puente Capuchinos
TO VALPARAISO (9km)
Esplanada

0   400 yards
0   400 meters

PACIFIC OCEAN

parallel to the river, are called **Norte** and are increase in number from south to north, so that **1 Norte** runs along the river. **Libertad,** the main thoroughfare for buses and *colectivos*, runs north-south and intersects Plaza Vergara. Streets running parallel to Libertad are called **Poniente** (west) and **Oriente** (east), and are numbered increasingly as the streets get farther from Libertad. **San Martín** runs along the beach, intersecting Von Schroeders in the south.

Tourist Office: on Marina (☎269 330; fax 269 332), at Plaza Latorre on Puente Libertad. Helpful staff provides maps of the city and tons of information. English spoken. Open Jan.-Feb. M-F 9am-9pm, Sa-Su 10am-9pm; Mar.-Dec. daily 9am-7pm. **Branch** on the corner of Av. Valparaíso and Villando (☎713 800). Open daily 10am-9pm. Smaller **tourist information posts** are set up Jan.-Feb. on Playas Acapulco, Caleta Abarca, and Los Marineros. **Sernatur,** Av. Valparaíso 507, #303 (☎683 355 or 882 285), provides information on Region V. Open daily 8:30am-7pm. **Conaf,** 3 Norte 541 (☎970 108 or 689 267). Open M-Th 8:45am-5:45pm, F 8:45am-4:45pm.

Tours: The tourist office provides an exhaustive list of tour operators in Viña. Most agencies in town offer tours of Viña and Valparaíso as well as excursions to nearby beach towns like **Isla Negra** and **Zapallar. Terranova Turismo,** Libertad 17, local 15 (☎975 092; fax 884 244), also goes to **PN La Campana. Valparaíso Travel,** 2 Oriente 945 (☎681 459), does **boat tours** of Valparaíso.

Banks: Banks line Av. Valparaíso and Arlegui. **Scotiabank,** Plaza Vergara 103 (☎600 670 0500; fax 683 215), at the corner of Arlegui, has a **24hr. ATM.** Open M-F 9am-2pm. **Banco Santander,** Plaza Vergara 108 (☎714 125), at the corner of Arlegui across from Scotiabank, also has a **24hr. ATM.** Open M-F 9am-2pm.

Market: Santa Isabel, Valparaíso 740 (☎684 145), across from Plaza Vergara. Open M-Th 8:30am-10:30pm, F-Sa 8:30am-11pm, Su 9am-10pm. MC/V.

Police: ☎133. 4 Norte 320 (☎689 268), at the corner of 4 Poniente. **Policía de Investigaciones de Chile,** Simón Bolivar 415 (☎677 861), are better suited to handle any problems travelers may encounter.

Pharmacy: Cruz Verde, Av. Valparaíso 404 (☎714 044), a block off Plaza Vergara. Open M-F 9am-3pm and 4-7pm, Sa 9am-1pm. MC/V. **Farmacias Ahumada,** Libertad 335 (☎687 405), at the corner with Valparaíso. Open daily 8am-midnight. MC/V.

Hospital: ☎131. **Hospital Gustavo Fricke,** Álvarez 1532 (☎652 200).

Internet Access: Internet access is available at most *centros de llamadas* lining Av. Valparaíso (CH$600). **Ciberviñ@,** Valparaíso 651 (☎692 105), on the 2nd floor of the small shopping mall between Plaza Vergara and Quinta, has the cheapest access in town. 1st 15min. CH$200, CH$390 per hr. Open daily 9am-midnight. **Café Alavista,** Av. Valparaíso 196 (☎690 529), is also a quiet cafe and bar. CH$500 per hr. Open M-F 10am-1am, Sa 11am-2am, Su 3-11pm.

Post Office: Arlegui 561 (☎695 482), next to the tourist office on Libertad. *Lista de Correos* available. Open M-F 9am-6pm, Sa 9:30am-1pm. **Branch office,** Libertad 1348 (☎800 362 236). Open M-F 9am-6pm, Sa 9:30am-1pm.

■ ACCOMMODATIONS

An 8-page listing of Viña's accommodations, available at the tourist office, is especially useful in the summer months when hotels and hostels fill up. Budget accommodations line Av. Valparaíso and Von Schroeders, while higher-end options are available along Arlegui and San Martín.

▨ **Siesta de las Poetas,** 9 Norte 843 (☎979 788). Though its name means "the poets' nap," this hostel wouldn't figure in the dreams of Shakespeare or Blake, unless they were on acid. Everything is painted in varying neon shades, and sombreros and giant cutouts of fruit dot the walls of the common room and patio. Free Internet. Private bath. Breakfast included. Singles CH$10,000; doubles CH$14,000; triples CH$21,000. ❸

Hotel Asturias (HI), Av. Valparaíso 299 (☎711 565), at the corner of Traslaviña. A popular choice with backpackers, Asturias is centrally located and has attractive rooms, all with private bath and cable TV. Breakfast included. Singles CH$16,000; doubles CH$22,000; triples CH$27,000; quads CH$32,000. HI members singles CH$7100; doubles CH$14,200; triples CH$21,300; quads CH$28,400. ❸

Hotel Capric (HI), Von Schroeders 39 (☎978 295 or 697 718; hotelcapric@123.cl or hotelcapric@yahoo.com), between Marina and Arlegui. The small rooms are quiet and bright, with private baths and low beds. Good place to meet other backpackers. Located near the beach and downtown. Breakfast included. Singles CH$12,000; doubles CH$15,000. HI members singles CH$6000; doubles CH$12,000. ❸

Hotel Balia Casino, Von Schroeders 36 (☎978 310), just off Marina. Although this hotel resembles a castle from the outside, the interior is much more modest. Large sunny rooms in an ideal location. All rooms have private bath and cable TV. Breakfast included. Free Internet access. Jan.-Feb. singles CH$20,000; doubles CH$25,000; triples CH$30,000; quads CH$35,000. Mar.-Dec. singles CH$16,000; doubles CH$20,000; triples CH$24,000; quads CH$28,000. ❹

Hotel Jardine del Mar, Av. Valparaíso 107 (☎697 952), at the corner of Von Schroeders. Good rooms in a great location, all with private bath and cable TV. Kitchen available for guest use. Doubles CH$10,000; triples CH$15,000. ❸

Residencial Ona-Berri, Av. Valparaíso 618 (☎688 187; fax 882 620), 1 block from Plaza Vergara. Most rooms are bright and airy, but others feel like cramped boxes. Ask to see what's available before committing. Breakfast included. Jan.-Feb. CH$7000 per person, with bath CH$10,000. Mar.-Dec. CH$6000 per person, with bath CH$8000. ❷

Hotel Ankara, San Martín 476 (☎465 500; www.hotel-ankara.co.cl), between 5 Norte and 6 Norte. Conveniently situated near the beach and nightlife hot spots, but rates are steep for those traveling on a budget. Rooms are very comfortable but small. All rooms have private bath, cable TV, and telephone. Breakfast included. Singles and doubles CH$67,000. Suites CH$89,000; CH$16,000 per additional person. AmEx/MC/V. ❺

🍴 FOOD

Viña's culinary scene is an amalgam of cafes, ethnic restaurants, and seafood stops. **Av. Valparaíso** is lined with cafes, and **San Martín** is the best place to find fresh fish. Kiosks on the beach sell ice cream and other snacks. Those tired of Chilean fare will want to head to the area between **2 Norte** and **6 Norte,** west of Libertad, where you can find everything from *tapas* to tacos to sushi.

🍴 **Fellini,** 3 Norte 88 (☎975 742), at the corner of 6 Poniente. Fellini's creative Italian menu will make your mouth water. Huge portions are large enough for 2 people. Many dishes are vegetarian. Entrees CH$4590-5490. Open Jan.-Feb. daily 1-5pm and 8pm-1am; Mar.-Dec. M-Sa 1-5pm and 8pm-1am, Su 1-5pm. AmEx/MC/V. ❸

Deli Planet, 5 Norte 315 (☎686 134), between 3 Poniente and 4 Poniente. Small and unassuming, Deli Planet has earned its reputation for serving delicious vegetarian food. English spoken. Sandwiches CH$1500-3000. Open daily 11am-3pm and 6-10pm. ❶

Club Unión Árabe, Marina 50 (☎621 403), between Playa Abarca and Castillo Wulff. This seafront mansion/restaurant specializes in pan-Arabian cuisine. The *menú* (CH$5500) includes Middle Eastern dishes. Open Tu-Su 9:30am-1am. AmEx/MC/V. ❸

Samoiedo Restaurant, Av. Valparaíso 637 (☎684 610), 1 block from Plaza Vergara. Sit inside for a little calm in the midst of the city, or grab a table outside to watch the bustling crowd. Cocktails CH$2100-4500. Vegetarian sides CH$800-1500. Entrees

CH$3400. *Menú* M-F CH$3100, Sa-Su CH$6100. Open daily 7:30am-midnight. AmEx/MC/V. The cafe, next door to the restaurant, serves coffee (CH$600-950), fruit juices (CH$600-1150), and sandwiches (CH$800-1200). Open daily 8am-midnight. ❷

Cap Ducal, Marina 51 (☎626 655; www.capducal.cl), right on the ocean. A Viña landmark since it was built in 1936, this ship-like seafood restaurant sits overlooking the coast, offering spectacular views from its elegant dining room. Entrees CH$3000-6500. Open 7am-midnight. AmEx/MC/V. ❸

⭕ SIGHTS

◼**MUSEO FONCK.** If a ticket to Easter Island seems too expensive, head to Museo Fonck for the next best thing. A large stone *moai* (indigenous sculpture from Easter Island) looms over the lawn, and inside the museum is a thorough exhibit on the island and its culture. The rest of the museum displays artifacts from Chilean natural history and is organized by region. *(4 Norte 784, at the corner of 1 Oriente. ☎686 753; www.museofonck.cl. Open Jan.-Feb. Tu-Sa 9:30am-6pm, Su 9:30am-2pm; Mar.-Dec. Tu-F 9:30am-6pm, Sa-Su 9:30am-2pm. CH$1000, ages 12 and under CH$200.)*

RELOJ DE FLORES. No tour of Viña would be complete without the requisite photo beside the exquisite "flower clock," the city's quintessential sight. The clock's face is made entirely of carefully arranged blooming plants. The displayed photos of women in bikinis pointing to the clock are tacky, but the clock is itself impressive. *(Across the street from Playa Caleta Abarca, where España meets Marina.)*

QUINTA VERGARA. The beautiful wooded paths of the Quinta Vergara are some of Viña's hidden treasures. In the heart of the city's urban sprawl, this impressive expanse of exotic and native trees feels like another world entirely. **Palacio Vergara,** a beautiful mansion in the park near the entrance to the Quinta, houses the **Museo de Bellas Artes.** A look at the palace itself is almost worth the entrance fee, but the collection inside, including 17th-century Italian paintings as well as some 20th-century Chilean works, makes it a must-see. *(Errázuriz 563, at the corner of Grove. ☎738 438 or 738 436. Museum open Tu-Su 10am-1:30pm and 3-5:30pm. CH$500; children, students, and seniors CH$300. Park open daily 7am-6pm. Free.)*

PALACIO RIOJA. Declared a historic monument in 1985, Palacio Rioja retains the grandeur of its origins. This French Neoclassical mansion was built between 1906 and 1910 for Don Fernando Rioja, a wealthy Spanish banker and tobacco investor. The palace's main floor has been preserved in its original style, and all visitors are forced to don ridiculous felt boots to protect the floor. The curved marble staircase leads to a large entrance hall where private city functions are still held. A conservatory in the basement houses a classical concert series; check at the tourist office for schedules. *(Quillota 214, at the corner of 3 Norte, 3 blocks from Libertad. ☎483 664. Open Tu-Su 10am-1:30pm and 3-5:30pm. CH$300, children CH$100.)*

⭕ BEACHES

Viña's beaches draw crowds in the summer, making them a great place to see and be seen. Most beaches are in the northern part of town, running alongside San Martín north of 8 Norte. To get to the northern beaches from Plaza Vergara, follow Libertad over the river and turn left onto 1 Norte until it intersects San Martín. **Playa Acapulco,** between 8 Norte and 10 Norte, and **Playa El Sol,** between 10 Norte and Muelle Vergara, are the most packed. Crowds are thinner on **Playa Blanca,** between Muelle Vergara and 15 Norte, and **Playa Los Marineros,** from 15 Norte stretching north. **Playa Caleta Abarca** is the only beach south of the river.

🎵 ENTERTAINMENT

Viña provides cultured fare for the discriminating—including art exhibitions and repertory theaters. For those who need a little more of the new world, catch the latest Hollywood blockbuster or take a seat at one of the tables in the casino.

Cine Arte, Plaza Vergara 142 (☎882 798), between Av. Valparaíso and Arlegui on the side of the Plaza nearer to the ocean. Repertory theater playing art films. Shows 3-10pm. CH$2500, students and seniors CH$1500; special events CH$5000/CH$4000.

Cinemark, Libertad 1348, #301 (☎688 188), in Mall Marina Arauco, at the corner of 4 Norte. Eight screens playing first-run movies. Shows noon-10pm. CH$5500. MC/V.

Centro Cultural, Libertad 250 (☎269 708), in the Palacio Carrasco. The Centro Cultural holds exhibitions, lectures, concerts, and more; check at the tourist office for schedules of exhibitions and events. Open M-F 9:30am-1pm and 2-6:30pm, Sa 10am-1pm.

Teatro Municipal, Plaza Vergara (☎681 739), on the side of the Plaza farther from the ocean. A local landmark since 1930, the Teatro Municipal hosts plays, concerts, and ballets. Check at the tourist office for calendar of events. Prices vary by event.

Casino Viña del Mar, San Martín 199 (☎500 600), near the mouth of the river. This pink romanesque building dominates the block, inviting adventurous gamblers upstairs to pull the arms of its many slot machines. Cover CH$3000. Formal dress required. Open Jan.-Feb. Su-Th 6pm-5am, F-Sa 24hr.; Mar.-Dec. Su-Th 6pm-4am, F-Sa 6pm-5am.

🎭 NIGHTLIFE

Viña's nightlife can be raucous in the summer, but it quiets down as the crowds disperse. On weekends throughout the summer the **Paseo Cousiño,** off Av. Valparaíso between Quinta and Plaza Sucre, shakes to the beat of its *discotecas*. The center of the action is in the area between **San Martín** and **4 Poniente**.

🍸 **The Happy Viking,** 6 Norte 318 (☎736 077), between 3 Poniente and 4 Poniente. Opening the blue metal and glass door leads you into a small but lively bar popular with expats and backpackers. Beer CH$1500-3000. Cocktails CH$1800-4500. Happy hour 9-11pm. Open Tu-Th 6pm-1am, F-Sa 6pm-3am, Su 6pm-midnight.

🍸 **Café Journal,** at the corner of Agua Santa and Álvarez (☎666 654). Hipsters come here for the electronic music. Beer CH$1000-3000. Open M and Th 9am-4pm, F-Sa 9am-5am, Su 7pm-3am.

Barlovento, 2 Norte 95 (☎687 472), at the corner of 5 Poniente. A large, relaxed *tapas* bar that picks up as the night goes on. *Tapas* CH$4500-8400. Beer CH$1500-3000. Cocktails CH$1700-5000. Open daily 11pm-4am. AmEx/MC/V.

Alcazaba Pub, 4 Norte 131 (☎680 879). A karaoke bar popular with the jet-set crowd that migrates from Santiago and Europe during the summer. Beer CH$2000-3000. Cocktails CH$3000-5000. Happy hour 7-10:30pm. Open M-Sa 11pm-4am. MC/V.

Bartolo, 4 Norte 147 (☎697 472). The place to go to salsa on hot summer nights. Beer CH$1800-2800. Cocktails CH$1800-5000. Open Tu-Su 11pm-3am. AmEx/MC/V.

🧭 DAYTRIPS FROM VIÑA DEL MAR

REÑACA

To get to Reñaca from Viña del Mar, take one of the frequent micros *that travel north up Libertad. The beige-colored Sol de Reñaca* micros *are the easiest to spot (CH$240).*

Near Viña del Mar, the *litoral central* is characterized by scrubby hillsides and rocky coastline punctuated by enclaves of civilization, which are actually some of Chile's finest resorts. For the Chilean elite who can't stand Viña's summer crowds, the nearby enclave of Reñaca is a popular retreat. The condominiums that rise up its hills are owned by those *que traen la plata* (who bring the silver), as locals say, and scores of expensive boutiques await them. Despite this ritzy background, however, the public beach at Reñaca plays host to all types and income brackets, with its fair share of schlocky souvenirs and neon discos. This mix of the ritzy and the rowdy makes the town a fun place to hang out and explore.

Perhaps the only non-chain dining option in town is the rustic-style **Entre Masas ❷**, Central 75 (☎839 888), just across from Hotel Piero. With adobe walls, a bookshelf of old magazines, and a tree growing up through the stone floor, the restaurant has character—a much needed change from the sterile restaurants nearby. Try the *Disco Entre Masas* (CH$13,000), a huge plate of meat, shrimp, cheese, and stuffed artichokes, or choose from the huge selection of *empanadas*.

Reñaca has few hotels, and all are pricey. With its proximity to cheap lodging in Viña, this makes the town more of a daytrip than an overnight destination for budget travelers. If you decide to stay to watch the stars come out over the water, try **Holiday Reñaca Hotel and Cabañas ❺**, Angamos 367, up the hill from Borgoño, which lets you combine two vacations in one, with private two- or four-person *cabañas* that give the feel of a mountain vacation only steps from the beach. But you'll be far from roughing it: the spotless cabins come with a porch, living room, cable TV, and kitchenette. (☎830 005 or 832 822; www.holiday.cl. Breakfast CH$2200. Doubles CH$57,000; quads CH$96,000. Extra bed CH$13,000. AmEx/DC/MC/V.)

Just after entering town on Borgoño, buses turn right and head uphill Calle Angamos. To get to the beach, ask to be let off after the turn, before the bus heads up the hill. If you need cash before starting the day, **Banco de Chile,** Borgoño 14675, has a **24hr. ATM,** as does **BBVA,** Borgoño 14611, closer to the drop-off.

CONCÓN

Micros to Concón leave Viña del Mar from Libertad on a regular basis and say "Concón" in the window. From Reñaca, board at the base of Angamos.

Fifteen kilometers from Viña del Mar, Concón follows Reñaca in the string of beach towns climbing up the coast. Concón's major beaches span 12km along the coast, in a setup ideal for a leisurely walk. From east to west, you'll pass **Playa Las Bahamas,** not so much a beach as a pile of slick rocks worn smooth by the ebbing tide; **Playa Negra,** a pile of larger rocks; and **Playa Amarilla,** the prime spot for swimming and sunbathing. Near Amarilla, new-age condominiums are built into the hill like stairs, and during the summer, kiosks selling snacks are all around. Next you'll go through **Concón Sur, Barrio Parque,** and **Concón Viejo.** At the southern end of Concón, in **Higuerillas,** is the **Higuerillas Yacht Club** (☎816 831; www.higuerillas.cl), on Borgoño, where sailboat rental is possible in the summer.

While you can sample the catch of the day at many little shacks along Concón's coast, there are a few more formal options. At **Aquí Jaime's ❸**, Borgoño 21303, the menu is decorated with dried starfish specimen and aquariums line the walls. Some of the prices seem raised to finance the gilded decor, with a ¼-lobster at CH$19,000. (☎812 042. Open Su-M 2-4pm, Tu-Sa noon-2am.) Other great eats can be found past the *caleta,* at **Restaurant Bellamar ❸**, Borgoño 21550. This eclectic restaurant features fish gurgling in the tanks and cartoonish pelicans. The menu is eclectic as well, with standard seafood dishes like *paella* (CH$4500) mixed in with squid salad (CH$3850) and other less-common fare. (☎811 351. Open 12:30pm-1am.) Beyond Playa Amarilla, **Caleta La Boca** houses some ramshackle restaurants and *pescaderías* selling fresh fish. If you want to spend the night in town, try the

MIDDLE CHILE

waterfront **Hostal Taitao ❺**, Borgoño 23100, on Playa Amarilla. (☎816 611 or 816 029. Large bathrooms and cable TV. Breakfast included. Doubles CH$30,000, with kitchenette and no breakfast CH$40,000; quads CH$40,000. AmEx/DC/MC/V.)

There are two roads from Viña to Concón. One follows the coast on Borgoño, and the other, more frequently traveled by **buses**, heads inland from Reñaca, behind large rolling dunes. At the northern edge of Concón, at Caleta La Boca, there is a **rotary**. Buses circle here before returning to Viña or crossing the Río Aconcagua to head north to other beaches. If you arrive here, as is most likely, follow the coastal road away from the industrial plant, and you will reach **Playa Amarilla** after passing by **Caleta La Boca**. You might first want to visit the town's **Oficina Comunal de Turismo** (☎810 980), which has a hut here.

QUINTERO

To get to Quintero, catch a bus in Viña del Mar. Buses leave from Libertad or from the bus terminal. From Concón, you can grab a bus to Quintero at the rotary (CH$400).

Quintero stands out from the other beach towns in the *litoral central* because of its beautiful path along the water and its tiny, sheltered beaches. This is a great town to visit during the low season, when the paths aren't crowded and the beaches feel like your own private getaway.

Quintero's famous path begins from the pier at the end of the main road, 21 de Mayo. The unmistakable **Waikiki Disco** is at the beginning of the path. As you conitnue, your surroundings become woodsy—birds (sounding remarkably like wild pigs) call from the tall cypress trees and sea lions sometimes sun themselves on nearby stones. Small, beautiful white-sand beaches, sheltered by rocky outcroppings, also line the path until it comes to an end at the **Cueva del Pirata**, where graffiti paintings on the rocks depict Pablo Neruda, Bob Marley, and Gandhi, among others. Walking the full path takes less than an hour if you resist the temptation to wander off onto the rocks or one of the beaches—but why resist?

If you meander away the hours and decide to stay in Quintero, two inexpensive hostels on 21 de Mayo are happy to oblige. **Hotel Monaco ❶**, 21 de Mayo 1530, is worn but decent. Try to get the pretty wood-paneled room near the balcony. (☎934 690. Dorms CH$5000 per person. Doubles with private bath CH$10,000.) There are several unspectacular **pubs** along 21 de Mayo serving seafood and beer.

ZAPALLAR ☎33

Seventeen kilometers from Viña del Mar lies Zapallar, considered one of the most beautiful beach towns on the Pacific coast. Though its two white-sand beaches, Playa Chica and Playa Larga, are popular destinations, the town still manages to retain a quiet, residential charm, with turn-of-the-century mansions and tall groves of trees. As such, walking around Zapallar feels a little like trespassing in a gated community. The major tourist activities here are strolling along the streets of Zapallar admiring the homes or enjoying the coastal paths and sheltered beaches.

While there are no real tourist accommodations in the town proper (although in summer it may be possible to rent rooms in private homes), a few slightly more upscale hotels are on the highway where buses pass, such as the pricey **Hotel Isla Seca ❺**, located on Camino Costero. (☎741 224; fax 741 228; reservashis@hotelislaseca.cl. Dec. 15-Mar. 31 singles US$95; doubles US$135, with ocean view US$160; suites US$185; suite apartments US$270.) A great restaurant by the tiny *caleta* is **Restaurant César ❸**, on La Rambla, where the locals descend from their holiday homes to dine on fresh seafood. (☎741 507. Open daily.)

ALGARROBO ☎ 35

During the summer, Algarrobo is swamped by *Santiaguinos* looking for a little white sand, while during the winter even the locals seem to abandon the town. The central beach, Playa Las Cadenas, is good for swimming, but the better beach, tiny Playa El Canelo, is on the southern end of town.

Restaurants specializing in seafood line Alessandri. ◪**Entre Nos ❶**, Alessandri 1508 #2, is a relaxed cafe serving light meals, real coffee, and delicious ice cream. (☎09 821 0865. *Empanadas* CH$700. Coffee CH$650-1890. Smoothies CH$1890. Ice cream CH$590-1790. Open daily 10am-1am.) **Restaurant Cecconi ❸**, Alessandri 1870, is a popular hangout in the evenings. (☎481 647. Happy hour daily Jan.-Feb. 9pm-midnight. Appetizers CH$4300-6800. Entrees CH$2500-7900. Pizza CH$2400-4200. Cocktails CH$1700-4800. Open daily 10am-2am. AmEx/MC/V.)

Budget accommodations run along the beach on Alessandri, the town's main strip. If everything is full in the summer, look for signs reading "Arrienda." **Residencial Vera ❸**, Alessandri 1521, has simple rooms off a courtyard that opens directly onto Playa Las Cadenas. (☎481 131. Breakfast included. Jan.-Feb. singles CH$10,000, with bath CH$13,000; doubles CH$20,000/CH$26,000; triples CH$30,000/CH$39,000. Mar.-Dec. singles CH$8000, with bath CH$10,000; doubles CH$16,000/CH$20,000; triples CH$24,000/CH$30,000.) **Hotel del Pacífico ❺**, Alessandri 1930, on Playa Las Cadenas in a giant orange and purple building, is an upscale option with a pool, sauna, restaurant, and bar. All rooms have private bath. (☎482 855. Breakfast included. Jan.-Feb. singles CH$35,900; doubles CH$46,400; triples CH$53,400; quads CH$58,500. Mar.-Dec. singles CH$32,600; doubles CH$42,200; triples CH$48,600; quads CH$53,200. AmEx/MC/V.)

During the summer there's a small **tourist post** on Alessandri in a gazebo on Playa Las Cadenas. (☎09 497 8349. Open daily Jan.-Feb. 11am-9pm.) **BCI**, Alessandri 1870, next to Restaurant Cecconi, has an **ATM**. (☎482 362. Open M-F 10am-2pm.) An **artisan's market** on Alessandri sets up shop during the summer. (Open Jan.-Feb. daily noon-midnight.) The **police**, at the corner of El Pinar and El Mercado (☎481 140), are off Toribio Larraín, uphill from Playa Las Cadenas. **Patricia Contreras,** Mücke 952, across from the bus station, runs an anonymous **laundromat** and also offers **Internet access.** (☎489 325. Laundry CH$4000 per 5kg. Internet CH$700 per hr. Open daily 11am-10pm.) **Farmacia Algarrobo,** Alessandri 1990, is on Playa Las Cadenas. (☎481 194. Open daily 9:30am-10:30pm. AmEx/MC/V.) The **Consultorio General,** El Retamo 2249 (☎481 187), offers medical services.

Buses depart from the tiny Terminal Pullman Bus on Mücke. **Pullman Bus** (☎481 105) sends buses to Santiago (1½hr., every 30min. 4:50am-10pm, CH$2400) and Valparaíso (1½hr., every 20min. 5:30am-10pm, CH$1500). *Micros* and *colectivos* wait at the bus station and stop along Alessandri. **Micros** and **colectivos** run to Cartagena (30min., CH$400-800), El Quisco (10min., CH$250-300), Isla Negra (20min., CH$350-500), Punta de Tralca (15min., CH$250-300), and San Antonio (45min., CH$400-800). **Taxis** run all over town (☎482 202 or 481 075).

EL QUISCO ☎ 35

As another beach town with a long white-sand beach, during summer, El Quisco becomes standing-room only, and would-be bathers at its *playa* compete for swimming space. Despite the importance of tourism here, there's little infrastructure, and little to do other than lie on the beach. In the middle of the beach is a rocky outcrop with a cactus; facing the ocean, the section left of the cactus is good for swimming, but the section to its right is generally too rocky to swim in safely.

Strewn like Incan ruins on a hillside in **Punta de Tralca,** the part of town approaching Isla Negra, are several large stone faces. These blocks of granite, now graffitied, were carved by Chilean sculptors in honor of Pablo Neruda, serving as lonely witnesses to the flow of the tide. There is also a rocky outcropping extending into the ocean here, which can be fun to explore. With almost no sign of human disturbance, there's nothing out here but peace and quiet. Ask a bus driver to let you off at Punta de Tralca. Walk 20min. down the road and bear left at the fork. To reach the sculptures, follow the road to the left to its end and head up the hill.

As in most coastal towns, seafood is the local specialty. **Restaurant El Cordovés ❸**, Dubournais 296, comes highly recommended by locals. (☎471 573; elcordoves@elquiscoeltabo.cl. Appetizers CH$2650-4550. Entrees CH$1950-5850. Salads CH$1150-2800. Open daily Jan.-Feb. 9am-1am; Mar.-Dec. 10am-midnight. AmEx/MC/V.) **Restaurant Mastique ❶**, Dubournais 190, is a popular restaurant also serving lighter fare. (☎471 919. Entrees CH$1800-4950. Salads CH$850-2400. Sandwiches CH$850-2300. Pizza CH$1600-1900. Cocktails CH$1200-4000. Open daily noon-midnight.) **Restaurant Pub Bossa Nova ❷**, Dubournais 109, is notable for its vegetarian *menú*. (☎471 391. *Caipiriña* CH$2000. *Pisco* sour CH$1000. *Menú* CH$2500. Open daily 11am-1am. AmEx/MC/V.)

Budget accommodations line Dubournais, but places fill up quickly in the summer. If everything's full, head to the tourist post for help finding a place to stay. **Residencial León del Quisco ❸**, Durbournais 405, at the corner of Costanera Norte, has clean rooms, all with cable TV. (☎471 362. Breakfast included. Doubles CH$14,000, with bath CH$16,000.) **Gran Hotel Costanera ❸**, Costanera 18, at the corner of Dubournais, has slightly upscale rooms, all with private bath and TV. (☎471 242; www.hotelcostanera.cl. Breakfast included. Jan.-Feb. singles CH$20,000; doubles CH$24,000; triples CH$35,000; quads CH$40,000. Mar.-Dec. singles CH$16,000; doubles CH$19,200; triples CH$28,000; quads CH$32,000. AmEx/MC/V.)

There is a small **tourist post,** on Dubournais across the street from Restaurant Pub Bossa Nova, focused on helping visitors find accommodations. (☎474 224. Open M-Tu 10:30am-2pm and 4:30-9pm, W 10:30am-2pm, Th-Su 10:30am-2pm and 4:30-9pm.) **Banco Santander,** Dubournais 391 #3, at the corner of Francia, has an **ATM.** The **police,** on Dubournais (☎471 155), are between the bus station and the beach. **Farmacia Costamar,** Dubournais 235, has the longest hours in town. (☎471 238. Open daily 9am-2pm and 4-10pm. AmEx/MC/V.) **Automed Médicos Domicilios,** Dubournais 525 (☎09 716 5016), provide medical services. **La Play@.net,** Aguirre 50C, has **Internet access.** (☎474 976. CH$300 per 15min., CH$900 per hr.; 2-6pm CH$600 per hr. Open daily Jan.-Feb. 10am-1:30am; Mar.-Dec. 10am-9:30pm.)

Buses depart from the town's small bus station, **Terminal Hualilemu,** on Dubournais at the corner of Hualilemu. **Pullman Bus,** Dubournais 1255 (☎471 094), six blocks from the bus station toward the beach, sends buses to Santiago (1½hr., every 30min. 5am-10pm, CH$2400) and Valparaíso (1½hr., every 20min. 7:20am-10pm, CH$1500). **Micros** and **colectivos** wait at the bus station and along Dubournais, and go to other area beach towns. **Taxis** run all over town.

ISLA NEGRA   ☎35

Isla Negra is the home of Chile's patron saint of poetry, Pablo Neruda. This small town has remained largely underdeveloped since Pablo Neruda bought his house overlooking the ocean in 1939. The same cannot be said for the house, now the **Casa Museo Pablo Neruda de Isla Negra,** on Camino Vecinal. Neruda's collections of shells, ashtrays, ship figureheads, and insects can be found in every nook and cranny. He spent most of his later years writing here, and it's easy to see why: the view is inspiring, with white-capped waves crashing on the rocky beach.

Most visitors move on after visiting the museum and the trinket shops above it. Those who, like Neruda, are lured to stay can ask at the tourist post for information on renting *cabañas*. ▇**Casa Azul ❷**, on Santa Luisa off Central, has cheap, comfortable rooms harboring other wandering souls, all with shared bath, as

Demythologizing Chile's Mythical Icon

As a Nobel Prize winner, Communist supporter, and undying romantic, Pablo Neruda stirs up a sense of pride and national identity in Chileans that few others can. Born Neftalí Ricardo Reyes Basoalto in 1904 in the town of Parral, Neruda spent most of his childhood in Temuco. After studying French and pedagogy at the Universidad de Chile, Neruda began a career in politics. Literature, politics, and women would occupy the next five decades of his life.

By age 20, Neruda published two of his most widely read anthologies, *Crupusculario (Dusk)* and *Veinte poemas de amor y una canción desesperada (Twenty Love Poems and a Song of Despair)*. While not regarded as his best literary achievements, they served to establish him as a major literary force—and a hopeless romantic.

In the years between 1927 and 1935, Neruda ended a torrid love affair to marry Maria Antoineta Hagenmaar, a Dutch woman who did not speak Spanish. Despite Neruda's amorous disposition, love could not conquer this linguistic divide, and the couple divorced in 1936.

The years Neruda spent in Madrid and Barcelona launched him into the *Generación de '27*, an eccentric artistic circle. While rubbing shoulders with painter Salvador Dalí, filmmaker Luis Buñuel, and poet Federico García Lorca, Neruda produced one of his more esoteric publications, the Surrealist masterpiece *Residencia en la tierra (Residence on Earth)*, in 1933. Neruda not only fit into this group of friends and artists, he lorded over it. Weekly *tertulias*, artsy intellectual chats in his Madrid apartment, were the central social activity of the *generación*.

Not just a talented writer himself, Neruda also brought out talent in others. One evening, while wandering the streets of Madrid, Neruda encountered an illiterate Andalusian asleep on a bench. Under Neruda's tutelage, this unlikely protégé, Miguel Hernández, became one of the most mesmerizing poets of the 20th century.

With the onset of the Spanish Civil War in 1936 and the murders of García Lorca and Hernández, Neruda fled to France. There, while working as a Spanish consul, he dabbled in communism, and published *España en el corazón (Spain in the Heart)* before being transferred to Mexico. There he wrote one of his greatest works, *Canto general (Common Song)*.

In 1943, Neruda married Argentine painter Delia del Carril. Rarely known by name in Chile, she is more often called *la Hormiguita* (the little ant), or, more commonly and more derisively,

"the poet's second wife." Although the couple returned to Chile that same year, they separated in 1955, in part due to Neruda's carryings-on with his future third wife.

Returning to Chile a full-blown literary celebrity after 15 years of government service put Neruda in position to run for office. In 1945, he was elected senator, and joined the Communist Party. He served as senator until 1949, although he had to live in hiding from 1947 to 1949 due to political differences with then-president González Videla.

Although they had been involved for many years, it was not until 1966 that Neruda married his third wife, singer Matilde Urrutia, or *la Chascona* (the messy-haired), as he affectionately called her. His constant companion at their homes in Valparaíso, Isla Negra, and Santiago, Matilde was the inspiration for some of his most famous love sonnets, including *Cien sonetos de amor (100 Love Sonnets)*, published in 1959. Matilde is respectfully acknowledged as the love of Neruda's life and the woman to whom tourists are greatly indebted—only through her generosity may travelers visit the couple's three homes and gain insight into Neruda's life.

In 1970, President Salvador Allende appointed Neruda ambassador to France. However, his tenure as ambassador was short-lived due to Neruda's own failing health as well as a declining political environment. According to legend, Neruda lost the battle against leukemia on September 23, 1973, the same night Pinochet's forces headed to his home in Isla Negra to arrest him.

Indeed, the violence that defined recent Chilean history is brutally manifest in Neruda's homes. After his death, Pinochet's forces raided and robbed his houses. The smashed grandfather clock in the study of Museo La Chascona is but one of the visceral reminders of the toll taken by violence on Neruda's life. These troubling traces are juxtaposed with numerous awards, including his Nobel Prize for Literature. Still, what makes Neruda's homes so remarkable is not the collection of glorious artifacts. Rather, a stroll through one of Neruda's residences produces an almost indecent feeling of intimacy and familiarity with this icon of Chilean culture. Perusing Neruda's eclectic collection of objects gives one an insight into his endearing eccentricities: odd splotches of green ink; profiles of himself embedded within Matilde's wild hair in his portraits of her; shrines to Walt Whitman, his literary father; and intentionally squeaky floors, which reminded Neruda of the sea. These quirky relics bring to life the man behind the myth.

Sarah Kenney was the editor of Let's Go: Barcelona 2002.

well as a *cabaña* and space for camping. (☎461 154. Kitchen available. Book exchange. English spoken. Breakfast included. Camping CH$3500 per person, without breakfast. Singles CH$7000; doubles CH$14,000; triples CH$21,000. *Cabañas* Jan.-Feb. CH$25,000; Mar.-Dec. CH$15,000.) **Hostería La Candela ❹**, Hostería 67, has well-decorated, comfortable rooms with private bath. (☎461 254; www.candela.cl. Breakfast included. Singles CH$22,000; doubles CH$38,000, with view and fireplace CH$48,000. AmEx/MC/V.)

Most restaurants in town serve light meals. **Café Calú ❶**, Dubournais 4380, is one of those restaurants. (☎462 400. Sandwiches CH$950-2100. *Empanadas* CH$600-900. Open daily 9am-10pm.) **Casa de las Flores ❶**, Dubournais 4325, is a colorful cafe during the day and a lively pub at night. (☎469 537. Internet access CH$700 per 30min. *Churrasco* CH$2000. Coffee CH$600-1800. Beer CH$900-1300. Cocktails CH$1800-3000. Open Su-Th 11am-8pm, F-Sa 11am-3am. AmEx/MC/V.)

There's a small **tourist post**, on Dubournais at the corner of Bajada de Las Gaviotas, that has maps of town. (☎461 846. Open Jan.-Feb. daily 10am-8pm; Mar.-Dec. Tu-Su 10am-8pm.) There are **no banks, ATMs, or currency exchanges** in Isla Negra. There's a small **clinic** on Dubournais (☎09 219 5973), but the closest **hospital** is in San Antonio. **Internet access** is available at Casa de las Flores (see below). The **post office** is in the Casa Neruda. (☎461 284. Open Jan.-Feb. Tu-Su 10am-7:30pm; Mar.-Dec. Tu-Su 10am-4:30pm.)

To get to Isla Negra from Valparaíso, find the tourist post on Dubournais at bus stop #20, follow Bajada de Las Gaviotas two blocks past the small artisan's market. (☎461 284. Reservations required. Open Jan.-Feb. Tu-Su 10am-7:30pm; Mar.-Dec. Tu-Su 10am-4:30pm. CH$2500, students and seniors CH$1300. English tours CH$3100.) Buses depart from the intersection of Dubournais, the town's main road, and Central. **Pullman Bus,** Dubournais 4226 (☎461 272), runs to Santiago (1½hr., every 30min. 5:15am-10:15pm, CH$2400) and Valparaíso (1½hr., every 20min. 5:45am-10:15pm, CH$1500). **Micros** and **colectivos** wait along Dubournais and go to other area beach towns. **Taxis** are found all over town (☎461 090).

CARTAGENA ☎35

Like Algarrobo and El Quisco, Cartagena is a popular in the summer with vacationing Chileans, who fill the multitude of hostels that cling to the hills overlooking the sea. The resort became stylish at the end of the 19th century as a summer retreat for wealthy Santiago families. Today, the town hosts mostly working-class families looking for a little fun in the sun. The town's two beaches get extremely crowded during the summer with swimmers and sunbathers, making the ocean feel almost claustrophobic; this is not the place to get away from it all.

Seafood is the name of the game in Cartagena, and the countless **restaurants ❶** lining both beaches and the boardwalk between them serve the regional specialty, *paila marina* (CH$1800). **La Manzana ❷**, Suspiros 118B, on Playa Grande, is the local favorite, serving meat dishes as well as lighter fare in its bright dining room. (☎450 220. Appetizers CH$1980-6500. Entrees CH$1500-4200. *Empanadas* CH$1980-6500. Cocktails CH$800-3000.)

Budget accommodations line the beaches and their side streets, particularly near Playa Chica. **Hotel Bella Vista ❷**, Ricardo Santa Cruz 216, one block uphill from Playa Chica, is a comfortable choice offering rooms with private bath. (☎451 216. Breakfast CH$1000. Singles CH$7000; doubles CH$10,000, with TV and view CH$14,000; triples CH$18,000; quads CH$24,000.) **Hotel Castillo ❷**, Ejército 82, two blocks uphill from Playa Chica, looks like a castle, but with a much more modest interior. (☎450 241. Breakfast included. TV CH$2000. Jan.-Feb. singles CH$6500, with bath CH$8000; doubles CH$13,000/CH$16,000. Mar.-Dec. singles CH$5000, with bath CH$6000; doubles CH$10,000/CH$12,000.)

The central **Plaza de Armas** is between the town's two beaches on Casanova. Directly downhill is a rocky bit of shore with a boardwalk connecting the beaches. The boardwalk is crowned by a statue of the **Virgen del Suspiro.** To her right is **Playa Chica,** ; to her left is **Playa Grande.** A small **tourist center,** Casanova 266, across from the plaza, provides listings of accommodations (☎200 736. Open Jan.-Feb. M-F 9am-8pm; Mar.-Dec. M-F 9am-2pm and 2:30-6pm.) **BancoEstado,** on Almirante Latorre next to Pullman Bus, has a **24hr. ATM.** (☎451 412. Open M-F 10am-2pm.) The **police,** Cartagena 755 (☎450 613), are just up from the plaza. **Farmacia San Sebastián,** on Casanova between Nieto and Cartagena, has the longest pharmacy hours in town. (☎459 364. Open daily 9:30am-10pm.) There's **no hospital** in Cartagena; the closest one is in San Antonio. **Centro de Fotocopiado,** at the corner of Esmeralda and Casanova, offers **Internet access.** (☎451 947. CH$500 per 30min. Open M-Sa 9:30am-9pm, Su noon-8pm. AmEx/MC/V.) The **post office,** Casanova 266, across from the Plaza de Armas, is in the *municipalidad.* (☎451 933. Open M-F 9am-2pm and 3-6pm, Sa 9am-12:30pm.)

Buses stop at Playa Grande or the Plaza de Armas. From Playa Grande, follow Suspiros around the coast to Playa Chica. To get to Playa Chica from the plaza, follow Casanova downhill toward the ocean and veer left at the road's end. **Pullman Bus,** Almirante Latorre 98 (☎450 913 or 450 708), on the plaza, sends buses to Santiago (1½hr., every 30min. 5:20am-9:50pm, CH$2000) and Valparaíso (2hr., every 20min. 5:20am-9:50pm, CH$1700). *Micros* and *colectivos* run along the beaches and also stop at the Plaza de Armas, and go to other area beach towns.

PARQUE NACIONAL LA CAMPANA ☎33

La Campana found fame in 1834 when Darwin scaled the park's namesake mountain and admired the views that extend to Valparaíso. Following in Darwin's footsteps, thousands of visitors make the ascent every year for a glimpse of the sea to the west and the high peaks of the Andes to the east. The park's 80 sq. km enclose stands of *roble* (the northern-most growth of this tree in Chile) and forests of native Chilean palms, which are considered a vulnerable species. Campana's wildlife is mostly of the small variety, but visitors occasionally see foxes and mountain cats. Eagles, hawks, and giant hummingbirds soar—or flitter—through the air, and lizards, toads, and the *rana grande* hide among the rocks.

 WHEN TO GO. Granizo is the only sector open year-round. Both **Cajón Grande** and **Ocoa** are open only January through February. The best time to visit the park is during the summer when, on clear days, the view extends from the Andes in the east to Valparaíso and the Pacific Ocean in the west. Winter months can bring heavy rains, so it's a good idea to check conditions with **Conaf** (see below) before heading out.

▐ **TRANSPORTATION. Micros** stop on the outskirts of Olmué (p. 264), about 1km from the park's main entrance at **Granizo** (labeled "45 Granizo," stops at bus stop 45; 15min., CH$200) and about 3km from the second entrance at **Cajón Grande** (labeled "40 Narvas," stops at bus stop 40; 10min., CH$200). The third entrance at **Ocoa** is accessible by taking a bus to Hijuelas, where you can catch a *micro* along the highway to Escuela Las Palmas, near the Ocoa entrance (40min., CH$900).

▐▐ **ORIENTATION AND PRACTICAL INFORMATION.** The park has three sectors, each with a Conaf ranger station and campgrounds. Sectors Granizo and Cajón Grande are accessible from Olmué (p. 264) and Sector Ocoa is accessible from Escuela Las Palmas. (www.parquelacampana.cl. Open M-Th 8:45am-5:45pm,

F 8:45am-4:45pm, Sa-Su 9am-5pm.) In case of emergencies, call ☎443 067. **Conaf,** on Granizo, at bus stop #43 in Olmué, has simple, but sufficient maps of La Campana as well as information on current conditions in the park. (☎441 342 or 442 922; www.conaf.cl. Open M-Th 8:45am-5:45pm, F 8:45am-4:45pm.) Or check out the office in Viña del Mar (p. 253). The cost of entry is CH$1500, CH$500 for ages 6-17 and over 65, and free for children under 6. There's no food available in the park itself; stock up beforehand in Olmué.

🏕 **CAMPING.** Conaf runs campgrounds in each of the park's three sectors. There are 23 sites at **Segundo Puente** in Granizo, 700m from the Granizo ranger station; 22 sites at **El Belloto** in Cajón Grande, 100m from the Cajón Grande ranger station; and 16 at **La Buitrera** in Ocoa, 1km from the Ocoa ranger station. Amenities at all campgrounds include bathrooms and showers, a table and bench, and a stove. It's best to boil water at the sites or treat it with iodine before drinking it. Sites are given out on a first-come, first-served basis. Camping is only permitted on Conaf's sites. (CH$6000 for up to 6 people, CH$1000 per additional person.)

🥾 **HIKING.** La Campana's trails are well-marked, and all but El Andinista can be successfully hiked by healthy adults without much hiking experience. The park's Conaf office and the ranger stations at each of the park's three entrances have simple maps of the trails. Summer is the best time to go hiking in La Campana, although spring and autumn are also pleasant. Winter can bring heavy rains.

In Sector Granizo, **El Andinista** (7km, 7hr. round-trip), is a steep climb leading to Cerro La Campana (1990m), and the only trail of interest to serious hikers. Those planning to attempt the climb should check with Conaf about current conditions before going. Only experienced hikers are encouraged to attempt the hike. Hikers must be at the Granizo ranger station, a 30min. walk from bus stop 45 in Olmué, by 10am in order to make it back before the park closes. For those looking for a more relaxed walk, try **La Canasta** (800m, 1hr. round-trip), which is popular with vacationing Chilean families. In Sector Cajón Grande, **El Plateaux** (1km, 1½hr. round-trip) offers some lovely forest views and passes by natural pools formed by the *estero*, while **Sendero Cajón Grande,** home to Pozo El Coipo, 800m from the Cajón Grande ranger station, is suitable for bathing. Finally, in Sector Ocoa, **Portezuelo Ocoa** (5½km, 4hr. round-trip) passes by a waterfall (elevation 35m) and the Chilean palms for which the park is known.

OLMUÉ   ☎33

Olmué is the principal gateway to **Parque Nacional La Campana,** offering access to both the Granizo and Cajón Grande sectors of the park. The tiny town itself is pleasant but pricey, and offers visitors little in the way of basic services. Still, Olmué offers accommodations to visitors on their way to or from the park.

There are a few noteworthy eateries in town. **La Cafeta ❶,** Prat 4900, just up from the plaza at bus stop 25, is a relaxed cafe serving real coffee and light meals. (☎09 507 9582. Coffee CH$400-1000. Fruit juices CH$1200. Sandwiches CH$1000-1500. Open daily Jan.-Feb. 9am-midnight; Mar.-Dec. 10am-noon and 4-9pm.) **Parilla Restaurant ❷,** Portales 2166, directly off the plaza at bus stop 24, has more substantial fare. (☎08 507 0411. Soups CH$900-1800. Sandwiches CH$900-1800. Entrees CH$2500-4900. Open daily Jan.-Feb. 10am-1am.)

Accommodations in town cater to vacationing Chileans who are willing to splurge a bit. **Camplejo Turístico Las Montañas ❺,** Granizo 9139, near the park entrance at bus stop #43, is a forested complex complete with a tennis court, pool, and playground. All *cabañas* have kitchen and private bath. (☎441 253. *Cabañas* for up to 5 CH$35,000, CH$5000 per additional person up to nine.) **Hostería Scala de**

Milán ❹, Prat 5058, a block from the main plaza at bus stop #25, has decent rooms and *cabañas.* (☎441 414. Singles CH$20,000; *cabañas* CH$30,000.)

The town is centered around a small plaza at the corner of Prat and Portales. A block from the plaza Portales intersects Eastman, which runs to nearby Limache. Between Limache and Olmué, *micros* run along Eastman and Prat, both of which have numbered bus stops making it easy to get around town. **There are no banks, ATMS, or currency exchange** in Olmué. It's a good idea to buy food here before heading to the park. There's a small **open-air market** on the plaza selling fruits and vegetables, as well as artisans' work. (Open daily 8am-6pm.)

Olmué is accessible only from neighboring **Limache,** which is easily accessible from Valparaíso and Viña del Mar. Most buses traveling along the Panamerican will stop at **Hijuelas,** a small town just north of the park's third entrance at Ocoa. From Hijuelas, catch a *micro* along the highway to La Calera (15min., CH$250), where you can take another *micro* from the corner of Aldunate and 21 de Mayo to Limache (1hr., CH$400). Ask to be let off in Limache at the train station at the corner of Urmeta and Prat, from where **Agdabus** *micros* run to Olmué (15min., CH$250). Look for signs indicating how far the bus will go. "24 Olmué" is the plaza, "45 Granizo" is the park's main entrance at Granizo, and "40 Narvas" is the entrance at Cajón Grande. *Micros* to and from Limache stop on Prat at the plaza (to PN La Campana 15min., CH$200; to Limache 15min., CH$250).

LA LIGUA ☎33

La Ligua is a small farming community just off the Panamerican. In the main square, men and women wearing long white jackets loiter with baskets filled with *dulces de La Ligua,* the caramel-filled sweets for which the town is famous. Other than sweets, La Ligua's principal attraction is the archaeological **Museo La Ligua,** Pedro Polanco 698, a 10min. walk downhill from the Plaza de Armas past the post office toward the outskirts of town. Small but well-organized, the museum is dedicated to regional history. One of its best displays consists of artifacts discovered between 1977 and 1989 by a group of local teens who called themselves "Yacas" and traveled through the countryside in search of archaeological remains. The eclectic highlights of this museum include a recreated Diaguita burial site, a whale skeleton initially believed to be a dinosaur, and old *escudos,* the original Chilean currency. (☎761 315. Open Tu-F 9:30am-1pm and 3:30-6:30pm, Sa 10am-2pm. CH$500, children CH$100.)

SWEET HOME LA LIGUA

Even if you don't get off at La Ligua, you'll notice as you pass by the town vendors standing along the Panamerican, and sometimes boarding buses, holding large baskets covered with white cloths. They are selling the town's namesake sweets, Dulces de La Ligua (CH$100-200, any 3 for CH$500, any 7 for CH$1000). These super-sweet pastries are filled with *manjar,* a caramel made from condensed milk. Although *manjar*-filled pastries are widely available in Chile, it is La Ligua that put the *dulces* on the map, and vice-versa.

Most vendors wait at the bus station, in the Plaza de Armas, and in small shops all over town, dressed in long white jackets and white caps. The pastries have become an important source of income to many families in this quiet farming community. Visitors pass through town in a steady stream just to buy some Dulces de La Ligua. The sweets themselves range from simple cakes topped with a dab of *manjar* to elaborate pastries made of layered phyllo dough and *manjar.* One of the most popular *dulces* is a cone made of phyllo dough filled with *manjar,* and it's eaten like an ice cream cone.

Take a peek into the baskets; the *dulces* make a great snack, although they can leave your hands a bit sticky. Vendors often also sell more standard *confitería* wares, but it's the Dulces de La Ligua that draws the crowds.

Most restaurants are directly on the **Plaza de Armas. Café Macalú ❶,** Polanco 279, is a popular cafe half a block from the plaza serving light meals, real ground coffee, and natural fruit juices. (☎711 428. Coffee CH$500-1500. Juice CH$500-1500. Sandwiches CH$300-1900. Open M-Sa 9am-9:30pm, Su 10am-9pm.) **Restaurant Parraguez ❷,** Esmeralda 264, is a relaxed eatery with vegetarian side dishes during the day, and a local gathering place for an evening beer. (☎712 599. Sandwiches CH$900-1500. Entrees CH$1000-6000. Sides CH$400-500. Beer CH$400-800. *Menú* CH$2000. Open daily 9am-1am.) Budget accommodations are located in the area around the bus station and the Plaza de Armas. **Residencial Aconcagua ❶,** Esmeralda 173, one block from the plaza toward the museum, is a quiet hostel with immaculately clean rooms, all with shared bath. (☎711 145. Breakfast CH$1000. CH$3000 per person.) **Hotel Chile ❷,** Polanco 7, at the corner of Papudo across from the bus station, offers airy rooms near the plaza, all with shared bath. (☎712 000. Singles CH$4000; doubles CH$8000; triples CH$12,000.)

The center of town is the Plaza de Armas, bounded by Polanco, Ortiz de Rosas, Serrano, and Portales. **BancoEstado,** on the plaza, has a **24hr. ATM. Eco Farmacia,** Ortiz de Rosas 494, on the corner of Polanco, is across from the plaza. (☎713 273. Open M-Sa 9am-10pm.) **Todo Compu,** Galería Lucumos 452, on the second floor of a small shopping plaza, has **Internet access.** (☎718 363. CH$600 per hr. Open daily 10am-11pm.) The **post office,** El Miralda 460, at the corner of Polanco, is a block past the plaza. (☎711 704. Open M-F 9am-1:30pm and 3-6pm, Sa 9am-noon.)

Buses depart from the **Terminal de Buses,** Papudo 485, between Polanco and Uribe. **Tur Bus** (☎712 712) runs to Pichidangui (1hr., 3 per day 9:45am-5:15pm, CH$1000) and Santiago (2½hr., every hr. 6:45am-7:45pm, CH$3000) via Hijuelas (45min., CH$1000). Buses into town stop on the Panamerican just outside town, from where *colectivos* head to the Plaza de Armas (CH$350). **Taxis** (☎712 734) line up along Ortiz de Rosas on the plaza.

THE ROUTE TO MENDOZA

From Valparaíso or Viña del Mar, many visitors choose to take a bus along the scenic Ruta 62 and across the Andes to visit nearby Mendoza, Argentina. Some travelers choose to stop in various towns along Ruta 62 before continuing onto Mendoza. To stop in one of these destinations, take a direct bus from either Valaparaíso or Viña del Mar, or simply let your driver know where you would like to be let off. Just make sure to find out when buses will be passing through town again.

QUILLOTA   ☎32

Only 65km from the bustle of Viña, the quiet streets and orchards of Quillota seem to be from a different time. They are, for the city was once an indigenous administrative hub, and later, one of the first settlements of the Spanish conquest. The sun-soaked fruits and wine that drew the original inhabitants continue to attract visitors, and local museums contextualize the path that the valley has taken.

Though many towns in Chile are heirs to a storied past, Quillota is particularly in touch with its roots, and its main attractions reflect the connection. In the center of town is the **Plaza de Armas,** where several monuments bear the names of forefathers and, unfortunately, graffiti artists. From there, walk two blocks toward where the bus dropped you off. At Blanco 241 is the **Casa y Museo del Huaso de Quillota,** which houses a huge collection of cowboy artifacts and agricultural machinery. (☎269 007. Open Tu-F 10am-1pm and 3-6pm, Sa 10am-1pm and 3-4pm, Su 10am-2pm. Free.) From here, walk toward the plaza on Maipú and take your first right onto Merced. The **Museo Histórico Arqueológico Quillota,** Merced 175, works to educate the public about the history of Quillota and the Aconcagua Valley, from its glacial creation, through indigenous times, the Spanish conquest, into the twentieth century. (☎291 273. Open M-Sa 8:30am-1:45pm and 3:15-5:30pm. Free.)

Though Quillota can be traversed in a leisurely day, it offers options for those who want to linger longer. **Bar-Grill O'Higgins ❶**, O'Higgins 85, serves *parrilla* and *comida típica* like grilled chicken and rice (CH$1700) just north of the Plaza de Armas. If you find the slightly dark interior more eerie than authentic, the supermarket, **DarMax**, is just across the street. **Hostal Alemán ❷**, El Milagro Parcela 3 (☎352 306; w_bogs@muchomail.com), has simple rooms with private bath. (Breakfast included. Camping CH$1500. Rooms CH$5000-10,000.) A more upscale option is **Hotel Bostón ❸**, 21 de Mayo 468, which offers cable TV and a restaurant/bar, but nothing to reference the city for which it is named. (☎316 500; hotelboston@entelchile.net. Doubles CH$25,000-30,000; suites CH$30,000-35,000.) If you have the time and transportation, consider a short trip to **Centro Turístico El Edén ❹**, 5km northwest of town on Balmaceda. This complex has gorgeous landscaping, views of the valley, a pool, sauna, and restaurant. (☎312 342. Doubles CH$20,000; triples CH$25,000; quads CH$30,000. All CH$5000 less without kitchenette.)

The **Cámara Informe**, a bright-orange hut at the far side of the Plaza de Armas on Maipú, can give you a clear map. (☎505 140. Open M-F 9:30am-12:30pm and 2:30-5pm.) Across the street, at the corner of O'Higgins and Chacabuco, is a **BCI Bank** with a **24hr. ATM**. The **library** attached to the Museo Histórico y Arqueológico (see above) has free **Internet access**. (Open M-F 10am-2pm and 3:15-7pm, Sa 10am-1pm.) To get to Quillota, take a *micro* from the eastern side of Av. Libertad in Viña del Mar (CH$350). Once in Quillota, get off at Maipú and walk three short blocks down to the Plaza de Armas. The ride is a bumpy hour from the coast, but vistas of lines of fruit trees against smog-free sky provide ample in-seat entertainment.

LOS ANDES
☎34

This tidy little town is the last stop on Ruta 62 before the Andes, and every inch of the horizon is dominated by their looming presence. The town's sights are located on the town's main road, Santa Teresa. Heading from the bus station, on the left, you'll come to the **Museo Arqueológico**. Its high wood-beamed ceilings, adobe walls, and dirt floors make great ambience for the collection of indigenous and colonial artifacts, including a mummified woman, in a glass case, whose braids are still attached to her peeling scalp. (Santa Teresa 398, at the intersection with O'Higgins. ☎420 115. Open Tu-Su 10am-8pm. CH$700.) Across the street is the equally eerie **Museo Antiguo Monasterio del Espíritu Santu**. This old convent was converted into a museum and is now abandoned—sort of. The old cells are glassed-in and peopled with mannequins praying, reading, and on their deathbeds. Photos of dead nuns are also mixed in with the requisite collection of glistening priestly frocks. The echo of your footsteps on the hardwood floors will creep you out. (Santa Teresa 389. Open daily 10am-6pm. CH$250.)

Seven kilometers west of Los Andes, through San Esteban, are the **Termas el Corazón** (☎481 371), thermal baths where you can soak in 27°C (80°F) water while gazing at the icy Andes. The **hotel ❺** is expensive (CH$67,000-112,000), but don't worry about breaking the bank—the Termas are an easy daytrip from town.

If you're only in time long enough for takeout, **La Pizza ❶**, Esmeralda 273, steps from the Plaza de Armas, serves pizza with more toppings and thicker crust than you'll find elsewhere in Chile. (CH$400 per slice. Open daily 10am-11pm.) Around the corner, **Masnick ❶**, Maipú 332, on the Plaza de Armas, is spotless for a restaurant serving *comida típica*, with marble floors and a terrace where you can lunch on 21 types of pizza (CH$1490), sandwiches (CH$1600), and *completos*. (☎422 385. Open daily 10am-1am. AmEx/DC/MC/V.) If you are staying in town, a good option is **Hotel Estación ❶**, M. Rodríguez 389, where the only trains nearby are the models on wall-bound tracks. (☎421 026. Rooms CH$3000 per person, CH$6000 with shared bath.) **Hotel Los Andes ❹**, Argentina 1100, on the main road into town, is more expensive, but is cleaner and more efficient. (☎428 484. Internet access and breakfast included. Private bath. Singles CH$20,000; doubles CH$28,000.)

Los Andes is small enough that you may not need aid, but there is a **tourist kiosk** on Santa Teresa, near the museum. Other amenities are clustered around the Plaza de Armas. There are several **banks** with **24hr. ATMs,** including **Banco de Chile**, Maipú 350, on the corner of Esmeralda. For **Internet** access, **Coffeenet**, Santa Rosa 213, serves up milkshakes (CH$600) with the megabytes. The **post office** is down Esmeralda on the corner of Santa Rosa. To get to Los Andes from the coast, there are only departures from Valparaíso (2hr., CH$1400) with companies like **Tur Bus** (☎212 028), **Pullman Bus** (☎256 898), and **Empresas Dhino's S.A.,** which also run from Santiago. *Micros* also run from Quillota (or any town along Ruta 62) and arrive at the **Terminal de Buses Los Andes,** at the end of Carlos Díaz, just off of the rotary. Companies with departures to Mendoza (CH$6000), passing by Portillo Ski Resort (CH$5000), include **ALSA Chile** (10, 10:20, 11:15am), **CATA International** (8:45, 10:30, 11:30am), **Chilebus S.A.** (10, 10:15, 11am), and **TAC** (10, 10:30, 11:30am, 1:30pm). The **radio taxi** service in town is **Radio Inkamar** (☎460 460).

BORDER CROSSING INTO ARGENTINA: MENDOZA

Crossing between Chile and Argentina is done by hundreds of people every day and has become nearly routine. The twisting mountain road that runs between the cities is paved, well-maintained, and heavily traversed by cars and buses. The **customs** process has many steps but is pretty straightforward. Buses and cars are stopped just before the tunnel and passengers must disembark. There is one kiosk for Chile and one for Argentina, where your passport and temporary visa will be stamped. Save the latter, since you need it to get back into Chile. Next, passengers go to a different area to claim their luggage, which may be x-rayed or searched for contraband and various food products. (see **Essentials: Border Crossings,** p. 35, for info on visas and fees).

MENDOZA, ARGENTINA   ☎0261

Located closer to Santiago than to the Argentine capital of Buenos Aires, Mendoza is almost an honorary Chilean city. You might even say it's Chilean by birth, founded in 1561 by a group of *Santiaguino* explorers led by García Hurtado de Mendoza. Still, through the years, Mendoza has cultivated a uniquely Argentine identity, suffused with a culture of *gauchos, bodegas,* and *parrilla.* Especially with increased purchasing power, more Chileans than ever before have been inspired to recreate Mendoza's original trans-Andean journey, and this million-strong suburb has evolved from a sleepy outpost into a popular, cosmopolitan tourist destination. Yet Mendoza's wide, welcoming avenues offer plenty of room for all, and its savory steak, sun-soaked wines, and convenient alpine locale continue to attract visitors from both over the border and beyond.

▐ TRANSPORTATION

Flights: All flights go to **Aeropuerto El Plumerillo** (☎448 7128), 10min. northeast of Mendoza proper. **Buses** from the airport run to the Omnibus terminal on the southeast side of town (every 30min., ARG$1.50. Purchase a *tarjeta* at the airport info booth). **Taxis** to the city center ARG$8-10. **LanChile,** Rivadavia 135 (☎425 7900), and

Mendoza Centro

⌂ ACCOMMODATIONS
Break Point Hostel, 10
Campo Base, 9
Hostelling International, 17
Hotel Petit, 1
Hotel Zamora, 6
Las Uvas Hostel, 12
RJ Hotel del Sol, 2
Savigliano Hostel, 16

🍴 FOOD
Azafrán, 3
Facundo, 7
Las Tinajas, 5
Los Tres Mosqueteros, 15
The Green Apple, 13

🍸 NIGHTLIFE
Apeteco, 18
Café del Teatro, 4
Drugstore Most, 11
El Cuervo Pub and Pool, 14
Por Acá, 8

Southern Winds, Rivadavia 209 (☎0810 777 7979 or 420 4827), are the 2 airlines that connect directly with Santiago and offer unrestricted round-trip fares (US$120-200). Fares are much lower with 3 weeks advance notice.

Buses: The local **Omnibus** system operates throughout Gran Mendoza. The two numbers in each window indicate the bus route—the top number indicates the general area of town serviced and the lower number marks the specific route. Consult bus maps for details. Fares generally run ARG$0.80. Magnetic swipe cards are available at kiosks or tourist information centers. **Regional** and **international** buses leave from the **Terminal del Sol** on Pedro de Palacios, at Mendoza's eastern border. Numerous companies run buses to **Santiago** (7hr., ARG$20-25), including **Tur Bus** (☎431 1008; 9:45am and 2pm); **Tas Choapa** (☎431 2140; 9am, 2pm.); **O'Higgins Internacional** (☎431 5946; 8:30am, 2:30pm.); **CATA Internacional** (☎431 0782; 10:30am and 1:30pm.); **TAC** (☎431 1039; 8:30am and 12pm); **El Rápido Internacional** (☎431 5271; 7:30, 10:30am, 1:30pm). Direct buses to **Valparaíso** and **Viña del Mar** run only once a day with Tur Bus and TAC (ARG$20-25). Connections to **Buenos Aires** (15hr., ARG$50-65) are available with TAC, AndesMar, and **Central Argentino** (☎431 3112; 6:45pm). **Ski shuttles** are not commonplace, as various tour agencies organize transportation to the slopes, but **Expreso Uspallata** (☎431 3309) sends a daily bus to **Penitentes** (6 and 10:15am; ARG$12). To get to **Las Leñas,** try TAC buses (6am, ARG$24).

MIDDLE CHILE

Taxis: Base rate is ARG$1.10, ARG$1.60 at night, and ARG$0.07 per 200m. Fare from the bus terminal to the airport in metered taxis is ARG$8.50. **Radio taxis** with pick-up service include **Coria Taxis** (☎445 5855) and **RadioMovil Taxi** (☎432 5055).

Car Rental: Several agencies operate at the airport, but tend to be expensive. **Andina Rent-A-Car,** Paseo Sarmiento 129 (☎438 0480; www.andinarentacar.com.ar.), in town, has more reasonable rates (from ARG$25-35 with insurance).

■ ▐ ORIENTATION AND PRACTICAL INFORMATION

Mendoza is a big, sprawling city in which streets change names with alarming frequency as they cross the city. All street signs in the city's boundaries have a number and direction, indicating the distance from the central intersection of **San Martín** and **Colón.** San Martín, with its abundance of shops, banks, amenities, and agencies, serves as the functional thoroughfare of the downtown area. **Paseo Sarmiento,** 4 blocks north of Colón, has a bevy of attractive sidewalk cafes east of Plaza Independencia. **Plaza Independencia** is the ad hoc center of town, as outlying mini-parks surround it within a two-block radius: **Chile** to the northwest, **San Martín** to the northeast, **España** to the southeast, and **Italia** to the southwest. **Parque General San Martín** borders central Mendoza to the west.

PHONE CODES	The international calling code for Argentina is ☎ **54.**

Tourist Offices: Mendoza's information network is very visible, and the tourism industry here is very focused on sales. A **tourist stand** at the airport (☎448 0017) and one at **Terminal del Sol** (☎431 3001) greet incoming visitors. However, the best place for comprehensive information, reams of brochures, and reliable advice is the central office of the **Subsecretaria de Turismo,** San Martín 1143 (☎420 2800), a huge marble building between Garibaldi and Catamarca. Open M-F 8am-10pm, Sa-Su 9am-10pm. Nearby, on the northeast corner of San Martín and Sarmiento/Garibaldi, a small **info shack** is more crowded but also very helpful. Open daily 9am-9pm. Farther south, a hut at Virgen del Carmen de Cuyo and España also gives information. Open M-F 8am-1pm.

Tours: The plethora of tour companies, especially in the Sarmiento/San Martín area, makes it easy to plan trips. Several companies compete for the tamer and more conventional bus-tour market. **Turismo Mendoza,** Las Heras 543 (☎429 2013), **Turismo Sepean,** Primitivo de la Reta 1088 (☎420 4162; mendoza@sepean.com), and **Saint Germain Tours,** Colón 126, 7th fl. (☎429 6202; sgtours@lanet.com.ar), all specialize in city circuits (ARG$18), mountain tours to the **Penitentes** and **Aconcagua** area (ARG$48), and **wine tours** (ARG$20). All 3 can accommodate English speakers, although the first 2 companies are more geared toward that market. For river-specific tours, **Betancourt Rafting,** Lavalle 35, in Galería Independencia, local 8 (☎429 9665; www.betancourt.com.ar), offers a fine selection of trips varying in difficulty and duration (2hr., from ARG$45). Hostels and hotels can also set you up with tour operators.

Consulate: Chile, Paseo de los Andes 1147 (☎425 5024). The office stays busy, as many people come here to renew Chilean visas. Open M-F 8:30am-2pm.

Banks and Currency Exchange: Banks are peppered along San Martín and near Plaza Independencia. Most have functional **ATMs** in the foyer. At San Martín and San Lorenzo there's a **24hr. Red Banelco ATM.** The best spot for changing currency is the corner of San Martín and Catamarca. Of the 3 *cambios* here, **Cambio Santiago,** San Martín 1199 (☎420 0277), has the latest weekend hours. Open M-F 8am-8pm, Sa 8:30am-1:30pm and 4:30-8:30pm. **Western Union,** España 1152 (☎420 5070). Open M-F 8am-9pm, Sa 9am-2pm. Services also available at the **post office** (see below).

PESOS (ARGS)		
AUS$1 = ARG$2.16		ARG$1 = AUS$0.46
CDN$1 = ARG$2.30		ARG$1 = CDN$0.44
CH$1000 = ARG$4.75		ARG$1 = CH$210.69
EUR€1 = ARG$3.71		ARG$1 = EUR€0.27
NZ$ = ARG$1.97		ARG$1 = NZ$0.51
UK£1 = ARG$5.54		ARG$1 = UK£0.18
US$1 = ARG$3.03		ARG$1 = US$0.33

Bookstore: Centro Internacional de Libros, Lavalle 14 (☎420 1266) carries trashy novels and syllabi-studders in English, French, German, and Spanish (around ARG$10). Open daily 8:30am-1pm and 4:30-8:30pm.

Shopping: The incredible exchange rate makes shopping a fabulous tourist attraction. The best line-up of stores is on San Martín and Paseo Sarmiento. There's also a mall at the outskirts of town, **Mall Plaza Mendoza,** Acceso Este 3280 (☎449 0100). Called **El Shopping** by locals, it has department stores, bowling, an arcade, and the largest movie theater in the city (☎421 0700). The best transportation is a cab from the city or bus # 50/51, 80/88, 120/125, or 160/162. Open daily 11am-10pm.

Laundromat: Try the self-service **Lava Center,** Mitre 1623 (☎423 4509), or **Lave Mas,** Garibaldi 142 (☎420 3960).

Police: ☎101. Belgrano and Peltier (☎429 4444).

24hr. Pharmacies: Less common than in Chile. **Mitre** at San Martín 701 (☎423 7123) and **Del Puente,** Las Heras 201 (☎425-9209).

Hospital: Emergency ☎107. **Central** (☎420 0600 or 429 7100), at the corner of Alem and Salta, just across from the bus terminal.

Internet: Rates are usually around ARG$1 per hr. **Internet Webhouse,** 219 Paseo Sarmiento (ARG$1.25 per hr.), and **LaRed Ciberbar,** at the corner of Alem and San Juan (ARG$1 per hr.), are open 24hr.

Post Office: Correo Argentino, at the corner of Colón and San Martín. Open M-F 8am-7:30pm, Sa 9am-1pm.

Postal Code: 5500.

ACCOMMODATIONS

As the base camp for hordes of young skiers and mountaineers, Mendoza is home to some of the best hostels within a huge radius. What's more, the decline of the Argentine *peso* has made accommodations in Mendoza very affordable.

Savigliano Hostel, Pedro B Palacios 944 (☎423 7746; www.savigliano.com.ar), just west of the bus terminal, through an underpass below Palacios. A quiet, Mediterranean-style house with an anomalous, neon orange common room, TV, and super-helpful, dedicated owners who somehow manage to defy Mendoza's hectic pace. All rooms have free lockers. Simple breakfast included. 4-6 bed dorms ARG$12-15; doubles ARG$35, with private bath ARG$40; triples with private bath ARG$45. ❶

Las Uvas Hostel, San Lorenzo 19 (☎420 4158; www.uvashostel.com.ar). Las Uvas means "the grapes," and the rooms are even named after different varieties; you could sleep in "Malbec" or "Cabernet." A huge TV with DirecTV, a DVD player, and fresh pastries at breakfast might make you feel a little buzzed. If not, the free wine tastings will. Dorms ARG$18; doubles ARG$25; 5-person suite ARG$120. ❷

As visitors will find, in Chile they don't speak "Español," but "Castellano," a dialect characterized by a clipped pace and the omission of various word endings. Once you've become accustomed to the particularly Chilean formulation, you might be surprised to find that right over the border in Argentina a different dialect has developed. Argentine Spanish is considered quite beautiful, marked mainly by the habit of accenting final syllables. As one Chilean argued, "It's just because they want to grab your attention — it's not that they're speaking it wrong; we're the ones that drop all our S's." In any case, in Mendoza, you'll be greeted with "ho-LA" not "HO-la." You'll also most likely be addressed not with the common Spanish "usted," but as "vos." Though the verb endings are the same, you may initially be confused by the designation.

Many other words have also developed differently on the opposite sides of the Andes. If you're looking for the Chilean favorite *manjar*, caramelized milk, in Mendoza, it'll be called *dulce de leche*, milk candy. What *Santiaguinos* call *escalopa*, lightly fried breaded beef cutlet, is *milanesa* in Mendoza's *tenedores libres*. Just be careful with the words you pick up. A carton of cigarettes in Mendoza is *cajetilla*, but don't ask for one in Santiago, where it's slang for male genitalia.

-*Melissa Cronin*

Break Point Hostel and Bar, Aristides Villanueva 241 (☎423 9514), is right in the thick of Mendoza's nightlife district, but there's just as much action inside as out. The crowd by the outdoor pool can get boisterous, especially with the hostel's bar attached. Breakfast, kitchen access, and Internet service are all included. Dorms with shared bath ARG$18, with private bath ARG$20; doubles with private bath ARG$50. ❷

Campo Base, Mitre 946 (☎429 0707; www.campobase.com.ar), just south of Plaza Independencia, 7 blocks from the bus terminal either by foot or on the #20 bus. Management caters to the outdoorsy crowd, as the cartoon mascot—a stuffed backpack—suggests. They offer an Aconcagua guiding service, and also run a sister hostel up at Penitentes. 15min. free Internet for guests. Kitchen facilities and laundry service available. 4-8 bed dorms and doubles ARG$10-13 per person. HI discount ARG$2. ❶

Hostelling International, España 343 (☎424 0018 or 424 8432; www.hostelmendoza.net), 8 long blocks south of Paseo Sarmiento and 2 blocks west of San Martín. A bit set back from the center, but with free bus station pickup, this hostel compensates with lots of amenities, a friendly staff, and a large sleeping capacity. Book exchange, kitchen facilities, laundry services (ARG$5), TV, a climbing wall, and lots of fun events and BBQs are part of the deal. Internet ARG$1 per hr. Bike rental ARG$8 per half-day. Breakfast included. Dorms ARG$15; doubles ARG$45. ❶

Hotel Zamora, Perú 1156 (☎425 7537; www.hotelzamora.netfirms.com), just north of the intersection with Paseo Sarmiento. Zamora is a step up from most hostels, with tiled decor, huge paintings, chandeliers, and more character than most moderate hotels in the area. Breakfast included. 2-4 bed rooms with bath ARG$28 per person. ❷

Hotel Petit, Perú 1459 (☎423 2099; www.petit-hoteles.com.ar), just south of Las Heras and north of Plaza Chile. This hotel really isn't as mini as the name suggests, but the knock-off French furniture speaks to its European pretensions. All rooms have phone, private bath, and A/C. Internet access available. Buffet breakfast included. Singles ARG$25; doubles Jan.-Mar. ARG$45, Apr.-Dec. ARG$60. ❸

RJ Hotel del Sol, Las Heras 212 (☎438 0218), on the southwest corner of the intersection with España. The halls here sport pristine, marble-like flooring and worn carpets. Rooms are spacious and come with TV, private bath, and A/C. Breakfast included. Singles ARG$42; doubles ARG$55; triples ARG$80; quads ARG$100. ❹

🖸 FOOD

Unleash the carnivore within—most visitors who journey to Mendoza will want to feast on various cuts of juicy, delicious, and cheap Argentine beef. The abundance of *parrillas* (grill-type restaurants) testifies to this culture's meat-eating.

🖫 Las Tinajas, Lavalle 38 (☎429 1174; www.lastinajas.com), just east of San Martín. All-you-can-eat usually doesn't mean custom-made crepes, fresh stir-fry, and choice cuts of rotisserie, but at Las Tinajas, it does. Combined with marble floors and an attendant at the door, this restaurant's cuisine rises above the other spots in this Mendoza dining genre. Lunch M-F ARG$7, Sa ARG$9, Su ARG$11; dinner Su-Th ARG$9; F-Sa ARG$11. Open daily noon-3:30pm and 8pm-1:30am. ❶

The Green Apple, Colón 458 (☎429 9444), is the vegetarian alternative to Mendoza's cult of the carnivore. They even offer a modified *tenedor libre* (ARG$8.50). Takeout is ARG$9 per kg. Open daily 8am-midnight, Su 8am-3am. ❶

Azafrán, Paseo Sarmiento 765 (☎ 429 4200) Less of a restaurant than a combination wine-bar and South American "deli," this place is a tastebud-tickler. A platter of olives, cheese, crackers, and other relishes (ARG$10) goes down well with a 300-label selection of wines, conveniently sold by the glass (ARG$3). Traditional *tapas* sold in the evenings. Open M-Sa 10am-2pm and 6pm-1am. ❷

Facundo, Paseo Sarmiento 641 (☎420 2866), west of Plaza Independencia. The arched doorways, warm wood, and yellow hues create the feel of a Mediterranean villa, but the flesh-filled menu is all Argentina. A favorite with couples, who get closer over a *parrilla* for 2 (ARG$27). Cheaper options include *milanesa* (ARG$7.50) or salmon (ARG$15). Salad bar ARG$5 per plate. Open daily noon-3pm and 8pm-1:30am. ❶

Los Tres Mosqueteros, Costanera 980 (☎423 2633), near the corner of Alem and Palacios. The pink concrete walls and plaid tablecloths halt the decor uncomfortably close to a themed ambience. And we've yet to think of a connection between the French countryside and *churrasco* (ARG$2). *Menú* ARG$3. Open 9am-11pm. ❶

🖸 🗾 SIGHTS AND OUTDOOR ACTIVITIES

ÁREA FUNDACIONAL. History buffs will want to make this area, 15 blocks north of the bus terminal west of Palacios, their first stop in Mendoza. **Plaza Pedro del Castillo** was the site of Old Mendoza, the first location of the city's government and markets before the devastating earthquake of 1861, which leveled most of the city. Two sights remain, however. The **Museo del Área Fundacional** shows the active excavation of Old City Hall, which was buried by the earthquake, then covered over by a slaughterhouse, and finally, a market. *(Beltrán and Videla Castillo on the Plaza Pedro del Castillo. ☎425 6927. Open Tu-Sa 8am-2pm, Su 2-8pm. ARG$1.50, students ARG$1.)* On the northwest side of the plaza, the **Ruinas de San Francisco** are the only pieces of Old Mendoza left standing 150 years after the earthquake, and even still, the rock and mortar are heavily scaffolded and covered with wood and metal support beams. *(On Beltrán and Ituaingo. Call the museum to set up guided visits M-F 9am-2pm.)*

PARQUE SAN MARTÍN. A popular weekend getaway for picnic-toting *Mendocinos,* this large, manmade park at the western limits of the city has enough attractions to fill a day. **Bikes** are a good way to see more of the park more quickly and with less effort, but **VIP buses** will save you the steep climb up to the **zoo** and **Cerro de la Gloria.** *(Main entrance at Emilio Civit. Bike rentals available at second roundabout from the main entrance. Open Sa-Su. ARG$4 per hr. Buses in front of the info center. ☎428 4515. 1hr. tours ARG$3.50. Zoo 3km from the east entrance. Take the #110/112 bus from the city center* *that says "Favorita-zoológico" in the front window. Open daily 9am-5pm. ARG$3.)* Regardless of how you decide to spend your day in the park, the **information center** can handle your recreational queries and give you a free map. *(☎ 420 5052. Open 8am-6pm.)*

BODEGAS AND WINE TOURS. Argentine wines are famous for their bold, fruity, flavor. Since up to 70% of Argentina's wine is produced at the abundant vineyards in this area, the best way to sample the wines is on one of the many available wine tours. Hard-core wine tasters should seek maps and guidance at the **visitor information centers** of vineyards they deem worthy of a visit. Those tourists who taste wine more for the flair of the action than the flavor of the product might appreciate the half-day tours, given three times a week, of an assortment of *bodegas* that include an ever-important tasting or two (see **Tours,** p. 270). Apart from offering well-organized tours, **La Rural** is known to have one of the largest and best facilities for independent visitors, including an entire museum devoted to *vino*. *(☎ 973 590. www.bodegalarural.com.ar. From the terminal, take bus #170/173; 30-45min. to the location in Maipú. Open M-F 9am-5pm, Sa-Su 9am-1pm.)* Also notable for its proximity and charming staff and ambience is the smaller facility, **Bodegas López.** *(Carril Ozamis 375, in Maipú. ☎ 497 2406. Bilingual tours every hr. M-F 9am-5pm with lunch break at 1, Sa 9:30am-12:30pm.)* Other vineyards to consider are **Bodega Salentein,** with its breathtaking location in Godoy Cruz. Salentein is constructed in the shape of a giant cross, with four separate wineries joined together in a central ampitheater. *(☎ 424 1845; www.bodegasalentein.com. Tours Tu-Sa 10am-4pm.)* If you simply can't get enough of Argentine wine, check out boutique-sized **Viña el Cerno,** in Maipú *(☎ 439 8447).*

> **FINE ARGENTINE WINE.** Although the best way to appreciate Argentina's particularly fine vintages is to experiment by sampling from the wide array of nuanced options, it does pay to follow some guidelines. First, the most acclaimed grapes grown in this region are **Cabernet Sauvignon** and **Malbec,** the former also being well-regarded in Chile. An extensive yet fair list of high-quality, good-value labels is impossible to assemble, but some amateur wine drinkers recommend the **Trapiche** and **Peñaflor** wines among the moderate ARG$12-25 bottle price range. **Flichman** is purportedly the way to go for a more expensive treat. **Azafrán** (see **Food,** p. 273) is a great spot to get a sense of your taste buds' fancy while you savor wines of disparate calibers.

SKIING. In the winter, busloads of travelers hit the eastern slopes of the Andes for first-rate skiing. Farthest from the city of Mendoza, **Las Leñas** has the best ski facilities in the country, but is prohibitively expensive by Argentine standards. Opened in 1983, the resort has over 65km of trail and nearly 2000 sq. km of off-trail skiing. It also has facilities for snowboarders and cross-country skiers. To add to its impressiveness, Las Leñas can hold over 3000 guests in lodgings that are all "ski in, ski out"—within 200m of a lift. *(☎ 114 313 1300; www.laslenas.com. Vertical drop 1230m. 13 lifts serve 55 trails. 5% beginner, 30% intermediate, 25% advanced, 40% expert. Open June-Nov. 9am-5pm.)* In contrast, **Vallecitos,** 79km from Mendoza, offers a short season and affordable lift tickets. The oldest ski resort in the area, it does offer respectable facilities and trails suited for both skiers and boarders. *(☎ 06 250 972. Vertical drop 2400m. 7 lifts serve 16.5km of trail. Open June-Sept.)* **Penitentes** is the unanimous choice for value, with a longer season, more snow, and stunning views of Aconcagua. *(☎ 424 8641 or 424 8633; www.lospenitentes.com. Vertical drop 2023m. 8 lifts serve 23.5km of trails. Open June 15-Oct. 15.)* Also at Penitentes is the HI-run **Refugio Penitentes ❶,** the cheapest lodging option in any of the Mendoza-area resorts. *(☎ 429 0707; info@campo-base.com.ar. CH$18,000-24,000 depending on the season.)*

OTHER SIGHTS. Perhaps the best unsung sight in Mendoza is the city's plaza system. The fountains and manicured gardens of **Plaza Independencia** are a free visual treat, but the theater and the **Museo de Arte Moderno** with its three-week exhibition rotation add depth to the visual appeal and make a day spent strolling through the city more substantive. (☎425 7279. *Open M-Sa 9am-1pm and 4-9pm, Su 4-9pm. Free.*) The most intriguing of the smaller plazas is **Plaza España,** which hosts an impressive monument and a collection of peddling artesans on weekends. The entire plaza is tiled, and each tile is decorated with some kind of colonial emblem—a horse, a crown, a tower. You'll be tempted to take pictures of the ground.

FESTIVALS. Mendoza's biggest event, the sparkling **Fiesta de la Vendimia,** during the first weekend of March, would make even Dionysus proud. Marking the grape harvest for autumn wine production, the three-day party is marked by wine paraphernalia, lavish food displays, and zany song-and-dance routines. Accommodations fill up well in advance, so plan ahead if you want to join in the merriment.

◙ NIGHTLIFE

Just because the wine's divine doesn't mean that *Mendocinos* don't just knock back for the buzz of it. Mendoza parties hard, and locals don't get their party started until many towns are already asleep. Dinner hours extend past 11pm, and many clubs don't open their doors until at least midnight. The greatest concentration of centrally-located nightlife is on **Aristides Villanueva,** the western extension of Colón. The dress code is fairly lax, and jeans are fine except in the priciest spots, but nice shoes and dressier pants will get you in if your pretty smile doesn't.

◙ **Por Acá,** Aristides Villanueva 557, at the corner of Granaderos. This trendy bar doesn't even need a specific name, other than "over there," because its beautiful young patrons are all in the know. Chill, jazzy music and understated decor set the ambience, but bar fare like *empanadas* (ARG$1) and individual pizzas (ARG$5-8) keep it from being uncomfortably pretentious. 1L beer ARG$3. Open Su-Th 8pm-4:30am, F-Sa 8pm-6am.

Apeteco, San Juan 199 (☎424 9220), at Barraquero. The only mark on this club's black facade is a giant metal logo of two stick figures, one with its legs straddling the other's head. It could be an encouragement to give piggy-backs to drunken friends, or it may hint at illicit behavior on far-flung corners of the dance floor, but it's hard to tell through the smoky fog. DJ plays disco, dance, and pop. Cover Tu-Th and Su ARG$3, F-Sa ARG$7. Open Tu-Th and Su midnight-3am, F-Sa midnight-7am.

El Cuervo Pub and Pool, at the corner of Pedro Molina and San Martín (☎425 1892). Cafe by day, this street-level pool hall morphs into a lively pub and disco on weekends. Pool ARG$3 per game. Expect a long wait during peak hours. Pub cover ARG$7. Pool hall open Su-W until late, Th-Sa 24hr. Pub open F-Sa midnight-7am.

Café del Teatro, at the corner of Av. Chile and Espejo (☎423 661), hosts different comedians, musicians, and lecturers each night. The clustered tables and dark lighting could make the time between acts just as engaging. Call ahead for schedule.

Drugstore Most, Montevideo and 9 de Julio (☎420 1954), on the northeast corner across from Plaza España. Nominally involved with real pharmaceuticals, Most supplies beer in copious quantities. A great place for a chill *cerveza* in a brightly-lit fishbowl room with stool seating—just don't reach for codeine by accident. Beer ARG$2. Open 24hr.

THE CENTRAL VALLEY

RANCAGUA ☎72

Rancagua is a vital resource for the regional economy, functioning as a market for the produce of the outlying countryside and as the source of much of the labor that keeps the nearby El Teniente copper mine humming. The city is not much to

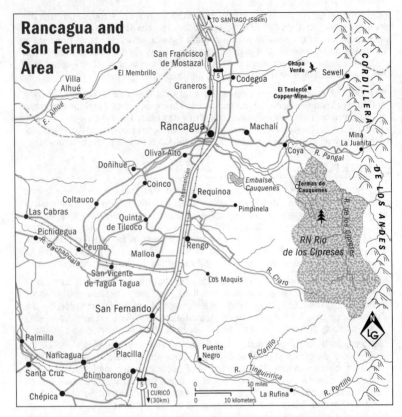

Rancagua and San Fernando Area

TO SANTIAGO (58km)

San Francisco de Mostazal

El Membrillo

Villa Alhué

Graneros

Codegua

Chapa Verde

Sewell

El Teniente Copper Mine

Rancagua

Machalí

Mina La Juanita

Olivar Alto

Coya

R. Pangal

Doñihue

Coinco

Embalse Cauquenes

Termas de Cauquenes

Coltauco

Requinoa

Las Cabras

Quinta de Tilcoco

Pimpinela

Pichidegua

R. Cachapoal

Peumo

Rengo

RN Río de los Cipreses

Malloa

R. de los Cipreses

San Vicente de Tagua Tagua

Los Maquis

R. Claro

San Fernando

Palmilla

Puente Negro

R. Clarillo

Nancagua

Placilla

Santa Cruz

Chimbarongo

R. Tinguiririca

Chépica

5 TO CURICÓ (30km)

La Rufina

R. Portillo

CORDILLERA DE LOS ANDES

Panamerican

0   10 miles
0   10 kilometers

look at, however—modern shopping centers, graffitied adobe buildings, and local complaints of crime in the dimly lit streets make it a more ideal stopover than a destination. The city throws off its shackles of banality for a week every year during Chile's **Rodeo Nacional,** but for the rest of the year, Rancagua is most popular among tourists as a jumping-off point for excursions to the Termas de Cauquenes, Chapa Verde ski center, Reserva Nacional Río de los Cipreses, and Lago Rapel.

TRANSPORTATION

Trains: Rancagua Station (☎230 361 or 238 530), on Estación between O'Carrol and Pinto, on the western edge of the city. Trains go to: **Chillán** (4hr.; 8:45am, 2:45, 7:45pm; CH$4200); **Concepción** (8hr., 10:50pm, CH$5800); **San Fernando** (50min.; M-F 6 per day 7:55am-10:30pm, Sa-Su 5 per day 11:15am-10:30pm; CH$630); **Santiago** (1¼hr.; M-F 20 per day 6:05am-10pm, Sa-Su 16 per day 7:15am-10pm; CH$1100); **Temuco** (11½hr., 9:09pm, CH$8000).

Buses: Tur Bus leaves from its terminal at O'Carrol 1175 (☎241 117), on the northeast corner of O'Carrol and Calvo. Buses go to: **Santiago** (1½hr., M-F every 15min. 5:50am-9:45pm, CH$1600); **Temuco** (8hr., 5:45am and 11:20pm, CH$6000). DC/MC/V. Other bus companies leave from the **Terminal Rodoviario,** on Doctor Salinas between Av. Viña del Mar and Calvo. **Buses al Sur** (☎222 669 or 230 340) goes to **Santiago**

Rancagua

⌂ ACCOMMODATIONS
Hotel Águila Real, **7**
Hotel Camino del Rey, **4**
Hotel España, **5**
Hotel Palace, **10**
Hotel Rancagua, **1**
Hotel Turismo Santiago, **8**

🍅 FOOD
Bavaria, **2**
Centro Chung Hwa, **3**
Daky, **6**
Max Sabor, **9**

(1½hr., M-Sa every 30min., CH$1300). **Gal-bus** (☎240 579) goes to **El Manzano** (3hr., every 15min. 6:25am-9pm, CH$1200) and **San Fernando** (1¼hr., every 16min. 6:08am-6:40pm, CH$700). **Sextur** (☎231 342) has service to **Lago Rapel** (2½hr.; 6 per day 6:25am-4pm; CH$1500) and **Pichilemu** (4hr., 6:40am, CH$2500).

Taxis/Colectivos: Rancagua is small enough to walk to most places, but try **Radio Taxi Arides** (☎216 175 or 219 728) for cheap, reliable service. Taxi fare from the train station to city center CH$650-1000. *Colectivos* CH$350 for trips within Rancagua.

ORIENTATION AND PRACTICAL INFORMATION

Eighty-seven kilometers south of Santiago on the Panamerican, Rancagua was originally designed as an 8-by-8 grid extending from **San Martín** in the west to **Freire** in the east, and from **O'Higgins** in the north to **Millán** in the south. At the center of the grid is the **Plaza de los Héroes,** where you can find Rancagua's City Hall, the provincial government office, and regional capitol building. Despite the original plan, however, Rancagua's commercial life has shifted to the west, closer to the city's train and bus terminals. Important commercial thoroughfares include San Martín, pedestrian mall **Independencia,** and **Brasil.** Keep in mind that you'll need to keep a map in hand. Few streets in town are labeled, so navigation can be very difficult.

MIDDLE CHILE

Tourist Office: Sernatur, Germán Riesco 277 (☎/fax 230 413; sernatur_rancag@entelchile.net). Open M-F 8:30am-5:15pm.

Tours: Turismo Dakota, Mújica 605 (☎228 166 or 228 165; fax 228 165; tdakota@cmet.net), arranges tours of **El Teniente** copper mine, which include transportation, tours of the mine and neighboring town of **Sewell,** and lunch (half-day excursion CH$18,000). Open M-F 9am-1:45pm and 3:30-7:30pm, Sa 10am-1pm. AmEx/DC/MC/V. A variety of tours are also offered by **Turismo Terrasur,** Astorga 230 (☎229 161; fax 229 149; terrasur@chilesat.net), including the **Ruta del Vino** winery tour (CH$68,000; includes lunch and a short course in wine tasting) and separate guided tours of El Teniente and Sewell (CH$30,000 for each excursion; includes lunch).

Currency Exchange: Forex, Astorga 369 (☎235 273). Cashes Thomas Cook and American Express traveler's checks. Has currency exchange, courier, wire, private postal box, photocopying, and fax services. Open M-F 9am-2pm and 4-7pm, Sa 10am-2pm.

Banks/ATMs: BancoEstado, Independencia 666 (☎239 823), has a **24hr. ATM.** Open M-F 9am-2pm. **Banco Santiago,** Mújica 577, on the corner with Astorga, has another 24hr. ATM. Open 9am-2:30pm.

Work Opportunities: Max Sabor (p. 279) hires waitstaff in Nov. **Granja Amanda,** Carrelea de la Fruta, El Manzano (☎198 2346), hires long-term, full-time workers in landscaping. For more info, see **Alternatives to Tourism,** p. 91.

Market: On Brasil, between Santa María and Independencia, a long line of street vendors have set up shop. In their stalls you can find just about anything—from fruit to handbags to Los Angeles Lakers headbands. Open daily 9am-10pm.

Police: ☎ 133. The *carabineros* have their **central office** (☎222 382) at the corner of O'Carrol and Bueras, and a branch office at San Martín 174 (☎221 122), between Cáceres and Mújica on the eastern side of the street.

Pharmacy: Farmacias Ahumada, Independencia 799 (☎228 342). Open daily 8:30am-midnight. **SalcoBrand Farmacéutica,** Independencia 784 (☎231 785). Open daily 9am-midnight.

Hospital: Ambulance ☎131. **Hospital Regional Rancagua,** O'Higgins 611 (☎200 200; emergency 207 253), where Astorga meets Alameda.

Fax Office: Services available at **Forex.** See **Currency Exchange,** above.

Telephones: Telefónica Mundo 188, San Martín 440 (☎227 595). Open M-F 9am-6pm, Sa 10am-1pm.

Internet Access: Servi@net, Centro Comercial Rodoviario, local 58-59 (☎220 814 or 09 226 4972; servi01@hotmail.com). M-F 9am-noon CH$600 per hr., all other times CH$800 per hr., students CH$700. Open M-Sa 9am-10pm.

Post Office: Correos is at Campos 322 (☎222 898 or 230 927). Open M-F 9am-1:30pm and 2:30-6pm, Sa 9am-12:30pm.

▟ ACCOMMODATIONS

Accommodations in Rancagua are somewhat limited, and generally reflect the atmosphere of the rest of the town. As crime is of huge concern in Rancagua, make sure to check the security of your accommodations upon arrival.

▧ **Hotel Rancagua,** San Martín 85 (☎232 663; fax 241 155; www.hotelrancagua.galeon.com). This hotel has the homey feel of a bed and breakfast, and a grandmotherly owner whose friendly demeanor will make you feel comfortable during your stay. Cable TV and Internet access available. Breakfast included. 24hr. reception. Singles CH$16,200; doubles CH$22,000; triples CH$29,000. ❹

Hotel Águila Real, Brasil 1045 (☎222 047; fax 223 002; Hsamour@ctcinternet.cl). This upscale hotel is rather sterile, but it makes up for its lack of pizzazz with an outdoor pool, ping-pong and billiards tables, private parking, and adequate (if somewhat small) mattresses dressed in plaid comforters. Cable TV. Breakfast and laundry service included. 24hr. reception. Singles CH$22,000; doubles CH$33,000. ❹

Hotel Turismo Santiago, Brasil 1036 (☎230 860 or 230 855; fax 230 822; hotels@gotolatin.com). In this stately hotel, rooms are smaller than you'd expect for the price, but it has large, comfortable beds, a full-service restaurant, and an outdoor pool. Cable TV. Breakfast included. Singles CH$28,600; doubles CH$41,600. ❺

Hotel España, San Martín 367 (☎230 141; fax 234 196). This century-old hotel has seen better days, as evidenced by the chipped paint and the ancient wooden doors that are difficult to lock. Still, Hotel España has a nice atmosphere and a cozy inner courtyard. Cable TV. Breakfast included. Singles CH$15,000; doubles CH$20,000-24,000. ❹

Hotel Palace, Calvo 635 and Estación 628 (☎224 104). The sign out front announces "Atención Las 24 Hrs," and red hearts flank the hotel's name. Continental breakfast CH$950. 24hr. reception. *Matrimoniales* CH$14,000; with space heaters, bath, and cable TV CH$22,000. ❸

Hotel Camino del Rey, Estado 275 (☎232 314 or 239 765; fax 232 314; hotelcaminodelrey@terra.cl). Though its name speaks of royal grandeur, this hotel is actually somewhat bland, despite its many amenities. Cable TV, minibar, security safe, private parking, central heating, and A/C. Breakfast included. 24hr. reception. Flexible check-out. Singles US$51; doubles US$76; triples US$102; suites US$92. Foreigners are exempt from the 18% IVA tax. AmEx/MC/V. ❺

🗋 FOOD

As with accommodations, food options in Rancagua are sparse, with many shops selling bread and *empanadas*, and not much in the way of restaurants.

Max Sabor, San Martín 422, 2nd fl. (☎220 088). A painting of a smiling waiter directs you carefully up the dark staircase into the bright eating area, where you'll find cheap specials, such as *pollo asado* (comes with soup, beverage, and a cup of diced fruit; CH$1000). Vegetarians can try the pizza with tomato, cheese, asparagus, and paprika (CH$900), and everyone loves a jug of Cristal beer (CH$2200). Open daily 9am-1am. ❶

Bavaria, San Martín 255 (☎233 827; www.bavaria.cl). This branch of the popular chain offers some of the best dining in Rancagua. One of its specialties is a roasted leg of lamb (CH$3100). To go with the delightfully unhealthy array of barbecue (CH$11,900), there is a variety of salads (CH$850-1950). Open M-Sa 9:30am-11pm, Su noon-10pm. ❸

Centro Chung Hwa, Cuevas 559 (☎244 705), between Astorga and Campos. Looks like any other mid-range *chifa*, with velvet-lined chairs, crimson tablecloths, and Chinese characters and watercolors decorating the walls. The food has a distinctively Chilean influence, however, with dishes like mandarin *parrilla* (CH$3000). Lunch *menú* CH$2800. Open daily 11:30am-3pm and 7:30pm-12:30am. DC/MC/V. ❷

Daky, San Martín 340 (☎243 813). The Budweiser babe meets the Cristal chick at this salt-of-the-earth *fuente de soda* downtown, where the pin-up pictures vie for your attention, along with equally glamorous photos of cheeseburgers and hot dogs. But forget the aesthetics—you can get a giant jug of Cristal for CH$2100. Open daily 6pm-3am. ❷

◉ SIGHTS

PLAZA DE LOS HÉROES. At the center of the city, in the **Plaza de los Héroes,** typical *bravura* statues glorify heroes of the city's past. One site of their remembered deeds is at the **Iglesia de la Merced,** Cuevas 399. In October 1814, the church (then a convent), was Rancagua's tallest building, and from its tower, O'Higgins kept close watch of the Spanish army as it crossed the Cachapoal River and headed north to smash the rebel movement. When they demanded surrender, he hung a black priest's robe in defiance. (☎ 221 456. Open daily 9am-1pm and 4-7:30pm. Mass M-Sa 7pm; Su 10am, noon, 7pm. Free.) On the southern edge of the plaza at O'Carrol 535 sits the **Iglesia Catedral.** Though small compared to the Catholic flagships in larger cities, the cathedral can be magnificent on a sunny day, its walls a gleaming gold. (☎ 230 048. Open M-Sa 9am-1pm and 4-8pm, Su during mass at 8, 11am, 12:30, 8pm. Free.)

ALONG CALLE ESTADO. Heading down Estado, the street next to the cathedral, you'll find the **Museo Regional,** Estado 685, to your right, and the **Casa del Pilar de Esquina,** Estado 682, on your left. These two buildings are the only structures still standing from the time of Santa Cruz de Tirana, the village that became Rancagua. (Museo Regional ☎ 221 524; fax 221 524; museo@chilesat.net. Both Museo Regional and Casa del Pilar open Tu-F 10am-6pm, Sa-Su 9am-1pm. CH$600, under 18 CH$300, includes both museums. Tu and Su free. Pay at the offices in Museo Regional.)

After leaving the twin museums, head farther south to where Estado meets Millán. The **Casa de la Cultura,** on Cachapoal, is across the street on the left. When the land north of the Río Cauquenes was a huge estate by the name of Los Cipreses, stretching out to the national reserve out east, this was the masters' **casa patronal.** All that remains from that day are portions of the original wall, thick adobe some 300 years old; the sienna-red roof and mixed-stone patio have been reconstructed. In addition to its tranquil groves of palm and pine trees, the *casa* showcases local art and houses a music school. The **library** is a good place for those escaping the city's bustle. (☎ 230 976 or 231 577. Casa open M-Sa 9am-8pm. Library open M-F 9:30am-1:30pm and 2:45-7:30pm, Sa 9:30am-1:30pm. Free.)

RODEO. The Central Valley is known as the *tierra huasa*—land of the cowboy—and Rancagua is the place where Chile's *huasos* gather for the national **rodeo championships,** which take place every year at the end of March or during the first week in April. The event is held at the city's grand **medialuna,** about a kilometer north of the city center. Here, rows of wooden benches ring a half-moon-shaped dirt space, framed in the distance by towering mountains. Even when the *huasos* aren't in action, however, they impress crowds with their splendid costuming—colorfully woven ponchos *(chamantos)*, wide-brimmed hats *(bonetesas huicanos)*, and silvery steel spurs. (To get to the medialuna, follow San Martín, which becomes España, and keep walking north until you hit Germán Ibarra—the yellow adobe complex is on your left across the street. Rodeo season begins after Independence Day, September 18. Call the Federación de Rodeos office in Rancagua at ☎ 221 286 for dates of local rodeos.)

DAYTRIPS FROM RANCAGUA

EL TENIENTE COPPER MINE

Codelco arranges tours to the area (50km east of Rancagua) through several local travel agencies. Call the Codelco offices (☎ 690 3000) for the most up-to-date list.

The largest underground mine in the world, El Teniente is the flagship of Chile's copper industry, a 1500km maze of tunnels burrowed into the Andes, 50km northwest of Rancagua. Founded in 1905, it now employs over 6000 workers. Tourists can visit the mine and take a guided tour through the tunnels. The required safety gear—plastic flashlight helmet, reflective jacket, gumboots, ventilator, safety belt, and goggles—will bring out your inner child. *(Tours cost around CH$7000 per person, last from 9am-3pm, and include excursions to the mine, its smelter, and the abandoned company town of Sewell. Some even include lunch deep inside the mine's recesses. See **Tours**, p. 278 for a listing of Rancagua agencies that offer El Teniente packages.)*

CHAPA VERDE SKI CENTER

The road to Chapa Verde is blocked to anyone without a permit (CH$80,000 per year), so catch the shuttle at the Lider Vecino supermarket, Miguel Ramírez 665, in Plaza América, east of the Plaza de los Héroes.

While outclassed by other ski resorts in the Andes, Chapa Verde offers a respectable array of 22 slopes, less than an hour by bus from Rancagua. Codelco, the corporation in charge of the nearby El Teniente copper mine, originally established the ski center for its workers, but the public is now welcome. The ski center offers slopes at all difficulty levels, serviced by five lifts (three 1200m, two 300m). There are restaurants at the middle and bottom of the mountain, serving snacks, international cuisine, and barbecue. *(☎ 217 651 or 294 255. Buses leave M-F 9-9:30am and Sa-Su 8-9:30am and return from the resort at 4:30pm. M-F US$5.70, Sa-Su US$6. Ski center ☎ 294 255; www.chapaverde.cl. Fully-appointed cabañas at **Hoya Blanca Resort** US$57-140 per day. Open June-Sept. 9am-5pm. Lift tickets M-F US$17, students US$13; Sa-Su US$22/ $17. Skis, boots, and poles US$19, snowboards and boots US$20.)*

LAGO RAPEL

Chile's largest artificial lake, Lago Rapel is a haven for backpackers looking for a not-so-wilderness experience and water sport enthusiasts seeking a place to take their jet skis out for a spin. The 40km long lake emerged in its present form in 1968 with the damming of the Cachapoal and Tinguiririca Rivers. Most buses and *colectivos* to the area run along the Carretera de la Fruta to the village of **El Manzano,** located on the southern shore of the lake's upper arm. Near its center, there is a *carabineros* stand that can assist you. For an impressive view, head north along the Carretera de la Fruta—a good 30min. walk to a bridge that spans the lake.

If you need help, visit the El Manzano *carabineros*, east of the town center on the *carretera*. A list of campsites and a map of the lake are available at **Las Cabras,** the nearby municipality. *(☎ 501 028 or 501 250; lascabrasmuni@entelchile.net).*

Many campgrounds and *cabañas* cover the lake's shores. Neaby El Manzano is **Granja Amanda ❷,** on the southeastern edge of the lake's upper arm, along the *carretera* as it heads north, 800m from the Puente el Durazno. Amanda has 66 10m-by-10m sites along the lakeshore with thatched-roof huts for picnicking under, and separate shower and bathroom facilities. *(☎ 198 2352; Dec.-Mar. 5-person campsites CH$25,000, each additional person CH$3000; Apr.-Nov. CH$15,000. Free use of windsurfing equipment, sailboats, and catamarans.)*

TERMAS DE CAUQUENES ☎ 72

Perched on a high bluff alongside the winding Río Cachapoal is the **Hotel Termas de Cauquenes ❺,** a hot springs resort where Chilean patriot Bernardo O'Higgins once rested, and one that continues to draw weary travelers looking for some pampering. The thermal baths are in the hotel's *sala de baños*, a high-ceilinged wooden hall decorated with stained glass and fresco paintings. There are 26 private stalls, each with a marble tub (the originals were installed in 1856) or a modern jacuzzi, all running the same pungent, mineral- infused waters. For some, the experience may be no more than a hot bath in smelly water, but it certainly soothes a weary back. (CH$3000 for marble baths; CH$5000 for jacuzzis. Massages CH$15,000.) A wooden bridge stretched between two stone arches leads across the river's small, rumbling rapids into a park, where cacti grow alongside towering trees.

French and Central European cuisine is served in the hotel's Mediterranean-style **restaurant** ❺, which provides a view of the snow-dusted Andes in the distance. (☎297 226. Breakfast CH$6000; lunch CH$13,000; dinner CH$17,000. AmEx/DC/MC/V.) The hotel's rooms are nothing special. (☎899 010; www.termasdecauquenes.cl. Breakfast included. Singles US$70; doubles US$72; triples US$165; quads US$164.) The hotel also offers day-tours to nearby **Reserva Nacional Río de los Cipreses,** a vast stretch of wilderness which offers scenic hikes past waterfalls, lakes, and glacial valleys.

SAN FERNANDO   ☎72

A small, sleepy town hidden among crop fields, San Fernando has no grandiose ambition to be a tourist mecca. Perhaps embodying the slow-paced *campo* lifestyle or the all-too-obvious lack of resources, San Fernando has not aesthetically recovered from a devastating 1985 earthquake; many of the victims, including once-soaring colonial churches, still remain shattered. San Fernando is, however, ringed by a scenic route that cuts right into the heart of Chile's *huaso* culture and ends at nationally-loved beaches. As a result, San Fernando's tourists continue to pass through on their way to more appealing attractions.

▐ TRANSPORTATION

Trains: The **train station** (☎711 087) is on Quechereguas. Trains go to: **Chillán** (3½hr., 5 per day 8:50am-7:50pm, CH$4500-6000); **Concepción** (10hr., 12:20am, CH$6500-8000); **Rancagua** (45min., M-F 5 per day 5am-9pm, CH$550); **Santiago** (2¼hr., M-F 5 per day 5am-9pm, CH$1650-13,200); **Temuco** (12hr., 7:30am and 7:30pm, CH$16,000-18,000).

Buses: Terminal de Buses, Manso de Velasco 1009 (☎713 912), 1 block east of the corner with O'Higgins. Information booth open daily 6am-10pm. **Buses Nilahue** (☎711 937), **Tur Bus** (☎712 929), and **Rutamar** (☎723 400) send buses to: **Bucalemu** (2½hr., 4 per day 10:15am-5:15pm, CH$2000); **Chillán** (4hr., every hr. 7am-8pm, CH$3100); **Concepción** (5hr., 12 per day 7:10am-12:30am, CH$4000); **Curicó** (1½hr., every 30min. 6am-midnight, CH$1000); **Pichilemu** (2½hr., 25 per day 8am-9:40pm, CH$2000); **Santa Cruz** (1hr., every 30min. 6am-11pm, CH$700); **Santiago** (2hr., 40 per day 5am-10pm, CH$2000); **Temuco** (7hr., 8 per day 9:30am-12:45pm, CH$5000); **Termas del Flaco** (4hr., Dec.-Mar. daily 3:30 and 4pm, CH$4000).

Taxis: *Colectivos* circle between the bus station and the hospital, along Velasco and Manuel Rodríguez. CH$200 anywhere in town.

✦ ▐ ORIENTATION AND PRACTICAL INFORMATION

San Fernando sits alongside the Río Tinguiririca. **Manso de Velasco** marks the northern boundary, running from the **bus terminal** in the southeast to the city's hospital and its two national monuments in the northwest. It is connected by the north-south **O'Higgins** to the east-west **Manuel Rodríguez**—this intersection forms the commercial heart of the city. The city's nondescript **Plaza de Armas** sits forlornly several blocks northwest of the O'Higgins/Rodríguez intersection.

Tourist Office: The closest thing San Fernando has to a tourist office is **Centro de Fotocopiado PSC,** Valdivia 754 (☎713 072), which sells detailed, unwieldy maps of the town (CH$600). Open M-F 9am-8pm, Sa 10am-1pm. For information, the best bet is to ask your hotel owner or stop at the tourist office in Rancagua (p. 278).

Bank: Banco de Chile, Manuel Rodríguez 864 (☎712 033), at the southwest corner of O'Higgins and Manuel Rodríguez, has a **24hr. ATM.** Open 9am-2pm.

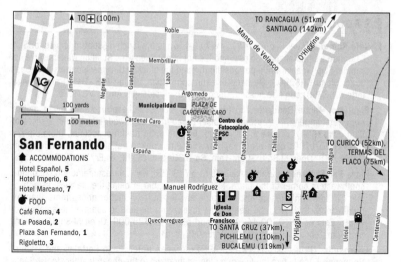

San Fernando

ACCOMMODATIONS
Hotel Español, 5
Hotel Imperio, 6
Hotel Marcano, 7

FOOD
Café Roma, 4
La Posada, 2
Plaza San Fernando, 1
Rigoletto, 3

Work Opportunity: Hotel Termas del Flaco (☎711 832), employs 70 seasonal hotel workers. See **Alternatives to Tourism**, p. 91.

Police: ☎133. *Carabineros* at Manuel Rodríguez 625, right across from the Iglesia de San Francisco, beside the plaza.

Pharmacy: Farmacias Ahumada, Manuel Rodríguez 902 (☎729 895), at the intersection with O'Higgins. Open daily 8am-midnight. AmEx/MC/V.

Hospital: Ambulance ☎131. **Hospital San Juan de Dios,** Negrete 1401 (☎209 400), at the northwestern end of Manso de Velasco, 1 block south of the corner with Carelmapu.

Fax Office and Telephones: Entel, Manuel Rodríguez 999 (☎715 941), on the corner with Rancagua. Domestic CH$350 per page, international CH$490 per page. Open M-F 8:30am-9pm, Sa 9am-6pm. AmEx/MC/V.

Internet Access: Matrix, Manuel Rodríguez 660, inside the courtyard. CH$500 per hr. Open M-Sa 10am-11pm, Su 3-9pm.

Post Office: Correos, O'Higgins 545 (☎711 051), in a small storefront. Open M-F 9am-1pm and 2:30-5pm, Sa 9am-noon.

ACCOMMODATIONS

Hotel Marcano, Manuel Rodríguez 968 (☎714 759), 1 block east of O'Higgins. Rooms vary greatly in price and quality, but tend to be clean and heated with gas-burning stoves. Cable TV. Breakfast included. Singles CH$12,000-18,800, with private bath CH$16,200-27,200; doubles CH$25,300-29,300; triples CH$37,700. IVA discount for foreigners. AmEx/MC/V. ❺

Hotel Español, Manuel Rodríguez 959 (☎711 098), between O'Higgins and Rancagua. This aging hotel has faded somewhat over the last several decades, but still offers plump beds and tastefully decadent rooms, with red carpeting and leafy ferns in the inner patio, and plaster sculptures of nymphs all over. Cable TV. Breakfast included. Singles CH$16,500; doubles CH$23,600. ❹

Hotel Imperio, Manuel Rodríguez 770 (☎714 595), 2 blocks west of O'Higgins. Simply adequate; the place is clean and the furniture simple. All rooms have private bath. Breakfast included. Reception 24hr. Singles CH$13,000; doubles CH$18,000. ❸

🟦 FOOD

🟦 **Café Roma,** Manuel Rodríguez 815 (☎ 711 455), is the lunching spot of choice for San Fernando's small business class, and it's not hard to see why. Bustling waiters serve up simple, filling meals, while patrons flip through the stack of daily newspapers from Santiago. *Menú* CH$2500. Desserts like the *copa italia* sundae (CH$1650) and orange torte (CH$750) can't be missed. Open daily 9am-midnight. AmEx/MC/V. ❷

Rigoletto, Manuel Rodríguez 751 (☎ 711 396), between Chacabuco and Chillán, across from Hotel Imperio. The *escalopes kaiser* (deep-fried steak wedged between 2 slices of ham; CH$3600), is sure to fill you up. For the more health-conscious, there's pizza (CH$1400-1700) or a *plato vegetariano* with cooked veggies that includes ham (CH$2700). Open M-Sa 8:30am-1am, Su 8:30am-midnight. AmEx/MC/V. ❷

Plaza San Fernando, Carampangue 787 (☎ 713 456; www.plazasanfernando.cl), on the southwestern corner of the plaza. Making a strong bid at being the classiest establishment in town, this restaurant unfortunately depends on higher prices more than on quality food. Still, you'll be treated like royalty and be able to sample the area's finer wines. Entrees CH$2700-4400. Seafood platter CH$28,000. Open M-Sa 10am-4pm and 6pm-2am, Su 2pm-midnight. AmEx/MC/V. ❸

La Posada, O'Higgins 651 (☎ 723 398), between Hotel Diego Portales and Manuel Rodríguez. Posada has the feel of a diner, right down to the cheap leather stools. Sandwiches CH$350-1650. Beer CH$400-1200. Open daily 8:30am-1am. ❶

👁 SIGHTS

The **Casa Lircunlauta,** Juan Jiménez 1595 (☎ 713 326), is at the northwestern end of Manso de Velasco. The name of this newly restored villa means "beautiful entry" in Mapuche, and it is a good place to start any tour of San Fernando—mainly because it's the only site that actually lets visitors walk inside. The white-adobe *casa patronal* was the home of wealthy landowner Juan Jiménez de Léon, who in 1742 donated part of his *hacienda* to the governor for the formation of San Fernando. Today, it is a brand-new museum spotlighting local natural history and *huaso* culture, as well as San Fernando's 15 minutes of international fame: local *carabineros* rescued Uruguayans stranded in the nearby Andes and brought them back to San Fernando to recuperate—a story best known from Frank Marshall's 1992 film, *Alive!* (*Casa* open Tu-Su 9am-1pm and 4-7pm. CH$500, students CH$100.)

🟦 DAYTRIPS FROM SAN FERNANDO

MUSEO DE COLCHAGUA

The Museo de Colchagua is in Santa Cruz, 37km southwest of San Fernando. Take a bus from San Fernando to Santa Cruz and ask to be let off at the Museo, Errázuriz 145.

Locals speak of the 🟦**Museo de Colchagua** with awe, claiming that it takes nearly a day to visit the museum in its entirety—and they aren't far off. This is the largest privately run museum in the country, and easily one of Chile's finest. In 1994, the **Fundación Cardoen** opened the Museo de Colchagua in an old colonial house with the purpose to exhibit "the wealth of creation...born into this land."

The museum begins with both minute and large—although all impressively delicate—fossils from around the Americas. The collection then moves through regional and national history, beginning with rich textiles, jewelry, and artifacts from the pre-Colombian cultures of South America to the present-day Colchagua Valley and its *huaso* culture. The exhibits are outdoors, in a peaceful courtyard adorned with turn-of-the-century viticulture equipment and a fully reconstructed Mapuche *ruca*. (☎821 050. Open Tu-Su 10am-6pm. CH$2500, students CH$500.)

LA RUTA DEL VINO

To organize a scheduled wine-tasting tour, contact La Ruta del Vino de Colchagua, Plaza de Armas 298, Santa Cruz. To reach the office from San Fernando, take a bus to Santa Cruz and ask to be let off at the Plaza. To reach the Viu Manet Winery, take a bus from San Fernando to Santa Cruz and ask to be let off at "Viña Viu."

The overlooked Colchagua Valley, cutting through the Coastal Range between San Fernando and Pichilemu, doesn'tt produce large quantities of any of Chile's well-known wines. Instead, the beautiful vineyards, nestled among arid hills, produce specialized, premium wines. Still, the family-run vineyards of the Colchagua Valley, nestled in the heart of Chilean *huaso* country, have refused to separate themselves from the valley's unique heritage, and make their wines—mostly Malbec and Cabernet Sauvignon—the old-fashioned way. Ten wineries in the relatively small Colchagua region have organized a vineyard and wine-tasting tour through **La Ruta del Vino de Colchagua** (☎823 199; www.rutadelvino.cl. Open M-F 9am-1pm and 3-6pm. Full-day tour, including transportation to 3 wineries, with English guide and lunch for 1 person CH$90,000; 2 people CH$58,000 per person; 3-5 people CH$45,000 per person; 6 or more people CH$34,000 per person. Express tour, including transportation to 2 wineries, with English guide for 1 person CH$56,000; 2 people CH$35,000 per person; 3-5 people CH$25,000 per person; 6 or more people CH$18,000 per person. Reservations required at least 24hr. in advance.)

You need not shell out wads of cash to tour the vineyards of Colchagua, however. Almost all lie along the road between San Fernando and Pichilemu and most buses will be happy to leave you at the vineyard of your choice. If you arrange for your own transportation, you should still contact La Ruta del Vino de Colchagua, as they can provide information on each vineyard, including tour times, and book tours for you. Each tour costs CH$6000 per person, includes a tasting, and must be reserved 24hr. in advance. The **Viu Manet Winery,** 5km east of Santa Cruz, offers an excellent, detailed tour of both viticulture and its own production. The 1hr. tour includes tasting of wines at different stages of the production process. (☎72 858 751; www.viumanet.cl. Tours Tu-Su 11am, 12:30, 3:30, and 5pm.)

PICHILEMU   ☎72

The brainchild of Scottish-Chilean businessman Agustín Ross Edwards, Pichilemu emerged in the late 19th century as a European-style luxury resort with a grand hotel, casino (Chile's first), and palm-studded park. Since then, Pichilemu's luxury has faded into the modest lodgings that now line the beach and surround the abandoned casino. This, however, gave Pichilemu a second lease on life. Today, the city draws a younger, hipper crowd—surfers hailing from Australia, Brazil, the US, and elsewhere now pack the hotels and *cabañas* in Pichilemu and nearby Punta de Lobos during the summer, raising rents—and also quite a bit of ruckus. The excellent waves aren't the only draw to Pichilemu; its beautiful vistas and *tranquilo* way of life also attract plenty of middle-class Chilean families looking to spend their vacation time on reasonably priced relaxation. Even so, the *surfistas* insist you won't get to know Pichilemu until you've taken a good headlong plunge just beyond the rocks of the *puntilla*. Don't forget your wetsuit.

▐ TRANSPORTATION

Buses: Buses stop along Pinto, 1 block south of the intersection with Ortúzar, in the commerical center of town. Separate booths on Pinto and Ortúzar sell tickets for each line. **Andimar** and **Pullman del Sur**, Pinto 213 (☎843 118), have buses to: **Curicó** (3hr., 10am and 10pm, CH$2500); **Rancagua** (3hr., every 30min. 6am-7pm, CH$2000); **Santa Cruz** (1¼hr., every 30min. 6am-9pm, CH$1200); **San Fernando** (2½hr., every 30min. 6am-7pm, CH$1500); **Santiago** (5hr., every 30min. 6am-7pm, CH$2500).

Car Rental: Puerto Piedra, Ortúzar 369 (☎09 562 220), rents a Toyota 4X4 for CH$35,000 per day. Call 24hr. in advance. Open M-Sa 10am-2pm and 4-7pm.

▰ ▐ ORIENTATION AND PRACTICAL INFORMATION

Pichilemu, 110km west of San Fernando, lies along the Pacific Ocean. The commercial heart of town is in the north, at the intersection of **Pinto** and **Ortúzar.** Pinto enters town from the north, crosses Ortúzar, and continues south, turning into **Ross.** Both Ross and **Costanera,** the beachside street, connect the north to the residential south and the *puntilla,* the main destination for visiting *surfistas.*

Tourist Office: Oficina de Turismo, Ángel Gaete 365 (☎841 257 or 842 532; www.pichilemu.cl), in the *municipalidad* building. Supplies maps of the city and coastal region. There is at least 1 English speaker among the helpful staff; ask for María Elena Arraya. Open M-F 8am-1pm and 2-5:30pm.

Banks: BancoEstado, Errázuriz 397 (☎841 091), 3 blocks south of Ortúzar along Pinto. **24hr. ATM.** Open M-F 9am-2pm. Or try **Banco del Desarollo,** Ortúzar 472 (☎842 858), between O'Higgins and Prat. **24hr. ATM.** Open daily 9am-2pm.

Rentals: Surf Shop, Ortúzar 305 (☎841 236), is a small boutique inside the Farmacia Nacional (see below). Buy surf gear or rent a surfboard for CH$6500 per day. Open daily in summer 9:30am-1am; in winter 9:30am-1:30pm and 4-9:30pm. A tiny shop to the left of Balaustro (p. 287) also sells surfing and skating gear and beachwear.

Surfing Schools: Lobos del Pacífico (☎09 9773 9580 or 09 9718 0255; lobosdelpacifico@hotmail.com), on Costanera. With the ocean on your right, walk down Costanera toward the *puntilla;* once you pass Merino, you'll see a wooden shack with an "Escuela de Surf" sign. Private and group lessons CH$10,000 (includes two 2hr. sessions). Open daily 9am-7pm. **Towia Big Wave** (09 401 1352), 6km south of town, is Punta de Lobos's new surf school. The owner gives surfing, windsurfing, and kitesurfing lessons at this surf mecca. Call 24hr. in advance.

Police: ☎133. Ortúzar 609 (☎841 034 or 841 939), at the corner with O'Higgins.

Pharmacy: Farmacia Nacional, Ortúzar 305 (☎841 236), at the corner with Pinto. Open daily in summer 9:30am-1am; in winter 9:30am-1:30pm and 4-9:30pm.

Hospital: Ambulance ☎131. The local hospital (☎841 022) is on Jorge Errázuriz between Valderrama and Jaramillo.

Telephones and Internet Access: SurfNet, Pinto 105 (☎/fax 841 324; www.surfnet.cl), 2 blocks south of Ortúzar. Calls to US CH$290 per min., to Canada CH$350 per min., to Australia and Europe CH$500 per min. Internet CH$800 per hr. Open daily 9am-11pm.

Post Office: Correos, Ortúzar 568 (☎842 131). Open M-F 9am-1pm and 3-5pm.

█ ACCOMMODATIONS

Because of Pichilemu's century-old tradition as a vacation spot, there are plenty of options for lodging here. Thanks to the town's price-conscious vacationers, rates are reasonable. Many foreigners staying several days rent a *cabaña*. Call the real estate agency in the Farmacia Nacional or the tourist office to arrange a rental.

Hotel Bar Rex, Ortúzar 034 (☎841 003). Right on the shore, Rex makes a jaunt to the beach all but effortless. But with plump new mattresses, hot water, and fine (if pricey) dining, you may be inclined to spend the day lazing at the hotel instead. Reservations recommended 2 days in advance Dec.-Mar. Breakfast included. Dec.-Mar. singles CH$10,000; doubles with cable TV CH$18,000. Apr.-Nov. CH$8000/CH$16,000. ❸

Hotel Asthur, Ortúzar 540 (☎841 072; fax 842 545; asthur@starmedia). As Pichilemu's humble attempt at luxury, Hotel Asthur is simply comfortable. Large rooms radiate off an impressive, sun-drenched main hall. All rooms have private bath and cable TV. Breakfast included. Dec.-Mar. singles CH$19,000; doubles CH$20,000; triples CH$30,000. Apr.-Nov. CH$18,000/CH$19,000/CH$30,000. AmEx/MC/V. ❹

Hotel Chile España, Ortúzar 255 (☎841 270; fax 841 314), toward the ocean, under the hot-pink neon sign and various country flags. As you might guess from the posters of Pichilemu's surfing championships and the surfboards littering the hallways, this is a top lodging choice among surf nomads. Internet CH$1000 per hr. Breakfast included. Rooms CH$7000 per person, with bath CH$9000 per person. AmEx/MC/V. ❷

Residencial Plaza, Ángel Gaete 109 (☎841 000), 1 block south of Ortúzar and down the hill. The small, hardwood rooms on the 2nd fl. look out over the beach and are warmed by the late afternoon sun. 1st fl. rooms look out onto a small courtyard where drying wetsuits and stray dogs collect. Shared bath. Breakfast included. Dec.-Feb. CH$4000 per person; Mar.-Nov. CH$3000 per person. ❶

█ FOOD

Most visitors to Pichilemu stay for a length of time, or are on a budget, resulting in a high ratio of grocery stores to restaurants. Pichilemu does, however, have places to eat out, with extensive seafood menus at affordable prices. Many restaurants also double as bars and stay open late to fuel hot summer nights.

Delirium Tremens, Ortúzar 215. With blaring music, a dance floor, and a young, rowdy crowd, Delirium Tremens's menu almost gets overlooked. Their pizzas (CH$1500-2000) are not to be ignored. Beer from CH$1200. Open daily 6pm-3am. AmEx/MC/V. ❷

Restaurant Donde Pin-Pon, Ross 96 (☎842 820), on the corner of Ross and Errázuriz, across from Banco de Chile. This is the consummate seafood restaurant—right down to the seashell necklaces hanging from the ceiling and the flies buzzing over your salsa. Try the *paila marina* (CH$2200) for a real shellfish rush—a savory, soupy blend of clams, mussels, crab, fish, cilantro, and other secret ingredients. Open 9am-midnight. ❷

Balaustro, Ortúzar 289 (☎842 458; info@balaustro.cl). Highly recommended by locals for a reason, Balaustro serves up excellent seafood in an elegant setting. The lunch *menú* (CH$2500) is a good pick, but doesn't compare to the wine-marinated clams (CH$3000). Live music on some nights. Open daily 9am-2am. AmEx/MC/V. ❸

Hotel Bar Rex, Ortúzar 34 (☎841 003). At this hotel restaurant, napkins are crisply folded, wine bottles are displayed artistically, and an old piano stands in the corner. Try the *Congrío Rex* (conger eel broiled with stuffed tomatoes, cheese, and *choricillo;* CH$3500). Open daily 8am-midnight. AmEx/MC/V. ❹

◉ SIGHTS

■ **PUNTA DE LOBOS.** The long, narrow Punta de Lobos pricks deeply into the Pacific's rough hide, helping to form one of the longest, most consistent left-points in South America. For non-surfers, the titanic waves crashing against the point and the wide **Playa Hermosa,** stretching all the way back to town, make the trip extremely worthwhile. The point is owned by a French-Chilean, Jean-Ro Pistone, who is completing construction on a shell-ornamented hostel, restaurant, and surf school (p. 286). *(Punta de Lobos is located 6km south of Pichilemu and may only be reached by private transportation. From town, follow Pinto as it turns into Ross, Merino, and finally, Comercio—the only road heading south out of town.)*

LA PUNTILLA. Punta de Lobos's smaller sibling and Pichilemu's own seaward-pointing toe, **La Puntilla,** is a wide, downward-slanting beach, ringed with squat black rocks, that has become one of the surf crowd's favorite spots for setting out into the Pacific. Waves here swoop down upon bathers with relentless force. To place yourself between a rock and that hard fist of water you'd have to be as crazy as…well, a surfer. *(Go down the long set of stairs to the bluff's edge and you will hit Costanera; turn left and follow Costanera down for a few minutes to reach La Puntilla. Beach open 24hr.)*

PARQUE MUNICIPAL AGUSTÍN ROSS EDWARDS. Originally built and planted by Pichilemu founder Agustín Ross Edwards, the eponymous park, on a bluff overlooking the sea, retains some of its original palms, as well as a host of smaller trees pruned in the shape of mushrooms. From the park's edge you can see the ocean stretching out before you. On one end of the park is the once-grand casino, the first gambling operation in the country. The card sharks have long since gone elsewhere, and nowadays the casino is just a historical monument in a sad state of disrepair. The *municipalidad,* in fact, is seeking sponsors to fund its renovation. *(Gates heading out to Ross open 9am-6pm; stone steps to the beach open at all times. Free. Casino open mid-Dec. to Feb. 10am-11pm. Free, donations suggested.)*

BUCALEMU   ☎ 72

The tiny fishing vilage of Bucalemu, standing firm against the ravages of the Pacific Ocean, is testing the waters of tourism. With little more to the town than a string of small seafood restaurants and a wide, black-sand beach that stretches to the horizon, Bucalemu is the more economical option for beach-going Central Chileans. A town of no more than 500 people, 112km southeast of San Fernando, quiet Bucalemu sits on a hillside literally at the end of the road. The houses on top of the hill—"Bucalemu Alto"—peer over a rocky cliff into the depths of the sea. At the bottom, where all the restaurants are, windows face north toward the cove and gently curving beach. During most of the year, the only activity in town is mending nets, but during the summer, sun-seekers on a budget flock to Bucalemu, taking advantage of its cheap lodging and fresh seafood. Most try their hand at windsurfing, though activity is limited since there are no places in town to rent equipment.

Bucalemu is well-stocked with seafood restaurants, although they all tend to be small, nondescript, and quite similar—perhaps it is because they all just either fry or boil whatever is caught that day. The restaurants line the main road into town, and all face the beach. **Restaurant Capri ❷,** near where the main street meets the sea, after the turnoff up the hill, not only provides variety, serving pizza, but also has a gut-busting portion of *corvina* (sea bass) with bread and a side (CH$3500). Glasses of Colchagua Valley wines cost CH$700. (☎825 949. AmEx/MC/V.)

There are two hotels, one at the bottom of the hill overlooking the beach, and the other at the top of the hill, within earshot of the waves crashing against the rocks. Both are large, sunny places with clean rooms at a value. **Hotel Rocha ❷,** along the

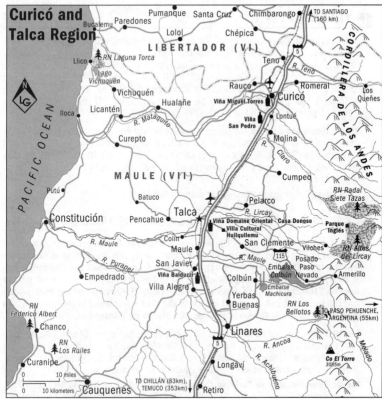

Curicó and Talca Region

Pumanque · Santa Cruz · Chimbarongo · TO SANTIAGO (160 km)
Bucalemu Paredones · Lolol · Chépica
LIBERTADOR (VI) · Teno
Llico · RN Laguna Torca · 5 · R. Teno
Lago Vichuquén · Rauco · Romeral
Vichuquén · Hualañe · Viña Miguel Torres · Curicó · Los Queñes
Iloca · Licantén · R. Mataquito · Viña San Pedro · Lontué
Curepto · R. Claro · Molina
PACIFIC OCEAN · MAULE (VII) · Cumpeo
Putú · Batuco · Pelarco · RN Radal Siete Tazas
Constitución · Pencahue · Talca · R. Lircay · Viña Domaine Oriental · Casa Donoso · Parque Inglés
R. Maule · Colín · Villa Cultural Huilquilemu · San Clemente · RN Altos del Lircay
R. Purapel · Maule · R. Maule · 115 · Vilches
Empedrado · San Javier · Posado · Paso
Viña Balduzzi · Colbún · Embalse Colbún Nevado · Armerillo
Villa Alegre · Embalse Machicura
RN Federico Albert · Yerbas Buenas · RN Los Bellotos · TO PASO PEHUENCHE, ARGENTINA (55km)
Chanco · Linares
RN Los Ruiles · 5 · R. Ancoa
Curanipe · Longaví · R. Achibueno · Co El Torro 3085m
0 10 miles · 0 10 kilometers · Cauquenes · TO CHILLÁN (83km), TEMUCO (353km) · Retiro

main road before the hill, has large rooms off a sun-drenched courtyard with great views of the beach. (☎ 825 923. Cable TV. Breakfast included. CH$6000 per person, with private bath CH$9000 per person. AmEx/MC/V.) **Hotel Casablanca ❷**, at the top of the hill, has cozy—if a bit dark—rooms off a long hallway. Luxurious suites have private bath and cable TV. (☎/fax 825 999. Breakfast included. With shared bath and no TV CH$5000 per person; suites CH$8500 per person. AmEx/MC/V.)

The town's one street enters from the west and goes up the hill, stopping at the cliff. The restaurants and beach are at the bottom of the hill. **Rutamar** (☎ 723 400) has buses that arrive and depart in front of the Bocamar Restaurant. Buses go to San Fernando (2½hr., 4 per day 11:30am-6:30pm, CH$2000). In summer, buses go directly to Santiago (5-6hr., 8 per day 6am-6pm, CH$3000).

CURICÓ

☎ 75

Founded in 1743, Curicó (pop. 104,000) has become a center for communications and agricultural commerce. It does not, however, have much in the way of a tourist industry, unless you count the perpetual throng of bleary-eyed business travelers passing through. Outside the peaceful Plaza de Armas, Curicó seems to be a city with much commotion but little spirit. That said, the view of the city from the hill nearby is impressive, proving that anything, from a distance, can seem worthwhile. Even though it's not much of a tourist hot spot, Curicó is an easy jumping-off point to enjoy nearby wineries and Reserva Nacional Radal Siete Tazas.

▐ TRANSPORTATION

Trains: Estación Curicó, Maipú (☎310 028), at the western end of Prat, 4 blocks west of the Plaza de Armas. Trains go to: **Chillán** (2¾hr., 5 per day 9:20am-1am, CH$3500-5600); **Concepción** (6½hr., 5 per day 9:20am-1am, CH$5500-7200); **Rancagua** (1¼hr., 5 per day 4:30am-8:30pm, CH$1500-1900); **San Fernando** (40min., 5 per day 4:30am-8:30pm, CH$1500-4000); **Santiago** (2½hr., 5 per day 4:30am-8:30pm, CH$1500-3500); **Talca** (45min., 5 per day 9:20am-1am, CH$1500-3500); **Temuco** (10hr., 5 per day 9:20am-1am, CH$5000-8500).

Buses: Terminal de Buses, on the corner of Maipú and Prat, 4 blocks west of the Plaza de Armas. Several bus lines operate out of Curicó, including **Andimar** (☎312 000) and **Talmocur** (☎ 311 360). Buses go to: **Molina** (30min., every 30min., CH$300); **San Fernando** (40min., every hr. 5am-midnight, CH$2000); **Talca** (1¼hr., every 30min. 6am-11pm, CH$1200).

Colectivos: *Colectivos* run throughout town for CH$150.

▗▘ ▐ ORIENTATION AND PRACTICAL INFORMATION

Curicó is situated just beyond the arterial flow of the Panamerican Highway. Its downtown is a 7x7 grid, with the **Plaza de Armas** at the center. **O'Higgins** marks the western edge of the square, although the **train** and **bus terminals** are one street farther west, on Maipú. The commerical sector of the city lines the east-west streets connecting the Plaza and O'Higgins, most notably **Merced** and **Arturo Prat,** which end at the terminals in the west. The rest of the grid is bordered to the south by **San Martín,** to the north by **Camilo Henríquez,** and **Manso de Velasco** to the east.

Tourist Office: There's no real tourist office in Curicó, despite the "Oficina Turismo" sign on the provincial government building. The post office has a section that is supposed to deal with tourist matters, but they'll likely tell you to just buy the **Turistel** travel guide. For basic info, hotel or hostel staff are generally the greatest help.

Tours: Eden Undurraga Turismo, Merced 225, Of. 203 (☎313 126 or 320 292; aeben@entelchile.net), in the Edificio La Merced complex, upstairs and to your left. English spoken. Open M-F 9am-1:30pm and 3-7pm.

Currency Exchange: Forex, Yungay 649 (☎311 518), cashes traveler's checks and changes currency from the English-speaking world, as well as from Japan and South America. Open M-F 9am-2pm and 4-7pm, Sa 10am-1pm.

Banks: Banks with **24hr. ATMs** surround the Plaza de Armas, including **Banco BHIF,** Yungay 655 (☎310 036), near the plaza. Open M-F 9am-2pm.

Luggage Storage: In the train station, on Maipú at the western end of Prat. CH$300 per bag. Open M-Sa 9-11:30am and 2-9pm.

Laundromat: Lavaseco, Membrillar 521, 1 block east of the plaza (☎324 588). Wash or dry CH$1000 per kg. Open M-F 9am-8pm.

Police: ☎ 133. *Carabineros* central office, San Martín 610 (☎324 123). Walk south on Manuel Rodríguez all the way to its end; the station is across the street on your right.

Pharmacy: Farmacias Ahumada, Peña 724 (☎329 769), 1 block west of the Plaza de Armas. Open 24hr. AmEx/MC/V.

Hospital: Ambulance ☎131. **Hospital Base Curicó,** Chacabuco 121 (☎206 200, emergency 206 206), at the corner with Buen Pastor.

Telephones: Entel, Camilo Henríquez 414 (☎317 415), on the corner with Yungay. Calls to Argentina and the US CH$400 per min., to Europe CH$500 per min. Open daily 8:30am-10pm.

Fax Office and Internet Access: Internet parlors line Yungay and Prat. For a late-night fix, try **Internet y M@s,** Yungay 665 (☎09 979 3719), next to Banco BHIF. CH$500 per hr. Domestic faxes CH$350 per page. Open 10am-1am.

Post Office: Carmen 556 (☎310 001), to the left of the *municipalidad*, on the eastern edge of the plaza. **Western Union** desk inside. Open M-F 9am-6pm, Sa 9am-noon.

♠ ACCOMMODATIONS

Curicó is filled with budget hotels and *residenciales*. Cheaper accommodations are found near the bus and train terminals on Maipú and O'Higgins, as well as on the way to the Plaza de Armas, along Montt and Merced.

Residencial Mobel, Merced 461 (☎324 717), 1 block west of the Plaza de Armas. The front of this *residencial* is a furniture workshop, ensuring that a fresh, woody fragrance permeates the rooms. The rooms, large and empty, are kept cheerful with fresh paint, polished floors, and cartoon bedspreads. CH$4000 per person. ❷

Hotel Comercio, Yungay 730 (☎312 443 or 310 014; www.curicochile.cl/hotelcomercio), 2 blocks north of the Plaza de Armas. With its all-business, no-frills decor and competent service, Comercio makes a strong case for comfort. Hot water and radiators are much appreciated in winter. Cable TV. Internet CH$600 per hr. Car rental CH$25,000 per day. Breakfast included. Singles CH$13,000, with bath and heater CH$19,000; doubles CH$28,000; triples CH$36,000. IVA discount for foreigners. AmEx/MC/V. ❸

Hotel Turismo, Carmen 727 (☎310 823; www.chilehotels.com), on the corner with Prat. One of Curicó's ritzier offerings, Turismo has palm trees near the entrance and a lush garden in the inner courtyard. Rooms have private bath and balconies overlooking the garden or street below. Cable TV. Breakfast included. Singles CH$28,600; doubles CH$33,000; triples CH$45,500; quads CH$56,000. IVA discount for foreigners. ❺

Residencial Maipú, Maipú 570 (☎311 126), 1 block south of the bus and train terminals. Conveniently located near the town's transportation centers, Maipú takes cozy to a new extreme, with low ceilings and beds nearly stacked on one another. But clean and warm means comfort to many a weary traveler. Shared bath. Breakfast included. CH$4500 per person, with cable TV CH$5000. AmEx/MC/V. ❶

♠ FOOD

Curicó is no culinary capital, but you can easily find decent meals at bargain prices here. Even the more upscale restaurants offer meals at reasonable prices—unless, of course, you wish to sample the region's fabled export wines.

☒ Los Ricos Pobres, Rodríguez 747 (☎336 6010). These "wealthy poor" don't bother with formalities like menus or professionalism, just good food and a raucous attitude. Choose from among the 4 food groups—beef, pork, chicken, or fish—and you'll get an excellent meal accompanied by rice or french fries. Meals around CH$1700. Open M-Sa noon-midnight, Su 1pm-11pm. ❶

A Casa Tua, Prat 395 (☎336 899), 1 block north of the Plaza de Armas. One of the few new, trendy spots in Curicó. It aims straight at the heart of youth with a sure shot: pizza. The extensive range of pizzas is sophisticated, including veggie (CH$3600) as well as salmon and other fishy treats (CH$4600). Open M-Sa 4pm-2am. AmEx/MC/V. ❸

Club de la Unión, Merced 341 (☎310 026; www.rubentapia.cl), on the northern end of the Plaza de Armas. You too can dine with Curicó's high society at this social club/restaurant, housed in a white building with elegant pillars and balconies. The salon and dining hall have high ceilings, with numerous windows to illuminate your luxurious glass

**STOP YOUR WINING:
A USER'S GUIDE TO
WINE-TASTING**

I had been anxious for my first wine tour since before my arrival in Chile. I was anxious, however, about the wine-tasting, since I knew nothing about wines and much less about the ritualistic antics behind tasting it. Unfortunately, because my tour leader was feeling ill, the experience was less than ideal.

To begin, I was the only person on the tour, and when the tour guide and I reached the part of the tour when the glasses were brought out, things got awkward. She had been quite unhappy that I showed up, which automatically put me in an uncomfortable position. And when she poured out five glasses of wine with a snide look on her face, I was unsure of what to do. So, I did the only thing I knew how to: drink. After half-hearted attempts at swirling and smelling, I downed each glass in complete silence, thanked the tour guide, and stumbled back to the waiting taxi.

Fortunately, I was not defeated. At the second winery I visited, I admitted my complete ignorance and asked the tour guide to teach me how to taste wine. So, for all my *cerveza*-phile brethren, here's the secret:

First, gripping the glass at its base, swirl by rotating your wrist, not your hand. This releases the aroma of the wine. Stick your

of Chilean wine (CH$3800-42,000). Grilled chicken breast CH$1800. Fish dishes CH$2000-6000. Lunch *menú* CH$2500. Open daily 10am-midnight. ❸

Restaurante El Alemán, Peña 879 (☎09 262 2441), between Camilo Henríquez and Montt. Except for the stout German in overalls and a feathered cap on the restaurant's storefront sign, this restaurant's food is not so much German as it is excessively cholesterol-saturated. Try the *lomo a la plancha,* a slab of beef draped in fried eggs and sauteed onions (CH$2500). For those with a less-than-Bavarian palate, there is a selection of pizzas, including a vegetarian option (CH$2500). Open daily 9am-4am. ❷

🔅 SIGHTS

When not populated by shrieking, uniformed teenagers just unleashed from school, Curicó's **Plaza de Armas** is a tranquil place to spend an afternoon. Located at the center of the city, the plaza is well-known and much-admired throughout Central Chile. Around the perimeter, stoic palm trees tower over neighboring buildings. On the plaza's eastern edge, a wrought-iron bandstand stands looking forlorn, oblivious to its newfound status as a National Monument. Near the southern edge of the park is a tree trunk carved into the likeness of **Toq Lautaro,** the Mapuche leader who defeated conquistador Pedro de Valdivia.

The **Iglesia Matriz** sits in ruin on the northwestern corner of the plaza, a testament to the city's efforts to fashion for itself a more aesthetically pleasing image. Destroyed in a 1985 earthquake, the church has been nearly restored; one can see how the scarred facade was kept, but the nave turned into an elegant courtyard. The fluted white pillars and balconies of the **Club de la Unión,** Merced 341, on the other hand, survived the earthquake intact. You can still enter the 120-year-old building, which houses a social club and upscale **restaurant** (see above).

To escape the heavy urban air for a bit, take a walk down Prat heading east, and cross the grand avenue of Manso de Velasco. You'll find a path leading up to the top of a small hill, **Cerro Carlos Condell.** Enjoy the view of the city from its 99m summit or walk around the hill's western ridge, along the Avenida, to find the local swimming pool, tennis courts, and playground.

🏃 DAYTRIP FROM CURICÓ

LA RUTA DEL VINO
To schedule an organized wine-tasting tour, contact La Ruta del Vino Valle de Curicó, Merced 341, on the north-

ern edge of the Plaza de Armas. The San Pedro Winery is 14km south of Curicó, off Km205 on the Panamerican. Take the bus from Curicó to Talca and ask to be left off at San Pedro. The Miguel Torres bodega is located off Km195 on the Panamerican; take the bus from Curicó to Molina and ask to be left off at Miguel Torres.

The most visible vineyards of Chile are to be found in the Valle de Curicó. South of Curicó, the distance between the Andes and the Coastal Range grows, creating a broad, flat, open valley that remains warm and dry—perfect for Cabernet Sauvignon and Sauvignon Blanc. The Panamerican slices through the heart of the valley, giving the bus-confined traveler an idyllic view. From Curicó, it's possible to arrange a visit to the endless sea of vines and cutting-edge wineries.

Seventeen wineries around Curicó have created **La Ruta del Vino Valle de Curicó,** and almost all can be visited by booking through the central office, on Curicó's Plaza de Armas. Tours should be arranged 24-48hr. in advance. (☎328 972 or 328 967; www.rvvc.cl. Open M-F 9am-1:30pm and 3-7:30pm. Tour, tasting, lunch, and transportation to 2 wineries CH$42,000. A flat rate of CH$4000 applies to nearly all the vineyards for an individual tour and wine tasting.)

A majority of the wineries in the Curicó Valley are right off the Panamerican, making an organized tour a luxury option. If you choose to go it alone, head to **San Pedro,** Chile's second-largest producer of wine, which offers an extensive tour of its massive operations, complete with look-out point where its vineyard stretches—literally—as far as the eye can see. Tours are conducted in English, French, and Spanish. (☎491 517; www.sanpedro.cl. Tours 1½hr., 11am and 3pm, CH$4000; must be booked through La Ruta del Vino Valle de Curicó.)

An even easier option is the **Miguel Torres Winery,** just south of Curicó. Although you will have to settle for a less in-depth tour, guests are free to drop by throughout the day. (☎564 100; mgarcia@migueltorres.cl. Tours 30min., 10am-6pm. Free.)

RESERVA NACIONAL RADAL SIETE TAZAS

The jewel in Middle Chile's verdant crown, Reserva Nacional Radal Siete Tazas is best known for the otherworldly beauty of its "seven teacups"—a chain of silver-blue mountain pools punctuated by short waterfalls descending into the depths of a narrow canyon. A steep wood-and-stone walkway meanders

nose fully in the glass—don't be shy—and enjoy the smells. Whites wines have the most pleasant aromas and smell fruity. Identifying "pear" and "peach" is always a safe bet.

Next, swirl some more and notice how the wine drips down along the side of the glass. If it takes a few moments for the "legs" to start to appear, the wine has good "body." At this stage you can also appreciate the colors and remark how this wine is more maroon than ruby while that one is more burgundy than red.

Finally, the tasting. If a spitoon is provided, take a small sip, swirl it around all parts of your mouth, and spit. Then, take another small sip, this time, swallowing, and notice where on the tongue and mouth flavor appears and also which flavors appear later. Reserve wines have complex layers of flavors and, with reds, the aftertaste differs on whether it has been aged in an American oak barrel versus a French oak barrel (the French oak has a more subtle wood flavor due to its less porous nature).

In the end, wine tasting is a social event—something to do while having good conversation and enjoying a pleasant atmosphere. I found it best to take it a little light-heartedly, and make it my own experience, even if I did end up a little red in the face.

-Danny Koski-Karell

around the lip of the mostly submerged teacups. From here, you can view almost the entirety of the Siete Tazas' churning course: water from melting glaciers pours out of holes in the rock face, cascading downward and then disappearing around a cavernous bend in the cliff wall. On hot summer days, visitors can leap into the teacups to cool off. Some intrepid kayakers even bounce their way through to the very bottom. Be aware that *Santiaguinos* flock here in droves during the summer. Fall and spring visits are ideal, though finding transportation during these periods can be difficult.

AT A GLANCE	
AREA: 51.5 sq. km	**WILDLIFE:** Forests of cypress trees; many species of singing birds, including *zorzal* and *tenca*; pumas.
CLIMATE: Warm climate with a prolonged dry season. Coldest temp. in July (8.4°C); warmest in Jan. (22°C). Annual rainfall 98cm, falling mostly Feb.-Apr.	**GATEWAYS:** Curicó or Talca via Molina.
	CAMPING: Sites inside park at Los Robles and outside entrance to park (CH$3000-12,000).
HIGHLIGHTS: The 7 teacup-shaped pools connected by waterfalls, including Velo de la Novia (the Bride's Veil).	**FEES:** CH$1300, children CH$300.

TRANSPORTATION. To get to the reserve, take a bus from Curicó or Talca to Molina, a small town along the Panamerican. Then catch a bus at the terminal headed for Radal. **Buses Hernández** in Molina (☎75 491 607) has frequent service to the park entrance during January and February (2½hr.; M-Sa 7 per day 8am-7pm, Su 5 per day 9am-6:30pm; CH$1000). From March to December, there is only a 5:30pm shuttle taking workers back to the town of Radal, 9km short of the reserve. If you use this method of transport, plan to stay two nights: you will arrive after dark and will have to wait until the day after to take the shuttle when it leaves Radal. Be forewarned—it's a 60km journey over a poorly maintained, steep dirt road. Rather than braving the park in a rental car in the low season, a good option is to contact Luis Rosales (☎493 847; crimas76@hotmail.com), who runs a tourist information office in Molina, and can arrange transport to the park for US$40.

ORIENTATION AND PRACTICAL INFORMATION. The reserve is open year-round, but during the winter, snowfall often blocks the roads leading up to it. At the entrance you must stop at a control post overseen by *carabineros*, who will ask to see your identification, and also how long you plan to stay in the reserve.

After the park entrance, 4km up from the Siete Tazas Vista (see **Hiking,** below) is **Parque Inglés,** a tranquil camping area nestled between the snow-dusted peaks of the Andes. Here you'll find an information center run by **Conaf,** which occasionally arranges free educational talks and guided walks. (Open daily Jan.-Feb. 9am-11pm; Mar.-Dec. 9am-1pm and 2-6pm.) For information on the reserve, call or visit the larger Conaf office in **Talca** (p. 296). Groups can arrange free guided tours.

ACCOMMODATIONS AND FOOD. For those who don't particularly enjoy rustic living, there is a privately run inn, the **Hostería La Flor de Canela ❹,** at the very end of Parque Inglés. The *hostería* burned down in 2001, but now, brand-new rooms, accompanied by gleaming toilets and sinks, are ready for reluctant campers. (☎491 613. English-speaking staff in summer. Reception 24hr. Singles CH$15,000, with bath CH$20,000; doubles CH$25,000.)

There are two kinds of **camping** available at **Camping Los Robles ❶**, in the reserve. Choose from sites with showers, hot water, and lighting (CH$8000 per site, max. 6 people), or more basic backwoods living with bathrooms but cold showers (CH$1000 per person). The price of camping gets you into the Siete Tazas Circuit.

Hostería La Flor de Canela has a **minimarket** that sells toiletries, food, drinks, and other necessities. The on-site **restaurant ❶** is housed in the in a small wooden hall with sliding-glass doors and plastic lawn chairs. The selection includes pizzas (CH$1500-3000), sandwiches (CH$800-1800), and a surprising assortment of wines (CH$1800-8000) for you to choose from. (Open daily 7am-11pm.)

🔟 **HIKING.** Not a very large reserve, Reserva Nacional Radal Siete Tazas's selection of hiking trails is limited, but what it lacks in quantity is made up for in quality. The **Sendero Paseo Salto de la Leona** is a short walk through an oak- and *araucaria*-laden patch of forest in the heart of the reserve. The first stop is the **Siete Tazas Vista,** a view of the nationally renowned rock formations thought to represent seven teacups, connected by crystal blue cascading waters. The path continues to the **Salto de la Leona,** a waterfall jetting out from a marbled cliff wall (1000m, 45min.). Just beyond the park entrance is the **Velo de la Novia** (the "Bride's Veil") waterfall. This easily accessible, 50m high fall untangles into a fine mist much like bridal lace, shrouding the receiving pool. **Mountain biking** is allowed in the park and is a popular method of seeing the area, although in the summer months it may be difficult, as crowds from Santiago choke the trails.

TALCA ☎ 71

Talca is the Mapuche word for "thunder"—an apt name for the bustling chaos of the streets surrounding the city's bus terminal, which on a typical afternoon are jam-packed with buses, taxis, and *colectivos*. Talca (pop. 209,000) feels like a small town with a big-city attitude. Most tourists, however, come for what lies beyond the city. Talca is not only a launching point for the renowned Reserva Nacional Radal Siete Tazas and the Villa Cultural Huilquilemu, but it also sits at the heart of Chile's largest wine-producing region. Containing over 30% of the nation's vineyards, the surrounding Valle del Maule is easily accessible, and its citizens are delighted when tourists come explore the cellars, admire the vines, and enjoy the all-important free tastings.

▬ TRANSPORTATION

Trains: Estación Talca, 11 Oriente 1000 (☎226 254), at the intersection with 2 Sur. Trains go to: **Chillán** (2hr., 5 per day 10am-1:40am, CH$4500-14,000); **Concepción** (5½hr., 5 per day 10am-1:40am, CH$6000-13,000); **Curicó** (1hr., 5 per day 3:45am-7:50pm, CH$1500-13,000); **Rancagua** (3hr., 5 per day 3:45am-7:50pm, CH$3000-14,000); **Santiago** (4hr., 5 per day 3:45am-7:50pm, CH$3500-16,000); **Temuco** (9hr., 1pm and 1am, CH$9000-24,000).

Buses: Terminal Gherardi, 12 Oriente 900 (☎243 270), at the intersection with 2 Sur. Dozens of bus lines service all points south of Santiago, including **Pullman del Sur** (☎243 431) and **Tur Bus** (☎245 029). Buses go to: **Constitución** (2hr., every hr. 5:40am-10pm, CH$1300); **Curicó** (1hr., every 15min. 5:30am-8:45pm, CH$1000); **Molina** (1¼hr., every hr. 7am-8:30pm, CH$3000); **Puerto Montt** (12hr., 9:50pm, CH$5000); **Santiago** (3½hr., every 15min. 5:30am-8:45pm, CH$3000); **Valparaíso** (4½hr., 5 per day 12:30pm-2am, CH$4500).

Local Buses: Heading downtown from the terminal, buses use 2 Sur—look for "Plaza de Armas" in the windshield. Buses heading back to the terminal use 1 Norte or 2 Sur and have "Terminal" in the windshield. CH$250.

Taxis and Colectivos: Taxis (CH$400 plus CH$80 per 200m) are ready to pounce outside the bus terminal, train station, and Plaza de Armas. Call **Taxi Plaza de Armas** (☎ 231 231), on the corner of 1 Sur and 1 Oriente, for pick-up. **Colectivos** cost CH$290 for anywhere in the city. Those headed down 1 Norte are usually labeled "Terminal"; those on 1 Sur and 12 Oriente, outside the terminal, say "Centro" or "Plaza."

Car Rental: Rent-a-car Rosselot, San Miguel 2710 (☎ 247 979 or 800 021 298; www.rosselot.cl), along the Panamerican. Rentals from CH$20,000 per day including basic insurance. 22+. ID and credit card required. AmEx/MC/V.

■ 7 ORIENTATION AND PRACTICAL INFORMATION

Talca is conscientiously organized, with its streets laid out in a numbered grid. The grid originates at the **Plaza de Armas** in the western half of the town; the four streets forming the square of the plaza are labeled 1 Norte (north), 1 Sur (south), 1 Oriente (east) and 1 Poniente (west). The numbers of the streets increase with respect to their distance from the plaza. 1 Sur runs east from the plaza to 12 Oriente (12 blocks east of the plaza) and the **bus terminal.** As Talca's commercial strip, 1 Sur is home to everything from banks to hotels to fried chicken.

Tourist Office: Sernatur, 1 Poniente 1281 (☎ 233 699; fax 226 940; infomaule@sernatur.cl), 1 block north of the Plaza de Armas, has a wealth of brochures and maps about the city and Maule region. Open M-F 8:30am-5:30pm. A smaller branch is at the corner of 1 Sur and 3 Oriente. Open M-F 8:30am-6:30pm. **Conaf,** 3 Sur 564 (☎ 228 029), has information on the region's parks and reserves. Open M-F 8:30am-6:30pm.

Currency Exchange: Forex, 2 Oriente 1133 (☎ 210 838), 1 block east of the plaza. Open M-F 9am-2pm and 3:30-6:30pm, Sa 10:30am-1:30pm. **Exchange,** 1 Sur 898, Of. 15 (☎ 221 768), inside the mall. Open M-F 9:30am-8pm, Sa 10am-2pm.

Banks: Dozens of banks line 1 Sur. **Banco de Chile,** 1 Sur 998 (☎ 206 215), between 2 Oriente and 3 Oriente, 1 block east of the Mercado Central. Open M-F 9am-2pm. **Banco del Desarrollo,** 1 Norte 901 (☎ 223 086), down the street from the Museo O'Higginiano. Open M-F 9am-2pm. Both branches have **24hr. ATMs.**

Market: San Brisas, on the corner of 1 Norte and 5 Oriente. Open daily 9am-10pm. AmEx/MC/V.

Police: ☎ 133. *Carabineros* at O'Higgins 687 (☎ 226 246 and 226 915), at the corner with 1 Poniente.

Pharmacy: Pharmacies abound on 1 Sur. **Farmacias Ahumada,** 1 Sur 1191, is at the corner with 5 Oriente. Open M-Sa 9am-11pm, Su 10am-9pm.

Hospital: Ambulance ☎ 133. **Hospital Regional,** 1 Norte 1990 (☎ 209 100), on the eastern side of the railroad tracks, along 12 Oriente.

Fax Office and Telephones: Entel, 1 Sur 908 (☎ 230 728), 2 blocks east of the plaza. Open M-F 8:30am-9pm, Sa 9am-2pm and 4-8pm. Domestic faxes CH$350 per page, international CH$1000 per page. **Telefónica CTC,** 1 Sur 1156 (☎ 229 862). Open M-F 10am-2pm and 3:30-6:30pm, Sa 10am-1pm. Domestic faxes CH$350 per page, international CH$990 per page.

Internet Access: Puntocom, 2 Sur 1014 (☎ 218 205), inside the courtyard. CH$400 per hr. Open M-Sa 9am-midnight, Su 3pm-midnight. **Phonecenter,** 3 Oriente 1109, 3 blocks east of the plaza. CH$500 per hr., Su CH$400. Open M-Th 9am-11pm, F-Sa 9am-midnight, Su 3-10pm. AmEx/MC/V.

Post Office: Correos, 1 Oriente 1150 (☎227 271), on the eastern edge of the Plaza de Armas. Open M-F 9am-1pm and 3-6pm, Sa 9am-1pm.

ACCOMMODATIONS

Talca is rife with hotels, and almost all can be found along the length of **1 Sur.** Unfortunately, they increase with quantity and quality as 1 Sur moves west, away from the bus and train terminals, which means that travelers have to hop on a city bus, *colectivo*, or taxi to get back to the Plaza de Armas.

▨ **Hostal del Río,** 1 Sur 411 (☎/fax 225 448; hostaldelrio@hotmail.com), at the very western end of 1 Sur. This newly remodeled hotel has soft, cheerful rooms with all the trimmings—and at the right price. Rooms have cable TV, private bath, and central heating. English spoken. Internet CH$800 per hr. Breakfast included. Singles CH$10,000; doubles CH$15,000; triples CH$18,000; quads CH$20,000. ❸

Hostal del Puente, 1 Sur 407 (☎/fax 220 930; hostaldelpuente@terra.cl), at the very western end of 1 Sur. Even when half of the hotel broke away to form the Hostal del Río, Hostal del Puente managed to hold onto its leafy, quiet ambience, albeit keeping it the less modern of the two. Private bath, cable TV. English spoken. Breakfast CH$1000. Singles CH$10,000; doubles CH$16,000; triples CH$20,000; quads CH$24,000. ❸

Hotel Terranova, 1 Sur 1026 (☎239 608; hotelterranova@entelchile.net). Set in the heart of the city, Terranova caters to businesspeople passing through town with comfortable rooms. Cable TV, central heating, and private bath. Breakfast included. Singles CH$24,600-28,600; doubles CH$32,600-38,600; triples CH$49,600. IVA discount for foreigners. AmEx/MC/V. ❹

Residencial Ortiz, 4 Oriente 1213 (☎714 286). Once a grand 19th-century hotel, Ortiz is bright and spacious, but by no means cozy. Plain beds are lost in giant rooms with high ceilings and hardwood floors. Cable TV in the common space. Breakfast included. Singles, doubles, and triples with shared bath CH$7000 per person. ❷

Hotel Terrabella, 1 Sur 641 (☎/fax 226 555; terrabella@hotel.tie.cl). Uncreative decor, soft jazz on the radio, and a meticulous daily cleaning make Terrabella a safe, if unexciting, night's stay. Cable TV, small outdoor pool, and free parking inside the hotel. Breakfast included. Reservations recommended. Singles CH$38,800; doubles CH$46,500; suites CH$63,000. IVA discount for foreigners. AmEx/MC/V. ❺

FOOD

Cafeterías and *fuentes de soda* dominate the storefronts of 1 Sur, and for the most part, you won't be disappointed with the large portions at low prices. Fine dining is also possible, though the finery has its limits in such a small city, and you might pay more than the food deserves. For especially cheap eats, head to the **Mercado Central,** on 1 Sur between 4 Oriente and 5 Oriente. There, you'll find a medley of meat and produce markets, as well as numerous hole-in-the-wall eateries.

Restaurant Chilote, 1 Sur 706 (☎215 267), on the southwestern end of the Plaza de Armas. This is one of the classier seafood restaurants in town, as you can tell from the attentive service, fine wines, and the napkins folded in the shape of seashells. If you try the insanely flavorful house specialty, you'll know why they call them "locos" (shellfish in a *salsa verde;* CH$6000). Wines range from the house table wine (CH$800) to fine creations by Miguel Torres (CH$11,000). Open M-F 10am-midnight, Su 10am-4pm. ❸

Casino Cuerpo de Bomberos, 2 Sur 1160 (☎212 903), inside the firehouse. This place doesn't mess around and gets straight to work filling you up. Pull a plastic chair in front of the TV and stock up on the *lomo a lo pobre* (CH$250) or huge *chuletas* (pork chops; CH$1800). Open M-Sa 10am-midnight, Su 10am-6pm. ❷

Fuente de Soda Germana, 3 Oriente 1105 (☎221 689), 2 blocks east of the plaza. Bigger means better at Germana, where sandwiches cause the tables to buckle under the load. Order the "Cocodrilo" (beef, tomato, guacamole, green beans, ham, melted cheese, and mayo; CH$3200) to hold you over for a week. Open daily 9am-1am. ❷

Pirandello, 1 Sur 835 (☎223 525). This small eatery matches its food to its decor: simple and elegant. The pizzas, while small, are filled with taste. An individual *Española* has fresh peppers and spicy sausage along with tomatoes (CH$1200). Open M-Sa 9am-midnight, Su 11am-11pm. AmEx/MC/V. ❶

Bavaria, 1 Sur 1330 (☎227 088; www.bavaria.cl). This local franchise of the popular restaurant chain offers sandwiches (CH$1350-2550), salads (CH$950-1850), and potatoes (CH$600-1200). On weekdays, there is a special lunch *menú* (12:30-3pm; CH$3000). Open M-Sa 9am-11pm, Su noon-10pm. AmEx/MC/V. ❷

🖸 SIGHTS

There is little to do in Talca, as most activities center around its endless commerical strip and the equally endless—though more picturesque—vineyards surrounding the city. Visitors tend to stay in town, then head for the *viñas* after breakfast.

MUSEO BOMBERIL BENITO RIQUELME. A single room in the city's main firehouse, the Museo Bomberil Benito Riquelme bursts at the seams with relics of Talca's bravest. Three antique fire engines, complete with carriage wheels and red painted water buckets, are crammed together in the room's center. On the surrounding walls are ancient fire extinguishers, personal effects, and a pictorial history of Talca's dashing firemen, with the 1850 crew competing closely with that from 1976. (*2 Sur 1160, between 4 Oriente and 5 Oriente. ☎231 599. Open M-Sa 10am-7pm.*)

MUSEO O'HIGGINIANO. The Museo O'Higginiano y de Bellas Artes, housed in a colonial-style 200-year-old house, is deceptively small and plain. Inside, large rooms hold a collection of grand paintings, mostly of evil-looking Mapuche or gallant Chilean peasants. The striking oil painting, *Caupolicán Prisionero*, depicts the Mapuche *cacique* about to be executed by the Spanish. To balance out the 19th-century paintings, a small gallery exhibits work by contemporary local artists. The main room gives honor to Bernardo O'Higgins, with a portrait in full military regalia, and a signed copy of the Act of Independence. (*1 Norte 875. ☎227 330. Open Tu-F 10am-7pm, Sa 10:30am-2:30pm, Su 3-7pm. CH$600, students CH$300.*)

PLAZA DE ARMAS. The city's rather lackluster Plaza de Armas is dedicated to Colonel Carlos Spano, the "hero of Talca," who died in combat in 1814 with a Chilean flag in his hands. Nowadays, the only action you're likely to find here is the noisy enthusiasm of gaggles of children, who pedal through the park in steel-framed race cars. A bandstand topped with iron spikes sits on the plaza's eastern edge, while graffitied white-stone statues—the spoils of war with Peru from two centuries ago—line the tree-shaded walkways. In the northwest corner of the plaza, a stone statue of one of Talca's past bishops stares toward his old cathedral, the **Catedral de Talca.** The impressive red-brick structure, built in 1954, features a long, dagger-like belltower. (*Catedral at 1 Norte 650. ☎231 412. Open M-Sa 8:30am-1:30pm and 3:30-9:30pm. Mass Su 10:30am-1pm and 6-8pm. Free.*)

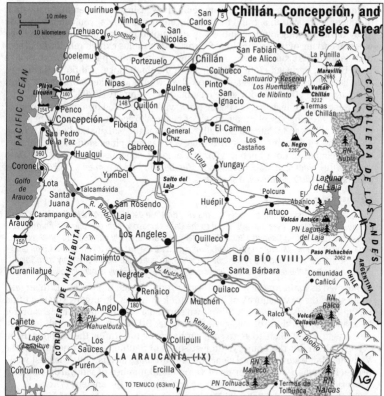

Chillán, Concepción, and Los Angeles Area

MERCADO CENTRAL. The city's hulking Mercado Central once had a resplendent fountain at its center. Now, there's just a circle of mossy, crumbling, worn stones in the fountain's place. Business, however, goes on as usual—you'll find fruit, meat, and fish for sale alongside stands hawking bags, wallets, and other handicrafts. *(On 1 Sur between 4 Oriente and 5 Oriente. Head north 1 block from the Museo Bomberil. Open M-F 8:30am-5:30pm, Sa-Su 8:30am-2pm.)*

🔀 DAYTRIPS FROM TALCA

VILLA CULTURAL HUILQUILEMU

Huilquilemu is 10km east of Talca. From the terminal in Talca, board a bus to San Clemente (CH$380), and ask to be dropped off at the villa, which is right on the highway.

Universally acclaimed as Middle Chile's greatest cultural attraction, the ◪**Villa Cultural Huilquilemu** has come a long way from a 19th-century *patronal*. While the name, "Huilquilemu," means "forest of the *zorzal* bird" in Mapuche, the villa has known little sylvan tranquility. Constructed in 1850 as the home of one of Chile's most influential families, the Donosos, the villa was once the base of operations for a huge agriculture enterprise. However, in 1966, when the country was in communist-inspired political upheaval, *campesinos* seized the estate and divided it among themselves. Finally, in 1974, the **Universidad Católica del Maule** purchased the property and began restoring the old estate.

MIDDLE CHILE

The villa now has a new life as a museum showcasing the university's collection of religious art. Within a grand hall supported by oak pillars, you can find a wide array of oil paintings and sculptures of devotional inspiration, including a huge wooden carving of the crucifixion of Christ. Other rooms exhibit religious and secular handicrafts from all over South America, including painted dragon masks from Bolivia, Peruvian cloth dolls depicting the three kings, and flowers made of dyed horse hair. See artisans at work on clay, wool, and wicker crafts in the villa's workshop, and go home with some handmade souvenirs (CH$200-20,000).

The estate itself features a majestic brick walkway shaded by a thick covering of *flor de la pluma*, as well as a number of peaceful tree-lined courtyards hemmed in by oak pillars and white-adobe walls. Walk along the path marked out by pruned shrubs and you'll come across towering sequoias and pines alongside more delicate specimens of flora, such as vibrantly colored camellias. (☎/fax 242 474. Open Jan.-Feb. Tu-F 9am-6pm, Sa-Su noon-6pm; Mar.-Dec. Tu-F 9am-1pm and 3-6:30pm, Sa-Su noon-6pm. CH$500, children and students CH$200.)

LA RUTA DEL VINO

To plan a wine-tasting tour, contact Ruta del Vino del Valle del Maule, at their office in the Villa Cultural Huilquilemu (see above). To get to the Casa Donoso Winery on your own from Talca, take the road to San Clemente for 2.4km until you reach the only intersection, which is just past the Pro Terra building on your right. Turn right onto the dirt road and follow it 3.5km until you see grape fields and the red adobe hacienda. To get to the Balduzzi Winery from Talca, take a bus from the terminal to San Javier or drive there. The winery is right in town.

Renowned as Latin America's finest wine producer, and the world's fifth largest, Chile ships the vast majority of its aged stock overseas. Strangely, you can't find the better brands of *vino* in Chile's own supermarkets, as many Chileans prefer beer and various kinds of sugar water to wine. Other than fancy hotels and restaurants, the best place to go to get your hands on the stuff is the *bodegas* themselves, which dot the countryside just south of Santiago—most notably in the Valle del Maule surrounding Talca. The area around Talca is Chile's largest wine-producing region, both in terms of volume and number of vineyards, and also has a rich and storied cultural tradition growing from the ancient *viñas*.

The **Ruta del Vino del Valle del Maule,** which has tour packages of 15 wineries in the Valle del Maule, has an office in the Villa Cultural Huilquilemu. Though the region's wines can be tasted at the office bar, going to the wineries is far more fun. Packages start at US$22 per person for two vineyards, guide, and transport (4hr., 9am-1pm or 2:30-6:30pm). There are also two-day weekend tours ranging US$90-120. (☎246 460; www.chilewineroute.cl. Open M-F 9am-6pm, Sa-Su noon-6pm.)

Of course, you don't have to shell out money for a decadent tourist package in order to sample the wines. Many *bodegas* allow visitors to stop by, although they appreciate an advance phone call. Guests get a brief tour, a wine tasting, and the obligatory walk past the shelves of bottles for sale (tours and tastings can range from free to CH$5000). Near Talca, a grand red adobe *hacienda* once owned by the powerful Donoso family now houses the **Casa Donoso Winery,** specializing in Cabernet Sauvignon. This is one of the better tours and higher quality wine producers in the area. (☎242 506; www.casadonoso.com. Open M-Sa 9am-6pm. Free.)

The **Balduzzi Winery** is one of the more popular wineries to visit, mostly because it is easily accessible, being situated in the small town of San Javier, 25km south of Talca. The disjointed tour offers a glance at Don Balduzzi's private reserve. (☎73 322 138; www.balduzzi.cl. Open M-Sa 9am-6pm. CH$2000.) The vineyards in the Valle del Maule center around the two towns of San Clemente (20km east of Talca) and San Javier (25km south of Talca.) Most tourists head to San Javier because the number of vineyards there is greater and they are relatively close to one another. A taxi from Talca will be happy to drive you to the wineries of your

Chillán

▲ ACCOMMODATIONS
Hostal Canada, **4**
Hostal Libertador, **1**
Hotel de la Avenida
  Express, **3**
Hotel Las Terrazas, **5**

🍴 FOOD
Arco Iris, **6**
Café Paris, **7**
Ficus, **2**
Fuente Alemana, **8**

choice (4hr. CH$10,000-15,000; 7hr. CH$20,000-25,000). For a complete listing of all the wineries in the region contact the Sernatur office in Talca (p. 296) or Santiago (p. 102).

CHILLÁN
☎ 42

Chillán, "*la silla del sol*" (the seat of the sun), fancies itself the cultural and tourist capital of central Chile; and indeed, this city (pop. 200,000) is quite comfortable in its tourism skin. Seemingly oblivious to the steady stream of visitors using Chillán as a transport hub and launching point to the luxurious Termas de Chillán—considered among the country's finest mountain resorts—the city remains as calm as the broad trees in the elegant central plaza. While a 1939 earthquake razed the majority of the city and killed a large portion of its population, thanks to its convenient location, great weather, and hospitable spirit, Chillán has fully recovered, and today is a vibrant center for business, tourism, and culture.

◰ TRANSPORTATION

Trains: Estación Chillán (☎222 424), on Brasil, at the western end of Libertad. Trains to: **Concepción** (3½hr., 3:40am, CH$4200); **Santiago** (6hr., 7:30am-2:45am, CH$9000); **Talca** (2hr., 5 per day 1:45am-4:30pm, CH$4500); **Temuco** (6½hr., 1:40am, CH$7000). Ticket window open daily 7am-10:30pm.

Buses: Tur Bus (☎212 502) and **Línea Azul** (☎211 192) run similar routes at comparable rates from the city's 3 major bus terminals:

Terminal de Buses Interregionales, Constitución 1 (☎221 014), at the western edge of the city center. To: **Concepción** (1½hr., 16 per day 8am-10:45pm, CH$1800); **Santiago** (5hr., 21 per day 7am-midnight, CH$3500); **Talca** (2hr., 14 per day 7am-6:30pm, CH$2000). Línea Azul goes to **Las Trancas** (1¼hr., 8am and 4pm, CH$1000) and **Termas de Chillán** (1½hr., 8am and 4pm, CH$1500).

Terminal de Buses de María Teresa, Panamericana Norte 10 (☎212 149 or 231 119), north of Ecuador, on O'Higgins. Provides same service as the Terminal de Buses Interregionales. Some buses coming from the north also discharge passengers here.

Terminal de Buses Paseo La Merced, Maipón 890 (☎223 606), at the corner with Sargento Aldea. Small buses service rural locations around Chillán, including **Yumbel** (1hr., CH$1500). The Línea Azul bus bound for **Termas de Chillán** stops here daily at 8:15am.

Taxis and Colectivos: Colectivos cost CH$250 throughout the city center. Taxis from the train station or Terminal De Buses Interregionales to the Plaza de Armas run CH$500-1000. **Radiotaxi Libertador,** Claudio Arrau 809 (☎212 020), and **Radiotaxi Flotana,** Libertad 170 (☎212 121), offer 24hr. call-based service.

Car Rental: Econorent (☎229 262) has a small office in the train station. Rentals from CH$25,000 per day. Open M-F 8am-7pm. AmEx/MC/V.

⚡🛈 ORIENTATION AND PRACTICAL INFORMATION

The city centers around the **Plaza de Armas** and its adjacent cathedral, flanked by two main east-west thoroughfares, **Libertad** and **Constitución.** The downtown forms a 12x12 grid, with the plaza at its center. **Argentina** forms the eastern boundary, **Ecuador** the northern, **Brasil** the western, and **Collín** the southern.

Tourist Office: Sernatur, 18 de Septiembre 455 (☎223 272), has free maps, brochures, and a wealth of information about the city and region. Open M-F 8:30am-6pm.

Currency Exchange: Money Exchange, Constitución 608 (☎238 638), at the southeastern end of the plaza. Cashes traveler's checks and exchanges American, Australian, British, and Canadian currencies, as well as euros. Some English spoken. Open M-F 10am-2pm and 4-6:30pm, Sa 11am-2:30pm.

Banks: Banks surround the plaza and line Constitución. **Banco de Chile,** Constitución 580 (☎219 434), at the southern edge of the plaza. **24hr. ATM.** Open M-F 9am-2pm.

Work Opportunity: Hostal Canada, Libertad 269 (☎234 515), hires 1 English-speaking tour guide to take guests on 4hr. excursions around the Chillán area. For details, see **Alternatives to Tourism,** p. 91.

Luggage Storage: At the Terminal de Buses Interregionales (see above). 24hr. storage. CH$500 for a backpack, CH$600 for a hiking pack or suitcase.

Markets: Feria de Chillán, on the corner of Maipón and 5 de Abril, southeast of the plaza. Open 9am-7pm. **Mercado Techado,** across the street from the feria, to the north. **Santa Isabel,** a large supermarket in the towering mall along El Ruble, southeast of the plaza. Open daily 9am-10pm. AmEx/MC/V.

Police: ☎133. Carabineros, 27 de Abril (☎211 118). Other offices are situated in the block bounded by Vegas de Saldra and Bulnes, between Claudio Arrau and Carrera.

Pharmacy: Farmacias Ahumada, 5 de Abril 702 (☎216 984), on the corner of Robles and 5 de Abril, near the Mercado Central. Has an **ATM.** Open M-F 8:30am-9pm, Sa 9am-5pm. AmEx/MC/V.

Hospital: Ambulance ☎131. **Hospital Herminda Martín** (☎203 000, emergency 208 221, ambulance 212 205), at the intersection of Libertad and Argentina.

Fax Office and Telephones: Telefónica CTC, Arauco 625 (☎215 443), 1 block south of the plaza. Domestic faxes CH$330 per page, international CH$1500 per page. Open M-Sa 9am-9pm, Su 10am-9pm.

Internet Access: Nethouse Cibercafé, Constitución 637, 2nd fl. (☎246 712), east of the plaza. CH$500 per hr. Open M-F 10am-10:30pm, Sa 11am-10:30pm, Su 4-10:30pm. **Servicio de Internet,** 18 de Septiembre 458 (☎221 650), across from the *municipalidad.* CH$500 per hr. Open daily 10am-10pm.

Post Office: Libertad 501 (☎222 388), at the northwestern edge of the plaza. Has a **Western Union** counter. Open M-F 8:30am-6:30pm, Sa 9am-12:45pm.

▟ ACCOMMODATIONS

The universal overnight stop for tourists traveling Chile, Chillán has a multitude of accommodations with quality surpassing that of other Panamerican towns. Cheap *hosterías* surround the train station, while pricier hotels ring the Plaza de Armas.

Hostal Canada, Libertad 269, 2nd fl. (☎234 515). Other than the bold red maple leaf on the sign, there's actually nothing Canadian about this small hostel—the owner hasn't been there and there's no Molson in the fridge. Still, the crowded rooms are a great deal. Cable TV and heaters. Shared bath. Breakfast CH$1000. Laundry service and parking are available. Singles CH$4000; doubles CH$8000; triples CH$12,000. ❶

Hotel Las Terrazas, Constitución 644, 5th fl. (☎227 000; www.lasterrazas.cl), 1 block east of the plaza. Sunny rooms outfitted in polished wood look out over Chillán from their 5th- and 6th-story perches. Unfortunately, in this case, that means plenty of rusty rooftops, trash-strewn lots, and tacky signs. Cable TV. Breakfast included. Reservations recommended. Singles CH$41,500; doubles CH$45,800. ❺

Hostal Libertador, Itata 288 (☎214 879). The rooms may be plain and drab, beds stuffed into every possible corner, but this large hostel is one of Chillán's best values. Offers free laundry facilities, full kitchen, and spacious communal dining room with cable TV. Shared bath. Breakfast CH$500. Dorms CH$4000 per person, students CH$3000. ❶

Hotel de la Avenida Express, O'Higgins 398 (☎230 256), on the corner with Bulnes. Hotel de la Avenida feels like home—if your home happens to have polished wooden night stands and headboards. Cable TV, private parking, and laundry service available. Breakfast included. Singles CH$19,800; doubles CH$23,000; triples CH$35,400. Low-season prices 10-15% lower. IVA discount for foreigners. AmEx/MC/V. ❹

▐ FOOD

For food with a distinctly local flair, head to the **Feria de Chillán,** where small eateries cram the pedestrian mall and sidewalks. (Open M-Sa 9am-7pm, Su 9am-4pm.) For a tamer, more touristy scene, go north a block to the **Mercado Techado,** where restaurants are a bit swankier. (Open M-Sa 8am-6pm, Su 8am-2pm.)

▨ **Arco Iris,** El Roble 525 (☎227 549). This vegetarian restaurant has tried hard to calm the business-lunch rush with New Age music, soft, unfinished wood, and dreamcatchers, but even the superb food cannot pacify the hungry crowds. The all-you-can-eat lunch buffet (CH$3400) is a must, with mini-*empanadas,* fresh salad, veggie quiche, and homemade lemonade. Open M-F 9am-9:30pm, Sa 10am-5pm. AmEx/MC/V. ❸

Café Paris, Arauco 666 (☎223 881), just south of the Plaza de Armas. The leafy balcony is a good place to sip *café irlandés* (Irish coffee; CH$2000) or *café con leche* (CH$600) while watching the world drift by on Chillán's streets. Besides the snack bar downstairs, a classy 2nd fl. restaurant offers reasonably priced lunch specials (CH$2800-3500), including a vegetarian option (CH$3200). Snack bar open M 9am-2am, Th-Su 24hr. Restaurant open noon-midnight. AmEx/MC/V. ❷

Ficus, Rosas 392 (☎212 176 or 233 522), on the northwest corner of Rosas and Bulnes. Paper napkins in a table dispenser are set down by vested waiters in black bowties. Locals recommend Ficus for its filling meat portions (CH$2000-3400) and pastas (CH$1600-3000). Open daily 12:30pm-2am. AmEx/MC/V. ❷

Fuente Alemana, Arauco 661 (☎212 720), 1 block south of the Plaza de Armas. If you want to see Chileans dressed up in bright red-and-green bonnets and aprons, visit this *cafeteria*-style diner near the central plaza. Choose from a range of meats and salads showcased behind the counter (CH$1500-3000), greasy sandwiches (CH$1000-2400), or pizza (CH$2000). Open daily 8:30am-11:30pm. AmEx/MC/V. ❷

◉ SIGHTS

▧ IGLESIA CATEDRAL DE CHILLÁN. This cathedral's predecessor was leveled by the 1939 earthquake, and the grieving city set about with determination to commemorate the victims. A huge cross of concrete and iron stands to the left of the new cathedral, a solemn reminder of the disaster. The church itself is a wonderfully realized combination of form and function: its concrete arches, built to represent two hands curled in prayer, descend deep into the ground to complete their arc and form a structurally sound foundation to prevent high death tolls in case of future emergencies. Inside, the space is austere and largely unadorned: small windows filter sunlight onto the marble floors, and a huge crucifix, carved from Italian wood with the image of Christ nailed to its trunk, hangs at the far end of the hall. The cathedral faces the city's spacious Plaza de Armas, where a statue of Bernardo O'Higgins watches over the city while Chilean soldiers scamper about the base of his pedestal. *(Arauco 503, on the eastern edge of central plaza. ☎ 212 071. Open M and Th-Sa 8am-9pm, Tu-W and Su 8am-1pm and 3-9pm. Mass M-F 12:15pm; Sa 12:15 and 7pm; Su 8:30, 10am, 12:30, 8pm. Free.)*

IGLESIA SAN FRANCISCO. This church, built in 1903, is one of Chillán's few living pre-1939 relics. Having miraculously survived the earthquake with only the loss of its once-towering dome, Iglesia San Francisco has changed little since the early 20th century, giving visitors an eerie time capsule—a window into the *gravitas* of frontier Catholicism. The pale adobe facade features a mural of St. Francis and his animals, while inside, the **Museo San Francisco** features pictures of the devastating earthquake, grand 19th-century devotional paintings, and a magnificent wood carving of the archangel Michael slaying a demon. *(Sargento Aldea 265, northeast of the plaza. ☎ 211 634. Museum open Tu-Sa 9am-1pm and 3-6pm, Su 1-2pm. CH$600, students CH$200. Mass Tu-Sa 7:30pm; Su 8, 10am, noon, 7:30pm.)*

ESCUELA MÉXICO. Visitors from around the world routinely brave screaming students and raucous hallways to see one of Chillán's worthwhile treasures—hidden in a local high school. Built after the earthquake with money donated by the Mexican government, the Escuela México was decorated with murals by Mexican artists David Alfonso Siqueiros and Xavier Guerrero, both friends of Pablo Neruda. Siqueiros's masterpiece, "Death to the Invaders," painted on the walls of the school library, was completed in 1942. Guerrero's murals are emblazoned on the walls of the stairwell and entry hall, and include an image of a Mexican woman caring for a Chilean child injured in the great earthquake. *(O'Higgins 250, northeast of the train station. Ask any adult milling about to let you into the locked library. ☎ 212 012. Open 10am-noon and 3-5pm. Free, donations accepted.)*

FERIA DE CHILLÁN. This ever-bustling locale is a mecca for bargain shoppers. Also called the **Mercado Descubierto**, the *feria* spans an entire block, with stores and carts lined up along an X-shaped walkway, centered at the tiny Plaza Sargento Aldea. Kiwis sell for CH$100 per kg at the fruit stands, while boisterous vendors at the multitude of cheap, hole-in-the-wall eateries and craft shops hawk *empanadas*, woolen scarves (CH$1500), and *huaso* outfits. *(Open daily 9am-7pm.)*

CHILLÁN VIEJO. A tour of the stately **Parque Monumental Bernardo O'Higgins,** in the old part of town, features a mosaic depicting the life and wondrous deeds of Chile's *libertador*. The park marks the site of the house where O'Higgins was born. Nearby, you'll find the chapel where O'Higgins's mother and sister are buried. *(On O'Higgins. Take a colectivo or bus from the Plaza de Armas. Open 8am-7pm.)*

▓ DAYTRIP FROM CHILLÁN

TERMAS DE CHILLÁN ☎42

Buses depart from Chillán daily 8am and 4pm, and return from Termas de Chillán 9:30am and 5:45pm. Buses from Las Trancas return to Chillán at 9:45am and 6:30pm. Transportation can be arranged in Chillán or directly through the hotels in Las Trancas (see below).

Some 80km east of Chillán, Volcán Chillán, a 3122m peak shrouded in snow and ice, stands among the Andes. On its western face perches one of Chile's most popular and luxurious resorts, the **Termas de Chillán.** This mammoth resort features sulfur-and-iron-infused thermal baths, as well as some of South America's finest skiing, with 29 runs and a 1100m vertical drop. In the valley below is an expansive series of hostels and *cabañas* along the main road, known as **Las Trancas.** The accommodations here are more reasonable and provide access to a diverse assortment of activities, including trekking, horseback riding, and mountain biking.

Volcán Chillán and its lesser mountain neighbors offer plenty to do year-round. A stay at the resort facilitates skiing, although daytrippers can also use the lift for CH$20,000 per day. The HI hostel (see below) rents skis for CH$5000, and snowboards for CH$7000. During the spring, summer, and fall, many accommodations provide guided treks, horseback riding (CH$2000 per hr.), and mountain bikes (CH$5000). Depending on the length of the rental, prices can be negotiated.

An easy and beautiful hike (2-3hr. round-trip) can be done unguided in an afternoon. From the **Shangrila Hotel,** at Km73, turn down the dirt road and follow it 6km as it deteriorates into a rocky trail. The path leads through a moss-covered alpine forest to a desolate lava moonscape, and ends at the wooden skeleton of the area's first *refugio*, long abandoned. The magnificent isolation of the Shangrila Valley, with its gorgeous views of the volcano, rivals that of any Chilean national park.

While the accommodations near the summit, including the **Grand Hotel ❺** (☎278 100; www.termaschillan.cl), are far beyond the range of budget travel (doubles US$990-2000 per week; includes lift ticket and daily session in the *termas*), nearby Las Trancas has a multitude of cheaper options. Most notable is the cozy and hip **HI Las Trancas ❷,** Km73.5 (☎243 211; www.hostellinglastrancas.com). **Aguas del Fuego ❸,** Km68 (☎197 3610), has *cabañas* with full kitchen and TV (doubles CH$10,000-20,000; 4-6 person *cabañas* CH$20,000-40,000). All lodgings have on-site **restaurants**—although a cheaper option is to buy provisions at the roadside **market stalls.** Getting to the volcano is simple. A road heads east out of Chillán, becoming a steep gravel road past Las Trancas; the last 6km to the *termas* may be icy in winter. **Línea Azul** has **buses** to Las Trancas and the *termas* year-round.

CONCEPCIÓN ☎ 41

Concepción (pop. 220,700), beats with a strong, often frenzied pulse. The mixture of students, workers, artists, and businesspeople creates an atmosphere that smacks of both determined commerce and wild nightlife. Just to the south, the solid Río Bío Bío pushes its way into the crashing of the Pacific—fittingly representing the culture of the city perched at its headwaters. Today, Concepción stands as a cultural crossroads, as the proud Chilean city where O'Higgins declared the country's independence in 1818, and the gateway to the still-untamed south, the heart of Chile's indigenous culture. A city of commerce, this tension now plays out in the sprawling commerical district as European *haute couture* vies for attention with handmade crafts from the south and towering new department stores are fronted by Concepción's street vendors.

▄ TRANSPORTATION

Flights: Aeropuerto Carriel Sur (☎ 732 005), in Talcahuano, 16km (15min.) northeast of Concepción. **F&S Transit** (☎ 935 083 or 09 799 9801), a van shuttle service, charges CH$3000 per trip. **LanChile,** Barros Arana 600 (☎ 229 138 or 600 526 2000). Open M-F 9am-6:15pm, Sa 10am-1:15pm. Flies to: **Arica** (3½hr., 5 per day starting at 7am, CH$127,000); **Puerto Montt** (1hr., 10:30pm, CH$48,000); **Punta Arenas** (6hr., 1:45pm, CH$135,000); **Santiago** (1hr., 8 per day starting at 7:15am, CH$40,000); **Temuco** (1hr., 3:40pm, CH$39,000). **American Airlines,** Barros Arana 348 (☎ 521 616), arranges international flights through Santiago. Open M-F 9am-2pm and 3-6:30pm, Sa 10am-1pm.

Trains: Estación Concepción (☎ 226 925), on Nuevo Prat, at the end of Freire, behind the giant Lider supermarket. Ticket office at Barros Arana 164. ☎ 226 025. Open daily 8am-10pm. Trains to **Santiago** (daily 10:45pm; M-Th CH$8000, F-Su CH$9000).

Buses: Tur Bus (☎ 315 555), **Bío Bío** (☎ 310 764), **Eme Bus** (☎ 312 610), **Igi Llaima** (☎ 312 498), and **Línea Azul** (☎ 311 126) depart from 2 bus terminals in town.

Terminal de Buses Camilo Henríquez, Camilo Henríquez 2565 (☎ 315 036). Catch a Rengo Lientur bus #44 along Rengo or Chacabuco (CH$300). To: **Chillán** (1½hr., every 30min. 7am-midnight, CH$1300); **Los Angeles** (2hr., 4 per day 7:45am-11:15pm, CH$1800); **Santiago** (6hr., every 30min. 7am-midnight, CH$5000).

Terminal de Buses Collao, Tegualda 860 (☎ 749 000). From San Martín, catch a Chiguayate Sur bus #14 with "T. Collao" in the front window (CH$300). Buses to: **Chillán** (1½hr., every 30min. 6:40am-9pm, CH$1800); **Los Angeles** (1¾hr., 31 per day 6:30am-8:45pm, CH$1850); **Puerto Montt** (11hr., 6 per day 10am-9pm, CH$6000); **Santiago** (6hr.; 12 per day 8am-11:45pm; CH$5000, *salón cama* CH$7000); **Temuco** (4½hr.; Su-Th 18 per day 6:30am-8:15pm, F-Sa 21 per day 6:30am-9:15pm; CH$3700).

Buses: The silver-and-blue **city buses** cost CH$300 and stop anywhere—flag them down. By day, buses run throughout the city and suburbs, but service stops late at night.

Taxis and Colectivos: Taxis are found near the Plaza de la Independencia and train and bus stations. Taxi from the central plaza to the bus terminals CH$2500. Taxi to the airport CH$5000. Try **Taxi Catedral** (☎ 236 241) or **Taxi O'Higgins** (☎ 234 394). **Colectivos** can be found on Freire, Roosevelt, and Chacabuco. CH$300, 9pm-7am CH$500.

Car Rental: Econorent, Castellón 134 (☎ 225 5377 or 600 200 0000; www.econorent.net), or at Aeropuerto Carriel Sur (☎ 732 2121). Rentals start at CH$25,000 per day, including insurance. 24+. Concepción office open M-F 9am-1pm and 3-7pm. Airport office open 8am-10pm. AmEx/MC/V. **Rosselot Rent-A-Car,** Chacabuco 726 (☎/fax 732 030; airport office 732 010; www.rosselot.cl). Rentals from CH$24,000. Open 24hr. AmEx/MC/V.

Lautaro

Janequeo

Paicaví

Ongolmo

Orompello

Tucapel

Castellón

Colo Colo

Aníbal Pinto

Caupolicán

Rengo

Lincoyán

Angol

Salas

Serrano

Arturo Prat

Nuevo Prat

Maipú

Freire

Barros Arana

O'Higgins

San Martín

Lautaro

Pedro Aguirre Cerda

PLAZA
PERÚ

Larenas

Beltrán Mathieu

Cochrane

Chacabuco

Victor Lamas

Arco Universidad
de Concepción

Casa
del Arte

Campanil

Universidad
de Concepción

TO SUMMIT

Econorent

Rosselot Rent-a-Car

Club de Tenis

CERRO CARACOL

Parque Ecuador

Veteranos del 79

Galería de la Historia
de Concepción

200 meters
200 yards

TO TERMINAL
DE BUSES C.
HENRÍQUEZ (4km)

TO TERMINAL
COLLAO (5km)

Parroquia de la Merced

Palacio
de Justicia

Mercado
Municipal

PLAZA
DE LA
INDEPENDENCIA

Museo de Arte
Sagrado

Catedral

LanChile

Manzano

Afex

American
Airlines

Instituto Chileno
Norteamericano de Cultura

Instituto Chileno
Británico

Wall Street
Institute

Lave Rap

Argentina

Train Ticket
Office

Estación
Concepción

PLAZA
ESPAÑA

Líder

TO (1km),
(16km),
MONITOR HUÁSCAR (18km),
LOTA (37km)

Chacabuco

Cochrane

Chacabuco

San Martín

O'Higgins

Barros Arana

Maipú

Freire

Concepción

ACCOMMODATIONS
Hotel El Dorado, 6
Hotel Alonso de Ercilla, 14
Hotel Bío Bío, 5
Hotel San Martín, 15
Hotel San Sebastián, 9
Residencial O'Higgins, 12

FOOD
Javiera's Restaurant, 4
Marmut, 7
Rich, 13
Rincón Marino, 10
Stromboli, 3

NIGHTLIFE
30 y Tantos, 11
Choripan, 2
Havana Club, 8
Katango Planet, 1

MIDDLE CHILE

✈ ❼ ORIENTATION AND PRACTICAL INFORMATION

Concepción centers around the **Plaza de la Independencia,** which is flanked by its cathedral, government offices, and banks. Concepción's layout itself is symbolic of its hybrid and contentious past: many northwest and southeast downtown streets are named after Mapuche chieftains—Caupolicán, Colo Colo, and so on—while the streets that they cross bear the names of Chilean independence fighters including O'Higgins and San Martín. A pedestrian mall heads east on **Barros Arana,** and is always bustling with activity. The **mercado municipal,** another good place for bargain shoppers, lies two blocks north of the plaza. Northeast of downtown lies the **Universidad de Concepción** in the **Barrio Universitario,** where you'll find the city's bohemian scene amid a smattering of bars and cafes. At the southeastern edge of the city is a tree-topped ridge, **Cerro Caracol;** at its foot is a pleasant park.

Tourist Office: Sernatur, Aníbal Pinto 460 (☎227 976; fax 229 201; infobiobio@sernatur.cl), on the northeastern edge of the Plaza de la Independencia, has free city maps. Open Dec.-Feb. M-F 8:30am-8pm, Sa 10am-2:30pm; Mar.-Nov. M-F 9am-1pm and 3-6pm. **Conaf,** Barros Arana 215 (☎238 504), near Barrio Estación, offers info about the region. Open M-F 9am-1pm and 3-5pm. **Copias Casanueva,** San Martín 663 (☎244 093 or 234 049), sells maps of the city and surrounding suburbs (CH$1000).

Consulates: Argentina, San Martín 472, 5th fl. (☎230 257; fax 910 183). Open M-F 9am-1pm and 3-6pm.

Currency Exchange: Afex, Barros Arana 565, local 57 (☎239 618; fax 210 590), in the Gutería Internacional. Changes currency and cashes traveler's checks. Open M-F 9am-2:30pm and 3:30-6:30pm, Sa 10am-1:30pm.

Banks: Banks and ATMs surround the plaza. **Banco Santander,** O'Higgins 560 (☎264 800), near the Plaza de la Independencia. **24hr. ATM.** Open M-F 9am-2pm.

Work Opportunities: Restaurant Da Giovanni, Caupolicán 346, local 3 (☎241 936), hires 2 waiters for work Dec.-Jan. Contact owner Gilda Carnese for information. **Havana Club,** Barros Arana 1356 (☎224 006), hires 5 waiters and 4 bouncers Jan.-Mar.

Teaching English: Wall Street Institute for English, Caupolicán 299 (☎910 791; www.wsi.es), seeks part-time or full-time English instructors year-round. For more info on teaching English, see **Alternatives to Tourism,** p. 89.

Cultural Centers: Instituto Chileno Norteamericano de Cultura, Caupolicán 315 (☎225 506). **Instituto Chileno Británico,** San Martín 531 (☎234 044).

Market: The **mercado municipal,** on the corner of Freire and Caupolicán, has a wide variety of items, from produce to clothing. Open daily 8am-8pm.

Supermarket: Lider, on the corner of Freire and Prat. Open daily 9am-10pm.

Laundromat: Laundromats are hard to come by in Concepción, but most hotels and *residenciales* provide laundry service. **Lave Rap,** Caupolicán 334 (☎234 826), 1 block east of the plaza. Wash or dry CH$1500. Open M-F 9:30am-8pm, Sa 9:30am-3pm.

Police: ☎133. *Carabineros* at San Martín 171 (☎235 011), at the corner with Salas.

Pharmacies: Farmacias Ahumada, Barros Arana 726-740 (☎255 540), next to the Mamul restaurant. Open daily 8am-midnight. **Salcobrand,** Barros Arana 611 (☎227 477), on the Plaza de la Independencia. **Open 24hr.**

Hospital: Ambulance ☎133. **Hospital Clínico Regional de Concepción,** San Martín 1436 (☎237 445 or 208 500), at the corner with Janequeo.

Fax Office and Telephones: Entel, Barros Arana 541 (☎911 449), near the Plaza de la Independencia. Domestic faxes CH$350 per page, international CH$1600 per page. Open M-F 8:30am-10pm, Sa 9am-9:30pm, Su 10am-5pm.

Internet Access: Internet, Barros Arana 439, 2nd fl. CH$500 per hr. Open daily 9am-10:30pm. **Cyber Café,** Caupolicán 588 (☎238 394), between Freire and Barros Arana. CH$900 per hr. Open M-Sa 9am-11pm, Su 11am-11pm.

Post Office: Correos, Colo Colo 417 (☎235 666), 1 block from the Plaza de la Independencia. **Western Union** wire service available. Open M-F 8am-7pm, Sa 8am-1pm.

ACCOMMODATIONS

Concepción offers every type of accommodation within walking distance of the Plaza de Armas. Most hotels and *residenciales* tend to be worn in, but they still provide a comfortable place to hang your hat in the heart of the city's busy center.

Hotel Alonso de Ercilla, Colo Colo 334 (☎227 984; www.hotelalonsodeercilla.cl). If you are willing to pay a bit more, this hotel offers modern rooms without the intimidating excess of pricier establishments. Cable TV. Breakfast included. Laundry service available. Singles CH$22,500-28,900; doubles CH$36,700; triples CH$49,900. IVA discount for foreigners. AmEx/MC/V. ❹

Hotel San Martín, San Martín 949 (☎/fax 981 282). One of the city's best values. Bright, spotless rooms are plain yet spacious. Walls are thin and bathrooms are down the hall, but the price is right. Cable TV. Breakfast included. CH$7000 per person. ❷

Hotel San Sebastián, Rengo 463, 2nd fl. (☎956 719), between Barros Arana and O'Higgins, has clean rooms with carpeting and comfortable beds. Cable TV and laundry service available. Breakfast included. Reservations recommended 3-4 days in advance Dec.-Mar. Singles CH$16,000, with bath CH$20,000; doubles CH$22,000/CH$26,000; triples CH$28,000; quads CH$34,000. AmEx/MC/V. ❹

Residencial O'Higgins, O'Higgins 457 (☎221 086). In this *residencial*, incense fills the air, and trinkets, posters, and relics from the 60s and 70s comically fill every nook and cranny. Rooms are dark, but a cheerful atmosphere prevails due to the energetic owner and the stream of backpackers passing through. Shared bath. CH$6000 per person. ❷

Hotel El Dorado, Barros Arana 348 (☎229 400; eldorado@entelchile.net). Concepción's bright, shiny, luxury hotel. Has large rooms with dark, polished wood furnishings and plaid sofas. Cable TV and heaters. Breakfast included. Singles CH$33,000; doubles CH$36,000; triples CH$44,000. IVA discount for foreigners. AmEX/MC/V. ❹

Hotel Bío Bío, Barros Arana 751 (☎228 018; www.contactoconce.cl), off the northern edge of the pedestrian walkway. This once-luxurious hotel has faded from its glory days, with stained carpets and cracked bathroom tiles, but rooms are big, warm, and quiet. A favorite of traveling businesspeople. Cable TV. Breakfast included. Laundry service available. Singles CH$12,000, with bath CH$14,000; doubles CH$16,000/CH$21,000; triples CH$22,000. IVA discount for foreigners. AmEx/MC/V. ❸

FOOD

Concepción doesn't have much in the way of local specialties, but as the only big city around, it boasts a wide range of culinary options. You will find lots of great seafood here, as well as a host of decent sandwich and dessert shops along Barros Arana, catering to the business and evening crowds. The cheapest and freshest meals are found in the food stalls of the **mercado municipal,** on the corner of Freire and Caupolicán, where set meals are served for under CH$750.

Liberarte, Barros Arana 244 (☎09 931 5562). Go through the walkway with a yellow sign—Liberarte is the restaurant in the green barn. The huge, airy dining space radiates a wholesome ambience, the ideal setting for enjoying the all-vegetarian menu and small library at the center of the restaurant. During the day, enjoy the buffet lunch; at night

STRANGER IN A STRANGE LAND

Mexican educator José Vasconceles called Latin America the birthplace of *la raza cósmica*, the "cosmic race." Emerging from the fusion of Spanish and indigenous cultures, the people of Latin America were the future of humanity, believed Vasconceles—a beautiful mixture of physiognomy and folklore that represented a world steadily losing all boundaries. I was hoping to find such forward thinking when I came to Chile. Instead, I encountered a disturbing amount of racial intolerance and ignorance.

With some exceptions, the Chilean propensity for xenophobia was commonplace. Wherever I went, from small towns to large urban centers, I met stares, heckling, and harassment, prompted by the mere sight of an Asian person. In Rancagua, a boy popped his head out of a car to shout "chino!" In Curicó, a man began making "kung-fu" yelps and shrieks when I approached. Concepción was the worst place for racial harassment—I was often accosted by men chanting "China! China!" Well, at least they got the ethnicity somewhat right: most would-be bigots would shout "japonés" or "correano."

In profound moments of self-pity, I talked to some of the more understanding locals, and they had theories about my problems. Some believed that Chileans were just not used to foreigners. After

the "Leaves of Grass" (veggie-filled omelette with yogurt sauce; CH$1800) is one of the best meals in town. Open M-Sa noon-4pm and 7pm-midnight. AmEx/MC/V. ❷

Javiera's Restaurante, Barros Arana 337 (☎228 207). One of Barros Arana's classier establishments, Javiera's is the place for international cuisine and tasty steaks (CH$5000). Most notable for its wide selection of salads (CH$1500-2200). The 3-course *menú* (CH$2500), cloth napkins, and Bing Crosby draw in the business lunch crowd. Open daily 8am-2pm and 6pm-midnight. AmEx/MC/V. ❸

Rincón Marino, Colo Colo 454 (☎230 311), up the stairs just to the right of the small mall, marked by a small sign. The big model fishing boat and the sign that reads "Gone Fishing" should tip you off that this is a place that takes seafood seriously. Try the *plato americano* (CH$4500), a large plate with all sorts of maritime mollusks, served cold with a drizzling of *salsa verde* and mayo. Open M-Sa noon-midnight. AmEx/MC/V. ❸

Rich, Colo Colo 325 (☎245 829), across from Hotel Alonso de Ercilla, in the pink building. Locals say this place serves the best burgers in Concepción (CH$900-1800), which come with a wide range of toppings, from *palta* (avocado pureé) to sunny-side-up eggs. Try the "Promoción Rich," a value meal including a hamburger, *papas fritas*, and a soft drink (CH$2800). Open M-Sa 10am-10pm. ❶

Stromboli, Manzano 548, down the small street off of Barros Arana. This shabby hole-in-the-wall restaurant, governed by a cohort of grandmotherly women, does not look like much, but you hardly notice when they bring out the big bowl of freshly cooked pasta. *Menú* CH$1100. Open daily noon-4pm and 7pm-midnight. ❶

Marmut, Barros Arana 744 (☎912 037), on the pedestrian mall near the plaza. Locals flock here for exotic dishes like grilled Alaskan salmon (CH$2250), New Orleans steak (CH$2290), and oriental chicken salad (CH$1490). 2-for-1 *Schop* during happy hour 6-8pm. Open M-Sa 9am-midnight, Su 10am-1am. AmEx/MC/V. ❶

🜨 SIGHTS

PLAZA DE LA INDEPENDENCIA. The only place livelier than the Universidad de Concepción is Concepción's **Plaza de la Independencia.** The place for street theater, summer weekend festivals, and—after dark—necking high-school students, the plaza is the city's public face. The walkways, crowded with people and all sorts of majestic trees, seem a fitting place for Chile's most grandiose act of patriotism. On a spot marked by a nondescript stone, Bernardo O'Higgins, standing before his Army of the South, declared the independence of Chile on January 1, 1818.

IGLESIA CATEDRAL DE CONCEPCIÓN. On the southwestern edge of the plaza, this gray-stone edifice has central doors made of bronze, decorated with scenes from the Old and New Testament. This cathedral centers around an Italian marble altar, behind which lies a huge, pastel-colored mural, depicting the Holy Trinity, Christ's birth and crucifixion, the Garden of Eden, and the Virgin Mary stamping the head of the serpent. (*Caupolicán 451. ☎ 223 701. Open M-F 9am-7:30pm, Sa-Su 9am-1pm. Mass M-F 10am; Sa 10am and 7pm; Su 10, 11am, 12:15, 7pm. Free.*)

MUSEO DE ARTE SAGRADO. This museum boasts a repository of religious art owned by the Universidad Católica de la Santísima Concepción. Its collection of objects and ornaments used in Catholic liturgy over the last six centuries includes extravagant amounts of gold, silver, and marble. (*Caupolicán 441, adjacent to the Catedral. ☎ 735 060; gvarela@ucsc.cl. Open Nov.-Mar. Tu-F 10am-1:30pm and 4-8pm, Sa 11am-2pm; Apr.-Oct. Tu-F 10am-1:30pm and 3-7pm, Sa 11am-2pm. CH$300.*)

UNIVERSIDAD DE CONCEPCIÓN. Chile's second-largest university, the Universidad de Concepción, lies in relative seclusion along a forested ridge at the eastern edge of downtown. No trip to Concepción would be complete without a prolonged gaze at the awe-inspiring *Presencia de América Latina*, a huge, fiery-red mural by Mexican artist Jorge González Camarena that stretches along the entire back wall of the university's ◪**Casa del Arte.** Painted in 1965, the mural depicts the whole of Latin America as a single entity: flags from each country flutter across the top of the mural, while the *pareja original*—an armored conquistador and a naked indigenous woman—watch from one end, their joined bodies representing the fusion of native and Spanish blood. The Casa del Arte also houses Chile's largest collection of paintings outside Santiago, including 19th- and early-20th-century paintings by both Chileans and foreign artists. (*On Paicaví, at Chacabuco. ☎ 204 290. Open Tu-F 10am-6pm, Sa 10am-4pm, Su 10am-1pm. Free.*)

Upon leaving the *casa*, turn right and head down Chacabuco until you reach the university's signature arch, the **Arco Universidad de Concepción.** Situated between the two halves of the university's medical building, the towering arch features a relief with images from Greek mythology. The university's elegant

all, those tall mountains to the east kept out visitors. And the Pinochet regime had not exactly been a wellspring of progressive, cosmopolitan thought. One Chilean ventured that Asians were singled out because Korean immigrants were reputed for mistreating Chilean employees who worked in the ubiquitous *chifas*. It also doesn't help that the average Chilean's knowledge of Asian culture comes from martial arts flicks—the most vivid image I had of Asians during my stay came from an antiperspirant commercial in which an Asian dude karate chops his way through a slew of bad guys only to marvel at the lack of sweat collected under his arm.

After mulling over the issue myself, I realized that I shouldn't be so hard on Chileans for being ignorant about my race or culture. It's not like bigotry is unique to Chile, for as Juan, a waiter in Pichilemu, observed, "To a Chilean, your eyes say japonés. People here don't know the difference between Japanese and Chinese. But it's the same thing in the US. If North Americans saw a Chilean, they won't think 'Chilean,' rather, they'd think in generalities like South American or Hispanic." I guess things are difficult for all strangers in strange lands, not just Asians in Chile. And there is something to be said for keeping a thick skin and not letting scattered ignorance make you close yourself to a whole society.

-Victor Tan Chen

campanil, a clock tower of white stone, sublimely unadorned, lies before the arch. Its steps lead down to the **plaza estudiante,** a space dominated by skateboarders. Around the plaza you'll find a few small lagoons and a variety of trees, some exotic.

◪ NIGHTLIFE

Laid-back bars with throbbing, packed clubs abound in the **Barrio Estación,** the city's official hangout for hard drinkers, partiers, and ne'er-do-wells. You'll find whatever poison suits your fancy here—whether it's a smoky bar scene with rock-star wannabes at the mic, a sweaty dance floor with little wiggle room, or piping-hot *empanadas.* Be careful, though—this neighborhood is reputed to be the city's most dangerous area. For a more sedate, but still hard-drinking, neighborhood, head to the **Barrio Universitario,** the sector abutting the Universidad de Concepción.

▨ 30 y Tantos, Prat 402, south of the Plaza España. This is the place to go do *empanadas* (CH$1080). In addition, there's a chill bar atmosphere, with light radiating from naked bulbs and candles, old transistor radiators stacked on wall shelves, and loud and lively music. Beer CH$850-1200. Mixed drinks CH$900-4800. Open daily 7pm-2am.

Kantango Planet, Prat 1354. Take a bus up Prat from the station, get off right before the bridge, and go down the small side road to the right. Several blocks north of Barrio Estación, Kantango is perhaps the city's most happening (and most exclusive) club. Be careful in this neighborhood at night. Open Sa-Su until late.

Choripan, Arturo Prat 542-546 (☎253 004), at the eastern end of Plaza España. A mellow bar that features live music on some nights—usually a Chilean rock band trying out your favorite American riffs. Try the *ponche* (red wine mixed with strawberry juice, or white wine mixed with punch) to really get that distortion buzzing in your head. (CH$500). Mixed drinks CH$1600-3900. Open daily 7:30pm-3:30am.

Havana Club, Barros Arana 1356 (☎224 006), 4 blocks east of the Palacio de Justicia. Despite its location, far from both Barrio Estación and Barrio Universitario, Havana Club offers 2 floors of dancing. Latin music and techno play on most nights, while Th is 80s night. Live acts make occasional appearances. Semi-formal attire required. Beer CH$500. Mixed drinks CH$1000-2000. 18+. Cover Th CH$1500, F and Su CH$3000, Sa CH$1000. All ages permitted Sa-Su 5-10pm. Open Th-Su 5pm-5am.

◪ DAYTRIPS FROM CONCEPCIÓN

CHIFLÓN DEL DIABLO

Catch a "Parque de Lota" bus at the northwest corner of Tucapel and Carrera (1hr., every 10min., CH$500), and get off at the painted "Chiflón del Diablo" sign at the top of the large hill upon entering into Lota.

Beneath Lota, a small, impoverished town 37km south of Concepción and smack in the middle of Chile's Costa del Carbón, is the mine of ▨**Chiflón del Diablo.** Here, at the only mine in the world that goes beneath the ocean floor, visitors descend 40m in a rickety cage and make their way along exposed coal veins, splintering wood abutments, and abandoned equipment. Tours are led by ex-miners struggling to find a living through tourism since the mines were closed. They sing of the heroics and struggles of generations of miners while cursing the pit mines of Colombia that put them out of business.

While the tour, which uses leftover lamps and other equipment, is as budget as the mine was, it provides a window into the lives and souls of Chilean coal miners. A must-see. (☎871 565; www.lotasorprendente.cl. Open daily 9am-5pm, tours leave whenever people show up. CH$4000 per hr.)

MONITOR HUÁSCAR

From O'Higgins and Castellón, catch the micro run by Buses Base Naval with a sign reading "Base Naval" in the windshield (45min., every 10min., CH$300). Upon arrival, you'll have to leave your passport and any bags at the gate with the guard.

Naval buffs and young children will gladly make the trip out to the Talcahuano naval base, 16km northeast of Concepción, to see the (still-floating) ironclad *Huáscar.* Built in England in 1865, with an 11cm thick hull of riveted steel and a double-cannon turret capable of rotating 180 degrees, this Peruvian gunship terrorized the relatively weak Chilean navy for more than a decade, until October 8, 1879, when two Chilean ships were finally able to batter it into submission with heavy cannon fire, but not, however, before the *Huáscar* took the lives of Chile's two greatest naval heroes, Captain Arturo Prat and Sergeant Juan de Dios Aldea. In one of history's most courageous (and pointless) acts of heroism during the War of the Pacific, Captain Prat leapt from his sinking wooden ship, the *Esmeralda,* onto the deck of the *Huáscar,* sword in hand. He was promptly shot to death. With such a glorious history, it's no wonder that the Peruvian government is still wrangling with Chileans over the boat which they claim is stolen property.

The ship is kept meticulously well-preserved; cleaning occurs every morning 8:30-9am, and all day on Monday. The uniformed sailors on board will happily explain the intricacies of the ship's turret system and engine room. *(At the Talcahuano naval base. ☎ 745 061. Open Tu-Su 9:30am-noon and 2-5pm. CH$1000.)*

LOS ANGELES ☎43

A small city with a big-city attitude, Los Angeles (pop. 140,000) has been rushing to transform itself into a center of transportation, culture, and industry. The one main obstacle, however, is a lack of any visible history. Founded as a fort in 1739 and used as a summer camp by the Spanish *Ejército de la Frontera* (Frontier Army), Los Angeles was destroyed and rebuilt several times and was later used as a timber-processing center. Now, with that industry less dependent on an urban center, Los Angeles is furiously changing. With a sparkling plaza dedicated to Bernardo O'Higgins, who owned a nearby *hacienda,* and easy transport to spectacular natural attractions, Los Angeles hopes to draw—and keep—tourists. Virtually anything can be purchased in the sprawling commercial sector and frequent buses run to Chile's highest waterfall and one of its premier parks. In the end, however, it all becomes clear: convenience reigns where character is lacking.

▐ TRANSPORTATION

Buses: Local bus routes are reliable. Hail a bus at Villagrán to get to the bus terminal (CH$220); buses from the terminal to the *centro* run on Almagro. The 4 main bus terminals in town are serviced by **Buses ERS** (☎322 356), **Buses IGI Llaima** (☎363 100), **Buses Bío Bío** (☎363 145), **Jote-Be** (☎363 037 or 363 174), **Tur Bus** (☎363 136), and **Unión del Sur** (☎363 045).

Terminal Rodoviario, Sor Vicenta 2051 (☎363 066), 3km north of the city center. A gaggle of companies service this terminal with similar rates, competing discounts, and schedules that cover dawn to midnight. Bus tickets can be arranged in town at a universal **ticket office,** Caupolicán 526. Open M-F 9am-1pm and 3-7pm, Sa 3-7pm. To: **Angol** (1¼hr., 9 per day 9am-9:30pm, CH$1100); **Chillán** (1¾hr., 13 per day 7:30am-9:30pm, CH$1300); **Concepción** (1¾hr., 29 per day 7:30am-10pm, CH$1850); **Osorno** (6hr.; 10, 11:45am, 1:50, 11pm; CH$4500); **Puerto Montt** (7½hr., 4 per day 10am-11pm, CH$4500); **Santiago** (7hr., every hr. 8am-1am, CH$3000); **Temuco** (2½hr., 20 per day 7:30am-11pm, CH$2500).

Terminal de Buses Vega Techada, San José 146 (☎324 080). To **Salto del Laja** (1½hr., every 30min. 5am-8pm, CH$600). Last bus returns to Los Angeles at 8:10pm.

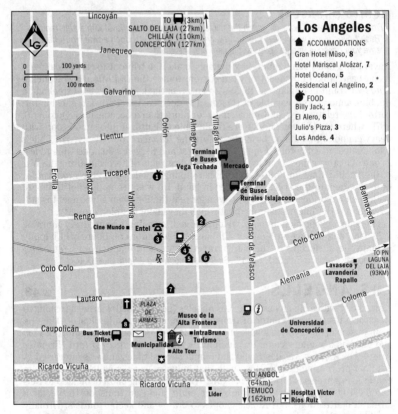

Los Angeles

▲ ACCOMMODATIONS
Gran Hotel Müso, **8**
Hotel Mariscal Alcázar, **7**
Hotel Océano, **5**
Residencial el Angelino, **2**

🍴 FOOD
Billy Jack, **1**
El Alero, **6**
Julio's Pizza, **3**
Los Andes, **4**

Terminal de Buses Rurales Islajacoop Ltda., Villagrán 501 (☎313 232 or 315 128; fax 315 128), at the corner of Rengo. Buses go to **Antuco** (1hr.; M-F 8 per day 7:15am-7:45pm, Sa 6 per day 9am-7:15pm, Su 7:15, 10am, 3, 7:15pm) and **El Abanico** (1½hr.; M-Sa 5 per day 8:30am-7:15pm, Su 8, 10am, 3, 7:15pm; CH$1000).

Taxis/Colectivos: Taxis and *colectivos* can be found around the bus terminals and the Plaza de Armas. *Colectivos* CH$200 within town. Taxis between Terminal Rodoviario and *centro* CH$1500. Call **Taxi Rengo** (☎321 226) for door-to-door service.

Car Rental: InterBruna Turismo (see **Tours,** below) rents cars starting at CH$20,000 per day, including insurance. No automatic transmission. **AlteTour** rents cars as well (see **Tours,** below).

✳ 🛈 ORIENTATION AND PRACTICAL INFORMATION

Los Angeles sits just off the Panamerican. **Sor Vicenta** leads away from the highway, passing the Terminal Rodoviario and then heading to the **Plaza de Armas** (the street becomes **Almagro** heading south). **Colón** is the main commercial avenue. **Villagrán,** a block east of Almagro, heads back north, merging into Sor Vicenta and returning to the Panamerican. **Alemania** (known as **Lautaro** to the west) goes east from the plaza and will take you all the way to Parque Nacional Laguna del Laja.

Tourist Information: The **municipalidad** has a small tourist office in the Oficina de Proyectos, on the 2nd fl. of the blue O'Higgins building, on the corner of Caupolicán and Colón. Has maps and brochures of Los Angeles and nearby scenic attractions. Open M-F 8:15am-1:45pm and 2:45-5pm. **Conaf,** José Manso de Velasco 275 (☎321 086 or 321 130) has maps of the national parks in Region VIII. Open M-F 8am-2pm.

Tours: InterBruna Turismo, Caupolicán 350 (☎313 812; fax 325 925; interbruna@hotmail.com). Handles flight-booking and travel arrangements continent-wide. Open M-F 9:30am-1pm and 3-7:30pm, Sa 10am-1pm. AmEx/MC. **AlteTour,** Colón 139a (☎/fax 325 692), has similar services. Open M-F 9:30am-1pm and 3-6pm. AmEx/MC/V.

Currency Exchange: InterBruna Turismo (see **Tours,** above), cashes traveler's checks and changes foreign currency, as does **AlteTour** (see **Tours,** above).

Bank: Dozens of banks ring the Plaza de Armas. **BancoEstado,** Colón 160 (☎314 120), down from the corner with Caupolicán. **24hr. ATM.** Open M-F 9am-2pm.

Library: Biblioteca Pública Roberto Espinoza, 1st fl. of the O'Higgins building, on the corner of Caupolicán and Colón. Free Internet. Open M-F 8am-7pm, Sa 9am-1pm.

Market: The city's **mercado,** located around the Terminal de Buses Vega Techada, sells fruit, vegetables, and handicrafts. Open daily 8am-8pm. The shiny new "hipermarket," **Lider** has its own phone code. On the corner of Ricardo Vicuña and Almagro. Open M-Th 8:30am-10:30pm, F-Sa 8:30am-11pm, Su 8:30am-10pm. AmEx/MC/V.

Laundromat: Lavaseco y Lavandería Rapallo, Alemania 355 (☎326 222). Dry cleaning available; machine wash CH$800 per kg. Open M-F 9am-8pm, Sa 9am-2:30pm.

Police: ☎133. *Carabineros* on Colón (☎312 595), 1 block south of the plaza.

Pharmacy: Pharmacies line Colón north of the plaza. **Salcobrand,** Colón 412 (☎327 542), has the longest hours. Open daily 9am-11pm.

Hospital: Ambulance ☎131. **Hospital Víctor Ríos Ruíz,** Ricardo Vicuña 147 (☎409 600), at the corner of Los Carrera.

Telephones: Entel, Colón 462, has phones for national and international calls. Open M-F 8:30am-9pm, Sa 9am-9pm, Su 10am-2pm. AmEx/MC/V. International calls also at Internet parlor (see below).

Internet: Parlor half-way down the creekside plaza between Colón's and Almagro's 400 block. CH$500 per hr. Open daily 10am-10pm. For late-night connections, try **Cyberland,** Valaso 292. CH$500 per hr. Open M-Sa 9:30am-2:30am.

Post Office: Correos, Caupolicán 460 (☎321 041), on the southern edge of the Plaza de Armas. **Western Union** wire service available. Open M-F 9am-7pm, Sa 9am-1pm.

ACCOMMODATIONS

In one way, Los Angeles seems to imitate its famous sister on the northern half of the globe: those with thick wallets stay at glitzy hotels, while the rest make do with *residenciales* at a distance from the central plaza. All in all, Los Angeles has a dearth of mid-range options—and the better hotels are not really worth the price. In fact, many hotels have sprung up along the Panamerican, ensuring that tourists have a clear path to Salto del Laja without having to set foot in the city at all.

Hotel Océano, Colo Colo 327 (☎342 432; hoteloceanola@hotmail.com). Océano offers bright, well-furnished rooms with cable TV and clean bathrooms. Space heaters and free parking. Reservations recommended in summer. Singles CH$10,000; doubles CH$16,000, with bath CH$21,000; *matrimoniales* CH$22,000. Low-season CH$8000/CH$15,000/CH$18,000/CH$19,000. ❷

Residencial El Angelino, Almagro 497 (☎317 786), has large, sunny rooms off a dim stone hallway. If these are taken, however, you might get stuck with a cell-like "matrimonial suite." Rooms are kept clean by the kind manager, but 24hr. reception keeps the bell buzzing all night. That, thin walls, and the location on busy Almagro, make earplugs almost a necessity. Shared bath. Breakfast included. Rooms CH$6000-15,000. ❷

Hotel Mariscal Alcázar, Lautaro 385 (☎311 725; www.hotelalcazar.cl). Unfortunately, the rooms do not live up to the sparkling reception area and lounge, but are quite comfortable regardless of the cheap wooden furniture and worn hardwood floors. Central heating and cable TV. Breakfast included. Singles CH$32,000-35,000; doubles CH$40,000-44,000; triples CH$51,000; suites CH$55,500-66,600. AmEx/MC/V. ❹

Gran Hotel Müso, Valdivia 222 (☎313 183; www.hotelmuso.cl). This aging hotel has comfortable rooms off a main plaza. All the trimmings included—cable TV, breakfast, and laundry service—but plain suites and dim atmosphere make you question the value. Singles CH$30,300; doubles CH$40,000; *matrimoniales* CH$40,400; triples CH$56,100. AmEx/MC/V. ❹

▐ FOOD

Los Angeles prides itself on its hearty traditional fare—beef-filled *empanadas*, tenderly grilled *parrilladas*, and *pollonas* (boiled chicken served with *papas fritas* and fried eggs). For cheap eats, head to the **mercado ❶**, where you will find *empanadas* galore (CH$300-400), along with other typical dishes like *porotos* (beans; CH$1200) and various *cazuelas* (CH$1500). Open 8am-late.

Julio's Pizza, Colón 452 (☎314 530). This sit-down pizzeria features delicious pizzas—a welcome break from the typical meat-and-potato options—although those are available. Those with an iron stomach can try the *piña* (mozzarella, pineapple, cream, and cherries); otherwise, play it safe and enjoy the quality pies. Slices around CH$2500; whole pies around CH$8000. Open M-Sa 9am-1pm, Su 11:30am-midnight. AmEx/MC/V. ❷

El Alero, Colo Colo 235 (☎320 058). Here, hearty, meat-themed meals are served in a dark yet spacious dining room at a reasonable price. *Ofertas* (meat entree, salad, side dish, and drink) are a steal (CH$1400-1600), or try the *parrilladas* (CH$3050) and *braseros* (CH$3900). Soup CH$500. Salads CH$500-1200. Open M-Sa noon-1am. ❷

Los Andes, Paseo Ronald Ramm 348 (☎344 155). Los Andes provides entertaining dining: either choose to people-watch outside or head indoors for the cable TV. On the menu, the choices are diverse, including lentils (CH$800) and *gnocchi* with chicken (CH$1600). Upstairs is a popular hangout that gets rowdy after dark on the weekends. Open M-Sa 10am-midnight. AmEx/MC/V. ❶

Billy Jack, Colón 592 (☎320 594). This hybrid fast-food joint and sit-down family restaurant smells suspiciously like a greasepit, although the logo of a smiling bull wearing a cowboy hat and enjoying a hot dog will draw you inside. The value meals are a steal: a hamburger and a drink is only CH$890. Open daily 9am-9pm. AmEx/MC/V. ❶

◉ ▐ SIGHTS AND ENTERTAINMENT

Los Angeles tries to capture the many tourists passing through on the way to PN Laguna del Laja and Salto del Laja with its oversized commercial center and modernized public face. In 2001, Los Angeles overhauled its central plaza, and recently, it unveiled the **Plaza de Armas Libertador Bernardo O'Higgins,** a splendid, strikingly modern space complete with wheelchair-accessible ramps. The center of the square, where various stone paths cross a ring of water and converge, represents the union and intermingling of Mapuche and Spanish culture. Other than the plaza, Los Angeles presents the **Museo de la Alta Frontera,** located on the second floor of the O'Higgins building on the corner of Caupolicán and Colón. Beyond the cache of foreign rifles used on the frontier, the museum showcases a resplendent array of Mapuche silver jewelry, as well as work by local artists. (☎408 641. Open M-F 8:15am-2pm and 2:45-6:45pm. Free.) For something a little flashier, head northwest to the brand-new **Mall Plaza Los Angeles.** On the fourth floor is the town's movie theater, **Cine Mundo,** Mendoza 477, which screens contemporary movies in English with Spanish subtitles. (☎343 311. Shows daily noon-10pm. CH$2900.)

⚑ DAYTRIP FROM LOS ANGELES

SALTO DEL LAJA

*To get to Salto del Laja, take a Jote-Be bus heading north from the Terminal de Buses Vega Techada (see **Transportation**, p. 313). The falls are also easily accessible by car— 30min. north on the Panamerican. Take the turnoff that says "Salto del Laja," about 1km before the falls. (Cars CH$400 to enter.) The entrance to the Salto Principal walkway is a bit hidden; it's to the left of the Feria Artesanal Stall.*

Twenty-seven kilometers north of Los Angeles, crowned by the largest waterfall in Chile, **Salto del Laja** thunders with a vengeance through a three-ringed gorge. Here, just off the Panamerican, the broad width of the Río Laja uncoils from a 50m precipice, its marbled white waters descending in a torrent of foam and mist. Visitors can walk close to the waterfall, on a flat stone plane, right into the churning remnants of the falls' impact. In the summer, tourists inundate Salto del Laja—be careful not to drown in either the gushing water or the vast sea of sightseers.

Accommodations, food stalls, and trinket vendors line the Panamerican as it crosses in front of the falls, completing the spectacle's kitschy atmosphere. On the south bank, closest to Los Angeles, sits the sprawling **Hotel y Hostería Salto del Laja ❸,** Km480 on the Panamerican (☎321 706 or 313 956; fax 313 996). Occupying the whole of Isla del Laja, this secluded spot offers rooms with stunning views of the mist-shrouded falls. Also available is a horseback-riding tour of the island, in which visitors encounter 50 species of trees and a pool with river water in which to bathe. (Breakfast included. Singles CH$32,000-40,000; doubles CH$25,000-48,000; triples CH$32,000-49,000; 4-person *cabañas* CH$40,000. AmEx/MC/V.) A cheaper alternative sits directly across on the north bank (Santiago side). **Parque Salto de Laja ❷** (☎09 354 1255) offers grassy sites with picnic tables, a fire pit, and hot-water baths at a prime location—right on the *salto*'s drop-off. (Picnic sites CH$800. Camping Dec.-Mar. CH$8000, Apr.-Nov. CH$6000. *Cabañas* CH$8000-20,000.) Every hotel on the strip has a restaurant, but the best values are at the *empanada* stalls (CH$300-500).

PARQUE NACIONAL LAGUNA DEL LAJA ☎43

▨**Parque Nacional Laguna del Laja** belongs on another planet. Volcanic activity, along with a cold, arid climate, has created a virtual moonscape with black soil and jagged boulders. With a sharp contrast of texture and color, the **Laguna del Laja** jumps out of the desolate lava fields like an ice-blue jewel. The lake, its volume significantly drained away by the damming of the Río Laja, is nestled among prickly Andean peaks at the base of the majestic **Volcán Antuco,** a 2985m slumbering giant wrapped in a mantle of snow. Aside from gentle ripples along its surface caused by wind, the Laguna is eerily motionless, the snowbanks on its edge imposing an other-worldly silence. The park, although not terribly diverse, provides well-maintained paths and a full day's worth of visual stimulation.

AT A GLANCE

AREA: 119 sq. km

CLIMATE: Cool and dry. Temperatures range from 13°C in Jan. to 0°C in Aug.

GATEWAYS: Los Angeles via Antuco/El Abanico.

HIGHLIGHTS: Laguna del Laja; lava fields; Salto de las Chilcas.

FEATURES: Laguna and Río Laja, Volcán Antuco (2985m), and the twin peaks of the Sierra Velluda (3200m and 3585m).

FEES: Entrance CH$700, children CH$300.

CAMPING: Campsites in Sector Lagunillas CH$5000. *Cabañas* CH$25,000.

E TRANSPORTATION. To get to Parque Nacional Laguna del Laja, the best bet is to get your hands on a car—preferably with sturdy tires and a good set of shocks, as the road becomes a rock-strewn dirt path east of Antuco (23km from the park entrance). Public transportation stops short of the park, with regular bus service from Los Angeles to El Abanico, 8km from the park entrance and another 6km to the lake (see **Transportation,** p. 313). The last bus leaves El Abanico at 5:30pm.

■▪ 🔊 ORIENTATION AND PRACTICAL INFORMATION. The only entrance to the park (not counting crossovers from Argentina) is 93km east of Los Angeles, at its northwestern corner. The park is bordered to the north by the *laguna*, to the east by the Andes, to the southwest by the fearsome **Sierra Velluda,** and held down in the center by **Volcán Antuco.** Most activity revolves around the park's northwest sector where information center is located, as well as the campgrounds in the Río Laja valley and the popular trail leading to the Saltos de las Chilcas and del Torbellino. The park's only road heads east from the entrance, past the ski center, skirts the lake's south shore, and then cuts southeast, passing a *carabinero* checkpoint, Los Barros, 29km down, before heading into Argentina via Paso Pichachén.

The park entrance, in **Sector Los Pangues,** collects the entry fee of CH$700 for adults and CH$300 for children. (☎321 086. Open June-Sept. 8:30am-9pm; Oct.-May 8:30am-6pm. Last entry 2pm.) **Sector Chicay,** 3km farther along, holds the park's administration and information center. The **Centro de Esquí Antuco** offers basic, sun-drenched slopes at either 1800m or 600m up. (Ski center office in Los Angeles ☎322 651. Open July to mid-Sept. Lift tickets M-F CH$7000, Sa-Su CH$10,000. Ski rental CH$10,000. Ski lessons CH$12,000 per hr. No snowboard rentals, although snowboards are permitted on the slopes.)

🔊 ACCOMMODATIONS. A kilometer northeast of the entrance lies **Sector Lagunillas,** where campsites and *cabañas* are located. There are 22 **campsites ❷** in a tree-shaded valley near the Río Laja, which offer electricity, grills, and bathrooms with showers. Hot water is only available during the summer; the rest of the year it's "tepid." (Camping CH$5000 per site.) Four double-level *cabañas*, each with five beds (1 *matrimonial*), kitchens with fridges and stoves, and bathrooms with hot-water showers are available. They are heated by wood-burning stoves or gas-burning space heaters. (Reservations recommended a week in advance Jan.-Mar., 1 day in advance in July. 6-person *cabañas* CH$25,000.) The campgrounds also have a **24hr. market,** which stocks food, drinks, toiletries, and other basic goods. For information or reservations, call **Conaf** (☎321 086).

🔊 HIKING. There are four trekking options of varying intensity. One circumvents the park, leading south from Sector Chacay up into a pass (2054m) between the volcano and the Sierra Velluda. The trail then heads east to **Sector Los Barros,** at the lake's southeast tip, then leads back to Chacay along the lakeshore; this last part, 23km, is a popular drive. The entire circuit takes 2-3 days, but the ascent to the pass, with its glacier and spectacular view, is 8-10hr. round-trip. A shorter, easier hike heads up the Río Laja valley, from the campgrounds to the majestic falls of Las Chilcas and Torbellino, the source of the Río Laja (5-6hr. round-trip).

Volcán Antuco (2985m) is a relatively easy ascent. Beginning at the ski area (1400m), safe routes head up the volcano's north face (5hr. to summit). An attempt, however, should only be done by experienced climbers. The **Sierra Velluda** (3585m) is exclusively for skilled mountaineers—several summit attempts have ended in fatalities. The treacherous twin peaks can only be ascended during the winter, when an ice bridge forms to allow passage to the summit.

ANGOL ☎ 45

Although Angol (pop. 50,000), lies isolated from the main flow of Panamerican travelers and commerce, it has somehow found an edge of hipness. Trendy cafes and raucous street vendors surround a surprisingly green central plaza, and the streets are much livelier than they should be for an out-of-the-way *pueblo*. The town, founded by Pedro de Valdivia in 1553, was razed six times by disgruntled Mapuche before the settlement took root. Today, Angol owes its survival to the forest industry's exploitation of the surrounding pine forests. Most tourists come here, if they come at all, to escape the kitsch of the Panamerican's tourist offerings and push on to the trails of Parque Nacional Nahuelbuta, 37km to the west.

▊ TRANSPORTATION

Buses: From Angol, buses depart to several regional destinations.

Terminal Thiele (☎ 711 854) is Angol's bright, new, main terminal inconveniently located outside of town. From the tourist office, head 1km away from the plaza down José Luis Osorno; to get to town, exit the terminal and turn left down Osorno. Bus lines service: **Concepción** (3¼hr., 16 per day 6:30am-7pm, CH$2500); **Los Angeles** (1¼hr., every 30min. 7am-8pm, CH$800); **Puerto Montt** (8hr., 8am and 10:55pm, CH$4800); **Santiago** (8hr.; 8:30am, 10, 11pm; CH$5000-8000); **Temuco** (2¼hr., 26 per day 6am-8pm, CH$1000).

Bío Bío Terminal (☎ 711 777), on the corner of Caupolicán and Sepúlveda, 1 block northeast of the plaza. Before leaving for the main terminal, buses pick up passengers at this more convenient in-town terminal. To: **Concepción** (3¼hr., 16 per day 6:30am-7pm, CH$2900); **Los Angeles** (1¼hr., every 30min. 7am-8pm, CH$800); **Temuco** (2¼hr., 26 per day 6am-8pm, CH$2300).

Terminal de Buses Rurales (☎ 712 021), where Lautaro runs into Ilabaca, near the tourist office. Buses depart daily for **Vegas Blancas** (1hr., 6:45am and 4pm, CH$1000).

Taxis/Colectivos: Taxis anywhere in the city cost CH$1500. *Colectivos* run throughout the city, many of them passing down Lautaro, by the central plaza, along O'Higgins, and then back again. Rides CH$200, 9pm-midnight CH$250, midnight-7am CH$300.

Car Rental: Turismo Christopher (see **Tours,** below) rents cars starting at CH$25,000 per day. Insurance included. 18+. Valid driver's license required. Jeeps CH$60,000. Manual transmission only. **Nahueltour** (see **Tours,** below) has minibuses for rent from CH$40,000 per day. Manual transmission only.

▊▊ ORIENTATION AND PRACTICAL INFORMATION

The Río Vergara splits Angol in two, with the residential zone and main bus terminal to the southeast and the center and commercial zone to the northeast. **Ilabaca** is the easternmost north-south border of the area, and **Lautaro,** running past the **Plaza de Armas,** is the commercial street. All points in the city are easily walkable.

Tourist Office: Oficina de Turismo, Lado Puente Vergara 1, Edificio Cena Chile (☎/fax 201 571; contactour@hotmail.com), at the end of the bridge farther from the Plaza de Armas. The helpful staff has a wealth of information, brochures, and maps of the city, region, and PN Nahuelbuta. Open M-F 8:30am-1pm and 2:30-5:20pm. **Conaf,** Prat 191 (☎/fax 711 870 or 712 328; hlucero@conaf.cl). Open M-F 9am-2pm.

Tours: Turismo Christopher, Ilabaca 421 (☎715 156; christop@entelchile.net), down the street from **Banco de Chile** (see below). Offers tours of local sites, including **Parque Nacional Conguillío,** the **Siete Lagos,** and various indigenous locales (starting at CH$35,000 per person). Open M-F 9:30am-2pm and 4-9pm. **Nahueltour,** Aguirre 307 (☎/fax 715 457; nahueltour@hotmail.com), off Lautaro. Makes international and domestic travel arrangements, and has offerings on regional tours for comparable prices. Open M-F 9am-1:30pm and 3:30-7:30pm, Su 10am-1pm.

Currency Exchange: Both **Nahueltour** and **Turismo Christopher** cash traveler's checks and change Argentine, Australian, Canadian, and US currencies, as well as euros.

Bank/ATM: Banks surround the Plaza de Armas, but down the street is **Banco de Chile,** Lautaro 02 (☎712 746), on the corner with Ilabaca. **24hr. ATM.** Open M-F 9am-2pm.

Market: Tucapel, on the east side of the bridge along Osorno. Open M-Sa 9am-9:30pm, Su 9:30am-8pm. AmEx/MC/V.

Police: ☎133. Also, Dieciocho 340 (☎711 124), between Tucapel and Coihue.

Pharmacy: Farmacia Ahuile, Lautaro 20 (☎711 828), between Sepúlveda and Ilabaca. Open M-Sa 9:30am-9pm. Up the street is **Salcobrand,** on the corner of Lautaro and Aguirre. Open M-Sa 9am-9pm. AmEx/MC/V.

Hospital: Ambulance ☎131. **Hospital Mauricio Heyerman,** Ilabaca 752 (☎711 001), between Covadonga and Jarpa.

Telephones and Internet Access: Netcafé and **Info.com,** 381 Ilabaca, side-by-side in the same building. CH$300 per hr. Open M-F 9am-11pm, Sa 10am-2pm and 4-11pm, Su 10am-9pm. The **public library,** on the corner of Lautaro and Vergara, has free Internet daily 10am-3pm and 5-10pm.

Post Office: Lautaro 202 (☎716 232), alongside the Plaza de Armas. Open M-F 9am-1pm and 3-6:30pm, Sa 9am-12:30pm.

ACCOMMODATIONS

While short on accommodations, what Angol does have provides comfort at a good value. Almost all options are in the town center, near the Plaza de Armas.

Hotel Angol, Lautaro 176 (☎714 170). Right in the bustling heart of Angol, here you will find a surprising calm. Rooms are plain but warm with carpeting, hearty bedspreads, heaters and private bath. Find your way to the sun-soaked top floor. Cable TV. Breakfast included. Singles CH$13,000; doubles CH$15,000. AmEx/MC/V. ❷

Hotel Millaray, Prat 420 (☎/fax 711 570; www.angolturismo.cl). Sterile, no-nonsense rooms are perfect for the passing traveler; Millaray's main clientele seem to be traveling salesmen. Still, rooms are clean, and beds are firm—and sometimes there is a TV hidden in the closet. Cable TV. Breakfast CH$1500. Singles CH$7500, with bath CH$12,000; doubles CH$12,000/CH$16,500. AmEx/MC/V. ❷

Residencial Olimpia, Caupolicán 625 (☎711 162), parallel to Lautaro, at the end farthest from the river. Angol's cheapest and most modest lodging. Spartan rooms have hardwood floors and spongy mattresses, lit by naked bulbs and tiny lamps. Private parking and kitchen access. Breakfast included. Dec.-Mar. singles CH$7000; doubles CH$12,000; triples CH$18,000. Apr.-Nov. CH$5000/CH$8000/CH$15,000. ❷

Hostal El Vergel (☎712 103), on the grounds of the agricultural institute of El Vergel, 5km south of downtown. At the entrance to the school grounds, go down the dirt road and turn left at the fork; the hostel is on your left after a sharp bend in the road. Among this hostel's rooms, the singles are cramped, but the larger doubles are quite pleasant, with views of the extensive grounds. TV, laundry, parking. Breakfast included. Reservations recommended in summer. Nov.-Mar. singles CH$8000; doubles CH$16,000, with bath CH$18,000; suites with bath CH$22,000. Apr.-Oct. CH$6000/CH$14,000/CH$16,000/CH$20,000. Dec.-Feb. MC/V; low season cash only. ❸

🍴 FOOD

La Rueda, Lautaro 176 (☎714 170), on the ground floor of Hotel Angol. While serving the typical cuisine, it manages to make its steak moist and delicious, not fried and charred. *Churrasco* dishes include the *Diplomático* (steak, egg, and cheese sandwich; CH$1600) and the classic dish of steak with all the trimmings (CH$2000). Open M-Sa 8am-1am, Su 8am-midnight. AmEx/MC/V. ❷

Sparlatto, Lautaro 418 (☎716 272). With soft jazz, layered tablecloths, and silver trinkets, this is Angol's leap into elegance. Sparlatto brings international flavor to a town with an impressive range of pizza options. Pizza is a bit uninspiring, but totally hearty—and with over half of their options meatless, this restaurant is vegetarian-centered. Individual portions from CH$2500, full pizzas from CH$3500. AmEx/MC/V. ❸

Lomito'n, Lautaro 145 (☎717 675), between Sepúlveda and Chorrillos. The photos of smiling customers on the walls may be a little tacky, but the food of this chain is reasonable, for lack of more gourmet options. All sandwiches are smeared with *palta*, a mashed avocado sauce that many Chileans are crazy about. Meals CH$1300-2000. Open M-Th 10am-8pm, F-Sa 10am-8:30pm, Su noon-8:30pm. AmEx/MC/V. ❶

👁 SIGHTS

Angol's most beautiful and fascinating locale, **El Vergel,** peacefully lies 5km from the city center. Established in 1919 by the Methodist Church, this agricultural institute is hidden underneath an array of towering flora, creating an arborist's dreamscape—more specifically, the dream of US-born agricultural specialist Dillman Bullock, who served as director of the school. A museum in his honor,

ALLEYS TO SPARE

In Chile, sports are so beloved that they've acquired an almost other-worldly quality. When speaking of *deportes*, you cannot help but think of the Chilean passion for *fútbol*, the traditional elegance of rodeo, the thrilling suspense of...bowling?

Though it doesn't seem to fit in with its historically-revered peers, bowling is seeing a strange burst of popularity throughout Chile. Though more than five years ago, the sport was practically unheard of, the years after 1999 saw a 20,000% increase in the rate of alley construction.

Many propose that bowling's popularity is largely based on its appeal to urban families. When families began to move away from the more rural areas, the family unit, an important part of Chilean culture, was subjected to a new stress—different, busy schedules. The once-intrinsic unity of the family became something that had to be strived for. Now, with the concept of structured "quality time," families have continued to seek opportunities for recreation.

Furthermore, it's much easier to fit a bowling alley onto a busy city street than a soccer field. All of these factors have caused the number of alleys in Chile to grow from one or two to over 200. Industry heads confidently predict double that number within a few years. And, with the possibility of spectatorship, before long, you might hear a TV announcer shriek with glee, "Strrrriiiiiiiiiiiiiiikkkkke!"

the ▣**Museo Dillman Bullock,** sits just beyond the hostel, and is easily one of the best museums in southern Chile. Its eclectic collection—ranging from a mastadon fossil to Confederate States of America currency—is capped off by a mummified Kofkeche woman and the giant urn she was buried in. *(To reach El Vergel, take colectivo #2 from downtown to the end of the line. Museum ☎ 711 142 or 712 395; fax 719 303; elvergel@ctcinternet.cl. Open M-F 9:30am-7pm, Sa-Su 10am-7pm. CH$450, children CH$200.)*

In Angol itself, there is little to see or do, though the town sports a surprisingly attractive **Plaza de Armas Benjamín Vicuña Mackenna.** The plaza, bursting with mammoth trees and amorous teenagers, encircles a pool with four small statues at its corners, symbolizing the four corners of the earth.

PARQUE NACIONAL NAHUELBUTA   ☎ 45

Although one of the country's smallest parks, weighing in at a mere 69 sq. km, Parque Nacional Nahuelbuta encompasses a high crest of the Coastal Range, with peaks around 1500m. The crown jewel is the **Piedra del Águila**—Eagle's Rock—from which, at 1379m, one can take in the whole breadth of Chile, from the ocean to the Andes, and even glimpse the snow-capped Volcán Villarrica in the far south. The high crest traps rain coming from the ocean, which has led to a one-of-a-kind stirring of rain forest and mountain ecosystem. The park provides shelter for both parakeets and other rainforest birds as well as the monolithic *araucaria* trees of the Andean slopes. The rare flora and fauna take advantage of Nahuelbuta's relative isolation, which also provides visitors refuge from the stampeding hordes of tourists at other, larger parks during the summer.

The two most popular viewpoints in Parque Nacional Nahuelbuta are the **Piedra del Águila** (Eagle's Stone) and **Cerro Anay,** farther to the south. A trail leads from the Centro de Información around and up the granite hill known as Piedra del Águila, passing by ancient *araucaria* and *coihue* trees before looping back to its point of origin (4.5km, 2hr.). Along the way, you should pass by some of the park's larger monkey puzzles, more than 50m in height and covered in rich green moss. **Cerro Anay** (1402m) is another hilltop with breathtaking views of the country, and is reached by two trails in succession—**Sendero Estero Los Gringos** (5km, 2½hr.) and then **Sendero Cerro Anay** (0.8km, 30min.), passing through pure forests of *araucaria* and *lenga* trees. If you're lucky on these trails, you might spot one of the park's several species of fox, including the *chilote*, a species from the island of Chiloé that inexplicably found its way here. There are also plenty of woodpeckers.

Nahuelbuta is located 35km west of Angol, up a dirt road. There is public transportation to the park only in January and February, when **Buses Angol** offers Sunday full-day tours from the Terminal Rural, at the corner of Ilabaca and Lautaro. (☎ 712 021. 1½hr.; 6:45am, returns 6pm; CH$1150, round-trip CH$2300.) The buses drop off at the **Conaf** station, where tours of the park begin. Visitors should bring food, as none is available in the park. Another option is to take a bus from Angol to the town of Vegas Blancas and walk the remaining 7km to the park entrance. Two companies run buses out of the Terminal Rural in Angol: **Buses Angol** (☎ 712 021; 1hr.; M, W, F 6:45am and 4pm, returns 9am and 6pm; CH$1000) and **Buses Nahuelbuta** (☎ 714 611; 1hr.; Tu, Th, Sa 6:45am and 4pm, returns 9am and 6pm; CH$1000).

The paved road from Angol to Parque Nacional Nahuelbuta ends at Vegas Blancas. From here, a dirt road enters the southern edge of the park and reaches the **Centro de Información** about 12km from Vegas Blancas. (Entrance CH$2000, children CH$500.) To reach the information center and the nearby campground, turn left at the fork after the entrance.

LA ARAUCANÍA AND LOS LAGOS

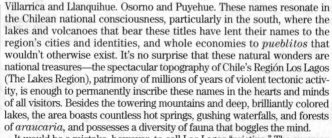

Villarrica and Llanquihue. Osorno and Puyehue. These names resonate in the Chilean national consciousness, particularly in the south, where the lakes and volcanoes that bear these titles have lent their names to the region's cities and identities, and whole economies to *pueblitos* that wouldn't otherwise exist. It's no surprise that these natural wonders are national treasures—the spectacular topography of Chile's Región Los Lagos (The Lakes Region), patrimony of millions of years of violent tectonic activity, is enough to permanently inscribe these names in the hearts and minds of all visitors. Besides the towering mountains and deep, brilliantly colored lakes, the area boasts countless hot springs, gushing waterfalls, and forests of *araucaria*, and possesses a diversity of fauna that boggles the mind.

It would be a mistake, however, to call Los Lagos "pristine." The summer months bring overwhelming tourist traffic, mainly from within Chile. Chileans flock to Los Lagos in January and February to lounge on sunny beaches, nap in lakeside *cabañas*, and linger at late-afternoon barbecues. Most international visitors, on the other hand, can find little time for relaxation between gaping at smoldering craters, hiking forested trails of immense arboreal diversity, rafting on turbulent, teal-green rivers, and counting stars on clear nights.

While the culture of the region still retains a large Mapuche influence, much of the region is also characterized by a distinctly German flair, left behind by German "pioneers" of the 19th century. Some Chileans even claim that the area is more German than it is Chilean—and indeed, the famous Chilean *huaso* (cowboy) seems to be fast disappearing from the region. Still, local festivals, seemingly celebrated endlessly from the end of January to the middle of February, continue to feature traditional rodeos, casual horse races, and the ever-popular *cueca*.

The area covered by La Araucanía and Los Lagos begins just south of **Los Angeles** and runs all the way to the industrial port of **Puerto Montt.** Dotted with tiny towns and mid-sized cities, the region plays host to some of the country's most celebrated **parques nacionales,** including the breathtaking **Vicente Pérez Rosales,** wrapped around **Lago Todos los Santos** in the shadow of **Volcán Osorno.** In addition, Los Lagos is home to **Parque Nacional Puyehue,** famed for its luxurious hot springs, and **Parque Nacional Villarrica,** where Chileans and foreigners alike crowd the fuming crater of the park's volcanic namesake. Summertime brings crowds to **Puerto Varas, Frutillar,** and the increasingly popular **Pucón,** but there are still several less-developed towns, including **Coñaripe, Ensenada,** and **Puerto Octay,** from which visitors can enjoy a quiet, undisturbed glimpse of natural wonders.

HIGHLIGHTS OF LA ARAUCANÍA AND LOS LAGOS

CLIMB up to the fiery crater of Volcán Villarrica in **Parque Nacional Villarrica** (p. 345).

ESCAPE from crowds in the awe-inspiring valley near **Cochamó** (p. 373).

RELAX in the soothing *aguas calientes* of **Parque Nacional Puyehue** (p. 361) and the **Termas de Coñaripe** (p. 349).

WONDER at the sheer majesty of Lago Todos los Santos in **Parque Nacional Vicente Pérez Rosales** (p. 375).

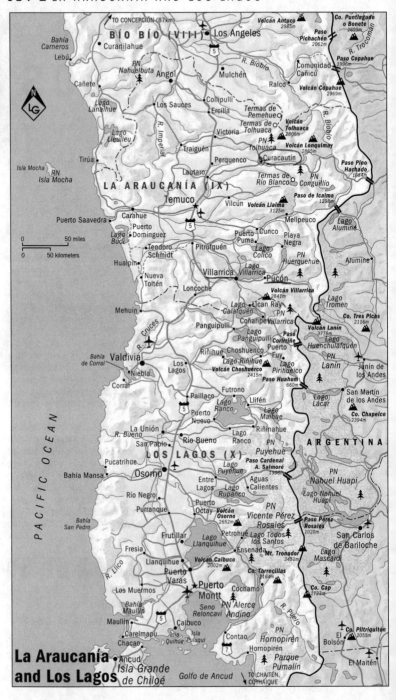

La Araucanía
and Los Lagos

TEMUCO   ☎ 45

Although it offers little to the tourist, Temuco is proudly growing into one of Chile's largest cities and—as the capital of the La Araucanía province—into one of the south's major economic and cultural centers. Situated along the Río Cautín, the Panamerican, and a major rail line, Temuco has been attracting both Chileans and foreigners since the 19th century. Today, however, Temuco struggles to match its appearance with its storied past; a few Mapuche relics hide in a small museum and squat, concrete buildings have long replaced any 19th-century frontier architecture. Being the site of several universities and corporations has only led to a city-wide graffiti decoration scheme and a choked *centro*. Even its convenient location does little to please visitors, and most—just like the Mapuche of old— make for the alluring hills to the east, using Temuco only as a point of transit.

⌐ TRANSPORTATION

Flights: Aeropuerto Maquehue (☎ 600 526 2000, ext. 8), 7km southwest of town, with domestic and international flights. **Transfer & Turismo de La Araucanía** (☎/fax 339 900; www.transtouraraucania.cl) will get you there in 15-20min. for CH$1000-3000. **LanChile,** Bulnes 687 (☎ 272 313), on the corner with Varas, facing the east side of the Plaza Aníbal Pinto. Open M-F 9am-1:30pm and 3-7pm, Sa 10am-1:30pm. Flights to: **Concepción** (40min., 8:35pm, CH$42,600); **Punta Arenas** (5hr., 6:15pm, CH$120,000) via **Puerto Montt** (45min., CH$15,600); **Santiago** (1¼hr., 5 per day 10:25am-8:35pm, CH$106,600).

Trains: Estación Temuco, Barros Arana 191 (☎ 233 416), at the eastern end of Lautaro. Ticket office open M-Sa 9am-7pm, Su 9am-2pm. To: **Chillán** (7½hr.; daily 8:30pm; economy CH$2300, tourist CH$2800, *salón cama* CH$3400); **Santiago** (13hr.; daily 8:30pm; economy CH$5400, tourist CH$6800, *salón cama* CH$8400); **Talca** (9½hr.; daily 8:30pm; economy CH$3400, tourist CH$4600, *salón cama* CH$5000).

Buses: Terminal Rodoviario de la Araucanía, Vicente Pérez Rosales 01609 (☎ 225 005 or 404 040), near the intersection with the Panamerican, 5km from the city center. Has private bus lines servicing all of Chile, with select service to destinations in Argentina. Among these options, a bus should be leaving to any given destination within the hour.

Bío-Bío (☎ 258 331) goes to: **Angol** (6 per day 8:40am-8:10pm, CH$2300); **Concepción** (6 per day 7:55am-7:40pm, CH$4200); **Los Angeles** (6 per day 7:55am-7:40pm, CH$2900).

Tur Bus (☎ 258 338) goes to: **Angol** (2hr., 2:35 and 7:20pm, CH$1400); **Osorno** (4hr., every hr. 1am-6pm, CH$3300); **Pucón** (2hr., 8 per day 6:35am-7:50pm, CH$2300); **Santiago** (9hr., every 30min. 7am-1pm and 8pm-12:15am, CH$5000); **Villarrica** (1½hr., 8 per day 6:35am-7:50pm, CH$1350).

Cruz del Sur (☎ 730 310) services points south. To: **Chillán** (4hr., 9 per day, CH$3700); **Osorno** (4hr., CH$3000); **Puerto Montt** (6hr., CH$4000); **Punta Arenas** (CH$41,000).

Express Buses to Pucón/Villarrica leave from the corner of Aldunate and Balmaceda. (6 per day 8am-6pm. **Pucón** CH$1300; **Villarrica** CH$1000.)

Terminal de Buses Rurales, Pinto 032 (☎ 210 494), on the corner of Balmaceda and Pinto, serves locations in the countryside around Temuco. To: **Curacautín** (2hr., 4 per day 7:15am-2pm, CH$1000); **Puerto Saavedra** (2hr., every hr. 7am-8pm, CH$1100).

Colectivos/Taxis: *Colectivos* are frequent and are found throughout the city. *Colectivos* #7, 9, and 11b run to the Terminal Rodoviario de la Araucanía. Stops are posted on front windshield. CH$250, students CH$100. Taxis are also easily found all over the city. Rides to: the **airport** (CH$3000-4000); **Terminal Rodoviario** (CH$2000-3000); **Pucón** (CH$35,000); **Villarrica** (CH$30,000).

Car Rental: Avis, Mackenna 448 (☎ 237 575 or 238 013 in Temuco, 02 331 0121 nationwide; fax 238 013; www.avischile.cl). Rates range from CH$33,990 per day and CH$211,000 per week for a Ford Fiesta to CH$74,800 per day and CH$455,900 per week for a 4x4 pickup. Also has a branch at Aeropuerto Maquehue (☎337 715). Both branches open M-F 8:30am-8pm, Sa-Su 9am-1pm and 3-8pm. **Turismo Christopher** (see **Tours**, below) also rents cars starting at CH$25,000 per day.

✦ 7 ORIENTATION AND PRACTICAL INFORMATION

With a grid of one-way streets, Temuco is cut in half lengthwise by the Panamerican (Hwy. 5), known as **Caupolicán** within the city center and **Rudecindo Ortega** north of the city center. The main bus terminal is northwest of **Ortega**, down **Rosales**. The *centro* is bordered to the north by **Balmaceda**, with the train station at its east end, and on the south by **O'Higgins**. To the east is **Barros Arana**, the railroad, and the **Río Cautín** a bit farther afield. In the center of town lies the **Plaza Aníbal Pinto** and the main commercial street, **Manuel Montt**, which runs to the west and turns into **Alemania** once it crosses Caupolicán. Besides the *centro*, the main centers of activity are the **Feria Libre Aníbal Pinto** northeast of the city center, and the large university and student neighborhood along Alemania, west of the city center.

Tourist Offices: Sernatur, Claro Solar 897 (www.temuko.cl), on the corner with Bulnes, has a wealth of useful information and brochures, as well as free maps of Temuco and La Araucanía province. Open M-Th 9am-5:30pm, F 9am-3:30pm. **Conaf,** Bilbao 931 (☎298 100; www.conaf.cl), has an office on the 2nd fl. of the Department of Agriculture office complex. The helpful, knowledgeable staff has maps of PN Conguillío for sale. Open M-F 8:30am-1:30pm and 2-5:30pm.

Tours: Turismo Christopher, Bulnes 667, Of. 202 (☎211 680; www.turismochristopher.cl), on the eastern edge of Plaza Aníbal Pinto. Offers tours of **PN Conguillío** (CH$35,000), **PN Huerquehue** (CH$35,000), **Pucón, Villarrica,** other scenic areas around **Lago Villarica** (CH$35,000), **Siete Lagos** (CH$45,000), and **Chol-Chol, Isla Huapi,** and **Lago Budi** (CH$35,000). Open M-F 9am-7:30pm, Sa 10am-5pm.

Banks: Are plentiful in Temuco, as are ATMs. **Banco de Chile,** Varas 818 (☎207 911), at the corner with Prat, cashes traveler's checks and exchanges currency. Open M-F 9am-2pm. **24hr. ATM.**

Currency Exchange: Turacamb, Claro Solar 733 (☎237 829), changes foreign currency and cashes traveler's checks. Open M-Sa 9am-2pm and 4-8pm. **Turismo Christopher** (see **Tours**, above) is one of the many money changers on Bulnes.

Laundromat: Marva, Montt 415 (☎952 201), 1 block east of Caupolicán. Wash and dry CH$3000. Open M-F 9am-8:30pm, Sa 9am-7pm.

Police: ☎133. *Carabineros* are at Claro Solar 1284 (☎211 604) and in the middle of the intersection of Balmaceda and Pinto (☎211 029), across from the Feria Libre.

Pharmacies: Farmacias Ahumada, Bulnes 413 (☎237 066 or 211 119), on the corner with Portales. Open daily 8am-11pm. **Salcobrand,** Montt 701-703 (☎237 321), on the corner with V. Mackenna. Open M-Sa 9am-10pm.

Hospital: Ambulance ☎131. **Hospital Regional de Temuco,** Montt 115 (☎296 100), between Blanco and Prieto Norte.

Fax Office and Telephones: Turacamb (see **Currency Exchange,** above) has telephone service through **Telefónica CTC.** International faxes CH$1200 per page, domestic CH$300. Open M-Sa 9am-2pm and 4-8pm. **CTC,** Montt 629 (☎239 472; fax 239 473), between Lagos and V. Mackenna. International faxes CH$1000 per page, domestic CH$250. Open M-Sa 8am-10pm.

Internet Access: Internet parlors proliferate along Montt, from Caupolicán to the *centro*. **888 Rodríguez** has fast service at CH$500 per hr. Open daily 9am-11pm. At the corner of Montt and Lynch is cheaper (CH$400), but has slower Internet. Open 24hr.

Post Office: Portales 801 (☎295 100), on the corner with Prat. Open M-F 9am-1pm and 3-7pm, Sa 9am-1pm.

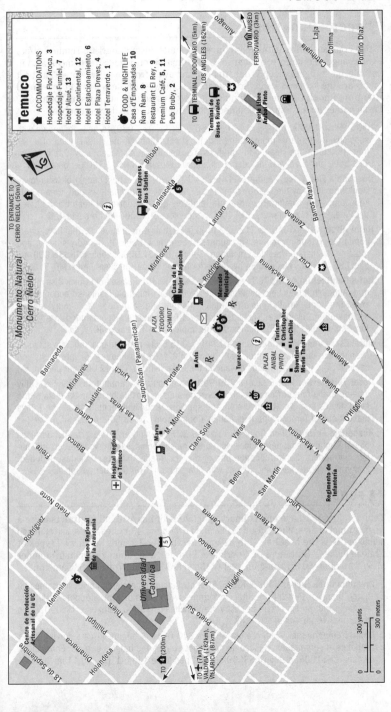

Temuco

▲ ACCOMMODATIONS
Hospedaje Flor Aroca, 3
Hospedaje Fumiel, 7
Hotel Aitué, 13
Hotel Continental, 12
Hotel Estacionamiento, 6
Hotel Plaza Dreves, 4
Hotel Terraverde, 1

● FOOD & NIGHTLIFE
Casa d'Empanadas, 10
Ñam Nam, 8
Restaurant El Rey, 9
Premium Café, 5, 11
Pub Bruby, 2

ACCOMMODATIONS

With a constant influx of business travelers, students, and tourists, Temuco offers a wide range of options for lodgings. Unfortunately, crowded streets mean a comfortable, quiet night's sleep is only to be found away from the city center. The best values are the *hospedajes* in the residential zone west of the *centro*. For personal attention, knock on one of the many private residences advertising "pensión." These homes have rooms to rent and line O'Higgins and 18 de Septiembre.

Hotel Plaza Dreves, O'Higgins 449 (☎260 008; fax 260 030). A new *hospedaje* with spacious, comfortable rooms along a quiet street. Although the hotel is a bit of a trek from downtown, the clean rooms and warm owner ensure a pleasant stay. Cable TV, private bath, and breakfast included. Call ahead to reserve. CH$14,500 per person. ❸

Hospedaje Flor Aroca, Lautaro 591 (☎234 205). One of the best budget picks in town. Don't be put off by the shabby exterior, as the inside is not nearly as bad. Clean, well-kept rooms are comfortably worn and relatively quiet. A universal heater and shared bath make for cozy quarters. CH$4000 per person, CH$5000 with breakfast. ❷

Hotel Aitué, Varas 1048 (☎212 512 or 329 191; www.hotelaitue.cl). This hotel offers comfortable, modern rooms with spotless bathrooms. Cable TV, laundry service, and radiators available. Breakfast included. Singles CH$31,000; doubles CH$36,000; triples CH$40,900. IVA discount available for foreigners paying cash. AmEx/MC/V. ❺

Hotel Continental, Varas 708 (☎238 973; fax 233 830), across from Quick Biss restaurant. Although it may be it past its prime, if you don't mind old-fashioned accommodations, the Continental's rooms are quite charming. Radiator heating, laundry service, and restaurant available. Breakfast included. Reservations recommended in advance Jan.-Feb. Singles US$26; doubles US$38; triples US$46. AmEx/MC/V. ❹

Hotel Estacionamiento, Balmaceda 1246 (☎215 503), near the bus and train stations. A bright exterior masks small, dark rooms, but each has heating, private bath, and cable TV. The parking lot lures drivers off the Panamerican. CH$12,000 per person. ❸

Hotel Terraverde, Prat 0220 (☎239 999; www.panamericanahoteles.cl). Peacefully located at the foot of Cerra Ñielol, Terraverde aims to provide business travelers with a good night's rest. An attentive staff and spacious, sparkling rooms with all the fixings make it one of Temuco's premier hotels. Rooms from CH$38,500. AmEx/MC/V. ❺

Hospedaje Furniel, Claro Solar 625 (☎313 327). Behind an impressive facade hides one of Temuco's cheapest places, with drab, musty rooms, sagging mattresses, and forlorn bathrooms. Central location one of the few quality aspects. Breakfast included. Parking CH$2000 per night. Rooms with shared bath CH$4000 per person. ❶

FOOD

Temuco does not have any culinary specialties of its own, but it attracts quite a few national chains, cheap food stalls, and *cafeterías*. For cheap eats, the **mercado municipal ❶** is the best bet, with its innumerable food stands serving all types of Chilean dishes. (Entrances on Rodríguez, Portales, and Aldunate. Open in summer M-Sa 8am-8pm, Su 8:30am-4pm; rest of the year M-Sa 8am-7pm, Su 8:30am-4pm.)

Premium Café, Bulnes 539 (☎402 626). A bustling cafe frequented by businessmen on lunch break or thirsting for after-work drinks. Also popular with shoppers looking to recharge with an ice cream or pastry. Sandwiches CH$3000. Entrees CH$6000. Open daily until 10pm. AmEx/MC/V. ❷

Casa d'Empanadas, V. Mackenna 687 (☎640 051). A brightly-lit cafe serving 1001 varieties of *empanadas*. If these do not entice you, try the burgers or pizza. *Empanadas* around CH$1000, pizzas CH$3000-5000. Open M-Sa 11am-11pm, Su 11am-3pm. ❶

Simone, on the corner of V. Mackenna and Balmaceda. The dark, well-worn interior should not deter you from sampling the cheap and greasy, yet delightfully filling pub fare. Sandwiches CH$1000. Meal platters CH$3000. Bar open after dark. ❷

Restaurant El Rey, Portales 874. This local watering hole offers the Temuco Special: fried meat with french fries. Blessedly quick and cheap, as the wood-paneled interior and blasting disco conspire to fuel a torrid 70s flashback. Most dishes under CH$5000. Open daily until 11pm. ❸

Ñam Ñam, Portales 802 (☎316 282), on the corner with Prat. Sit in the old-fashioned, leather-lined booths of this bustling sandwich shop and you'll find yourself wreathed in cigarette smoke within minutes. Still, it's a good place to go for *churrasco* (CH$1250-2350), hamburgers (CH$750-1550), and other sandwiches (CH$630-2850). Lunch specials CH$1290-1590. Open daily 9am-midnight. AmEx/MC/V. ❶

🎵 🎬 ENTERTAINMENT AND NIGHTLIFE

The nightlife scene in Temuco revolves around early-morning pitchers of beer in dark, smoky bars. Most *cafeterías* also double as watering holes. After dark, though, stay in the *centro* or west of Caupolicán, as other parts of the city have a bad reputation. For a rockin' university hangout, check out **Pub Bruby,** on the corner of Alemania and Thiers. This is the place to go if you want to practice Spanish, engage in a lively debate with Chilean youths, or simply sit back and enjoy the university spectacle. (1L beer CH$1400. Open daily until 4am.) For those looking for a less uproarious time, check out the **Showtime Movietheater,** on Varas, near the south side of Plaza Aníbal Pinto. Showtime has a decent variety of new releases in English with Spanish subtitles. (Last showing around 10pm. CH$1700 per person.)

📷 SIGHTS

As Temuco is waking up to the possibility of being a tourist draw, it is slowly adding tourist attractions—though they tend to be rather limp and somewhat far from the *centro*. The heart of the city is **Plaza Aníbal Pinto,** bounded by Bulnes, Prat, Claro Solar, and Varas. In the center of the plaza, ringed by palm trees, is the **Monumento a la Araucanía,** which pays homage to the many threads of culture that have been woven into modern Temuco, from Mapuche warriors to Chilean soldiers.

MONUMENTO NATURAL CERRO ÑIELOL. This heavily forested hill, rising to 200m above sea level, provides splendid views of the city and surrounding countryside. Rambling trails criss-cross the hill, all leading to the crest, which holds a monument to the Mapuche peace treaty signing ("Patagua"), a restaurant and bird sanctuary, and the Observatorio Volcanológico de los Andes del Sur (☎270 700; not open to the public). Cerro Ñielol also houses a native forest of *lingüe,* laurel, *raulí, coihue,* and oak trees. Among them, you might be able to spot the *copihue,* Chile's national flower. Considering the park's proximity to downtown, there is an amazing assortment of wildlife hiding in the woods—buff-necked ibises, foxes, and even the *monito del monte,* the smallest marsupial in the world. *(Park entrance located at the north end of Prat, several blocks north of the city center. Park open daily 8:30am-10pm. Environmental Information Center open daily 8:30am-6pm. CH$700, children CH$200.)*

MUSEO REGIONAL DE LA ARAUCANÍA. Surrounded by towering trees, this museum is worth a visit, even if just for its peaceful setting. On the first floor you will find a sizable collection of Mapuche pottery, wooden masks, and weavings—although they are all outdone by the remarkable reconstruction of a Mapuche home. The second floor is devoted to the long, bloody history of conquest. Unlike many other museums in Chile, this museum has stylish, professional-looking interpretive signs in Spanish with *mapudungun* (the Mapuche tongue) translation for the exhibits on the first floor. *(Alemania 084. Head down Montt—which turns into Alemania—away from the city center. The museum is just past the Universidad Católica.* ☎730 062. *Open M-F 9am-5pm, Sa 11am-5pm, Su 11am-2pm. CH$600, children CH$300. Free Su.)*

MUSEO NACIONAL FERROVIARIO PABLO NERUDA. Set in an appropriately gritty restored railroad yard, the locophile will marvel at the beautifully redone locomotives, while everyone else can still appreciate the power of the imposing relics. Amidst ghostly whistles, steam, and steel sits the town's only homage to Pablo Neruda, housed in the Coal Bunker Building. This museum succeeds at putting Temuco's smoky industrial image to good use and that, in itself, is more than enough reason to make your way here. *(Barros Arana 565, 3km northeast of the* centro. *www.temucochile.com. Open Tu-Su 9am-6pm. CH$1000, children CH$300.)*

▢ SHOPPING

Temuco is a great place to find Chilean pottery, wood carvings, and wool items. The **mercado municipal** (p. 328) is a good place to start: an entire block full of handicraft shops and food stands, it is one of the largest and liveliest municipal markets in all of Chile. If you're looking for fine indigenous craftsmanship, head to the **Casa de la Mujer Mapuche**, Prat 283, on the eastern edge of Plaza Teodoro Schmidt, a collective run by Mapuche women from throughout the region who work in clay, wool, and cloth. (☎233 886. Open M-F 9:30am-1pm and 3-6pm; in summer also open Sa 10am-6pm.) The **Centro de Producción Artesanal de La Universidad Católica,** Alemania 0442, on the corner of 18 de Septiembre and Alemania, is another excellent place to look for Mapuche craftsmanship, especially for silver and ceramic works. (☎212 081 or 205 306. Open M and W 9am-1pm and 3-6pm, Tu and Th-F 9am-1pm and 3-7pm; longer hours in summer.) For a wilder shopping experience, head out to the **Feria Libre Aníbal Pinto,** along Pinto near the train station. Among the swirling crowds you'll find row upon row of stands selling produce, meats, dairy products, and crafts. (☎210 968. Open M-Sa 8am-6pm, Su 8am-4pm.)

PARQUE NACIONAL TOLHUACA ☎45

Tolhuaca means "Front of the Cow" in Mapuche. The name might seem rather bizarre until you make the 50km drive from the Panamerican to the park's secluded entrance. The sometimes rock-strewn, sometimes muddy, and always treacherous path will lead you past several curious bovine observers, just about your only company for the one and a half hours of automobile rattle-and-hum. More than 60 sq. km of forest sprawl over hills and along the banks of the **Río Malleco,** featuring a terrific diversity of fauna, from Andean condors to the *pudú,* the smallest deer in the world. *Araucaria* line the hills while *coihue* and oak trees thrive at lower elevations. The center of the park lies around its serene **Laguna Mal-**

AT A GLANCE	
AREA: 65 sq. km	**HIGHLIGHTS:** Hiking into the Malleco National Reserve; Andean condors; *pudús; coihue; araucaria;* Salto Malleco, Laguna Malleco, and Laguna Verde. Lookouts of Volcán Tolhuaca.
CLIMATE: Jan.-Feb. Cool and dry; Mar.-Dec. cool and wet. 250cm of rain per year. Average annual temp: 14°C.	
	FEES: CH$1700, children CH$600.
GATEWAYS: Curacautín from Temuco or Victoria and Inspector Fernández from Los Angeles and Victoria.	**CAMPING:** Sites at Laguna Malleco, and in the Malleco reserve, CH$7200.

leco, whose western edge unravels into a 49m high waterfall, ■Salto Malleco. Seven well-marked trails, ranging from 1.5km to 8.6km in length, wind their way around the park from the base camp at the lagoon; some trace a course within view of **Volcán Tolhuaca** (2806m), or along the flight path of the Andean condors.

▐ TRANSPORTATION. There is no public transportation to Parque Nacional Tolhuaca, and even with private 4WD the route is tricky, as the dirt roads are poorly maintained and damaged by logging trucks and washouts. One way to drive there is to follow the Panamerican to the exit marked "Inspector Fernández" and "Parque Nacional Tolhuaca," 98km south of Los Angeles (make sure to exit at the blue sign that says "Salida"—not the service road before it). Once you exit the highway, the bumpy dirt-and-sharp-rock road begins, and will take you over wooden bridges and muddy hills for 50km. It's especially dangerous at night, when there's absolutely no lighting. An alternate route follows the paved road from Victoria east to the town of Curacautín. Drive 39km north on that dirt road to the Termas de Tolhuaca, and continue 9km west to the park entrance. Remember to drive slowly and watch out for the cows. For those without private transportation, the best bet is to head to Curacautín and take a taxi up the 30km dirt road.

▐▐ ORIENTATION AND PRACTICAL INFORMATION. Parque Nacional Tolhuaca, 50km east of the Panamerican, spreads east to west, with the Reserva Nacional Malleco to the north and logging lands and the town of Curacautín to the south. The road from Victoria/Inspector Fernández brings you to the center-south of the park, marked by Laguna Malleco. This, the main entrance, has the administration center with plenty of maps, and also has access to the trailheads of the park's five main trails. The park can also be entered from the southeast via Curacautín, with access to three trailheads and Laguna Verde. More information can be obtained at **Conaf's** Temuco branch (p. 326), or the smaller branch in Curacautín, O'Higgins 565, 2nd fl. (☎882 702 or 881 184), one block south and one and a half blocks west of the bus drop-off. (Open M-F 8:30am-2pm.)

▐ ACCOMMODATIONS. At the park's main entrance are **campgrounds ❸** nearby both **Laguna Malleco** and Salto Malleco. Privacy reigns at the heavily wooded grounds (CH$7200 per site, with showers and toilets). A second campsite is hidden in **Reserva Nacional Malleco,** north 12km over a 1300m ridge. To the east of the main entrance, 9km down the dirt road, is a privately run **campground** at the **Termas de Tolhuaca,** as well as *cabañas* and a luxury hotel. (☎881 211. Open Dec.-Mar.) *Hospedajes* line Curacautín's Av. M. Rodríguez, where the bus drops off.

▐ HIKING. Several trails of all difficulty levels radiate out from the park's main entrance. The premier trail, **Sendero Mesacura,** marked by orange posts, climbs into a pass thick with *araucaria* trees, and over the next 15km reaches a height of 1250m (5-7hr. round-trip). By the end of the trail, you are northwest of the entrance in Reserva Nacional Malleco. Splitting north from the Mesacura trail is the **Sendero Lagunillas,** marked by purple posts, the park's steepest and most scenic trail, with lookout points at 1600m and a terminus at a series of small *lagunillas.* (8.6km one-way, 6-8hr. round-trip.) Farther along the Mescura trail is the **Sendero Tolhuaca Niblinto,** which heads north over a pass (1150m) and ends at the administration building for Reserva Nacional Malleco. More than half of the 12km, lilac-posted trail is in the remote national reserve (7-8hr. round-trip).

The easiest and most popular trails in the park hug its southern perimeter. The **Sendero Salto Malleco** heads west of the entrance and curves around Laguna Malleco's north shore closing in on the din of ■Salto Malleco, a 49m powerhouse of a waterfall (1.7km, 1½hr. round-trip). East of the entrance is the yellow-posted **Sen-**

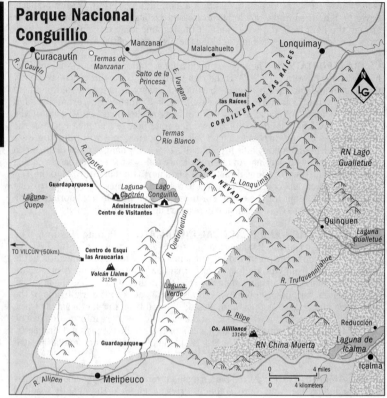

Parque Nacional Conguillío

dero **Laguna Verde,** a 4km flat road through varying vegetation and the most sightings of the Andean condor. This well-used path—the park's most popular—becomes a swift stream during and after the slightest rainfall (3-4hr. round-trip). At the end of this trail is the short, uphill **La Culebra Laguna Verde,** which, after 2km, deposits you on the shore of an electric green lake amidst a forest of *araucaria* (1½-2hr. round-trip). At the park's easternmost tip, past the thermal baths, is the **Sendero Chilpa,** a steep climb from 1250m to 1450m over 1.5km that connects the thermal bath road to its northbound arm, heading deeper into wild logging lands.

PARQUE NACIONAL CONGUILLÍO   ☎ 45

The most prominent features of ◫**Parque Nacional Conguillío** are a smoking volcano and its neighbor to the north, a serene, crystal-blue lake. Its 603 sq. km of unspoiled wilderness embody vivid contrasts: on its northern shores lie dense thickets of *araucaria* and the small **Sierra Nevada** mountain group; while toward **Volcán Llaima** (3125m) in the south sprawls a wasteland of hardened lava, evidence of the still-active volcano's periodic outbursts (its last major eruption was 1957). The fantastical diversity of landscape, flora, and fauna translates into an impressive range of hiking options, making the park a must-see of Chile's south.

The bulk of the area of Parque Nacional Conguillío spreads east and north to include Lago Verde and Lago Conguillío, and also the Sierra Nevada mountain group in its northeast corner. The western entrance to the park ends at a ski resort and *cabañas*

AT A GLANCE

AREA: 609 sq. km

CLIMATE: Temperate. Nov.-Mar. average 15°C; June-July average 6°C; annual rainfall 200cm.

GATEWAYS: Temuco via Curacautín, Melipueco, or Vilcún.

HIGHLIGHTS: Hiking the Sierra Nevada; climbing Volcán Llaima; *araucaria*.

FEATURES: The mountain peaks of the Sierra Nevada, Volcán Llaima, Lagos Conguillío and Verde.

FEES: CH$2800, children CH$800.

CAMPING: Plentiful sites at Lago Conguillío and Laguna Captrén (CH$15,000).

on the volcano's western face. More frequently used are the northern and southern entrances. The park's only road connects these two and provides access to the administration buildings and the main campgrounds on the south shore of Lago Conguillío.

With luck, the park is accessible year-round from the west and south; rains and snows ruin the northern portion of the road. The park itself is open November through April 8:30am-6pm. (CH$2800, children CH$800.) A small ski center is located on the western edge of the park, accessible through Vilcún. **Centro de Esquí Las Araucarias** is open June to September, snow permitting. More information about the park can be obtained at Conaf's Temuco office (p. 326) or at the Curacautín branch (see **Orientation and Practical Information**, p. 331).

The park has a popular 90-site **campground and cabaña complex ❷**, complete with restaurant and lava-sand beach, at the southern edge of Lago Conguillío. A smaller and more densely-forested 11-site campground also claims the south shore of swampy Laguna Captrén. Campsites have hot showers, toilets, and sinks; *cabañas* have kitchens, private baths, and hot water. (Camping CH$15,000. Call Conaf's Temuco office for reservations. *Cabañas* CH$35,000 for groups of 8 or fewer and CH$50,000 for groups of 9-12. Open Nov.-Apr.) *Hospedajes* line Av. M. Rodríguez in Curacautín, the same street as the bus drop-off.

The park is difficult to access by public transportation. Bus lines reach each of the three closest towns: Curacautín, 42km north of the park; Vilcún, 50km west of the park; and Melipueco, 22km south of the park. Each is accessible from Temuco and Los Angeles. To close the distance from these towns, it's best to rely on private transportation to negotiate the dirt roads. In the summer, a bus leaves from Curacautín at 6am; a taxi costs CH$10,000. The northern road to the park is usually closed by rains and snow from April to November.

LAGO VILLARRICA

VILLARRICA ☎ 45

Villarrica has long sat in the shadow of its more picturesque sister, Pucón—and even locals admit that their neighbor across the lake is a little more aesthetically pleasing. Nevertheless, Villarrica is worth the trouble for those looking for more than pricey thrills: not only is it easier on the wallet than Pucón, but it is also quieter, with smaller mobs of carousing tourists in the summertime and a magnificent view of Lago Villarrica. Villarrica, home to a significant Mapuche population, is also an excellent place to learn about indigenous culture, and also to pick up some authentic handicrafts. Beware the months outside of December through February, though—it is decidedly wet, and when it rains in Villarrica, it rains for weeks.

LOS LAGOS

Villarrica

🏠 ACCOMMODATIONS
Cabañas El Morro, **10**
Cabañas Nancy Astora, **11**
Hostería Hue-Quiney, **4**
Hotel El Ciervo, **1**
Hotel Valentíno, **2**
La Torre Suiza, **12**

🍴 FOOD
50 Locales, **8**
Alternativo, **7**
Café-Chito, **6**
El Rey del Marisco, **3**
Tabor, **13**
Tejuelas, **9**
The Travellers, **5**

◧ TRANSPORTATION

Buses: The 2 major bus lines are **Tur Bus** and **JAC,** which have terminals facing each other across Anfión Muñoz, 1 block south of Pedro Valdivia. **Tur Bus,** Anfión Muñoz 657 (☎413 625), and **JAC,** Bilbao 610 (☎411 447), offer expensive services to points beyond Temuco. It is cheaper to catch an express bus to **Temuco** (CH$1000) or **Pucón** (CH$400) from the corner of Muñoz or León Gallo, 1 block south of the bus terminals. Buses leave every hr. 7am-7pm.

Taxis/Colectivos: Although walking the length of Villarrica is quite easy, taxis are abundant and cost CH$800 for anywhere in town (CH$1000 after midnight). *Colectivos* (CH$200, students CH$80) run a circuit through the city center.

Car Rental: Castillo Rent-A-Car, Anfión Muñoz 415 (☎411 618; fax 411 076; hugo77@ctcreuna.cl) has trucks for CH$30,000 per day and cars for CH$28,000 per day. **Valentino,** Henríquez 394 (☎415 862), is located on the 2nd fl. of the hotel. Trucks CH$28,000 per day, cars CH$26,000 per day.

Bike Rental: La Torre Suiza (p. 336) rents bikes for CH$5000 per day.

◪ PRACTICAL INFORMATION

Tourist Office: The *municipalidad* has its **Oficina de Turismo** at Valdivia 1070 (☎206 619 or 206 618; fax 206 641; www.villarrica.co.cl), next to the museum and public library. They offer maps and event schedules for Villarrica and the Lago Villarrica area. Open M-F in summer 8:30am-9pm, in winter 9am-6pm.

Tours: Villarrica is flush with tour agencies ready to provide you with your next outdoor adventure. **Familia Ríos,** San Martín 256 (☎412 408), at the very western edge of San Martín, offers fishing tours in rowboats on **Lago Villarrica** (CH$5000 per hr.) and at selected spots along the length of the Río Toltén. The fishing season begins the second week of Nov. and lasts until the first week of May. Tour rates are for 2 people accompanied by a guide. Open daily 8am-9pm. **Politur Villarrica,** Anfión Muñoz 647 (☎092 652 752; www.politur.com), and **Trancura,** Henríquez 455 (☎447 498 575; turism.tran-cura@entelchile.net), both offer packaged tours for similar prices. An ascent of the smoldering **Volcán Villarrica,** including guide and all necessary clothing and equipment, runs

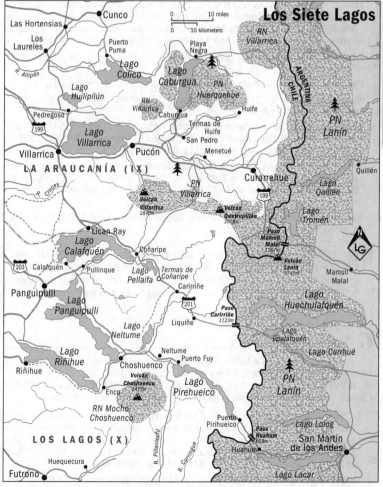

Los Siete Lagos

about CH$25,000. **Whitewater rafting** for varying skill levels CH$5000-20,000. Other options include **hot springs** (CH$5000), **horseback riding** (CH$12,000), and **Parque Nacional Huerquehue** (CH$15,000).

Currency Exchange: Currency exchanges line Henríquez between Vicente Reyes and Valdivia. The booth at Henríquez 544 changes Argentine pesos, euros, and US dollars. Open M-F 10am-2:30pm and 3-7pm, Sa 10am-3:30pm.

Banks: Found along Henríquez and Valdivia. **Banco de Chile,** Valdivia 799 (☎411 668). Open M-F 9am-2pm. **24hr. ATM.**

Work Opportunity: Politur Villarrica (see Tours, above) looks for guides and office workers during the busy summer months. All hires, however, are done through the Pucón branch. For more information, see **Alternatives to Tourism,** p. 91.

Library: Biblioteca Pública Dictino Niño de la Horra, Valdivia 1050 (☎412 445). Free Internet access. Open daily 9am-1pm and 3:30-7pm.

Market: There are traditional craft stores scattered all throughout the downtown area. One of the better ones is **Feria Artesanal Huimpay,** Julio Zegers 570 (☎410 003), on the corner with Valdivia. Sells all sorts of objects fashioned by local artisans—from wooden toys to woolen scarves and leather purses. Open daily Jan.-Feb. 9am-midnight; Mar.-Dec. 10am-6pm.

Police: ☎133. *Carabineros* headquarters, M. A. Malta 230 (☎411 433), on the eastern end of the Plaza de Armas.

Pharmacy: Farmacias Ahumada, Henríquez 561. Open daily 9am-11pm. AmEx/MC/V.

Hospital: Ambulance ☎131. **Hospital Villarrica,** San Martín 460 (☎411 169), on the northern end of the Plaza de Armas.

Fax Office and Telephones: Centro de Llamadas, Henríquez 590 (☎410 965 or 410 961), just north of Valdivia. Offers telephone service through **CTC.** International faxes CH$1500 per page, domestic CH$300. Open daily Dec.-Mar. 8:30am-midnight; Apr.-Nov. 8:30am-10pm.

Internet Access: If you are starved for cash and quite patient, enjoy the free access at the **Public Library** (see above). Otherwise, **PuntoNet,** 755 Letelier, charges CH$400 per hr. Open M-F 9:30am-10:30pm, Sa 11:30am-10:30pm, Su 2-10:30pm. **Politur Villarrica,** Anfión Muñoz 647, also charges CH$400 per hr. (see **Tours,** above).

Post Office: Anfión Muñoz 315 (☎412 860). Open M-F 9am-2pm and 3:30-7pm, Sa 10am-1pm. AmEx/MC/V.

TRAVEL WARNING. Crime in Villarrica has risen sharply in the past few years. Only recently have tourists been targeted, involving incidents of rape and murder. Almost all crimes happen after dark, on Villarrica's dark side streets. If you venture out in the dark, travel only in large groups and be sure of your way.

ACCOMMODATIONS

Almost every block of the town, especially near the lake, has cheerfully painted signs advertising *cabañas* and *hospedajes,* and the prices tend to be well below what you'll find just across Lago Villarrica. The road to Pucón, especially along Letelier outside of town, is speckled with well-worn lakeside campsites.

La Torre Suiza, Bilbao 969 (☎411 213; www.torresuiza.com). This creaky wooden "tower" is the epicenter for the Villarrica backpacker scene. With a trove of information and bright, cozy accommodations, this is your place—unless you are looking to escape *turistas.* Sept.-May dorms CH$5000 per person; doubles CH$12,000, with private bath CH$15,000. June-Aug. CH$4000/CH$10,000/CH$12,000. ❷

Hotel Valentino, Henríquez 394, 2nd fl. (☎415 862; www.hotelvalentino.enynter.net). This hotel's cozy apartment-style accommodations rise above its neighbors', with great views of the lake and a comfortable common space. Privae bath. Breakfast included. Rooms CH$11,800-28,500. AmEx/MC/V. ❹

Hostería Hue-Quiney, Letelier 1030 (☎411 462). This lake-front wooden lodge offers one of the best views in Villarrica. The front of the house has a spacious restaurant, while clean, sunny, romantic rooms have scenic views. Cable TV, private bath. Rooms Nov.-Mar. from CH$15,000; Apr.-Sept. from CH$10,000. AmEx/MC/V. ❸

Hotel El Ciervo, General Körner 241 (☎411 215; www.hotelelciervo.cl). The mahogany furniture and aroma of potpourri in this converted German mansion give the rooms a homey feel. Gleaming white bathrooms and views of Volcán Villarrica add to the experience. Central heating,. English spoken. Internet CH$500. Breakfast included. Dec.-Feb. singles CH$33,000; doubles CH$44,000; suites CH$62,700. Mar.-Nov. CH$25,000/CH$33,000/CH$46,000/CH$12,000. AmEx/MC/V. ❺

Cabañas El Morro, Bilbao 950 (☎412 601; tycelmorro@hotmail.com). 2 large, well-kept *cabañas* house up to 6 people each and can be rented out indefinitely; including full kitchens and baths. In the main residence are 2 private rooms and a shared bath—all kept immaculately clean. Breakfast included. Private rooms CH\$5000. *Cabaña* prices negotiable depending on stay. AmEx/MC/V. ❷

Cabañas Nancy Astora, Federico Trapp 157 (☎419 558). Señora Astora has a spacious, 2-story *cabaña* for up to 5 people with 2 rooms, full kitchen, and bath. She and her daughters make sure you feel right at home. Located near the lakeshore and *centro* in a quiet, residential neighborhood. Jan.-Feb. CH\$15,000; Mar.-Dec. CH\$12,000. ❸

 FOOD

Seafood is an obvious specialty for a lakeside town like Villarrica, but locals also pride themselves on their savory *cazuelas*—rich beef stews laden with sweet potatoes and a creamy mush of rice. The quickest and cheapest local treats can be found at the **50 Locales** ❶—a cooperative of local food vendors on the corner of Valdivia and Aviador Acevedo. (Open M-Sa 10am-7pm.) **Supermarkets** and local produce vendors line Alderete between Valdivia and Bilbao.

The Travellers, Letelier 753 (☎413 617). Probably the most cosmopolitan restaurant south of Santiago, The Travellers provides a delightful mix of cultures, with everything from *gyros* to *pad thai*. One of the few veggie places in the province. Entrees CH\$3250-6000. Open daily Dec.-Mar. 9am-3am; Apr.-Nov. 10:30am-1am. AmEx/MC/V. ❸

El Rey del Marisco, Letelier 1030 (☎412 093), on the shorefront near Julio Zegers. This cozy restaurant, set against the striking blue backdrop of Lago Villarrica, has fabulous seafood. Even a simple dish like *crema de espárragos* (CH\$1200) is heavenly. Try the *parrillada marisco* (CH\$5200), a medley of shellfish, calamari, and salmon. Fish dishes CH\$3100-5300. Open M-Sa 11am-4pm and 7-11pm, Su 11am-4pm. AmEx/MC/V. ❸

Alternativo, Vicente Reyes 737. Warmed by an open fire, this restaurant-bar specializes in authentic Mexican food. Alternativo—true to its name—draws a raucous, artsy crowd during the 10-11pm nightly happy hour. Try the hearty quesadillas (CH\$1800). Entrees around CH\$3000. ❷

Café-Chito, Vicente Reyes 665 (☎416 265). With flannel, exposed logs, and mounted animal heads, Café-Chito is the local effort to hold on to the frontier atmosphere that once reigned in these here parts. Dishes like steak, 2 fried eggs, french fries, and a basket of fried bread (CH\$2100) ain't for the faint of heart. Open daily until late. ❷

Tabor, Saturnino Epulef 1187 (☎411 901), between Acevedo and Rodríguez, 3 blocks south of Valdivia. Seashell chandeliers hang from the ceiling and fat wooden fish decorate the walls at this fine seafood restaurant. The adventurous should try the *erizos al mático* (CH\$4900), sea urchins doused in lemon juice, diced onions and cilantro Fish entrees CH\$3800-5200. Open daily 11:30am-midnight. AmEx/MC/V. ❸

Tejuelas, Alderete 632 (☎410 619), near the corner with Valdivia. Tejuelas serves sandwiches (CH\$1600-2200) and pizzas (CH\$2900-4500). Also try the bizarre mix of orange Fanta and beer, the *Fanschop* (CH\$800). Open Nov.-Mar. daily 9am-midnight; Apr.-Oct. M-Sa 9am-midnight, Su 7pm-midnight. ❷

 SIGHTS

Villarrica's most breathtaking scenic attractions are, of course, Lago Villarrica and Volcán Villarrica. The latter, though some 30km away, is visible in all its fuming glory throughout the town. To enjoy the lake, head out to **Playa Pucara,** at the intersection of General Urrutia and Julio Zegers. Once a volcanic black-sand beach, it's now more a muddy grass field than a beach. Nevertheless, it's still a great place to admire the huge expanse of softly undulating water. Head farther north along the lake's edge and you'll eventually reach the **Embarcadero Municipal**, a wide, concrete dock where locals tie up their boats. Here, you can appreciate the mist-shrouded mountains in the distance and the incredible array of blues that paint the horizon.

Villarrica also has an active indigenous community and, during the summer, the town draws Mapuche from all over the area, who congregate at the **Muestra Cultural Mapuche** at the corner of Valdivia and Julio Zegers. There, Mapuche artisans sell handmade crafts and clothing and also have demonstrations of their centuries-old traditions of weaving, jewelry, and craft making. (Open from first M of Jan.-Feb. 25 daily 9am-11pm. Free.)

Just down the road, on the top floor of the public library, you'll find the small but enthusiastically run **Museo Histórico y Arqueológico Municipal de Villa-Rica**, Valdivia 1050. On display is a wide assortment of Mapuche paraphernalia, including grinding stones made from volcanic rock, ceremonial wood and leather drums, pouches made of animal scrotums and bladders, and a fascinating selection of silver stirrups. (☎413 445. Open Jan.-Mar. 15 M-Sa 9:30am-1pm and 6-10pm, Su 6-10pm; low season M-F 9:30am-1pm and 3:30-7pm. CH$100.)

PUCÓN ☎45

The charming town of Pucón looks like it was made to be on a postcard—quaint wooden cabins line leafy streets at the ashen lip of a vast, still lake in the shade of mist-ringed mountains. Towering over everything is the picturesque Volcán Villarrica, the most active volcano in South America, a smoldering core of pent-up geological angst, just minutes away from downtown. As Central Chile's most visited town, and appropriately, Pucón has learned how to cater to its visitors' every whim. Innumerable tour agencies hawk trips up the volcano, down river rapids, and to thermal baths. Once you try some of Pucón's international cuisine, enjoy a few glittering sunsets on its lakeside beach, and lose several weeks wages at Hotel del Lago's gleaming casino, you'll want to leap into one or many of the nearby natural attractions—enough to keep even the most hardened adventurer busy.

⌐ TRANSPORTATION

Flights: Aeropuerto Necluman (☎878 8914), 6km east of Pucón. Necluman operates only during summer and for special holiday flights. Purchase tickets at the LanChile office, General Urrutia 104 (☎443 516). Open Dec.-Feb. daily 10am-2pm and 6-10pm.

Buses: Tur Bus, O'Higgins 910 (☎443 328), has an inconvenient depot 2km east of the city center. Other companies line Las Américas south of O'Higgins. In the middle of town is **JAC,** Uruguay 505 (☎443 693). To: **Lican Ray** (every 30min. 6am-9pm, CH$400); **PN Huerquehue** (8:30am, CH$1500); **Santiago** (8:15pm, CH$8900; 8:45pm, CH$21,000; 9pm, CH$13,100); **Temuco** (every 30min. 6am-9pm, CH$3800); **Valdivia** (5 per day 6am-6pm, CH$4900); **Villarrica** (every 30min. 6am-9pm, CH$400). **Condor,** on the corner of O'Higgins and Las Américas, heads frequently to: **Lautaro** (CH$2000); **Santiago** (9:15am, 6:30, 8pm; US$9); **Temuco** (CH$1300); **Valparaíso** (7:50 and 8:15pm, CH$2500). Open M-Sa 8:30am-1pm and 3-7:50pm, Su 8:30am-12:30pm and 5-7:30pm.

Taxis/Colectivos: Taxis can easily be found on O'Higgins and the Plaza de Armas. CH$1000 anywhere in town. *Colectivos* run along O'Higgins and elsewhere throughout town (8am-9pm CH$250, 9pm-midnight CH$350).

Car Rental: Hertz, Ansorena 123 (☎441 664; www.hertz.cl), is well stocked with a variety of vehicles. Compact cars CH$20,000; 4x4 trucks CH$38,000; SUVs CH$79,000. Weekend and weekly rates available. Open daily 9am-8pm. AmEx/MC/V. **SUP Rent-A-Car,**

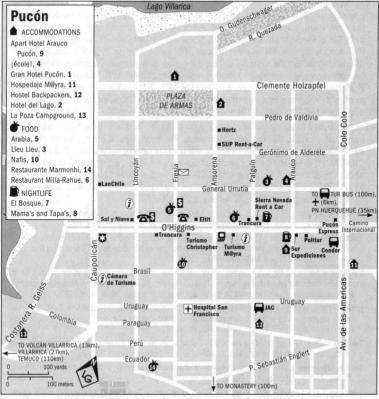

Pucón

🏠 ACCOMMODATIONS
Apart Hotel Arauco
  Pucón, **9**
¡école!, **4**
Gran Hotel Pucón, **1**
Hospedaje M@yra, **11**
Hostel Backpackers, **12**
Hotel del Lago, **2**
La Poza Campground, **13**

🍴 FOOD
Arabia, **5**
Lleu Lleu, **3**
Nafis, **10**
Restaurante Marmonhi, **14**
Restaurant Milla-Rahue, **6**

🍸 NIGHTLIFE
El Bosque, **7**
Mama's and Tapa's, **8**

Lago Villarica
O. Gudenschwager
R. Quezada
Clemente Holzapfel
PLAZA DE ARMAS
Pedro de Valdivia
Colo Colo
■ Hertz
■ SUP Rent-a-Car
Gerónimo de Alderete
Lincoyán
Fresia
Ansorena
Palguín
Arauco
■ LanChile
General Urrutia
Sierra Nevada Rent a Car
TO TUR BUS (100m),
(6km),
PN HUERQUEHUE (35km)
Sol y Nieve ■
O'Higgins
■ Eltit
■ Trancura
Pucón Express
Camino Internacional
Caupolicán
■ Trancura
Turismo Christopher
Turismo M@yra
Sur Expediciones
Politur
Condor
Brasil
Cámara de Turismo
Uruguay
Uruguay
Av. de las Americas
Costanera R. Geiss
Colombia
Paraguay
Hospital San Francisco
JAC
TO VOLCÁN VILLARICA (13km),
VILLARRICA (27km),
TEMUCO (110km)
Perú
Ecuador
P. Sebastián Englert
0   100 yards
0   100 meters
TO MONASTERY (100m)

Ansorena 191 (☎ 444 485), offers mini Fiats (CH$20,000), 12-passenger vans (CH$35,000), and everything in between. Open daily 8:30am-7pm. AmEx/MC/V.

Bike Rentals: Sierra Nevada Adventure, O'Higgins 524a (☎ 444 210; sierranevada@entelchile.net) has sturdy mountain bikes (CH$2500 per half day, CH$6000 per full day). Open daily 9am-8pm. AmEx/MC/V. **SUP Rent-A-Car** (see **Car Rentals,** above) also does bikes at CH$1000 per hr., CH$3000 per half day, CH$5000 per full day.

Ski Rental: Sol y Nieve (☎ 441 070), on the corner of O'Higgins and Lincoyán, rents skis for CH$9000 per day and snowboards for CH$13,000 per day. Open daily 9:30am-8:30pm. AmEx/MC/V. **Turismo M@yra,** O'Higgins 447 (☎ 444 514), rents skis for CH$5000 per day and snowboards for CH$12,000 per day.

🔆 🔢 ORIENTATION AND PRACTICAL INFORMATION

Pucón lies on the eastern edge of Lago Villarica, at the foot of Volcán Villarica, 25km from the town of Villarica. **O'Higgins** is the town's main thoroughfare, which during busier months looks like a catwalk for all the 4WD pickups and SUVs to strut their stuff. Along this strip you'll find a horde of adventure tour outfits and upper-end retail stores—the best that corporate America and Europe have to offer. Three blocks north of O'Higgins is the **Plaza de Armas,** flanked by the ritziest hotels in town—just around the Gran Hotel Pucón is Pucón's black-sand beach.

Tourist Offices: The signs that say "Oficina de Turismo," right off the highway, lead to the privately run **Cámara de Turismo,** Brasil 115 (☎441 671; www.puconturismo.cl) on the corner with Caupolicán. The English-speaking staff offers maps and an extensive price list of Pucón's accommodations. Open daily 10am-9pm. In the center of town is the *municipalidad*'s **Oficina de Turismo,** O'Higgins 486 (☎293 003; fax 293 001; ofturismo@municipalidadpucon.cl), on the corner with Palguin. Extensive collection of free brochures and helpful maps. Open daily Dec. 15-Feb. 28 8am-10pm; Mar.-Nov. 8:30am-7pm. **Conaf,** Lincoyán 336 (☎/fax 443 781; pnvillarrica@conaf.cl), 1 block north of O'Higgins, has maps and other information on PN Huerquehue and PN Villarrica. Open M-F Dec.-Feb. 8:30am-6pm; Mar.-Nov. 9am-4pm.

Tours: Countless tour agencies line O'Higgins. Each offers similar services with some individual twists to differentiate themselves. The most popular outing, summitting **Volcán Villarrica,** runs about CH$25,000; **whitewater rafting** ranges from CH$10,000 to CH$18,000 depending on difficulty of rapids; an evening's trip to **thermal baths** is about CH$8000 (not including CH$3000 entry fee); a guided tour of **PN Huerquehue** at CH$5000; a **horseback tour** of the area is around CH$12,000; and "hidrospeed" (boogie-boarding down Class III rapids) is CH$12,000.

Trancura, O'Higgins 211 (☎443 436; www.trancura.com), is one of the largest and most outfitted operations. Open daily Dec.-Feb. 9am-midnight; Mar.-Nov. 9am-8pm. AmEx/MC/V.

Politur, O'Higgins 635 (☎441 373; www.politur.com), offers an extra guide for extra safety on its volcano trips as well as complimentary beer and hot chocolate upon return. Open daily Dec.-Feb. 7am-10pm; Mar.-Nov. 7am-8:30pm. AmEx/MC/V.

Sol y Nieve (☎441 070; solnieve@entelchile.cl), on the corner of O'Higgins and Lincoyán. One of the older and more reputable operations, but also one of the more expensive. Also offers summitting excursions to other volcanoes in the area. Open daily 9am-8:30pm. AmEx/MC/V.

¡école!, General Urrutia 592 (☎441 675; www.ecole.cl). Has exclusive access to Cañi, a private nature reserve run by a foundation of ecological organizations. Day-long trip is CH$10,000; in winter, snowshoe rental CH$15,000. AmEx/MC/V.

Turismo M@yra, O'Higgins 447 (☎444 514). Run by an amiable Frenchman, M@yra has some of the cheapest prices in town as well as extensive rental options. AmEx/MC/V.

Sur Expediciones, on the corner of O'Higgins and Arauco, has canopy ziplines in the forest outside of town. Trips leave daily at 11am, 2, 4pm. CH$13,000.

Currency Exchange: Multiple options line O'Higgins. **Turismo Christopher,** O'Higgins 335 (☎/fax 449 013) cashes traveler's checks and changes US dollars, euros, and other foreign currency. Open daily Jan.-Feb. 9:30am-3am; Mar.-Dec. 9:30am-7:30pm. **Telefónica Pucón** (see **Fax Office and Telephones,** below) changes US dollars.

Banks: Banco de Chile, Fresia 223 (☎442 718), has a **24hr. ATM. BancoEstado,** O'Higgins 240 (☎441 100), also has a **24hr. ATM.** Open M-F 9am-2pm.

Work Opportunity: Turismo M@yra (see **Tours,** above), hires secretaries and salespeople to work in their office Dec.-Feb. **Hostel Backpackers** (see **Accommodations,** below) looks for speakers of both English and Spanish to act as sales representatives. For more info on working, see **Alternatives to Tourism,** p. 91.

Language Lessons: ¡école! (see **Tours,** above) offers Spanish classes starting at CH$9000 for a 2hr. class. 1-on-1 instruction also available. For details see **Alternatives to Tourism,** p. 88.

Market: Among the many *bodegas* on O'Higgins is the **Eltit Supermarket,** O'Higgins 336 (☎441 103 or 441 342) between Fresia and Ansorena. Open daily Jan.-Feb. 9am-11pm; Mar.-Dec. 9am-9:30pm. **Pucón Express,** on the corner of O'Higgins and Colo Colo is open 24hr. in summer.

Police: ☎133. *Carabineros* at O'Higgins 135 (☎441 196), at the corner with Caupolicán.

Hospital: Ambulance ☎131. **Hospital San Francisco,** Uruguay 325 (☎441 177), on the block between Fresia and Ansorena.

Fax Office and Telephones: Telefónica Pucón, O'Higgins 312 (☎442 052 or 442 054), between Fresia and Ansorena. Offers telephone service through Entel. International faxes CH$500 per page, domestic CH$350. Open M-Sa 10am-2pm and 4-8pm. **Centro de Llamadas,** O'Higgins 480, charges CH$200 per min. to the US and CH$300 per min. to most of Europe. Open daily 8:30am-11pm.

Internet Access: Most tour agencies offer free Internet in their office if you sign up for one of their tours. Otherwise, try **Cyber Unid@d,** store L-B in the complex at the corner of O'Higgins and Ansorena. CH$800 per hr. Open daily until midnight.

Post Office: Fresia 183 (☎441 164), on the corner with Alderete. Open M-F 9am-1pm and 3-6pm, Sa 9am-12:30pm.

ACCOMMODATIONS

As a premier destination for tourists around the globe, Pucón has some of the most luxurious (and most expensive) hotels in Chile. These are mostly located near Playa Grande, along the Plaza de Armas. Luckily, many *hospedajes* cater to the needs of the young backpacking crowd, so rates can be quite reasonable, especially outside the high season. Many *hospedaje* owners and workers are also tapped into the adventure tour business, so they can be a great source of advice.

¡école!, General Urrutia 592 (☎441 675; www.ecole.cl). All "Friends of the Earth" will enjoy this *hospedaje*/cafe's cheerful rooms—named for trees—and the gleaming shared bathrooms—named for birds. In the summer, be quick to stake out a spot in one of the hammocks under the grapevine trellis. Dec.-Mar. dorms CH$3500, with sheets CH$7500; singles CH$12,000; doubles and singles with private bath CH$17,000; triples with bath CH$23,000. Apr.-Nov. CH$3500/CH$6500/CH$9000/CH$15,000/CH$21,000. IVA discount for foreigners. 10% HI discount on dorms. AmEx/MC/V. ❷

Hostel Backpackers, Palguín 695 (☎442 412; www.politur.com/hostel). Masterfully managed by mountain-guide Claudio, Backpackers is the pleasant, low-key place that quickly becomes home. This old, creaky house is kept spotless by cooperative guests and the living room warm by a wood stove. Full kitchen, communal cable TV. Rooms with shared bath CH$5000-7000; doubles with bath CH$14,000. ❶

Gran Hotel Pucón, Hozapfel 190 (☎441 001; www.granhotelpucon.cl). You'll probably want to spend your time in this palacial hotel's huge plaza, with the best views of Pucón's amazing sunsets, or at the plentiful spa facilities. Singles CH$64,000; doubles CH$85,000; single junior suites CH$109,000; double junior suites CH$144,000. Low-season CH$52,000/CH$70,000/CH$92,000/CH$122,000. AmEx/MC/V. ❺

Hospedaje M@yra, Colo Colo 485 (☎442 745; myhostel@hotmail.com). This comfortable and relaxed *hospedaje* is on every backpacker's radar and they soon become like family in this cozy alpine lodge. Full kitchen. 10% discount on tours with Turismo M@yra. Nov.-Feb. rooms CH$5000 per person, with bath CH$7000 per person; Mar.-Oct. CH$4000/CH$5000. AmEx/MC/V. ❷

Hotel del Lago, Ansorena 23 (☎291 000; www.hoteldellago.cl). This is the place where Pucón's high rollers go to live it up. The hotel houses Pucón's casino and movie theater, and the huge entry hall, equipped with the requisite glass elevator, is indubitably one of Pucón's modern wonders. Rooms CH$126,000-201,000; in winter CH$33,000-159,000. AmEx/MC/V. ❺

La Poza Campground, Costanera Roberto Geiss 769 (☎441 435). The only campground in town, La Poza tries hard to replicate the area's natural wonders with tall, powerful trees and lakeside property, but it cannot hide its location. A busy road passes nearby and tourists arrive in busloads. Still, you are guaranteed privacy. Camping CH$4000. AmEx/MC/V. ❶

Apart Hotel Arauco Pucón, Arauco 440 (☎/fax 441 711; www.araucopucon.itgo.com), has private *cabaña*-like lodgings off a brightly-lit walkway. The owners are adamant about keeping the place quiet after 10:30pm and between 2:30 and 5pm for the afternoon *siesta*. Dec.-Mar. 2-person apartments CH$25,000; 4-person CH$35,000. Apr.-Nov. CH$12,000/CH$18,000. IVA discount for foreigners. AmEx/MC/V. ●

🍴 FOOD

As central Chile's premier tourist town, Pucón guarantees visitors overpriced cosmopolitan menus. Almost any dish you like can be found along O'Higgins, but your tastebuds will most likely be left wanting: Pucón has favored quantity over quality.

▨ Arabia, Fresia 354B (☎443 469), between General Urrutia and O'Higgins. A tiny restaurant that cooks up fantastic Middle Eastern dishes. Try the vegetarian sandwiches (CH$2900-3300) named after various Arab countries—the "Qatar" is stuffed with falafel, hummus, and tabouleh (CH$3300), and the "Jordania" has cheese, tomato, avocado, and mayo (CH$2900). Wrap up the meal with an Arabian coffee, *Kahue* (CH$900). Open daily 9am-2am; low season 10:30am-3:30pm and 7-10:30pm. ❸

Lleu Lleu, General Urrutia 520. Loved by locals, Lleu Lleu serves up serious *empanadas* ready to burst with full meals packed inside. Typical Chilean options are joined by the "vegetarian" and heart-choking "Neopolitan." Small CH$250, large CH$500. Open M-Th and Su 10am-midnight; F-Sa 11am-2am. ❶

¡école!, (p. 341), serves meatless dishes in a chill atmosphere, amid leafy plants and peacefully soporific tunes. There is a wide range of meal-sized salads (CH$2500) and omelettes (CH$2500-4400) to choose from. Try the *tabruli* (CH$1000), made of Andean *quinoa*, tomatoes, parsley, mint, and herbs, or one of the quiches (CH$3500-4800). Open daily 8am-midnight; low season 8am-10pm. AmEx/MC/V. ❸

Nafis, Fresia 477 (☎443 440), serves authentic, tasty Middle Eastern dishes, all certified kosher. Omelettes, pita sandwiches, and meal-sized salads all under CH$2000, although the portions equal the price. Open Dec.-Feb. 8:30am-midnight, Mar.-Nov. 8:30am-10pm. AmEx/MC/V. ❶

Restaurant Milla-Rahue, O'Higgins 460 (☎441 610). A pleasant restaurant shod in pine wood, perfect for a reasonably priced night out. Large windows give a great view to the milieu of O'Higgins while enjoying a wide selection of soups and fish, from Mexican trout (stuffed with spicy bits of chicken; CH$4800) to Sicilian salmon (with mushrooms; CH$4800). Open daily Jan.-Mar. 8am-1am; Apr.-Dec. 10am-11pm. AmEx/MC/V. ❸

Restaurante Marmonhi, Ecuador 175 (☎/fax 441 972), between Caupolicán and Lincoyán. Locals congregate here for inexpensive, filling lunches and pricier dinners. English menus. Soups CH$1000-2900, fish CH$3900-4980, other meat dishes CH$2500-4980. *Menú* with soup, entree, and dessert CH$3880. Open Jan.-Feb. daily 10am-midnight; Mar.-Dec. M-Sa 10am-10pm, Su 10am-6pm. Accepts US dollars. ❸

👁 SIGHTS

While Pucón does not offer many sights within city limits, the main attraction is Pucón's beach, **Playa Grande,** on the northern end of town, behind the Gran Hotel Pucón. The "beach" is really a dark-gray collection of crushed volcanic rock—not very suitable for building sand castles. Still, the view of the lake, flanked by snow-capped mountains, is impressive. The waters of Lago Villarrica, are wondrously still, shimmering softly in the light breezes of the valley. You can rent **boats** or **jet skis** here if you want to make some waves of your own. Just be sure not to miss the breathtaking sunsets, when the blues of the lake waters drain away into fiery red.

On the opposite side of town, on a hill overlooking Pucón, sits the **Monasteria Santa Clara.** This aged monastery is little more than a few rooms and a small chapel, but its stone patio offers a breathtaking view of the lake and mountains. The monastery can be reached by a narrow, steep ascent through the woods, beginning a little beyond the gate at the end of Ansorena.

📷 NIGHTLIFE

Nightlife in Pucón starts inexplicably late—past midnight—which does not bode well for early starts to the volcano and surrounding parks. The late-night scene centers along O'Higgins, as many restaurants are also bars.

Casino del Lago, inside Hotel del Lago (p. 341). This popular 2-story casino is no less exciting than the smoking lip of Villarrica. TV screens, flashing lights, and the jingling bells of slot machines dominate the 1st fl. For true players, the 2nd fl. beckons with the finest gaming tables in the Andes, but access will make you (at least) CH$2000 poorer. Open Jan.-Feb. 24hr.; Mar.-Dec. daily 11am-4am, card tables 8pm-4am.

Mama's and Tapa's, on the corner of Arauco and O'Higgins, is the new, hip bar on the block. The dark, smoky interior has pulsating beats and live music on weekends. Draws almost exclusively from deep-pocketed tourists. Open daily 8pm-late. AmEx/MC/V.

El Bosque, O'Higgins 524. The multi-sensory experience of El Bosque involves house trance music, projections of extreme surfing and skiing footage, and scantily-clad tourists. All housed in a spacious transplanted ski lodge. Popular with tourists and locals alike. *Schop* CH$1500. 2-for-1 happy hour daily 9pm-11pm. Open daily 4pm-late.

PARQUE NACIONAL HUERQUEHUE

Parque Nacional Huerquehue is easily the most beautiful place in the Lago Villarrica area. Often overshadowed by the more visible Volcán Villarrica and the more exciting activities of whitewater rafting and "hidrospeed," Huerquehue has yet to be overrun by the thousands of tourists visiting Pucón each month. Even so, it is easily accessible, has serene places to overnight, and boasts a well-maintained trail perfect for a one- or three-day hike through jaw-dropping, pristine country.

A steep, densely forested trail climbs 750m from the park entrance, past two raucous waterfalls and two *miradores* of Volcán Villarrica, to Lago Chico, kept still by towering granite cliffs to the north. The trail continues 1200m to the aptly-named Lago Verde. The trail then splits: one branch continues north 1450m into an *araucaria* forest with two more hidden lakes, while the shorter branch cuts east to Lago el Toro before looping back. The northern route eventually loops back and forms a 20km, 6½hr. hike, while taking the Lago Verde-Lago el Toro cutoff forms a 16km, 5½hr. hike. To reach the campground at Renahue, take the northern branch to Lago Huerquehue (the second lake) and head east on the blue trail. (The turnoff is well-marked with a sign.) From this turnoff, the campground is 3km down the trail, under the shadow of San Sebastián. Ten kilometers beyond the campground is the privately-run **Termas de Río Blanco,** with food, accommodations, and, of

AT A GLANCE	
AREA: 125 sq. km	**GATEWAYS:** Pucón, Villarrica.
CLIMATE: Temperate; warm summers; wet, cold winters. Annual rainfall 2000cm almost all during May-Sept.	**HIGHLIGHTS:** Hiking to the Five Lakes and secluded thermal baths; *araucaria* trees. Views of Volcán Villarrica; 2 waterfalls, Cerro San Sebastián (2000m).
CAMPING: Sites at Conaf's Refugio Renahue, CH$5500.	**FEES:** CH$2500, children CH$600.

Or, How to Impress Friends While Hiking Through *Parques Nacionales*

Chile's *parques nacionales*, from Torres del Paine to Vicente Pérez Rosales to Volcán Isluga, are the highlights of any trip to Chile. A hike through any of these spectacular reserves is only enriched by a knowledge of and appreciation for Chile's diverse flora, which results from its unique topography. Spanning over 40° of latitude, and a huge range of altitudes, gives rise to distinct plant communities. Any attempt to characterize the country's varied flora as a whole is futile. Instead, an introduction to the more conspicuous and interesting native plants, found in different habitats—from deserts to rainforests—is enough to bring out the botanist in anybody.

The deserts of northern Chile are some of the driest in the world, with rain falling only once a decade. Consequently, they are largely devoid of vegetation, except near streams or areas of frequent fog. Nonetheless, many different plants are adapted for life in these deserts, with over 20 species of cactus in the genus *Copiapoa* found in the Atacama desert. One of the strangest natural sights in Chile, in fact, is the *Copiapoa columna-alba*. All cacti of this variety lean markedly northward, leading to the illusion that the entire landscape is tilted. This behavior has been explained as a tactic by which the cactus minimizes the surface area exposed to the direct rays of the sun. In this environment where light is not limited but water is, plants must avoid excess exposure to intense sunlight. Thus, the sun hits the bent-over top of the cactus at a 90° angle, with the long trunk receiving only indirect light.

Farther south, these cacti give way to more verdant yet similarly unusual species of flora. Central Chile was once home to luxuriant forests of the Chilean wine palm, *Jubaea chilensis*, but now they are found only in isolated and mostly inaccessible populations in the wild. The beautiful palm tree grows to 6ft. in diameter and has a gray trunk that is smooth in appearance but bears diamond-shaped leaf scars. Known locally as the *coquito*, this tree has fruits that resemble small coconuts, both in appearance and in taste. The harvesting of the fruits does the tree little harm, but it has suffered extensive decline due to the harvest of its sweet sap, harvested by cutting the crown of leaves, which causes the sap to rise. A single full-grown tree can house up to 90 gallons of harvestable sap, which is released over the course of a few months. The sap nourishes the tree; thus, trees cannot survive many such harvests. Once collected, the sap is either fermented to make wine or boiled to make a sweet syrup called *miel de palma* (palm honey).

Perhaps the most recognizable native Chilean tree is the monkey puzzle tree, *Araucaria araucana*, which grows in southern Chile at mid-elevations. These conifers are popular garden and arboretum specimens the world over. Juveniles are covered with hard, triangular, spiky leaves, even on the trunk. It was this anti-herbivore protection that led a Cornish gentleman in the 19th century to remark that attempting to climb it would puzzle even a monkey. In the wild, *araucaria* can reach heights of over 180 ft. Trunks are straight and typically devoid of branches for ¾ or more of their length. Branches are long and straight, covered in leaves, and slightly pendant. Where they coexist with other species, *araucaria* overshadow all others in height, making the canopy look like an even layer punctuated by strange toothpicks topped by a pyramid of green.

The trees, called *pehuén* by some natives, served as a major food source for many of the indigenous peoples, particularly the Pehuenche. The tree's seeds, *piñones*, are delicious and quite abundant. Female cones are so massive that many places prohibit the planting of female trees for fear of falling cones braining passersby. The seeds can be eaten raw, but are typically dried, roasted, and eaten whole or ground into flour.

One of the best places to see large populations of the monkey puzzle is Santuario Cañi, a private reserve dedicated to promoting local guide training and sustainable interactions with the remaining forests. There are no roads, so be prepared to hike. If you reach the high *mirador*, you will be afforded a simultaneous view of four spectacular volcanoes and an old *araucaria* forest.

Foreigners made several failed attempts to grow the tree abroad until the success of Englishman Sir Joseph Banks. Fascination with the tree has not, however, prevented its declining numbers. The straight trunk and huge size make it a valuable lumber product and, despite nominal protection, illegal logging continues at a high rate.

Venturing still farther south, you may be lucky enough to see the majestic *alerce*, which resembles the giant redwood, but is actually related to the cypress. While not as tall as the sequoia (only reaching 150 ft.), it can live over 3500 years and grow to 4m in diameter. The wood contains protective resins that made it popular timber for exterior structures like shingles and decks. Only 15% of the area originally forested by *alerce* remains, but the recent creation of Parque Pumalín will hopefully go a long way toward ensuring the long-term survival of this unique species.

Amity Wilczek was a graduate student in evolutionary biology at Harvard University.

course, hot baths. A second, less-traveled route, splits off just after the park entrance and climbs 2000m up **Cerro San Sebastián** where, at the summit, you can gaze at the stunning landscape, including 10 lakes and 9 volcanoes. (8km, 6½hr.)

The park is open year-round and entrance costs CH$2200 for adults, CH$600 for children. The trails are steep, so during or after heavy rains, much of the park is inaccessible. There are picnic grounds and a parking lot immediately behind the entrance to the park. Two kilometers farther down the road is the privately-run **Refugio Tinquilco ❷** (☎09 539 278; www.tinquilco.cl). Set beside Lago Tinquilco, this modern *refugio* offers the best accommodations in the park. The owners are ecology-minded and strive to ensure a peaceful stay to "restore your balance." (Breakfast CH$1800, lunch or dinner CH$3800. Bunk beds CH$5900, with sheets CH$6900. Payment in US dollars has 19% discount.) In the middle of the park, 13km from the entrance, is Conaf's **Refugio Renahue ❷**, with just a few campsites for CH$5500 a night. At the complete other end of the park, 20km from the entrance, is the privately run **Termas Río Blanco ❸**. (CH$6000 per night.)

The park is accessible from Pucón. **JAC buses** (Uruguay 505) leave daily at 8:30am from Pucón and from PN Huerquehue at 10am and 5:30pm. Buses ride directly from the JAC depot to the park entrance. (1hr., round-trip CH$3000.) PN Huerquehue can also be reached by car, although turns on a series of unmarked roads necessitate a map—inquire at Pucón's **Conaf** office (p. 340). Almost all the tour agencies in Pucón also offer guided tours of the park.

PARQUE NACIONAL VILLARRICA

The most active volcano in South America, Volcán Villarrica (2847m), dominates the skyline for miles around with its distinctive, smoldering crown, visible on clear days from across the lake in Villarrica. The volcano has erupted more than 30 times since 1558. Its last major outburst was in 1971, when a violent explosion triggered avalanches and unleashed a blizzard of ash upon Lagos Villarrica and Calafquén. However, since its last minor eruption in 1984, the mountain has been fairly quiet. Today, scores of tourists make the ascent hoping to see a pit of hot magma—though they are often thwarted by thick sulfur clouds blanketing the crater or dark rain clouds over the entire area. Still, Volcán Villarrica is quite accessible, and it's worth the 5hr. hike to gamble on seeing the impressive lava.

Though the celebrity status of the volcano tends to eclipse all else, the park's 630 sq. km offer much more in the way of breathtaking beauty. Formed around a spur jutting from the spine of the Andes, the park is home to three other major volcanoes—Volcán Quetrupillán (2360m), Volcán Quinquilil (2022m), and the mammoth Volcán Lanín (3747m). Along the southern slopes of the four sibling volcanoes, stretches a thick forest of monkey puzzle *(araucaria)* trees, some that have seen as many as three millennia. Natural reservoirs of alpine runoff also dot the park, providing a placid counterbalance to the lava-spewing volcanoes.

AT A GLANCE	
AREA: 630 sq. km	**HIGHLIGHTS:** Volcanes Villarrica, Quetrupillán, and Lanín; *araucaria.*
CLIMATE: Average annual rainfall 250-350cm of rain Mar.-Aug. Average high temp. Jan.-Mar. 23°C; average low temp. May-Aug. 4°C.	**FEES:** No park entrance fee; trail entrance fees CH$1500-CH$3200, payable at the park entrances.
GATEWAY: Pucón.	**CAMPING:** Near entrance to Quetrupillán; CH$5000 per 8-person site.

TRANSPORTATION. There is **no public transportation** to the Rucapillán or Quetrupillán sectors, where the most popular hikes begin. A **taxi** from Pucón to the beginning of the trail to the volcano, in sector Rucapillán, runs CH$10,000-12,000. **Buses JAC** (☎ 443 693) runs from Pucón to the easternmost park entrance at Sector Puesco (1¾hr.; M, W, F 6:10pm, returning M, W, F 7am; CH$1400). Many tour operators in Pucón offer transportation-inclusive ascents of Volcán Villarrica.

ORIENTATION AND PRACTICAL INFORMATION. Conaf administers the park from its office in Pucón (p. 340), where visitors can find the most comprehensive information, on the park's three different sectors. Within the park, there are three **guardaparques** outposts: one at the entrance of **Sector Rucapillán**, at the western end, where ascents to Volcán Villarrica begin and the ski center is located; one at the entrance of **Sector Quetrupillán**, in the center, between Volcanes Villarrica and Quetrupillán; and one along the route through the mountains to Argentina, at **Sector Puesco**, between Volcanes Quinquilil and Lanín. (*Guardaparques* stations open Jan.-Feb. 6am-6:30pm; Mar.-Dec. 8:30am-1pm and 2:30-6:30pm.)

HIKES. The park's most frequented sector, **Sector Rucapillán**, has two principal **trails**—one up the volcano (5km, 6hr., CH$3200), and one around its southern edge (23km, 12hr., CH$3000). The trip up the volcano begins at the Conaf office at the park entrance, where those brave enough to make the ascent without a guide must show proof that they have sufficient climbing experience (alpine club ID or the like) and the proper equipment, including all-weather clothing, crampons, an ice pick, and appropriate climbing gear. Each person intending to ascend in a private group must show credentials. All climbers must bring a gas mask (provided by tour agencies) to fend off the poisonous fumes from the perpetually burning crater. A good pair of shades are also a must. (5hr. up, 2hr. down. Ascents must begin between 7 and 10am.) The trek then starts on the road to the ski center covering the slopes of Villarrica. There is a **ski lift** (CH$3000) that cuts 1-1½ hr. off the hike; however, it only runs 8-9am outside the ski season. After getting beyond the ski center, it's another 3-4hr. up the snow-covered slopes to the lip of the crater.

Getting down the volcano slopes can be a refreshing change of pace. Walking will take you 2hr., but many tour agencies will lend you **slides** so you can shimmy down a bit more playfully than you came up. Some tour agencies will also let you climb the slope **ski randonee,** wearing skis specially modified so that you can walk uphill and ski back down (must be intermediate skier). **Snowboards** are also allowed—but you have to haul one to the top yourself.

The trail around the volcano, **Sendero Challupen Chinay,** offers stunning views of the volcano wrapped in ice and Lagos Calafquén and Villarrica, all glinting in the sunlight. In all, the 12hr., 23km hike brings you to the Conaf office at **Sector Quetrupillán,** an often overlooked, but abundantly rewarding, swath of pristine forest stuck between two volcanoes. The shortest trail in Quetrupillán is **Sendero Pichillancahue,** an easier jaunt through an *araucaria* forest, with views of Volcán Choshuenco to the south and Volcán Quetrupillán to the north. It also gives you the opportunity to observe the glacial movement of ice on Volcán Villarrica (3.3km, 1¼hr. one-way). Longer trails stretch around Volcán Villarrica's far end to the west, and to Volcán Quetrupillán to the east, eventually ending up, some 32km of hiking later, at Sector Puesco, on the other side of the volcano. (*Trail access CH$3000. 4WDs allowed on the 9km stretch of muddy dirt road, accesible only in summer. The park's camping facilities are located near the entrance to Quetrupillán and are open only in summer; bathrooms and showers; no hot water. Max. 6 people. CH$5000 per site).*

Just before the highway cuts through the Andes at Paso Mamuil Malal, the gateway to Argentina, it passes through the park's most secluded sector, **Puesco.** A customs post (☎ 171 2196 8592; open Dec.-Mar. 8am-6pm) stands guard at the entrance here, where you'll have to show identification and vehicle registration. Those who want to visit the park will have to hand over their passports, which they'll give back when you leave the park. Within the next few years, Chile intends to build a new customs station at the actual border, hence obviating the need to surrender your passport just to enter the park.

The trails in Sector Puesco lie in the shadow of the massive Volcán Lanín. At 3747m, it's a few heads taller than its more famous brother to the west and sits only partially in Chile. There are numerous shorter trails—**Sendero Lagos Andinos** (12km, 6hr., CH$3000) makes a lazy circuit around several small Andean lagoons replete with wildlife, while **Sendero Momolluco** (10hr. round-trip) heads west toward Sector Quetrupillán alongside the southern slopes of the volcano, then loops back upward to end at the Puesco entrance. *(The entrance to Sector Puesco is 69km from Pucón, with another 18km of road leading to the mountain pass and international border. To get there, take a bus from Pucón.)*

🎿 **SKIING.** Situated on the slopes of Volcán Villarrica inside Sector Rucapillán is **Ski Pucón Chile.** It boasts 12 trails serviced by nine ski lifts in a wide range of difficulty levels. Lava flows have carved out channels into the mountain face, creating natural half-pipes that will challenge expert skiers and snowboarders. Most trails sit at 1200m above sea level with a few lifts taking you up to 1800m. (☎ 441 901, in Pucón 441 001; www.granhotelpucon.cl. Season passes CH$120,000, children CH$85,000. Full-day lift tickets CH$14,000. Open July-Sept.)

LAGO CALAFQUÉN

LICAN RAY   ☎ 45

For the Chileans who flock here each summer, Lican Ray has it all: long beaches along Lago Calafquén's placid bays, plenty of seasonal restaurants and *papas fritas* stands for eating, bars for drinking (or dancing) away the end-of-summer blues, and plenty of *cabañas* for sleeping it off. For all these reasons, Chilean teenagers and families inundate the place during January and February—and then quickly disappear, leaving Lican Ray deserted and almost ghostly. Even during the high season, the town has precious few services; visitors should stock up before coming, then plan to languish here for a few days and soak up some sun.

📠 **TRANSPORTATION.** Buses JAC, Tur Bus, and **InterBus** (☎ 431 260) pull into and out of the east side of the plaza at Urrutia, where the three companies share an office and terminal. They serve Coñaripe (30min.; Jan.-Feb. every 30min. 7:45am-9:45pm, Mar.-Dec. every hr. 7:45am-7pm; CH$300) and Villarrica (30min.; Jan.-Feb. every 30min. 7:45am-9:45pm, Mar.-Dec. every hr. 7:45am-7pm; CH$400). Buses to Panguipulli can be caught in Coñaripe. **Transtur,** Urrutia 400 (☎ 09 200 9914 or 09 846 9726), offers day-long tours to the Termas de Coñaripe (9am, CH$2800), as well as direct transportation to the **airport** in Pucón or Temuco (CH$30,000).

📑 **ORIENTATION AND PRACTICAL INFORMATION.** The town's main road (and also the only paved one) is **General Urrutia,** which runs east from the main road between Villarrica and Coñaripe, passes the **Plaza de Armas,** and ends at **Playa Chica,** on **Lago Calafquén.** Urrutia runs parallel to and two blocks inland from **Playa**

Grande, the larger and more popular of Lican Ray's two beaches. **Cacique Punulef,** home to many hostels and *cabañas,* lines Playa Grande, connected by a series of side streets to the more restaurant-oriented Urrutia.

A small **tourist kiosk** is located on the corner of the Plaza de Armas; here you'll find a wealth of pamphlets and a helpful staff. (☎431 516. Open Jan.-Feb. daily 9am-11pm; Mar.-Dec. M-F 9am-1pm and 3-5pm.) **Bikes** can be rented at **Hospedaje Cristóbal,** Millañanco 145. (☎09 571 4220. CH$1000 per hr.) Like many of its rural, lakeside neighbors, Lican Ray **has no ATMs, banks, mail services, or car rental agencies;** be sure to take care of these details before leaving larger outposts. The **Posta de Salud,** on Catrini, east and south of the Plaza, is a small clinic which is always open for emergencies, but has fewer hours for visits to the doctor. Look for the **Entel** *centro de llamadas,* Huenuman 270, on the plaza's western edge. (Open 9:30am-midnight.) **Internet access** is available at two terminals in the tourist office or directly across the street from the Posta de Salud (both CH$500 per hr.)

⚑ ACCOMMODATIONS. **Hotel Refugio Inaltulafquén ❸,** Punulef 510, has the laid-back atmosphere of a tropical *cabaña,* complete with a lakefront restaurant and bar. Many of the large, bright rooms feature lake views. (☎431 115. Breakfast included. Singles CH$10,000, with bath CH$15,000.) Just down the road, **Hospedaje Victor's Playa ❷,** Punulef 120, at the eastern end of the street, offers somewhat less expensive accommodations at a less expensive price, and manages to maintain a relaxed lakefront ambience. (☎09 523 9549. Breakfast included. CH$5000 per person, with private bath CH$7000 per person.) **Residencial Temuco ❸,** Gabriela Mistral 515, is another cheap stay farther from the water. The warm, caring staff maintains basic rooms and spotless, if slightly forlorn, bathrooms. (☎431 130. CH$5000 per person.) Quality **cabañas** abound in Lican Ray. Hit the tourist office for an updated list of what's open and to make a price comparison. For a solid spot close to the water, head to **Cabañas Lican Ray ❶,** Urrutia 135, where 5-person cabins go for CH$25,000. (☎09 998 4286; polisur@telsur.cl.) **Camping is not allowed** on either Playa Chico or Playa Grande, but just off the road, toward Coñaripe, there are sites on the lakefront such as **Camping Vista Hermosa ❷,** 4.5km away.

⬛ FOOD. Winter travelers be warned—most of Lican Ray's eateries shut down from March to December. If you're here in summer, though, you're in luck, as restaurants and food stands cover the tiny town. When in doubt, head for any number of *papas fritas* and *pollo asado* stands that line Urrutia near the plaza (Chicken CH$2800; bucket of fries CH$1000). For more formal dining, **The Ñaños ❸,** Urrutia 105 (☎431 021), is the most popular spot in town—some diners travel from other towns just for its food. Classic fare ranges from hamburgers (CH$2000-3000) to *pastel de choclo,* which can be prepared with or without chicken (CH$3800). Just across Urrutia from the plaza, a nameless **Restaurant ❷,** Urrutia 315 (☎431 154), offers one of the cheapest *almuerzos* around (CH$1600). The *porotos granados* (lima and string beans in soup) make for a healthy, satisfying lunch. **Cábala ❸,** Urrutia 201 (☎431 653), is Lican Ray's attempt at an Italian pizzeria. Patrons enjoy gourmet pizzas (CH$3500-8100) and pastas (CH$4000) in an elegant deck setting.

◩ ⬛ SIGHTS AND ENTERTAINMENT. Between **Playa Grande** and **Playa Chica** lies a grassy, forested peninsula. Stroll through this welcoming splash of green that provides respite from the sunny beaches (not to mention from the sunburned beach crowd). The **Semana de Lican Ray** typically takes place the 2nd week of February, and the festivities promise to be great—in past years, the town has broken records for world's largest barbecue. And while this grilling en masse is dwindling, the week is still full of not-to-be-missed beach events—for more details, check with the tourist office after November. **Boat rentals** are a fun way to explore the lake, and are generally cheaper on Playa Chica (paddleboats CH$2000 per hr.; individual kayaks CH$4000 per hr.; banana-boat rides CH$11,000). **Transtur** (see **Transportation,** p. 347) runs tours in the summer to various lakes and cities in the region, as well as to the nearby hot springs. (Valdivia tour CH$12,500; Puerto Montt tour CH$28,500; Villarrica and Pucón tour CH$4500; Termas daytrip CH$2800.)

For such a tiny town, Lican Ray has some surprisingly serious nightlife during its peak months. **Desibelius,** a hip disco, lies a short 3km drive out of town on the road to Villarrica. Jam-packed with grooving youths in the summer, the *discoteca* only runs on weekends during the rest of the year. (☎431 019. Cover CH$3000 in summer. Open 11pm-4am.) Many locals start the night off at the popular **Donde el Flaco,** near the Plaza de Armas. Scheduled to open its doors for the 2005 season, **Partido la Mitad,** Urrutia 590, should add to the midnight mayhem in Lican Ray.

COÑARIPE ☎63

Nestled along the banks of Lago Calafquén, the tiny town of Coñaripe offers pristine, undisturbed views of the lake and Volcán Villarrica. Until recently, Coñaripe was overlooked by Chilean students in favor of the more flamboyant party town of Lican Ray. But quiet Coñaripe has begun to steal away some of those tourists, and the spectacular views, serenity, and particularly, the development of the Termas de Liquiñe are making Coñaripe and the less-frequented Lago Calafquén a more tranquil alternative for visitors to the Villarrica region.

Pub La Terraza ❷, Luis Roza 32, on the waterfront, offers clean, affordable dining with beach and volcano views. Sample the *cazuela* (CH$1500) or a classic *bife a lo pobre* (CH$2700) while you watch the beach bums frolic outside. (Open in summer from 9am.) Up the road, there's **Restaurant Chumay ❷,** attached to the hostel of the same name. (☎09 458 9640. Meals CH$1500-2500. Open in summer from 9am.)

Hostal Chumay ❷, Las Trepas 201, across the plaza from the tourist office, is the best budget option in town, with tidy (if somewhat bare), well-ventilated rooms and impeccable bathrooms. Owner Leo speaks some English and leads tours to the nearby *termas.* (☎09 458 9640; turismochumay@hotmail.com. Breakfast included. CH$5000 per person, low-season CH$3000 per person.) **Hotel Entre Montañas ❷,** Beck 496, has somewhat darker, less appealing rooms. Nevertheless, all rooms have private baths, and at CH$6500 per person, it's a deal. (☎317 298. Breakfast included. Singles CH$6500; doubles CH$13,000.) Otherwise, pitch a tent at any of the myriad campsites lining the beach. **Camping Millaray ❶,** a few sites down on the beach from the end of the road, with hot showers and bathrooms. (☎09 825 3467. 5-person sites CH$8,000).

Upon arriving in town, the road from Lican Ray turns into **Guido Beck de Ramberga,** the main thoroughfare in Coñaripe. The road passes by the **plaza** (on the right as you come in from Lican Ray) and the **bus station,** 200m farther along on the left, just before the road forks right toward Panguipulli. The curvy and scenic road continues left to the refreshing Termas de Coñaripe and farther down to the **spa** at Liquiñe. The **Oficina de Turismo** is located in a kiosk on the plaza. (☎317 378. Open in summer 9am-10pm, closes earlier in winter.) The nearest **banks** are in Panguipulli or Villarrica, so make sure you have enough cash with you before you arrive. The **health clinic,** across from Chumay, is always open for emergencies. The **police** are found on the road into town just before the plaza. (*Guardia* open 24hr.)

Buses leave for Lican Ray (30min.; Jan.-Feb. every hr. 9:30am-9pm, Mar.-Dec. schedule varies, ask drivers for info on times; CH$400) and Panguipulli (1¼hr.; M-Sa 6 per day 7:30am-2pm, Su 10am and 7pm; CH$900). From either of these towns, board other buses to Valdivia and Osorno. Buses to the **Termas de Coñaripe** and **Liquiñe** leave less frequently, but still make for relatively easy transport (30min.; 5 per day 9:15am-5:45pm, last bus returns from Liquiñe at 5:30pm; CH$500).

LOS LAGOS

A variety of hot springs locations can be found about 15km southeast of the town of Coñaripe along a slow, uphill gravel road. Budget travelers who have been passing up the opportunity to take a dip in more expensive soothing baths will be glad to finally pamper themselves without breaking the bank. The least expensive options, **Eco Termas Vergara** (☎09 457 7656) and **Eco Termas Pellaifa** (☎09 458 1768), at Km14 and Km16, respectively, charge a CH$2000 entrance fee. The more expensive **Termas de Coñaripe** will be worth the splurge for those who seek a secluded, all-inclusive resort. (Entrance CH$6000, children under 10 CH$3000.) The attached **hotel** ❺ offers pricey accommodations, as well as a gym, horseback riding facilities, and a massage parlor. (☎431 407. Rooms and *cabañas* CH$33,000-80,000 per person, depending on meals and amenities included.)

Mid-range *termas*-seekers will also appreciate the slightly more remote **Termas de Liquiñe.** Here, an emphasis on the purely natural makes up for the somewhat harrowing ride up along a winding dirt road. The accommodations, however, are expensive; staying in Coñaripe may be the best option. (☎230 004. Baths CH$3000. Cabañas CH$28,700 per person.)

WEST COAST

VALDIVIA   ☎63

Surrounded by the rich, fertile hills of the Coastal Range, Valdivia (pop. 124,000) is often called the most attractive city in all of Chile, and with its annual rainfall of 230cm, it is also definitely the wettest. Locals here sum up the weather with the simple phrase, *pura lluvia*—nothing but rain. Nonetheless, the city itself is pleasant enough: neat, bustling streets give way to broad "coastal" (riverfront) areas that line Valdivia on three sides. An abundance of university students keeps the city's services in a convenient state of readiness, and the town's attractions, while not famous or overwhelming, make for a day of relaxed sightseeing. If you're not in a hurry, Valdivia constitutes a nice stop.

▐ TRANSPORTATION

Flights: The airport, 40km north of the city, has flights on **LanChile,** Maipú 271 (☎246 493; open M-F 9am-1:30pm and 3-7pm), to **Santiago** (2 per day, CH$70,000).

Buses: Long-distance buses run from the **Terminal de Buses,** Anfión Muñoz 360. Consult with the **information desk** (☎212 212; open 8am-10:30pm) downstairs for up-to-date schedules. The staff has a general departure chart and can tell you when the next bus leaves. **Cruz del Sur** (☎213 840), **Buses Norte** (☎212 800), **Tur Bus** (☎226 010), and **Buses JAC** (☎212 925), among others, have multiple departures each day. They serve: **Bariloche, ARG** (6hr.; M-Tu, Th, Sa 9:30am, W, F, Su 12:30pm; CH$10,000-13,000); **Futrono** (2hr., every 15min. 6:50am-9:10pm, CH$1300); **Lago Ranco** (2¼hr., 8 per day 8am-7pm, CH$1500); **Panguipulli** (2½hr., every 15min. 6:30am-8:50pm, CH$2000); **Puerto Montt** (3hr., every 15-30min. 3:45am-9:15pm, CH$2800) via **Osorno** (2hr., CH$1500); **Santiago** (12hr., every 15-30min. 7:05am-11:55pm, CH$18,500); **Temuco** (3hr., every 20min. 5:45am-1:40am, CH$2500).

Local Buses: Buses to **Niebla** can be found along Prat, especially near Sernatur (30min., every 30min. 8am-9pm, CH$400). Inexpensive city buses also pass through the plaza area frequently and go by the bus station as well.

Colectivos: *Colectivos* linger around the same area as buses to Niebla (CH$500).

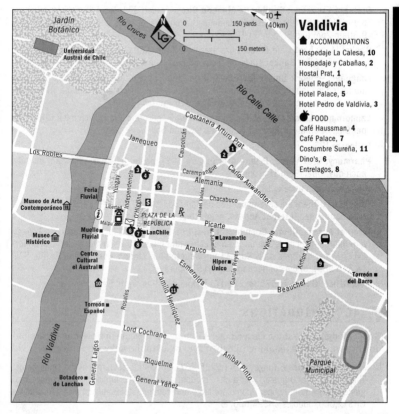

Valdivia

▲ ACCOMMODATIONS
Hospedaje La Calesa, **10**
Hospedaje y Cabañas, **2**
Hostal Prat, **1**
Hotel Regional, **9**
Hotel Palace, **5**
Hotel Pedro de Valdivia, **3**

🍎 FOOD
Café Haussman, **4**
Café Palace, **7**
Costumbre Sureña, **11**
Dino's, **6**
Entrelagos, **8**

▟ ▟ ORIENTATION AND PRACTICAL INFORMATION

Three rivers meet in Valdivia. The **Río Calle Calle** runs northwest along the eastern border of the city until it meets the **Río Cruces** coming south and turns into the **Río Valdivia.** The Río Valdivia heads southwest to the Pacific Ocean, separating mainland Valdivia from Isla Teja to the west. From the bus station on the eastern side of the city, **Prat** (also known as Costanera) runs along the Río Calle Calle. When it reaches the northern tip of the city at the confluence of Calle Calle and Cruces, Costanera turns south and ducks under the **Puente Pedro de Valdivia,** the bridge to Isla Teja, and ends on the edge of downtown.

Two blocks to the east, the **Plaza de la República** is the center of activity. Bordered by **Henríquez** to the east, **O'Higgins** to the west, **Maipú** to the south, and **Libertad** to the north, the plaza stretches two blocks. **Picarte** heads east from the center of the plaza and is the most commercially developed street in town, with many budget hotels along the way to the bus station. In the opposite direction, at the entrance to the bridge to **Isla Teja,** is a smaller plaza with the *municipalidad* and the grand Hotel Pedro de Valdivia.

Tourist Offices: Sernatur, Prat 555 (☎ 242 300), south of the Feria Fluvial, has tour boats and tours waiting just outside its doors. English-speaking staff always available in summer. Open M-F 8:30am-7pm, Sa-Su 10am-7pm; low season M-Th 8:30am-5:30pm, F 8:30am-4:30pm. A **kiosk** in the bus station provides quick info for needy travelers.

Currency Exchange: Cambio de Moneda Giros, Arauco 331, local 24 (☎212 177), in the mall south of BancoEstado, changes traveler's checks as well as cash. Open M-F 9:30am-2pm and 3-7pm, Sa 10am-2pm.

Banks: Many **banks** are in the plaza area and **24hr. ATMs** are scattered all across the *centro,* including **BancoEstado** on the southeast corner of the Plaza.

Language Schools: Universidad Austral de Chile, Casilla 567 (☎213 911). Students interested in learning Spanish can enroll directly in the university, or arrange private lessons. For more information see **Alternatives to Tourism,** p. 88.

Laundromat: LavaMatic, W. Schmidt between Picarte and Arauco, charges CH$2700 per 5kg. Open M-F 9:30am-7:30pm, Sa 9:30am-6pm.

Police: ☎133.

Pharmacy: Cruz Verde, Picarte 404 (☎254 705), posts the 24hr. pharmacy-on-duty each day. Open 9am-10:30pm.

Hospital: Ambulance ☎133.

Telephones: There are several *centros de llamadas* around the plaza, and **Centro Comunicaciones** (see **Internet Access,** below) offers public phone services.

Internet Access: Centro Comunicaciones, Libertad 127 (☎341 054), between Yungay and Independencia, is a great Internet cafe with phones, faxes, printers, and a scanner. CH$700 per hr. Open daily 9am-11pm. Near the bus station, **Lospri.com,** Picarte 877 (☎346 589), offers connections at CH$500 per hr.

Post Office: O'Higgins 575 (☎212 167). Open M-F 9am-7pm, Sa 9am-noon.

▐ ACCOMMODATIONS

Budget lodging in Valdivia is average. A number of upscale options cluster around downtown, offering tempting (if expensive) relief for hostel-weary travelers.

Hospedaje La Calesa, Yungay 735 (☎225 467), above the restaurant of the same name. This is a pearl of a hostel, with a chic, modern paint job and furnishings ensconced in a grand old riverfront house. Rooms are large and comfortable. Breakfast included. Singles CH$12,000; doubles CH$24,000. ❸

Hospedaje y Cabañas, Carampangue 626 (☎217 910), may be nameless, but the owners are still working on that, and it doesn't detract from the bright, fragrant garden and clean, new accommodations. All rooms have private bath and cable TV. Singles CH$14,000; doubles CH$25,000. ❸

Hostal Prat, Prat 595 and Carampangue 692 (☎222 020), comes highly recommended by locals. Sitting right on the waterfront, the living room, dining room, and several of the guest quarters look out over the Río Calle Calle. Simple but clean rooms all have private bath. Breakfast included. Singles CH$15,000; doubles CH$20,000. MC/V. ❸

Hospedaje Libertad, Libertad 150, may appear a bit spartan, but the rooms are large and the paint jobs are new and bright, as are the palatial bathrooms. The location, mere steps from the Costanera, is hard to beat. CH$7000 per person. ❷

Hotel Regional, Picarte 1005 (☎216 027), opposite the bus terminal. Rooms are fairly clean, though the wallpaper has seen better days. Sinks and mirrors in each room make up for a lack of decor. Singles CH$4500, with bath and breakfast CH$6500; doubles CH$9000/CH$13,000. ❷

Hotel Pedro de Valdivia, Carampangue 190 (☎212 931), is among Valdivia's most distinctive landmarks. This is fitting, because the fine accommodations within provide for a distinctive, 5-star stay. Many guests like to lounge in the elegant courtyard. Cable TV and breakfast included. Singles CH$38,000-42,000; doubles CH$48,000-53,000. AmEx/MC/V. ❺

Hotel Palace, Chacabuco 308 (☎213 319), at the corner with Henríquez, is bigger than it looks from the crowded street below, though its lobby and breakfast room are a bit crowded. Some rooms have street views. Singles CH$23,000; doubles CH$27,000; triples CH$34,700. AmEx/MC/V. ❹

🄵 FOOD

Like that of most Chilean towns, Valdivia's cuisine is nothing to scream about. Travelers from more cosmopolitan locales will no doubt be disappointed by everything here—with the possible exception of the chocolate.

Costumbre Sureña, Henríquez 746 (☎249 155), located in a high-ceilinged, airy, German colonial house, prides itself on well-made traditional dishes. Friendly service and welcoming ambience make up for relatively small portions. Each day brings a new list of choices for an *almuerzo* (CH$2500-4000). Open daily noon-4pm and 7-11pm. ❸

La Calesa, Yungay 735 (☎213 712), is a fine dining experience featuring Peruvian cuisine. The pretty garden and river views are enough of a reason to eat here—and that's even before sampling the food. The real specialty, however, is the seafood (CH$4000-6000). Open M-F noon-3:30pm and 8pm-midnight, Sa 8pm-midnight. AmEx/MC/V. ❸

Entrelagos, Rosales 640 (☎218 333), is perfect for travel-weary tourists. They have some menus in English, and serve familiar dishes including sandwiches (CH$2000-4000), salads (CH$2000), and fajitas for 2 (CH$5000). Don't leave without trying the specialities—fine chocolates and aromatic coffee. If you just can't get enough, head next door to the *chocolatería*, where endless varieties of delectables await. ❷

Café Haussman, O'Higgins 394 (☎213 878), 1 block north of the plaza, is somewhat of a local tradition, daily serving hundreds of *crudos*—slices of bread slathered with uncooked beef, onions, an herbal dressing, and fresh lemon juice—an unlikely combo which actually works quite well, as evidenced by the locals who pack the joint around lunchtime. (*Crudos* CH$1050). AmEx/MC/V. ❶

Dino's, Maipú 191 (☎213 061), at the corner with O'Higgins. This branch of the Dino's chain actually has a high-quality buffet room downstairs (CH$4500). Upstairs, the cafe serves sandwiches (CH$2000) and hot drinks (CH$500-1000) all day long. Buffet room open Apr.-Dec. noon-3:30pm and 8pm-midnight. ❸

Café Palace, Rosales 580 (☎213 539), is a Chilean diner popular with Valdivian students. Notable items include Spanish-style *tortillas* (CH$2200) and tempting desserts. Sandwiches CH$2000-3000. Entrees CH$3000-4500. ❷

🄶 SIGHTS

DOWNTOWN. Most of Valdivia's main attractions lie across the river on Isla Teja. A stroll along the **Costanera,** however, where locals like to jog, provides relaxation and pleasant breezes off the rivers. Follow the path long enough and you'll come to the **Feria Fluvial,** where vendors come to hawk fresh seafood catches. Unmistakable due to its strong seafood smell, the *feria* plays host to fish merchants loudly hawking their wares, children running underfoot, tourists and locals poking about the merchandise, and seals who swim upriver in search of food scraps. From here you can also catch frequent and popular boat tours, which troll up and down the river, some stopping at points of interest (CH$10,000-18,000). It's best to bargain for a tour package that includes food and landings. Tour lengths vary, with the longest ones reaching the ocean (near Niebla) before returning.

Farther south and a block inland from the river, one of the two **Torreones de Valdivia,** built in the 1600s, continues to stand guard over the city's seaward ramparts. The other Torreón lies near the bus station, far to the east. Neither is much to look at, but romantics will appreciate the faint air of the Conquista that hangs around each of them. A block north of the more western Torreón is the **Centro Cultural el Austral,** Yungay 733 (☎213 658), a lovely building with free entry to view its art galleries. Painting lessons are offered by the artists-in-residence and a calendar of cultural events is available as well.

ISLA TEJA. Thousands of people walk across the Pedro de Valdivia bridge to Isla Teja every day, although most are students heading to the **Universidad Austral de Chile,** at the center of the island. Teja does, however, boast other attractions for a day of sightseeing. The first of these, the **Museo Histórico,** is an interesting stop—if only for the view. The old mansion has nice views of Valdivia, the river, and the university crew teams that row along it. The contents and displays in the museum itself are somewhat interesting. All labels are in Spanish. Many visitors stop to marvel at the "platería mapuche," a room featuring ornamental jewelry from the pre-Conquest days. *(On Los Laureles. Cross the bridge and take the first left, then follow the signs.* ☎212 872. *Open 10am-1pm and 2-8pm. CH$1200, children CH$300.)*

MUSEO DE ARTE CONTEMPORÁNEO. Intriguingly ensconced in the ruins of an old factory, this second of Isla Teja's museums offers views comparable to those of the Centro Cultural on the mainland; the artwork is interesting, but not worth a trip out of your way. *(Next to the Museo Histórico. Open 10am-2pm and 3-9pm. CH$1500.)*

PARKS. Behind the university are the **Botanical Gardens** and the **Parque Saval.** Both make for a lovely walk in nice weather with thousands of species of plants and flowers, many of them well-labeled. *(Open until dusk. Free.)*

NIEBLA ☎ 63

Lying at the mouth of the Río Valdivia, Niebla serves primarily as a summer haven for *Valdivianos* wanting to escape the city for a while to languish in a *cabaña* by the beach and soak up some sun. The rest of the year, the only attraction here is the nearly 400-year-old **fort** built (in 1643) by Spanish colonizers to guard the mouth of the Río Valdivia from seafaring invaders. While the fort itself is not the most exciting sight in the region, if you have the time for a tour, haggle a fair price with a guide (CH$1500) and learn the interesting history of Valdivia and the surrounding area. (Open Nov.-Mar. 10am-7pm; Apr.-Oct. 10am-5:30pm. CH$600, children CH$300.) If forts are not your cup of tea, stroll over to the cliffs, which offer picturesque views over the crashing waves below.

If you're hungry, stop by *empanada* stands at the fairgrounds (next to the bus terminal, by the road to the public beach) and pick up a dozen *empanadas* (CH$1800), or an *anticucho* (shish-kebab of beef and sausage with onion; CH$700). **Restaurant los Castellanos ❸,** Antonio Dulce 865, near the center of town, offers a more refined dining experience. True to its name, it serves *paella* (CH$4900), *tortillas* (omelettes with potato and onion; CH$3200), and other Spanish specialties. (☎282 082. Open 12:30-3pm and 7:45-11pm. AmEx/MC/V.)

Niebla features a short yet pleasant waterside walkway. Speckled with a few seafood restaurants and budget *hospedajes*, the otherwise-quiet town gets lively and brims with energy in the summer. Splurge and enjoy the biggest Niebla draw, a spacious and comfortable *cabaña* suitable for families or groups of friends. **Cabañas Parador ❸,** Del Castillo 975, right next to the plaza in front of the fort, offers well-equipped cabins elegantly built in the style of ships. Second-floor balconies overlook the fort and the ocean below. (☎282 080. 2-person *cabañas* CH$40,000 per night; 6-person *cabañas* CH$50,000 per night.) **Cabañas El Paso ❷,** 1125 Conde de Castellar, set farther back from the ocean and across the street from the fairgrounds, has standard *cabañas* at lower prices. (☎282 257. 5-person *cabañas*

CH$20,000.) **Camping ❶** is available throughout Niebla; just look for the signs that say "carpas," and break out the tent. (CH$1500 per person.)

All **buses** to or from Niebla stop by the fort, then continue to the beach and the hamlet of Los Molinos before returning to Valdivia (30min. from the Sernatur office, CH$400).

LAGO RANCO

Lago Ranco looks very much like a broad, deep-blue plain, with expansive, calm waters radiating tranquility into the small towns all around it. The lake, on the edge of the Andean foothills, offers gracious vistas of the transition from rough and mountainous to flat, central-valley terrain. Relatively under-touristed (as compared to some of its sibling-lakes in the region), Ranco has relatively few services and even fewer foreigners. Most visitors are avid Chilean anglers or wealthy *Santiaguinos* looking for a little relaxation. As a result, budget tourist infrastructure lacks the ease and convenience of much of the rest of Los Lagos.

FUTRONO ☎ 63

Arriving in Futrono early in the morning, you'll find it deserted and peaceful—that is, until roaring SUVs full of *Santiaguinos* take to the streets in search of food and supplies for days of fishing, tanning, or puttering about the lake. Futrono's one main street plays host to a string of "supermercados" (read: *bodegas*), which supply the needs of Futrono's resort-seeking summertime residents. Though this is the biggest town on Lago Ranco, there's little else here; despite the bustling main street, the town's beautiful setting makes for a nice stroll on a sunny day.

⌸ TRANSPORTATION. All **buses** to Futrono originate in Valdivia or Paillaco. **Buses Futrono** (☎ 481 279) services Valdivia (2hr.; M-Sa 13 per day 6:30am-7:30pm, Su 10 per day 7:55am-7:30pm; CH$1300) via Paillaco (1hr., CH$900). In Valdivia, connections can be made to cities farther afield. Otherwise, **Tur Bus** and **InterBus** (☎ 481 402) send buses to Santiago (12hr.; 7:30, 7:45, 8:30pm; CH$9000-12,000).

⬛▮ ORIENTATION AND PRACTICAL INFORMATION. Balmaceda is the main strip, with a ¼ mi. stretch of *supermercados, fruterías,* and restaurant/bars. The helpful **tourist office** is at the intersection of Balmaceda and O'Higgins, near the western end of town. Buses pass by it on the way in from Valdivia and Paillaco. This is a good place to consult

IN RECENT NEWS

ALL FALL DOWN

Visitors to Chile soon learn that one of the country's largest industries is logging—half the terrain is ideal for lush hardwood forests. The timber industry alone generates nearly $300 billion per year, more than 10% of Chile's total exports; 120,000 Chileans are employed directly by the timber industry. In south-central Chile, logging provides the lifeblood of economic development, especially in the regions of La Araucanía and Bío Bío.

This juggernaut, however, has recently come to head with another: the Mapuche. These indigenous people of southern Chile, famed for their ferocity and valor, have never sat idly as their traditions and lands have come under attack. Recently, as logging intensified, groups of Mapuche occupied several tracts of land owned by logging companies. The occupations drew in the Chilean Parliament and judicial system and were eventually resolved peacefully. Yet the issue remains.

Chileans are sharply divided over the question: some see the Mapuche as asserting their ancestral claims while others see them as hindering economic development. For many of Chile's one million Mapuche, however, this is a question of land rights dating back 500 years, when European settlers overran ancient Mapuche soil. Hopefully for the Mapuche, this time the result will not be the same.

LOS LAGOS

for up-to-date information on local tour guides and resorts. (☎482 636; turiftrn@telsur.cl. Open Dec.-Feb. M-F 9am-9pm, Sa-Su 10am-9pm; low season daily 9am-5pm.) The nearest **banks** are in Valdivia, so make sure to withdraw cash there before heading to Futrono. The **police**, Balmaceda 10, have a **24hr. guardia** at the *carabineros* station just a little bit fuather out of town (☎481 233). For those in search of **telephones**, try **Fotocentro**, Balmaceda 247, which houses a *centro de llamadas*. Fotocentro also has **Internet access**. (☎481 327. Open daily 8:30am-11pm. Internet CH$500 per hr.)

⌂⌂ ACCOMMODATIONS AND CAMPING. Though set back from the lake on Balmaceda, **Hospedaje Futronhue ❷**, Balmaceda 90, offers clean, airy rooms and surprisingly spacious bathrooms. (☎481 265. CH$4000 per person.) Or splurge at the luxurious **Caja Compensación Los Andes ❹**, a hotel complex on Acharán Arche, right behind the Plaza Municipal. Possibly the nicest place to stay in Futrono, the complex has posh rooms with balconies that overlook the lake and the lush Parque Futronhue, as well as an indoor pool and sauna, free for guests. At night, vacationing families relax in the billiard room and bar downstairs. (☎481 208. Doubles Jan.-Feb. CH$43,000; Mar.-Dec. CH$20,000.) **Camping ❷** by the lake may just be the best option for budget travelers; look for signs or simply knock on a door and ask where you can park your tent. (Sites CH$5000-10,000.)

⬛⬛ FOOD AND ENTERTAINMENT. The most chic restaurant in town, with a DJ and *tapas*-style menu, **Las Terrazas ❸**, Leo Degario 15, offers all the style of big-city fine dining, enhanced by gorgeous views from the restaurant's patio. Spanish-style cuisine includes traditional *tortillas*. (☎481 667. Open Dec.-Mar. Entrees served 12:30-3:30pm, CH$4000-6000. *Tapas* served 8pm-1:30am.) A cheaper, homestyle meal can be enjoyed at **Restaurant Don Floro ❷**, Balmaceda 114 (☎481 271). Hearty *almuerzos*, served Monday through Saturday, run about CH$3500, while the house specialty, *longaniza* sausage, costs CH$2500. The nearby **Restaurant Donde Chamullo ❷**, Balmaceda 565, specializes in shellfish and other seafood delicacies. They fry almost everything on the menu, but if you're feeling adventurous enough, sample from their diverse raw bar. (☎481 343. Fish entrees CH$2400-4500. *Paila marina* CH$2000. *Empanadas de mariscos* CH$3000 per dozen.) On weekends, the **Discoteca Osiada** on Gastón Guarda opens its doors to townies and tourists alike, and stays thumping until the wee hours of the morning.

⬛ OUTDOOR ACTIVITIES. Several parks and beaches can be accessed from Futrono via the 121km dirt road around Lago Ranco. Bus service here is irregular and sometimes non-existent, so it is best to rent (or have) a car. Even so, the road is not always passable, and sometimes the only option for cars other than 4WD vehicles is to return to the Panamerican and get at the lake from a different point. Nearby **Parque Futronhue** is a neatly manicured reserve with clearly labeled signs describing the flora to be found here. **Fishing, horseback riding, trekking, boating, rafting trips,** and other ecological excursions can be booked between November and April, but the schedules and offerings vary frequently, so consult with the tourist office to plan a trip (see **Orientation and Practical Information**, p. 355). Also ask about trips to **Isla Huapi**, a small island in Lago Ranco populated by native inhabitants (CH$35,000).

Coique, just west of Futrono, is a lakefront resort with various housing complexes on the water. The best known is **Bahía Coique ❺**, an expensive, all-amenities-included resort for wealthy Chileans. Coique's **beach** is the best on Lago Ranco and is consequently crowded during summer months. Six-person **camp-**

sites ❶ are available here for CH$15,000. Nearby **Llifén** is a natural and peaceful beach. Massive **Cerro Huequecura** (1584m) looms over the beach, making it a picturesque place to spend an afternoon swimming, picnicking, and fishing.

LAGO RANCO
☎ 63

Locals will tell you to go to Lago Ranco (the town—not to be confused with the lake of the same name) to get away from it all...and they do mean it *all*. This *pueblito* is little more than a few buildings lining a dusty highway. Travelers will enjoy the rustic attractiveness of the town and its backcountry setting. The addition of a few good budget lodgings make it a good place to just relax and enjoy all that the lake has to offer. Be forewarned: bus service is infrequent, and there is a palpable dearth of amenities.

If driving to Lago Ranco, turn off the highway that circuits the lake at the Río Bueno exit. The road into town winds downhill past the **municipal building** to the left, passing Calle Temuco and ending at Calle Viña del Mar on the lakefront. Coming east through town on the main road, the "highway" from the Río Bueno, veer left at the sign for the **tourist office,** a helpful shack full of info. (Open Dec.-Mar.) There is nowhere to change money in town, so get cash in Valdivia or Osorno.

If you decide to stay in town, try **Casona Italiana ❷,** Viña del Mar 145, a collection of six nice *cabañas* overlooking the water. The amiable owners permit barbecuing on their property, making for some festive summer nights. (☎491 225. Breakfast included. *Cabañas* CH$15,000-25,000.) For food, the lively dockside restaurant, **Ruca Ranco ❶,** cooks up good set meals for a pittance (CH$1500), but if you really want to hold on to your cash, try barbecuing at the park along the beach, 50 yards away from Casona Italiana.

OSORNO
☎ 64

Deep in the heartland of Chile, Osorno (pop. 105,000) has too few attractions to constitute a destination in and of itself. It does, however, boast a density of conveniences and transportation options unmatched in the surrounding area, making it a popular quick-fix stop for those who need to stock up on supplies or catch bus connections. A walk through the lively streets of Osorno's bustling downtown will also rejuvenate those who have grown weary of travels in cow country.

▐ TRANSPORTATION

Flights: Aeropuerto Carlos Hott Siebert, 7km east of town. **Taxi** from downtown CH$3500. **LanChile,** Ramírez 802 (☎600 526 2000, ext. 8), has flights to **Santiago** (CH$101,500) and **Temuco.**

Regional Buses: Long-distance buses leave from the **Terminal de Buses,** Errázuriz 1400 (☎234 149).

Cruz del Sur (☎232 777) and **Turibus** share a window, offering trips to: **Castro** (14 per day 6:30am-6:45pm, CH$5300) via **Ancud** (CH$3900); **Frutillar** (7 per day 7am-7:30pm, CH$1000); **Puerto Montt** (12 per day 7am-11pm, CH$1500); **Puerto Varas** (11 per day 7am-9:30pm, CH$1300); **Santiago** (8:30, 10:15, 11pm; CH$13,000, *salón cama* CH$23,000).

Bus Pirehueico departs for: **Bariloche, ARG** (5hr., 11:20pm, CH$10,000); **Panguipulli** (4hr.; 4 per day 8:20am-5:40pm, Su 3 per day 2:30-9pm; CH$3000) via **Valdivia** (M-Sa 7 per day 8:20am-9:40pm, Su 3 per day 3:30-8pm; CH$1500); **Puerto Montt** (M-Sa 7 per day 9:10am-7:45pm, Su 3 per day 10:45am-7:45pm; CH$1500).

Intersur sends buses to **Chillán** (8hr.; 9:30, 11:30am, 12:40pm; CH$8700); **Concepción** (9hr.; 8:35, 11am, 12:20pm; CH$7500); **Los Angeles** (5 per day 7:45am-midnight, CH$6600); **Santiago** (7 per day 7:15am-11:30pm, CH$10,000. *Salón cama* 8, 9, 10, 10:05pm; CH$13,200).

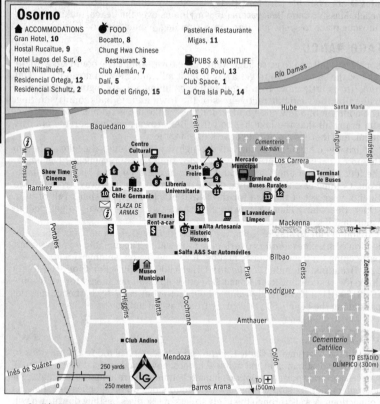

Osorno

🏠 ACCOMMODATIONS
Gran Hotel, **10**
Hostal Rucaitue, **9**
Hotel Lagos del Sur, **6**
Hotel Niltaihuén, **4**
Residencial Ortega, **12**
Residencial Schultz, **2**

🍴 FOOD
Bocatto, **8**
Chung Hwa Chinese Restaurant, **3**
Club Alemán, **7**
Dalí, **5**
Donde el Gringo, **15**

Pastelería Restaurante Migas, **11**

🍺 PUBS & NIGHTLIFE
Años 60 Pool, **13**
Club Space, **1**
La Otra Isla Pub, **14**

Queilén Bus heads to: **Coyhaique** (21hr.; Su-M, W, F 1:45pm; CH$20,000); **Punta Arenas** (28hr., 12:45pm, CH$38,000); **Santiago** (9:15pm, CH$10,000).

JAC serves: **Puerto Montt** (2hr., 7 per day 7:45am-10:45pm, CH$1500); **Santiago** (12hr., 8 per day 9am-11:30pm, CH$13,200); **Temuco** (4½hr.; 10am, 1:15, 5pm; CH$3600); **Valdivia** (1½hr., 4 per day 10am-6:10pm).

Bus Norte goes to: **Puerto Montt** (8:15 and 9:30am, CH$1500); **Santiago** (7:30 and 9:30pm, CH$10,000); **Valdivia** (7:30pm, CH$1500); **Valparaíso** (13hr., 7:30pm, CH$13,000).

Vía Octay heads to **Puerto Octay** (1hr.; M-Sa 15 per day 7:20am-8:30pm, Su 14 per day 8am-8pm; CH$700).

VíaTur runs buses to **Santiago** (12hr.; 7:30, 9, 10pm; CH$12,000).

Vía Bariloche serves **Bariloche, ARG** (4:30pm, CH$10,000).

Local Buses: Leave from the **Terminal de Buses Rurales** behind the Mercado Municipal, on the corner of Prat and Errázuriz. **Expreso Lagos Puyehue** (☎243 919) runs to: **Aguas Calientes** (1½hr., 9 per day 8am-7:15pm, CH$1200) via **Entre Lagos** (1hr., every 30-40min. 6:50am-9pm, CH$800); **Anticura** (min. 2 passengers; 10:30am, 3, 7:15pm; CH$5000). **Buses Río Negro** (☎249 682) serves **Río Negro** (M-Sa every 30min. 7am-9pm, Su every hr. 7am-9pm; CH$700).

Car Rental: Salfa A&S Sur Automóviles, Bilbao 992 (☎240 124 or 240 119), rents cars of varying sizes for CH$18,500-50,000 per day, including basic insurance. AmEx/MC/V. Across the street, **Full Travel Rent-a-car,** Mackenna 939 (☎235 579), offers similar prices. AmEx/MC/V.

AT A GLANCE

AREA: 1067.72 sq. km

CLIMATE: Temperate with a cool annual average temperature of 8°C.

HIGHLIGHTS: Hiking Sendero de Excursión al Volcán Puyehue and Volcán Casablanca. Hot springs at Aguas Calientes.

GATEWAYS: Osorno; Entre Lagos; Bariloche, ARG.

CAMPING: Camping and picnicking grounds are scattered throughout the park. Several *refugios* and *cabañas* are available along the trails.

◢◣ ◪ ORIENTATION AND PRACTICAL INFORMATION

The **Plaza de Armas** is in the center of town, bordered by **Ramírez** to the north, **Matta** to the east (where a tall, latticed cathedral faces the plaza), **Mackenna** to the south, and **O'Higgins** to the west. Banks surround the plaza, and several money exchanges operate just off the plaza on Ramírez. The long distance bus terminal exits onto Ramírez; reach the Plaza de Armas (less than 500m away), by turning right (to the south) out of the terminal and passing the municipal market and Plazuela Yungay (at Av. Prat), a busy little plaza with benches and foosball tables.

Tourist Office: Sernatur, O'Higgins 667 (☎234 104 or 237 575), offers some printed material and will try to answer questions. Open M-F 8:30am-6pm. Also has a **summer kiosk,** on the Plaza de Armas (open Jan.-Feb. 10am-8pm). There is another office at the **main bus terminal,** 2nd fl. (☎234 149). Open M-F 9am-1pm and 4-8pm. **Conaf,** Martínez de Rozas 430 (☎234 393), has limited information on PN Puyehue.

Tours: Club Andino, O'Higgins 1073 (☎232 297), can help arrange transportation to and within PN Puyehue for those interested in skiing at the Antillanca resort. (7-day all-inclusive ski packages US$640-930, depending on accommodations.) **Conaf** *guardaparque* Luis Santibáñez and his son, Gerardo (☎09 253 9150; raihuenecotour@hotmail.com) provide more convenient and friendly service, offering trips within the park as well as tours from Osorno and Puerto Montt. **Osorno-Aguas Calientes** CH$25,000; **Osorno-Antillanca** CH$55,000. Van to **PN Puyehue** from CH$20,000.

Currency Exchange: Cambiotur, Mackenna 1004 (☎234 846), is a good, reputable money exchange. Helpful staff also provides travel services. Other money changers are on Ramírez, off the plaza. Open M-F 9am-1pm and 3-7pm, Sa 10am-1pm.

Banks: Banks surround the Plaza de Armas. **Banco Santander** has 2 locations, at Matta and Ramírez and Mackenna and O'Higgins. Both have **24hr. ATM.** Open M-F 9am-2pm.

Bookstores: Librería Universitaria, Cochrane 545 (☎232 613), has a wide selection of novels and textbooks (open 9am-1:10pm and 3-7:30pm).

Outdoor Supplies: Climent Pezca y Caza, Angulo 603 (☎233 248), across the street from the bus station, has equipment for many different outdoor activities. Open M-Sa 9am-1pm and 2:30-7:30pm.

Laundromat: Lavandería Limpec, Prat 678 (☎238 966), just south of Plazuela Yungay. Wash and dry CH$3600. Turnaround 2hr. Open M-F 8:30am-7:30pm, Sa 8:30am-1pm.

Police: ☎133.

Hospital: Ambulance ☎131. **Hospital Base** (☎235 572) is 10 blocks south of the plaza on Buhler, in the southern part of the city center.

Telephones: Many *centros de llamadas* are around the plaza and on Ramírez. Travelers in the bus station can take advantage of the convenient **Duguet Centro de Llamadas,** (☎316 229), on the 2nd fl. Open daily 8am-midnight.

Internet Access: Fast, cheap connections can be found all over town. **Sagittarius Express,** Los Carrera 930 (☎316 584), 2 blocks north of the Plaza de Armas, charges CH$350 per hr. Open M-Sa 9am-2am, Su 9am-1am. **GEA.com,** Mackenna 1140 (☎09 067 3488), charges CH$500 per hr. Open daily 9am-midnight.

Post Office: O'Higgins 645 (☎235 176), next to Sernatur, just west of the plaza. Open M-F 9am-1pm and 2:30-6:30pm, Sa 10am-12:30pm.

ACCOMMODATIONS

Most comfortable places in Osorno will cost you a pretty penny. There are a few passable budget options near the bus station. In winter, however, Osorno can get quite cold, so consider paying extra for a room with a heater.

Residencial Ortega, Colón 602 (☎232 592), 1 block from the bus terminal. This *residencial,* which houses many truckers and traveling salesmen, is the best budget deal in town, with cheap prices and continental breakfast. CH$6000 per person. ❷

Residencial Schultz, Freire 530 (☎237 211), between Los Carrera and Ramírez, has hot water and heaters in the small, clean rooms. If no one answers the bell, knock on the wooden door next to the main entrance. Breakfast included. Singles CH$12,000; doubles CH$15,000. ❸

Hotel Niltaihuén, Los Carrera 951 (☎232 356 or 234 960), between Cochrane and Matta. Apartment-style rooms with complete kitchen and heating make this one of the best mid-range values in town, particularly for triples. Breakfast (CH$1600) can be served to your room. High-season singles CH$21,500; doubles CH$32,000; triples CH$31,700. Prices halved in low season. MC/V. ❹

Hostal Rucaitue, Freire 546 (☎239 922), has immaculate, elegant rooms with TVs and hot baths. A pleasant cafe serves up sandwiches (CH$1200-1800), and a small bar behind the cafe has draught beers (CH$700). Breakfast included. Singles CH$15,000; doubles CH$20,000. AmEx/MC/V accepted with 5% surcharge. ❹

Gran Hotel, O'Higgins 615 (☎232 171), on the corner with Ramírez. This classy, old hotel definitely needs some refurbishing, but still has some of its classic charm. Many rooms have balconies overlooking the plaza. Breakfast included. Singles CH$18,500; doubles CH$26,500. MC/V. ❹

Hotel Lagos del Sur, O'Higgins 564 (☎243 244). This upscale venue offers private bath, cable TV, laundry and room service, and central heating. Singles CH$33,700; doubles CH$42,700. AmEx/MC/V. ❺

FOOD

Osorno's questionable "city" status lends some cosmopolitan quality to its restaurants, which range from typical Chilean dives to upscale establishments.

Pastelería Restaurante Migas, Freire 584 (☎235 541), has the most tempting pastries in town. The gregarious owner, is of German descent and loves to practice English with patrons. Sandwiches, pizzas, baked *empanadas* CH$600-3000. *Tarteleta* of coconut, strawberries, and fresh cream CH$750. *Almuerzo* CH$1900-2400. Open 8am-9pm. ❷

Club Alemán, O'Higgins 563 (☎232 514), is a palpable vestige of German influence in the area. Patrons are greeted by a homey lobby behind which are 3 separate rooms that house the restaurant, cafe, and bar (also labeled Fogón Bar at a separate entrance). Meals are a fusion of German and Chilean cuisine. Entrees CH$3000-6000. *Almuerzo* CH$4600. Beer CH$800-1200. Open daily 11am-3:30pm and 7;11:30pm. MC/V. ❸

Dalí, Freire 542 (☎201 080), in the rear of Patio Freire. An elegant, relatively new addition, Dalí significantly elevates the city's offerings. Salmon with papaya and sage chutney and a side of polenta CH$6200. "Vegetarian" special includes hearts of palm, asparagus, cheese, mushrooms, and shrimp (CH$3600). Open noon-3pm and 7:30-11pm. AmEx/MC/V. ❹

Donde el Gringo, Mackenna 1027 (☎242 797), between Cochrane and Freire. Specializes in fine meat dishes such as succulent wild pig (CH$5000) and has the largest wine selection in Osorno. Steak and fish CH$3000-5000. Open daily noon-4pm and 8pm-midnight. AmEx/MC/V. ❸

Chung Hwa Chinese Restaurant, Matta 517 (☎243 445). No self-respecting Chilean city would be caught *chifa*-less, and Osorno is no exception. Tasty meals for 2 CH$6000. Entrees CH$2500-5000. Open daily noon-4pm and 7pm-midnight. MC/V. ❷

Bocatto, Ramírez 938 (☎238 000), between Cochrane and Matta, has sandwiches and pizzas (CH$1000-2000). *Helados* CH$650-1600. Open 10am-10pm. AmEx/MC/V. ❶

🗿 SIGHTS

Osorno has precious little to offer the sight-seer. That said, the pervasive Germanic influence is still very present in some of the city's buildings, particularly along Mackenna, south of the plaza, where a **Feria Artesanal** appears to have been built to attract tourists. A walk down this street will bring you past some of the oldest establishments in town, most built in 19th-century Victorian style. The section between Cochrane and Freire has been well-preserved, and has some quaint boutique stores and restaurants, including an exquisite handicraft store, **Alta Artesanía.** (Mackenna 1069. ☎232 446. Open M-F 9am-1pm and 3-5:30pm.)

The other potential attraction in Osorno is the **Museo Municipal,** Matta 896, on the corner of Bilbao. Although the collection is a little eclectic, it has some marginally interesting pieces. Keep an eye out for the classic Wurlitzer jukebox from Germany and the gorgeous old pipe organ. (☎264 358. Open M-Th 9:30am-6pm, F 9:30am-5pm, Sa 2-7pm. Free.)

🎭 🎷 ENTERTAINMENT AND NIGHTLIFE

As in many Chilean cities, the main event is always the goings-on of the local soccer team. Catch a game at the **Estadio Olímpico** (☎233 211). **Show Time Cinema,** Ramírez 650, local 16 (☎233 890), at the back of the mall, plays subtitled and dubbed English films (CH$2400). To get your **shopping** fix, head to the **Plaza Germania,** on the northern end of the Plaza de Armas. A tribute to Osorno's love of shopping malls, it offers all the chain-stores you've been missing. **Patio Freire,** on Freire south of Los Carrera, offers similar features, around a well-manicured central garden. Nightlife options are few, but nonetheless worthy of a night on the town.

La Otra Isla Pub, Freire 677 (☎09 203 6391), on the corner with Mackenna, has a log-cabin exterior and a fun, lively atmosphere inside. The owner has been known to cover the floor with sand for "beach" parties. The well-stocked bar tends to draw a fairly professional crowd. Beer and mixed drinks CH$1500-3000. Open W-Sa 8pm-5am.

Club Space, Los Carrera 620 (www.space.telsur.cl), near the corner with Portales. The rowdy downstairs attracts mostly university students, while upstairs is a chill bar scene. Drinks CH$2000-3000. Cover F-Sa CH$2000.

Años 60 Pool, Colón 599, has a bright, fun atmosphere and stays open late enough for you to play a few games. Pool CH$1100 per hr. Open daily 10:30am-1am.

PARQUE NACIONAL PUYEHUE

Nestled in the foothills of the Andes, this park is one of Chile's most developed and visited for two reasons: the hot springs in Aguas Calientes and the skiing in Sector Antillanca. While *Santiaguinos* come to escape the city and enjoy the luxury of spa and/or ski resort lifel, the park does contain volcanoes, a wealth of fauna, and a gorgeous expanse of forest that is home to over 600 species of flora, while its trails snake through verdant *bosque* to emerge on jagged peaks.

📛 TRANSPORTATION. The park lies on Ruta 215, which runs from Osorno over the border to Bariloche, Argentina. At Km76, highway U-485 splits off to the south, passing through the main *guardaparque* at Aguas Calientes before continuing another 18km to the ski resort at Antillanca. Buses run regularly into the park from Osorno (see **Transportation,** p. 357). **Club Andino** in Osorno (see **Tours,** p. 359) can help arrange transportation within the park for guests of the ski resort.

⛄🏂 ORIENTATION AND PRACTICAL INFORMATION. The park is divided into three sectors—Aguas Calientes, Sector Anticura, and Sector Antillanca. Aguas Calientes's main attraction is the renowned hot springs. Sector Anticura, traversed by the Río Gol-Gol, is best suited to hiking, with trails extending from the entrance to Volcán Puyehue (10km), Los Baños (20km), Pampa Frutilla (20km), and Lago Constancia (28km). Sector Antillanca is home to Volcán Casablanca, a high-end resort, and some of the best skiing in the area. The park's ski center sits at the base of Volcán Casablanca.

The main **Conaf** office (☎197 4572) for the park lies in Sector Aguas Calientes, although Sector Anticura and Sector Antillanca also have central Conaf outposts. **Information centers** are located in Aguas Calientes and Anticura. A small **store** resides next to the concessionary restaurant in Aguas Calientes, but selections are extremely limited, so it's best to bring your own supplies. (Open daily 9am-1pm and 2-9pm.) There are public **telephones** in Aguas Calientes, but they do not accept coins; cards must be purchased at the kiosk in front of the Conaf headquarters. (Open daily 10am-1:30pm and 3-7:30pm.)

The **ski resort** (☎235 114; antillanca@telsur.cl) in Antillanca can be reached year-round, although winter is obviously the busiest season. For those looking for package deals to the park's snowy slopes, check out Club Andino in Osorno.

🏠🍴 ACCOMMODATIONS AND FOOD. Most established lodgings in the park lie in Aguas Calientes; less expensive options can be found nearby on Ruta 215 between Osorno and the park, particularly in Entre Lagos. **Cabañas Nilque ❹,** Km65 from Osorno, rents cabins for relatively affordable prices, and offers discounts for long stays. (☎371 218. *Cabañas:* 1 person US$35; 2 people US$50; 3 people US$65; 4 people US$80; 5 people US$953. Prices halved Mar.-Nov.) Reservations can be made at the travel agency below the hotel (☎232 356; turismonilque.cl).

At Aguas Calientes, a Conaf-contracted **concessionary ❸** offers expensive, resort-style *cabañas* and limited camping. (☎331 700. Camping max. 4 people CH$14,000; additional persons CH$2500 each. *Cabañas* CH$77,000-91,000; low- season CH$37,000-69,000. AmEx/MC/V.) There are similar campsites and *cabañas* in Sector Anticura; contact the Aguas Calientes location for reservations. (Camping max. 4 people CH$10,000; *cabañas* CH$20,000-40,000.) **Termas Puyehue Resort with Gran Hotel and Spa ❺** resides just outside of the park, within easy reach of the Aguas Calientes entrance. This gorgeous hotel is connected to a beautiful, modern spa, slightly more expensive than that inside the park, but also of better quality. Rooms in the newer section of the hotel have cable TV and are more expensive, as are those with views of the volcano to the north. (☎232 157. Breakfast and hot springs entrance included. Singles US$55-108; doubles US$88-140. AmEx/MC/V.)

There aren't many options for food outside the resorts. The Aguas Calientes facility has a **cafe ❶** that serves sandwiches (CH$600-1000), drinks, and ice cream. The more upscale **Restaurant Las Canelas ❸,** also run by the resort, lies across the road. The menu is a montage of traditional Chilean dishes and a few more international selections. (Entrees CH$2000-6000. AmEx/MC/V.) Right behind Las Canelas lies **El Quincho ❹,** a concession to Chilean meat-worship. This eatery is devoted to serving as much meat as possible, grilled and mixed together in traditional *parrilladas* of chicken, beef, lamb, veal, and sometimes seafood. (*Parrilladas* for 2 CH$10,500. AmEx/MC/V.) For budget travelers, the only worthwhile option is to bring food and eat where you can find a spot. There are two official **picnicking sites** in the park; but these will cost you as well. (CH$3000 per table.)

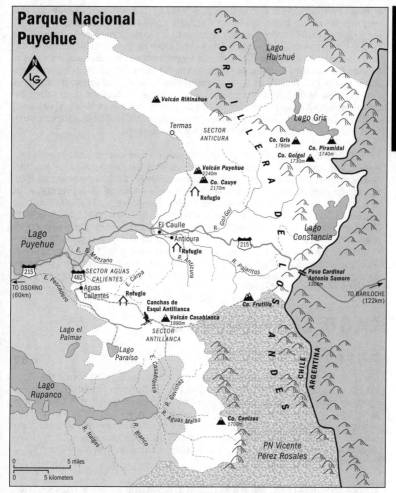

Parque Nacional Puyehue

HIKING. Sector Aguas Calientes is is home to the main **Conaf** station and several short hikes. The longest of these is **Sendero Berlín** (11km, 5hr. round-trip), which winds its way all the way to Lago Berlín and terminates at a small *refugio*. **Sendero Pionero** (1.8km, 1¼hr. round-trip) climbs its way up tallest hill in the sector with a great view of Lago Puyehue and the Río Chanleufú; **Sendero El Recodo** (380m, 15min.) is less of a trail than a short jaunt to the picnic grounds. **Sendero Los Rápidos,** across the bridge over the outdoor *termas*, leads to a short stretch of rapids on the nearby Río Chanleufú (1.25km, 40min.).

Sector Anticura has the most extensive trail system. For those wanting to start off easier, there are several **miradores** that can be easily accessed from the *guardaparque* in this sector. Across from the Conaf office are trails to **Salto del Indio** (900m) and **Salto de Fla Princesa** (1.2km); each takes at most 15min. each way. For those who want to take on some more serious trekking, there are several excursions. **Sendero de Excursión**

al Volcán Puyehue starts at Fundo el Caulle (on Ruta 215, Km89, west of Anticura) and runs through private land to a 12-person *refugio* at the rim of Volcán Puyehue (5km, 6hr. one-way; CH$7000 to enter trail), then continues to the *termas* at Azufreras (3km farther, 4hr. one-way). From here, a 1½-day trail leads northward to Riñinahue, on the shores of Lago Ranco, where buses depart for civilization. The other major venture is **Sendero de Excursión a la Pampa de Frutilla** (20km, 2-3 days). From Ruta 215, Km94, near Anticura, the trail follows an ancient road through a stretch of forest, then ends at Cerro Frutilla, in the park's southeastern region. Sector Antillanca in the south of the park does not have much hiking, other than an excursion between Volcán Casablanca and Lago Rupanco. A short trail leads up to a crater on Casablanca's western side, from which visitors can enjoy views of the surrounding area.

▲ OUTDOOR ACTIVITIES. At Aguas Calientes, thermal waters, suffused with iron sulfate, sodium chloride, and lithium, come bubbling out of the ground at a steamy 75°C, providing one of the park's main attractions. Visitors flock to the resort for luxurious treatments ranging from a simple dip in one of the thermal pools (maintained at 40°C) to massages and aromatherapy. (☎331 700. Indoor hot pool CH$4500; outdoor hot pool CH$1200; hot tub treatments CH$5000; massage CH$12,000; mudbath CH$10,000; aromatherapy CH$7000. Indoor pool open 8:30am-8pm; outdoor pool open 8:30am-7pm.) The resort also has four-person **cabañas ❺** that it rents out to guests with a little advance notice (see **Accommodations and Food,** p. 362). The Osorno office, O'Higgins 784 (☎232 881), runs daytrips. If booking through the office, opt for the package deal including lunch and pool fees to get the best value (with open-air pool CH$8000, indoor pool CH$10,000).

LAGO LLANQUIHUE

PUERTO OCTAY ☎64

Comfortably situated on the quiet side of Lago Llanquihue, an hour's ride from Puerto Varas or Frutillar, Puerto Octay sees drastically fewer tourists. Here, there's space to enjoy the lake and brilliantly colorful German colonial architecture with some modicum of peace. Appropriately, Puerto Octay also serves as a convenient departure point for wilder destinations in and around Volcán Osorno and Parque Nacional Vicente Pérez Rosales; those who find their way here generally stay a few days, relax at the beach, and enjoy relatively crowdless hikes on the volcano's less-frequented northern side.

▣ TRANSPORTATION. Buses depart from a station atop the hill, at Balmaceda and Esperanza, to Osorno (1hr.; M-F every 15-30min. 6:30am-8pm, Sa-Su every 15-30min. 8am-9pm; CH$700) and Puerto Montt (1½hr, 5 per day 8:05am-6:05pm, CH$1400) via Puerto Varas (1hr., CH$1200) and Frutillar (45min., CH$700).

▣▣ ORIENTATION AND PRACTICAL INFORMATION. Esperanza and **Germán Wulf** serve as the main thoroughfares, running north-south, intersected by Independencia at the lakeshore and Balmaceda and Amunátegui farther uphill, where the **Plaza de Armas** marks the center of town. The **tourist information kiosk,** next to the municipal offices on Esperanza to the east of the Plaza de Armas, has a map posted to help travelers find important municipal services. (☎391 750. Open Dec.-Mar. Tu-Su.) **BancoEstado,** Pedro Montt 345, north of Independencia, has a **24hr. ATM.** (☎391 425. Open M-F 9am-2pm.) Conveniently located below the Hospedaje Teuber (see **Accommodations and Food,** below), **Supermercado Teuber** offers the best selection of groceries in town. (☎391 438. Open daily 8:30am-4pm.)

Emergency services include a 24hr. **police** station, Germán Wulf 797 (☎391 615), on the northern end of town across from the Shell station, and a **hospital,** Pedro Montt 601, across the diagonal street northeast of the Plaza de Armas. (☎259 265, emergency 259 260. Primary care open M-F 8am-4:30pm. Emergency room open 24hr.) A small **centro de llamadas** in the bus station (open 9am-10pm) supplements the **Entel** center, Pedro Montt 387, north of the bank. (☎391 554. Open 9am-10pm.) The municipal **library,** Independencia 591, on the corner of Esperanza, provides the only public **Internet access** in town. (☎391 523. 30min. free. Open M-F 9:30am-1pm and 2-7pm.) The **post office,** Esperanza 555, resides within the municipal building. (☎391 429. Open M-F 9am-12:30pm and 2:30-5:30pm, Sa 9am-12:30pm.)

▐▓ ACCOMMODATIONS AND FOOD. Probably the best reason to stay in Puerto Octay is ▓**Zapato Amarillo Backpacker ❷,** 2.5km north of town on the road to Osorno. Frequent buses run this way and will know where to stop if you ask. Look for the yellow boot, follow the driveway past the first cluster of houses, and go right at the gate. The multilingual family is a great travel resource, offering all sorts of perks from their warm, cozy, grass-roofed chalet. A brand-new building next to the main home houses a dormitory and a dining room where the lovely Nadia serves up what are probably the best dinners in all of Region X (CH$4500). This is *the* place to stay in Puerto Octay (and maybe in all of Llanquihue), so reserve ahead. (☎391 575. Call from town for pickup. Bicycles, canoes, laser sailboats, and mountaineering equipment for rent. Tours and transport around the lake offered. Internet, kitchen access, and breakfast included. Dorms CH$6000; doubles CH$14,000.) A cheaper, plainer option is **Hospedaje Teuber ❶,** Germán Wulf 712, above the grocery store. (☎09 641 5300 or 09 644 0240. Kitchen access. Shared bath. Breakfast CH$500. Rooms CH$3500 per person.)

The delicious smells of **Baviera ❶,** Germán Wulf 587, coyly tempt passersby, many of whom stay for a thoroughly satisfying *almuerzo* (CH$3000) of *cazuela, segundo,* and dessert. The bar next door offers Cristal to wash it all down. (☎391 460. Open daily 10am-11pm.)

◙▟ SIGHTS AND OUTDOOR ACTIVITIES. For historical background on Llanquihue's 150-year-old German colonization, check out the **Museo el Colono,** Independencia 591. During the low season, only one room is open, but aficionados of the *colonización alemana* will find it worth a visit. (☎391 523. Open Dec.-Mar. Tu-Su 10am-1pm and 3-7pm; Apr.-Nov. M-F 8:30am-12:30pm and 1:45-6:30pm. Dec.-Mar. CH$500; Apr.-Nov. free.) The walking-tour brochure, **Histórico Paseo de Puerto Octay,** will direct you to the town's oldest and most colorful buildings. Find copies of the brochure at the museum or at Zapato Amarillo (see above).

Puerto Octay claims more deserved fame, however, for its proximity to some of Lago Llanquihue's most appealing attractions. At **Las Cascadas,** on the eastern side of the lake between Puerto Octay and Ensenada, a short 30min. trail leads to a lovely 90m waterfall. Buses generally run every hour or so from the highway intersection 9km north of Puerto Octay (accessible by any bus bound for Osorno). The last bus returns early in the evening. Ask bus drivers for confirmation.

The northern escarpment of **Volcán Osorno,** also conveniently near Puerto Octay, tempts climbers and hikers alike. A 3hr. trail leads from the Conaf *refugio* down to Petrohué, and offers extensive views of Lago Todos los Santos; ask at Zapato Amarillo for details on transportation to and from the trail. Those hoping to conquer the volcano should also inquire at Zapato Amarillo, where up-to-date information can be found on less-frequented (and sometimes less technical) ascents.

FRUTILLAR ☎65

Ten blocks long and two blocks deep along a crescent-shaped shoreline, fashionable **Frutillar Bajo** is a resort town that exists for about four months per year. From December through March, the town hops with wealthy Chilean visitors. Almost every residence puts out a *"hospedaje"* sign, and festivities peak with the **Semana de Musical Frutillar,** a celebration of classical music and jazz in late January or early February (see www.semanasmusicales.cl for current details). For the rest of the year, however, the town is not known for rocking 'n' rolling—even sports and picnics are prohibited on the inviting shoreside park. Peaceful, quiet, and perhaps unnervingly picturesque, this historic German settlement offers rest and relaxation to those who flock to its sheltered shores.

Frutillar Alto, 4km west of Frutillar Bajo, is indisputably the more rowdy and practical of the towns, offering **supermarkets,** a **police station,** a **medical center,** and **buses** to the outside world.

◘ TRANSPORTATION. Frequent **buses** (CH$200) and **colectivos** (CH$250) connect Frutillar Bajo and Alto; pick one up on Philippi in Frutillar Bajo, or anywhere along Carlos Richter. From the **bus station** at the top of Carlos Richter, *micros* run to Puerto Montt (every 15min. 8:30am-9pm, CH$1000) via Puerto Varas (CH$700), as well as to Puerto Octay (every 2hr. 7:15am-7:15pm, CH$600).

▌▐ ORIENTATION AND PRACTICAL INFORMATION. The two towns are connected by **Carlos Richter,** which runs perpendicular to the shoreline. In Frutillar Bajo, the main drag along the shoreline is **Philippi,** with **Vicente Pérez Rosales** one block from the lake.

The **visitor information kiosk** (☎420 198), in the middle of town on the Plaza de Armas, operates from December 22 through February 22. **Banco Santander,** Philippi 555, at the north end of town, has a **24hr. ATM.** (☎421 228. Open M-F 9am-2pm.) The **police station** (☎422 435) stands on Carlos Richter. **Internet access** is only to be found in Frutillar Alto's call centers. **Servitel Centro de Llamadas,** Philippi 883, charges CH$900 per hr. (Open Jan.-Mar. daily 9:30am-11:30pm.) More connections can be found at the small **post office,** Vicente Pérez Rosales 172, at the corner with San Martín, one block north of the *municipalidad.* (☎422 479. Postal services open M-Sa 9am-4pm. Internet available M-Sa 9am-11:30pm. CH$1000 per hr.)

▐▌ ACCOMMODATIONS AND FOOD. In summer, it pays to reserve accommodations well in advance, especially around the music festival. *Hospedajes* in town charge a premium for the scenery and small-town ambience. **Turismo el Arroyo ❸,** Philippi 989, operates a spacious, year-round *hospedaje* that offers one of the best values in town. (☎421 560. Breakfast included. Rooms with shared bath CH$6000 per person, low-season CH$4000; *matrimoniales* with private bath CH$15,000.) **Hotel Trayen ❸,** Philippi 963, above the restaurant of the same name, makes a great deal for mid-range shoppers. Rooms have private bath, personal heaters, cable TV, and balconies overlooking the lake. (☎421 346. Singles CH$10,000; *matrimoniales* CH$20,000.) **Hostería Winkler ❹,** Philippi 1155, a gracious German colonial mansion near the south end of town, smells of roses (from the prolific garden outside) and makes up for small rooms with spotless private baths and ample breakfasts. (☎421 388. Singles CH$10,000; *matrimoniales* CH$20,000.) **Hotel Am See ❺,** Philippi 539, north of the town center, is among the town's most luxurious accommodations, with grand views. Not surprisingly, it is also among the most expensive. (☎421 539; fax 421 858; ciberg@123mail.cl. Cable TV. Private bath. Breakfast included. Singles CH$30,000; doubles CH$40,000. Low-season CH$14,000/CH$20,000.) Shaded tent sites are available about 1.5km south of town at **Camping Los Ciruelillos ❶,** visible from town with its long, cookie-cutter hotel building and pre-fabricated *cabañas.* (☎420 163. Showers and kitchen. 2-person sites CH$5000; 6-person sites CH$10,000; *cabañas* for 6 CH$30,000.)

Tourist prices are also applicable to many of Frutillar's restaurants. A notable exception is **Café Al Paso ❶,** Jorge Montt 93B, a small stand where sandwiches and hamburgers go for CH$700-1200, and an *"empanada* + té" combo will set you back just CH$500. (Open daily 8:30am-10pm.) **Trayen Salón de Té ❶**, Philippi 963, offers affordable *kuchen* (a German fruit tart) and *churrasco con palta y tomate* (grilled meat with avocado and tomato; CH$1900), as well as unbelievably tempting cakes in the display case. (☎421 346. Open Jan.-Feb. 8am-10pm; Mar.-Dec. 8am-8pm.) Those looking for a bit heavier fare will be welcomed at bright, trendy **Café Restaurant Colonos del Lago ❷**, Philippi 883, at the corner with Jorge Montt. A sedate setting provides pleasant ambience to accompany an ample selection of omelettes (CH$1000-3000), aperitifs, and more traditional salmon entrees (CH$4000-6000). (☎421 110. Open Jan.-Mar. 10am-midnight.)

🆆 **SIGHTS.** The **Museo Colonial Alemán**, on Vicente Pérez Rosales at the north end of town near Richter, provides some insight into the German colonial exodus to the Llanquihue area following the Democratic Revolution of 1848 in Germany; in fact, it's probably the best museum of its kind in the area. A small house with a working waterwheel houses a textual record of the history of Germans in Chile, while the two outlying houses replicate the abodes of both wealthy and modest German settlers. (☎421 142. Open Jan.-Feb. daily 10am-8pm; Mar.-Dec. Tu-Su 10am-2pm and 3-8pm. CH$1600, children CH$500.) The **Bosque Nativo Chile**, at the Centro Experimental Forestal Edmundo Winkler on the extreme north end of town, is a sort of woodlands observatory, home to a group of friendly, informative naturalists who "just love this land." A short nature trail (800m) exists to illustrate the diversity and qualities of various local arboreal species, but also serves as an excellent afternoon stroll; the trees provide a meditative, seductively beautiful retreat from Frutillar's jaunty tourism. (☎422 307. Open daily 10am-7pm or sunset. CH$1000, children CH$500.) Should you tire of both tourists and trees, you can check out the gargantuan chess set right in front of the *municipalidad*. Two-foot-tall pawns make for a game that's strenuous physically as well as mentally.

PUERTO VARAS ☎65

Unlike industrial Puerto Montt, 20km to the south, Puerto Varas is not really much of a *puerto*. In fact, it has only one pier, which supports a visitor information stand and souvenir shop, rather than a fleet of fishing boats. Puerto Varas may be a bit too touristy for some—tour agencies hang carved wooden signs on nearly every square foot of the downtown grid. Nevertheless, with plentiful *hospedajes* and all the conveniences of home, this German colonial town makes a great jumping-off point for exploration of the surrounding region. On sunny days, Puerto Varas is brilliant; locals call their home "the city of roses," after the flowers that bloom in its well-manicured gardens. And if you should tire of smelling the roses, you need only look up to enjoy stellar views of Volcán Osorno, just across the lake.

▐ TRANSPORTATION

Flights: The **airport** is 45km away, beyond Puerto Montt, but **LanChile,** Granado 560 (☎234 799), operates an office in town. Open M-F 10am-1:30pm and 3-8pm, Sa 10am-2pm. To get to the airport, take a *micro* to Puerto Montt (see below; CH$700) and then board a big, blue **Pullman** airport bus (CH$1000). A taxi to the airport costs CH$11,000-12,000.

Buses: Long-distance buses do not leave from a single terminal; 5 different companies maintain offices in town.

Tur Bus, San Pedro 210 (☎233 787). To: **Santiago** (6, 8, 9:10pm; CH$13,400; *Salón cama* 6:30, 7:45, 8:50pm; CH$27,100); **Temuco** (6hr., 8 per day 10:15am-9:10pm, CH$4700) via **Osorno** (1hr., 11 per day 10:15am-9:10pm, CH$1400) and **Valdivia** (3hr., 7 per day, CH$2800).

Tas Choapa, W. Martínez 230 (☎233 831), goes to: **Bariloche, ARG** (M, W, F 10am; Tu, Th, Sa 1pm. CH$10,000); **Osorno** (CH$1300); **Santiago** (6:15, 8:15pm; CH$10,000; *Salón cama* 8:30pm, CH$18,000).

Cruz del Sur, W. Martínez 299B (☎231 925), departs from a terminal southeast of town at San Francisco 1317, near the bus station. To: **Bariloche, ARG** (daily 8:50am, Th and Su 11:15am; CH$10,000); **Castro** (5 per day 9:15am-9:55pm, CH$4000) via **Ancud** (CH$2900); **Santiago** (12hr.; 6:50, 8:35, 10:15pm; CH$14,000; *salón cama* 6:45, 9pm; CH$24,000); **Temuco** (10 per day 7:20am-10:15pm, CH$4000) via **Osorno** (CH$1300) and **Valdivia** (CH$2000).

Andina del Sud, Del Salvador 72 (☎232 811; www.crucedelagos.cl), is the only operator that runs the expensive hybrid bus/boat trip to **Bariloche, ARG,** including 3 bus legs and 2 lake crossings. (Jan.-Feb. 12hr.; 9am; US$140, not including lodging and food. Mar.-Dec. 2 days, 1 night in Peulla; US$210.) Office open Jan.-Feb. 8am-8pm; Mar.-Dec. 8:30am-1pm and 4-7pm.

Micros: The *micro* system, chaotic and variable, is mediated somewhat by the fact that all east-, north-, and Puerto-Montt-bound *micros* stop in front of Restaurant Don Jorge (p. 371), at the corner of San Bernardo and W. Martínez, across from Supermercado O'Higgins. **Expresos** run to **Llanquihue** (every 5-10min., CH$300) and **Puerto Montt** (every 5-10min., CH$700). **Thaebus** goes to **Frutillar** (every 10-15min. until 7:30pm, CH$600) via **Llanquihue** and **Puerto Octay** (every 2½hr. until 6:20pm; CH$1000). **Interlagos** (☎257 015) goes to **Ensenada** (every 30min., CH$1000) and **Petrohué** (every hr., CH$1200). **Buses Fierro** (☎253 022) goes to **Ensenada. Suyai** also runs buses to **Puerto Chico** and **Puerto Montt.** Fares are fixed. Look for the destination on the windshield and flag down the bus.

Taxis: Can be found at the taxi stand across from the Vyhmeister supermarket (see below) and at the intersection of Santa Rosa and Del Salvador. **Radio Taxi** (☎310 870) offers call-based service. *Colectivos* run to **Puerto Chico** and other neighborhoods.

Bike Rental: Informatur (see below) rents bikes for CH$1000 per hr.

▓✱❷ ORIENTATION AND PRACTICAL INFORMATION

It's fairly easy to get oriented downtown—look for the main lakeside quadrant, the **Plaza de Armas.** The major northwest-southeast thoroughfare is **San Francisco,** which continues south to access **Ruta 5 Sur** to Puerto Montt. Running northeast-southwest, **San José** and **Del Salvador** extend beyond town to **Ruta 5 Norte** toward Osorno. **Costanera,** along the shoreline, heads east through Puerto Chico along the south side of the lake to Ensenada and Petrohué. **San José** becomes **Granado** beyond San Bernardo, but the changeover is unmarked and somewhat confusing.

Tourist Office: Informatur (☎338 542), at the corner of San José and Santa Rosa. Its status as a subscription-based tourist promotion agency undermines its quantity and quality of information. Open Nov.-Mar. 8am-11pm, Apr.-Oct. 9am-2pm and 3-7pm. **Información Turística** (☎237 956), on the pier, has less biased info and better maps. Open 9am-10pm.

Tours: There are at least a dozen adventure tour operators in town, but two of them handle most of the walk-in, independent traveler business. **Al Sur Expeditions,** Del Salvador 100 (☎232 300; www.alsurexpeditions.com), on the lake side of the Plaza de Armas, offers **rafting** on the Petrohué (5hr., CH$20,000), **horseback riding** (half-day CH$30,000; full-day CH$55,000), and an **ascent of Osorno** (12hr., 5am, US$220 including climbing equipment). They also offer hard-to-find trips to **Parque N3acional Pumalín.** (6-day, 5-night kayaking trips US$990; 4-day, 3-night trekking tours US$690. AmEx/MC/V.) **Tranco Expediciones,** San Pedro 422 (☎311 311), offers similar trips and prices. AmEx/MC/V. **Ko' Kayak,** San José 320 (☎346 433; www.paddlechile.com), offers lake and **river kayaking** as well as trips on **Estuario Reloncaví.**

Currency Exchange: Exchange Ltda., Del Salvador 257, local #11 (☎232 019), cashes traveler's checks and changes cash. Open Dec. 15-Mar. daily 15 9am-8:30pm, Mar. 16-Dec 14 M-F 9am-2pm and 3-7pm. **AFEX,** San Pedro 414 (☎232 377), offers the same services. Open daily Dec.-Mar. 9am-9pm; Apr.-Nov. 9am-6pm.

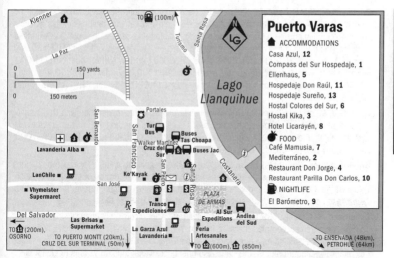

Puerto Varas

⌂ ACCOMMODATIONS
Casa Azul, 12
Compass del Sur Hospedaje, 1
Ellenhaus, 5
Hospedaje Don Raúl, 11
Hospedaje Sureño, 13
Hostal Colores del Sur, 6
Hostal Kika, 3
Hotel Licarayén, 8
🍴 FOOD
Café Mamusia, 7
Mediterráneo, 2
Restaurant Don Jorge, 4
Restaurant Parilla Don Carlos, 10
🌙 NIGHTLIFE
El Barómetro, 9

LOS LAGOS

Banks: There are a host of banks in the downtown area, most with **ATMs. BancoEstado,** Santa Rosa 414 (☎232 296) has a **24hr. ATM.** Other options include **Banco Santander,** San José 291 (☎235 670), on the corner of San Pedro.

Bookstore: El Libro del Capitán, 418 W. Martínez (☎234 501), boasts a stack of books in English and German. Exchange possible. Open M-Sa 10am-1:30pm and 4-9:30pm.

Supermarkets: Vyhmeister, Granado 565 (☎232 831), just past San Bernardo. Open M-Sa 8:30am-10pm, Su 9am-9:30pm. Also **Las Brisas,** Del Salvador 451 (☎346 400), across from the Esso station. Open daily 8:30am-10pm.

Laundromat: Lavandería Alba, 511 W. Martínez (☎232 908), has wash and dry services for CH$1500 per kg. **La Garza Azul Lavandería,** San Pedro 563 (☎09 458 3677), washes and dries for CH$1500 per kg.

Police: ☎133. Also at the northern end of San Francisco (☎237 449 or 237 455), past W. Martínez on the right.

Pharmacy: Salcobrand (☎234 544), at the corner of Del Salvador and San Francisco. A rotating 24hr. pharmacy list is posted here. Open daily 9am-11pm. AmEx/MC/V.

Hospital: Ambulance ☎133. **Clínica Alemana/Hospital San José,** Otto Bader 810 (☎232 336), has 24hr. urgent care. Another option is **Centro Médico,** W. Martínez 576 (☎232 792).

Telephones: For relatively convenient hours, try **Entel** (☎234 905), near San José and San Francisco. Open M-Sa 9am-9:30pm.

Internet Access: Internet centers cluster around the intersection of San Pedro and Del Salvador; it's best to shop around for competitive pricing. For a sure thing, head to **Red-Tel,** Granado 560 (☎232 775), where prices hover around CH$500 per hr. Open M-Sa 10am-2pm and 4-7pm.

Post Office: San José 242 (☎232 304), at the corner of San José and San Pedro. Open M-F 9am-1pm and 3-6pm, Sa 9am-1pm.

🏛 ACCOMMODATIONS

Puerto Varas's accommodations boast some of the best variety and most consistent quality in Los Lagos. Consequently, many travelers sleep here and take daytrips to the smaller, more expensive outlying communities along the lake. In summer, reservations are advised, and prices rise with the tourist tide.

Compass del Sur Hospedaje, Klenner 467 (☎232 044; mauro98@telsur.cl). Mauricio, the friendly English- and German-speaking owner, will help you get your bearings in this gracious German colonial house on the west side of town. Comfortable beds, a spacious, well-supplied kitchen, and a multilingual crowd make stays a pleasure. Owner rents out his car (CH$35,000 per day). Internet CH$900 per hr. Bike rental CH$6000 per day. Airport shuttle CH$11,000. Continental breakfast included; full breakfast CH$1000. Laundry CH$3500. Camping CH$6000 per tent. Dorms CH$7000; singles CH$11,000; doubles CH$18,000; triples CH$24,000. ❸

Casa Azul, Manzanal 66 (☎232 904; www.casaazul.net), at the intersection with Del Rosario. This bright blue, newly renovated hostel lives up to its name, standing out in a rather tame suburban neighborhood. Has a kitchen, book exchange, and central heating. Dorms CH$7000; singles CH$10,000; doubles CH$14,000. ❷

Hotel Licarayén, San José 114 (☎232 305). If you are going to splurge for accommodations in Puerto Varas, this is your place. Rooms are bright and well-decorated, with cable TV, balconies, palatial bathrooms, and views of the lake. "Superior" lodgings have large bathtubs. Breakfast included. "Standard" singles US$60; "superior" US$75. ❺

Ellenhaus, W. Martínez 239 (☎233 577; ellenhaus@yahoo.com). Ellenhaus's simple exterior houses an extremely complex, mazelike interior. Within the labyrinth, however, you'll find stellar common spaces, including a large kitchen, cable TV, and a ping-pong table, all accompanied by relatively standard rooms. The Haus also offers occasional tours to various Region X destinations. Breakfast CH$1500. Laundry CH$1000 per kg. Dorms CH$4500; singles CH$5000; doubles CH$11,000; *matrimoniales* with bath CH$20,000; triples CH$15,000. ❷

Hostal Colores del Sur, Santa Rosa 318 (☎231 850). Even more vibrant than neighboring Caza Azul to the south, this *hostal* welcomes visitors with its colorful exterior and friendly red, green, and blue interior. All the brightness helps to make up for the fact that the rooms, like the homey kitchen, are cramped. An aesthetically-gifted pragmatic touch has brought convenient stalls to the common bathroom. Internet CH$600 per hr. Dorms CH$5500; doubles CH$11,000. ❷

Hostal Kika, W. Martínez 584 (☎234 703). A solid, mid-range value for Puerto Varas, Kika has 5 rooms upstairs with basic private baths. Downstairs, however, is far from basic: the large living room houses a cozy hearth with an English book exchange. Reservations necessary in high season. Singles CH$18,000; doubles CH$25,000; triples CH$28,000. ❹

Hospedaje Sureño, Colón 179 (☎232 648). Tucked away in the south of the city near the Cruz del Sur bus terminal, Sureño offers squeaky-clean facilities. Kitchen and parking available. Breakfast included. Singles CH$6000, with bath CH$7000; doubles CH$12,000/CH$14,000. 5-person *cabañas* from CH$25,000. ❷

Hospedaje Don Raúl, Del Salvador 928 (☎234 174), a brisk jaunt west of town center. With the cheapest accommodations in town, Don Raúl is first-come, first-served. Simple rooms house as many beds as can fit. Full, if dingy, kitchen available. Camping CH$2500. Singles CH$4000; doubles CH$8000. ❶

◖ FOOD

Perhaps in response to its international tourist clientele, Puerto Varas boasts some relatively elegant, failsafe eateries. For inexpensive *comida típica*, there is a row of hole-in-the-wall joints south on San Francisco, near the church.

Mediterráneo, Santa Rosa 068 (☎237 268). An innovative menu will please the *típica*-weary at this waterfront restaurant. Large *tapas* menu includes delicious *salmón ahumado* (CH$3600). As a main course, try one of the pasta dishes (CH$6600) or the house suggestions, which have been known to include *tilapia* with shrimp and clam sauce (CH$8000). Open Oct.-May 10am-1am, June-Sept. 7pm-midnight. ❸

Café Mamusia, San José 316 (☎233 343). The chocolates displayed out front (CH$800-1000) are just part of the allure here. The lunchtime feast ($3300), with a dessert and an espresso, will keep you going all day. Tackle the *Volcán Osorno* (cheeseburger with onions and pickles) for CH$3900. Open daily 8:30am-midnight. ❸

Restaurant Parilla Don Carlos, on the corner of Santa Rosa and Del Salvador (☎338 530), across from the Plaza de Armas. Don Carlos runs a tight, bright ship, with generous *parrilladas* that include beef, pork, chicken, and sausage, sandwiched with appetizers (*empanadas* and a soup du jour) and fries. *Parrilladas* for 2 CH$11,400, for 3 CH$17,500, for 4 CH$27,700. Open daily noon-4:30pm and 6-11:30pm. ❷

Restaurant Don Jorge, San Bernardo 240 (☎312 427), kitty-corner from Supermercado O'Higgins. The TV may be blaring, and the waitress glaring, but it's the best deal in town for a solid *almuerzo* (CH$1800). It's also conveniently located, as buses to points east and south stop right outside. Open 11am-midnight, depending on business. ❶

👁 🎵 SIGHTS AND ENTERTAINMENT

For a city so deeply involved in the tourist trade, Puerto Varas is surprisingly short on sights and attractions. Most people simply use the attractive city as a base for day **excursions** to points along and near Lago Llanquihue. A few downtown locales do, however, merit attention. The **Plaza de Armas** spans some impressive lakeside real estate in the center of town, good for lingering on a nice day.

For some peace and quiet, hike up the short path to the top of **Cerro Calvario,** a hilltop park on the southeast side of town next to the hospital. Signs here read, "Zona de Meditación," and the park delivers on this promise. Fascinating (if somewhat gruesome) altars to Jesus Christ may distract some visitors from the impressive view of Osorno, which here can be appreciated in blissful solitude.

For a night out on the town, try **El Barómetro,** San Pedro 418. Well-known for its summertime *fiestas*, this bar rises to the occasion, pumping music, Latin and otherwise, into the early morning hours. Special event notices are posted all over town. (☎346 100. Open daily 4pm-late, low season M-Sa 7pm-late.)

🏔 OUTDOORS

The extensive list of outdoor activities available in the Lago Llanquihue vicinity could overwhelm even the most active traveler. Puerto Varas is the headquarters for many local adventure travel outfitters. Among the most popular summer excursions are **rafting** the Río Petrohué, **horseback riding, trekking,** and **climbing** the nearby volcanoes. **Al Sur** (see **Tours,** p. 368) employs guides for these activities and others, including **canyoning** and **fly-fishing.** Consult companies individually to choose your own adventure. independent-minded, budget-conscious travelers can skip the packaged tours and find their own way to the eastern side of the lake, using Puerto Varas as a stopping point for supplies, inspiration, and advice. Just about any point along the lake can be a daytrip from town.

A more expensive but nonetheless relaxing and popular way of experiencing the lakes is the **Andina del Sud** (see **Transportation,** p. 367) ferry/bus combination across the lakes that passes to **Bariloche, ARG.** A bus runs from town to Petrohué, where a boat crosses to **Peulla,** on the other side of **Lago Todos los Santos.** After two more boat trips and two more bus legs, the trip pulls into Bariloche late in the evening (during summer). For those intent on going to Bariloche, daily buses from Puerto Varas also reach the city for about 10-20% of the cost of Andina del Sud. If you'd rather **cruise** only the beautiful Lago Todos los Santos, buying only the leg from Petrohué to Peulla and back is much cheaper (from CH$17,000) and can be arranged from the small office in Petrohué (p. 374).

LOS LAGOS

ENSENADA   ☎ 65

Proximity to several natural wonders and panoramic views of Lago Llanquihue make peaceful Ensenada an enjoyable stopover for those en route to Petrohué. A smattering of decent accommodations and services have sprung up to oblige travelers passing through the town, which is really little more than a string of lakeside properties along the highway. Many travelers also set up on the pebble-filled beach to watch the sunset light up Lago Llanquihue and the snow-covered slopes of Volcán Osorno. Activities nearest to Ensenada include hiking the Laguna Verde Trail and climbing or skiing the slopes of Volcán Osorno. For more information on activities around Ensenada, see **Hikes,** p. 376.

While culinary choices are less than plentiful, particularly in winter, good food and good cheer can be found year-round at **Restaurant Bordelagos Donde el Español ❸,** where delicious smells tempt passersby into a warm dining room that is nearly overwhelmed by commanding views of the lake and volcano. Soups include a scrumptious *crema de choclo* (cream of corn; CH$1800), while lovingly prepared entrees run about CH$4000-6000. (☎212 083. Open daily 9am-midnight.) **Restaurant Toqui ❷,** a short walk to the west, serves slightly cheaper fare in a less grandiose atmosphere. A *plato vegetariano* (CH$5500) consisting of grilled and fresh produce will tempt attention-starved veggie travelers, but be advised that it includes salmon. (☎212 063. Open daily Dec.-Mar. 8:30am-midnight; Apr.-Nov. 8:30am-9pm, depending on business.)

The string of accommodations along the lake varies widely in price and quality. Comfortable rooms and self-contained (yet surprisingly reasonably priced) lakeside *cabañas* can be procured, breakfast and all, at **Brisas del Lago ❸,** Casilla 24, next to Supermarket Bellavista. (☎212 012; briensen@telsur.cl. Jan.-Feb. singles US$51; doubles US$59; triples US$60; *cabañas* for 1-3 people US$55; for 4-5 people US$60. Mar.-Dec. US$29/US$35/US$42/US$28/US$42. AmEx/MC/V.) **Hospedaje Yessely ❷,** at Km43, offers small singles, doubles, and quads, plus access to a nice kitchen; one room has a private bath. (☎212 009; yessely@entelchile.net. Breakfast CH$1500. Reservations recommended in summer. Rooms CH$5000 per person.) **Hospedaje Ensenada ❷,** east of Yessely, has a somewhat more gracious atmosphere at a reasonable price, and breakfast is included. (☎212 050. Singles CH$6000 per person; *matrimoniales* with private bath CH$10,000.) In-town camping options include **Camping Trauco ❶,** with an outdoor toilet and small cooking shelter. (☎212 033 or 212 006. Sites CH$3000-4000 depending on view and proximity to road.) Another more remote campsite lies 2.5km from town at Puerto Oscuro in Parque Nacional Vicente Pérez Rosales (CH$4000 per tent).

Kiñuhuen Excursiones, just north of the fork leading to Petrohué and Cochamó (☎212 086), offers all the usual adventures: Osorno ascents (CH$100,000), kayaking (lake trip CH$18,000; river trips CH$30,000), horseback riding (5hr., CH$40,000), and bike rentals (CH$7000 per day). **Supermarket Yessely,** in the southwest end of town, is the best-stocked market, but still has only the very basics. (☎212 009. Open daily 9am-9pm, Jan.-Feb. until 11pm.) Other services include a **police station,** at the fork on the east side of town (☎212 057 or ☎212 060; open 24hr.), and a **post office,** next to the Copec station. (☎212 038. Open Sa 2pm-6pm.)

A fleet of **Interlagos micros** departs from Ensenada for Petrohué (every 1-2hr. Jan.-Feb. 8:30am-5:30pm; Mar.-Dec. 7am-4pm; CH$500) and Puerto Varas (Jan.-Feb. every 30min; Mar.-Dec. every hr. 8am-7pm, CH$700). **Buses Fierro** goes to Cochamó (3 per day, CH$1500). The town spans a 3km stretch of highway ending in a fork that splits the road in two—one branch heading south to Petrohué and Cochamó, and the other north along the eastern edge of Lago Llanquihue. Buses will drop you off or pick you up anywhere along the main highway.

COCHAMÓ

☎ 65

Looking around Cochamó, you'll wonder which is more miraculous—the stunning view of the adjacent peaks, or the fact that the town's ravenous huskies don't devour the clucking fowl all around them. But in Cochamó, everybody just seems to get along. Maybe it has something to do with the placid waters of the estuary or the vigilant eye of Volcán Yates, which surveys the town from the southern end of the turquoise and jade waters of the Estuario Reloncaví.

Much of Cochamó's excitement and activity takes place 5km south of the town's center at a fabulous eco-resort. **Campo Aventura ❶**, at the mouth of the Cochamó River, has its entrance on the south side of the bridge, about 200m up the driveway. An all-inclusive stay at Aventura may seem a bit pricey, but this refreshingly eco-friendly complex (complete with water heated by burning processed driftwood) is well worth the money. Budget travelers can also opt to enjoy any independent part of the facilities' offerings. The base camp at the mouth of the river offers sites with access to shower facilities (CH$3500 per person) or lodge accommodations (private bath; CH$10,500 per person) with vegetarian breakfast (CH$600), lunch (CH$3500), and a three-course dinner (CH$9800) available.

A 17km hike or horseback ride separates the base camp from **La Junta** lodge facility, which offers equally top-notch service in a spectacular glacier-carved, granite-dome-studded valley. Most people come for guided horseback riding trips (1½-3½ days) or packages including kayaking, canyoning, hiking, fishing, and farm visits, all which can be arranged from Aventura's office in Puerto Varas. Popular tours include a 3½-day option that takes travelers by horseback up to the beautiful upper valley, with a full day to appreciate it (1 night at river mouth, 2 nights at mountain lodge; sumptuous meals included; US$349) and a 1½-day shorter trek that remains in the picturesque lower valley. (1 night at river mouth. Full meals included. US$97.) The trip can be shortened to a 9am-5pm daytrip (US$60) if one has a car and can arrive early enough. (☎232 910; www.campo-aventura.cl. Reserve ahead. Bike rentals available for CH$5000 per day. Free access to library and beach. Driftwood-burning sauna CH$5000. Laundry CH$840 per kg.) Independent **hikers** and **climbers** can also attempt to reach the glacial valley, but should definitely consult first with Campo Aventura. Unpredictable weather and frequent river crossings makes hiking these trails alone a risky undertaking; many times of year they are impassable for all but the most expert denizens.

Hospedaje Edicar ❷, on coastal Arturo Prat, is the best year-round accommodation in town, with clean, relatively modern rooms and a common balcony overlooking the water. (☎216 156. 19 beds in 8 rooms. Breakfast included. CH$6000 per person.) Slightly uptown, **Cabañas Montymar ❷**, Av. Catedral 20, has comfortable, well-equipped 5-person cabins for CH$20,000, as well as a single with private bath (CH$12,000) and the occasional *hospedaje*-style room for CH$5000 per person. (☎216 208.) In-town camping is possible at **Posada Campesina ❶**, on the southern end of Av. Cochamó. (☎09 130 4665. 2-person site CH$5000.) For food, there's just one option, but luckily it's a good one: **Restaurant Reloncaví ❷**, Catedral 16. The menu varies day-to-day, but a seafood *almuerzo* can generally be had for about CH$2800-3000. (☎216 253. Hours vary; call ahead to see if they are serving.)

On the main street, **Avenida Cochamó**, visitor information can be gleaned from the **municipal offices** near the northern entrance to town. (☎216 205. Hours vary.) Also on Av. Cochamó are a well-marked **police station** (☎216 233; *Guardia* 24hr.), **public telephone,** and tiny **post office** (☎216 285; open M-F 3-6:30pm). The only **call center** in town is on Av. Catedral, just past Restaurant Reloncaví (see below), at the **centro de llamadas.** (☎216 289. Open 9am-10pm.)

FROM THE ROAD

MARLBORO MAN

It's 5km from the town of Cochamó to the mouth of the Cochamó River. Next bus out is in three hours. I think I'll walk. With dust on my shoes and grit in my eyes, I look up and notice him—a menacing figure moseying along on a stalwart horse. This *caballero*'s at home in the wasteland—my fleece jacket and notebook say I don't belong. I'm crunching gravel as I walk; he half-turns at the sound of my footsteps. There's a rifle laying across his lap. No big deal. This *huaso* doesn't have Old-West vigilantism in him. Besides, I'm from Texas.

I slow down. It's not high noon, but the next best thing—2pm. Sun glints off his shooter. He brings his horse to a dead stop. I keep walking. He looks me up and down. He slowly lights a cigarette and takes a long drag. There's sweat in my eyes, cotton in my mouth, and a good-for-nothin' cowboy packin' a firearm sizing me up. It's time for a showdown. I say "Buenas tardes." He coolly brings his hand to his hat and nods slightly. Sun moves across the sky and out of my eyes. The *caballero*'s got a baby-face. His well-worn boots are covered in camouflage pants. The wide-brim hat is grunge, not Wild West. The bright red Limp Bizkit sweatshirt shakes the yellow belly out of me. This fella's a rocker. Guess that's why they keep 'em in silhouette in the Marlboro commercials.

-Tom Mercer

Cochamó lies 20km south of **Ralún** and is only accessible from the north, along a hard-packed, somewhat narrow dirt road. **Buses Fierro** is the only company running this route, from Puerto Montt (3hr.; Su-Th 8:30am, 12:30, 5pm, Sa 8:30am, 12:30, 4pm; CH$2500) via Puerto Varas (2½hr.; Su-Th 9am, 1, 5:30pm, Sa 9am, 1, 4:30pm; CH$2000), and returns three times per day (6:45am, 2, 4:45pm).

PETROHUÉ ☎ 65

The road east from Ensenada leads across a short but spectacular land bridge, spanning the area between Lago Llanquihue and Lago Todos los Santos. Following the turquoise waters of the Río Petrohué, the pavement road becomes dirt just east of the (rightfully) acclaimed **Saltos de Petrohué.** Most travelers continue their bumpy journey in awe, staring up at the peaks and forested granite walls around them, to emerge on the edge of heart-wrenchingly beautiful **Lago Todos los Santos.** Here, the "town" of Petrohué is home to a hotel, an adventure tourism office, a dock, a Conaf station—and nothing else. In the high season, crowds of tourists are a fixture, as are a flotilla of small motorboats, ready to shuttle hikers and sightseers to and from trailheads and picnic spots around the lake. Although there are a good number of guides and locals to offer information from December through March, there is little in the way of formal community services and infrastructure.

A large cruise boat operated by **Andina del Sud** runs to Peulla, on the east side of Lago Todos los Santos. Another boat takes 30min. "tours" of the west side of the lake (read: crowded jaunts around the beach area) and longer trips to the picnic-friendly Isla Margarita. (☎ 232 811. Peulla trip 11:30am, returning at 5:45pm; CH$19,000 per person. Isla Margarita trip departs 1 and 3pm, CH$5000 per person. Frequent lake tours CH$5500. 30min. ride around western lake CH$1800.)

From a small outpost next to the Petrohué Hotel (see below), **Expediciones Vicente Pérez Rosales** operates canyoning (US$65 per half-day), rafting (US$36 per half-day), and fly-fishing trips (US$30-200 depending on length). They have recently added an "EcoExtreme" trip that incorporates kayaking, trekking, climbing, rapelling, and a zipline. (☎ 212 045; www.petrohue.com. "EcoExtreme" trip 3hr.; US$35. Mountain bike rentals US$12 per day; fly-fishing equipment rentals also available.) **Conaf** has its park administration office in town. (☎ 09 375 8388; pprosal@conaf.cl. Open M-F 8:30am-1pm and 2-6:30pm; Sa-Su 9am-1pm and 2-6pm.) Other services include a **public telephone,** in front of the Conaf office.

There are only two options for indoor accommodations in Petrohué, and only one budget choice: **Hospedaje y Camping Familia Küschel ❷**, only a rowboat ride across the mouth of the lake. Very basic rooms are first come, first served, and go quickly in summer. (Breakfast included. CH$7000. Camping CH$2000 per tent. Other meals offered for CH$3000.) **Hotel Petrohué ❺**, on the other hand, is a full-scale luxury hotel. (☎212 025. Breakfast included. Singles US$77; doubles US$139; triples US$156. 4-person *cabañas* US$132; 7-person US$168; 8-person US$180. AmEx/MC/V.) Camping is also available at the Conaf location. (1-4 person sites CH$7000, 5-8 person sites CH$12,000.)

Interlagos buses depart for Puerto Varas (1½hr.; Jan.-Feb. every 1-2hr. 8:30am-5:30pm, Mar.-Dec. 5-6 per day 7am-4pm; CH$2000) via Ensenada (CH$500). A small number of independent **water taxis** shuttle to trailheads all over the lake and take fishermen out to catch salmon and trout (CH$10,000-50,000).

PARQUE NACIONAL VICENTE PÉREZ ROSALES

Established in 1926, this sprawling national park is one of Chile's most visited and most breathtaking. An intricate sequence of relatively recent geological events have sculpted the area, guiding the path of the **Río Petrohué** away from **Lago Llanquihue** and placing **Volcán Osorno** and **Volcán Puntiagudo** prominently on the topographical map. Glacial scouring and melting has also left its mark on the sheer walls and hanging valleys around **Lago Todos los Santos.** The results are nothing short of astounding. Even the crowds of summer can do little to detract from the majestic setting that greets visitors stepping off the bus at Petrohué.

Summer brings swarms of two kinds: pesky *tábanos* (horseflies) and tourists, who come to raft, hike, cruise, and climb in and around Volcán Osorno and environs. In the center of all this is the spectacular Lago Todos los Santos. A first glance will no doubt explain to newcomers why the Chilean park service protects the area all around this gem. Crumbling Calbuco and stately Osorno dominate views from all parts of the lake, while dramatic Puntiagudo graces only the northern shore with its nearly conical volcanic pinnacle. The lake also acts as a hydro-highway, ushering a steady stream of cars, buses, and boats along its banks, up to the toothy corridor of the Andes and beyond. Despite the warm-weather influx of visitors, crowds are not much of a problem—those with a little advice from Conaf and an adventurous spirit can easily blaze their own trail into the mountains.

■🏻 **ORIENTATION AND PRACTICAL INFORMATION.** For basic information about the park, trails, and services, contact **Conaf**, either at its park **headquarters** in Petrohué (p. 374) or at its one-man **branch office**, just outside Ensenada on the road to Las Cascadas. (☎212 036. Open daily 9am-1pm and 2-6pm.) There are also more specialized offices at **Centro de Esquí la Burbuja** and **Saltos del Río Petrohué.** In an **emergency,** try the Conaf cell (☎09 375 8388) or dial ☎138 for "air rescue."

AT A GLANCE	
AREA: 2537.8 sq. km.	**GATEWAYS:** Ensenada, Puerto Frías.
CLIMATE: Humid and temperate. Average annual rainfall of 250-400cm. Temperature ranges from about 16°C in summer to 6.5°C in winter. Snow at highest points.	**HIGHLIGHTS:** Natural wonders such as Volcán Osorno, Lago Todos los Santos, the Petrohué waterfalls, and Río Negro; more than 100 species of birds and 30 species of mammals.
CAMPING: 2 Conaf locations: Playa Petrohué and Puerto Oscuro.	**FEES:** Free, except for Saltos del Río Petrohué (CH$1200).

LOS LAGOS

☞ **CAMPING.** Conaf offers two camping areas in the park. The biggest and most popular is the expanded **Playa Petrohué ❶**, whose 24 sites have great views across the lake. (Toilets, water, cooking shelter, and parking available. Up to 4 people CH$7000; 5-8 people CH$12,000; day use CH$3000.) Just 2.5km north of Ensenada on Lago Llanquihue, near the turnoff for the Osorno Refugio and ski area, is the more rustic **Puerto Oscuro ❶**. (10 sites. Toilets, shelter, trash disposal. Up to 4 people CH$4000; day use CH$2000.)

🥾 **HIKING.** Hikers should be well-prepared for cold, wet weather at all times of year and should expect rapid weather changes, as storms coming off of the Pacific slam right into these mountains without much advance warning. It is advisable to consult Conaf about your intentions before you leave on a longer excursion. Many of the trails from remote Lago Todos los Santos are very isolated; carry plenty of extra supplies and be sure to arrange a water taxi back. The best readily-available topographical **map** of the area is the red JLM trekking map #15, available in Puerto Montt and Puerto Varas bookstores.

For a short, accessible jaunt, try the **Laguna Verde Trail** (200m; 20min.). Beautiful at sunset, the trail leads from the Ensenada Conaf outpost to a bright green, algae-colored pool, which is separated by a thin neck from the main body of Lago Llanquihue. The most scenic beginner hike on Volcán Osorno is the **Paso Desolación Trail** (12km; 5-6hr. round-trip; only one water source en route), extending from Petrohué up to the pass, then onward to where Refugio La Picada, now abandoned, used to be located. (Hike from Petrohué to the former site takes 7hr. one-way.) Along the way, views open in the direction of the lake and Mt. Tronador, as well as toward the peak of Osorno. A pleasant alternative to the bus, the **El Solitario Trail** (6km; 2hr. one-way; no water) goes from the Las Cascadas road near Puerto Oscuro to the Petrohué road 1km south of Saltos del Río Petrohué. Finally, the **Rincón del Osorno Trail** (10km; 4hr. round-trip) winds from Petrohué along the lake, offering variations on the lake-and-peaks theme.

Hikes from the remote shores of the lake and Peulla generally require a bit more effort, time, preparation, and gear. Most of these trails should be done as multi-day trips and some don't follow established trails. From Peulla, the well-established **Laguna Margarita Trail** (16km; 8hr. round-trip) ends at a nice pond in a grove of native trees. Along the lake, the most popular backcountry route in the park, **Termas de Callao** (2-3 days), can be done as either a round-trip or one-way hike, leading up the **Río Sin Nombre** and coming out the other side on Lago Rupanco at Las Gaviotas, a remote farming and agro-tourism community. There is a simple cabin at the springs, though it may be full in the summer (use of the springs and cabin CH$4000). A bus from Osorno has access to near Las Gaviotas at a cheaper price than the negotiated water-taxi price (CH$40,000) to the Río Sin Nombre trailhead.

A worthwhile trail leads up the **Río León** (5-7hr.) to a grove of *alerce* trees, a popular destination for canyoning operators. A more remote and undeveloped **river valley route** (50km, 2-5 days) loops from Cayutúe to the Río Blanco, passing Lago Cayutúe on the south side, heading up the Río Conchas, then the Río Quitacalzones to the valley containing the natural Baños de Bariloche, where the trail heads down the Río Blanco back to the lake. Check conditions with Conaf before leaving, as the route can be quite messy after heavy rains. From the Cayutúe trailhead, a relatively easy trail leads south from Lago Cayutúe over beautiful **Paso Cabeza de Vaca** (6-7hr. one-way) to a gravel road just north of Ralún.

▲ **OUTDOOR ACTIVITIES.** Most other outdoor activities must be undertaken through guides or outfitters, because equipment and/or experience may be necessary. **Rafting** trips on the Río Petrohué are popular in the summer. Most operators are located in Puerto Varas. **Fly-fishing** is another opportunity; those interested should contact **Expediciones Vicente Pérez Rosales** (see **Petrohué**, p. 374).

Parque Nacional Vicente Pérez Rosales

PN Puyehue

Co. Patojo
2024m

Co. Sarroso
1630m

TO OSORNO
(70km)

Lago
Rupanco

Puerto Rico

Volcán Puntiagudo
2493m

Co. la Picada
1710m

R. Escape

R. Sin Nombre

SIERRA
EL RINCÓN

Co. Techado
1890m

R. Peulla

Peulla

Paso de Pérez
Rosales 1022m

Las Cascadas

Volcán Osorno
2652m

Lago Todos
los Santos

Centro de
Esquí la Burbuja

Petrohué

Isla
Margarita

Co. Tronador
3320m

Saltos del
Petrohué

Lago
Llanquihue

Ensenada

225

R. Blanco

TO PUERTO VARAS
(20km)

R. Petrohué

Cayutúe

Lago Cayutúe

Volcán Calbuco
2003m

0   5 miles

0   5 kilometers

Ralún

TO COCHAMÓ (15km)

CORDILLERA

CHILE

ARGENTINA

R. Negro

DE

LOS

ANDES

In addition to the Lago Todos los Santos area, much of the park's outdoor activities take place on the slopes of **Volcán Osorno.** Companies based in Puerto Varas, Ensenada, and Petrohué offer guided trips to the peak, which is a technically challenging ascent. If you have experience and want to do the trip solo, contact Conaf by phone or in person at the **Centro de Esquí La Burbuja** (☎ 252 571). Be prepared to show mountaineering club membership and appropriate equipment. After the climbing season, powder buries the peak, and the ski season runs from June to September. The ski center has one T-bar lift and one surface lift in operation. Call the center for details about schedule, tickets, and rentals.

BARILOCHE, ARGENTINA   ☎ 2944

Argentina's original ski destination, Bariloche has grown from its humble beginnings as an exclusive alpine village to its present place as the nation's premier mountain resort. Being on top has its cost, though: rampant population growth and tourist-fueled overdevelopment have largely overwhelmed Bariloche's small-town charm. The mountains and lakes surrounding town, on the other hand, retain all the majesty that first brought wealthy Argentines to the area more than half a century ago. Today, Bariloche serves as a northern gatekeeper to Patagonia, a perfect jumping-off point for the Argentine Lakes District, and a guaranteed good time for the young at heart. For info on border crossing into Bariloche, see p. 469.

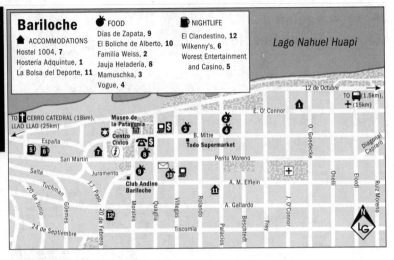

Bariloche

🍅 FOOD
Días de Zapata, **9**
El Boliche de Alberto, **10**
Familia Weiss, **2**
Jauja Heladería, **8**
Mamuschka, **3**
Vogue, **4**

🏠 ACCOMMODATIONS
Hostel 1004, **7**
Hostería Adquintue, **1**
La Bolsa del Deporte, **11**

🍸 NIGHTLIFE
El Clandestino, **12**
Wilkenny's, **6**
Worest Entertainment
and Casino, **5**

Lago Nahuel Huapi

📠 TRANSPORTATION

Bariloche serves as a transportation hub for travelers headed east from Chile or south down the Patagonian steppe to destinations like El Calafate. The major routes into and out of Chile are through Peulla to Osorno and Puerto Montt and through Esquel to Fuatalefu and Coyhaique.

Flights: Aerolíneas Argentinas, Mitre 185 (☎422 425; www.aerolineas.com) flies direct to El Calafate Nov.-Feb. Tu, Th, Sa-Su (one-way ARG$438). Flights to **El Calafate** connect to **Ushuaia** for an additional ARG$326. Aerolineas also flies daily to **Santiago, Chile** through **Buenos Aires** for around ARG$1077. (Open M-F 9am-1pm and 4-8pm; Sa-Su 9:30am-1pm and 5-8pm.) **Southern Winds,** Quaglia 262 (☎423 704; www.sw.com.ar), flies to **El Calafate.** (W and F-Sa, ARG$335 one-way. Open M-F 9am-1pm and 4-8pm; Sa 9am-1pm.) A *remisse* to or from the airport runs ARG$15. City bus #72 makes the trip from the airport to the city center (every 2hr. 8:50am-9:50pm, ARG$1), and also from the corner of Mitre and Quaglia starting at 6:45am.

Buses: Purchase bus tickets at virtually any travel office in town—just look for the logo of the company that you want to travel with. The bus station is about 2.5km east of town on Rte. 237 (Av. 12 de Octubre) and is served by city buses #10, 11, 20, 21, and 22 (ARG$1). **Vía Bariloche,** Mitre 321 (☎429 012), travels daily to **Puerto Montt** (7hr., ARG$40) and is open daily 9am-9pm. **Andesmar** offers the same service and has an in-town representative office at Mitre 385 (☎430 211; open daily 9am-9pm). Several companies also offer trips along Patagonia's famous Rte. 40 from Bariloche to El Calafate. A good one, organized by the **Alaska Hostel** (p. 380), takes 4 days, allows ample time to explore, and puts passengers up at remote *estancias* (ARG$600).

Boat/Bus: The **Cruce de Lagos** delivers passengers to **Puerto Montt** (12hr.) from the shore of Lago Nahuel Huapi. On the way, passengers take in tremendous and remote mountain scenery as they transfer between 3 boats and 4 buses en route. **Catedral Tourism** (p. 379) has a package for US$140. Between mid-Apr.-mid-Sept., shorter daylight hours necessitate an expensive overnight at **Peulla** (doubles around US$150).

Taxis/Remisses: Blue cabs cruise downtown frequently, and, taken with friends, are a good bet for getting back to your hostel at 6am. For a *remisse,* try **Angostura Taxi and Remisse** (☎494 218).

Car Rental: A-Open Rent-a-Car, Mitre 171 (☎426 736), rents economy-sized vehicles starting at ARG$70 per day (100km included). Weekly rates available from ARG$426.

Bike Rental: Aire Sur, Elflein 158 (☎522 135). Half-day rental ARG$12; full-day ARG$15. Rentals for Circuito Chico include map, helmet, tire tube, and air pump. Open M-F 9:30am-1pm and 4:30-8:30pm; Sa closes at 8pm. If no one's in the shop, ring the hostel next door.

■ ⚹ 7 ORIENTATION AND PRACTICAL INFORMATION

For a sprawling Andean mini-metropolis, Bariloche is remarkably easy to navigate. Most services, restaurants, and stores occupy ten bustling blocks of **Mitre** and **Perito Moreno** east of the Centro Cívico. Radiating south and west of the Centro, **San Martín** and **20 de Febrero** also host bars, shops, and restaurants. To reach the mountains, as well as many of Bariloche's more upscale hotels and restaurants, head west out of town on **Avenida Bustillo.** A frequent and inexpensive (ARG$1-1.50) network of local buses serves most destinations; pick up a route map and schedule from the tourist office. For a somewhat commercial, but rather handy, take on local activities, pick up a copy of the free *Guía Busch* from most businesses in town.

Tourist Office: Bariloche's primary tourist hub is front and center in the Centro Cívico (☎429 850; www.bariloche.com.ar), but there is also a satellite office located at the bus station. On summer days, the line at the main office may extends out the door, but friendly, English-speaking attendants make the wait worthwhile. Open daily 8am-9pm.

Trekking Information: Helpful and well-organized **Club Andino Bariloche,** 20 de Febrero 30 (☎527 966), is an indispensible resource for all of the area's trails. Open late Nov.-Mar. M-Sa 9am-1pm and 4:30-8:30pm. In Jan., also Su 9am-1pm and 4:30-8:30pm.

Tours: Mitre and Moreno are choked with tour agencies. Most sell a variety of half-day tours to local sites like Cerro Catedral and Llao Llao, as well as longer day-tours to other towns in the region like El Bolsón and San Martín de los Andes. For adventure tourism, visit **Active Patagonia** (www.activepatagonia.com) at the Club Andino Bariloche (see **Trekking Information,** above); **Huapi,** San Martín 61 (☎522 438; www.huala.com.ar; open M-Sa 9am-noon and 5-9pm, Su 6-9pm); or **Patagonia Outdoors,** Elflein 29 (☎426 768; www.patagonia-outdoors.com). For more serious mountaineering excursions, check out **Aukache** on the web (www.aukache.com). For conventional tours, try **Vivir Viajes,** Palacios 141 (☎522 038; open daily 8am-10pm); **Turisur,** Mitre 219 (☎426 109; www.bariloche.com/turisur; open daily 9am-10pm); or **Catedral Tourism,** Palacios 263 (☎425 444; open daily 6:30am-9pm). **Baruzzi Fly Shop and Outdoors,** Urquiza 250 (☎424 922; www.baruzzi.com; open M-Sa 9am-1pm and 4-9pm) runs a variety of fly-fishing excursions starting at US$120 for 1 or 2 people, transportation and food included, equipment US$20 extra. A non-resident fishing pass costs ARG$30 per day, ARG$150 per week, and ARG$200 for the entire season.

Currency Exchange: Sudamerica Exchange, Mitre 63 (☎434 555), exchanges any amount of traveler's checks for a US$2.78 fee. Open M-F 9am-9pm, Sa 9am-1pm and 4-8pm, Su 10am-1pm and 5-8pm.

Bank/ATM: ATMs are clustered around Mitre and San Martín. The Link ATM at **Banco de la Nación Argentina,** 158 Mitre, accepts AmEx/Cirrus/MC/V.

Bookstore: Librería Cultura, Elflein 78 (☎420 193), boasts an excellent selection of Patagonian tomes as well as a small but provocative corner of English titles. Open M-Sa 9:30am-9pm.

Camping/Fishing Equipment: Martin Pescador, Rolando 257 (☎455 955), sells anything an angler or trekker could want, including fishing licenses and all varieties of fuel for camp stoves. Open daily M-F 9am-1pm and 4-9pm.

Market: Todo, Mitre 281 (☎527 974). Large market with convenient downtown location. Open M-Sa 9am-11pm, Su 9:30am-10pm.

Laundromat: Lavadero, Villegas 292. ARG$7 per sizable basket; washed, dried, and folded. Next-day pickup. Open M-F 8am-10pm, Sa 9am-9pm.

Emergency: ☎101.

Police: In the Centro Cívico (☎ 423 434).

Pharmacy: Farmacia Dr. Eslustondo, Mitre 379 (☎ 423 025). Open M-F 9am-10pm, Sa 9am-1:30pm and 5:30-10pm; Su 10am-1:30pm and 5:30-10pm. A sign posted on the door reveals which of Centro's many pharmacies will be open **24hr.** on any given day.

Hospital: Dr. Ramon Carillo Regional Hospital, Moreno 601 (☎ 426 119).

Telephones and Internet Access: Per capita, Bariloche may well be the most well-connected city in Argentina. In the downtown area, telephone offices and Internet cafes crowd nearly every block. For Internet, try moody **La Lomo,** Villegas 360 (☎ 422 494; ARG$2 per hr.; open M-Sa 10am-2am, Su 2pm-2am) or central **Refugio,** Mitre 106 (☎ 428 596; ARG$2 per hr; open M-Sa 9am-2am, Su 10:30am-1am).

Post Office: Correo Argentino, 175 Perito Moreno (☎ 423 100). Open M-F 9am-7pm, Sa 9am-1pm.

ACCOMMODATIONS

Bariloche boasts one of the world's most iconic luxury hotels, **Llao Llao ❺,** where foreign dignitaries assemble and a high-season bed costs more than US$200 per night. It also has at least a dozen hostels and an overwhelming array of options in-between. Despite the glut, beds fill quickly (especially Dec.-Feb. and July-Aug.), so be sure to phone ahead.

La Morada, Cerro Otto, Km5 (☎ 442 349; www.lamoradahostel.com). Don't try to find this secluded haven on your own or you may wind up lost halfway up Cerro Otto. Instead, catch the free 4x4 shuttle from Hostel 1004 (see below). Once you arrive, the intimate and immaculate house, the excellent barbecue, and the views will leave your jaw gaping. The remote location is perfect for couples and solitude-seekers, but inconvenient for nightlife. Internet $3 per hr. 4-bed dorms ARG$16; doubles ARG$38-46. ❶

La Bolsa del Deporte, Palacios 405 (☎ 423 529; www.labolsadeldeporte.com.ar), on the corner of Elflein and Palacios. The quirky and cozy chalet offers backpackers premium perks like free Internet, satellite TV, a VCR (the video store's just down the street), and a secure, pleasant garden area. Bolsa attracts trekkers, so if you're seeking mates to explore Nahuel Huapi, it's a good bet. Bunk beds ARG$15; doubles ARG$34. ❶

Hostería Adquintue, O'Connor 766 (☎ 527 974; www.noticiasdebariloche.com.ar/adquintue), a short walk east from the Centro. Close enough to be convenient, yet far enough to be quiet, Adquintue offers pleasant rooms with televisions and private baths to couples or backpackers eager for respite from the hostel scene. Breakfast is included in the light-filled dining area and there's a hearth-side lounge for taking in a novel, newspaper, or Argentine magazine. Singles ARG$69; doubles ARG$94. ❸

Alaska Hostel, 328 Lilinquen (☎ 461 564; www.alaska-hostel.com). Take city bus #10 or 20 to Bustillo Km7.5, follow Palo Santo uphill, turn right onto Laura Street and then left onto Lilinquen after one block. Although farther from town than most, this secluded hostel has perks worth the trip, including a jacuzzi and sauna (ARG$5 per day). During the winter, the extra distance just puts guests closer to the slopes. Alaska offers an ARG$8 round-trip shuttle service to Cerro Catedral in winter and also coordinates discount ski-rental packages for guests (ARG$33). Reception 9am-midnight. Dorms ARG$16, with HI ARG$14; doubles ARG$40. ❶

Hostel 1004, San Martín and Pagano, 10th fl. (☎ 432 228; www.lamradohostel.com). Take the elevator and turn right down the dim corridor. The rooms and kitchen of 1004's top-floor penthouse suite feel tired, but the view from the balcony is astounding. An excellent place to meet other hard-partying backpackers, many of whom will end the night at 5am crashed on the living room floor. Laundry ARG$7. Sleep on the floor after midnight for ARG$8. Dorms ARG$14; doubles ARG$35. ❶

La Selva Negra, Bustillo, Km3 (☎441 013). A Bariloche retreat for more than 30 years, this pleasant campground offers excellent lake views, well-maintained grounds, and convenient proximity to town. Catch Boca Junior on the bar TV or just kick back and enjoy the solitude. ARG$8 per person; multi-night stays ARG$7. ❶

☐ FOOD

Low-carb devotees, welcome to dietary nirvana. Nearly every restaurant in town serves some variety of grilled meat in no-need-for-dinner-rolls portions. Just beware of Bariloche's renowned dessert: chocolate. The best of Bariloche's chocolate venders is **Mamuschka,** Mitre 216 (☎432 294).

▧ **Jauja Heladería,** Moreno 18 (☎437 888). If the buzz on the street makes you suspect hype, don't be fooled: this is the best ice cream in town. Sculpted in seductive waves beyond the glass case, more than 20 flavors, including 5 varieties of *dulce de leche,* await. On a hot summer day, the *limón* is divine. Regular-size cone ARG$3; large ARG$4. Open Dec.-Feb. daily 10am-1am; irregular low-season hours. ❶

Días de Zapata, Morales 362 (☎423 128). Fresh, piquant Mexican food has never been more a breath of fresh air than in this town full of grilled meat, breaded meat, and meat with potatoes. Zapata serves the expected assortment of tacos (ARG$12-13.50), fajitas (ARG$15.50), and burritos (ARG$11-13) along with zesty specials like the *Crepes de Mole* (ARG$14). Open daily noon-3pm and 5pm-midnight. ❷

El Boliche de Alberto, Villegas 347 (☎431 433). A standout amongst Bariloche's plentiful *parrillas,* Alberto's has earned its travel-buzz celebrity thanks to unimaginable portions at negligible prices. Vegetarians beware: the cowhide-covered menu offers only grilled meats as main courses, so if you accompany your carnivorous friends, expect to eat french fries for dinner. The full portion *asado* runs ARG$14, but a half portion (ARG$9) will more than suffice for most. Open daily noon-3pm and 8pm-midnight. ❶

Vogue, Palacios 165 (☎431 343). One of many among Bariloche's pizza parlors, Vogue takes the prize for the sheer volume of its options: more than 5 pages of pizzas fill the menu. Small pizzas are cheap (ARG$6-15) and filling for one, so it's wise to have everyone at the table pick an odd variety and swap slices. Otherwise, who would order the onion, tuna, and egg? Open daily noon-3pm and 8pm-2am. ❶

Familia Weiss, Palacios and O'Connor (☎435 789). This family-owned eatery offers excellent regional dishes and stellar lake views. Known throughout Argentina, the Weiss family often hosts a substantial tourist crowd, but locals swear by the food. Try the trout with herbs (ARG$16) or a Weiss specialty, smoked salmon and trout (ARG$8). Open daily noon-midnight. ❶

☉ SIGHTS

There's little to see in Bariloche proper beyond souvenir shops and vacationing families. A quick stroll around the **Centro Cívico** provides a glimpse of Bariloche's architectural heritage. Designed during the 1930s under the guidance of architect Ezequiel Alejandro Bustillo, the elegant stone structures incorporate local materials to evoke a European alpine style. While strolling, be sure to stop at the **Museo de la Patagonia,** in the northeastern corner of the square. This tidy museum houses the best collection of natural history, prehistory, ethnography, and European history exhibitions on Patagonia. It's an excellent first stop before any adventures farther south into the heart of Patagonia, or farther inland into mountains of Nahuel Huapi. With little more than one look at the confused early maps of Patagonia, you'll understand why the region remains so mysterious today. (☎422 309; www.bariloche.com.ar/museo. Open M 10am-

THE HIDDEN DEAL

CAN I BUY AN LL?

When the Argentine *peso* was detached from the US dollar in 2001, the doors opened to a flood of gringos descending on the country with only an awkward ¡Hola! in their Spanish repertoire. Argentina, traditionally a very expensive place to travel, had suddenly become a backpacker's bargain dream. As the hordes arrived, wise Argentines and foreign nationals realized that if the gringos wanted to hack it in their immense country, they'd have to learn a thing or two in Spanish.

In the last three years, informal Spanish language schools have sprung up all over Argentina. While the bargains are not as good as those found in Central American countries like Guatemala (which can be half as expensive), Argentina's schools are an excellent option for independent travelers who want to acquire language skills but can't afford courses in their home countries. What's more, most of the schools are located in popular tourist destinations like Buenos Aires, Bariloche, and Ushuaia, allowing backpackers to sample sights they'd intended to see while brushing up on their conjugation.

Argentine Spanish has its idiosyncrasies, chief among them being variant pronounciations of "y" and "ll." In Buenos Aires, "y" sounds like a soft English "g"; in the rest of the Spanish-speaking world it just sounds like a "y." The

1pm, Tu-F 10am-12:30pm and 2-7pm, Su 10am-1pm. ARG$2.50, children under 12 free. An English guide to the museum—everything's in Spanish—costs ARG$2.50.) Once you've seen the Centro, get out of town (see **Outdoor Activities,** below).

◖ NIGHTLIFE

For its size, Bariloche rivals Argentine giants like Buenos Aires and Córdoba as a party town. After a *siesta* and a 10pm dinner, bars begin to fill around midnight and don't empty until sunrise. If pounding techno suits your fancy, try the row of discos on **J.M. de Rosas** west of the Centro Cívico. Or to pace yourself, catch a late flick at **Cine Arrayanes,** Moreno 39 (☎433 860; ARG$5) and *then* hit the bars.

Wilkenny's, San Martín 435 (☎424 444). Love it or hate it, Wilkenny's is where you'll find the crowd—mostly young, single, and looking for fun. Argentines and foreigners alike pack this Irish pub from wall to wall, enjoying ARG$3.50 *schop* and the latest pop and dance rhythms. Other drinks, like an ARG$8 pint of the house beer, can get rather pricey. Live music Tu-Th, mostly rock but occasionally Celtic. Open daily 11am-5am.

El Clandestino, 20 de Febrero 510, near the corner with Gallardo. If you're lucky enough to find it, this remarkable bar will bring new meaning to the phrase "underground music." There's no sign out front and only a surreptitious knock on the door will gain you admittance. Once inside, grab a liter of Quilmes (ARG$4) from the bar and head downstairs where, in 2 rooms packed with locals, there's excellent live music nightly all summer. Th tango, F folk, Sa reggae, Su Latin. Open daily 1-7am; low season Th-Sa 1-7am.

Worest Entertainment and Casino, España 476 (☎424 421), between Wilkenny's and the discos. If this casino feels chintzy to you, don't worry—it is. But don't be fooled by the name; there's plenty of late-night entertainment to be had at Worest, which features poker, blackjack, Roulette, slots, and craps. There's also a bar and a dance floor that begins to crowd around 1am. Open M-Th 10am-4am, F-Sa 10am-5am, Su 10am-4am.

◮ OUTDOOR ACTIVITIES

CIRCUITO CHICO/LLAO LLAO. Bariloche's classic tour, this 65km circuit follows routes #77, 79, and 237, departing from the Centro Cívico and heading west to where towering Andean peaks collide with

Lago Nahuel Huapi. It takes about 10km to escape Bariloche's far-reaching tendrils of tourist development, but once free, the views get better and better. After 25km, the circuit passes through the pleasant mountain hamlet of **Llao Llao,** home to the internationally renowned hotel of the same name. Visitors are allowed to stroll the hotel grounds for free and, on Wednesday at 3pm, take a free informative tour of the main corridor and other hotel facilities (hotel ☎448 530). Across the street from the hotel is **Puerto Pañuelo,** a pleasant harbor from which boats to Isla Victoria, Puerto Blest, and Los Arrayanes depart. Passing the hotel, the road winds through the shady glades of Llao Llao Municipal Park and on to Bahía López. From the shores of this scenic bay, the circuit turns west directly beneath towering Cerro López back toward Bariloche, which is 25km off.

Nearly every tour office in town offers a half-day circuit of the Circuito Chico for ARG$15-20. It is also possible to complete most of the tour by city bus (the #20 runs on the half-hour to Llao Llao and the #10 to Bahía López). Completing the entire loop via public transportation is impossible, however. From where the #20 stops to where the #10 starts lie 8-9km of walking. It's also possible to rent a bicycle and complete the hilly and challenging circuit in 5-6hr.

ON THE LAKE. Nahuel Huapi's Lacustrine Zone rivals its mountains in splendor, but you'll need a ship to see it. **Isla Victoria,** the lake's largest, serves as a nature reserve protecting an uncut forest and indigenous birds, including an extremely rare colony of fresh-water cormorants. Short hiking trails and several lunch options make for a pleasant daytrip. Boats depart from Puerto Pañuelo for the daytour (tour ARG$38; entrance fee ARG$12). Reservations are available from various travel agents in town. Most excursions to Isla Victoria include a brief stop at **Parque Nacional Arrayanes,** home to a unique forest of cinnamon-colored trees in the eucalyptus family. While the trees grow elsewhere as shrubs, the national park is the only place in the world where they grow to tree-like heights. Finally, similarly-priced excursions from Puerto Pañuelo travel into the secluded **Blest Arm** of Lago Nahuel Huapi, where the mammoth lake reaches its maximum depth and where pristine waterfalls cascade through the luxuriant Valdivian forest.

WILDERNESS TOURS. From whitewater rafting to world-class climbing and from glacier mountaineering to sea kayaking, Bariloche's got it and there's a company in town offering to take you to it.

letter "ll" sounds like "ch" instead of "y." Argentines also replace the second-person pronoun "tú" with a ubiquitous "vos" that leaves many visiting Spanish-speakers confused. In general, though, Argentines speak clearly, and once you grasp the ticks of the accent, you'll be keeping up with the best of *ellos*.

The following schools provide lessons in towns covered in the Patagonia section of this guide. At most schools, classes occupy 4hr. in the morning, with afternoons free for leisure, school activites, or studying. Programs can be hit or miss, so arrive at your destination town early, and visit a few schools first. *¡Suerte!*

In Bariloche:
La Montana Spanish School (☎2944 524 212; www.lamontana.com) offers an intensive 4-week program that includes 3 weeks' homestay for US$775.

CLB (☎2944 523 105; www.clbariloche.com.ar) offers a similar course for US$550, US$850 with 4 weeks' homestay included.

ABC Spanish School (☎2944 529 911; www.abcspanish.com) provides a 4-week survival Spanish course for US$460. Homestays are US$110 per week.

In Ushuaia:
Finis Terrae Spanish School (www.finisterrae.8m.com) teaches classes in two-week segments. A two-week course (4hr. per day) runs US$350, including lodging at the school.

For many activities, sticking with the long-established and well-reputed **Club Andino Bariloche** (p. 379) is the way to go. Through their guiding service, **Active Patagonia** (www.activepatagonia.com), they offer rock-climbing trips that range from a half-day near town (ARG$130) to a 3-day basic rock climbing course (ARG$350). They can also arrange guides to take you to the summit of Mt. Tronador (ARG$380 per person; min. 2 people), or to lead you on a less-intense half-day of ice walking (ARG$90; min. 2 people). A half-day vertical ice-climbing lesson costs the same.

At least three companies in town offer one-day rafting trips on the **Río Manso** which are easily booked from any tour office in town. The river offers two options: a tamer Class II and III section, and a wilder Class III and IV stretch of rapids. Either way, the trip lasts all day, but be prepared to spend much of it in transit between Bariloche and the river. **Rafting Adventure,** Morales 362 (☎432 928; www.raftingadventure.com), runs trips on both segments (ARG$90 for Class II and III, ARG$120 for Class III and IV). For a more placid aquatic experience, **Patagonia Outdoors** (p. 379) offers half- and full-day sea kayaking trips on area lakes through Extremsur (half-day ARG$90, full-day ARG$120).

Horseback riding excursions, available at virtually any tourist office in town, begin at around ARG$35-40 and rapidly get more expensive, especially for multi-day horsepacking trips into the Andes.

WINTER ACTIVITIES. Cerro Catedral was Argentina's first ski resort, and while it is no longer regarded among the best of international ski destinations, it remains a premier place to enjoy powdery runs. The slopes boast 20 sq. km of downhill trails (30% easy, 45% intermediate, 25% expert) and more than 15 different ways up the mountain. The high percentage of easy and intermediate trails makes the mountain an excellent place for beginners. Lift tickets run ARG$46-80 per day depending on the season, and equipment is available for ARG$15-70 depending on the set desired and the season (☎423 776; www.catedralaltapatagonia.com). Other winter activities include nordic skiing (the area around Refugio Frey is excellent) and winter trekking. **Patagonia Outdoors** organizes daytrips for both (nordic skiing at Cerro Otto ARG$55 per person per day; winter trekking ARG$85-120).

PARQUE NACIONAL NAHUEL HUAPI

Argentina's first national park, Nahuel Huapi was established in 1934 on lands donated by the famous Patagonian explorer Francisco Pascasio Moreno. Its 7050 sq. km stretch from Parque Nacional Lanín in the north to the Río Manso in the south, unfurling along the Andes-studded border in towering peaks and glacial lakes. Since its founding, Nahuel Huapi ("Tiger Island" in Araucán) has been a favorite of outdoor-lovers, and the park's well-maintained system of trails and *refugios* remains as scenic and accessible as ever. An excellent place for day-hiking, backpacking, rock climbing, glacial mountaineering, and downhill and nordic skiing, Nahuel Huapi requires at least a few days to explore and enjoy.

■ **TRANSPORTATION.** Getting to the most popular parts of the park is as easy as hopping on a city bus. Fares to destinations outside of town generally cost ARG$2. For Cerro Catedral and the hike to Refugio Frey, pick up the "Catedral" bus from the bus stop on San Martín behind the Centro Cívico. For Refugios Jakob and Cerro López, take the #10 bus toward Colonia Suiza and ask the bus driver to drop you near the trailhead. Reaching Mt. Tronador requires a bit more effort. Most companies in town offer round-trip bus tours to the mountain (2¼hr. each way; ARG$25-35). **Expreso Meiling,** available through the **Club Andino**

AT A GLANCE	
AREA: 7050 sq. km	**GATEWAY:** Bariloche (p. 377).
CLIMATE: Dry in the east toward the glacier; foggy and damp toward the west.	**CAMPING:** Permitted in designated areas near *refugios; refugios* serve food and cost ARG$8-14 per night.
HIGHLIGHTS: Tronador Volcano, excellent hiking, Isla Victoria, Pelugian Lakes.	**FEES:** Admission to the Southern Zone near Bariloche is free. Entering the park near Tronador or or visiting the park's Lacustrine Zone costs ARG$12.
WILDLIFE: *pudu-pudu;* the Andean Condor.	

Bariloche, is a good choice. (Departs daily mid-Dec.-Jan. 8:30, 10am; Feb.-Nov. 8:30am only. Buses return 4pm and 5pm Dec.-Jan., only at 4pm Feb.-Nov. Book at Club Andino Bariloche. One-way ARG$15, round-trip ARG$25.)

■ ORIENTATION. Because of its massive size and its location atop the continental divide, Nahuel Huapi protects a remarkable diversity of landscapes and ecosystems. The park's main geographical feature is Lago Nahuel Huapi, which covers more than 600 sq. km. Glaciers scoured this splendid lake so deeply that the floor of the Blest Arm is 464m below the surface. At least a dozen other glacial lakes speckle the parklands; the rivers that drain them flow into both the Atlantic and Pacific. East of the continental divide, the vegetation is sparse and the climate dry. At the park's western edge, however, near the Chilean border, the lush plant life of the Valdivian "jungle" fills the mountainsides with towering *coihue* and the luxuriant underbrush of moss and ferns. Wildlife highlights include herds of *guanacos* and the occasional puma at higher altitudes, the world's smallest deer (the *pudu-pudu*), and high-flying Andean Condors.

The park is divided into three administrative sections. The **Southern Zone,** just west and south of Bariloche, contains the vast majority of trails and outdoor activities. Access to the dry **Northern Zone** is best found through Villa La Angostura, 85km north of Bariloche. To explore the **Lacustrine Zone,** you'll need to book a boat tour with one of Bariloche's many tour companies (p. 379). In the Southern Zone, popular activities include day-hiking to **Refugio Frey,** near Cerro Catedral, rock climbing at Refugio Frey, hut-to-hut backpacking, and exploring Nahuel Huapi's most famous peak, the heavily glaciated 3554m **Mt. Tronador.**

◪ HIKING. The **Club Andino Bariloche** (p. 379) has excellent trekking information, maps (ARG$8), and the very helpful *Infotrekking Patagonia Nahuel Huapi Guide* (ARG$15). The **National Park Office,** San Martín 24 (☎ 423 111) also has excellent brochures (in Spanish) and information, but they do not have as many English speakers on staff as the CAB. (Open M-F 8am-4pm; Sa-Su 9am-3pm.)

Cerro Catedral/Refugio Frey. (160km round-trip, 6-7hr., easy to moderate). The area around Refugio Frey is Nahuel Huapi's most popular backcountry destination, surrounded by jagged peaks and towering spires that draw rock climbers from all over the world. From the Cerro Catedral parking lot (elevation 1082m), the trail traverses an open slope with excellent views of Lake Gutiérrez before dropping into the drainage of Van Titter Arroyo. Near the head of the valley it climbs steeply to the *refugio* (elevation 1760m). An alternative hike begins from the parking lot with a ARG$17 chairlift to the ridge. The 4 mi., 3hr. hike between the end of the lift and the hut offers extravagant views of the Nahuel Huapi backcountry, with Mt. Tronador in the distance.

Refugio López/Tourist Summit. (6.4km round-trip to Refugio López, 6 mi. to summit, 5-8hr. round-trip; moderate to difficult). Beginning from the road to Bahía López, this trail heads nearly straight up the mountain to Cerro López. Just past the *refugio*, it breaks out of the trees for a difficult scramble to the top, but once there, the views of the far reaches of Lake Nahuel Huapi are well worth the effort. The steep climb should not be attempted by those in poor physical condition.

Refugio Meiling/Tronador's Glaciers. (9.6km one-way, 4-6hr., moderate). From the Park Ranger Office at Pampa Linda, the hike to this popular *refugio* winds through lush forests en route to the glacial talons of Tronador. If the 1100m climb to the *refugio* seems stiff, imagine going the next 1500m to the top. The *refugio* itself enjoys a terrific location, situated on a spur between the Castano Overo and Alerce Glaciers. Many trekkers spend a night at the *refugio* (ARG$12) in order to enjoy a pre-booked excursion out onto the ice the following day (see **Outdoor Activities,** p. 382).

Hut-to-Hut in Nahuel Huapi. (36km one-way, 4-5 days, difficult). Sometimes called the "Nahuel Huapi Traverse," this classic backpacking trip alternates between exposed ridges and breathtaking glacial valleys as it winds its way from the Cerro Catedral parking lot to Bahía López. Most sections are moderately challenging, with the exception of the steep and difficult-to-follow route between Refugio Jakob and Refugio Italia. Fortunately, each of the *refugios* has its own access trail to the main road, so it's possible to go hut-to-hut for just two or three days if time is limited. To travel light, leave the tent behind and stay in *refugios* (ARG$8-14). The *refugios* serve excellent, if pricey, food.

PUERTO MONTT ☎ 65

As the transportation hub and gateway to the south for both travelers and 18-wheelers, Puerto Montt has an unmistakably industrial feel. Visitors on their way to the fjords, surrounding wilderness, or the Carretera Austral tend not to linger here. However, the vibrant streets and bustling port boast a charm of their own, particularly in summer, when the plaza and Talca fill with shoppers, vendors, and street performers. With more restaurants, shops, hostels, markets, and amenities available than in other cities and towns in the area, Puerto Montt is a good place to take advantage of the services and facilities of city life before heading into the beauty and tranquility that lie ahead.

▊ TRANSPORTATION

Flights: Aeropuerto El Tepual, about 20min. north of town, accessible by bus from the bus station. **LanChile,** O'Higgins 167 (☎600 526 2000, ext. 8), flies to: **Balmaceda** (10am and 3pm, CH$64,000); **Concepción** (5pm, CH$35,500); **Punta Arenas** (4 per day, CH$104,000); **Santiago** (9 per day 8am-9pm, CH$113,000); **Temuco** (5:25pm, CH$34,500). Flights can also be purchased at **Eureka Turismo** (see **Tours,** p. 388).

Buses: A state of orderly confusion persists at the **bus station,** just west of downtown on coastal Diego Portales. Different bus companies all serve the same locations, with small variations in price and schedule. Although hordes of people rush about searching for the right bus at the right price, crowded buses roll in and out punctually. **Minibuses** to **Frutillar, Llanquihue,** and **Puerto Varas** leave from the station, but can also be waved down on **Portales;** just look for the signs in the windshield. Low season brings cheaper prices to **Santiago,** advertised by large posters with times and lowered prices.

Tur Bus (☎253 329) goes to **Concepción** (10hr., 9 per day 7:05am-10:10pm, CH$9000; *salón cama* 9:15pm, CH$15,700) and **Santiago** (14hr., 16 per day 8am-10:15pm, CH$14,500; *salón cama* CH$16,700).

ETM (☎256 253) serves the **airport** (1½hr. before every flight out, CH$800) and **Maullín** (M-Sa every 30min. 7:30am-9pm, Su every hr.; CH$900).

TransChiloé has buses to: **Ancud** (2½hr., 7 per day 7:45am-8:15pm, CH$2000); **Castro** (every 1½hr. 7:45am-6:50pm, CH$3200); **Quellón** (every 2hr. 7:45am-4:45pm, CH$4500).

LOS LAGOS

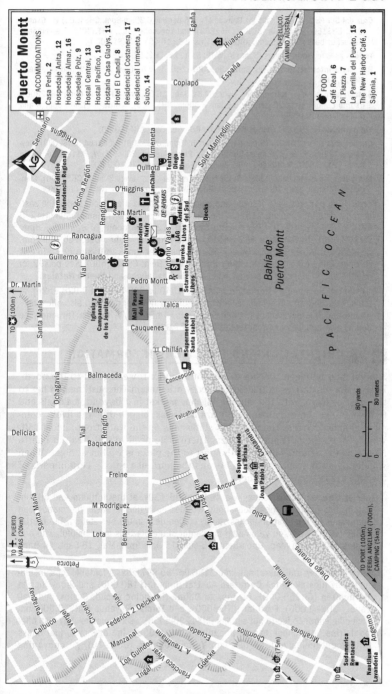

Puerto Montt

▲ ACCOMMODATIONS
Casa Perla, 2
Hospedaje Anita, 12
Hospedaje Almar, 16
Hospedaje Polz, 9
Hostal Central, 13
Hostal Pacifico, 10
Hostaria Casa Gladys, 11
Hotel El Candil, 8
Residencial Costanera, 17
Residencial Urmeneta, 5
Suizo, 14

◆ FOOD
Café Real, 6
Di Piazza, 7
La Parrilla del Puerto, 15
The New Harbor Café, 3
Sajonia, 1

Cruz del Sur (☎254 731) goes to: **Temuco** (7hr., 6 per day 6:30am-8pm, CH$4000) via **Osorno** (2hr., CH$1500), **Valdivia** (3½hr., CH$2800), and **Loncoche** (4hr., CH$3300). The company also sends buses to **Bariloche, ARG** (7hr., Th and Su 10:45am, CH$10,000).

Turibus goes to **Punta Arenas** (32hr.; M, W-Th, Sa 11am; CH$25,000).

Bus Norte Internacional serves **Bariloche, ARG** (7hr.; daily 8:30am, also M-W and F-Sa 9am; CH$10,000).

Buses Fierro goes to: **Hornopirén** (4½hr.; M-Sa 8am, 1:30, 3pm, Su 3 and 6pm; CH$2800); **Osorno** (1¾hr., M-Sa 20 per day 6:30am-8:30pm, CH$1500); **Santiago** (13hr., daily 8 and 8:30pm, CH$10,000).

Vía Bariloche (☎253 841) serves **Bariloche, ARG** (7hr., 3pm, CH$10,000).

Queilén Bus serves: **Castro** (8 per day 8:20am-6:40pm, CH$3200) via **Ancud** (CH$2000); **Coyhaique** (22hr.; Su-M, W, F noon; CH$20,000); **Punta Arenas** (30hr.; M, W, F 11am, Tu, Th, Sa noon; CH$28,000); **Santiago** (14hr., daily 7:40 and 9:15pm, CH$10,000).

Minibuses leave regularly 7:30am-9:30pm for: **Frutillar** (1hr., every 30min., CH$1000); **Llanquihue** (45min., every 30min., CH$800); **Puerto Varas** (35min., every 10min., CH$700).

Ferries: The **port** lies west of town, and all company offices are directly inside the easternmost gate, at Angelmo 2187, in the middle of the market. **Transmarchilay** (☎270 430, 270 431, or 270 432) goes to **Chaitén** (12hr.; M noon, Tu 8pm, Th-F 8pm; CH$12,000). **Navimag** (☎432 360) goes to **Chaitén** (10hr., Dec.-Feb. Su 1pm, CH$12,000). **Aisén Express** (☎437 599) sends **catamarans** to **Castro** (2hr., Tu and Th 6pm; CH$12,000) and **Chaitén** (4hr.; M, W, F 9am; CH$21,500). See p. 392 for information on longer ferry excursions to **Puerto Chacabuco** and **Puerto Natales**.

Car Rental: Sudamerica Rentacar, Miraflores 1540 (☎348 585 or 09 926 2526), at the intersection with Angelmo, rents cars for CH$22,000 per day, and also offers telephone and Internet services. Open 9am-9pm. AmEx/MC/V. **Eureka Turismo** (see below) also arranges daily car rentals for CH$27,000.

◼▓ 🔂 ORIENTATION AND PRACTICAL INFORMATION

Sandwiched between the sea to the south and a towering hill to the north, Puerto Montt's narrow grid makes for easy orientation. The bustling **port** lies to the west of town, with the vibrant **Angelmo market** just beyond it. Locals and tourists mingle at the downtown **Plaza de Armas**, bisected by the lively, commercial **Antonio Varas**. The noisy **bus station** sits on the waterfront almost halfway between the port and the plaza. There is no need to hail a cab in Puerto Montt, as the 25min. walk from the port to the plaza is well-lit at night. When wandering away from the water, beyond the port, use a taxi—certain parts of the area are less safe than others.

Tourist Offices: Conaf, Ochagavia 464 (☎486 120), at the northern end of Rancagua, has printed information about facilities in Region X. Basic information can sometimes be found at an inconsistently-staffed desk in the bus station. The **tourist office** (☎281 823), on Varas near the center of the plaza, is more helpful, with brochures and a town map. Open Sept. 15-Mar. 15 9am-9pm; Mar. 16-Sept. 14 9am-1pm and 3-7pm.

Tours: Travellers and Tours, Angelmo 2186 (☎295 997), has affordable trips, including 6-day trips along the **Carretera Austral** (from CH$180,000) and 2-day trips to **Hornopirén** (CH$55,000). Daytrips to **Chiloé** (including Ancud, Castro, and Dalcahue; CH$10,000), **Frutillar** (CH$5000), and **Termas Puyehue** (CH$10,000, not including entrance fee to hot springs CH$1200-5000) also available. They also offer **boat trips** from Chiloé to visit **penguins** (CH$15,000). The agency further books equipment-inclusive trips to climb **Volcán Osorno** (US$220), go **canyoning**

(CH$30,000), or **fly-fish** (US$250), all of which depart from Puerto Varas. Their newest tour includes **zip-lining** (3hr., CH$25,000). The slightly upmarket **Eureka Turismo,** Gallardo 65 (☎250 412), tailor-makes packages to suit clients' needs, facilitates car rental, and sells tickets for domestic and international flights.

Currency Exchange: Clearly labeled currency exchange offices cluster around Antonio Varas and Talca. **Eureka Turismo** (see **Tours,** above) exchanges traveler's checks, as does **Trans Afex,** Diego Portales 516. Those pressed for time can try **La Moneda de Oro,** in the bus terminal.

Bank: Banco Santander, on the corner of Varas and Gallardo, has a **24hr. ATM.** Cirrus/MC/Plus/V. Most banks are located 1-2 blocks north on Gallardo.

Bookstore: Sotavento Libros, Diego Portales 580 (☎256 650), boasts the town's best collection of regional information and English literature. Open M-F 10am-1:30pm and 3:30-8pm, Sa 10am-2pm and 5:30-8pm. **LAG Libros,** Varas 462 (☎232 318), has less of a selection but a more convenient location. Open M-Sa 9am-8pm.

Supermarket: Las Brisas, on the corner of Lota and Portales, across the street from the bus station, stocks most conventional items. Open daily 8:30am-midnight. Across the small square in front of the bus station, **Full Fresh Market** is even larger and sells some items more cheaply. Open M-Sa 9am-10:30pm, Su 10am-10:30pm.

Laundromat: Lavandería Narly, San Martín 165 (☎311 528), charges CH$1000 per kg. Open M-F 9am-1pm and 3-7:30pm. **Lavandería San Ignacio,** Lota 117A (☎343 737), offers the same service at the same price. Open M-Sa 9:30am-1pm, 3-8:30pm.

Police: ☎133. Also, Gallardo 519 (☎431 355 or 431 349).

24hr. Pharmacy: A rotating pharmacy system prevails here. **Cruz Verde,** Varas 952 (☎312 012; open M-F 9am-9pm, Sa 9am-8pm), and **Salcobrand,** Varas 549 (☎259 440; open M-Sa 9am-10pm), display the latest schedule.

Hospital: Ambulance ☎131. **Hospital Regional** (☎261 134), on Seminario.

Telephones: *Centros de llamadas* can be found all over town, most notably inside the bus station (on the 2nd fl.) and the strip mall across the street.

Internet Access: Internet, within the strip mall connected to Supermarket Las Brisas (see above), near the bus station. Fast and reliable service CH$800 per hr. **New-Cyber,** San Martín 230 (☎350 339), charges CH$1000 per hr. Open daily 9am-midnight. **Ciber Cost@nera,** Diego Portales 736, costs CH$700 per hr. Open daily 10am-10pm.

Post Office: Rancagua 126 (☎252 719). Open M-F 9am-6:30pm, Sa 9am-12:30pm.

▐ ACCOMMODATIONS

The cheapest (and most squalid) choices are located at sea level, between the bus station and town center. More expensive options with immaculate service dot the downtown area near the plaza. Finally, east of the town center, as well as in the western hills, cleaner, more moderate options abound.

▨ **Suizo,** Independencia 231 (☎252 640). Easily the most creative hostel in town, Suizo is decorated exclusively with the owner's art, which is all for sale. The bright rooms and distinctive architecture are sure to delight, while vivacious guests make an evening spent lolling about the porch a great treat. Dorms CH$8000-10,000 (depending on view and bath). Doubles with bath CH$20,000. Large cabin without beds but with a kitchen and space for 10 sleeping bags CH$5000 per person. ❷

Hostal Central, Huasco 71 (☎263 081), on the eastern side of town. Prices here seem a bit random: a spot in a 6-bed dorm costs the same as a single with cable TV. This place is a stand-out, however, for providing clean, comfortable, efficiently-run accommodations in a town where these qualities (particularly the former) can be quite elusive. CH$6000 per person. ❷

Hospedaje Almar, Chorillos 1379 (☎254 332). It's a bit of a walk from downtown, but this nondescript *hospedaje* matches tidy rooms with a palatial, sparkling common bathroom. Open Dec.-Mar. only. Doubles CH$10,000; triples CH$15,000. ❷

Hostal Pacífico, Mira 1088 (☎256 229). Despite the somewhat dingy upholstery, this slightly upscale option should suit those returning from less hospitable accommodations in the great outdoors. Privacy, in-room telephones, and cable TV add extra allure for the homesick. Singles CH$15,000; doubles CH$26,000; triples CH$30,000; quads CH$32,000. 18% discount for guests with a foreign passport. ❹

Casa Perla, Trigal 312 (☎262 104; casaperla@hotmail.com), south of the intersection with Crucero, a 10-15min. walk from the bus station. From the bus station, catch the #5, 50, 55, or 57 *colectivo*. Dorm rooms are somewhat cramped, but in this warm and clean house, no one's complaining; in fact, Perla's popularity makes reservations a necessity. Kitchen, laundry, and Internet access available. Breakfast included. 6-day, 7-night package (US$190 per person) includes a room, 18hr. of Spanish lessons, 1hr. Internet per day, and sea-kayaking excursion. Singles CH$5000; doubles CH$10,000; triples CH$15,000; quads CH$20,000. ❷

Residencial Urmeneta, Urmeneta 290 (☎253 262). Despite its central location, Urmeneta's prices remain slightly lower than those of its neighbors. Skylights flood most 2nd fl. rooms with warm sunlight. Welcoming owners make guests comfortable in the high-ceilinged kitchen. Doubles CH$12,000, with bath CH$17,000. ❷

Residencial Costanera, Angelmo 1528 (☎255 244). A large, plushly upholstered downstairs living room gives way to crowded, somewhat noisy 2nd fl. doubles. Large bathrooms counterbalance small rooms, but can't quite make up for the noise of busy Angelmo outside. Breakfast included. Doubles with shared bath CH$12,000. ❷

Hospedaje Polz, on the corner of Ancud and Juan José Mira (☎252 851). A long, spiral staircase leads up to slightly overpriced, cramped rooms. The central location compensates, particularly for those looking to be near the bus station. CH$7000 per person. ❸

Hostería Casa Gladys, Ancud 112 (☎260 247). Clean, neatly trimmed, and well-lit rooms almost make up for the moldy ceilings in the bathroom at this centrally-situated hotel. The price, however, is reasonable, considering the large size of the rooms. CH$5000 per person. ❷

Hospedaje Anita, Mira 1094 (☎315 479). The massive stairway leads up to small rooms with bunkbeds and drab shared bathrooms. It may be basic, but it's about as close to the bus station as you can get, and friendly Doña Griselda allows guests to use her kitchen. CH$4000 per person. ❶

Hotel El Candil, Varas 177 (☎253 080). 2nd fl. rooms in this hotel seem overpriced given that some don't have windows, but *matrimoniales* on the 3rd fl. have new furnishings and views of the water. Central hot water makes this a good bet for comfort. Breakfast CH$1000. Singles CH$12,000; doubles and *matrimoniales* CH$18,000. ❸

FOOD

Those looking for a break from the omnipresent Chilean "meatery" will find some relief in Puerto Montt. Pizza joints lurk on side streets, and vegetable vendors own the city's sidewalks. Carnivores should hit the Angelmo market for an obligatory *curanto* plate: a combination of meats and seafood. The nicer restaurants that line the market tend to be pricier. Andrés Bello, several blocks in front of the bus station, has many small eateries serving daily lunch specials for CH$1500.

Sajonia, Gallardo 231. This fine restaurant caters to Puerto Montt's corporate clientele, but remains moderately priced, with a selection of crepes (CH$1800-4000) and house specialties (CH$3900-5900). *Menú* (CH$2300) includes soup and an entree. Open M-Sa 10am-midnight. ❷

La Parrilla del Puerto, Independencia 165 (☎258 197). Despite a lack of natural light, the open grill and wood-paneled dining room create a pleasant atmosphere for dining on perfectly grilled meat selections. The basic *lomo* comes with a side dish of your choice (CH$3000), while zesty sauces like the *pimienta* can spice up your meal for a little more (CH$3500). If you can't decide, order the complete *asado*, a mélange of chicken, sausage, pork, and beef (CH$8500). Open 11am-midnight. ❸

Café Real, Rancagua 137 (☎253 750). A central location and hearty dishes make locals and visitors gravitate to this bright and open cafe. Start with a salad (CH$700-1400) or a heaping bowl of *cazuela* (CH$1900) before attacking a thick *lomo* (CH$4600) or *paella* (CH$4500). Downstairs rocks with live music M-Sa after 10pm. Check the sign on the door to see who is playing. Open daily 8am-12:30am. ❸

Di Piazza, Gallardo 119. Great pizzas and pasta draw crowds to this bright, clean pizza joint. Thin-crust pizzas and a variety of toppings make for an interesting meal; a large easily serves two people (CH$2000-4200). Open 11am-11pm. ❷

Restaurant La Nave, Ancud 106. This large, cafeteria-style dining room may not look as inviting as some of its neighbors. Still, the *pastel de choclo* (CH$2500) comes out piping hot and utterly divine. Open 9am-11pm. ❷

The New Harbor Café, San Martín 185 (☎293 980), is a hip spot to have a drink and catch some live music any night except Su. The house specialty is a variety of alcoholic coffees, from Irish and Italian coffee to "Buccaneer coffee" (with rum and cacao). Coffees CH$2500. Open M-Sa 8:20am-2am. ❷

SIGHTS

ANGELMO MARKET. West of the port, this artisanal market brings the street to life. The market stretches from the port to the cul-de-sac, where a busy fish market and a cluster of restaurants attract locals and tourists alike. Fine woolen and leather goods, crafted by regional artisans, include *huaso*-style hats and antique boot spurs. The fish market is always bustling as the latest catch is cleaned and prepared in front of hungry customers. As you peruse the line of restaurants, enjoy playful banter with white-aproned women who will wink, smile, and gesture coyly to cajole you to their restaurant. *(Though the 15min. walk from downtown is relatively easy, local westbound buses service the area; look for "Angelmo" signs on windshields. CH$200.)*

PUEBLITO DE MELIPULLI. West of the bus station, on the way to Angelmo market, lies this tiny museum, coffee shop and craft center. Colorful paint jobs and kitschy *artesanía* lend the whole place a festive atmosphere, and it's not a bad place to take a break during the walk to Angelmo or the port. Featured artwork by

THE *ALERCE* MAFIA

On the black market, a cubic meter of *alerce* wood can fetch US$5000. With its intricate grain and extreme rot-resistance, this giant tree (also called the Chilean Larch) has become one of the world's most coveted. It's also one of the world's rarest. Rampant logging in the early 20th century led to international recognition of the *alerce* as an endangered species. The Chilean government declared the tree a national monument and banned its cutting in 1976. The ban, however, has been ineffective.

In May of 2004, Conaf director Carlos Weber was arrested for questioning in illegal trade of Alerce trees. Although authorities then released him for lack of evidence, this event precipitated a heated debate in the press about the Chilean government's commitment to protecting the *alerce*. Sources in Chile allege that government officials have been complicit in allowing the export of *alerce* trees to the United States, where they are often used to build luxury homes.

Data provided by NASA clearly show the disappearance of large, remote groves of *alerce*. The trees, visible on satellite images taken in 1976, have disappeared in images taken in 2004. Because the listing of the *alerce* as endangered flora occurred in 1976, the

Pablo Fierro depicts "Casas Antiguas" from the area, and merits a look. *(With your back to the bus station, cross the street and turn left. Continue straight ahead until you see the brightly-colored "museo" on your right. Hours vary. Free.)*

◪ DAYTRIPS FROM PUERTO MONTT

SAIL THE SOUTH

The Puerto Eden *and the* Magallanes *are similar boats that traverse the glacial south. Jan.-Feb. 4-day trips to Glaciar San Rafael US$310 per person; Mar. and Sept.-Oct. US$280 per person. Oct.-Apr. 3-day trips to Puerto Natales US$275; May-Sept. US$200. All voyages include food and lodging aboard the ship (more luxurious berths can be negotiated for 30-50% more) and stop in Puerto Chacabuco. 10% discount for students with ID. For more information or to purchase tickets, contact a Navimag office: Coyhaique, Presidente Ibáñez 347 (☎233 306); Puerto Montt, Angelmo 2187 (☎432 360), in the shipyard; Puerto Natales, Manuel Bulnes 533 (☎414 300); Punta Arenas, Magallanes 990 (☎200 200); Santiago, El Bosque Norte 0440, 11th fl., Las Condes (☎442 3120).*

In the last decade, Puerto Montt has emerged as a gateway to the desolate beauty of the ice-encrusted passages, nameless glaciers, and frosty waterfalls of the far south. Even in the summer, some hills in the region appear to be trapped in an endless winter as snow creeps down as low as 400m above sea level. Enterprising companies have recently refurbished ships to carry foreign and domestic travelers into the icy tundra. Despite the close quarters on board, the boats allow travelers to enjoy a meditative journey through a frozen world. Large public decks are a respite from the cabins and provide opportunities to socialize with boatmates.

Most travelers begin in Puerto Montt and take the three-day trip to **Puerto Natales.** After passing Chacabuco's sea lions and lone albatrosses, the ships enter exposed waters. The massive cargo ship remains unfazed by increased waves until the **Golfo de Penas** (appropriately, the "Gulf of Struggle"), where the force of the Pacific swells and surges. As the passage narrows, magnificent glacial vistas and unchartered land pass by in a never-ending reel of ice.

Advance bookings are required for trips taken in January or Feburary, since the cruise has become increasingly popular among Chileans who plan summer trips. Still, last-minute purchases may be possible even in high season, so if acting on impulse, don't hesitate to give it a shot. Meals on board are basic—chicken, seafood, or beef with pasta and soup are standard. Vegetarians receive little attention, and are often served the same meal without meat. If you plan to end your evenings on deck with a glass of port with fellow passengers, stock up on wine or spirits before setting sail—alcohol is available at the bar, but it is expensive.

Accommodations are better than at most basic hostels, but the cramped living quarters can get stifling. Some bunks on lower decks get hot, and the floors may collect water. Comfortable beds come only with a fitted sheet, so a sleeping bag or blanket is necessary. Security is very good—all passengers have personal locked cupboards, although some don't have enough space to hold an entire backpack.

A popular alternative to this journey south is a visit to spectacular **Laguna San Rafael,** which leaves from Puerto Montt or Puerto Chacabuco and avoids the Golfo de Penas.

PARQUE NACIONAL ALERCE ANDINO

Check in with park officials in Puerto Montt before starting out. Smaller park offices are available on the Río Chaica and in Correntoso. Buses Fierro goes from Puerto Montt to Hornopirén (4½hr.; M-Sa 8am, 1:30, 3pm, Su 3 and 6pm; CH$2800) via Río Chaica (2hr.). There is no public transport to Correntoso; if driving, take the 46km V-65 from Puerto Montt to reach the guardería here. To drive to the Río Chaica sector, head southeast from Puerto Montt on the Carretera Austral until the road brings you to Lenca (36km), where a road (passable by 4WD vehicles) leads eastward along the river into the park (8km). Basic camping (CH$3000) available at Correntoso, Río Chaica, and Lago Chaiquenes.

Southeast of Puerto Montt and bordering on Estuario Reloncaví, Alerce Andino preserves a host of *alerce* stands and scores of rugged, bush-covered peaks. Infrequent public transportation makes access virtually impossible without a car. However, diligent backpackers can quench their thirst for wilderness on satisfying trails through these unique, virgin forests.

The most popular and worthwhile trail is **Laguna Fría,** which commences at Lago Sargazo and passes through millennia-old stands of *alerce* to arrive at a rustic *refugio* on Laguna Fría (9.5km, 5hr.). Conaf also recommends the trail from the Río Chaica park entrance to Laguna Triángulo (9.5km, 6hr.) via Laguna Chaiquenes (5.5km, 4hr.) On a map, you may see a trail between the Laguna Fría and Lago Triángulo trails; in reality, this route has long been overgrown.

taking of these trees was clearly in violation of the International Trade in Endangered Species. In some cases, as many as 70% of the trees were cut after 1976. In most cases, the area where the trees were cut shows burn damage.

Southern Chile is exceptionally wet and fires seldom occur naturally. Fires caused by man burn only briefly and rarely spread. But Chilean law stipulates that partially burnt *alerce* trees can be cut, thus giving would-be tree smugglers a foolproof strategy: arson. Impoverished residents of the region can sneak into *alerce* forests, ignite the trees, and then, once the forest has burned, legally cut the wood and sell it to lumber-trading middlemen.

With recorded ages surpassing 3000 years, *alerce* trees are the second longest-lived species of tree in the world—only the gnarled, North American bristlecone lives longer. According to some Chilean environmental activists, Conaf has only one employee per 900,000 acres dedicated to protecting native forests. That's one Conaf employee per region nearly the size of Rhode Island, and most of these employees are behind desks in urban centers. Without a substantial increase in vigilance, the next NASA satellite images may be bereft of *alerce* trees altogether.

CHILOÉ

In stark contrast to the spectacular, rough *cordillera* to the east, the terrain directly south of Puerto Montt melts gradually into the sea, creating an archipelago of gentle hills, verdant meadows, and muted natural splendor. Such is Chiloé, a collection of islands whose geographic tranquility matches the temperament of its denizens. The *Isla Grande* and the surrounding lesser isles are famous for a slower, rustic lifestyle, one that thrives on tradition, on wresting subsistence from the clutches of a harsh environment, and on isolation from the outside world.

Indeed, isolation is what most visitors first notice when coming to Chiloé. Crossing from the mainland by ferry, newcomers step back in time, to a place where many folks have never left the tiny islands on which they were born; where livestock block dirt roads for hours; where the daily catch is what's for dinner; where there are no movie theaters or McDonald's; and where local folklore maintains that mythological creatures stalk the woods and seas both day and night. Chilotes are fiercely proud of their unique culture, and seem to accept tourists as passing oddities, nothing more.

Yet the tourists keep on coming, in increasing numbers, drawn by mouth-watering fresh seafood, quiet harbor towns, picturesque fishing villages, and fascinating examples of the ongoing merging of pre-Hispanic Huilliche and Chonos cultures with their Spanish Catholicism. Chiloé does not promise the adrenaline rushes of the mainland: the archipelago answers the Andes' craggy peaks and spectacular highlands with rolling hills and quiet farmland. Voyages here are about taking time out from the rush of mainstream tourism and appreciating the patience and stolidity that characterize Chilotes. Here, tourists stroll slowly along dusty roads to see *palafitos* (houses built on stilts over the water) and rustic wooden churches, relics of a Jesuit past. Hostels house more Chileans, escaping from hectic northern regions, than foreigners, most of whom are too busy running around the mountains to the east and south. Chilotes often speak of their island as a separate nation, and modern daily life here stubbornly maintains striking similarities to that of past decades and even centuries. Just ask the people who live and work here, many of whom call the journey through their homeland *"la ruta de las tradiciones."*

HIGHLIGHTS OF CHILOÉ

CHOW DOWN on fresh oysters by the bucket in **Curaco de Velez** (p. 405).

SCALE sand dunes to gape at the grand Pacific in **Parque Nacional Chiloé** (p. 414).

PUTTER around the archipelago in a pastel-colored launch in charming **Chonchi** (p. 402).

RELIVE the Spaniards' last stand at Fuerte San Antonio in **Ancud** (p. 394).

MARVEL at two different species of penguins at the **Pingüineras de Puñihuil** (p. 394).

ANCUD ☎ 65

Since travelers to Chiloé generally seek a small-town charm, Ancud, the largest of the island's municipalities, is often overlooked. Some lament the absence of a traditional Chilote church; others merely pass through too quickly to notice. Regardless, Ancud has a unique and infectious life of its own. The **Plaza de Armas** comes alive on Friday and Saturday nights to demonstrate the town's combination of

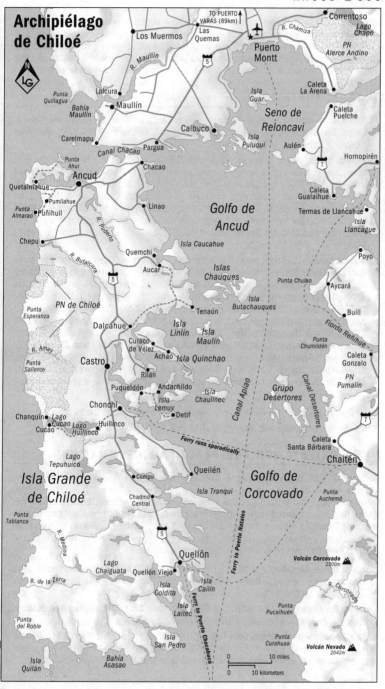

Archipiélago de Chiloé

TO PUERTO VARAS (89km)

Correntoso

Lago Chapo

R. Chamiza

PN Alerce Andino

Los Muermos

Las Quemas

Puerto Montt

R. Maullín

Isla Guar

Seno de Reloncavi

Caleta La Arena

Caleta Puelche

Punta Quillagua

Bahía Maullín

Lolcura

Maullín

Calbuco

Isla Puluqui

Aulén

Hornopirén

Carelmapu

Canal Chacao

Pargua

Chacao

Quetalmahue

Ancud

Punta Ahui

Caleta Gualaihue

Termas de Llancahue

Pumilahue

Puñihuil

Punta Almarao

Linao

Golfo de Ancud

Isla Llancague

Poyo

Chepu

R. Pudeto

Quemchi

Isla Caucahue

Aycará

Punta Chuleo

R. Butalcura

Aucar

Islas Chauques

Buill

Punta Esperanza

PN de Chiloé

Tenaún

Isla Butachauques

Fiordo Reñihue

Dalcahue

Isla Linlín

Isla Maullín

Punta Chumildén

Caleta Gonzalo

R. Amay

Punta Saliente

Castro

Curaco de Vélez

Achao

Isla Quinchao

PN Pumalín

Rilán

Puqueldón

Andachildo

Isla Chaulinec

Grupo Desertores

Canal Desertores

Chonchi

Isla Lemuy

Detif

Canal Apiao

Chanquin

Lago Cucao

Huillinco

Lago Huillinco

Cucao

Ferry runs sporadically

Caleta Santa Bárbara

Chaitén

Lago Tepuhuico

Isla Grande de Chiloé

Queilén

Golfo de Corcovado

Compu

Isla Tranqui

Punta Auchemó

Punta Tablanca

Chadmo Central

R. Medina

Volcán Corcovado 2300m

Quellón

Lago Chaiguata

Quellón Viejo

Isla Cailín

Isla Coldita

R. Corcovado

R. de la Zorra

Isla Laitec

Punta Pucaihuén

Punta del Roble

Isla San Pedro

Punta Curahuaa

Volcán Nevado 2042m

Isla Quilán

Bahía Asasao

0   10 miles

0   10 kilometers

Ferry to Puerto Natales

Ferry to Puerto Chacabuco

urban and rural life. Street mimes amble around packs of stray dogs and vendors hawk local produce in front of restaurants where families, raucous teenagers, and sedate senior citizens linger together long into the night. Rest and relaxation are plentiful here, as easy daytrips to **Peninsula Lacuy,** the small town of **Caulín,** and the penguined Pacific coast complement the town's closer-to-home attractions.

▐ TRANSPORTATION

Flights: The nearest **airport** is in Puerto Montt, and **LanChile** offices are located there and in Castro. **Austral Adventures,** on Lord Cochrane next to Hostal Lluhay (☎ 625 977) sells tickets for domestic travel. Open M-Sa 9:30am-7pm.

Regional Buses: Known locally as *buses rurales.* Based out of a dusty lot behind the Feria Municipal (entrance on Colo Colo, or just walk around the Feria), **Buses del Río** goes to **Chepu** (M-Sa 8am, CH$800) and **Quemchi** (1hr.; M-Sa 7:15, 11:45am, 4pm, Su 8am, 1:30pm; CH$1000), and **Bus Caulín** goes to **Caulín** (M-F 7am, noon, 4pm, Sa 7:10am, 2pm; CH$700). From a lot on Anibal Pinto between Goycoleta and Pedro Montt, **Buses Mar Brava** heads out along the Lacuy Peninsula, stopping at various destinations (ask the driver for specific stops) and ending in **Fuerte Ahui** (1¼hr.; M, W, F 6:45am, noon, 4pm, Tu and Th 6:45am, 4pm, Sa 6:45am, 1:30pm; CH$1200).

National Buses: Leave from the central terminal, a 15-20min. walk east of the city on Arturo Prat. Take any *colectivo* (CH$150) or taxi (CH$2500) to travel between the town and the terminal. **Buses Cruz del Sur,** Chacabuco 193 (☎ 622 265), between Pudeto and Ramírez, has updated schedules and tickets to: **Puerto Montt** (2hr., 16 per day 7:15am-9:40pm, CH$2600); **Quellón** (2½hr., 8 per day 7am-4:30pm, CH$3200) via **Castro** (1½hr., 21 per day, CH$1500) and **Chonchi** (2hr.; 7am, 2:30, 6:30pm; CH$2000); **Santiago** (6:40pm, CH$16,500; *salón cama* 5:15pm, CH$28,000); **Temuco** (8 per day 8:45am-7:10pm, CH$6900) via **Osorno** (CH$3900) and **Valdivia** (CH$5400). **Buses Trans Chiloé** (☎ 622 876) goes to **Puerto Montt** (8 per day, CH$2000) and **Quellón** (4 per day 7:45am-6:50pm, CH$2800) via **Chonchi** (CH$1700). **Queilén Bus** (☎ 621 140) may have cheaper fares to **Castro, Puerto Montt,** and **Santiago.** It's best to check schedules close to your travel days.

Taxis: Pudeto 210, east of the Plaza de Armas, or call ☎ 623 434.

Car Rental: There is no car rental agency in town—to get a car, head to **Castro** (p. 406).

Bike Rental: Hospedaje San Jose, Pudeto 619 (☎ 622 467). CH$3000 per day.

▐ ▐ ORIENTATION AND PRACTICAL INFORMATION

Many of downtown Ancud's amenities are two to three blocks from the shore. **Avenida Arturo Prat,** the city's main thoroughfare, leads east from the ocean, through town, and out to the bus station. Municipal offices, **Sernatur,** and the **Museo Regional de Ancud** surround the **Plaza de Armas,** located on a hill two blocks south of Prat and a block east of the water. **Calle Pudeto,** lined with many of the town's shops, restaurants, and bars, runs east from the Plaza to the inland hills and west to **Avenida Costanera,** which follows the shoreline.

Tourist Office: Sernatur, Libertad 665 (☎ 622 800; fax 622 665; chiloe@sernatur.cl), offers friendly advice and a wide range of information. This office also serves as Sernatur's regional headquarters for Chiloé. Open M-F 7am-7pm, Sa 9:30am-6:30pm.

Banks: Banco de Chile, Libertad 621 (☎ 621 166), has a **24hr. ATM,** as does **BancoEstado,** Eleuterio Ramírez 229 (☎ 624 102). There are no *cambios* in Ancud.

Work Opportunities: Fundación con Todos, Eleuterio Ramírez 207, 2nd fl. (☎ 622 604; contodos@entelchile.net), works with a network of farmers in Chiloé in an attempt to include tourists in environmental work. For details, see **Alternatives to Tourism,** p. 90.

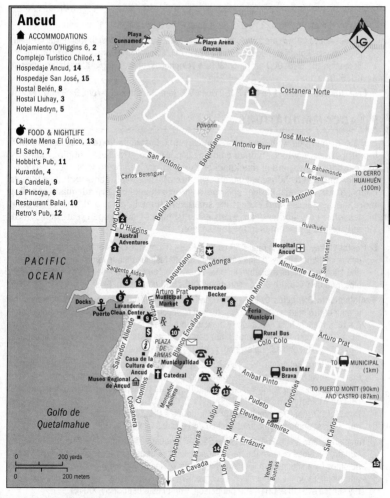

Ancud

ACCOMMODATIONS
Alojamiento O'Higgins 6, **2**
Complejo Turístico Chiloé, **1**
Hospedaje Ancud, **14**
Hospedaje San José, **15**
Hostal Belén, **8**
Hostal Lluhay, **3**
Hotel Madryn, **5**

FOOD & NIGHTLIFE
Chilote Mena El Único, **13**
El Sacho, **7**
Hobbit's Pub, **11**
Kurantón, **4**
La Candela, **9**
La Pincoya, **6**
Restaurant Balai, **10**
Retro's Pub, **12**

PACIFIC OCEAN

Golfo de Quetalmahue

CHILOÉ

Playa Cunnamed
Playa Arena Gruesa
Costanera Norte
Polvorín
José Mucke
Antonio Burr
San Antonio
Baquedano
Carlos Berenguer
N. Bahamonde
C. Gesell
TO CERRO HUAIHUÉN (100m)
San Antonio
Bellavista
Lord Cochrane
O'Higgins
Austral Adventures
Huaihuén
Hospital Ancud
San Vincente
Sargento Aldea
Covadonga
Baquedano
Almirante Latorre
Docks
Lavandería Clean Center
Puerto
Arturo Prat Municipal Market
Supermercado Becker
Pedro Montt
Feria Municipal
Arturo Prat
Liberdad
Blanco Encalada
Rural Bus Colo Colo
TO MUNICIPAL (1km)
Salvador Allende
PLAZA DE ARMAS
Casa de la Cultura de Ancud
Municipalidad
Buses Mar Brava
TO PUERTO MONTT (90km) AND CASTRO (87km)
Museo Regional de Ancud
Catedral
Aníbal Pinto
Goycolea
Chonllos
Costanera
Monseñor Aguirela
Maipú
Pudeto
Mocopulli
Eleuterio Ramírez
San Carlos
Chacabuco
Los Las Heras
Los Cavada
Los Carrera
F. Errázuriz
Yerbas Buenas

0   200 yards
0   200 meters

Markets: Mercado Municipal, between Arturo Prat and Dieciocho, to the east of Libertad. Buckets of crabs, fish, and shellfish are fresh and ready for purchase, along with bundles of seaweed and wood-carved crafts. Stands open approximately 9am-8pm. Across Pedro Montt, the recently-built **Feria Municipal** offers similar wares in a white-tiled, brand-new setting. Stands open approximately 9am-9pm.

Laundromat: Lavandería Clean Center, Pudeto 45 (☎623 838). Wash and dry CH$1100 per kg. Turns loads around in 2hr. Open M-Sa 9:30am-1pm and 3-7:30pm.

Police: ☎133. Plaza Centenario (☎628 655 or 628 656), at the corner of Blanco Encalada and O'Higgins. **Guardia** open 24hr.

Pharmacy: Farmacia Buseyne, Libertad 566 (☎622 281). Open M-Sa 9:30am-11pm. **Farmacia Ancud,** Pudeto 289 (☎623 369). Open M-Su 9am-9pm. AmEx/MC/V.

Hospital: Ambulance ☎131. Almirante Latorre 301 (☎622 355), off Pedro Montt.

Telephones: *Centros de llamadas* are plentiful, including at Aníbal Pinto 301 (open 9am-11pm). **Entel,** Pudeto 123 (☎623 839; open M-Sa 9am-8pm, Su 11am-6pm).

Internet Access: There are a few connections in town, but check first with your hostel, as many offer access. **ZonaNet,** Pudeto 396 (☎621 571). Open daily 10am-3pm, CH$700 per hr.; 3pm-midnight, CH$1000 per hr. **Entel** (see **Telephones,** above), CH$800 per hr.; noon-6pm, CH$500 per hr.

Post Office: Pudeto 201 (☎624 843). Open M-F 9am-1:30pm and 3-7pm, Sa 9am-12:45pm.

▐ ACCOMMODATIONS

For those equipped with tents, the scenic avenue **Costanera Norte** offers several cliff-top properties on which summer camping is permitted. If you are camping alone, try to negotiate a one-person, backpacker rate. Otherwise, the town's countless *hospedajes* manage to house the summer influx of Chilean students and their foreign counterparts. Ancud's budget accommodations, in general, are adequate—nothing more, nothing less—and except for small variations in price and amenities, most hostels offer very similar deals. Many establishments remain open year-round, occasionally offering discounts in the low season.

▨ **Hostal Lluhay,** Lord Cochrane 458 (☎622 656). Panoramic views of the *bahía* supplement unassuming hospitality, a limitless breakfast, and tasteful antique furnishings. Private baths and kitchen facilities available. Internet access free and fast. Singles from CH$9000; doubles from CH$14,000; 3-4 person rooms CH$7500 per person. ❷

Alojamiento O'Higgins 6, O'Higgins 6 (☎622 266), on the corner of Lord Cochrane. The interior of this stately old house is just short of spectacular, and exudes an old-world charm. A sweet, friendly host and a lovely breakfast nook help to keep travelers fully satisfied. The shared bathroom is a bit cramped, but bargain prices certainly make up for any disappointment. Singles, doubles, triples, and quads CH$4500 per person. ❷

Hotel Madryn, Bellavista 491 (☎622 128; hotelmadryn@hotmail.com), on the corner of Prat. Madryn has tidy, spacious, pleasingly private rooms. Tight staircases and low door frames enhance the mariner theme. Cable TV, private baths, Internet access, and breakfast (8-10am) included. Nov.-Mar. singles CH$10,000; doubles CH$14,000; triples CH$18,000. Apr.-Oct. singles CH$8000; doubles CH$12,000; triples CH$14,000. Separate 7-guest apartment includes kitchen and 2 baths for CH$35,000. ❸

Hospedaje San José, Pudeto 619 (☎622 467; rocarmu@telsur.cl). While a hike up steep Pudeto, San José is worth the trek. A new building out back provides rooms of varying sizes, adjoined by a sitting room with sweeping views of Ancud and the bay. Downstairs a kitchen and dining room make the place as convenient as it is charming. Internet access and laundry service available. CH$4000 per person, with private bath CH$7000. ❷

Complejo Turístico Chiloé, Costanera Norte 285 (☎622 961). A popular choice among backpackers, this campground is a fun and lively place to hang your hat in the summer. Cooking shelters, Internet access, and phone service available. Sites for up to 5 people CH$8000; spacious *cabañas* for up to 5 CH$30,000, low-season CH$20,000. ❷

Hospedaje Ancud, Los Carrera 821 (☎622 296; marcriser@latinmail.com), just south of the corner of Errázuriz. The amiable, retired teacher who runs this small *hospedaje* will gladly sit you down for an informative lesson on the region. A warm kitchen, complete with the aroma of fresh baking, combined with a clean shared bath make for a quality stay. Breakfast included. Singles, doubles, and triples CH$5000 per person. ❷

Hostal Belén, Arturo Prat 269 (☎622 343; hostalbelen@entelchile.net), above Supermercado Becker. In a central location, Hostal Belén is amazingly tranquil, with pink and red tones enhancing a plush wood interior. Rooms are small. Some have private bath. Singles CH$7000 with breakfast; doubles and triples CH$5000 per person. ❷

🌓 🔊 FOOD AND NIGHTLIFE

A multitude of well-stocked stores and cheap market stands will well serve those who cook for themselves. For basic ingredients, try **Supermercado Becker,** Arturo Prat 271 (☎ 627 100; open daily 8:30am-10:30pm). **Fruits** and **vegetables** can also be purchased from smaller shops on Pedro Montt, between Arturo Prat and Dieciocho (open daily 9am-8pm). **Fish** and **shellfish** are available in the **Mercado Municipal** and the **Feria Municipal** (see **Markets,** p. 353).

🦐 **La Candela,** Libertad 599. A breath of fresh air in the midst of Ancud's endless *curanto*-hawkers, this corner restaurant combines fresh, delectable cuisine, attractive presentation, plentiful vegetarian options, and quality service in a homey setting. Sandwiches CH$1500-1950. Salads CH$800-2700. Entrees $1900-4000. Open daily. ❷

La Pincoya, Arturo Prat 61 (☎ 622 613 or 622 511), near the port. Diners enjoy appealing views, excellent service, and delectable cuisine in 2 stories of semi-elegant dining. The *curanto* (CH$3800) is an obvious favorite, but *salmón papillón* (CH$3800), salads (CH$1000-1500), and *pastel de choclo* (CH$3300) complete the balanced menu. Open daily noon-11pm. Schedule may vary in low season. ❷

Chilote Mena El Único, Pudeto 318 (☎ 625 835 or 626 944). *Comida típica* with good ambience during all business hours. Reliable stand-bys like *churrasco con palta* (CH$1200) and *italiano* (with tomato and avocado; CH$1300) served up daily. The pastry display case is extremely tempting. Open M-F 11am-10pm; Sa-Su 24hr. ❶

El Sacho (☎ 622 260), located in the central courtyard of the Mercado Municipal. Despite being busy and bustling, this laid-back eatery will satisfy any fish craving. *Corvina* and *congrío* (CH$2000-3000) with heady sauces (CH$2000), served *a la carte,* are tasty options. *Menu* CH$1500-2000. Open daily 9am-midnight. AmEx/MC/V. ❸

Kurantón, Arturo Prat 94 (☎ 622 216). Friendly staff serve a wide variety of seafood dishes in this intimate, boutique-like restaurant. Although Kurantón is famed for its *curanto* (from CH$4500), the ceviche seems an equally succulent choice. Open 10:30am-11pm; liable to close early if customers don't linger. MC/V. ❷

Restaurant Balai, Pudeto 199 (☎ 629 089), adjacent to the plaza. If you're getting sea-sick from all the *mariscos* you've been sampling, stop by for a wider selection, including pizzas (CH$3300), *lomo* and *filete* options (CH$3600-4000), and salads (CH$2000). 3-course lunch specials CH$2600. Open daily 10:30am-1am. AmEx/MC/V. ❷

ON THE MENU

FISH FOOD

From the moment tourists set foot in Chiloé, all the restaurants they come across will invariably offer them one thing: *curanto.* It's the be-all and end-all of Chilote dishes, a no-holds-barred stew-like collection of meats, potatoes, vegetables, and spices, all served piping hot. Most folks come to Chiloé, however, expecting to have a bowl of ready-to-eat deliciousness set in front of them.

But no—eating *curanto* the traditional way is a very personalized, do-it-yourself experience. In most cases, the items are served separately, though all at the same time: chicken, beef, pork, and sausage on one plate, *mariscos* in a bowl, soup in a smaller dish, and potatoes and mixed vegetables off to the side. So, in this case, "buen provecho" doesn't mean "dig in"—a more accurate translation might be "start making your meal before it gets cold!"

The beauty of this, of course, lies in the fact that diners get to mix and match to their own satisfaction, choosing from a variety of delectable ingredients. Those who don't like seafood can order their *curanto* without it; they'll just get the same as everyone else, only without the *mariscos* bowl. Be careful, however, not to offend locals, to whom *curanto* is an art; the fruits of the sea are a major part of life here, and you may just have to suck it up and chow down on some fishy foods.

BRIDGE TO NOWHERE

The passage from Pargua, the last mainland town before Chiloé, to Chacao, just east of Ancud, seems a fitting initiation for travelers to the Grand Isle. In the course of the short journey, a certain quiet falls over bus-, car-, and foot-borne passengers who choose to sample Chilote life. Perhaps it's the refreshing sea-spray, which here tastes—not unpleasantly—of salt and fresh kelp. Perhaps it's the sobering sight of the Andes towering over the coast off the port side. Then again, maybe it's the great mouth of the Pacific stretching out interminably to the west. Whatever the case, the ferry brings calm to its passengers, and indelibly incorporates itself into memories of Chiloé.

For some, though, the trip is a nuisance, a hindrance to Chiloé's advancement into modernity. Occasionally, in winter, the weather is so bad that the ferry cannot run, hampering business-people and residents alike; some ordinary Chilotes also genuinely desire a firmer connection to the outside world, if only in the name of progress. Those most irritated by the lack of a bridge, however, appear to be industrialists, truckers, and public officials, many of whom have vested interests in the construction of a 2.3km section of highway across the channel. Indeed, such a bridge is supposedly on the way—as of 2002, the Chilean government had awarded a foreign contractor the rights to build it, hoping that the subse-

Retro's Pub, Maipú 615 (☎626 410), between Pudeto and Ramírez. This pub may not be very retro, but it's still a great place to chill and down a beer or two (CH$800-1300). In the summer, 70s and 80s music gives way to live jazz and rock acts. Burgers CH$1300. Happy hour M-F 7:30-9pm. Open daily 11am-4am. AmEx/MC/V. ❶

Hobbit's Pub, Pudeto 263, 2nd fl., between Maipú and Goycolea. You'll be greeted by the large mural of Gandalf in the doorway; the undaunted proceed upstairs for a drink and some company. Laid back and perfect for people-watching, Hobbit's gathers an eclectic mix of locals and young Chilean tourists, all of whom stick around for long nights of *cerveza* (from CH$800) and *pisco sours* (CH$1800). During the day, stop in for a cheap lunch special (CH$2000). Open M-Sa 11am-3am. ❶

🔅 SIGHTS

On sunny days, Ancud lends itself well to sightseeing, best started on the colorful and lively **Plaza de Armas.** Proceed to the **Museo Regional de Ancud,** Libertad 370, a few buildings south of Sernatur, easily visible with its striking blue base and turreted courtyard. The second-floor displays offer an insightful and comprehensive look at the Grand Isle's history, culture, and geography through ceramic and textile relics, a 1774 edition of the Spanish crown's *Recopilación de los leyes de los indios,* and pictures of the 1960 earth-quake's devastating impact on Ancud. There's even a picture of Ancud's Cathedral, designed by Eiffel (of Eiffel Tower fame), which had to be dismantled after the quake. Outside, a *fogón* (Chilote cooking hut) and various intriguing marine flotsam adorn the courtyard. (☎622 413. Open daily Jan.-Feb. 10am-7:30pm; Mar.-Dec. M-F 10am-5:30pm, Sa-Su 10am-2pm. CH$600, children and seniors CH$300.) While the museum's displays on Spanish colonialism will bring out the historian in you, a stop at **Fuerte San Antonio** will exercise your imagination. On the site where Spanish colonial troops were defeated and expelled from Chile in 1826, the grounds of the fort hold seven cannons. From the fort, walk east a block, then one block north on Baquedano, and continue east on Antonio Burr following the path to the top of **Cerro Huaihuén,** for the best view of town. In bright, sunny weather, expect panoramic views of the main-land with its peaks and volcanoes. Once the sightseeing is over, amble over to the **Mercado Municipal** (p. 397) for dinner or souvenir shopping.

In January and February, Ancud comes alive with a variety of gastronomic, cultural, and com-memorative events. These include the **Musical Days** of Chiloé, a loose confederation of classical music concerts in the second week of January, and the **Annual Meeting on Folklore**, in the third week of January, when respected scholars gather on the beach to discuss witches and mutants. Contact Sernatur (p. 396) for up-to-date information on these events.

DAYTRIPS FROM ANCUD

Ancud's outlying areas boast attractions that range from relaxing to fascinatingly unique. North of town, the **Lacuy Peninsula** curves out eastward in the shape of a fish hook, ending at Ahui, the point clearly visible opposite the town center. Created by the 1960 maremoto (the earthquake-generated tidal wave that transformed the plain between Ancud and Puente Ahui into a bay), the peninsula promises an incomparable combination of lush beauty and isolation. At **Piedra Run**, 24km from Ancud on the peninsula, intricate volcanic rock formations stand on a beach with undulating sand dunes. On the north side of the peninsula, **Faro Corona** will please lone rangers and lighthouse enthusiasts with its remote location 45km along the Canal de Chacao. **Fuerte Ahui**, at the eastern tip of the peninsula, 40km from Ancud, attracts many history buffs. Constructed in 1779, its ruined battlements are more intricate than those of its San Antonio counterpart, and it boasts 14 impressive cannons. The large ruin in the center of the fort is all that's left of the armory, while the underground stairs embedded in the hill on the site's inland boundary lead to the remains of the dungeon. The **Amadeus** (☎9643 7574), a small boat leaving from the muelles on Arturo Prat, makes trips out to the fort in January and February (3hr.). Call ahead to check schedules. Destinations on the peninsula may also be reached by land on **Buses Mar Brava** (p. 396).

Southwest from Ancud lies one of the area's (and the world's) most unusual sites. **Pingüinera Puñihuil,** an island preserve off Chiloé's western coast, hosts a significant population of Humboldt and Magellan penguins. This is one of the only places on the globe where two species of penguins coexist. A boat trip (CH$3000) takes visitors to the island from a nearby beach, but the best way to visit from Ancud is by catching an all-inclusive minibus tour with **Tour Pingüineras.** (☎9501 5594. Buses run daily late Nov.-early Mar. 9, 10:30am, 2:30, 3:30pm. CH$6000.) Supermarket Andrea, at the corner of Costanera and Arturo Prat, sells tickets, though buses leave from Sernatur.

quent decrease in transit time would increase the efficiency of commerce and development in this relatively rural sector of the country. Paralyzing snags, however, have held up the process to the point that no one can offer a confident response on whether or not the project will ever go forward. Indeed, many Chilotes resent the idea of a bridge, stating that it will spoil the island's terrain and culture. Some opponents counter that only a fraction of the apportioned funds would be necessary to improve the ramps leading to the ferries, an upgrade which would similarly decrease the duration of the passage. The rest of the funds, it is said, should be used to improve the road network that the bridge would connect to the mainland; the Chilote section of the Panamerican stands in relative disrepair, and many of the island's other "roads" are mere dirt paths.

The 3-year stagnation of the project, however, has made indifference the opinion *du jour* on the bridge. In keeping with the laid-back pace of life here, most Chilotes seem to think that things will turn out for the best; no one seems worried about waking up tomorrow to find *camionetas* from Santiago rumbling down the dirt road to Puñihuil. There are some who ardently support construction; those who have been buying up land near the proposed terminus of the bridge, for instance, consider the project urgent. For everyone else, it's *toda política*—so why bother worrying?

Caulín, 26km east of Ancud, not far from the ferry dock at Chacao, is a small town known for its oysters, handicrafts, and black-necked swans. A bike ride from Ancud to Caulín along the coast can be immensely rewarding, but watch out for the high tide—water rushes over the coastal road, making it almost impassable.

For those craving a more in-depth introduction to the area, **Austral Adventures,** Lord Cochrane 432, boasts a variety of tours on the island of Chiloé and the **Pumalín Fjords. Kayaking** daytrips with professional naturalists (who also double as guides) give travelers the chance to see the Grand Isle and surroundings from another perspective. (☎625 977; www.australadventures.com. CH$17,000-22,000 per person). Austral's crown jewel is the *Cahuella*, a luxurious vessel that takes tourists on all-inclusive four-, six-, or seven-day cruises (starting from Ancud, Puerto Montt, or Puerto Varas) to the spectacular waters, valleys, and hot springs of the Pumalín Fjords. (4 days, US$775; 6 days, US$1400; 7 days, US$1600.)

QUEMCHI ☎65

This small, sandy bay city (pop. 9800) with pastel-patterned boats lies at the end of a hilly 22km split that runs eastward from the Panamerican Highway. On sunny days, residents come out to drink, dance, and stroll along the docks, while visitors marvel at the impressive view across the Gulf of Ancud to the volcanoes of the **Hornopirén** area, which rise up beyond the nearby island of **Caucahué**.

Though not as grandiose as some of the island's other churches, Quemchi's is worth a visit if you are in town; to take a look, ask for Doña Maria in the brown-and-green house across Pedro Montt. In the summer, along the water there are **boats** for hire, in which you can explore **Caucahué,** home to **Morro Lobos,** a fascinating seal colony. To organize a trip in advance, call Nolberto Ampuero (☎691 260). A one-hour trip should cost about CH$3000 per person. For the boat-wary, a bridge connects the mainland to **Isla de Aucar,** 4km south of Quemchi and 500 yd. off the coast; during low tide, it is possible to walk out to the island and visit the pretty botanical garden. You can also hire boats to take you to the island. The **coastal road** from Dalcahue through San Juan and Tenaún via a detour at Quicavi, and on to Quemchi, is one of the most beautiful rural roads in Chiloé; it does, however, require access to a car, as regular Castro bus service only runs via the inland route to Quemchi. Renting a **bike** from one of the *hospedajes* in Castro is a cheaper option, but plan for a couple of days of travel each way. The views are infinitely better if you're traveling northeast. Be sure to check the forecast ahead of time.

Most locals will steer travelers toward the clean, bright, and reasonably-priced **Hospedaje Costanera ❷,** Diego Bahamonde 141. With your back to the bus station exit, turn left, walk past the central plaza, and two blocks later, 141 will be on the right. Ring the bell at the house. (☎691 230. Singles and doubles CH$5000 per person, low-season CH$4000; 6-person *cabañas* CH$16,000.) For the cheapest room in town, **Hospedaje Yungay 71 ❷,** across from the bus terminal, has adequate doubles with low ceilings. (☎691 285. CH$3000 per person.) Perhaps Quemchi's most heartwarming feature, **El Chejo Restaurant ❶,** on the Costanera between the Hospedaje Costanera and the bus terminal, serves mouth-watering local specialties, including *empanadas* made from just about anything. Be sure to sample the spicy *ají salsa* served with the *empanadas de carne* (CH$400). A hearty *almuerzo* (CH$2000) includes local catches and sometimes salmon.

The **information kiosk,** open daily noon-8pm, is on the waterfront in front of the town's church. In the event of an emergency, the **police** are available daily 24hr. at Puerto Montt 430, just a block north of the plaza (☎691 233). The Quemchi **public library,** Pedro Montt 431 (☎691 467; open M-Sa 8:30am-5pm), offers free **Internet access. Public phones** may be found at the *centro de llamadas* found in the **post office,** on the Costanera at Diego Bahamonde 450 (open daily 9am-3pm). **Minibuses** service the route to **Ancud** (1½hr., 9 per day 7:30am-6pm, CH$1000) via the Pan-american. **Buses Quemchi** heads to **Castro** (1½hr., 6-9 per day, CH$1000). All buses leave from the bus terminal at the far north of town on the Costanera, known as Diego Bahamonde in its southern stretches and Yungay on the north end.

DALCAHUE
☎ **65**

Dalcahue (pop. 3000) seems somehow oblivious to the crowds of tourists tramp-ing through it each summer. With relatively few *hospedajes*, no tourist office, and little in the way of amenities, this tiny hamlet doesn't exactly cater to travelers. In fact, it's the kind of place where folks will still stop and stare when they see *extranjeros*. Nonetheless, many outsiders pause here, either as a daytrip from Castro or as a pit stop on the way to Isla Quinchao. The famous Sunday market draws the most visitors, but quality crafts and delectable cuisine can be found in Dalcahue any day of the week.

TRANSPORTATION AND PRACTICAL INFORMATION. Regular **ferry** ser-vice to **Isla Quinchao** (10min.; every 20min. 7am-9pm; passengers free, CH$1500 per car) is offered at the dock. To reach the loading ramp, follow Ramón Freire toward Castro and veer off to the left (toward the water) at the fork just before the road leaves town. Regular **buses** run to **Castro** (35min.; M-F every 15min. 7am-9pm, Sa-Su every 15min. 8am-9pm; CH$600) from right in front of **Supermercado Ariztía,** Ramón Freire 114. To catch a bus for **Achao** (every 30min., CH$900), walk down to the docks and hail the next bus that comes down the ramp. **Taxi colectivos** to Castro (CH$600) leave from in front of the **consultorio general** (24hr. rural medical clinic; ☎641 295) at Ramón Freire 302, and tend to stop running around 6-7:30pm. Three blocks inland from the **Dalcahue channel,** the main street, **Ramón Freire,** runs paral-lel to the water and **Ana Wagner,** while **Pedro Montt** traces the coast, passing the market, municipal building, and cultural center toward the eastern edge of town. One block inland on **Calle Manuel Rodríguez** and slightly to the east lies a sizeable plaza fronting the town's *alerce*-shingle church. **BancoEstado,** Freire 645, has a **24hr. ATM,** and claims to change money and cash traveler's checks. Open M-F 9am-2pm. The **police,** Mocopulli 102 (☎641 748; **Guardia** open 24hr.), one building north of the intersection with Ramón Freire, are often friendly and willing to provide information to orient visitors. **Internet access** is available at a blue-and-yellow stand at the entrance to town, on Ramón Freire. Just walk along Ramón Freire westward past the spit leading down to the docks (keep going straight at the fork) and look for the signs reading "Internet." (CH$500 per hr. Open 11am-8pm.)

ACCOMMODATIONS AND FOOD. Although value accommodations do not abound in Dalcahue, **Residencial San Martín ❷,** on the southwest corner of the plaza in front of the church, boasts tidy rooms, a motherly owner, and low, low prices. (☎641 207. Singles CH$3000; doubles CH$8000; triples CH$10,000.) **Residen-cial La Fiera ❷,** M. Rodríguez 017, two blocks west of the *iglesia*, is also a good bet, but be sure to bring your own toilet paper. A range of rooms is offered on the second and third floors while the restaurant downstairs serves as the only main common area. (☎641 293. Kitchen access in the winter. Singles or dorms CH$5000; doubles CH$10,000, with bath CH$14,000; low-season singles CH$4000; doubles CH$8000/CH$12,000.) Down the street at **Restaurant Playa ❷,** M. Rodríguez 09, excellent waitstaff serve remarkably well-made dishes. The *cazuela de ave* (CH$1600), a Chilean favorite, incorporates a delicate blend of curry, cilantro, gar-lic, and onion for a mouthwatering, bowl-licking result. (☎641 397. Open 9:30am-midnight.) Cheaper **Palafito Las Brisas ❶,** behind the *mercado*, offers a variety of fish including *ceviche* and *comida típica*. (CH$1600-2800. Open 10am-midnight.) For groceries, relatively large and new **Supermercado Trahuel,** Ramón Freire 410, offers the best selection in town. (☎641 266. Open daily 9am-10pm. MC/V.)

◙ SIGHTS AND OUTDOOR ACTIVITIES. The famous ◙**Sunday market** livens up the waterfront in the winter, but only lasts until mid-afternoon. In the summer, people pour in from Castro, Ancud, and other outlying areas to keep both market and town as a whole bustling late into the evening. The lesser-known Thursday market also has some interesting items, but does not match Sunday's more extravagant affair. The **Iglesia de Nuestra Señora de Los Dolores,** north of the open plaza on the east side of town, built in 1858, mimics the style of earlier cathedrals on a more grandiose scale. Inside, a small, unmanned "museum" offers documents, scriptures, vestments, and hymnals from the history of the church. Just east of the municipal building, the **Centro Cultural Dalcahue,** Pedro Montt 105, displays a collection of models and artifacts focusing on the history and traditions of local people. (☎642 375. Open Dec.-Mar. daily 8:30am-5pm; Apr.-Nov. M-F 8:30am-5pm.) The **docks** are worth a walk any day of the week—watch fishermen pull in bags of shellfish and piles of fish and transport them to the market or to nearby canning factories, and be glad you're on vacation.

Three kilometers north of town, in an even smaller hamlet named **Astillero,** a *palafito* lodge houses **Altue Expeditions,** which guides upscale **sea kayaking** trips in the fjords across the gulf and to the outer islands of the Chiloé archipelago. Guests spend a night in the spotless, communal bunkroom before leaving for distant waters. Archipelago trips paddle through the **Mechuque** and **Chauque Islands;** guests stay in family houses for a full cultural and culinary experience. Trips are scheduled months ahead of time, but call last-minute for available spots. (☎641 110, in Santiago 2 233 2964; www.seakayakchile.com.)

ISLA QUINCHAO

Whereas much of Chiloé is still in the process of rebuilding and developing, Isla Quinchao represents the picturesque repository of all that is pure and alluring about Chilote life. Towns here lack the amenities of Isla Grande, but they make up for it with simple, unspoiled charm and the raw beauty of the nearby countryside. Ostra stands in Curaco de Velez welcome visitors on their way to Achao, where a long and glittering beach frames the nine lesser islands that lie off Quinchao's eastern coast. Visitors seeking the quiet and slow pace that have put Chiloé on the tourist map will certainly find satisfaction in the trip backward in time from Dalcahue to Achao, a route that Quinchao natives call "La Ruta de Las Tradiciones."

CURACO DE VELEZ ☎ 65

At low tide, the channel separating Curaco de Velez (pop. 3520) from Isla Grande recedes 200 yd. or so, creating a huge, black-sand plateau framed by rolling green hills and a tiny hamlet, whose name in Huilliche means "water over the rocks." The enlarged beach practically begs picnicking; this works out quite well, as there are a cluster of oyster vendors near the waterfront with signs that read "Ostras...para servirse y llevar" ("Oysters...Take 'em and go!").

The main reason to come to Curaco is to eat—preferably at lunchtime, since there are no *hospedajes* in town. Famous for their unparalleled oysters, townsfolk do their darnedest to live up to their reputation. A stroll down by the waterfront yields numerous finds: just look for signs that say "Ostras." **Don Carlos Oyarzun,** Errázuriz 20, sells fresh catches for CH$120. Follow the dirt path around the side of the green house; Don Carlos can be found in the yard behind it. (Open daily Dec.-Mar.) Standing on the steps of the church facing the street, head right on Av.

F. Bohle, down the hill and across the bridge, where the street becomes Avenida del Mar; here you will find a cluster of restaurants and *ostra* stands, including **Restaurant Los Troncos,** where visitors relax outdoors in a pleasant stand of trees, feasting on buckets of oysters and downing cheap but tasty wine. (Open 8am-9pm. Oysters CH$100-250. Fries CH$250-350. Wine CH$1800 per bottle.)

Continuing into town away from the highway, the first crossroad one encounters is Gabriela Mistral, home to the **Municipal Building,** 10 Gabriela Mistral, in which the **tourist office** occupies a small back office. (☎667 223. Open M-F 8:30am-5:30pm.) Gabriela Mistral runs parallel to Errázuriz, a block farther into town, which runs down to the water, passing along the north side of the town's **Plaza de Armas.** Bounded on the north side by Curaco's traditional church, the plaza pays homage to Curaco's most famous son, Galvarino Riveres Cardenas, a hero of the War of the Pacific. Visitors can find more information on Cardenas in the tiny **Centro Cultural,** directly across the plaza from the *iglesia.* (Open Jan.-Mar. 9:30am-6:30pm. Free.) A **post office,** at Errázuriz 7, offers basic services, but may not be able to send large packages. (Open M-F 9am-1pm and 2-6pm.)

Curaco is a stop for buses going both directions on the route between **Achao** (20min., every 15min. 8am-8pm, CH$500) and **Castro** (50min., every 15min. 8am-7:30pm, CH$1000) via **Dalcahue** (15min., CH$500). Buses drop off and pick up passengers on the road into (and out of) town from the highway.

ACHAO ☎65

Although Achao is one of Isla Quinchao's largest settlements, the town nonetheless remains relatively unspoiled. Fishermen (many of whom have never been further than Achao itself) from the outlying islands come in to market once a week, where elderly gentlemen stop and smile on the street, and where locals vend produce and crafts to one another, rather than to tourists.

Most houses in town boast traditional shingle architecture of various styles, with the shape and size of the shingles indicating the era in which a house was constructed. The beautiful **Iglesia Santa María** crowns a plaza on the east side of town. Built in 1767, the church is Chiloé's oldest, and boasts a breathtaking, ruggedly intricate interior, carved and painted in bright blue and white. Local artisans often gather on the plaza to sell wares, and are happy to chat with visitors about the town and its surroundings. Those with an appetite for further exploration report hitching rides (for a fee) with local fishermen at the docks, though *Let's Go* does not recommend this practice. Be sure, however, to secure a way of getting back before leaving; these islanders often come to town only on Monday, Wednesday, and Friday, arriving early in the morning and leaving in early afternoon (1-1:30pm). If you do head out to the islands, you may be forced to wait until the next market day to come back, or you may find yourself paying an arm and a leg to return on your desired date. Ask at the tourist kiosk for up-to-date information on visiting and lodging on the islands.

Restaurant **Mar y Velas,** Serrano 02A, on the second floor of the large red building at the dock, is a great place to enjoy a snack, a meal, a cocktail, or the view. (☎661 375. *Caipiriñas* CH$2000. Sandwiches CH$800-2900. Entrees CH$3000-5000. Open 9am-1am.) A few blocks inland, **El Medán,** Serrano 018, offers a daily *menú* (CH$1800) at a slightly lower price. (☎661 409. Open daily 10am-midnight.) For accommodations, try the seaside **Hostería La Nave ❷,** Sargento Aldea 01, at the intersection with coastal Arturo Prat, which offers a quiet *hospedaje* with fantastic views, as well as a tasty seafood menu boasting excellent oysters (CH$2500), both raw and on the half-shell. (☎661 219. High-season singles CH$5000; doubles CH$10,000, with bath and TV CH$17,000. Low-season singles CH$4000; doubles CH$6000/CH$13,000.) True to its name, **Hospedaje y Lavandería Armac,** Serrano 065, offers laundry and lodging. Rooms here are bright and seem to be the best bargain in town. A large hot water tank out back ensures 24-hour shower comfort. (☎09 619 2328. Laundry $1000 per kg, day-long service. Open to public M-F 9am-noon and 3-6pm. *Hospedaje* singles CH$3000, with breakfast CH$3500.) **Hospedaje Sol y Lluvias ❸**, Ricardo Jara 09, the green-and-yellow house on the way into town, offers standard rooms of above-average neatness. (☎661 383. Breakfast included. Singles CH$6000; doubles CH$10,000, with bath CH$16,000.)

The single road into town, **Serrano,** is home to a **tourist information kiosk,** Serrano 060, located near the entrance to town, which enthusiastically provides information and small maps and can help organize *agroturismo* ventures to the nearby islands. (Open Dec. 15-Mar. 15 9am-8pm.) One block from the coast, Serrano crosses **Delicias.** To get to **BancoEstado,** on the corner of Delicias and Miranda Velásquez, take a right off Serrano onto Delicias. One block away, you will find a **24hr. ATM.** (☎661 243. Bank open M-F 9am-2pm.) The first cross-street on Serrano, **Ricardo Jara,** is home to the **police station,** Ricardo Jara 012 (☎661 662), where those in need can find **24hr. guardia assistance.** Across the street lies **Ciber Zon@Net,** Serrano 061, an **Internet cafe** with reasonable speed and most standard plug-ins. (☎661 608. Open daily 10:30am-11pm. CH$500 per hr., CH$300 per 30min.) Regular bus service makes the town an easy daytrip from Castro or Dalcahue. *Expresos* (buses) to **Castro** (1¼hr., every 15min., CH$1200) via **Dalcahue** (CH$800) leave from the center of town; catch one in front of the police station on Ricardo Jara.

CASTRO
☎65

Jumbled, touristy, and slightly chaotic, Castro is characterized by a grid pattern of crowded sidewalks, traffic-jammed streets, and overwhelming commercialism. Prior to the earthquake of 1960, the city's topography reflected its history as a Spanish outpost established in 1567. Today, however, little remains of that illustrious past. Rebuilding efforts have not retained colonial charm, and as a result, Castro can feel much like any other nondescript city in Chile. Nonetheless, Castro's role as a transit hub often makes it a necessary stopover, and once here, most travelers wisely stray from the city center out toward the waterfront, where broad vistas, relative quiet, and traditional *palafitos* (houses built on stilts that rise out of the littoral flats) distinguish Castro's shoreline neighborhoods from their rather grungy inland counterparts. Having seen the *palafitos* and trolled along the quay, however, it's best to move on into the countryside, where Chiloé's slow, sweet loveliness can be better appreciated.

█ TRANSPORTATION

Flights: There is **no airport** on the island, though **LanChile,** Blanco Encalada 299 (☎635 254), on the southeast corner of the Plaza, books flights out of **Puerto Montt.** Open M-F 9am-1:30pm and 3-6:30pm, Sa 10am-1pm. AmEx/MC/V. Next door, **Turismo Pehuén** (see **Tours,** p. 408) also sells domestic tickets.

Buses: Buses rurales to destinations in central Chiloé leave from the **Terminal Municipal,** San Martín 681, just north of the intersection with Sergeant Aldea and set back from the street through a small *paseo.* **Queilén Bus,** also housed here, has departures to destinations farther afield. This terminal can be confusing inside—if you're bound for central Chiloé, you'll do best by walking out back, finding a bus with your destination in the window, and asking the driver for a fare quote. The information booth inside the terminal has a general schedule of all departures. **Buses nacionales** leave from the **Terminal Cruz del Sur,** San Martín 486, at the corner of Sotomayor, less than a block north of the church. **Luggage storage** available (CH$700 per day).

Castro

⌂ ACCOMMODATIONS
Hospedaje Casa Particular, **14**
Hospedaje Central, **3**
Hospedaje Chiloé, **2**
Hospedaje El Mirador, **6**
Hospedaje El Molo, **7**
Hospedaje Mansilla, **1**
Hostal and Hospedaje
   Quelcun, **5**
Hostal Chilote, **13**
Hostal Costa Azul, **9**

🍴 FOOD & NIGHTLIFE
Brújula del Cuerpo, **10**
Octavio, **4**
Ottoschop, **11**
Restaurant Años Luz, **8**
Sacho, **12**

Terminal Cruz del Sur (☎ 632 389 or 635 152), serves: **Ancud** (1½hr., 26 per day 6:25am-8:10pm, CH$1500); **Chonchi** (30min., 12 per day, CH$600); **Osorno** (CH$5300); **Puerto Montt** (3½hr., 26 per day 6:25am-8:10pm, CH$3700); **Punta Arenas** (36hr.; Tu, Th, Sa 7:00am; CH$38,000); **Quellón** (2hr., 17 per day 7am-10:30pm, CH$1300); **Santiago** (17hr.; 3:45 and 5:15pm; CH$17,500, *salón cama* CH$29,000); **Valdivia** (7 per day 7am-3:30pm, CH$6500).

Terminal Municipal: Various buses to: **Achao** (1¼hr., M-F every 30min. 7:30am-9pm, CH$1200) via **Curaco de Velez** (1hr., CH$800) and **Dalcahue** (30min., every 15min. 7:30am-9pm, CH$500); **Chonchi** (every 15min. 7:30am-9pm, CH$600); **Cucao** (1½hr., 5 per day 10:30am-7:30pm, CH$1300); **Huillinco** (45min.; M-F 12:10, 3:20, 7:20pm, Sa 12:10, 3:10pm); **Puqueldón** (1hr.; M-Sa 7am, 1:20, 3:45, 6:45pm, Su 9am); **Quemchi** (1½hr.; M-F 7 per day 7am-6:15pm, Sa 5 per day 11am-7:30pm, Su 9:30am-4:15pm); **Tenaún** (1hr.; M-Sa 11:45am, 1, 6:30pm, Su 6pm; CH$1300). **Bus Quellón** serves **Quellón** (1½hr.; M-F every 30min. 6:30am-8:30pm, Sa every 30-45min. 6:55am-7:55pm, Su every 30-45min. 8am-7:55pm; CH$1000) via **Compu** (1hr., CH$800) and **Chadmo Central** (1hr., CH$800). **Queilén Bus** serves **Puerto Montt** (4hr., 10 per day, CH$3200) via **Ancud** (2½hr., CH$1200); and **Santiago** (17hr., 3:15 and 5pm, CH$15,000). **Tur Bus** serves **Bariloche** (11hr., Su 7am, CH$13,700).

Ferries: TransMarChilay, Lillo 111 (☎630 630), offers passage from Castro to **Chaitén** (6½hr.; Jan.-Mar. M, Sa, Su 6:20pm; CH$12,000 per passenger, CH$65,000 per car), as well as information and bookings for trips from **Puerto Montt** and **Quellón.** Open M-F 9am-1pm and 2:30-6pm, Sa-Su 10am-1pm and 3-6pm.

Taxis: Taxis and *colectivos* running city routes cluster along San Martín. Look for signs that say "Parada" or a cluster of taxis. Call-based service is available (☎632 273). *Colectivos* to **Chonchi** (CH$600) are south of the Terminal Municipal east of San Martín on Ramírez. *Colectivos* to **Dalcahue** (CH$600) are located just east of San Martín, a block north of the **Terminal Municipal** (see **Buses,** p. 396).

Car Rental: Juan Andrade G, Los Carrera 480 (☎632 227), behind the large Goodyear building, charges CH$25,000 per day for cars and CH$29,500 per day for trucks.

Bike Rental: Casa de las Bicicletas, 274 Thompson, right next to the Bakania Planet Internet cafe (p. 398).

✦❷ ORIENTATION AND PRACTICAL INFORMATION

Castro is fairly small and easy to navigate. The downtown area follows the typical Chilean grid pattern and is bounded by **Costanera Pedro Montt** to the east, by **Freire** to the west, **Lillo** to the south, and **Magallanes** to the north. The **Panamerican** splits into the southbound **O'Higgins** and the northbound **San Martín** as it enters town. These two streets form the **Plaza de Armas** when they intersect with **Gamboa** and **Blanco Encalada.** A block to the west, **Serrano** runs from the Terminal de Buses Rurales in the northwestern part of town.

Tourist Offices: The **information kiosk** is in the Plaza de Armas. Open Dec.-Mar. 10am-8pm, Apr.-Nov. 11am-3pm. **Conaf,** Gamboa 424 (☎532 500), just west of the Plaza, has some info on **Parque Nacional de Chiloé,** but they generally limit their assistance to travelers planning trips of four or more days. Open M-F 9am-1pm and 2-5:45pm.

Tours: Trips to locales all over the island originate from Castro. **Turismo Pehuén,** Blanco 299 (☎635 254, www.turismopehuen.com), offers 8hr. daytrips to **Achao, Dalcahue, Isla Lemuy, and Parque Nacional Chiloé,** as well as a visit to the penguins and seals (CH$18,500 per person, min. 2 people; CH$30,000 for one person). **Turismo Queilén,** Gamboa 351 (☎630 670) offers bargain-basement daytrips to **Isla Lemuy, Isla Mechuque, Isla Quinchao,** and **Parque Nacional Chiloé** (CH$10,000-15,000). **Turismo Quelcún,** San Martín 581 (☎632 396), operating out of Hostal Quelcún (p. 410), has more budget-oriented full daytrips (10am-9pm; 2-3 person min.) Offerings include trips to **Parque Nacional Chiloé** (CH$10,000), the **pingüineras of Puñihuil** (CH$15,000), **Isla Lemuy** (CH$12,500), and boat trips around **Isla Mechuque** (CH$15,000). Quelcún also offers **sea kayaking** trips through the **fjords** near Castro (1 person, CH$28,000; 2 people, CH$17,500 per person; 3 people, CH$11,500 per person; 4 people, CH$8500 per person; 5 people, CH$7000 per person).

Banks: BancoEstado, San Martín 397 (☎632 251), on the Plaza de Armas, and **Banco de Chile,** Blanco Encalada 201 (☎635 331), both have **24hr. ATMs.** Both open M-F 9am-2pm.

Bookstore: Librería El Tren, Thompson 229 (☎633 936), has a lovely atmosphere, and a hearth for those cold, rainy, curl-up-with-a-book days. Open M-Sa 9:30am-10:30pm.

Laundromat: Clean Center, Balmaceda 230 (☎633 132). CH$1100 per kg; CH$1300 with ironing. Turnaround 2hr. Open M-Sa 9:30am-1pm and 3-7:30pm.

Police: ☎133. Diego Portales 457 (☎631 850), west of the plaza. **Guardia** open 24hr.

Hospital: ☎131. Freire 852 (☎632 444), north of the intersection with Mistral.

Pharmacy: Salcobrand, San Martín 449 (☎633 589), on the plaza, is well-stocked.

Telephones: *Centros de llamadas* are easy to find all along San Martín. **Entel**, Gamboa 267, is close to the plaza. Open daily 9am-10:30pm. Farther uptown, **CTC Mundo**, San Martin 783, offers similar services. Open daily 10am-10:30pm.

Internet Access: *Banda ancha* (broadband) connections abound in Castro. **Bakania Planet**, Thompson 256 (☎532 810; open M-F 10am-11pm, Sa 11am-10:30pm, Su 11:30am-9:30pm) and **Gyganet**, Sotomayor 279 (☎530 237; open M-Sa 10am-11pm, Su 4-11pm) both offer connections for CH$500 per hr. Check your hostel first.

Post Office: Bernardo O'Higgins 326 (☎632 725). Open M-F 9am-1:30pm and 3-6pm, Sa 9am-12:30pm.

ACCOMMODATIONS

As a tourist hub, Castro has *hospedajes* in every nook and cranny. Unfortunately, very few of these constitute good bargains. Mid- to upper-range accommodations that merit their prices are hard to come by, and budget options vary widely in terms of comfort and value. Travelers will find the highest density of rooms with a view on **Barros Arana**, the pedestrian-only stairway extension of Sotomayor. A word to the wise: *hospedaje* proprietors throughout Castro change prices at the drop of a hat, depending on day-to-day demand. Given the abundance of options, it's usually possible to shop around for a deal, but in high season (Jan.-Feb.), reservations are advisable for those who wish to find convenient, inexpensive lodging.

Hospedaje El Mirador, Barros Arana 127 (☎633 795; maboly@yahoo.com). This towering 3-story mansion has fjord views from some of the rooms. The lovely family of owners makes a stay in these spotless, well-maintained rooms a delight. Internet access available (and free in low season). Breakfast included. Dorms and doubles CH$5000 per person, with private bath CH$7500. ❷

Hospedaje El Molo, Barros Arana 140 (☎635 026). Right across from El Mirador, the space here is communal, with a bigger kitchen and a larger dining room for summertime meals. Front rooms with clean wooden floors may have the best views on Barros Arana—as well as one of the nicest *dueñas* in Chiloé. Internet access. Breakfast included. Singles, doubles, and triples Dec.-Mar. CH$5000 per person; Apr.-Nov. CH$4000. ❷

Hospedaje Mansilla, San Martín 879 (☎635 613). The kind woman here must be the most motherly *hospedaje* owner in town—with a stern demeanor barely

THE BIG SPLURGE

CHILOÉ'S PINK ELEPHANT

This hotel can't be missed—literally. It's big, bright, beautiful, and pink. Originally constructed in 1910 as the home for a large, powerful, native Chilote clan, the hotel is nothing short of breathtaking. Once inside, turn right and enter the turret, climbing its antique spiral staircase with panoramic views of the bay; you may want to pause after reaching the highest floor to sit on the small viewing couch that gracefully tops the tower. Straight down the corridor is a broad, red-carpeted staircase that leads even higher and farther up the hill, offering views on either side down to the hotel's base, hundreds of feet below. The staircase ends in a long corridor whose tempting depths are too much for one person to explore.

If nothing else, the view from this level encourages romantic ruminations, perhaps on the inspiration for the hotel's name: Silvio Rodríguez's famous *canto, Mi Unicornio Azul*, a heartbreaking ballad about lost dreams and dwindling hope. The name reflects, perhaps, the fate of the family who once called this place home; they moved out at the hotel's inception in 1986, though their spirits linger on in this grand old dream of a residence.

Hotel Unicornio Azul, Pedro Montt 228 (☎632 359; hotelunicornioazul@surnet.cl). Doubles CH$27,000. Salmon dinner, including appetizer CH$4000. ❺ masking her warm hospitality. Wooden floors, a clean bathroom, and a large dose of TLC make up for a dimly-lit hallway and the lack of ocean views. Hearty breakfast included, often with fresh-baked bread. Jan.-Mar. singles and doubles CH$4000 per person. ❷

Hostal Costa Azul, Lillo 67 (☎632 440; costazul@chiloeweb.com). The open staircase and skylight brighten the mood in this practically flawless hotel, the best mid-range accommodation in town. Cable TV, phone, private bath, breakfast included. Twins and doubles Dec.-Mar. CH$10,000 per person; Apr.-Nov. CH$7000 per person. ❸

Hospedaje Chiloé, Monjitas 739 (☎635 136), just off San Martín. Cheery, economical and hospitable. A spacious downstairs bathroom is kept clean. Internet access included. Breakfast CH$1000. Singles CH$4500; triples CH$3500 per person.

Hostal Chilote, Aldunate 456 (☎635 021). A two-in-one in a quiet neighborhood, hotel-type rooms are upstairs in the main house, while hostel-style rooms are out back in a separate building. Private baths and cable TV make up for the cooking odors in the full units. Homestyle breakfast included. *Hospedaje* singles and doubles CH$5000 per person, some with private bath; hotel singles and doubles CH$8000. ❷

Hospedaje Central, 527 San Martín (☎633 028), close to the bus station on San Martín. This *hospedaje's* brand-new rooms are located at the rear so as to shut out noise. An equally new kitchen makes guests quite comfortable. Ask for a room with a window, as a few interior rooms have no access to light and ventilation. Singles CH$5000. ❷

Hostal and Hospedaje Quelcún, San Martín 581 (☎632 396; quelcun@telsur.cl). Quelcún's tropical-themed courtyard lies adjacent to the upstairs dorm-style rooms. Quiet *hostal* rooms are complete with private bath and TV, but feel a little cramped—and overpriced. The *hospedaje* rooms are the better bet. Breakfast included. For details on excursions offered see **Tours** (p. 408). *Hostal* singles CH$14,000; doubles CH$18,000. *Hospedaje* singles CH$5000; doubles CH$8000. ❷

Hospedaje Casa Particular, Lillo 159 (☎637 431). Nestled among the more garish *hospedajes* along the waterfront, this house advertises itself with only an unassuming *"Hospedaje"* sign. Although a good budget option with newly-painted rooms and some solid views, the seasonal rate flexibility may facilitate over-pricing for unsuspecting foreigners. Kitchen access only in the winter. Beds CH$4000-6000 per person. ❶

🍴 FOOD

For groceries, visit the massive, two-story **HiperBeckna** at O'Higgins 711, at the intersection with Sargento Aldea. (☎637 100. Open daily 8:30am-10pm. AmEx/MC/V.) A wider selection of **fruit and vegetable** stores can be found on Aldea and along San Martín. In Castro, as in the rest of Chiloé, seafood is the victual of choice, although much of it is brought in from other ports. The tourist dining hot spot is down at the **palafitos restaurants,** behind the *feria.* All establishments offer cheap lunches featuring seafood (CH$2000-2500) and keep similar hours. (Sept.-Mar. 9am-midnight, Apr.-Aug. 9am-6pm, depending on availability of patrons.)

Octavio, Pedro Montt 261 (☎632 855), a block north along the coast from the eastern end of Barros Arana. The decoration is a pleasant mélange including yellow-and-orange tablecloths, Chilote neo-primitivist paintings, and nets draped dramatically over support poles. The family kitchen's food is equally remarkable. The savory *salmón Octavio* (CH$3400)—grilled fillet dressed with a fiery red sauce accompanied by your choice of rice or potato sides—is highly recommended. Terrestrial delights prove equally delectable: *Fillete à Champignon* (CH$3600) includes a savory mushroom sauce and also comes with a side dish. Open 10am-midnight. ❷

Sacho, Thompson 213 (☎632 079), a steep walk up Thompson from the southern end of Lillo and the waterfront. In the rarified air of the hill over the waterfront, the prices rise, but so does the complexity of the cuisine. The creamy crab-based *carapacho* (CH$1900) and *almejas Sacho* (clams; CH$3000) are great. Be forewarned—the place is often packed during dinner hours. Open noon-4pm and 8pm-midnight. ❸

Brújula del Cuerpo, O'Higgins 308 (☎633 229), on the southwest corner of the Plaza de Armas. Service here is perfunctory, and the ambience is reminiscent of a Denny's, but those elements are overshadowed by the reasonably priced food and huge selection. The salads (CH$2500) may be one of the best options for vegetarians in a town with a crippling dearth of non-seafood options. Hamburgers CH$1500, personal pizzas CH$2000. Open 9:30am-1:30am. AmEx/MC/V. ❷

Restaurant Años Luz, San Martín 309 (☎532 700), on the east side of the Plaza de Armas. Sit back, relax, and enjoy the U2 and Duran Duran while you sample the creative cocktails at this colorful watering hole. Creatively-named dishes (like the *Mar y Tierra* salad, which incorporates tuna and a variety of vegetables and legumes; CH$2500) add a California-cuisine flair to more Chilean standards, including fixed lunches (CH$2500) and *küchen* (CH$2000). Open 10am-midnight or later in summer; hours shortened in winter. AmEx/MC/V. ❷

Ottoschop Pub, Blanco 356 (☎636 281). A sign in the window reads *"El Rey de los Pitchers"* (the King of Pitchers), great for those who like beer cheap, cold, and easy to share. Pitchers of various beers go for CH$2900, and sandwiches (from CH$1000) and pizzas (CH$1200) are available for when those munchies set in. Open 10am-2am. ❶

◱ SIGHTS

Most attractions in Castro are actually outside of Castro, as the town is generally a stopover on the journey to points more remote. Still, there are a few activities to keep one busy within the city limits. A stroll along the shoreline, starting south from Octavio restaurant, will lead you immediately to a relic from Castro's distant past: a locomotive from the little railroad that could, at least until the 1960 earthquake. Continuing past some of the *palafitos*, you will come to the *feria artesanal*, a bazaar featuring traditional Chilote products; these include weavings, pottery, and woodwork. Turning right up Thompson, you'll head back to the town center, where Castro's 1906 cathedral towers over the plaza. Though not representative of Chiloé's more traditional *iglesias*, this church's bright color and large size make it a popular photo opportunity. Snap a photo, then linger on the plaza. On sunny days, musicians and vendors create a lively atmosphere, while locals and tourists congregate to slurp down huge ice cream cones.

Heading south again, away from the church down Esmeralda, you'll come to the **Museo Regional de Castro,** Esmeralda 255, where you can meander through displays of photos and artifacts relating to Chilote traditions and architecture. A maze of oddly partitioned space has displays on Catholic vestments, boat building, and the unique Chilote tradition of uprooting houses and hauling them to new locations. (☎635 967. Open M-F 9:30am-1pm and 3-6:30pm, Sa 10:30am-1pm; in summer M-Sa until 7pm. Free, donations requested.) Three hours north of town, housed in a done-up *fogón*, the **Museo de Arte Moderno** features Chilote artwork that incorporates traditional themes and modern aesthetics. Look for a bus or *colectivo* that includes Parque Municipal on its route; the museum is just beyond the park on the right. (☎635 454. Open mid-Jan. through mid-Mar. 10am-7pm. Free.)

Castro's well-known festivals are consistently the best on the island. The **Festival Costumbrista Chilote** in the second week of February is the largest bash, celebrating all things Chilote with traditional food, culture, and myth on display. Various other eclectic festivals are peppered throughout January and February, when the party never ends down in Chiloé.

CHONCHI ☎ 65

The heavens have good reason to be jealous of Chonchi—quiet and idyllic, this hilly *pueblito* is little more than a cluster of colorful homes around a flowery, well-kept plaza. Perhaps that's why, two years ago, the gods took their revenge here: 2002 brought Chonchi more than its share of small-scale natural disasters. First, a huge patch of the northern waterfront burned down in a massive early-morning fire. Then, a freak gust of autumn wind toppled the town's church steeple, leaving an unsightly wooden gash in its place. With reconstruction underway, however, town life ambles on: salmon boats pack the main pier to unload their profitable cargo, and area farmers herd their livestock among passing buses in the town center. Among the more attractive and traditional of the handful of authentic Chilote towns that surround more commercial and sterile Castro, Chonchi is also central, making it a convenient base for visitors making daytrips around the island.

⬛ TRANSPORTATION. From their office on Pedro Montt, the street bordering the plaza on the north, **Cruz del Sur** and **Trans Chiloé** (☎671 218) go to **Castro** (30min., every 45min. 8am-9pm, CH$500) and **Quellón** (1½hr., every 45min. 7:30am-9pm, CH$1000). From a kiosk about 20m down the street, **Queilén Bus** heads to **Queilén** (1½hr.; M 6 per day 7:30am-8pm, Tu-Th and Sa 5 per day 7:30am-8pm, F 7 per day 7:30am-8:15pm, Su 5 per day 8:45am-8:15pm; CH$1000). This hutch also serves as a stop for buses headed to **Puqueldón,** on **Isla Lemuy** (2-3 per day, prices and times vary). From the orange bus "terminal" situated between Cruz del Sur and the kiosk, **Buses Arroyo** and **Ojeda** offer a notoriously variable service to **Cucao** (1hr., Dec.-Mar. 6 per day, CH$1000) via **Huillinco** (CH$400). From Centenario, next to the church, minibuses (CH$500) and *colectivos* (CH$600) head to **Castro.**

⬛ ORIENTATION AND PRACTICAL INFORMATION. Candelaria, the road into town on the way from Castro, ends at a T-intersection with Centenario, which heads north past the Plaza de Armas to the port. A small, sheltered **tourist information kiosk** is located at the corner of Centenario and Candelaria. (Open Jan.-Feb. 10am-8pm.) Walk downhill to reach the plaza, around which most municipal offices are clustered. Other services include: a **24hr. ATM** at **BancoEstado,** Centenario 28 (☎671 226); **police,** Cerda 224 (☎671 845); **24hr. medical consultorio,** at Candelaria and Andrade (☎671 643); and **Internet access,** at the small "playstation" center next to Cruz del Sur, on the plaza. (CH$200 per 15min., CH$600 per hr. Open M-Sa 10am-1pm and 2:30-10:30pm, Su 2:30-10:30pm.) The **post office** is at Candelaria 134. (Open M-F 9am-1:30pm and 3-6pm, Sa 9am-12:30pm.)

⬛ ACCOMMODATIONS AND FOOD. By far the best lodging in Chonchi for independent travelers is **⬛Esmeralda by the Sea ❷,** which hugs the beach only 100m southeast of the *mercado* and the terminus of the Irarrázaval Costanera road. After seven years here, the Canadian-born Carl(os) is a true *chonchino* and proves to be a great source of info regarding all things Chilote. Sit back, relax and let Carl regale you with stories of Chilean history, legend, and current events; grab your camera and request one of the many excursions that he organizes to nearby locales, or slip on your boots and ask him to draw you a map to points more remote, including a pirate fort left over from Chonchi's headier days. A stay at

Esmeralda comes complete with a homestyle breakfast, full kitchen privileges, laundry (hand-wash) facilities, use of the Internet (CH$300 per hr.), rowboats, and bicycles (CH$6000 per day). Camping equipment and fishing gear available for a small contribution. Stick around long enough and Carlos will cook up a fresh fish dinner for CH$2500. Dorms CH$5000; doubles with private bath CH$10,000. Coming in a distant, yet commendable, second place, is **Hospedaje El Mirador ❷**, Ciriaco Alvarez 198, down the street beyond the fire station, southeast of the Plaza de Armas. A kind and hospitable owner maintains cheap rooms with clean bathrooms. (☎671 351. Breakfast CH$700. Singles CH$4000; doubles CH$7000.)

For basic food needs, large and new **Supermercado Economar**, Irarrázaval 49, on the waterfront next to the port, sells most standard groceries. (☎671 944. Open M-Sa 9am-9:30pm, Su 10am-2pm. AmEx/MC/V.) While Chonchi's diminutive size keeps the number of restaurants in town relatively low, there is still good seafood is to be found, including at the friendly, family-run **El Trébol ❸**, Irarrázaval 187, just a few buildings down from the *mercado*. Try the *Trébol del Mar* (CH$3600), a decadent fish and shellfish sampler. (☎671 203. Open M-Sa 10am-11pm.) Meanwhile, **Restaurant Alerce ❷**, Candelaria 308, on the second floor of a large brown building across from the *consultorio*, focuses its fare on fowl and beef. The menu depends on what the kitchen has in stock, and prices are determined by the chef's mood, but a tasty *churrasco* with a side order and a drink averages about CH$2000-3000. (☎671 346. Open 11am-midnight.) Top off any sort of meal with a visit to **Angélica Patricia's Pastelería**, Irarrázaval 61, where tempting baked goods range from ring-shaped *chonchinas* to artisanal chocolates (CH$100-500), all of which delight the tongue and the eye. (☎671 496. Open 10am-8pm.) Wash it all down with a shot of *licor de oro*, Chonchi's famous creamy aperitif, distilled from milk and distinctly flavored and sweetened.

◪ SIGHTS. Chonchi may be small, but getting around it proves to be a stiff task. Known as the "city of three levels," steep roads between the Plaza de Armas and the Costanera lead farther uptown. Fortunately, along Centenario, on the way to the town center, the **Museo de las Tradiciones Chonchinas** provides a good stop halfway up the hill. Opposite the intersection with Cerda, this is no ordinary small-town museum. The colonial mansion is decorated in period style and is artfully cluttered with old knick-knacks and colorful artifacts. The attic harbors a collection of local tools and photographs, canvassing a wide array of Chonchi activities and experiences. (Open M-F 10am-1pm and 3pm-7pm, Sa-Su 10am-1pm and 3pm-5pm. CH$500 "donation.") Any trip to Chonchi should include a visit to the **Iglesia San Carlos**, which, although temporarily maimed, has quite a beautiful wood interior and adds an imposing presence to the west side of the Plaza de Armas. Since the meaning of "chonchi" is "slippery earth," you may want to investigate the almost annual phenomenon along the northwest end of the Costanera, where a small **landslide** occurs, threatening the same building near the pier—try to find the spot, which may be quite "freshly slid" in the autumn and winter. Or if you're passing through town in the second week of February, eat, drink, and be merry at the **Fiesta Criolla de Chonchi**, one long party flaunting music, crafts, and *curanto* feasts.

▶ DAYTRIP FROM CHONCHI: ISLA LEMUY. Even if you don't catch the excursions that Carlos runs from Esmeralda by the Sea (see **Accommodations and Food**, p. 412), Chonchi's convenient location facilitates a relaxing independent daytrip to **Isla Lemuy** (pop. 42,480), the third-largest island in the Archipelago de Chiloé. A ferry, will have you on Lemuy in a jiffy. Much like slightly larger Isla Quinchao, Lemuy is home to a culture that has nearly faded from the Grand Isle; without paved roads, supermarkets, or a regular bus service, Lemuy feels like a world unto itself. Once on the island, walk (or bike) the road to **Ichuac** (3km), a tiny hamlet whose beautiful church stands across the road from its brilliantly colorful cemetery. A 5km stroll farther down the road will bring you to **Puqueldón,** the "capital" of Lemuy. The town has two restaurants, **Restaurant/Shopería Lemuy** and **Café/Restaurant Amankay** (☎ 677 207), both located just east of the central plaza on Carreras. In keeping with Lemuy's ultra-rural ethic, both eateries open occasionally (depending on demand), and offer a daily menu selected from a range of classic Chilote fare. After munching or relaxing at the beach, catch the last bus back to Chonchi, which usually leaves at 6:30pm. The **carabineros,** located on the road into town, are professional and helpful as usual, and can offer information to helpless wanderers. (☎ 677 233. **Guardia** open 24hr.) The **ferry** landing, located 4km west of Chonchi, can be accessed by bus or on foot (15min.; M-Sa every 30min. 8am-9pm, Su every hr. 8am-9pm; passengers free, CH$3000 per car). **Boats** from the Chonchi waterfront may also be available for transport to the other side of the channel, as well as to **Castro** (CH$5000). Carlos can also recommend various walking or biking tours, depending on your interests and time constraints.

PARQUE NACIONAL CHILOÉ ☎ 65

The road there may be long, hot, and dusty (or long, cold, and muddy, depending on the weather), but when buses arrive in Cucao, travelers step out into a magical world where white-capped lake meets glittering ocean, lushly forested mountains tumble into staid rivers, and beaches stretch into gargantuan moonscapes. Such is Parque Nacional Chiloé. This 430 sq. km swath of rugged terrain showcases the spectacular, if uninhabitable, beauty of the Grand Isle's seaward territories. Only Conaf's constant machete maintenance is able to keep the creeping vegetation from enveloping established trails. Roaring coastal storms frequently cause flooding, landslides, road washouts, and general misery among stubborn hikers who think trekking trails here is just another "walk in the park."

It's possible to "do" the park as a day's excursion from Castro or Chonchi, but many visitors spend several days here, daytripping from Cucao into the park or hiking up from town to the campsites and *refugios* at Anay or Cole-Cole. Despite the intimidating and seemingly impenetrable terrain, the experience of conquering the Chilote wilds is worth the trouble. The sheer variety of flora and fauna, coupled with the view along the weathered coastline, is awe-inspiring. Even Charles Darwin could not resist the temptation to tackle this backcountry. Traversing the trans-island route in 1834, he stopped in the small Huilliche settlement of Cucao and wrote a famous account of his impressions of the landscape. However, Darwin's little town of native villagers has long been replaced by a sprightly town that opens its doors to tourists in the busy months of January and February.

◨ TRANSPORTATION

Bus service to the park is available from Ancud to Chepu (see **Transportation,** p. 396) and from Castro (see **Transportation,** p. 406) via Chonchi to Cucao, on a daily basis. **Buses Ojeda,** which runs from Cucao to Castro, has been known to cancel service if the bus isn't full. (1½hr., 3-6 per day 7:30am-5pm.)

◪ ◪ ORIENTATION AND PRACTICAL INFORMATION

The park is divided into two main sectors open to visitors. The northern **Sector Chepu** is accessible from the settlement of **Puerto Anguay** only by boat across the Río Chepu. From the river, follow the trail south along the coast to the park's borders. **Sector Anay,** also known as Sector Cucao or Chanquín, is the most reasonably accessible part of the park, and the sector most frequented by visitors. The town

AT A GLANCE	
AREA: 430 sq. km	**HIGHLIGHTS:** Lago Cucao, the coastal bluffs, horseback riding on the sparkling beaches.
CLIMATE: Warm and humid with frequent and sudden storms.	
FEATURES: Hilly terrain covered in rainforests and groves of *alerce* marked by cliffs and sandy beaches.	**CAMPING:** Chanquín, Cole-Cole, and various other *refugios*.
	FEES: CH$1000.
GATEWAYS: Cucao and Puerto Anguay.	

of **Cucao** offers access from the south along coastal trails. The smaller, restricted sectors of **Metalqui,** an island haven for marine wildlife, and **Abtao,** a northern adjunct to the Cucao area, are so remote and fragile that access is both naturally and legally restricted. The gravel road to Cucao from the east runs alongside two lakes—**Lago Cucao** and **Lago Huillinco.** The lakes are connected by broad river channels and the water level is often affected by storms. Lying behind the coastal dunes, most of the town of Cucao is on the southern side of the bridge straddling Lake Cucao's outlet stream. However, several campgrounds and *hospedajes* are located on the northern side of the bridge, where the road continues into the park.

Although the main **park administration** (☎ 532 502) is in Castro (p. 408), the most helpful information can be found at the **Chanquín visitor's center,** 500m north of the bridge from Cucao. The center also houses modest displays about the flora, fauna, culture, and agriculture of the area. (☎ 09 932 9193. Open Jan.-Feb. 9am-8pm; Mar.-Dec. 9am-1pm and 2-7pm.) For safety reasons, it is recommended that visitors register their trip with **Conaf** officers. Conaf maintains an additional outpost near the northern border of the Chepu sector at the **Río Lar.**

ACCOMMODATIONS AND FOOD

Outside park boundaries in Cucao, there is a proliferation of small *hospedajes,* ranging from clean and friendly to basic and squalid. You should always see your living and sleeping space before committing for the night. On the town side of the bridge, along the main road, the bright pink **Hospedaje y Camping El Paraíso ❷** remains the best bet in town. With thirty years in the business under her belt, the garrulous owner keeps neat (if cramped) rooms and spotless bathrooms. (☎ 09 296 5465. Breakfast included, other meals available for extra. Camping CH$1000. Rooms Dec.-Mar. CH$5000 per person; Apr.-Nov. CH$4000.) Just next door, the clearly-labeled **Supermercado Elena** (open 9am-11pm) is attached to **Posada Cucao ❷,** which offers rooms comparable to those of El Paraíso, and perhaps a bit more spacious. (☎ 09 219 3633. Singles and *matrimonales* CH$5000 per person.) A cheaper but less attractive alternative lies on the right side of the road just past the bridge heading north, at **Cocinería and Hospedaje Las Luminarias ❶,** whose prices reflect a dingy interior and cramped bathrooms. Bring your own lock. An *almuerzo,* updated daily, is available for CH$2000. (☎ 09 775 0193. Restaurant open 8am-11pm. *Empanadas* CH$200. Singles CH$3500, low-season CH$3000.) Across the bridge, **El Fogón de Cucao ❸** provides a full-service experience (including a restaurant with a reputation for excellent *corvina*). Here Don Miguel Ángel, a transplant from Santiago, maintains some of the finest accommodations around, at appropriately higher prices. Horseback tours and boating excursions are available. (☎ 09 946 5685. Breakfast included. Laundry CH$2500 per load. Camping CH$2500. Singles CH$7500; doubles CH$15,000; *matrimoniales* with private bath CH$25,000.) Even if you aren't hiking or camping, it pays to **bring your own food supplies** because the selection available in town is severely wanting.

While campgrounds in town abound, many take advantage of Cucao's friendly, business-minded residents, who often rent their space to travelers across the river. After finding a site, locate the owner and offer to pay CH$1000-1500 for a night there. Or look for houses with "camping" signs out front. The official **Conaf concession ❶** at Chanquín is more luxurious than some *hospedajes* in town, with access to toilets, showers, and cooking shelters. More expensive *cabañas* are also available. (☎09 932 9193. Sites CH$3000 per person; 6-person *cabañas* CH$25,000.) Primitive camping at **Cole-Cole ❶** includes pit toilets and a basic shelter (CH$1000 per person). A range of **refugios ❶**, usually equipped with a cooking shelter or stove, can be found at the Río Anay, Cole-Cole, and the Río Refugio, in Sector Chepu (CH$1000 per person).

🏃 HIKING

The network of trails in the park is not very extensive, but the trails that do exist are well maintained and provide wonderful opportunities to see the coastal rainforest in all its glory. Depending on the weather, bridges may wash out, trails may become overgrown, and campsites may flood—all in a matter of hours. Check with Conaf for trail conditions before you leave, but be prepared for anything. Big storms can turn a weekend getaway into an exercise in survival. If you're not a wilderness expert, don't brave the weather if there's a bad forecast or if it looks ominous. For those who venture into the park, a sturdy pair of waterproof boots, good raingear, and warm clothes are extremely important. Hiking off-trail in Parque Nacional Chiloé is not just inadvisable, it's suicidal, and would require a chainsaw.

SECTOR ANAY. This sector, also known as Sector Cucao or Chanquín, can be reached from the visitor's center along a number of trails of varying lengths and difficulty levels. The **Sendero Interpretivo El Tepual** (1km, 45min.-1hr.) leads through bog and forest, with eye-catching flora along the way. It's a good way to get acquainted with the forest when you're under time constraints. The **Sendero Dunas de Cucao** (1.7km, 45min.), also an easy circuit, showcases the area cleared of vegetation by the tidal wave of 1960. **Lago Cucao** is said to be layered with saltwater on the bottom and fresh water on the top from the tidal influx. Fishermen report that both salt-water and fresh-water specimens can be caught in the lake. The stark beach between the lake and ocean is daunting on a gray, windy day, and stunning on a clear one. Access to the beach is also available from the road leading through Cucao. One kilometer to the south of town lies a large expanse of pristine *playa*, while within the park the road reaches the beach at a small Huilliche town three kilometers farther north, west of the bridge over the outlet river from Lago Huelde. There are trails around **Lago Huelde,** but it's more practical to hire a boat that runs to trails on the other side of the water. From here, a trail (12km, 4hr. one-way) leads northeast to the **Rancho Grande,** an *alerce* forest at a 600m high point in the park (ask at the visitor's center if the trail is open). Farther north, car access becomes difficult and the hardcore walking trail really begins. The path goes north to **Río and Playa Cole-Cole** (24km, 6hr. one-way) and continues to **Río Anay** (10km, 3hr. one-way). In bad weather, allow more time for the obligatory wading and splashing around. Some water crossings may be necessary regardless, depending on the maintenance of the trail. Follow the trail until it terminates on the beach, then follow the beach until it ends at the cliffs. At this point, the trail enters the forest and heads up and over **Punta Chaiquil** and down to Cole-Cole. From here the hike to Anay is straightforward.

OTHER SECTORS. South from Cucao, a trail (2-3 days round-trip) leads through private land to a popular sea lion hangout called **Punta Pirulil.** Locals or Conaf officials will be able to tell you about the condition of the trail and nearby campgrounds. In the northern Sector Chepu, the esteemed **Chepu-Lar-Refugio Trail** leads from the southern banks of the Río Chepu to the Conaf ranger station at **Río Lar** (14km, 4hr. one-way) and farther on to the mouth of the **Río Refugio** (6km, 1½hr. one-way). The trail is less frequented than Cole-Cole and lends itself well to a tranquil day in the great outdoors. Plus, the beaches along the way are stunning. There is also a trail along a dirt road between Dalcahue and Castro to the **Sector Abtao** (18km, 8hr. one-way), where a *refugio* is open and maintained. However, ask a ranger before attempting it, as the trail is often overgrown and impassable.

 THE HIKING BUG. Some portions Parque Nacional Chiloé's trails are not as well-maintained as others. This can make hiking difficult at times, due to overgrown vegetation, which may cause visitors to lose their way along the trails. Maps given to visitors also provide little help, so be sure to keep your bearings at all times. Additionally, in the height of the Chilean summer, many trails are populated by rather large *tábanas* (horseflies). Be sure to spray yourself thoroughly with bug spray containing DEET before you head out.

◪ OUTDOORS AND TOURS

If hiking isn't your forte, other outdoor activities are available. The Chanquín campsite rents **kayaks** (CH$3000) for use on Lake Huelde. **El Fogón de Cucao** (p. 415) organizes horseback tours to points of interest in the park, including **Lago Huelde** and sea lion hangout **Punta Pirulil** (2hr. daytrips CH$15,000 per person.; 2 day, 1 night tours CH$70,000 per person). In addition, a number of tour companies in Castro offer all-inclusive trips to the park (See **Tours,** p. 408).

QUEILÉN   ☎ 65

At first glance, Queilén may seem little different from any other quiet Chilote pueblito…but look up. Towering in the distance, an ineluctable reminder of mainland Chile's grandeur, **Volcán Corcovado** and its surrounding peaks provide a surreal backdrop for Queilén's long, peninsular black-sand beach. As if the view itself weren't enough, Queilén also beckons with sprightly, pastel-colored houses set in neat gardens, one of the finest beaches in Chiloé, and an unbelievable tranquility. Forty-four kilometers from Chonchi over a bumpy, unpaved (and very dusty) road, this town adds new meaning to the word "isolation," even here in Chiloé. Slow, sunny days and cool, quiet nights make Queilén's summers just about perfect.

◪ ◪ **ORIENTATION AND PRACTICAL INFORMATION.** Of Queilén's two main roads, each leading from the eastern side of the peninsula to the western shore, the more heavily traveled is actually the end of the highway into town. Once inside the town limits, this road becomes **Avenida La Paz** and then **Pedro Aguirre Cerda**, which ends in the docks. On the way it passes the bus station, where buses leave for **Castro** (2hr.; M-Sa 5-6 per day 7am-5pm, Su 4 per day 10:30am-7:45pm; CH$1500) via **Chonchi** (1½hr., CH$1000). One block west, **José Manuel Balmaceda** lines the southern side of the Plaza de Armas, then runs all the way west to the coastal **Teniente Merino.** Unsurprisingly, Queilén is fairly bereft of services; however, a **tourist information kiosk** located right at the entrance to town can point visitors to necessities and attractions. (Open Jan.-

Mar. 10am-8pm.) Barring help from this tourist-friendly outpost, the **carabineros,** Balmaceda 083, also provide good advice. (☎611 233. **Guardia** open 24hr.) A few doors down Balmaceda, a **medical consultorio** opens its doors to those in need. (☎611 231. Open M-F 8am-5:25pm.) All contact with the outside world will have to go through the proprietor of **Grandes Tiendas y Centro de Copiados "Camila,"** Pedro Aguirre Cerda 268, where travelers can find a **call center** and **postal services.** (☎611 229. Open M-Sa 9am-1pm and 2:30-10pm.) There is **no bank or ATM** in Queilén.

Ⅱ◻ ACCOMMODATIONS AND FOOD. Places to stay don't come easily in Queilén, but one good bet is **Hotel/Restaurant Plaza,** Bernardo O'Higgins 093, located on the plaza across from a small church. Adequate rooms come at an average price; the real draw is that you can walk outside to linger on the plaza while admiring Corcovado across the bay. (☎611 567. Breakfast and internet access included. Singles and doubles $4000 per person.) Should you chance to tear your eyes away from the view, you'll notice a convenient restaurant downstairs, where a complete *almuerzo* (*entrada, cazuela,* and entree) will set you back just CH$1500. Sandwiches (CH$500-2000) and *a la carte* entrees (CH$1500-3000) are also available. If the three-block walk from the bus station to the plaza is too much for you, there's **Hospedaje Ensueno,** Aguirre 259, just down from the station. Overpriced rooms include breakfast and a shower. (☎611 521. Singles and doubles CH$8500 per person.) Also very close to the bus station, **Lugga's Cafe, Restaurant, and Shopería** offers classic fare at low prices. (☎09 777 2170. Daily *almuerzo* CH$1500. Open 9am-midnight, or as demand dictates.)

◧ SIGHTS. Besides that which can't be missed with a simple glance (i.e., the huge peaks rising from across the water), Queilén's waterfront has a small but worthwhile **Centro Cultural y Museo,** Presidente Alessandri, just north of the docks, featuring images and implements from the town's (and, curiously, Valparaíso's) turn-of-the-century past. Long-dead prominent citizens gaze out from scratchy photographs neatly labeled and posted along each wall. Look out for people with the two identical *apellidos* (last names, generally the paternal grandfather's and the maternal grandfather's family names, respectively); rumor has it that Queilén's isolation has led, by necessity, to a certain degree of inbreeding. (☎611 460. Open daily 8:30am-6pm. Donations requested.) After scrutinizing the photos, climb up Avenida Presidente John Kennedy to the **mirador** overlooking the town and the bay for a different perspective on Queilén's stunning panorama.

QUELLÓN ☎65

As the sun sets behind Quellón, a soft orange tinge creeps into the perennial snow that smothers the Andes, which lie opposite town across the Golfo Corcovado. For a moment, all is still, and one can hear the water lap against the fishing boats in the harbor...but soon Quellón comes roaring back to life. For a small town, Quellón has more than its share of drunken sailors, aggressive beggars, and belching buses. Perhaps this results from the fact that, unlike its ancient neighbors, Quellón was born in the early 1900s as a commercial port; then again, maybe it's the town's pivotal position at Chiloé's southernmost extreme, which makes it a fishing, ferry, and naval center. Still, locals are hard at work trying to change Quellón's rough 'n' tumble feel, and the *zona urbana* boasts a number of conveniences (including a huge, gleaming supermarket) that soon-to-be ferry passengers will appreciate.

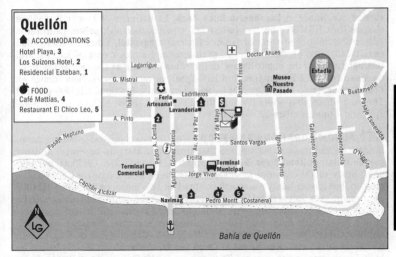

Quellón

🏠 ACCOMMODATIONS
Hotel Playa, 3
Los Suizons Hotel, 2
Residencial Esteban, 1

🍴 FOOD
Café Mattías, 4
Restaurant El Chico Leo, 5

CHILOÉ

🔲 **TRANSPORTATION.** From the **Terminal Comercial,** Pedro Aguirre Cerda 052, **Cruz del Sur, Regional Sur,** and **Transchiloé** serve Puerto Montt (6hr., 15 per day 6:50am-7:30pm, CH$4500) via Ancud (3hr., CH$2800), Castro (2¼hr., CH$1000), and Chonchi (CH$900). (☎ 681 284. Office open daily 8am-8pm.) **Minibuses** to Castro, reputedly faster and sometimes cheaper than the larger companies, leave from the **Terminal Municipal** on Alonso de Ercilla near the intersection with 22 de Mayo (M-F every 20-30min. 6:35am-7:45pm, Sa every 30-45min. 6:40am-7:45pm, Su every 40min. 8:20am-7:45pm). **Ferry** times can change drastically (sometimes at a day's notice) and oftentimes won't run in the winter due to low demand. **Navimag,** Pedro Montt 457, on Costanera just east of Gómez García, sends ships to Chaitén (15hr.; F 10am, Sa noon; CH$12,000, cars CH$65,000), with connections available to Puerto Montt. (☎ 680 511. Open M-Th 9am-1pm and 3-7pm, F 7am-1pm and 3-7pm, Sa 9am-noon.) **Aisén Express,** located on the bottom floor of the Hostel Romeo Alfa at the corner of Pedro Aguirre Cerda and Costanera, offers faster, passenger-only **catamaran** service to Chacabuco (9hr., W and F 1:45pm, CH$27,000) and Puerto Montt (5hr.; Th 5:30pm, Su 4:30pm; CH$18,000) via Chaitén (2½hr. ☎ 680 047. Open M, Tu, Th 9am-1pm and 3-7pm; W and F 9am-12:30pm and 4-7pm.)

🔲🔲 **ORIENTATION AND PRACTICAL INFORMATION. Avenida Pedro Montt** (known to locals as **Costanera**) follows the coast in an east-west direction. Most of the town's attractions and services lie within three blocks of the coast between the north-south streets of **Pedro Aguirre Cerda** and **Ramón Freire.** When Ruta 5 Sur comes within city limits, it becomes the east-west **Avenida Juan Ladrilleros,** the main commercial stretch in town. Accessing Costanera is difficult because three of the north-south streets don't reach the coast east of **Avenida A. Gómez García,** although there is a stairway down to Costanera near the end of **Avenida 22 de Mayo.**

The small **information kiosk** on the Plaza de Armas, at the corner of Santos Vargas and Gómez García, houses a staff whose exceptional eagerness to help will leave tourists laden with information. (Open Dec. 15-Mar. 15 M-F 9am-9:30pm, Sa-Su 11am-7pm.) **BancoEstado,** 22 de Mayo 399, at the corner of Ladrilleros, has a **24hr. ATM** (MC only) and exchanges and cashes checks—for a premium. (☎ 681 266. Open M-F 9am-2pm.) Other amenities include **laundry** service, available at **Lavandería Ruck Zack,** Ladrilleros 399, which washes clothes for CH$4500 a basket. (☎681 787. Open 9am-9pm.); **police,** Ladrilleros 461 (☎682 865), just west of Gómez García; a **hospital,** Eduardo Ahues 305 (☎681 243), two blocks north of Ladrilleros and a block east of La Paz; and **Internet access** at the **public library,** in the same building as the **post office** on 22 de Mayo (open M-F 9am-1pm and 2:30-7pm), or next door at **Capacitación en Computación.** (☎681 011. Open M-Sa 9am-1pm and 2-11:30pm. CH$500 per hr.) The post office also offers **Western Union** services. (☎681 862. Open M-F 9am-1pm and 3-6pm, Sa 9am-12:30pm.)

⬛⬛ ACCOMMODATIONS AND FOOD. With few exceptions, Quellón's accomodations and restaurants are less than promising. Bargain-basement housing can be found at **Hotel Playa ❶,** Pedro Montt 427. (☎681 278. CH$3500 per person.) Some might consider **Residencial Esteban ❷,** Pedro Aguirre Cerda 355, a step up, but it's probably not worth the buck or two more. (☎681 438. CH$4000 per person.) **Los Suizos Hotel ❹,** Ladrilleros 399, at the southeast corner with La Paz, is definitely a step up, with well-appointed rooms and friendly service. (☎681 787. Private bath and cable TV. Breakfast included. Singles CH$15,000; doubles CH$18,000; *matrimoniales* CH$22,000.) **Camping** can be found south and west of the city. **Restaurant El Chico Leo ❷,** Pedro Montt 325, is hailed by locals as the best lunch in town. The *curanto* (CH$3500) might strike the fancy of more culinarily ambitious folk. *Menú* (CH$1900) includes *cazuela* and an entree. (☎681 567. Open 7am-midnight. AmEx/MC/V.) Down the street, **Café Mattías ❸,** Pedro Montt 227, also serves a daily *almuerzo* (CH$2500), or entrees *a la carte* for around CH$2000. (Open 11am-midnight.)

◪ SIGHTS. Quellón does not offer any in-town activities worth missing the ferry for. If you have some time on your hands, however, the **Museo Nuestro Pasado,** Ladrilleros 225, east of the center, includes a striking sculpture and arboreal garden. The real draws are reconstructions of the ubiquitous *fogón*, the *companaría*, and the primitive mill. (☎681 213. Open Dec.-Mar. during daylight. CH$500.) The **feria artesanal,** on Gómez García, features carved and knitted wares, but doesn't compare with its counterparts in Castro and Dalcahue. For a nice day not too far away, head for the (quite swimmable) beach opposite town, known as **Punta de Lapa.** At the very tip of this peninsular outcropping, a monument marks the end of Highway 5, the Panamerican. Municipal buses from town head to the Punta. Just grab any west-bound bus on Ladrilleros that reads "Punta de Lapa."

Tours to nearby Isla Cailín can be arranged through the **Cámara de Turismo de Quellón,** in the *feria artesanal* at the fifth stall from the top of hill. Eight-hour tours include two guides (one of whom is a local Huilliche chieftain), and are a steal at CH$10,000 per person. (☎682 440; leclerc@hotmail.com.)

 ALL ABOARD...OR NOT. While traveling by boat from local docks may be an inexpensive and exciting method of travel to nearby islands, boat travel is often undependable, with rides back to the Grand Isle often being hard to come by. Travelers from Quellón to surrounding islands should arrange tours with the local **Cámara de Turismo** (see **Sights,** above) to ensure round-trip service.

AISÉN AND THE CARRETERA AUSTRAL

Aisén—over 1000km of wild, rugged, mountainous terrain—is Chile's least developed region. Indeed, with less than 100,000 people inhabiting this untamed land, it is almost entirely *un*developed. In colonial days, Spanish and British sailors making the journey through the Straits of Magellan reported that Aisén was an inhospitable land lacking any trace of human civilization. Even after subduing the fierce Mapuche in the 19th century, few Chileans ventured south of Puerto Montt. The reason is not hard to fathom. Just beyond Puerto Montt, the lush valley running through Middle Chile and Los Lagos plunges into the Pacific Ocean, creating a mazelike coastline of channels, inlets, fjords, and archipelagos, while the interior is dominated by snow-capped mountains, thick forests, and raging rivers.

Aisén is one of the poorest regions in Chile and the government has frequently subsidized development efforts in the area. In the 1960s, government incentives inspired a minor migration southward, which resulted in the uncontrolled clearing of many forests for lumber and farmland. In 1976, General Pinochet worried that Chile's archrival, Argentina, could attack through this totally undefended region. He initiated a project to improve communication and infrastructure in the south, which entailed the construction of the grand Carretera Austral, an audacious public-works project intended to create a vital highway corridor for exploiting the region's resources and connecting its isolated people. Despite the road's smooth beginnings in Puerto Montt, this road tripper's dream-come-true quickly turns into a rough, partially maintained dirt road that disappears entirely in some places when the terrain becomes unruly.

The best place to begin an exploration of the area is in **Chaitén,** just south of Puerto Montt and reachable by flight or ferry. Nearby, the incredible Parque Pumalín introduces travelers to the ruggedness of the region. Once accustomed to dense forests, dirt roads, and stark mountains, head south to **Futaleufú.** This hot spot is the center of adventure tourism in Aisén and home to the famous and ferocious rapids of the **Río Futaleufú.** South of Futaleufú, the road gets rougher, winding around hairpin turns and raging torrents while passing tiny frontier towns. Stay a day in **Puyuhuapi** checking out its unique German heritage, **Parque Nacional Queulat,** and the local thermal spa. Then proceed south again to the bustling regional hub, **Coyhaique.** The ride isn't over here: south of Coyhaique, the scenery continues to increase in splendor as the Carretera winds toward **Cochrane** and its termination point, **Villa O'Higgins,** where the bold can continue on to Argentina. Along the way, don't miss tranquil **Tortel,** a charming, boardwalked fishing village that opened to the world with the completion of the first road to it several years ago.

HIGHLIGHTS OF AISÉN AND THE CARRETERA AUSTRAL

BATTLE the raging rapids of the mighty **Río Futaleufú** in a fragile kayak (p. 426).

GAPE at the incredible hanging glacier, suspended over the placid waters of a blue-green lake in **Parque Nacional Queulat** (p. 430).

WHILE away the hours fly-fishing in the rolling river of **Reserva Nacional Río Simpson** (p. 435) outside of **Coyhaique** (p. 431).

MEANDER through the largest private park in the world, **Parque Pumalín** (p. 426).

AISÉN

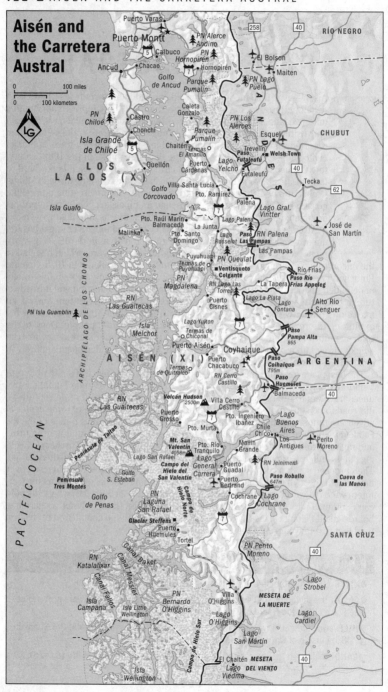

Aisén and the Carretera Austral

0 — 100 miles
0 — 100 kilometers

RÍO NEGRO

Puerto Varas
Puerto Montt
PN Alerce Andino
Calbuco
Ancud
Chácao
Hornopirén
PN Hornopirén
Hornopirén
El Bolsón
Maiten
Golfo de Ancud
Parque Pumalín
PN Lago Puelo
Caleta Gonzalo
PN Chiloé
Castro
Chonchi
PN Los Alerces
CHUBUT
Isla Grande de Chiloé
Parque Pumalín
Esquel
Chaitén
Termas El Amarillo
Trevelin
Welsh Town
Paso Futaleufú
Puerto Cárdenas
Lago Yelcho
Quellón
Futaleufú
L O S L A G O S (X)
Tecka
Golfo Corcovado
Villa Santa Lucía
Pto. Ramírez
Palena
Lago Gral. Vintter
Isla Guafo
Lago Palena
José de San Martín
Pto. Raúl Marín Balmaceda
La Junta
Paso Las Pampas
RN Palena
Malinka
Pto. Santo Domingo
Lago Rosselot
Las Pampas
Puyuhuapi
PN Queulat
Río Frías
Termas de Puyuhuapi
Ventisquero Colgante
Paso Río Frías Appeleg
PN Magdalena
RN Lago Las Torres
La Tapera
PN Isla Guamblin
RN Las Guaitecas
Puerto Cisnes
Lago La Plata
Alto Río Senguer
Lago Fontana
Isla Melchor
Lago Yulton
Termas de Chiconal
Puerto Aisén
Coyhaique
Paso Pampa Alta 865
A I S É N (XI)
Puerto Chacabuco
Paso Colhaique 795m
ARGENTINA
Termas de Quitralco
RN Cerro Castillo
Paso Huemules
RN Las Guaitecas
Volcán Hudson 2500m
Villa Cerro Castillo
Balmaceda
Puerto Grosso
Pto. Ingeniero Ibañez
Lago Buenos Aires
Pto. Murta
Chile Chico
Perito Moreno
Mt. San Valentín 4058m
Pto. Río Tranquilo
Malín Grande
Los Antiguos
Lago San Rafael
Campo del Hielo del San Valentín
Lago General Carrera
Puerto Guadal
RN Jeinimeni
PN Laguna San Rafael
Campo de Hielo Norte
Puerto Bertrand
Paso Roballo 647m
Cueva de las Manos
Glaciar Steffens
Cochrane
Lago Cochrane
Puerto Huemules
Tortel
SANTA CRUZ
PN Perito Moreno
RN Katalalixar
Canal Baker
Canal Messier
PN Bernardo O'Higgins
Villa O'Higgins
MESETA DE LA MUERTE
Lago Strobel
Isla Campana
Isla Little Wellington
Lago O'Higgins
Lago Cardiel
Campo de Hielo Sur
Lago San Martín
El Chaltén
MESETA DEL VIENTO
Lago Viedma
Isla Wellington

PACIFIC OCEAN
ARCHIPIÉLAGO DE LOS CHONOS
Península de Taitao
Península Tres Montes
Golfo S. Esteban
Golfo de Penas
Isla Guafo

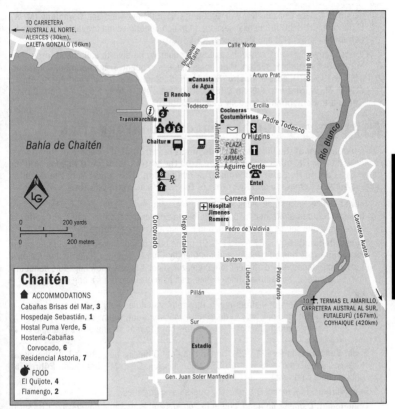

TO CARRETERA AUSTRAL AL NORTE, ALERCES (30km), CALETA GONZALO (56km)

Calle Norte

Diagonal Portales

Arturo Prat

Río Blanco

■Canasta de Agua

El Rancho

Todesco

Ercilla

Transmarchile

Cocineras Costumbristas

Padre Todesco

Río Blanco

Bahía de Chaitén

Almirante Riveros

O'Higgins

Chaitur■

PLAZA DE ARMAS

Aguirre Cerda

Entel

Carrera Pinto

Corcovado

Diego Portales

Hospital Jimenes Romero

Pedro de Valdivia

0   200 yards

0   200 meters

Lautaro

Libertad

Piloto Pardo

Carretera Austral

TO ✈, TERMAS EL AMARILLO, CARRETERA AUSTRAL AL SUR, FUTALEUFÚ (167km), COYHAIQUE (420km)

Pillán

Sur

Chaitén

🏠 ACCOMMODATIONS
Cabañas Brisas del Mar, **3**
Hospedaje Sebastián, **1**
Hostal Puma Verde, **5**
Hostería-Cabañas Corvocado, **6**
Residencial Astoria, **7**

🍴 FOOD
El Quijote, **4**
Flamengo, **2**

Estadio

Gen. Juan Soler Manfredini

AISÉN

CHAITÉN   ☎ 69

This rugged town serves as a regional port, receiving local flights and crowded ferries from Chiloé and Puerto Montt. The popular and well-serviced Parque Pumalín lies just to the north, providing visitors with a rare peek into the region's inaccessible wilderness. Chaitén lies between the striking Volcán Michinmáhuida to the northeast and the subtler Volcán Corcovado to the southwest. In between, in town, the paucity of services suggests that visitors are wise to pass through.

TRANSPORTATION

As a port with many transportation options, Chaitén serves to unite sea, land, and air travel efficiently.

Flights: The local airport is located 6km south of town. **Aero Taxis del Sur,** Riveros 479 (☎731 315), flies to **Puerto Montt** (M-Sa 1pm; CH$32,000, including airport shuttle). Same-day tickets occasionally discounted. Contact **Chaitur** (see below) for information on other air options.

Buses: The **bus station** is at the **Chaitur** office on O'Higgins. Chaitur manages most local departures. Schedules are highly variable depending on season and demand, so be sure to contact Chaitur in advance of the planned travel day. In high season, buses generally depart to **Caleta Gonzalo** (M, W, F 9:30am; CH$3500 one-way) and **Coyhaique** (M, W, F, Su 9am; CH$15,000). In high season, afternoon departures are available most days to **Futaleufú** (CH$6000) and **Puyuhuapi** (CH$8000).

Ferries: Ferry prices and schedules change frequently. Be sure to call ahead, especially outside of the summer season when boats are less frequent. **Transmarchile,** Corcovado 266 (☎731 272), goes to **Castro** (8hr.; M, W, Su 9am; CH$10,000) and **Puerto Montt** (12hr.; M, W, Su 9pm, F 9am; CH$12,000). Jan.-Feb., a ferry also runs from **Caleta Gonzala** to **Hornopirén** (6hr., daily 9am, CH$9000).

 ORIENTATION AND PRACTICAL INFORMATION

Two blocks east of the bay, the **Plaza de Armas** is surrounded by some of the town's basic services. The main street running from the water to town is **O'Higgins,** and on it lie the Parque Pumalín office and the bus station. The road along the coast is called **Avenida Corcovado** and has most of the town's accommodations.

Tourist Office: In a small glass booth on Corcovado, near Padre Juan Todesco. Offers basic brochures and a helpful staff member to answer questions. Nicolás at **Chaitur** is also a valuable source of information and English-language guidance.

Tours: Chaitur, O'Higgins 67 (☎731 429), in the bus station. Owned and operated by an American expat named Nicolás and his friendly Chilean family, Chaitur is the region's most comprehensive and efficient tour organizer. Nicolás is very knowledgeable about the Carretera Austral, and with advance notice, can help organize tours along its length.

> **TIP** Small numbers of visitors mean that tour schedules vary with demand, so don't count on being able to do exactly what you want, when you want to, without paying through the nose, as you may have to rent an entire bus yourself.

Bank: BancoEstado (☎731 260), on the corner of O'Higgins and Libertad, on the plaza. Changes traveler's checks with a US$12 commission. Open M-F 9am-2pm. **24hr. ATM** only accepts cards with MC or Cirrus affiliation.

Supermarket: El Rancho, 90 Todesco, stocks basic groceries.

Laundromat: Canasta de Aqua, corner of Portales and Prat. Same-day service. CH$3500 per kilo.

Police: ☎133.

Pharmacy: Farmacia Austral, Corcovado 442 (☎731 078). Open M-Sa 9am-1:30pm and 2:30-9pm, Su 10am-2pm and 4-9pm. For **24hr. service,** call ☎09 840 5326.

Hospital: Jiménes Romero, Ignacio Carrera Pinto 153 (☎731 244).

Telephones and Internet Access: Entel (☎731 603), on the corner of Libertad and Cerda. Offers Internet (CH$700 per hr.) and reasonable rates for calls to the US and UK. Open daily 9am-1pm and 2:30-10pm. Also try **Cibernet** (☎731 890) for fast and inexpensive (CH$650 per hr.) Internet connections. Open daily 10am-10pm.

Post Office: O'Higgins 253 (☎731 481), in the municipal building on the park. Open M-F 9am-12:30pm and 3-5pm, Sa 9am-1pm.

ACCOMMODATIONS

Be sure to check your bed before committing to a stay, as some accommodations can be run-down. The hotels and hostels on the waterfront charge a little more, but in the low season most establishments are willing to give guests a discount.

Hostal Puma Verde, O'Higgins 54 (☎731 184). Designed by former Patagonia Clothing CEO Kris Thompkins, this intimate boutique hotel is polished to the finest detail, containing a serene garden, airy kitchenette, and rustic, elegant furnishings. When it's frosty outside, enjoy the down duvets and raging fire. The attentive and helpful staff serves a hearty continental breakfast each morning. Single beds in a triple room CH$25,000; *matrimonales* CH$35,000; 5-person cabins CH$60,000. ❸

Residencial Astoria, Corcovado 442 (☎ 731 263). The spacious living room on the 2nd fl. makes up for the cramped bedrooms. With a view of the bay, a small restaurant, and basic breakfast, Astoria is an easy place to pass a day or two. Breakfast included. Doubles CH$12,000, with bath CH$15,000; triples CH$18,000/CH$22,500. ❷

Cabañas Brisas del Mar, Corcovado 278 (☎ 731 284). 8 efficient cabins with cable TV, kitchenettes, and clean bathrooms. Most cabins have 1 double bed and 2 twins; some have 4 twins. In all, the living space is cramped, but perks, like an excellent in-house restaurant and free Internet, will keep you out of your room. CH$35,000 per cabin. ❸

Hostería Sebastián, Almirante Riveros 163 (☎ 731 225), has an immense, well-run restaurant, homey rooms, transportation service, and excursion planning. Spacious doubles and triples fill up with both Chilean and foreign guests looking to enjoy nearby adventures every summer. Lunch or dinner CH$3000. Breakfast included. Doubles CH$16,000; triples CH$24,000. ❷

Hostería-Cabañas Corcovado, Corcovado 408 (☎ 731 221). Tight rooms with large beds overlook the bay. The small restaurant downstairs only serves a few people a day, but they can whip up almost anything with warning. Breakfast included. Doubles with bath CH$14,000. ❷

◨ FOOD

Chaitén's culinary offerings are limited, so most accommodations offer simple fare from in-house restaurants. If you plan to eat at your *residencial*, be sure to notify the manager and maybe even pre-order so that they can shop and prepare your meal later. If you're after a quick and culturally-interesting bite, try **Cocinerías Costumbristas ❶** on Portales near the corner with O'Higgins. Local mothers vend home-cooked meals in an open-air food court while they supervise their sons playing basketball on the adjacent court.

El Quijote, O'Higgins 42 (☎ 09 183 4054). While the pseudo-rustic decor feels a bit eclectic and the menu is short, the enthusiastic owner will be happy to talk about Chaitén, Pumalín, and growing numbers of visitors. Try the salmon (CH$3800) or a sandwich (CH$2000-3000). El Quijote doubles as one of few places in town to guzzle a beer (CH$700) or sip a *pisco* sour (CH$1500). Open daily 11am-9:30pm or later. ❶

Flamengo, Corcovado 218, serves up a variety of locally-caught fish and other seafood with sauces (CH$4000-6000). If *merluza*'s on the menu, give this white, oily fish a try. Chicken and steak dishes (CH$3500-5000) round out the menu. Regardless of whether you understand Spanish, you'll have difficulty keeping your eyes off the latest soap opera playing on the enormous TV. Open 11am-9pm. ❸

◪ OUTDOOR ACTIVITIES

Tourist activities around Chaitén are underdeveloped, making a do-it-yourself attitude essential to exploring the region. Nicolás, of Chaitur, is an excellent resource and can arrange trips north into **Parque Pumalín** and south to the Glaciar Yelcho and the turbulent **Futaleufú.** Pumalín's famous **alerce** forest is the area's most popular and convenient attraction. The massive, 4000-year-old trees are a humbling sight. The nearby **Volcán Michinmáhuida** is accessible as well, but time, some foresight, and a dash of persistence are necessary to arrange this trip. Call or stop by **Chaitur** to customize a trip.

PARQUE PUMALÍN

Parque Pumalín contains 3000 sq. km of virgin wilderness that stretch between the Argentine border and the Pacific coast, effectively slicing Chile in half. It protects remote valleys, sparkling rivers, pristine fjords, and the wildlife that frequent them. Pumalín is the pet project of Douglas Tompkins, an American environmental activist who made a fortune as founder of the Espirit and North Face clothing lines, and began acquiring property in Chile in 1991. Through his purchases and the acquisitions of his non-profit foundation, the Conservation Land Trust, Pumalín is now the largest private park in the world. Its size and scope have attracted concern from Chileans, especially those who want to develop lumber and hydroelectric interests in the area. Others express concern about the strength of national sovereignty when a foreigner controls such a vast tract of land. Despite its critics, Pumalín is one of the most forward-thinking conservation projects in the world and, furthermore, a beautiful place to visit.

The development of tourist facilities in the park has proceeded slowly, partially because Tompkins remains unsure of how much of the park should be left entirely wild. Four well-traveled day-hikes, however, facilitate an exploration of the park. A perfect picnic spot is along the **Sendero Cascada,** just south of **Caleta Gonzalo,** the small port 56km north of Chaitén where the bulk of public access facilities are available. The path carves through rainforest before reaching the impressive waterfall (3hr. round-trip). Thirteen kilometers south of town, the **Laguna Tronador** trail winds uphill to a lake with gently trickling streams near a welcoming campground (3hr. round-trip). Another kilometer farther south, the short **Sendero Alerce** offers an inspiring stroll through the ancient giants, some of which are thousands of years old. The **Hidden Falls Trail,** 14km south of Caleta Gonzalo, passes three spectacular waterfalls along a wet, idyllic path (1½hr. round-trip). It's possible for the curious to arrange tours of Pumalín's agricultural projects near Renihue. For information on all park resources and activities, stop by the friendly Visitors Center in Chaitén, O'Higgins 62 (☎731 341), before departing for the park.

Plan to spend the night in Chaitén, as accommodations in Caleta Gonzalo are expensive. The **Cabañas Caleta Gonzalo ❺** offer excellent service in small rooms. (☎09 256 6624. Doubles CH$55,000.) Three hundred meters south of Caleta Gonzalo lies **Camping Río Gonzalo ❶,** with good facilities and plenty of sites (CH$1500 a night; camping under rainproof shelters CH$5000). The campground at the trailhead of the **Hidden Falls** consists entirely of covered shelters perfect for car camping or for keeping your tent dry (CH$5000 per person). Food is only available in the small cafe at Caleta Gonzalo. The food is pricey (*menú* CH$6500) but of very high quality. Most of the vegetables served are grown on Pumalín's organic farms. If you're not planning to travel all the way to Caleta Gonzalo, pack what you'll need and take it along with you.

FUTALEUFÚ ☎65

Branching off the Carretera Austral, the road to Futaleufú quickly reaches the shore of turquoise Lago Yelcho, fed by the mighty Futaleufú River. The powerful waters of the "Fu" carve through the lush mountain landscape, descending tumultuously in some of the best whitewater in the world. The Futaleufú is revered among professional river guides—most guides running the river spend years honing their skills on big North American rivers in preparation. Rafting is the main draw, but adventure junkies drawn to the big whitewater can now bike, fish, and hike in the valleys and ranges surrounding the centerpiece, Fu. Most of this tiny town's services are highly seasonal: everything's open in January and February, and almost everything's closed by early April. If you're visiting outside of high season, be prepared to ask around to find what you need.

TRANSPORTATION

Buses: Transportation Cordillera, Prat 236 (☎721 249), goes to **Chaitén** (4hr., M-Th 7am, CH$6000) and the **Argentine border** (20min., M and F 8am and 5:30pm; CH$1500), where buses going on to **Esquel** and **Trevalin** are available. **Transportation Ebenezer,** Balmaceda 511 (☎721 288), also heads to **Chaitén** (4hr., M-Sa 7am, CH$5500). In the summer, buses leave for **Puerto Montt** on Tuesdays if there is enough demand. The 33hr. ride through Argentina departs on an irregular schedule, so have your passport handy and call for more information.

ORIENTATION AND PRACTICAL INFORMATION

Futaleufú sits on a plateau and is laid out on a grid system. Most services are scattered throughout the few blocks nearest the central plaza. Buses from other parts of Chile enter from the west and the road to Argentina is on the east side of town. Your best bet is riding a bus from Futaleufú that will meet an Argentine bus from Trevalin. Once in Trevalin, connections to Bariloche are easily to come by.

Tourist Office: O'Higgins 536, on the square. Offers little more than a regional map.

Tours: Expediciones Chile, corner of O'Higgins and Mistral (US ☎888 488 9082; www.exchile.com), is the premier guiding service in town. They've been running the river commercially for nearly 20 years—much longer than any other company. They offer everything from single-day trips to week-long packages, and their website is an excellent source of information on the Futaleufú area even for those not attempting the river. The **Patagonia Adventure Center,** O'Higgins 397 (☎721 320; www.pacchile.com), in the Hostería Río Grande (see **Accommodations,** below), is run by a Chilean family originally based in Puerto Varas. They provide safe rafting, kayaking, and sea-kayaking activities, as well as a range of other adventure-sport offerings. For a professional locally-run company, try **Guías Nativas,** Cerda 697 (☎721 281). Other operators have offices along the river, which are most easily contacted by stopping by **Sur Andes,** Cerda 308 (☎09 824 3180). The helpful owner also runs a variety of combination trips in the area, including a 4-night horseback riding tour of a valley that stops at secluded villages in the wilderness (US$330 per person).

Bank: BancoEstado, on the park at the corner of Rodríguez and O'Higgins. Changes US dollars and traveler's checks at fair rates with a US$11 commission. Open M-F 9am-2pm. There are currently **no ATMs** in Futaleufú.

Supermarket: Supermercado Flores had two locations: Balmaceda 434 (☎721 213) and Prat 268 (☎721 417). Both open daily 9am-10pm.

Police: ☎133.

Hospital: Ambulance ☎131. **Hospital de Futaleufú,** Balmaceda 382 (☎721 231), offers basic services, but lacks English-speaking staff.

Telephone: Ruly Call Center (☎721 425), look for the Telefónica on the square. Calls to the US or UK cost CH$250. Open daily 8am-midnight.

Post Office: On the corner of Rodríguez and O'Higgins in the municipal office, opposite the bank. Open M-F 9am-12:30pm and 2:30-6pm, Sa 9am-12:30pm.

ACCOMMODATIONS

During the summer season, *hospedajes* spring up north and east of the plaza, offering cheap accommodations with kitchen facilities. The following is a list of quality standby establishments that remain open year-round.

ON THE ROAD AGAIN

It's appropriate that as Herman, a local trucker, cruises home to Coyhaique, he croons to the music of John Denver. Like Denver and Willie Nelson (the driver's top picks for sing-alongs), Herman appreciates the value of a good road. As a southerner in Chile, Herman is personally invested in the difficult history of the infamous highway he drives along—the Careterra Austral.

Over a jovial chicken dinner set to rocking 60s tunes, Herman explains that although the flourishing lumber industry and the growing population of the Far South should ensure that a city like Coyhaique is fully connected to the rest of the nation, fluidity of transportation is not something he takes for granted.

The Carretera Austral was Pinochet's major project, integral to his vision of a homogeneous, united Chile. The first to admit that the rough-cut road is an incomplete venture (ferry rides are still necessary to traverse the breaks in the road), Herman is well-aware that his persistent allegiance to the ruthless dictator is a tense issue. However, Herman's explanation of the road's real benefits for the people of the region—electricity, water, schools, hospitals, effective police services, a standard of life on par with the rest of Chile—makes the citizens' loyalty to the deposed tyrant seem a little less absurd.

-Alex Leary

Hostería Río Grande, O'Higgins 397 (☎721 320). With its central location and amiable, professional staff, Río Grande sets the standard for nicer hotels in town. The small restaurant serves select dishes and wonderful grilled meats. All rooms have private bath and simple decor. Singles CH$30,000; doubles CH$50,000; triples CH$60,000. ❺

Cabañas Aguas Blancas, Carreras 702 (☎721 335; aguasblancas@hotmail.com). Two tidy cabins await traveling groups. In both, sturdy ladders climb past the small but well-apportioned downstairs kitchens to upstairs beds. The cabins are very popular with traveling Argentine and Chilean families; if you're planning to stay Dec.-Feb., call several weeks ahead to reserve a place. Both cabins CH$35,000. ❹

Hospedaje Adolfo, O'Higgins 302 (☎258 633). Soft beds, a warm fire, and a filling breakfast are standard issue at Adolfo. The kind and meticulous schoolteacher/owner welcomes guests with the same winning warmth she extends to her pupils. Beds are upstairs; downstairs, the comfortable lounge doubles as a class-prep office, but the sofas are open on rainy days. Singles CH$5000; 4-bed cabins CH$25,000-30,000. ❷

Hospedaje Canete, Mistral 374 (☎721 214). Wins high marks for hospitality and low marks for ceiling height. If you're taller than 6 ft., either bring a helmet or look elsewhere. Shorter guests will delight in the familiar atmosphere, comfortable beds, and personal attention. Breakfast included. Dorms CH$5000, with bath CH$6000.

Residencia Carahue, O'Higgins 332 (☎721 221). The massive dining area with satellite TV is a perfect escape from the slightly run-down bedrooms. Kitchen use is sometimes available, and cheap, basic meals are made with some advance notice for CH$3000. Breakfast CH$1000. Doubles CH$10,000; triples CH$15,000. ❷

◖ FOOD

The number of seasonal restaurants in Futaleufú is growing rapidly. Those listed below are long-standing, locally-run options. If you're in town in January or February, ask around to find the best of the season's exciting new dining options.

Futaleufú, Sargento Aldea 265 (☎721 295). The salmon, beef, and chicken dinners (CH$3600-4000) are simple yet filling meals, served up in a large, unadorned space. Nightly specials include the favorite *curanto,* an overflowing plate of mussels, sausage, pork ribs, and chicken. Open daily 8am-10pm, low-season hours vary. ❷

El Encuentro, O'Higgins 653 (☎721 247). White tablecloths and gentle lighting lend Encuentro a classed-up feel, but the friendly service will make you feel right at home. Cuisine is unsurprisingly typical. Try fresh salmon in cream sauce (CH$3000) or a ¼-chicken (CH$2000). Open daily in summer 8am-10pm. ❷

Escorpio, Gabriela Mistral 255. In high-season, ravenous rafters crowd Escorpio for hearty bar grub, sloshing pints, and good company. A favorite of river guides and clients alike, Escorpio's an excellent place to unwind from a day of anxious paddle-clenching. Open daily 11am-10pm. ❷

OUTDOOR ACTIVITIES

The tumbling Futaleufú is the region's star attraction. River rats all over the world esteem its rapids as among the globe's most challenging. However, other rivers that spill into the Fu, including the scenic Espolón, make the Futaleufú valley a perfect training camp for kayakers of all ability levels. One-day rafting excursions on the Fu generally run the "bridge-to-bridge" route, which features Class III and some Class IV water (all companies start at US$85). Trips down more powerful stretches of the river start at US$100. **Expediciones Chile** (Exchile) offers multi-day packages that start with the Fu's tamer sections and, as clients gain confidence, begin tackling the more daring sections. Rafting on the Espolón is less expensive (US$50) and significantly less exhilarating—unless you've got a serious fear of whitewater, you'd be remiss to travel to Futaleufú and not try the Fu.

Kayak lessons are also available at all levels and programs start around US$200. Exchile has the most kayak experience in town (their owner, Chris Spelius, is a former Olympic kayaker and the first to run commercial trips on the Fu). In all aquatic pursuits, don't underestimate the river's potential to get vicious. Clients have died on commercial rafting trips. Put yourself in safe hands by going with a reputable company and make sure to ask about safety precautions. Avoid any trips that don't include a rescue catamaran and at least one safety kayak.

The Futaleufú valley is a scenic wonderland even for those not wanting to be flung around by the Futaleufú. Several operators in town offer a range of alternative adventure activities, from **horseback riding** to **canyoning** and **mountain biking.** Exchile offers nearly every activity available. (Horseback riding US$80, guided trekking US$40-80, fly-fishing US$215.) **Guias Nativas** offers a variety of rafting trips priced slightly under Exchile and PAC. Both Exchile and PAC offer sea-kayaking on lakes and slower rivers in the area; visit their websites for current packages and prices (see **Tours,** p. 427). There are also a variety of outfitters located on the road between Futaleufú and Villa Santa Lucia that offer adventure activities. Travelers with vehicles may find better deals outside of town. For river activities, stick with the established outfitters with offices in town.

Day-hikes from town are a simple way to enjoy the woodlands and impressive rivers. A relaxing trail starts at the town center; go west on Balmaceda down to the bridge. The road curves out of town and continues up the hill that looms over Futaleufú. From here, visitors who choose not to test the river can at least have a peek at its tumult. Trail development around Futaleufú is proceeding rapidly—be sure to check with your hostel owner for recommendations on pleasant strolls.

PUERTO PUYUHUAPI ☎67

German settlers left their mark on this small town, which hugs the northern edge of **Parque Nacional Queulat,** 220km from Coyhaique. Most travelers who stop at Puyuhuapi are looking to enjoy the nearby hot springs, located 11km and a boat ride away from town. While there are extensive plans underway to develop Puyuhuapi's tourist resources, the town remains a challenging place to visit. Outside of town, fabulous trails await, but no transportation currently serves them. In town, nascent tourist enterprises offer varying degrees of service and quality.

Once an inauspicious getaway where locals could soak away worries, the baths at the **Termas de Puyuhuapi** are now operated as a five-star resort with five-star prices. **Hotel Termas de Puyuhuapi ❺** charges CH$78,000 for a single bed. If that sounds excessive, a day visit is CH$17,000. (☎325 103. Transportation included. Towel rental CH$2000.) The springs are across the bay from the Carretera. A boat leaves for the pools every 2hr. in summer, but you're wise to call ahead to arrange a pickup. There is currently no public transportation to reach the departure point, 11km south of town. In summer, a small **cafeteria ❸** serves sandwiches (CH$3500) and expensive lunches (CH$14,000).

Choices for accommodations appear limited within Puyuhuapi due to a lack of signage. Most families in town, however, are happy to convert their houses into *hospedajes*—just don't expect amenities. There are a few standouts. **Casa Ludwig ❹**, on the eastern side of town, offers quaint and clean rooms in a peaked farm house built by the original settlers. The real treat is the massive sunlight-filled living room with comfortable couches and an enormous dining table. (☎325 5220; www.contactchile.cl. Breakfast included. Singles CH$20,000; doubles CH$40,000.) **Residencial Marily ❷**, on the Carretera Austral in the middle of town, offers comfortable beds in slightly crowded rooms. (☎325 201. CH$6000.) Local fish and the lunch of the day are available for CH$3000, but there are options for food outside the *hospedajes* as well. Puyuhuapi's finest dining is found at cozy, family-run **Lluvia Marina ❸**, on the Carretera at the southern end of town (☎325 219. Open daily Jan.-Feb. 10am-11pm.) **Café Rossbach ❷**, on Aisén at the northern end of town, is run by the meticulously attentive daughter of one of the founding settlers. The menu varies depending on what's fresh, but it's generally German-influenced and seafood-focused. (☎325 118. Specials CH$4800. Open daily 11am-11pm.)

Any minibus headed north or south can easily drop travelers off at Puyuhuapi, since the Carretera Austral runs through the heart of town. Make sure you check the schedule for the next bus headed in your direction when you stop—schedules can be irregular, especially outside of January and February. **Buses Becker** stops at the **post office** in the middle of town on the Carretera en route to Chaitén. (☎325 195. M-Tu and Th-F 3:30pm; Tu and F buses connect with a minibus to Futaleufú. CH$8000 for both destinations.) For **tourist information,** visit the kiosk on Aisén, near the Fábrica de Alfombras. While there is no transportation from Puyuhuapi to natural sites in the region such as Parque Nacional Queulat, there are plans for a shuttle service to begin in 2005. Contact Eduvino Mayorga (☎325 105) for details.

PARQUE NACIONAL QUEULAT ☎67

The thick, temperate rainforest of Queulat limits visitors to the two major marked trails, one of which leads to an increasingly rare "hanging" glacier. The astounding **Ventisquero Colgante** hangs over a silty lake, spewing torrents, rocks, and ice chunks into the water. To reach the hanging glacier, enter the park through the southern entrance, 22km south of Puerto Puyuhuapi. Follow the valley path of the **Río Guillermo** for 1½hr. before climbing onto the glacial moraine. No public transportation heads directly to the park, but any northbound or southbound transportation on the Carretera Austral will drop you off at the park entrance— just be attentive, as drivers can pass it without a second thought. **Camping ❶** is permitted, but there are no facilities or shops for food. (Camping CH$4000. Entrance to park CH$1500.)

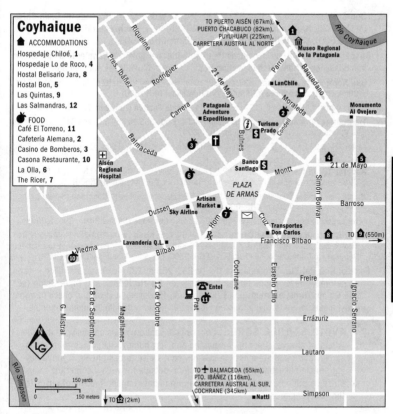

Coyhaique

▲ ACCOMMODATIONS
Hospedaje Chiloé, 1
Hospedaje Lo de Roco, 4
Hostal Belisario Jara, 8
Hostal Bon, 5
Las Quintas, 9
Las Salmandras, 12

🍴 FOOD
Café El Torreno, 11
Cafetería Alemana, 2
Casino de Bomberos, 3
Casona Restaurante, 10
La Olla, 6
The Ricer, 7

TO PUERTO AISÉN (67km),
PUERTO CHACABUCO (82km),
PUYUHUAPI (225km),
CARRETERA AUSTRAL AL NORTE

Río Coyhaique

Museo Regional
de la Patagonia

Riquelme
Pres. Ibáñez
Rodríguez
21 de Mayo
Carrera
Balmaceda
Parra
Baquedano
Moraleda

■ LanChile

Patagonia
Adventure
■ Expeditions

(i) Turismo
Prado

Condell

Monumento
Al Ovejero

Bulnes

Aisén
Regional
Hospital

Banco
Santiago

Montt

21 de Mayo

Simón Bolívar

Barroso

PLAZA
DE ARMAS

Artisan
Market ■

Dussen Sky Airline

Horn

Cruz

Transportes
■ Don Carlos
Francisco Bilbao

Lavandería Q.L. ■
Viedma
Bilbao

TO 9 (550m)

Cochrane

Eusebio Lillo

Freire

Ignacio Serrano

18 de Septiembre
Magallanes
12 de Octubre
Prat

Entel
11

Errázuriz

G. Mistral

Lautaro

N

Río Simpson

0   150 yards
0   150 meters   TO 12 (2km)

TO ✈ BALMACEDA (55km),
PTO. IBÁÑEZ (116km),
CARRETERA AUSTRAL AL SUR,
COCHRANE (345km)   ■ Natti

Simpson

AISÉN

COYHAIQUE   ☎ 67

As a hub of transportation and commerce, Coyhaique is, effectively, Region XI. Most of Aisén's population lives in this unpolished town. All buses travel through it, and all flights land near it. What Coyhaique lacks in the glitter of destinations such as Punta Arenas or Puerto Natales, it makes up for with an authentic, working-class look at hardscrabble life in Chilean Patagonia. While most travelers stop in Coyhaique just to transfer elsewhere or refuel, the town has a thriving culture of its own, displayed in youth-filled discos, young and enterprising fishing guides, and a forward-looking tourism board. Come to Coyhaique to depart for the fabulous wilderness surrounding it, but while you wander through town, plan on discovering the unexpected.

▐ TRANSPORTATION

Flights: There is no airport in Coyhaique, but local flights use the airport in **Balmaceda**, 45min. away and accessible by minibuses (CH$2500). **LanChile** (☎231 300), on the corner of Parra and Moralada, books flights to **Santiago** (CH$100,000) via **Puerto Montt** (CH$50,000) and **Punta Arenas** (CH$31,000). **SKY Airlines,** Prat 203 (☎240 825), has daily flights to **Puerto Montt** (CH$56,000) and **Santiago** (CH$110,000). **Transportes**

Don Carlos, Subteniente Cruz 63 (☎231 981; www.doncarlos.cl), heads to: **Chile Chico** (M, W, F-Sa 10am, Tu and Th 2:30pm; CH$25,500); **Cochrane** (M and Th 9:30am, CH$43,000); **Villa O'Higgins** (M and Th 9:30am, CH$64,000).

Buses: These tend to be minibuses that can better navigate the Carretera Austral. Some minibuses leave from the **bus station** at the corner of Magallanes and Lautaro.

Bus Norte C. Austral, Parra 337 (☎232 167), has buses to **Chaitén** (M-Tu and Th-F 8am, CH$15,000) via **La Junta** (CH$8000) and **Puyuhuapi** (CH$7000).

Buses Daniela, Baquedano 1122 (☎231 701), goes to **Chaitén** (Tu-W and Su 8am, CH$15,000).

Transportes Terra Austral, at the bus station and at Pardo 368 (☎254 335 and 346 757), travels to **Puerto Cisnes** (M and Sa 3:30pm; CH$6,000).

Javier Ali (☎09 313 1492) travels to **Cerro Castillo** (1½hr.; M, W, F 5pm, returns Tu, Th, Sa 7am; CH$3000).

Acuario 13, in the bus station (☎522 143), has tickets to **Cochrane** (6-7hr., W-Sa 10am, CH$9500) and connects from Cochrane to **Tortel** (3hr.; Tu, Th-F, Su; CH$5500).

Buses Don Carlos, Subteniente Cruz 63 (☎231 981), sends buses to **Cochrane** (8-10hr., generally Tu-Th and Sa 9:30am, CH$9000.)

Inter Lagos, in the bus terminal (☎240 840), goes to **Cochrane** (Su-M 9:30am, CH$10,000).

Other Buses: Dario Figueroa Castro (☎233 286), **Tour Aisén** (☎09 898 2643), **Minibus Don Tito** (☎250 280), and **Yamil J. Ali. M.** (☎250 346) depart daily for **Puerto Ibáñez** to catch the 9am ferry to **Chile Chico.** All shuttles cost CH$3500. Call ahead for departure schedule.

Ferries: Mar del Sur, Baquedano 146A (☎231 255 or 233 466), has an office in town that can make reservations for the ferry between **Puerto Ibáñez** and **Chile Chico** (see **Chile Chico: Transportation,** p. 437). Especially for drivers, it is wise to check for room in Coyhaique before traveling to Puerto Ibáñez as the ferry can fill in summer months.

AVOID SADDLE SORES. Choose your seat on buses carefully, as the ride is almost always longer than expected and very bumpy. Schedules change seasonally and month-to-month in season, so it's wise to call ahead. If you're having trouble collecting bus information from outside the area, contact the tourist office by phone or e-mail; they keep an up-to-date transport listing of buses for the entire region.

ORIENTATION AND PRACTICAL INFORMATION

It seems that Coyhaique's founders were fed up with the grid system that characterizes most Chilean towns—instead, they formed a pentagonal **central plaza** which makes for extremely confusing navigation. Only a couple of blocks out from the plaza, however, the city returns to the conventional format with perpendicular streets. From the manicured plaza, **Avenida Horn** meets **Arturo Prat** to form a lively strip of restaurants and shops, while in the opposite direction from the center, **Condell** harbors many banks and travel services.

Tourist Office: Bulnes 35 (☎231 752; www.aisen.org). Extensive written materials and maps, and a small but helpful staff. The best resource in town for navigating the complicated and variable bus services along the Carretera Austral. Open in summer M-F 8:30am-8:30pm, Sa-Su 10am-6pm.

Tours: Patagonia Adventure Expeditions, Riquelme 372 (☎214 894; www.adventure-patagonia.com). This British- and American-run operation specializes in **kayaking** (US$100) and **river rafting** (from CH$16,000) on bulging Patagonian rivers. They also offer **horseback riding** trips around Coyhaique (CH$30,000), **fly-fishing,** and **extended guided hikes** (see website for prices and details). **Andes Patagónicos,** inside the **Ricer** restaurant (☎216 712; www.ap.cl), is a good tour agency with a friendly English-speaking staff. They can arrange scenic flights and cruises to the **San Rafael Glacier**, local area tours, and last-minute **car rentals**. Open daily 8am-10pm. **Sandy,** the owner of **Las Salamandras** (see below), runs a variety of excursions: **PN Queulat** (min. 4 people, 2 days, US$192 per person); day-tour to **Cerro Castillo** (min. 4 people, 1 day, US$50); rafting the **Río Baker** (min. 4 people, 2 days, US$221).

Currency Exchange: Turismo Prado, 21 de Mayo 417, exchanges traveler's checks. Open M-F 9am-1:30pm and 3:30-7pm, Sa 9am-1:30pm and 5-7pm.

ATM: Beginning at the park, Condell has many large banks with **ATMs,** including **Banco Santiago,** Condell 141. Cirrus/MC/Plus/V.

Supermarket: Hiper Multimas, Lautaro 331 (☎234 600), has a wide variety of goods, including excellent produce and peanut butter. Open daily 9am-10pm.

Market: Just west of the central plaza, a small collection of booths sell regional wool crafts and leather goods at negotiable prices.

Laundromat: Lavandería QL, Bilbao 160 (☎670 318). Wash and dry CH$1800 per kg. Open M-F 8:30am-1pm and 3-7pm, Sa 8:30am-1pm.

Police: ☎133.

Pharmacy: Has a rotating 24hr. pharmacy. Check the central **Salcobrand,** 326 Bilbao (☎210 465), on the corner with Horn, for the list of 24hr. pharmacies.

Hospital: Ambulance ☎131. **Aisén Regional Hospital,** on the corner of Ibar and Carrera.

Telephones and Internet Access: Entel, Prat 326, is usually very busy, but offers several phones and fast Internet access for CH$1000 per hr. Open M-F 8:30am-10:30pm, Sa 10am-10:30pm, Su 11am-7pm. **C-Sur,** Prat 347, 2nd fl. (☎233 824), provides fast Internet service (CH$500 per hr.) and can burn CDs. Open daily 10am-midnight. On the other side of the square, **Puerto Pat@goni@,** Condell 23 (☎231 961), also has connections (CH$500 per hr.). Open M-Sa 10am-midnight, Su 3pm-midnight.

Post Office: Cochrane 226. Open M-F 9am-12:30pm and 2:30-6pm, Sa 9am-12:30pm.

ACCOMMODATIONS

Coyhaique has a severe shortage of quality budget accommodations. There are plenty of family homes to stay in, but they offer little more than a too-squishy mattress and the feeling that you're in someone else's place. The traffic of high-end fly-fishermen in town tends to push nicer accommodations to the expensive side.

Las Salamandras, on Teniente Vidal (☎211 865; www.salamandras.cl), 2km outside of town. Region XI's only true backpackers' hostel, this hand-built lodge is perfect for its surroundings. Run by a knowledgeable Spanish couple who also do tours (see above), the hearth is warm and the bathrooms are spotless. Breakfast included. Dorms CH$6000; *matrimoniales* with bath CH$16,000; 6-person *cabañas* CH$40,000. ❷

Las Quintas, Bilbao 1208 (☎231 173). A step above Coyhaique's *hospedajes,* Las Quintas has the feel of an efficient continental motel. Rooms are clean and well kept, and a small lounge/dining area provides a pleasant common space. All rooms come with TV and include breakfast. Singles CH$12,000; doubles CH$18,000; triples CH$23,000. ❸

Hostal Belisario Jara, Bilbao 662 (☎234 150), boasts pristine decor, marvelous views, an apple tree garden with great apples, and excellent service. Guests enjoy a glimpse of rustic Patagonian living with a touch of luxury. The lookout spire and charming TV-equipped bedrooms with private bath complete the aesthetic experience. Breakfast included. Singles US$58; doubles US$75; triples US$88. ❺

THE LOCAL STORY

WILD AISÉN

Judd Rogers, the NOLS Patagonia Branch Director, has been a Coyhaique resident since 1992.

When I showed up, there wasn't a pub in Coyhaique. There were whorehouses and a disco. Now, in the summer months, things are cooking at half a dozen bars in town. There are many, many more tourists, but compared to a place like Pucón or Puerto Natales, it's not quite at that level. Coyhaique's off the beaten path and there's no guarantee of good weather. But every year, more and more people think, "This place is pretty cool."

Outside Coyhaique, most travel down here is exploratory. We just look at a map and say, "let's see if this valley goes." Sometimes, we hit the most thick, dense vegetation and we get shut down. Other times, we run into a big trail that a *pueblador*'s cut to get his animals to summer pasture. It's not cataloged. It's not mapped; the maps that are available are really outdated. The land's really raw and new and interesting that way.

o The most grueling trip I've had was in the Queulat National Park. I remember crossing the ice field from Argentina and being pummeled by storms. We spent a month working our way across Chile and, one morning

Hostal Bon, Serrano 91 (☎231 189; hostalbon@patagoniachile.cl). The fly-fisherman owner cooks and services this quiet and clean establishment. Both the hotel-style rooms in the main building and smaller rooms for traveling students have TVs and big, soft beds. Breakfast included. Lunch and dinner CH$4000-4500. Dorms CH$8000; singles CH$16,500; doubles CH$24,000; triples CH$35,000. ❸

Hospedaje Lo de Rocco, 21 de Mayo 668 (☎231 285). Common spaces and a clean kitchen are adorned with bright paintings and matching bedspreads. Breakfast included for all rooms and for campers. Camping CH$3000 per tent. Singles CH$7000, with bath CH$9000; doubles CH$14,000/CH$18,000; triples CH$21,000/$27,000. ❸

Hospedaje Chiloé, Baquedano 274 (☎251 381), is an affordable choice for groups that cook—the apartments include a small kitchen. They're scheduled for remodeling and need it. 4-bed apartments CH$20,000; 6-bed CH$25,000. ❷

🍴 FOOD

For a small town, Coyhaique has a surprisingly hopping nightlife to go along with its cuisine. On Thursday, Friday, or Saturday, check out the bars on Moraleda to join in the melding of international travelers and Coyhaique youth culture.

Casona Restaurante, Obispo Viedma 77 (☎238 894). Hidden in an out-of-the-way neighborhood, this restaurant is where Coyhaique families go for a nice night out. The dining area is unadorned, with small tables and simple artwork, but the service is excellent and the food superb. Try the succulent *salmón cecilia* (CH$4000) or the bacon-wrapped *lomo casona* (CH$4000). For lunch, the *menú* (CH$3000) competes with other midday bargains in town. Open daily noon-3pm and 7:30pm-midnight. ❸

Casino de Bomberos, Parra 365 (☎234 037). Tucked into a cramped, windowless space behind the fire station, Bomberos fills with local families and businessmen looking for the heartiest, and most affordable, lunches in town. A packed house may make for slow service, but the people-watching is great. *A la carte* options include local seafood (fried *merluza* CH$3800) and a heaping *bistec a lo pobre* (CH$4600). *Menú* CH$3000. Open daily 11am-4pm and 7pm-midnight. ❸

Cafe El Torreno, Prat 470. After Bomberos, the best place for slice-of-life Coyhaique. Boisterous locals crowd in to enjoy *fútbol* games and some of the finest lunch specials in town (CH$2500). The lunch business is so brisk that tables come pre-set with the first course of the lunch *menú*. For a power lunch, Coyhaique style, gulp a ½-liter of beer (CH$1000) with your meal. Open daily 10:30am-11pm. ❷

The Ricer, Horn 48 (☎216 711). Unmistakably touristy but renowned for its fabulous sandwiches, this cafe is a reliable bet day or night. The lodge decor includes fur-covered seat backs and rough-cut wood, and while the service isn't always sparkling, the food is terrific. Try the *ave completa* (chicken, veggies, and guacamole; CH$3950). Breakfast CH$3500-4000. Traditional dinners CH$5000-6000. Open daily 8:30am-2am. ❸

Cafetería Alemana, Condell 119 (☎231 731). The German-influenced menu contains a few surprises (bratwurst CH$2800) in addition to the standard assortment of local dishes, pizzas (CH$2000-2800), and gargantuan sandwiches (CH$1500-4000). The dining area has sturdy wooden chairs and buzzing tables. Open M-Sa 9am-midnight. ❷

La Olla, Prat 176 (☎234 700). La Olla has a curious past-its-prime feel, but it remains a cut above most Coyhaique eateries. Maroon drapings and white tablecloths attempt elegance, but you'll feel fine in road-worn jeans and a t-shirt. The cuisine is Spanish-influenced and the *paella* (CH$4000) is a highlight. Open daily 11am-9pm. ❷

🔳 DAYTRIPS FROM COYHAIQUE

RESERVA NACIONAL COYHAIQUE. This small reserve offers visitors good views of the bustling town and a few simple walks along two small lakes. Proximity has made this wooded area popular among locals looking to relax, but it remains relatively secluded. Since the park is within the city limits, it can be reached by a 1½hr. walk north along Baquedano. Once you cross the bridge over the Río Coyhaique, the Reserva will be on your left. *(Conaf collects a CH$600 fee at the entrance and offers basic information for Laguna Verde and Laguna Venus. Camping sites are available around both lakes for CH$3500 a night for up to 6 people; basic bathrooms and fresh water are available but you will need to bring all food and other provisions.)*

RESERVA NACIONAL RÍO SIMPSON. This reserve's namesake river and its tributaries hold many trout and attract many fly-fishers. The evergreen forest veils a majestic waterfall, the **Cascada La Virgen,** where the river meets the Río Correntoso. Thirty-seven kilometers from Coyhaique toward Puerto Chacabuco, a **visitors center** has a small museum and botanical garden. *(Take any bus from Coyhaique to Puerto Chacabuco and ask to be let off at the park entrance. Camping CH$7000.)*

toward the end of our traverse, we could smell the ocean and hear trucks on the Carretera. We were with our students and told them, "Okay guys, we'll meet you at the roadhead at 3 o'clock this afternoon." We were literally 2km away. We split into groups, commenced our journey, and found ourselves trapped in dense brush. By 9pm, we decided to set up camp.

The next day, 7am to 9pm, we moved all day and didn't make it. The next day, 7am to 9pm, we hiked all day, going, raining, bushwacking through the *coihue*, the *nalca*, and still didn't make it. It took us three and a half days to go 2km. But on the journey we came across the most amazing places, down this river valley, places where no human's ever been before. No humans were stupid enough to even get themselves into that situation. I think that's a pretty typical Patagonia experience. You look at a map and you think, okay, we can do that. Then you end up doing a tenth of what you thought. In Aisén, you've got one person per square mile, but it's mostly concentrated in Coyhaique.

In the US, we think about Alaska, or the Yukon—places that, even if we don't go, just the thought of them makes us feel that the world's a better place. I'd like Aisén to be that for Chile and certainly for the world.

PARQUE NACIONAL LAGUNA SAN RAFAEL. Located in the northern region of the frozen, desolate Chilean fjords, the national park harbors many birds and marine life. The real attraction, however, is the famous **Glaciar San Rafael.** Hanging fog and ominous peaks set the backdrop for the impressive ice sheet as it calves into the sea. Most visitors access the park by plane from Coyhaique for a short 1-2hr. tour of the glacier and lake. Other visitors take one of the cruise ships from Puerto Chacabuco that navigate the narrow opening connecting the lake to the ocean. *(Contact any of the travel agents in Coyhaique to arrange transportation. Min. 4 passengers. US$250 per person. 1-day catamaran cruises US$275, but are a better option for solo travelers because of minimum passenger limitations on scenic flights.)*

VILLA CERRO CASTILLO, PUERTO RÍO TRANQUILO, AND PUERTO BERTRAND ☎ 67

South of Coyhaique, the Carretera Austral winds on well-maintained, two-lane pavement through rolling pastures and into the craggy mountains surrounding Cerro Castillo. Passing through the reserve, the paved road descends into an enormous valley and then, at Villa Cerro Castillo, it ends. From here, the remaining 500km of road consist mostly of dirt, gravel, and pesky washboard bumps. While the going may be slow, the scenery is marvelous: mountains get bigger, trees grow taller, and rivers run wider.

> Both northbound and southbound buses along the Carretera can make stops on request in Villa Cerro Castillo, Puerto Río Tranquilo, and Puerto Bertrand, although bus-bound travelers generally have little reason to stop, especially because schedules are erratic and disembarking can mean a several days' stay.

These three villages provide waypoints to Carretera travelers in need of simple food, fuel, or a night's lodging. **Villa Cerro Castillo** is the termination point for the popular backpacking trip around **Cerro Castillo,** the jagged, basaltic summit that lords over this section of the southern road. The trek commences at **Las Horquetas Grandes,** where there is little more than a sign—you'll need to ask your Puerto Ibáñez or Cochrane-bound bus driver to stop for you—and travels for 4 days through rugged alpine areas. While the weather in this range of mountains is often fickle, a clear day affords tremendous views of unforgettably craggy and forbidding terrain. The **tourist office** (p. 432) or the staff at **Las Salamandras** (p. 433) in Coyhaique can provide additional details on making the trek. Upon completing the hike, many trekkers choose to hitchhike back to Coyhaique, although traffic along the Carretera can be scarce and *Let's Go* does not recommend hitchhiking. **Buses** between Cochrane and Coyhaique stop in **Villa Cerro Castillo** (pop. 300), where there's little more than a few worn but friendly *hospedajes.* Be sure to ask around town for when and where the bus is stopping, as schedules change frequently.

South of Cerro Castillo, the Carretera climbs through dramatic cliff bands, winding toward the shores of **Lago General Carrero,** Chile's largest lake. On the western lakeshore, it arrives at **Puerto Río Tranquilo,** the last fuel before Cochrane and home of the **Capilla de Marmol,** a fantastic series of grottos formed by the action of Lago General Carrero's waves undercutting a marble bank near town. The caves can only be explored by boat, and César Vargas (☎411 121), the gas-station owner, will happily guide a 1½hr. excursion there for CH$20,000. Other than the grottos, there's little in town beyond a few *hospedajes* and small grocery stores. A pleasant exception is the hostel **El Puesto**

❹ (☎02 196 4555; www.elpuesto.cl), where well-kept rooms start from CH$30,000 with breakfast. A less-expensive option is **Residencia Costanera** ❸ (☎411 121), right on the Carretera in the center of town.

Rounding the southern limit of Lago General Carrera, the Carretera crosses the dramatic bridge at El Desague where in a narrow gap between sheer faces, hanging glaciers dip toward Lago Bertrand. The road then passes exclusive fishing lodges and arrives at Puerto Bertrand, a tiny hamlet situated at the origin of the Río Baker, the most voluminous river in Chile. If you're strapped for fuel, the small **Supermercado Eca** on the lakefront sells overpriced but life-saving bottles of gasoline. Simple accommodations are available in the **Hostería Puerto Bertrand** ❷, on the lakeshore. Rooms are cramped and drafty, but the newer, kitchen-equipped cabins next door are a deal for groups. (☎419 900; all businesses in town have this same number, the Hostería has the town's only telephone. Breakfast included. Rooms CH$8000; cabins CH$35,000.) Rooms are cheaper up the hill at **Residencia Coighae** ❷, Esparsa 265, where you'll stay in the home of a local family. Bring your Spanish language skills and willingness to substitute hospitality for amenities (CH$6000; call the Hostería Puerto Bertrand number for reservations.) At **Campo Baker** ❷, along the Carretera, a Hare Krishna family serves vegan meals (CH$6500, includes appetizer and dessert!) to passersby. **Patagonia Adventure Expeditions** (p. 432) runs its rafting trips on the Río Baker from a barn on the waterfront. Although it's advisable to make arrangements for a rafting trip in Coyhaique, it is sometimes possible to arrange a last-minute trip. Stop by the barn in the evening, because trips tend to leave in the morning.

BORDER CROSSING INTO ARGENTINA: CHILE CHICO
Sitting just 3km from the border, Chile Chico provides easy access to Argentina from where you can start your trek southward to the glacier parks and Tierra del Fuego. A rough road runs across the Chile-Argentina border to **Los Antiguos** 10km on the other side, where it becomes Ruta 43. Sixty kilometers later it runs through Perito Moreno, where it meets Ruta 40, the unpaved road to El Calafate. The pass remains open unless Chile Chico itself is buried in snow. The customs office at the border is open 8am-9pm. The process is fairly simple and involves no more than a passport stamp and a brief search of your luggage for contraband and various food products (see **Essentials: Border Crossings**, p. 35, for info on visas and fees).

CHILE CHICO ☎67

Chile Chico's ubiquitous poplars barely hinder the powerful winds that blow over from the adjacent Patagonian plains. This quiet town remains a pleasant getaway, with its dramatic blue water and nearby secluded parks, paying little attention to the stream of tourists on their way to Argentina. Chile Chico's greatest claim to adventure fame is the westbound road to Cochrane that mountain bikers hail as the most inspiring in the region, despite the difficult climb and tight curves.

⧉ TRANSPORTATION. Minibus Padilla, O'Higgins 420 (☎411 904), rolls to Los Antiguos, ARG (1½hr.; M-Sa 9am and 1:30pm, returns 10am and 2:30pm; CH$4000). **Condor,** O'Higgins 420 (☎411 904), goes to Puerto Río Tranquilo (4¼hr., M-Tu and Th 5pm, CH$7000) via Puerto Guadal (2½hr., also F 5pm, CH$5000). **ALE,** Rosa 880 (☎411 739), near the stadium, goes to Cochrane (7hr., 2 per week, CH$11,000). ALE offers additional service on Saturdays during the summer. **Transportes Don Carlos** (☎411 490) flies to **Coyhaique** (M-Sa, CH$25,500). **Ferries** go to Puerto Ibáñez, leaving from beneath the cliff in the northwest corner of town. The small **Mar del Sur** office at the docks sells tickets. (☎411 864. Open M-F 9am-1pm and 3-7pm, Sa 2-6pm, Su noon-3pm.) Ferry scheduling is highly variable; try to call ahead. Ferries run infrequently in low season. (2¼hr.; departs Chile Chico M-Tu and F 8:30am, W 4pm, Su 2:30pm, returns from Puerto Ibáñez M and F 6pm, W-Th 10am; CH$2200). Several minibus companies leave directly from Puerto Ibáñez upon arrival of the ferry, heading to **Coyhaique** (2½hr., CH$3000). There are few tourist attractions in Puerto Ibáñez and transportation can be difficult to arrange when the ferry is not running, so travelers are wise to transfer to Coyhaique upon arrival.

■ ■ **ORIENTATION AND PRACTICAL INFORMATION.** Most basic services can be found on the main street, **Avenida O'Higgins**. The **tourist office** (☎411 268), on the corner of O'Higgins and Lautaro, lists local events and has a simple regional museum. **ALE** (☎411 739) arranges transportation and fishing and horseback-riding trips to nearby parks including **Lago Jeinimeni**, but is best for groups. **BancoEstado,** González 112, changes US dollars at poor rates and has a **24hr. ATM** that accepts only cards with MC affiliation. (☎411 258. Open M-F 10am-1pm.) For emergencies, contact the **police** (☎133) or the **hospital,** Lautaro 275, (☎131). The local **Entel** office can be found at O'Higgins 420 (☎411 904). The **post office** is at Rodríguez 121.

■ ■ **ACCOMMODATIONS AND FOOD.** Chile Chico is simple but friendly. **Eben-Ezer ❸,** Rodríguez 302, has doubles and triples with low ceilings but good company and a living room. (☎411 535. Breakfast included. CH$5000 per person.) Although known predominantly for transportation and tours, **ALE ❷** continues to expand its services, offering cozy beds and an outdoor grill for guest use. Breakfast included. (Singles CH$5000.) The hearty plates of grub served at **Elizabeth y Loly ❷,** González 25, are satisfying for lunch or dinner. The lunch specials at **Café Refer ❷,** O'Higgins 416 (☎411 225), featuring only local meats and fish (CH$3500), are a great pick.

COCHRANE   ☎67

The only settlement of significance south of Coyhaique, Cochrane has a rough-and-tumble outpost feel. It serves as a hub of civilization for fishermen at the area's fishing lodges and a provisioning post for kayakers bent on exploring the wild rivers. Unless you're very serious about your fishing or do-it-yourself wilderness exploring, though, Cochrane's just another stop on the highway—a chance to refuel on gas, coffee, or sleep before another day bouncing off along the road.

For good food and a familial atmosphere, try **El Fogón ❷,** San Valentín 653. Fried *merluza* (CH$3600) and the *lomo fogón* (steak served in a piquant tomato broth, CH$4200) are specialties. (☎522 240. Open daily 11am-midnight.) At **Nirrantal ❷,** O'Higgins and Esmeralda, chop suey (CH$3500) and curried chicken (CH$3200) highlight a surprising Asian menu. (☎522 604. Open daily 11am-late.) Excellent accommodations are available at **Hostal Lago Esmeralda ❷,** San Valentín 141. (☎522 621. Singles CH$6000; doubles with bath CH$15,000.) The **Latitud 47 Sur Hostel ❷,** Lago Brown 564, offers clean rooms and excellent breakfast. (☎522 401. Singles CH$7000; doubles CH$20,000.)

A small **tourist office**, located in the square on the corner of Esmeralda and Steffens, is staffed infrequently. If no one is attending, walk across the street to friendly **Latitud 47 Sur,** Dr. Steffens 576 (☎522 280), a travel agency. They can offer complete advice on local activities, transport tips, and general Cochrane know-how. The **Río Baker Tourism Network,** San Valentín 438 (☎522 646), is also an excellent link to locally-owned tour operators offering trips that range from horseback riding to glacier cruises. **BancoEstado,** on Esmeralda on the Plaza de Armas, has a **24hr. ATM** that accepts MasterCard only. The **Casa Melero Supermarket,** Las Golondrinas 148 (☎322 141), stocks basic groceries. The **police** office (☎131) is at the corner of Esmeralda and Merino, and the local **hospital** is located on O'Higgins. To mail a letter from the Carretera, visit the **post office,** Esmeralda 398 (☎522 282).

Transportes Don Carlos, Prat 344 (☎522 150), and **Acuario 13,** Río Baker 349 (☎522 143), handle air and bus transportation to and from Coyhaique several times per week. **Inter Lagos** (p. 432) makes the trip daily, stopping at Cerro Castillo, Puerto Río Tranquilo, and Puerto Bertrand.

CALETA TORTEL AND POINTS SOUTH   ☎67

> In 2004, boat service across Lago O'Higgins was infrequent and irregular, making the crossing possible only for those determined and with time to burn. For information on the current schedule and feasibility of the crossing, contact the tourist office in Coyhaique. The tourist kiosk in Cochrane is likely to have even more up-to-date information.

Until the connecting road to the Carretera opened in 2003, Tortel was a sleepy, backward fishing village accessible only by boat and consisting entirely of multi-colored buildings and cedar boardwalked footpaths. Now, tourists drawn to the buildings and boardwalks make the town feel much less sleepy, though it's still quite simple. Tourism is developing rapidly, with most families eager to get a piece of town's lucrative new industry. Expect makeshift restaurants in family living rooms, bedrooms shared with local children, and an overwhelming warmth and charm that will make you both glad about the opening of the road and sad that town will never feel quite so quaint again.

Tortel is located directly between the northern and southern **Patagonian Icefields,** and will eventually be a hub for visiting tidewater glaciers flowing from both. Other attractions include the **Isla de los Muertos,** a mysterious island cemetery covered with 36 crosses and surrounded in local legend, and the **Cerro la Bandera Trail,** a 2-3hr. hike that offers spectacular views of the Río Baker's mouth.

If you're hungry, try simple **El Mirador ❷,** near the public phone (open daily 9am-11pm), or seafood-haven **Delicious del Mar ❷,** on the boardwalk just before the town center. For accommodations, the **Hostal Costanera ❸,** above the town center, has clean rooms and a mini-kitchen. (Breakfast included. *Matrimoniales* CH$8000.) The **tourist office,** just beyond the square, has information on boat trips to **Glaciar Montt** (5hr., CH$140,000), **Glaciar Steffens** (3hr., CH$80,000), and **Isla de los Muertos** (45min., CH$25,000). There is only one **telephone** in town and it is used to reach all residents and businesses (☎234 815). There's free **Internet access** in the bright, barn-like **public library. Actuario 13** runs buses to Cochrane. (☎232 067. Tu-Su 2:30pm, CH$6000.)

South of Tortel, the road continues to get wilder, terminating at **Villa O'Higgins** after about 120km. There's little reason to visit Villa O'Higgins, except for the honor of having reached the end of the Carretera Austral—and the novelty of traveling back in time to 1960s-era Chile. Many travelers reach Villa O'Higgins intending to travel south to El Chaltén in Argentina. This crossing requires time, patience, and several boat connections.

MAGALLANES AND TIERRA DEL FUEGO

Patagonia is big in every way imaginable. Granite towers rise thousands of feet into clouds, barren steppe lands envelop millions of acres, and gargantuan ice fields stretch for miles. It's been legendary since European explorers grappled with its hostile natives and harsh shores, and the region still retains fabled status as one of the world's wildest and most scenic natural areas. Technically, "Patagonia" includes everything south of 40°S latitude, but the southernmost tip encompassed by the regions of Magallanes and Tierra del Fuego boasts the greatest concentration of Patagonian icons. Here is where you'll find the mountains, fjords, steppe, and glaciers worth traveling to the end of the earth to see.

If you have a passion for backcountry trails, an infatuation with paddling through pristine fjords, or a penchant for scaling famous peaks, look no further. But even those with little enthusiasm for the outdoors will find plenty to do in these southern lands. Literary junkies will enjoy rediscovering Bruce Chatwin's journeys to places like the Cueva del Milodón and culinary savants will delight in a hearty but sophisticated regional cuisine. There are charming frontier towns to explore, working *estancias* to visit, and a rich history full of exploration and outlaws (including Butch Cassidy and the Sundance Kid) to learn from. Chances are, too, that even if you arrive with a mortal fear of fresh air, you'll succumb to the seductions of this inimitable landscape.

Punta Arenas is the regional hub, served by regular LanChile flights and buses from most towns in the region. Most travelers make a quick transfer to Puerto Natales, the winsome village that serves as the jumping-off point for **Parque Nacional Torres del Paine.** Just across the border lies one of Argentine Patagonia's most charismatic sights: **Glaciar Perito Moreno.** Aggressively promoted by Argentina's tourist board, the glacier now rivals the Buenos Aires obelisk as a symbol of national pride. North of Perito Moreno, the tiny hamlet of **El Chaltén** welcomes visitors eager to hike beneath the towering **Mt. Fitz Roy** and the eerie spire of **Cerro Torre.** To see some of the region's most under-visited but deserving sights, you'll have to head south to Tierra del Fuego. There, you'll find **Ushuaia,** renowned for its colorful buildings, and **Parque Nacional Tierra del Fuego,** a testament to the power of the elements at the earth's extremity. To see the farthest reaches, though, you'll have to cross the Beagle Channel and check out **Puerto Williams** on Isla Navarino, a Chilean naval town that's on its way to becoming a tourist hub.

HIGHLIGHTS OF MAGALLANES AND TIERRA DEL FUEGO

MARVEL at the blue-green lakes, sparkling glaciers, and twisted towers that sit atop the Paine Massif in **Parque Nacional Torres del Paine** (p. 452).

GAPE at enormous falling pillars of ice as **Glaciar Perito Moreno** (p. 461) calves into Argentina's second-largest lake.

SLIP across fields of ice as you hike the Andean glaciers of **Parque Nacional Los Glaciares** (p. 466) above **El Chaltén, Argentina** (p. 462).

CAMP along the **Los Dientes de Navarino Circuit** (p. 479) and be the southernmost person on land in the Western Hemisphere.

INDULGE in decadent king crabs and Argentine wine in **Ushuaia, Argentina** (p. 470).

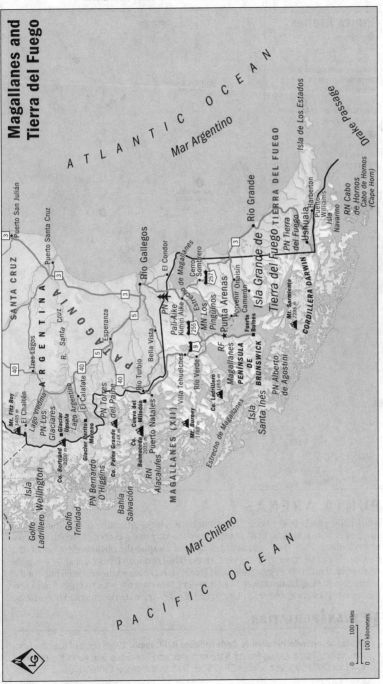

Magallanes and Tierra del Fuego

ATLANTIC OCEAN

Mar Argentino

Drake passage

Isla de Los Estados

Isla Cabo de Hornos (Cape Horn)

RN Cabo de Hornos

Navarino

Isla

Puerto Williams

Harberton

Ushuaia

PN Tierra del Fuego

TIERRA DEL FUEGO

Río Grande

Isla Grande de Tierra del Fuego

CORDILLERA DARWIN

Mt. Sarmiento 2235 m

PN Alberto de Agostini

Isla Santa Inés

Popenir Onaisin

Cameron

Estancia de Magallanes

Cerro Sombrero

El Condor

Río Gallegos

Puerto Santa Cruz

Puerto San Julián

SANTA CRUZ

ARGENTINA

PATAGONIA

R. Santa Cruz

Tres Lagos

Lago Viedma

Mt. Fitz Roy 3405 m

El Chaltén

Lago Argentino

PN Los Glaciares

Glaciar Upsala

Glacier Perito Moreno

Co. Bertrand 3270 m

El Calafate

PN Torres del Paine

Esperanza

Río Turbio

Bella Vista

Villa Tehuelches

Co. Paine Grande 3248 m

Balmaceda 2035 m

Cueva del Milodón

RN Alacalufes

Puerto Natales

MAGALLANES (XII)

Mt. Burney 1758 m

Co. Ladrillero 1665 m

Río Verde

Estancia de Magallanes

PN Pali-Aike

Kimiri Aike

MN Los Pingüinos

Punta Arenas

Fuerte Bulnes

RF Magallanes

PENÍNSULA DE BRUNSWICK

Golfo Ladrillero

Isla Wellington

Golfo Trinidad

PN Bernardo O'Higgins

Bahía Salvación

Mar Chileno

PACIFIC OCEAN

40 · 5 · 3 · 9 · 255 · 257

0   100 miles

0   100 kilometers

Punta Arenas

⌂ ACCOMMODATIONS
Hostal al Fin del Mundo, 11
Hostal de la Avenida, 4
Hostal de la Patagonia, 1
Hostal del Estrecho, 8
Hostal del Rey, 12
Hostal la Estancia, 5
Hotel Calafate, 9
Residencial Roca, 7

🍎 FOOD
Damiana Elena, 3
La Luna, 10
La Natta Pizza, 2
Puerto Viejo, 13
Sandino, 6

TIERRA DEL FUEGO

PUNTA ARENAS
☎ 61

Until 1914, nearly every vessel traveling between the Atlantic and Pacific Oceans stopped in Punta Arenas, making this out-of-the-way city a center of wealth and cosmopolitanism. Then the Panama Canal opened. Despite the obvious drawbacks of a new inter-oceanic route, "Sandy Point" (named by Lord John Byron, a slightly less agile wordsmith than his poet-grandson Lord Byron) has remained the essential hub for the resource-rich Magallanic region. Most travelers, however, are wise to enjoy Punta Arenas for what it's always been: a place to linger a day or two between grander journeys.

▐ TRANSPORTATION

Flights: Aeropuerto Presidente Carlos Ibáñez del Campo, 19km north of the city. From the airport, Punta Arenas-Puerto Natales buses and Pancheco Bus go to the center of town for CH$1500. Van service CH$2500. Taxis to the center CH$6000.

Airlines: DAP, O'Higgins 891 (☎223 240; www.aeroviasdap.cl). There's often space available even if the flights are "full," so keep asking. Sends small planes to: **Cabo de Hornos** (mostly Tu, US$300); **Porvenir** (12min., 2 per day M-Sa, US$26); **Puerto Williams** (1hr.; Nov.-Mar. Tu-Sa variable times, Apr.-Aug. Tu, Th, Sa 1pm; US$71); **Río Grande** (45min., F 9am, US$90); **Ushuaia, ARG** (45min.; M, W 9am; US$108). **Lan-Chile,** Lantaro Navarro 999 (☎241 232, at the airport 213 211), flies to: **Concepción** (US$123); **Puerto Montt** (US$98); **Santiago** (4hr., US$230); **Temuco** (US$105). Office open M-F 9am-1pm and 3-7pm, Sa 10am-1pm.

Buses: Punta Arenas has no central bus station; buses leave from companies' offices.

Bus Sur, José Menéndez 565 (☎227 145), travels to: **Castro** (32hr.; M-Th, Sa 8:30am; CH$38,000) via **Osorno** (CH$28,000) and **Puerto Montt** (CH$28,000); **Coyhaique** (20hr., M 10:30am, CH$30,000); **Puerto Natales** (3hr., 5 per day 9am-7pm, CH$3000); **Ushuaia, ARG** (12hr.; M, W, F 9am; CH$21,000). Connections from Puerto Natales to **El Calafate, ARG** (M, W, F 9am; CH$15,000).

Pancheco Bus, Colón 900 (☎242 174), goes to: **Osorno** (32hr., W, CH$38,000); **Puerto Natales** (3hr.; 3 per day 7:30am-7:30pm; CH$3500 one-way, CH$6000 round-trip); **Río Gallegos, ARG** (4hr; Tu, F, Su 11:30am; CH$6000); **Ushuaia, ARG** (12hr., M-Sa 7:30am, $20,000) via **Río Grande** (8hr., CH$13,000).

Bus Transfer, Magallanes and Colón (☎229 613), has the best price to **Puerto Natales** (3hr., 6pm, CH$2500).

Buses Fernández, Samueza 745 (☎242 313), goes to **Puerto Natales** (3hr., 8 per day 8am-8pm, CH$4000).

Buses Techni Austral, Lautaro Navarro 975 (☎222 078), also travels to **Ushuaia, ARG** (12hr.; Tu, Th, Sa 9:30am; CH$19,000).

Taxis: There are always a few waiting around the central plaza or cruising Colón, Magallanes, and Bories. Fares start at CH$200, CH$220 at night, and CH$250 Sundays.

Colectivos: #15 goes to **Tres Puentes** for ferries to **Los Pingüinos** and **Porvenir.** Most destinations are CH$200.

■ ⑦ ORIENTATION AND PRACTICAL INFORMATION

The central plaza, **Plaza Muñoz Gamero,** was named for the governor who first proposed a city plan for Punta Arenas, and it's the heart of the city. To the west, streets climb into the hills; to the east, they run into the Strait of Magellan. Thankfully, Gamero's plan was for a grid, and navigating Punta Arenas is simple. Important streets include **Magallanes** and **Bories,** both of which flank the plaza and change names (to **21 de Mayo** and **Nogueria**) upon crossing the plaza. Nearly all important shops and services lie within a four-block radius of the square.

Tourist Office: (☎200 610; informacionturistica@puntaarenas.cl) Victorian-style kiosk in Plaza Muñoz Gamero. Has transportation and accommodations information for Punta Arenas and Puerto Natales. English spoken. Open M-F 8am-7pm, Sa-Su 9am-2pm.

Tours: Many tour operators are scattered east of the central plaza on Lautar Navarro between Errázuriz and José Menéndez. The tourist office has a list of other tour operators in the area. English-speaking staff available at all tour offices. Nearly every office offers the tours listed below, and cooperation between agencies keeps prices nearly constant. If there's anything you want to do in Patagonia, **Comapa,** Magallanes 990 (☎200 200; www.comapa.com), can book it for you. They specialize in booking sailing trips of Patagonian fjords and islands, including on the popular Navimag ship, but can also coordinate a variety of overland excursions and adventures. Open daily 9am-8pm. **Turismo Viento Sur,** Faguano 585 (☎225 930), offers tours near Punta Arenas, in Torres del Paine, and to the islands at the limit of the continent. Mountain bike rentals available (half-day CH$7000, full-day CH$9000). Ask about short kayak daytrips in the area (US$38, 3hr.) and fly-fishing excursions (US$100, min. 2 people).

Consulates: The tourist office has a complete list of consulates. Consulates in the area include **Argentina,** 21 de Mayo 1878 (☎261 912); **Brazil,** Arauco 769, (☎241 093); and the **UK,** Cataratas del Niagara 01325, (☎211 535).

Currency Exchange: Cambios Scott, Colón and Magallanes (☎220 967), is among many exchange offices near the Plaza that change cash and travelers checks at good rates. Open M-Sa 9:15am-8pm; Su 10:30am-5pm.

ATM: Many large banks with **24hr. ATMs** circle the central plaza. **Banco de Chile,** Roca 864, accepts Cirrus/MC/Plus/V. Open 24hr.

Western Union: Pedro Montt 840 (☎228 462). **DHL** express mail service available. Open M-F 8:30am-7:30pm, Sa 9:30am-2pm.

Supermarket: Listo, 21 de Mayo 1133, near the central plaza. Open M-Sa 9am-9pm, Su 10am-2pm. DC/MC/V. Or try mammoth and always crowded **Abu Gosch,** Bories 647. Open M-Sa 9am-10pm, Su 10am-9pm. DC/MC/V.

Laundromat: Josseau, Ignacio Pinto 766 (☎228 413). Same-day service before noon. CH$1300 per kilo. Open M-F 8:30am-7:30pm, Sa 8:30am-2pm. AmEx/MC/V.

Police: ☎133.

24hr. Pharmacy: There is a rotating system between local pharmacies of staying open 24hr. The current rotation is posted on the front door of each of the pharmacies in town.

Hospital: Ambulance ☎131. **Hospital Regional,** Angamos 180 (☎205 000).

Telephones: Call centers fill the blocks surrounding the Plaza, with several on Bories heading north from the center. For good rates on phone calls to the US, try **Solber Ltd.,** Bories 801 (☎235 142). CH$400 per minute. Open daily until midnight.

Internet Access: Calafate Internet, Magallanes 922 (☎241 281). Central location, fast connections. CH$700 per hr. CD-burning stations and digital photography facilities. Open M-F 8am-1:45am; Sa-Su 9am-12:35am.

Post Office: Bories 911 (☎222 796).

▗ ACCOMMODATIONS

There's no shortage of places to stay in Punta Arenas. In fact, competition is so tight that would-be hosts stumble over each other to greet passengers arriving by bus. There is, however, a shortage of quality budget accommodations. Beware of proprietors offering to drive you to "look" at their out-of-town accommodation. No matter what they promise, they're likely to be peeved if you don't like what you see and request a ride back to town. The accommodations listed below are generally within six blocks of the central plaza.

Hostal de la Patagonia, O'Higgins 730 (☎249 970; www.ecotourpatagonia.com). Recently remodeled, this squeaky-clean *hostal* provides spotless rooms, cable TV, and an in-house tour office, all at bargain rates. The foyer and dining area have an unshakable retirement-community feel, but once you've stretched out on the plush beds and had an excellent shower, it's no bother. Singles CH$15,000; doubles CH$20,000. ❸

Hostal de la Avenida, Colón 534 (☎/fax 247 532). Treat yourself to quiet rooms with private bath, a small garden, and immaculately attentive service. Avenida is one of the most comfortable and well-appointed hostels in town and the prices and demand for beds show it. Be sure to book ahead. Breakfast included. Singles CH$25,000; doubles CH$35,000; triples CH$38,000; quads $45,000. ❺

Hostal La Estancia, O'Higgins 765 (☎249 130). Just around the corner from Pancheco Bus, this friendly hostel offers pleasant rooms, reliable Internet access, and an excellent included breakfast. Kitchen use available; free storage. Dorms CH$5000; singles CH$10,000; doubles CH$15,000. ❷

Hostal del Estrecho, José Menéndez 1045 (☎/fax 421 011; www.chileanpatagonia.com/estrecho). The friendly owner takes excellent care of the bright and clean rooms. Breakfast included. Singles CH$15,000, with bath CH$20,000; doubles CH$20,000/CH$25,000; apartment for 3-4 people CH$30,000. ❸

Hotel Calafate, Magallanes 926 (☎241 281; www.calafate.cl), just north of the plaza, above the popular Internet cafe. Concealed amidst its labyrinthine halls and poorly decorated common spaces, Calafate offers clean hotel rooms at reasonable rates. The proximity to the plaza and services can't be beat, and cable TV, telephones, and included breakfast are all pleasant perks. Singles US$22, with bath US$35; doubles US$33/US$45; triples US$42/US$61. ❸

Hostal al Fin del Mundo, O'Higgins 1026 (☎710 185; www.alfindelmundo.cl). Upstairs, past the dark reception room and dorm-like living room, lie clean and comfortable doubles and shared rooms. The bathrooms are among the brightest and cleanest budget lavatories in town, and kitchen access, a DVD player, and breakfast service secure a pleasant stay. Bike rentals available. Dorms and doubles CH$7000 per person. ❶

Residencial Roca, Magallanes 888 (☎/fax 243 903). Despite squeaky floors, cluttered common spaces, and cramped bathrooms, Roca offers one of the best bargains near the plaza. Enthusiastic owners will fill your ears with travel advice. Continental breakfast included. CH$5000 per person, with bath CH$10,000. ❷

Hostal del Rey, Fagnano 589 (☎223 924; www.chileaustral.com/hdelrey), 2 blocks west of the central plaza. Family-run and group-oriented. Rooms are small and eclectic, but like the communal bathrooms, are clean and well-kept. Cable TV. Doubles CH$10,000; apartment for 3-4 guests CH$21,000-25,000. ❷

🍴 FOOD

Cuisine isn't Punta Arenas's strong suit, but there are a few restaurants and bars that shouldn't be missed. Try the king crab and other seafoods to escape *milanesa* malaise, and although it may go without saying, avoid at all costs any restaurant near the harbor billing itself as a "*restaurante turístico.*"

🦐 **La Luna,** O'Higgins 974 (☎228 555). Exactly as the menu promises: good food, best prices. This unassuming eatery, a favorite of both locals and travelers, specializes in seafood. The *chupe de centollas* (CH$4600) is not to be missed, nor are the local scallops (CH$2850). When you're finished, join the ranks of visitors who make their mark on the wall of world maps. Open M-Sa noon-3pm and 7-11:30pm, Su 7-11pm. ❸

BEAVER PROBLEMS

Since beavers were introduced to Tierra del Fuego 45 years ago, their population has grown to 60,000. They're busy beavers: every stream on Isla Navarino has been permanently altered by beaver construction, and beaver dams drown the surrounding *lenga* forest, leaving apocalyptic hillsides of dead, bleached trees.

As summer director of the Omaru Foundation, a non-profit organization committed to the preservation of the unique forest south of the Beagle Channel, Steven McGehee also finds himself defending species few people care about. Isla Navarino possesses a forest unlike any in the world: while short of biodiversity in macrofauna and macroflora, it's a Eden of mosses, lichens, and liverworts. Despite this important diversity, it's difficult to defend liverworts when other places have grizzlies, *guanacos*, and great spotted owls.

In the face of challenges, Omaru has petitioned the United Nations to have Isla Navarino declared a World Biosphere Reserve. The timing of their petition couldn't be better: with the Chilean Navy reducing its base and regional authorities pressing to develop the island, Navarino's mosses need defenders.

To support Omaru, try the beaver steaks at Cabo de Hornos Restaurant. Then, visit the foundation's website: www.omaru.org.

Damiana Elena, O'Higgins 694 (☎222 818). Inside, a warm, country-house ambience hosts locals who crowd in for inexpensive home cooking. A large fillet of salmon runs CH$3600 and pastas (CH$3600-4000) and *milanesas* (CH$3900-4100) fill out the menu. There's always an extensive list of daily specials and exhaustive wine list, just to haunt the indecisive. Open M-Sa 7:30pm until the last patrons wander out. ❸

Sandino, Colón 576 (☎220 511). Packed with Punta Arenas's young movers and shakers late at night, this new bar/restaurant serves excellent light meals. On the brick walls, striking black-and-white photos of *gauchos* mix with 1920s- and 1930s-era relics and a wooden ceiling gives the space a seemingly endless depth. Try the standard *lomo* and seafood fare (CH$3500-4800) while you warm up for the evening with one of the many choices of cocktails (CH$1800-3500). Half-price drinks at happy hour 6-9pm. Open daily 6pm-3:30am. ❸

La Natta Pizza, Bories 601 (☎240 310), next to Abu Gosch supermarket. A clean and friendly greasy spoon/pizzeria close to the center of town, perfect for grabbing a quick, cheap bite and catching the latest *fútbol* scores on the television. Sizable small pizzas run CH$2400-5500 and include a seafood option topped with Magallanic king crab (CH$5500). A real bargain for an empty stomach is the half rotisserie chicken (CH$1900). Open Su-Th noon-midnight, F-Sa noon-2am. ❷

Puerto Viejo, O'Higgins 1205 (☎225 103), at the port. A great stop for a seafood luncheon, this fresh eatery offers a variety of seafood dishes, like king crab (CH$7000) and locally caught scallops (CH$4300). And, of course, they also offer the requisite list of pastas (CH$3500-4200) and *milanesas* (CH$3800-4000) in case you're not feeling fishy. The brightly painted walls and smart wooden tables and chairs create a sense of class missing at other places in town. Open daily noon-3pm and 8pm-late. ❸

◎ SIGHTS

MUSEO REGIONAL DE MAGALLANES. Also known as the Casa Braun-Menéndez, this decadent residence of the Menéndez family has been restored to reveal the prosperous lifestyle of late 19th-century Punta Arenas. The mansion, declared a national monument in 1974, remains largely as it was in the heyday of Punta Arenas. The rooms, visible only from the threshold, bring a bit of French royal style to Patagonia. Just past the restored home, another series of rooms document the discovery and settlement history of the Magallanic region. *(Magallanes 900 block, north of the central plaza. ☎244 216. Open M-Sa 10:30am-5pm, Su and holidays 10:30am-2pm. CH$1000, children CH$500. CH$1000 extra to use cameras.)*

MUSEO REGIONAL SALESIANO. In 1881, Salesian missionaries arrived in Patagonia with grand hopes of rescuing the immortal souls of the region's many indigenous peoples. They had little time for success, however: European-introduced diseases like smallpox rapidly decimated the native populations just as the missionaries sought to bring them into the fold. The missionaries did succeed, however, in documenting and recording indigenous traditions and practices before they disappeared. The Salesian Museum presents the story of these missionaries, and the native tribes they lived with, in four floors of exhibits. Interspersed with the indigenous and missionary histories are basic displays on natural history and other regional sites, like the *Cueva de Milodon* and the *Cueva de las manos*. *(Bulnes 336. ☎245 866. Open Tu-Su 10am-6pm. CH$2000, children CH$200.)*

CLUB DE LA UNIÓN. Built in 1895 by Sara Braun, the widowed wife of local leader José Noguiera, this ornate building is one of Punta Arenas's architectural wonders. For many years after Sara's death, the palace was maintained by local socialites for private use. Although an exclusive group of local citizens still meets in the marble-floored salons and wood-paneled music room, the club—named a national monument in 1982—is open to the public. If it is particularly quiet, the guard may allow access to the terrace and dining rooms now used by the new five-star hotel that shares the building. *(Plaza Muñoz Gamero 716. ☎241 489; clunion@entelchile.net. Open Tu-Su 10am-1pm, 5-10pm. CH$1000.)*

CEMENTERIO MUNICIPAL. An easy 15min. walk from the center of town, this well-maintained burial ground tells the story of Punta Arenas with funerial monuments. There are opulent vaults housing the remains of former residents like José Menéndez and Sara Braun and simple tombstones etched with ethnic names that reveal the town's immigrant heritage. A visit makes for a pleasant morning or afternoon stroll, and is especially worthwhile for visitors who have yet observe the elaborate ornamentation of a Chilean or Argentine cemetery. *(Bulnes 949, 10 blocks north of the central plaza. Open dawn to dusk. Free.)*

▶ DAYTRIPS FROM PUNTA ARENAS

MONUMENTO NATURAL LOS PINGÜINOS. In 1892, Marta and Magdalena Islands were established as a national monument, protecting the breeding habitat for more than 50,000 pairs of Magallanic penguins. These flightless birds, sometimes known as "jackass" penguins because of their distinctive bray-like call, congregate en masse between November and the end of February. After the 2hr. ferry to the island, visitors are given nearly an hour to watch the penguins struggle overland and roam about the shore. The real treat, however, is back on the boat where the elevated position allows for splendid views of these adorable aquatic animals as they return from the sea. *(For information, contact Conaf, Bulnes 0309. ☎238 581. Purchase tickets at any tour office. Boats leave daily from Tres Puentes Port, easily accessible by colectivo 15 that passes Magallanes every few minutes. Tours CH$20,000, children CH$10,000.)*

SENO OTWAY. One hour north of town, Seno Otway allows for good viewing of the "jackass" penguin, but it is noticeably smaller and less personal than the more popular Monumento Natural Los Pingüinos. Despite the smaller penguin population here, it may be better for those short of money or time. *(If you're quoted a higher price at your hostel, try an agency. Most tours to Seno Otway cost CH$10,000 including entrance fee and bilingual guide.)*

FUERTE BULNES. Founded in 1843, Fuerte Bulnes was the first Chilean settlement along the Strait of Magellan, meant to establish Chilean sovereignty over the region. The bases, however, only lasted a few years before citizens moved 55km north to Punta Arenas for better soil and protection. The present-day reconstruction of the settlement includes a chapel, horse stalls, a jail, and an ominous fence of sharpened stakes. The real gem of a visit, though, is the coastal walk and expansive view across the Strait of Magellan. In total, an excursion to Fuerte Bulnes takes about three hours, with an hour at the site itself. An on-site cafe has reasonably priced food and is a great place to enjoy a picnic. *(Tickets can be purchased from any tour office in town for CH$10,000 per person. Some hostels will also arrange trips, although prices can vary greatly. Taxis will make the round-trip journey for CH$25,000.)*

RESERVA FORESTAL MAGALLANES. Just west of town and overlooking the bay, the reserve is a forested escape from Punta Arenas's gusty winds. Local families often come up to enjoy a barbecue or a calming walk in the picturesque forest, but this is no spectacular highlight for most travelers seeking Patagonia's natural wonders. The mountain, given over to cheap (though unexceptional) skiing in the winter, doubles as a hiking site during the summer. A 1hr. circuit trail and a 45min. hiking trail to the peak provide a great view of town. *(Turismo Viento Sur offers trips to*

Puerto Natales

▲ ACCOMMODATIONS
AguaTerra, **10**
Casa Cecilia, **5**
Concepto Índigo, **12**
Danicar, **1**
Magallania, **8**
Patagonia Adventure, **7**
🍴 FOOD
Concepto Índigo, **11**
El Asador Patagonia, **3**
El Cristal, **4**
El Living, **2**
El Marítimo, **13**
La Oveja Negra, **6**
Restaurant Última Esperanza, **9**

TO ✈, PN TORRES DEL PAINE (150km),
PUNTA ARENAS (247km),
EL CALAFATE (362km)

Canal Señoret

0   100 yards
0   100 meters

the reserve's ski club at 10am and 1pm that return at 1:30 and 5pm. CH$2000 each way. Lift tickets and rental equipment CH$22,000. In the summer, Viento Sur rents bikes with helmets; half-day CH$7000, full-day CH$9000. To reach the park, ride 9km west along Independencia.)

PUERTO NATALES   ☎ 61

Founded in 1911 as a sheep-herding settlement, Puerto Natales now attracts flocks of tourists and trekkers. Its proximity to Parque Nacional Torres del Paine and Cerro Balmaceda makes this an ideal place to stock up on camping equipment and supplies for heading out into the wilderness. But, for a town largely oriented toward tourism, Puerto Natales maintains a remarkably charming, small-town feel. It's one of the finer places in the region to spend a day or two resting and recuperating, lounging in excellent cafes and restaurants, or just gazing aimlessly out onto the scenic waters of the Seno Última Esperanza (Last Hope Sound).

🖵 TRANSPORTATION

Flights: The small local airport, 6km west of town, is usually very quiet, with almost no major airlines. **DAP**, represented in town by Path@gone (see below) has the only regular service to **El Calafate, ARG** (45min., M-Sa 9am, US$54). Taxis to the airport cost about CH$5000. **LanChile** does not fly to Puerto Natales, but their representative, **Comapa** (see below) can answer questions, book flights, and rearrange itineraries.

Buses:

Bus Sur, Baquedano 558 (☎411 325), goes to: **Coyhaique** (20hr., M 8:30am, CH$30,000); **El Calafate, ARG** (5hr.; M, W, F 9am; CH$15,000); **Osorno** (34hr., M and Th 7am, CH$35,000) via **Puerto Montt** (32hr., CH$35,000); **Punta Arenas** (3hr.; 5 times per day M-F, 4 times per day Sa, 3 times per day Su; CH$3500); **Río Gallegos, ARG** (6hr., M and F 6:30am, CH$8000); **Río Turbio, ARG** (1hr.; M-F 8:30am and 6pm, Su 9pm; CH$2000). Most buses leave from the office, but confirm ahead of time, as some early ones leave from the plaza.

Cootra, Baquedano 244, also heads to **El Calafate, ARG** (5hr.; M-F 8:30am, Sa-Su 8am; CH$13,000).

Pancheco Bus, Baquedano and O'Higgins (☎414 513), goes to **Punta Arenas** (3 per day, CH$3500).

Buses Fernández, Eberhard 555 (☎411 111), has the most frequent service to **Punta Arenas** (3hr., 7 per day 7:15am-8pm, CH$3500).

Ferries: Navimag, Costanera Pedro Mont 380, runs 2- and 4-day boats to **Puerto Montt** and **Puerto Chacabuco.** Visit the Comapa office (see below) for inquiries.

Taxis: Although they are generally unnecessary because most things are within walking distance, taxis can be found around the plaza. Fares start at CH$700.

Car Rental: Prices for day-tours of the park are so expensive that groups short on time that have credit cards for the security deposit should consider renting a car for the day. **Patagonia Infinita Turismo,** Bulnes 469 (☎415 018) rents Jeep 4x4s for CH$45,000 per day.

Bike Rental: Sendero Aventura, Tomás Rogers 179 (☎415 636), rents bikes for CH$10,000 per day, and will deliver rented bikes to the National Park for CH$15,000.

✈ 🛈 ORIENTATION AND PRACTICAL INFORMATION

Around the manicured **Plaza de Arturo Prat,** Puerto Natales' streets extend in a standard grid system. Most of the town's services line **Avenida Bulnes,** which runs from the waterfront to the outskirts of town, one block from the plaza. North of the square, the intersection of **Blanco Encalada** and Bulnes is also a center of activity.

Tourist Office: Inside the friendly Puerto Natales Historical Museum, Bulnes 285 (☎411 263), is the municipal **tourist office.** Open daily in summer 9am-12:30pm and 3-8pm. Most hostels and hotels, however, can book everything from their reception desks.

Tours: Most offices offer similar packages.

Path@gone, Eberhard 595 (☎/fax 413 291; www.pathagone.com), is extremely helpful, offering ice hiking, sailing, trekking, and combination packages. It also administers most of the *refugios* in the park and is an excellent place to book lodging for a trek. Open 9am-10pm.

Big Foot, Bories 206 (☎414 611 or 413 247; www.bigfootpatagonia.com), runs a top-notch adventure guiding outfit with tours of the national park, sea kayaking, glacier trekking, and rock- and ice-climbing. Their sea kayak trips on the Serrano River are extremely popular; for a challenging day excursion, try a day of climbing the knobby conglomerate at Laguna Sofia (US$110). With advance notice, they can coordinate more serious climbing and kayaking expeditions.

Chile Nativo, Barros Arana 176 (☎411 835; www.chilenativo.com), runs excellent horse-packing and bird-watching trips in the region.

Comapa, Bulnes 533 (☎414 300), handles Navimag (www.navimag.com; to Puerto Montt US$275) bookings. Inquire also about their lodge at Rincón de Tenerife and guided climbs of Cerro Tenerife (US$155, min. 2 people).

Estancia Travel, Bulnes 241 (☎411 841), features horse-packing and fly-fishing.

Currency Exchange: Mily Travel Agencies, Blanco Encalada 277 (☎411 262), exchanges US dollars and traveler's checks. Open M-Sa 10am-1pm and 3:30-7pm.

ATM: Banco Santander, on the corner of Bulnes and Blanco Encalada. AmEx/MC/V.

Laundromat: Catch, Bories 218 (☎411 520), takes about 2-3hr. CH$3500 for a 3kg load. Open daily 9am-11pm.

TIERRA DEL FUEGO

Supermarket: Don Bosco, Baquedano 358 (☎411 582), is centrally located with a good selection. Open M-Sa 9am-10pm, Su noon-8pm.

Equipment/Bike Rental: Many hostels offer reasonable equipment at fair prices. **Sendero Aventura,** Tomás Rogers 179 (☎415 636), rents stoves (CH$1000 per day), sleeping bags (CH$1000 per day), and tents (2-person CH$3500 per day), among other things. If no one is attending the shop, stop into Patagonia Aventura next door. **La Maddera,** Prat 297 (☎413 318), is a good place to buy white gas and other camp stove fuels, even on Su when most other shops are closed. Open daily 8am-11pm.

Police: ☎133. Local police ☎411 133.

24hr. Pharmacy: Puerto Natales runs on a rotating system of 24hr. pharmacies, so check the schedule at any one. **Farmacia Puerto Natales,** Esmeralda 701 (☎411 306), is centrally located. Open 9:30am-1pm and 3-10:30pm.

Hospital: ☎131. Pinto 537, ☎411 582.

Telephones: Telefónica, Blanco Encalada 298 (☎415 728), is great for phone calls. Open M-F 9am-11pm, Sa-Su 10am-11pm.

Internet Access: Internet access is widespread, but there are no broadband connections in town. **Cyberplay,** Baquedano 480 (☎412 301) has the fastest connection, for CH$800 per hr. Open M-Sa 10am-11pm, Su 3-8pm. **Fortaleza,** Blanco Encalada 170, is popular and usually has fast connections. CH$1000 per hr. Open daily 10am-11pm.

Post Office: Correos de Chile, Eberhard 429, on the plaza. Open M-F 8:30am-12:30pm and 2:30-6pm, Sa 9am-12:30pm.

ACCOMMODATIONS

Natales has loads of excellent budget accommodations. For January and February, prior bookings are essential to ensure a bed, as some double rooms are booked more than six months ahead.

Casa Cecilia, Tomás Rogers 60 (☎/fax 411 797; redcecilia@entelchile.net). A staple of Natales's budget travel crowd, Cecilia's offers professional service at affordable prices. The new mattresses, open kitchen, inviting lounge areas, and excellent showers are a perfect welcome to guests back from a week in the park. Quality camping equipment for rent. English and German spoken. Breakfast included. Reservations essential. Dorms CH$7000; doubles with bath CH$23,000. ❷

Patagonia Adventure, Tomás Rogers 179 (☎411 028; www.patagonia-adventure-lodging.com). Each morning, the homey downstairs kitchen churns out fresh bread for the included breakfast while upstairs, happy guests catch some final zzz's in cozy bunkrooms and doubles. Built almost entirely with wood, Patagonia Adventure has a rustic, lodgy feel, and the excellent equipment rental and trekking advice make it a good stop for Torres-bound travelers. Dorms CH$5000; doubles CH$12,000. ❷

AguaTerra, Bulnes 299 (☎412 239; www.aguaterrapatagonia.cl). Brand-new and refined, this pleasant boutique lodge is an excellent option for couples seeking a splurge after a gritty week in the park. Plush beds, down duvets, and immaculate showers compliment the refined lounge and restaurant spaces. Singles US$30; doubles US$35, with bath US$50; triples US$45. ❹

Magallania, Tomás Rogers 255 (☎414 950; www.chileaustral.com/magallania). Run by two bachelor brothers, Magallania makes up for its tight bedrooms with a lounge complete with cable and DVDs, luxurious mattresses, and carefree feel. Kitchen facilities, free storage, tour information, and camping available. Camping CH$2000. Dorms CH$3000, with breakfast CH$5000. ❶

Concepto Índigo, Ladrilleros 105 (☎413 609). Hostel rooms available above the popular cafe/restaurant/bar. The colorful doubles and bunks at Índigo offer some of the best waterfront views in town. There's an excellent restaurant and cafe (p. 451) downstairs, where guests often while their afternoons away sipping Chilean wine and watching the wind kick up the Canal Senoret. Breakfast and Internet included. Free storage. Dorms CH$12,000; doubles CH$25,000, with bath CH$28,000.

Danicar, O'Higgins 707 (☎412 170). This central hostel is managed by an entire family—mom, dad, and three daughters. The rooms are well kept and some *matrimoniales* include free cable TV. Breakfast included. Doubles and *matrimoniales* CH$10,000. ●

🍴 FOOD

Options abound in Puerto Natales, from light vegetarian fare to hearty plates for post-trail gluttony.

▨ **El Living,** Arturo Prat 156 (☎411 140), on the plaza. One of few places around here where you'll find a curried chickpea casserole (CH$3800) and notice a conspicuous absence of *lomo*. This hip veggie cafe could be in London or Berkeley, but luckily for Torres visitors, it offers its excellent sandwiches (CH$1800-2800) and salads (CH$1800-2600), superb coffees, and magnetic atmosphere a bit farther south. The book exchange and extensive selection of international magazines will keep you for hours. Open Nov.-Apr. 11am-10:30pm. ●

▨ **El Asador Patagonia,** Arturo Prat 158 (☎413 553). As if the laws of food karma commanded it, this new entry into Puerto Natales's restaurant scene serves the exact opposite menu of its neighbor, el Living: only grilled chicken, beef, pork, and lamb. Sure, you can have a side salad (CH$1500) with your show-stopping grilled lamb chops (CH$6000), but if you're hunting something other than bulky, perfectly-prepared hunks of flesh, you've missed the point. Reservations strongly recommended—the place brims with trekkers just off the trail and locals out for a special dinner. Open daily 12:30-3pm and 7-11:30pm. ❸

El Marítimo, Pedro Montt 214 (☎/fax 414 994). El Marítimo feels exactly like a family-owned, harborside restaurant should. The food is delicious and comes in ample and affordable portions, and the interior is unadorned and welcoming. The biggest challenge may be finding a table. Try the *Palta Victoria* appetizer (king crab and avocado, CH$3000) or the heaping *salmón a la pobre* (CH$3800). Open noon-midnight. ❸

Concepto Índigo, Ladrilleros 105 (☎413 609; www.conceptoindigo.com), at the port. The large windows overlooking the bay make this a picturesque spot for an afternoon coffee (CH$1000) or early evening beer (CH$1000). The rest of the menu, while pricey, is delicious and elegantly presented. The evening *menú* costs CH$10,000 and includes stew, chef's choice of entree, and dessert. Outdoor climbing wall. Open 11am-11pm. ❸

La Oveja Negra, Tomás Rogers 169 (☎415 711). Taking its name seriously, "The Black Sheep" of Natales restaurants puts unexpected twists on traditional Patagonian dishes. The lamb chops (CH$4200), for example, come with an Asian-influenced sweet-and-sour sauce and are excellent paired with a side of curried rice (CH$1000). Or, enjoy the relaxing music and homey decor while you sample the specialty, *Chupe de Centolla* (CH$6000). Open Oct.-Mar. M-Sa noon-4:30pm and 6-11:30pm, Su 6-11:30pm. ❸

Restaurant Última Esperanza, Eberhard 354 (☎413 626 or 411 630). Esperanza serves good portions of some of the best seafood in town in a slightly upscale, albeit staid, atmosphere. The lunch *menú* (CH$3500) is the best deal, but the king crab platter (CH$8000) and salmon (CH$4000) should not be missed for a filling *cena*. Open daily noon-3:30pm and 6:30pm-midnight. ❷

El Cristal, Bulnes 439 (☎411 850). Local families crowd around the long tables at cozy Cristal for the hearty lunch *menú* (CH$3000 with appetizer and dessert), and while it may be full of tourists at night, they come for good reason. The menu is basic, but the food is delicious. If you've got the appetite, sample the enormous *picada,* a pile of french fries, beef and chicken chunks, *chorizo,* and sausage, all smothered with cheese and fresh tomatoes (CH$4200 for 2). Wash it down with a mammoth draft of Austral (CH$1000). Open 11am-11:30pm daily. ❷

🔍 SIGHTS

The sights around Puerto Natales are rather limited, but one particularly fascinating attraction is the **Cueva del Milodón,** where, in 1890, Hermann Eberhard discovered the skeleton and some intact flesh of a prehistoric ground sloth, setting off international speculation that the sloth was still alive. Today, a tacky plastic Milodón towers over visitors to the cave. The **Museo de Sitio** offers further information about the harmless beast and the native humans who hunted it. Some tour companies offer trips to the cave, but taxis are more flexible. (Open 8am-8pm. Cave entrance CH$3000, CH$10,000 for up to 4 people.)

A wide variety of **guided tours** are available in Puerto Natales. A relaxed full-day bus tour of **Parque Nacional Torres del Paine** provides a glimpse of the dramatic Paine Massif, but allows next to no time to get out and explore the park. (Tours 7:30am-7:30pm. CH$22,000 plus CH$8000 park admission.) It's also possible (and more exciting) to reach the park via a ferry through the Seno Última Esperanza and a zodiak ride up the Serrano River (CH$56,000). A tour to **Perito Moreno** glacier and **El Calafate, ARG** is a grueling 14hr. trip—a 12hr. round-trip bus ride with an unfortunately short 2hr. to observe one of the most magnificent glaciers in the world. (Tours 7am-9pm. CH$35,000 plus ARG$20 park entrance fee.) Starting in 2005, regular flights with **DAP** to El Calafate will make day-tours of Perito Moreno more comfortable (approximately US$71 each way; inquire with Path@gone for details). The two trips offered to the **Estancia Rosario,** just across the bay, give a good taste of life on a Patagonian ranch. The lunch trip includes a full *asado.* (Tours 12:30-4:30pm. CH$12,500.) Some trips only have a snack, but leave more time for exploring the ranch. (Tours 2-6pm.)

For more fast-paced tours, **Big Foot** (p. 449) has a variety of kayaking tours in and around the national park. A two-day sea-kayak tour of the Seno Última Esperanza and the Serrano Lagoon allows you a chance to paddle between massive icebergs (CH$180,000). For a more challenging excursion, set out on a thee-day descent of the Serrano River (CH$280,000). Or for the less-time, less-*dinero* option, consider a day paddle near Puerto Natales (CH$68,000). All trips require a minimum of two people.

PARQUE NACIONAL TORRES DEL PAINE

As the tour bus rattles along the dirt road north of Puerto Natales, there will come a moment when you look out the window and think, "This is what I came to Patagonia to see." In front of you, the three granite towers of the Paine Massif jut high above the surrounding steppe, dominating the landscape as far as the eye can see. And if the Torres themselves are not enough, the park named in their honor also contains the Valle Francés, the sparkling Glaciar Grey, and the equally impressive Cuernos del Paine, whose tan- and black-banded cliff faces are as distinctive as the neighboring Torres. What's best about the scenery, though, are the more than 200km of trails threading through it. Just lace up your boots and get off the bus.

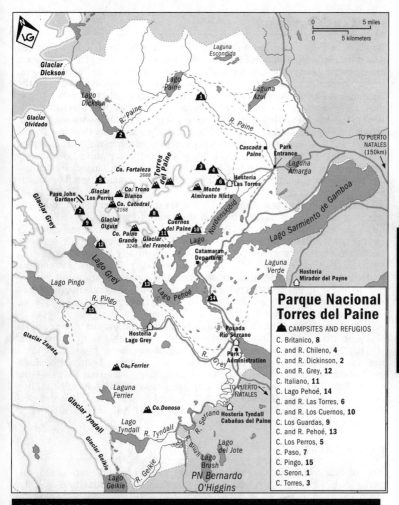

Parque Nacional Torres del Paine

▲ CAMPSITES AND REFUGIOS

C. Britanico, **8**
C. and R. Chileno, **4**
C. and R. Dickinson, **2**
C. and R. Grey, **12**
C. Italiano, **11**
C. Lago Pehoé, **14**
C. and R. Las Torres, **6**
C. and R. Los Cuernos, **10**
C. Los Guardas, **9**
C. and R. Pehoé, **13**
C. Los Perros, **5**
C. Paso, **7**
C. Pingo, **15**
C. Seron, **1**
C. Torres, **3**

TIERRA DEL FUEGO

AT A GLANCE

AREA: 2422 sq. km

CLIMATE: Strong winds throughout the year. Mean summer temperature is 11°C. Average rainfall 70cm per year. Altitude from 50m to 3000m.

CAMPING: Various privately-owned campsites throughout the park. Free camping in designated areas.

FEES: Park entrance CH$8000; children CH$5000.

GATEWAYS: Puerto Natales, Punta Arenas.

HIGHLIGHTS: Wildlife including *guanacos*, *ñandús*, condors, pumas, foxes, and a variety of birds. Glaciers, lakes, lagoons, rivers, and the famous granite towers.

FEATURES: Paine Massif, Paine Grande, Cuernos del Paine, Salto Grande, Salto Chico.

┌═ TRANSPORTATION

Buses from Puerto Natales only travel the park road via strictly prescribed schedules, twice per day in high season. Transport is also pricey: buses are nearly twice as expensive as a transfer from Punta Arenas to Puerto Natales. From November to mid-March, local bus companies travel once early in the morning and again in mid-afternoon (in low season, only the earlier trip is made). The morning trip arrives at Laguna Amarga around 10am and then heads west to the Administration office. The same bus leaves the office around 1:30pm, arriving at Laguna Amarga around 3:30pm and departing from there for Puerto Natales. In peak season, a second bus departs Natales around 2:30pm, arrives at Laguna Amarga around 5pm, travels the park road, and returns immediately from the Administration Office at 6:15pm, passing Laguna Amarga for Natales around 7:30pm. Round-trip tickets (CH$11,000) are discounted and there's little sense in buying a one-way.

Visitors wishing to travel the park road via motor power must catch their bus company headed in the direction they want to go; otherwise, the only other transport is sore feet on a dusty road. Other companies will generally charge passengers of competitors a few dollars for in-park shuttle services, but since all the transport companies run essentially the same schedule, switching companies offers little additional flexibility. There are also shuttles that meet arriving and departing buses at Laguna Amarga to transport passengers to and from **Hostería y Camping Las Torres.** (CH$3500 round-trip, includes a night of camping at any one of Fantástico Sur's three *refugios:* Las Torres, Chileno, and Los Cuernos.)

By **boat,** the folks at Path@gone will happily arrange transport to the park via ferry on the Seno Última Esperanza and zodiak up the Serrano river (CH$53,000). Inside the park, the **Hielos Patagónicos** crosses Lago Pehoé three times per day in the summer, less frequently in low season. Leaving from **Refugio Pudeto,** the boat offers amazing views (30min., 3 per day 9:30am-6pm, CH$10,000). From the **Hostería Lago Grey** (see below), a 3hr. tour of Lago Grey goes to the glacier and back (CH$35,000), but this trip is more weather-dependent. **Horses** are available for rent at the **Conaf** Administration Office (CH$15,000 per hr).

▦ ORIENTATION

The mountains of Torres del Paine erupt magnificently from the surrounding terrain 150km north of Puerto Natales. The three major park attractions—Glaciar Grey, Valle Francés, and the Torres themselves—are accessible either via the Torres Circuit trail (8-10 days, see below), which circumscribes the entire Paine Massif, or via the "W" circuit (4-6 days), which creates a Torres del Paine "greatest hits" trail by eschewing the walk around the park's northern periphery.

Heavy tour-bus traffic along the road from Puerto Natales arrives first at the park's eastern guard post, **Laguna Amarga,** where passengers disembark to pay the entrance fee (CH$8000). From there, the dirt road continues along the southern edge of the Paine Massif to the catamaran dock at Lago Pehoé and then on to the park office. Key access routes to the "W" and Circuit treks begin with either a minibus transfer from Laguna Amarga to **Hostería Las Torres,** via a catamaran ride to **Refugio Pehoé,** or by a 5hr. hike in from the Administration Office there. Kayaking excursions on the Serrano River begin at the Administration Office, where shuttles are also available to **Hostería Lago Grey** and the ferry service to Glaciar Grey.

ACCOMMODATIONS

There are four types of accommodations within the park, listed in order of decreasing grime and increasing glamour: backcountry camping, *refugio* camping, *refugio* bunks, and luxury rooms. Moving clockwise from the entrance at Laguna Amarga, free camping is available near the Torres Mirador at **Torres Campsite** (not to be confused with the **Hostería y Camping Las Torres**), above Glaciar Grey at **Paso Campsite** and **Los Guardas Campsite**, and in Valle Francés at **Italiano** and **Británico** campsites. Continuing clockwise, *refugios* with camping include **Las Torres**, at the end of the Laguna Amarga road (camping CH$3500; bunk CH$14,000); **El Chileno**, halfway up the trail to Mirador Torres (camping CH$3500; bunk CH$14,500); **Serón, Dickson**, and **Los Perros**, all on the northern stretch of the Torres Circuit (camping CH$3200; bunk CH$10,500); **Grey**, at the terminus of Glaciar Grey (camping CH$3200; bunk CH$10,500); **Vertice Pehoé**, destination of the popular catamaran and essential "W" link (camping US$5; bunk US$17); and **Los Cuernos**, 2hr. east of the head of Valle Francés (camping CH$3500; bunk CH$14,500).

For those who require pre- or post-trail pampering, there's plenty to be had at **Hostería Las Torres ❸**. (☎710 050. Private bath. Breakfast included. Free parking. Internet, laundry services available. Singles US$155, low-season US$89; doubles US$176/US$109.) Also try **Hostería Lago Grey ❺** at Lago Grey. (☎410 172. Private bath. Breakfast included. Free parking. Internet, laundry services available. Singles US$173, off-season US$82; doubles US$199/US$95; triples US$228/US$109.)

The park's surging popularity and unpredictable weather mean that *refugio* beds are often full, so make sure to reserve ahead. Most tour offices and hostels in Puerto Natales can make reservations for you, or you can contact the concessionaires directly. **Fantástico Sur**, Magallanes 960 in Punta Arenas (☎226 054), manages El Chileno, Las Torres, Los Cuernos, and camping at Serón. **Andescape**, Eberhard 599 in Puerto Natales (☎412 592), owns Dickson, Grey, and Los Perros. **Turismo Comapa** (p. 449) handles reservations for **Vertice Pehoé.**

HIKING

"W" TRAIL. Designed to make the park's most splendid scenery accessible through a series of day-hikes, the "W" can be walked in either direction. The eastern starting point is Hostería Las Torres, accessible by shuttle bus from **Laguna Amarga.** Starting from the west, hikers either wander in (5hr. from the Park Administration Office) or take the catamaran (see above) from the Pehoé Guard Station to **Refugio Pehoé.** There's little difference between an east-west hike and a west-east hike, but if the weather is good at the time of your entrance to the park, it is wise to begin in the east to catch the Torres when they're not clouded in. The minimum amount of time required to complete the trek is four days, but to truly soak in the scenery, five or six days is more appropriate. The following description assumes a five-day trek from east to west.

From the east on day one, trekkers disembark at Laguna Amarga and shuttle to Hostería Las Torres (CH$3500 per person, includes a free night of camping at any of Fantástico Sur's three campsites; likewise, purchasing a night's camping at one of the campsites comes with a free shuttle transfer from Las Torres back to Laguna Amarga). From the Hostería, it's a stiff 2hr. climb to the **Refugio Chileno,** or a 3hr. climb to the free camping at **Torres Campsite.** From both, what follows is a 1-2½hr. scramble over loose talus to the crown jewel, **Torres Mirador.** Many hikers depart early on day two for the Mirador to catch the rusty hues of the Torres as the sun first strikes them. Some trekkers choose to set up camp at **Camping Las Torres** (near the Hostería) and climb to the Mirador as a long day-hike.

On day two, proceed along the shortcut trail (not marked on the park map, but clearly indicated by signs) departing from the Torres Mirador Trail about 30min. below Refugio Chileno to either **Refugio Los Cuernos** (5-6hr.) or **Italiano Campsite** (7-8hr.). The following day, grab your daypack and proceed up to Valle Francés, or carry your tent up to **Británico Campsite** (2½-3hr. from Italiano; 5-6hr. from Los Cuernos) for scenic sites in a breathtaking alpine bowl.

Start day four by trekking to **Refugio Pehoé** (2-4½hr.) and then proceed on to **Refugio Grey** (another 4hr.), where you can spend the evening watching the sun set over the Southern Patagonian Icefield from a *mirador* (outlook), just 15min. past camp. The following day, hike back to Pehoé to catch the catamaran (6:30pm, summer only) and your bus connection to Puerto Natales.

TORRES CIRCUIT. The classic **Torres Circuit** hike begins at **Hostería y Camping Las Torres** and travels clockwise around the Paine Massif. Ambitious trekkers can tackle the circuit in 7-8 days, but because of the vagaries of weather and blistered toes, 10 days is a more reasonable allowance. While such a long trek is very time-consuming, the chance to beat the crowds and experience Torres del Paine's true backcountry is well worth the extra days.

Circuit hikers generally begin with a 7hr. day hike to the **Mirador Las Torres** from Hostería Las Torres, but if the weather's bad, save the viewpoint for last. Traveling around the northern side of the Paine Massif can take 3-5 days, depending on how demanding a regime of walking you choose. The campsites and *refugios* (Serón, Dickson, and Los Perros) are spaced 4-6hr. apart and the trail between them generally traverses flat (if muddy) terrain. The walk from Las Torres to Los Perros can generally be accomplished in three days. After Los Perros, the going gets rougher: a 12km, 6hr., 3000 ft. ascent passage through Paso John Gardner. Descending the pass, most trekkers camp at the free **Paso Campsite** and then travel to **Lago Grey** the following day. From Grey, the Torres Circuit becomes a "W" from the west, terminating back at Hostería Las Torres. The park's most traveled footpath, this trail is the thoroughfare to the finest viewpoint of the Torres. The trail begins and ends at Hostería Las Torres, winding up alongside the **Río Asencio.** The climb, which is steep at times, takes about 2hr. before flattening out and contouring along exposed scree slopes to Refugio Chileno. Then, entering the trees, it climbs moderately for 1hr. before reaching the last, most difficult leg: a long scramble up a loose talus slope. Extra caution should be afforded to this final section, as the boulders are not secure and the incline is challenging. At the *mirador*, break out your lunch and your camera and take in one of Patagonia's finest views.

SENDERO MIRADOR CUERNOS AND OTHERS. This short hike offers quite a bang for little effort, since it places visitors in the glow of the Central Horn after only a 1hr. walk. The hike begins just above the catamaran dock after a short walk along a dirt road. The trail to the thundering **Salto Grande** waterfall, only 15min. from the dock, also begins at the end of the dirt road. Many daytrips to the park are sure to include these easily accessible sights. Other hikes in the park include the three-day trip to **Lago Pingo,** west of Lago Grey, and the short trip to **Laguna Verde.**

EL CALAFATE, ARGENTINA ☎ 02902

El Calafate is literally in the middle of nowhere. Surrounded by steppe for hundreds of miles to the east and bounded by the Andes in the west, it's also the closest place to one of Patagonia's most celebrated sites, the Glaciar Perito Moreno, and an excellent jumping-off point for an excursion to the impressive Mt. Fitz Roy

El Calafate

🏠 ACCOMMODATIONS
Albergue Buenos Aires, **12**
Calafate Hostel, **3**
Hostal del Glaciar Libertado, **10**
Hostal de Glaciar Pioneros, **13**
Hostel de las Manos, **1**
Lago Argentino, **11**
Los Dos Pinos, **2**
🍎 FOOD AND NIGHTLIFE
Casablanca, **6**
La Lechuza, **7**
La Tablita, **9**
Pura Vida, **4**
Rick's, **8**
Shackleton, **5**

and Cerro Torre. What's more, the combination of Argentine President Kirchner entertaining high-profile visitors in the area and a massive marketing effort has catapulted the town into a top destination for domestic-traveling Argentines. The middle of nowhere has suddenly become the place to be. As a result, Calafate's thoroughfare may feel touristy and crowded, but there are plenty of friendly hostels, smart restaurants, and packed bars to keep visitors entertained when they're not gaping at Perito Moreno.

▟ TRANSPORTATION

Flights: El Calafate's new **airport** is about 15min. from town. **Manuel Tienda León** (☎ 493 766) meets incoming flights and shuttle passengers to town for ARG$12. Shuttles to the airport cost the same. **Aerolíneas Argentinas,** 9 de Julio 57 (☎ 492 815), to: **Bariloche, ARG** (W and Sa 8:30pm, ARG$131); **Buenos Aires, ARG** (7:15pm, ARG$108); **Trelew, ARG** (M-Tu and Sa 7:15pm; ARG$140); **Ushuaia, ARG** (3:15pm, ARG$78). Open M-Sa 9am-2pm and 3-9pm, Su 3-9pm. The only international flight is with **DAP** to **Puerto Natales** (M-F 10am in summer, US$54). Buy **DAP** tickets in town at Libertador 761 (☎ 491 726). There is a **departure tax** of ARG$24 for international flights and a tax of ARG$8 for domestic flights, paid at the airport.

(side margin) TIERRA DEL FUEGO

PATAGONIAN PEACE

After a 6hr. bus ride, I arrived in El Calafate with a friend I had met in Puerto Natales. Hours staring across the lonely Patagonian plains on the rocky road had put me in a daze. I sat down for a coffee while my friend went to check email. While I waited, I watched the lazy clouds tumble and unfold under the merciless winds.

"This is a great place to be alone," the waiter broke in, as he placed my cup on the table. Although I explained that I was with someone, he continued, "No, you haven't been here long enough—you'll see."

Looking back on my time in Tierra del Fuego and Torres del Paine, I can begin to understand what he meant. Although buses and hostels were full of other adventure-seekers, the landscape of the Far South had impressed upon me a peaceful solitude—the unrelenting winds and glacial rivers seemed to have swept everything else away. I now understand why European pioneers who came to this region are often depicted as weathered, weary, and almost always alone: their distant stares were an attempt to reconcile the massive expanse around them with their loneliness, and accept the task of summoning the personal endurance required to survive within it, making Patagonia *the* place where adventurers are forced to discover what they are really made of.

-Alex Leary

Buses: Buses arrive and depart from the orderly **bus station** on Julio Roca, just off Libertador. All bus companies have desks in the terminal; many have offices in town as well. **Cootra** (☎491 444) goes daily to **Puerto Natales** (5½hr., 6am, ARG$45). **Bus Zaahj** (☎491 631) makes the same trip (W, F, Su 8am; ARG$45). **Interlagos** (☎491 179) heads to **Río Gallegos, ARG** (2½hr., Su-F 2:30pm, ARG$30). Ask for the 10% student discount. **Chaltén Travel** (☎491 833) sends buses to **El Chaltén, ARG** (4-6hr.; 8am and 6:30pm, returns at 6:30am and 6pm; ARG$45) and along **Ruta 40** to **Perito Moreno, ARG** and **Los Antigos, ARG** (15hr.; northbound on odd-numbered days, southbound on even days at 8am; ARG$193). The northbound bus connects in **Perito Moreno** for **Bariloche** on even-numbered days (11hr.; ARG$130). **Cal Tur** (☎491 842) travels daily to **El Chaltén** (4-6hr., 7:30am and 6pm, ARG$45).

◼◼ ORIENTATION AND PRACTICAL INFORMATION

The main avenue, **Avenida del Libertador General José de San Martín,** is locally known simply as Libertador. A majority of the town's services line this street, and nearly everything else worth seeing is within easy walking distance. The **bus station** sits atop this hill with convenient access to town. A new lakeside promenade is set to open in 2004-2005, which will provide for scenic strolls along Lago Argentino.

Tourist Office: Roca 1004 (☎491 090), in the bus terminal. Has helpful pamphlets and books of hostels and restaurants to peruse. Open 9am-9pm.

Tours: Many hostels and bus companies will sell tickets for trips to **Glaciar Perito Moreno** and other excursions. **Sur Turismo,** Libertador 1226 (☎491 266; www.surturismo.com.ar), has a wide range of options. **Mundo Austral,** Libertador 1114 (☎492 365) runs afternoon tours to the glacier daily with an English-speaking guide (6hr., 3pm, ARG$60 plus park entrance). Most popular "minitrekking" excursions are run by **Hielo y Aventura,** Libertador 935 (☎492 205).

Currency Exchange: Many large shops on Libertador offer poor to moderate rates for US dollars and traveler's checks. Try **Thaler,** Libertador 1309. Open M-F 10am-3pm and 6-8:30pm, Sa 10am-1pm and 6-8:30pm, Su 6-8:30pm.

ATM: Banks with ATMs line Libertador and adjoining streets. **Banco de la Nación Argentina,** Libertador 1133 (☎492 536), is closest to the bus station.

Supermarket: ALAS, 9 de Julio 71, has a wide selection. Open 8:30am-10pm. For trail goodies, check out the store with the mysterious Marlboro sign next door.

Laundromat: Lavandería, 25 de Mayo 43 (☎492 183), in back of the shopping area, cleans a load in about 2hr. for ARG$9. Open M-Sa 8:30am-12:30pm and 3-8:30pm, Su 4-8:30pm.

24hr. Pharmacy: The rotating system of 24hr. pharmacies prevails here, so check the list at **Farmacia El Calafate,** San Martín 1192 (☎491 407). Open daily 7:30am-11pm.

Hospital: Albertal Formente, Roca 1487 (☎491 001), is near the bus terminal.

Telephones: The large and busy **Telefónica Locutorio,** San Martín 996, is open daily 7:30am-11pm.

Internet Access: For Internet, try **El Cyber,** Espora 44 (☎493 750; ARG$3 per hr.).

Post Office: Correo Argentina, San Martín 1102, at the foot of the stairs to the bus terminal. Open M-F 9am-4pm, Sa 9am-1pm. Most tourist shops that sell postcards also sell stamps.

▶ ACCOMMODATIONS

In the dog-eat-dog world of budget travel, hostel managers at times feel compelled to ensure a completely full house, regardless of prior reservations. El Calafate's recently surging popularity and the caliber of its budget accommodations make for overwhelming demand, so if you're showing up late to claim your bed, chances are decent that it will be gone. For January and February, reserve a spot at popular hostels at least a month in advance, and be sure to reconfirm your reservation before arrival. Several hostels do not take reservations for dorm beds, preferring clients at the desk with cash in hand to those who may or may not show up. If you show up in town without a reservation, be persistent: hostel owners can generally call around to find you a bed, so you don't have to sleep in the bus terminal.

▨ **Hostel de Las Manos,** Egidio Feriglio (☎492 996; hosteldelasmanos@cotecal.com.ar). Walk away from the bus station on 9 de Julio, cross the wooden footbridge, veer right on the dirt path, take the first left, then turn right onto Feriglio. A small, secluded haven still quite close to the center of town, Las Manos offers 24 beds in 6 bunkrooms. Huge picture windows open onto a calm lounge/bar area perfect for reading Bruce Chatwin or scribbling a postcard when the wind is too fierce to brave. Internet access ARG$6 per hr. Bunks ARG$25, with breakfast ARG$30. Reduced rates in low season. ●

Calafate Hostel, Moyano 1226 (☎492 450; www.hostelspatagonia.com). Often filled with Argentine youths and weary Europeans, the long halls and sunny common space of this log-cabin hostel are always clean and buzzing. With reasonably-priced promotions for trips to Perito Moreno and El Chaltén, the friendly front desk staff doubles as a budget travel agent. Kitchen, Internet access, affordable in-house restaurant, free shuttle from airport for advance bookings. 4-bed dorms ARG$22; doubles and *matrimonales* with bath ARG$80-100. HI discount. ●

Hostel del Glaciar (Pioneros and Libertador), Los Pioneros 255 and Libertador 587 (☎491 243 and 491 792; www.glaciar.com). These two hostels are the budget Trump Towers of Calafate. Pioneros, the older of the two, is often packed with young backpackers looking to meet each other over beers in the aptly-named on-site restaurant "Punto de Encuentro." Libertador offers plush doubles and shared quads spread over 3 floors of a Victorian-style building. If they're overbooked, a spot at the *refugio* where you can crash on the floor in a sleeping bag runs ARG$12. Bunks ARG$22-25; doubles with bath ARG $100-150; triples with bath ARG$120. HI discount at Pioneros only. ●

Los Dos Pinos, 9 de Julio (☎491 271; www.losglaciares.com/losdospinos). Sprawling over a large lot just north of the town center, Pinos feels like a cross between a roadside motel and a campground. Clean but bare rooms line one arm of the building while in the

THE LAST OF THE GREAT ICE DAMS

Watching enormous chunks of ice slough from the face of the Perito Moreno glacier is so transfixing that, before the construction of boardwalks to keep onlookers a safe distance away, 34 people were crushed by falling ice. Building-sized chunks of ice fall from the glacier's 70m face daily, but every once in a while, there's a break that makes all others look puny. It's a release of icy energy violent enough to inspire one Buenos Aires news agency to publish the headline: "Perito Moreno set to explode."

It used to be that every eight years, the Perito Moreno glacier would advance across a narrow stretch of Lago Argentino to the Magallanes Peninsula, forming a dam that separated Argentina's second-largest lake into two halves. Fed by rains and glacial rivers, the southern half of the lake would rise as much as 60 ft. higher than the northern half, placing more and more pressure on the ice dam. Then, some morning, unannounced, the dam would yield to the hydraulic force and come crashing down, letting forth a gush of southern lake water and equalizing Lago Argentino's level.

The last occurrence of such a crash happened in 1988, but after the dam broke, many experts believed that the slowing rate of the glacier's advance meant that it would never happen

adjacent yard, campers pitch tents near small, 4-person dorms. Kitchen access. Camping ARG$8. Dorms ARG$18; doubles ARG$50, with bath ARG$120. ❶

Albergue Buenos Aires, Buenos Aires 296 (☎491 147; www.argentinahostels.com). Close to the bus station and with a friendly owner, Buenos Aires offers hotel-style rooms with private bath and 8-bed dormitories. While the corridors are tight and the rooms a bit dark, the well-lit common area has a cable TV and the advice on local travel couldn't be clearer. Free bike use. No reservations accepted for bunks. Dorms ARG$22; doubles ARG$100; triples ARG$120. ISIC and HI discounts. Most credit cards accepted. ❶

Lago Argentino, Campaña del Desierto 1050 (☎491 423; www.losglaciares.com/lagoargentino). Just around the corner from the bus station, Argentino occupies two buildings. The backpackers building is cramped and barracks-like (there are better dorms in town for around ARG$20), but the private rooms across the street are delightful; situated around a garden and near a sunny lounge. Breakfast included for all private rooms. Laundry and tourist bookings available. Reserve several weeks ahead in high season. Doubles with bath ARG$120; triples ARG$150; quads ARG$180. ❸

🎭 🎵 FOOD AND ENTERTAINMENT

Fashionable restaurants and bars keep popping up in El Calafate as its popularity grows. While there's plenty of *parrilla* to be had, shop around for more innovative (and less artery-clogging) options. On Tuesday nights, locals crowd into **La Tolderia,** Libertador 1177, for impromptu cinematic events.

Pura Vida, Libertador 1876 (☎493 356), about a 5min. walk west of town. Part lounge, part bar, and mostly restaurant, this chic eatery serves excellent regional food in a sleek, art-inspired setting. The *cazuela de cordero* (ARG$22) is an excellent choice to warm glacier-chilled limbs. There's also an excellent selection of vegetarian cuisine, like baked, stuffed pumpkin (ARG$15). Enjoy the lake views and laid-back aura, and when you're done eating, improve your taste in music by asking your waiter for the playlist. Open M-Tu 7pm-midnight, Th-Su 12:30-3pm and 7pm-midnight. ❸

La Lechuza, Libertador 1301 (☎491 610), across from the park information office. Calafate's favorite pizzas, served in a dazzling array of varieties, including the namesake "Owl" (with ground beef, ARG$21) and an excellent mushroom pizza (with Patagonian fungi, ARG$21). Locals pack the eatery for lunch and late dinners, and during summer months, patio dining allows patrons to take in some rare Patagonian sun. Sandwiches ARG$6.50-10; pizzas big enough for two ARG$10-21. Open daily 11am-11pm. ❸

Shackleton, Libertador 3287 (☎493 516), a long walk or short cab ride from the center of town. Self-consciously and unapologetically cool—the chef moonlights in Ibiza in the low season—this "landscape bar" combines cocktails (ARG$7-10), beers (ARG$6), and tremendous views of Lago Argentino (best at sunset and on full-moon nights) to create a surprisingly relaxed and unpretentious scene. A limited menu of food (pizzas ARG$15-19, lamb and chicken pot pies ARG$14) and a collection of books and movies on Ernest Shackleton will keep you entertained even if friendly locals and your fellow hostelers don't. Open M, W-Su 5pm-2am. ❷

La Tablita, Rosales 28 (☎491 065), just across the bridge east of town. The locals' (and visiting *porteños'*) pick for *parrilla,* La Tablita has crowded tables and excellent fare. *Parrilla* for two (ARG$36) comes out on a sizzling grill and the full-portion tenderloin (ARG$16) is an immense and unforgettably delicious taste of Argentina. Call ahead to reserve a window table; otherwise, be prepared to wait upwards of 30min. Open daily 12:30-2:30pm and 7:30pm-midnight. ❸

Casablanca, Libertador 1202 (☎491 402). Right in the heart of town, this versatile cafe is a convenient stop for a quick lunch, an afternoon coffee, or an early-evening glass of wine. The decor is a schizophrenic combination of Humphrey Bogart paraphernalia and Patagonian landscape photos. Sandwiches ARG$5-10. Pizza ARG$9-22. Specialty "*lomo* complete" sandwich ARG$12. Open M-Sa 10am-1am, Su noon-midnight. ❶

Rick's, Libertador 1091 (☎492 148). One of several *tenedores libres* in town, Rick's gaudy, textured yellow exterior can't be missed. Inside, the buffet *parrilla* (ARG$17) includes a somewhat limited salad selection and free dessert. While there are other options on the menu (pastas, ARG$12; trout, ARG$20), if you're looking for more than all-you-can-eat *carne,* there are better options in town. Open daily noon-midnight. ❶

◉ SIGHTS

GLACIAR PERITO MORENO. As one of the world's few stable glaciers, **Perito Moreno** is the main show in town. More than 4km wide and as high as 70m, Los Glaciares National Park's feature attraction is inspiring, ennobling, and ultimately humbling. Argentine President Nestor Kirchner has hosted international dignitaries at its face, and recent tourist promotions have vaulted Perito Moreno nearly ahead of the Buenos Aires again. They were wrong. On March 15, 2004, thousands of onlookers witnessed the dramatic collapse of what may be, truly, Moreno's last ice dam. While it took 16 years this time around, the effect was the same: deafening cracking noises, crumbling chunks of ice, rushing waves of water from the southern half of the lake. Parts of El Calafate were flooded.

It's long been claimed that the Perito Moreno is one of the world's few advancing glaciers. This claim, however, depends on the speed of advance compared with the amount of ice sloughing off. In recent decades, the glacier has pushed forward faster than its face has crumbled, but in the last several years, the glacier has stalled. It's not quite retreating, but, according to Los Glaciares park officials, it's no longer safe to say that it's advancing either. Many experts blame global warming, shifting weather patterns, and unreliable precipitation for changing the pattern that the glacier had followed for so many years.

Though the dam may never form again, visitors to Perito Moreno still haven't lost the look of wonder and excitement that arises when sheets of ice come crashing down into the water. For them, the significance of the dam is lost in wonderment at what survives. And for their sake, we hope that park officials keep that barrier far from the crash zone.

obelisk as a national icon. The ice itself, located 80km (1½hr.) west of town, attracts buses and buses of national and international visitors, all eager to watch gigantic ice chunks calve off into **Lago Argentino.**

Simple transportation to the glacier costs ARG$20 (round-trip) and can be booked through nearly any office or hostel in town. Pricier tours that include an English-speaking guide run ARG$60. Most tours leave around 8am and spend all day at the glacier, but some leave at 3pm and return at 9pm for a shorter afternoon excursion. So-called "alternative" tours take a more leisurely and scenic dirt road to the park, stopping along the way to hunt for local fauna, but if you're mostly interested in getting to the ice in a hurry, stick with conventional tours along the paved road. All tours offer the option of a boat excursion to the ice face (ARG$25 on the south side of the glacier; ARG$20 on the north). Besides the boat trip, the viewing area only contains a few short boardwalked paths from which to watch for "the big one," so depending on your tolerance for beauty, a full-day excursion will either seem boring or scarcely long enough. Simple food is available at the cafeteria, but most visitors pack lunch and eat while watching the glacier. Inquire at the park office about the campground 8km from the viewing area. Photographers take note: the front of the ice is best lit early in the day; the top, in the afternoon. *(For more information on flora, fauna, and natural history in Los Glaciares National Park, visit the Park Information Office, Libertador 1302. ☎ 491 005. Open M-Th 8am-8pm, F 8am-9pm, Sa-Su 9am-9pm. Park entrance ARG$20.)*

RESERVA LAGUNA NIMEZ. The new **Reserva Laguna Nimez,** a short walk north of town, protects an enormous population of local birds. On sunny days, the lagoon glistens while more than 80 species of swans, ducks, flamingos, geese, and hawks feed in a perfectly intact habitat. To see them, visitors can follow an easy 45min. circuit around the reserve. *(Head away from town on Ezéquiel Bustillo for 3 blocks, go left on Los Gauchos for half a block, and cross the only bridge. Continue north another 5min., take a right onto Brown and a quick left, then continue for another block. ARG$2.)*

OTHER TOURS. 4x4 tours for 3hr. (ARG$75) or 7hr. (ARG$150 with lunch) ride along the tough terrain, but usually don't pass by much flora or fauna. The longer tour arrives at the South Face of Perito Moreno. To see a well-polished ranch, visit **Estancia Alice** for ARG$60 (lunch included) or pretend to be a *gaucho* on full-day horse rides around **Cerro Frías** for ARG$95 (dinner included). **"Minitrekking"** is the most popular guided tour available, as it takes you across the southern Brazo Rico lake and up on the Perito Moreno glacier for a 5hr. tour of icy rivulets, pools, and axe-carved paths. While the trek does require crampons, it is accessible to visitors of all fitness levels between the ages of 10 and 60. *(11hr., daily 8am, ARG$150 plus ARG$20 park admission.)* For a more extensive tour of the park's glaciers, consider the Glacier Navigation boat tour to **Glaciares Upsala** and **Onelli.** This all-day cruise departs early in the morning and winds among the glaciers that feed Lago Argentino (ARG$180, including transport to the departure dock at Punta Bandera).

EL CHALTÉN, ARGENTINA ☎02962

Born as a town in 1985, El Chaltén maintains an unshakable frontier ambience. Its low buildings appear braced for the relentless winds that rip along the imposing bluffs surrounding town, and its 300 residents remember a time when cows crowded the streets like tourists do today. El Chaltén (the "National Trekking Capital") is the only departure point for hikes into Parque Nacional Los Glaciares and tourism there is taking off, with the numbers of national and international visitors multiplying every year. When you plan your own visit, allow at least three days: two to explore the remarkable trails, and one to wait out the weather—there *will* be bad weather at least one day. Don't worry, rainy days are easily passed with a favorite book in one of town's many pleasant hostels and restaurants.

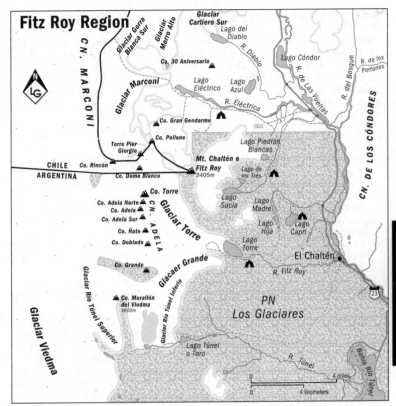

Fitz Roy Region

TRANSPORTATION

Most buses head to and from El Calafate (p. 456), so many visitors book return trips there before leaving for El Chaltén. This is especially important in January and February, when most buses run full. If you have an open return ticket, be sure to notify your bus company when you plan to leave, as far in advance as possible.

The following companies go to El Calafate: **Chaltén Travel** (☎ 493 022), from Rancho Grande Hostel (6:30am and 6pm, ARG$45); **Cal-Tur** (☎ 493 062), from the Fitz Roy Inn (6am and 5:30pm, ARG$45); and **Los Glaciars** (☎ 493 063), from the corner of Güemes and Lago del Desierto (6pm, ARG$45). Chaltén Travel also goes north to Perito Moreno and Lagos Antiguos (15hr., leaving on odd-numbered dates and returning on even-numbered dates 8am, ARG$165). From Perito Moreno, the bus connects north to Bariloche, ARG on the following day (9am, ARG$130). While there is discussion of a route from El Chaltén to Lago del Desierto, across to Lago O'Higgins and Villa O'Higgins in Chile, this service is irregular and unreliable. For information, contact **Mermoz** (see below) regarding transportation to and across Lago del Desierto (ARG$25 for transport to the lake, ARG$45 for a boat cruise on it) or contact one of the operators in Villa O'Higgins (see **Cochrane,** p. 438).

✦ ❓ ORIENTATION AND PRACTICAL INFORMATION

Güemes, the main street running through the heart of town, is perpendicular to **Lago del Desierto** (named for the lake 37km north of town). Most services lie on these two streets. A block east of their intersection is the beginning of the other main stretch, **San Martín,** which passes several hostels and terminates at trailheads to Mt. Fitz Roy and Cerro Torre. Nearly every address is *sin número* (without a number), but friendly locals know where to find most shops and offices.

Tourist Office: First building on the left on Güemes (☎ 493 001). Has most basic information. Open in summer daily 8am-7pm.

Tours: Mermoz, San Martín 493 (☎ 493 098). Very helpful, with a wide range of tours. If anyone in town will know about crossing the Andes to Villa O'Higgins, Chile, this is the place. Open M-Sa 8:30am-12:30pm and 5-9:30pm. Also try **Fitz Roy Expeditions,** on Güemes (☎ 493 017; www.fitzroyexpediciones.com.ar), for tours onto the Glaciar Grande below Cerro Torre and for serious expeditions onto the Southern Patagonian Ice Field. The helpful team at **Chaltén Travel** (☎ 493 022; www.chaltentravel.com) also offers glacier tours and other excursions from their office at the corner of Güemes and Lago del Desierto. Open daily 9am-9pm. For multi-sport adventures, check out **N.Y.C. Adventure,** on Güemes (☎ 493 185; www.nyca.com.ar).

Currency Exchange: There is **no bank, ATM,** or **currency exchange** in El Chaltén. There is talk of an **ATM** opening for the 2005 season, but don't bank on it. **Rancho Grande** exchanges traveler's checks, but at poor rates.

Supermarket: Supermercado Jerónimo, on San Martín near the hostels (☎ 493 090), has a decent selection, with fresh fruits and veggies and long hours. Open daily 8am-midnight. For a better selection, try **El Gringuito,** near the corner of Antonio Rojo and Cerro Solo (☎ 493 065). Open daily 9:30am-2pm and 5-10:30pm.

Equipment Rental: Viento Oeste, at the trailhead end of San Martín (☎ 493 021), rents sleeping bags (ARG$7 per night), stoves (ARG$3), tents (ARG$15), and serious climbing equipment like plastic boots and climbing ropes. The only gas station, near the visitor's center in town, has white gas for camp stoves.

Laundromat: Most accommodations in town provide laundry service for about ARG$12.

Emergency: ☎ 101. Radio emergency frequency: 155.835.

Police: ☎ 133. Also, on Vueltos ☎ 493 003.

Pharmacy: Farmacia del Cerro, Halvor Halvorsen (☎ 493 911), has limited selection. Open M-Sa 10am-1pm and 3:30-8:30pm.

Hospital: El Chaltén Hospital, on De Agostini near Adalas (☎ 493 033).

Telephones: Try **Telefónica,** on Güemes (☎ 493 091), but expect to wait almost a minute to make the initial connection. Rates to the US are remarkably inexpensive (ARG$0.90 per min.). Open daily 9am-2pm and 4-11pm.

Internet Access: Both the **Zafarrancho** bar (p. 466; Internet open 24hr. in high season) and the **Chaltén Travel** tour office (see **Tours,** above) offer satellite connections at ARG$12 per hr. Office open 9am-midnight for Internet.

Post Office: The tourist office doubles as a stamp vendor and can also send out packages, but souvenir shops that sell postcards also sell stamps.

ACCOMMODATIONS

Parque Nacional Los Glaciares maintains the primitive, free **Campground Madsen** near the Mt. Fitz Roy trailhead, allowing well-equipped trekkers to forgo the often crowded indoor lodging. The hostels in El Chaltén, however, are generally pleasant and fun and the weather, generally, is unpredictable and harsh, so booking ahead for a bed is prudent.

Albergue Patagonia, on San Martín (☎493 019), a 5min. walk north of the town center. While the rooms are on the smaller side, the common areas and hospitality couldn't be more inviting. Has a well-stocked kitchen, a comfortable common area, and a comprehensive library. Knowledgeable staff provides information on area activities. Reserve far ahead in summer. 4-6 person dorms ARG$22; HI members ARG$18. ❶

Rancho Grande, on San Martín (☎493 005; www.chaltentravel.com). The massive common space doubles as a popular restaurant with large portions and a comfortable living room. At the reception desk, friendly staff members answer guests' questions with some of the best information in town. Dorms are clean and spacious. Laundry service ARG$12. 4-bed dorms ARG$25; doubles ARG$100. HI discount ARG$5. ❶

El Base, on Lago del Desierto, west of Güemes (☎493 031). The cabin-like accommodations are excellent for couples and groups, due to private bathrooms and a brand-new common kitchen. Some cabins enjoy views of Mt. Fitz Roy, and on rainy days, there's an extensive video collection to help while away the hours. Doubles ARG$100; triples ARG$120; quads ARG$150. Low-season discounts available. ❹

Hostería Posada Lunajuim, on Trevasin (☎493 047; www.elchalten.com/lunajuim). A perfect treat for the trail-weary, this upscale *hostería* offers top-notch luxury service with prices to match. Comfortable rooms, down duvets, and a welcoming hearth are staples. Full American breakfast included. Singles US$80; doubles US$90; triples US$120. ❺

Condor de los Andes, at the corner of Río de las Vuelatas and Halvorsen (☎493 101; www.condordelosandes.com). Often filled with Argentine students, the Condor is a hopping option for visitors from the world over. Space, in general, is cramped, both in the 6-bed dorms and the front lounge/dining/kitchen area, and you'll likely be spilling over onto your roommates (which, considering the youthful clientele, is perhaps not an unpleasant prospect). Several new, sparkling *matrimonial* rooms are a great catch for couples. Dorms ARG$22; *matrimoniales* ARG$100. HI members 10% discount. ❶

Hostería Los Nires, on Lago del Desierto (☎493 009; www.elchalten.com/losnires). Most of the basic motel-ish rooms with private bathrooms have views of the Fitz Roy peaks. The starker dorm rooms have kitchen access and more limited views of the range. In front, a cavernous, tiled-floor dining area greets guests with included breakfast. Dorms ARG$20, HI members ARG$18. Doubles and *matrimoniales* with bath ARG$100; triples ARG$140; quads ARG$180. ❶

Albergue del Lago, on Lago del Desierto (☎493 010; www.lagodeldesierto.com). In lieu of a common area, most visitors spend time hanging out in the open kitchen. Rooms are small and there are lines for the bathrooms, but the jovial manager keeps everyone happy with advice. Camping ARG$8 per person. 4- to 6-bed dorms ARG$20. ❶

FOOD

Joking about El Chaltén's rapidly ascending popularity, Argentines like to claim that the tiny hamlet has six artisanal ice cream shops. In fact, it only has one. Still, the variety and quality of food found in El Chaltén is exceptional for a town of only 300 year-round residents.

La Estepa, Cerro Solo and Antonio Roco (☎493 069). Step inside and tiny El Chaltén suddenly feels trendy. This slick eatery has quickly become a local favorite for its pleasing variations on regional favorites. The *cordero estepa* (ARG$20) is bathed in a sweet *calafate* berry sauce, and the vegetables in the *carbonata criolla* (pumpkin stuffed with minced lamb and veggies; ARG$15) will leave you marveling at how on earth so much fresh produce travels up the bumpy road from El Calafate. Open daily 7pm-1am. ❷

Ruca Mahuida, 1 block west of San Martín at the start of Lionnel Terray (☎493 018). Widely heralded as El Chaltén's best restaurant, this intimate eatery fills a compact space with good cheer and delicious eats. Try the potato-dusted trout with citrus and fennel (ARG$27) or, for something simpler, the delicious salmon-filled ravioli (ARG$18). There are only a handful of tables; reservations are essential. Hours vary. ❸

Patagonicus, at Güemes and Madsen (☎493 025). In a lodge-like setting with photos of local mountains and mountaineers, the welcoming staff serves good pizzas (large ARG$9-16) and pastas (ARG$8-11). The immense and delicious *bife de chorizo* (ARG$10) goes well with their wines (ARG$6-80). Open 10:30am-midnight. ❶

Fuegia, on San Martín (☎493 025). Just before Albergue Patagonia, its affiliated hostel, this simple eatery offers some refreshing options, especially for vegetarians. Don't be shocked at the appearance of chicken tandoori (ARG$16) or tabouleh (ARG$7) on a Patagonian menu. Peruse the vegetarian options (eggplant lasagna ARG$15). If nothing exotic suits you, there are staples like lamb (ARG$16). Open daily 7:30am-11pm. ❷

Zafarrancho, on Lionnel Terray (☎495 005). Hostel Rancho Grande's rustic backyard restaurant/bar serves up hearty Argentine cuisine (meat), cans of *Quilmes* (ARG$3), and semi-current movies on Tu, F, and Su nights. Friendly hosts offer lamb ravioli (ARG$16), roquefort trout (ARG$22), and an assortment of pizzas (ARG$13-19) on sturdy wooden tables. A lounge area fills up late on busy summer nights, when Zafarrancho is the only place to be. Open daily noon-midnight, later on busy nights. MC/V. ❶

◎ SIGHTS

PARQUE NACIONAL LOS GLACIARES. Dominated by the massive Southern Patagonia Icefield, this 730,000 sq. km national park is more for gazing than exploring. Dangerous glaciers and difficult terrain make for a scarcity of accessible trails. The few trails that do enter the park, however, are spectacular. Even better, they are all clustered conveniently around El Chaltén and offer easy access to some of Patagonia's most astounding scenery.

Topping the list are footpaths to robust **Mt. Fitz Roy** and tendril-like **Cerro Torre.** Both summits rise from the surrounding terrain like triumphant monuments. When planning a trip to El Chaltén to hike around these icons, be sure to allow yourself several days. While most trails can be hiked in a single day, bad weather often clouds both peaks in. The longer you can afford to stay in town, the better your chances of finding an unforgettable, dazzlingly clear day.

Since water in the park is generally considered to be potable, visitors are asked to stay 100m away from water when using the bathroom or washing dishes in order to keep the water clean. The best source of information on area trails is the incredibly efficient and friendly Los Glaciares Park Office. They meet most incoming buses and provide visitors with a handy trail map. *(Park Administration Office, across the bridge just south of town.* ☎ *493 004. Open in summer daily 8am-10pm. No entrance or camping fee.)*

CERRO TORRE MIRADOR (LAGO TORRE). An easily tackled daytrip, this rolling trail ambles up the Río Fitz Roy valley, headed for Lago Torre and the arresting pinnacle of Cerro Torre. Trails depart west from nearly every section of town for the footpath—just make sure you're not following signs for Mt. Fitz Roy and you'll be on the right track. The trail climbs gently from town, traversing grassy slopes and passing bulging granite humps before attaining a high point after approximately an hour. From here, it's possible to predict your fate: on clear days, you can see all the way into the head of the valley; on most days, Cerro Torre and the surrounding peaks are shrouded in cloud. Either way, proceed another hour up the valley to the junction with the **Madre y Hija Trail** (2hr. one-way), a connector that links the Cerro Torre route with the

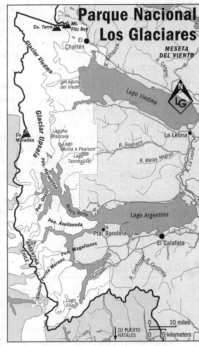

popular trail to the base of Mt. Fitz Roy. The path then moves toward the river, skirting another hill before opening to a massive rock field. To the left among the trees is **Camp D'Agostini**, an excellent but sometimes busy campsite, where glacial rivers sing guests to sleep. Just before D'Agostini on the northeast side of the lake is **Camp Thorwood**, the commercially-run campground where trekkers arriving early for morning glacier walks spend the night. Another 15min. past D'Agostini will bring you to Laguna Torre. Many follow the ridge on the north side of the lake to get a closer look from *Mirador Maestri*. Because Cerro Torre is often cloaked by wispy clouds even on crystal blue days, spending a night at D'Agostini increases your odds of catching a glimpse.

FITZ ROY LOOKOUT. Imposing Mt. Fitz Roy lords over the region like a king. Its majestic and stately face tops out at 3405m and has long been considered one of mountaineering's most daunting climbs. You don't need ropes, a harness, and a few loose mental screws to experience the peak, however; an excellent day-hike allows visitors to depart from El Chaltén, reach a stunning viewpoint, and return to town in a single day. The trail begins at the far end of San Martín, climbing and curving along a steep wooded trail until it contours across a ridge that provides stellar views of the broad glacial valley extending north toward Lago del Desierto. After approximately 2hr., a spur trail diverges to the campsite at **Laguna Campri**, a retreat for those seeking to escape town. Descending through more forest and traversing alpine meadows, the trail approaches **Camp Poincenot,** which has sheltered campsites with access to the Río Blanco for water. Nearby, **Camp Río Blanco** waits for mountaineers attempting to summit some of the park's major peaks; casual hikers should not camp here. Emerging from the final thicket surrounding Poincenot, a challenging stack of boulders greets hikers for the final 1½hr. of scrambling before the vista. Take the scramble slowly, as the stones are not always stable and there is no single path. From the crest of the boulder field, Mt. Fitz Roy up close seems impossibly, mindnumbingly immense. On the exposed boulder field, winds can blow fiercely. Be sure to carry along extra layers to keep warm.

OTHER HIKES IN FITZ ROY. Some visitors travel to both Fitz Roy and Cerro Torre in one multi-day trip without returning to El Chaltén, by using the **Madre y Hija Trail**, a 2hr. walk through lush forests and along lake shores that connects the park's two best day-hikes. It's also possible to push down the riverbed of Río Blanco from Camp Poincenot before cutting up to the Río Eléctrico and making a half-circle around Fitz Roy. The final portion of this three- to four-day trip is on private property, but you are welcome to use the path and make a one-night stay at **Piedra del Fraile**. This trek can also begin after a ride up to the meeting of the Río de las Vueltas and the Río Eléctrico and then down to Camp Poincenot before returning to town. Finally, park rangers strongly recommend the **Loma del Pliegue Tumbado** trail, a 7-8hr. day-hike that offers superior views of the entire range and allows photographers to capture both Cerro Torre and Mt. Fitz Roy in a single frame.

🔊 GUIDED TOURS

The most exciting and popular excursion in town is the ice-trekking and climbing under Cerro Torre. The pros at **Fitz Roy Expeditions** (p. 464) begin the full-day adventure by hiking hours up the valley, traversing a glacial river on a Tyrolean, and finally setting out for ice-walking and climbing. Begin in El Chaltén at 7:30am or camp below Laguna Torre at Camp Thorwood in the Fitz Roy megatent for free. (Tours ARG$125. All-inclusive tour including lunch, dinner, and a sleeping bag to use for camping the night before ARG$230.) For the serious (or budding) mountaineer, Fitz Roy Expeditions also conducts ice-climbing schools and multi-day expeditions into the remote backcountry on the Southern Patagonia Ice Field. Excursions from **Mermoz** (p. 464) include buses to the pristine **Lago del Desierto** to see and explore the beautiful lake (9am, ARG$25 round-trip). Once there, a boat cruise around the lake costs ARG$45. From the south shore of the lake, an easy 2hr. hike climbs to the spectacular **Glaciar Huemel**. The trail crosses private land and requires a ARG$5 usage fee. Horse rides to the Río Blanco take the work out of seeing the park (ARG$80). Mermoz also sells vouchers for a transfer/cruise/ice-trekking combo to Glaciar Viedma. The trip departs El Chaltén at 8am, cruises the lake at the glacier terminus, and guides guests for 2hr. exploring the ethereal blue glacier surface (ARG$170). **Albergue Patagonia** (p. 465) also rents mountain bikes that are great to bring on the bus to Lago del Desierto (ARG$40 per day).

🏃 DAYTRIP FROM EL CHALTÉN

RUTA 40

During the 2003-2004 season, regular bus service opened along Argentina's lonely Ruta 40, a remote interior road previously reserved for travelers on exclusive "backroads Patagonia" tours and those with budgets capable of covering rental car costs. The new bus service makes possible a connection, albeit

BORDER CROSSING INTO ARGENTINA: PASO PAJARITOS
Ruta 215, the road that leads from Osorno through Entre Lagos into Parque Nacional Puyehue, continues on to **Bariloche, Argentina**. Within the park itself, the road runs through Sector Anticura before arriving at **Chilean customs**, 22km from the border. From there, the road continues just north of the majestic Cerro Frutilla before winding up eventually in Bariloche. From Bariloche, many travelers choose to continue on to points south in Tierra del Fuego (see **Bariloche: Transportation**, p. 378). The customs office at Pajaritos station is open Jan.-Feb. 8am-9pm; Mar.-Dec. 9am-8pm. The process is fairly simple and involves no more than a passport stamp and a brief search of your luggage for contraband and various food products (see **Essentials: Border Crossings**, p. 35, for info on visas and fees).

a long and arduous one, between Los Lagos and Southern Patagonia's highlights, including Mt. Fitz Roy and the Torres del Paine. The trip has quickly become popular with travelers hoping to avoid the rough roads and irregular bus schedules along Chile's Carretera Austral, and advanced bookings for summer months are now essential.

The every-other-day bus service is provided by **Chaltén Travel** (p. 464) and leaves El Calafate at 8:30am on odd-numbered days, headed for Perito Moreno and the Argentine border town Los Antiguos. Another bus departs El Chaltén around 10am to meet the Calafate bus, allowing passengers in both towns to connect with the northbound buses. Passengers spend the night in either Perito Moreno (for those headed to Bariloche) or Los Antiguos (for those headed to Chile Chico in Chile). For those staying in Perito Moreno, check out the **Hotel Belgrano ❷**. (Singles ARG$28; doubles ARG$45.) The following morning (on even-numbered days), the bus leaves from Perito Moreno at 9am for a 10hr. ride to Bariloche.

From Los Antiguos, shuttles provided by **Jorge Vargas** (In Los Antiguos, mobile ☎156 252 702; in Chile Chico ☎411 524; ARG$10 or CH$2000) travel across the border to Chile Chico, Chile. **Chaltén Travel** goes from: El Calafate to Perito Moreno or Los Antiguos (15hr., ARG$198); El Chaltén to Perito Moreno or Los Antiguos (13hr., ARG$165); Perito Moreno to Bariloche (10hr., ARG$130). Ruta 40 is long and rough and stops are few and far between, so passengers should prepare ahead with reading material, comfortable clothing, and a sack of groceries to snack on.

Passengers traveling from the north should visit the office of **Andes Patagónicos**, Mitre 125 in Bariloche (☎431 777), for details and tickets. The bus headed south for Perito Moreno (and Los Antiguos) departs on odd-numbered days at 8am.

Along the way, there's little to see on Ruta 40 other than the very picture of desolation, sublime though it be. Miles and miles of dusty steppe stretch as far as vision can reach. Between Bajo Caracoles and Perito Moreno lies the much-discussed and little-visited **Cueva de las Manos**. The cave, famous for its indigenous cave paintings and inspiringly human handprints, lies east of Ruta 40 and is extremely difficult to reach without ample amounts of money or private transportation. **Perito Moreno Travel**, located at San Martín 1779 in Perito Moreno (☎432 720), arranges tours to the cave for a hefty ARG$240 per trip (max. 4 people). Plan on the trip taking a day and pack your own lunch.

TIERRA DEL FUEGO

USHUAIA, ARGENTINA ☎2901

Welcome to the *"fin del mundo."* Once a remote frontier outpost, then a prison community and fishing town, Ushuaia has remade itself as the gateway to Antarctica. And a charming gateway it is. Far out on South America's extremity, Ushuaia has an endearing against-the-elements character that's as appealing as its friendly citizens. There's excellent day-trekking nearby in Tierra del Fuego National Park, wonderful wildlife viewing in the Beagle Channel, and more than a few pleasant distractions to keep you around town. Once you've reached the end of the road, you'll find yourself asking: why go anywhere else?

▐ TRANSPORTATION

The road ends in Ushuaia, so if you plan on descending farther south, you'll be aboard a ship or plane. The tourist office (see below) maintains a comprehensive list of up-to-date transport information. Be sure to reserve as far ahead as possible for northbound travel; buses fill up rapidly.

Flights: Aeropuerto Internacional Malvinas Argentinas is one of the country's newest airports. The only transportation to or from the airport is by taxi (ARG$4-5). **Aerolíneas Argentinas,** Roca 116 (☎421 218; www.Aerolíneas.com.ar), flies to **Buenos Aires, ARG** (3½hr., 2-4 per day) and **El Calafate, ARG** (1¼-2hr., 2-4 per week). **LADE,** San Martín 542 (☎421 123), flies to **Buenos Aires** M and F, and **El Calafate** M, W, F, often at lower prices than Aerolíneas Argentinas.

Buses: Techni Austral, Roca 157 (☎431 408), goes to **El Calafate, ARG** (14hr., M-Sa 6am, ARG$115) and **Punta Arenas** (12hr.; M, W, F 6:30am; ARG$80). **Bus Sur** also goes to **Punta Arenas** (10hr.; Tu, Th, Sa 8am; ARG$90). **Lider,** Paz 1056 (☎424 200), makes daily runs to **Río Grande** (3½-4hr.; 7 per day starting 6am; ARG$25).

Car Rental: ARG Tagle Rent-a-Car, San Martín 1199 (☎422 744), rents compact cars for 3 days with unlimited mileage, starting at ARG$285. **Hertz** and **Avis** rentals are also available at the airport at higher prices.

Bike Rental: 7Deportes, San Martín 802 (☎437 604). ARG$30 per day. Open M-Sa 10am-1pm and 4-9pm.

❄▐ ORIENTATION AND PRACTICAL INFORMATION

Ushuaia occupies a tiny parcel of land squeezed between the southern limit of the Andes and the Beagle Channel. The 75 sq. block area of most interest to visitors lies upon a hill with streets arranged in cardinal directions. Most businesses are on **San Martín,** located one block up from the gusty **Maipú,** which is situated directly on the port. Be particularly cautious of traffic going up or down the hill, as stop signs are rare and traffic has the right of way.

Tourist Office: San Martín 674 (☎424 550). Plentiful information on the city and region, with excellent info in English. Be sure to get your free certificate proving you've been to the southernmost city. English spoken. Open M-F 8am-10pm, Sa-Su 9am-8pm.

Antarctic Tour Office: Tierra del Fuego Tourism Board, Antarctic Unit, at the tourist port on Maipú (☎423 340). Dream about traveling to Antarctica (US$4000 or more) as you pore through comprehensive materials. They also offer information on activities around Ushuaia. English spoken. Open daily 9am-5pm, closed Sa-Su in winter.

Tours: For outdoor activities and to dodge the traditional tours for cruise passengers, head first to **Canal Tours,** Rivadavia 82 (☎437 395. Open M-Sa 9:30am-1pm and 5-8pm, Su 5-8pm). They do daytrips that combine kayaking, trekking, and penguin viewing (ARG$250 includes food and equipment) near Estancia Haberton, east of town. They also

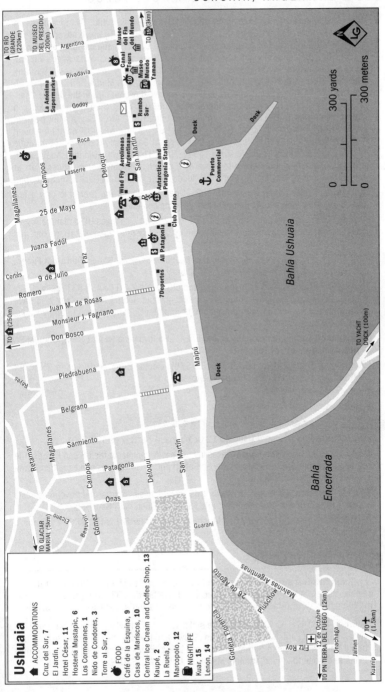

TIERRA DEL FUEGO

Ushuaia

▲ ACCOMMODATIONS
Cruz del Sur, **7**
El Jardín, **5**
Hotel César, **11**
Hostería Mustapic, **6**
Los Cormoranes, **1**
Nido de Condores, **3**
Torre al Sur, **4**

◆ FOOD
Café de la Esquina, **9**
Casa de Mariscos, **10**
Central Ice Cream and Coffee Shop, **13**
Kaupé, **2**
La Ruela, **8**
Marcopolo, **12**

■ NIGHTLIFE
Kuar, **15**
Lenon, **14**

offer adventurous off-road excursions (ARG$180) to Lago Fagnano. For adventures on foot and on belay, contact **Compañía,** Campos 795 (☎ 437 753), which advertises a collection of day multi-day treks, ice- and rock-climbing excursions, and **camping equipment rental.** For more conventional tours, most offices in town sell identical packages. **All Patagonia,** Juana Fadul 60 (☎ 433 622), is centrally located and helpful. Open M-F 9:30am-1pm and 3-8pm, Sa 10am-1pm and 5-8pm. **Rumbo Sur,** San Martín 350 (☎ 422 275), is also a good agency. Excursions include: half- and full-day boat trips in the Beagle Channel to see sea lions, penguins, and other wildlife (ARG$60-130); canoeing and trekking in the national park (ARG$120-130); horseback riding (2hr., ARG$60); glacier trekking (2hr., ARG$140); scenic flights (US$70 per person per hr.); and 4x4 daytrips around Lago Fagnano (ARG$180). Most longer trips begin at 9am, but will only go if 2 or more people sign up. **Wind Fly,** 25 de Mayo 143 (☎/fax 431 713; www.windflyushuaia.com), organizes fly-fishing excursions to the area's excellent fishing holes. Prices start at ARG$360 for a one-day trip. Equipment included. Store open M-Sa 9am-9pm, Su 3-9pm.

Consulates: Chile, Jainen 50 (☎ 430 909). Open M-F 9am-1pm. There are only a few European consulates and none for English-speaking countries.

Currency Exchange: Thaler, San Martín 788 (☎ 421 911), changes US dollars to Argentine pesos and will cash traveler's checks, though at lower rate. Open M-F 10am-3pm and 5-8pm, Sa 10am-1pm and 5-8:30pm, Su 5-8:30pm.

ATM: Most banks at the eastern end of San Martín have ATMs. **Banco Tierra del Fuego,** San Martín 388, accepts AmEx/Cirrus/MC/Plus/V.

Bookstore: Antarctica and Patagonia Station, 25 de Mayo 30 (☎ 430 537) sells mostly English books on Patagonia, Antarctic exploration, and natural history. They also have trade paperbacks and English translations of important South American literary works. Open M-Sa 10am-9pm, Su 5-9pm.

Supermarket: La Anónima, on the corner of Paz and Rivadavia (☎ 421 304). Open M-Sa 9am-10pm, Su 9:30am-2pm.

Laundromat: Qualis, Deloqui 368 (☎ 432 578), cleans, dries, and folds in 2½hr. for ARG$12. Some hostels offer cheaper services.

Emergency: ☎ 101.

Police: ☎ 421 416.

24hr. Pharmacy: Andina, San Martín 638 (☎ 423 431).

Hospital: Hospital Regional Ushuaia 12 Octubre and Fitz Roy (☎ 423 200).

Telephones: The many **Telefónica** offices in town easily connect to the US and Europe. The office at Belgrano 97 is a good choice and often not as crowded as offices farther downtown. Open daily 9am-midnight.

Internet Access: Café Net, San Martín 565, serves basic snacks and beverages while offering reliable Internet connections. ARG$3 per hr. Open daily 8am-5am.

Post Office: Correo Argentino, San Martín and Godoy (☎ 421 347). ARG$4 to send a postcard to the US. Open M-Sa 9am-7pm, Su 9am-1pm.

ACCOMMODATIONS

As Ushuaia has transformed from Fuegian backwater to international boomtown, hotels and hostels have multiplied to comfort the hordes. The result: a nearly dizzying list of accommodations, available for free, in English, at the tourist office.

▨ **El Jardín,** Paz 1478 (☎ 422 044). If the sinks seem low, they're meant to be. This converted daycare center has glorious views of town and the channel. Massive dorm rooms, board games, and clean bathrooms are appealing. Breakfast included. Closed to hostelers and open to kindergarteners Mar.-Nov. Dorms ARG$20. ❶

Nido de Condores, Campos 793 (☎437 753; www.nidodecondoresush.com.ar). An excellent choice for couples or traveling duos seeking tranquility, this *posada* features a large dining and lounge area, top advice on local activities, and an impressive included breakfast. Reservations recommended. Doubles ARG$60, with bath ARG$85. ❷

Hotel César, San Martín 753 (☎421 460). Surprisingly clean and classy for one of the cheapest rates in town. The downtown location, on San Martín in the thick of the shopping and tourist agencies, can't be beat. Perks like cable TV, VCRs, and included breakfast offer a wisp of luxury. Reservations recommended 2 weeks in advance. Singles ARG$65, with bath ARG$75; doubles ARG$90/ARG$100. ❸

Torre al Sur, Paz 1437 (☎430 745; www.torrealsur.com.ar). Stunning views, clean dorms, friendly staff, and Internet access (ARG$3 per hr.) help this HI affiliate fill up fast. Despite its many beds and tiny kitchen, reservations are usually needed. 2- to 4-bed dorms ARG$17, HI members ARG$15. ❶

Los Cormoranes, on the corner of Kamshen and Alem (☎423 459; www.loscormoranes.com). It's a steep walk up from the center of town, but the kitchen facilities and lounge areas will make you forget your sore legs. Besides, if you reserve in advance, you're entitled to a free transfer from bus or airport. The dormitory complex has a summer-camp feel designed for groups. Upstairs, there's free Internet and a superb view of the town. Breakfast included. Dorms ARG$20. ❶

Cruz del Sur, Deloqui 636 (☎423 110). Trekking maps and information line the walls of this friendly youth hostel. Free coffee or tea, cable TV, Internet access, and a communal atmosphere sweeten the deal. The cozy quarters may deter some visitors, however. 4- to 8-bed dorms ARG$20. ❶

Hostería Mustapic, Piedrabuena 230 (☎421 718). When Mustapic opened in 1972, Ushuaia was scarcely on the tourist radar. Little has changed at Mustapic since then, but despite feeling dated, this *hostería*'s rooms are remarkably well kept and its owners are delightfully friendly. Breakfast included in top-floor dining area with amazing views across the Beagle Channel. Singles ARG$45, with bath ARG$70; doubles with bath ARG$82; quads ARG$120. ❸

▐ FOOD

The central blocks of San Martín are lined with mostly indistinguishable cafe and *parrilla* establishments, with a few exceptions listed below.

▩ Kaupe, Roca 470 (☎422 704). This intimate restaurant offers some of the finest dining in the region, and if it fits the budget, it shouldn't be passed over. *Kaupe* is an indigenous word meaning "to be at home." In this case, the home belongs to Ernesto Vivián, his wife, and their daughters who dutifully prepare and serve delicious regional food while guests gaze out on the Beagle Channel. The king crab, served *au naturel* or in a creamy tomato broth (ARG$42), is a house specialty, as is the local scallop ceviche (ARG$36). Reservations recommended. Open daily 6:30-11pm. ❹

Central Icecream and Coffee Shop, 25 de Mayo 50 (☎430 264). This tastefully hip diner combines the two quintessential of any pleasant afternoon: caffeine and ice cream. There are plush, white leather armchairs for curling up with a book and a selection of English-language newspapers to peruse as you lunch on a gourmet sandwich (ARG$3-8). Grab a small ice cream (ARG$5) and don't miss the superb selection of fresh fruit flavors. Open daily 8am-1am. ❶

La Ruela, San Martín 193 (☎436 540). Pack it in with La Ruela's local-favorite *tenedor libre* for only ARG$19, but you will have to purchase a beverage (ARG$1-2.50). Take your time enjoying the extensive salad bar and full range of grilled meats. Don't overestimate your appetite, though—there's a ARG$2 surcharge for wasting food. Fish and other entrees also available. Open Tu-Su 7:30-11pm. ❶

Marcopolo, San Martín 748 (☎430 001). This refined restaurant/cafe offers *haute* cuisine and elegant decor at reasonable prices The set lunch (ARG$15) includes wine, appetizer, entree, and dessert and is a nice break from *lomo* and pasta. A breakfast of coffee and 3 filling croissants runs ARG$5. Open daily 7:30am-1am. AmEx/MC/V. ❶

La Casa de Mariscos, San Martín 232 (☎421 928). Small and unaffected, this local favorite serves Fuegian seafood at some of the most reasonable prices in town. The region's king crab specialty (ARG$31) is prepared a number of ways, while the hearty *cazuela de pulpa* (octopus casserole; ARG$32) combines tough octopus with delicate crab in a seafood melange. Some non-seafood dishes also available (half-chicken ARG$16). Open daily 11:30am-3pm and 6pm-midnight. ❷

Café de la Esquina, San Martín 601. This tourist-friendly cafe serves a basic menu of *milanesa* (thinly sliced, breaded meat; ARG$12) and sandwiches (ARG$4.50-6) and is a functional spot for a quick and tasty bite. The ever-changing set lunch (ARG$8-10) is usually served within minutes. Open M-Th 7:30am-3:30am, Sa 9am-3:30am, Su 4pm-1:30am. AmEx/MC/V. ❶

🔘 SIGHTS

MUSEO DEL PRESIDIO AND MUSEO MARÍTIMO DE USHUAIA. Like another famous place down under, Ushuaia earned its first renown as a prison, when Argentina moved its military jail from Isla de los Estados to a site just outside Ushuaia in 1902. Around the same time, the state decided to found a second, civilian prison in Ushuaia, and in 1911 the two penitentiaries merged. Prisoners built their own cells from locally quarried rocks, and the prison complex grew and grew. Eventually, it topped over 380 cells and held more than 800 prisoners. In 1947, Argentine authorities shut the prison down. Within the walls of the now defunct building are two museums and other frequent expositions. The smaller but very detailed **Museo Marítimo** houses numerous models and descriptive maps that thoroughly highlight the exploration and defense of Argentina's extensive coastline from as early as 1520. The **Museo del Presidio** begins in one of the five arms of the prison complex, with many separate displays set up in the rows of cells, detailing prison history and the biographies of important prisoners. Be sure to visit the middle arm of the prison, which remains largely unchanged and gives visitors a more chilling impression of the dreary existence of Argentina's worst convicts. The center Rotunda contains a small cafe where you can refuel for more exhibits, and on Friday nights at 10pm, the Ushuaia Cinema Club plays movies in the former prison bakery. *(Within the naval base, access museum from the Paz and Yuganes entrance. ☎/fax 437 481; www.ushuaia.org. Open daily 9am-8pm. ARG$15. Cinema club movies ARG$1.)*

MUSEO DEL FIN DEL MUNDO. Housed in a stately, waterfront building, this museum meticulously exhibits the human and natural histories of Tierra del Fuego. There are rooms documenting the island's early exploration, its settlement, and its use as penal facility. Another room features a large exhibit devoted to the birds of Tierra del Fuego, 180 species in all, stuffed and preserved in glass cases. Finally, the "Grocery Store" exhibit pays tribute to Ushuaia's early vendors. *(Maipú 175. ☎421 863; www.tierradelfuego.org.ar/museo. Open daily in summer 9am-8pm; in winter M-Sa 1-8pm. Guides available in English. ARG$10, under 14 free.)*

MUSEO MUNDO YAMANA. Full of interesting factoids, the Yamana Museum presents the fascinating origins and customs of Tierra del Fuego's original human inhabitants. Where else would you learn that only the Yamana women could swim, or that the men would conduct night raids on cormorant colonies, killing the birds by biting them in the neck? The information is presented with descriptions in both English and Spanish. *(Rivadavia 56. ☎422 874; mundoya-mana@infovia.com.ar. Open daily in summer 10am-9pm; reduced hours in low season. ARG$5; students ARG$3.)*

🔳 NIGHTLIFE

Though a calm city, Ushuaia does offer a few options for nightlife. Catch a cab (ARG$3) to **Kuar,** Perito Moreno 2232 (☎437 396), about 5min. out of town. One of Patagonia's few microbreweries, this stylish bar brews dark, amber, and golden varieties. The prices are as expected for artisanal quality (ARG$8 per pint), but the views of the Beagle Channel and the glimpses of Ushuaia's trendy scene justify the price. (Open daily 12:30pm-5am in high season.) Closer to town, try stylish, popular, misspelled **Lenon,** Maipú 263 (☎435 255), where a *schop* of Quilmes runs ARG$4 and tables feature sketches of the Beatles icon. (Open daily 6pm-6am.)

🔳 OUTDOOR ACTIVITIES

GUIDED TOURS. Don't get confused if it seems as if the tourist industry in Ushuaia is managed by one company—collaboration between companies ensures that one office provides all the services offered, at the same prices. Canal Tours, Compañía, Rumbo Sur, and Wind Fly (see **Tours,** p. 470) are reliable companies that run most of the tours they sell. The **city tour** (1½hr., ARG$15) is a ride through town in either a van or a double-decker bus. Coffee and tea are served between frequent stops at easily accessible sights and local museums. **Boat excursions** are tours that reach combinations of destinations within the bay, including the sea lion colony, bird sanctuary, lighthouse, Magellan penguins, and the historic Harberton Estancia. (5½hr., 9:30am, ARG$60-130.) **Tourist flights** over the Beagle Channel in 8-person planes last only 30min., but afford majestic views (US$35 per person).

WILDERNESS TOURS. There are few guided tours through Parque Nacional Tierra del Fuego because much of the park is easily navigable without help. The **bus tour** is informative, although slightly removed from the natural surroundings (ARG$40). Canal Tours offers a combination canoe/trekking excursion to the park for ARG$120. The **Train to the End of the World** is a small-track locomotive that recreates the route along which lumber was transported out of the park. It is, however, a slow journey that can easily be skipped. (Estación del Fin del Mundo, Ruta 3. ☎431 600; www.trendelfindelmundo.com.ar. ARG$50, under 12 ARG$18.) The more serious mountains surrounding Ushuaia, however, invite all range of daring outdoor pursuit. **Compañía** guiding service offers day-treks to Cerro de Medio (near Ushuaia, ARG$140), glacier Viniciguerra (includes some ice-climbing, ARG$140), and a two-day ice-climbing school at Cerro Alvear (ARG$350, equipment included). Well-organized **fly fishing** trips including all equipment, transport, and food are also available from Wind Fly (ARG$360 per day; p. 470).

WINTER ACTIVITIES. The winter season in Ushuaia is not as happening as the summer, but the tourism board is developing attractions in an attempt to maintain interest despite the bleak days and meager snowfall. The **Festival of the Longest Night** at the end of June kicks off the winter season and is soon followed by the **End of the World Car Rally** in July. August ushers in the **Snow Sculptors Meeting** and the cross-country **White March** competition to keep up spirits in Ushuaia. Otherwise, mediocre downhill skiing and cross-country skiing will keep visitors busy at **Cerro Castor** (27km from town, hourly shuttle ARG$10, rentals and lift ticket ARG$50).

⚡ DAYTRIP FROM USHUAIA

GLACIAR MARIAL. This scenic 3hr. hike 7km from town rewards industrious visitors with excellent views of Ushuaia. The chairlift runs until 6:15pm and saves an hour's walk, but is not necessary (ARG$7). To get to the base of the hike, take a van with Pasarela from the corner of Maipú and 25 de Mayo that leaves every hour on the half-hour 9:30am-5:30pm, and returns on the hour (ARG$5 one-way, ARG$8 round-trip). Taxis are also available (ARG$5-6 for up to 4 people).

PARQUE NACIONAL TIERRA DEL FUEGO

Comprising the tip of the Subantarctic Southern Beach Forest, this stunning park invites visitors to experience the wild at the world's end. The experience itself is ephermal—with irregular weather patterns, a sunny day turns in minutes into a rainy one, and finally a windy one. The recreational area of the park (only a fraction of the total acreage) is very well maintained and easily accessible to day-hikers, car-campers, and other recreationalists. Enjoy a day or two walking through soft, fragrant undergrowth, tracing the shore of the Beagle Channel, or cutting up to a craggy peak for an expansive view that seems to stretch on to Antarctica.

■ ORIENTATION

Trails commence at either **Lago Roca, Bahía Enseñada,** or **Bahía Lapataia,** the drop-off sites for most tour companies. Although all the marked trails take only half a day to complete, there are a handful of rustic campsites for hikers who would like to spend a night at the park. There's always more to explore at **Black Lagoon** (400m from Rte. 3), named for its dark color caused by the presence of peat; the **Island** (800m of coast along the Lapataia and Ovando rivers); and **Lookout Point** (through the *lengas* wood at Bahía Lapataia). Although Parque Nacional Tierra del Fuego may not attract swarms of hardcore hikers like other national parks in the region, its quality sights and easy access make for relaxing outdoor adventures.

🔄 TRANSPORTATION AND PRACTICAL INFORMATION

To access the park, use the **shuttle service** provided by most tour companies in Ushuaia. Buses leave from the corners of 25 de Mayo and Maipú and J. Fadul and Maipú every half-hour. There are half a dozen companies making the trip for ARG$15 round-trip (to Lago Roca, ARG$5 more to Bahía Lapataia). Be sure to note the return schedule for your company and be prepared (with food and warm clothes) to wait. The last bus for most companies is at 8pm. The tourist office has

---

AT A GLANCE

AREA: 630 sq. km

CLIMATE: Humid.

HIGHLIGHTS: Black Lagoon, viewing the grand panorama from Lookout Point, meeting the beavers 400m upstream from Los Castores.

FEES: Park admission ARG$12. Round-trip shuttle services ARG$8-14.

GATEWAY: Ushuaia.

WILDLIFE: Diverse wildlife including white *cauquenes* (mackerel), black eye-browed albatross, diving petrel, *chun-gungo* (a rare otter), and a particular variety of Tierra del Fuego red fox.

CAMPING: Camping is permitted in designated areas; free campsites available (campsites with services ARG$2-4).

Tierra del Fuego

adequate information on the park, but stop by the **main park office** for more information. (San Martín 1395. ☎421 315. Open M-F 9am-4pm.) Pay park admission (ARG$12) at the park entrance, where free maps are available.

📷 CAMPING

Camping is available at **Lago Roca** near a friendly *confitería* with showers and bathrooms. Free camping can be found on the island at the mouth of the **Lapataia River** and at the beginning of the **Costera Trail,** but neither site has any services.

🥾 HIKING

Cerro Guanaco Trail (4km; 4-5hr. to top, 2½hr. to return; difficult). This, the only summit trek in the park, begins at Lago Roca and heads straight up to the top of Guanaco (elevation 970m). The arduous ascent is interrupted by 2km of mountain pasture that is extremely soggy, and slow going. The summit is almost totally exposed, so wear layers to stay warm. Despite the challenge, you'll be rewarded with a view of the city and the mountains surrounding it, and of the Beagle Channel across to Isla Navarino.

Hito XXIV Trail (4km one-way, 3hr. round-trip, medium). Also starting from Lago Roca, this path follows the northern shore of the lake, skirting in between surrounding trees. The pleasant breeze over the lake and the variety of small birds and rabbits make this a relaxing and enjoyable hike. It ends at the Argentine-Chilean border.

Costera Trail (6½km, 3hr. one-way, medium). An excellent choice for a leisurely walk, this footpath traces the shore of Bahía Lapataia, climbing small outcroppings and affording view after view of secluded coves. The trail begins on Rte. 3 near the turn for Lago Roca and ends at Bahía Ensenada, where you can walk the access road to Rte. 3 and find transport back to town.

Pampa Alta Trail (4.9km, 1hr. one-way, medium). An optional extension of the Costera Trail, the Pampa Alta follows lazy bends of the Pilato stream, eventually reaching an open plain with a panoramic view of the Beagle Channel.

**BORDER CROSSING INTO ARGENTINA: PUERTO WILL-
IAMS** Finding a way to cross the Beagle Channel between Puerto Williams and Ushuaia may seem difficult at first, as boats heading west to Punta Arenas or Puerto Natales cannot stop by Ushuaia on their journey because of geopolitics and border worries on both sides. Your best bet for finding passage across the channel is to contact the **Fuegian Association for Subaquatic and Nautical Activities (AFASYN),** located at the yacht dock near the municipal airport (☎435 805). Through them, you can negotiate with a yacht captian for passage (one-way US$80, but it is often possible to broker a better deal). If the need to cross is urgent and you're having trouble finding a boat, the **Aeroclub Ushuaia** (☎421 717) flies to Puerto Williams M, W, F for US$100 per person, one-way. No matter how you get across, it is essential to have your paperwork in order. Most captains will arrange the paperwork with border control for you, but it is a good idea to contact border control a few hours before you depart to ensure that everything goes smoothly (see **Essentials: Border Crossings,** p. 35, for info on visas and fees).

ISLA NAVARINO

PUERTO WILLIAMS

This fascinating little town of about 2000 residents, founded as a naval base in 1950, is in a curious state of flux. Border tensions with Argentina have relaxed and the navy is diminishing its presence. At the same time, every summer brings more tourists eager to sample the impressive wilderness at the end of the world. While still primarily a military town and poorly equipped with tourist amenities, Puerto Williams is quickly changing to better accommodate its new popularity: in 2004, the local bank opened the island's first ATM. Catch Navarino fast while it's still a backwater, before long tours include this pleasantly out-of-the-way destination.

⌐ TRANSPORTATION. Planes from Punta Arenas arrive at **Aerodromo Guardima-rina Zañartú. DAP,** in the commercial center, is the only commercial airline servic-ing Puerto Williams, and flights departing at varying times go only to Punta Arenas (M-Sa, US$71). Puerto Williams has one taxi which does not always meet incoming flights; fortunately, DAP provides a free shuttle to the center of town. Some pri-vate **boats** take passengers to Ushuaia and and there are also regular Monday, Wednesday, and Friday flights offered by the Ushuaia Aeroclub (see **Border Cross-ings,** p. 478). **Austral Broom,** east of town before the river, has a weekly **ferry**

between Punta Arenas and Puerto Williams, but it is often choppy, and always expensive and long. Contact Sr. Godoy to arrange ferry trips from Puerto Williams. (In Puerto Williams ☎621 015. Punta Arenas office, Bulnes 05075 ☎218 100. 36hr.; departs W returning F or Sa; US$120, with bed US$150. Children ½ price.)

⑦ **PRACTICAL INFORMATION.** Nearly all services in Puerto Williams lie within a 5min. walk of the Plaza de Armas, just up the hill from the naval dock. Adjacent to the Plaza in the north is a small commercial center that hosts many services important to travelers. For **tourist information,** head to **Turismo Sea, Ice, and Mountain (SIM) Ltda.** (☎621 150), Ricardo Maragaño 168, inside Refugio Coiron (see below), half a block east of the Plaza. Abundant information about the town and plane ticket bookings is readily available, as well as excellent advice on hiking the Los Dientes de Navarino Circuit. With advance notice, they can arrange sailboat trips to Cabo de Hornos (7 days) and Antarctica (29 days). **Banco de Chile,** one block north of the plaza at Yelcho 140, changes a minimum of US$100 to Chilean pesos. (☎621 105. Open M-F 9am-2pm.) They also have an **ATM** machine that accepts Visa, and is accessible during business hours and by knocking on the door Monday through Friday between 4 and 6:30pm. Stock up on trail food or grab an *empanada* at **Simon and Simon** grocery store, Piloto Pardo 157. (☎621 146. Open daily 8am-1am.) If arriving on the weekend, be sure to bring enough Chilean pesos to cover your expenses; trying to pay with Argentine money here could be insulting. The **police** can be reached at ☎621 035. There are two **telephone offices** in the commercial center. **Turismo Akainij,** in the commercial center, offers the most reliable Internet service in town, but expect to spend much of your CH$1500 per hr. waiting for pages to load. (☎621 195. Open daily 10am-8pm.) To mail a post card from the end of the world, visit the **post office** in the commercial center, open M-F 9:30am-2:30pm and 4:30-6:30pm, Sa 10:30am-2pm.

🍴⃞ **ACCOMMODATIONS AND FOOD.** ▨**Refugio Coiron ❸**, Ricardo Maragaño 168, is the place to stay in Puerto Williams, with excellent local information, a warm and welcoming wood stove, and free kitchen access. It's also a great place to meet other trekkers from the Los Dientes circuit. (☎621 227. Dorms CH$8500.) **Hostal Pusaki ❸**, east of the Plaza de Armas at Piloto Pardo 222, has friendly service and dinner is available on request. (☎621 116. Breakfast included. Dorms CH$8500.) Or just stop by **Cabo de Hornos ❷**, on the plaza at Ricardo Maragaño 146 (☎621 067), which serves hearty meals, including locally-hunted beaver with fries (CH$4900), but maintains irregular hours. Last, be sure not to miss **Yacht Club Micalvi Bar ❷**, housed waterfront about 1km west of the commercial center in the aging ship used to bring founding supplies to Puerto Williams. Amidst tacky 70s decor and over CH$1000 glasses of Austral, you'll meet sailors preparing for all varieties of wild Antarctic adventures. (Open daily from 8pm.)

IN AND AROUND PUERTO WILLIAMS

While the town of Puerto Williams itself offers travelers little in the way of attractions, a quick visit to the free **Martín Gusinde Museum,** Aragay 1 (☎621 043), is an hour wisely spent. Inside, well-composed exhibits and striking photographs document the history and final days of Navarino's often misunderstood indigenous peoples. The second floor provides a taxonomic tableau of stuffed wildlife from the area, just in case you're not planning to get out and see some yourself. Another pleasant afternoon excursion near Puerto Williams is the **Omora Ethnobotanical Park,** 6km east of town (☎621 305; www.omora.com), where the dedicated efforts of volunteers have created an attractive and informative trail through native forest that documents flora, fauna, and indigenous forest use. Afternoon tours are available for CH$5000 per person.

The real draw of Puerto Williams, however, is the increasingly popular **Los Dientes de Navarino Circuit,** a 4-5 day trek around the island's signature jagged mountain range. Because of bad weather, minimal facilities, and a difficult-to-follow trail, the circuit should only be undertaken by well-equipped trekkers who possess skill at route-finding. Although difficult at times, Los Dientes delivers the remote wilderness feel now gone from places like Torres del Paine, the chance to view the Cape Horn Islands from high in the Dientes range, and the novelty of being on the southernmost hiking trail in the world. The trail is marked by cairns and red-striped blazes and travels along high talus slopes, through uncut forests of *lenga* and *coihue*, and into some of the finest habitat for Canadian Beavers in the world. Without natural predators, the beavers grow to unimaginable sizes and have successfully dammed every stream on the island. While the 54km circuit can be covered in less than 4-5 days, it's best to allow extra time because bad weather (or a summer snowstorm) can make travel along the exposed route dangerous.

In 2001, Chile's Ministerio de Bienes Nacionales published a comprehensive trail guide to the Circuit, complete with route descriptions in English and photographs that correspond to red numbers painted along the trail. However, the brochure is no longer available in print form, even from the ministry's office in Punta Arenas. Luckily, **Turismo SIM,** at Refugio Coiron, has an original of the guide that they are happy to lend to trekkers who can have it photocopied at the DAP office. There is little available in Puerto Williams in the way of camping supplies (no gas canisters or white gas—only gasoline), so arrive well-prepared. Before leaving, be sure to register with the Puerto Williams police (✆621 035), on Piloto Pardo past Simon and Simon, for aid in the event of an emergency.

EASTER ISLAND

Foreigners have called it Easter Island, *Isla de Pascua*, and *Ile de Paques*, but to locals, it's Rapa Nui. The center of the universe, their tradition claims, is this speck of land, 3700km off the Chilean coast, a five-hour flight from Santiago. The center of the universe—but maybe not ours.

For it seems that mysterious Easter Island is in fact from some other world, fallen through the sky to its current location in the middle of the Pacific Ocean. Its rolling slopes are devoid of large vegetation, and coated in neon green. Volcanic hills such as **Rano Raraku** and **Rano Kau** are jagged outlines of gray and orange against the uninterrupted horizon. The turquoise sea sparkles with sunlight that blinds in whatever direction you look. And the inhabitants of the island are giants, petrified by some unknown force, staring defiantly at the sky, some drowning in the grass.

In fact, the island wasn't part of our world, or of our maps, for centuries. Its isolation allowed the Polynesian settlers to flourish as the Rapa Nui, developing unique and advanced cultural practices. The giant stone statues—the *moai*—are the most famous of their achievements, but many others are just as singular. Visitors will find the Rongo Rongo—tablets of cryptic ideograms whose meaning has long been lost—to be both incredible and mystifying. Additionally, **petroglyphs** across the island depict an intricate ancient competition, one which after three months would crown a leader—the Birdman.

During this period of development, Easter Island was a land that time forgot; but it was soon remembered—and with a vengeance. Clan warfare and foreign expeditions to the island destroyed much of the native land and culture. As a result, today, parts of the island have the eerie feel of a graveyard, with hidden stories and centuries behind each stone.

As more people are drawn by the thrill of the unknown, Easter Island is a slowly growing tourist destination. The central (and only) town of **Hanga Roa** is gradually morphing from a tropical hideaway to an Internet- and cell phone-accessible retreat. The beaches of **Anakena** and **Ovahe** are often packed with radio-toting revelers. Still, when the sun goes down in a psychedelic blaze, the sky fills with points of light even older than the relics on the ground. You are reminded of those first Polynesian navigators, who discovered and developed this dreamland. And as you look at the stars, you can't help but think that only they know all of its secrets.

HIGHLIGHTS OF EASTER ISLAND

FLOAT in the warm waves of the ultimate desert island beach, **Anakena** (p. 498).

WANDER through the final resting place of hundreds of unfinished *moai* in the deserted quarry at **Rano Raraku** (p. 497).

CHANNEL the mystical energy of the magnetic stone at **Ahu Te Pito Henúa** (p. 498).

BASK in the singular, spectacular sunset at **Tahai** (p. 495) after a day of exploration.

FEEL the power of the gaze of the fifteen *moai* at **Ahu Tongariki** (p. 497).

HISTORY

PREHISTORIC ARRIVAL ON THE ISLAND AND THE CONSTRUCTION OF THE MOAI (AD 400-1722). Current international perceptions of Easter Island as one of the most isolated and mysterious islands in the world are indicative of a history dominated by intrigue, uncertainty, and legend. While the exact origin of the Rapa Nui (the Polynesian name by which the island and its natives are known) is unknown, it is believed that the island was first inhabited by travelers from the Marquesas. These travelers, supposedly, were led there by the legendary first king of Easter Island, Hotu Matu'a, who landed on the northern beach of Anakena, naming the island "Te Pito o Te Henúa" ("The Earth's Navel"). Others, such as Norwegian explorer Thor Heyerdahl (who traveled to the island in the mid-1950s), hypothesize that the first travelers to Easter Island came from South America, more specifically, from the Tiahuacano peoples of modern-day Bolivia and Chile.

In either case, it is believed that the first settlers arrived between AD 400 and 800, known as the Population Phase of the island. From 800 to 1680, Rapa Nui culture was at its peak, during what is referred to as the Ahu Moai Phase, in which most *moai* were constructed. While not much is certain about the years after that peaceful time, archaeological and anthropological evidence suggests that the years before the arrival of the Dutch in 1722 were characterized by continuous warfare. Many believe that this was due to dwindling resources on the island as clans (Ure) competed to build bigger and better *moai*. *Moai* were toppled and vegetation was burned as the clans fought for land and food. After the king of the island, Ariki Mau, was killed in battle, the famed Tangata Manu or "Birdman" ceremonies at Orongo began as a means of finding new leadership.

FOREIGN VISITORS (1722-1895). On Easter Sunday of 1722, Dutch explorer Jacob Roggeveen arrived on the island. While Roggeveen is purported to have spent only 11 hours on the island, he still managed to kill more than a dozen natives. The next to visit were the English, under the supervision of Captain James Cook, in 1774, followed by the French in 1786 and the Russians in 1804. After Cook's visit, the island received a number of visitors, each bringing with them a new (and often unfortunate) consequence for the natives. The next to arrive were Peruvian labor-seekers in the early 1860s, who proceeded to attack the islanders, kidnapping thousands for use in the Peruvian slave trade. Ultimately, only 15 native islanders were repatriated, bringing back with them smallpox and other diseases previously nonexistent on the island. By 1877, of the several thousand natives thought to have resided on island in the early 19th century, only 111 remained, their small numbers only adding to the dearth of knowledge surrounding the history of the Rapa Nui and their mysterious island.

In 1888, Easter Island received yet another visit—from Chilean Captain Policarpo Toro, who was easily able to conquer the island's vastly reduced population. Toro proceeded to annex the island in the name of Chile, and only seven years later, the island was rented out as a ranch to a British sheep-farming company, Williamson and Balfour. The 40,000 sheep brought over further contributed to the deterioration of already burned vegetation.

UNDER CHILEAN RULE (1895-PRESENT). As a result of the conversion of the island into a ranch, all native Rapa Nui were forced to reside in the small western village of Hanga Roa, which remains Easter Island's single city. In 1935, the Chilean government decided to open up "Parque Nacional Rapa Nui," incorporating much of the lands and archaeological sites, and charging admission (at present, US$11) to visitors. In 1952, the Chilean Navy took control of the island, leading to much resentment, and ultimately, revolt from the Rapa Nui. In 1965, led by Alfonso Rapu (later the first Rapa Nui elected mayor of the island by the six councillors elected every four years by the Rapa Nui), their revolt was successful. The island was granted the status of "civil department," and a government similar to those of Chile's mainland provinces was estab-

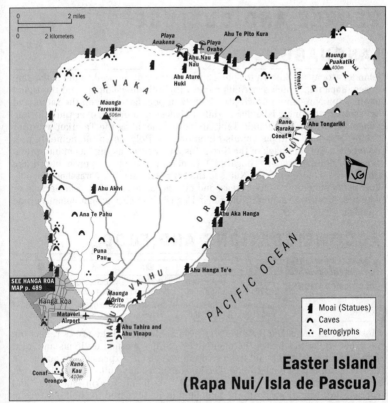

**Easter Island
(Rapa Nui/Isla de Pascua)**

Moai (Statues)
∧ Caves
∴ Petroglyphs

lished, headed by an appointed governor. In 1984, Sergio Rapu (younger brother of Alfonso) received this appointment, becoming the first native governor of Easter Island.

TODAY

With over 15,000 visitors traveling yearly to Easter Island from both Santiago, Chile, and Papeete, Tahiti, Easter Island is faced with a unique challenge. With tourism as the main industry and the resulting growing influx of tourists to this isle of intrigue and tropical mystique, the threat of loss of cultural identity looms on the horizon. Since the annexation of 1888, the Spanish language and foreign currencies have begun to permeate the island more and more.

Additionally, natives of the island are currently involved in a struggle to obtain land rights for the island—more specifically, of the government-owned, Conaf-operated Parque Nacional Rapa Nui. Given the lack of trees on the island, the land itself is susceptible to mineral leeching and coastal erosion; and the solution of soil restoration through careful agricultural management is easier said than done. Nonetheless, this solution would allow islanders to grow various items, including certain fruits, spices, and flowers (whose extracts could be used for various commercial goods, such as perfumes), that would help revolutionize the economy of the island in a manner that would help to ease the current cultural and geographical strain experienced by the island.

PEOPLE AND CULTURE

LANGUAGE

Islanders today are known to speak **Spanish** primarily, as well as the native language, **Rapa Nui,** which shares its name with both the islanders and the island itself. Rapa Nui can be heard prominently in popular music on the radio, and occasionally amongst islanders. While Polynesian in origin, over time the language has evolved to include Tahitian words, including the Tahitian word for "hello" ("iorana"). Rapa Nui also includes the Polynesian phoneme, ŋ, pronounced at the very back of the throat (usually written as "ng," as in interpretations of "Hanga Roa" or "Tongariki"). Generally, though, it is pronounced like Spanish. For more on Rapa Nui, see the **Let's Go! Rapa Nui Phrasebook,** p. 506. **English** is common in tourist areas, and menus can also be found in German or Japanese. Tours are generally offered in English, French, German, Japanese, and Spanish.

ACCOMMODATIONS AND FOOD

EASTER ISLAND	❶	❷	❸	❹	❺
ACCOMMODATIONS	Less than CH$16,000	CH$16,000-CH$27,000	CH$27,000-CH$38,000	CH$38,000-CH$48,000	CH $48,000 and up
FOOD	Less than CH$3100	CH$3100-CH$6400	CH$6400-CH$9500	CH$9500-CH$13,000	CH$13,000 and up

Most food on the island is flown over from Santiago, and the prices reflect the fact that you're paying for the plane ticket. Still, supermarket items and local fare, like tropical fruits and fresh seafood, are just as expensive, so maybe it's just a case of tourist exploitation. The free breakfast at your lodging will help cut costs, but climbing all the volcanic hills will make it hard to skip a meal now and then. Either bring food from the mainland or be prepared to shell out for the short time you're on the island. Most dishes are similar to those on the mainland (*empanadas, churrasco, ceviche*) but the fresh fruit juices are really delicious and distinctive.

CUSTOMS AND ETIQUETTE

The most important local custom to be aware of is the **flexibility and unpredictability of schedules.** While your tour will definitely be on time, most restaurants, bars, stores, and businesses operate on the whim of the owners. They open when they get there, close when they're bored, and take days off to watch the fútbol game. We've listed the hours we could eke out of staff, but you'll probably find that "island time" isn't just a cliché to put on souvenir t-shirts.

Another very common custom that visitors might have trouble getting used to is **bargaining.** It's very common throughout the island's institutions, from artesanía stands even to rental car places, so don't be afraid to give it a try. If you feel guilty, remember that islanders are shrewd businesspeople, and no one will sell anything at a loss. For more information on bargaining, see **The Art of the Deal,** p. 19.

Finally, it may seem as if all residents of the island know one another, and you'll hear constant shouts of salutation wherever you go. This friendliness extends to tourists, as locals will invariably smile, nod, and say "hola" while passing in the street. Don't be a stranger: drop the city mindset, look up, and return the greeting.

SMART SHOPPERS. Shopping for souvenirs on Easter Island may require some forethought, since many pieces are quite an investment, at US$100 and up. Woodwork, especially carvings of the endemic *Mako'I*, is the most expensive genre. Check to make sure that your country will allow in natural products (Australia does not) before splurging on that seven-foot Polynesian oar. Also, onyx and lapis lazuli are not native to the island, so don't be fooled by claims of their "authenticity"—they are shipped in from the mainland to be sold at higher prices to gullible, non-*Let's-Go*-reading tourists.

HOLIDAYS AND FESTIVALS

In 1975, islanders developed the **Tapati Rapa Nui** festival in order to attract tourists. Today, the festival,which takes place every year at the end of January and beginning of February (the height of the summer—and subsequently, tourist—season) includes native singing and dancing throughout the island, as well as recreations of historic events, such as the arrival of Hotu Matu'a on Anakena beach over 1500 years ago. In addition, the festival is characterized by athletic and dance competitions, as well as the yearly "crowning of the queen," an extremely popular and competitive event among natives which takes place in moonlight on the final Saturday of the festival. Be warned: the Rapa Nui know how to party.

Another important cultural event on the island is **The Day of the Language.** Originally conceived as an exposition of the works of the Department of Rapa Nui Language, each year artistic presentations from woodworking to body painting to literature are presented on November 22 in the gymnasium on Te Pito o Te Henúa. A similar exposition is held July 14-18 in the same gymnasium. Organized by the **Municipality of Easter Island** (☎ 100 226), **Tokerau** is a presentation of Rapa Nui song and dance that is meant to conserve the island culture.

With strong Catholic foundations imposed by European missionaries, Islanders celebrate religious holidays fervently. All are organized by Hanga Roa's Santa Cruz Church (☎ 100 357). On **Holy Friday,** two days before Easter, there is a huge mass and procession around Hanga Roa. On June 29, there's a celebration to honor **Saint Peter** and **Saint Paul** in the Hanga Roa Cove, with food and festivities for all. **Christmas** is another huge event, with processions, food, and generally good weather.

ADDITIONAL RESOURCES

CURRENT EVENTS, HISTORY, FICTION, AND FILM

Te Rapa Nui, www.rapanui.co.cl. An online version of Te Rapa Nui: The Gazette of Easter Island. Contains current news concerning local events, in both Spanish and English.

The Kon-Tiki Expedition, by Thor Heyerdahl (1950). Heyerdahl's account of his expedition to the island is as riveting as it is historically informative. It was a huge bestseller and can still be found in many of the island's souvenir shops. He also published a sequel, **Aku Aku, the Secrets of Easter Island** (1957).

Ethnology of Easter Island, by Alfred Métraux (1971). A detailed study of the history and culture of Easter Island, with an attempt to unravel the mysteries surrounding the island's piecemeal, uncertain history.

Easter Island, by Jennifer Vanderbes (2003). A fictional account of the life of English archaeologist Katherine Routledge, often known as the first scientist who, in her work, **The Mystery of Easter Island** (1917), sought to solve the enigmas created by the various cultural artifacts left behind on the island throughout the centuries.

EASTER ISLAND

Rapa Nui, directed by Kevin Costner (1994). Though it flopped in the US and harmed some of the archaeological sites, this movie remains the most ambitious depiction of the island's mysteries. Islanders still remember when Hollywood took over Rapa Nui.

Ogú y Mampato en Rapa Nui, directed by Alejandro Rojas (2002). The young daughter of a native Rapa Nui, transplanted from the island, returns to discover more about the island's seemingly mystical past.

EASTER ISLAND ESSENTIALS

TRANSPORTATION

BEFORE YOU GO
Passport/Visa: As virtually all travel to Easter Island is through Santiago, Chile, no additional documentation other than what is needed to enter Chile is needed to enter Easter Island (see **Before You Go,** p. 13). However, a departure tax of US$8 is required for those traveling to the island. The departure tax from the island is US$7.
Required Vaccinations (p. 7). No inoculations are required.

Opened in 1967, Mataveri Airport (☎ 100 277 or 100 278) in the south of Hanga Roa is Easter Island's only airport. LanChile is currently the only airline offering service to Easter Island (US$800-1000). Service to and from Mataveri is limited, with two to four Boeing 767 flights per week from Santiago to Easter Island, depending on the season (5hr.; mid-Oct.-Mar. Tu-W and Sa-Su; Apr.-early Oct. W and Su. Schedules may vary. Make sure to have return tickets before arrival on the island. Purchase in advance.) To save money, residents of Australia and Europe are occasionally able to include Easter Island as part of a customizable, multi-destination "around-the-world ticket," while residents of the US and Canada can have Easter Island added to their ticket to Santiago for an additional fee as part of a "VC Chile Pass," which must be purchased before departure to Chile. (VC Chile Pass US$269 in each direction. 14-day max. stay in Santiago before departure to Easter Island.)

There is **limited public transport** on Easter Island. **Taxis** are a good choice for those wishing to see the sights of the island, and are easily found throughout the streets of Hanga Roa. While *Let's Go* does not recommend hitchhiking, locals have also been known to give rides to travelers. In addition, **rental cars, motorbikes,** and **bicycles** are all popular means for sightseeing at your own pace, and are available at many hotels and local rent-a-car services (p. 488). Car rentals can get slightly expensive, however, costing anywhere from US$40 to US$100 per day. **Horses,** a marginally less reliable means of transport, are also available for rental. For those renting cars and motorbikes, make sure to have an **International Driving Permit.**

TOURIST SERVICES AND MONEY

Sernatur (p. 489) has an office in Hanga Roa. Ask about accommodations, food, car rentals, and the many **tours** (p. 490) around the island, including sightseeing tours of the **moai,** trips to **Anakena, boat tours,** and **diving excursions.** Tours range US$25-US$90. For those more interested in outdoor activities, information on **camping** and **hiking** around the island is available at the local **Conaf** office (p. 489). For additional info, check out the local **Cámara de Turismo de Isla de Pascua** (p. 489).

The official currency of Easter Island is the Chilean *peso,* though islanders will also accept **US dollars** and **traveler's checks. Credit cards** (AmEx/MC/V) may be used in certain establishments, though cash is preferred due to the time lag associated with credit card use. Some restaurant and hotel owners may charge a service fee for those wishing to use credit cards. **Currency exchange** can involve a tiresome, complicated process, so it's best to change money in Santiago. Tourists using US dollars will almost invariably pay more, so asking first for a price in pesos is a good idea. While there is a **24hr. ATM** on the island (p. 490), make sure to bring enough of both currencies with you to the island, as many visitors have experienced problems with it. Be prepared: prices on Easter Island are noticeably higher than in much of Chile. Budget travelers can expect to pay at least US$35 for a day's accommodations and food (including the customary 10% tip for restaurant meals).

HEALTH AND SAFETY

EMERGENCIES In case of medical emergencies call ☎ **100 215** or **100 217.**

MEDICAL EMERGENCIES AND HEALTH. Medical facilities are limited on the Island, with only one hospital, **Hospital Hanga Roa** (p. 491). Make sure to bring your own aspirin, antibiotics, bandages, and sunscreen. Don't forget insect repellant. Mosquitoes are found throughout the island, and black widow spiders are common on the northern coast. While food and water are generally safe, be careful when eating fish and seafood. When traveling around the island, be sure to bring your own food and water, as these are scarce outside Hanga Roa.

SAFETY. Native islanders are generally friendly and welcoming. Occasionally, visitors can even expect a traditional greeting from locals upon arrival to the island. Nonetheless, tourists must be aware that they are easily recognizable to the natives. A small **police** force exists on the island, divided between airport security and the local **guardia** stationed in the south of town on Manutara, near the airport.

WEATHER AND PACKING CONCERNS

In general, Easter Island has a subtropical climate, with annual average temperatures of 20°C (67°F). The island's coldest month is August, with average temperatures of 15°C (59°F), though wind chill during the winter months of June through August can make it seem colder. The island's hottest month is February, with average temperatures of 25°C (77°F). May and June are considered to be Easter Island's rainy season. Make sure to bring boots and a flashlight to explore the island's caves. A light shell or jacket is essential, as there isn't much shelter to wait out the surprise downpours. Most tourists come between November and March. To avoid crowds and sweltering temperatures, plan a trip during the low season.

KEEPING IN TOUCH

PHONE NUMBERS The country code for Easter Island is ☎ **56.** The regional code for all Easter Island is ☎ **32.** Note: all phone numbers on the island begin with either "100" or "551."

Like other amenities on Easter Island, communications are also somewhat limited. **Public phones** and **fax machines** are available at call centers in Hanga Roa (p. 491) and in many local businesses. The only type of phone card that can be used on the island is **Entel.** Finally, buildings in Hanga Roa do not have street numbers; therefore, all regular mail, which comes in through Chile (see **Keeping in Touch,** p. 41), arrives at the **post office** (p. 491). In general, the fastest way to find a person or establishment is to ask around. Most locals are friendly and always ready to help.

E A S T E R   I S L A N D

HANGA ROA   ☎ 32

The city of Hanga Roa on the southwest coast is the only inhabited place on Easter Island, home to its 4,000 inhabitants. For one of the most isolated spots in the world—free from tourists until the 1960s—Hanga Roa has a level of modernity that will surprise you. There's an ATM and Internet service, and the city even recently received cell phone service. Still, the unpaved streets, low-slung tropical buildings, and horses galloping right down the sidewalk give it the air of an age past. Furthermore, Hanga Roa's concentrated area means that you'll constantly run into the same people, making you feel at home in the place farthest from it.

▐ TRANSPORTATION

Taxis: Most travelers will find everything in Hanga Roa on foot. For those who just can't face another muddy hill, however, **taxis** are a reliable presence throughout the city. **Radiotaxi Avareipua** (☎ 100 700) is by far the best option, with a large number of clean and well-kept cars. A trip to **Anakena** costs about CH$8000 round-trip.

Car rentals: Or more specifically, 4WD rentals, which are best for longer journeys. You'll see advertisements in store windows, on the streets, and in the windows of homes for rentals from US$40 to US$100. The most organized and official outfits are **Oceanic Rent a Car** on Atamu Tekena (☎ 100 985), **Haunani Rent a Car** on Atamu Tekena next to the supermarket (☎ 100 353 or 100 225), and **Comercial Insular** at the very south of Atamu Tekena (☎ 551 276 or 100 480), which offers delivery. Be aware that the vehicles generally have manual transmission. Also, definitely fuel up and check your oil before leaving Hanga Roa, since there are no other service stations on the island. All of these outfits also offer **motorbikes** (CH$45-60 per day), though looking at the tiny arcade-style tires after bumping over the treacherous roads outside of Hanga Roa might make you think twice. In any case, demand a helmet.

DRIVE SAFELY. Even driving on Easter Island can be an adventure. If you venture outside of Hanga Roa, be prepared for spine-jangling dirt roads that turn to soup in even the slightest rain. On top of that, the local method for avoiding potholes often involves driving on the wrong side of the road. Drive slowly—not that your ancient manual Jeep would allow you to do otherwise.

Horse Rentals: Horses were the original form of land transport on Easter Island, and continue to pervade the island today. Eating dinner on the outdoor terrace of a pub, you might be shocked to see a local gallop right down the sidewalk, and even on the highest point of Rano Raraku, you can see wild steeds grazing. You can hop on the bandwagon with rentals from **Pantu** (☎ 100 577), a reputable guide on the island. An 8hr. rental costs US$35.

✦ ❓ ORIENTATION AND PRACTICAL INFORMATION

The layout of Hanga Roa is a far cry from the municipal grid of most cities in Chile. There are no street numbers, and street names, if marked, are written in peeling paint on the side of the curb. Luckily, due to its small size, getting lost isn't that different from carefree wandering. You'll know to turn around once you stop seeing souvenir shops, which will never be more than ten minutes from the center.

Located on the island's southwest corner, the town is generally bounded by three streets. **Avenida Policarpo Toro** runs along the western coast from the south of town to Tahai in the North. When it passes Caleta Hanga Roa on the left, it

Hanga Roa

⌂ ACCOMMODATIONS

Chez Cecilia, **6**
Hostal Manavai, **1**
Mahina Taka-Taka Georgia, **3**
Martín y Anita, **15**
Residencial Puka Rangi
  Uka, **13**
Residencial Vai Ka Pua, **14**
Taura'a Hotel, **17**
Vai Moana, **9**

🍴 FOOD

Ariki o Te Pana, **18**
Café Ra'a, **8**
El Cuerito Regalón, **4**
Restaurant Ava Reipua, **11**
Restaurant Bar Tavaka, **7**
Restaurant Pea, **12**
Te Moana, **5**

🎵 NIGHTLIFE

Aloha Bar & Pub, **21**
Banana Pub, **20**
Piriti, **19**
Pub Tupuna, **16**
Topa Tangi Pub, **2**
Toroko, **10**

Map labels: Toki Tour; Te Pito o Te Henúa; Super-mercado Kai Nene; Sebastian Englert Anthropological Museum; TO DOS VENTANAS CAVE; TAHAI; Tahai; Feria Municipal; Moni Tau; Atamu Tekena; Avareipua; Mike Rapu Diving Center; Orca Diving Center; Caleta Hanga Roa; Policarpo Toro; Petero Atamu; Te Hoe Manu; Ara Piki; Aku Aku Tours; Mercado Artesanal; Ara Hoa Rakei; Playa Pea; Ahu Tautira; Te Pito o Te Henúa; Apina; Hetereki; Oceanic Rent-a-Car; SEE INSET ABOVE; Avareipua; Manutti; Simón Paoa; Rongorongo; Puku Rangi Uka; S. Englert; Atamu Tekena; Tuki Haka Hevari; Tu'u Koihu; Molina Luco; Make Make; Kaituoe; SEE INSET BELOW; Pont; Gas Station; Hotu Matu'a; Manutara; Mataveri Airport; TO ORONGO & RANO KAU; TO ANAKENA, RANO RARAKU & VAIHU

Moai (Statues)

Inset (bottom left): Oceanic Rent-a-Car; Lavanderia Tea Nui; Kia Koe Tours; Cámara de Turismo; LanChile; Atamu Tekena; S. Englert

EASTER ISLAND

intersects **Te Pito o Te Henúa,** which runs straight up a hill from the bay to the church and the **Mercado Artesanal.** Halfway up, Te Pito o Te Henúa is intersected by **Avenida Atamu Tekena,** the town's main drag, which goes all the way from the airport in the south to Tahai in the north. If all else fails, just remember that the sea is on the west and the airport is in the south.

 STAYING ON SOLID GROUND. In addition to taking care to avoid the "souvenirs" left behind in the streets by Hanga Roa's many horses, visitors must always take care to watch their steps. The main streets of Hanga Roa are lined with drainage ditches that are covered to serve as sidewalks in some areas. At night, it all looks the same, so especially if you've had a few, walk only on the grass and don't ever cross directly from the road to the curb without checking your footing first. Volcanic rock doesn't exactly cushion a fall.

Tourist Office: Sernatur has an office on Tu'u Maheke (☎100 255; sernatur_rapanui@entelchile.net), at the intersection with Apina, and at the airport, to the left of the baggage claim exit. **Conaf** also has an office near Mataveri Airport, down the road to Rano Kau (☎100 236; fax 100 827), and another at the base of Rano Raraku.

PRISCILLA EDMUNDS

Prisclla Edmunds is 25, and is the host of an environmental TV show on the island. She was born on the island, left at age 3 to live on the mainland, returned for a few months each summer, and last year moved back for good.

LG: Why do you think your parents left the island?

A: My father was born here and lived here almost 30 years. Most of my family went to the mainland to study. My mother is from Chile, and she came here to work. Then she met my father and got married. They went to live in Santiago because of work.

LG: Is that why most people leave? Do most people stay?

A: People leave for work, or to go to university. They study for a year or so, then come back. It's hard for people to get used to life on the mainland.

LG: Is that why you came back to the island?

A: Yes. It's not easy to get used to life there. I came here mainly to build a home, because on the island there is a law that the land is just for the people. A Chilean can't own a piece of land here. You have to inherit it—my grandmother is going to give me a piece of land to build my house on. Or, if you are Rapa Nui, you can submit your name, wait three or four years, and you get a piece of land for free.

You can also find info at the local **Cámara de Turismo de Isla de Pascua** on Atamu Tekena (☎550 055; camararapanui@entelchile.net).

Tours: Kia Koe Tour on Atamu Tekena, across from the Aloha Pub (☎100 282; kiakoe@entelchile.net), and **Aku-Aku** Tour on Hotu Matu'a (☎100 770), are the largest and most efficient outfits. They offer tours in many languages, including English, French, German, and Japanese. **Ile de Paques Sejours** on Av. Pont (☎550 375) has a French emphasis, and **Archaeological Travel Services** on Policarpo Toro (☎100 284) is a good choice for those more serious about their sightseeing. **Tokitour** offers trips to the more inaccessible parts of the island (☎551 295), for those who've seen enough of the tour-group vans. Yet the breathtaking views from Easter Island's heights are rivaled by those at its depths. **Diving** here is quite excellent, due to the clear water, tropical marine life, looming caverns, and numerous shipwrecks off coast. **Orca Diving Center,** Caleta Hanga Roa Otai at the base of Te Pito o Te Henúa (☎550 375; www.seemorca.cl) and **Mike Rapu Diving Center** to its right (☎551 055; www.mikerapu.cl) both offer excursions for licensed divers from US$45-$60, with all gear included. Mike Rapu runs a scuba certification class for US$70, but for other watersport enthusiasts, Orca has more options. They offer a $25 snorkel trip, and rent kayaks (US$15-25 a day), surfboards (US$10-15 for 3hr.), snorkeling equipment (US$10), and bodyboards with fins (US$10) in **Hare Orca,** the adjacent shop.

Currency Exchange: The **BancoEstado** exchanges American dollars and traveler's checks of different currencies, and also gives cash advances on Visa cards. **Moni Tau,** on Atamu Tekena next to Te Moana (☎100 265), offers those services, and will also exchange euros for a 15% commission. Open M-F 9am-5pm, Sa 9am-1:30pm.

Bank: There's one bank on the island, the **BancoEstado,** on Tu'u Maheke next to the market (☎100 688 or 100 679). Open M-F 8am-1pm. The only **24hr. ATM** is located to the left of the bank, farther down toward the coast. Its cash, however, often runs out before the end of the day, so go early. Also, some people report difficulty using the ATM with anything but MasterCard.

English-Language Bookstore: Some souvenir stores, including the gift shop of the Archaeological Museum, sell English-language guides and histories of the island, but they are ridiculously expensive (CH$18,000-60,000). It's best to buy books on the mainland before or after you visit the island.

Library: Open since October 2002, the **William Mulloy Specialized Archaeological Library** at the Sebastian Englert Museum is the first and only collection on the island. Its 2000 titles and 3000 photographs are a great resource to delve further into the history, geography, and anthropology of the island. Its lecture hall occasionally hosts small talks. Open Tu-F 9:30am-12:30pm and 2-5:30pm, Sa-Su 9:30am-12:30pm.

Cultural Center: Aukara Center of Art and Culture (☎ 100 539 or 551 128) houses expositions on traditional carvings and printings and offers occasional classes on Rapa Nui history and traditional dance. Open M-Sa 10am-1pm.

Market: The **Mercado Artesanal** at the top of Te Pito o Te Henúa, to the left of the church, is a huge, multi-vendor crafts market housed inside a multi-wing wooden structure. Open M-Sa 10am-7pm. The vendors at the **Feria Municipal** on Atamu Tekena at the intersection with Tu'u Maheke sell fresh meats, fruits, and vegetables, as well as the typical variety of local crafts. Open M-Sa 8am-7pm. From 7 to 11am you can get cooked fare at the little cafe in its center. The *empanadas* (CH$1000) and *churrasco* (CH$1500) are by far the cheapest in town.

Laundromat: Aside from the occasional friendly favors of hostel owners, the only option for washing away volcanic dust is the **Lavandería Tea Nui** on Atamu Tekena (☎ 100 580). Call to arrange free pickup and delivery.

Film Developing: You can buy film almost anywhere, but you can only get it developed at **Rapa Nui Lab** on Te Pito o Te Henúa across from the school (☎550 989).

Hospital: Hospital Hanga Roa on Simón Paoa (☎ 100 215 or 100 217) is open 24hr. Its **pharmacy** is the only 24hr. pharmacy on the island. For access, ask at urgent care.

Fax: Hare PC on Te Pito o Te Henúa in the LipiGas office (☎ 100 829) has a public fax .

Telephones: Entel Telephone Services on Policarpo Toro (☎ 103), near Sernatur, offers the most complete range of assistance, while **Rapa Call Center** on Atamu Tekena (☎551 600) is good for quick calls home.

Internet Access: Internet access on the island is slower and much more expensive than on the mainland, running about CH$4000 per hr. **Rapa Call Center** on Atamu Tekena (☎551 600) has the most terminals, and is the only place with DSL. Open M-Sa 10am-7pm. **@**, the blue building across the street, has fewer terminals and is slower, but has a CD burner. Usually open until at least 9pm. **Café Ra'a** on Atamu Tekena (☎551 530) is the cheapest, at CH$2800 per hr. Open M and W-Su 10:30am-2:30pm and 7-9pm.

Post Office: The only post office is located on Te Pito o Te Henúa, just up from the soccer field. Though small, it is efficient and offers all standard services. Open M-F 9am-1pm and 2:30-6pm, Sa 9am-12:30pm.

LG: You have a daughter here. What's it like to be a kid on the island? What do they do for fun?

A: Well, my daughter is only two and a half years old. But the kids here swim, play soccer, ride horses, and bike.

LG: Do you think parents here are strict?

A: No. Not at all. That's the problem. Kids are too free. Then they grow up and go wild. I think for that reason, it's good to raise your kid here, but only until 8 or 10 years old. Teenagers are always looking for something to do. So you have drinking, smoking, parties every night. It's too small. That's the hardest thing about living on the island.

LG: What is the best thing about living on the island, though? Do people appreciate the sights?

A: Being close to all the traditions and the culture. You have two big groups of people, though. One wants technology, the other wants to continue like this, to have this be enough. But I think they're both fighting for a better life for people, while staying near to the culture, without losing it.

LG: Has the island changed a lot in the past couple years?

A: Yes. Cell phones! I think it's stupid. People live so close together—cell phones are useless. They have been around for a month. Now they want to put towers everywhere. I guess that's the price of having people who want technology.

ACCOMMODATIONS

Most accommodations on Easter Island are disappointing for the inevitably expensive price, and higher rates don't really buy you a substantially better room. In fact, they're all pretty much the same: tile floor, gray walls, and floral bedspread, all slightly musty from the ocean breeze. Still, the natural beauty surrounding it all makes up for it. You'll probably only need to reserve ahead if you're coming in July, August, January, or early February, when prices will be US$10-20 more expensive. Budget establishments have representatives at the airport and offer on-the-spot discounts. Breakfast is included, unless otherwise noted.

Taura'a Hotel, Atamu Tekena (☎ 100 732). With 22 siblings, owner Edith has an inside connection to anything you might need during your stay, and she'll make you feel like part of her family. Bright rooms with private bath. The restaurant serves fruit smoothies at breakfast. Singles US$45; doubles US$80; triples US$100. AmEx/DC/MC/V. ❸

Residencial Tahai, Simón Paoa and Tu'u Koihu (☎ 100 395; mariahey@latinmail.com). Though a bit of a walk from the center of town, this simple budget option is ideal for sunset views. All rooms have a private bath, and there's a TV in the lobby. Free transfer from airport. Singles US$20; doubles US$40. ❶

Residencial Vai Ka Pua, Tu'u Koihu at Te Pito o Te Henúa (☎ 100 377; vaikapua@entelchile.net), has no-frills lodging on a quiet street near the church. The lush plant life will make you feel like you're in a real Polynesian paradise. Jeep rentals US$40. Singles US$20; doubles US$40. ❶

Mahina Taka-Taka Georgia, on Tahai (☎ 100 452; riroroco@entelchile.net). The sparse rooms might not make up for the 10min. walk from town, but the price is right and rooms come with private bath. Singles US$25; doubles US$45. ❶

Hotel Residencial Puku Rangi Uka, Puku Rangi Uka (☎ 100 405; puku-rangiuka@entelchile.net). English-speaking owners Marta and Luis are welcoming, and keep their hotel very clean. TV in the lobby and Internet available for US$4 per hr. Free transfer from the airport. 4-bed dorm with shared bath US$15 per person; singles US$30; doubles US$50; triples US$60. ❶

Martín y Anita, Simón Paoa (☎ 100 593; hmanita@entelchile.net). This spot feels just like you are being let into someone's home—and you are. Rooms are larger than elsewhere, with private bath and A/C. Restaurant and kitchen available. Free transfer from airport. Singles US$39; doubles US$79; triples US$89. AmEx/DC/MC/V. ❷

Chez Cecilia, Policarpo Toro (☎ 100 499), offers many amenities for its small size, including a bar, restaurant, fax, TV, and private bath. The ocean view, however, is really the best feature. Singles US$40; doubles US$65; triples US$90. AmEx/DC/MC/V. ❷

Vai Moana, Atamu Tekena (☎ 100 626; vai_moana@entelchile.net), rents hillside cabins with a view of the famous Tahai sunset. Rooms have hand-crafted decor. The on-site restaurant and bar make the 10min. walk less of an issue. Free transfer from airport. Singles US$40; doubles US$60; triples US$90. AmEx/DC/MC/V. ❷

Chez María Goretti, Atamu Tekena (☎ 100 459; mariagoretti@entelchile.net), is really beautiful, with spacious rooms spread across verdant gardens. The modern restaurant is a relaxing place to start the day before making the 10min. walk to town. Free transfer from airport. Singles US$50; doubles US$70; triples US$100. ❸

Hostal Manavai, Te Pito o Te Henúa (☎ 100 670). The rooms here are a little small, but the pool, restaurant, bar, and 24hr. room service make up for it. All rooms have private bath. Singles US$55; doubles US$80; triples US$113. AmEx/DC/MC/V. ❸

FOOD

Food on Easter Island is surprisingly expensive, even when bought in the store. Several *mercaditos* on Atamu Tekena sell fresh bread, yogurt, cookies and drinks. **Supermercado Kai Nene** on Atamu Tekena has a wider range. Note that supplies are shipped in with the tourists, so come by after your flight for the best selection. Despite the prices, however, restaurants seem geared toward a younger crowd, with good, greasy fare. Beyond that, fresh seafood dominates the menus. The tuna is delicious, but don't bother splurging for the miniscule and overpriced lobster.

Café Ra'a, Atamu Tekena (☎551 530), bills itself as the most isolated coffee shop in the world, but its coziness and quality mean you'd never guess it. Light eats like *gazpacho* (CH$2000), salad (CH$2500), or sandwiches (CH$3000) can all be packed up for a picnic, but the free games, toys, and books might convince you to stay. Internet CH$2800 per hr. Open M and W-Sa 10:30am-2:30pm and 7-9pm. ❶

Restaurant Pea, Policarpo Toro (☎100 382). The ocean view and hand-crafted decorations make Pea one of the most impressive restaurants in town. There's a range of fresh *empanadas* (CH$800-1500) and sandwiches (CH$2500) that can be accompanied by unique fried sweet potatoes (CH$2500), but save room for the *panqueque Alaska* (CH$3000), a crepe baked around rum raisin ice cream. Open daily 11am-11pm. ❶

Ariki o Te Pana, Atamu Tekena (☎100 171), calls itself "Queen of the Empanadas," and the large, flaky pockets definitely don't disappoint (CH$1200-1800). The pizza (CH$4500) has a similarly great crust. Both go well with beer, of course (CH$1500). Open 11am-3pm and 7-10pm. ❶

Merahi Ra'a, Te Pito o Te Henúa (☎551 125), serves huge portions of several different kinds of fresh fish. In fact, you might see the owner bringing them in right from the bay. Tuna, *Kana-Kana,* and *Herui* are among the offerings (CH$5500 each). Steak (CH$6500) and spaghetti (CH$4200) are available for those uncomfortable with meeting their meal before it's on their plate. Open daily from 5pm. ❷

Restaurant Ava Reipua, Policarpo Toro (☎551 158). The view of the bay makes Ava Reipua a great place for a relaxing lunch of Chilean fare like *churrasco* (CH$3000), *lomo al pobre* (CH$3200), or *barros luco* (CH$2800). Make sure to ask for some *ají chileno.* Open M and W-Su 1pm-midnight. ❷

THE BIG SPLURGE

A SOUVENIR FOR TRAVELING LIGHT

From heavy basalt *moai* to giant mahogany sceptres, the souvenirs of Easter Island are generally too big for backpackers. But that doesn't mean you have to resign yourself to a keychain. For a few extra bucks, you can buy a souvenir that reflects the heart of Rapa Nui culture. What's more, you can carry it with you, it's not very heavy, and—so long as you consider the risks of infection in a clear, sober state of mind—it'll never fade: a Polynesian tattoo.

Tattooing is an important part of all Polynesian cultures, and Rapa Nui is no exception. Most locals have some kind of marking, from small armbands to full-facial designs. In ancient days, there was a unique repertoire of designs on the island, but this too is shrouded in uncertainty. Slave raids and clan warfare killed off all the tattoo experts, and the only knowledge of the old designs comes from photos and sketches of pre-20th century explorers. Some *moai* have carvings indicative of tattoo designs, and the work of modern tattoo artists reflects those early influences. **Moko Mae Tattoo** on Atamu Tekena (☎551 554) is the best choice on the island. Their work blends traditional artistry with modern techniques and sanitation, not the Tahitian method of bamboo and ink. A square inch rendition of the Birdman petroglyph costs US$30. No matter what design you choose, this souvenir will help you brag about your trip for the rest of your life.

Restaurant Bar Tavake, Atamu Tekena (☎100 300), serves no-frills greasy fare like *empanadas* (CH$2000), pizza (CH$2500), and fries (CH$2000). The fruit shakes are a welcome anomaly (CH$1500). Service can be a little slow, but who's in a rush? ❷

El Cuerito Regalón, Atamu Tekena (☎551 232). The macramé lamps and plastic flowers of this sidewalk cafe don't seem to mesh with the gigantic, 3-room assortment of alcohol out back, but the market and the restaurant are tecnically one and the same. The open-air terrace is popular with locals, who dine on the lunch *menú* (CH$4000), salads (CH$2500), *churrasco* (CH$3000), or pastries (CH$2500). ❷

Te Moana, Atamu Tekena (☎551 578). Though slightly more expensive, Te Moana has an authentic Polynesian atmosphere, and what seems to be the only non-salad vegetarian option on the island—a delicious and filling chop suey (CH$6000). Sandwiches (CH$5000) like the multi-layer club are a cheaper option and come with free fries, which is a rarity. Open from 5pm. ❷

ENTERTAINMENT

The **Kari Kari Group** performs traditional dances and Rapa Nui songs at the Hotel Hanga Roa. (☎100 767 or 551 064. Performances M-Tu and F-Sa 10pm. US$15.) The **Polynesia Group** has a similar show at the Kopakavana Restaurant near the top of Te Pito o Te Henúa. (☎551 152. Shows Tu and F 10pm.) A less professional, but still impressive show is put on at the **Restaurant Te Henúa** on Tu'u Maheke. (☎551 704. Shows M and F 10pm.) You can catch the cheesy American take on the island when the **Hotel Manavai Cinema Bar** on Te Pito o Te Henúa across from the post office screens its only option, Kevin Costner's *Rapa Nui*. (☎100 670. Film in English. Screenings M-Tu and Th 9:30pm. CH$3000 or US$5.) You'll marvel at the fact that the ancient Rapa Nui spoke with clipped British accents.

NIGHTLIFE

In general, nightlife fits in with the rest of the island's character: laid-back and somewhat unorganized. Pubs along Atamu Tekena sporadically showcase live music, posting signs out front as the occasion arises. **Aloha Bar and Pub,** on Atamu Tekena (☎551 383), is the cleanest and is lit by romantic candlelight. **Banana Pub** has a pool table, **Topa Tangi Pub** has the best live music, and **Pub Tupuna** has a collection of feathered headdresses that at least one person ends up wearing every night. Everything's dead on Sundays and Mondays (when most restaurants close), and before at least 11:30pm on other days. On Wednesday nights, when the Lan-Chile flight leaves for Papeete and the other half of the tourist population is leaving in the morning, the pubs host more of a quiet local scene.

There are only two nightclubs on the island. **Toroko,** on Policarpo Toro, is right near the center of town. On Thursdays it seems to house everyone that arrived the night before from Tahiti. Fewer tourists make it out to **Piriti,** on Hotu Matu'a near the airport. Both clubs play a mix of reggae, English pop, and Polynesian covers of each. Expect to hear a lot of Bob Marley hybrids. (Cover CH$2500 at both clubs).

OUTDOOR ACTIVITIES AND DAYTRIPS

Technically an open-air museum, the island is full of potential sightseeing stops. In fact, there are 887 *moai* dotting the island, or just over 8 per square mile. Only 388 ever made it out of the quarry and onto an *ahu* (platform), and coupled with the relatively small amount of restoration done, the number of major sites is limited. Still, there are probably many islanders who have never seen all the isle has to offer. Our listings reflect the most impressive and most frequently visited sites, but it's important to be aware of the truly overwhelming possibilities of the island.

PICTURE THIS! Locals in traditional garb set up shop at the many archaeo-logical sites and charge US$2 for a picture. Don't try to sneak one from afar, as they are surprisingly aware—and may be irritated by the intrusion.

HANGA ROA AREA

Even as Easter Island's "urban hub," the town of Hanga Roa is home to several archaeological sites. A short afternoon walking tour serves as a good intro to the kinds of things you'll see outside the city center. Start at around 2pm to reach Tahai by sunset. On Policarpo Toro just south of Te Pito o Te Henúa, begin your trip at **Pea Beach.** This rocky inlet is small and you'll have to put your towel on the grass above, but you can take a dip in the calm waters or watch surfers farther out.

Farther down Policarpo Toro, keeping the water on your left, you'll come to **Ahu Tautira.** This 100m platform holds two restored *moai*, which even today suppos-edly transmit their *mana* to the soccer field across the street. Continuing past is **Hanga Roa Tai,** the city's main bay. It bustles throughout the afternoon as fisher-men bring in dinner for the island on brightly colored wooden boats.

About 15min. north on Policarpo Toro is the sweeping **Tahai** complex, the best archaeological site near the city. There are traces of *hare paenga* (canoe houses) throughout, but the *ahu* are the real attraction. There are three moving north along the coast: **Vai Uri, Taha,** and **Kote Riku.** Aside from the restored *moai* they hold, these *ahu* are quite unique. Vai Uri marks the burial site of archaeologist Wil-liam Mulloy, who led several restoration efforts on the island. Kote Riku holds one of the only *moai* on the island with eyes, added by the island elders' council. Orig-inally, every *moai* was fitted with eyes of white coral with obsidian or scoria pupils. It was the very last step in their creation, and completed only when the *moai* was placed on the *ahu.* The insertion of the eyes made the statue an *aringa ora* (living face), and began the transmission of *mana* from the statue to the vil-lage. All of the eyes either broke or were stolen during the clan warfare, and today only hollows remain in some *moai*, marking those that actually made it to an *ahu*.

Past Tahai, take a right on the dirt road up to the **Sebastian Englert Anthropologi-cal Museum** on Tahai. Since 1973, this small museum has worked to preserve Rapa Nui history and culture. Its artifacts and explanatory posters are worth a look if you have the time, but aren't essential stops if you've taken a tour. (☎551 020. CH$1000, children 8-18 and ISIC holders CH$500. Open Tu-F 9:30am-12:30pm and 2:30-5:30pm, Sa-Su 9:30am-12:30pm.) Then head back to Tahai and sit back on the low wall to the east to watch its famed sunset, which is by far the most impressive (and the cheapest) sight on the island. Streaks of vibrant color fill the sky and uninterrupted expanse of sea, all as motive backdrop for the looming *moai*.

ORONGO AREA

This cluster of sites sits in the area southeast of town. It's a four- or five-hour loop, depending on how long you linger at each spot, and serves as a good introduction to the experience of driving on Easter Island. For walkers, it's a daytrip. Head out toward the airport and follow the road up the hill toward **Rano Kau** volcano. Just before you reach the summit, you'll see a pull-off area on your right, worn down by tourgroup vans. Stopping here rewards you with a sweeping view of the island. Hanga Roa lies spread out to the left, and the island's 70 volcanic hills look almost computer-generated, as they curl in a perfect vista of green. You can also see the three volcanic corners of the island—**Rano Kau, Rano Raraku,** and **Rano Poike.**

Continue up the road to Rano Kau crater and look out. The volcano last erupted 2.3 million years ago, leaving this crater to mark the spot. The 1.6km diameter cra-ter, about 300m deep, is breathtaking. Its freshwater lagoon, the island's main res-ervoir, is filled with an archipelago of reeds that make it look as if you are gazing

THE LOCAL STORY

A GUIDE TO THE SIGHTS

Ahu, ceremonial sites for the community, are common to many Polynesian cultures. On Rapa Nui they took three shapes: *ahu poepoe* are boat-shaped caskets, semi-pyramidal *ahu* are rough prisms of stone, and *ahu moai* are the famed *moai* pedestals. These were originally made from slabs of ventricular basalt and some were later fitted with decorative scoria panels. Though they are most known for holding the *moai*, *ahu* were important in funerals and other ceremonies before and after their prevalence. Over 200 dot the island.

Ana, caves, are the result of the island's early volcanic activity. Rapa Nui who were too poor to pay for homes took shelter in them, as did those hiding from later slave raids. Today, intrepid campers occasionally repopulate them, living among the crumbling stoves and other structures.

Hare Paenga, or canoe houses, are traditional Rapa Nui homes named for their elliptical shape. The stone foundation held up bamboo shoots that supported a palm frond roof. Traces of these structures remain throughout the island, especially near *ahu*.

Mana Vai are gardens developed by resourceful Rapa Nui. Plants and flowers are still surrounded by stone walls to pro-

down at another planet. There is a path to the bottom from the lookout point, but it is very rugged and the bottom is very muddy. Just don't forget that you have to get back up. A *Tangata Manu* (Birdman) petroglyph is located right at the lookout, speaking to this site's importance in the competitions. Hopu Manu is said to have used the crater's reeds as floats to the nearby island of Motu Nui.

The very heart of the *Tangata Manu* competitions, however, was the nearby village of **Orongo,** farther up the road. There is a hut at the entrance where you will have to pay US$10/CH$5000, good for the duration of your stay. This village, perched on a sweeping green expanse perilously high above the sea, was *tapu* ("sacred") for the Rapa Nui. Only the nobility (numbering 200) were allowed to enter, and even then, only from June to September, during *Tangata Manu*. Its 53 houses were built for that purpose. Though destroyed by early explorers, all but two were restored by Sebastian Englert in 1935 and William Mulloy in 1960, and today they sit, like little stacks of black coins, spackled by barnacles, overlooking the sea. Petroglyphs of Birdmen abound and there's a commanding view of the sea, spotted only by three islands below: **Motu Nui, Motu Ipi,** and **Motu Kau Kau.**

Heading back toward Hanga Roa on the western coast is a cave, **Ana Kai Tangata**—"the cave of the cannibals." Especially during times of war, cannibalism was a reality on the island, and this cave was the residence of the last human-eating holdout. Of the many caves on the island, this is by far the most incredible. It is a gaping black enclave right at the sea, and huge turquoise waves crash just outside its mouth. The walls are covered with traditional paintings, somewhat dimmed from the bright lights used during the filming of Kevin Costner's *Rapa Nui.*

Closer to town, at the western end of the airport strip, are **Ahu Tahiri** and **Ahu Vinapu.** The six *moai* here are toppled with their faces to the ground. What's most impressive is the construction of Ahu Tahiri, on the left. The wall that faces the sea is known as the "Inca wall" because of its tight construction, similar to the murals of Cuzco. This was often cited by Heyerdahl as evidence of Rapa Nui's South American connection, but many think it's just coincidence. Ahu Vinapu is not as well-constructed, but is unique as the site of one of the only female *moai*, marked by its breasts. Early sketches showed the statue as having two heads, which means it was probably a goddess statue. When a missionary was killed here and hung from the head, his peers smashed its top half.

SOUTH COAST TO ANAKENA

The south coast is home to over 90 archaeological sites, including the most impressive ones to be found on the island. Starting out to the east you'll come to **Ahu Hanga Te'e,** where there are eight toppled *moai* and some *pukao* (smaller decorative stones used as headdresses for the *moai,* or "topknots") lined up against the sea and the small bay, **Hanga Te'e.** The island's subterranean springs exit here, so at low tide islanders can gather fresh water at the mouth of the bay. This confused early Europeans, who believed the Rapa Nui could drink sea water.

Farther up the coast is **Ahu Aka Hanga,** distinctive for its more modern fitting of red scoria decorative tablets on top. There are traces of *hare paenga, mana vai* (gardens), and *paina* (stones). Also, on the ocean side of the *ahu,* there is a small rectangle of stones where cremations were done. **Ana Aka Hanga,** a small cave you can enter, is carved into a hill to the right of the *ahu* and back toward the street.

Next, follow signs northeast to **Rano Raraku,** the abandoned *moai* quarry. When Poike erupted to the east, it spewed out ashes and volcanic rock that petrified into Rano Raraku. It was the only site on the island for such rock, and so all clans came here to make their *moai,* staking out different sites across its surface. When the quarry was abandoned due to warfare or famine, the clans left the *moai* in progress, and so today basically every rock you can see is a statue, in various stages of completion. This makes it easy to see how it was done. First, *moai* were carved to the angle of the rockface. **El Gigante,** at 22m the largest *moai* on the island, lies face-up in this stage. The other *moai,* drowning in the grass hills, had already been cut out and were having their backs finished for transport.

To see the major sites, take the path around the hill. You'll pass a bearded *moai* uncovered by Heyerdahl on a ledge looking out to **Ahu Akivi.** El Gigante is next, and then you'll come to a *moai* with a European ship carved on its front by a graffiti artist. There's also one *moai* with Polynesian tattooing on its neck. You can see it all in an hour, but could easily spend a day wandering if you bring food and water.

The next stop along the coast is **Ahu Tongariki,** which is definitely the most impressive *ahu.* Its 15 *moai,* backed by open sea, were restored in 1992-95 with backing from a Japanese company. There are several huge red *pukao* lined up to the side, but only one tops a *moai.* Archaelogists didn't want to replace the *pukao* because they couldn't tell for sure which *moai* had worn them. Locals were for it, however, and one morning, they hijacked a crane before the crew arrived, giving just one *moai* a top-

tect them from the island's fierce winds.

Moai are undoubtedly the most famous, yet most mysterious, aspect of the island. These huge statues were carved from basalt at Rano Raraku. *Tiki moai* were the earliest form, made in tribute to gods. They have round faces, and legs in a kneeling position. In the later classic *moai* style, the body is long, the head is rectangular, the lips are defined, and the nose is long and snubbed.

Most agree that the *moai* were constructed to visually demonstrate the genealogy and the organizational power of a clan as they looked out from the *ahu,* transmitting their *mana* (power) down onto the village. What no one really knows, however, is how they got there. Scientists have posed and tested many theories, involving various configurations of ropes and logs, but the truth is, we'll never know for sure.

Paina can be found in front of most *ahu.* Corpses were left within these circles of stones until only bones remained, as clan members marched or sat around the circle in tribute.

Pukau, or "topknots," are red scoria cylinders found atop a few *moai* and throughout the island's landscape. They were most likely developed to reflect the hairstyle of the *Ariki Mau,* who was never allowed to cut his hair because it was thought to hold *mana.*

knot. It was never removed, and remains quite distinctive. The hollowed eyes, tied arms, sealed lips, and defiantly-tipped chins of this row are haunting, as if they are awaiting a firing squad.

Continue on the coastal road until you come to **Ahu Te Pito Henúa.** On the way you'll pass several stone pillars. Called *pipi hureko*, they were ancient boundary lines. **Ahu Te Pito Kura** is the site of the largest *moai* to make it onto an *ahu*. At 11m, and weighing eight tons, currently, it lies toppled. To the left side of the *ahu*, closer to the sea, you'll come to the center of the universe—at least, that's what the Rapa Nui call "the spot," marked by a large, perfectly round stone. The stone is surrounded by smaller rocks, on which Rapa Nui would sit as they pressed their head and hands to the rock to siphon its *mana*. Though we can't confirm the spiritual bit, the rock is in fact magnetic. If you place a compass on top, it will spin indefinitely. Putting your head and hands on it, will give you a strange kind of charge, perhaps not entirely from the blood rush to the head.

Farther along the coast you'll pass the small volcanic beach of **Ovahe.** It has golden sands and is usually less crowded than its more spectacular neighbor to the northwest, **Anakena.** With white coral sands, palm trees, and views of turquoise sea to eternity, Anakena is at once one of the world's most beautiful and most isolated beaches. Hotu Matu'a is said to have landed here in ancient times. **Ahu Ature Huki,** to the right side facing the sea, holds one *moai* that was the first island restoration done by Heyerdahl in 1956. **Ahu Nau Nau,** at the back of the beach, was restored by Sergio Rapu in 1978. Its seven *moai* are very well-preserved because of the sand, and you can even make out intricate tattoo designs on their backs. Spend whatever time you have left enjoying the beach. There are bathrooms for changing at the rear of the palm tree side, and also a small snack stand closer to the water.

ROIHO AREA

Puna Pau, to the east of Hanga Roa, was once the *moai* topknot quarry. It is much smaller than Rano Raraku because only one clan carved the *pukao* in this quarry. There are a few giant *pukao* here, and the smallish crater is an easy hike, but the main feature is its looming view of Hanga Roa. You'll hear roosters crowing and dogs barking across the landscape spread below.

Close to Puna Pau is **Ahu Akivi,** which was the first scientific restoration on the island done in 1960 by William Mulloy. To raise funds, the archaeologists sent American and British donors videos of the progress, creating perhaps the first tourist interest in the island. The most distinctive feature of Ahu Akivi's seven *moai* is that they seem to be facing the sea. As *moai* always faced the village, to project the protective *mana*, many wonder if Mulloy goofed up. The village, however, does lie down in the direction of the sea, so his theory has not been altogether discarded. Also, some theorize that the Rapa Nui did this as tribute to the first navigators on the island. Oral tradition holds that Hotu Matu'a's priest had a dream one night in which his soul flew over the ocean and discovered the island of Rapa Nui. Hotu Matu'a sent navigators to find it before they returned to bring settlers. Seven of the navigators remained on the island waiting for the king, and it is thought that these seven *moai* face out toward Polynesia in tribute.

Near Ahu Akivi is **Ana Te Pahu,** a cave that was originally a lava tube created by the eruption of Terevaka, until part of its roof collapsed, making the subterranean caves accessible. The lava flow also made the soil particularly rich, and the area between the two entrances below ground level, has an explosion of plant life, with banana trees, tobacco, ferns, and even clovers. Make sure to bring a flashlight.

APPENDIX

SPANISH QUICK REFERENCE

PRONUNCIATION

Each vowel has only one pronunciation: A ("ah" in father); E ("eh" in pet); I ("ee" in eat); O ("oh" in oat); U ("oo" in boot); Y, by itself, is pronounced the same as Spanish I ("ee"). Most consonants are pronounced the same as in English. Important exceptions are: J, pronounced like the English "h" in "hello"; LL, pronounced like the English "y" in "yes"; and Ñ, pronounced like the "ny" in "canyon." R at the beginning of a word or RR anywhere in a word is trilled. H is always silent. G before E or I is pronounced like the "h" in "hen"; elsewhere it is pronounced like the "g" in "gate." X has a bewildering variety of pronunciations: depending on dialect and word position, it can sound like English "h," "s," "sh," or "x." Z is pronounced like the "s" in "sky."

Spanish words receive stress on the syllable marked with an accent ('). In the absence of an accent mark, words that end in vowels, "n," or "s" receive stress on the second to last syllable. For words ending in all other consonants, stress falls on the last syllable. The Spanish language has masculine and feminine nouns, and gives a gender to all adjectives. Masculine words generally end with an "o": él es un tonto (he is a fool). Feminine words generally end with an "a": ella es bella (she is beautiful). Pay close attention—slight changes in word ending can cause drastic changes in meaning. For instance, when receiving directions, mind the distinction between *derecho* (straight) and *derecha* (right).

LET'S GO! SPANISH PHRASEBOOK

ESSENTIAL PHRASES

ENGLISH	SPANISH	PRONUNCIATION
Hello.	Hola.	OH-la
Goodbye.	Adiós.	ah-dee-OHS
Yes/No	Sí/No	SEE/NO
Please.	Por favor.	POHR fa-VOHR
Thank you.	Gracias.	GRA-see-ahs
You're welcome.	De nada.	DAY NAH-dah
Do you speak English?	¿Habla inglés?	AH-blah een-GLACE
I don't speak Spanish.	No hablo español.	NO AH-bloh ehs-pahn-YOHL
Excuse me.	Perdón.	pehr-DOHN
I don't know.	No sé.	NO SAY
Can you repeat that?	¿Puede repetirlo?	PWEH-day reh-peh-TEER-lo

SURVIVAL SPANISH

ENGLISH	SPANISH	ENGLISH	SPANISH
Again, please.	Otra vez, por favor.	I'm sick/fine.	Estoy enfermo(a)/bien.
What (did you just say)?	¿Cómo?/¿Qué?	Could you speak more slowly?	¿Podría hablar más despacio?

ENGLISH	SPANISH	ENGLISH	SPANISH
I don't understand.	No entiendo.	How are you?	¿Qué tal?/¿Comó está?
What is your name?	¿Cómo se llama?	Where is (the center of town)?	¿Dónde está (el centro)?
How do you say (dodgeball) in Spanish?	¿Cómo se dice (dodgeball) en español?	Is the store open/closed?	¿La tienda está abierta/cerrada?
Good morning/night.	Buenos días/noches.	I am hungry/thirsty.	Tengo hambre/sed.
How much does it cost?	¿Cuánto cuesta?	I am hot/cold.	Tengo calor/frío.
Why (are you staring at me)?	¿Por qué (está mirándome)?	I want/would like...	Quiero/Me gustaría...
That is very cheap/expensive.	Es muy barato/caro.	Let's go!	¡Vámonos!
What's up?	¿Qué pasa?	Stop/that's enough.	Basta.
Who?	¿Quién?	What?	¿Qué?
When?	¿Cuándo?	Where?	¿Dónde?
Why?	¿Por qué?	Because.	Porque.

YOUR ARRIVAL

ENGLISH	SPANISH	ENGLISH	SPANISH
I am from (the US/Europe).	Soy de (los Estados Unidos/Europa).	What's the problem, sir/madam?	¿Cuál es el problema, señor/señora?
Here is my passport.	Aquí está mi pasaporte.	I lost my passport.	Perdí mi pasaporte.
I will be here for less than six months.	Estaré aquí por menos de seis meses.	I have nothing to declare.	No tengo nada para declarar.
I don't know where that came from.	No sé de dónde eso cuando vinieron.	Please do not detain me.	Por favor no me detenga.

GETTING AROUND

ENGLISH	SPANISH	ENGLISH	SPANISH
¿How can you get to...?	¿Cómo se puede llegar a...?	Is there anything cheaper?	¿Hay algo más barato/económico?
Does this bus go to (Tierra del Fuego)?	¿Va este autobús a (Tierra del Fuego)?	On foot.	A pie.
Where is (Mackenna) street?	¿Dónde está la calle (Mackenna)?	What bus line goes to..?	¿Qué línea de buses tiene servicio a...?
When does the bus leave?	¿Cuándo sale el bús?	Where does the bus leave from?	¿De dónde sale el bús?
I'm getting off at...	Bajo en...	I have to go now.	Tengo que ir ahora.
Can I buy a ticket?	¿Podría comprar un boleto?	How far is...?	¿Qué tan lejos está...?
How long does the trip take?	¿Cuántas horas dura el viaje?	Continue forward.	Siga derecho.
I am going to the airport.	Voy al aeropuerto.	The flight is delayed/cancelled.	El vuelo está atrasado/cancelado.
Where is the bathroom?	¿Dónde está el baño?	Is it safe to hitchhike?	¿Es seguro pedir aventón?
I lost my baggage.	Perdí mi equipaje.	I'm lost.	Estoy perdido(a).
I would like to rent (a car).	Quisiera alquilar (un coche).	Please let me off at the zoo.	Por favor, déjeme en el zoológico.
How much does it cost per day/week?	¿Cuánto cuesta por día/semana?	Does it have (heating/air-conditioning)?	¿Tiene (calefacción/aire acondicionado)?
Where can I buy a cellphone?	¿Dónde puedo comprar un teléfono celular?	Where can I check e-mail?	¿Dónde se puede chequear el email?
Could you tell me what time it is?	¿Podría decirme qué hora es?	Are there student discounts available?	¿Hay descuentos para estudiantes?

DIRECTIONS

ENGLISH	SPANISH	ENGLISH	SPANISH
(to the) right	(a la) derecha	(to the) left	(a la) izquierda
next to	al lado de/junto a	across from	en frente de/frente a
straight ahead	derecho	turn (command form)	doble
near (to)	cerca (de)	far (from)	lejos (de)
above	arriba	below	abajo
traffic light	semáforo	corner	esquina
street	calle/avenida	block	cuadra

ACCOMMODATIONS

ENGLISH	SPANISH	ENGLISH	SPANISH
Is there a cheap hotel around here?	¿Hay un hotel económico por aquí?	Are there rooms with windows?	¿Hay habitaciones con ventanas?
Do you have rooms available?	¿Tiene habitaciones libres?	I am going to stay for (four) days.	Me voy a quedar (cuatro) días.
I would like to reserve a room.	Quisiera reservar una habitación.	Are there cheaper rooms?	¿Hay habitaciones más baratas?
Can I see a room?	¿Podría ver una habitación?	Do they come with private baths?	¿Vienen con baño privado?
Do you have any singles/doubles?	¿Tiene habitaciones sencillas/dobles?	Can I borrow a plunger?	¿Me puede prestar una bomba?
I need another key/towel/pillow.	Necesito otra llave/toalla/almohada.	My bedsheets are dirty.	Mis sábanas están sucias.
The shower/sink/toilet is broken.	La ducha/pila/el servicio no funciona.	I'll take it.	Lo tomo.
There are cockroaches in my room.	Hay cucarachas en mi habitación.	They are biting me.	Me están mordiendo.

EMERGENCY

ENGLISH	SPANISH	ENGLISH	SPANISH
Help!	¡Socorro!/¡Ayúdeme!	Call the police!	¡Llame a la policía/los carabineros!
I am hurt.	Estoy herido(a).	Leave me alone!	¡Déjame en paz!
It's an emergency!	¡Es una emergencia!	They robbed me!	¡Me han robado!
Fire!	¡Fuego!/¡Incendio!	They went that way!	¡Fueron en esa dirección!
Call a clinic/ambulance/doctor/priest!	¡Llame a una clínica/una ambulancia/un médico/un padre!	I will only speak in the presence of a lawyer.	Sólo hablaré en presencia de un abogado(a).
I need to contact my embassy.	Necesito contactar mi embajada.	Don't touch me!	¡No me toque!

MEDICAL

ENGLISH	SPANISH	ENGLISH	SPANISH
I feel bad/better/fine/worse.	Me siento mal/mejor/bien/peor.	I have a stomach ache.	Me duele el estómago.
I have a headache.	Tengo un dolor de cabeza.	It hurts here.	Me duele aquí.
I'm sick/ill.	Estoy enfermo(a).	Here is my prescription.	Aquí está la receta médica.
I'm allergic to...	Soy alérgico(a) a...	I think I'm going to vomit.	Pienso que voy a vomitar.
What is this medicine for?	¿Para qué es esta medicina?	I haven't been able to go to the bathroom in (four) days.	No he podido ir al baño en (cuatro) días.

ENGLISH	SPANISH	ENGLISH	SPANISH
Where is the nearest hospital/doctor?	¿Dónde está el hospital/doctor más cercano?	I have a cold/a fever/diarrhea/nausea.	Tengo gripe/una calentura/diarrea/náusea.

EATING OUT

ENGLISH	SPANISH	ENGLISH	SPANISH
breakfast	desayuno	lunch	almuerzo
dinner	comida/cena	drink (alcoholic)	bebida (trago)
dessert	postre	bon appétit	buen provecho
fork	tenedor	knife	cuchillo
napkin	servilleta	cup	copa/taza
spoon	cuchara	Do you have hot sauce?	¿Tiene salsa picante?
Where is a good restaurant?	¿Dónde está un restaurante bueno?	Table for (one), please.	Mesa para (uno), por favor.
Can I see the menu?	¿Podría ver la carta/el menú?	Do you take credit cards?	¿Aceptan tarjetas de crédito?
This is too spicy.	Es demasiado picante.	Disgusting!	¡Guácala!/¡Qué asco!
I would like to order the eel.	Quisiera el congrio.	Delicious!	¡Qué rico!
Do you have anything vegetarian/without meat?	¿Hay algún plato vegetariano/sin carne?	Check, please.	La cuenta, por favor.

MENU READER

SPANISH	ENGLISH	SPANISH	ENGLISH
a la plancha	grilled	kuchen	pastry with fruit
al vapor	steamed	leche	milk
aceite	oil	legumbres	vegetables/legumes
aceituna	olive	lima	lime
agua (purificada)	water (purified)	limón	lemon
ajo	garlic	limonada	lemonade
almeja	clam	locos	abalone (white fish)
arroz	rice	lomo	steak or chop
arroz con leche	rice pudding	macedonia	syrupy dessert
ave-palta	sandwich with chicken and avocado	maíz	corn
Barros Luco	sandwich with beef and cheese	mariscos	seafood
Barros Jarpa	sandwich with ham	miel	honey
bistec	beefsteak	naranja	orange
bundín de centolla	crab with onions, eggs, cheese	nata	cream
café	coffee	paila marina	soup of various shellfish
caldillo de congrio	eel and vegetable soup	pan	bread
caliente	hot	pan amasado	a common heavy bread
camarones	shrimp	papas	potatoes
carne	meat	papas fritas	french fries
cazuela	clear broth with rice, corn, and chicken or beef	parrillas	various grilled meats
cebolla	onion	pasteles	desserts/pies

SPANISH	ENGLISH	SPANISH	ENGLISH
cerveza	beer	pastel de choclo	corn cassarole with beef, chicken, raisins, onions, and olives
chacarero	sandwich with beef, tomato, chili, and green beans	pebre	mild or spicy salsa eaten with many foods
chupe de marisco/locos	sea scallops/abalone with white wine, butter, cream, and cheese	pernil de chanco a la chilena	braised fresh ham with chili sauce
churrasco	steak sandwich	pescado	fish
chorizo	spicy sausage	picoroco	dish using barnacle meat
coco	coconut	pimienta	pepper
congrio	eel	pisco sour	drink made with pisco (from grapes) and egg whites
cordero	lamb	plato	plate
curanto	hearty stew of fish, chicken, pork, lamb, beef, and potato	pollo	chicken
dulces	sweets	porotos granados	cranberry beans with squash and corn
dulce de leche	caramelized milk	puerco	pork
empanada	dumpling filled with meat, cheese, or potatoes	queso	cheese
ensalada	salad	sal	salt
entrada	appetizer	tragos	mixed drinks/liquor
gaseosa	soda	vino tinto/blanco	red wine/white

SPANISH GLOSSARY

aduana: customs
agencia de viaje: travel agency
aguardiente: strong liquor
aguas termales: hot springs
ahora: now
ahorita: "now in just a little bit," which can mean anything from 5 minutes to 5 hours
aire acondicionado: air-conditioned (A/C)
a la plancha: grilled
al gusto: as you wish
al tiro: immediately
alemán: German
almacén: (grocery) store
almuerzo: lunch, midday meal
alpaca: a shaggy-haired, long-necked animal in the camelid family
altiplano: highland
amigo/a: friend
andén: platform
anexo: neighborhood
araucaria: monkey puzzle trees
arroz: rice
arroz chaufa: Chinese-style fried rice
artesanía: arts and crafts
avenida: avenue
bahía: bay
bandido: bandit
baño: bathroom or natural spa

barato/a: cheap
barranca: canyon
barro: mud
barrio: neighborhood
biblioteca: library
bistec/bistek: beefsteak
bocaditos: appetizers, at a bar
bodega: convenience store or winery
boletería: ticket counter
bolivianos: Bolivian currency
bonito/a: pretty/beautiful
borracho/a: drunk
bosque: forest
botica: drugstore
bueno/a: good
buena suerte: good luck
buen provecho: bon appétit
burro: donkey
caballero: gentleman
caballo: horse
cabañas: cabins
cajeros: cashiers
cajeros automáticos: ATMs
caldera: coffee or tea pot
caldo: soup, broth, or stew
calle: street
cama: bed
camarones: shrimp
cambio: change
caminata: hike
camino: path, track, road
camión: truck
camioneta: small, pickup-sized truck
campamento: campground
campesino/a: person from a rural area, peasant
campo: countryside
canotaje: rafting
cantina: drinking establishment, usually male-dominated
carne asada: roast meat
capilla: chapel
caro/a: expensive
carretera: highway
carro: car, or sometimes a train car
casa: house
casa de cambio: currency exchange establishment
casado/a: married
cascadas: waterfalls
casona: mansion
castellano: Castilian (Spanish spoken in Spain)
catedral: cathedral
centro: city center
cerca: near/nearby
cerro: hill
cerveza: beer
ceviche: raw fish marinated in lemon juice, herbs, and veggies
cevichería: ceviche restaurant
chico/a: boy/girl, little
chicharrón: bite-sized pieces of fried meat, usually pork

chifa: Chinese restaurant
chuleta de chancho: pork chop
churrasco: steak sandwich
cigarillo: cigarette
cine: cinema
ciudad: city
ciudadela: neighborhood in a large city
club: club (usually strip club)
coche: car
colectivo: shared taxi
coliseo: coliseum/stadium
comedor: dining room
comida criolla: regional, Spanish-influenced dishes
comida típica: typical/traditional dishes
con: with
consulado: consulate
correo: post office
cordillera: mountain range
corvina: sea bass
croata: Croatian
criollos: people of European descent born in the New World
crucero: crossroads
Cruz Roja: Red Cross
cuadra: street block
cuarto: a room
Cueca: Chilean national dance
cuenta: bill/check
cuento: story/account
cueva: cave
curandero: healer
damas: ladies
desayuno: breakfast
descompuesto: broken, out of order; spoiled/rotten food
desierto: desert
despacio: slow
de turno: a 24hr. rotating schedule for pharmacies
dinero: money
discoteca: dance club
dueño/a: owner
dulces: sweets
edificio: building
email: email
embajada: embassy
embarcadero: dock
emergencia: emergency
encomiendas: estates granted to Spanish settlers in Latin America
entrada: entrance
estadio: stadium
este: east
estrella: star
extranjero: foreign/foreigner
farmacia: pharmacy
farmacia en turno: 24hr. pharmacy
feliz: happy
ferrocarril: railroad
fiesta: party, holiday
finca: a plantation-like agricultural enterprise or a ranch

friajes: sudden cold winds
frijoles: beans
frontera: border
fumar: to smoke
fumaroles: hole in a volcanic region which emits hot vapors
fundo: large estate
fútbol: soccer
ganga: bargain
gobierno: government
gordo/a: fat
gorra: cap
gratis: free
gringo/a: North American
guanaco: animal in the camelid family
habitación: a room
hacer una caminata: take a hike
hacienda: ranch
helado: ice cream
hermano/a: brother/sister
hervido/a: boiled
hielo: ice
hijo/a: son/daughter
hombre: man
huaso: Chilean cowboy
iglesia: church
impuestos: taxes
impuesto valor añadido (IVA): value added tax (VAT)
indígena: indigenous, refers to the native population
isla: island
jarra: 1L pitcher of beer
jirón: street
jugo: juice
ladrón: thief
lago/laguna: lake
lancha: launch, small boat
langosta: lobster
langostino: jumbo shrimp
larga distancia: long distance
lavandería: laundromat
lejos: far
lente: slow
librería: bookstore
lista de correos: mail-holding system in Latin America
loma: hill
lomo: chop, steak
madre: mother
malo/a: bad
malecón: pier or seaside thoroughfare
maletas: luggage, suitcases
maneje despacio: drive slowly
manjar blanco: a caramel-like whole-milk spread
Mapudungun: the Mapuche language
mar: sea
mariscos: seafood
matas: shrubs, jungle brush
matrimonial: double bed
menestras: lentils/beans
menú del día/menú: fixed daily meal often offered for a bargain price

mercado: market
merienda: snack
mestizaje: crossing of races
mestizo/a: a person of mixed European and indigenous descent
microbus: small, local bus
mirador: an observatory or look-out point
muelle: wharf
muerte: death
museo: museum
música folklórica: folk music
nada: nothing
niño/a: child
nightclub: strip club
norte: north
obra: work of art/play
obraje: primitive textile workshop
oeste: west
oficina de turismo: tourist office
padre: father
pampa: a treeless grassland area
pan: bread
panadería: bakery
panga: motorboat
parada: a stop (on a bus or train)
parrilla: various cuts of meat, grilled
paro: labor strike
parque: park
parroquia: parish
paseo turístico: tour covering a series of sites
payaso: clown
pelea de gallos: cockfighting
peligroso/a: dangerous

peninsulares: Spanish-born colonists
peña: folkloric music club
pescado: fish
picante: spicy
pisa de uvas: grape-stomping
pisco: a traditional Chilean liquor made from grapes
pisco sour: a drink made from pisco, lemon juice, sugarcane syrup, and egg white
plátano: plantain
playa: beach
población: population, settlement
policía: police
pollo a la brasa: roasted chicken
pudú: a Chilean wild goat
pueblito: small town
pueblo: town
puente: bridge
puerta: door
puerto: port
queso: cheese
rana: frog
recreo: place of amusement, restaurant/bar on the outskirts of a city
refrescos: refreshments, soft drinks
reloj: watch, clock
río: river
ropa: clothes
sábanas: bedsheets
sabor: flavor
sala: living room
salchipapa: french fries with fried pieces of sausage
salida: exit
salto: waterfall

salsa: sauce (can be of many varieties)
seguro/a: lock, insurance; adj.: safe
semáforo: traffic light
semana: week
Semana Santa: Holy Week
sexo: sex
SIDA: the Spanish acronym for AIDS
siesta: mid-afternoon nap; businesses often close at this time
sillar: flexible, white, volcanic rock used in construction
sol: sun/Peruvian currency
solito/a: alone
solo/a: alone
solo carril: one-lane road or bridge
soltero/a: single (unmarried)
supermercado: supermarket
sur: south
tarifa: fee
tapas: bite-size appetizers served in bars
telenovela: soap opera
termas: hot mineral springs
tienda: store
tipo de cambio: exchange rate
trago: mixed drink/shot of alcohol
triste: sad
trucha: trout
turismo: tourism
turista: tourist
valle: valley
vicuña: a llama-like animal
volcán: volcano
zona: zone

RAPA NUI QUICK REFERENCE

LET'S GO! RAPA NUI PHRASEBOOK

ESSENTIAL PHRASES

ENGLISH	RAPA NUI	ENGLISH	RAPA NUI
Hello/Goodbye	Iorana	Thank you.	Maurur
How are you?	Pehe koe.	You're welcome.	O te aha no.
Fine.	Riva riva.	Please.	Ana hanga koe.

NAVIGATING THE SIGHTS

ENGLISH	RAPA NUI	ENGLISH	RAPA NUI
Bay	Hanga	Moon	Mahina
Boat house	Hare Paenga	Mountain	Maunga
Bird	Manu	Platform	Ahu
Burial chambers beneath certain *ahu*	Avanga	Star	Hetu'u
Cave	Ana	Stone	Paina
Crater	Rano	Sun	Ra'a
Earth, land	Henua	Topknot (headdress for *moai* carved from red scoria)	Pukao
Horse	Hoi	Tree	Miro
Large, stone figures	Moai	Water	Vai

MISCELLANEOUS

ENGLISH	RAPA NUI	ENGLISH	RAPA NUI
Banana	Maiku	Father/old man	Koro
Beer	Pia	Fish	Ika
Big	Rapa	Little	Iti
Chicken	Moa	Man	Tangata
Cigar	Potu	Mother/old woman	Nua
Day	Otea	Night	Po
Eat/food	Kai	Woman	Vahine

INDEX

ABOUT LET'S GO

GUIDES FOR THE INDEPENDENT TRAVELER

At Let's Go, we see every trip as the chance of a lifetime. If your dream is to grab a machete and forge through the jungles of Brazil, we can take you there. If you'd rather bask in the Riviera sun at a beachside cafe, we'll set you a table. We write for readers who know that there's more to travel than sharing double deckers with tourists and who believe that travel can change both themselves and the world—whether they plan to spend six days in London or six months in Latin America. We'll show you just how far your money can go, and prove that the greatest limitation on your adventures is not your wallet, but your imagination. After all, traveling close to the ground lets you interact more directly with the places and people you've gone to see, making for the most authentic experience.

BEYOND THE TOURIST EXPERIENCE

To help you gain a deeper connection with the places you travel, our researchers give you the heads-up on both world-renowned and off-the-beaten-track attractions, sights, and destinations. They engage with the local culture, writing features on regional cuisine, local festivals, and hot political issues. We've also opened our pages to respected writers and scholars to hear their takes on the countries and regions we cover, and asked travelers who have worked, studied, or volunteered abroad to contribute first-person accounts of their experiences. We've also increased our coverage of responsible travel and expanded each guide's Alternatives to Tourism chapter to share more ideas about how to give back to local communities and learn about the places you travel.

FORTY-FIVE YEARS OF WISDOM

Let's Go got its start in 1960, when a group of creative and well-traveled students compiled their experience and advice into a 20-page mimeographed pamphlet, which they gave to travelers on charter flights to Europe. Four and a half decades later, we've expanded to cover six continents and all kinds of travel—while retaining our founders' adventurous attitude toward the world. Our guides are still researched and written entirely by students on shoestring budgets, experienced travelers who know that train strikes, stolen luggage, food poisoning, and marriage proposals are all part of a day's work. This year, we're expanding our coverage of South America and Southeast Asia, with brand-new *Let's Go: Ecuador*, *Let's Go: Peru*, and *Let's Go: Vietnam*. Our adventure guide series is growing, too, with the addition of *Let's Go: Pacific Northwest Adventure* and *Let's Go: New Zealand Adventure*. And we're immensely excited about our new *Let's Go: Roadtripping USA*—two years, eight routes, and sixteen researchers and editors have put together a travel guide like none other.

THE LET'S GO COMMUNITY

More than just a travel guide company, Let's Go is a community. Our small staff comes together because of our shared passion for travel and our desire to help other travelers see the world. We love it when our readers become part of the Let's Go community as well—when you travel, drop us a postcard (67 Mt. Auburn St., Cambridge, MA 02138, USA) or send us an e-mail (feedback@letsgo.com) to tell us about your adventures and discoveries.

For more information, visit us online: www.letsgo.com.

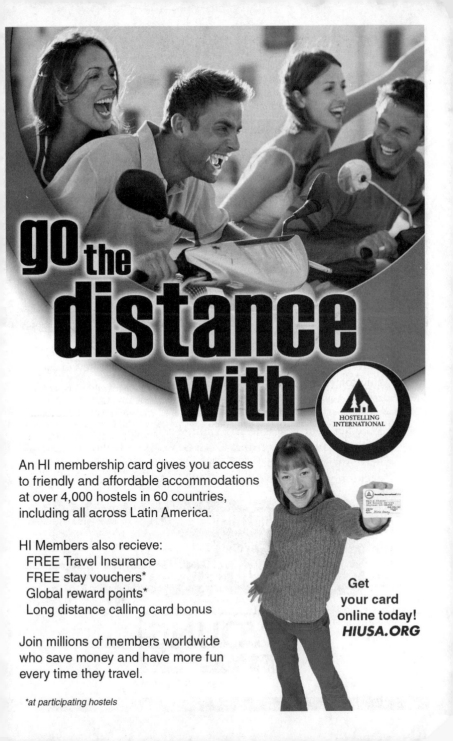

LONG ON WEEKEND. SHORT ON CASH.

The fastest way to the best fare.

AP INDEX

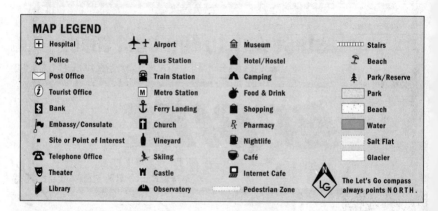

MAP LEGEND

✚ Hospital	✈ Airport	🏛 Museum	ⅢⅢⅢ Stairs
✪ Police	🚌 Bus Station	🏨 Hotel/Hostel	⚲ Beach
✉ Post Office	🚆 Train Station	⛺ Camping	🌲 Park/Reserve
ⓘ Tourist Office	Ⓜ Metro Station	Food & Drink	Park
$ Bank	⚓ Ferry Landing	Shopping	Beach
Embassy/Consulate	🕆 Church	℞ Pharmacy	Water
■ Site or Point of Interest	Vineyard	Nightlife	Salt Flat
☎ Telephone Office	⛷ Skiing	☕ Café	Glacier
Theater	♜ Castle	Internet Cafe	The Let's Go compass always points NORTH.
Library	Observatory	Pedestrian Zone	